THE LIVES AND TIMES OF

THE GREAT COMPOSERS

MICHAEL STEEN

This revised edition published in the UK in 2010 by Icon Books Ltd,
Omnibus Business Centre, 29–41 North Road, London N7 9DP
email: info@iconbooks.co.uk
www.iconbooks.co.uk

Original edition published in 2003 by Icon Books

Sold in the UK, Europe, South Africa and Asia
by Faber & Faber Ltd, Bloomsbury House,
74–77 Great Russell Street, London WC1B 3DA
or their agents

Distributed in the UK, Europe, South Africa and Asia
by TBS Ltd, TBS Distribution Centre, Colchester Road,
Frating Green, Colchester CO7 7DW

This edition published in Australia in 2010
by Allen & Unwin Pty Ltd, PO Box 8500,
83 Alexander Street, Crows Nest, NSW 2065

Distributed in Canada by
Penguin Books Canada, 90 Eglinton Avenue East,
Suite 700, Toronto, Ontario M4P 2YE

ISBN 978-184831-135-0

Typesetting by Wayzgoose and Marie Doherty

Printed in Great Britain by Clays Ltd, St Ives plc

For all who want to know more

ACKNOWLEDGEMENTS

The sources, upon which this book is wholly dependent, are generally quoted in the section entitled 'Sources and Further Reading'. I cannot overstate the extent to which I have depended on them.

I am grateful for assistance at the City of London Libraries and the Royal College of Music Library. I have also been helped by the Bodleian Library and the Library of the Royal Opera House, Covent Garden. Whereas the content of libraries may be different, their staff seem to share the same sense of dedication and to display a degree of courtesy, helpfulness and speed of response which is both exceptional and exemplary.

Others to whom I am most grateful for pointing me in the right direction, advice, information, or just help and support, are Dr Roland Aubrey, Nigel Blackwell, Nicholas Boggis-Rolfe, Jenny Brown, Peter Byrom, The Rev. Anthony Chambers, Sophie Chessum, Paul Collen, Peter Collett, Christopher Collier, Sarah Dodgson, Miles Emley, Alex Findlater, Dr Brian Gilmore, Jenny Haimes, Geoffrey Hodgkins, Sir Jeremy Isaacs, Nigel Jaques, many of my former partners at KPMG, Richard Macnutt, Dr Robert Manning, Robert Meekings, Dr Janet Morgan, Roger Munnings, Provost Nicholson and his colleagues at Oriel, Dr Caitríona Ó Dochartaigh, Christopher Paterson, Sir Joseph Pilling, Dame Janet Ritterman and her colleagues at the Royal College of Music, Clive Ryder Runton, Dr Amar Sabberwal, Yvonne Scott, Daniel Snowman, Sue Sturrock, Pamela Thompson, Nicholas West, Paul Whitfield and Peter Willett. These are just some of those with whom I have corresponded.

I am deeply grateful to those who commented on specific excerpts and early drafts, in full or in part: Dr Guy Deutscher, Dr David Maw, Andrew Robinson, Dr Esther Schmidt and Dr Janie Steen. Jonathan Price and David Vaughan gave me unstinting help and support. Because I did not act on all their suggestions, they cannot be assumed to agree with the final text, and responsibility for any errors that remain is entirely mine. But without their input, whatever shortcomings the book may have would have been more considerable.

The team at Icon, led by Peter Pugh and Jeremy Cox, has been tremendously helpful, and I must especially thank the editors Duncan Heath and Ruth Nelson, Jenny Rigby, and the designer Christos Kondeatis.

This book could not have been written without considerable effort by, and encouragement from, Professor Robert and Mrs Elizabeth Steen, and Sir Stanley Cochrane, Bart. I owe Rosemary my wife a special word of thanks for her skill, for reading drafts and for unswerving support. She is now expert in locating a Geburtshaus, a Casa Natale, a museum or a ruined house.

Contents

ABOUT THE AUTHOR

Michael Steen OBE was born in Dublin. He studied at the Royal College of Music, was an organ scholar at Oriel College, Oxford, and then spent 30 years in a successful career in the City of London. He is Treasurer of the Open University, and has been chairman of the Royal College of Music Society and the Friends of the Victoria and Albert Museum. He is also the author of *Enchantress of Nations: Pauline Viardot: Soprano, Muse and Lover* (Icon, 2007).

List of Colour Plates

MAP OF PRESENT-DAY EUROPE SHOWING COMPOSERS' BIRTHPLACES

KEY TO BIRTHPLACES
OF THE COMPOSERS

BIRTHPLACES	**COMPOSERS**
Bergamo	Donizetti
Bergen	Grieg
Berlin	Meyerbeer
Bonn	Beethoven
Busseto	Verdi *(Le Roncole)*
Catania	Bellini
Cologne	Offenbach
Cremona	Monteverdi
Down Ampney	Vaughan Williams
Eisenach	Bach
Halle	Handel
Hamburg	Mendelssohn, Brahms
Hämeenlinna	Sibelius
Hukvaldy	Janáček
Kaliště	Mahler
Karevo	Mussorgsky
La Côte St André	Berlioz
Leipzig	Wagner
Liège	Franck
Litomyšl	Smetana
Lowestoft	Britten
Lucca	Puccini
Moscow	Scriabin
Munich	Richard Strauss
Nagyszentmiklós	Bartók
Nelahozeves	Dvořák
Novgorod	Rachmaninov, Rimsky-Korsakov *(nearby)*
Pamiers	Fauré
Paris	Bizet, Saint-Saëns, Debussy, Poulenc
Pesaro	Rossini
Raiding	Liszt
Rohrau	Haydn
Salzburg	Mozart
Smolensk	Glinka *(nearby)*
St Petersburg	Borodin, Shostakovich, Stravinsky *(nearby)*
St-Germain-en-Laye	Debussy
St-Jean-de-Luz	Ravel *(Ciboure)*
Vienna	Schubert, Johann Strauss
Vilnius	Cui
Worcester	Elgar *(nearby)*
Żelazowa Wola	Chopin
Zwickau	Schumann

Tchaikovsky was born 600 miles east of Moscow

KEY TO MAPS

◆ **Birthplaces of composers**

MAP OF MID-19TH-CENTURY ITALY

KEY TO MAP

SAVOY Old regional names

Old regional borders

MAP OF SAXONY AND CENTRAL GERMANY

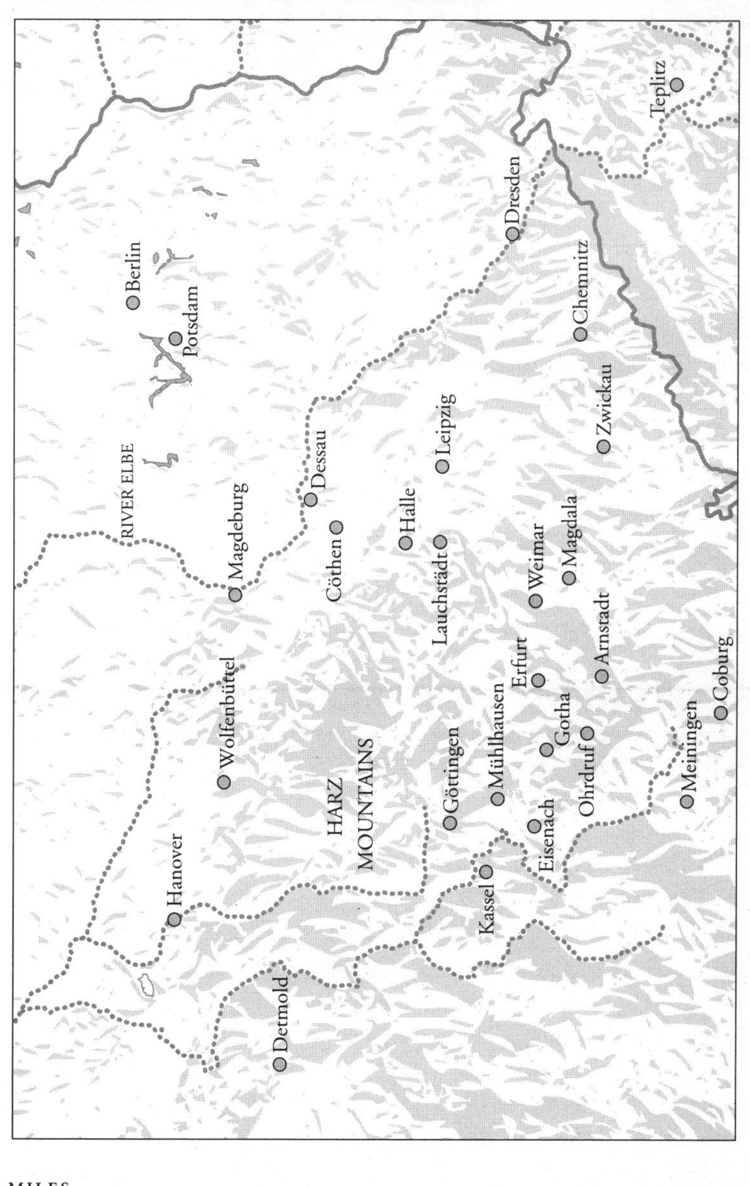

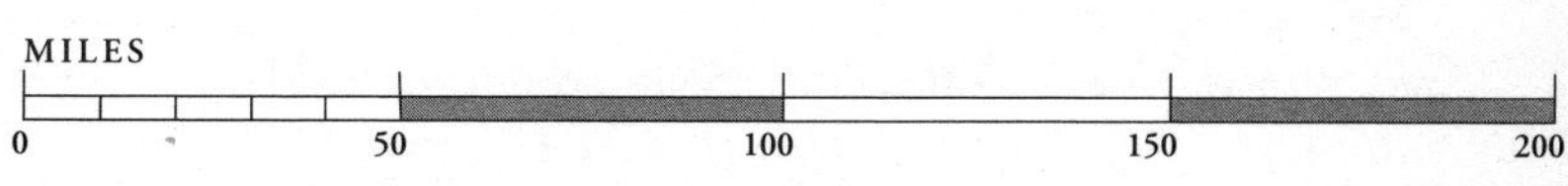

Preface

'Mr Lely, I desire you would use all your skill to paint my picture truly like me, and not flatter me at all; but remark all these roughnesses, pimples, warts, and everything as you see me; otherwise I will never pay a farthing for it.'

– Oliver Cromwell[1]

This book provides sketches of some of the great and popular classical composers, their world and their lives. It is for those who have neither the time nor the inclination to read the many enjoyable and excellent, but longer, individual biographies that are available.

I have accepted that:

The art of Biography
Is different from Musicography.
Musicography is about Cellos
But Biography is about Fellows.[2]

Readers wanting the analysis of individual works, so necessary for good performance, should turn to the longer studies or to programme notes.

This book emphasises the context, the setting in which the composers lived, what was going on at the time, some of the things that they might have talked about. Some readers might protest: surely, of all the arts, music is above all this mundane stuff. Of course, they might say, many novelists, dramatists and poets, Austen, Dickens, Ibsen, Brecht, to name but a few, deliberately described or reflected the world in which they lived; painters like Goya, Delacroix and Picasso responded to the events of their time. But musicians have always been rather different. Did not Sibelius claim that music is on a higher plane than everything else in this world?[3] To this I would say: music may be, but composers are not. They lived, and do live, on Earth. Mozart did not write an opera for eternity, or for an ideal, but when there was a demand for one.[4] Even though Beethoven was in a position to compose music for the sake of art alone, nobody would deny that events in France affected where he chose to live and influenced his 'Eroica' Symphony.

Many composers have been caught up directly in the events of their time: Michael Wise, a 17th-century English composer, was killed by the night watch for 'stubborn and refractory language'[5] during a brawl in Salisbury. In Austria, 250 years later, three shots fired by an American sentry tragically killed Anton Webern when he emerged from the house to smoke a contraband cigar.[6] Wagner made a sensational escape from Dresden in 1848, was sheltered by Liszt, and was subsequently exiled for over a decade.

However, it is far beyond the scope of this book to explore the relationship between the works of a composer and his environment. That is a complex matter: Prokofiev's Classical Symphony and Shostakovich's Seventh Symphony were each composed at times of great upheaval, the one, the most momentous revolution, and the other, the longest siege in history. Yet they are entirely different in character.

I shall not tread on such dangerous territory. I merely aim to turn up the lights on some selected aspects of the background scenery. By illuminating them, I necessarily and deliberately reduce the spotlight on the individual.

When to begin and end? I chose to start in the 1680s with Handel and Bach, and to finish with a selection of composers who were already well established in the first half of the 20th century. There is an underlying rationale to my choice, partly musical, partly just based on convenience.

By the time Handel and Bach were born, a number of familiar features of classical music were securely in place. The most obvious of these is the sense of key, or tonality, which enables listeners to recognise an obviously 'wrong' note, and feel comfortable when the music has ended on the 'right' one. Much of the pleasure in listening to music is actually provided by the tension as the music moves away from the initially established key and reverts back to it.[7]

I chose to draw to a close when that sense of key broke down. An outraged Camille Saint-Saëns thought he saw the end coming with Richard Strauss, who was then considered avant-garde. 'The completest liberty reigns', Saint-Saëns complained. 'While one group of instruments covers one tonality, another has no scruples about battling with its neighbour, while the voices travel along elsewhere.'[8]

As it happens, our ears sense that conventional tonality survived, in one form or other, long beyond Saint-Saëns, and thus I continue for some time after Strauss. However, the decision to exclude those composers whose main works are called 'atonal' enabled me to draw a line in the first half of the 20th century. I did this with relief: I did not relish the considerable challenge of doing sufficient justice to the 20th century and the times and lives of Schoenberg's group and its successors. But I felt that I should include several whose principal compositions are 'tonal' in character, who were active in the early decades of the 20th century and lived long into it. So, in the end, my line became increasingly blurred as I wandered on. I do not think that matters.

Having drawn some boundaries, albeit arbitrary, I faced the question: which composers to include? What about Henry Purcell, England's renowned master, the composer of Dido's Lament, 'When I am laid in earth'? He was at his height in the 1680s. He 'began to shew his Great skill before the reforme of musick, *al Italliana*, and, while he was in warm pursuit of it, Dyed, but a greater musical genius England never had'.[9] However, unfortunately, we know little about Purcell, this 'amazing shadowy musical figure'.[10] Only at the beginning of the 18th century, with Handel and Bach, do the lives of most of the individual composers emerge in something approaching full colour.

Or I might have been tempted to begin with 'the shrewd avarice and great pomp'[11] of Jean-Baptiste Lully who died in the 1680s. The glittering but mind-numbingly rigid court of Louis XIV, the Sun-King, could have made a good story with a contemporary flavour. Imitating the rapacity of his monarch, Lully secured, for himself and his heirs, a complete monopoly over opera. He thus became one of the richest musicians there has ever been. He augmented his earnings with real-estate speculation.[12] He was bisexual. Being fleet of foot in every sense (like his monarch, he was a skilled and graceful ballet dancer),[13] his end was appropriate. In his day, and long afterwards, conductors beat time by banging the floor, or a desk, with a cane. Fate caught up with Lully, when conducting a Te Deum: he missed the floor and stabbed his foot; it turned gangrenous;[14] so he died. But Lully's monopoly constrained the progress of music in France, and to start with him would have given him undue prominence. Hence, my first chapters are about Handel and Bach.

For chapter headings, I have somewhat arbitrarily chosen composers who are generally regarded as 'popular'. So Puccini qualifies, but Gluck and Weber, to name but two, who on any measure of excellence should have deserved a full chapter, do not. With the twentieth century, I become increasingly selective. The more glaring omissions, I have mentioned *en passant*.

What to include? I have had to be ruthless in my choice of background material, cultural, social, military and political. If I were not, this book would turn into a comprehensive history of Europe. Certain chapters, particularly the earlier ones, require more background material to 'get the story going'. Equally, various parts of the scenery must be painted in some detail if those sitting in the audience are to gain a reasonable impression of what is being portrayed on the stage. So, I make liberal use of footnotes to relegate information which might otherwise impede the flow of the narrative. This detail, which readers can read or ignore at their choice, provides a counterpoint to the main themes in the text.

A caveat is necessary. In some cases, considerable mythology has grown up around the lives of composers, Mozart's death being an obvious example. Stories have been handed down and gained credibility. Biography is often written by people who want to force their version onto the record. Fanny Burney's *Memoirs* of her father Doctor Burney, author of the four-volume *General History of Music* published towards the end of the 18th century, is a notorious case of this.[15] As to accuracy, I enjoyed one 19th-century biographer's admission: 'I should not be in the least surprised to discover some thirty or forty inaccuracies among the countless masses of minute detail which go to make up this biography.' A footnote provided by the translator adds acidly 'perhaps a hundred would be nearer the mark'.[16] Autobiography, particularly by a 'Romantic' such as Berlioz, is arguably even more untrustworthy, which will be of no surprise to modern readers familiar with autobiographies of politicians and others.

I have sometimes drawn on material from contemporary literature. For example, I found the novels of Stendhal and Balzac helpful in looking at France in the first half of the 19th century, and Zola subsequently. The background portrayed by those authors is intended to be reasonably authentic, even if they too have wanted 'to make a point'. And their perceptions are contemporary. I have, however, regarded historical novels as unreliable: because they portray a period much earlier than the time at which the novel was issued, there is more room for confusion between fact and fiction.

Some readers may feel that much of my material is too earthy. For this I make no apology, although I emphasise that this is not intended to be a book about composers' sex lives. Just as it is interesting to know that Schubert and Scriabin, Mozart, Mahler and Ravel were tiny, it is relevant that Scriabin seduced a fifteen-year-old schoolgirl,[17] Janáček and Bartók married pupils who were almost (although not quite) 'under age' under current British definitions, and Tchaikovsky's taste in boys would be suspect at a time when the press focuses so much on paedophilia. Sex, of varying sorts, plays such a part in most people's lives that it cannot be ignored. If, for some, this tarnishes the image, too bad; it makes the individual human.

The achievement of the composers makes me very humble. Put aside art, for a moment. Handel's enormous output includes more than 2,000 arias. The first page of Bach's manuscript of the St Matthew Passion contains less than twenty seconds of a work lasting two and a half hours. On that page alone are at least 450 individual notes written on 24 staves. This is just the first item in the work. Twenty pages later, there is a page of music which lasts about two seconds longer: it contains about 800 notes, countless sharps, flats, naturals, rests and words.

Imagine, if you can, the effect of the delay between conceiving the music in the ear and writing it down. Imagine the sheer physical effort needed to write this, to obtain and rule the paper, with none of our modern facilities such as electric light to lengthen the working day. The Bach-Gesellschaft edition amounts to around 50 volumes and that does not include Bach's compositions which never survived beyond his own lifetime. The piled up volumes of the Mozart edition on display in Salzburg measure over six feet high. Mozart also wrote voluminous correspondence. Grieg is said to have written more than 17,000 letters.[18]

Or, travel forward in time from Mozart and imagine Berlioz struggling to put on concerts in Paris in the 1830s 'with no telephone, no secretary, no publicity machine, no regular backers, no permanent orchestra and nobody to assemble the players but himself'.[19] How did the composers have the time to do it, or to relax? These were people I would love to have met. This, to a limited extent, is what I have tried to do.

One of the interesting aspects of getting to 'know' them has been to see where so many of them lived and worked. I sometimes have been asked why that has been necessary. I can find no better answer than to quote some words of the leading conductor Bruno Walter: 'I once saw at Stefan Zweig's Salzburg home Beethoven's wooden desk, to the eye a soberly uninteresting object without distinguishing features. But it caused a hardly bearable tumultuous onrush of imagination, pictures, memories, thoughts and sentiments.'[20]

It has been a privilege for me to visit places where the composers lived.

It seemed incredible to be high up in the old city of Bergamo and hold the original manuscript of Donizetti's *L'Elisir d'Amore*; and to sit in a Russian Conservatoire and hold an autograph book containing entries from most of the leading mid- to late-19th-century composers. It was thrilling to find the country house in Slovakia where Schubert stayed for two summer vacations, to find the farm in Moravia which Smetana's father wanted him to run, to see the miniature palace on the Ukrainian steppe where Liszt wooed his princess.

Although my bibliography shows considerable breadth of coverage, I cannot claim to have done any significant primary research. Even then, there is a vast corpus of literature about these composers and the world in which they lived; I can only claim to have touched the tip of the iceberg. I am totally indebted to my sources. I trust I have acknowledged them all.*

Sadly, so much of all that the composers knew and left behind has been destroyed. Joseph II, Holy Roman Emperor in the 18th century, said that war was a 'horrible thing ... much worse than I had imagined ... the ruin of so many innocent people'.[21] The cultural damage has also been appalling, whether in the Leipzig of Bach, Mendelssohn and Schumann; the Vienna of Haydn, Mozart, Beethoven, Schubert, Brahms, Mahler and Bruckner; the Warsaw of Chopin; the Weimar of Bach and Liszt; or the Dresden of Weber and Wagner. At this distance in time, it is difficult to comprehend why the asylum near Bonn in which Schumann died, or the monument over his grave, should have been wrecked in the Second World War; presumably there was some good military reason. There is a poignancy about the war memorials in the great church in Lübeck, a city that figures in the lives of Handel and Bach. There, one can see a memorial for the Germans killed in the Franco-Prussian War of 1870–71; also, the two bells which had sounded over the city for 434 and 273 years now lying shattered on the ground where they fell on the night before Palm Sunday 1942. The human and cultural loss stands as an awesome reminder that requiems for war are many-sided.

In the mid 1700s, the peer and poet Lord Cornbury asked Lady Mary Wortley Montagu, known for describing her travels through Europe, for her 'sincere opinion' of his poetry. She wrote: 'I was not so barbarous to tell

*Many of my sources have provided quotations which it would be foolish to try to paraphrase. Their attribution in the narrative would break the continuity. To find the source, readers should turn to the References.

him that his verses were extremely stupid (as God knows they were) … I contented myself with representing to him … that it was not the business of a man of quality to turn author, and that he should confine himself to the applause of his friends, and by no means venture on the press.'[22] I hope that even those of my friends who look askance at a claim by me to be a man of quality will concede that I have written something which readers will enjoy, and which will help them learn a bit more about the history of music, the people involved and the times they lived in. Readers may even feel that 'Plus ça change, plus c'est la même chose'?

PREFACE TO THE SECOND EDITION

This edition incorporates several minor improvements. Also, hopefully, it gives due credit to the much-derided Emperor Joseph for his patronage of Mozart, patronage which has recently been emphasised by Derek Beales in his magisterial second volume *Joseph II: Against the World 1780–1790* (Cambridge, 2009). To the emperor, the world should be eternally grateful; to the professor, I must add my own thanks.

Michael Steen, Mattingley

Prelude

The Italian and German Background

Allegro, ma non troppo, un poco maestoso. These tempo markings at the start of Beethoven's Ninth Symphony, and words such as *sonata*, *concerto* and *opera* remind us of Italy's enduring influence on music. Handel and Mozart both went there to gain experience. Bach and Haydn never visited Italy, but Haydn composed numerous Italian operas and Bach's first biographer dared to claim that he began to 'think musically' only after he had studied and transcribed some of Vivaldi's violin concertos.[1] So, if we wish to look at the Continental European setting for the late baroque period,* clearly it is in Italy that we should start. Besides, as Joseph Addison, journalist of *The Tatler* and *The Spectator*, observed around 1700, 'there is certainly no Place in the World, where a Man may travel with greater Pleasure and Advantage than in Italy'.[4]

Addison added that in Italy is 'the great School of Musick and Painting'.[5] Indeed, when he was there, Antonio Vivaldi was based in Venice, and Alessandro Scarlatti in Naples. Rome was home of Arcangelo Corelli, known as 'Il Bolognese' because he was trained in Bologna, which was famed for the quality of its instrumental music.[6] In Florence, the birthplace of opera,** Bartolomeo Cristofori had recently manufactured the first

* Handel and Bach are sometimes called late baroque composers. Baroque was a term of abuse (like 'gothic'), meaning a 'mis-shapen pearl'.[2] It ridiculed the way in which, in the visual arts, painters had no respect for beauty or tradition: art was now full of pathos and the sensational; the strict rules of the Greeks and Romans had been replaced. For music, the phrase is not particularly enlightening. Sometimes an analogy is drawn between the virtuoso coloratura singers and the gilded, splendidly ornate interiors of baroque churches; but there were also coloratura singers two centuries later. When music became mannered, as in the delicate works of François Couperin, it has been called rococo, by analogy with the parkland scenes of Antoine Watteau, where it never rains, and 'the life of the shepherds and shepherdesses seems to be a succession of minuets'.[3] Rococo is derived from the word rocaille, the artificial rockwork and pierced shellwork, seen in pavilions, pagodas and garden-houses.

** The first dramatic work with continuous music was Jacopo Peri's *Dafne*, composed just before 1600.[7]

piano; and in Cremona, about 50 miles from Milan, Antonio Stradivari was making violins. Handel and Bach were but teenagers.

Italy in the 17th century was very different from the nation we think of today. As a country, it did not exist. The peninsula was divided by the Papal States, the 'seamless garment of Christ',[8] ruled by the Pope. The States were a large area, and cut right across the middle, from the mouth of the River Po to a point some 80 miles south of Rome. Further to the south, the Spanish Habsburgs ruled in Sicily and in Naples, which was then Europe's fourth largest city, somewhat smaller than Paris. To the north, there were several small states. There were republics in Venice and Genoa. There were decaying duchies, such as Tuscany, Parma and Modena, which were ruled by relicts of the formidable families of a bygone age, the Medici, the Farnese and the d'Este. From Turin, then the capital of Piedmont, the Duke of Savoy ruled territories which reached up to Lake Geneva. The Spanish Habsburgs ruled in Milan.

The complicated components of Italy were relatively straightforward compared to the ragbag of territories over the Alps, which owed allegiance to the Viennese branch of the ubiquitous Habsburg family. The head of this German branch had a grandiloquent and confusing title, the 'Holy Roman Emperor'. It was in his 'Empire' that so many leading composers were born; there, to a great extent because of the Habsburgs, or despite them, several made their career. So, as well as looking briefly at the background in Venice, Rome, Florence and Naples, we must also visit Germany. We shall conclude this Prelude by looking at some aspects of the music of the period and particularly at the Italian Opera, which could be attended by those gentlemen like Addison when doing the Grand Tour, and which followed them back to London. We shall meet some musical celebrities including the castrati whose presence is, to us, such an extraordinary aspect of the time.

Venice

Our usual image of Italy in the 18th century is of Venice, the city of Canaletto. We picture St Mark's Square, the lagoon, gondoliers in bright clothes plying their trade along the Grand Canal near the Rialto Bridge. We think of the Carnival and the magnificent festivals, such as Ascension Day, when the ruler, the Doge, sailed out in his ornate barge to drop a ring into the sea, thereby signifying the marriage between the Republic and the

Adriatic. The reality was more reminiscent of Canaletto's picture of *The Stonemasons' Yard*, with its labouring stonemasons, its women at work, washing, spinning, shouting, and nursing a bawling, urinating child (see colour plate 1).[9] The odour from the canals, sewers of filth, was indescribable. It was easy to slip on the paving and fall in, because there were no railings on the bridges. Visitors were therefore advised to beware of the four Ps: 'Pietra bianca, Putana, Prete and Pantalone', which, translated, are 'a white stone, a whore, a priest, and the last P may denote either mountebanks and jugglers, or the nobility themselves, that being a nickname given them by the vulgar'.[10] Like most major cities at the time, Venice was full of beggars and prostitutes.

This 'great Town half floated by a Deluge'[11] had a magnificent musical tradition, especially at St Mark's. In the 16th century, Andrea Gabrieli had directed its music. His nephew Giovanni* had studied under the Flemish master Orlando di Lasso, and on his return was a magnet attracting others to come to Venice. Claudio Monteverdi, whose *Orfeo*, produced in 1607, was 'unquestionably the first masterpiece of operatic history',[13] spent the second half of his life working at St Mark's.** Venice became pre-eminent in opera.

Monteverdi died in 1643. The next Italian composer whose name most of us recognise today is that of Antonio Vivaldi, memorable for *The Four Seasons*. He was born in Venice in early 1678. He became the leading concerto composer of his time and boasted that he could compose a concerto

* Giovanni Gabrieli is credited with first coining the word *sonata* to warn performers that, as opposed to a *cantata*, the composition is intended for instrumentalists rather than singers. His publication in 1587 of concertos, as a tribute to his equally distinguished uncle, represents the first use of that term.[12]

** *Orfeo* was performed at the court of the Duke of Mantua, where Monteverdi at first worked and for whom he wrote many secular songs, called madrigals. His avant-garde style, including the use of prolonged dissonance, was publicly attacked by a theorist, thus providing an element of *succès de scandale*. Monteverdi was born on 15 May 1567 in Cremona. After the death of both his wife and his leading *prima donna*, and feeling undervalued at Mantua, he had a nervous breakdown. At this time, he wrote the *Vespers*. Soon after being dismissed from Mantua, he was appointed to Venice, where his services were well remunerated. In his last years he composed *L'Incoronazione di Poppea* and *Il Ritorno d'Ulisse in Patria*. Monteverdi's long life included surviving the Venice plague of 1630–31, fending off a highwayman and extricating his son from the Inquisition. He was also in the duke's retinue when he went to Hungary to fight the Turk, and to take the waters in Flanders.[14]

faster than it could be copied.* He composed 500 concertos[16] and also claimed to have composed 94 operas.[17]

Among the entertainments attended by those doing the Grand Tour were the weekend concerts at the Pietà, where Vivaldi first worked as a brilliant *maestro di violino* and as an ineffectual priest. The number of foundlings abandoned by their parents or by desperate unmarried mothers was one of the bleakest aspects of 18th-century society. Unwanted girls were placed in the Pietà which was one of the four *conservatorio* or orphanages. The Pietà specialised in music and also accepted girls who were not orphans. 'I assure you, there is no more delightful sight than a pretty young nun wearing a white robe and a bouquet of pomegranate flowers in her hair, leading an orchestra with incomparable grace and with the proper feeling', wrote one visitor.[18]

Despite its musical accomplishments, Venice and much of the rest of Italy were in decline. Venice was no longer a supreme maritime power, dominating the trade in the Eastern Mediterranean. It was not the first, nor the last, great power to become a mere resort for tourists.

The discovery of America and the sea-route to the Indies had caused this decay. Also, as Addison recorded, 'the Venetians are in continual Apprehensions from the Turk',[19] the vast Ottoman Empire ruled by the Sultan in Constantinople. In the opening storm scene of *Otello*, Verdi's Moor of Venice arrives in Cyprus proclaiming 'Esultate!' at a Turkish defeat.** In the middle of the 17th century, the Turk was still a significant threat: Venice's treasury was depleted by over 90 per cent as a consequence of a 24-year war about Crete, one of the Republic's oldest possessions.[21] The defeat was publicly presented as a success, in pictures of valour and heroism.

Rather than crushing Venice, the Turks headed north. In 1683, led by 'the scourge of mankind',[22] Grand Vizier Kara Mustapha, they ravaged a large area of Hungary and Austria, and committed dreadful atrocities. An

* Music was sold more often in the form of manuscript copy than as a printed edition. Since there was no copyright, the distribution of manuscript copies could be better controlled than that of printed ones; also manuscript was easier to read than printer's type, where the short notes were troublesome, since the beams were seldom continuous. The printing of chords was clumsy.[15]

** For the Italian, the Turks were defeated by Otello. The Englishman's explanation was slightly different: the Turkish fleet of possibly 200 galleys 'bearing up to Cyprus' came to grief because a 'desperate tempest hath so bang'd the Turks that their designment halts'.[20]

army of 200,000 men besieged Vienna for 60 days. Other Christian countries felt threatened. So, an alliance led by the King of Poland defeated the Grand Vizier, who was renowned for his cruelty and appetites: he possessed 1,500 concubines who were guarded by 700 black eunuchs.[23] But, no more; he was strangled; his head was chopped off and sent back to the Sultan in Constantinople.

The frontier between Christian and Infidel was in the Balkans, a short distance across the Adriatic from Venice. It was settled with Serbian Christian refugees,[24] bred to resist the Turk. Territory in the Balkans, particularly the area around Belgrade, changed hands frequently and ferociously.[25] One glorious Christian victory was celebrated by Vivaldi with a cantata, *Juditha triumphans.*[26] But the Turkish problem persisted and continued to destabilise Europe until, in 1922, the British finally picked up the last expense account of Sultan Mehmet VI, amounting to £484.7s.4d.[27] The legacy has remained.

The unpleasant realities of life in Venice, as in Italy generally, were relieved by Carnival, a bacchanalian relic of pagan times, meaning 'farewell to flesh meat'.[28] It ran for around eight weeks from the day after Epiphany, 7 January, until midnight on Shrove Tuesday, the day before the fasting season of Lent began. Carnival was a time for entertainment such as opera; there were races on the canals; bets could be placed at twenty different casinos. There were masked balls. Addison observed: 'These Disguises give occasion to abundance of Love-Adventures … and I question not but the secret History of a Carnival would make a Collection of very diverting Novels.'[29]

Rome

While those on the Grand Tour went to Venice for Carnival, amusement and sex, they went to Rome for culture. 'Whoever beholds the ruinous remains of ancient Rome may well say "Rome is no more"; but whoever turns his eyes towards the splendid palaces of new Rome, may justly say "Rome still flourishes".'[30] Grasping their classical texts, such as those by Horace, Virgil and Ovid, the visitors would gaze at a temple 'parcelled into several divisions and let out by the Apostolic chamber to graziers as an inclosure for their bullocks &c.', or at some granite object in the Forum, now used 'for a drinking trough for sheep and oxen'.[31] The visitors could languidly criticise the administration for allowing the inside of the decayed

Coliseum to be 'overrun with grass and weeds'.[32] They could admire St Peter's and moralise about the splendid palaces of the rich nobility, such as the Colonna and Barberini families, who were related to previous popes. They could speculate about the amount of Rome's pecuniary wealth contributed by Roman Catholics in far-off lands.

Rome, like Venice, was smelly and unpleasant. The water of the River Tiber was 'so thick and foul that it is not fit for horses to drink till it has been in flood two or three days'.[33] In the summer months, when the heat was insufferable, most people stayed indoors during daytime. There was a saying at the time: 'None but dogs, idiots and Frenchmen walk the streets in the day-time.'*[34]

To distract the masses, Rome also had its Carnival. This tended to be confined to the week before Lent. One could watch the horses being raced riderless along the Corso. A great prelate, such as Cardinal Ottoboni, would have operas performed in his private theatre, to which he allowed public access. The Popes took an ambivalent attitude to the lewder aspects of Carnival. One, at the end of the 16th century, raised gibbets and whipping posts to overawe his subjects. On the other hand, Pope Clement IX wrote librettos and authorised the building of a large theatre. In the 1720s, Benedict XIII, a reforming Pope, found it easiest to turn a blind eye to it all and shut himself up in a monastery for the season.[35]

Florence and Naples

In the magnificent city of Florence, there were fewer inhibitions: it was said of Cardinal Gian Carlo de Medici that 'if there was a beautiful woman to be had in Florence, he was determined to enjoy her favours at any time and cost'.[36] Although this might cast doubt on the proposition that 'the old Medici line was spent',[37] the descendants of Lorenzo the Magnificent, who had recently brought the scientist Galileo to Florence, were actually reaching the end of the road. The prim Grand Duke Cosimo III now aped King Louis XIV, with whom he had nothing in common, 'being arrogant, pretentious, extravagant and not very intelligent'.[38] The only bright spot was his homosexual son,[39] Ferdinando, a connoisseur and composer, whose patronage attracted several musicians to Florence, including Alessandro Scarlatti, his son Domenico and Handel.[40]

* More recently, Noel Coward expressed a similar view about Englishmen.

Naples was praised for its grandeur, 'the Beauty of its Pavement, the Regularity of its Buildings, the Magnificence of its Churches and Convents'.[41] There were few antiquities of any value to be seen because the Roman remains at Pompeii and Herculaneum had yet to be discovered, and anything good had been sent back to Spain.[42] But tourists could marvel at the Bay of Naples and go on an expedition up Vesuvius. They were advised to carry firearms in Naples: 'few cities are more dangerous after dark' and many of its people were 'trained up to rob and murder'.[43] The Neapolitans were anyway a disputatious lot, and the city was full of lawyers. Addison tells of a Pope asking a Neapolitan marquis 'to furnish him with thirty thousand Head of Swine'; the marquis answered 'that for his Swine, he could not spare them, but if his Holiness had occasion for thirty thousand Lawyers, he had them at his Service'.[44]

Among the unattractive aspects of Italy, none was more noticeable than the poverty. In Naples, it was exacerbated by high taxes, levied particularly regressively on the coarser meat eaten by the poor. Addison observed that the people in Parma and Modena 'would live in great Plenty amidst so rich and well cultivated a Soil, were not the Taxes and Impositions so very exorbitant; for the Courts are much too splendid and magnificent for the Territories that lie about them'.[45] He also said that 'this Desolation appears no where greater than in the Pope's Territories'.[46] He continued: 'His State is thin of Inhabitants, and a great Part of his Soil uncultivated. His subjects are wretchedly poor and idle, and have neither sufficient Manufactures nor Traffick to employ them.'[47] For a good Protestant and Englishman, this could readily be blamed on a Church which 'shuts up in Cloisters such a Multitude of young and lusty Beggars, who instead of increasing the common Stock by their Labour and Industry, lie as a dead Weight on their Fellow-Subjects, and consume the Charity that ought to support the Sickly, Old and Decrepid'.[48] Brigandage was obviously attributable to the many pilgrims, that is, foreigners.

Germany: the Holy Roman Empire and the Habsburgs

Whereas Italy may appear to have been fragmented, Germany was kaleidoscopic: it comprised around 360 individual states, 1,800, if all the estates of the Imperial Knights of the south-west are included.[49] This agglomeration was ruled by bishops and abbots, dukes, margraves and counts, and the like. Lands were often divided between sons, rather than being bequeathed to the eldest. Thus, by 1618, in the little state of Anhalt, itself hardly larger than Essex, there were four principalities,[50] one of which was Cöthen, where Bach would spend over five years of his life.

Germany was held together by the 'Holy Roman Empire', which goes back to the coronation of Charlemagne in Rome in 800 AD, and which became a national political entity around the time of the first millennium. Centuries later, it was to be described by the French writer and wit Voltaire as neither Holy, nor Roman, nor an Empire. By the 1600s, the Emperor* was elected by three spiritual princes, the Archbishops of Mainz, Cologne and Trier, together with four secular princes from Bohemia, the Palatinate, Brandenburg and Saxony.

The Elector of Bohemia, the area within a hundred miles radius of Prague, was a Habsburg. He was also Archduke of Austria and, in his capacity as King of Hungary, he had the right to exercise a veto in the conclave which chose the Pope.[51] The Elector of the Palatinate, based in Heidelberg, ruled territories on the upper reaches of the Rhine and Danube; the Elector of Brandenburg, whose chief city was Berlin, had recently inherited Prussia with its fine city of Königsberg (today, Kaliningrad); and the Elector of Saxony resided in Dresden. There were two 17th-century electoral creations, the Elector of Bavaria, in 1620, and the Elector of Hanover, in 1692.

The Empire came under the sway of the Habsburgs who controlled it by using already well-honed techniques, particularly the careful choice of appointments, a euphemism for cash, and the residual threat of force. The Habsburgs, whose family tree can be found on page 970, ran a kind of global family property concern, whose managers were focused on growth and on passing the group of subsidiaries and related companies to the next generation. The family had concluded some acquisitive marriages in the 15th century.** These brought in Burgundy with the Netherlands, Castile and Aragon in the Spanish peninsula, and Hungary. Naples and Granada were conquered, as were swathes of America.[53]

France was beyond the Habsburgs' control, regrettably. But they surrounded it, a factor which might be said to have affected the French psyche

* 'Salic' law did not permit a female to be elected.

** The Habsburg principle was expressed in the hexameter, 'Bella gerant alii, Tu, felix Austria, nube', (let others wage war, you, happy Austria, marry!).[52]

until today. The French Bourbons (whose family tree may be found on page 969) stood in the way of the Habsburgs getting from their southern territories in the Mediterranean to their northern territories. The Habsburgs had to go round the outside, hence the strategic importance of the Alpine route through the Grisons in Switzerland, the Rhineland and Bavaria. The French impediment then suited other countries, such as England, which was concerned with maintaining the delicate, fragile balance of power in Europe.

In 1556, the mighty Emperor Charles V retired to a monastery (for us, to re-emerge three centuries later in Verdi's opera *Don Carlos*). He divided his vast possessions.* The Netherlands, Italy and Spain went to his ascetic son Philip II, who had recently married, as his second wife, 'Bloody' Mary Tudor. He gave the Holy Roman Empire to his brother Ferdinand and his descendants.

Occasionally, family concerns like the Habsburgs face a crisis, as they did when Emperor Matthias died childless in 1619. This event unleashed religious differences and a struggle for power. The three other secular electors were by then Protestant, as was much of the nobility of Bohemia, while the Habsburgs were Catholic. The family backed one of their members, Ferdinand of Styria,** on the understanding that he would permit Spanish troops to pass through his lands on their way north. The Jesuit-educated Ferdinand refused to guarantee the arrangements for Protestant worship in Bohemia, and his legates were thrown out of the window of Prague castle, only to be saved almost miraculously by landing on the soft dung-heap outside. The Elector of the Palatinate was then given the crown of Bohemia by the Protestant rebels, but his forces were defeated by Ferdinand at the Battle of the White Mountain, near Prague. It was a bloody business: for a week after the battle, Ferdinand's troops were given licence to do what they wanted. At the behest of the Jesuits, there was then a massive expulsion of Protestants.†

* The portraits by Velasquez and other painters in the Habsburg courts show the protuberant jaw which Charles V and his father also bequeathed to so many descendants on both sides of their family.

** The area around Graz in Austria, later to be much loved by Schubert.

† Around this time, the Bohemian nobles who figure prominently in some later chapters, such as the Lobkowitz family, which supported Beethoven, were granted their lands.[54] The defeat at the White Mountain gave a body blow to Bohemian national identity, a matter felt acutely by Smetana and Dvořák, among other Czech composers in the 19th century.

The Thirty Years War

So began the Thirty Years War, one of the most devastating wars in the history of Germany.[55] Onto the stage stepped generals whom we would now regard as no better than thugs. There was Ferdinand's predatory henchman, a Jesuit-educated convert from Protestantism, Adalbert von Wallenstein. He was known for 'his ungovernable temper, his disregard for human life, his unsteady nerves, his immutable chastity, his faith in astrology'.[56] There was Gustavus Adolphus of Sweden, the golden king, the Lion of the North, laying waste as he went, in order that the land could not support another army. And there was the cruel Bernard, Duke of Saxe-Weimar, a part of Germany that was to figure prominently in the lives of Bach and Liszt.

There are stories of Ferdinand's troops slaughtering children in the cellars, throwing women out of the upper windows of the houses, and boiling a housewife in her own cauldron; stories of the Swedes sprinkling gunpowder on their prisoners and setting fire to their clothes; of the Bavarians shutting the gates of a town, firing the walls, training guns on the gates and shooting at the people as they tried to escape the flames. Both sides made it their business to burn everything they passed in hostile country. One of the worst atrocities was at Magdeburg, on the River Elbe: fire destroyed the city even though its burghers had wished to surrender it. Only about 5,000 of its 30,000 inhabitants survived, mostly women whom the victors had abducted to their camp.* With war came dreadful disease, particularly bubonic plague.[58]

The peace congress at Westphalia in 1648 at which the Thirty Years War was eventually concluded had been sitting for nearly a year when the delegates found that they were still unclear about the reasons for the war. When a treaty was finally agreed, Germany experienced the consequences of demobilisation: the Swedes, for example, had to demobilise nearly 100,000 soldiers, mainly Germans without hope for the future. On the Habsburg side, about 200,000 men and women were robbed of their sole means of existence. In some cases, the soldiers took to the hills and formed robber bands.[59]

* The numbers compare with contemporary horrors in, say, Ireland. At Wexford in October 1649, with Cromwellian soldiers out of control, it seems likely that 1,500 actual inhabitants were killed. At Drogheda, where Cromwell ordered the massacre, somewhere between 2,000 and 4,000 people died.[57]

While the religious wars lasted, music could not prosper. Heinrich Schütz, arguably the leading figure in 17th-century German music, had been recruited to Dresden after studying in Venice with Giovanni Gabrieli. He managed to escape to work in Denmark at various times during the war. Other distinguished composers whose lives were severely disrupted were Samuel Scheidt at Halle, and Johann Hermann Schein at St Thomas' Church in Leipzig. Leipzig was besieged six times and it was occupied four times by hostile troops. There was so little food for the choristers that they had to be sent home.[60]

The limited scope for culture in Germany at this time is perhaps illustrated by Heinrich Schütz's 'boss', Elector Johann Georg of Saxony, whose main form of relaxation was to carouse, box his dwarf's ears, gorge homely foods and swill beer. If necessary, he would pour the dregs of his tankard over a servant's head as a signal for more.[61]

The Habsburgs in Vienna, however, were cultured and musically talented; this boded well for the future. Emperor Ferdinand III, who ruled from 1637, in the second half of the Thirty Years War, wrote instrumental music and opera. His son, Emperor Leopold I, wrote an oratorio, and his *Sacrificio d'Abramo* established the form for the oratorio used in Holy Week. Both emperors are accorded the accolade of 'Master' by a 20th-century expert on baroque music.[62] Leopold's son Charles VI, it was said at the time, 'not only plays on several instruments, but is also a perfect master of the rules of composition'.[63] His family, possibly the most important patrons of music, were unlikely to be well-disposed towards 'taking any nonsense' from some 'upstart' like Mozart.[64]

Some Aspects of Music in the 'Late Baroque'

Even at the risk of considerable oversimplification, it is helpful to appreciate some of the features of the music of the late 17th century which distinguish it from earlier music. In Palestrina's *Missa Papae Marcelli*, written in the 1560s, or the *Miserere* of Gregorio Allegri, written half a century later, we hear equally balanced lines being played or sung in an ensemble: the rhythms are very subtle and the music seems almost to float. Later, in the works of Corelli and Vivaldi, there is more obvious propulsion: the bass propels the music forward and both treble and bass provide an increased sense of key.[65]

In this later period, we often hear separate groups of musicians, perhaps string bands or trumpets, sometimes located in different galleries, echoing each other, alternating, even competing with each other. It is said that the term concerto is derived from the Italian word 'concertare', to compete. By the time of the classical concerto, the virtuoso soloist and orchestra converse back and forth about the same themes.[66]

Also, in this new style, each composition or number, such as an aria, was intended to reflect a single, specific and usually somewhat exaggerated emotion or feeling. As well as being consistent with the pathos of the baroque visual arts, this mood provided a sense of unity without which the music risked becoming diffuse and unco-ordinated.* The single mood might portray, say, violent pain, deep sorrow, exuberant joy, passionate love or anger. Individual instruments were associated with certain moods: there were pompous horns, proud bassoons, harsh cornets, modest flutes, heroic kettledrums, flattering lutes, grumbling bass fiddles.[68]

Unity was also provided by the use of imitation, the repetition of a melody. Although this technique was not new, the imitation now became more structured, as in the fugue, in which the same 'subject' enters in each voice successively and is then developed further. Occasionally, composers used considerable ingenuity in writing 'canons' in which the same theme may perhaps be played lengthened, shortened, backwards or upside down, or backwards *and* upside down, by different voices or instruments all at the same time.[69] Bach was particularly skilled at exhausting all the imitative possibilities and usually, at the same time, producing a beautiful work.[70]

Contrast was often provided by combining different movements, perhaps slow and fast, together in one overall work. Dances would be assembled in one suite. The French suite was a free anthology; the German suite contained only three basic movements, the allemande, the courante and the sarabande, with the gigue appearing optionally.[71]

Many of these aspects are found in the instrumental works of Vivaldi. The virtuoso violin would alternate with repeats of similar material played by the string orchestra. He used this structure for the outer movements, recognisable for their drive and verve, and he placed a slow movement in

* The mood was known by the curious term 'affection'. The beauty of music and all art depends on both form and content. Coleridge, the English poet, praised Raphael's paintings for the 'balance, the perfect reconciliation, effected between the two conflicting principles of the *free life*, and of the confining *form*!' He continued: 'How entirely is the stiffness that would have resulted from the obvious regularity of the latter, fused and almost *volatilized* by the interpretation and electric flashes of the former.'[67]

the middle. He was himself perhaps the first virtuoso violinist, amazing his listeners with his skill, playing 'at unbelievable speed, astonishing everyone'.[72]

Vivaldi is best known to us by his concertos which he called *The Four Seasons*.* They are descriptive and portray something non-musical, such as a hunt, a storm, the murmuring of waves, the blowing of zephyrs, or sleep. Vivaldi preceded each of the four concertos by a short poem in which he described the images and events depicted.**[73]

Claudio Monteverdi, or perhaps Antonio Stradivari / Antonio Vivaldi

Italian Opera – the Business

Some might say that the development of opera was the most important achievement of the Italian composers of the time. Opera received considerable support from the authorities. It is 'the most easily assimilable of musical genres and can be enjoyed without the need for any great appreciation

* *The Four Seasons* are examples of the 'concerto grosso', in which the orchestra divided into the *tutti* on the one hand and the solo, or *concertino,* on the other. Vivaldi enlarged the solo passages until the violin became the dominant instrument of the whole ensemble; the *tutti* would often repeat a section on different scale steps of the home key, while in between, the virtuoso violin soared and modulated. The repeated sections were called *ritornellos,* or 'little returns'.

** Nineteenth-century composers, such as Liszt and Richard Strauss, went further and wrote 'programme' music which purports to develop a narrative.

of music'.[74] It was thus a suitable means of entertaining royalty and the aristocracy; he who pays the piper calls the tune.*

Opera was also politically correct, because tragedy taught virtues such as obedience, heroism, loyalty; comedy ridiculed misbehaviour. Indeed, the shape of the opera house reinforced the social structure. The theatre of St John Chrysostom, the largest in Venice, had five tiers of 35 boxes for the upper classes, the floor below being filled with the middle class and visitors. Venice was the first city to allow admission just on payment for a ticket. Gondoliers were admitted free of charge to the empty seats on the floor.[76]

By 1700, Venice had at least six opera houses; apparently 1,274 operas were performed there during the 18th century.[77] The ambitious court of Hanover, whose elector would eventually become King of England, even maintained a permanent box at the opera in Venice. The other main centre for opera was in Naples. Rome had a leading opera house until Pope Innocent XII, against the protestation of his cardinals, razed it in 1697.

The opera performance usually began at 7 pm and ended at 11 pm. In Venice, the audience was often attired in cloaks and masks, so there was usually no need to dress up. At Carnival or Ascension-time, many would go on afterwards to a masked ball.

A special charge was made for the printed libretto, which was sold with a little candle to enable the buyer to read it in the darkened theatre. The opera would usually begin with an energetic first movement, or overture, to notify the audience that the opera was about to start. But watching the performance was ancillary. 'Every lady's box is the scene of tea, cards, cavaliers, servants, lapdogs, abbés, scandal and assignations.'[78] Thus, there was no point in composing a work which demanded constant attention; it was better to write one during which two or three arias grabbed attention and stopped conversation. Some opera houses had other purposes. Naples' Teatro della Pace had to be closed in 1749 because it was deemed a threat to public morals.[79]

An opera house was usually leased by a nobleman to an impresario who took the considerable commercial risk of promoting operas and managing all the artistic and business aspects. The box-office receipts rarely covered more than 75 per cent of the outgoings, so the operating loss had to be

* This is consistent with Richard Strauss' observation in prosperous Berlin just before the First World War: concert audiences comprised connoisseurs, whereas opera audiences were pleasure seekers, 'nothing but bankers and shopkeepers'.[75]

financed by sales of merchandise.[80] An important source of revenue was the casino business run in the front of the house.

Whereas the composer was comparatively poorly paid, the impresario had the chance to make a fortune, as Vivaldi found and did, becoming vain and conceited in the process. Equally, the impresario could lose the lot, as Vivaldi also discovered when, laden with financial commitments to stage managers and others, he quite suddenly ceased to be popular. When he was spurned and his productions were cancelled or flopped, he blamed the disaster on his reputation for being a lapsed priest, and his reputed affair with his *prima donna*, Anna Girò, who had 'a very slim waist, beautiful eyes, lovely hair, a charming mouth'.[81] However, an equally probable cause of his downfall was the bane of the entertainment world, fashion. Vivaldi had been superseded in Italy by Johann Adolph Hasse, Il Sassone (the Saxon), husband of the international soprano Faustina Bordoni. Hasse commuted between Dresden, Naples and Vienna.

Italian Opera – The Content

What was Italian opera like at that time? The opera consisted of arias using expressive melody, known as baroque *bel canto*, which enabled the different qualities of the voice to be demonstrated and the mood and sentiment of the character to be expressed. Sometimes there was an instrumental section called Sinfonia which depicted a storm or provided a funeral march. Speech-like recitative, often very beautiful, was used to take the action forward. The chorus, an ensemble of soloists, was usually restricted to the finale.*

Sometimes sections were borrowed from other operas by the same composer, or other composers. And some operas, known as pasticcios, had each act or section composed by a different composer.

The story usually involved heroes drawn from Greek, Roman and Biblical history and legend, such as those portrayed by the French dramatists Corneille and Racine, and the Flemish painter Rubens.** The players

* The aria was usually in three parts, the first two followed by a more ornamented repetition of the first, known to us as 'Da Capo'. A familiar example is Handel's 'Why Do the Nations?' An example of *bel canto* is his 'I Know that my Redeemer Liveth'.

** These operas were known as *opera serie*. Comic opera, *opera buffa*, the text sometimes written by a dramatist such as Goldoni, became increasingly popular, and was much enjoyed by all classes. By the end of the 1740s, *opera buffa* and *opera serie* were equally popular.[82]

were often transported through the air by expensive machinery which was also essential for simulating apparitions, sea storms, conflagrations and miracles. The English dramatist John Gay jeered in his spoof, *The Beggar's Opera,* saying 'an opera must end happily … no matter how absurdly things are brought about'.[83] A '*deus ex machina*' would appear suddenly in the final act and bring about the happy conclusion.

The singers were desperate to grab the attention of the noisy audience. They did this by demonstrating virtuosity in three styles: the cantabile, the grazioso and the bravura. Thus, the music tended to reflect standard moods, such as rage, triumph, or jealousy, rather than the personality of the character being portrayed.[84]

The opera soon degenerated into something like a costume concert. The voices competed with flute or cornet in virtuosity; a scene would be ended with an 'exit aria', aimed more at creating an opportunity for applause than at unfolding the drama. If a singer did not approve of an aria, he or she simply substituted another from the repertory, regardless of its irrelevance. In the 1700s, a leading poet, Pietro Metastasio, and the slightly older Zeno, began to institute improvements. But Metastasio's dramas nevertheless still 'swarm with impossible heroes of magnanimity and renunciation … heroic sons and daughters; intriguers and conspirators, who are inevitably pardoned; with attempts at suicide as invariably frustrated'.[85]

Addison protested: 'The Poetry of 'em is generally so exquisitely ill, as the Musick is good. The Arguments are often taken from some celebrated Action of the ancient Greeks and Romans, which sometimes looks ridiculous enough, for who can endure to hear one of the rough old Romans squeaking thro' the Mouth of an Eunuch.'[86]

The Stars and the Castrati

The works were often specifically tailored to individual 'famous' singers, stars, who operated internationally. They were paid spectacular sums and had correspondingly inflated egos.[87] Once the particular star had moved on, the opera was shelved, because the work was no longer relevant or a commercial proposition.

The stars included Francesca Cuzzoni, Faustina Bordoni and the castrati Annibali, Bernacchi, Senesino and Farinelli. One traveller summed them up. 'Some of these Singers, however, seem to despise all œconomy', he wrote. 'And they get large Sums without much trouble, so they lavishly

CELEBRITIES: SOPRANOS AND CASTRATI IN HANDEL'S TIME

Faustina Bordoni (1) – this portrait of the Venetian soprano and wife of Hasse can be seen at the Handel House, London. The castrati such as 'Farinelli' (2), Giovanni Carestini (3) and 'Senesino' (4) aroused much ribaldry: 'Senesino' was once mistaken by Horace Walpole for a fat old woman. The relative size of the male and female is lampooned in the caricature (5) of Senesino with Francesca Cuzzoni, the soprano from Parma, and another castrato Gaetano Berenstadt. Their vanity was equal.

spend them by keeping elegant Tables, wearing rich Dresses, and other extravagances; but throw away still more by Gaming.'[88] Farinelli went on to become director of royal entertainments in Spain. Another castrato, Caffarelli, purchased a dukedom.[89]

To us, the castrati are one of the more surprising features of musical life in this period. Their volume, range and dexterity were considerable: Carestini could sing from the A below middle C, up to top A.[90] The timbre was described as 'clear and piercing as that of choir boys and much more powerful; they appear to sing an octave above the natural voice of women ... their voices have something dry and harsh, quite different from the youthful softness of women; but they are brilliant, light, full of sparkle.'[91] A modern author says that Farinelli's vocal cadenzas 'appear to have been lifted out of a violin concerto'.[92]

Poor parents, with a son aged between seven and twelve, could easily be tempted with the prospect of a son becoming a celebrity. A few castrati did, but most just became drudges in churches. The chances were poor. It has been estimated that about 4,000 boys were given the operation in Italy between 1600 and 1800.[93] The doctors in Bologna were particularly specialist in the technique. The child was usually drugged with opium and put in a hot bath; alternatively, he would be knocked out by compressing the carotid arteries. A bath of milk might be used to soften the organs. Then the spermatic cord was severed and the boy probably plunged into a bath of icy water to slow the bleeding. Unlike the experience of a eunuch in the Turkish harem, full removal does not seem to have been applied. The estimates of the rate of mortality from the operation are so wide that one cannot draw meaningful conclusions, other than to suggest that there was probably about an even chance of survival.[94]

Following a successful operation, the child might be sent to the castrati training school in Naples. Apart from having a high voice, the boy, as he grew up, would be distinguishable from a normal adolescent by having abnormally large breasts, hips, thighs and neck, and by having no Adam's apple and little body hair, except perhaps in the pubic area. They often grew very tall, and this made them well suited to act the part of a god or hero. Some apparently got married: they could ejaculate but they were infertile. We do not hear the wives' views on this aspect of their career.

One may well wonder why this mutilation was undertaken. The answer is that eunuchs were necessary to supply the Church's requirements. Small boys normally lacked the breath control, range and sustaining power, versatility and colour to perform the complex ornamentation required in church music in the last quarter of the 16th century.[95]

The obvious alternative, the adult female, was unavailable. The Church would not allow women to act or to sing in choirs:[96] since St Augustine's time, female theatrical performers and singers were associated with prostitution and loose living. In the chapter in the Bible which follows the much-read words about Love and Charity, St Paul wrote: 'Let the women keep silence in the churches. For it is not permitted unto them to speak; but let them be in subjection, as also saith the law.'[97] A recent Dean of Westminster resolved this embarrassment, even if selectively, by saying, candidly: 'St Paul got this quite wrong!'[98]

Although the Church generally condemned mutilation (except for criminals),[99] castration was sanctioned in a Papal Bull of Sixtus V as a practical expedient, especially if done for medical reasons, say 'following an attack by a wild boar' or 'with' the consent of the boy.[100]

The wide use of castrati in churches soon extended into opera. Thus the role of Orfeo, which we may associate with Kathleen Ferrier or Janet Baker, was actually written by Gluck for a castrato. It was first heard in Vienna in 1762. Mozart wrote parts for castrati;[101] and one was a regular visitor to the family home in Salzburg. For 300 years, until 1898, there were castrati in St Peter's in Rome.[102]

The use of castrati was interrupted when, in Napoleonic times, laws were enacted forbidding it. This coincided with a change of taste away from the highly stylised and formal Italian opera towards the more realistic dramatic works of Rossini and Meyerbeer. *Opera buffa*, about real people, also forced a return to the proper type of voice for the part. An early work of Meyerbeer, written in 1824, seems to have been the last opera with a castrato role.

The soprano-male concept endured in roles such as Cherubino in *The Marriage of Figaro*, Prince Orlovsky in *Die Fledermaus* and Octavian in *Der Rosenkavalier*. The prohibition on women singing in churches lasted well into the 19th century: the performance of Mozart's Requiem by solo sopranos at Chopin's funeral in Paris in 1849 needed special permission, which was only obtained with difficulty and some publicity.[103] Even as late as 1903, Pius X, by some standards an enlightened Pope, in an attempt to restore the dignity of church music, tried to ban women in the church choir, and the use of instruments and even the organ, although with little success.[104]

The castrati, the stars, such were the actors who performed Italian opera at the start of the 18th century, and such was the stage upon which they sang. It was a fragile existence. After Vivaldi, once so popular, fell from grace, he went to Vienna where he died in 1741 in complete obscurity and poverty. Hasse had superseded him in the top position.

Who was Hasse? He was idolised as 'the undisputed ruler of Italian opera'.[105] The wheel of fortune has turned again, and few of us would know a work by him. He was a contemporary of Handel and Bach, whose lives we shall now consider. For most musicians, including the castrati, Macbeth was surely right when he said:

> Life's but a walking shadow; a poor player,
> That struts and frets his hour upon the stage,
> And then is heard no more: it is a tale
> Told by an idiot, full of sound and fury,
> Signifying nothing.[106]

Only the reputation of a few has survived. Even for them, their reputation has, in many cases, had to be revived.

Johann Adolf Hasse

Handel

CHAPTER 1

One composer whose reputation is surely assured is Handel, whose corpulent, sombre figure towered over the musical scene in the 18th century.

Under the full-bottomed wig, behind Handel's dour image, there was, according to the 18th-century musical historian Dr Burney, a smile, 'bursting out of a black cloud … a sudden flash of intelligence, wit and good humour, beaming in his countenance, which I hardly ever saw in any other'.[1] Without this sunny side to his character, Handel surely could not have been successful in English showbusiness, at the pleasure gardens, or at the Italian opera for which he wrote 36 works and which occupied such a large part of his professional life.[2] Handel's shows offered a venue at which London's privileged classes could meet and his music provided a momentary means of escape from the city's poverty and sordidness.

It did not matter that Handel's audience did not understand what was being sung, even though this aspect contributed to the ultimate failure of Italian opera in London. One journalist observed that 'our great Grandchildren will be very curious to know the Reason why their Forefathers used to sit together like an audience of foreigners in their own Country, and to hear whole Plays acted before them in a Tongue which they did not understand'.[3] Handel's operatic ventures such as The Royal Academy prospered and his success enabled him to afford a house in Brook Street in modern Mayfair, where we shall go to see his *ménage*. We shall also travel abroad with him to recruit new stars.

When Handel's opera business ground to a halt, ever resilient, he developed a new product, the oratorio. This was less expensive to mount and thus far less risky financially. His best-known oratorio is surely *Messiah*, which was first performed in Dublin. In his final two decades, he continued to write oratorio and took an increasing interest in charitable works, but suffered very bad health and became blind. He was very wealthy when he died, aged 74.

Early Days in Germany and Italy

We must start with Handel's early career in Germany and Italy. He was born on 23 February 1685, in Halle, some twenty miles from Leipzig, at the centre of the European trade routes. Halle had a strong musical tradition: it had been the home of Samuel Scheidt, one of the trio of important Saxon composers in the early 17th century, Schütz, Scheidt and Schein.[4] In the wake of the devastating Thirty Years War of 1618–48, Halle was passed around. At first, it was administered under the Elector of Saxony; then it was detached and became a distant outpost of the Elector of Brandenburg-Prussia. The family of the previous Saxon ruler, who had resided in the city and underwritten its prosperity, moved the court to nearby Weissenfels. No wonder Halle was in decline.

Handel's elderly father (he was in his 60s when Handel was born) was the son of a coppersmith; like Monteverdi's father, he was both a barber and a surgeon, a combination customary before the 18th century. He had prospered under the Saxon duke, and he lived in a house in the centre of the city. With his first wife, he had six children; with the second, Handel's mother, the daughter of a local Lutheran pastor, he had four. Georg Friedrich was at first destined to become a lawyer, a job suitable for the upwardly mobile; but, during a family visit to his step-brother, who worked in Weissenfels, he was heard playing the organ by the duke, who persuaded his father to let him study music. Handel learnt the Italian and German musical styles by studying music primers and by relentless copying.[5] He was also taught by the organist at Halle's Marienkirche, a pleasant man who enjoyed knocking back a 'chearful glass'.[6]

Handel went to the university in Halle, founded a few years earlier in

1694, like other universities, in order to train the growing ranks of state officials.[7] The nearby 'reformed' cathedral, smaller than the Marienkirche, and today noticeably run down, needed an organist. It could not find an appropriate Calvinist to do the job, so it employed the Lutheran Handel. His emoluments included his lodgings, a few paces from where he was born, in the Moritzburg. This was a forbidding, moated and partly ruined fortress, which had been a residence of the Archbishop of Magdeburg, until he was ejected at the time of the war.[8]

Halle was not an ideal location for a highly ambitious young man to stay. It is said that the Elector of Brandenburg-Prussia offered to send Handel to study in Italy, but he shrewdly knew that this would be conditional on taking up a permanent post in Berlin, with little or no flexibility to get away. It seems that he was spotted at the ducal court by the director of the Hamburg Opera House, Reinhard Keiser. So, at the age of eighteen, Handel set out for the metropolis of Hamburg, 200 miles away. This was in the same year as Vivaldi joined the staff at the Pietà and Bach took up his first job in the small town of Arnstadt.

Hamburg, the leading North Sea port and financial centre, had largely avoided the depredations of the war and was booming (see colour plate 3).[9] It was positioned at the gateway to the inland, up the Elbe; it provided a short-cut to the Baltic through its sister city, Lübeck, some 40 miles overland. It was staunchly Lutheran. Consistent with its dignity, it had its own opera. Keiser, probably the first 'big-time' impresario, was a big-spending mass producer: he wrote seventeen operas during his four-year directorship.[10] Germans took the parts; and, as there were no castrati that far north, 'market women and dames of more than questionable reputation sang the female roles'.[11] The more pious and orthodox Protestant merchants were unhappy with this state of affairs, and resented the fact that Hamburg's secular music had eclipsed the sacred music at which it had excelled some 50 years before.[12]

The bustling city, with its population of over 70,000,[13] must have been a change for young Handel. We do not know whether he took as dim a view of the weather as Brahms did many years later: on one occasion, Brahms wrote that 'the weather is vile as only Hamburg weather can be, and is, on 360 days a year. It is difficult enough to hit the other five'.[14] During the winter three years before Handel arrived, the Elbe was so frozen that coaches could travel on the river.

Handel teamed up with Johann Mattheson, formerly a musical infant prodigy, the son of a tax collector. In many ways the two young men were very similar: both were ambitious, highly gifted and also intended originally for the legal profession. They went off to Lübeck's Marienkirche to compete in an audition to succeed the elderly and renowned organist, Buxtehude.[15] But neither liked the terms, which included marriage to his daughter. This was not a bad deal: frequently, it was the widow who came with a vacancy like this. As Bach also turned down the position two years later, Fräulein Buxtehude has always been assumed to have been plain. At least, she must have been of riper years, because eventually she found a widower 'ten years younger'. Her husband succeeded her father in 1707; he survived her and married again. This was a normal pattern at the time; Buxtehude himself had married his predecessor's daughter.[16]

The friendship between Handel and Mattheson could be tempestuous. They literally crossed swords: Handel only survived the duel because Mattheson's thrust struck a button on his coat.

Handel did well for himself. When he was twenty, his first opera *Almira* ran for twenty nights with Mattheson as the principal tenor. The opera *Nero* followed and then *Florindo*. Handel was able to send a remittance home to his mother. Experience in Italy would be the next step. He is said to have been invited to Florence by the musical Prince Ferdinando de Medici. The invitation was possibly transmitted by Prince Gian Gastone, the last of the Medici line, who was in Hamburg in 1703–4 escaping from his wife, a lady described as 'a surprising mound of bosom and belly – a female colossus that might well inflate a Turk but freeze a Florentine of Gian Gastone's refinement'.[17]

So, farewell to Mattheson, who went on to become conductor, composer, translator, publisher of the first German musical periodical, and a leading author of musical textbooks much in vogue at the time. He was an expert on the aesthetics of music and also compiled a Who's Who of around 150 composers.*[19]

* Mattheson stressed the importance of music expressing the 'Affection', that is, the emotion, the feeling, the mood. His views contrasted with those of Andreas Werckmeister, for whom music was a mathematical expression of Creation and of the spirit of God. It was to Werckmeister, the expert on the science of tuning instruments, that some say we owe the division of the octave into twelve equal intervals, 'equal temperament', instead of the natural intervals which are sounded if a reverberating string is shortened.[18] Mattheson's *Der Vollkommene Kapellmeister*, a compendium of information that every director of music should know about, was one of his most important works.

Going south, Handel needed to skirt round the armies fighting the war arising from the most recent succession crisis in the Habsburg family. In 1700, Carlos II, the Habsburg King of Spain, retarded and childless, died. The younger son of the Austrian branch, Archduke Charles, laid claim to the throne, as did Philip, Duke d'Anjou, the younger son of the Bourbon house of France. A union between France and Spain would have upset the balance of power in Europe, which of course troubled the English among others. So the War of the Spanish Succession followed. In August 1704,

Young Handel, a man of fashion, so different from Bach (see page 76)

Marlborough for the English and Prince Eugene for the Austrians defeated the French and the Bavarians in a resounding victory at Blenheim on the Danube in Bavaria. The Austrians went on to besiege Turin.*

Around this time, we find Handel, a fashionable young man, in Florence with his first Italian opera, *Rodrigo*. He then went to Rome, under the patronage of various cardinals. He played at the Marquess Ruspoli's regular Sunday afternoon salons, where Corelli led the orchestra. He also

* When Charles' brother died in 1711, the balance was upset again. Charles VI became Emperor; eventually Philip V was confirmed as King of Spain.

attended an exclusive circle of noblemen artists and musicians, who affected to live in an idyllic atmosphere, remote from reality, appropriately called the Arcadians.[20] He amazed his listeners with his skill at improvisation. A contest was held between Handel and Domenico Scarlatti. Handel won on the organ, whereas Domenico won at the harpsichord.

Since opera was then forbidden in Rome by papal decree,[21] oratorio was in vogue. Intended for concert performance, this differed from opera only in that the content was moral and devout, and used a narrator to take the action forward.* For Easter Sunday 1708, Handel wrote his first oratorio. The part of the Magdalen was sung by Margherita Durastanti, a regular performer at Ruspoli's, who joined Handel as a singer in London some years later. Her participation resulted in Marquess Ruspoli receiving a papal rebuke for allowing a woman to take part.[22]

Handel moved back and forth between the major centres, while war rumbled alarmingly around him. In Naples, he wrote a one-act *serenata*, *Aci, Galatea e Polifemo*; in Venice, his *Agrippina* was performed for 27 successive nights during the Carnival.

It is possible that Handel fell briefly in love with some Florentine lady at this time. Vittoria Tarquini, a leading singer known as La Bombace, who was already familiar with the bedrooms of the grand duke's palace, reputedly fell for him.**[23] Whatever happened, we do not know and there are differing views of Handel's inclinations; certainly there was every kind of experience to be had in Florence, as well as elsewhere.[25]

Being a Protestant, Handel had no lasting future in Italy. The famine and disease which followed the particularly cold winter of 1709, and the war, meant that Italy was in bad condition. Handel was by now 'a polished and fully equipped artist'[26] and the British ambassador tried to head-hunt him; however, he was persuaded instead to go to Hanover, by Prince Ernst, and by the elector's deputy master of the horse.

Hanover, the capital of an up-and-coming, ambitious German principality,

* The first extant oratorios are those of the Roman, Giacomo Carissimi, in the mid-1600s. They were used in Italy for many years, particularly as a form of religious propaganda, by the Congregation of the Oratory founded by St Phillip Neri.

** This could be risky. Only a century earlier, Duke Vincenzo Gonzaga of Mantua (for whom Monteverdi subsequently worked) attacked and ran through his tutor, the prodigiously brilliant Scottish disputant known as 'the Admirable Crichton', possibly because he had attracted the attentions of the duke's mistress.[24]

was in tune with Handel's own aspirations. Handel went as Kapellmeister, a job much broader than being in charge of chapel music; the Kapellmeister was director of the whole musical establishment (the 'Kapelle') of a court, and was expected to compose for it. Composers only created a separate role for themselves in the 19th century, when it was generally considered that it was better to leave the art of composition to 'men of genius'.[27]

Handel immediately negotiated a year's leave; so, with a sure eye for the 'Big Time', he left for London, visiting his mother in Halle on the way. London must have seemed ideal, half-way between the narrow Protestantism of northern Germany and the unacceptable Roman Catholicism of the south. For this visit, he stayed only eight months. We should consider some aspects of life in London during the five decades he would live there.

Eighteenth-century London

The year before Handel arrived, Sir Christopher Wren's St Paul's Cathedral had been completed at a cost of £1,167,474, paid for largely by the import duty on coal.[28] Sir Isaac Newton, the great scientist, was still at work. London, with its sounds of wheels rumbling on cobbles and cries from the street vendors, was well into a century of commercial and cultural prosperity: the country's population grew by 71 per cent over the century;[29] its merchant fleet more than doubled in tonnage between 1702 and 1776.[30]

Behind its superficial prosperity and elegance, London was overcrowded, squalid and full of beggars. People had fleas, lice and few teeth.[31] Most people defecated in nooks and crannies, or used public lavatories built over rivers such as the Fleet. For the more refined, with a small fee, the 'human lavatory' would provide a pail and extend its large cape as a screen.[32] Lavatory paper did not exist, the alternatives ranged from a sponge on a stick in a container of salt water, to stones, shells and bunches of herbs.

Curiously, in larger towns at the time, there were many more women than men, around five women for every four men.[33] In the country, there was little for women to do; men were more at home there, with their agricultural pursuits and, for the upper classes, 'the Chace, the Green and the Assemblée'.[34] Also, service in a town house was an attractive form of employment for the lower classes.

The political outlook was uncertain. Queen Anne, who was in her late 40s, had borne seventeen children; mostly still-born, none had survived. For Protestants, the throne was destined for Sophia,* a granddaughter of King James I. In return for helping the Habsburgs against the Turk, her husband, the scion of the Dukes of Brunswick, had recently been created Elector of Hanover. This was a highly prestigious position and, importantly, with access to many remunerative offices and perquisites.

Not surprisingly, Queen Anne disliked Hanoverians. Handel's position must have been difficult. Londoners also disliked foreigners, too many of whom were successful businessmen. In February 1710, following the trial of Dr Sacheverell, who had preached a sermon attacking the government for betraying the Church and state to dissenters (particularly non-Anglican Protestants), a rampaging mob, of perhaps 3,000, burnt and looted for several days. An enormous bonfire was held in Lincoln's Inn Fields.[35]

To maintain a semblance of law and order in this unruly society, the authorities dangled the noose. A person could be hanged for such offences as pickpocketing anything worth a shilling or over, for stealing a fish out of any river or pond, for impersonating the out-pensioners of Greenwich Hospital, or, as a bankrupt, for failing to attend for examination within 42 days.[36] Later in the century, the eighteen-year-old Mary Jones, who had been evicted after her husband was press-ganged 'on the alarm about the Falkland Islands',[37] was caught shoplifting a small piece of linen. She was hauled to the scaffold with one of her children sucking at her breast.**

Handel lived close to the Oxford Road along which the condemned were taken from Newgate, near the Old Bailey, to Tyburn, now Marble Arch. The roar of the vast crowd which attended the eight hanging days each year would have been clearly within earshot of his house. The condemned travelled in the same carts as their coffins, but were usually sedated with liquor. These festivals, which continued until 1783, involved much rioting, thieving and whoring.[39]

* Electress Sophia was the mother of George I, who eventually became king.

** Between 2.5 and 7 per cent of those indicted, and about 10 per cent of those tried for serious crime, were actually executed.[38] Rather more than half of those sentenced were reprieved. Prisoners were not given access to evidence or counsel, on the footing that the judge would look after their interests. 'Justice' was quick: even 100 years later, trials lasted on average only eight and a half minutes. Speed was important perhaps because gaol fever (typhus) easily spread from the dock across the courtroom floor.

Life was short: disease was rampant. Smallpox was 'always present, filling the churchyards with corpses, tormenting with constant fears all whom it had not yet stricken, leaving on those whose lives it spared the hideous traces of its power, turning the babe into a changeling at which the mother shuddered, and making the eyes and cheeks of the betrothed maiden objects of horror to the lover'.[40] A few years after Handel arrived, Lady Mary Wortley Montagu launched a campaign for smallpox inoculation, which she had seen practised in Turkey; there was a row, caused by those who claimed that such prevention was in defiance of God's will.

Statistically, for every four children baptised under the age of five, there were three burials. 'It was impossible and undesirable to make a heavy emotional investment in each one as it was born.'[41] But this did not prevent grief. Books such as Elizabeth Rowe's popular book *Friendship in Death: Twenty Letters from the Dead to the Living* encouraged the notion that much greater joy was to be had hereafter, thus softening the blow for the young when their parents died.[42]

For the ordinary person the anaesthetic to all this horror was gin, flavoured with cordials – as depicted in Hogarth's engraving 'Gin Lane'. In the London of 1725, there were over 6,000 places retailing spirits, not including the City and Surrey side of the river. A spoonful of gin also did as a medicine, even for babies, who usually died as a result.[43]

The more prosperous escaped by ferry* to Vauxhall Spring Garden or, later in the century, to Ranelagh. At Vauxhall, once you got through the hubbub at the landing stage, you could enter into the full blaze of the gardens, lit with a thousand lamps. The Gardens were in twelve acres, 'part laid out in delightful walks, bounded with high hedges and trees and paved with gravel; part exhibiting a wonderful assemblage of most picturesque and striking objects, pavilions, groves, grottos, lawns, temples and cascades; porticos, colonnades, and rotundas; adorned with pillars, statues and paintings; the whole illuminated with an infinite number of lamps, disposed in different figures of suns, stars and constellations; the place crowded with the gayest company ranging through those blissful shades, or supping in

* London Bridge was then the only bridge across the Thames, which teemed and bustled with river traffic. Westminster Bridge was opened in 1750, after which it became an object of interest as we can see from the London paintings of Canaletto. The Pool of London was full of sail. Ranelagh Gardens were next to the Royal Hospital, Chelsea, where the annual Flower Show is held today.

different lodges on cold collations, enlivened with mirth, freedom and good humour, and animated by an excellent band of music'. You could enjoy chicken, ham and beef: even if 'the thinness of the slices was proverbial'.[44]

In the centre, there was a 'temple for the musicians, which is encompassed all round with handsome seats, decorated with pleasant paintings, on subjects most happily adapted to the season, place and company'.[45] By the 1730s, there were two statues in Vauxhall, one of Apollo the God and one of Mr Handel, the Master of Musick. Neither apparently attended very regularly.[46]

The concert would begin at 5 or 6 pm and last until 9 or 10 pm. 'It consisted of sixteen pieces, songs alternating with sonatas and concertos ... an overture on the organ always formed part of the entertainment.'[47] The songs consisted chiefly of sentimental ballads and of a few more sprightly ditties, for example, Miss Stevenson's song 'You tell me I'm handsome. All this has been told me by twenty before; but, he that would win me must flatter me more'.[48]

Another form of enjoyment was the masquerade or masked ball. Participants came in disguise, fancy dress, and masked. Dancers passed from one person to another asking, 'Do you know me? Who are you?',[49] until partners were chosen and the unmasking took place; then one discovered whether the experience with one's partner would be pleasurable or horrifying. The notorious Elizabeth Chudleigh, later Duchess of Kingston and tried for bigamy, appeared at a masquerade in 1749 at Ranelagh 'as Iphigenia for the sacrifice, but so naked, the high priest might easily inspect the entrails of the victim'.[50]

English Music and Theatre

When Handel arrived in London in 1710, its musical world was facing a relatively lean time. More than 80 years before, the elderly William Byrd, Orlando Gibbons and the lutenist John Dowland had all died within the space of a few years. Then there was the Civil War. A brief and patchy revival after the Restoration in 1660 came to a halt with Purcell's premature death in 1695. Jeremiah Clarke, the composer of the Trumpet Voluntary, died twelve years later. Handel's English contemporaries were Croft, Crotch and then Greene, Arne and Boyce, among a host of lesser men. They were centred on St Paul's, Westminster Abbey and, especially, the Chapel Royal, which was based in Kensington Palace, where it provided Divine Service for the royal family. Outside the organ loft, only Arne,* who composed 'Rule Britannia', makes an impact today.

The focus of Handel's work at the time was court entertainment, the theatre. The aristocracy increasingly congregated in the capital and it has been suggested that 'the opera house represented the main venue, save the Houses of Parliament' where the élite met.[51] The opera was served mainly by foreign musicians, especially by Italians, even though local musicians had for some time composed incidental music for straight plays.

Theatre in London was tightly controlled under the Lord Chamberlain** so as to ensure that it was orderly and did not spread sedition.[52] For long, there had only been two theatres, both established under royal patent, one in Drury Lane, and the other at first in Lincoln's Inn Fields and subsequently in Covent Garden. The dramatist and architect Sir John Vanbrugh designed the King's House in the Haymarket, 'in the Second Stable Yard going up the Hay Market'.†[53] This opened in 1705 as the Queen's Theatre, operating by virtue of a special licence. It had a capacity a little less than 700, but if necessary could pack in over 900. It became the home of Italian opera and the large majority of Handel's operas and oratorios were premièred there.[54]

The stage was lit with candles held in brackets or hoops; patent lamps were only introduced at Drury Lane in 1785. The threat of fire was ever-present: all of those theatres mentioned were destroyed at some stage. Facilities were of course very limited: a French visitor said that 'the auditorium is small and in very poor taste; the stage is quite large with poor scenery. There is no amphitheatre, only a pit, with large curved benches right down to the orchestra, where the gentlemen and ladies are crowded uncomfortably together.' He added: 'the King has two boxes at the side of the stage, and he came twice with the Queen. The Princesses were opposite, in another box. Everyone applauds when the King arrives, and cheers when they leave.'[55]

The behaviour in the theatres was very rough: the habit of spitting and throwing objects into the parterre made it desirable to take seats well out

* Arne seems to have disliked Handel, although one of Handel's favourite singers was Susanna Cibber, Arne's sister.

** He was also responsible for looking after the queen's swans.

† Vanbrugh was architect of Blenheim Palace and Castle Howard near York. The origin of the present London theatres is complex: the Theatre Royal, Haymarket descends from the Little Theatre in the Haymarket, founded in 1720. Her Majesty's descends from Vanbrugh's theatre.

into the middle. At one of Signora de l'Epine's appearances a servant of Mrs Tofts, a rival star, was taken into custody after hissing and throwing oranges at her.[56]

The attitude of 18th-century theatre-goers generally is satirised by the novelist Fanny Burney, later in the century. She describes a fop saying: 'one merely comes to meet one's friends, and shew that one's alive. I confess I seldom listen to the players: one has so much to do, in looking about, and finding out one's acquaintance, that, really, one has no time to mind the stage. Pray, – what was the play tonight?'[57]

Early Days in England

By the time Handel arrived in London, Italian opera was firmly established there. The invasion began some years before: in 1693, an Italian lady was giving concerts at York Buildings every Tuesday and in Cornhill every Thursday. In the summer season of 1703, Signora de l'Epine gave a series of 'positively last' appearances.[58] Despite this, she remained in England for many years thereafter. Being the best singers, the Italians squeezed out the English; soon, it became the rule that no other language than Italian was acceptable.[59] The audience could obtain the text in dual language word-books.

Handel's Italian opera *Rinaldo* was a hit, even though some of the complex stage effects did not work quite as planned: during the aria 'Little birds', sparrows were let loose causing some inconvenience to the audience below. After this, Handel went back to Hanover, but soon obtained leave for a second visit to London, provided he returned in a reasonable time. He stayed first in Barnes, writing *Il Pastor Fido*. He then mainly lived at Burlington House as part of the establishment of the Earl of Burlington.

Handel would meet his musical friends at the Queen's Arms tavern near St Paul's. He also became friendly with the queen's physician, Dr Arbuthnot, and may have slipped useful information about her health back to Hanover: the elector knew he had to move very quickly indeed to stake his claim, once the queen died. Through Arbuthnot, Handel would have become acquainted with many journalists* and writers blossoming in

* The first daily paper, a kind of fact sheet, was printed in 1702, although there had been weekly gazettes and political journals for some time: the press as an engine of public opinion took off in the following year under Daniel Defoe, whose *The Review* was usually issued three times a week. (*Robinson Crusoe* was later; it began to be published in 1719.) By 1782, eighteen newspapers were being published in London; in France there were 169 papers by 1789.[60]

London at the time, including John Gay the dramatist and Jonathan Swift, the author of *Gulliver's Travels* and shortly to become dean of St Patrick's Cathedral in Dublin. Also he would have known Alexander Pope, the poet, 'a delicate, deformed stooping creature only four feet six inches tall';[61] and the Lübeck-born portrait painter, Sir Godfrey Kneller, a mass producer of portraits.

Handel wrote an ode for the queen's birthday and a Te Deum and Jubilate for the service in St Paul's to celebrate the Treaty of Utrecht, which ended the War of the Spanish Succession, and gave Gibraltar, Canada and Minorca to Britain. Queen Anne gave him a generous pension of £200 per annum.* She died on 1 August 1714. Legend has it that Handel, having absconded from Hanover, was in trouble with her successor. But this is unlikely: his Te Deum was played at the Chapel Royal on the first Sunday after King George arrived. The story about *The Water Music*, that he tried to regain the king's favour by serenading him, uninvited, is untrue: the music was written later.[63] Besides, water music serenading revellers on the Thames was not unusual: Handel's friend Mrs Delany** subsequently described an evening picnic during which her party were rowed from Whitehall Stairs up to Richmond, 'and were entertained all the time with very good musick in another barge. The concert was composed of three hautboys, two bassoons, flute, allemagne, and young Grenoc's trumpt ... we ate some cold meat and fruit, and there was a variety of wines'.[64]

When King George arrived, the scene was very unsettled, all over the country. There were riots, mobs supporting either the pro-Hanoverian Whigs or the pro-Stuart (Jacobite) Tories.† The new monarch and his

* The top salary for an English actor was £150 per annum. £50 per annum was the minimum income at which one could aspire to be middle class. A shopkeeper might perhaps earn £1 per week, a skilled worker marginally more. £20 per annum, around the income of a lowly manual worker and his wife, was necessary for mere subsistence; a ticket to the gallery at the opera (five shillings) would represent around two-thirds of their weekly income. Inflation only picked up in the third quarter of the century. (A guinea was one pound and one shilling, i.e. £ 1.05.)[62]

** Born Mary Granville, she was then the widow of the bedraggled, florid Mr Pendarves, MP for Launceston, whom she was forced to marry. Twenty years after his death, she married Dr Delany, Dean of Downpatrick.

† The Jacobites were the supporters of 'The Old Pretender', the putative son of the ousted Roman Catholic King James II, reputed 'at birth' to have been smuggled into the queen's bed in a warming pan. Italian musicians, being Roman Catholic, tended to be suspected as Jacobites.[65]

government were unpopular. In Scotland, there was a rising by supporters of The Old Pretender. This coincided with the death of Louis XIV, as a result of which French support was not forthcoming; besides, the rebels lacked leadership and determination. The Old Pretender was 'a man anyway better fitted to reinforce failure than to turn it into success, his only effect on the morale of his followers was to lower it'.[66] So the immediate threat fizzled out, although it remained ever present.

Handel, however, prospered sufficiently to invest £500 in the South Sea Company, although this was soon drawn down to pay for a visit to his family. In mid-summer 1716, he recruited Johann Christoph Schmidt as his treasurer and copyist. On returning to London, his operas *Rinaldo* and *Amadigi* were revived, and he was employed, for £600 per annum, to teach music to the princesses and the king's daughter by the Duchess of Kendal.

Life at court in London soon settled down. George I disliked crowds and formality; he lived quietly with his dull duchess, known disrespectfully as the Maypole, and two Turkish attendants, Mehemet and Mustapha.*[68] Indeed, performances of Italian opera ceased completely in 1716–17. In contrast, the Prince and Princess of Wales lived 'in style' at Hampton Court. Soon, the king was forced to be more public, to the advantage of the musicians.

During the lull in the fortunes of Italian opera, Handel came under the patronage of the Earl of Carnarvon, subsequently created Duke of Chandos, who had made a fortune while Paymaster of the Army during Marlborough's campaigns. Cannons, his stately home near Edgware, was described by Defoe as the most magnificent palace in England.[69] It appears that Handel was the equivalent of Kapellmeister, the employee in charge of the musical establishment, although this is not clear: his role may have been more like that of a resident visiting composer.[70] He composed eleven anthems, the 'Chandos' anthems, for the earl's private chapel. The masque (in effect, a short opera) *Acis and Galatea* was performed there in May 1718.

The 'Royal Academy of Music'

Handel returned to London, largely to promote his own opera. It was recognised, then as now, that a successful opera house cannot cover its

* Some years earlier, the king's wife had been locked up following a scandal; her lover, the handsome and fast-living Count von Königsmarck, was assassinated. Her name was not allowed to be mentioned.[67]

enormous outlays by box office receipts, and so he sought a government grant to establish an opera company. The king promised £1,000, for five years, and around 50 others subscribed £200 per share.[71] The company, called the 'Royal Academy of Music', made a profit in the first year, and even declared a dividend. Then as now, however, 'the opera enjoyed enormous social glamour, but the economics did not really make sense'.[72] It has been calculated that the gross loss could be of the order of 25 per cent on a box-office turnover of about £11,000 per annum, for a season of 50 nights. The singers accounted for nearly 50 per cent of the cost.[73]

Handel went at first to Dresden to recruit singers, making a stop-over in Halle. At first, he only managed to engage Durastanti, whom he had met in Rome. Later, the Italian alto castrato Senesino was engaged at £3,000. This seemingly spectacular remuneration may not have been too far from the 'going rate': de l'Epine was said to have amassed a fortune of 10,000 guineas in perhaps four years.[74]

Opera was at the height of fashion. Gay wrote to Swift: 'Everybody is grown now as great a judge of music, as they were in your time of poetry, and folks, that could not distinguish one tune from another, now daily dispute about the different styles of Handel, Bononcini*, and Attilio … Senesino is daily voted to be the greatest man that ever lived.'[76]

In the 1720s, Handel composed a new opera on average almost every nine months. They were dashed off in a hurry. As was customary, he plagiarised other composers' work and swapped numbers between works.[77] It was relatively easy to swap music around in Italian opera where the characters, however virtuous or nasty and of whatever age, status or origin, sang much the same sort of music. In those days, before Gluck 'reformed' opera, most composers gave comparatively little thought to the dramatic meaning of an opera as a whole. Modern experts, however, eloquently distinguish the artistic achievement and effectiveness of many of Handel's operas and rightly refer to their potential to provide 'powerful theatrical experiences' for a modern audience.[78]

* Giovanni Bononcini was Handel's main rival. An Italian Roman Catholic, he came into disrepute when he was linked with the Jacobites at the time of an abortive plot inspired by Bishop Atterbury of Rochester. He was ultimately seen off, at the end of the 1720s, when he fraudulently claimed to have written a madrigal for the Academy of Ancient Musick: he had actually copied a work by another composer. Plagiarising others' work was quite usual, but Bononcini must have gone 'over the top' in this case.[75]

The singers 'competed strenuously with each other for the favour of the arbiters of taste and fashion'.[79] As in Italy, the public went to the opera to hear an exhibition of vocal prowess; the scenery, costume and stage effects were incidental. The audience 'demanded at all costs that it should not be bored', and composers satisfied the public. Their predicament was well put in a Dublin paper some years later when it announced that Mr Arne, 'intends between the Acts of his Serenatas, Operas, and other Musical Performances, to intermix Comic Interludes ... intended to give Relief to that grave Attention, necessary to be kept up in Serious Performances'.[80]

Handel had to write arias which built upon the strengths of his singers; Faustina Bordoni excelled in agility, and Francesca Cuzzoni's* strength was in the *cantabile*. He also had to manage them and to deal with their tantrums. Writing early in the 20th century, one commentator noted: 'the musical world has never seen a race of men and women whose outlook was so entirely bounded by the horizon of their own little vanities as the great vocal stars of the early eighteenth century; solo singers have indeed been, as a rule, up to a time that is within living memory, artistically the lowest class of musicians, but the full-blown tyrannously selfish conceit of the *prima donna* and *prio uomo* of Handel's day was something quite unique'.[83] There was such rivalry that when the supporters of one applauded, the supporters of the other began to hiss and cat-call. This behaviour took place even in the presence of the Princess of Wales.

Senesino was dismissed from Dresden when he refused to sing an aria which he did not like, and tore up another singer's music. In London, when Handel was rehearsing his opera *Ottone*, Cuzzoni, who had been engaged for 2,000 guineas, refused to sing. So Handel threatened to drop her out of the window. On another occasion, when a tenor threatened to jump on the harpsichord and smash it, Handel coolly replied, 'Let me know when you will do that and I will advertise it: for I am sure more people will come to see you jump than hear you sing.'[84]

Handel was short-tempered and intolerant.[85] He fell out with the most eminent and gifted English composer, Maurice Greene, it would seem because he was also a friend of Bononcini. Once Handel shouted at Burney for singing a wrong note. When Burney nervously pointed out that there

* It was said of Cuzzoni that 'her acting was somewhat cold, and her figure was not too favourable for the theatre'.[81] She was subsequently in and out of the debtors' prison. Her penurious old age was spent in Bologna sewing buttons.[82]

was some mistake in the copying, Handel, 'with the greatest good humour and humility, said, "I pec your barton – I am a very odd tog: – maishter Schmitt is to plame."'[86]

Many of the subscribers to Handel's Royal Academy were hit by the South Sea bubble, the widespread financial speculation which crashed in 1720. The South Sea Company, which owned substantial monopoly rights, had concentrated its activities on the provision of financial services, buying at a discount the IOUs given to sailors in lieu of pay earned during the War of the Spanish Succession. As it prospered, its stock value increased by around 1,000 per cent.

This encouraged speculation generally, whereupon 'any impudent impostor, while the delirium was at its height, needed only to hire a room at some coffee house, or other house, near the Exchange, for a few hours and open a subscription book for something relative to commerce, manufactures, plantations, or some supposed invention newly hatched out of his brain'.[87] By the time of the crash, there were 185 bubbles, including, for example, Item No 86: 'Pinder's invention for the more effectual making of an Equinoctial Instrument for the Convenience of Ladies' Hoop Petticoats'; there were other fanciful items as well as more normal items, No 176: 'Bleaching of Hair' or No 23: 'Wild's Insurance against Highwaymen'.[88] 'Persons of rank of both sexes were deeply engaged in these bubbles ... the gentlemen going to the taverns and coffee houses to meet their brokers and the ladies to their milliners' and haberdashers' shops for the like purpose.'[89]

The South Sea Company foolishly caused the bubbles to burst by applying to the courts to enforce the trading monopoly it possessed over all these crazy activities. The bubbles, and it as well, crashed. The primary cause of the collapse of the Academy was, however, the cost of the imported singers. It was so extravagant that one Frenchman wrote, in 1728, 'When I left London people were saying that it would break the opera'.[90] But before continuing with Handel's increasingly fraught opera activities, we should explore in more detail the backdrop to his life in London.

The West End

The theatres in which Handel operated were in what we might call the red light district, and full of 'thieving shops for the reception of highwaymen, bullies, common assassins and affidavit men'. Many courts and lanes around about were unsafe. The writer John Gay wrote in 1717:

O may thy virtue guard thee thro' the roads
Of Drury's mazy courts and dark abodes
The harlots guileful paths who nightly stand
Where Catherine Street descends into the Strand.[91]

There was a thriving trade in sex: both in London and on the Continent, a vast amount of erotic literature was written.*[92] Even in the previous century, the diarist Samuel Pepys bought a book called *L'Ecole des Filles*, 'a lewd book, but what doth me no wrong to read for information's sake';[93] and '*passo tempos* for the amusements of single ladies' were imported from Italy and first became available in the 1660s. By 1750, there was a fortnightly pornographic magazine.

Even among 'respectable' people, pre-marital intercourse was by no means unknown. Charles Burney met his first wife at one of the dances organised by his brother, a dancing master; he married her very shortly after their baby was born in 1749.[94] They were both in their early 20s. Similarly, at the end of the century, the composer Samuel Wesley only married his wife when she became pregnant: he subsequently left her for a teenage servant on whom he sired S.S. Wesley, the leading composer of Victorian church music.[95]

Handel never married. Of itself, this may not be significant. In 1773, the *Lady's Magazine* complained that nowadays 'the men marry with reluctance, sometimes very late, a great many are never married at all'. The explanation it offered was the 'fear of expense, now rendered insupportable by women's passion for caprice and extravagance'.[96] Companionship and sexual satisfaction could be obtained, if one wanted them, far more cheaply with a lower-class mistress. Condoms – 'clumsy affairs, made of sheep gut … secured to the wearer at the base with a red ribbon'[97] – could be obtained at The Sign of the Cross in St James' Street. Their purpose was

* In 1741, fashionable ladies at Vauxhall had to be seen reading Samuel Richardson's excellent novel *Pamela*, a series of letters chronicling, in considerable and thus compelling detail, the lubricious experiences of a servant who resists her employer's attempts to seduce her. He eventually marries her, thus giving cause for a colossal argument with his sister. Fielding, better known to us for the lascivious *Tom Jones*, lampooned this in *Joseph Andrews*, a book about a chaste servant who has to run away because his female employer attempts to seduce him.

largely protective (against venereal disease) rather than contraceptive. They could be useful in extra-marital affairs: but Boswell, Dr Johnson's biographer, was prepared to risk the cost of having to support a baby, rather than use a contraceptive; provided, that is, he was confident about the woman's health.

With the theatres and opera at the centre of this somewhat sleazy world, Handel must have been easily attracted to escape to one of the new housing developments being constructed to the west. They were reasonably accessible. Getting home after work could be tricky: London was the worst-lit capital in Europe and walking was dangerous: the 'Linkmen' employed to help pedestrians avoid potholes and dunghills had a bad reputation for taking their customers down dark alleys, and robbing them. Handel probably used the hackney coach or the modern invention, the sedan chair, provided the chair-men were not harvesting or hop-picking.* Not being a particularly social person, he did not want to keep his own carriage.[99]

25 Lower Brook Street

Handel took an annual lease** on 25 Lower Brook Street, a relatively modest house near Cavendish, Hanover and Grosvenor Squares and New Bond Street. One of his neighbours was an MP, another a colonel, another would be the talented Mrs Delany, who over ten years created nearly 1,000 pictures of plants assembled from tiny mosaics of pieces of paper.[101]

Handel's house had its main reception room on the upper floor above the dusty ground floor. The bedroom was on the floor above. The museum at 25 Brook Street displays rooms which have been carefully reconstructed by the Handel House Trust. They are remarkably small, considering that there is reliable evidence that he held rehearsals in the house, to which a select number of patrons were invited.

Being a prosperous district, street lighting might have been provided by lamps with cotton wicks, burning whale oil.† They were suspended over

* The public chairs could be an insanitary means of transport, the last occupant being unknown; they were used to transport fever patients to the workhouse. Besides, the chairs were easily overturned.[98]

** A foreign national could not own property such as a long lease. Handel's rent in 1742 was £50 per annum.[100]

† A pilot gas system was started in 1792, and by 1842 most streets were gas-lit. The Lyceum theatre was lit with gas in 1807.

the entrance to the houses or from an occasional lamp hung from a wall or pole and protected by a glass bowl. Water was piped in from Islington or York Buildings through lead or oak pipes by one of the privately run water companies, but nobody would have dreamt of drinking it. The privy was in the garden.*[102]

Handel might have furnished the house from one of the furniture makers established in St Martin's Lane or Long Acre. French Huguenot craftsmen had fled there in 1685 after Louis XIV had revoked the Edict of Nantes which had guaranteed their religious rights. Mahogany imported from the West Indies was increasingly supplanting walnut as the favourite wood, although Handel seems to have preferred the latter; the activities of the East India Company also promoted a taste for oriental-style lacquering and ceramics.[103]

No doubt Handel had a sizeable domestic staff who slept in the attic. Moderately well-to-do gentry employed six or seven servants. A friend of Horace Walpole, the writer and probably the youngest son of the former prime minister, estimated that in order to live comfortably one needed three menservants and four women. Many domestic servants were from the country, domestic service being the largest employer, apart from agriculture.[104]

Handel would have selected his cook carefully: he particularly enjoyed his food, and might have made purchases from Fortnum and Mason, which was founded in 1707. He would have drunk tea, coffee or chocolate for breakfast, with some whigs (rich bread rolls) and buttered toast and cake; for dinner, he might have had 'a fine piece of beef roasted, a currant pond pudding, a currant suet pudding and butter pudding cake'.[105] This would be washed down with some Portuguese or Spanish wine, French wines being rare because of the wars with France. Pies were filled with beefsteak, giblets, pigeon, duck; or fruit, currants, or just butter. Improved transport would have enabled him to eat sea fish or regional specialities such as Scotch salmon, Newcastle salted haddock, and cheeses from Cheddar, Gloucester, Cheshire and Stilton.

When visiting the aristocracy, he might have enjoyed grapes, peaches and even pineapples from their hothouses; he could have had ice cream made with ice stored in ice-houses. His main diet would have been roast

* The chamber pot was the most popular device in the home and remained so well into the 18th century.

beef, puddings and pies, with lashings of butter on everything, all consumed with far too much wine. He might have had a few olives from the Mediterranean, particularly as in Germany they were recommended as an antidote to alcohol and to counter drunkenness.

The food would possibly be cooked in a modern brick stove heated with baskets of charcoal, a considerable improvement on the open grate, but still not as manageable as the iron ovens with grates underneath, 'the perpetual oven', which were gradually introduced during the century.

It seems that meal times slipped back in the middle of the century. Breakfast, which had been at half past eight, was at ten or eleven. Other meals slipped a couple of hours: dinner, which had been at two, might be at four; supper might be at ten or eleven, rather than at eight. Heavy drinking and gambling late into the night was normal. The more refined played whist,* which Horace Walpole said had 'spread an opium over the nation'.[107]

In 1717, Twining opened the first Teashop for Ladies, to match the coffee shops for men. Tea could cost ten shillings a pound, or sometimes as much as three guineas. Tea was so expensive that the servants might sell used tea-leaves to be re-coloured and sold on. It was therefore locked in the caddy.[108]

Handel's wardrobe would have contained his knee-breeches, stockings, buckled shoes, a waistcoat and a full coat reaching down to the knees, flared at the bottom into a wide arc. In it also would have been his white, soft linen shirts with lace at cuffs and neck. Somewhere, he would have placed his three-cornered hat which he either wore or carried, and the sword which, being a gentleman, he would have worn. Handel relaxed at home in an Indian nightgown or banyan; his wig was removed, his closely cropped hair being covered by an embroidered cap. By the end of his life, his large wig, costing around £30, a temptation and amusement for pickpockets, would have been unfashionable: fashionable people tied their wigs at the back with ribbons, and ultimately enclosed them at the back in a silk bag.[109] He would have had several snuffboxes. Snuff was taken, and in quantities, by men of consequence, whereas smoking was considered appropriate to labourers and sailors.[110]

* As the most popular game, whist superseded quadrille, which in turn had superseded ombre. Another popular game was loo (lanterloo), in which the knave of clubs is the highest trump.[106]

The women around him would have been noticeable for their absurdly high headdresses, creations 'like Steeple Bow or Grantham Spire',[111] supported by a wire frame, covered with lace and ribbons. Their faces were painted with compounds of white lead, rice and flour, with washes of quicksilver boiled in water, and with bismuth. These habits caused some amusement and much satire; in one play the maid observes: 'Your ladyship has frowned a little too rashly, madam. There are some cracks discernible in the white varnish.'[112] Some of the more fashionable of both sexes would have worn patches on the face, pieces of velvet or silk in all sorts of shapes, including dogs, horses, foxes and even jumping fleas: one placed close to a man's eye was an indication of love.

The woman's shape was that of 'an equilateral triangle resting securely on a wide base'.[113] Around 1730, hooped petticoats, some enormous, were reintroduced, and persisted until the French Revolution. Two women could not walk abreast in the narrow streets or occupy a carriage together in comfort. Women were tightly laced up at the back,* forcing the breasts upwards and outwards. There was even a concern that too much tight lacing of 'wasp-waisted ladies'[115] could cause women to swoon and 'Mean while, an Am'rous Youth may steal a kiss, Or snatch, unfelt, perhaps a greater Bliss'.[116]

Underneath, there were no underclothes, at best a shift. The limbs were naked except for the stockings which reached to just above the knee and were fastened by garters just below it. *The Ladies' Dictionary* of 1694 observed that 'as for their looser parts, them they let loose ... Their breasts lay open like two fair apples'.**[117] Out of doors, ladies wore a long scarlet coat called the cardinal, as worn by Little Red Riding Hood. This was frowned upon by some as it could conceal stolen goods or a pregnancy.[118]

Ladies would carry a fan, like the snuff box, an essential accessory. In mid-century, the possession of a monkey or a green parrot was a sign of luxurious refinement and those who could afford it – Mrs Delany was one – purchased a little black boy as a personal attendant. Dressed in bright clothes, he would be intended to match the toilette, while contrasting with

* The French did it from the front. Lace from Flanders was very costly and much of it was smuggled in. The philosopher Bishop Berkeley asked 'Whether it be true that Two Millions are yearly expended by England in foreign Lace and Linnen?'[114]

** The bra came only in the early 20th century.

the white skin, of his mistress.* A woman of fashion was surrounded from the moment she got out of bed by a crowd of admirers, dressmakers, furniture vendors, musicians, dancing masters and dependents.**[120]

Of course, our image of the Georgian period is this superficially elegant one. It is easy to overlook the fact that the dirt and filth was such that a person of Handel's status would have had to have his shoes cleaned at least four or five times a day. The daughters of George II† had to be provided with a new pair of shoes each week, at six shillings a pair.[121]

A New Company and Travels Abroad

As we have seen, the finances of the Italian opera were in a dire state. Then, in January 1728, there was the first performance, at the theatre in Lincoln's Inn Fields, of *The Beggar's Opera*. The libretto, written by John Gay, was set to a pastiche of popular melodies by the husband of Signora de l'Epine, John Christopher Pepusch.[122] He was a Prussian residing in England, who had already composed several masques and operas. Its enormous success led to four other ballad-operas in 1728 and eleven in 1729,[123] in all around 50 successors over the next seven years; one, *The Devil to Pay*, was even performed in Berlin.[124]

The Beggar's Opera ridiculed the pomposity of Italian grand opera, for which it provided an alternative 'which the English middle classes could enjoy without feeling out of their depth'.[125] It was also an attack on the sleazy ministry of Sir Robert Walpole: it suggested that his dealings were indistinguishable from those of thieves and highwaymen. 'There is in it such a labefactation [weakening] of all principles as may be injurious to morality', complained Dr Johnson, the author of the *Dictionary of the English Language*.[126] Gay's sequel, *Polly*, was banned on political grounds the following year. As a consequence, the Stage Licensing Act of 1737 was passed, giving the Lord Chamberlain the official role of censor.††

* In Richardson's novel *Pamela*, a little Negro boy, of about ten years old, is sent from Jamaica as a present to wait upon a small child. 'But he was taken ill of the Small-pox, and died in a Month after he was landed.'[119]

** The scene in the first act of Richard Strauss' *Der Rosenkavalier* is reasonably authentic.

† George II was crowned in 1727 to the accompaniment of Handel's 'Zadok the Priest'.

††The law and practice was consolidated in the 1843 Act, which gave the Lord Chamberlain the power to forbid any play 'whenever he shall be of the opinion that it is fitting for the preservation of good manners, decorum, or the public peace so to do'. Opera was within the definition, but until 1865 ballet was excluded. The Lord Chamberlain retained the censorship role until 1968.

At the end of the 1727–8 season, the company went bankrupt and disbanded. Handel seems to have survived this financially, and he started a new Academy in December 1729. He prospered; his venture was presumably underwritten by patrons. When his mother died in 1730, the family could afford for the funeral sermon to be specially printed.[127]

Handel's energy must have been boundless. He went to Bologna, Rome and Venice in order to recruit stars. Travel to Italy was exhausting and time consuming: London to Dover took two days; the traveller dined at Rochester and slept at Canterbury. Throughout the latter years of the 18th century, the speed was about 5–6 mph; there were ruts and potholes everywhere, and the passenger was much shaken. Turnpike Trusts had taken over the maintenance of various roads and charged a fee for usage; but this attempt at privatisation had made little difference.[128]

Assuming one was avoiding Paris, the route to Italy was through St Omer and Rheims to Dijon, a journey lasting four to five days. The traveller sailed down the Saône from Chalon to Lyon, 'a disagreeable but cheap trip'[129] through wonderful wine country. From there, the journey was by road to the French border with Savoy, then a separate and down-at-heel country. This frontier was just beyond Pont de Beauvoisin, about twenty miles to the west of Chambéry. It was 80 miles further, behind what is now the Trois Vallées ski region, to the Alpine pass crossing to Turin. As the carriage climbed gently, with increasingly dramatic scenery, past Les Forts de l'Esseillon guarding the valley, the gorge narrowing, snow capped mountains rising above the mists, even the most hardened of travellers would be apprehensive about what lay ahead.

Until Napoleonic times, crossing the Alps was a challenge. Much of the journey up to the plateau on the Mont Cenis was done on the back of the stubborn mule, the carriage having been left behind at the bottom. At the top, horses or mules would pull the traveller over the plateau on a sledge. Then the descent to Novarese was very steep with precipices and cascades. The mule could not be relied upon, so quarrelsome chairmen carried the traveller down in a low-backed straw chair. 'A corpulent Englishman … was obliged to make use of twelve chairmen'. (See colour plate 11.)[130]

Coming back the other way, there was one particularly difficult place where travellers 'ascended ladders placed on the face of the rock, to the height of one hundred feet; then they entered a cavern and after climbing more than eighty feet through it, regained the day, in a deep cleft of the mountain'. 'This was an undertaking dangerous to the unskillful, and often impracticable, for the cavern was the embouchère of the waters from the ravine above.'[131] But the descent was not so steep as on the Piedmontese side, so sledges were used to go downhill. 'These sledges hold only two, the traveller and the guide who sits forward steering with a stick. On each side he has an iron chain; which he drops like an anchor, either to slacken the course of the sledges, or to stop it ... Some travellers, especially the English and the Germans, are so delighted with this expeditious descent, that they ride up again on the mule ... for the enjoyment of that pleasure a second time.'[132]

The alternative was to get to Nice, considerably further by land, and then take a boat rowed by ten or twelve 'stout' mariners. This took two and a half days provided the gale was not fresh; with a favourable wind, it could be done in fourteen hours. And, of course, there were the many hazards of the sea. We do not know how Handel did the journey. Lady Mary Wortley Montagu used the Mont Cenis route.

Some years later, it took Burney seventeen days to travel from Paris to Naples. Rome to Naples in 1730 took five days, via Monte-Cassino. There was much bureaucracy to cope with along the way. Between Rome and Naples, a passport was needed which could be obtained quite easily from the imperial minister or the cardinal-agent; and on return to Rome another passport had to be obtained from the viceroy.[133] Customs in France and the Italian states were particularly troublesome, particularly in respect of books: Burney's were detained for a fortnight before he could recover them. He was later told that if a single book was found in his *sac de nuit*, its whole contents would be forfeited.[134]

Competition

We return to London. Soon, Handel faced further competition from a new opera company, the 'Opera of the Nobility' who set up in the new theatre built in Covent Garden. This company brought in Nicola Porpora, court composer at Dresden, to be resident composer. Some of Handel's singers absconded to Porpora, possibly out of pique because Handel was hard to work with. Also, Handel's own works were put on by his competitors. The rivalry was intense. Porpora staged *Arianna in Nasso*; Handel responded with *Arianna in Creta* with a new castrato, Carestini; the following year, he put on the virtuoso French dancer Salle who appeared like a Greek statue 'without a pannier skirt or bodice'.[135]

The opera world reflected some of the tensions in the royal family. Handel was sponsored by the Princess Royal, Princess Anne; the Opera of the Nobility was sponsored by the cello-playing Frederick Prince of Wales, the father of George III. However, the prince redirected his support to Handel after he composed an anthem for the prince's wedding.[136] Princess Anne remarked that she 'expected in a little while to see half the House of Lords playing in the orchestra in their robes and coronets'.[137]

There were, however, changes afoot in public taste which did not bode well for the future of Italian opera. While the aristocrats on the Grand Tour in Europe might collect Canalettos and Poussins and import 'shiploads of dead Christs, Madonnas and Holy Families',[138] the landed squirearchs and growing middle class of England, people like the Burneys, looked for a plainer down-to-earth style: we can see it from the portraits set in parkland, with horses or ships as background.

There was a growing freedom of thought and speech, a sense of scepticism and tolerance, to an extent which surprised foreigners. These trends were illustrated in William Hogarth's engravings of *The Beggar's Opera* in 1730, and in his engravings of *The Harlot's Progress*. In 1738, the philosopher David Hume published his *Treatise on Human Nature*. Around this time, John Wesley, an Anglican clergyman, who had been a missionary in Georgia, began the Methodist movement. Soon, he and George Whitefield were travelling the countryside, preaching. Wesley travelled 224,000 miles and preached over 40,000 sermons.[139] He was joined by his brother Charles, for whose hymn, 'Rejoice the Lord is King', Handel wrote a tune. It is hard to imagine Hogarth, Hume, the Wesleys, or John Howard who agitated for prison reform, standing beside the stylised gods and heroes of the opera.

Social, not musical, reasons were the cause of the downfall of Italian opera in London.[140] The nobility could not support one, let alone two, opera companies; and the middle class was not interested in an aristocratic activity nor in being entertained in a foreign language. By 1736, the Opera of the Nobility was in financial difficulty and closed down. Handel may have known that he had them on the run: he ran a particularly heavy season, a repertory of twelve works of which five were new to the London audience. But he is reputed to have lost £9,000 and almost bankrupted himself in the process. The business stresses and strains were such that his health gave way, and he had to go to Aix for the vapours, where 'his sweats were profuse beyond what well can be imagined'.[141]

He was amazingly resilient and bounced back. He returned in the autumn and staged *Faramondo* and *Xerxes* (which includes the ode to a tree, known as the Largo). He seems to have given up promoting operas as an entrepreneur, and was now just composing them. *Deidamia*, early in 1741, was his last opera.

Handel's Oratorios

Handel hit on the idea of running oratorios on Wednesdays and Fridays in Lent, a season during which stage performance was forbidden. As we have seen, he had come across oratorios in Rome, and also in his earlier days in Protestant Hamburg, where his friend Mattheson developed the practice of using women singers from the opera house in the oratorios, a custom permissible in a Protestant environment. Oratorio became virtually indistinguishable from opera, except for the presence of a narrator. Today, *Theodora* is presented as one. The secular oratorio *Semele*, which includes the well-known 'Where e'er you walk', is based on an opera libretto by the playwright Congreve.*[143]

Handel's first masterpiece oratorio was *Athalia*, which was first performed in the Sheldonian Theatre in Oxford in 1733, when he was offered an honorary degree. There was then a pause in writing oratorio until *Saul* in 1738–9.

After this, Handel rolled them off. It took only about a month for him to write one. Many are now forgotten by other than specialist audiences: for example, *Belshazzar*, *Joshua* and *Jephtha*. Some excerpts are still very popular, such as 'Let the Bright Seraphim' from *Samson*. Not all were successful at the time: *Israel in Egypt* was a flop, perhaps because 1739–40 was the very cold winter in which the Thames froze over, and attendance levels were poor.

Handel devoted the summer of 1741 to the composition of *Messiah* and *Samson*. *Messiah*, which was more meditative in style, was drafted between mid-August and mid-September; and *Samson* was drafted by 29 October. Two days later, Handel attended the first night of the new opera

* Most of Handel's oratorios are forceful choral dramas based on Old Testament themes: 'monumental characters in a monumental setting'.[142] Some of the others, such as *L'Allegro* and *Alexander's Feast*, are choral cantatas about allegorical subjects. Performances often included organ concertos played between the acts. The organ concerto is an innovation attributed to Handel.

company in the King's Theatre. Three weeks later, he was in Dublin at the invitation of the Lord Lieutenant.

Swift, on his way to Dublin, has described the coach journey to Chester, which left Aldersgate at 3 am:

> Roused from sound sleep – thrice called – at length I rise
> Yawning, stretch out my arm, half close my eyes.
> By steps and lanthorn enter the machine
> And take my place – how cordially – between
> Two aged matrons of excessive bulk
> To mend the matter, too, of meaner folk.
> While in like mood, jammed in on t'other side
> A bullying captain and a fair one ride
> Foolish as fair, and in whose lap a boy –
> Our plague eternal, but her only joy ...
> When soon, by every hillock, rut and stone,
> Into each other's face by turns we're thrown.
> This granddam scolds, that coughs, the captain swears,
> The fair one screams and has a thousand fears; ...
> Sweet company! Next time, I do protest, sir,
> I'd walk to Dublin ere I'd ride to Chester.[144]

Because the wind was blowing in the wrong direction, Handel waited at Holyhead for five days, only arriving at Dublin on 21 November.

Dublin boasted an active cultural life with theatre companies and concert societies. Many of London's best performers found it good business to do an occasional season there. It was then a gracious city of elegant town houses, although Dr Johnson, no fan of Ireland, and no music lover, would write: 'Dublin, though a place much worse than London, is not so bad as Iceland.'[145]

Mrs Delany, who had married an Irish clergyman, gives an indication of genteel life in Dublin. The social round, including enormous meals, centred on Dublin Castle, the seat of government, and her first duty was to call on the viceroy there.[146]

Music was not really appreciated. Mrs Delany mentioned a concert which she attended with the Lady Lieutenant: 'The great ladies and their attendant peers were so impatient to get to their cards and to their dancing, that a message was sent to [the performer] to "shorten the musical entertainment".'[147] The Irish were energetic dancers; there might be 36 dances, and the event might begin at seven, and go on all night, with supper at twelve.*

On 10 December 1741, Handel's 'Utrecht' Te Deum and Jubilate and a Coronation anthem were performed at St Andrew's Church. After this, Handel set up in Abbey Street soliciting subscriptions for his six concerts. This series was a considerable success and, before the first six were over, he launched an invitation for a second six. A new venue, Mr Neale's Great Musick Hall in Fishamble Street, up the hill from the River Liffey, had opened the previous October. Jonathan Swift, Dean of St Patrick's Cathedral, prohibited his choirmen from performing there, possibly because it was of doubtful respectability, or perhaps because it was so close to the rival Christ Church Cathedral.

On Friday 9 April 1742, *Messiah* was publicly rehearsed and was first performed the following Tuesday, a day later than originally planned. This was a charity performance 'for the Relief of the prisoners in the several gaols and for the support of Mercers Hospital in Stephen Street and of the charitable Infirmary on the Inns Quay'. It was attended by 700 against a capacity in the hall of 600. The audience were asked to come without swords or hooped dresses, in order to maximise the seating. It was a great success. For the 3 June performance, the audience was reassured that the top panes of glass would be removed from the windows, because of the hot weather.[149]

Poor Health, Charitable Works and Decline

Handel left Dublin on 13 August with plans for a further season in twelve months' time. When *Messiah* was put on in London in February 1743, the reception was less enthusiastic. A number of people felt that concert performances of religious works were inappropriate. But there is no doubt that Handel had started a new trend.

Handel then became ill again, perhaps from the poor food as a result of bad weather conditions in Britain during 1743–5. Horace Walpole said: 'We are likely at last to have no Opera next year: Handel has had a palsy, and can't compose.'[150] But Handel recovered quickly and he wrote *Semele*. He annoyed the Prince of Wales and the nobility by refusing to compose for the Middlesex opera company; but it collapsed, and he moved back

* She also said that 'the poverty of the people as I have passed through the country has made my heart ache'.[148]

into the King's Theatre with an oratorio series. This was not a success: *Hercules*,* which opened on 3 November, conflicted with a performance at the Drury Lane of *Richard III*, starring David Garrick, who had made his début as an actor in this role a couple of years before. As a result, Handel had to offer back three quarters of the subscription money. He salvaged something by revivals in Lent of *Samson*, *Saul* and *Joseph*.

Also around this time he composed an anthem and Te Deum to celebrate Dettingen in June 1743, a battle in the War of the Austrian Succession which arose from a succession crisis faced by the Habsburgs in 1740, about which we shall hear more in connection with Haydn. Dettingen is noteworthy because it was there that King George II became the last King of England to lead his troops in battle. He commanded, very bravely, disregarding the risk of death or capture, an army of 40,000 men against 60,000 French.[152]

In June 1745, Handel went to the home of the Earl of Gainsborough in Rutland, and then visited Scarborough and Dorset. In the autumn of 1745, he was ill again, 'a good deal disordered in the head'.[153] As a Hanoverian in London, he may have felt particularly insecure. Many years earlier, in 1715, there had been the abortive rising in Scotland, immediately after the accession of George I; and there was a Spanish-inspired one in 1719. But now, in February 1744, there was something altogether more threatening. At Dunkirk, Marshal Maurice de Saxe,** one of the leading military commanders of this period, had begun to embark 10,000 troops to invade England. There was a violent storm and Saxe called it off. Bonnie Prince Charlie, son of the 'Old Pretender', decided to proceed without foreign support, landing at Eriskay in the Outer Hebrides, off the west coast of Scotland, at the end of July 1745. He and his small army of 5,000 men reached Derby, 125 miles from London, in December. An invasion from France was imminent.

London panicked. The novelist Henry Fielding observed: 'When the Highlanders by a most incredible march got between the Duke's army and the metropolis, they struck terror into it scarce to be credited.'[154] Business came to a standstill; shops shut. There was a run on the Bank of England

* *Hercules*, 'which has a strong claim to be the finest of all eighteenth-century dramatic works to an English text with continuous music',[151] is a personal tragedy of jealousy.

** He will reappear later as the great-grandfather of Chopin's lover, George Sand.

which, to gain precious time, paid out in sixpences which were deliberately heated to such a pitch as to be too hot to handle.[155] Soldiers were posted in the main squares. The guards camped at Finchley Common and Highgate. King George, it was said, had given orders for his yachts, laden with his more precious personal belongings, to be kept anchored off Tower Quay, ready to sail at any moment. But Prince Charles' army was hopelessly extended and had not picked up the support it had hoped for. It was trapped between three Hanoverian armies totalling 300,000 men. His generals advised retreat. 'Of few moments in history can it more justly be said that there is a tide in the affairs of men than of the Jacobite decision to turn back from Derby.' Back they went, and after the disastrous defeat at Culloden, a most scenic battlefield a few miles from Inverness, Prince Charles escaped, eventually settling in Rome, where he took to playing the French horn in between shooting and much drinking; he died in 1788. Handel celebrated the 'Forty-Five' with 'Stand round, my brave boys' and the Occasional Oratorio. After Culloden, he wrote *Judas Maccabeus*, a tribute to the Duke of Cumberland, the victor.[156]

Also celebrating the achievement of 'Butcher' Cumberland was Christoph Willibald Gluck, who wrote an opera which compared the duke's victory to that of Jupiter over the rebellious giants.[157] Gluck, the son of a forester on the Lobkowitz family estates near Mannheim, was then in London struggling to write Italian opera for the King's Theatre. More successful, however, were his performances on Bohemian musical glasses, 26 glasses filled with varying amounts of water; these were played either by stroking them with the fingers or by using two sticks.[158] He seems to have been friendly with Handel, who took a dim view of his professional abilities, saying that he 'knows no more of contrapunto as mein cock'.[159]

In summer 1746, as an alternative to visiting the lions on display in the Tower, or the madhouse at Bedlam,* it was interesting to take a boat down the Thames to see the hulks where the Jacobite prisoners were confined.[160] There had been so many that it was arranged that they should draw lots, with one in every twenty standing trial for his life, the others being transported overseas. At the end of July, the hanging, drawing and quartering began on Kennington Common. This attracted immense crowds, with people queuing from the evening before in order to get a good view.[161] At

* Recently, the Imperial War Museum.

the same time, in Westminster Hall, the trial of some of the leading Jacobite Lords took place before their 136 peers, resplendent in coronets and ermine. There were special boxes for the Prince and Princess of Wales, the Duke of Cumberland and foreign ambassadors and ministers. A cockney woman shrieked at Lord Lovat as he left the hall, 'You'll get that nasty head of yours chopped off, you ugly old Scotch dog', to which he replied, 'I believe I shall, you ugly old English bitch'.[162] At his execution, one of the stands collapsed with the weight of the people who had come to see him die, killing many. This was the sort of competition the entertainment industry could do without.

By January 1747, Handel seemed to have recovered from his sickness and Lord Shaftesbury wrote: 'Mr handel call'd on me tother day. He is now in perfect health and I really think grown young again. There is a most absurd and ridiculous opera going forward at present and, as it is not likely to meet with success, he is delighted.'[163]

Handel was doing well out of his Lenten oratorio, which involved far less effort than staging risky opera. Tickets for the pit and boxes seem to have been priced at around the same level as opera; the gallery was cheaper. The cost base was far lower. *Solomon*, from which is taken the 'Arrival of the Queen of Sheba', was composed at this time.[164]

Handel was an excellent businessman. He is said to have made £2,000 out of the Oxford visit. After the performances of *Judas* he deposited £600 in his bank account and at the end of the 1748 season he bought himself £4,500 worth of annuities. A year later he was depositing £8,000 in his bank account and buying a Rembrandt for £39.18s. He would visit the city 'for the purpose of investing his money … under the direction of Mr Gael Morris, a broker of the first eminence, who he used to meet and confer with at Garraway's or Batson's coffee-house'.[165]

He went to take the waters at spas such as Aix-la-Chapelle, Bath, Cheltenham, and at Tunbridge Wells where 'all ranks are mingled together without any discrimination … so long as you behave with that decorum which is ever necessary in genteel company'.[166] And he probably stayed with Princess Anne, now wife of the Dutch King, at Het Loo. During one of his Continental trips, he was injured when his coach overturned between Haarlem and The Hague.

He wrote the *Fireworks Music* to celebrate the Peace of Aix which concluded the War of the Austrian Succession. An audience of more than 12,000 attended the public rehearsal at Vauxhall. Although one end of the building at Green Park went on fire, the celebration seems to have been a success.*[167]

In his later years, Handel became conspicuously pious, regularly attending St George's Church in Hanover Square, near his house. He also took a particular interest at this stage in The Hospital for the Maintenance and Education of Exposed and Deserted Young Children, which had been recently founded by Thomas Coram.

Because of the large number of foundlings, the demand for this charity was considerable, and it received much support. At one stage, between 1756 and 1760, the Hospital opened its doors to all who brought children to it. But the gates were besieged; almost 15,000 children were taken in.**[168] Only 30 per cent of these lived to be apprenticed. Concerts were held in aid of the charity, one attended by the Prince and Princess of Wales. A concert including *Messiah* became an annual event.† For the 1750 concert, the hospital authorities had made careful preparations, but were overwhelmed by the size of the audience. One thousand people managed to cram into the chapel. Handel had to do a further repeat performance and nearly 2,000 tickets were sold for the two performances. The Foundling Hospital suggested that, by Act of Parliament, they should receive proprietary rights over *Messiah*; the minutes, however, record that when the idea was put to the composer 'the same did not seem agreeable to Mr Handel for the present'.[170]

For Handel, spring 1749 had been unusually busy, and there was a visit to Bath in the summer. He completed *Theodora* in 1749, but it was not a success, perhaps because of rumours of earthquakes. Handel said: 'The Jews will not come to it (as to Judas) because it is a Christian story; and the Ladies will not come, because it is a virtuous one.'[171] On New Year's Day, 1751, he began a new organ concerto and in February, he started work on *Jephtha*, for the forthcoming season. On 13 February, when he was setting the words 'all hid from mortal sight', in the chorus 'How Dark, O Lord,

* Fire was always a threat in London, particularly in the docks area: in 1716, 150 houses were burnt down in Wapping and a further 70 in 1725.

** Enlightened parishes, such as St James' Westminster, boarded out their children with carefully selected cottagers on Wimbledon Common.

† These performances led to the monster performances put on in Westminster Abbey. From 1859, they were held in Crystal Palace, the last one being in 1926. At the 1883 one, 4,500 performers entertained 88,000 people.[169]

are Thy Decrees', the sight in his left eye deteriorated suddenly.[172] Still, he was soon at work on *Jephtha* again. Between the end of February and the beginning of April, he had deposited nearly £2,300 in his bank account.

On 17 August 1752, London's daily paper, the *Public Advertiser*, announced: 'We hear that George-Frederick Handel, Esq; the celebrated Composer of Musick was seized a few Days ago with a Paralytick Disorder in his Head, which has deprived him of Sight.'[173] On 3 November, he was operated on for cataracts by the surgeon to the Prince and Princess of Wales, no doubt an excruciating experience,* and by the end of January 1753, he was blind.

Handel's Death

It was a long run in to the finish. Four years later, in February 1757, Lord Shaftesbury reported: 'Mr Handel is better than he has been for some years and finds that he can compose Chorus's as well as other music to his own (and consequently to the hearer's) satisfaction. His memory is strengthened of late to an astonishing degree.'[176]

Shaftesbury, on the last day of 1757, reported him 'pretty well'. He was in Tunbridge Wells in August 1758. Again, he had an eye operation by Mr Taylor, an oculist who had also operated on Bach. It was unsuccessful. After the season, Handel planned to go to Bath, but he never got there and never performed at the Foundling *Messiah*, as advertised, in May. On 11 April, he dictated a codicil to his will. He left £1,000 to the Society for the Support of Decay'd Musicians and allowed up to £600 for his monument in Westminster Abbey. On Saturday 14 April 1759, he died having said his farewells.

His 'private' funeral at Westminster Abbey was attended by bishops, prebendaries and 3,000 people. He apparently died worth £20,000.** His niece, the wife of the Rector of the University of Halle, and other German relatives received £9,000. His art collection was sold by auction and comprised 67 lots, a considerable volume for a house the size of Brook Street.

Among the most prized possessions of George III, who succeeded to the

* The fortitude of earlier generations is amazing. Samuel Pepys had a gallstone of over two inches diameter removed in 1658.[174] Dr Burney's daughter, the novelist Fanny, had a mastectomy without anaesthetic in 1811. She describes 'a terror that surpasses all description, & the most torturing pain ... I began a scream that lasted unintermittently during the whole time of the incision – & I almost marvel that it rings not in my ears still! So excruciating was the agony.'[175] She survived until January 1840.

** His publisher was worth twice as much when he died six years later.[177]

throne in the following year, were a harpsichord which had once belonged to Handel and the scores of some of his early and unpublished operas. A Roubiliac bust of Handel occupied a prominent position in the Japan Room at the Queen's House (now Buckingham Palace), and the king was occasionally to be seen wearing a Handel medal on his coat. When, every month, he attended the Concert of Ancient Music, known as a King's Concert, and it was the monarch's turn to choose the programme, he was almost certain to choose a work by Handel.

Much of Handel's large output of instrumental music tends to be overlooked, the pieces for harpsichord, the many organ concertos, the chamber sonatas and the concerti grossi for strings. The Italian operas are now increasingly revived. He has always been remembered for various numbers from them such as the so-called 'Largo', and for the suites such as the *Water Music* and *Fireworks Music*. But Handel's oratorios have commanded the greatest respect. These, especially *Messiah*, are the works the public has loved and revered. Indeed, Handel idolatry in England reached such a pitch that, even before the turn of the century, Dr Burney was concerned that it was preventing the English from 'keeping pace with the rest of Europe in the cultivation of Music'.[178]

It is perhaps not surprising that Wagner, during one of his few visits to England, observed that 'everyone holds a Handel vocal score as if it were a prayer book'.[179]

The Apotheosis of Handel. Later to be joined by Mendelssohn, his influence was the dominant force in English music until Elgar

BACH

CHAPTER 2

A FEW DAYS after Handel was born, less than 100 miles away, Maria Elizabeth Bach gave birth to Johann Sebastian, the latest in a large family and a long line of musicians. Several Bachs had been town musicians in the area, calling the hours, acting as lookouts for troops and for fires. The family was so involved with music that the words 'musician' and 'Bach' were almost interchangeable.

Eisenach, where Bach was born, is in Thuringia, sandwiched between the forest to the south and the Harz Mountains to the north, in a beautiful yet out-of-the-way part of Saxony, which borders on Hesse. Bach's father was in charge of music for the town council, responsible for twice-daily performances from the balcony of the town hall and for performing at services in St George's Church.[1]

Bach's background was socially and geographically very different from Handel's. This goes some way to explaining the difference in their careers, output and subsequent reputation. Bach, 'parsimonious and prudent' and with a reputation for being obstinate, immersed himself in narrow-minded Lutheran Saxony.[2] Handel, the Italian-trained extrovert, became a risk-taking entrepreneur on an international scale.

Bach is sometimes criticised as 'an unintelligible musical arithmetician',[3] composing 'more for the eye than the ear'.[4] Indeed, this is how he was often viewed at the end of the 18th century by the small number of people who knew the very few works then in circulation. A century and a half later, Fauré, although an admirer, said that some of his fugues were 'utterly boring'.[5] Debussy put it more graphically: 'When the old Saxon Cantor hasn't any ideas, he starts out from any old thing and is truly pitiless. In fact he's only bearable when he's admirable … If he'd had a friend – a publisher perhaps – who could have told him to take a day off every week, perhaps, then we'd have been spared several hundreds of pages in which you have to walk between rows of mercilessly regulated and joyless bars, each one with its rascally little "subject" and "countersubject".'*[8]

Often, Bach may give much more pleasure to the performer who will be fascinated by his art, than to the audience disconcerted by his complexity. However, with a little patience, most of his works are totally absorbing and, to some people, he provides almost daily pleasure. Some of his works, the St Matthew Passion being the obvious example, are almost Wonders of the World.

We shall start with Bach's tough upbringing. After his education, he became organist and choirmaster in two staunchly Protestant towns near his birthplace, first in Arnstadt and then very briefly in Mühlhausen. He then spent nearly ten years working at Weimar, an almost pantomime court. By the time Bach was 30, Handel's friend Mattheson was talking about 'der berühmte Bach', the famous Bach.[9] For a short time, he worked in the Frenchified court at Cöthen, away from church music. But church music was his vocation, so he returned to the Lutheran baroque as 'Cantor' of St Thomas' Church in Leipzig. Here, he spent his last three decades, living comfortably, but up a backwater and greatly unappreciated. It is no wonder that he showed signs of having a large chip on his shoulder.

Bach's achievement was to synthesise laborious German part-writing with the styles of the light French dances and the Italian concertos and sonatas. His works represent a culmination: by the time he was finished, there was musically nothing more anyone could do in his style, except to write exercises and answer examination questions; he had taken it to the limit.[10]

* Bach was the greatest exponent of counterpoint, the art of combining melodies.[6] It has not always been popular. The leading philosopher Rousseau believed that the combination had the effect of neutralising the merits of each individual melody.[7]

The music which we have been fortunate to inherit is awesomely beautiful. By the time of his death, however, tastes had changed. For royalty and the aristocrats who led taste and fashion, solid oak furniture had long given way to ormolu, thin veneer and chinoiserie.

Bach's Youth in Thuringia and North Germany

Johann Ambrosius Bach, an identical twin, had married the daughter of a furrier and a municipal councillor in Erfurt, where he worked. By the time their son Johann Sebastian was born on 21 March 1685, they had moved to Eisenach, 30 miles away. This part of Germany is steeped in history, particularly Lutheran. Above Eisenach is the Wartburg, the castle where Martin Luther had taken refuge after being declared a heretic at the Diet of Worms. In it, disguised as 'Junker Georg' (Squire George), Luther began to translate the New Testament into German; and, as legend has it, he threw an inkpot at the Devil who was attempting to weaken his resolve.[11] Long before, in the Middle Ages, there had been a song contest at the Wartburg between the Minnesinger, or poet-musician, 'Der Tanuser' and 'Her Wolveram', the writer of *Parzival*; this was immortalised for those who enjoy music by Wagner.[12]

The Wartburg is so high above Eisenach that one doubts if the young Bach would ever have been allowed to climb up to its ruins. Now restored, the visitor can ponder that here in 1817 was held the first student protest, against the repressive regime of the Habsburg chancellor, Prince Metternich; the visitor can also look at the murals painted by Schubert's friend Moritz von Schwind; and imagine Franz Liszt conducting the St Elisabeth Oratorio with which he celebrated the Wartburg's 800th anniversary.

As with all children at the time, Johann Sebastian was lucky to be alive. Half of all babies born in the 17th century died within twelve months of birth. With both disease and war ever present, the average life expectancy was 22 years, with the wealthy and well-fed perhaps living until their early 50s.[13] There were exceptions, of course: Jan Reinken, the organist at Hamburg, died only five months short of his 100th birthday.[14]

Bach's great-grandfather died of plague in 1626. Eighteen months before Bach was born, plague struck the wife and baby son of the family friend and teacher Johann Pachelbel, who is known to us for the *Canon*.[15] A bad harvest, leading to famine, could be another cause of devastation.

Only in Britain, with its increasing and productive agriculture, its great merchant marine and foreign trade, and growth in industry, could the population feel reasonably safe from famine.[16]

The Thirty Years War had ended less than 40 years before Bach's birth. So, stories of bloodshed, rape, robbery, torture and famine abounded at the time. Had he been older, he might have heard of the Thuringian father who sought justice against a soldier who had raped and killed his daughter: the father was heartlessly and crudely told that the girl would still be alive, had she not been so reluctant. The Bachs might have associated the nearby city of Weimar with Duke Bernard, one of the Protestant generals, who, when on campaign, burnt everything around him.[17]

The staunchly Protestant Bachs would probably have looked back to that war as a religious war, a righteous one, Protestant fighting Roman Catholic. In reality, these wars were about power. The Continent's royal families were quite happy to change their religion when it suited their purpose. At a high level, it was usually possible to be flexible.*

To the Bachs, the Lutheran hymns (chorales), such as 'Wenn wir in höchsten Nöthen sein', 'When in the hour of utmost need, we know not where to look for aid ... and cry, O faithful God, to Thee', would have had a deep significance. However, life was not all doom and gloom, as we can hear from the sheer joy expressed in other chorales such as 'Jesu meine Freude', 'Jesu my joy, my priceless pearl and treasure, Sunshine of my heart!'[19]

Bach benefited from the education which in most of Lutheran Germany was compulsory for children between five and twelve years old.[20] He learnt the catechism, the psalms, the Bible, history, writing and Latin. Literacy levels in that part of Germany were far higher than those elsewhere: in England, for example, even in the middle of the next century, about a third of men and two thirds of women were unable even to sign their own name.[21]

He studied music with his father and played with the two journeymen musicians and two apprentices who lived in the house. He also studied with his distinguished cousin, the most successful Bach so far, Johann

* Augustus the Strong, Elector of Saxony and King in Poland, with whom Bach later 'corresponded', became a Roman Catholic in order to become King. A more celebrated case was the protestant King Henry of Navarre who said that 'Paris vaut bien une messe' (Paris is well worth a mass).[18]

Christoph, town organist and harpsichordist in the court of the Duke of Eisenach.

When Bach was nine, his mother died. This was not particularly unusual. In the second half of the 18th century, it was normal for children aged fourteen to have lost one or both parents.*[22] Since the family was the basis of society, it was crucial to remarry quickly. So, six months later, Bach's father married the already twice-widowed daughter of the burgomaster of nearby Arnstadt, a town where many of the family had been employed as musicians. But, the marriage did not last long: three months later, his father died. The family was broken up; while his sisters remained with their stepmother, Johann Sebastian and his elder brother travelled the 22 miles along the edge of the Thuringian Forest to Ohrdruf to live with his eldest brother Christoph, a past pupil of the family friend, Johann Pachelbel.**

The Ohrdruf school, close to the stream that flows fast through the town, had 300 pupils and 6 masters. It boasted that peasants were better educated there than noblemen elsewhere. Bach, despite his sorrow at losing his mother, was resilient and determined. He did well at his studies. He is also supposed to have copied, by moonlight, a book of clavier† pieces.[24]

Although Johann Sebastian would have been paid for singing in the choir, and contributed to his keep, Christoph's own family was expanding. There was no room; the adolescent had to move on. He could have just become an apprentice, but he chose instead to go to St Michael's Church, at Lüneburg, about 30 miles from Hamburg, and join its distinguished Matins Choir.

So, aged fifteen, with his classmate Georg, Bach made his way 200 miles northwards to Brunswick and on to Lüneburg. The first leg of their journey would have necessitated bypassing the sombre Harz mountains, which lie in the way. The densely forested Harz was then infested with robbers, and even today[25] it is a forbidding place during early March, the time

* Death, rather than divorce, terminated the average marriage, which lasted twenty years. Less than one in ten lived to over 60; those over 65 made up 4–5 per cent of the population.

** Pachelbel's son, Charles Theodore, was perhaps the most distinguished professional musician in America before 1750. He began New York's public concert life when he arrived from Boston in 1736. He died in Charleston, where he was organist at St Philip's Church and very active in promoting music; he started an annual concert on St Cecilia's Day there.[23]

† 'Clavier' was a generic term for several types of keyboard instrument.

when they travelled: the temperature even at midday is sometimes only 6–7°C; mist swirls ominously through the dripping, creaking trees; the melting snow freezes hard at night; any wagon would have slipped on the ice or got stuck in the mud. It was an arduous journey however they went, whether on foot, or by hitching a lift; unfortunately, there was no navigable river to provide a more comfortable and faster means of transport.

Their conversation, as they went, might have touched on the extraordinary changes being made to the calendar: in a year when anyway the century had changed, the dates between 18 February and 1 March had simply disappeared.*

When these country bumpkins got to Lüneburg, they must have been astonished by the size of St Michael's, and its mighty organ. The church towered over the small houses in their crooked streets. Bach continued his academic studies, Latin, Greek, Hebrew, arithmetic and probably some French and Italian as well. He also studied all the leading composers by copying, the traditional mode of learning; and he had organ lessons from Georg Böhm, one of the three leading organists in Germany at the time, the others being the Swedish-born Buxtehude in Lübeck and Pachelbel, who by now was based in Nuremberg.[26]

The choristers might have gossiped about a scandal, about five years earlier, involving the daughter and heiress of the ruling Duke of Brunswick-Lüneburg-Celle. Her lover, a count, was found murdered.**[27] But, even if they had heard of this, Bach, being a serious boy, will surely have been more interested in the potential for visiting nearby Celle, a minor Versailles, and for going to Hamburg.

In summer 1701, he walked the 30 miles to Hamburg.[28] Whereas Handel had been attracted by the opera, Bach wanted to hear Jan Reinken, then the youthful 80-year-old organist of the 13th-century St Catherine's Church down by the inner harbour. When he approached the church for the first time, Bach must have been astonished at the bustling activity with lighters unloading the big sea-going ships on the Elbe.

In August 1702, Bach left school and returned southwards to apply for

* See Note on Money, Dates and Names.

** She was the mother of the future King George II of England and the grandmother of Frederick the Great of Prussia. The lover was Count von Königsmarck. The great military leader Maurice de Saxe, the great-grandfather of George Sand, Chopin's lover, was sired (by Augustus the Strong) on the lovely Aurore, the count's sister.

jobs. He was turned down for one, and possibly may have filled in time as a farm hand. On Easter Day 1703, he was enrolled as a violinist in the service of the younger brother of the Duke of Weimar, whom we shall meet later.[29]

Jobs in Arnstadt and Mühlhausen

He did not stay long in Weimar, on this occasion. A new organ was being built for the Church of St Boniface, near the market place in Arnstadt, about twenty miles from Ohrdruf. Bach was asked to be one of the inspectors, so he must already have acquired a considerable knowledge of organ construction. After the public inauguration, in August 1703, the eighteen-year-old was appointed to the well-paid job of organist to this church, which had a capacity for over 1,000 people.[30] He was certainly young for the job, but he had good connections in the town, and the castle organist was married to a cousin.

Arnstadt was a small walled town, populated with tanners, cloth-makers, brewers and potters. It had a castle occupied by a local count. It could be a jolly and festive place, for example, when the schoolboys put on their plays at Carnival time.[31] Bach was now in charge of an excellent organ.* He could spend time composing for it.

At this early stage, the young Bach showed a trait shared, it seems, with his successful cousin at the court in Eisenach: he was pedantic about what he was employed to do. He claimed that he was only appointed for accompanying chorales on the organ and not for the more elaborate orchestral and choral ('concerted' or 'figural') music-making, such as the performance of cantatas.[33] This attitude seems somewhat perverse as the church authorities were critical of his embellished accompaniments, so obviously he enjoyed elaboration. Also, we begin to see signs of Bach's poor interpersonal relations. In 1705, he was criticised by the authorities for being involved in a brawl with a student who had thrashed him in the market place in the presence of his girlfriend.[34] Bach, superior and highly educated, had referred, idiomatically and unwisely, to the bleating noise his attacker made when attempting to play the bassoon.

* To practise, one needed to pay a bellows operator; later, Bach could afford a harpsichord with pedals attached which facilitated practice in the home. The organ in St Paul's Cathedral was still being blown by treadmill in the time of Sir John Stainer, in the 1870s. Around that time, the army of bellows operatives (male and female) at Notre-Dame-de-Paris was pensioned off.[32]

In 1705, he was granted four weeks' leave of absence and set off again 300 miles to the north to Lübeck to hear Buxtehude's evenings of oratorio, which were held on either side of Advent Sunday. In that year, there were two extra performances, one lamenting the death of Emperor Leopold I and one hailing his successor Joseph I.[35] Lübeck's Marienkirche has, even today, the highest brick nave in the world;[36] for Bach it must have been an awesome sight compared to his own relatively small church at Arnstadt.

Young Bach. Bernd Göbel's monument in Arnstadt, for the 1985 Tercentenary, suggests a completely different character from Handel (see page 37)

By the time he returned to Arnstadt in February 1706, he had been away for much longer than planned, and he was reproved by the church authorities, who continued to complain about his elaborate and confusing accompaniments. He was in trouble again in November for not playing orchestral music; on this occasion, the church authorities also asked him by what right he had recently allowed a 'strange maiden' into the choir loft and let her make music there.[37]

With all this bickering, it may have seemed just as well that in Mühlhausen, the Church of Divi Blasius* was looking for an organist, as theirs had died. Bach accepted the post, which also included playing the

* Previously Saint Blasius, but the Lutherans did not recognise the saint, so the church was downgraded at the Reformation.[38]

organ at a girls' convent, and involved an increase in pay. He also had a sudden windfall: his aunt left him a legacy, a sum of 500 thalers,* amounting to more than half his annual stipend. He could afford to get married. In October 1707, he married his cousin Maria Barbara. At 22, he was slightly young to marry: men typically married at 28, women at 25.[40]

Mühlhausen, a large walled town of wool merchants and weavers who carefully guarded their very ancient privileges, is not far from Eisenach. Staunchly Protestant, it had experienced terrifying upheavals when the Protestants splintered into various sects at the time of the Reformation, 200 years before. People had become more literate, so they erroneously believed that they were entitled to interpret the Bible themselves, rather than accepting what the authorities told them to believe.[41] Thomas Münzer, an 'Anabaptist' preacher, prophesied the end of the world, and incited a peasant revolt in the 1520s. He was executed in the town.

By Bach's time, Mühlhausen was dominated by 'Pietists', a wing of the Lutheran church. They expressed with saintly simplicity a very personal faith and relationship with God and Christ. They had clear-cut views about what was appropriate as church music, rumblings about which we have already heard in Arnstadt. Protestants in general were particularly concerned about the nature of church music because they had forsworn many of the means of inspiring and expressing religious devotion available to the Roman Catholics, such as its evocative art, architecture and certain of its sacraments.[42] We should spend a moment on Lutheran music.

Lutheran music comprised two principal items, firstly the chorale, the German hymn sung in unison by the congregation. This was much loved by the 'Pietists', for whom congregational participation was the essence of worship. More orthodox Lutherans, however, wanted the subject matter preached in the sermon, the central item in their worship, to be amplified by 'figural music', that is, *art* music such as the cantata or passion. Pastor Neumeister from Hamburg, author of many cantata texts, intended cantatas to be played before and/or after the sermon, thereby enhancing its impact. Much to the concern of the Pietists, this cantata music was beginning to predominate. With its arias and recitatives, it seemed to them to be dangerously operatic, and inappropriate for church use.[43]

* A barber was paid an annual salary of 70 thalers; a pastor 175 thalers. A ream (480 sheets) of paper would cost about 0.85 thalers.[39]

This was not a calm debate of the type familiar to us in the 20th century: Pastor Neumeister regarded the Pietists as the equivalent of Turks or papists. They thundered back. They produced a flood of devotional songbooks with chorale-like arias based on sentimental and ecstatic texts, many about the flesh, blood and wounds so dear to them. The leader of the Moravian Brethren who had emigrated to Bethlehem, Pennsylvania, himself wrote 2,000 such songs.[44]

Bach fitted uneasily and contrarily into this scene. Having tried to restrict himself in Arnstadt to accompanying chorales, he now wanted to perform cantatas. But his church in Mühlhausen was run by a Pietist pastor who did not want cantatas. Bach did, however, write one for the inauguration ceremony for the burgomaster, the text being written by the somewhat bigoted pastor of the rival orthodox Lutheran church nearby.

Bach's biographers are by no means unanimous about the extent to which he was concerned about being out of step, as indeed he must have been in each location. However, when in 1708, an opportunity arose at Weimar, with better musical resources and pay three times what he had been earning in Arnstadt, he jumped at it. He did not fall out with the Mühlhausen authorities: he continued to supervise their organ rebuild, and he returned in 1709 to play the new organ at the annual civic service.

Weimar

Weimar, 50 miles from Leipzig, with all the elegance of a miniature capital, is today remembered for an age long after Bach, the Golden Age of German Literature: Goethe, the German poet of Shakespearean stature, author of *Faust*, settled there in 1775. Through him, Weimar acted as a magnet for other poets such as Wieland, and the playwright Schiller, the author of *Don Carlos*, *Wallenstein*, *Maria Stuart* and *William Tell*. The German cultural philosopher Herder lived there, as did Liszt. More recently, the German national assembly, which preceded Hitler's regime, convened in Weimar: the politically unstable 'Weimar Republic' is remembered for presiding over an inflation such that, by November 1923, it took a million million marks to equal the purchasing power of one 1914 mark.[45] Nearby is the notorious Nazi concentration camp at Buchenwald.

With this history, Bach does not feature much on today's tourist map of Weimar, even though here he wrote a large amount of his well-known organ music, and developed his technique for writing cantatas. This is partly because most things relating to him were destroyed in a fire just before Goethe arrived.

In Bach's time, Weimar was ruled by Wilhelm Ernst, a precociously serious duke who, at the age of seven, had preached an Ash Wednesday sermon before his courtiers.[46] The centre of court ceremonial was the castle chapel, with its grotesque pyramid-shaped altar-canopy adorned with cherubs reaching the three stories to the roof. In the ceiling was the organ and musicians' gallery.[47] From below, the music must have sounded truly ethereal. However, there was no scope for letting the mind wander: the duke tested his servants on their attention and understanding of the sermons.

The duke was descended from one branch of the Saxon royal family. In the 1400s, the Elector of Saxony had divided his lands between his two sons Ernst and Albert. The Albertine line came out on top, while Ernst's descendants, who had supported Luther, retained just a few scattered territories in Thuringia, such as Weimar and Gotha. Weimar itself had a curious constitution in which the eldest son inherited the ducal authority, but his brothers were given a consultative voice.[48] This was typical of the confusion in Germany at the time and led to trouble for Bach, as we shall see.

One aristocrat wrote in 1738: 'Germany today teems with princes, three quarters of who are completely devoid of common sense.'[49] The Elector of the Palatinate had a grand admiral to command the few boats he maintained on the Rhine.[50] 'A sort of shabby finery' was the impression received by Lady Mary Wortley Montagu in 1702: 'a number of dirty people of quality tawdered out; narrow nasty streets out of repair, wretchedly thin of inhabitants, and above half of the common sort asking alms'.[51] The typical ruler 'contented himself of an evening playing at bassett* or being amused by the court dwarf'.[52]

The rulers had regal pretensions and usefully provided a source of suitable spouses for the British royal family in the 19th century. But in Bach's time, the focus was on France, for language, clothes, food, furniture: 'French dances, French music, the French pox … perhaps there is also a French death.'[53] A French groom in Celle was paid almost twice what a German one was paid; a French coachman was paid about the same as a German doctor. The respect was not reciprocated: the French regarded the Germans as gross and ignorant. Voltaire, writer, wit and thinker, summed

* An obsolete card game.

it up in 1750 when he arrived at the court of Frederick the Great: 'I find myself in France here; our language alone is spoken. German is only for soldiers and horses.'[54]

To travel the 50 miles from Eisenach to Weimar, one had to pass through two other sovereign territories, first Gotha, the capital of the Duke of Saxe-Gotha-Altenburg, forebear of Prince Albert of England; then Erfurt, a possession of the Archbishop of Mainz. One would turn off the main road near Erfurt, for the final ten miles of the journey, occasionally making a detour through the fields when the rutted road was impassable. The Castle at Weimar occupied about a third of the town; everything revolved around the court, which, at the time of Goethe's arrival 50 years later, 'expressed its existence by eating'.[55] Those not directly involved with the court, the tailors, shoemakers, bakers, blacksmiths and apothecaries, were dependent on it. The town was full of pigs and chickens and peasants' carts. Cattle were kept within the walls and led out to the pasture in the daytime. The place would have smelt like a farmyard. Other than a small amount of stocking weaving, there was no industry; and there was no trade with the outside world. There was no middle class of merchants, manufacturers or professional men, the class of people with whom Bach wished to consort.[56]

Here, Bach was just another servant. His role was Konzertmeister and court organist. He worked for the Kapellmeister, the director of music, who was assisted by his son as vice-Kapellmeister.[57] The orchestra, in which Bach played, wore a livery similar to a hussar's uniform. The duke was very keen on his hussars; he had around 40 of them, a kind of ducal police force whose responsibilities ranged from tax collection to ejecting illegal immigrants such as deserters from the Prussian army next door. 'It is wise not to form too idyllic a picture of peaceful Weimar. Petitions from districts ravaged by fire or flood are legion, as are complaints about ruthless seizure of tax arrears.'[58]

Bach's work was appreciated and he was given a succession of pay rises which eventually took him above the pay level of the Kapellmeister.[59] But Bach's way of life was a far cry from Handel's, and indeed from the exceptional position Goethe was to occupy in the future. Goethe slept in the duke's chamber, he dined with the duke and they bathed together; and he was treated as a guest, riding, shooting, attending balls and masquerades. Both Goethe and Schiller were ennobled.[60]

Bach's daughter Catherina Dorothea was born at the end of 1708; Wilhelm Friedemann was born in November 1710; and, in February 1713, he had twins, a boy and a girl who appear to have died on the same day. Carl Philipp Emanuel (C.P.E. Bach), destined to be an outstanding musician, was born in March 1714.

In 1713, Handel's teacher in Halle died, and Bach, who by now had built up an excellent reputation, was tempted to move. But the duke increased his stipend and promoted him, so he stayed at Weimar, much to the disappointment of the Halle authorities, who had invited him there and 'looked after' him very well: his brandy and tobacco were charged to the expense account. They suspected that Bach had used their invitation as a lever to extract promotion and get a better salary.[61]

Until this event, Bach's main focus had been on composing organ works. He had also arranged, for clavier and organ, Vivaldi's concertos which had been published as *L'Estro Harmonico* in 1711.[62] Possibly they were brought back by the younger duke when he returned from his Grand Tour.

However, with the renegotiation of his terms of employment, Bach was at last able to do what he had wanted to do when he went to Mühlhausen, namely to write vocal music. He wrote cantatas, largely amatory or pastoral, mostly for the birthday, name-day* or accession of a royal or aristocratic person, or for some academic ceremony. The one composed for Duke Christian of Weissenfels includes the aria, 'Sheep may safely graze where a good shepherd is watching'. When we listen to it today, we are often unaware that the good shepherd was Duke Christian.[63]

Clearly, Bach's reputation was growing. He was invited to visit Dresden, capital of Saxony, to compete with the 'conceited, improvident, arrogant'[64] Louis Marchand, court organist at Versailles. Marchand had marital problems, and his wife arranged for half his salary to be paid to her. So in the middle of a service at Versailles, he closed the organ, and said: 'If my wife gets half my stipend, let her play half the service';[65] and was dismissed. On the morning of the contest, he decamped, and Bach performed, receiving 'praise in abundance',[66] but apparently not the prize of 100 Louis d'Or. This story about Marchand 'did the rounds' in Germany right up to the end of the century.[67]

The Duke of Weimar got on badly with his younger brother, and

* The name-day, much celebrated, was the day of the saint after whom a person was named.

subsequently with his widow and her two sons. Ominously, this was the household for whom Bach had worked before going to Arnstadt. As the relationship within the ducal family deteriorated, so did the relationship between Wilhelm Ernst and Bach. The duke started fining any member of his household who served his brother's family. This possibly explains why Bach was not promoted to the position of Kapellmeister when the previous one died, even though he was performing many of the old man's duties. The son, rather than Bach, got the job.[68]

Early in 1716, the younger duke's son married the sister of Prince Leopold of Anhalt-Cöthen. The prince offered Bach a salary which involved a pay rise of about a third, together with a substantial 'golden hello'. Wilhelm Ernst refused to allow Bach to go and locked him up 'for too stubbornly forcing the issue of his dismissal'.*[73] He was released from gaol almost a month later and grudgingly allowed to leave for Cöthen. It is sometimes suggested that he wrote the *Little Organ Book* of chorale preludes during his detention, in order to while away the time.

Cöthen

Cöthen, 25 miles north of Halle, was another typical tiny German principality which had fragmented from an earlier larger one. It had a history of culture; in the early 1600s, the first society for the encouragement of the German language was founded there. When Bach arrived, the moated castle was being renovated in the French style as a gracious château, with three fine baroque towers outside, and superb furnishing within. It had beautiful gardens in which the duke was about to build an orangerie.[74]

The court was Calvinist, so there was no church music, other than the singing of chorales. Bach conducted an 18-piece orchestra and maintained the prince's harpsichords. The orchestra had been augmented with instru-

*Other composers brushed with the authorities. Weber was imprisoned after he repaid money embezzled by his father. (To finance this, he was implicated in a scam whereby pretty young men avoided conscription by buying positions at court.) Earlier, he had been imprisoned when he directed to the King's private room an old woman asking where to find the court washerwoman.[69] Samuel Wesley was imprisoned for failing to pay his debts; Berlioz, for failing to attend National Guard Duty;[70] Schumann and Stravinsky for being involved in minor 'student' disturbances;[71] and Poulenc spent ten days in a military prison for overstaying leave in 1918.[72] The most culpable, Richard Wagner, avoided imprisonment, but he was prominently political.

mentalists made redundant when the Prussian orchestra was closed on the accession of the militaristic Frederick William I.

In Cöthen, Bach was in clover. He was writing for a patron who had recently been to Italy on the Grand Tour and who loved and understood music, an accomplished string player, competent on the clavier and as a singer. Bach wrote chamber music, such as sonatas, concertos and the English, French and German suites. He followed the trend for writing educational works: he wrote the first 24 preludes and fugues of the *Well Tempered Clavier*, the *Inventions* (designated by him as 'an honest guide to the lovers of the clavier'[75]), and composed the *Klavierbüchlein* for his son, Wilhelm Friedemann. From here, he could also visit Hamburg, Berlin and Leipzig to inspect the new organs. Here, for the first time, he seems to have been content, although this was not to last.

In May 1720, Bach accompanied the duke on a visit to take the waters at Carlsbad, the fashionable spa.* On his return, Bach found his wife dead and buried, although seemingly he had left her in good health. Death, as we have seen, was ever present.

Bach was now left with four children, Catherina Dorothea, the eldest, aged twelve, and Friedemann, Emanuel and Bernhard, aged ten, six and five respectively. His wife's elder sister Friedelena, who had lived with the family for some years, must have been a godsend at this difficult time.[77] Bach clearly needed a second wife. On 3 December 1721, he married Anna Magdalena Wülcken, the daughter of the court trumpeter at Zeitz and Weissenfels.[78] Anna Magdalena was aged twenty, and was already a singer on the Cöthen payroll. For her, Bach wrote the *Little Clavier Book* and, later, the *Notebook*.

Bach reflected on his domestic circumstances: he was concerned about the children's education and the large class sizes at the Lutheran school.[79] He also wanted to compose church cantatas. Besides, Cöthen was far from anywhere; and the prince's budget was tight, especially after the prince's marriage left less resource available for music. So, Bach considered applying to be organist at Pastor Neumeister's church in Hamburg. But the job

* It seems likely that during this visit, he was asked by the Margrave of Brandenburg to provide him with the six *concerti grossi*, which he wrote in the style of Vivaldi. Although Bach probably performed them at Cöthen, there seems to be no record of any acknowledgement from the margrave, and the condition of the manuscript shows that they were never performed by him. They were assembled with other manuscripts after the margrave's death and sold as a job lot.[76]

went to someone prepared to pay for it, leading Mattheson to observe that 'even if one of the angels of Bethlehem should come down from Heaven, one who played divinely and wished to become organist of St Jacobi, but had no money, he might just as well fly away again'.[80]

The Appointment as Cantor in Leipzig

Bach continued to look elsewhere for positions. In June 1722, Johann Kuhnau, 'Cantor' of St Thomas' in Leipzig, and one of the leading writers of church cantatas, died. Bach knew him well: he had worked with him on the inspection of the organ at the Marienkirche in Halle in 1716,[81] and they had presumably dined together at the banquet to celebrate its opening.

The church, with its excellent Thomasschule, had a long musical tradition. The prominent composer of the early 1600s, Hermann Schein, previously briefly at Weimar, had been Cantor during the Thirty Years War. The church's musical establishment had subsequently gone through a rocky patch when Johann Rosenmüller, a 'composer of unquestionable genius'[82] and potential Cantor was, with several others on the staff, gaoled on suspicion of homosexuality. Rosenmüller escaped to Venice.[83]

Leipzig was the second city in Saxony. Virtually in the middle of Europe, it was a prominent commercial centre, well known for its Easter, Michaelmas and New Year Fairs, which dated from medieval times. It had acquired leadership in the publishing trade when, at the end of the 17th century, Frankfurt introduced severe censorship. Breitkopf, the publishers, had been there for about three years.[84]

It was also another of the centres of Lutheranism, with a proud tradition. There, after attending a service in St Thomas', Luther had publicly supported certain aspects of the teaching of Jan Hus, the Bohemian heretic. This gave rise to the papal bull 'Exsurge Domine' which Luther burnt and which was followed by his excommunication, and appearance at the Diet of Worms.[85]

The city was redolent of Nuremberg in the days of *Die Meistersinger*, with its patrician families and its guilds which jealously guarded their monopoly rights.[86] At the start of the 18th century, it experienced a considerable boom with nine banks opening.[87] These merchants were proud of the notion that their city should properly be regarded as a great cultural centre, the 'Klein-Paris' of Germany.[88]

The appointment of Kuhnau's successor as Cantor was thus an important one for these self-important burghers to make, and proved difficult and contentious. The city council first selected Georg Telemann,[89] who had previously worked in Leipzig: he was now in Hamburg where he had been very proactive and introduced public concerts; but, after he got a pay rise, he withdrew his application. Bach was then one of several contenders for the post, but was still not the first choice. Graupner from Darmstadt, an alumnus of St Thomas', was approached, but his employer, the Landgrave of Hesse-Darmstadt, would not let him go, tempting him with a salary increase and a pension for his dependants.

The council then reconsidered the nature of the job. This partly involved teaching the 55 resident pupils, and around 100 non-resident pupils, in non-musical subjects as well as music. The council discussed separating the teaching and musical roles. Councillor Dr Platz raised the temperature by saying that 'since the best man could not be obtained, mediocre ones would have to be accepted'.[90] The subsequent comments at this meeting are not recorded, because the clerk of the city council was told not to take any further minutes. This was an unpropitious start to Bach's appointment which he accepted ten days later, having been given a theological examination and found sound. Councillor Dr Steger adjured Bach to 'make compositions that were not theatrical'.[91] The composer duly gave several undertakings. He agreed not to leave the city without the burgomaster's consent. He also undertook to 'set the boys a shining example of an honest, retiring manner of life',[92] and to instruct them conscientiously, and 'so to arrange the music that it shall not last too long, and shall be of such a nature as not to make an operatic impression but rather incite the listeners to devotion'.[93] All was now in order.

At the end of May 1723, two carriages and four wagons full of belongings left Cöthen along the flat road to Leipzig. This was to be the family home for the remaining 27 years of Bach's life. There was a formal induction ceremony on 1 June, held by a representative of the city council, the pastor, the school rector and the chief town clerk. The schoolboys performed a piece outside the door, and then filed in. Although the event went off with due decorum, there seems to have been some confusion about the procedure, with some bickering between the church authorities and the city council about who should perform the installation.[94]

Life in Leipzig, Second City to Dresden

Bach lived in the inner city, which had a quaint medieval aspect; there were fortified walls, and leafy suburbs and fine gardens outside, where we can imagine him, relaxing and sketching, which he enjoyed so much,[95] and walking with Anna Magdalena who loved flowers.[96]

Lady Mary Wortley Montagu, writing less than ten years earlier, described the fashions of Leipzig: The women 'are very genteely dressed, after the French and English modes, and have generally very pretty faces, but they are the most determined minaudières* in the whole world. They would think it a mortal sin against good-breeding, if they either spoke or moved in a natural manner. They all affect a little soft lisp and a pretty pitty-pat step.'[97] It was in Leipzig that the Viennese obtained their shoes, and bargains could be had: pages' liveries and gold stuffs could be bought at half the price of those in Vienna, partly due to the customs duties and partly to the relative skills of the craftsmen.

Leipzig's university was the largest in the German-speaking world. One of its alumni, who studied there in Bach's time, was Empress Maria Theresa's powerful chancellor, Prince Kaunitz.[98] He was a typical example of someone who chose to travel north to obtain his university education, rather than go to one of the southern universities whose teaching had been dominated by the Jesuits.[99]

Another alumnus was Lord Chesterfield's illegitimate son Philip.** His father's exhortations give one an indication of customs in the top echelons of the city. 'There is a great deal of good company in Leipzig, which I would have you frequent in the evenings', wrote the lord. 'There is likewise a kind of court kept there, by a Duchess Dowager of Courland, at which you should get introduced. The King of Poland and his Court go likewise to the fair at Leipsig twice a year.' He added: 'I shall write to Sir Charles Williams, the King's Minister there, to have you presented, and introduced into good company.' Philip was to 'observe and imitate the manners of the people of the best fashion there; not that they are … the best manners in the world; but because they are the best manners of the place where you are, to which a man of sense always conforms'. As well as reminding him to clean his teeth and dress well, Chesterfield admonished him thus:

* Simpering manners.

** Chesterfield was an English diplomat, politician and peer.

'Having mentioned laughing, I must particularly warn you against it: and I could heartily wish that you often may be seen to smile, but never heard to laugh while you live. Frequent and loud laughter is the characteristic of folly and ill-manners.'[100] One hopes that the Bachs managed an occasional laugh despite the dour Lutheran precincts of St Thomas'.

Leipzig was a contrast to the backwater at Cöthen and the tawdry elegance of crumbling Weimar. Of even more contrast, however, was the capital of Saxony, Dresden, some 65 miles away, the seat of Elector Augustus I who was also King Augustus II in Poland. Being a recent convert to Roman Catholicism,* his court was keen to show its enthusiasm by doing everything Italian.[102] It thus became the centre of Italian in Continental northern Europe, attracting considerable talent, a recruiting ground for Handel. Its music would soon be dominated by Johann Adolf Hasse and his wife, the international soprano, Faustina Bordoni, who were friends of the Bachs.

The court at Dresden was a compound of exquisite culture and rank corruption. Augustus the Strong (see colour plate 8) was addicted to collecting porcelain, particularly from the Far East. A few miles down the Elbe from Dresden was the Meissen porcelain factory, started around 1710.** A few miles upstream, Augustus could step from his gondola on to the magnificent landing stage at Pillnitz, his pleasure palace built in the Chinese style, for China was then regarded as a paradise on earth, a land of carefree living and luxury.[103] The palace was being completed at the time Bach arrived in Leipzig, and would soon be the scene of the three-week-long celebrations for the wedding of one of the king's daughters. Augustus was also renovating the Moritzburg castle, the Zwinger Palace, and creating for himself some baroque gardens in the hills above the Elbe. The Protestant burghers of Dresden were not to be left out: the city architect was completing his plans for a new church, to be called the Frauenkirche.†

Underneath this veneer, Augustus was 'Lutheran by birth, Catholic by ambition (the Poles were violently Catholic) and Mahometan in his

* In the year after Bach arrived in Leipzig, Augustus executed the Protestant leaders at Thorn (now Toruń) in Poland in what was known as the 'Bloodbath of Thorn'.[101]

** The Meissen porcelain factory was the first in Europe; its products would soon be copied at Sèvres.

† Bach played the Silbermann organ at the Frauenkirche even before the outer shell of its dome was completed in December 1736.

habits'.[104] 'In the matter of morals the court of Augustus was possibly the most corrupt establishment in Europe. An observer might just as well have attempted to define the interrelationships in a warren of [rabbits] as to give a name to the multifarious couplings of lovers, mistresses, sons and daughters.'[105] When he died, he left a legitimate heir and 354 illegitimate children, one of whom was General Maurice de Saxe.[106]

Dresden was a social and cultural world distant from the precincts of St Thomas' Church and its school where Bach worked and lived. It was a world in which Handel could have thrived because the opportunities for the entrepreneurial musician were enormous. Bach's circumstances were different.

Bach had 'dropped a rung in the social ladder' from his position in Cöthen. His job was arduous, and he was misled at the outset into thinking that the emoluments were around the same as the combined salary which he and Anna Magdalena had received at Cöthen. He was required to supervise the music in the four civic churches. At St Thomas' and St Nicolas',* the principal churches, Bach had to rehearse the Sunday cantata and direct the first choir on alternate Sundays. The main Sunday service began at 7 am and lasted until midday, with a sermon for an hour in the middle. On the great feast days, the same service was repeated in the other principal church. The cantata would have been performed at 7.30 am, hardly the best time for young choristers and instrumentalists to perform; boys who left before the service ended were birched.[107]

One can picture Bach striding across from St Thomas' to St Nicolas' Church, past the City Hall and the Exchange, not a great distance. The two other churches, the New Church and St Peter's, were served by the less competent singers: the choir at St Peter's could 'only just barely sing a chorale'.[108] They would have attracted less of Bach's time.

The Cantor's principal colleagues were the Rector, the Conrector, both of whom also had teaching responsibilities at the university, and the Tertius.** Each week, Bach farmed out five of his twelve hours of non-musical teaching duties to Magister Pezold, the Tertius. Every fourth week,

* Protests held in St Nicolas' Church were an important contributor to the fall of the East German communist regime.

** The German Gymnasium at full strength included eight masters, the Rector (teaching the Primaner, the top form), the Conrector (teaching the Secundaner), Subrector, Quintus, Quartus, Tertius etc.[109]

Bach was duty master, responsible for discipline, ensuring that the boys were up at 4 am in summer and 5 am in winter, saying morning prayers a quarter of an hour later, supervising the meals in the refectory. After the evening meal, prayers were at 8 pm.

As well as doing all this, Bach managed to write a massive amount of music, particularly in his first year. His vocation was to write church music. He seems to have set out in Leipzig to provide a five-year cycle of cantatas and passions: more than half the volumes in the Bach-Gesellschaft edition are devoted to this. He composed 265 cantatas;[110] all but a few were written during his first five or six years, at the rate of about one a week. In addition, he wrote motets; these were performed at vespers on Sunday afternoons, at the beginning of the main morning service or during communion, funerals or memorial services. In Lent, there was no cantata music and this gave him time to write the Passions.* The St John Passion was written in 1724 and the first version of the St Matthew Passion in 1727.

Bach's work extended beyond the confines of St Thomas'. For around twelve years from spring 1729, he directed the secular Collegium Musicum which Telemann had founded. Meetings were held on Friday evenings usually at Zimmermann's coffee house,[111] which held 150 people, or in summer in the garden just outside the city. The coffee house is probably where the 'Coffee' Cantata was performed. After 1741, the larger Grand Concerts begun by a group of Leipzig aristocrats increasingly eclipsed the Collegium. Bach was involved, but on the sidelines.

The secular cantatas are the nearest Bach came to writing an opera. He took his children to the Dresden opera several times 'to hear the lovely Dresden ditties'.[112] He attended Hasse's *Cleofide* in September 1731 and played an organ recital the following day.[113]

After Augustus the Strong died in 1733, there was a compulsory period of court mourning during which cantatas were not allowed in church. Court mourning was a disaster for musicians. Bach's predecessor Kuhnau said: 'nobody will pray more devoutly for a long life of his sovereign than the instrumentalists'.[114] Bach, however, took this opportunity to write the B minor Mass.

* Bach's obituary says that he composed five Passions but only the two have survived complete. There is a libretto for the St Mark Passion; the St Luke Passion is not thought to be by Bach.

He composed a cantata for the new king, when he visited Leipzig. Six hundred students formed a torchlight procession to the market place where Bach's Collegium performed. The king was not much better than his father: one of his favourite amusements was shooting dogs from the windows of his palace in Warsaw.[115]

Domestic Life

Bach's sister-in-law, Friedelena, continued to live with the family until her death in 1729. In 1731–2, the Bachs' apartment was renovated and they moved to temporary lodgings. By the standards of the time, the Cantor's premises were large, although not very private: there was a throughway to the classroom and dormitories through the middle.[116]

Bach's possessions at his death enable one to envisage his lodgings. His study was full of books: there were 80 theological ones. His dining room was furnished with heavy black leather chairs; on the wall was a portrait of his father. The kitchen, where no doubt Anna Magdalena spent a considerable amount of time with the children, was bright with copper and brass; on a shelf they placed their silver cutlery and candlesticks, and the silver tea and coffee service. Bach ran a kind of music shop on the side, which involved organising the sale or hire of instruments. In his lodgings, he had several harpsichords, violins, violas, cellos, gambas and a lute. His clothes included eleven shirts and he had a silver mounted stick and even a silver dagger. With his glass of rosehip brandy and his pipe, he must have conveyed the image of a comfortable, religious, very respectable burgher. One can speculate that the Hasses from Dresden would have regarded him as a bit too respectable, almost dull.[117]

The Bach family atmosphere was busy and highly cultured. The family unit formed a vocal and instrumental ensemble, which was augmented by the resident apprentices. It also pitched in to help Bach with his work; Anna Magdalena and the older children made fair copies of his compositions.[118] Compared to today, the labour necessary to create a score was considerable: Bach had to rule his own paper, and sharpen his quills with the knife which was also used for erasing mistakes. Working in candlelight must have considerably tired and strained the eyes.

In most years, Anna Magdalena bore a child: they had thirteen. In the early years, many died, some either in or just after childbirth, but several aged three or four. Hardly eighteen months went by without a funeral:

children died in June 1726, November 1727, September 1728, January 1730 and August 1732. The year 1733 was particularly sad with deaths in April and November. But this was not unusual. Even a few years later, a quarter to a third of all infants still failed to survive their first year; half would die before the age of ten.[119]

As we have seen in the London of Handel, the frequency of death, sudden and unpredictable, did not permit the wrenching emotions of today. This perhaps helps one understand why Jonathan Swift, Dean of St Patrick's Cathedral in Dublin, could chide a mother grieving for the loss of a daughter, urging her against 'too strong attachments' to her children, 'a weakness God seldom leaves unpunished'.[120] It was a hard and sad world. If one did not escape into the fleshpots of Dresden, one took one's solace from the deep and devotional Lutheran religion.

Some of Anna Magdalena's children survived. The best known is Johann Christian, who went to live in London. He was born in 1735. Heinrich, born eleven years earlier, had some learning disability. Elizabeth was born in 1726, Christoph Friedrich in 1732 and Johanna Carolina in 1737. There was an after-thought in 1742, Regine Susanna, who survived into the 19th century: she died in 1809, when she was said to be 'starving'. There was an appeal for her to which Beethoven responded. The Bach line died out in 1845 when Wilhelm Friedrich Ernst, harpsichordist to the Queen of Prussia, died; he turned up, rather to everybody's surprise, in 1843 when the memorial to Bach was unveiled in Leipzig.[121]

Protracted Disputes

Bach was not happy or contented; he became enmeshed in the tensions between the university, St Thomas' and the city council. In September 1725, he had his first row, a 'turf' dispute about his entitlement to play at, and be remunerated for, services at the university church. Bach appealed to King Augustus who, we may assume, had other things on his mind. The pleadings went back and forth several times. Bach wrote his own at considerable length, referring to the historical role of the Cantor, stipulating the amounts involved, which were trivial, well below ten per cent of his annual salary. The king, or some diligent civil servant, confirmed Bach's responsibility for the festival and academic services, but upheld the right of Gottlieb Görner, the university organist, to play at the routine services.[122]

This was not the end of it: about twenty months later, when Augustus' wife died, a young noble at the University commissioned Bach to write a funeral ode, and Görner objected.[123] The noble had to buy Görner off, Bach being asked, and refusing, to sign an undertaking not to encroach on his territory in future. Surprisingly, during all this, Bach and Görner managed to stay on reasonably friendly terms.

There was a row the following year about the choice of hymns for Vespers.[124] The ecclesiastical authorities wanted the preacher to choose the hymns before and after the sermon, whereas Bach said that this had always been the prerogative of the Cantor.

The city council took Bach to task about his disinclination to teach non-musical subjects, because Magister Pezold, the Tertius, does not seem to have been much good at the work delegated to him. Councillor Steger gives one a clear indication of Bach's reaction: 'Not only did the Cantor do nothing, but he was not even willing to give an explanation of that fact.'[125]

Meanwhile, Bach was preparing a lengthy memorandum about the difficulties of finding sufficiently talented singers and instrumentalists. He pointed out that at Dresden 'the musicians are relieved of all concern for their living, free from chagrin, and obliged each to master but a single instrument',[126] whereas he had seventeen usable musicians, twenty not yet usable and seventeen unfit, largely because his recommendations for admissions had been overruled. His predecessor had similarly complained about the new opera house attracting singers away from St Thomas'.

It is not surprising that, a couple of months later, Bach was in touch with the school friend who had accompanied him to Lüneburg, by now the imperial resident agent in Danzig. Bach was looking for another job. In his letter he said that he had to live amid 'almost continual vexation, envy and persecution'. The money was not up to the level he had expected when appointed and the cost of living was high; also, as he put it, 'when a healthy wind blows', the level of fees from funerals is disappointing.[127] But no job was forthcoming.*

Yet, all of this was just the prelude to a much larger drama, baroque in its intricacy. A new Rector, August Ernesti, was appointed who was 22

* This was probably just as well, as Danzig was besieged in the War of the Polish Succession in 1734 which followed the death of King Augustus. The Polish Diet elected Stanislas Leszinski, father-in-law of Louis XV, but a Russian invasion of Poland enabled Augustus' son to succeed his father as King Augustus III.

years younger than Bach, a brilliant teacher, an innovator, and unsympathetic with the traditions of St Thomas':*[128] consistently with the trend at the time, he regarded the musical side of church worship as an impediment, and ticked off boys found practising: 'so you mean to be a fiddler in a pub?', he reputedly asked one boy who was trying to practise his violin.[129]

Each of Bach's choirs had a prefect, more like a junior master, one of whose roles was to deputise as conductor when the Cantor was absent in another church. In August 1736, the prefect of the first choir had beaten one of the younger boys who had misbehaved at a wedding service; the boy complained to the Rector, who ordered the prefect to be flogged before the whole school. The prefect, who was aged 22, would not submit and asked to leave, but was refused his customary certificate of discharge; when he absconded, Ernesti seized his belongings and money.[130]

Ernesti nominated another to be prefect, who Bach thought was a poor musician and therefore not up to the position at St Thomas'. To accommodate the Rector, Bach appointed Ernesti's nominee as prefect of the New Church choir where, as we have seen, the musical tradition was less demanding. The protagonists and their nominees became entrenched. On two consecutive Sundays, there were scuffles in St Thomas' gallery when the two rival appointees turned up. Bach would not have had any conductor, had not Krebs, a university student and pupil of Bach, stood in.

There was voluminous correspondence with the city council, with Ernesti pointing out venomously that if Bach had not been absent from the wedding, the whole saga would never have arisen. The city council upheld Bach's nomination of prefects, but did not criticise Ernesti. Yet, instead of stopping there, Bach appealed to the ecclesiastical authorities, and then to the king, requesting them to uphold him in his office and impress on Ernesti that he should cease telling the school boys to ignore his instructions.

Although Ernesti had severely undermined Bach's authority, it is not clear for what 'pound of flesh' Bach was looking. He cannot realistically have expected to oust Ernesti, a highly-regarded scholar: in future years Goethe attended his lectures at the university. The king's officers, who must have begun to regret that Bach had recently been appointed to the honorific position of Electoral Saxon and Royal Polish Court Composer,

* The immediately preceding Rector was a friend of Bach's from Weimar days.

wrote to the Church authorities requiring them to take such measures 'as you shall see fit';[131] an example of diplomacy, which Bach could well have practised in the first place. Whereas one can have much sympathy for Bach's right to be satisfied with the musical ability of his deputy, one wonders whether, had he sought to discuss the appointments with Ernesti in the first place, all of this might have been avoided.

THE BACKWATER

As the years went by, Bach's children with his first wife gradually drifted away, leaving a gap in the family ensembles, and reducing the number of assistants available for copying. Bach obtained good positions for his sons. Friedemann went to Dresden's Sophienkirche. Carl Philipp Emanuel went to the university at Frankfurt an der Oder. Johann Gottfried Bernhard, with his father's support, went to Mühlhausen's Marienkirche and then Sangerhausen. Bernhard was a bad sort, incurring debts everywhere he went, and in the end he disappeared; he eventually turned up at Jena University, where he died of fever. On a happier note, in 1738–42 a cousin, Elias, came to lodge with the Bachs. He acted as Bach's secretary and tutor to the younger children.[132]

In the eyes of his contemporaries, Bach was getting increasingly 'out of date' and isolated from the newly fashionable *galant* style. This had a much thinner texture and a clear melody with symmetrical phrases and regular rhythms, a style we associate with France and Couperin Le Grand. The knife was stuck in when the fortnightly publication *Critischer Musikus* criticised Bach for 'taking away the natural element in his pieces by giving them a bombastic and confused style' and suggested that he should 'not darken their beauty by an excess of Art'.[133] The accusation, which enrages Bach supporters, was written in 1737 by Scheibe, whom Bach had rejected for the post of organist at St Nicolas'. Scheibe was an acquaintance of Gluck.

Bach increasingly found himself up a backwater in a city where tastes were changing. A decade later, the burghers of Leipzig would be watching a travelling opera group performing Scalabrini's *Demetrio* and *Merope* and attending a concert at which 'arias by a great maître from Italy were sung'.[134] They preferred this entertainment to Bach's 'dual unity of absolute mathematics and absolute poetry'.[135]

Dresden saw the double royal wedding between, on the one hand,

Elector Max Joseph of Bavaria and a daughter of King Augustus, and on the other, the Saxon Prince Christian and a Bavarian princess. The sumptuous celebrations included, as one might expect, a festival opera by Hasse. Bach, the so-called 'court composer', was not involved; Gluck was.[136]

Against this uncomfortable background, Bach plodded on at his duties. His productivity dropped. His output in the middle Leipzig years was small. In some of his works, such as the Christmas Oratorio and the B minor Mass, he borrowed extensively from earlier compositions. He completed the final 24 preludes and fugues for *The Well Tempered Clavier* in 1742. And between 1731 and 1742 he also compiled the four educational volumes of the *Klavierübung.** The fourth volume includes variations composed, it is said, for an insomniac nobleman who wanted a piece with which his harpsichordist Goldberg could soothe him to sleep.

The third volume illustrates Bach's 'difficulty' only two well. This was one of the first of his works to be circulated. It includes several chorale preludes for the organ, that is, music which would typically serve as an introduction to the congregational singing of a chorale; the preludes are framed between the well-known Prelude and Fugue known as 'St Anne'. As always, with sufficient patience, Bach's meticulously crafted pieces please the performer; but there are pieces that are far more enjoyable to play elsewhere. With a few exceptions, these *Klavierübung* chorale preludes are rarely performed today.

It appears that Bach was frequently away from home, doing recitals, and advising on organ building. Early in 1740, the council appointed an extra master to instruct the school in musical theory. 'If the Council frowned, it had learnt by experience that the cantor was not to be coerced.'[138] In 1741, he visited Berlin, where, in the previous year, Emanuel Bach was appointed harpsichordist at the court of Frederick the Great. This visit was disturbed by news that Anna Magdalena was unwell, although she recovered.

Bach visited Berlin again in 1747 in order to meet Emanuel's wife, the daughter of a wine merchant. At night, after supper, King Frederick the Great usually required his courtiers to listen to a concert: he would play the flute, accompanied by his long-standing flute teacher, Johann Joachim

* Part I sold for 2 thalers, Part III for 3 thalers; the same price as a violin and a spinet respectively.[137]

Quantz.[139] When Bach arrived at the palace in Potsdam, twenty miles from Berlin, Frederick was notified and invited him to play his new Silbermann pianos and develop a fugue on a theme ('subject') which he would provide. The following day Bach gave an organ recital, and again, at the palace, improvised a six-part fugue. On return to Leipzig, he developed the *Musical Offering*, based on Frederick's fugal subject, and the *Art of Fugue*.

This story, no doubt embroidered over the years, gives us a politically correct picture of the 35-year-old king making music with the elderly but distinguished commoner. Frederick (see colour plate 7) was a talented musician, but it is as well to remember that, following a childhood scarred by a ferocious father, he was by then well into his career as the exponent of *Realpolitik*. When the Habsburg Emperor died without a male heir, Frederick took the opportunity to seize the rich area of Silesia; he was now determined to crush Saxony. Shortly before Bach's visit, one of Frederick's warriors, accredited with inventing the practice of troops marching in step,[140] led a surge of soldiers into Leipzig. One cannot imagine that the precincts of St Thomas' Church were immune from the extortion of the billeted troops. Shortly afterwards, the Prussians were victorious at Kesselsdorf, just outside Dresden, where combined armies of 61,000 men sustained an appalling casualty rate of 25–33 per cent.[141] So much for the flute.

Frederick became an explicit role model for Hitler, who hoped to possess his knack for surviving against all the odds. If it had not been for some visits by Voltaire and Bach, Frederick might be seen by posterity in a rather different light.[142]

It is Bach's son Emanuel, not the king, who deserves the lasting fame. Had he not subsequently been overshadowed by his father, he would surely now be in the pantheon of great composers. C.P.E. Bach provides the bedrock on which Haydn and Mozart built their structures;* he also evolved an expressive piano style which they emulated and then took forward. We can surmise that, during his father's visit, Emanuel will have shown his father the rococo summer palace which Frederick was having

* The sonata movement of the 18th century normally has two identifiable parts, the second reworking the material of the first. In C.P.E. Bach's sonatas, there is a clear recapitulation of opening material within the second section. This was an important step towards 'sonata form', which by the 19th century became a three-part structure in which, generally speaking, the first section sets out a number of themes (the exposition), which are then developed in the second section, called the development, and returned to in the final section, known as the recapitulation.[143]

built on the hill above Potsdam. It would be completed in the following year and would be called Sanssouci, meaning 'free of care'.

Bach's visit to Berlin was his last journey. In 1749, the year which saw the marriage of his daughter Elizabeth to the organist at Naumburg, the city council took the apparently unprecedented step of nominating Bach's successor, while Bach was still in post. At the end of that year, his eyesight was so troublesome that he consulted the English eye doctor, John Taylor,

Bach's church by Mendelssohn

who later treated Handel. Taylor operated.[144] When Bach's eyesight permitted, according to tradition, he assembled the Eighteen Chorales; an amanuensis had to write the 16th and 17th. He headed the 18th, 'Vor deinen Thron tret ich', 'Before thy throne I come'. Bach's manuscript ends in the 26th bar. On 18 July, he rallied and saw a bit. He then relapsed. He died on 28 July 1750. The cause of death is not clear, since eye diseases are not normally fatal. Years later, a coffin was found which was matched to him; it was eventually placed in the chancel of St Thomas', where the tomb may now be seen.

There was no minute of regret from the city council. Bach was replaced by one Gottlob Harrer. Privy Councillor of the War Office and

Burgomaster Stieglitz announced that 'the school needs a Cantor, not a Kapellmeister'.[145] Harrer died five years later; his successor Doles was almost as obscure, and is only remembered for his statement that the fugue was an antiquated form of scholastic exercise. Doles' own successor condemned cantatas for arousing 'disagreeable emotions of boredom and disgust, if not utter annoyance'.[146]

Bach's style was thought to be 'harmonious and full-voiced, but not melodious and charming'. He 'sought more to compose in an artistic than in a comprehensible and pleasing manner'.[147] Four years after his death, none of his works were included in the catalogue of the library at Cöthen. His works were occasionally performed in St Thomas'; and individual copies were to be found, usually in organ lofts. A few of his works, mainly those used for teaching, were engraved and in circulation. These were not his best advertisement: works such as the *Klavierübung* and the *Art of Fugue*, for the amateur at least, are not always the most pleasurable. So, six years after he died, a travel writer in Leipzig does not even mention Bach.[148] This was at a time when Handel's *Messiah* was receiving its annual performance before vast audiences in Westminster Abbey.

Anna Magdalena died ten years after Bach and appears to have survived on alms.[149]

HAYDN

CHAPTER 3

TO BERNARD SHAW, the Irish playwright and critic, the Inferno will be like a performance of an oratorio in a vast Royal Albert Hall: in the galleries, choristers will sing 'All that hath life and breath, sing to the Lord'; in the arena below, the condemned will sit in their evening dress, while demons force them to stay awake.[1]

Yet surely we could do worse than to be obliged to hear a continuous loop of Haydn's *The Creation*? We would get such pleasure from the chorus 'The Heavens are Telling the Glory of God' and from the air 'With Verdure Clad the Fields Appear'! We would enjoy the horn chorus from *The Seasons*. We could happily listen to 'Heyday, the liquor flows, raise your cups and let us merry be', provided of course that the bar would open and we had the cash to pay. Eternal tedium would be relieved by Haydn's delightful sense of humour as, in *The Creation*, he imitates the roaring lion and observes how 'in long dimension, creeps with sinuous trace the worm'. Haydn's contemporaries appreciated his light touch: one, an Englishman, thought that listening to his music was like hearing a conversation at afternoon tea; listening to Handel's music was, by contrast, more like hearing a sermon delivered from the pulpit. Doubtless, the Englishman had not heard of Johann Sebastian Bach.[2]

Haydn was born when Bach was working on the B minor Mass; he died when Beethoven had written his Fifth and Sixth Symphonies. He lived at a time when Vienna had become *the* centre for music in Europe.[3] Composers were pouring out sonatas, quartets and symphonies* to meet the demand created by an increasing number of public concerts. The earliest symphonies listened to by most of us are those by Haydn. His genius was to bring together several styles and to compose something entirely personal and individual. He blended the light *galant* style of Couperin le Grand and Sammartini with the heavier textures of Bach's son, Emanuel.**

We shall follow Haydn from his birthplace on the Hungarian border to Vienna, only 25 miles to the west. Although on a war footing and with an empty treasury, Vienna was about to be uplifted by Empress Maria Theresa's glittering reign. The middle 30 years of Haydn's life were spent, however, away from the centre, secluded and constrained in the service of the fabulously rich Prince Esterházy. While Haydn was there, momentous changes were taking place outside: Western civilisation was being transformed by the Enlightenment. We shall look at two developments which were part of this: the wide-ranging reforms of Emperor Joseph II, and the transformation of opera by Gluck and his colleagues. Then we shall travel with Haydn to London, where he was tempted to settle among friends. However, he returned to Vienna for his old age, and died while Napoleon's troops rained down shells upon that most beautiful and cultured city.

Early Days in Rohrau

Franz Joseph Haydn, the second of twelve children, was born on 31 March 1732 in a small thatched cottage in Rohrau, a few hundred yards from the Leitha, the small river which marked the border between Lower Austria and Hungary. The countryside is rather flat, although on a clear day a snow-capped mountain is visible in the far distance. The cottage was on

* Symphonies were now being composed in a form which we would recognise. Starting from something like an overture, a structure with three movements, fast-slow-fast, developed. In the middle of the century, we find composers beginning to include a minuet and also a slow introduction to the first movement. We hear these in Haydn's symphonies. Mannheim was an important centre for symphonies. There, the Elector of the Palatinate spent a fortune on his orchestra, and its director, the Czech émigré Johann Stamitz. The orchestra was reputed to be capable of performing a crescendo so dramatic that people rose in their seats.[4]

** François Couperin le Grand, from Paris, died eighteen months after Haydn was born; G.B. Sammartini lived in Milan and was a generation older than Haydn.

the estate of the Harrach family, who lived in a castle a stone's throw away. The Harrachs combined the thuggery and taste so typical of the aristocracy: a forebear had been Lord Chamberlain to Wallenstein, the sinister and ferocious general of the Thirty Years War; others, more cultured, had been in the foreign service of the Habsburgs in Madrid, Naples and Brussels. This had enabled the family to assemble the magnificent art works now on display in Rohrau.[5]

Matthias, Haydn's father, made wagons for the horses and bullocks to pull. He was also responsible for the upkeep of the roads. A pillar of the traditional and conservative serf establishment, he dispensed justice in the village court, and handled cases of adultery, excessive gambling or failure to attend church. Haydn's mother Anna had been a cook with the Harrachs, whose moated castle, although not large, would have been a comfort and means of defence in times of trouble: her father had lost all his possessions when a Hungarian peasant army had plundered Rohrau some 30 years earlier.[6]

Life was hard. Serfdom varied throughout the Habsburg Empire, in some parts being indistinguishable from slavery. Two, if not three, days' compulsory labour were required per week; children, on reaching the age of fourteen, were required to work full-time for three to seven years.[7] This work was called 'robot', and the mechanical, unenthusiastic way in which the serfs toiled is at the root of the modern word with which we are familiar. In Rohrau, the Haydns might have commuted the required services with a cash payment;[8] but almost certainly they could not leave the estate, marry or choose their occupation without Harrach consent. They seem to have leased their own land, had their own cattle and wine cellar. Times were relatively good: the price of agricultural produce was rising, and Anna, a good *Hausfrau*, insisted that everything was neat and tidy. Matthias played his harp in the evenings. No doubt the domestic scene was comfortable and cosy.[9]

The standard of living of the Haydn family was considerably higher than that of the peasant whose main diet was rye bread washed down with water.[10] However, Anna's domestic economy could not sustain twelve children, so Joseph, or Sepperl as he was then known, had to be pushed out of the nest. His uncle suggested that he should join him in Hainburg, the local big town about eight miles away where he was headmaster and precentor at the church of St Philip and St James. Aged just five and a half, the boy was sent away, never to return to his family home except for rare and brief visits.

He was surely too small even to notice the gate and walls of Hainburg, or to appreciate its beauty with the Danube flowing below and the hill above. Had he, he would have learnt that this tranquil setting was illusory: less than 50 years earlier, at the time of the siege of Vienna, the Turks had massacred the inhabitants, including his great-grandfather. There was now yet another war with the Turks, with the Habsburgs supporting their Russian allies in a dispute over territory in the far-away Caspian region.[11] The 'Türkenglocken' bells rang out each morning, calling people to pray and reminding them of the horrors of a Turkish invasion.

Haydn learnt the clavier, violin and kettledrum, and played in the church orchestra. 'I was a regular little ragamuffin', he said many years later. There were lots of floggings and little food. He was soon to move on.[12]

The Chorister

St Stephen's Cathedral in Vienna was described by the musical historian Dr Burney as 'a dark, dirty and dismal old Gothic building … In it are hung all the trophies of war, taken from the Turks and other enemies.' This gave it 'the appearance of an old wardrobe'.[13] Be that as it may, the cathedral needed a regular flow of new choristers, and George Reutter, who had recently succeeded his father as choirmaster, included nearby Hainburg in his search for suitable talent. This recruitment drive must have been a distasteful and undignified experience for someone so obsequious and vain.

In his time, Reutter was successful and thus important, or at least self-important. He reduced the court musical establishment by implementing the economies requested. He married the daughter of a court functionary; he held many appointments; he was knighted. His 80 Masses were very popular: one was even used during a visit of the Pope. For all this, however, Burney described his work as 'great noise – little meaning',[14] and today we are spared the noise.

Reutter's signal achievement, in later years, was to destroy the far-sighted Count Durazzo, the director of theatres who was working with Gluck to raise the standards in the opera. Reutter complained that the Count was poaching some of his church musicians, and carrying out rehearsals in unsuitable places; he objected when the Count invited Gluck to be composer of court and chamber music. A master of the turf dispute, he got Durazzo dismissed.[15]

But Reutter's successes are forgotten. Posterity just remembers his poor treatment of Haydn, who, aged only eight, moved into his house next to the cathedral, where he joined the other five choristers, the sub-cantor and two preceptors. Whether his treatment was worse than that of any similar choirboy one does not know: Reutter's cardinal error was not to recognise genius, something history never forgives. We can imagine that, rather than looking after choirboys, Reutter must have found it more congenial to trot along to give little Archduke Joseph his music lessons at 6.30 pm on Mondays and Wednesdays.[16]

Haydn received virtually no formal education from Reutter. But he did get a considerable amount of practical experience. The choristers had to perform High Mass and Vespers each day, besides performing on great feast days when the cathedral was visited by the Imperial Court. These occasions were frequent: the court had 78 ceremonial attendances at church service every year.[17] A particularly solemn annual occasion was the equivalent of the British Remembrance Sunday, the commemoration of the lifting of the Turkish siege of 1683.

Vienna and the Court

Like Venice, Vienna was smelly, with the added disadvantage that the 16,000 carriages and their horses stirred up the dust, which irritated the eyes and chest. It had some fine new buildings, including Prince Eugene's Belvedere and the St Charles' Church, designed by Lukas von Hildebrandt and Fischer von Erlach. The magnificent palace at Schönbrunn was still being built. Haydn apparently climbed the scaffolding and was ticked off by the empress.[18]

Vienna was in some ways the Manhattan of the 18th century: its buildings were unusually high, most being five or six storeys, and the streets were narrow. It was considerably more crowded than London. According to an English traveller, almost 50,000 inhabitants were compressed into 1,233 houses.[19] The dusty ground floor was kept empty for the billeting of court servants, but, on the mezzanine and first floors, the rich and successful lived in considerable splendour.[20] Above this, there were further floors and the garret at the top: 'the apartments of the greatest ladies and even of the ministers of state are divided but by a partition from that of a taylor or shoemaker', it was said.[21]

The real purpose of the city was to support the Habsburg Court.[22] An English visitor drily observed that 'no sooner is a man a master of a moderate fortune, but his head is turned with the thoughts of a patent of nobility; and none sets out lower than with the title of a baron'.[23] The importance of the Crown was exemplified in the dying words of Prince Schwarzenberg when shot by the emperor in a hunting accident: 'It was always my duty to give my life for my sovereign', he gasped.[24]

The Court employed hundreds of master artists, including 243 goldsmiths.[25] There were few shops: traders sold their wares from building to building. Burney observed that 'a stranger is teased to death by these chapmen, who offer to sell wretched goods, ill-manufactured and ill-fashioned. In old England, it is true, things are very dear, but if their goodness be compared with these, they are cheap as dirt.'[26] He also criticised the Viennese penchant for cruel sports: he describes dogs being set upon a wild ox which had crackers festooned to its head and body and fire secured under its tail. There were lots of dogs.[27]

The city was noticeably international,* as evidenced by the colourful costumes of Hungarians, Poles, Serbs, and the Croats 'with black tubs balanced on their heads'.[29] The considerable presence of the Church was on display, with many religious processions at which a foreigner would be well-advised to genuflect if he did not want to be roughed up.[30]

The 'monstrous' fashions of the aristocracy were observed by Lady Mary Wortley Montagu,** and must have amused little Haydn. 'They build certain fabrics of gauze on their heads about a yard high, consisting of three or four stories, fortified with numberless yards of heavy riband. The foundation of this structure is a thing they call a Bourle … This machine they cover with their own hair, which they mix with a great deal of false.' She added: 'their hair is prodigiously powdered to conceal the mixture, and set out with three or four rows of bodkins, wonderfully large.' The dresses were monstrous too. 'Their whale bone petticoats out do ours by several yards' circumference, and cover some acres of ground.' Yet, in spite of this physical disadvantage, the normal routines of life prevailed: ''Tis the established custom for every lady to have two husbands, one that bears the name and another that performs the duties', Lady Mary wrote.

* It has been suggested that one needs fourteen languages to write the biography of a Habsburg emperor, at the very least French, German, Latin and Italian.[28]

** Lady Mary visited Vienna early in the 18th century. Dr Burney's visit was in 1770.

In the customary English style, she observed that the Austrians were 'not commonly the most polite people in the world or the most agreeable'.[31]

The War of Austrian Succession

Haydn arrived in Vienna in 1740, around the same time as Vivaldi died there in obscurity. The court was in turmoil. The Habsburg family suddenly faced a most serious crisis with the death of Charles VI. Like other members of his family, he indulged in blood sports on an enormous scale, heron-baiting being his favourite pastime.* In October 1740, he caught a chill after a day's shooting. He then consumed a large pot of mushrooms stewed in his favourite Catalan oil, and died. He had no male heir. His only son had died in infancy, and his repugnance at his empress' obesity, together with his preference for a combination of his Spanish mistress and young men, precluded any resolution of this difficulty.[33]

To succeed him, he left only a daughter, the Archduchess Maria Theresa, thus breaking the direct line of male succession which could be traced back at least 23 generations. Women rulers were unknown in Central Europe. The young Archduchess of Austria, then aged only 23, could in theory be elected Queen of Hungary, but not to the throne of the Holy Roman Emperor. Charles' predecessor, his elder brother, Joseph I, had sired two daughters before he had managed to give his wife a recurring venereal infection.[34] These two girls, properly excluded from succeeding their father when he had died, were now married to the powerful Electors of Saxony and Bavaria, and they arguably had superior claims to Maria Theresa. Besides, they also had six sons between them, whereas, until her son Joseph was born on 13 March 1741, Maria Theresa had borne only daughters. There were five particularly tense months after her father's death until Archduke Joseph was born. Meanwhile, the other Habsburg heiresses and their husbands saw this as an excellent opportunity for acquisition; other nations of Europe, particularly France and England, watched for any move that might change the delicate balance of power.** Such succession

* In a shoot in 1729, 'the falcons killed two hundred and eighty herons, twenty-seven hares, seven kites, nineteen wild ducks, fifty-eight magpies, twenty-nine ravens'.[32]

** Charles had ostensibly secured his daughter's position by requiring his nieces, in their marriage settlements, to renounce their superior claims. He had also got foreign rulers to sign up to his Pragmatic Sanction. But this provided little security; after all, the Habsburgs had taken no notice of the will left by the last Spanish king, bequeathing his throne when he died.

problems were grist to the mill of all rulers in Europe, and inevitably led to war.[35]

The archduchess was in a parlous position. Her husband Francis Stephen, formerly Duke of Lorraine, was unpopular and ineffectual. Her father had squandered his fortune on wars with Turkey and on the magnificent baroque buildings of Vienna. She had less than 100,000 florins in her treasury, an army depleted to half-strength after the wars with Turkey, and a council of state whose members 'appeared to be embalmed'.[36] Before she knew where she was, the Elector of Brandenburg, the Prussian King Frederick, seized her lands in Silesia* on the specious grounds that, in return, he would help defend her against her foes.

The War of Austrian Succession spread and continued for almost all the time that Haydn was a chorister at St Stephen's. The Elector of Bavaria staked his claim and was crowned the first non-Habsburg Holy Roman Emperor for centuries. Prague fell, and only the onset of winter prevented the occupation of Vienna. Cartoons of the period describe Maria Theresa's predicament: one shows the octogenarian Cardinal Fleury of France demanding 'Let me handle it' as his hands grope at her scantily clad body.[38]

But Maria Theresa was tough. She got herself crowned Queen of Hungary in Pressburg (now Bratislava), resplendently riding a black charger to the top of a mound and pointing her sword to all four points of the compass. Although there were defeats still to come (Prague changed hands three times in three years),[39] she was crowned Queen of Bohemia. After the death of the former Elector of Bavaria, she ensured that her beloved husband Francis Stephen was crowned Emperor. The thirteen-year-old Haydn must have watched the colourful celebrations for this event, including the big military parade held near St Stephen's Cathedral.

Although that war ended in October 1748, there was continuing instability. Frederick attacked Dresden in 1756, inflicting enormous damage. The peasants in Bohemia suffered terribly. To keep warm, soldiers would set a dwelling on fire and sit round it: the fire gave out good heat and lasted a long time.[40] War again ebbed and flowed, with perhaps 850,000 men lost

* Silesia was the area around Breslau (now Wroclaw) in modern Poland. Rich in coal and other minerals, and with a flourishing textile industry and excellent water communications, it yielded 25 per cent of the revenues of the Habsburg's Austrian and Bohemian lands. Its loss strengthened the Prussian position and weakened the adjacent economies of Bohemia and Moravia. It also put Prussians within 100 miles of Prague and 130 miles of Vienna.[37]

in action in these campaigns: Prussia itself lost a tenth of its population.[41] Musical talent drained from the war-torn areas. One immigrant to England was Zumpe, the inventor of the square piano and father-in-law of John Broadwood, the prominent English piano maker.[42]

Destitution, then Luck

Meanwhile, young Joseph Haydn was singing in the cathedral, where his brother Michael, five years younger, joined him. But this position was on a short lease, unless he was castrated, and his father put a stop to that suggestion. So his treble voice began to break. He was expelled, ostensibly for refusing to accept a beating for cutting off the pigtail of another chorister. It is said that on a cold November day in 1749, Haydn, with three ragged shirts and a worn coat, was turned onto the streets. Fortunately, a singer in St Michael's Church invited him into his poor garret, where he lived with his wife and nine-month-old baby. Haydn earned money playing where he could, at dances, churches and in particular as a street musician serenading at night.[43]

We have a description of these Viennese serenades at the end of the century: 'During the summer months ... one will meet serenaders in the streets almost daily and at all hours ... They do not, however, consist as in Italy or Spain of the simple accompaniment of a vocal part by a guitar or mandolin ... but of trios, and quartets ... frequently of an entire orchestra, and the most ambitious symphonies are performed ... one soon discovers people at their open windows and within a few minutes the musicians are surrounded by a crowd of listeners who rarely depart until the serenade has come to an end.'[44]

With the accession of Maria Theresa, Vienna had become a much livelier place, a radical change, because nobody had ever seen her father smile. The young royal couple* discarded his stiff Spanish ceremonial; masked balls were reinstated; a form of waltzing began, called the Deutsche.[47] The nobility and the royal family staged their own amateur dramatics.

Regardless of wartime austerity, Maria Theresa had insisted that 'shows must go on; without them one cannot stay here in such a great residence'.[48]

*Maria Theresa and her husband were genuinely in love. 'Only the onset of the menopause ended the constant parade of new archdukes and archduchesses.'[45] Of course, he had affairs, causing her to observe: 'Never marry a man who has nothing to do.'[46]

The court theatre, the Burg theatre, had opened on the site of the old tennis court close to the Hofburg palace, very near to Haydn's garret. It was open to anyone who could afford to buy a seat: the cheapest were either in the top balcony (known as the Paradis), or in the rear parterre, segregated from the front 'parterre noble' (known as the ox-pen) reserved for aristocrats, officers and officials.[49] During Lent, the theatre was transformed into a concert hall. As there was a lot of chatter during the performances, one does not know how much of the performance Haydn could hear: on some occasions the performers could not even hear each other.[50]

Haydn borrowed and scrimped. But when his hosts were expecting another baby, he had to move on. He went to a sixth-floor garret where he had an 'old worm eaten clavier' and was able to study music theory such as Fux's *Gradus ad Parnassum*, a primer widely used, and works by C.P.E. Bach.[51]

We have seen that in Vienna all classes lived cheek by jowl. By an extraordinary stroke of luck, on the third floor of Haydn's building lived Pietro Metastasio, the poet laureate of the Habsburgs and author of countless opera librettos. Also living in the same building was one of the Esterházy princesses.[52]

Metastasio shared his apartment with some Spanish friends, the Martinez family. He must have heard sounds from above, because, in return for free board, Haydn was engaged to teach Marianne Martinez, then aged ten. She was talented: Mozart used to attend her *soirées* many years later.[53] Of course, Metastasio knew all the important people, and he arranged for Marianne to have singing lessons from the elderly and distinguished Nicola Porpora, doyen of Neapolitan opera. Porpora, said to be the greatest vocal teacher of his time, formerly taught the castrato Farinelli, and was an erstwhile rival impresario to Handel in London.[54]

Haydn, who accompanied Marianne at these lessons, asked to study with Porpora, in return for 'cleaning shoes, beating his coat and arranging his antique periwig'.[55] Haydn learnt the fundamentals of composition, singing and Italian. He accompanied Porpora on his trips to the spa, and, crucially, became noticed by others. One such influential person invited Haydn to his country home, where he wrote his first string quartets. Through Porpora, he also met successful composers such as Giuseppe Bonno and Gluck, and G.C. Wagenseil, the empress' music teacher, a leading writer of symphonies and the most important musical figure in Vienna in the 1750s. Bonno and Gluck at this time were working for the Prince of Saxe-Hildburghausen who had his own orchestra, giving magnificent concerts for the music-loving Viennese nobility.[56]

Haydn took an increasing number of pupils and worked hard, from sixteen to eighteen hours a day. He must have eyed somewhat jealously the success of his brother Michael, who, at the age of twenty, was appointed conductor to a Hungarian bishop.[57] Joseph was the archetypal slow developer, but his turn came when he was about 27: he was recommended to Count Morzin, a connection by marriage of Count Durazzo. Haydn worked at Morzin's imposing baroque palace,* twelve miles south of Pilsen (now Plzeň) on the road north to the Bohemian spas such as Karlsbad, Teplitz and Marienbad.[58] The long journey from Vienna must have gone quickly as Haydn contemplated his pay of 200 fl plus board and lodging,** even though he earned less than half what a ballet dancer in the theatre would have been paid.[60] Here he composed his first symphony.

Haydn fell in love with the daughter of a hairdresser, who sadly (for him) preferred to become a nun; he wrote an organ concerto for the ceremony of her profession. Then, on 26 November 1760, in what was a disastrous move, Haydn married the elder sister, Maria Anna. She was aged 31, priest-ridden, unattractive and not even a good *Hausfrau*; worse, she showed no interest in his work. As Haydn put it later: 'She doesn't care a fig whether her husband is an artist or a cobbler.'[61] She is the first in our series of apparently difficult wives: Constanze Mozart, Harriet and Marie Berlioz, Félicité Franck, Geneviève Bizet, Antonina Tchaikovsky, Pauline Strauss, Elvira Puccini ... For differing reasons, rightly or wrongly, each of these gets a bad press. As Zdeňka Janáček, Alma Mahler and Lina Prokofiev would find, being married to a great artist was no bed of roses; and often we do not hear the wife's side of the story.

A month before Haydn's wedding, Vienna saw a royal wedding. A magnificent procession of 106 coaches accompanied Isabella of Parma to her wedding to Archduke Joseph, the heir to the Habsburg Empire.[62] We do not know whether Haydn saw this, but he was soon back in Vienna.[63] Apparently, Morzin could not afford to keep his musical establishment going; perhaps he had spent too much on his palace. It has also been suggested that Haydn was sacked for having married without consent.

* The palace, now empty and in sad condition, was close to a Benedictine shrine to Our Lady of the Assumption, visited by pilgrims. The large baroque church was then in the course of construction.

**A factory worker might earn between 50 and 60 fl per annum; a coachman 20 fl with food.[59]

Starting with the Esterházys

Haydn was then recruited by Prince Paul Anton Esterházy. Around May Day 1761, he began a 30-year period of service, at first in the Esterházys' splendid four-square castle at Eisenstadt. The castle reigned over a substantial town, also known as Kismarton, only around 30 miles from Vienna. It is set on the side of the Leitha hills with magnificent views over the wine country nearby, and has a delightful park and orangerie behind. It was on an altogether different scale to the relatively modest castle of the Harrachs or Morzin's palace.

The Esterházys were an old Hungarian family who had made the Habsburgs hereditary kings of Hungary and defended them from the Turks. Consequently, they were created princes of the Holy Roman Empire. The Esterházys augmented their vast fortune by judicious marriage and by ensuring that the family wealth was not divided up but remained with the eldest son.[64] In Hungary, 50 noble families owned the greater part of the country's wealth; and as part of the deal to support the succession of Maria Theresa, they paid no taxes.[65] An Esterházy descendant, a crony of King George IV of England, appeared at Queen Victoria's coronation, in 'a scene of unsurpassed magnificence ... covered in jewels from head to heels. When the sun caught him, he turned into a dazzling rainbow of light.'[66] The saddle cloth of the prince in Haydn's time was even encrusted with diamonds. In 1918, the Esterházys owned 21 castles, 60 market towns and over 400 villages in Hungary, as well as a number of castles and lordships in Austria, and a whole county of Bavaria.[67]

Haydn was a house officer rather than a servant, and he was provided with a fine livery. He eventually acquired a little house in the town, the present-day museum. He had to attend twice a day in the prince's antechamber. He was conductor, composer and in charge of the library and instruments. He was also responsible for the music staff, settling disputes such as the incident when a cellist damaged the oboist's eye during a brawl in a tavern. He was paid initially 400 fl per annum plus a food and board supplement; this rose to 600 fl after the first year.[68] For five years he had to put up with his elderly and abusive predecessor.[69] As a result of his complaints, Haydn was rebuked for 'indolence and lack of discipline among the musicians'. This spurred him on to list his compositions, showing that he had been far from idle.[70]

Less than a year after Haydn joined the Esterházy staff, the prince died and was succeeded by his brother Prince Nicholas, who became known as 'the Magnificent'. One of his sisters-in-law was in Archduke Joseph's closest circle; another was married to Count Durazzo, the head of the court theatres; a brother was Count Franz ('Quinquin') Esterházy, Durazzo's predecessor.[71] Prince Nicholas himself played the baryton, an unusual cello-like instrument with six main strings and eighteen reverberating strings.* Dr Burney called it an 'ungrateful' instrument, and described the additional strings sarcastically as an 'admirable expedient in a desert, or even in a house, where there is but one musician'.[72]

Beneath the cultural surface of the Esterházys, however, was a ferocious and formidable prince who had greatly distinguished himself in the recent Seven Years War.** The Esterházys had a private army of six-footers. The year before Haydn went into service, the prince had been in command of Austrian forces who had entered the palace of Frederick the Great at Potsdam.[74]

Field Marshal Prince Nicholas Esterházy de Galanta, Count of Forchtenstein

* The reverberating strings resonated the harmonics and thus enriched the sound; they also gave a special effect when plucked with the left thumb.

** Goethe said that the prince was 'not tall, but well built, vivacious and distinguished, and at the same time without haughtiness or coldness'.[73] A print in the Beethoven memorial museum in Vienna shows him with a long nose and a small mean mouth, although there are portraits which give him a pleasanter expression with a bit of a twinkle in his eye. He distinguished himself at the battle of Kolin (June 1757), where his name appears on the monument depicting Frederick the Great running away following his defeat.

Not surprisingly, the prince was very severe with his servants, and when a tenor was caught with his hand up the skirts of a soprano, he was jailed for two weeks and received 50 lashes from the Esterházy executioner. Conditions were extremely tough for the musicians, and, no doubt, the other servants. Haydn was fortunately exempted from the rule, instituted later, that the servants were not allowed to have wives. This was somewhat ironic, as Haydn said: 'My wife was unable to bear children and for this reason I was less indifferent towards the attractions of other women.'[75] How he achieved his objectives without suffering the same fate as the tenor, we know not.

In later years, the discipline must have been relaxed. In 1779, the Esterházy establishment was joined by a lively nineteen-year-old mezzo-soprano, Luigia Polzelli, and her elderly violinist husband, Antonio.[76] Possibly Haydn fathered her son, born four years later. This dark-eyed brunette perhaps had a predecessor as, late in life, Haydn thought of leaving some money to one of the waiting women in the Esterházy household. 'Papa' Haydn's fatherly tenderness may well have developed into something more serious. Equally, his affairs could have resulted from sheer desperation. Besides, Signor Polzelli may not have objected to the arrangement. He and his wife were such indifferent musicians that without Haydn's intervention they would have been sacked.[77] Haydn also went out of his way to simplify some of the works Luigia was to sing, so as to bring them within her limited competence.[78]

Esterháza

The prince decided to upgrade his hunting lodge at Süttör, at a cost of some thirteen million florins. This is located about fifteen miles from Eisenstadt, on the southern end of the Neusiedlersee.* This period saw a considerable amount of building activity: at the northern end of the twenty-mile long lake, the Harrachs were converting the inner courtyard of their castle at Rohrau into an elegant château. One imagines that Haydn heard about this, and also learnt that the church in Hainburg, where he had started, was having a baroque tower added.[79]

The prince's plans were on an altogether more magnificent scale. The hunting lodge was turned into a kind of Versailles, painted with ochre,

* The long, shallow, reedy, salty Neusiedlersee can sometimes be seen on the left hand side, when flying in to Vienna airport.

and renamed Esterháza. On arriving there, one enters a large horseshoe-shaped courtyard, to face an outside double-staircase leading up to the magnificent white and gold reception rooms on the first floor, scene of many of Haydn's performances. There are more than 126 gilded and panelled rooms, some with Chinese wall paintings, some Chinese lacquer, and large stoves to keep them warm. Behind, in those days, were the beautiful French gardens and park. Looking out to the park, on the right side was an opera house, built in 1768; on the left, a puppet theatre, built five years later. Designs for the opera house indicate that it had a frontage of around 60 feet; inside, a parterre with ten rows of seats, the prince's *loge* and a gallery above. Sadly, today one just has to imagine the park, the gardens and the theatres.[80]

Esterháza became the main scene of Haydn's activities. He lived in quarters on the edge of the park. He composed many works for the opera house and many pieces for the baryton for the prince. But he was also writing many symphonies, string quartets and piano sonatas and, once his predecessor was dead, church music. Some of this music from the early Esterháza years, such as the *Stabat Mater* and the string quartets, is noticeably expressive and intense. It is not known whether this was caused by some spiritual or personal crisis; it may have been a response to a deeper sense of emotion found in literature around this time, known as *Sturm und Drang* (storm and stress). The frothy but emotionless world of the *galant*, with its rustic cottages and shepherds, was beginning to pall.[81]

Maria Theresa, who cannot fail to have been jealous of the Esterházy family's enormous fortune, visited Esterháza in 1773. When the Prince showed her his newly built Chinese folly, she asked how much he was spending on it: 'a mere bagatelle', he replied. Her visit was marked by a firework display, which included a tableau of the coat of arms of Hungary, and a masked ball with the musicians dressed in Chinese costume. Haydn's burletta *L'infedeltà delusa* was performed for her, as was his opera for the marionette theatre, *Philemon and Baucis*.

Maria Theresa's arrival at the Esterházys must have been an exciting event. Preceded by postillions and trumpeters, she would travel in a procession of over 30 coaches and wagons (with a few spares in case of breakdown), powered by over 200 horses. She did not like slow speeds, so she would move at twelve miles per hour, perhaps for ten hours at a stretch.[82]

By the time of this visit to Esterháza, she was a widow, dressed in black. Eight years before, during a gala ballet performance to celebrate their son

Leopold's marriage to Maria Luisa of Spain, Emperor Francis Stephen collapsed; he died in the corridor a few moments later. Maria Theresa did not make a public appearance for eight months, during which time she calculated that she had been married precisely 385,744 hours.[83] Thereafter, until her death in November 1780, there was an uneasy co-regency: Joseph succeeded as Holy Roman Emperor, while she continued to make the decisions. Mediating between mother and son was their chancellor, the chillingly calculating but incorruptible Wenzel Anton von Kaunitz. Formerly ambassador to Paris, Kaunitz was the architect of the *renversement des alliances** by which Austria and France, former enemies, became allies. This was symbolised by the marriage in 1770 of the empress' daughter Marie Antoinette to the Dauphin, Louis-Auguste of France. Kaunitz was ultimately responsible for French theatre and opera being brought to Vienna, and he was also an important supporter of Gluck.**

The Enlightenment Outside

We should pause to consider the considerable changes that were happening in the world beyond the boundaries of the vast Esterházy estates. The world was experiencing what has been called 'the greatest cultural and spiritual re-orientation since Christianity supplanted the antique world'.[85] However isolated Haydn may have felt, information about trends and developments outside must surely have percolated back to him; also, he went into the wider world when he accompanied the Prince in his retinue.

'Man', which now included a growing middle class, had emerged from darkness into light, from baroque confusion into the Age of Reason. As the two Roman cities Herculaneum and Pompeii, destroyed by Vesuvius in 79 AD, slowly disgorged their classical treasures, the arts reached back to the serenity of antiquity, to simplicity, and to the realistic. Haydn lived at the time of Voltaire and Diderot, authors whose contentious works the authorities frequently had burnt. It was the age of Immanuel Kant, whose *Critique of Pure Reason* was published in 1781; and of Jean-Jacques

* Politically, the *renversement* was a disastrous policy: France, going fast downhill, was hardly a useful ally. Also, Austria now found itself part of a Catholic bloc pitted against Anglo-Prussian forces, known as the Protestant League. Kaunitz's support for music had an enduring influence.

** Kaunitz's manners were arrogant and eccentric. He received the Pope in his dressing-gown and shook the hand outstretched for him to kiss. After dinner, he would ceremoniously clean his teeth.[84] Amazingly, Dvořák became related to Kaunitz by marriage: his brother-in-law was the penultimate owner of the magnificent baroque château at Austerlitz (now Slavkov).

Rousseau, the first 'angry young man', a competent composer as well as a great philosopher.[86] For Kant, the source of all human knowledge was not just experience, but a combination of reason and experience: reason without experience is empty; experience needs reason or it descends to chaos. It was now the age of 'the universally cultured man'.[87]

An important event which had a significant effect on the thought processes of intelligent people was the Lisbon earthquake and fire of 1 November 1755. This killed 30–40,000 people and reduced the city to rubble. It caused the French King's mistress, Madame de Pompadour, to give up rouge for a week. The English, having attributed the disaster to the wrath of God, banned masquerades for a year; the gambling stakes at White's Club were substantially reduced.[88]

Joseph's Reforms

Emperor Joseph II (see colour plate 9) aimed to put some of the concepts of the Enlightenment into practice. Besides, he knew that, without reform, the Habsburg edifice, weakened by war, would collapse. His ideas were far in advance of his time: he tried to engineer from above the revolution which the French would achieve from below. He wanted a centralised state which would work for the greatest good of the greatest number, because that could achieve what the individual alone could not achieve.[89] He also maintained that all men were equal; and that everyone should contribute to the general good according to his wealth. There should be no kneeling, except to God; no bowing, except to the sovereign.[90] These notions naturally appalled the aristocracy who supported his throne.

Although the Esterházy family would surely have been discreet when talking in front of the servants, Haydn must have been aware of the pace of change as Joseph implemented these ideas. By 1780, the government in Vienna was relentlessly publishing around two decrees per day, whereas 40 years earlier the rate had been about three per month.[91] The Esterházys probably ignored many, hoping the whirlwind would blow over, but occasionally they did object, for instance when Joseph decreed that German should be the official language in his realm. Meanwhile, they were told to put away their saddle cloth.[92]

Joseph's catalogue of reforms affected everything and everyone. Here are just a few examples. He overhauled the tax system. Education was to be compulsory between the age of six and twelve, and parents should be punished for their child's truancy. Every community was to have a nurse and doctor employed by the state. Bureaucracy was cut, and training courses were introduced for bureaucrats and judges. Judges' pay was increased so that they would be less likely to take bribes. A civil service contributory pension scheme was set up which included schemes for widows and children.[93] Capital punishment was curtailed, torture abolished.[94] Free legal aid was to be provided for peasants in dispute against their lords. Censorship was reduced and centralised. Notoriously, the burial laws were changed, because Joseph observed that useful economies could be achieved, including the rapid re-use of the cemetery, by re-using coffins and burying people in sacks in common graves.[95]

Meticulously attentive to detail, Joseph, a control freak, was the consummate busybody. He banned ballet from court theatre because it was erotic. He prohibited the use of corsets, because they impaired childbearing ability.[96]

Joseph was like many a late 20th-century chief executive. Key words were 'commitment' and 'duty'.[97] Overweening and conceited, he would ridicule and humiliate people who had no recourse whatsoever. In a century when no British monarch visited Scotland, Wales or Ireland, Joseph was to be met on fact-finding missions in which he travelled 30,000 miles around his domains and abroad, from the Bay of Biscay to Moscow. His visit to Russia involved travelling 3,000 miles in less than four months.[98] As with royal visits generally, things were spruced up: cottages were quickly thatched before his arrival; some rustics had the sense simply to flee into the woods. A print was circulated showing the prince behind a plough: it has been described as 'a much depicted anticipation of the art of the photo-opportunity'.[99]

Joseph grappled with the mighty Roman Catholic Church in whose hands so much wealth was concentrated: it was on display at monasteries such as Melk above the Danube and St Florian near Linz. There were over 2,000 abbeys in the areas of his empire which were directly under his control. Joseph seized a third of these, especially those which served no useful function providing health or education, and reduced the numbers of monks and nuns by about 40 per cent. He issued an Edict of Tolerance for Protestants and Orthodox, and lifted various of the restrictions on the Jews. The Pope was so worried that he came to Vienna in 1782 and spent a month in direct and often bad-tempered negotiations with Joseph. No Pope since the early 15th century had crossed the Alps, so his visit caused sensation.[100]

Not having had the advantage of attending a course in 'change management techniques', he encountered resistance even from those such as the peasantry who, supposedly, would benefit from his edicts. He had to depend for his plans on a small group of officials in Vienna, but they were insufficient to break the resistance of the outraged Church, the nobility, the provincial estates and chartered towns. Besides, his ideas struck at the heart of his own legitimacy as emperor, whose title and position was essentially grounded in property ownership. There was so much disruption in Hungary that the Prussian King considered seizing the throne, or installing the Duke of Saxe-Weimar.

When dying from tuberculosis contracted while campaigning against the Turks, the emperor wrote his own epitaph: 'Here lies Joseph II, who failed in everything he undertook',[101] a confession which many a modern and over-remunerated chief executive could do well to make. Joseph's successor, his brother Leopold II, took a grip and reversed many of the reforms. One of Joseph's more productive achievements was, however, to explain the facts of life to his brother-in-law.*

Changes in Opera: Gluck

The period of the Enlightenment also saw some important changes in the nature of music. On 5 October 1762, Gluck's *Orfeo ed Euridice*** was first performed in the Burg theatre in Vienna; this was around the time that Haydn joined the Esterházy staff. *Orfeo* retains many features of Italian opera, such as long orchestral interludes (for ballet), the 'exit aria' at the end of which the hero leaves the stage in a flourish (ready for the applause), and the '*deus ex machina*' who descends from the skies and brings a happy ending. But Gluck's opera was far less stylised and much more realistic. The music was no longer just the latest accompaniment for a standard and absurd text: it now reflected the action and the emotions of the characters on the stage. Before Gluck's 'reforms', Metastasio's texts were set by numerous composers anything from twenty to a hundred times;[103] after Gluck, an

* He explained to Louis XVI that procreation requires movement as well as insertion. Prince Kaunitz's daughter-in-law said that Joseph looked at women in the way that people normally look at statues.[102]

** We particularly remember *Orfeo* for the dance of the Blessed Spirits and the aria 'Che farò senza Euridice?' which, although written for a castrato, we associate with the deep contralto voice of Kathleen Ferrier. She emerged from Second World War factory recitals to be one of the finest singers of her time; she died aged 41 in 1953.

opera was so integrated with its text that it was unique and that particular libretto could only rarely be used again.*

Gluck's librettist was Raniero Calzabigi, a colourful character whose chequered career involved a poisoning in Naples and a lottery in partnership with Casanova in Paris.[104] Calzabigi prepared a Preface to *Alceste* for Gluck to sign, in which he wrote: 'I have striven to restrict music to its true office of serving poetry by means of expression and by following the situations of the story, without interrupting the action or stifling it with useless superfluity of ornaments.' He continued: 'I did not wish to arrest an actor in the greatest heat of dialogue in order to wait for a tiresome ritornello, nor to hold him up in the middle of a word on a vowel favourable to his voice, nor to make display of the agility of his fine voice in some long drawn passage, nor to wait while the orchestra gives him time to recover his breath for a cadenza.' Gluck said: 'I have sought to abolish all the abuses against which *good sense and reason* have long cried out in vain ... I have felt that the overture ought to acquaint the audience of the nature of the action of the drama.' His punch-line was: 'I believed that my greatest effort should be devoted to seeking a beautiful simplicity.'[105]

Alceste was first produced in Vienna in December 1767. It has many of the old features: the chorus, the ballet interludes. But amid exquisite music, what really stands out is the way the recitative is made an integral and expressive part of the drama.**

In the early 1770s, in the wake of Marie Antoinette, Gluck went to Paris where his two *Iphigénie* operas were first staged; there we shall go in connection with Mozart. Meanwhile, under the auspices of Kaunitz and Durazzo, French theatre and ballet was brought to Vienna, where it was beloved by the Viennese aristocracy. Its dominance was not to last. As early as 1761, a German Society had been formed to popularise German literature. Emperor Joseph, of whom it was said that 'he will certainly employ no Frenchman until German plays are performed at Versailles',[106] led this crusade and stopped the subsidy to the French. When the French departed, the aristocracy first expostulated and then set up their own French theatre; but it failed.[107]

* *Orfeo* was also composed straight through, with the complete replacement of the unaccompanied *recitativo secco* with *recitativo accompagnato*, which Gluck had heard in France in works of Lully and his successor, Rameau.

** For example, when Alceste tells her husband the she must die for him, and when she enters Hades. We are beginning to hear a real music drama rather than the concert in costume, or a backcloth for vocal pyrotechnics.

In 1776, Joseph stopped all theatre performances except for plays in German. This led to the growth in the German-language opera, the Singspiel. Joseph also dismissed the staff at the Burg theatre, with a promise of three months' wages, and installed a German troupe instead. Performances at the Kärntnertor theatre,* which he wished to purge of its crude and vulgar comedians, were limited to those by travelling troupes; theatres were opened up in the suburbs. Haydn had a cellist friend who had been lured to Vienna by increased pay; now, he was very lucky to be re-employed at a reduced salary. Such were the upheavals of the time.[108]

Haydn's Operas

Haydn himself became increasingly involved with Italian opera, especially because Prince Nicholas became bored with playing his baryton. At Esterháza, between 1776 and 1784, there were typically two operas and two concerts a week, apart from the daily chamber performances and the occasional entertainments in honour of guests.[109] Even after fire destroyed the theatre – it had destroyed Haydn's house in Eisenstadt in 1768 – opera performances were not curtailed. In fifteen years, Haydn conducted more than 1,000 performances: in 1786, there were 125 opera performances of seventeen different works.[110]

Haydn's operas were still in the old style and did not reflect Gluck's 'reforms'. Much of Haydn's time went into modifying, to suit his available resources, compositions by prominent composers of the time, such as Piccinni or Salieri. His own works, such as *Lo speziale* and *Il ritorno di Tobia*, being in the old style, are mostly forgotten now, as is the incidental music he wrote for the acting troupes which visited Esterháza, which performed plays by Shakespeare, Lessing and Schiller.[111]

Service with the Esterházy family gave Haydn comparative security in an age when this was needed. He was protected from the effects of the devastating harvest failure of 1770–71 and from the peasant revolts which flared up sporadically in Bohemia and Transylvania.[112] No doubt the country location also had its attractions, and we can imagine him relaxing,

* The Kärntnertor Theatre which had been built in 1708–9 was next to the Carinthian Gate, leading out of the city to the south-west. It staged Italian and German operas and was noted for its outrageously coarse farces, much enjoyed by rich and poor alike. Joseph's theatre reforms were motivated by his desire to use the theatre to educate the people in the values of the Enlightenment.

fishing in the lake nearby, and enjoying the distinctive sounds from the large number of birds who made it their habitat. Being on the Esterházy staff also gave him a status which is reflected in some of the concert bills of the period: Haydn's position is stated, whereas Mozart by then has none.[113] Also, Haydn was now earning a lot more than his brother Michael received in a new post in Salzburg.[114]

But Haydn was stuck in the middle of nowhere. In the early years, obtaining leave was virtually impossible, and trips to Vienna could be made only in the Prince's retinue. In the 1780s, Haydn seems to have had more freedom to visit Vienna, perhaps to look for music to bring back. On one occasion, he heard one of his minuets being played badly in a tavern, criticised the playing and was nearly beaten up.[115]

When he managed to visit Vienna, he would see a circle of friends. This included Mozart, with whom he played chamber music. It also included the prince's doctor, Peter von Genzinger, and his wife Marianne, whose Sunday afternoon musical salons Haydn attended. One letter indicates his Sunday-evening reluctance to return to his duties: 'Here at Eszterháza nobody asks me "would you like chocolate with or without milk? Will you take coffee with or without cream? What can I offer you my good Haydn? Will you have vanilla ice or strawberry?"'[116]

Haydn's circle also included some musicians from the British Isles: the Dublin-born tenor Michael Kelly, the composer Stephen Storace,* and Nancy, his sister. Nancy Storace was a soubrette soprano, the first Susanna in *The Marriage of Figaro*. It was a lively group. Stephen was arrested for brawling at a Shrove Tuesday Carnival ball. Nancy and the officer with whom she was dancing fell on the floor after the officer's spurs got caught in her dress. Stephen, who had had too much champagne, accused the officer of the wrong thing and was put under lock and key in the guard-house, where he, of course, sent for more champagne.[118]

There were plans to get Haydn to England. London was then a Mecca for musicians in search of fortune, particularly foreigners, because music was increasingly considered an insufficiently masculine profession for Englishmen.[119]

* Storace is pronounced 'Storachi'. His father was a Neapolitan working in Dublin.[117]

'World' Fame and the Problems of Copyright

Although stuck at Esterháza, Haydn's fame had spread abroad. In 1780, Artaria* published a set of his piano sonatas, the first of over 300 Haydn editions published by them. Haydn was also included in their equivalent of 'Who's Who in Music'. The King of Spain had sent him a golden snuff-box set with diamonds, presented in person by the secretary of the Spanish legation.[121]

In the mid-1780s, Haydn was commissioned to write six symphonies for the Paris Concerts Spirituels.[122] This was the first real concert organisation,** a society which held concerts in Lent and on religious feast-days when the opera was prohibited. Around the same time, he resumed writing string quartets. Cadiz cathedral commissioned *The Seven Last Words*. This was performed in America as early as 1793. At Bethlehem, Pennsylvania, in 1795 a string quartet met regularly to play Haydn's music.[124] In England, well over 100 of his works were published.

Publication did not lead to an increase in riches. The growing 'mass' market called for printed works, but copyright law was generally chaotic both nationally and internationally. It was far from clear whether statutes designed to protect authors of *literary* works – that is, *words* – also extended to composers of music. Previously, this did not trouble composers too much, because a musical work, once performed, was usually not needed again: the small, aristocratic market was supplied by using cheap, impoverished copyists, a typical example being the philosopher Rousseau, who died when eking out a living as one. However, once printed, published works could easily be pirated abroad,† and, by 1764, editions of Haydn's works could be obtained in Holland and England. Bach's son Christoph successfully sued Longmans in the 1770s for unauthorised publication. In the 1780s, Stephen Storace also sued Longmans, establishing

*Artaria were the leading publisher in Vienna. Prints show the shop next to St Michael's Church, where Haydn had started out on his own. The firm operated on a subscription basis: half the price was paid in advance by the subscriber, and half on delivery.[120]

** Permission for the concerts had first to be obtained from Lully's heirs, who held a patent with complete monopoly over opera. So, restrictions were imposed: concerts could be held only when the Académie Royale de Musique was not in session; and they could not include even a fragment of French opera. The ban on French was tacitly overlooked in mid-century.[123]

† Until the Union in 1800, the English copyright statute of 1710, the 'Act of Anne', did not apply in Ireland, so Dublin provided a source of pirated editions selling at 10–15 per cent below the English price; the Irish did a healthy export trade to America.

that a composer had original title to the composition and confirming that sheet music was covered by the copyright legislation.[125]*

The difficulties went far beyond the issue of whether composers were entitled to the same protection as writers and poets. There was no coherent framework even for literary works. The German states were particularly chaotic, with different rules in each state, most of them being unwilling to protect works by foreigners, except where there was reciprocation in the foreigner's home state. The Habsburgs even encouraged piracy of works by foreigners as a means of importing know-how and technical skills. We can see the extent of the difficulty when we find Kant, at the end of the 18th century, publishing an essay, 'Was ist ein Buch?' Even though 38 states in Germany agreed in 1815 to do something about copyright, and expressed good intentions several times thereafter, nothing effectual was done to resolve the problems until 1870, when the German Empire was formed.

To protect their position as best they could, composers for a long time arranged for their works to be published simultaneously in the principal markets. Thus, Chopin, in the 1830s, published simultaneously in France, England and Germany. Stravinsky, being a Russian, experienced difficulty with copyright in the United States, at least until he became a French citizen; when in 1945 he became a citizen of the United States, he revised various works partly for copyright reasons.

In England, the legal profession thrived on copyright law.** Indeed, the second of the two court cases about *The Seasons*, the poem by James Thomson which Haydn later used for his oratorio, is described as 'the bedrock judicial decision in English law of copyright'.[127] And Thomson, a canny Scot, himself provided an early example of a device for extending copyright by adding to his poems so as to create a new edition and thus trigger a new date from which his copyright would apply.[128]

* Some publishers got around the law by publishing arrangements, or by providing new words for the popular tunes. Storace's 'Blithe as the hours of May' became 'Blest was the vernal day'.

** Although various Acts in the 19th century were designed to clarify copyright in the United Kingdom, cases about music continued to figure prominently. Their complexity is illustrated by the case about a foreigner who wrote a work overseas, which was first published in England. Could he claim the benefit of English copyright? The case turned on whether nine arias in Bellini's *La Sonnambula* could be deemed to have been published simultaneously, having appeared in Milan in 1831 at 9 am (that is, 8.20 am GMT), but in London at noon. The court found that the intention of the legislation was 'to promote the cultivation of the intellect of the Queen's subjects not to encourage the importation of foreign works and their first publication in Britain'.[126]

Off to London

The opportunity for Haydn to go to England arose in 1790, a year in which both Joseph II and Prince Nicholas died. The prince's heir abandoned Esterháza and returned to Eisenstadt; also, he was not so interested in music. The orchestra was disbanded and Haydn was allowed leave, on full pay. He moved swiftly to Vienna. He was on the point of going on to Naples, when the London-based violinist and impresario Johann Peter Salomon heard that he was 'free'. Salomon greeted him: 'My name is Salomon. I have come from London to fetch you.'[129] He engaged him to write an opera, six symphonies and twenty other pieces, and to conduct in as many concerts, for a minimum of £1,200.[130]* Haydn had two visits to London, in 1791–2 and 1794–5.

The cultural atmosphere in London had evolved considerably during the generation since Handel's death 30 years earlier. The artist Thomas Gainsborough had recently died; the architect Robert Adam, and Edward Gibbon, author of *The Decline and Fall of the Roman Empire*, were now close to the end of their lives. Adam Smith had published his *Enquiry into the Wealth of Nations* in 1776. As indicated by Joseph Wright's picture of the 'Experiment with the Air Pump', painted around 1768, important scientific and industrial developments had taken place. Watt invented the steam engine in 1769. Priestley isolated oxygen in 1774. A variety of scientists, including Dr Benjamin Franklin of Philadelphia, had taken forward our knowledge of electricity. At a more mundane and commercial level, the textile industry had been revolutionised in the 1770s by Arkwright's water frame, Hargreaves' jenny and Crompton's mule.[132]

It was onto this fast-changing stage that, on New Year's Day 1790, there stepped an incongruous pair: there was the elderly Haydn, aged 58, who – apart from his brief job at Count Morzin's establishment in Bohemia – had never been beyond a radius of 40 or 50 miles from Vienna;[133] and there was the international impresario Salomon.

The journey itself must have been a novel experience. No doubt Haydn was already familiar with some of the irksome aspects: there were customs posts between Hungary and Vienna, so he would have been used to delays

* There was some inflation in the third quarter of the century. £50 to £100 a year was now normal income for the petty bourgeoisie, while £300 per annum would keep a gentleman in style; Dr Burney was paid £100 per annum for teaching at Mrs Sheele's school in Queen Square. A thrifty family could hope to keep itself out of debt on a pound a week.[131]

while officials extorted duties and examined books and other writings 'lest they contain something prejudicial to the state'.[134] The pair travelled through Munich and Bonn, where Salomon had been born and where he knew the Beethoven family. They passed through France ruled by revolutionaries; it was a year and a half since the fall of the Bastille. On New Year's Eve, they arrived in Calais.

The delightfully dyspeptic Dr Tobias Smollett travelled the Calais to London route a few years earlier. Describing the ferry, he said that 'the cabin was so small that a dog could hardly turn in it and the beds put me in a mind of the holes described in some catacombs, in which the bodies of the dead were deposited, being thrust in with the feet foremost'. Dover was 'a den of thieves ... The people are said to live by piracy in time of war and by smuggling and fleecing strangers in time of peace.' As for the London to Dover road, 'I need not tell you this is the worst road in England with respect to the conveniences of travelling ... the chambers are in general cold and comfortless, the beds paultry, the cookery execrable, the wine poison, the attendance bad, the publicans insolent and the bills extortion'. Importantly, he noticed that there was 'not a drop of tolerable malt liquor to be had from London to Dover'.[135]

At least Haydn avoided being seasick. The two arrived safely at the music 'warehouse' in High Holborn run by John Bland, a publisher. Then Haydn moved to Salomon's house in 18 Great Pulteney Street, Golden Square.[136] Here, one could apply to him for tickets to his series of Friday concerts. The first, on 11 March at Hanover Square rooms, was a triumph, as were those which followed. An extra 'benefit' concert brought in £350.*

London had enjoyed regular subscription concerts for some time; they were a flourishing business, with as much snob appeal as the opera. The programmes performed at them were long – say, three hours; so the procedure was for people to move from one hall** to another.

*Nancy Storace received £10 per performance in 1789. Solo singers were entitled each to one personal benefit night per season. The beneficiaries were responsible for selling their own tickets and paying the substantial house charge, so there was some risk involved. At a benefit concert, a popular artist might gross £100; but Sarah Harrop, a soprano, crammed 2,101 people into the Pantheon and got £1,000.[137]

** There was considerable rivalry and competition between the various venues. The London Tavern seated around 800–1,000 people, about twice the capacity of the older halls such as York Buildings and Hickford's Rooms. The Pantheon, in which Burney had shares, was built in Oxford Street in 1772, but it was burnt down in 1792. In 1764, J.C. Bach and C.F. Abel took over a concert series started by Theresa Cornely[138] at the Assembly Rooms in Soho Square.

A week after his arrival, Haydn wrote to Marianne Genzinger: 'I could have an invitation every day; but first I must consider my health, and second my work.'[140] He seems to have enjoyed a musical evening at Carlton House, the residence of the chastened Prince of Wales: it was only just over eighteen months since the service of thanksgiving in St Paul's Cathedral for King George's recovery from his first attack of madness, a disease which at first was attributed to his wearing damp stockings and eating four large pears. As only a servant would, Haydn discovered that the recipe for the prince's punch was 'one bottle champagne, one bottle burgundy, one bottle rum, ten lemons, two oranges and a pound and a half of sugar'.[141]

Haydn visited Dr Burney at Chelsea College, where he was organist. There was much to talk about. Burney's son had been with Captain Cook on his second and last journey around the world in 1776.* Burney's friends included the portrait painter Sir Joshua Reynolds, and the diarist Boswell who was writing the life of Dr Johnson. Haydn used to go into the woods to study English. Hopefully, he did not have to read the works of Johnson, whose books 'are written in a learned language which nobody hears from his mother or his nurse, in a language in which nobody ever quarrels, or drives bargains, or makes love, in a language in which nobody ever thinks'.[143]

Haydn also caught up with his friends from Vienna, Michael Kelly and the Storaces. Their circle included the Drury Lane director Thomas Linley, whose talented son, accidentally drowned some time before, had met Mozart in Florence in 1770; and also the wild and colourful Irishman, Richard Brinsley Sheridan, author of *The Rivals* and *The School for Scandal*, who had eloped from Bath with Linley's beautiful sixteen-year-old daughter, a prima donna.**

Sheridan was, with Edmund Burke, one of the prosecutors in the impeachment of Warren Hastings, who had risen from impoverished circumstances to become the first governor-general of British India. Haydn

She was a former flame of Casanova; the masquerades she held were so disreputable that the magistrate wanted to close her operation down. J.C. Bach moved from there to Almack's and subsequently to the Hanover Square Rooms.[139]

* James served in the Navy from the age of ten. Anchored offshore of O'Why'he (Hawaii), where they had re-victualled, young Burney watched aghast from *Discovery* as Cook, who had gone back to the shore to sort out some thefts, was clubbed to death.[142]

** They set out for a nunnery in France and, on the way, 'got married'. Then he returned to fight two duels with another of her admirers. They got married properly a few years later.[144]

arrived in London when the lengthy trial in Westminster Hall, which had started as 'the greatest public sensation of the 1780s'[145] was bogged down in detail and technicalities and still less than half way through its seven-year run. The case was about misrule in India, then an El Dorado: young men in search of a fortune would join the East India Company. 'The business of a servant of the Company was simply to wring out of the natives a hundred or two hundred thousand pounds as speedily as possible, that he might return home before his constitution had suffered from the heat, to marry a peer's daughter, to buy rotten boroughs* in Cornwall and to give balls in St James's Square.'[147] Eventually in 1795, after a long and famous closing speech by Sheridan, Hastings was acquitted, although the cost of his defence cost him his vast fortune.

The Hastings impeachment must have been of great interest to the music industry, since the administrative ruling classes in India constituted a lucrative market into which to export musical instruments such as harpsichords and pianos, provided that they were specially reinforced to withstand both transport and climate. Instruments could be used by the large number of civil servants and their families, who needed to while away time spent on the long sea journey and also to relieve the boredom on arrival. John Bland, Haydn's acquaintance in Holborn, would offer naval officers a quantity discount for taking such items in the stowage assigned individually to them on board the East Indiamen: it was normal for earnings to be supplemented with a little such business on the side.[148]

Oxford University conferred a Doctorate on Haydn. He attended the Handel commemoration concert, at which the massed choir and orchestra were raked so steeply that one of the performers fell, and disappeared into a double bass with only his legs protruding. He went to the annual meeting of Charity Children in St Paul's, at which 4,000 children sang: no doubt they would have enjoyed the incident with the double bass. Meetings of the Music Clubs** were more frequent. At these, there was an

*A parliamentary constituency with only a handful of voters, and thus easily corruptible; typically, Old Sarum, 'a green mound and a wall with two niches in it'.[146]

** Music Clubs had long been prominent in English music-making (see picture on page 858). Amateurs met to perform madrigals, glees, catches and chamber music. The Noblemen and Gentlemen's Catch Club was founded in 1761, to dine in a tavern, listen and then join in the singing. In a provincial town such as Romsey in Hampshire, the music society included a scrivener, a tallow-chandler, a hairdresser and a minor canon; the easily-playable concertos of Corelli were particularly popular in these groups.[149]

increasing taste for 'ancient' music, then defined as any piece at least twenty years old. However, Haydn did not confine himself to music: he also went to the horse-races* at Ascot Heath.

London Opera and Fashions

Haydn had agreed with Salomon to provide an opera for the King's Theatre in the Haymarket, the home of Italian opera. He composed *L'anima del filosofo*, based on the story of Orpheus. But Haydn's opera was not performed. The theatre had burnt down, a fate that befell so many theatres. In 1791, a year in which Drury Lane was condemned as unsafe and demolished, the King's Theatre reopened with an opera by Paisiello, not by Haydn.[151]

The failure to stage *L'anima del filosofo* must have been disappointing, if only because there was much money to be made in London with opera. Storace received £400 for his opera *The Haunted Tower*, and 500 guineas for *The Siege of Belgrade*. He was often paid 50 or 100 guineas for a single vocal composition.[152]

Storace's method now seems very suspect. Out of 29 numbers in *The Siege*, nine were adapted from *Una Cosa Rara* by the Vienna-based Spanish composer Martin y Soler. For part of the overture, he borrowed a large amount of Mozart's 'Alla Turca', the last movement of the Piano Sonata in A. It was quite normal to raid other works in this way. Storace's uncle wrote: '… an author is no more to be censured for embellishing his work with any valuable papers which he has met with in his readings, than a traveller for ornamenting his house with pictures he has picked up on his Tour.'[153]

For the composer, opera was an important way to make money; for the audience, it was an important component of the London social scene. Not surprisingly, Haydn fitted easily into this. His appearance – sturdy, small, dark, pock-marked with a large aquiline nose and noticeably short legs[154] – is almost straight out of one of the caricatures of Thomas Rowlandson or James Gillray.

These characters could also be seen at the Gardens at Ranelagh and Vauxhall. There, men and women also paraded the latest fashions. Swords

* Horse-racing was popular and had grown greatly in the 17th century; by 1722, over 122 towns and cities were holding race meetings. Gambling was endemic: people bet on cock-fighting, dog-baiting and bear-baiting, and on cricket.[150]

no longer had to be carried, nor was it necessary to wear the extremely high wigs and tiny hats of the 1770s, a style taken to an extreme by the Macaroni Club, some young men who had recently travelled in Italy. Men now wore cocked hats and a double-breasted tail-coat, with, to facilitate movement, the front cut away so as to show a fancy waistcoat. Ladies' fashions had also changed, much to the satisfaction of those like Burney, whom the caricaturists considered had an eye for the girls. Following a fashion created by Queen Marie Antoinette, some dressed delightfully as milkmaids, sometimes with their dresses decorated with straw. However, unlike in France, transparent dresses were not normally worn in London. By the time of Haydn's later London visit, women were wearing enormous ostrich plumes and carrying handbags, the latest in accessories.[155]

Despite the veneer of politeness and elegance, London was still a violent place, and at times particularly uncomfortable for Roman Catholics such as Haydn. Five years before, there had been rumours of civil war. And only ten years before, there had been the anti-popery riots incited by the wildly eccentric Lord George Gordon. Then, there had been rumours that 20,000 Jesuits were hidden in tunnels under the Surrey bank of the Thames, aiming to blow it up and flood London, and also that all the flour in Southwark had been poisoned.* Nevertheless, Haydn enjoyed London so much that he decided to stay for a second season, and was even tempted to settle there.

Much of his time was spent teaching. One of his pupils, the 40-year-old Mrs Rebecca Schroeter, set her cap at him. Once an heiress, she had eloped fifteen years before with Queen Charlotte's music master, whom she married despite one relative making a dramatic attempt, in the vestry of St Martin's-in-the-Fields, to have the wedding stopped. She forfeited her inheritance of £15,000 which was contingent on the consent of her father's executors; this led to litigation. Her husband had died a couple of years before Haydn arrived in London.[157]

In his second season, Haydn's concerts faced some competition from Ignaz Pleyel, once his lodger and pupil in Eisenstadt. Pleyel had a successful career,

*A crowd of 60,000 got out of hand: the damage was appalling. Chapels were burnt, Newgate and other prisons opened and set on fire, much of Holborn destroyed, including a papist-owned distillery which exploded. The Bank of England was attacked, and houses burnt. Between 800 and 1,000 people died. Twenty-one ringleaders were hanged, of whom seventeen were under eighteen, one a boy aged fifteen and another a girl of sixteen. The jury acquitted Gordon.[156]

first as director of music in noble houses, then in London and finally as a publisher, piano manufacturer and gentleman farmer in and near Paris.*

Meanwhile, events were moving on in Vienna. Leopold II died, after a short reign of two years. The Esterházys called Haydn back: his music was bound to be needed when they celebrated the coronation of Francis II. Haydn's departure from London was a great disappointment to Mrs Schroeter. He travelled back via Bonn, where he had a talk with Beethoven and made arrangements for him to go to Vienna and study with him.

Vienna, London, Vienna

Haydn arrived in Vienna on 29 July 1792, around seven months after the death of Mozart. There, for Haydn, life was much quieter than in London: nobody in Vienna was particularly interested in him. He bought a small house in the suburb Auf der Windmühle (On the Windmill) in which to lodge his wife. She characteristically said that it would do her well when she was widowed. He turned to Marianne Genzinger for solace, but six months later she died. When his wife died in 1800, Luigia Polzelli reminded Haydn of a former promise to marry her; but he did not want to. So she extracted a written promise giving her first refusal and a pension after his death; she then went off and married an Italian.

In January 1794, Haydn departed again for London. By this time, the spread of republican principles, especially the events in France, were causing considerable concern in England: clubs such as the 'Friends of the People' and the 'London Corresponding Society' had sprung up. There was a crack-down on security, aliens and immigrants. One doubts, however, if anyone would have worried about old Haydn.

His second London visit was less sensational. He took part in the weekly concerts in the spring season; he wrote and performed his twelve London symphonies; he arranged for his music to be published, and he travelled around the South. Haydn also appeared again in royal circles: King George invited him to Windsor. He was in England at the time of the royal wedding which took place in April 1795, when the Prince of Wales made his disastrous marriage to Princess Caroline of Brunswick.

The symphonies written for his English visits in the early 1790s repre-

* Pleyel's music could be heard in George Washington's household, where it was much enjoyed by his stepdaughter. It was popular partly because it was easy to play.[158]

sent the peak of Haydn's symphonic output, and carry the names which are so familiar to us: the *Surprise*, the *Clock*, the *Drum Roll*, the *Oxford* and the *London* symphonies. What is perhaps less well known is that at this time he wrote 445 arrangements of Scottish, Welsh and Irish folksongs, many of them for George Thomson, who later commissioned similar works from Beethoven and Weber. Thomson's intention was neither romantic nor scholarly: he was simply trying to save these old melodies from oblivion.[159] In 1793 he had published his first set of Scottish songs, and he continued to publish up until 1841. A craze for folk music had been inspired to a large extent by a best-seller of 1760 entitled *Fragments of Ancient Poetry collected in the Highlands of Scotland, and translated from the Gaelic or Erse Language*. The fragments were supposedly* the work of the bard Ossian, and recounted the deeds of Gaelic heroes, including Ossian's father Fingal.[160]

In August 1795 Haydn had to return to Vienna. Prince Anton Esterházy had died, and his son, another Nicholas, wanted him to revive the princely musical establishment. But since the new prince was less obsessed with music than his grandfather, Haydn was able to spend much of his time in the capital; his main obligation was to write an annual Mass for the name-day of the prince's wife.

Haydn's experience of the Handel Commemoration concert, together with his friendship with the influential Gottfried van Swieten, a supporter of Mozart, inspired the two masterpieces, *The Creation* and *The Seasons*. Swieten, the son of the empress' doctor,** was a champion of the works of Handel and J.S. Bach; he had met Emanuel Bach when in the diplomatic service in Berlin. An oratorio enthusiast, Swieten promoted a choral version of *The Seven Last Words* and arranged the text for *The Creation*, based on Genesis and Milton's *Paradise Lost*. The two private performances of

* The translator was James Macpherson, a teacher from Ruthven, Inverness. The publication contained a preface by Dr Blair, a professor of the University of Edinburgh who was convinced of its authenticity. Macpherson had actually made up many, although not all, of the poems. On the back of his deception, Macpherson built a very successful career and became an MP. He lies in Poet's Corner in Westminster Abbey.

** Baron Gottfried was the head of the Imperial library, and ran the education commission which implemented Emperor Joseph's education reforms. He was amoral, proud, disagreeable and frosty. However, during diplomatic service in Paris and Prussia, his staff assessment recorded that 'la musique lui prends le meilleur de son temps'. Swieten's father, a liberal Dutchman, had been the inspiration for the Vienna medical school. He assisted Empress Maria Theresa with education and censorship, and curbed the influence of the Jesuits.[161]

The Creation in 1798 were a considerable success: 'Perhaps no other piece of music has ever enjoyed such immediate and universal acceptance.'[162] Haydn had been nervous that it might not be well received by a wider audience, but it was an ideal composition to be performed at the regular public concerts now run by the Musicians' Society. *The Seasons*, which Swieten based on the poem by James Thomson, followed in 1801.

In 1800, Haydn wrote the *Nelson* Mass to mark the visit of Nelson to Eisenstadt. Nelson was accompanying his mistress Emma Hamilton, who was in the entourage of the Queen of Naples. He was on a leisurely trip back to England after one of the more inglorious episodes in his career when, urged on by the queen to 'treat Naples as if it were a rebellious Irish town',[163] he summarily executed even those who only under compulsion had supported the rebels. The composer Cimarosa was lucky only to suffer imprisonment.[164] In Vienna, the hero seems to have been oblivious to the scandal he was creating as Lady Hamilton, fat but still beautiful, fawned on him. The British representative in Vienna recorded: 'he does not seem at all conscious of the sort of discredit he has fallen into, or the cause of it.'[165] Haydn, it would appear, accompanied her ladyship, who sang a cantata in a 'clear strong voice'.[166] However, on another occasion, when Haydn was performing with an orchestra, she preferred to chat and play at cards rather than listen to the music. Emma rarely gets a good press.

As an international celebrity, Haydn received medals and accolades from Paris, Russia and Sweden. But Vienna still treated him with relative indifference. An attempt to get an honour conferred upon him, the Leopold Order, failed: his achievement did not meet the narrowly defined qualifications for the award.[167]

In December 1803, Haydn conducted in public for the last time. Five years later, Antonio Salieri conducted a performance of *The Creation* to celebrate Haydn's 76th birthday. Beethoven attended this concert and 'knelt down before Haydn and fervently kissed the forehead of his old teacher'.[168]

A nasal polyp caused Haydn discomfort. He became run down and depressed by 'the melancholy sentiment that life was escaping him'. But in his shaky handwriting, he was able to record that he had acquired a new fortepiano for 200 ducats.[169]

In early 1809, Napoleon's army closed in on Vienna. They occupied the palace at Schönbrunn, and on 11 and 12 May they bombarded the city (see colour plate 4). The city walls were only about a mile away from Haydn's house, which was in the suburbs, half-way out to Schönbrunn. Either he must have been surrounded by the French batteries, or the shells must have been screaming overhead. In the distance, he would have seen the city burning.

Apparently, Napoleon placed a guard of honour at his house. Haydn is supposed to have been moved to tears when an officer of the hussars turned up and sang the aria from *The Creation*, 'In native worth'.* On 31 May 1809, shortly after midnight, Haydn died. At his funeral, 'high ranking French generals, officials and officers as well as the whole cultural world of Vienna were present'. Mozart's *Requiem* was played.[170]

With such an unpropitious start, such slow development, and such an unhappy home life, it is surprising that Haydn could say of himself that he was often 'seized by uncontrollable humour'. 'A secret feeling within me whispered: "There are but few contented and happy men here below; grief and care prevail everywhere; perhaps your labours may one day be the source from which the weary and worn, or the man burdened with affairs, may derive a few moments rest and refreshment."'[171]

Haydn had that sense of balance, warmth and gaiety which finds its way into his compositions. He personified those typical features of man at the time of the Enlightenment: propriety, style and wit.[172] That is surely why his music is so popular.

* The words in the second half of this aria are: 'With fondness leans upon his breast, The partner for him formed; A woman, fair and graceful spouse. Her softly smiling virgin looks, Of flow'ry spring the mirror, Bespeak him love and joy and bliss.' As Frau Haydn was dead, perhaps it is too irreverent to suggest that it was Haydn's sense of humour that caused his tears to flow.

Mozart

CHAPTER 4

In 1899, Alma Mahler, shortly before she married Gustav, went to a concert at which Mozart's Jupiter Symphony was performed and 'got frightfully bored'. She added: 'I felt it wasn't exciting but merely long-drawn-out. Times have changed. Nowadays nobody wants such hyper-naïve themes.'[1] The young lady, a very talented musician, had fallen into a familiar trap. Because Mozart's music is so easy to listen to, and often so light, we can easily think of him largely as a composer of background music fitted to complement champagne and strawberries at a *fête champêtre,* or to relax one when waiting for an aeroplane to take off.

Mozart's lightheartedness and his 'inexhaustible capacity for love'[2] enabled his music to transcend the seriousness of his personal struggle. Yet, we should not think of him as a mere adjunct to powdered wigs, silk stockings, flunkeys and marzipan. Mozart could 'look straight into the human heart'.[3] In that sense, he was like Rembrandt, although the painter preceded the composer by more than a century.

It can be instructive to join Mozart and Rembrandt in the same sentence, however much it may seem odd to do so: for it can remind us that, until Mozart, probably no composer conveyed such deep perception. In his operas, for the first time we meet and hear people as they are, not as they

Above: THE PICTURE HAS BEEN CALLED THE MOST LIFELIKE OF ALL THE MOZART PORTRAITS

ought to be. They express themselves from the bottom of their hearts. The conductor Bruno Walter, who recognised 'behind a seemingly graceful playfulness, the dramatist's inexorable seriousness and wealth of characterization', called Mozart 'the Shakespeare of the opera'.[4] It was through his music that Mozart achieved this: 'the drama is there only to give music opportunities; it is absorbed and completely recast in the music which remains supreme'.[5]

Mozart's achievement was astonishing; we have entered a new world. If one compares his operas with Gluck's *Orfeo*, performed only 24 years before, much of it suited to the plangent tones of the castrato, the contrast is almost incredible.* Possibly Mozart's struggle to be the first freelance musician gave him a deeper insight into human behaviour than others possessed. Others too have had 'a hard time', but who has produced compositions of the same quality or which give such pleasure? Try to compile a list of 'highlights' from *Figaro* or *Don Giovanni*. What will you leave out?

Wolfgang Amadeus Mozart's short life of almost 36 years began in Salzburg, on 27 January 1756. He was, famously, the infant prodigy whose cash flow potential had to be maximised before he grew up and ceased to be a novelty. This meant relentless touring as a small child, first to Munich and Vienna, and then away on a three-and-a-half-year trip to Paris and London. After this, he went three times to Italy. The circus act was soon played out; he was soon regarded as just another professional in the market for a job.

He was desperate to break away from the confines of the typical 'musician in service', but his timing was wrong, and the circumstances were particularly inhospitable. He had a disastrous attempt at finding a job in southern Germany, and also in Paris, which was more interested in arguments about different types of opera than in him. After kicking his heels for a couple of years, he went to Vienna. Although supported by Emperor Joseph, the Viennese aristocracy found his music puzzling and disliked, one guesses, his character, his bumptious, boasting manner. His position cannot have been helped by a 'bad' marriage. For some reason, he seems always to have been broke, despite working himself to exhaustion. There have been many rumours as to why he died so young, one of which is

* Even Gluck's *Iphigénie en Tauride*, less than a decade earlier, retains some of the antique features: the ballet, the pantomime, and the '*deus ex machina*', Diana, who comes to provide the happy ending. It can be instructive to listen to CDs of *Iphigénie* and *Figaro*, consecutively.

portrayed in the drama by Peter Shaffer, *Amadeus*. Here, we can only touch on this conundrum.

Early Days in Salzburg

Salzburg, one of the most beautiful cities of Europe, mixes German earnestness and Italian brilliance. Until Napoleonic times, its population of 16,000 was ruled by the Roman Catholic prince-archbishop. He was a prelate of considerable importance because his principality and the Habsburg Holy Roman Emperor were mutually dependent on each other for support. The Archbishop's revenues, principally from the salt industry, enabled him to sustain a court with a chief minister, master of the horse, lord steward, lord chamberlain, lord marshal, cupbearer, lords of the bedchamber plus 22 canons, all counts or lords.[6]

Salzburg was then a city of contrasts. The archbishop's palace was 'magnificent, abounding with fine pictures, tables of inlaid marble, and superb stoves of all colours and ornamented with statues ... In the menagery are to be seen some cranes, a pelican, which is in effect nothing but a kind of bittern, with a large bag at his throat, in which he can lay up a store of provision. There are also rock eagles, lynxes and two bevers.'[7] The Getreidegasse, where Wolfgang was born, was in the narrow streets. Here a nightwatchman kept law and order and called out the hours. The house would have been pervaded with smells from the earth closet, which led into a cesspit in the courtyard; the street reeked from the sewer running down the middle, the Salzach River stank from the filth thrown in. These smells had the merit of concealing the odour of the people who never washed, but rubbed themselves clean and occasionally doused themselves with perfume. On Saturdays, garbage was removed: the canal sluices were opened and the Getreidegasse was flooded.[8]

The people of Salzburg were notable beer-drinkers, but were not particularly prosperous. The city's resources had been depleted by the expulsion of its Protestant population in the 1730s.[9] Crop failures and the Seven Years War had also led to inflation, which had weakened the economy.

Leopold Mozart, the son of a bookbinder, had moved to Salzburg from Augsburg, some twenty years before his son was born. He was employed first as a valet and musician to one of the canons and then in the Archbishop's court, where he progressed to become deputy Kapellmeister. Unlike his son, he was a thrifty administrator; he might even have made a good accountant. But he was also a skilled musician.[10] His most famous piece, the Toy Symphony, was long attributed to Haydn.[11] He was also the author of a textbook on violin playing, which remained a respected primer for almost a century.[12] He handled all the marketing of this himself: he kept a stock at home; periodically he sent copies to German booksellers.

The court music department naturally swarmed with intrigue and gossip.[13] It was dominated by Italians, who came and went. Sometimes they left the local girls pregnant – surprisingly perhaps, since the Salzburg government determined the clothing one had to wear in bed, the bedclothes one could have, the times of getting up, and at what age one might share a bedroom with one's children. The day-to-day work in the music department was done by Germans such as Leopold and Haydn's brother Michael, who was despised as a tippler. Leopold wanted the top job, but there was as much chance of that as of a German being appointed head chef.

Leopold's wife Maria Anna was a local girl, the daughter of an impecunious widow who supplemented her income by lace making, the traditional means whereby impoverished, but respectable, widows eked out an existence.[14] The Mozarts had seven children. Only Maria Anna 'junior', known as Nannerl, and Wolfgang, who was four and a half years younger, survived.

From the age of three, Wolfgang (Wolferl, as his family called him) dabbled on the clavier. He progressed fast: when he was five, he composed a minuet and trio; by the time he was seven, he also played the violin.[15] Musical prodigies were not wholly unusual. To the considerable benefit of her father's teaching practice, Hetty Burney, the doctor's eleven-year-old daughter, had played complex Scarlatti harpsichord pieces on the London stage only three years before the Mozarts appeared in London.[16] Twenty years after Mozart, J.N. Hummel read music at four, played the violin at five, and the piano at six. There were others, now forgotten, including Nannerl herself. The poet and playwright Goethe suggested that instrumental skills could develop much earlier than literary or other artistic ability, because 'music is something innate and internal, which needs little nourishment from without, and no experience from life'.[17] The ultimate test is whether the child possessing those early mechanical and aural skills actually matures into an artist. Most do not.

On the Road

Prodigies open up all sorts of commercial possibilities for promoters. Wolfgang made his first appearance in September 1761 at Salzburg University, before he was six. In January, he was whisked off to Munich, 90 miles away, where he played before Elector Maximilian Joseph. One can imagine the family discussions during the subsequent months, as they planned an autumn visit to Vienna. On 18 September 1762, they set out, probably down river, to join the Danube at Passau.[18] Wolfgang played before the prince bishop, but was only given a few florins. This stinginess disappointed Leopold. How he coped with the continual stress of waiting for flunkeys to arrive with a bag of gold, we do not know. But he was a good man genuinely devoted to his children's best interests. Success for Wolfgang could eventually provide a good marriage for Nannerl, without which she would be doomed to an impoverished future.

Leopold wrote regularly to his landlord, Lorenz Hagenauer. Not only did he want to get news of his children back to Salzburg: Hagenauer, a successful grocer, was his banker, and 'had connections as far as Hamburg, Rotterdam, Marseilles and Venice'.[19] He provided the Mozarts with letters of credit which enabled them to draw cash in distant places. If Hagenauer had no direct trading contact at their next destination, the initial credit could be extended by a letter from the first contact to a further business acquaintance. The debts then bounced back to Hagenauer along the mercantile credit network.[20] It is important to impress one's banker; and Leopold usually put a good spin on what he said.

The Mozarts travelled on down the Danube, possibly in one of those well-appointed boats, 'having in them all the conveniences of a palace, stoves in the chambers, kitchens etc.',[21] rowed by twelve men, which went down the river at high speed. At Linz, the powerful Count Palffy heard the Mozarts play, and passed on news about them to Archduke Joseph (as Emperor Joseph II was then). The archduke asked his mother to invite the Mozarts to appear at the palace at Schönbrunn.

They arrived in Vienna some two and a half weeks after they had set out. Then they performed before the Imperial Vice-Chancellor: Leopold played the violin, Nannerl played the clavier and sang, while Wolfgang, with fingers spanning only five keys and feet not touching the ground, played the clavier and the violin.* Leopold wrote back, as one might expect, 'All the ladies are in love with my boy'.[23]

A few days later, they appeared at Schönbrunn, the first of two visits there, and they also played at the Hofburg, the imperial palace in Vienna. The empress, who only a week earlier had heard the first performance of Gluck's *Orfeo ed Euridice*, was musical,** like her ancestors. She played the clavier and had been taught singing by Hasse, the leading opera composer of his day. When she was young, the Italian castrato Senesino was, sensibly no doubt, reduced to tears by her singing.[24]

But she was tough. Only a couple of years before, the Prussians were winning the wars against her, there was administrative chaos, and her treasury was nearly bankrupt; her son and heir called their position 'terrifying'. She was practical: her criterion for whether an altarpiece was good was whether it was easy to dust.[25] She was also matronly: in the nineteen years before Mozart's birth she had borne sixteen children, the youngest a future Archbishop-Elector of Cologne, being about Wolfgang's own age.

She allowed the children to romp together; Wolfgang jumped up on the empress' lap and kissed her, fell on the floor and was picked up by Archduchess Marie Antoinette, who was about a year older than him. Wolfgang commanded the distinguished composer Wagenseil, who was in attendance on the empress, to turn the pages for him.[26] Poisonous child.

We may surmise that the empress felt that Wolfgang would help to keep her children entertained for that afternoon. Afterwards, she sent him one of their cast-off coats, lilac and gold, which would have been very expensive to acquire; the emperor sent Leopold 100 ducats, the equivalent of about fourteen and a half months' salary. The coat was worn by Wolfgang when he performed; the money was deposited in Hagenauer's bank account in Vienna.

Presumably, it was later that the empress formed her devastating dislike of the Mozarts. Eight years later, she would discourage one of her sons from taking Wolfgang into his service, saying: 'If however it would give

* A few years later, Grétry, composer of an early Romantic masterpiece, the opera *Richard Coeur de Lion*, noticed that Wolfgang did not seem to follow the text he was given to read, but substituted his own improvisations, once he had got going.[22]

** Her son Joseph played the cello and harpsichord, and listened to music for half an hour on most days.

you pleasure, I have no wish to stop you. I just want to prevent you burdening yourself with useless people and giving titles to people of that sort. If they are in your service, it degrades that service when these people go about the world like beggars.' She added a telling comment in times when courts found that they could be burdened with dependants: 'Besides he has a large family.'[27] 'Thumbs down' from Empress Maria Theresa was likely to be disastrous.

After the royal performances, Leopold experienced a serious hitch: Wolfgang was covered in spots. The cash flow stopped; but thankfully he recovered. They travelled on to Pressburg (now Bratislava) where Leopold could buy himself a four-seater coach, a sign of considerable upward momentum, even if horizontally, as we shall see, it was to be rather less effective. They left for Salzburg on New Year's Eve, having done some more performances in Vienna. We can picture the proud Leopold, as he drew up in the tiny square in the Getreidegasse in his new coach.[28]

More than Three Years on the Road

Within six months, they were off on their travels again. One wonders how the children had time to practise, and how Leopold found time to give them a general education. Wolfgang of course missed his friends from Salzburg. But the show had to go on.

No sooner had they set off on 9 June 1763 in their smart carriage than a back wheel broke. The replacement turned out to be too small, and it was well past midnight before they arrived at their first scheduled halt. It then took two days to fix. When they got to Munich, Leopold hung around the Nymphenburg Palace gardens, ingratiatingly, hoping to be noticed. Fortunately they were. Their performance that evening in the palace yielded 100 ducats from the elector, 75 from his brother, and, crucially, letters of recommendation to other dignitaries further along their route.[29]

When the party arrived at Augsburg, Leopold's birthplace, they could afford to buy a clavier from the celebrated maker, Stein. On they went, down the Rhine. In Heidelberg, they did some sightseeing, and saw the ruined castle and the Great Tun, the enormous barrel which holds 221,726 litres of wine. When they reached Mainz they parked the coach and went by market boat to Frankfurt. Goethe later recalled seeing there 'the little fellow with his coiffure and his sword'.[30]

As well as cash, they received presents, a fashionable English hat and embroidery for Nannerl and a porcelain snuff-box for Wolfgang.* The coach must have got increasingly cluttered: Leopold wrote, 'With snuff boxes and trinkets and such stuff, we could furnish a stall.'[33] Indeed by the end of the tour they had collected nine gold watches, twelve gold snuff-boxes, earrings, necklaces, knives, toothpicks, toothpick boxes and swords, all amounting to a value of about 35 times Leopold's annual salary.

Some of the journey was by boat, although this was expensive: they had to travel '*noblement*' to keep up appearances,[34] and they were badly held up by the weather. On they went, past the castles of the robber knights through that beautiful reach of the Rhine, with the S-bend, rapids and vertical cliff, subsequently called the Lorelei. In Coblenz, it rained for two days and Wolfgang caught a chill. So Leopold had a chance to do his accounts. They pressed ahead if the local dignitary was indisposed or away; they performed and collected if he was there.

In modern Belgium, they twice lost iron hoops off their coach wheels. On the second occasion, while the coach was being repaired, they lunched in an inn. There, Leopold recorded, 'we often had the honour of pigs grunting around us and hens paid us a visit'.[35] They stopped for six weeks in Brussels, the seat of the emperor's brother. There, Wolfgang wrote the Sonata in C for Piano and Violin.

PARIS

After this, the Mozarts set off into France along its good roads constructed with local forced labour but surrounded by desperate poverty. Then, on 18 November 1763, they arrived in the muddy and congested streets of Paris.[36] The city was growing rapidly; the Place Royale, between the gardens of the Tuileries and the wooded Champs Elysées, was about halfway through its construction. A foreigner in Paris would find it necessary immediately 'to send for the taylor, perruquier, hatter, shoemaker, and every other tradesman concerned in the equipment of the human body'. A husband observed that 'it is enough to make a man's heart ake to see his wife surrounded by a multitude of cotturieres, milliners, and tire-women. All her sacks and negligees must be altered and new trimmed. She must

* Snuff-boxes were a common accessory; Frederick the Great had 1,500; one stopped a bullet killing him in battle.[31] They were a preferable gift to the two performing bears which Liszt received from the tsar.[32]

have new caps, new laces, new shoes, and her hair new cut. She must have her taffaties for the summer, her flowered silks for the spring and autumn, her satins and damsks for winter'.[37] Leopold cooled his ladies' enthusiasm with the comment: 'This disgusting make-up makes even a naturally beautiful woman look unspeakable in the eyes of an honest German.'[38]

There were considerable disparities of wealth.[39] Beggars were driven in from the countryside as a consequence of the poverty caused by the stagnant agrarian economy and the rising population. There were the rich: some of the richest being the 40 *fermiers généraux* who bought the right of collecting the indirect taxes. One of these, Le Riche de la Pouplinière, who had died the previous year, had his own private orchestra where Jean-Philippe Rameau, now aged 80, had worked.[40]

The Mozarts had a valuable introduction to Friedrich Melchior Grimm, secretary to the Duc d'Orléans, cousin of the King. Grimm also had excellent contacts among the cultured: he had assisted Diderot with his work on the *Encyclopaedia*, and he knew the philosopher Jean-Jacques Rousseau. The Mozarts played in private houses and palaces, and in two public concerts, known as the Concerts Spirituels.[41] The opera at the Académie Royale de Musique, run as a monopoly by Lully's heirs, would have been inaccessible to them.

The Mozarts' appearance at Versailles was initially delayed because of the death of Archduke Joseph's first wife, who was the granddaughter of King Louis XV. When the Mozarts appeared there on Christmas Eve, Wolfgang stood behind the queen, Marie Leszinska, at a meal, while she periodically passed him morsels to eat. One presumes that he peered over the 'monstrous headdresses that erected such a heavy burden over such light heads'.[42] The food thrown to him must have been delicious, even if not quite what a boy of his age would want: this was the time when French cuisine was developing, and the great wines and cheeses were beginning to emerge.[43]

The Queen of France was the daughter of a King of Poland. She was plain and prudish. Her father once said that 'the two most boring queens in Europe are my wife and my daughter'.[44] So, as an indefatigable hunter of animals and women, Louis enjoyed his mistresses, the most famous being the now matronly Mme de Pompadour (née Poisson) and the delicious Mme du Barry. When Mme de Pompadour became too old to meet his needs – heating, stimulating drugs and aphrodisiacs proved insufficient to halt the march of time – Louis had a private brothel set up which he would visit in the disguise of a Polish nobleman. 'How is it that at 65 you have the same desires as at 25?', the king asked one of his more notorious courtiers. 'Sire', was the reply, 'I frequently change the object; novelty produces the desired result.'[45] Louis' preference was for young girls, so as to avoid catching syphilis.

Mme de Pompadour placed Wolfgang on a table to inspect him but recoiled when he tried to kiss her. 'Who is this woman who will not kiss me?', demanded the brat. 'Why, the Empress herself kissed me', he expostulated.[46] This was unlikely to cut any ice with the formidable Madame. She was still a powerful confidante of the king and important to the now friendly relationship between France and Austria. She was also a person of exquisite taste. It was she who had the state china factory moved from Vincennes to Sèvres, so that it was closer to her château. When she died, it took two notaries a whole year to catalogue her art collection.[47] One of her most favoured artists was Boucher, whose sophisticatedly erotic paintings eulogised women: he painted pictures of lithe goddesses and nymphs, 'their delicate bodies not yet fully developed, yet aware that life throbs within them and knowing something of its secrets'.[48]

London

In April 1764, the Mozarts moved on to London, where they stayed for eighteen months. The routine was similar to Paris. They gave four public concerts: one in the Spring Gardens on the day after the king's birthday; this was a good time as much of the nobility was in town.[49] There was a charity concert in Ranelagh,* and there were two further concerts, the final one being eleven months after they arrived. They also appeared in drawing-rooms, gaining an entrée through a very popular castrato they had befriended. They appeared at Lady Clive's magnificent house in Berkeley Square, bought with prize money and other revenues her husband had

* Ranelagh had opened in 1742. 'My Lord Chesterfield is so fond of it that he says he has ordered all his letters to be directed thither.' In 1774, 'the people of the true tone come in at about eleven, stare about them for half an hour, laugh at the other fools who are drenching and scalding themselves with coffee and tea … despise all they have seen, and then they trail home again to sup … The citizens on the other hand come to stare at the great … They come to see how the great folks were dressed, how they walked and how they talked'.[50] There were no glossy magazines in those days.

obtained in India. It may have been the suggestion that they might play at Mrs Cornely's disreputable joint that prompted Leopold to remark: 'I will not raise my children in this dangerous place, where most people have no religion and where one sees nothing but bad examples.'[51]

They performed at Buckingham House. The young royal couple were musical.[52] George III played the violin, flute and harpsichord. Queen Charlotte, a German then aged only around twenty, was apparently no beauty, having too wide a mouth,[53] but sang nicely and played the glockenspiel as well as the harpsichord. Wolfgang played to them works by Handel and by J.C. Bach, who had settled in London five years before and was the queen's music teacher.

King George, who was soon to lose his American colonies and go mad, was then jolly, popular and dowdy. When told that a courtier was about to give birth to her twentieth child, he said that he hoped that she would have twins, 'the more the merrier'.[54] But alongside this apparent lightheartedness, there was a protocol so strict that it drove one of the queen's keepers of the robes, Fanny Burney, almost to anorexia nervosa.[55] She sent her sister 'Directions for coughing, sneezing or moving, before the King and Queen'. Even ladies in waiting were not allowed to walk past the open door of a room where a member of the royal family was present; and they had always to remain standing, sometimes for hours on end. No doubt, for all the superficial informality of the royal couple, the Mozarts had to watch their own behaviour most carefully.

The king was exceptionally good at recognising people. So, when he came across the Mozarts in the park, he pulled down the window of his carriage to acknowledge them. Leopold was delighted; but, financially, it was less satisfactory. The king was notoriously thrifty; and the queen reputedly sent out servants to buy her books more cheaply from secondhand bookstalls.[56] Leopold was dismayed to be paid only about half what they got from the French court.

To start with, the Mozarts lived at a haircutter's in 19–21 Cecil Court, off St Martin's Lane. Then Leopold became unwell with bronchial problems so they moved out for seven weeks to Dr Randall's house at 180 Ebury Street, Chelsea.

This gave Wolfgang the chance to practise his composition and learn from the works of J.C. Bach. Wolfgang's health was also noticeably poor: one aristocrat noted that 'we have got the little German boy here ... he is really the most extraordinary effort of nature, but our professors of physick don't think he will be long lived'.[57]

They returned to Frith Street, Soho. By now, the Mozarts' circus act in fashionable West End circles had been played out. So Leopold opened up his lodgings from midday to 3 pm every day, where, for a reduced fee of five shillings, the public could enjoy a private recital and see Wolfgang improvising and playing with his hands covered with a cloth. Copies of his compositions were sold at the door. Wolfgang would also play for half a crown at the Swan and Hoop, Cornhill, where Leopold could tap the prosperous middle classes in the City. The Mozarts had the opportunity to relax, and they went on sightseeing trips to the Tower, Greenwich, Kew, Richmond, Westminster Hall, Kensington Gardens and the British Museum.[58]

On 24 July 1765, they left London. They had a brief stop at a private house near Canterbury, and attended the horse-races. They crossed to Calais and soon took possession of their own coach again.

The Dutch envoy had asked them to go to Holland, where they stayed for about nine months. Wolfgang performed, composed and played the organ in churches. They almost faced catastrophe: Nannerl developed typhoid, and was given the Last Rites. They switched doctors and she recovered. Then Wolfgang also got typhoid.

In July 1766, they were back in Paris, where they had wisely stored much of their luggage, and stayed briefly in Versailles. Leopold subscribed to an appeal to support the Calas family, Huguenots from Toulouse who had been persecuted and had suffered a serious miscarriage of justice. They travelled on to Dijon and Lyon. Wolfgang saw a public execution. They went on to Geneva. They tried, without success, to see Voltaire who lived nearby. A few years later, Dr Burney had more luck, although Voltaire greeted him with, 'Well gentlemen, you now see me, did you take me for a wild beast or monster, that was only fit to be stared at as at a show?'[59]

On the way back through Munich, Wolfgang became very ill with rheumatic fever. They finally arrived back in Salzburg on 29 November 1766, a couple of months short of his eleventh birthday.

To Vienna and Italy

But there could be no let up. In September 1767, they were off again on their travels to Vienna, where an archduchess was about to marry the king of Naples, with all the pomp of a royal wedding. That the Mozarts went there illustrates the extent of Leopold's trust in Providence. It also indicates the almost reckless risks which he was prepared to take with his family. Vienna had been stricken with smallpox earlier that year: in May, the epidemic killed Emperor Joseph's second wife and almost took Empress Maria Theresa as well. The royal bride-to-be then succumbed on the day after she should have been married. Maria Theresa, at this stage, advised by her doctor, Gerard van Swieten, did not believe in inoculation.[60]

This epidemic put Leopold in a quandary. He was hoping at any moment to be summoned by the emperor. This was an opportunity not to be missed, yet disease was raging around him. It even attacked the household in which the Mozarts lodged. Leopold delayed as long as he dared. He then escaped with Wolfgang over 100 miles to the north, to Olmütz (now Olomouc), leaving his wife and Nannerl behind: he thought that they had already had smallpox and thus would be immune. For about eight weeks, while father and son were guests of the dean in the house next to the Olmütz cathedral, mother and daughter were left to deal with the 'call from the Palace', should it come. But Leopold had miscalculated on most counts: both Wolfgang and Nannerl caught the disease, luckily very mildly, and there was no summons.

Eventually, they were called. Wolfgang wrote an opera for the emperor, *La Finta Semplice*, but its performance was frustrated by intrigue on the part of the musicians, including the director of the theatres* and the French troupe.[62] Leopold realised that he would have to abandon its production. Dr Mesmer, whose healing techniques gave his name to the word 'mesmerise', commissioned a comic opera, *Bastien and Bastienne*, which was performed at his house.

The Mozarts returned to Salzburg, and planned a visit to Italy, although this time Nannerl and her mother were to stay behind. This trip was to be educational, particularly to study Italian opera and learn from Padre Martini, the leading teacher of his time. They left in December 1769. We can balk at the pressure, but Wolfgang was enjoying it, according to the letters which he sent home, many multilingual and full of spelling mistakes and puns.[63]

* The director, Giuseppe Affligio, subsequently got into trouble: Michael Kelly, the Irish singer, saw him in Italy, where he was a galley slave.[61]

Soon after setting off, he scribbled: 'My heart is filled with alott of joy because I feel so jolly on this trip, because it's so cozy in our carriage, and because our coatchmann is such a fine fellow who drives as fast as he can when the road lets him.'[64] Lombardy in Northern Italy was an important Habsburg possession, so the roads were good. Indeed, at this stage, the Brenner Pass was the only one which could be got across without the travellers having to leave their carriages. The trout from the lake at the top was a particular delicacy, but the charges were extortionate: a later traveller complained of one post-station where he was charged 'a franc and a half for a bed upon the end of which the author had incautiously sat for a minute'.[65]

Leopold and Wolfgang went to Milan and Bologna, where they met the castrato Farinelli, who was retired and living in style; they then went to Florence. They were in Rome by Holy Week. This is the occasion on which Wolfgang was reputed to have written down, from memory, Allegri's *Miserere*.[66] The Pope conferred on him the Order of Golden Spur, which had been conferred on Gluck.

In Rome, he met Prince Charlie who was then less than Bonny, and usually inebriated.[67] More happily perhaps, Mozart had already struck up a friendship with a prodigy, the violinist Thomas Linley, son of Haydn's acquaintance in London. No doubt Thomas enjoyed Wolfgang's story about the comedian he had seen in Cremona, who gave a fart every time he performed a jump.[68] The threat of highwaymen delayed the journey to Naples, a five-day trip with all the bureaucracy of passports and officials.[69] But, once there, Wolfgang enjoyed seeing the volcano puffing away and Leopold had the pleasure of meeting the British ambassador, Sir William Hamilton. On the return journey through Bologna, Wolfgang was admitted a member of the Accademia Filarmonica; the authorities had to change the rules to admit somebody aged fourteen.

The Mozarts were in Bologna for the summer, and delayed there because Leopold gashed his leg when the horse pulling their vehicle fell. Mozart must have explored the city with its ancient university, and the two leaning towers, one almost 100 metres high, the other about half that height. Bologna had seen better days. In the Middle Ages, it had been one of the ten largest cities of Europe; now it did little more than entertain and have carnivals. It had fallen on hard times: one quarter of the inhabitants seem to have lived by begging or public charity.[70] However, the church of

San Petronio still had a formidable reputation for the quality of the instrumental music accompanying its services.[71]

From there, they moved back to Milan where Wolfgang's opera *Mitridate* was successfully staged with 22 performances. Then to Venice, where, in the opinion of an Italian academic expressed to a reputable newspaper[72] in January 2001, the musical prodigy became a sexual prodigy: scarcely fifteen years old, his voice just breaking, Wolfgang sired a child. In Venice, they met Count Durazzo, who had been rusticated there as ambassador, having fallen from grace in his row with Haydn's teacher Reutter.[73] They eventually got home at the end of March, a year after they set out. Wolfgang had grown six inches.

The pace could not slacken, although Wolfgang was often absolutely exhausted. In August, they set off for Italy again. This time it was a four-month round-trip to Milan for the royal wedding of Archduke Ferdinand. For this, Wolfgang was asked to write *Ascanio in Alba*, an opera which was well received. He was now in search of a job; he was nearly sixteen. Salzburg was a backwater for musicians. Archduke Ferdinand asked his mother for advice about whether to employ the Mozarts; she gave the crushing reply, quoted earlier, a message which passed around the Habsburg family network. A third Italian trip took place the following autumn, when again he made an attempt to get a job in Florence, where another of Maria Theresa's sons was grand duke: this led to nothing. After this third trip, they went to Vienna. Nothing came of an audience with Maria Theresa who had just returned from her visit to the Esterházys; she did, however, say something which Leopold felt he could not put down in writing. Possibly this was a significant moment in the history of music?[74]

Archbishop Colloredo

The Mozarts had been able to get away on all these tours owing to the indulgence of Archbishop Sigismund Christoph, Count von Schrattenbach. But he died just as they returned from their second Italian trip. He was succeeded, after an election involving five days of intrigue and thirty ballots, by Hieronymus, Count von Colloredo.[75] Besides being very powerful by virtue of his position as archbishop, Hieronymus was impeccably connected: his family tree, covered with colourful escutcheons, some princes, some cardinals, reaches back to 1200. He was also at the centre of power: his father was Prince Rudolf Colloredo-Wallsee und Mels, Imperial

Vice-Chancellor, head of bureaucracy in Vienna, and policy adviser to the emperor. A Colloredo was usually in Joseph's suite on his travels.[76]

The appointment had considerable significance; the new archbishop was definitely not a man to cross. He implemented imperial reforms and policies, like his role model the emperor, without much sensitivity. Although strictly Roman Catholic, anything Jesuitical came under attack:* there were restrictions on the use of candles, statues, relics and church music. Some changes were sensible: the archbishop required that Mass

Count Hieronymus von Colloredo-Wallsee und Mels, Archbishop of Salzburg

should last no longer than three quarters of an hour; he also tried to purge the smaller and rural churches of 'miserable fiddling and horrible howling'.[78]

Music in Salzburg had centred on the cathedral, the court and the university theatre. Cathedral music was cut back. The university theatre company was closed, making the theatre dependent on travelling troupes.

* Salzburg had recently been a cradle for various influential 'Jansenist' prelates eager, in worship, for more austerity and less opulence. There was considerable upheaval: the Jesuits, bitter rivals of the Jansenists, had been expelled from Portugal in 1759, accused of subverting Spanish and Portuguese policy in South America and of an attempt to assassinate the king. Pope Clement XIII, who tried to protect them, died of apoplexy when threatened with war by Spain and France, who had expelled the Jesuits in 1767, and by the Two Sicilies. His successor, Pope Clement XIV, who received the Mozarts, eventually suppressed the Jesuits in 1773.[77]

Some music at court would continue: the archbishop enjoyed his violin; but what music there was would be led by Italians, and definitely not by the Mozarts, who were nevertheless bound to his service.[79]

Settling Down in Salzburg

Wolfgang was now just another of the many composers around: somebody has counted at least 16,500 symphonies composed between 1720 and 1810.[80] The conceited former prodigy aroused jealousy and opposition. His colleagues derided his Papal Order, when he was foolish enough to wear it.[81] They would of course be friendly and charming, but would give him no help: the best thing was to see him off. And no doubt it was quite satisfying to do so.

The family kept together in Salzburg from spring 1775 until autumn 1777.[82] Leopold took in resident pupils. Wolfgang had to be content with the post of Konzertmeister at a salary of 150 fl. He wrote the bassoon concerto, and, for the Munich carnival of 1775, *La Finta Giardiniera*. He supplemented his salary by composing works for notables in the city. Since there was less music at court, there was now more music in houses.[83] The Mozarts obtained work from wealthy traders like the Haffners, and nobility such as Countess Lodron, whose maiden name was Harrach. Her husband was high steward and lord chamberlain.

Although feeling increasingly resentful, the Mozarts led a pleasant life. They were sociable, and would invite round friends for music making, chat and gossip.[84] In 1773, they moved to an elegantly furnished apartment in the 'Dancing Master's House', on the other side of the river, looking out on the market place. This had a large ballroom in which they could make music and Leopold could store his stock of books and the instruments he bought and sold. They also used the room for shooting: between six and ten people would shoot with air-guns at an appropriate point on a drawing which reflected recent gossip, often lewd or irreverent.[85]

They would play chess and cards. They could go to tournaments held in the archbishop's riding school and to the ballroom in the town hall where there were twice-weekly balls in Carnival time. They would of course go to the theatre, to see the travelling troupes. There would be performances three days a week, usually of a play or a light opera, followed by a ballet. There was considerable variety: one troupe had a repertory of 25 operas and a melodrama. The Mozarts could also enjoy their own 'pop-up theatre', made of cardboard, and look through a lens at theatre scenes and places.

Even though visits, outings, churchgoings, bathing and shooting may have been pleasant, Wolfgang was very frustrated. In 1776, he wrote to Padre Martini: 'I live in a country where music leads to a struggling existence.'[86] He was worried about the quality of music in Salzburg as well as the lack of opportunity. The Mozarts were desperate to get away.

Change needs management: Wolfgang had to cast around, but not in a way that would give the impression of disloyalty; if it did, both father and son might be sacked. While they were away, the vulgar Frau Michael Haydn could stir up gossip about the extent of Mozart family commitment to Salzburg. To avoid disclosing that the family might decamp, Nannerl and her mother would stay behind. Anyway, dependants were an encumbrance when applying for a job: potential employers, as we have seen, would be alerted to future pension obligations.[87]

So, in 1777, Wolfgang applied for leave to travel. The formal, horrifying reply from the canny archbishop was that both 'father and son shall have permission to seek their fortune elsewhere'.[88] Chilled by this, Leopold compromised and stayed behind. Mozart went off with his mother, in Leopold's words, 'either to get a good permanent appointment, or, if this should fail, to go off to some big city where large sums of money can be earned';[89] a not untypical attitude, perhaps, for a father and his 21-year-old son.

The Disastrous Trip to Paris

On 23 September 1777, Wolfgang set off in high spirits, in a chaise bought for about 100 fl.* He was delighted at getting away from that 'prick' Colloredo. The epithet naturally alarmed his father. And the plan was hopeless. The strength of the Mozart team lay in Leopold's business acumen complementing Wolfgang's artistic skills. His mother, who had no entrée to the social occasions, merely went along to do the housework. On this trip, she would sit freezing in her lodgings, utterly miserable.

Things began to go wrong very quickly. There were no vacancies in Munich or Mannheim, the home of the magnificent orchestra built up by Stamitz. So, Mozart hung around in Mannheim inventing a number of hare-brained schemes: for example, with the help of an innkeeper, he

* This was around the same amount as the annual wages of an unmarried female singer[90]

concocted a plan whereby, in return for compositions, he would be paid 600 fl annually by a consortium, and 200 fl by a count.[91]

Cash drained away. They deceived Leopold in their correspondence, hoping that the future would come right. There was considerable scope for confusion and deception. The post took six days from Salzburg, so there was a minimum response time of twelve days. Leopold tried to sort out things, including arranging credits with merchants against which the travellers could draw. Increasingly concerned about the family reputation and status, he knew that finance for his retirement years depended on the success of his son; as did Nannerl's future, that is, if she were not to land up in penury like their lodger who eked out a living mending caps.[92]

Wolfgang planned to go to Paris in the spring with the court flautist. This particular scheme entailed their expenses, in the interim, being met from the commission on two flute quartets; there was also expected to be a sufficient surplus to enable Frau Mozart to return to Salzburg. In the event, the money from the flute music was less than expected and could not pay for her return trip. She had to tag along.

This shambles was not helped by the fact that by now the lively, fun-loving Mozart, at 21, had an eye for women. He was very attracted to Rosa, the thirteen-year-old daughter of the Mannheim conductor, Christian Cannabich.[93] In Augsburg, it seems probable that he had an affair with Leopold's niece, Maria Anna Thekla, known as the 'Bäsle', the little cousin. Their letters fascinate psychologists keen to diagnose and classify Mozart's behaviour. They reek of the lavatory,* although this was not unusual in this century: some of the writings of poets such as Alexander Pope and Jonathan Swift do not stand up to prudish scrutiny.

Mozart's first serious girlfriend was the sixteen-year-old Aloysia Weber, whose father Fridolin was a bass in Mannheim. Fridolin's brother, a string player in the Mannheim orchestra, who assumed noble ancestry (hence the 'von'), would later get his son into trouble by embezzling his boss' money. That son was Carl Maria von Weber now remembered for *Der Freischütz*, *Euryanthe*, *Oberon* and the *Invitation to the Dance*, among other great works. If it were not for the importance of Carl Maria one might think that

* Mozart's amusement at this extended to his music: he wrote a canon on 'Leck mich im Arsch' (Lick my arse).[94] The Bäsle's subsequent career does not help her reputation; she became a kept woman, explaining away her trappings by saying that they came from her rich uncle (Leopold!) in Salzburg; she then suffered the ultimate disgrace, when she had an illegitimate child.[95]

the Webers were generally a bad lot. Aloysia's mother had a reputation for being an alcoholic.[96]

Wolfgang went on a tour with Aloysia and her father in mid-January 1778. When the young couple hatched a scheme to go off to Italy together, Leopold was horrified.[97]

Problems in Germany and Paris

Apart from Wolfgang's antics, there were two serious reasons why this trip in search of a job was destined to be a failure. Firstly, a change of ruler meant that two key areas of opportunity, Munich and Mannheim, suddenly shrank to one. Secondly, the musical world of Paris was focused on the vexed question of the future of opera: this was more important and interesting than the career plans of someone from Salzburg.

On 30 December 1777, the Elector of Bavaria died without a son. The heir* to a substantial portion of his territory was his dissolute Wittelsbach cousin from the Palatinate, who decided to move his court from Mannheim to Munich. For employees such as musicians, there were now no opportunities in Mannheim and, with excess capacity, redundancies might be expected in Munich. For kings and electors, there was a considerable amount of wheeling and dealing to be done. Emperor Joseph tried to strengthen the Habsburg territorial position, thus disturbing the balance of power. War eventually broke out six months later.**[98]

For Mozart, all this disruption meant that the five Electorates of Brandenburg-Prussia, Bavaria, the Palatinate, Bohemia and Saxony had other more important matters to consider than hiring expensive musicians. The courts of the spiritual Electors of Mainz, Cologne and Trier, although magnificent in their own way, were no better prospects than Salzburg and the other small princelings in southern Germany. Mozart did think that

* The succession issue was so complicated that it reputedly gave rise to 288 treatises at the time. By February, Leopold was nervous about the deteriorating conditions in Bavaria.

** In the middle of 1778, Frederick the Great again took his chance and seized Bohemia. Two enormous armies faced each other across the Elbe between Prague and Dresden. Neither wanted to fight: Frederick was too old and Joseph, while keen to flex his muscles, was reined in by his mother who was extremely concerned that he was 'betting the firm'. The armies ravaged Bohemia and when the supply system collapsed, the soldiers lived on the potatoes which they dug from the sodden fields: hence its name, 'the Potato War'. With Russian intervention, peace was eventually made in May 1779, a date which marks the establishment of two new powers on the world stage, Prussia and Russia.

Cologne might be a possibility if the old archbishop were to die and the Habsburg nominee were to succeed. But, to all intents and purposes, unless he went to look for a job in Protestant Hanover or London, there was only one place to try: Paris. This was anyway the place to which Leopold had been urging his son to go.

The journey to Paris, at the end of March 1778, took nine days; the Mozarts reduced the cost by agreeing that their driver could keep their chaise when they got there.[99] They looked up Grimm, who had been so helpful on the earlier visit. He introduced them to a duchess in whose

Niccolò Piccinni. His row with Christoph Willibald Gluck about the nature of opera was a hot topic in 1778, when Mozart was in Paris

house Mozart played background music to the chatter of conversation and card playing. Mozart had already written to Leopold indicating that he was not prepared to teach.[100]

It was a particularly unpropitious time for a newcomer like Mozart to arrive in Paris. Both musicians and audiences were focused on a dispute between those who advocated the new more realistic operatic style of Gluck and those who preferred the old-fashioned, stilted Italianate style of Hasse, with his settings of libretti by the poet Metastasio. (Hasse was Bach's friend, and Metastasio helped Haydn to find his feet.)

Gluck had gone to Paris to replenish his fortunes lost in running the Burg theatre in Vienna; he also was a protégé of Queen Marie Antoinette.

With his opera *Iphigénie en Aulide*, he became a celebrity. He then staged *Orfeo* in French, followed by *Alceste*, and then in September 1777, *Armide*. Early the following month, a distinguished, but dogmatic, critic made a virulent attack on *Armide* in the press, only to be ridiculed by Gluck in another paper a week later. The row about opera began.[101]

To defend its cause, the anti-Gluck faction invited to Paris the Neapolitan composer Niccolò Piccinni, who had already about 300 operas to his name, including a 'world hit', *La Buona Figliuola*.[102] His opera *Roland* was performed a few weeks before the Mozarts arrived on 23 March 1778. Mozart met Piccinni, but Gluck was away during his stay.*

Then, suddenly Mozart's mother fell ill and died. He wrote home: 'Weep, weep, as you cannot fail to, but take comfort at last.' This letter crossed with a poignant one from Leopold writing to celebrate her name-day: 'it is only this separation which gnaws at my heart – to be separated from you, and to be living so very far off'.[103] She was already dead.

This was a heart-wrenching moment in Wolfgang's sad life. He seems to have underestimated the seriousness of her condition: when his mother was ill, much of his time was spent scheming with the Webers for them to join him in Paris. His relationship with his father deteriorated. His father blamed him for not getting a doctor earlier. To meet his mother's funeral and medical expenses, Wolfgang pawned her watch and gave her amethyst ring to the nurse who attended her, otherwise the nurse would have taken the wedding ring.

Grimm packed him off home to Salzburg, sending him, to the composer's fury and indignation, by the cheapest and most uncomfortable route. Instead of going straight home to face his father, if not console him, Wolfgang diverted to Mannheim and to Munich, where the Webers had moved. Clutching an aria as an engagement present, he met up with Aloysia. But she, who was about to become a highly successful singer, was no longer interested in this particularly small man, 'very thin and pale, with a profusion of fine fair hair, of which he was rather vain'.[104] So he seems to have drifted into Salzburg in January 1779, accompanied by his naughty cousin, the Bäsle.

* Leopold, who had warned Mozart off Gluck, was not to know that he would return to Paris with *Iphigénie en Tauride*. This, with its evocative music, lyricism and characterisation, seems to be in a different class from his *Orfeo*. It eclipsed Piccinni's version, which was not helped by the drinking habits of its *prima donna* and was referred to as *Iphigénie en Champagne*.

His father knew now that Wolfgang was totally unfit to hold the type of administrative musical appointment that he was aiming for, one which involved man management, leadership and teamwork. He had incurred debts of more than twice Leopold's salary; he had already borrowed almost one year's salary to fund the start of the trip. He may possibly have been offered the poorly remunerated post of court organist in Paris; equally, it is possible that canny Leopold just mentioned this to alarm the Salzburg nobility, who liked the Mozarts, to put pressure on them to offer Wolfgang a job. Leopold actually achieved Wolfgang's return to Salzburg at a combined family income of 904 fl compared with the previous figure of 504 fl. But Wolfgang had achieved nothing in the way of employment. He had lost his mother.[105]

In Salzburg Again

Mozart was back in Salzburg for the next couple of years, from January 1779 to November 1780. He had about twelve years to go, little did he know it. He was still a few months short of those truly 'vintage years', when so many of his best-loved works were written. But for now, he was forced to undertake some drudgery in order to earn his keep. Nannerl gave lessons and practised, attended daily mass, supervised the maid, did the ironing and needle work; she had her hair dressed at home several times a week and would take the dog, Miss Pimpes, for a walk.[106]

Mozart, however, put his experience of Gluck's style together with his knowledge of Italian opera to good use. During 1780, he was commissioned to write an opera for the forthcoming Carnival season at Munich. The result was *Idomeneo*, which was first performed in January 1781.

To Vienna, Breaking Loose

During that month, Archbishop Colloredo went to Vienna because his father was ill. He took with him a court in miniature, including a castrato, a womanising Italian violinist, and young Mozart. But he did not want his servants poached, so they were restricted to giving private concerts at the house of the Teutonic Order where Colloredo was lodging, and at the houses of some of the Viennese nobility. They ate with the valets and cooks.

Mozart resented this treatment. As soon as there was talk of returning to Salzburg, he was determined to stay and try his luck. Impetuously, he handed in his resignation but the archbishop's chamberlain, who was a friend of the Mozart family and may have had his best interests at heart, refused at first to accept it and tried to counsel him. After a couple of interviews, the chamberlain finally, in desperation, kicked him out of the palace. Mozart, whom the archbishop thought 'dreadfully conceited',[107] told his father that the chamberlain 'ought to have reasoned quietly with me, rather than throw such words about as "clown" and "knave" and hoof a fellow out of the room with a kick on the arse'.[108] The story of Mozart kicking over the traces of course did the rounds of Vienna; and if prying eyes read any of his subversive comments about the social structure, as expressed in his letters to his father, he will have done himself considerable harm.

Mozart did not want to be a servant. As we have seen, he had written arrogantly to his father that he did not want to teach, that he 'was not born for that kind of work'.* 'I can't be expected to have to keep an appointment, or to have to wait for someone at a house. I won't do it. That sort of work is for those who can't do anything else except play the keyboard. I am a composer, and was born to be a Kapellmeister.'[110]

Mozart was too impatient: Viennese society was not yet ready to encourage the notion of the emancipated artist. Poets and authors still depended on working as secretaries, or private tutors, at court or for a noble patron. There was no structure to enable a composer to strike out on his own. For a few years yet, musicians would still be servants: as late as 1798, there was an advertisement for a musician who would also act as *valet de chambre*. This would change: Mozart's contemporary, the virtuoso performer, Muzio Clementi, lived long enough to invest his earnings, from performance and his *Gradus ad Parnassum*, in a successful piano business. But this was some years later. Besides, Mozart seemingly was disliked by both the imperial family and the Archbishop of Salzburg, and his behaviour showed a contempt for authority which the aristocracy would definitely wish to discourage. He would be entirely dependent on this aristocratic support: of the 174 subscribers to his concert series in 1784, only eight per cent were middle class.[111] If the nobility did not like him, he did not stand a chance.

* This was at a time when, certainly in England, most composers survived on income from teaching, earning between a quarter and half a guinea an hour. Samuel Wesley, for example, complained of 'the Drudgery of more Dunces assaulting my Ears for six hours together';[109] but musicians had (and have still) to put up with this. Mozart's letter also took the opportunity to praise the 'merits' of Aloysia Weber: his father must have been furious.

Mozart's timing, again, was unlucky: when he broke loose, it was summer and the nobility was out of town. Poor Leopold, a practical man of the world, was very worried about the insecure future that awaited his son. He agreed with the chamberlain that Mozart allowed himself 'to be far too easily dazzled in Vienna'. A man's reputation there lasts a very short time: 'at first, it is true, you are overwhelmed with praises and make a great deal of money into the bargain – but how long does that last? After a few months, the Viennese want something new.'[112]

By the end of June, Mozart was teaching in return for meals, and at the end of the year there was a possibility of his becoming keyboard teacher to Princess Elisabeth of Württemberg, but this did not materialise: Antonio Salieri, six years older than Mozart, was appointed instead.[113]

At this time, Viennese opera, like Parisian, was in turmoil.[114] The Emperor was exceptionally knowledgeable about music and personally controlled court entertainment, issuing instructions even when away on his travels. He loathed stilted Italian theatre and French ballets. In the teeth of his nobility, he got rid of them and promoted German theatre, purged of its lewd aspects. Mozart's *Die Entführung aus dem Serail*, a 'Singspiel', was broadly what he wanted. His notorious observation that this had too many notes was probably a criticism of his courtiers' brainpower, rather than of Mozart.[115]

Still, *Die Entführung* was a considerable success, although even that was a mixed blessing: Mozart wrote to his father that 'because of my boasting and criticisms, the Professori of music and many others have become my enemies'.[116] By 1786, the opera had been performed in more than twenty cities. As well as being in German, it reflected a fashion for oriental and exotic things; aristocrats liked to be seen in the clothes of a sultan or that of the harem. Piccolos, cymbals and bass drums, typical instruments of a Turkish military band, were also much in fashion.[117]

Mozart tried to ingratiate himself with the emperor's influential valet, Strack. More successfully, he came to the notice of Baron Gottfried van Swieten, a key member of the team implementing Emperor Joseph's reforms,* an experienced diplomat, and, as we have seen, the author of the

* Joseph's relentless reforms (see page 115) seriously unsettled the aristocracy. Although capital punishment had been abolished, they saw one of their own class, convicted of forgery, joining the chain gang of shaven-headed convicts sweeping the streets, fed on a diet of bread and water and then sent to join the barge hauliers. In the first year of barge hauling, 75 per cent of the convicts died.[118]

poems for Haydn's *The Creation* and *The Seasons*. Van Swieten's father, now dead, had been the empress' doctor.[119]

Swieten hired Mozart to arrange Bach's and Handel's works and introduced him to the Imperial Library, of which he was the head. There, among 300,000 volumes, Mozart could find Bach's *The Well Tempered Clavier* and *The Art of Fugue*, C.P.E. Bach's works and Handel's oratorios. This taught him to graft counterpoint on to 'sonata form' and produce his unique style to which the Viennese did not warm, but which is so popular today. Mozart played in the salons of van Swieten, the Russian Ambassador Prince Galitzine and others; also, he played at public concert performances or academies (when the Burg theatre was closed for Lent, it could be booked for these), working closely with others such as Aloysia Weber, whose family had followed her to Vienna.

Marriage

Mozart had moved into the Webers' house. By now, Fridolin was dead and Aloysia had married an actor by the name of Lange.* Wolfgang fell in love with her younger sister, the eighteen-year-old Constanze (see colour plate 13). He began to think of marriage. In one of his many letters to his father, he wrote in December 1781: 'The voice of nature speaks as loud in me as in others, louder perhaps than in many a big strong lout of a fellow.'[120] He added somewhat sententiously, 'I simply cannot live as most young men do these days … I have too great a love of my neighbour and too high a feeling of honour to seduce an innocent girl; and … I have too much horror and disgust and too much dread and fear of diseases and too much care for my health to fool about with whores.'[121]

Constanze moved out of her mother's house to stay with a 33-year-old baroness, seemingly a shady character to whom Mozart wrote some tender letters and who lent him money, but with whom he did not fancy marriage. He described her to Constanze as being 'inclined to be promiscuous with her favours. I hope dearest friend that even if you do not wish to become my wife, you will never lead a life like hers.'[122]

Then Constanze's mother decided to force the pace. Frau Weber got Constanze's guardian to tell Mozart that he could not see her again unless he signed a marriage contract. He agreed to marry and accepted a

* Lange was a very highly regarded actor in the early 19th century.

considerable penalty of 300 fl per year* if the contract were not completed.[124] The Frau was good at negotiating these deals: she had already got a healthy lump sum of 900 fl with an annuity of 700 fl when Aloysia got married. She then clinched it. Possibly because Constanze was already living in Mozart's accommodation, she threatened to call in the police if they did not get married.**

Leopold was appalled. His son, like him before, needed a salaried position before he could marry. He also needed a rich wife to free him of economic worries and to give him the independence for which he craved. Gluck, the son of a woodcutter from Bohemia, had married into a well-to-do merchant's family: his sister-in-law was a lady-in-waiting to Maria Theresa; and her husband was the imperial inspector of court buildings and eventually became a privy councillor.[126] This was the sort of union Leopold must have had in mind for his son.

However, to no avail. In August 1782, Wolfgang and Constanze were married in St Stephen's Cathedral. The congregation consisted of just Constanze's mother, her guardian, the best man and a district councillor, who gave her away. Afterwards, they went back to a wedding feast at the baroness'.

Constanze, who seems to have been a bit of a trollop, has always had a bad press. Her husband found some of her antics unfortunate: 'Why in heaven's name did you not take the ribbon and measure your own calves yourself (as all self respecting women have done on similar occasions in my presence) and not allow a young rake to do so?'[127] However, Mozart seems to have been devoted to Constanze, although it is by no means clear that his devotion was reciprocated. They had six children, only two of which survived: Karl Thomas was born 1784, and Franz Xaver Wolfgang in 1791, just before Mozart died (see colour plate 12).

What seems indubitable is that Constanze did Mozart no good socially or musically. She spent a lot of time recuperating at the spa in Baden, from what, we know not. Set on the edge of the Vienna Woods, this is a delightful place with warm water sulphorous springs. There was the opportunity

* A middle-class gentleman in Vienna needed 464 fl to live in an 'unpretentious life style' in 1786, and 775 fl in 1793.[123] Mozart's finances indicate that his aspirations (and lifestyle) were considerably more costly.

**Leopold thought that Constanze's mother and guardian should be sent to sweep the streets.[125]

to go on outings to the beautiful Helenthal, where visitors could see the bridge over the river or look at ruined castles on the hills.* Although it became even more fashionable in Beethoven's time, for Constanze, it must have seemed a pleasant contrast to her father's lodgings in Mannheim. Mozart wrote to her in August 1789: 'I do wish that you would not sometimes make yourself so cheap. You are too free and easy with [name obliterated].'[129] We can only speculate what she got up to, but whatever it was, she must have been consuming cash.

It would not have been unusual for Mozart to keep a mistress. Beethoven, for one, thought that Mozart was having an affair with a pupil from whose husband he had borrowed money. The couple lived next door. Somewhat sensationally, the day after Mozart's death, the husband committed suicide, leaving his wife, five months pregnant, in a pool of blood, slashed across the face, neck, shoulders and arms. Newspaper reports suggest that the wife and baby survived the attack, but this incident added to the mystery of Mozart's death.[130]

It was some time before Mozart took Constanze, who was not exactly a trophy bride, home to meet his father and sister. There were many reasons for procrastinating. Being self-employed, he had to wait around in Vienna in case some opportunity came up; he also claimed that he might be arrested in Salzburg; then Constanze was expecting their first baby, who was born on 17 June 1783.[131] Six weeks after the birth, they left the baby behind and went to Salzburg where they stayed for three months. This seems to have been a very happy family visit: they socialised, and met Nannerl's escort, an army captain some twenty years older than her. They made music and went to the theatre.[132] On their way back to Vienna, the Mozarts stayed in Linz, where the Linz Symphony was written. It is not known when they discovered that their baby had died, suffering from intestinal cramp, two months earlier, on 19 August.[133]

* An English traveller was surprised that 'both sexes bath here without distinction, in the same bath and at the same time. The bathing clothes are made to cover the whole body; and those of the woman have lead at the bottom of them to keep them down. The company walk up and down in the bath conversing together.' Although this description might suggest some attributes of the modern health farm, at Baden the ladies were 'sometimes treated with sweat-meats'. There were separate changing rooms.[128]

Freemasonry and Finance

Shortly after the Salzburg visit, Mozart became an active freemason; a number of his cantatas were written for and performed at his masonic lodge. Freemasonry had been normal, indeed fashionable. Empress Maria Theresa's husband, Francis Stephen, had been a mason, as had Haydn, and at one stage around 80 per cent of higher public officials in Austria were masons.[134] In 1780, there were thirteen 'lodges' in Vienna with 700 members, around half of which were nobles.[135] The other half was made up of civil servants and army officers. The clergy were involved, including two abbots of the wealthy Benedictine monastery at Melk. Masonic ideals of Liberty and Equality were in tune with the Emperor Joseph's reforms, provided they did not undermine Church and state. But, by the time Mozart joined, masonry was being strongly discouraged, especially as the movement was by then thought to be subversive.[136] Almost immediately following the exposure of a conspiracy to undermine the Church-dominated government of Bavaria, there was a crackdown on masonic activity; many lodges were closed. By the end of the century, some were saying that the whole French Revolution had been a conspiracy of anti-Christian, anti-royal and anti-social freemasons bent on destroying civilisation.[137]

For Mozart, the masons seem to have been a useful source of the credit of which he was always in need. His personal finances have always been a mystery. For an opera, the composer would only be paid a single fee of 100 ducats (426 fl in 1782). Because there was no copyright, the composer received nothing for the copies produced by the theatre copyist, nor did he receive anything for further performances. The composer could, however, sell printed items to a publisher like Artaria: Mozart was paid 100 ducats for the 'Haydn' string quartets; he could also earn from arranging the sale of manuscript copies.

When, in February 1785, Leopold went to see Mozart in Vienna, all the evidence pointed to his being successful, living well,* and making a lot of money. Thrifty Leopold estimated that he cleared 2,000 fl out of the Lent concert series alone. He was enjoying meals of meat, oysters, glacé fruits, champagne and coffee. He was probably spending a lot and borrowing a lot.[139]

* He was sociable: he had a billiard table, and he held dances at home, one ending at 7 am. For one Carnival ball he dressed up as harlequin. Michael Kelly, the Irish singer, said that 'he was remarkably fond of punch, of which beverage I have seen him take copious draughts'.[138]

In the year in which he died, his income has been reckoned to have been between 5,000 and 6,000 florins, probably nearer six. His wardrobe at death was that 'of a well to do merchant'.[140] Although he lived in eighteen separate houses or apartments in Vienna, it is believed that the accommodation he occupied was comfortable, well furnished, and two servants waited on him.[141]

But by the time he wrote *The Marriage of Figaro* in 1786, Mozart was preoccupied by financial worries and what he called black moods.* He wrote sometimes desperate and poignant begging letters, particularly to Michael Puchberg, a merchant and fellow mason. The good life and, in particular, the need to keep up appearances, would have been a drain on his resources. Unlike her sister, Constanze earned no income. She was expensive, particularly when in July 1789 she, pregnant, became seriously ill with a leg or foot ulcer and went off to her health-spa in Baden.[142]

When his father died on 28 May 1787, the Salzburg authorities wound up the estate, and, after some meticulous accounting and an auction at the Michaelmas Fair, Wolfgang was sent 1,000 fl in Viennese currency.[143] But, as usual, major receipts seem to have gone straight to repay creditors. To improve his finances, Mozart actively looked for court appointments. He had written to his father about moving to Prague or England. He even took lessons in English.[144] His father had been doubtful about the economics; and when Leopold was asked if the children might be parked with him while Mozart looked around, he turned the suggestion down flat.

Gluck died in 1787 aged 73. The Emperor then appointed Mozart Court Chamber Composer, even though his spending on music was being squeezed because of military expenditure. (This honorific title, worth 800 fl for no specified duties, should not be compared with Gluck's full-time pension of 2,000 fl.) The appointment represented a breakthrough after more than six years of freelance work. And in the year of his death, Mozart was appointed to succeed the Kapellmeister of St Stephen's, a job worth a handy 2,000 fl per annum, before perks such as firewood and candles. However, the duties and salary were deferred until the present incumbent died. The sick man recovered and Mozart predeceased him.[145]

In April 1789, when the economic outlook was deteriorating, Mozart

* Mozart began to apply to become a member of the Composers' Society, which would have provided some support for widow and child when he died. This application did not go through, possibly because he may just not have got round to completing the formalities.

went off, presumably job-hunting, to Berlin, via Prague, Dresden and Leipzig.* He was accompanied on the first leg of this journey by Prince Lichnowsky, from whom he borrowed 1,435 fl. (Shortly before Mozart died, possibly having heard news of his illness, the Prince established this debt in a court judgement.)

Figaro, the Don, Così, and the Flute

In 1783, Emperor Joseph, instead of promoting German opera, had decided that he wanted Italian again.He favoured the librettist Lorenzo da Ponte and the Spanish composer Martin y Soler, from whose opera *Una Cosa Rara* Mozart quotes in the supper scene in *Don Giovanni*. The public preferred cheerful works such as Dittersdorf's *Doktor und Apotheker* and Cimarosa's *Il Matrimonio Segreto*; another popular opera was Salieri's *Les Danaïdes*, which had a murder scene and a vivid portrayal of the torments of Hades. Also, the public liked the waltz even though, rather like jazz in the twentieth century, it caused eyebrows to be raised: Dr Burney dreaded to think what an English mother would have thought if her daughter were seen waltzing.

So, *The Marriage of Figaro*, first performed in the Burg theatre in 1786, was, to our surprise, only a moderate success: it was even thought 'boring' by one aristocrat.[147] Joseph, who thought Beaumarchais' play offensive and subversive, only allowed it to be put on after assurances from Da Ponte that the text had been sanitised and that the music was wonderful. In Berlin, it was thought that *Figaro* was for experts. In provincial Prague, it was more successful: they liked to hear arrangements of the tunes for quadrilles and waltzes. Similarly, *Don Giovanni*, the following year, was a success in Prague, but the subsequent performance in Vienna flopped.

One of Mozart's greatest problems, which we may find incomprehensible, was that his music was not particularly liked. His works were thought difficult to play; it was said that 'the orchestra overpowered the singers';[148] Italian singers thought them too demanding. Also his operas did not really suit the 'star' system, as their casting usually requires a spread, rather than a concentration, of talent.[149] Of course, as modern audiences well know, where the quality of performance is not sufficiently strong to reinforce a weak or unsuitable production, the effect can be total failure. This may have been Mozart's experience, as well.

* Travelling around in this period must have been difficult: there was a lot of unrest, including peasant revolts. There had been a very poor harvest in 1787.[146]

Mozart's output was enormous and he worked frantically hard, whether composing or recasting the librettos which usually required a considerable amount of amendment. Despite his protestations, he had to teach.* As teaching filled his mornings, the only time for composing was in the afternoon. Yet in 1786, as well as composing *Figaro*, he wrote two keyboard concertos, the Horn Concerto K 495, and several other pieces, quartets, trios and sonatas. In two energetic months in the summer of 1788, he wrote the last three symphonies, the E flat, the G minor and the 'Jupiter', presumably for a concert.

But he was unlucky again with the timing. Audience numbers were significantly down, owing to war. The Habsburgs had allied themselves to Russia: if the Turks attacked, each was to come to the other's aid.

Antonio Salieri, surely no villain? / Emanuel Schikaneder, the businessman

Stirred by Russian ambitions far away in the Caucasus and the Crimea, the Turks declared war in 1787, and the Habsburgs were immediately involved. This war against a ferocioous adversary bled the country, and many of the aristocratic families were forced to go to their estates, to escape from the costly capital. In 1788, there was a seven per cent war tax; grain

* Ironically, one of his pupils was Archbishop Colloredo's niece.

prices rocketed; bakers refused to sell at fixed prices, there were riots in which bakeries and grain stores were looted. It is likely that the costs of the Turkish wars caused Joseph again to withdraw from sponsorship of the Italian opera in 1788. There was a fall off in public concerts: private soirées, in bourgeois rather than aristocratic circles, with smaller orchestras, became more normal. When news arrived of the capture of Belgrade in October 1789, there were joyous celebrations. Mozart, in his role as Court Composer, wrote some jingoistic songs to celebrate. But this did not help the cash position.

Perhaps to produce something more popular, Emperor Joseph commissioned Mozart to compose *Così fan tutte*.[150] As with *Figaro* and *Don Giovanni*, Da Ponte was the librettist. In this superficially light-hearted romp, considered indecent at the time and subsequently, Mozart's music takes the audience into the recesses of the human mind.* After *Così*, he teamed up with a fellow mason Emanuel Schikaneder, the impresario of the suburban Theater auf der Wieden, to produce *The Magic Flute*. Mozart had seen his works when his troupe was on tour in Salzburg. Schikaneder knew what his public wanted and he supplied it: 'My sole aim is to work for the box office and see what is most effective on the stage so as to fill both the house and the cash box.'[151] That Mozart managed to create such an enduringly successful opera from Schikaneder's curious libretto was in itself an astonishing achievement, and it has been authoritatively described as 'the supreme achievement of popular theatre in eighteenth-century Vienna'.[152] Its first performance, the first opera not written for the court, was on 30 September 1791. Mozart conducted from the forte-piano, Constanze's sister Josepha was the Queen of Night, Schikaneder was Papageno and his father was one of the priests. The show eventually became so profitable that Schikaneder could afford to build his own theatre, the Theater an der Wien.

A New Regime

Mozart's begging letters had become more desperate around July 1789. The outlook for him grew bleaker, linked, as it was, to the fortunes of the court. On 20 February 1790, his empire alarmingly out of control, orders still flying, ministers resigning, Joseph II died in excruciating pain from an

* Listen, for example, to the tensions and strains in Fiordiligi's aria before she is seduced in Act II.

anal abscess, and choking with the tuberculosis he contracted when leading his troops at the front.[153] His death meant that all the theatres were closed. While the immediate concern was that the run of performances of *Così fan tutte* had to be stopped, there was a much greater worry: Mozart's chief patron was gone; his brother and successor, Leopold, cut costs and his empress disliked Mozart's music.[154] Da Ponte was dismissed and Mozart received no further commissions from the court to write opera.

Emperor Leopold had detested his elder brother, his arrogance and his 'liberal' policies, which he set about reversing.[155] But Leopold's health was bad and his reign only lasted a couple of years. In the last months of Mozart's life, the crackdown began, a process intensified when very shortly after Mozart's death, Leopold's son Francis became emperor. Not wishing to share their French relative's experience, the Habsburgs set up an efficient secret police, directed by Count Pergen, a former educational reformer. Others were less nimble than Pergen: Mozart's patron Gottfried van Swieten, a creature of Joseph, was under pressure and eventually replaced. Mozart, a mason, was associated with the old régime: works such as *Figaro*, *Don Giovanni*, *Così fan tutte*, could be construed as subversive. Unlike the suave, fashionable and street-wise court composers such as Salieri, Mozart and his louche wife were potentially in dire trouble.[156]

While Mozart may not have recognised the extent of his peril, he knew that he had to build a relationship with the new court, so he travelled to Leopold's imperial coronation in Frankfurt in September 1790. He also went to the coronation in Prague, which was held to symbolise a return to de-centralised rule. Mozart went to Frankfurt, in style, expensively, in his own coach. To pay for this, he pawned his furniture. Only an incurable optimist could have expected this profligacy to provide positive returns.

With his world falling apart, Mozart must have been very depressed after his return. When Haydn and Salomon set off to London in December, Mozart said goodbye, and said prophetically, 'we are probably saying our last adieu'.[157] Haydn, who was elderly, thought this might be a rather tactless remark about his own age.

The offer to write an official opera for the Prague Coronation at first went to Salieri, who was senior to Mozart, but he turned it down.[158] Mozart must have been greatly relieved when he was sent the commission in mid-July, even though there was hardly any time left to write the opera, *La Clemenza di Tito*. Constanze gave birth to Franz Xaver at the end of

July. Mozart left for Prague with Constanze and their lodger Süssmayr on 25 August. The fast mail coach took three nights and four days.

As they were boarding the coach, someone 'plucked the hem of Constanze's travelling cloak'.[159] This was a messenger from whoever it was that had commissioned Mozart to write a Requiem.* Mozart said he would return to work on it as soon as he got back. The coronation festivities, largely conducted by Salieri, included many Mozart masses. But Empress Maria Luisa thoroughly disliked *La Clemenza di Tito*, and said so.

After returning from Prague, the messenger appeared again and gave Mozart a second instalment of money. Constanze went off to Baden. Mozart, on a high, wrote enthusiastically to her noting that *The Magic Flute* was being received with great acclaim, and in Prague *La Clemenza di Tito* was being performed with, in his view, considerable success.[160] He took Salieri and his mistress to *The Magic Flute*. He described this to Constanze: 'You can't believe how sweet they both were – and how much they enjoyed not only my music but the libretto and everything. Both of them told me it was an *opera* fit to be played at the grandest festivities, before the greatest monarch.' This was in October.[161]

Last Days

Mozart's final illness lasted fifteen days. His health had never been good; he was overworked and stressed. The story goes that the illness began with swellings in his hands and feet and an almost total inability to move. Sophie, Constanze's younger sister, wrote that she and her mother made him a night jacket which he could put on frontwards, since, on account of his swollen condition, he could not turn in bed. He was completely conscious until two hours before his death. On the day he died, he reputedly had the score of the *Requiem* brought to his bed. 'Didn't I say before that I was writing this Requiem for myself?', he apparently asked. There was a long search for the doctor, who was at the theatre. He ordered cold poultices for the patient. About two hours before Mozart died, he convulsed and became comatose. Then, an hour later, he attempted to sit up, opened

* There has been much speculation about the origins of the *Requiem*. According to Constanze, a messenger arrived with the commission. This is now thought to have been from Count von Walsegg, owner of big estates and a gypsum works, a passionate lover of music, whose wife Anna had died in February 1791. He commissioned many works for performances held at his house.

his eyes wide and fell back with his head turned to the wall; his cheeks were puffed out. It was 55 minutes past midnight on Monday 5 December 1791.[162]

Baron van Swieten organised the funeral on the following day. It was just a few yards to take the body from the house in Rauhensteingasse to the cathedral for the service, which was held in a chapel on the north side. Mozart's corpse was then conveyed to the cemetery of St Marx, a suburb at least one hour's walk from the centre, where he was given a standard burial. Although Joseph's requirement to use sacks had been discontinued, people were still buried away from the town centre in shaft graves with five or six coffins, the grave being reused nine or so years later. No mourners were allowed, so Constanze was not present at the burial.[163]

The Sequel, Fact and Fiction

Constanze, left with two sons aged seven and four months, surprisingly leapt to the front of the stage. The ulcerous leg had presumably healed in Baden. Within the week, on 11 December, she personally petitioned the emperor: eventually, she was granted a pension of a third of Mozart's 800 fl salary 'as a special favour and not to establish a precedent'.[164]

As Mozart had been employed by the court for less than ten years, Constanze was not entitled to a pension, and he had not joined the Composers' Society which would have assisted her.[165] So, she promoted memorial and benefit concerts, and even tried to launch the boy Franz Xaver as a prodigy. She sold several compositions for 3,600 fl to the king of Prussia. She also managed to pass off works by others as works by Mozart. At the time of his death, only one fifth of his compositions were in print, whereas by the 1820s nearly two thirds were. But we should not accuse Constanze of profiteering. There are precedents for widows marketing their dead husbands' works: Frances Purcell had done this too.[166]

Around five years after Mozart's death, Constanze's finances were so well under control that she could afford to lend a family friend 3,500 fl at six per cent. In 1799, Constanze took in a paying guest, Georg Niklaus von Nissen, a bachelor from the Danish embassy. He was two years older than her. They married and lived in Copenhagen where he worked in the censorship department for ten years, before retiring to Salzburg, where he died in 1826. She put him in Leopold's grave and erected a monument over it, more than she ever did for Wolfgang. By the time the musician and publisher Vincent Novello met her in Salzburg in 1829, she was a cultivated lady speaking three languages. She died in 1842, aged 79, and was buried in that grave. She had survived Mozart by half a century.[167]

Sorting out fact and fiction about Mozart's death is a veritable industry. The fictional drama starts with the weather: the night he died was said to have been stormy; at his burial, there was snow and rain; neither accords with the weather reports.

As early as January 1792, a Salzburg newspaper reported the story that Mozart thought that he was writing the *Requiem* for himself.*[168] This started the demand for anecdotes which was subsequently stoked by Breitkopf, the publishers, who knew that publicity of this variety would benefit their sales.[169] The suicide in the house next door, already mentioned, created a suitably suspicious background.

Nissen wrote a book on Mozart which would have one believe that the loving Constanze saw the composer's life ebbing away during the autumn. To relieve the gloom, they drove together to the Prater, the amusement park in Vienna. On the drive, Mozart told her that he was writing the *Requiem* for himself, and suggested that he might have been poisoned.[170]

If indeed he was poisoned, by far the most famous suspect is Salieri,** who confessed to this crime in a moment of senile dementia a third of a century later.[171] Like many courtiers, Salieri was a schemer, but he was fundamentally well meaning and tried hard to help other composers; he was, for example, the only teacher Schubert ever acknowledged; and he taught Liszt and Meyerbeer. Mozart's visit with him to see *The Magic Flute* was amicable. The myth that he murdered Mozart may reasonably be considered absurd.[172]

Others have suggested that Mozart was poisoned by the masons in revenge for his disclosure of masonic practices and secrets in *The Magic Flute*.† A masonic hit squad would surely have gone for Schikaneder as

* The *Requiem* was unfinished when Mozart died, so Süssmayr completed it. Much to the fury of the Count, it appears that Süssmayr and Constanze sent a copy to Breitkopf & Härtel, and the Count found that the work which he had commissioned had been published in Leipzig.

** Peter Shaffer's play *Amadeus* subtly suggests that Salieri deliberately, as an act of murder, broke Mozart psychologically rather than poisoned him.

† *The Magic Flute* is reputed to be full of masonic symbols, including the passage from Darkness into Light. The numbers three and eighteen are apparently particularly important. The opera has lots of 'threes': in the overture, the three-times-three chords; there are three boys, three ladies. It has lots of eighteens: there are eighteen priests; the chorus 'O Isis and Osiris' is eighteen bars long.[173]

well, had they wanted revenge. Yet he survived a further twenty years until 1812, when he died with both his business and his mind in a state of collapse.[174]

None of Mozart's doctors, who were highly qualified, mentioned poison. Yet, nearly 40 years after Mozart's death, Constanze claimed that he said on that drive to the Prater: 'Someone has given me *acqua toffana*'.*[175] Experts emphasise that many of the 'theories' are based on conversations or writings long after the event. Sophie's report of the last hours dates from 33 years after the event.[176] The story of the *Requiem* was recorded in 1827 and the details of the funeral in 1856.

All the stories are set against a very mixed background: on the one hand, Mozart's world was falling apart; on the other, his lifestyle was good, and *The Magic Flute* was going very well. One of the sources, Ignaz Arnold, was the author of gothic novels. A possibly more reliable source was the family in Prague where Karl Mozart lodged and was a pupil; and of course Constanze, but she is known to have been untruthful.

Anyway, we shall never know the cause of Mozart's death. He never had good health, and may have died of a kidney complaint or something arising from his earlier rheumatic fever. The usual treatments at the time, bleeding,** the emetics,[178] may have aggravated his condition and led to heart failure.

We do know that his early death was one of the greatest tragedies in the history of music.

Karl entered the civil service in Milan, and later, with profits made from performances of *Figaro*, retired to a country estate near Lake Como; he died in 1859. His younger brother studied composition with Salieri and Albrechtsberger and became a music teacher in Lemberg (now Lvov, in Poland); he died in 1844. Neither son married.[179]

* *Acqua toffana*, a mixture of white arsenic, antimony and lead oxide, was invented in the previous century by a Sicilian woman Teofania di Adamo; it was well known as a slow poison which gives the lie that the victim is dying of natural causes. Further enquiries to Sherlock Holmes, please.

** Bleeding was supposed to clean the body fluids. The veins were blocked and then opened with a special scalpel and blood was drawn. When a small quantity of blood was needed, a small warmed bleeding glass was pressed against the skin. As the glass cooled the pressure dropped and the blood was drawn out.[177]

Nannerl, seven years before Mozart's death, became the third wife of a 47-year-old magistrate, Berchtold von Sonnenburg. Her marriage was a step up for her: the Berchtolds were raised to the nobility in 1792 and became barons and baronesses. They lived in St Gilgen, a breathtakingly beautiful place about twenty miles east of Salzburg, but then very remote, inaccessible and lonely. Communication with Salzburg was generally by the weekly backpacker who did a round trip. The keys of the clavier which her father gave her as a wedding present would stick with the damp. After her husband died in 1801, she returned to Salzburg and became a piano teacher. She died some 30 years later.[180]

A brilliant keyboard player, Nannerl too had been an infant prodigy.[181]

Leopold, Wolfgang and Nannerl Mozart

Beethoven

CHAPTER 5

'He is perfectly entitled to regard the world as detestable, but that does not make it any more enjoyable for himself or anyone else.'[1] This could be an exasperated adult speaking about a difficult adolescent; but it is actually the suave, sophisticated poet Goethe despairing about the behaviour of Beethoven. When, strolling together in a park, so the story goes,* they saw the royal family coming towards them, Beethoven pressed on: he went through the throng of Habsburg princes and sycophants like Moses parting the Red Sea. He then turned around and, much to his amusement, saw Goethe stand aside, his hat in hand and bowing obsequiously, to let the procession proceed.[3]

This incident and much of Beethoven's life illustrate the extent to which, within a few years of Mozart's premature death, a talented artist could assert his independence and yet survive.[4] Although Beethoven often felt financially insecure, he did not have to hang about ingratiatingly and hope that some chamberlain would arrive with a bag of ducats. No longer was the musical composition on a shopping list of an aristocrat preparing the day's entertainment, or 'made to order' to embellish the worship of God.

* This story is sometimes said to have been concocted by Bettina von Arnim, who appears later.[2]

This argumentative, ugly, pockmarked and slovenly man could now make a reasonable living from creating his *own* works of art. Music had become an object in itself, each work entirely the inspiration of the individual.

The audience could still be ignorant and abusive, as on the occasion when an empress dismissed a Mozart opera as 'German hogwash'.[5] Or it could even be intelligently critical. But gone were the days when a Medici prince could interfere and require Alessandro Scarlatti to make an opera nobler and more cheerful; or a Habsburg emperor could be concerned with the number of notes in an opera by Mozart.*

Beethoven, Goethe and the Royal Family

This new environment was attributable not just to the French Revolution which weakened the rigid framework of social structures. There was now an entirely new attitude towards art. Goethe caustically described the constraints by which artists had previously been circumscribed: 'A good

* Sponsorship, but importantly 'without strings attached', has continued to be an important source of finance into the 20th century and beyond: the support of the Princesse de Polignac was crucial to Stravinsky; without Mr and Mrs Robert Woods Bliss we might not have the 'Dumbarton Oaks' Concerto; without Mrs Coolidge his *Apollo*.[6]

deal can be said of the advantages of Rules, much the same as can be said in praise of bourgeois society. A man shaped by Rules will never produce anything tasteless or bad, just as a citizen who observes law and decorum will never be an unbearable neighbour or an out-and-out villain.' He continued: 'On the other hand, the Rules will destroy the true feeling of Nature and its true expression!'[7]

So, while all great composers push out frontiers, Beethoven could break the rules in leaps and bounds. He remained fundamentally 'classical' in his style. Yet he surprised listeners of his First Symphony in C major by beginning it in F major.[8] He began the Fourth Piano Concerto with the solo piano, a complete change from all previous concertos. He started the 'Moonlight' Sonata unconventionally with a slow movement.[9] The final movement of the Ninth Symphony begins with a shocking chord. These are just obvious examples. Why did he do it? For his art. He went so far that his successors found that he had taken certain types of instrumental music almost to the limit, and he was virtually impossible to follow: Brahms just did not feel confident tackling a symphony until he was in his forties.[10]

Ludwig van Beethoven was born around 16 December 1770 in Bonn, the residence of the Archbishop-Elector of Cologne. A trivial consequence of the momentous French Revolution was that Bonn became an unbearable place in which to live. Beethoven moved to Vienna, a year after Mozart died. He withdrew increasingly into his shell as his sad life progressed, with his hopeless love life, his deafness and the family troubles with his nephew. His middle years, a period of great creativity, were accompanied by worries caused by the Napoleonic wars. By the start of the Congress of Vienna in 1814, other tastes and trends were developing, apparent in the operas of Rossini and heard in the new romantic sounds and textures coaxed out of the orchestra by Carl Maria von Weber.

At the end of his life, Beethoven lived in self-inflicted squalor, apparently drinking a bottle of wine with each meal.[11] Rossini was so appalled when he saw him that he tried fundraising to help him, but got no support. People gave Beethoven up as a lost cause. But, in those last years, he wrote the Ninth Symphony. He seems to have thrown down the gauntlet to the next generation, almost saying: 'try beating that!'[12] It was a long time, if ever, before anyone did, or could.

Bonn

We start far from Vienna. Beethoven's grandfather, the son of a baker, was choirmaster in a church in Louvain, close to Brussels, where the family had earlier been involved in the lace business. Archbishop Clemens-August of Cologne invited him to travel 100 miles to Bonn and join the court music staff. He rose to become Kapellmeister, in the year that the archbishop died, nine years before Beethoven was born. This appointment was the kind of prestigious position which Leopold Mozart craved for himself or his son.

The highly cultured Archbishop Clemens-August was the brother of the Elector of Bavaria who in the 1740s briefly interrupted the Habsburg succession and became emperor. The archbishop resided in Bonn, well away from the Free City of Cologne, with whose burgers he had a very shaky relationship. He built himself several palaces, including a large 'pleasure' palace in nearby Brühl. This had a magnificent rococo staircase, and, in the garden, a summerhouse called the 'Indian palace' even though its style was Chinese. He enjoyed falconing, riding on his English hunters and being entertained by his jester. He also played the viola da gamba. There is a picture of him at a masked ball in the 1750s with the musicians working away in two bands on either side.[13] (See colour plate 10.)

This relaxed and cultured life was spent against a background of rising prosperity.[14] The agricultural revolution caused a considerable boom in property values. There were improvements in diet and hygiene, with a relatively low incidence of disease. The population was growing fast. There was, however, unemployment and vagabondage. France, increasingly unstable, was not far away.

The Kapellmeister's son, Beethoven's father, sang in the choir. He married, beneath his status, the widowed daughter of the head cook in one of the palaces. He took to drink and it was an unhappy marriage. Beethoven's mother, who was never known to laugh, regarded life as 'a little joy – and a chain of sorrows'.[15] They had three surviving children, first Ludwig, then Caspar born in 1774, and Johann born two years later.

Beethoven was born at the back* of a modest house in the Bonngasse, a few yards from the market place and the gate leading out to Cologne, some sixteen miles away.[16] In later years, he was unclear of his exact age. He

* Today, one can visit the small attic with its low ceiling.

was probably born on the day before he was baptised, 17 December 1770. At any rate, baptism had to take place within three days of birth. Around sixteen months earlier, Napoleon had been born in Corsica.

Bonn was rich in musical talent. The Beethovens' neighbours included the violinist Franz Ries, a former infant prodigy; his son Ferdinand was one of the brilliant pianists in the first years of the 19th century. Nearby lived the horn-player and dealer in printed music and musical instruments, Nicolaus Simrock, who started one of the leading music publishing businesses of the 19th century. Also nearby was the family of Johann Peter Salomon, who at the age of thirteen had been appointed to the Bonn court orchestra.[17] By the time of Beethoven's birth, Salomon had become an impresario. The city continued to attract musicians. When Beethoven was fifteen, Anton Reicha from Prague came as a flute player in the court orchestra; he would eventually move to Paris where Liszt, Berlioz and César Franck became his pupils.

Beethoven showed early musical promise: he performed in his first public concert before he was nine and issued his first composition by the age of twelve. His father and local musicians taught him the violin, viola, horn and clavier. He was also taught by the court organist, Christian Neefe, a 'rare enthusiast for the music of JS Bach'.[18] He deputised for Neefe and, at twelve, he was harpsichordist with the court orchestra. Despite his technical competence, he was not presented as an infant prodigy.

Beethoven must have witnessed the colourful celebrations when the elector-designate visited Bonn in 1780. In an important move, the Habsburgs had arranged that on the death of the incumbent, Emperor Joseph's brother Max Franz would succeed to the archiepiscopal throne. A million florins had been scattered in order to secure the votes of the canons of Cologne and Münster, thus, as Frederick the Great acidly described it, 'making sure of the inspiration of the Holy Ghost'.[19] As Max Franz was already grand master of the Teutonic Knights, an ancient and noble order of knighthood which was still influential, he was set to become the most powerful ecclesiastic prince ever seen in the Holy Roman Empire. He had previously been destined to become military viceroy of Hungary; but several operations to cure knee trouble meant that this was not a realistic position for him to hold.

The new archbishop, who succeeded in 1784, wanted to reorganise his court and implement economies, like his Salzburg colleague. The music department of 49 musicians was reviewed.[20] Neefe's salary was halved, and it even seemed at one point as if Beethoven was going to supplant him. But this matter was resolved. Some years later, Beethoven wrote to Neefe: 'I thank you for the advice you have very often given me about making progress in my divine art. Should I ever become a great man, you too will have a share in my success.'[21]

When he was seventeen, Beethoven was sent to Vienna to improve his musical experience. He may have had a few lessons from Mozart. But within a fortnight, he heard that his mother's health – she suffered from consumption – was deteriorating badly, and he had to return home quickly. She died, and was closely followed by her daughter, aged a year and a half. After this, with his father suffering increasingly from alcoholism, Beethoven had to take hold of family affairs. He managed to get half of his father's salary assigned to him. When his father died at the end of 1792, the archbishop is said to have made some wry remarks about the adverse effect of the death on the archiepiscopal revenues from liquor tax.[22]

The next few years were spent in Bonn. Beethoven was one of the four viola players in the court orchestras. He wrote songs, piano music and chamber music. He frequented the Zehrgarten tavern in the market place, a meeting place for intellectuals. He studied philosophy at Bonn University and read the poetry and plays of Klopstock, Goethe and the young Schiller whose early play *Die Räuber* had recently been published. He imbibed the literature of the Enlightenment in a way in which no great composer before him had the opportunity to do.[23]

He was a frequent visitor to the house of the Breuning family, who held a middle-class salon for artists, musicians and writers. Helene von Breuning, whose husband had been killed when the archbishop's town residence had been burnt down in 1777, acted as a second mother to Beethoven. He fell in love with her daughter, Lorchen (Eleonore), although she, in the end, married Franz Gerhard Wegeler, a student who had lodged with them. In the year before he died, Beethoven wrote to Wegeler: 'I still have the silhouette of your Lorchen, from which you will see that all the goodness and affection shown to me in my youth are still dear to me.'[24] Just before he left Bonn, Beethoven and Lorchen had some bust-up, a 'fatal quarrel' of which he was ashamed. Was he too impetuous?

Haydn passed through Bonn on his way to and from London. Having looked over one of Beethoven's cantatas, possibly one written to mark the death of Emperor Joseph II, he invited Beethoven to Vienna to take lessons. Beethoven was encouraged and supported in this by another regular visitor to the Breunings, Count Waldstein, who was in Bonn as a novice of the Teutonic Knights.[25] So, aged 22, Beethoven set out for Vienna again. On his departure, his friends assembled an autograph album. Waldstein wrote in it: 'With the help of hard work, you shall receive Mozart's spirit from Haydn's hands.' Lorchen wrote, more poetically: 'Friendship with one who is good lengthens like the evening shadow until the sun of life sinks.'[26] And she gave him the silhouette.

European Upheaval

There were very good reasons for Beethoven to get out of Bonn and stay away. During the time that he had been playing the viola in the orchestra, Europe had entered a most turbulent period. He was seventeen when the first public events of the French Revolution took place in early 1787. With Bonn little further from the French border than London is from Birmingham, Beethoven will have become aware of the limitations, indeed the dangers, of remaining there.

There were many developments which brought France to revolution, not least the new thinking of the Enlightenment. The mention of a few of the stresses, strains and fast-moving events should be sufficient to describe the context for Beethoven.

The much-detested King Louis XV, before whom young Mozart had performed, died of smallpox in 1774.[27] He was succeeded by his grandson, who married Empress Maria Theresa's youngest daughter, Marie Antoinette. The French government's finances were chaotic, partly because of war in America: bankruptcy was declared in August 1788. The underlying economic situation was dire: in the 60 years before 1789, grain prices in France rose three times as fast as wages did. By 1789, the cost of bread absorbed nearly 90 per cent of a workman's resources.[28] A free trade treaty with England led to serious unemployment in major textile centres. In 1787–9 there were bad harvests.

Louis XVI tried to respond to demands for reform:[29] France had the best roads in Europe, Paris was being rebuilt, social welfare was being extended, national income and productivity were improving. And when the Bastille fell on 14 July 1789, there were actually only seven prisoners in it.[30] But it was too late. The most risky moment for a bad government is when it starts to reform.[31] The middle classes, which the *ancien régime* excluded from high office, felt deprived and therefore combined with the lower classes to seize power. Feudalism and aristocratic privileges were abolished and church property was nationalised. The disruption continued. In June 1791, the king and queen decided to run for it; but they were stopped in Varennes, a village halfway between Paris and Cologne.[32] A grocer aptly named Monsieur Sauce found them walking along the street knocking on doors to get a change of horses. The suspicion that Louis had fled in order to raise an invading army was one factor which led to his execution a year and a half later, and to Queen Marie Antoinette's nine months after that.

16 October 1793: Queen Marie Antoinette is taken to the guillotine

War was needed to deter foreign invasion and to put an end to the use of Coblenz, only 40 miles up the Rhine from Bonn, as a base for émigrés such as the king's brothers, the Counts of Provence and Artois.* War would also unite the disparate revolutionaries. At the end of 1791, the French gave the electors in the Rhineland an ultimatum to halt the émigré activity. After the Habsburgs offered to protect the electorates, France declared war. Shortly thereafter, the mob stormed the Tuileries Palace, and Louis

* The Counts subsequently became kings of France after the fall of Napoleon.

XVI effectively lost all authority. The following month, just a few weeks before Beethoven left Bonn, half the prison population of Paris, well over 1,000 people, were massacred.[33] The guillotining of Louis XVI sent shock waves through the courts of Europe, as did the subsequent Terror of 1793–4.*

The war waged by France evolved from a defensive one to an offensive one, as Napoleon progressed from being merely a senior officer to being first consul in 1799. Four years later, in Notre-Dame, he crowned himself emperor of the French in the presence of the Pope. Yet, less than ten years after his coronation, Napoleon's empire had collapsed. These tumultuous events were compressed within only 30 years; when Napoleon fell, Beethoven had a further thirteen years of his life left.

Beethoven in Vienna

It made sense for Beethoven to get out of Bonn. The plan to study with Haydn took him to Vienna. At the time he made the journey, French armies had overrun the entire Austrian Netherlands and the bishopric of Liège, not far from Bonn; Mainz and Frankfurt had just fallen. There was complete chaos. Ignoring 'camp followers', the French armies in the Rhineland required provisioning for about a quarter of a million people. They had to fend for themselves. They seized wine, coffee, cocoa, clothing, boots, shoes, mattresses, blankets, linen, soap; they would also force local labour to construct fortifications, build roads, make uniforms and join up.[34] They exacted forced loans. Beethoven found himself in the centre of all this.

In his diary, Beethoven recorded giving his driver a tip because 'he drove us like the devil, at the risk of a thrashing, right through the Hessian army'.[35] Although the fortunes of war ebbed and flowed, the economic life which supported the lavish courts of the ecclesiastical princes was simply shattered. Trade in the city of Cologne was badly hit by Napoleon's economic sanctions, and the closing of European ports to British goods: although it was upriver, Cologne was a city where trade in colonial goods such as tobacco was important.[36]

When Beethoven arrived in Vienna in late 1792, the atmosphere was jittery and remained so for several decades to come. Besides, there had

* The guillotine was tried out on a highwayman in April 1792 and used for a political victim four months later.

been a change at the top. Earlier that year, Emperor Francis II succeeded his father Leopold, who died after being bled excessively as a cure for a respiratory ailment. Fearful of the events overwhelming his uncle in France, Francis implemented reactionary policies. In summer 1794, a drunken army officer revealed a plot to overthrow the monarchy.[37] Forty-five others were arrested with him, although many of them were guilty of little more than inflammatory rhetoric. Several were executed, while the rest got lengthy prison terms. Beethoven wrote: 'Here many "important" people have been rounded up, it is said, to pre-empt a revolution. But I reckon that there won't be a revolution so long as the Austrian has his brown beer and sausage.' He added: 'You wouldn't want to speak too loudly here, or the police will lock you up.'[38]

Studying in Vienna

On his arrival in Vienna, Beethoven took advantage of introductions provided by Waldstein and Haydn. Musical life still owed much to phenomenally rich patrons, a number of whom were to figure prominently in Beethoven's life, such as the Lichnowskys, Archduke Rudolph (brother of Emperor Francis), and the Lobkowitz, Browne, Razumovsky and Kinsky families. Virtuoso performers, such as Beethoven, were much in demand in their drawing rooms.

Beethoven lived on the ground floor of the palace resided in by a connection of Waldstein's, Prince Karl Lichnowsky, the aristocrat who had proved a substantial debt against the dying Mozart less than a year before.[39] The Prince had his own string quartet, and organised regular musical salons, usually every Friday morning.[40] It is sometimes speculated that his support for Beethoven was in response to pangs of conscience about his action against Mozart.

Beethoven was disappointed with his lessons with Haydn, who was preoccupied with his second visit to London and thinking of taking his pupil with him as copyist and factotum. As evidence of progress, Haydn sent the Elector some of his pupil's pieces and requested reimbursement of money lent to him. The Elector's response, based on a misunderstanding, was negative: most of the pieces, he said, were composed before Beethoven left Bonn; he suggested that Beethoven was not progressing, rather he was just 'living it up' running up debts, as he had done on his first trip to Vienna.[41]

Both pupil and patron were unfair to Haydn. He introduced Beethoven to Handel's music and taught him counterpoint, the art of combining melodies. Like so many classical composers, he used the *Gradus ad Parnassum* of Johann Joseph Fux, a system for learning the style of great composers of the Renaissance, such as Palestrina and Lasso.[42] This dry and dreary method was much approved of in Beethoven's time, and indeed was still in use in the middle of the 20th century.[43]

Beethoven also took violin lessons three times a week from the leader of Lichnowsky's string quartet. He studied more complex counterpoint with Albrechtsberger, the Kapellmeister at St Stephen's.[44] Up to around the turn of the century, he also studied with Salieri,* to whom he dedicated three violin sonatas.[45]

It was as a virtuoso pianist that Beethoven performed at the two annual concerts run by the Vienna Philharmonic Society. The piano, having been around since the pianos of Cristofori of Florence in the 1720s, had become more prominent at the beginning of the 1760s, the decade before the founding of the Philharmonic Society. The harpsichord, with its plucked strings suitable for the more intimate salon style, faded from view. The piano could make the larger sound needed in a hall; it could also hold its own against an orchestra, rather than having to alternate with it in separate blocks of sound. Beethoven exploited it to its technical limits at the time.**[46]

A couple of years after the death of Mozart, Beethoven was earning enough for his two brothers to leave Bonn and join him. Caspar came in 1794 as a music teacher, and Johann in the following year, as an assistant to an apothecary. The general exodus from the Rhineland included the Breuning brothers, and also Wegeler, who came in order to complete his medical studies, before returning in 1796 to settle with Eleonore von Breuning in Koblenz.

In November 1795, Beethoven was commissioned to compose the minuets and other dances for the charity ball held in the magnificent Redoutensaal in the Imperial Palace. He also played at an interlude during a performance of *La Clemenza di Tito* organised by Constanze Mozart. In 1796, he went on an extended tour, similar to that undertaken by Mozart

* Salieri used to offer free tuition to impecunious musicians, especially in the setting of Italian words to music.

** Beethoven composed for a far less powerful instrument than the modern concert piano. The piano used by Liszt, with an iron frame, and a strain of some 20 tons, was only invented (in Philadelphia) in 1825. Steinway cast the first single-piece metal frame in 1855.

some six years earlier. He visited Prague, Dresden, Leipzig, Berlin and, later in the year, Pressburg.

He taught, he advertised, and he sold his works. His Opus 1, a set of piano trios, was sold by subscription: 123 subscribers ordered 245 copies, which were printed by the leading publishing house, Artaria. From this, Beethoven made a profit of 735 florins, the equivalent of one year's living expenses.[47] Many of his works were commissioned. After six months elapsed, he was allowed to publish them himself and obtain a fee from publishers. He would seek simultaneous contracts in several countries at the same time.[48]

Beethoven was a good businessman, and proud of his ability to earn an income sufficient to live in comfort.[49] From 1800 onwards, Lichnowsky granted him an annuity of 600 fl.* A couple of years later, Beethoven's brother Caspar helped him with his business affairs, and managed to push up the prices demanded from publishers. Whereas Beethoven sold the First Symphony for 20 ducats, Caspar got 38 for the String Quintet. Caspar also started getting earlier works published, which contributed to the cash flow. But it was not always plain sailing. Copyright was a continual headache: in 1802, we find Beethoven putting a notice in the papers denying that quintets published by a publisher in Vienna and by one in Leipzig were the originals.**

The Frustrated Composer and Lover

The First Symphony was performed on 2 April 1800 in a concert at the Burg theatre: tickets were available at Beethoven's lodgings for a programme that also included a Mozart symphony, some extracts from Haydn's *Creation*, one of Beethoven's Piano Concertos, a Septet and an improvisation. It is hard for us to imagine the effect that this concert had. The audience would have been surprised by the opening of the symphony and by the increased, unusual, emphasis given to the wind instruments.[51]

So, by the turn of the century, when Beethoven was almost 30, he was well established. But he became increasingly temperamental. He bust up with Stephan von Breuning when they set up house together. His other

* A reasonable midday meal of soup without wine or beer could cost less than a florin in 1790. There were between four and five florins to the ducat, depending on the location.[50]

** Around 1807, Caspar handed over the secretarial activity to Baron Ignaz von Gleichenstein. When the baron got married around 1811, the secretarial role was taken over by Franz Oliva.

Bonn friend Ferdinand Ries, whom he took in as a pupil, was horrified to find him fighting with his brothers in the street. To the composer and pianist Hummel, Beethoven wrote: 'Keep away. You are false and fit for the knacker.'[52] Later, he lost his temper when he was staying at Prince Lichnowsky's opulent castle at Grätz.* The prince asked him to play to some French officers. Clutching the 'Appassionata' and the Razumovsky Quartets, Beethoven left in a huff, in the rain, to the nearby city of Troppau (now Opava).** On his return to Vienna, he smashed a bust of the prince.[54] He patched up these quarrels and quickly made his peace. But there were other symptoms of his eccentricity. In 35 years, he lived in 33 lodgings,† 71 if one includes summer residences.

He would read deep into the night, letting candle wax drip onto the pages of his book, already blotched with coffee stains. The young Karl Czerny, today known for his volumes of piano exercises, climbed the many stairs to the fifth- or sixth-floor apartment in the Tiefen Graben to find Beethoven whose 'coal black hair, cut *à la Titus*, bristled shaggily about his head. His beard – he had not shaved for several days – made the lower part of his already brown face still darker.'[55]

Beethoven would get up very early, at 5 or 6 am, and then he worked. After breakfast, he strolled in the fields beyond the old fortifications, in the Vienna woods or along the Danube. Although he was very much a loner, he was 'always in love', according to Wegeler. He was really crying out for affection. He sometimes attempted conquests 'that an Adonis would have found difficult, if not impossible'. He fell for ladies who would have ruined themselves by falling for their music teacher. Despite the social changes, individuals were still expected to live and work within their divinely ordained class.†† Yet the temptations were considerable. An English colonel described the personal problems the male might feel: 'Formerly when women wore long stiff stays and cork rumps, you might as well sit with your arm round an oaken tree with the bark on, as around a lady's

* Grätz (now Hradec nad Moravici), also visited by Liszt, is almost on the Czech border with Poland.

** The 'Appassionata', with splodges of rain on it, was sight-read from the score by Marie Bigot, wife of Razumovsky's librarian. She later taught Mendelssohn and his sister in Paris.[53]

† A patron, Baron Pasqualati zu Osterburg, would put him up when he needed somewhere to go.

†† To do otherwise was seen as a challenge to the social order: a Prussian law of 1794 prohibited marriage between nobles and middle-class women unless with special government permission.[56]

waist; but now, as you have seldom any more covering but your shift and gown of a cold day, your waist is extremely warm and comfortable to the feel.'[57]

Ries wrote: 'Beethoven loved to see women, particularly pretty youthful faces.'[58] We have already met his first love, Eleonore von Breuning. He proposed to the singer Magdalena Willmann during the 1790s, but she refused him, because 'he was ugly and half crazy'.[59] Neither of these reasons would appear to be an impediment to marriage, however.

In 1799, two young countesses, Therese and Josephine Brunsvik, became pupils, and Beethoven stayed on their family estate in Hungary. He fell for Josephine, but she then married Count Deym, who, following exile after a duel, returned to Vienna, where he ran a waxwork museum under the pseudonym Herr Müller. When Deym died, Beethoven fell in love again with Josephine. But it would have been unrealistic for them to marry: she would have lost her status, title and the guardianship of her children.[60] By the time of her second marriage to Baron von Stackelberg, Beethoven's affections had drifted elsewhere. In the intervening period, he had fallen for the Countess Giulietta Guicciardi, a cousin of the Brunsviks, to whom he dedicated the 'Moonlight' Sonata. After she married a nobleman in 1803, Beethoven wistfully wrote: 'I was loved by her, and more than her husband ever was. Yet he was more her lover than I.'[61]

Later, aged 40, he proposed to the eighteen-year-old Therese Malfatti. She was the niece of his doctor, and sister-in-law of his 'secretary' Gleichenstein. Apart from inspiring him to improve his wardrobe, the romance came to nothing.[62]

He fell for the irresponsible, brilliant conversationalist, Bettina Brentano, whose mother had been the model for one of Goethe's characters in *Werther*. In her twenties, Bettina had chased the poet, by then almost 60. 'I have got to have a child by Goethe at all costs,' she exclaimed. 'Why, it will be a demigod!'*[64] Beethoven also fell for the guitar-playing

* Not surprisingly, Bettina had a row with Goethe's wife. Her brother Clemens worked with the man whom she was shortly to marry, Ludwig von Arnim, in assembling old popular legends and songs which were published as *Des Knaben Wunderhorn* between 1800 and 1808. The opening poem tells of a youth who brings a magic horn to the empress. This was one of Brahms' favourite books; Mahler set poems from it. Clemens married the half-sister of Marie d'Agoult, so Bettina pervades the musical world of the century even to the extent of being Cosima Wagner's half-aunt's sister-in-law![63]

Antonie Brentano, who had married Bettina's half-brother, Franz. There were others as well.

One lady from this catalogue was presumably the 'Immortal Beloved' referred to in a letter written in July 1812, from Teplitz, where Beethoven had gone for a health cure.[65] He wrote: 'In bed, my thoughts are with you, my Beloved ... you know my faithfulness to you; never can another possess my heart. Your love has made me one of the happiest and, at the same time, one of the unhappiest of men – at my age, I need a quiet steady life – is that possible in our situation? Ever thine, ever mine, ever each other's.'[66] Antonie Brentano is often the favourite candidate as addressee for this letter, which was found after Beethoven's death in a secret drawer of a cash box.[67]

A great friend was Countess Marie von Erdödy, from one of the important families in the Hungarian aristocracy. She was described as 'a very handsome, small, refined person five and twenty years old, who was married in her fifteenth year. Immediately after her first confinement, she contracted an incurable malady, so that, for ten years, with the exception of two or perhaps three months, she had been bedridden. Yet she gave birth to three dear healthy children who clung to her like creepers. Music is her sole enjoyment; she plays Beethoven's compositions extremely well, and with swollen feet limps from one piano-forte to another, but for all that is cheerful and friendly.'[68]

The Revolutionary Climate and Napoleon

In 1808, Beethoven lived in the same house as Countess Erdödy and her three children. But the countess was banished from Austria, for criticising the finance law of 1811. Banishments like this were not unusual in these unsettled times: the secret police were reputed to have 10,000 informers to assist in collecting information to pre-empt insurrection. Although actual policing seems to have been lax, the outspoken Beethoven might easily have found himself in gaol or banished.[69] Beethoven was trailed, but he was only once arrested, because he was mistaken for a tramp.[70] Possibly his friendship with the emperor's youngest brother, Archduke Rudolph, gave him protection.

It is understandable that the authorities had for long been nervous. In the mid-1790s, the 27-year-old Napoleon was given command of the army of Italy. It did not take him long to move into Piedmont and on to

Lombardy, the areas around Turin and Milan.[71] After showing great personal bravery leading his troops over the bridge at Arcola, he marched into Austria in 1797, sending the court and no doubt the whole of Vienna into a considerable panic. But his supply lines became increasingly extended, so he stopped at Leoben, about 90 miles to the south. The nobility, bourgeoisie, students and artisans offered themselves to defend the homeland. Beethoven wrote the 'Austrian Warsong' and the 'Song of Farewell to the Citizens of Vienna'. Haydn wrote his *Missa in Tempori Belli* and offered to write a National Hymn. But Napoleon accepted peace, and the troops returned into Vienna in triumph as if they had actually fought and won. Under the subsequent Treaty of Campo Formio, the left bank of the Rhine went to France, and, as compensation for giving up Belgium, Austria was given Venice, once Napoleon had sent many of its treasures back to France.

General Bernadotte was appointed French Ambassador in Vienna, bringing in his retinue Rodolphe Kreutzer, to whom Beethoven dedicated the Kreutzer Sonata for Violin and Piano.[72] At this stage in his career, the general flaunted his republican principles and Beethoven was a frequent visitor at the embassy.* According to a tale put about by Beethoven's amanuensis and biographer Anton Schindler, Bernadotte encouraged him to write a symphony in honour of the Republic and its virtues. This eventually led to the 'Eroica' Symphony, although it was not finished until 1804, several years later.[73]

The Austrians reoccupied northern Italy briefly when Napoleon was in Egypt and Palestine. But French control was resumed following Napoleon's victory at Marengo in June 1800. Six months later, following the battle of Hohenlinden, Beethoven took part in a concert organised in aid of wounded soldiers and was considerably peeved that his name did not appear in the advertisement. The French got to Melk, the magnificent Benedictine abbey, high above the Danube, 50 miles from Vienna. Mozart's sister Nannerl, living at St Gilgen just outside Salzburg, was in the war zone; her husband died while French soldiers were billeted on them.[74]

The situation was alarming. Since the Turks were defeated in 1683,

* Bernadotte was the son of a master tailor in Pau, near the Pyrenees. Renouncing his republican origins, he eventually was appointed to succeed the King of Sweden; he and his wife Desirée Clary, who had a romance with Napoleon (and some others), are ancestors of the present Swedish royal family.

Vienna had neglected its defences. The Habsburgs had to capitulate to Napoleon and this led to the Treaty of Lunéville in February 1801, under which the rest of Italy and the Rhineland passed into French control. Two years later, an imperial commission formalised the abolition of the ecclesiastical states, such as Cologne, and most of the lay principalities and free cities. Beethoven, however, had far greater anxieties on his mind.

Deafness

As early as 1801, Beethoven was writing to friends: 'My compositions bring me in a good deal; and I may say that I am offered more commissions than it is possible for me to carry out ... so you see how pleasantly situated I am.' The letter continued ominously: 'But that jealous demon, my wretched health, has put a nasty spoke in my wheel; and it amounts to this, that for the last three years my hearing has become weaker and weaker.'[75] His deafness started particularly in the left ear. He had written a few months earlier: 'Only think that the noblest part of me, my sense of hearing, has become very weak. Already when you were with me, I noted traces of it, and I said nothing. Now it has become worse.'[76] His doctors assured him that the complaint was temporary, and arose from an abdominal problem. He was apparently always suffering from diarrhoea: in 1797, a year of few compositions, he had been seriously ill.

He now took almond oil, cold and tepid baths, pills and infusions; his internal problems improved, but deafness persisted. He wrote to Wegeler: 'the humming in my ears continues day and night without ceasing. I may truly say that my life is a wretched one ... When at the theatre, I am obliged to lean forward close to the orchestra, in order to understand what is being said on the stage ... Often I can scarcely hear anyone speaking to me; the tones yes, but not the actual words; yet, as soon as anyone shouts, it is unbearable.' And again: 'I cannot, it is true, deny that the humming, with which my deafness actually began, has become somewhat weaker, especially in the left ear. My hearing however has not in the least improved; I really am not quite sure whether it has not become worse.'[77]

Some have attributed his deafness to syphilis. They point to his contemporary, the Spanish painter Francisco Goya who went stone deaf in 1792, and suffered from syphilis.[78] And they refer to Beethoven's earlier writings, such as: 'Keep away from rotten fortresses, for an attack from them is more deadly than one from well-preserved ones.'[79] From Prague, he had written to his brother: 'Do be on your guard against the whole tribe of bad women.'[80]

It is generally agreed, however, that he suffered from otosclerosis,* and the subsequent deterioration of the auditory nerves. For long, he used the brass ear trumpets such as those which can be seen in the Beethoven museum in Bonn. Deafness became total around 1818, when anyone communicating with him had to write down their remarks in a book. These are called the 'conversation books'. One hundred and thirty-seven of them survive.[82]

Like many other reasonably affluent Viennese, Beethoven spent part of the summer months in the country, staying in several different places, all now on the outskirts of Vienna. These included Baden, the spa enjoyed by Constanze Mozart, and Unterdöbling, Oberdöbling, Mödling, delightful places at the foot of the Vienna Woods, among trees and gardens full of birds. In 1802, he stayed in a small two-storey house amongst the woods and vines of Heiligenstadt, now to be found in a narrow street. He stayed for longer than usual, working on piano sonatas, and the Second Symphony. There, in October 1802, he poured his heart out in a letter of despair to his two brothers. This indicates that he had been troubled for the last six years by 'an incurable complaint, which has been aggravated by incompetent doctors. I cannot enjoy meeting people, talking to them, exchanging ideas with them. I can only risk meeting them when absolutely necessary, because I am so desperately worried that they will notice my condition. So I am condemned to a lonely existence, almost that of an outcast ... It has driven me to despair, even to the point of contemplating suicide. Only art held me back. So, Death, I look forward with Joy to meeting you. Come when you will; I will face you courageously.' He continues: 'Yes, I must now completely abandon the fond hope which I brought here that I would at least see some improvement. It has gone, withered like the leaves in autumn.' He asks providence to grant him a single day of Joy.[83]

This 'Heiligenstadt Testament' provided an emotional outlet for Beethoven and, thereafter, he was far less prone to self-pity and despair. Within eight days of it, after his return to Vienna, he was writing business

* Today, the fenestration operation would have resolved this. It produces a new window for the passage of sound waves that bypasses the problem caused by the development of excessive bone in the middle ear.[81]

letters to the publishers Breitkopf & Härtel about two sets of variations for the piano that he had composed.[84]

He went to the top Viennese doctors, including the staff surgeon to the emperor.[85] He considered trying miraculous cures through the use of Galvanism, named after Luigi Galvani who had observed what he called animal electricity in frogs' legs. For a few years, Beethoven tried a faith healer at St Stephen's, who prescribed pouring oil into the ears. This was at the time he was visited by the young Czerny who recorded that he 'had cotton, which seemed to have been steeped in a yellowish liquid, in his ears. At the same time, however, he did not give the least evidence of deafness.'[86]

Indeed, at first, his hearing got no worse. He launched into what is regarded as his 'middle' period,* 1803–12, years of astonishing creativity. In 1806, he was composing at the rate of one major work per month. These years heard the Third Symphony, and ended with the completion of the Seventh and Eighth Symphonies. They heard the Violin Concerto – the score was only just ready with two days to spare and the soloist more or less sight-read his part, interpolating some violin acrobatics of his own between the movements. They heard the 'Appassionata' and 'Waldstein' Sonatas, the Razumovsky Quartets, the overtures to *Coriolan* and *Egmont*.[88]

Beethoven worked on the Third Symphony when staying in a small farmhouse very close to the one in Heiligenstadt where he had despaired. The small white building with a tiny courtyard covered in vines provides a strong contrast to Prince Lobkowitz's palace with its magnificent staircase leading up to the grand saloon, in which the 'Eroica' was given a first, private run-through in December 1804. The symphony was not received too well at its first public performance on 7 April 1805: a man shouted from the gallery: 'I'll give another kreutzer if only the thing will stop.'[89] Had that man possessed modern equipment which allows one to play Mozart's last three symphonies, themselves masterpieces, and then listen to the 'Eroica' written only fifteen years later, he would have understood the significance of the occasion. The symphony has been called 'one of the incomprehensible deeds in art and letters, the greatest single step made by an individual composer in the history of the symphony and in the history of music in general'.[90] Another writer has described it as 'one of the wonders of music,

* It has been pointed out that Beethoven's three periods are no more than youth, maturity and old age: 'Opus 1 is the work of a finished master.'[87]

supremely alive in every detail yet completely unified, supremely clear yet most powerfully impulsive'.[91]

The Third Symphony was first dedicated to Napoleon. But Beethoven was furious when Napoleon declared himself Emperor of the French in May 1804. He ripped out the reference to 'Buonaparte', although he later reinstated it. By the time of the first printed edition, the symphony had been called 'Eroica', and dedicated to Prince Lobkowitz, who paid Beethoven a large sum for both the dedication and the exclusive rights to it for six months.[92]

Early in 1803, Beethoven had taken lodgings in Emanuel Schikaneder's Theatre an der Wien, where he was appointed composer to the theatre. Taking advantage of the choral resources, and possibly inspired by his own sufferings, he wrote the oratorio *Christ on the Mount of Olives*. Being essentially an instrumental composer, he first took advice from Salieri about vocal declamation.

Schikaneder wanted a new opera. The proposed work, *Vesta's Feuer*, proceeded slowly and was abandoned. Operas by the Paris-based composers Luigi Cherubini and Etienne-Nicolas Méhul, with their plots of heroism, rescue and escape, had been successful in Vienna. So Beethoven turned to a French work,* Bouilly's *Léonore, ou l'Amour Conjugal*. The story of Léonore, the ideal woman, suited Beethoven; Florestan, her husband whom she saves, seems to encapsulate Beethoven's own suffering. This would eventually become the opera we know as *Fidelio*.[93]

Napoleon again: Austerlitz

The dire political and military situation provided a chaotic background to this. The Habsburgs were very concerned that they were being lined up to become the next of Napoleon's puppet states, like those in Germany, Italy and Spain, so they concluded a defensive pact with Russia. War broke out again; Beethoven's friend Ries was 'compelled to shoulder a musket in this calamitous war'.[94] After a catastrophic surrender of the Austrian army at Ulm, Napoleon triumphantly entered Vienna in the second week of November 1805, just three weeks after the French naval defeat at Trafalgar. He stayed in Schönbrunn; but he did not relax. He had to protect himself

* He found a new librettist in Joseph Sonnleithner, archivist, secretary of the court theatres, uncle of the poet Franz Grillparzer, and supporter of Schubert.

from the approaching allied armies from Russia and Italy. It helped that he was facing 'a squabbling committee consisting of two sovereigns and their advisers'.[95]

By luring the Russians to attack him on 1 December 1805, before the arrival of the Austrian reinforcements from Italy, Napoleon won a decisive victory at Austerlitz, on the estate of Prince Kaunitz just outside Brünn (now Brno) in southern Moravia. Austerlitz was Napoleon's 'supreme professional performance'.[96] The French lost 8,000 men killed or wounded; on the allied side, 12,000 were killed and wounded, 150,000 prisoners and 133 guns were taken. 'This is the happiest day of my life',[97] said Napoleon after the battle, a remark which, one may conjecture, might be intelligible to someone with a military training. Talleyrand, the ubiquitous and obsequious French politician, crippled by falling out of a chest of drawers aged four, told him: 'Your Majesty can now eliminate the Austrian monarchy or re-establish it. But this conglomeration of states must stay together. It is absolutely indispensable for the future well-being of the civilised world.'[98] However, the thousand-year Holy Roman Empire was brought to an end.*

The first performance of *Fidelio* took place at the Theater an der Wien less than a fortnight before Austerlitz. Beethoven's patrons had fled, so it played to almost empty houses. It ran for only three nights and got bad reviews. Besides, an opera about oppression and political prisoners was untimely. A revised version in 1806 was poorly performed and failed also. Beethoven's 'propensity for writing long-drawn-out movements, which served him well in instrumental music, militated against him in a stage drama'.[100] In 1807, he applied for a permanent position as an opera composer, but was rejected. Perhaps it was just as well: his skill was at its best in instrumental and choral music, not opera.

Meanwhile, Beethoven had to live through the food shortage caused by the arrival of a vast French army. There were food riots. The cost of the war was enormous, paper money rolled off the printing presses, and the state debt increased, aggravated by the French, who spread around counterfeit banknotes. The cost of living had nearly trebled in just four years. People on fixed incomes, such as government employees, were particularly badly

* At the time Napoleon created himself emperor, Francis had the foresight also to create himself Emperor of Austria. So he did not lose his imperial title when he abdicated as Holy Roman Emperor in 1806.[99]

hit. One police report estimated that only one in five petty officials could afford to buy meat for their families. Others profiteered: the peasants and agrarian population benefited from land and grain price increases, especially those who had commuted their feudal obligations ('robot' – see page 101) into fixed liabilities, or who had borrowed. Industrial expansion, the manufacture of uniforms for the army and the blockade of Europe provided a huge captive market for some.[101]

Beethoven was conscious of the need for hard currency in concluding his business dealings. In 1806, he wrote to a publisher: 'I expect you to offer me £100 sterling, or 200 Vienna ducats in gold, and not in Vienna bank-notes, which under present circumstances entail too great a loss.'[102] He thought of accepting the position of Kapellmeister in Kassel, at the court of Jerome Bonaparte, King of Westphalia. This offer enabled him to negotiate a guaranteed annuity of 4,000 fl from his leading patrons. Archbishop Rudolph contributed 1,500 fl, Prince Lobkowitz 700 fl, and Prince Kinsky, a new and less reliable donor, the considerable sum of 1,800 fl.[103] This arrangement, whereby the nobility paid for him to be independent, was unprecedented.[104] There were some strings attached: almost twenty years later, Beethoven was giving Archduke Rudolph two-hour lessons each day. But the archduke was a magnificent patron; Beethoven dedicated to him the 'Emperor' Concerto, the 'Hammerklavier' Sonata, the *Missa Solemnis* and the 'Archduke' Trio.

With his increasing deafness, Beethoven continued to be obsessed with financial security. He was right: there was continuing inflation; and, after Kinsky was killed in a riding accident and Lobkowitz died, there were arguments with their heirs who wanted to cancel the annuity. Beethoven did not feel that it was in any sense assured.[105]

The flow of major compositions continued. A benefit concert on 22 December 1808 has been described as being surely 'one of the most fantastic displays of new music ever put on by a single composer'.[106] It included the first performance of the Fifth and Sixth Symphonies, the Fourth Piano Concerto, movements from the Mass in C and the Fantasy for Piano, Orchestra and Chorus. The 'Emperor' Concerto was written in the following year, but, owing to his deafness, Beethoven did not perform it himself.*

* The first performance was given in Leipzig in 1811. Czerny gave the first performance in Vienna.

NAPOLEON AGAIN: WAGRAM

Beethoven must have been horrified when hostilities were resumed yet again. When the French invaded Portugal in 1807, the emperor's brother Archduke Charles, a competent commander-in-chief and one of the more perspicacious members of the royal family,[107] summed up Napoleon's aims: 'There can no longer be any question what Napoleon wants – he wants everything.'[108] Intelligence reports from the ambassador in Paris, Clemens von Metternich,* indicated that Napoleon's continuing aggression was inspiring some opposition at a high level in the French government. So, plans for war began to be drawn up in May 1808. The Tyrolean peasantry successfully rose against the Bavarians, whom Napoleon had installed as their overlords. But, in the event, Napoleon crushed Spain and returned to Paris to suppress the opposition. On 14 April 1809, he left Paris to wage war against Austria for the fourth time.

Vienna was bombarded on the night of 11 May (see colour plate 4). Beethoven took refuge in his brother Caspar's house, covering his head with pillows. The city fell on 13 May; a fortnight later, Haydn died. Beethoven wrote: 'What a destructive disorderly life I see and hear around me: nothing but drums, cannons, and human misery in every form.'[110] It seemed that the Viennese were accepting that the French would take over; one observer reported that the eagerness with which the city's women rushed to accommodate the French soldiers 'made Vienna look like Sodom and Gomorrah'.[111]

Napoleon needed to destroy the Habsburg army led by Archduke Charles before he could afford to relax in the palace at Schönbrunn. In early July 1809, he decided to cross the Danube, six miles south of Vienna. When a small number of his soldiers were across, the archduke attacked and sent boats down to destroy his pontoon bridge, which was also hit by a tidal wave of flood water. The battle of Aspern, his first battlefield defeat, has been described as Napoleon's 'rashest military undertaking thus far; an act of recklessly bad generalship'.**[113] But the archduke, possibly fearing that a single defeat could destroy the Habsburg dynasty, did not pursue his advantage; Napoleon took the rest of his army across the Danube. On the

* Metternich was an imperial knight from the Rhineland in service at the imperial court. He disliked innovation. At this stage, he was said to be avenging Austerlitz by cuckolding the Grand Army: he was sleeping with the wives of two marshals of France, Caroline Murat (Napoleon's youngest sister) and Laura Junot.[109]

** The tenor who sang to Haydn just before he died was killed around this time.[112]

battlefield of Wagram, he faced more than 300,000 men and nearly 900 cannon. After a two-day battle, at least 32,000 of Napoleon's own troops and roughly a similar number of Austrians lay dead or wounded on the field. It has been said that Wagram 'proclaimed a new order of warfare; it looked ahead to such combinations of massed manpower and firepower as the battles of the American Civil War; as Verdun and the Somme; as Stalingrad'.[114]

And so the war ended again, for the moment. Emperor Francis ceded further lands, this time in Poland and along the Adriatic. Napoleon, anxious for an heir, married the emperor's daughter Marie Louise, a union arranged by Metternich, who had recently become foreign minister and now dominated the Habsburg Empire.[115] But first, Napoleon took up residence again in Schönbrunn, running his empire from there during the summer, and proving his virility by siring a child* on his Polish mistress Marie Walewska.

Conditions in Vienna were wretched and the burden of billeting the enormous army was considerable; sometimes 100 or more soldiers were required to be accommodated in one house. While the French were in occupation, there was very little food, and the Viennese ate bread made of barley left over from the breweries. Minor comforts such as tea and coffee could not be obtained.[117]

The government was forced to declare its first bankruptcy, by means of the finance patent of 15 March 1811: the nominal value of the florin was reduced to one-fifth of its previous value. Hence Beethoven's annuity of 4,000 fl reduced to 800 fl. The bankruptcy led to a highly complicated situation where two currencies were operating at the same time.[118]

Later, in September, the government decreed that contracts in fixed money should be divided by 2.48 rather than 5, making Beethoven's annuity 1,600 fl. It is no wonder that sponsors such as Lobkowitz and Kinsky, who were feeling the pinch, tried at first to pay him in the reduced currency. Eventually they settled for an annuity at 3,400 fl.**[120]

*The future foreign minister to Napoleon III. Napoleon had met the virtuous, religious wife of Count Walewice-Walewski on the way back to Warsaw, at a stop for a change of horses. She was told by the Polish nobility to close her eyes and think of Poland. Napoleon thought her 'the perfect woman, being docile, soft and lacking the disadvantages of a mind and will of her own'.[116]
** There was a further monetary reorganisation when the silver florin was reintroduced in 1818: the annuity was reduced by 60 per cent in the new currency, yielding 1,360 fl. Monetary comparisons are problematic, but Haydn's home was sold in 1810 for 6,840 fl (expressed in the new currency).[119]

Congress of Vienna

In one of the most famous campaigns in modern history, Napoleon was repelled from Russia, losing 570,000 men in the process. It was an exceptionally cold winter. He arrived at the Tuileries just before midnight on 18 December 1812, having travelled virtually non-stop, apart from several breakdowns, 1,400 miles in 13 days. With extraordinary energy, he raised a fresh army and, by April, he had 200,000 men in the field. He defeated the Russians and Prussians at Lützen and Bautzen. In August, the Habsburgs declared war, and Napoleon suffered a serious defeat at a four-day battle around Leipzig in October.* On the morning of 1 April 1814, the allied cavalry, commanded by the tsar, rode 30 abreast down the Champs Elysées, the first foreign armies to enter Paris since the 15th century. The Comte de Provence was installed as King Louis XVIII.** The Congress of Vienna, presided over by Metternich, began in October: its main objective was to settle territorial claims in the post-war period, with a view to maintaining the balance of power.[121]

Shortly before this, Beethoven worked with Maelzel, who had recently invented the metronome, to arrange a grand charity concert in aid of war victims; fundraising concerts, sometimes organised by a group of ladies, had begun about this time. Beethoven's 'Battle' Symphony, which celebrated Wellington's victory over Napoleon at Vittoria, was performed on a star-studded stage, which included Hummel, Salieri and the virtuoso violinist and composer Louis Spohr. Its success with the Viennese was 'stupendous' and it was given four performances in quick succession. This brought Beethoven considerable financial gain, and led to a bitter quarrel with Maelzel about the future rights to the work. An embarrassing amalgam of 'Rule Britannia', 'God Save the King' and so on, the 'Battle' Symphony thankfully only lasts about a quarter of an hour.[122]

Heads of five reigning dynasties and of 216 princely families flocked to Vienna, 'like peasants to a country fair', as Marshal Blücher (of Prussia and, nine months later, of Waterloo) put it.[123] Beethoven will have seen the Prater amusement park full of riders and carriages. The protagonists were Tsar Alexander, of whom Napoleon said that 'it would be difficult to have

* The British were not represented. This decisive battle has not figured greatly in British education.
** After the execution of Louis XVI, his second son was proclaimed Louis XVII, but remained in prison until his early death.

more intelligence than the Emperor Alexander; but there is a piece missing; I have never managed to discover what it is'.[124] There was the French minister, the unprincipled Talleyrand,* the Habsburg chancellor Metternich and the British Lord Castlereagh.** With them, there was an enormous influx of hangers-on. All interests were represented, down to a Herr Cotta of Augsburg, representing the publishing trade.[126] Mendelssohn's uncle was in the Prussian delegation.

Every night, dinner was laid at the Hofburg Palace in Vienna for 40 tables, and while the delegates were dining or carousing, there was a lot of rummaging in wastepaper baskets by housemaids. Baron Hager, the director of the state police, had covered the whole city with his network, and used this material to submit his voluminous reports to the emperor.[127] Most of the diplomatic couriers were in Austrian pay and all letters were opened and transcribed. 'The interception of letters remained a craft in which the Austrians had no equals.'[128]

As happens at conferences, a festival committee devised a varied programme of entertainment to distract the participants from the futility of their presence and also, in this case, from the activities of the housemaids. 'At times it seems that no other committee at the Congress worked so hard.'[129] For the VIPs, there was Metternich's masked ball, at which Lady Castlereagh wore in her hair her husband's garter (the strap normally worn below the knee, signifying the highest order of chivalry in England). The Castlereaghs had availed themselves of dancing lessons, but it was observed 'how sadly each of them had profited by such instructions'.[130]

There was an unending sequence of drawing rooms, balls, banquets and gala performances. Waltzes were all the rage. There were *tableaux vivants* at which the young ladies of Viennese society would give representations of Louis XIV at the feet of Madame de la Vallière, or Hippolytus defending his virtue before Theseus. There were sleighing expeditions to the Vienna

* Talleyrand, former Bishop of Autun, is a study in political intrigue and survival. He was described by Napoleon as 'a piece of dung in a silk stocking'. He played his cards deftly during the Revolution and later on. He was made a prince by Napoleon, played an active part in restoring the Bourbons, and worked for King Louis-Philippe who visited him on his deathbed when he was dying aged 84. His sex life was notorious.

** Castlereagh was a veteran British politician and manipulator, 'as cold as a fish'.[125] He suffered from melancholia and killed himself with a penknife in 1822. The mob cheered at his funeral, held in Westminster Abbey.

Woods; there were hunting parties and there was Kraskowitz's balloon ascent. The ballet *Fore et Zephire* was performed again and again at the Opera House with Signorina Bitottini in the principal part. On 28 October, there was a performance of *Fidelio*, which Beethoven had revised in the spring, using another librettist. On a weekday, instead of a Sunday, out of respect for the religious prejudices of the British delegation, the tsar and Frederick William attended a gala concert of the Seventh Symphony and the 'Battle' Symphony. Beethoven conducted, 'a short and stout figure waving his baton triumphantly'.[131] *Fidelio* was repeated fifteen times. Beethoven wrote several works specifically for the Congress, such as a cantata, 'The Glorious Moment', and a 'Chorus for the Allied Princes'.[132]

There were other diversions. The Castlereaghs continued to cause some amusement. Sometimes, it was the way they went window-shopping 'like a provincial on holiday'; on other occasions, it was their bourgeois domesticity, and their tendency to sing Anglican hymns in their house, to the accompaniment of a harmonium.[133] Others were more typical, according to the police reports. The King of Prussia went out in civilian clothes with a round hat pulled down over his eyes. The Grand Duke of Baden spent his nights in a brothel. The Prince de Ligne, in his 80th year, died from a cold contracted while waiting for an assignation at a street corner. The tsar and Prince Metternich swapped mistresses. A report to the emperor also states that a certain Mayer made his living by selling remedies against venereal disease.[134] What Emperor Francis made of all this detail, one cannot imagine: he was normally at his happiest 'when engaged in his workshop stamping seals onto sealing wax or merely cooking toffee at the stove'.[135]

The Congress was concerned about Russian expansion westwards and became bogged down over the partition of Poland, the country of the five-year-old Frédéric Chopin.[136] Then, proceedings stopped when Napoleon escaped from Elba. Although Napoleon landed on 1 March, Metternich only opened the packet from the consul in Genoa at 7.30 am on 7 March. Vienna emptied: 'A thousand candles seemed in a single instant to have been extinguished.'[137] It was observed that 'fear was predominant in all the Imperial and Royal personages'.[138]

Beset with Problems

The 'Battle' Symphony was composed at a low point in Beethoven's creative life. After 1812, his 'torrent of inspiration dwindled to a trickle'.[139]

The pressures on him were considerable. He wrote to Archduke Rudolph: 'I have been ailing, although mentally, it is true, more than physically.'[140] Also, his popularity began to decline after around 1815. And the waltz, with its energy, speed and human contact, was superseding group dances such as the stately and stationary minuet as the fashionable music.* Vienna now vibrated with music of a totally different variety to Beethoven's. As early as 1809, a German journalist noted that every evening 50,000 thronged to dance halls and calculated that one in four of the Viennese must have spent their evening waltzing.[141] The title of an anthology of dances published fifteen years later, *Halt's enk z'samm* ('Hold on tight'), tells us much about the nature of the dancing of the time.[142]

Artistically, Beethoven was out on a limb. In June 1816, Salieri celebrated the 50th anniversary of his arrival in Vienna with a public service in the cathedral, the award of a gold medal and an evening party at which his pupils, old and young, including Schubert, each made a contribution. Salieri gave his impressions of the reception: he praised the 'expression of pure nature, free of all eccentricities' in the works of his pupils, but he deprecated the extravagance and disregard of conventional forms for which 'one of our greatest German artists' was responsible.[143] By this, he meant Beethoven.

Although 1816 heard the song cycle *An die Ferne Geliebte*, there was a sharp decline in Beethoven's musical productivity in the following year: it is thought that he may have had some sort of debilitating illness. Certainly, his hearing deteriorated, so much that soon he was using the conversation books for people to write messages for him. At times, he was 'in the most deplorable condition'[144] and so ill-kept and unhygienic that guests at an inn avoided sitting near him.

Family problems were added to the professional, financial and health worries. In 1812, he forced his brother Johann, a successful pharmacist in Linz, to marry the woman he was living with. She already had an illegitimate daughter by another man. Then, in November 1815, Caspar died of

* To waltz means 'to turn'. The waltz was popular by 1800; 30 years later, it was said that 'the menuet in its old form reaps only laughs', an attitude that may be familiar today. The novel aspect was that waltzing couples held each other in an embrace. They usually danced a six-step turn clockwise and continuously moved round the room counter-clockwise. The picture then would have been different from the later crinoline version; the dance floor was sprayed with water to keep the dust down.

tuberculosis, leaving behind his wife Johanna, daughter of a well-to-do upholsterer, and their nine-year-old son Karl (see colour plate 14). A codicil to the will appointed Johanna as guardian, with precedence over Beethoven. Beethoven was obviously desperate for a child of his own, and Karl fitted the bill. His only chance of getting custody was to prove Johanna's unsuitability. So, he alleged that she had poisoned her husband, and he dragged up a four-year-old case in which she had been detained for stealing pearls.[145]

Johanna was also rumoured to have offered herself 'for hire'. Beethoven wrote: 'Last night this "Queen of the Night" was at the artists ball till 3 o'clock, not only wanting in sense but even in decency ... Oh terrible, and into these hands ought we, even for a moment, to entrust our precious treasure? No, certainly not.'[146] Karl was whisked off to a boarding school on the outskirts of Vienna. Beethoven wrote to his schoolmaster asking him not to allow Karl's mother to exert any influence over the boy.[147]

In 1818, Johanna began interfering in Karl's education, which was strict and severe, although possibly no more than was customary. At the end of that year, Karl ran away to her. There was a court hearing about the boy's future. Beethoven attempted to have the case heard in the court for the nobility because he was 'van Beethoven'.* Johanna appealed on the grounds that van Beethoven was a commoner and, to his chagrin, won. She was granted temporary custody, having claimed that Beethoven's deafness and poor health made him an unsuitable guardian. Beethoven attempted to have Karl sent to a top school in Bavaria, but the magistrate turned that down. The case dragged on, with Beethoven eventually winning in 1820 after four and a half years, around the time Johanna produced an illegitimate daughter, an event which may not have been so unusual given that 40 per cent of births in Vienna at that time were illegitimate.[149]

Apart from the emotional strain, the court case took up much of Beethoven's time: for the appeal, he had to prepare a memorandum 48 pages long.[150] And he was totally unsuitable as a surrogate father for a child of Karl's age, even if he tried very hard. We see him writing to the schoolmaster that Karl's 'boots are too narrow', and added that 'a thing of that

* The use of 'von' implied nobility, although there were a number of bogus ones around, Carl Maria von Weber being an example. Unlike 'von', however, 'van' had no status; it simply indicated Flemish ancestry.[148]

sort spoils the feet, so I beg you not to let him put on these boots any more until they have been stretched. As regards pianoforte practice, I beg you to keep him to his work, otherwise there is no use in him having a teacher.'[151]

A source of great practical and moral support to Beethoven, almost a mother figure, during these difficult years, was Nanette Streicher.* Some extracts from his letters to her indicate the tedious and intractable problems he faced, or thought he faced, with his domestics. 'The low behaviour of these persons [the two servants Nany and Baberl] is unbearable … for a housekeeper she has not sufficient training … the other does not really deserve a New Year's present.' And again, 'I have already found out that she [i.e. the cook] cannot cook daintily, nor in a way beneficial to health. She behaved at once very pertly when told about it, but in the sweetest manner I told her that she should pay more attention to it. I did not trouble any more about her, went for a walk in the evening, and on my return found she had gone, leaving this letter behind. As this is leaving without giving notice, the police perhaps will know how to make her return.' On another occasion, he wrote to Nanette: 'Concerning the future housekeeper, I wish to know whether she has a bed and bedroom furniture? By bed, I mean partly the bedstead, partly the bed, the mattresses etc etc.'[154]

Laundry seems to have been a particular obsession. He wrote to Nanette: 'I beg you only to say to him that you thought that a pair of socks has been lost, this is clear from the letter which you wrote to me about it; he is always telling me that you had found the socks again. The washerwoman received two pairs of stockings, as the two washing bills, yours and mine, showed; and this would not be so had she not received them. So I am convinced that she gave him the two pairs of stockings, as she certainly received them, so that they must have got lost only through him.' Again Beethoven writes: 'I also ask you kindly to see that the washerwoman delivers the washing at latest Sunday. I do not wish you to imagine that I think that in any way through carelessness on your part anything has been lost … I must have cooking for myself, for in these bad times there are so few people in the country that it is difficult to get a meal in the inns, still more

* Nanette, as an eight year old, had impressed Mozart with her talent, but also both amused and worried him with her antics at the keyboard.[152] Her husband together with her father, Andreas Stein the Augsburg piano manufacturer, developed the Viennese piano which had a lighter touch but less sonorous tone than the English and French actions.[153] Streicher also made ear trumpets for Beethoven.

to find what is beneficial and good for me.' He adds: 'I beg you to send to the washerwoman so that the washing may come home on Sunday.'[155]

That this genius was being diverted by such trivia is amazing. Beethoven must have been completely distracted. At least there is an occasional glimmer of humour. 'Yes, indeed all this housekeeping is still without keeping and much resembles an *allegro di confusione*.'[156]

There was 'business' correspondence to be attended to as well, whether writing to George Thomson of Edinburgh, for whom he arranged many Scottish, Welsh and Irish airs,* or to publishers about corrections to proofs. 'Frequently the dots are wrongly placed, instead of after a note, somewhere else', he wrote to Schotts in Mainz. 'Please tell the printer to take care and put all such dots near the note, and in a line with it.'[158] For all his slovenly appearance, his personal habits and the chaotic appearance of many of his autographs, Beethoven showed a meticulous attention to detail.

The Last Great Works

At the end of the decade, Beethoven's output picked up, and the quality improved. He started work on the 'Hammerklavier' Sonata, his first major project for many years. Shortly before he completed it, he received a Broadwood piano from London, where Clementi had been publishing his works. Now that war was over, several attempts were made to get Beethoven to visit London. He contemplated rearranging the 'Hammerklavier' Sonata to make it suitable for an English market, an interesting notion. A visit was planned for early 1818. But health and the problems with Karl seem to have got in the way.

In 1819 he started work on the 'Diabelli' Variations. The publisher and composer Diabelli had circulated a waltz theme to 50 or more composers around Vienna, including Schubert, Liszt, Czerny and Hummel, inviting them to submit a variation which would be combined into a 'union of artists of the Fatherland'. Beethoven naturally did not want to take part in a collective work, and in any case he thought the theme trivial. He eventually produced his own complete work with 33 variations.[159]

Also in 1819 he began the *Missa Solemnis*, which was intended for Archduke Rudolph's installation as Archbishop of Olmütz in the following

* We do not often associate Beethoven with Paddy O'Rafferty, Merch Megan, Norah of Balamagairy, Highland Harry or Polly Stewart! In the end, the canny Scot lost interest: 'He composes for posterity' was his perspicacious complaint.[157]

year. Beethoven decided to postpone printing the work, and to sell copies to the principal courts of Europe and to anyone else who might subscribe. This naturally entailed considerable correspondence, the canvassing of sponsors, letters to Goethe asking him to use his influence with the Duke of Weimar, and so on.

In the early 1820s he wrote the last three Piano Sonatas. But there was a pause in 1821, which coincided with bereavement and personal problems. His much-loved Josephine Stackelberg (née Brunsvik) died.[160] Also Beethoven seems to have had rheumatic fever and jaundice.[161] The doctors at least got him to reduce his consumption to one bottle of wine a meal.[162]

Around 1822, he was requested to write an oratorio for the Boston Musical Society. Prince Galitzine of St Petersburg commissioned some quartets; the London Philharmonic Society commissioned a symphony. He wrote to his friend in London, Ferdinand Ries: 'If only God will restore me to my health, which to say the least has improved, I could do myself justice, in accepting offers from all cities in Europe, yes, even North America, and I might still prosper.'[163] The Almighty ensured that the flow of masterpieces continued. In 1824, the Ninth Symphony was performed. In 1825–6 he wrote the *Grosse Fuge* and the final String Quartets.

Meanwhile, Karl helped his uncle with messages and accounts. He stayed with him at Baden, one of Beethoven's favourite country retreats, in summer 1823, and in Vienna during his university studies. But they quarrelled. Beethoven wrote in October 1825: 'My dear son! Only nothing further – only come to my arms, you shall hear no harsh word. For heaven's sake do not rush to destruction – you will be received as ever with affection – as to considering what is to be done in future … no reproaches, on my word of honour, for it would be of no use.'[164] At the end of the following July, Karl tried to shoot himself in the head at Helenenthal, a lovely beauty spot near Baden.* Karl blamed his attempted suicide on his uncle. Beethoven was appalled at the disgrace, and at the crime of suicide, particularly as it was a step he himself had struggled to resist taking. After being released from the city hospital, Karl joined the army.[165]

* This was Baden near Vienna, not the Grand Duchy. Some years later, near there, Crown Prince Rudolph was to be more successful in destroying himself and his mistress.

New Styles – Rossini and Weber

Beethoven's successors found his late works very difficult to understand. For Berlioz, Mendelssohn and Schumann, the influential works of Beethoven were the 'Eroica', 'Pastoral' and Fifth Symphonies, and the Sonatas Opus 53 and Opus 57. Most of the later works were received 'with disappointment and embarrassment, even by those who admired the composer and put forward the excuse of his deafness'.[166] 'If only we knew what

Carl Maria von Weber at work

you were thinking about in your music', the poet Grillparzer confessed to him in 1823.[167] The string quartet, the *Grosse Fuge*, is a good example: after its first performance in March 1826, it was not heard again in Vienna for 33 years.

While Beethoven was conceiving his great final works, new trends and new styles continued to develop, especially in opera. The first performance of Rossini's *Barber of Seville*, regarded by some as perhaps the greatest of all comic operas, had taken place in 1816. In 1822, there was a Rossini festival in Vienna, in which six operas were performed with considerable commercial success. Rossini 'fever' raged.[168] Also around this time, Carl Maria von Weber was transforming opera, orchestral performance and orchestration. We will meet Rossini again in a later chapter. Here, something should be said about Weber, who, with Beethoven, would exercise such a considerable influence on composers in the 19th century.

Weber visited Beethoven in 1823, when he came to Vienna for the first performance of *Euryanthe*, an opera which provided much inspiration for Wagner.[169] Weber, like Beethoven, was one of the most brilliant piano virtuosos of his age:* his concert pieces such as the *Invitation to the Dance* inspired both Liszt and Chopin.

Weber was a cousin of Constanze Mozart. Although small and with a limp, he was a formidable opera director. At work in Breslau, Stuttgart, Prague and Dresden, he implemented proper conditions of service, got rid of older players, improved the repertoire and revised rehearsal arrangements. There was uproar,** manifestos and open letters were issued; but he even went so far as to learn Czech, so as to be able to understand the grumbles. He paid great attention to detail, casting, production and lighting. He studied costume designs from old books and he himself supervised the scenery painting.[170]

Weber also transformed conducting methods. The Dresden orchestra was still seated in much the same way as it was in Hasse's time, when the conductor sat at the clavier in the middle, unable to see some of the players, a few of whom were peering at the music over his shoulder. Weber conducted from the front. We see this in the well-known picture of him conducting the orchestra in London, directing with a rolled up sheaf of paper. This was something entirely new.†[172]

Comparing Weber's operas with, say, the *Fidelio* of fifteen years earlier makes one appreciate the speed of change, both in content and in the use of instruments to create colour, whether individually or together. *Der Freischütz* was first performed in Berlin in June 1821. A contemporary described it evoking 'unbridled and hysterical enthusiasm'.[173] Critics and jealous competitors, such as Spontini and Spohr, dismissed it as pop-opera

* His technique benefited from an elongated thumb, which enabled him to play four-part chords covering a tenth without difficulty.

** Uproar was consistent with his colourful, short life, in which he even found time to begin writing a novel, the Tonkünstler's Leben. Early on, he nearly died from drinking from a wine bottle filled with engraving acid. Reference has been made in the chapter on Bach to Weber's imprisonment. He also spent considerable energy untangling himself from a series of love affairs. He announced his betrothal to his wife on the day of the total eclipse of the sun.

†Mozart conducted *Die Entführung* from the clavier. Gluck led the orchestra with the violin.[171]

for the masses. But, here was a truly *German* opera, the successor to the 'Singspiel' – opera with vernacular and music mixed, as in Mozart's *Die Entführung* and *The Magic Flute*.

It is based on the German folklore and country life in which, as a young man, Weber had immersed himself: he was one of the first composers to realise the potential of folk melody as a source of inspiration. There are jolly drinking and hunting choruses, lovely arias, and the Wolf's Glen scene, which is weird, phantasmagoric and reminiscent of *Macbeth*. For this, Weber insisted on having an 'owl with flaming eyes, and real fluttering bats'. 'Spare neither spectres nor skeletons', he wrote, 'and let the horrors increase crescendo with each bullet.'[174]

For the intellectuals, the mystery, superstition, legend and ghosts, and the emphasis on Nature, fitted in with the Romantic movement which was sweeping away Classicism. And ordinary people, such as soldiers returned from the Napoleonic Wars, 'imbued with the newly won pride of German patriotism', related easily to the ordinary humble village folk, 'the breeze of the German forests and mountains', and 'the horns and popping muskets of the huntsmen'.[175]

There were at least 30 different productions of *Der Freischütz* by the end of 1822. At one time during 1824, there were three productions running simultaneously in London, and there was one in New York in the following year.[176]

Weber's *Euryanthe* is a colourful tale of knighthood and romance. There are the choruses, like the Huntsmen's and Peasants' choruses; there is vengeance worthy of *Otello*; there are luscious and lyrical songs such as Euryanthe's 'Tinkling bells in the glen, the rippling brook'. But it was not a success at the time, partly because of the Rossini craze with which it coincided.

Then, at the start of *Oberon*, we seem to look through gauze, it is so light and fairy-like. The playbill described it as 'Oberon, or The Elf-King's Oath; with entirely new Music, Scenery, machinery, Dresses and Decorations'. It is very different from the others, almost a play punctuated by occasional music. The colour of the music is delightful, colour which only someone who totally understood the workings of an orchestra could reproduce.

In all three operas, Weber had created a new style of orchestration. Thus these works are landmarks; just as much as Beethoven's great works of the time. Debussy said that Weber 'scrutinises the soul of each instrument and exposes it with a gentle hand'.[177] Beethoven recognised that this was something new. He said of Weber and *Der Freischütz*: 'that usually feeble little man – I'd never have thought it of him.'[*178]

Beethoven – Towards the End

All this was happening at a time when Beethoven was considered completely eccentric. He could communicate solely by means of the conversation books. But in spite of all this, a journalist could say in 1822 that he 'radiated a truly childlike amiability … even his barking tirades … were only explosions of his fanciful imagination and his momentary excitement. They were uttered without any haughtiness, without any feeling of bitterness or resentment.'[179]

There was a disastrous rehearsal of *Fidelio* in 1822, at which the orchestra broke down completely; his amanuensis and faithful secretary Schindler persuaded him to abandon and return home. On the other hand, in May 1824, there was a historic concert at the Kärntnertor theatre at which the Ninth Symphony, the Kyrie, Credo and Agnus Dei from the *Missa Solemnis* and the overture, 'The Consecration of the House', were performed. Beethoven had to be turned round to witness the applause which he could not hear. Yet, even this occasion went sour: the financial outcome was not so good owing to the heavy expenses, and there was a row in public, when Beethoven accused Schindler of cheating him. Besides, Beethoven had had a struggle with the censors who maintained that the excerpts from the Mass should not be performed in a concert.

In 1826, Beethoven started work on a Tenth Symphony. After having had a genuine attempt at reconciliation with Karl, there was a further row. In December 1826, he visited his brother at Gneixendorf, along the Danube towards Melk; on the return journey, he caught pneumonia. 'I have been prostrated with the dropsy since the 3rd December', he

* Tragically, Weber showed early symptoms of the tuberculosis from which his mother had died. The bank in which he had invested his and his wife's savings collapsed. Desperate to provide for his family, and against medical advice, he accepted an invitation from Charles Kemble, the London theatre manager, to write an opera. He took 153 lessons in English, and set off via Paris, where Rossini tried to dissuade him from going on. In London, he conducted *Oberon*. On the morning of 5 June 1826, they broke into his room and found him dead. He was not yet 40.

recorded.[180] Dr Malfatti was called in, among other doctors, and prescribed iced punch. Beethoven wrote to London about a possible benefit concert: he was still, but unnecessarily, concerned about his finances.* The London Philharmonic Society sent him £100 through Rothschilds, and he asked Schindler to write and thank them for it. Schindler wrote: 'Even on the brink of the grave he thanked the Society and the whole English nation for the great gift.'[182] Beethoven wrote to the publishers Schotts at Mainz asking for some Rhine or Moselle wine which Dr Malfatti had prescribed. But it did not arrive until he was dying: 'Pity, Pity, too late', he commented. These seem to be some of his last words.[183]

He died, probably of cirrhosis of the liver,[184] on 26 March 1827, at a quarter to six in the evening. Ironically, the only actual witness at his death was Johanna, 'The Queen of the Night'.** An acquaintance of Schubert's viewed the body on the following day. It was in a room almost unfurnished apart from the six-octave Broadwood grand piano which the English had sent him, and a coffin. The acquaintance, who was with a friend, noticed that the smell of corruption was already very strong. They asked for a lock from Beethoven's head, but the attendant had to wait until three fops, tapping their canes on their pantaloons, had left; and, after he had been given a tip, the attendant gave them the hair in a piece of paper.[185]

Three days after Beethoven's death, 20,000 people crowded into the square in front of the house. 'The funeral, so different from Mozart's, was commensurate with the immense fame he had acquired in his lifetime.'[186] Hummel was a pallbearer and the torchbearers included Czerny, Schubert, the poet Franz Grillparzer and Schuppanzigh, a prominent violinist. An oration written by Grillparzer was read by an actor at the gates of the cemetery in Währing, where Beethoven was first buried.

Thus ended Beethoven's stormy, tempestuous life. For us, it is the sheer power and beauty of his music which is so overwhelming. The whirlwind Seventh Symphony; the 'Hammerklavier', the Agnus Dei of the *Missa Solemnis* ... it is pointless to provide examples, there are just so many.

* Beethoven's assets at death were over 10,000 fl, the equivalent of two years' salary for a leading singer at the opera, or a senior civil servant.[181]

** There is also a suggestion that the witness was just 'a maid'.

Schubert

CHAPTER 6

'Music has here entombed a rich treasure, but much fairer hopes', was Franz Grillparzer's epitaph to Schubert.[1] The poet was referring to the composer's premature death, aged only 31. Little did he realise the size of the hoard, which was gradually unearthed through the 19th century. Few had any inkling of how much Schubert had achieved in those few years, composing symphonies, quartets, quintets and masses, and the wonderful piano music.

We shall always associate Schubert with glorious melody, particularly with the *Lied*, the accompanied German song. Many composers at the time wrote songs.* A ready market for them was provided by the growing middle class, in whose houses there was often a piano to be found, and who considered that an ability to make music was a sign of social advancement.[3] Schubert's songs are not just 'settings' of poems by prominent contemporary poets, such as Goethe and Schiller. Rather, he used each poem to create an entirely new and balanced composition. It is almost as if the poem was the landscape, whereas the song was the landscape painting, the

* Sometimes composers used a group of poems to create a song cycle comprising songs with a common theme, perhaps by one poet. Beethoven did this with his song cycle *An die Ferne Geliebte*. On a lower plane, many composers also arranged extracts from operas.[2]

work of art. Leading composers of *Lieder*, such as Brahms, Hugo Wolf and Richard Strauss, would look back primarily to Schubert for inspiration and as an example to follow.

Even Schubert's instrumental music is 'bursting to be sung'.[4] The listener emerging from a performance of the Great C major Symphony will have its melodies ringing in his ears. For earlier composers, melody had been mainly a means of providing contrast. For his contemporary Weber, the object of melody was to provide colour. With Schubert, melody, pure lyricism, has become an 'end in itself'.[5]

Schubert's short life was spent almost wholly in his birthplace, Vienna, although he took occasional summer trips to Hungary or into the Austrian mountains. He was precocious: by the time he turned nineteen, he had already composed his Third Symphony and over 200 songs, including the two for which he used Goethe's poems 'Gretchen am Spinnrade' and 'Erlkönig'.[6] Much of Schubert's subsequent energy was wasted in a fruitless effort to write an opera, then seen as the crock-of-gold for all composers; he completed seven of them.[7] His final years were astonishingly creative. It is all the more incredible that some of his greatest works were produced when suffering from the symptoms of his fatal disease, chronic headaches and giddiness, for example.

Schubert died only around a year and a half after Beethoven, who, stone-deaf, slovenly and sodden in alcohol, had long been out of tune with life in the Habsburg capital. Vienna was a dazzling place, with lots of dancing, several theatres and much gaiety. Schubert himself provided a focus for a small circle of 'bohemian' friends whose main interests, music, drink and sex, were not particularly exceptional, other than in extent. The traditional picture of Schubert is, however, of a man who was unassuming and self-effacing. A story is told how, in the salon of Princess Kinsky, the audience applauded the singer but ignored the accompanist. The princess felt she should commiserate; however, Schubert, peering through his spectacles, said that he preferred being unnoticed, 'for it made him feel less embarrassed'.[8] One friend said: 'He disliked bowing and scraping, and listening to flattering talk about himself he found down-right nauseating.'[9]

Birth and Youth

Franz Schubert was born on 31 January 1797, in the Himmelpfortgrund, a slum area which the authorities had allowed to develop well back from the walls of central Vienna. The Schuberts lived in Nussdorferstrasse in a building which housed around 70 people in 16 tiny 'apartments'. From the small courtyard with its pump, a stone staircase leads up to the 25-square-metre tenement. Franz was the twelfth of fourteen children, of whom only four boys and a girl survived into childhood. Older than him were Ignaz, who was a hunchback, Ferdinand and Karl; Maria Theresa was born four years later.[10]

Franz's uncle had come to Vienna from Moravia to teach at the Carmelite School in Leopoldstadt, which is just behind the Prater amusement park and some distance from the birthplace. As so frequently happened then, he married the widow of his predecessor and became headmaster. The standard fee per child was very modest, but, because the school had a poor reputation when he took over, he sometimes received less than the standard rate.[11]

Franz's father joined his brother as his assistant in about 1783 and later had his own school in the Himmelpfortgrund. Franz's mother, Elizabeth, was in domestic service and her brother was a weaver. Her father had been fortunate to escape to Vienna from Silesia after he had been accused of embezzlement, a crime for which he could easily have been executed.[12]

It is often suggested that the first music which Schubert heard was the military music when, on Easter Day 1797, the troops went forth to face Napoleon. News that the French were marching on Vienna probably had little effect on the Schubert family: there was nothing they could do, unlike the court which was 'packing enormous trunks into carriages preparing to flee before the French advance'.[13] Franz's mother, who presumably had experienced the effects of the devastating wars in Silesia, must have been apprehensive for her newborn child. The deprivations arising from the Napoleonic wars, and which Beethoven lived through, must have made her task particularly difficult.

As he grew up, Franz was taught the violin by his father and the piano by Ignaz. He also studied with the organist at the parish church, who observed: 'If I wished to instruct him in anything fresh, he already knew it. Consequently I gave him no actual tuition but merely conversed with him and watched with silent astonishment.'[14]

When he was eleven, he was entered, in response to an advertisement, for a choral scholarship at the Imperial and Royal City College. One of the two examiners was the great Antonio Salieri himself. The scene reminds one of little Haydn: on the one hand, the smooth, international, highly successful courtier; on the other, the tiny boy accompanied by the humble father. So much was at stake.

The school, next to St Stephen's Cathedral, was run by Piarists, religious brothers dedicated to education. Although it was called unprepossessingly 'the Konvikt',* it was a prominent boarding school for commoners.[16] It had about 130 boarders, divided into 7 houses. Beethoven would later resist an attempt to get his nephew transferred there, because he thought that the supervision was inadequate.[17] But, for a boy with Franz's background, the school could provide a considerable leap forward: there, he would meet the sons of nobles, army officers and officials. The school uniform was a dark brown coat with a small gilt epaulet on the left shoulder, a white neck-cloth, knickerbockers, buckled shoes and a low three-cornered hat. Imagine the pride, the joy, the hopes, when little Franz won his scholarship! One wonders how the family could afford the clothes.

Soon after Franz joined the school, another attack by Napoleon caused some excitement. Several of the boys attempted to enrol in the army and were called back. Then, during the bombardment of Vienna, around the time that Haydn was dying, the school buildings were hit by a grenade, which exploded in the prefects' room; the little boys were disappointed that the prefects were not in the room at the time.[18]

Schubert was given good reports. His studies were 'good', his morals were 'very good', and he had 'a musical talent'.[19] He was taught by the court organist and by Salieri. It was not long before he was being commended. He became leader of the school orchestra, which was run by a young university student, Josef von Spaun, who was eight years older. Spaun obtained some manuscript paper for Schubert who was too poor to buy it himself. And he took him to the opera, where the boy was moved to tears by Gluck's *Iphigénie en Tauride*. Spaun, an official in lottery administration, became a lifelong friend, and was crucial in introducing Schubert to his widening circle of friends. In particular, he brought him in touch with the bureaucrats, intellectuals, doctors and so forth, the middle class of the time.**

Nevertheless, at this stage Schubert was a bit of a loner: 'He was silent and uncommunicative', wrote one of his friends. 'Even on the walks which

* This is based on the Latin word 'convictorium', a communal house. Mozart also wanted his son Karl to be registered at the Piarist school.[15]

** This was a different circle from the more aristocratic circle which was Beethoven's milieu, when he was not alone.[20]

the pupils took together, he mostly kept apart, walking pensively along with lowered eyes and with his hands behind his back, playing with his fingers (as though on keys), completely lost in his own thoughts.'[21]

During the school holidays, the Schubert family, which by then had moved to larger quarters not far from Franz's birthplace, formed their own string ensemble. Schubert wrote his early quartets for this. In later years, this family group became a mini-orchestra capable of playing Haydn symphonies.

When Schubert was thirteen, his musical creativity took off. His first complete work was a fantasie for four hands. He then wrote the Six Minuets for wind instruments and the song 'Hagar's Klage'. But this period was a sad one. When he was fifteen, his mother died of 'nervous fever'. His father remarried and fortunately Schubert acquired a stepmother who was sufficiently kind to lend him money in later years.[22]

Around the time of his mother's death, Schubert's voice broke and, after the performance of a mass, he scribbled on his part, 'Schubert, Franz, crowed for the last time, July 26th, 1812'.[23] In the following year, his future came up for review. The emperor, who has been described as 'one of the most influential mediocrities of modern times',[24] took a close interest in school matters. This possibly explains why Salieri wisely took a keen interest as well. In the week before the battle of Leipzig, and in the field, the Emperor of Austria, who was notoriously bad at delegating, and known to have as many as 2,000 reports piling up on his desk at any one time,[25] was dealing with endowments involving Schubert and three others. Then, a couple of days after the battle, still in the field, the emperor stipulated the terms on which Schubert could continue; he emphasised the primary importance of general studies, and observed that 'singing and music are a subsidiary matter'.[26]

But Schubert did not want to take the necessary examination in general studies, so he left the Konvikt in October 1813, and went to a teacher training school also near the cathedral. When, a year later, he passed the exam to qualify as a primary school teacher, he took over the responsibility for the infants' class in his father's school. This earned him 80 florins a year, which represented less than a fifth of the 450 fl salary typically earned by a fully qualified teacher or junior civil servant.*[27] The fact that Franz had

* In 1818 a gentleman would need 2,000 fl per annum to live well in Vienna. Rank and file musicians at the opera earned 480 fl. Cooks and butlers in a grand household might earn between 300 and 400 fl; a sedan chair bearer would do better, at 625–780 fl. In 1824, Beethoven charged his publisher 600 fl for the Ninth Symphony; Schubert's *Lieder* earned him about 20–25 fl each.

joined the school no doubt in some ways pleased his father, of whom he was very fond. Teaching in the small schools was a family affair; Ignaz took over from his father as headmaster, eventually.[28]

Meanwhile, lessons were continued with Salieri. They stopped when Schubert was nineteen, because Salieri disliked Schubert's growing interest in the poetry of the German Romantics. However, Schubert must have felt that he owed a lot to Salieri, because for his 50th jubilee in 1816, Schubert's contribution included the words, 'kindness and wisdom flow from thee, as God's own image thou'rt to me'.[29]

Towards the Middle Years

Schubert lived quietly at home in the schoolhouse. As a schoolmaster, he could avoid compulsory military service, which could last fourteen years and was applied to men aged from 18 to 45. Also, he was too short: he was only about five feet tall, and had poor sight.[30] Indeed, his spectacles, which are now in his birthplace museum, are notably small, and indicate that he had a small head as well.

Schubert's school duties probably left him with much spare time. He had enormous energy and his output of music in the next three years was astonishing.[31] Nearly half the works listed in the thematic catalogue of his works drawn up by Otto Deutsch belong to those years.[32] In his eighteenth year, he composed two symphonies, four operas, two masses and other liturgical works, several piano works, a string quartet in G minor and about 150 songs.

Spaun, his friend at school, claimed that the well-known song 'Erlkönig', with its urgency created by galloping triplets, and its dramatic end, was composed in just one afternoon; he walked into the schoolroom and found Schubert composing it.*[33] When, in due course, 'Erlkönig' was sent to the publishers Breitkopf & Härtel, they assumed that it was by the Franz Schubert who was a string player in Dresden.** They sent it on to him; he was furious at someone using his name and, unfortunately for his future reputation, described the work as 'rubbish'.[35]

* The last two bars sung by the soloist, 'In his arms the child was dead', are in the form of a recitative. Spaun's story seems improbable in view of the time necessary merely to copy out the work, let alone compose it.

** In later years, Clara Schumann used to play trios with his son, the violinist Franz Schubert, leader of the Dresden orchestra, and his cellist brother Friedrich.[34]

Spaun sent some of Schubert's settings to Goethe, who took no notice and just returned them. This behaviour was not unusual for Goethe and there was a later occasion when Goethe did not even reply. Schubert was not the only composer he overlooked: he kept Weber waiting in an anteroom, twice sending out to enquire what 'the man's' name was.[36] When eventually Weber was admitted into the presence, he was shown a chair, asked about a few acquaintances in Dresden and then summarily dismissed. Yet Goethe was quite capable of being gracious: Mendelssohn, as a boy, sent Goethe some piano music and received a fulsome letter of thanks. But Mendelssohn was a banker's son.[37]

Johann Wolfgang von Goethe, whose poetry inspired Schubert and so many songwriters

Schubert wrote the Mass in F for the centenary of his local church. Salieri attended the performance at which Schubert conducted and his brother Ferdinand played the organ. This coincided with the start of the Congress of Vienna. Ten days later, a performance of Schubert's mass was attended by several of the delegates to the Congress. It was held in the royal Augustinerkirche, just beside the palace, the Hofburg. Schubert's father was so proud that he is said to have presented his son with a piano, an enormous expense.

Schubert fell in love with his soloist, Theresa Grob, whose mother ran a silk business near the church. Theresa was 'not by any means a beauty, but well shaped, fairly buxom, with a fresh childlike little round face and a fine soprano voice'.[38] As an impecunious schoolmaster, Schubert was hardly looked upon as an eligible son-in-law. He applied, helped by a reference from Salieri, for a teaching post at Laibach (now Ljubljana). This would have paid him an annual salary of 450 fl.[39] But he was not appointed, so, a few years later, Theresa married a baker.

In autumn 1816, Schubert gave up teaching and began a career as a freelance composer. This seemed a viable proposition as he was beginning to obtain some recognition, even if it was in narrow circles. He was commissioned to write the cantata, 'Prometheus', which was performed on 24 July 1816, in the garden of the house in which he now lodged. Schubert received 100 fl and proudly noted in his diary: 'today I composed for money for the first time'.[40]

At the end of 1817, Schubert's father was appointed to another school, in the Rossau district, slightly nearer the Inner City but in much the same area. The previous master had been sacked for breach of discipline.[41] This more commodious accommodation became the base for the family, which now included two sons and two daughters of the second marriage.

Schubert's Circle of Friends: Schubertiads

'Prometheus' was written in honour of a music professor who taught some of Schubert's friends, including Spaun. This professor was what we might describe as being 'Leftist'. Schubert's circle widened to include several 'angry young men' who had the normal radical views of their years, but who were also arty and able.* None of them remotely reached the greatness of Schubert; they eventually went about their own different careers. Some of them settled down to become reputable artists, like Moritz von Schwind, the brilliant illustrator of German fairytales. Others, like the distant and aloof poet Johann Mayrhofer, had eventually to sell their souls: he became an official in the censorship department.

Some were typical of any middle-class group: Josef Hüttenbrenner, member of a very supportive family for Schubert, became his 'business manager'. There were several women in the circle, such as the four very

* Schubert was a member of the Nonsense Society, a secret men's club of intellectuals who met in 1817–18 for private weekly entertainment.

musical Fröhlich sisters at whose house Franz Grillparzer, who was to become the national poet of Austria, lodged. But, although one of the women taught at the Philharmonic Society's conservatoire, and another was a good mezzo-soprano, they were not especially prominent.[42]

As well as simply providing an audience, Schubert's friends raised his sights socially. Schwind was the son of a court secretary. The Fröhlich sisters were daughters of a 'nobleman, turned merchant'.[43] The poet Franz von Bruchmann was the son of a rich merchant and patron of the arts.

The friends also had an important artistic effect. Mayrhofer's poetry introduced Schubert to the notion of longing for the unreachable. And they helped him 'network', so crucial for a freelance. In the chorus for 'Prometheus' was Grillparzer's cousin, Leopold Sonnleithner. His uncle was Beethoven's first librettist for *Fidelio*, and his father had published music for Beethoven and was prominent in the formation of the Vienna Philharmonic Society. The Sonnleithners held a regular salon on alternate Fridays throughout the winter: up to 120 guests attended it. Schubert became a frequent visitor there and at other well-known middle-class salons where leading playwrights, poets and thinkers of the age were to be found.

In addition, the Sonnleithners helped Schubert to get some of his works published. This was an uphill struggle, because the key to getting a work published was to be well known as a virtuoso performer, which he was not. He never performed in public as a solo pianist other than as an accompanist for his own songs. Yet the Sonnleithners managed to achieve the publication of 'Erlkönig', 'Gretchen am Spinnrade', and altogether twenty songs by the end of 1821. This, and the salon appearances, meant that Schubert's reputation spread among the growing middle class of Vienna.[44]

The group of friends also provided friendship, fun and sometimes lodgings. Schubert lodged with Mayrhofer, who was almost certainly a homosexual,[45] although there is no reason to suppose that Schubert was other than heterosexual. He also lodged with the cultured law student Franz von Schober, son of a councillor. Just a bit older than Schubert, Schober had come from Malmö, where as a boy he had watched Nelson's bombardment of Copenhagen in 1801.[46]

Schober took Schubert to parties held at part of the Klosterneuburg monastery estate at the foot of the Vienna Woods, about seven miles from the city. He introduced him to J.M. Vogl, the first Pizzaro in the revised

Fidelio, and a leading baritone. Vogl – described as 'a gentleman, tall, well-educated and uncommonly well-read … somewhat gruff … his play with an eye-glass, when seated beside the piano, was a little foppish' – used Schubert as an accompanist in drawing rooms.[47]

The composition of the group of friends surrounding Schubert changed as people came and went, or disappeared into jobs or marriage. There were also the tensions typical in a small group, for example, when Schober went off with Bruchmann's sister.

These friends took part in reading parties which met two or three times a week. They also took part in what became known as Schubertiads (see colour plate 16). These were lively get-togethers, which combined Schubert's music with eating, drinking, literary discussions and dances. They also featured games, gymnastics and wild excursions into the countryside. The participants would eventually land up carousing in a pub. So we read: 'at first there was a Schubertiad, then supper, then a ball, then a drinking bout, all very jolly … It was 2 o'clock before we left, in the seventh heaven'.[48] 'On every Wednesday and Saturday evening we go to the ale-house … Nearly every day to Bogner's coffee-house.'*[50] The Schubertiads were eventually infiltrated by a hearty element, whom one friend described as 'our billiard-playing fraternity'.[51] It comes as no surprise that Schubert composed his best music for other occasions.

The behaviour at Schubertiads was consistent with the obsession for gaiety which prevailed in Vienna. Because our image of the capital at this time can easily be dominated by the dour, brooding figure of Beethoven, we can easily forget that it was a 'fun' place in which to be. From the start of the century, there was an almost non-stop craze for dancing and light music, a waltz mania.** The top echelons of society would compete ferociously to be included on the list of invitees to a dance. Restaurants offered dancing, especially in the Carnival season between Christmas and Lent, and, in the larger restaurants, one could hear the bands of Lanner and

*Even by 1770, Vienna had 21 cafés, 45 inns, 111 beer houses. Genuine coffee, unavailable during the Continental blockade, could be had again from 1813.[49]

** On one night in 1821, 1,600 balls took place. In the 1823 Carnival there were 772 balls attended by over 200,000 persons. Balls began about 8 or 9 pm and went on until 3–4 am. The next generation was not overlooked: in 1832, there were two children's balls. Dances were highly regulated, and they were also subject to a special tax. Dance halls could easily have their privileges revoked by the authorities.

Strauss. Itinerant harpists, zither players and folk singers performed in the taverns, the *Heurige*; street hawkers would even sell sheet music. Not surprisingly, Schubert earned fees for his contributions to anthologies of new dances.[52]

The Viennese were also very enthusiastic about the theatre. The upper classes would go to the Burg or Kärntnertor theatres, the lower classes flocked to shows of travelling troupes in the suburban theatres, the Theater an der Wien and the theatres in the Leopoldstadt and Josephstadt suburbs. Seats could not be reserved, so, to get a decent one, one had to push and shove. As with the dance halls, the theatres were strictly regulated, and, of course, the plays were subject to censorship. Encores and curtain calls were prohibited. However, enforcement in the suburbs seems to have been relatively lax.[53]

As well as dances and theatres, there were other 'attractions' such as firework displays and balloon ascents. In one year, Eskimos were on display, paddling and rolling their canoes; they were sited next to the skating lake of the Belvedere Palace, in the hope that they might feel more at home there.[54]

Maybe lightheartedness was sometimes taken too far. The Mass at St Stephen's Cathedral was more a social than a religious occasion. It was said that 'the priest who is able to do it in the shortest time, about twelve minutes, is surrounded by the greatest crowd'.[55] This applied not only at St Stephen's: Midnight Mass generally acquired the name Hurenmesse, since the ladies of the night found it best to advertise their services in the churches, thus avoiding the police who were patrolling the streets.

The Police

The wilder groups such as those frequented by Schubert attracted the attention of the police, whose activity was pervasive, as Beethoven had observed. To survive, one needed to be circumspect. Governments throughout Europe were concerned about an upsurge in liberalism, precisely of the kind for which Schubert's friends stood.* The new generation were 'enraged by the spectacle of the same old men creeping back into the same old positions … denying to youth those opportunities which, in the

* The regime lurched 'from complacency to paranoia'.[56] This neurosis was personified by the novelist Stendhal's portrayal of the Prince of Parma, 'a ridiculous tyrant, who gets up at night to look under his bed'.[57] Reactionaries, who still wore wigs and powdered their hair, were easily identifiable.

gay dawn of Liberation, had seemed so glamorous'.[58] Mayrhofer and some of Spaun's family combined to publish a literary journal under the innocuous title, *Contributions to the Education of Young People*: it was probably regarded as subversive.[59]

Some of the activity was particularly demonstrative. At the end of 1817, several hundred 'long-haired and bearded' students,[60] largely from Jena University, about 50 miles from Leipzig, organised a meeting in order to celebrate the tercentenary of the Lutheran reformation and the fourth anniversary of the battle of Leipzig. They met at the Wartburg near Eisenach and had a bonfire of reactionary books and pamphlets.

Two years later, a young theological student assassinated the prominent playwright and journalist Kotzebue, whose works Schubert used as libretti for some early operas.*[63] Kotzebue, who was in the pay of the tsar, had ridiculed the liberal ideas of the German students. The chancellor, the powerful Prince Metternich, who has been described as 'a pompous pedant who was constantly telling everyone that two and two made four, not five, and that all actions had consequences',[64] saw the assassination as the opportunity to crush the liberal movement in Germany. A meeting of German states was called at Karlsbad in Bohemia, where decrees were issued ordering the dissolution of student societies, the censorship of the German press, and the appointment of 'curators' to supervise the universities. Censorship was extended to include works such as Schiller's *William Tell* and Grillparzer's dramas.[65]

The disruption was not just confined to 'German' territories. A revolution in Naples was firmly suppressed. This was led by the Carbonari, whose ranks had been swelled by former Napoleonic officers and officials. The Carbonari advocated the assassination of despotic kings and wanted to establish an egalitarian republic. They had a structure and ritual similar to that of the Freemasons, and had branches in Spain and France, and contacts in England.**

In Manchester, there was a large demonstration, known subsequently as

* Jane Austen used an adaptation of one of Kotzebue's plays, *Lovers' Vows*, for the amateur theatricals which caused an uproar in *Mansfield Park*.[61] Kotzebue's plays also reached the provincial Russia featured by Gogol in his novel *Dead Souls*.[62]

** The cell structure evolved by the Carbonari ensured that no ordinary member knew anyone but the members of his own cell; deputies of twenty particular cells comprised a more senior cell, which sent a deputy to a yet higher cell, which reported to a directing committee.[66]

'the Peterloo Massacre', which was badly handled by the magistrates and the army, so that eleven were killed and hundreds severely wounded. In London, six months later, there was the Cato Street conspiracy, in which extremist reformers planned to assassinate ministers at a dinner party and to seize the Bank and the Tower of London. There were mutinies in the garrison in Cadiz, and in a crack regiment of the Russian Imperial Guard. An heir-apparent to the throne of France, the Duc de Berri, was assassinated outside the Paris Opéra.

The authorities were rattled, including the chief of police in Vienna, who was known as the 'dust on Metternich's soles'.[67] So it is not particularly surprising to find the police raiding the lodgings of one of Schubert's friends from Konvikt days. From the police report, one can picture the circumstances. Schubert's friend said that 'he did not care a damn about the police' and 'the government was too stupid to be able to penetrate into his secrets'. Others with him, including Schubert, described as the school assistant, 'chimed in, in the same tone ... with abusive language'.[68] They were taken in for questioning. Schubert seems to have escaped with a few bruises and 'a black eye'.[69] He might have regarded this as merely comical, had his friend not been imprisoned for fourteen months and then banished to the Tyrol.

Summer in the Country

Schubert got himself a nice summer job in the country, teaching music to the children of Count Esterházy, a distant relative of the prince for whom Haydn had worked for so many years. In the second half of 1818, with a travel permit from the police, he set off to Zseliz (now Želiezovce), then in Hungary, now in Slovakia. Perhaps surprisingly, the Hungarian tinge some listeners hear in Schubert's works has been attributed to his two short trips into modern Slovakia.[70]

Although occupied by an Esterházy, the Zseliz residence is tiny compared to the princely palace at Esterháza.[71] It was a small, elegant, single-storey country house a few hundred yards from a tributary to the Danube, about twenty miles north of Gran.* Schubert went there by coach, a long journey of fourteen stages.[72] It was twelve years before a steamboat service

* A fire had destroyed a large part of Gran in the April before Schubert went to Zseliz. Today Gran is called Esztergom. It is only about 25 miles from Budapest.

would be run by a couple of Englishmen along the Danube to Gran,[73] and three years before the building started on the colossal basilica, modelled on St Peter's in Rome, which was to feature in Liszt's life.

Schubert was delighted to get away to the countryside. Zseliz is located in rather a flat area, although there are the hills of the Danube Bend in the far distance. But the birds singing in the trees, the river, the whole environment must have been a welcome contrast from Schubert's squalid urban existence. He wrote that he was surrounded by a most beautiful garden, and one can still see mature trees and a little brook close to the ruined house; a river about the width of the Thames at Oxford flows by about 500 yards away. It is no wonder that he was enthusiastic at first.

The Esterházys were musical: the count sang bass, Countess Rosine, who called herself Heidenröslein (after Goethe's poem, before Schubert wrote the song), was a contralto. Marie was aged sixteen, Caroline was thirteen and Albert was seven.[74] Schubert was paid an exceptionally handsome fee of 76 fl per month.[75]

Schubert did not live in the main house, but was in the servants' annex. 'It is fairly quiet, save for some forty geese', he wrote, 'the cook rather a rake, the lady's maid thirty years of age.' He continued: 'The Count is rather rough, the Countess haughty but more sensitive; the little Countesses are nice children. So far I have been spared dining with the family.'[76]

This is when we first hear specifically of Schubert's fateful womanising. He had an affair with Pepi, the countess' chambermaid, who was 'very pretty and often my companion'.[77] Pepi ultimately married the valet.[78]

Schubert wrote to his friends, 'I compose like a God … Thank God I live at last, and it was high time.'[79] He wrote several piano duets, and composed a Requiem for his brother Ferdinand to pass off as his own. On a more prosaic note, he wrote home saying that he needed some handkerchiefs, scarves and stockings and two pairs of cashmere trousers; and he assured his family that his laundry was well looked after.

He was there for four months. It began to pall. 'Not a soul here has any feeling for true Art, except, at best, the Countess occasionally.'[80] When the Esterházys returned to Vienna for the winter, the vacation work came to a halt; but Schubert continued to give the children lessons, in the winter months. On his return, he lodged with the reclusive poet Mayrhofer in a single room on the third floor of a tobacconist's, close to the old town hall.

For his *Lieder*, Schubert used a large number of his poems: indeed Mayrhofer was almost his favourite poet, second only to Goethe.[81]

In the following year, Schubert, having obtained the necessary police permits, went on the first of several country holidays, which provided him with relaxation and inspiration. He went with the baritone Michael Vogl to Steyr, Vogl's birthplace 90 miles west of Vienna. Steyr was a prosperous provincial town, its merchants living in their fine houses decorated with stucco.* Schubert described the scenery as 'inconceivably lovely';[82] it is a different world from Zseliz. Steyr's castle stands at the confluence of two rivers, with swans sailing where the differently tinged waters merge. Looking up the river Enns, one's eye is attracted to the snow-capped mountains in the distance.[83]

Schubert and Vogl stayed in the house of a mining engineer. The doyen of the musical circle, the local manager of the mines who played the cello, commissioned the Trout Quintet: he apparently suggested using the tune of 'Die Forelle' as a theme. Schubert wrote a Piano Sonata in A major for the daughter of a local iron merchant. He clearly had an eye for pretty girls.[84]

A Search for an Opera

Schubert's attention now turned towards opera. For the rest of his short life, Schubert was to try his hand at this; but he had only around ten years left to live.

Rossini's operas showed that vast sums were to be made in Italian opera. Rossini was promoted by the Neapolitan impresario Domenico Barbaja (see page 244), who dominated what was to be a golden age for the impresario: he spotted Bellini and Donizetti as well. Starting as a waiter, Barbaja is reputed to have first made money out of patenting coffee or chocolate topped with whipped cream. He exploited the retail potential of opera house floor space, by using the front of the house as a casino, where the new game of roulette could be played. In 1821, he took over the Burg theatre in Vienna, and ran Italian opera there.[85] This coincided with the time that the efforts of composers to establish German opera came to fruition with Weber's successful *Der Freischütz* (see page 206). Barbaja asked Weber

* Towards the end of the century, Steyr would be a retreat for Bruckner, who composed his final works in a house next to the gothic parish church. Now it is the location of the Steyr-Daimler-Puch motor works. The breech-loaded rifle was invented at Steyr, which at one time was an important centre for the manufacture of armaments.

to write a German opera for the 1822–3 season. But Weber's *Euryanthe* had a very complicated story and could not compete with the Viennese craze for Italian opera.*

Schubert was among the composers who tried to create a German opera. In January 1819, he finished writing a one-act comic opera, *Die Zwillingsbrüder*. The management of the Kärntnertor theatre commissioned this for a staged-payment fee totalling 500 fl; but, because of the preferential treatment given to Italian opera, it was not produced until summer 1820, when Vogl performed in it, acting the roles of both the twin brothers; another part was taken by Constanze Mozart's brother-in-law. Constanze's son observed that the 'composition contains some quite pretty things but is kept a little too serious'.[86] It was withdrawn after a further five performances.

Like many great symphonic composers, apart from Mozart, Schubert was to find that composing opera was very difficult.[87] Reviews of *Die Zwillingsbrüder* suggested that his abilities lay more with tragedy than with comedy. His next opera, *Die Zauberharfe*, was thought to be too long; it was 'ineffective and fatiguing, the harmonic progressions are too harsh, the orchestration redundant, the choruses dull and feeble'.[88] It ran to eight performances only. The overture to *Die Zauberharfe*, known as the 'Rosamunde' Overture, is all that is remembered of it now.[89]

The waltzing Viennese much preferred to hear Italians such as Rossini or virtuoso performers such as the Italian virtuoso violinist Niccolò Paganini. A concert put on called 'Franz Schubert's Invitation Concert' received hardly a line in the press, although the net proceeds provided Schubert with 320 fl.[90] Of course, his earnings were a pittance compared to the receipts of the pop stars such as Paganini.** But, if 450 fl was the annual pay of a schoolteacher or minor civil servant, the money provided by the concert was perhaps not too bad for a local composer in his early

* The medieval romance about Euryanthe is set in France in the reign of Louis the Fat. It was not a good subject for a German opera. The librettist, a minor poet, rewrote the complicated libretto eleven times. At least she realised that it might be rather difficult to stage a scene where a mole on the heroine's breast is espied through a hole in the bathroom wall.

** Schubert was earning 1,500 fl per annum between 1826 and 1828. Paganini is said to have earned over 30,000 fl from his concerts in Vienna. Even if it is necessary to discount the Paganini remuneration to 12,000 fl to reflect the new currency, it may be best just to regard it as 'a very large amount'. People fainted during Paganini's concerts, although this may just have been from the heat. The Kärntnertor theatre was said to be 'tropical' inside, and the Burg theatre not much better.

twenties. Schubert also supplemented his earnings with some coaching work at the theatre.

In September 1821, Schubert and Schober worked together on an opera, *Alfonso und Estrella*, while staying in the castle of Schober's relative, the Bishop of St Pölten. It was finished in the following February, but was turned down by the theatre management. The audience just wanted to see Italian opera. Attempts to get *Alfonso* staged in other cities around Europe, including sending it to Weber, failed as well. Other works such as *Fierabras*, set in the time of Charlemagne, also got nowhere; as did incidental music to *Rosamunde*, a play by Weber's librettist for *Euryanthe*. Schubert's quest for opera continued until the end of his life: a couple of days before he died, he was talking about his opera venture *Der Graf von Gleichen*. At least not all his energy was going into opera. In 1822, he wrote, or started to write, many other works, including many songs. This was the year in which he wrote the 'Wanderer' Fantasy for Piano and the Unfinished* Symphony in B minor.[92]

Schubert's productivity was immense. He was climbing laboriously uphill, quite successfully for a composer who was not Italian. It seems that he was receiving some recognition in a relatively small corner of Vienna. However, on the whole, Schubert remained unknown and unaccepted in what has been described as an inglorious phase in German music publishing.[93] Even a few years later, an attempt to get Breitkopf to publish got a frosty reply preceded with the reservation: 'We are as yet wholly unacquainted with the commercial success of your composition.'[94] A similar response was received from the publishers, Peters. The Viennese publishing house, Artaria, responded with: 'our public does not yet sufficiently and generally understand the peculiar, often ingenious, but perhaps now and then somewhat curious procedures of your mind's creations. Kindly therefore bear this in mind on sending me your manuscripts.'[95] Schubert's works were thought to be too difficult, or they suffered from being poorly rehearsed when performed.[96]

Suddenly, though, there was a change in Schubert's behaviour. He no longer lodged with Schober, but was back at the Rossau schoolhouse. It is

* Schubert failed to complete several works; 'he reached the point where the invention stalls, temporarily one hopes, after repeated attempts to move forward, the stalling point becomes fixed and immutable, like a corroded screw'.[91]

reasonably certain that, at the end of 1822 or the beginning of 1823, he caught syphilis. Possibly, this is why the Unfinished Symphony was unfinished. B minor is a most unusual key for a symphony; it is a key associated in Schubert's mind with sadness and loneliness. Whatever, something was very seriously wrong.[97]

Disease

Forty years after his death, Schober said: 'Schubert was recklessly promiscuous.'[98] The French novelist Gustave Flaubert realised, when he had caught syphilis, that women, then, could be 'hell beneath a skirt'.[99]

The disease, now rare, was common in the 19th century: during a visit to just one of Vienna's hospitals in 1828, a foreign doctor counted 190 cases of venereal disease. It has been estimated that twenty per cent of Paris suffered from syphilis towards the end of the second half of the 19th century.[100] Mozart's correspondence indicates that he was well aware of the dangers. The list of great artists who caught it is long. As we shall see, Donizetti died of it in an appalling condition. It is likely that Schumann had it, and Delius certainly did. Others who suffered from it included Paganini, Keats, Nietzsche, Stendhal and Maupassant.* Although various remedies were tried, there was no satisfactory cure until penicillin treatment became available in 1943. Treatment with potassium iodide started in 1836, but patients in Schubert's time were just given mercury ointment to rub on. The mercury caused headaches.

Within ten days to ten weeks of infection, the patient experiences what is usually called the primary stage, a hard, painless swelling, which heals quite quickly. This is followed, perhaps four to eight weeks later, by the second stage, which 'produces clinical manifestations in about half the persons infected'. The ominous symptoms are usually fever and a rash of spots on the chest and abdomen and upper thighs. Later, there are pea-size spots and an acne-like rash covering the body, including the face and palms.[102]

This second stage, which lasts for several months, is followed by a latent period,** when there is little or no sign of the disease. One in four might

* Gluck is suspected of having had venereal disease caught off an opera singer in Hamburg, who had previously been the mistress of the English envoy. Also, Brahms' brother may have had it.[101]
** The latent period often lasts between three and ten years; but it could also last much longer, up to around 30 years, or be overtaken by death from another cause.

then be expected to develop tertiary syphilis. In half of those, it is relatively benign but, for the other half, it is incapacitating or fatal.[103]

After he was first diagnosed, Schubert would have been advised by his doctors to stay at home. The earliest evidence that he had the disease is in a letter of 28 February 1823. He says that the state of his health still does not permit him to leave the house.[104] He had been put on a strict diet and confined to his room.

Soon, he was suffering some of the symptoms of secondary syphilis: face rash, hair loss, hoarseness and pain in bones. He also could not bear bright light: he screwed up his eyelids.

By late spring 1823, he was desperately ill, and it seems that he was admitted to Vienna General Hospital. From now on, his medical expenses would have been a continual drain on his resources. He began to despair. He wrote a poem, called 'My Prayer':

> See abased in dust and mire,
> Scorched by agonising fire,
> I in torture go my way,
> Nearing doom's destructive day.
> Take my life, my flesh and blood,
> Plunge it all in Lethe's flood,
> To a purer, stronger state,
> Deign me, Great One to translate.[105]

One of the recommended cures was fresh air and exercise, so, in the summer, we find him in Steyr again. He wrote to Schober: 'Whether I shall ever quite recover, I am inclined to doubt. Here, I live very simply in every respect, go for walks regularly, work much at my opera and read Walter Scott.'*[106] Beethoven was told in one of his conversation books: 'they greatly praise Schubert, but it is said that he hides himself'.[107]

The Latent Period Sets In

At the end of 1823, when, one may suppose, the latent period set in, there was some optimism. Schwind wrote to Schober: 'Schubert is better, and it will not be long before he goes about with his own hair again, which had to be shorn owing to the rash. He wears a very cosy wig.'[108] His doctor, Dr

* There was a craze at the time for the works of the Scottish novelist and poet, Sir Walter Scott.

Bernhardt, joined his inner circle of friends. Schubert continued composing.

But Schubert's poor health returned, whether directly because of the disease, or because of the mercury treatment, we do not know for certain. In the first part of 1824, he wrote two string quartets, one of which was No 14 in D minor, known as 'Death and the Maiden'. In early April, Schwind wrote that Schubert was so unwell that he could not play the piano at all. Schubert's own letters tell of his despair: 'Think of a man whose health will never be right again, and who in sheer despair over this always makes things worse instead of better', he wrote. 'Think of a man, I say, whose brightest hopes have come to nothing; for whom the happiness of love and friendship have nothing to offer but, at the best, pain; whose passion for beauty (at least the sort that inspires) threatens to forsake him.'[109] Schubert would experience headaches, sickness, aching bones, nausea and giddiness for the rest of his short life. Yet, despite this, he wrote a whole series of masterpieces.

Back to Zseliz

In May 1824, Schubert heard the first performance of Beethoven's Ninth Symphony and parts of the *Missa Solemnis.* He then returned to Zseliz for a second time. His brother Ferdinand was asked to correct the proofs of *Die Schöne Müllerin,* which was published while he was away.

Either the Esterházys had no idea of his medical condition, or they had absolute confidence in the iron rigidity of the social framework: otherwise, surely, they would not have been prepared to allow Schubert close to their daughters. Music teachers were sometimes notorious for abusing their access to female pupils: there are cartoons satirising Dr Burney doing just this.[110]

At Zseliz, the terms and conditions were far better than on the previous visit. Schubert was paid 100 fl a month. He stayed in one of the guest rooms in the main house and dined with the family. With the help of another visitor, a mutual friend, a quartet could be assembled in the evening. 'Gebet', a prayer quartet, was ordered by the family at breakfast time and was ready for the rehearsal in the drawing room in the evening.

Pepi was relegated to taking the post to Vienna. Schubert developed a passion, probably a sort of romantic longing from afar, for the younger Esterházy daughter, Caroline. This love was to cause some drollery among his friends. But it inspired him, and his Fantasie in F minor was dedicated to her. He was giving her lessons nine months before he died.[111]

He was lonely in that open countryside. He wrote to Schober in late September: 'Now I sit here alone in the depths of the Hungarian countryside where I unfortunately let myself be enticed a second time without having a single person with whom I could speak a sensible word.'[112] In the middle of October, he drove back the two-day journey to Vienna. Schubert managed to smash the window at the back of the coach at the end of the first day; so the second day was draughty and cold.[113]

Great Creativity

He returned to the schoolhouse, where he had ups and downs. In early November, Schwind wrote to Schober: 'Schubert is here, well and divinely frivolous and rejuvenated.'[114] Yet, there were no major works between October 1824 and April 1825, and he appears to have become unsociable. Possibly he had another stay in hospital around this time. By April 1825, he was able to enjoy the *Heurige* (new wine) and enjoyed long walks with his brothers.

In that summer, Schubert went with Vogl to Steyr. They visited many friends and had some Schubertiads. He also stayed in Gmunden in a house in the narrow streets. Among the treasures in the nearby church is a porcelain Virgin, the Madonna of the Cloak. It comes as no surprise that, in this beautiful town, Schubert composed the *Ave Maria*, in which he used Sir Walter Scott's poem, 'Ellen's Song'. The place is idyllic and romantic: the carillon sounds beautifully over the magnificent Lake Traun, and the colours change on the water as the sun sets, the silvers, the greys until there is just a silhouette, the fuzzy line of the trees on top of the hills. Here, he also sketched the Great C major Symphony.

Schubert and Vogl then went on to Linz where they were enrolled as members of the Linz Philharmonic Society. They travelled on into the mountains and to Salzburg. They were in Bad Gastein at a time when Constanze Mozart and her husband Nissen were there, so perhaps they met, as she knew Vogl.[115]

When he returned to Vienna, there were Schubertiads and late night sessions at inns and coffee houses often until 2 or 3 am.[116] Professionally, Schubert was making progress: his picture could be bought at one of the main music publishers in Vienna; his piano duets brought him some income. He was elected a deputy member of the council of representatives of the Philharmonic Society. But his reputation was still confined to a smallish circle: when a young English musician, who was keen to imitate Dr Burney's travels, came to Vienna, he heard nothing of Schubert and made no reference to him.

Salieri died around this time, as did the court organist. This led to a scramble for musical posts, and Schubert, increasingly in need of security, if not income, applied for the position of court organist. He was not appointed.[117]

In 1826, he completed the Great C major Symphony, his ninth, and in mid-summer his last, some would say 'the greatest', string quartet, the G major. On 10 July 1826, he wrote: 'I cannot possibly get to Gmunden or anywhere else, for I have no money at all.'[118] Approaches to top publishers proved unsuccessful. Nevertheless, his works were gradually, albeit from a very low base, being published and being performed at Philharmonic Society concerts.[119]

In the following year, he composed *Die Winterreise*. He completed the first part in March, the month of Beethoven's death, and the second in the autumn. Although it received a good review in the Viennese press, its deep pessimism caused consternation among his friends. The cycle of 24 songs ends with 'Der Leiermann' – 'the pitiable hurdy-gurdy man'. Spaun said: 'For a time Schubert's mood became more and more gloomy and he seemed upset.'[120] There was much more desolation to come.

Shortly before Beethoven died, Schubert is reputed to have visited him. This is said to have been the only time they met. Schubert was one of 36 torchbearers at the funeral.[121]

Schubert's gloom continued to be anaesthetised by wild parties, at Bogner's coffee house, or the pubs around the cathedral, such as Zum grünen Anker or the Zum Schloss Eisenstadt. He was seen womanising.* The police activities continued and a group of artists, writers and intellectuals, which Schubert had applied to join, was raided at midnight and the members locked up.[122]

Schubert went to the large city of Graz for the summer of 1827, and stayed with friends, the Pachlers, who were brewers and patrons of the arts. He made the journey of 150 miles by express coach leaving at 9.30 pm and getting to Graz at 9 pm the following night. During this summer, he wrote Four Impromptus for the Piano and the 'Moments Musicaux'. There were

* Syphilis is not usually contagious in the latent period.

Schubertiads, but he was poorly and continued to suffer from headaches.[123]

Schubert started working on yet another opera: the impresario Barbaja was back in Vienna. One of Schubert's circle, Edward von Bauernfeld, house dramatist at the Burg theatre and later well known as a playwright and translator of Dickens and Shakespeare, wrote the libretto of *Der Graf von Gleichen.*[124] It is about a crusader who brings a Saracen princess home to set up a *ménage à trois* with his wife, a story hardly likely to appeal to the censors.[125] Nevertheless, Schubert sketched out 88 pages of it.

Schubert and his friends had a lively New Year's party as 1828 began. In March, he had a very successful public concert at the Philharmonic Society, where he made a profit of more than 300 fl. The carnival season was wild, even though his friends were gradually drifting away to settle down. Spaun, who had taken up the new sport of swimming, had recently got engaged to be married.[126]

Towards the End

Schubert's works poured forth. His energy was frantic. In the summer, he completed many songs, including 'Der Doppelgänger', and three Piano Sonatas in C minor, A major and B flat. He also wrote the String Quintet, the Adagio of which paints such a bleak and desolate scene.

There was insufficient money to afford a summer visit to the countryside. Throughout the last summer of 1828, Schubert was under the care of Dr Ernst Rinna, one of the top doctors in Vienna, who was about four years older than himself. Rinna had already been appointed personal medical adviser to the Emperor; and his fees were no doubt expensive. He advised fresh air and exercise. At the beginning of October, Schubert went on a brisk walking trip with Ferdinand and two companions to Haydn's grave at Eisenstadt.[127]

He wrote several sacred works,* the Mass in E flat, a setting of the 92nd psalm and other pieces. Possibly with a church job in mind, he arranged to brush up his technique of counterpoint with the court organist Simon Sechter, then a leading authority on fugue, and a future teacher of Anton Bruckner.

* Although a devout person, Schubert did not believe in all the details of Christianity.[128] Key phrases are notably omitted from his masses, such as the words in the Credo: 'Et in unam sanctam, catholicam et apostolicam ecclesiam.'

But, at the end of the month, Schubert was very poorly, after having a fish supper at the tavern Zum roten Kreuz with Ferdinand and some friends. Then he seemed to recover. When Spaun visited him, Schubert said that he felt so exhausted that he thought he would fall through the bed. On 12 November he wrote to Schober: 'I am ill. I have eaten nothing for eleven days and drunk nothing, and I totter feebly and shakily from my chair to bed and back again. Rinna is treating me. If ever I take anything, I bring it up again at once.'[129]

He asked for novels by Fenimore Cooper,* a very popular American novelist whose *Last of the Mohicans* had been published a couple of years earlier. The story of life on the Frontier at the upper reaches of the Hudson River during the French–British wars in 1757 must have been as fascinating to Schubert as it was to Cooper's readership generally, which included Berlioz. Pale-faces, red-skins, savages 'of gigantic stature and of the fiercest mien', whoopings and howlings, tomahawks and scalps** will all have been particularly exciting and intriguing in an age unfamiliar with the tales and films of the Wild West. Doubtless, Schubert will have been amused by the droll figure of the musician, a psalmodist, reminiscent of the religious groups who had migrated to America, whom Cooper uses to add some contrast and humour to the tale. Although told that 'Singing won't do any good with the Iroquois', the singer lives a charmed life and survives.[131]

On 1 September, Schubert moved into an apartment which his brother Ferdinand had recently taken, in a new development, next to the green fields on the edge of Vienna. By the standards of the time, it was a relatively large three-room apartment on the second floor of Kettenbrückengasse 6, not far from the house in which Haydn had lived, close to the River Wien.[132]

From 14 November, Schubert was confined to bed. He wanted to hear

* Fenimore Cooper, seen as America's equivalent of Sir Walter Scott, published his first of 33 novels in 1819. For a long time, he was the youngest student at Yale, having entered in his thirteenth year. He made 'American manners and American scenes interesting to an American reader'.[130] His novels are regarded as being of uneven quality, his best being those written in the early 1820s. Today analysts point to his racism. The heritage of Native Americans is now rightly said to be 'as impressive in its modern richness and variety as in its historical depth and continuity'. Of course, in Schubert's time, people would have been 'racist' in outlook, if one applies modern terminology and concepts.

** Here is a typical quote: 'Hist! Man, keep close! Or the hair will be off your crown in the turning of a knife.'

one of Beethoven's quartets and it was played to him in the room. Schober kept away, but others came to see him. Two days later, there was a consultation with two leading doctors, Rinna being ill. After this consultation, a male nurse was brought in to help Ferdinand's wife and Schubert's stepsister Josepha who were looking after him. He was fully conscious on 17 November when Bauernfeld came and talked to him about the opera. He soon fell into a coma and died at 3 pm on 19 November. His last words to Ferdinand were: 'Here, here is my end.'[133]

The funeral service was held in the parish church of St Joseph Margareten on Friday 21 November, a short way across the fields from the house. The burial was changed at the last minute from there to the Währing cemetery, where he was buried very near to Beethoven. In the night before his death, Schubert implored Ferdinand: 'Transfer me to my room and do not leave me here in this corner under the earth; do I then deserve no place above the earth?' Ferdinand answered him: 'Dear Franz, rest assured, believe your brother Ferdinand whom you have always trusted and who loves you so much. You are in the room where you have always been and lie in your own bed.' To this, the dying man replied: 'No, it is not true, Beethoven does not lie here.'[134]

On 23 December, a memorial service was held in the Augustinerkirche, the royal church, where his Mass in F had been performed fourteen years before with his girlfriend-to-be, Therese Grob, as a soloist.

Sequel

Schubert's death certificate lists his few possessions totalling a value of 63 fl.[135] This compares with liabilities of almost 270 fl. Obviously, his expenses towards the end must have been colossal, and, since he held no permanent appointment,[136] it is not surprising that he was poor. But he was neither a bohemian nor a pauper, as will be apparent from some of the earnings referred to already. He certainly ran into financial difficulties in 1822, and sold out many of his works to the publisher Diabelli. He was also a free and generous spender when money was available.

Ferdinand took considerable trouble to get his brother's music published. Immediately, he offered some songs, piano music and certain chamber work to Diabelli and they appeared between 1830 and 1851 in 50 instalments. When Robert Schumann visited Vienna around eight years after Schubert's death, he met Ferdinand and saw the piles of still unpublished music, the operas, symphonies and masses. As a result, Schumann enabled Mendelssohn to give the first performance of the Great C major Symphony at the Leipzig Gewandhaus in March 1839.

Some of Schubert's works were pirated: in 1847, Ferdinand handed the G major Mass over to Diabelli for publication only to discover that it had already appeared in print in Prague as the work of a certain Kapellmeister called Robert Führer. It was only towards the end of the century, between 1884 and 1897, that the complete works were published.[137]

There is some doubt that Schubert was actually killed by syphilis, although the disease must have contributed enormously to his weakening; and the mercury treatment itself was toxic. There was some suggestion that the sanitary conditions in Ferdinand's new apartment were poor and that he might have died of typhoid fever.*[139]

At the tertiary stage of syphilis, a chronic debilitating illness affects most organs of the body.[140] Usually there is paralysis coupled with rapidly progressive dementia (known as General Paralysis of the Insane) and often blindness and deafness. Schubert did not display these symptoms, although the exhaustion which he felt could have been as a result of syphilis affecting the brain.

For an illustration of what can happen to someone with syphilis, one need only turn to the portrait of Donizetti in his last days (see page 299). For a description, one can turn to the last days of Winston Churchill's father, Lord Randolph, whose syphilis was not spoken of by his biographers until the 1980s. People did not mention these things. In Lord Randolph's awful case, it was said of his final two years: 'there was no retirement, no concealment. He died by inches in public.'[141] When Lord Randolph spoke in the House of Commons, his 'shaking hands and dreadful articulation were too much for many, who quietly slipped out of the House … the speech was a waking nightmare … rambling incoherent speech'.[142] He also became deaf.[143]

Another example was the painter Edouard Manet who died in 1883, eight years after discovering that he had syphilis. Desperate for a cure, Manet eventually tried ergot, a rye-based fungus.[144] This drug constricts the blood vessels, so he got gangrene. His leg was then amputated and ten days

* His life, just short of 32 years, was actually only a little shorter than average, which was 36 to 40 years for a man.[138]

later he died in terrible agony. Another impressionist painter, Berthe Morisot, wrote: 'It was death in one of its most appalling forms.'[145]

Schubert's sad death was relatively less ghastly. Maybe his syphilis, like Aids, facilitated the illness, whatever it was, of which he eventually died. We should not be distracted by such morbid matters. We have the privilege of enjoying the legacy of his wonderful music.

Rossini

CHAPTER 7

We now step from the dingy backstreets of Vienna, in which the threadbare Schubert died, onto the polished, paper-thin veneer of opulent Second-Empire Paris, almost exactly 40 years later. Rossini, who was born almost five years before Schubert, is dead. The grand officier of the Légion d'Honneur, in every sense 'successful', enormously rich, gourmand and gourmet, has passed away.

The grandiose cortège, clad in black drapery and crêpery, wended its mournful way from his sumptuous villa in the suburb of Passy, to the funeral in the Sainte Trinité church, past his apartment in the rue de la Chaussée d'Antin and on to the Père Lachaise cemetery.[1] A few years before, the remains of Meyerbeer had been honoured in the same way. After 50 years, similar obsequies would be accorded to Camille Saint-Saëns, another composer whose melodies are enjoyed.[2]

There was no doubt about Rossini's stature: the greatest Italian composer, some said, before Giuseppe Verdi. In the 1820s, in what was possibly the first celebrity biography, the biographer and novelist Stendhal had, in uncharacteristically florid prose, trumpeted that: 'Napoleon is dead; but a new conqueror has already shown himself to the world; and from Moscow to Naples, from London to Vienna, from Paris to Calcutta, his name is constantly on every tongue.'[3] He was referring to Rossini.

Yet, by the time of his death in 1868, Gioachino (Joachim) Rossini was of largely historical interest. His best-known work, *The Barber of Seville*, was first performed in 1816, seven years before Beethoven wrote the Ninth Symphony. When Rossini was born in 1792 in northern Italy, Lieutenant Napoleon Bonaparte was still messing around in Corsican politics, and Mozart had been dead for less than three months.

After his initial success in Italy, Rossini's life was a blaze of glory, in Vienna, in London and in Paris. At least, to start with; but suddenly in 1829, with *Guillaume Tell*, the opera production line stopped. His health declined. He fell out with his wife, a former *prima donna*, and took up with a faded courtesan. She nursed him through a stressful time, when he was a physical and mental wreck. He learned to cope with the catheters and other medical contraptions. Despite this, he had a triumphant final few years. The *bon viveur*, enjoying his cigars, the breakfast of two soft-boiled eggs and a glass of claret, and the occasional Tournedos Rossini, was revered, honoured and visited by all the great and the good; he even wrote a little music.

Here, we shall focus particularly on the years up to the time he stopped writing opera. This coincided with a notable moment in French history, 'Les Trois Glorieuses', the three days which saw the Bourbon kings finally kicked out. To sense the atmosphere at that time, we shall draw on some contemporary novels, and we shall look at the opera world of Paris, dominated as ever by the stars. First, however, we must go back to Italy almost 40 years before.

Italy at the Time of Rossini's Youth

Italy, although it had long been a holiday destination for the rich in search of culture, was still nothing like the country we now know. As late as 1848, Prince Metternich, the Habsburgs' chancellor, still referred to it merely as 'a geographical expression'.[4] Most people spoke one of the main regional dialects rather than the élitist language which we recognise today. Even a couple of years after Rossini's death, only two and a half per cent of the population of Italy spoke Italian; and 69 per cent of those over six years of age were illiterate.[5]

In the year of Rossini's birth, the Italian peninsula, so long a beneficiary of relative peace, was disrupted by the French revolutionary war. Five years later, the 27-year-old Napoleon, then in command of the French army in northern Italy, created the Cisalpine Republic, a French clone, which penetrated as far as Bologna (around 130 miles to the south-east of Milan) and the Romagna on the east coast. After Napoleon advanced northwards towards Vienna, the Habsburgs conceded that, apart from Venice, he could take the whole of northern Italy.

There was a brief interlude when the Austrians returned and made life very difficult for anyone who had collaborated with the French. However, Napoleon was soon back, victorious at Marengo, calling himself King of Italy. The Pope was good enough to turn up for the imperial coronation in Paris, but Napoleon roughed him up, bundled him hither and thither, and annexed Rome and Venice. He put his brother Joseph, and subsequently his colourful marshal, Joachim Murat, into Naples. He handed out other realms to various other relatives to rule. French laws and bureaucratic procedures were introduced.

When Napoleon fell, the Austrians, known as the 'Germans',[6] returned again, and the clock was turned back. Italy was divided again into kingdoms and duchies, all firmly under the thumb of Metternich. The Austrians controlled Venetia and the duchies in Tuscany, Parma and Modena; until almost 1860, they also ruled Lombardy, the area around Milan.

In the centre of the Italian peninsula were the Papal States, which were ruled harshly by priests from Rome. The second largest city, with a population of 70,000, was Bologna, a 'legation' ruled by a cardinal legate.* As might be expected, only one religion was permitted in the states: Jews, for example, were forced to attend a Roman Catholic church service once a week.** There were some other bizarre aspects: vaccination was declared illegal; street lighting in Rome was not permitted. The countryside was impoverished.[9]

Further south, the Two Sicilies were then ruled by Nelson's friend, Queen Maria Carolina, a daughter of Empress Maria Theresa. The queen's husband Ferdinand, boorish and illiterate, provided her with seventeen children, but otherwise took a back seat. Naples, their capital, was now the third largest city in Europe, and twice the size of Rome. It was saturated with priests,

* These cardinals were often not actually priests, but Roman noblemen and administrators.[7]

** The persecution of the Jews was eased when the Pope needed to borrow from the Rothschilds in the 1850s.[8]

nuns and lawyers, and full of beggars. It was a sink of corruption.[10]

The Habsburgs knew that if anything went wrong in the Papal States or in the Sicilies, they could intervene. But, as it transpired, there was one loose cannon, known to us as Piedmont, the area around Turin, sandwiched between the Italian peninsula and France.[11] It was ruled by the King of Sardinia, a title acquired by the Duke of Savoy as a reward for helping the allies in the War of the Spanish Succession. His territories reached right up to the shores of Lake Geneva, and included Nice. He was given a second major seaport, Genoa, at the Congress of Vienna,[12] and so, for the present, provided a useful bastion to hamper any ambition by France to return to northern Italy.

As for music in Italy, Venice was in decline, like its economy: only the Pietà, where Vivaldi used to work, continued to teach on a substantial scale. Milan, more prosperous, was more fortunate: La Scala had opened in 1778. Rome's church music was controlled by the Congregazione dei Musici, which later became the Accademia di Santa Cecilia; Rome also had several theatres. Bologna was renowned for the teaching of Padre Mattei, the successor to Padre Martini, with whom Mozart had studied. Naples was about to see the return of Cimarosa whose opera *Il Matrimonio Segreto* was a considerable success in the year of Rossini's birth.[13]

Rossini's Early Years in Italy

But it was in Pesaro, another 'legation' in the Papal States, long renowned for its beautiful ceramics and delicious figs,[14] that Rossini was born on 29 February 1792.[15] His father, Giuseppe, an itinerant trumpeter and horn player from near Ravenna, south of Venice, had taken lodgings there. Today, the humans soaking up sunshine on the beach seem a world away from its quaint streets, the conservatoire and the Teatro Rossini; but beach and town enjoy the tangy, salty smell of the Adriatic. Giuseppe lodged in one of the streets close to the market square. His landlords were bakers, though one of their younger daughters had a reputation with the police for being a whore. It was the eldest daughter Anna, a very pretty nineteen year old, whom Giuseppe got with child: Gioachino was born five months after his parents were married.*

* Perhaps this was not unusual: the illegitimacy rate in Vienna was estimated at 40 per cent.[16] However imprecise, the figures were clearly 'large'.

Giuseppe unfortunately collaborated with Napoleon's Cisalpine Republic and was imprisoned when the Austrians resumed control. To make ends meet, and at what must have been a very difficult time, Anna became a successful singer. No doubt, young Gioachino saw life backstage in the various opera houses where she was performing. He was soon singing the boy's part in an opera in Bologna and was employed as continuo player and répétiteur.

Giuseppe was released after Napoleon's victory at Marengo, and the family moved to Lugo, near Ravenna. Gioachino was taught the horn by his father, and singing by a local priest, who may also have introduced him to the pleasures of food. Gioachino was a good singer: one of his uncles, a butcher by trade, suggested that he should be castrated, but his mother would have none of that.[17]

He made quick progress. He was admitted to membership of the Accademia Filarmonica of Bologna when he was fourteen, slightly younger than Mozart had been when he was admitted. In Bologna, Rossini studied cello, piano and counterpoint and particularly the music of Haydn and Mozart. Although he found the teaching of counterpoint somewhat technical, he won prizes with some of his compositions.[18]

One of his parents' friends, an impresario in Venice, was let down by a German composer who did not produce the new work which was required of him. Rossini stepped in and wrote a one-act farce, *La Cambiale di Matrimonio*. Other works followed, some more successful than others, particularly *L'Inganno Felice*, in Venice in January 1812. *La Pietra del Paragone*, premièred in September 1812 at La Scala, had 53 performances in its first season. Rossini was still only twenty.

Compulsory conscription into Napoleon's armies for four years was one of the serious disadvantages of French rule in Italy.[19] All young men over twenty who were fit, unmarried and not ministers of religion were liable unless they could afford a considerable payment. Rossini's operatic success enabled him to obtain the necessary exemption. This was possibly facilitated by one of his female admirers who was influential with the Viceroy, Prince Eugène de Beauharnais, the son of Napoleon's first wife Josephine.[20]

Around this time, Rossini caught gonorrhoea, a venereal disease in which, after a few days incubation, the urethra is obstructed and there is a recurring discharge. There is a painful burning when urinating.[21] For some, spontaneous recovery may occur, but in Rossini's case it was to be a curse for the rest of his life.

For the time being, the gonorrhoea does not seem to have affected Rossini's productivity. He was expected to write the music to any libretto he was given, adapt it to the needs of the singers and rehearse it, all within about five weeks.[22] *L'Italiana in Algeri* was composed in 27 days. At one stage, Rossini churned out new operas almost at the rate of one every other month; although, in doing so, he sometimes recycled various numbers between operas.[23] Beethoven observed that Rossini's music fitted in with the frivolous spirit of the times, adding that 'Rossini is a man of talent and an exceptional melodist. He writes with such ease that for the composition of an opera he takes as many weeks as a German would take years.'[24]

In 1813, *Tancredi* was produced at Venice's La Fenice. The song 'Di Tanti Palpiti' became a smash hit and was sung by gondoliers and aristocrats: it was even referred to by Lord Byron, the poet, in his *Don Juan*. Rossini was soon recognised as the leading Italian composer and his music was enthusiastically received almost everywhere. But his earnings were limited to the performances in which he himself was involved, because there were no copyright laws in the region.[25]

Domenico Barbaja, businessman

In 1815, when still only 23, Rossini began a partnership with Domenico Barbaja, the impresario whose sponsorship Schubert had been keen to attract. Barbaja and Rossini entered into a six-year contract.

Rossini was to write two operas a year for the Naples opera houses, and to direct revivals of older works, in return for a large payment and a share in the proceeds from the front-of-house gambling activities.[26]

The Barber

Also in 1815, Rossini wrote *Elisabetta Regina d'Inghilterra*. Then, in Rome, he was given short notice, certainly less than three weeks, to write an opera for the close of the Carnival.[27] This was *The Barber of Seville*, based on the play by Pierre Caron, known as Beaumarchais. A clockmaker by training, Beaumarchais was an adventurer and chancer, and, at one stage, an arms dealer acting for the American revolutionaries; he fortunately survived duels, and spells in and out of prison and love, to write *The Barber of Seville* and *The Marriage of Figaro*, and to concoct a scheme for supplying Paris with water.[28]

The first night of Rossini's *Barber*, 20 February 1816, was a fiasco. The Don Basilio tripped over a trapdoor and had a nosebleed; and a cat walked onto the stage. The jeering and booing has been compared with the reception of *Tannhäuser* in Paris and the first night of *Carmen*. Subsequent performances were more successful. Indeed Verdi wrote, at the end of the century: '*Il barbiere di Siviglia*, for the abundance of the musical ideas, for its comic verve and the accuracy of its declamation is the most beautiful *opera buffa* there is.'[29]

Another composer in Naples, the now elderly Giovanni Paisiello, a protégé of Napoleon, had also written an *opera buffa* using the same play, in 1782. This precursor to Mozart's *Figaro* was composed for Emperor Joseph. As Paisiello was still alive in 1816, albeit discredited because of his association with the Bonapartists, Rossini used the title *Almaviva, Ossia l'Inutile Precauzione* to distinguish his work. He also included in the libretto a eulogy to Paisiello, whom he described as the 'immortal composer'. He got that wrong; and some of Paisiello's supporters may have been responsible for the booing on the first night. The more common title was used when the opera was revived in Bologna later in the year.

In 1816, Rossini wrote *Otello*, which was very successful. This was followed by *La Cenerentola*, and *La Gazza Ladra* (the Thieving Magpie) in the following year; then, *Mosè in Egitto, Ermione*, *La Donna del lago* and, in 1820, *Maometto II*. Many of these were sensational successes.[30]

Rossini concentrated on writing for singers who specialised in florid singing.[31] One of his *prima donnas* was Isabella Colbran, Barbaja's Spanish mistress. She was, between 1806 and 1815, one of the most celebrated coloratura sopranos in Europe (see colour plate 17). 'Offstage she possessed about as much dignity as the average milliner's assistant', said Stendhal, 'but the moment she stepped on the boards, her brow encircled with a royal diadem, she inspired involuntary respect.'[32]

For these stars, Rossini had created a virtually new idiom, with the patter songs such as Dr Bartolo's 'A un dottor della mia sorte'. A 20th-century critic has written: 'Rossini goes so fast that he achieves the immobility of a top spinning round and round in the same direction.'[33] He also created his own unmistakable trademark, the immense but gradual crescendo.

Others were not always so enthusiastic, Berlioz, for example: 'Rossini's melodious cynicism, his contempt for the traditions of dramatic expression, his perpetual repetition of one kind of cadence, his eternal puerile crescendo, and his crashing big drum, exasperated me to such a degree as to blind me to the dazzling qualities of his genius and the real beauties of his masterpiece, the *Barbiere*, with its delicate instrumentation and no big drum.' Berlioz continued, 'I often used to speculate on the possibility of undermining the Théâtre des Italiens, so as to blow it and its Rossini worshippers into space.'[34]

The Princess

As the local celebrity, Rossini returned to his birthplace in Pesaro to inaugurate the theatre which had been restored. There, he had an altercation with Princess Caroline, the notorious wife of the even more notorious English prince regent. Pesaro was full of spies looking for evidence of Caroline's adultery so that the prince regent could engineer his divorce. A footman who gave evidence to the parliamentary commission of enquiry into her behaviour said, with that candour normally expected when answering questions at such enquiries, that the princess was 'very fond of fucking'.[35] She herself put it more clinically, 'I have a bedfellow whenever I like. Nothing is more wholesome.'[36] The 50-year-old princess rented an elegant villa on the Colle San Bartolo on the hill above Pesaro and moored her yacht in the harbour below. She lived with her lover Bartolomeo Pergami, handsome, well over six feet tall and with black curling hair.[37] After hearing of the death of both her daughter Charlotte and her grandchild, she decided to stay and bought her own villa, the Villa Vittoria, a name not to be confused with that of her niece, who was yet to be born.

Princess Caroline invited Rossini several times to evening receptions, but he declined, on the pretext that rheumatism prevented him making the necessary bow that her rank demanded. Being the very fastidious person that he was, Rossini may have been concerned about her personal problems as exemplified in the story of her first meeting with her fiancé, some 25 years earlier, who, on embracing her, 'retired to a distant part of the apartment' and called to Lord Malmesbury: 'Harris, I am not well; pray get me a glass of brandy.'[38]

The princess and her household did not take kindly to Rossini's refusal. When he returned the following May, Pergami's drinking companions disrupted his performance in the theatre. In high dudgeon, Rossini left Pesaro for Naples, escorted out by an unruly crowd, who then turned on the princess' villa and broke the windows. The story goes that peace was only restored after she left Pesaro. Rossini never returned there, although he remained sufficiently fond of his birthplace that he subsequently bequeathed a fortune to it.[39]

Naples, to which he went, was an uncomfortable place in which to be. An uprising took place in July 1820, started by the Carbonari, which today would surely be branded a terrorist organisation.[40] The king issued a constitution which he swore to defend. Ardent patriots like Gabriele Rossetti, father of the Pre-Raphaelite painter, proclaimed prematurely that Italian slavery was at an end, and the English poet Percy Bysshe Shelley wrote an 'Ode to Naples'. However, Metternich believed that to acquiesce in any gesture towards liberalism or nationalism would be disastrous. He got the international community to agree that any 'illegal' attempts at change should be suppressed. So, the Austrians intervened and entered Naples in March 1821. It was garrisoned with Swiss guards and 35,000 Habsburg troops. The minister of police, the Prince of Canosa, exacted a terrible retribution. There were public executions; other rebels were chained up in the Spielberg fortress at Brünn (now Brno) in Moravia.*

* 'Anything's better than the Spielberg', said one of Stendhal's fictional characters about this Habsburg prison for political detainees, redolent of *Fidelio*. A sentence to 'twenty years in the hulks, or to death – that is a great deal less terrible than the Spielberg, with a chain of a hundred and twenty pounds weight on each foot and eight ounces of bread for my sole nourishment'.[41] It must have been fearsome for its reputation for harshness, and its distance from Italy, rather than for its appearance: the white castle stands on its hill just above Brno; it contains plaques commemorating the Italian patriots.[42]

It was as well to get out of Italy; Gabriele Rossetti fled to London. In 1821, Barbaja took his Neapolitan company, including Rossini, to the Kärntnertor theatre in Vienna, where there was a Rossini festival from April to July 1822, with six of Rossini's operas being performed. There was a Rossini craze, the cash began to flow, and a music magazine reported that 'the entire performance was like an idolatrous orgy; everyone acted as if he had been bitten by a tarantula; the shouting, crying, yelling of "*viva*" went on and on'.[43] During this visit, Rossini met Beethoven; the meeting was stilted because Rossini's side of the conversation had to be written out in Beethoven's conversation books.

Marriage to Isabella

Around this time, Rossini took over Colbran from Barbaja. She was seven years older than Rossini. Professionally, she was going into a decline: Stendhal, in his *Life of Rossini*, described her singing at this time as 'what (in inferior mortals) would certainly have been termed execrable … soon it became an unparalleled piece of good luck to hear her get through an aria without disaster'.[44] She seemed to be unable to sing in tune.

In 1822, apparently under pressure from his mother, Gioachino and Isabella were married in Castenaso, a village about five miles from Bologna, on the road to Ravenna. Isabella was rich;[45] apart from her own success, her father was one of the new middle class who had benefited from the sale of church property in the Napoleonic period.[46] She brought a substantial dowry, including a property in Sicily; and, a couple of years later, she inherited the estate at Castenaso. The Rossinis settled there, having parted company from Barbaja and the Neapolitan opera; they also acquired a palazzo in Bologna itself.

Rossini was spectacularly successful. His works now accounted for half the repertoire and 80 per cent of the evenings at the Théâtre des Italiens in Paris.[47] He operated at the highest level. He wrote two cantatas for Metternich for the Congress of Verona at the end of 1822, both compiled from other works. There he met the emperor, the tsar and the Duke of Wellington.[48] He composed *Semiramide*, which considerably impressed Bellini, then a student at Naples. Rossini was 31 and he had already written 34 operas.

In autumn 1823, the Rossinis set off for London. They went via Paris, where Rossini was fêted at a large banquet for 150 people.[49] They were in

London in December and stayed until the following July. To create the desirable 'PR', Stendhal wrote his book, which was translated into English. He describes Rossini in the style of a modern glossy magazine: 'If you like Italy and things Italian, nothing is so delightful as Rossini's conversation. His mind is all fire and quicksilver, darting here, darting there.' He added, like a toad: 'It is Rossini's undying misfortune to be constitutionally disrespectful towards everything except genius.' Stendhal certainly had a positive journalistic style: 'Rossini has an incredible talent for mimickry ... Light, lively, amusing, never wearisome, but seldom exalted – Rossini would appear to have been brought into this world for the express purpose of conjuring up visions of ecstatic delight in the commonplace soul of the "Average Man".' Stendhal concluded: 'The sad, sighing beauty of Mozart has a quality which he could not dream of emulating.'[50]

An English Interlude

Within a few days, and after recovering from a rough crossing of the Channel,[51] this paragon was playing duets and singing Desdemona's willow song with King George IV, at the Royal Pavilion in Brighton.*[53] Had Rossini accepted Princess Caroline's invitation in Pesaro, these honours and the access to the drawing rooms of high society in London, from the Duke of Wellington down, might not have been accorded to him. Rossini now consorted with the important people painted by Sir Thomas Lawrence, lampooned in the lewd caricatures of Rowlandson.

London, lit by gaslight, was full of dandies, foppish clothes and absurd behaviour, with 'the Regent' as its role model. Its people were more interested in the result of horse races and prize fights than in music. Music was dismal: Mozart's *Don Giovanni* only reached the West End stage in April 1817, although the more enlightened City audience had staged an amateur performance a decade before.[54] In 1818, a version of *The Barber of Seville* was put on in Covent Garden, part Rossini's version, part Paisiello's, 'the overture and new music composed, and the whole adapted to the English stage by Mr Bishop'.[55]

The British had a reputation more for talent in literature than in music.

* The Pavilion had only just been completed. Rossini's visit coincided with one of the few times the king stayed there: he and his mistress, Lady Conyngham, did not like it, because the growth of the town affected his privacy; also, there were security problems. The King preferred using Windsor instead.[52]

Although Jane Austen was dead, the prolific Sir Walter Scott was at work. He provided stories for many 19th-century operas, such as *The Bride of Lammermoor* and *The Lady of the Lake* (*La Donna del lago*). The poet Shelley had recently been drowned off the Italian coast; also, his friend Lord Byron, the proud, contemptuous, oversexed Napoleon of the London drawing rooms, had died of fever while fighting, rather improbably, with a bunch of unco-ordinated freedom fighters on the west coast of Greece. Rossini, appropriately, held a concert in his memory.

In the London season of 1824, eight of Rossini's operas were performed. He amassed riches, tens of thousands of pounds; in our terms, millions.* He was offered 100 guineas (£105) an hour for singing lessons, whereas the current going rate was one guinea (£1.05) for the best music teachers. Indeed, a highly reputable musician such as Samuel Wesley probably earned around £390 per annum at this time, comparable to a moderately successful doctor or lawyer. The Rossinis' appearance fee merely for a single evening engagement was 50 guineas. Isabella Rossini sang in some of the productions. Her fees too were enormous: for *Zelmira*, one of Rossini's recent successes, it was £1,500.**[57]

At the other end of the social scale, reality was, however, rather different. Women and children in the coal mines and cotton mills were 'compelled to work fourteen hours a day, in a heat of eighty-four degrees', and were 'liable to punishment for looking out at a window of the factory'.[58] The famished cottager living in the countryside of enclosed fields, if caught poaching a rabbit, could be transported for seven years. Agricultural workers rioted in 1830 to support a wage of half a crown (£0.125) per day; three were hanged and 420 were transported to Australia.[59]

Even at the top, life was brittle; there was no safety net. As Thackeray showed in his novel *Vanity Fair*, the once affluent could easily fall into this abyss. Sir Walter Scott staved off ignominious bankruptcy arising from his unwise business and publishing transactions; his last years were spent exhaustingly earning money to pay off his creditors.[60] Ruin was never far away. 'Under the last two Georges, banks rose like mushrooms and went down like ninepins.'[61] Henry Manning, the future cardinal, accompanied

* The Philharmonic Society's generous gift, three years later, to the dying Beethoven was £100. Jane Austen received £110 in 1812 for *Pride and Prejudice*; she had hoped for £150.[56]

** The 'incredibly popular' Irish poet Thomas Moore was promised and received a sensational £3,000 from Longmans for his poem *Lalla Rookh*, published in 1817.

his father to the Guildhall to witness the 'humiliating spectacle of a former Governor of the Bank of England handing over his gold watch, chains and seals, the symbolic last possessions of a bankrupt'.[62] As a result, Manning's prospective marriage was scotched by his fiancée's parents. Similarly, the bank owned by the father of John Henry Newman folded. The family, with an aunt and grandmother, squeezed into a cottage in Norwood; the father became the manager of a brewery in Alton, Hampshire and then a tavern-keeper in Clerkenwell. The grandmother and aunt tried to make ends meet by opening a finishing school for young ladies.

These were some of the realities and pressures which the escapist dream world of entertainment could attempt to conceal. Opera was the 19th-century equivalent of the cinema: international, brash, violent or sentimental; appreciated particularly by the young; often based on contemporary novels. It was a source of hit tunes. It was also a magnificent spectacle, and had the added advantage that young ladies could safely attend, because the love scenes were sung in a foreign language.[63]

Paris

In February 1824, Rossini signed an exclusivity agreement for 40,000 francs. He undertook to live in Paris, working only at the Opéra and the Théâtre des Italiens. Some months later, he contracted to run the administration of the Théâtre des Italiens for 25,000 fr per annum,* although he quickly handed over the detailed responsibilities for this and devoted his attentions to the Opéra.[65]

Paris was different from the one we know. Between the heights of Montmartre to the north and Montrouge to the south, it was set 'in a valley of crumbling stucco and gutters black with mud, a valley full of real suffering and often deceptive joys' (see colour plate 5).[66] The Champs Elysées ended at Rond-Point, and was little more than a muddy lane dotted with taverns and temporary stalls selling lemonade. The Arc de Triomphe had been started in 1806 but was only completed 30 years later; beyond it, there was just heathland and the Bois de Boulogne. La Madeleine, with its impressive façade like an ancient temple, was

* In the mid-1830s, a student paid his 'daily' 40 fr per month to make his bed, clean his shoes and cook his lunch; for the rest of the day she earned 50 centimes turning the handle of a machine. Her husband, a cabinet-maker, earned four francs a day. With three children they had barely enough to live on.[64]

incomplete. It had been started as a hall of fame for Napoleon's Grand Armée in 1806; three decades later, when still unfinished, many thought it should be a railway station.

Paris was sometimes enveloped in a thick fog, made denser by the smoke from the fires warming the houses. At times, it would become so dark that 'the most precise and punctual people are led astray'.[67] Only in the 1830s did light from gas lamps enable the pedestrian to see an omnibus emerge from the encircling gloom, as it trundled along on the new tar-macadam surfacing.[68]

In the past few decades, France had been through the upheavals of the Revolution, the Empire, a Restoration, Napoleon's return from Elba, the Battle of Waterloo, and then another Restoration. Successful musicians, such as Cherubini, Le Sueur and Méhul, had joined in the shenanigans of the Revolution and tailored their behaviour to the continually changing circumstances. Cherubini had conducted a choir at the opening of the Council of Five Hundred on the third anniversary celebrations of the execution of Louis XVI (21st January), which the Opéra duly celebrated with a gala performance. For the Fête de l'Etre Suprème in 1794, with other eager colleagues at the Institut Nationale de Musique (subsequently the Conservatoire), Cherubini offered to set a hymn to the Eternal Being; he then coached the 'democratic' crowd so that they could participate in the performance.

'In the morning, the guillotine was kept busy and in the evening one could not get a seat in the theatre', said Cherubini's wife.[69] 'In the presence of the scaffolds, the theatres were filled as usual', complained the *littéra-trice*, Germaine de Staël.[70] But, in the next decade, Cherubini had to attune himself to the requirements of Napoleon: he organised concerts for him at Schönbrunn, although the emperor's preferred work was *Ossian, ou Les Bardes* by Le Sueur, on whom he bestowed the Légion d'Honneur, 6,000 fr and an engraved snuffbox. By contrast, Empress Josephine's favourite was the enormously successful and highly honoured Gaspare Spontini, who dominated Paris opera in the first two decades of the century. Spontini's *La Vestale* and his *Fernand Cortez* were regarded as the best works before Rossini.[71]

Of course, when Rossini arrived in Paris, there was more music being performed than just opera. In the home, the number of amateur musicians rocketed from 3,500 at the time of the French Revolution to 80,000 four decades later. In the concert hall, where non-vocal performances were rare, François-Antoine Habeneck, the conductor at the Opéra, conducted the twice-yearly Concerts Spirituels. He also ran end-of-term concerts at the Conservatoire, and formed his own orchestra in 1828, the Société des Concerts du Conservatoire. It was Habeneck who conducted the first performance of Berlioz' *Symphonie Fantastique* in 1830, and introduced Beethoven's music to France. Performances were somewhat unusual by our standards:* for its Paris première, Beethoven's Ninth Symphony was cut in two by interposing performances of works by Cherubini and Weber, and a Beethoven quartet.[72]

Operas were even more mercilessly hacked around by the producers. *The Magic Flute*, with modifications to the overture and Sarastro's big aria, was blended with excerpts from *Don Giovanni* and *La Clemenza di Tito* into a performance called *Les Mystères d'Isis*. Weber's *Der Freischütz*, relocated in England and 'improved',** was produced as *Robin des Bois* in 1826; similarly *Euryanthe* was re-presented as *Le Forêt de Senart*. Weber was appalled and wrote a letter of complaint to the press. When this was published, the editor responded contemptuously that what he had done was necessary to ensure the opera's success.[73]

The composer's views were largely irrelevant, because the audience did not go in order to see or listen to the show:[74] they went to meet their friends 'in so many little suspended drawing-rooms, the fourth wall of which had been removed'.[75] As in London, opera was at the centre of affluent social life. In one contemporary novel, when a young man confessed to his acquaintances that he had been to the Opéra only once, they were shocked: 'No one ever goes anywhere else', they said. 'Your first outing must be to the Opéra to hear *Comte Ory*.'[76] With its curtains and candles, the box provided a miniature stage on which these socialites could perform. We hear how, at the Opéra-Comique, a countess' face 'shone with inexpressible joy when, having directed her glass at all the other boxes and conducted a

* The quality of orchestral performance was said to be poor, despite the fact that appointment to the Opéra orchestra was by competitive audition, and half its members were trained at the Conservatoire, where most had won first prize. Importantly, there were strict rules on absenteeism. Orchestra and soloists were held together by tapping, perhaps on the candlesticks, or stamping.

** Even Berlioz agreed to provide recitatives for Weber's *Der Freischütz* at the Opéra. They were needed because the spoken word was not permitted on the stage of the Opéra.

rapid examination of all the women's dresses, she felt assured that she outshone the prettiest and most elegant ladies present by the beauty and the splendour of her costume'. The countess 'laughed to show off the whiteness of her teeth and tossed her flower-bedecked head to attract attention'.*[77]

However, behind this superficial glamour, the buildings were hot with candle or gaslight, and were smelly. So we hear how a lady, 'mindful of the sweaty odour of the working-class audience in this hall in which we would have to sit for several hours, regretted not having a nosegay'.[78] There was also a great risk of fire. In January 1838, the casualties at the fire which destroyed the Théâtre des Italiens included its director Severini, who was killed jumping from the blaze.

Restoration Politics

Rossini had come to Paris at a very difficult time when society was still polarised between those who supported the restored monarchy and those who did not. The brother of Louis XVI, the 60-year-old Comte de Provence, had been placed on the throne by the reluctant Allies:**[79] some would have preferred to retain a cowed and compliant Napoleon; but to do so was 'politically' impossible. The task facing the government was to reconcile the old nobility with the new élite created by Napoleon.† Feelings ran high. During the brief period before Waterloo, when Napoleon was confined to Elba, two men who shouted 'Vive l'Empéreur' in the Gardens of the Tuileries had been stabbed to death by some ladies with their umbrellas.[80] With the change in regime, officials, of course, easily jumped ship: after Waterloo, the police chief demonstrated his new loyalty by naming 54 people for exemplary execution.†† Talleyrand, the foreign minister, reviewed the list and commented sardonically: 'he has forgotten

* In Vienna, Emperor Joseph used to talk during the performance; in Milan at La Scala, the audience did not pay much attention. It is no wonder that something spectacular, in the form of Grand Opera, became necessary to attract attention.

** The son of Louis XVI had died of scrofula, in captivity.

† The nobility of the ancien régime had only lost around 20 per cent of their land and thus retained considerable power.

†† The police chief had already carefully hedged his bets before Waterloo by opening discussions with the royalist Comte de Flavigny, whose ten-year-old daughter would later become Liszt's mistress, and mother of Cosima Wagner.[81] Michel Ney, reputed to be one of the bravest of Napoleon's marshals, was shot. Cimarosa, who supported the French-inspired revolution in Naples, was lucky only to be imprisoned when the royalist government took control again in Naples.

none of his friends'.[82] In 1816, some men alleged to be involved in a conspiracy against the king had their right hands cut off and were then guillotined.

If this was not bad enough, a considerable deterioration in the political situation began at the start of the 1820s, with the assassination of the only attractive Bourbon, the sociable, pleasure-loving nephew of Louis XVIII, the Duc de Berri. He was stabbed with a seven-inch dagger by a 37-year-old saddlemaker. He had escorted his wife to her carriage halfway through a performance at the Opéra and was returning for the rest of the show (and for what he expected to follow it), when he was struck. When his assassin was guillotined, there were considerable political demonstrations, particularly by students. There was then a crackdown, involving a whole series of measures. Press censorship was tightened; the 23,000 wealthiest electors were given a double vote; the bodies of Voltaire and Rousseau were ejected from the Panthéon; a liberal revolt in Spain was crushed by French troops. An alliance between the Throne and Altar was a prominent feature of these times, so several professors were dismissed from the Sorbonne University and a priest was installed as rector. The Jesuits returned, in force. Irreligious literature was burnt, capital punishment was instituted for sacrilegious acts. Between 1815 and 1830, 1,000 new nunneries were founded, almost doubling the number.[83]

In this climate, it was inadvisable to express any enthusiasm for liberal principles. Political discussion in the salons, which had been lively after the Restoration, was curtailed. The stifling atmosphere in a royalist salon is depicted by one novelist:* 'Provided you did not treat God, the clergy, the King, or anyone holding public office as a matter for jest; provided you did not speak in favour of ... the newspapers of the opposite party, Voltaire, Rousseau, or anyone allowing himself freedom of speech; provided above all, that you never mentioned politics, then you were free to discuss anything you pleased.' He continues: 'Young people coming there to pay their respects, afraid of saying anything that might lay them under suspicion of having a thought of their own, or of having read some prohibited book, lapsed into silence after making a very few tasteful remarks on Rossini or the weather.'[84]

* Stendhal, in his novel *Le Rouge et le Noir*, published in 1830.

Paris Opera: the Structure

All rulers at the time were concerned that get-togethers of the rich and influential might easily become subversive. So, in Paris, the theatre was tightly run by the state. The rigid structure, which would have a considerable bearing on many composers in this book, had been specified by Napoleon. The companies who produced most of the now familiar operas were the Opéra (the Imperial Academy of Music), the Opéra-Comique and its former 'subsidiary', the Théâtre des Italiens, also known as the Opéra-Bouffe.*[86]

The Opéra and the Opéra-Comique had the right and obligation to produce works *in French*. So, for performances at the Opéra, Rossini adapted *Mosè in Egitto* into *Moïse et Pharaon* and *Maometto II* into *Le Siège de Corinthe*. The Opéra was required to be a showcase for French lyric art. The minister kept control by issuing a mandate to the director and enforced it by manipulating the level of government subsidy: the minister even specified the number of orchestra players and the size of the chorus. However, economy does not seem to have inhibited the production of Spontini's *Fernand Cortez* in which fourteen horses from Franconi's circus took part in the cavalry charge scene.[87] Soon, the Opéra would stage other spectacular Grand Operas, shows such as Auber's *La Muette de Portici* and Meyerbeer's *Robert le Diable* and *Les Huguenots*.

Alongside the Opéra was the Opéra-Comique, whose name can be misleading. Indeed one might have expected that the première of Rossini's humorous *Le Comte Ory* would have been the Opéra-Comique, whereas it was actually held at the Opéra. The crucial distinction was that whereas the Opéra was dedicated wholly to song and dance, *the spoken word, in French,* was permitted at the Opéra-Comique. In addition, works performed at the Opéra-Comique were not expected to be too serious or sad and they rarely portrayed death. Many years later, it did not help Bizet's *Carmen* that it was premièred there.

The Théâtre des Italiens performed Italian opera only. So, the works perhaps best known to us were staged at the Théâtre des Italiens, such as the operas in Italian by Bellini, Donizetti and Verdi.

The rules also prescribed the format of opera: the work had to have five

* The Opéra had a seating capacity of just under 2,000, and was located in the rue le Peletier, until burnt down in October 1873. The Opéra-Comique and the Théâtre des Italiens were in various locations, but settled in mid-century at the Salle Favart and the Salle Ventadour respectively.[85]

acts, include a ballet and, in fixed order, display a romance or ballade, a few cavatinas and arias for the female and male leads, and a passionate duet. The large chorus became an integral part of the production. It was obligatory, after at least two acts, to have a big tableau accompanied by the full orchestra, cast and chorus.[88]

Paris Opera: Librettists and Singers

As we have seen, the composers were relatively unimportant. The librettists were very powerful, the theatre directors were rude and overbearing, and if they wanted a change or cut, the composer simply had to agree, something, which in due course, would infuriate Wagner and Verdi. Many of the librettos were written by Eugène Scribe, whose texts fill 26 volumes.[89]

Success or failure depended on the stars, so each production had to be tailored to the individual celebrity's personal requirements.* If it was necessary to demonstrate technical skill, stars would interchange arias to suit their range; these were known as 'trunk arias' (*aria di baule*), because the stars carried them around with them. This even happened during the 1870s: one diva in Verdi's *Don Carlos* substituted an excerpt from *Les Huguenots* at one performance and a piece from *Macbeth* at another. As nobody was listening carefully, it probably did not matter.

Although the stars were celebrities, unlike today they were hardly 'respectable'. One of Balzac's characters, the provincial and timid Madame Grandet, exclaims: 'Go to the theatre to see actors! But, Monsieur, don't you know that's a mortal sin?'[91] Actors had long been linked with prostitutes: both sold their bodies (albeit in different ways) to provide pleasure.[92] In France, until 1849, actors were denied Communion, marriage, absolution and a Christian burial. However, the earthly compensation was considerable. The stars earned stratospheric sums of money and were followed by a throng of fans.[93]

Rossini said of the singers of his day: 'The most remarkable was Madame Pasta, Madame Colbran was the foremost; but Madame Malibran was unique.'[94] Berlioz said that Henriette Sontag 'played with notes as no Indian juggler has ever juggled with golden balls, but she also sang music, as musicians sometimes dream of hearing it sung'.[95]

* This applied generally: Mozart had to adapt *Figaro* for specific performances; Debussy similarly had to adapt *Pelléas*.[90]

Giuditta Pasta was Rossini's Tancredi, Desdemona and Semiramis, and Bellini's Norma. She created the title role and ensured the success of Donizetti's *Anna Bolena*. The mezzo-soprano Maria Malibran (see colour plate 18) was the daughter of the Spanish tenor Manuel Garcia, a violent bigamist, for whom Rossini wrote the part of Count Almaviva in *The Barber*. Maria was educated in a convent in Hammersmith. She had an enormous success in 1825 in New York, where she went with her father on

Adolphe Nourrit, the French tenor, and Henriette Sontag. Berlioz said that she 'sang music as musicians sometimes dream of hearing it sung'

a visit, which effectively gave the USA its first taste of Italian opera. There, she married a merchant and banker, Eugène Malibran. A couple of years later, aged just twenty, and single again, she returned to Paris. She was being paid 35,000 fr for a six-month season at the Théâtre des Italiens and 40,000 fr* for a three-month season in London, where she was praised for her skill at extemporisation, keeping to the score not being the main purpose of the performance.**

* This was at a time when a violin soloist received 3,000 fr per annum; the bass drum player in the orchestra of the Opéra, 600 fr. Pay was less at the Italiens, although there were 15 per cent fewer performances there; desk leaders there got 1,500 fr compared to 2–3,000 fr at the Opéra, whereas the other musicians got 8–900 fr at the Italiens against 1,200 fr on average at the Opéra. Cornélie Falcon, the creator of Halévy's *La Juive*, was paid 50,000 fr; a top singer such as the first Elvire in Auber's *La Muette* got 16,000 fr for a one-year engagement.[96]

** Malibran had a sad end, when aged only 28. She had a riding accident in Regent's Park, when

The pressures of stardom were considerable. When the leading tenor Adolphe Nourrit, a pupil of Garcia, was eclipsed in the 1830s, he became so depressed that he left Paris. Because he believed that the applause at a performance in Naples was insincere, he threw himself from the top floor of the Hotel Barbaja the following morning.[98]

Less tragically and more comically, stars would have tantrums, live flamboyantly and be intensely jealous. A theatre director confessed: 'I am weary, obsessed and disgusted by the harassment these ladies subject me to. My patience is at an end.'[99] On one occasion in the 1840s, Rosine Stoltz crossed the stage eating a plate of macaroni while a competitor was trying to perform her main aria. As might be expected, Stoltz was created a countess by the King of Württemberg; a few years later, she became a duchess, and, aged 63, she married a Spanish prince. A Russian aristocrat described 'Mme Stoltz's singing, or, rather, her shouting', adding that 'her vocal and bodily contortions are in the typical French style, a melodramatic genre in which passion is replaced by delirium, anger by rage, and love by something whose name cannot yet be found, as far as I know, in any dictionary'.[100]

The stars' success was dependent on the behaviour of the claque, an important ingredient of the Paris operatic scene. The claque were a group who were paid to applaud or hiss. *Rieurs* laughed during comedies; *pleureuses* wept during tragedies; *bisseurs* called for encores.[101] We hear of the claque 'loudly clapping, in time, like the rattle of gunfire'.[102] The claque leaders, who received monthly payments from the actors and free tickets from the management, were very influential.

'Les Trois Glorieuses'

Rossini was brought to Paris, in an attempt to raise standards, by the Directeur des Beaux Arts, Vicomte Sosthène de la Rochefoucauld, known as 'le Napoléon des arts'. Rossini's arrival 'had the effect of a whipcrack on the somnolent Théâtre des Italiens'.[103] It created what the composer Boieldieu described as 'notre convulsion musicale'.[104] But Rossini was a

she was thrown against a wooden fence. Against the advice of her homeopathic doctor, she carried on with a demanding schedule. Three months later, she was in Manchester, lodged in the Mosley Arms Hotel, where she died after a miscarriage. Liszt, recognising that the stars made their débuts too early and forced their voices, commented some years later that maybe it was just as well that she died young, because 'she might very well have finished up by going to St Petersburg and singing out of tune like La Pasta'.[97]

poor administrator, and it was only the patronage and financial support of the royal family that saved the theatre from financial collapse.

Rossini actually achieved little during his tenure of the directorship, although he did bring many stars to Paris and appointed Ferdinand Hérold, later to compose the ballet *La Fille Mal Gardée*, as singing coach. He attracted considerable flak. His 'self-satisfaction, his exorbitant income, and the noise and showiness of his orchestration and perceived overuse of percussion, brass and high instruments were fodder for constant criticism and mockery'.[105] It was said that 'M. Rossini will only compose for twenty francs per note'.[106]

In September 1824, at the time Rossini moved to Paris, Louis XVIII died and was succeeded by his 67-year-old younger brother, the Comte d'Artois. The new king, Charles X, although delightfully pleasant and charming, was 'a man of slender abilities with violent passions',[107] and 'a converted libertine who had found piety late in life'.[108] Rossini wrote *Il Viaggio a Reims* for the elaborate coronation at which the king was anointed with sacred unction from a phial, smashed in the Revolution, but now miraculously restored. The event cost 6 million francs.[109] It is said that the king was thoroughly bored by *Il Viaggio*: neither of these Bourbon kings was particularly interested in music or the arts. Louis XVIII had been keener on food, and his heavy diabetic body, paralysed with gout and gangrene, was not suitable for going in and out of the opera houses: he used to be conveyed in a wheelchair carried by eight men.[110]

After writing *Il Viaggio*, Rossini was ill for three months. After this, he wrote four works: the two adaptations from Italian, *Le Siège de Corinthe* and *Moïse*; then *Le Comte Ory*, in which he borrowed music from *Il Viaggio*, and *Guillaume Tell*, based on Schiller's play. *Tell*, premièred on 3 August 1829, was his last opera.

By then, the reign of Charles X was reaching its dénouement, accompanied by dire economic circumstances. The population increased by nearly 2.5 million between 1815 and 1830 without any significant increase in agricultural or industrial productivity. The grain and potato harvests failed in 1827 and this led to a protracted economic slump from 1828. Grain prices rose 50 per cent; and there were food riots.[111]

In March 1830, a large number of deputies in the parlement voted a critical 'address' to the monarch. When most of these were returned in an election held in July, King Charles introduced further controls on the press, and called for new elections based on an electorate of the wealthiest men in France. In this, he was advised by his prime minister, a papal prince, the Prince de Polignac,* whose mother Yolande had played at being milkmaids with Queen Marie Antoinette.[112]

Despite the diversion provided by a war against Algeria, this doomed regime was finished by 'Les Trois Glorieuses', the three days of fighting on 27, 28 and 29 July 1830.[113] In the disturbances in Paris, an estimated 200 troops were killed and 800 wounded; the insurgents suffered 800 dead and 4,000 wounded, a high proportion of which were artisans and skilled workers.[114] Charles was sent packing, back to Holyrood House in Edinburgh, where he had previously lived in exile. The revolution concluded on 31 July, when Lafayette, hero of the American and French revolutions, embraced, as king, a former French teacher at the Reverend George Nicholson's private school at Ealing.[115] This was Louis-Philippe, the descendant of Louis XIV's younger brother Monsieur, and son of Philippe-Egalité, the regicide Duc d'Orléans. These major events did not stop the show going on: *Guillaume Tell* was performed on 28 July, and the Opéra reopened its doors on 4 August with Auber's *La Muette* as if nothing had happened.

The July Monarchy

Rossini was on holiday in Italy when the July Revolution took place. In early September, he returned to Paris, to sort out his affairs. Shortly before King Charles fled, Rossini had negotiated an annuity. As a separate matter, he agreed to spend three months a year in Bologna, where he would compose a work, and nine months in Paris, where it would be staged; he offered five operas over a ten-year period.

After the July Revolution, the second half of the deal was irrelevant and there was only the annuity to sort out. Unfortunately for Rossini, there was a bitter purge. Polignac was arrested wandering around Normandy and condemned to life imprisonment; all those who had backed Charles' regime were suspect. Two years later, Charles' daughter-in-law, the Duchesse de Berri, bored with Scotland and yearning to be a Joan of Arc, staged an uprising.[116]

* Polignac is possibly of more interest to musicians as the father-in-law of the Princesse de Polignac who was an outstanding Parisian patroness of the avant-garde music in the first years of the 20th century. Such is the compression of history.

Meanwhile, Rossini was closely associated with the evicted regime.[117] Also, the new king, Louis-Philippe, wanted to implement savings and cut the civil list to a third of the previous amount. Besides, administration for the Opéra had been passed to the ministry of the interior, who had delegated it to a private group. So, the regime reneged on Rossini's annuity. It took six years of litigation before he got paid.[118]

Louis-Philippe's accession marked the start of the 'July Monarchy'. The 'King of the French', as he called himself, was much satirised for his corpulent figure and pear-shaped head. The pioneer of the walk-about, he had a propensity for holding his umbrella in one hand and shaking everyone's hands with the other. To increase his popularity, 'he also would sing the Marseillaise upon the slightest provocation'.[119] The king had no particular taste for music. He enjoyed sitting by the fire while Queen Marie-Amélie did her embroidery. The royal chapel was closed, but opera continued, even though the king's physique was not conducive to his attendance. The Opéra, privatised, thrived under the directorship of Dr Véron, who had formerly marketed chest ointment.[120]

The cosy royal domesticity concealed considerable change in the underlying social structure, which was described by Balzac in one of his novels: 'Political power has been transferred, as you know, from the Tuileries Palace to the newspaper offices, just as economic power has changed its address from the Faubourg Saint-Germain to the Chaussée d'Antin.'[121] Nevertheless, wives of bankers would 'stick at nothing' to gain access to the salons of the Faubourg Saint-Germain, where the old nobility lived: there 'the brightest constellations of their sex shone'.[122]

In this bourgeois-led society, everything became focused on money, 'the only god that people believe in nowadays'.[123] This is epitomised in Balzac's miser Monsieur Grandet, the cooper whose fortune was based on church property put up for sale during the Revolution. Even the noble and landed élites depended increasingly on commerce. Heaven help the unsuccessful. Balzac summed up the vulgar and distasteful situation: 'Death to the weak' is, he wrote, 'the watchword of what might be called the equestrian order, the wealthy class found in every country. That death sentence is deeply engraved on the heart of every nobleman or millionaire.'[124]

Rossini back in Italy

Rossini had made his fortune. *Guillaume Tell*, his 39th opera, was his last: there was virtual silence for 40 years. Between October 1836 and 1855 he lived in Italy doing little, but was chronically ill. This silence may have been a delayed reaction to his mother's death in 1827, or it may have been due to pressure from his father. 'He has toiled long and wearily enough', his father wrote to a friend.[125] Or maybe Rossini recognised that there was a new generation of composers, his successors, all of whom were then making their name, Meyerbeer, Bellini and Donizetti. Maybe the style of the new grand operas was something with which he simply did not wish to be involved or to compete.*

He was not ill all the time, however. Ferdinand Hiller, the virtuoso pianist and conductor, met him in Brussels in 1836, where Rossini had gone with Leopold Rothschild, whose family bank he used.[126] Rossini was so unnerved by the train journey that he never again used this novel means of transport.** Nevertheless, Hiller observed that he had 'lost the enormous corpulence of his former years', adding that he 'beamed with health and happiness'. He was 'a man of the world, dignified, graceful and charming and enchanting everybody with his irresistible amiability'.[128] He was good fun: listening to him singing the 'Largo al Factotum' from *The Barber* must have been hilarious. The composer Auber said that he heard him 'sing a most beautiful baritone with spirit and brio'.[129]

In the late 1830s, Rossini's medical condition certainly deteriorated: he was very poorly both physically and mentally, a manic-depressive. The gonorrhoea continued to produce secretions and blockages. His doctor's report mentions 'mucous matters, through the urethra, often white, often yellowish or greenish yellow';[130] he also had psoriasis on the scrotum that caused great itching; and, on top of all this, he had debilitating bouts of diarrhoea. Antibiotic treatment was 100 years away, so Rossini resorted to a catheter, and he dosed himself with a variety of medicaments: sweet

* Another composer whose flow of works stopped was Sibelius. For the last 30 years of his life he produced almost nothing.

** The development of the railway, a crucial change in technology, was not universally welcomed in the 19th century. It was feared that passengers would asphyxiate if carried at more than 20 mph. In March 1862, *The Lancet* published an investigation regarding 'The influence of railway travelling on public health'. The writer John Ruskin considered that railway travel 'transmutes a man from a traveller into a living parcel'.[127]

almond, mallow, gum, and flower of sulphur mixed with cream of tartar. He took warm baths, and drank castor oil and purgative broths. Leeches were applied to haemorrhoids and to the perineum.[131]

Olympe, the Courtesan

Rossini was nursed through his health problems by Olympe Pelissier, a former courtesan. Courtesans, later known as *les grandes horizontales*, were a feature of Paris life in the 19th century; they recur in later chapters of this book. They have tended to be glamorised, as in Verdi's *La Traviata*, while the sordid and practical aspects, whether reproductive or infectious, have had less attention. Except in their lifestyle, it is difficult to distinguish a courtesan from a prostitute. One author has made *choice* the distinguishing feature: 'A courtesan is less than a mistress, and more than a prostitute. She is less than a mistress because she sells her love for material benefits; she is more than a prostitute because she chooses her lovers.'[132]

For many in this era, prostitution was the only way out of the gutter, the money outweighing the dangers of disease and violence. In any one year in Paris, about 3,800 prostitutes were registered to work in the 180–200 licensed brothels, graded according to 'luxury' and cost. Those who were not licensed risked round-up, inspection and imprisonment in special prisons.* St Lazare prison, built in 1836, had over 4,800 inmates by the 1860s; they were segregated into those over and under 13 years of age, and also those with venereal disease and those free from it; lesbianism was rife.[134] This pathetic scene was far from the stage upon which Olympe played, but it represented one residual and very serious threat.

The other threat facing the courtesan was 'the sort of old age she could look forward to – abandoned, empty, dreary'.[135] Balzac depicts a former courtesan, living in a boarding house, wearing 'a dirty, green taffeta shade bound with iron wire, which would have frightened the angel of pity away. Her shawl with its scanty drooping fringe seemed to cover a skeleton, so angular was her body. What acid had consumed the feminine curves of this creature? She must once have been pretty and well formed … Was she expiating the triumphs of a flaunting youth when the world had run after

* The novelist Emile Zola describes the scene as the police rapidly close in on their prey: '"The cops!", she cried white in the face. "Oh hell, what rotten luck! Now we are in the shit!"' The police made them show their hands; if there were no signs of needle pricks, the girl did not have a job, and therefore must be a prostitute.[133]

her to offer pleasure, by an old age shunned by the passer-by? Her blank look chilled the blood, her shrunken face seemed a threat.'[136]

The editor of the *Revue de Paris* claimed that, shortly before Olympe took up with Rossini, Balzac, 'an enormous man whose ego easily matched the proportions of his physique',[137] had hidden himself in her bedroom to observe her. He then based a scene in his novel *La Peau de Chagrin* on the experience.[138] In that novel, the *primo uomo*, from behind the curtains,

Balzac

observes the courtesan entering, humming a phrase of an aria from Cimarosa's opera *Il Matrimonio Segreto*: 'the beauty of her voice was one more element of mystery in this pre-eminently mysterious woman', he records. 'It gave me ineffable pleasure to watch her movements, as delicate and graceful as those of a cat grooming herself in a sunny nook.' She looked at herself in the mirror and said out loud, as though crossly, 'I wasn't looking my best this evening … My complexion is fading so fast … Perhaps I ought to go to bed earlier and give up this dissipated life.' The voyeur 'was dazzled by the sight of her virginal bosom. Through her chemise her pink and white body gleamed in the candle-light like a silver statue shining through a wrapping of gauze.'[139] Balzac called Olympe 'the most beautiful courtesan in Paris'[140] and so had a brief affair with her, and even proposed to her.*

Others have been less complimentary about Olympe. Verdi found her on one occasion 'more disagreeable than usual', and a friend of his described her as 'a whore who took on anyone willing to pay her with small change … she has an income of 30,000 francs which she earned by moving her thighs back and forth'.[143] Olympe apparently disliked Italians (other than Rossini).

Olympe is a shadowy figure eclipsed by the corpulent frame of Rossini. If the courtesan in Balzac's novel is an indication of what she was like, she was feline, the incarnation of the hard-hearted and hard-faced Society, a vain and artificial woman 'whose heart demanded to be re-conquered every successive moment'. But she was also beautiful, worthy of the Venus de Milo: 'she was more than a woman: she was a romantic novel'. But 'her soul was a waterless desert'.[144]

An Unhappy Fallow Time

Rossini's relations with his wife Isabella had long been strained. She had taken to gambling. Rossini described her as 'a proud and disgraceful woman, a spendthrift … and she does not remember her birth, that she too was the daughter of a poor trumpet player like me'.[145]

So, early in 1837, Olympe left Paris to join Rossini in Bologna, although her presence there had to be handled carefully; there was no question of them living together. There was some relief that a lunch with Isabella went off well. Around this time, Liszt played at some of Rossini's soirées. Liszt's mistress, the Comtesse Marie d'Agoult, who was about to give birth to their daughter Cosima, was frosty towards Olympe. Whatever similarities there may have been in their way of life, they were from a different class.

Rossini's father died in 1839, aged 80. This seems to have caused a major setback to Rossini's health. Olympe took him to Paris for medical treatment for three months in 1843. At times, there was a queue of visitors outside his house in the place de La Madeleine.

After Isabella died aged 60, in October 1845, Rossini and Olympe

* Rossini enthusiasts claim that the bedroom scene is not documented; Balzac's seem less concerned.[141] It is also suggested that the courtesan was modelled on the Princess Belgiojoso, the Italian political activist, and a friend of Bellini.[142]

could at last get married. Their wedding took place on 16 August 1846, when he was aged 54 and she was 49.

Ill health continued to dominate Rossini's life, but he was sufficiently robust that he could visit the stock exchange and play the markets. He also virtually became director of what is now the Conservatorio G.B. Martini in Bologna. At one stage, he tried to persuade Donizetti to become professor of counterpoint there.[146]

Rossini's only new work at this time was the *Stabat Mater*, which was performed in Paris in 1842. Donizetti, back from attending the première of Verdi's *Nabucco* in Milan, conducted the Bologna performance; he reported: 'The enthusiasm is impossible to describe. Even at the final rehearsal which Rossini attended ... he was accompanied to his home by the shouting of more than five hundred persons.'[147] Rossini had actually begun the work about ten years earlier. At that time, he only wrote half the score, and asked a friend to finish it. It was dedicated to a Spanish state counsellor, on the footing that it would not be published. When the Spaniard died, the manuscript was about to be sold off and published with the rest of his estate. Rossini maintained that all rights remained with him as the composer; he reclaimed the work, and finished it. After this, however, anyone who wrote to Rossini asking to publish his work was liable to get a letter back threatening a legal suit.

His works continued to be performed in Paris, and a pasticcio of his work called *Robert the Bruce* was put on in 1846. In October 1848, *Andremo a Parigi?* (Shall we go to Paris?), an adaptation of *Il Viaggio* and *Le Comte Ory*, was staged there.

The years 1848–9 saw turbulence and revolutions across Europe. Wagner, the revolutionary, fled from Dresden; in France, the king was replaced by a president. These stories will be told in later chapters. In Italy, Rossini's position was difficult. He was tainted by the music he had provided in support of the Congress of Verona, a quarter of a century earlier. He may well have been viewed as representative of the much-resented middle class which had profiteered in the period of French rule and thereafter. Payment of sufficient protection money to the Republicans might have helped his cause, but he did not volunteer enough. There was a nasty demonstration against him outside his house. The mob booed and shouted: 'down with the rich reactionary'. So he left Bologna for Florence, where he took up permanent residence. To placate the Bolognese, he sketched a nationalistic hymn and sent it to Bologna to be performed. When the authorities recovered control, he was invited back, but he declined, only returning (in 1850) with a police escort. He must have got a considerable fright in Bologna, and may even have thought that he was on a hit list. He sold the villa at Castenaso and left Bologna for ever in May 1851.

An Improvement: the Return to Paris

In 1854, Olympe had to deny a report in the *Revue et Gazette Musicale* that her husband was mad. In 1855, in desperation for a cure, Rossini returned to Paris. The change in environment and a few trips to spas worked wonders. The improvement was remarkable. Rossini never went back to Italy.

The Rossinis rented the second-floor flat on the corner of the boulevard des Italiens and the rue de la Chaussée d'Antin. Although apparently on the same site as the building in which Mozart lodged after his mother died, this area, as we have seen, was now the financial and banking district, housing the *nouveaux riches*. The portrait painter Winterhalter also lived in the building, which is very close to the site where, five years later, work began on building the Opéra Garnier. Today, Rossini's flat is opposite a cinema.

The boulevard des Italiens, which begins at the rue de la Chaussée d'Antin, was the hub of operatic and theatrical life, especially on the north side where the pedestrians, and prostitutes, promenaded. There, the Opéra had moved after the assassination of the Duc de Berri. There, the Café de Paris had the best food; Tortoni, the ice cream maker, served punch and sorbets, and no doubt the ice cream reminded Rossini of Italy. It was said that 'it was necessary to be rich to dine at the Café Hardy and hardy to dine at the Café Riche'.[148]

In March 1859, the cornerstone was laid for Rossini's new villa in the suburb of Passy, on the edge of the Bois de Boulogne. This is almost opposite the Eiffel Tower, close to the Trocadéro and now a district reminiscent of Kensington. Rossini enjoyed visiting and supervising the works: it took fifteen months to build; of it, there is now not a trace. When he was in residence in Passy, a gilt lyre used to be mounted on the entrance gate.

Samedi Soir

It was particularly appropriate that the rich, bourgeois, and by no means aristocratic Rossinis should reign over a salon. Salons had long been an aspect of upper-class cultured life in Paris, and much sought after: 'To be admitted to these gilded salons was equivalent to being awarded a patent of nobility.'[149]

A salon was essentially 'open house' for a lady's acquaintances who wished to attend on the appointed evening each week. Thus, after dinner, around 9.30 pm, Parisians in the top social echelon would move, on a casual basis, from one salon to another. The Princesse de Vaudémont would serve tea, ices and, at the end of the evening, some punch.[150] But there was no obligation to serve food, the main purpose being conversation. For the ground rules, we can turn back to Madame Récamier, doyenne of the aristocratic salon, the most celebrated beauty of her age. Surrounded by leaders in the literary world, including notably Chateaubriand, she generally spoke very little but 'she would listen and smile intelligently, and from time to time throw in some observation to show that she understood the person who happened to be speaking'.[151] Although an excellent raconteuse, she would call on someone else who knew the particular tale to tell it. She also gave weekly musical parties, and she invited any distinguished foreigners who happened to be in Paris. Rossini, one might assume, had attended one of these.*

Under the July Monarchy, the *nouveaux riches* followed suit and opened their houses too. By the last decades of the century, the practice had spread to people of a lower social sphere and taste. Proust describes a salon which was 'beneath the lowest rung of the social ladder':[153] the principal regular guests of the vulgar pipe-smoking host and his awful wife were people 'sublime in their bourgeois mediocrity':[154] a second-rate painter, a second-rate doctor. A courtesan acted as a magnet and a second-rate pianist played occasional music. Access to the exclusive, top salons of the Faubourgs Saint-Germain and Saint-Honoré, to people of 'real social brilliance',[155] was not available to them.

The Rossinis held their first '*Samedi soir*' on 18 December 1858; the

*Madame Récamier had held salons under the Directory and Empire. After the Restoration, somewhat impoverished, she revived her salon in a room in an old Paris convent. She said that she would know she was no longer beautiful when the little chimney sweeps no longer turned to look at her in the street. Chateaubriand, her constant companion, was one of the finest Romantic writers and the most conspicuous figure in French literature during the Napoleonic period. He was also ambassador and foreign minister. In the 1820s the especially fashionable salons included those of Countess Merlin, the Duchess of Duras, and the highly fashionable portrait painter François Gérard; and, after 1830, the salons of the Princess Belgiojoso, and of Liszt's lover, the Comtesse Marie d'Agoult.[152]

last on 26 September 1868. Those invited included many of the great artists and public figures living or passing through Paris. Invitations were prized. Their salons were attended by such as Liszt, Rubinstein, Verdi, Meyerbeer, Auber, Gounod, Bizet, Saint-Saëns, as well as artists, politicians and diplomats.

The influential Viennese music critic Eduard Hanslick noticed that 'rows of ladies glittering with jewels occupy the whole of the music room'.[156] To imagine them, one can look at the portraits of the top salon hostesses painted by Jean-Auguste-Dominique Ingres, who was about twelve years older than Rossini: he painted the fabulously rich Betty de Rothschild and Madame Moitessier, dressed in enormously expensive silks from Lyons and arrayed in priceless jewels. Hanslick, however, dismissed Olympe with: 'I have nothing to say about the present Mme Rossini, except that she is well off and once was beautiful. A haughty Roman nose, like some tower that has escaped the ravages of time, rises from the ruins of her former beauty; the rest is covered with diamonds.'[157]

It seems that often there were too many guests at these soirées. According to Hanslick, 'the men stand, so jammed against one another that they cannot move … the heat is sometimes intolerable and the crowd so thick that a singer is literally forced to fight her way to the piano to sing'.[158] Rossini himself avoided the crowd by sitting in the dining room, where he was usually attended by his crony Michele Carafa, professor of composition at the Paris Conservatoire.*[161]

Rossini, now totally bald, received people either in a wig or swathed in a huge coloured handkerchief. Stories are told about his wigs. He had one for each day of the week (it was said) and two for Sunday: 'When he goes to Mass, he puts one wig on top of the other, and if it is very cold he puts still a third one on, curlier than the others for the sake of warmth.'[162] On one occasion, Rossini touched Liszt's hair to see whether it was real; pointing to his own, he said: 'See, there's nothing left there now, and I have hardly any teeth or legs.'[163]

* Carafa (see page 277) was a nobleman, a veteran of the Napoleonic Russian campaign, and a conductor for Barbaja in Vienna. He was well known in the Paris boulevards, where he rode on a horse so ancient that Rossini, alluding to *Don Quixote*, asked him on one occasion: 'Have you noticed, Don Michele, that your Rosinante is walking with appoggiaturas?'[159] When Cherubini, by then the director at the Conservatoire, appointed Carafa professor, he asked him to study counterpoint and fugue before teaching it to others.[160]

The Grand Old Man

All who met Rossini enjoyed his wit, often caustic. The soprano Adelina Patti was brought down to earth with a bump, when Rossini followed her over-ornamented account of Rosina's 'Una Voce Poco Fà' with 'Very nice my dear, and who wrote the piece you have just performed for us?'[164] Speaking of the London-based conductor Michael Costa, Rossini said: 'Kind Costa sent me the score of an oratorio and a stilton cheese; the cheese was excellent.'[165]

Rossini's knowledge of food was great. 'He shocked an expatriate Italian grocer by returning to him some Neapolitan macaroni on the eminently justifiable ground that it clearly came from Genoa.'[166]

He would be courteous, except about Wagner. 'Do you know what Wagner's music sounds like to me?', he asked the daughter of Pauline Viardot.* 'Here; this is how the music of the future sounds', and he opened the piano and sat down heavily on the keyboard.[167] He served *turbot à l'allemande* at dinner on one occasion; the sauce came, but no fish: 'the fisherman forgot to bring it. It's the same with Wagner's music. Good sauce but no turbot, no melody.'[168] Another of his *bons mots* was: 'Wagner has some good moments, but bad quarters of an hour.'[169]

In his last years, Rossini wrote small pieces, the first being *Musique Anodine*, dedicated to Olympe in gratitude for her support during the years of illness. He also composed around 150 piano pieces, songs and small ensembles. Occasionally, he emerged to write a work such as the 'Hymn to the Emperor and his Valiant People', which included military effects such as gunfire. This was written for the 1867 Paris Exhibition, supplanting a winning cantata by Saint-Saëns.[170]

He wrote the *Petite Messe Solennelle* for the consecration of the private chapel of a countess. It could not be performed in church because of the ban on female singers. This led Rossini to ask Pope Pius IX to rescind the papal bull forbidding mixed choirs in church. The word 'Petite' was a Rossini joke, for it is a monumental work. Rossini wrote on the manuscript, to be seen today at La Scala: 'Dear God ... I have finished this poor little mass. Have I written musique sacrée or sacrée musique?' He continued, 'You know I was born for opera buffa which contains little

* Pauline Viardot was Malibran's much younger sister. A brilliant mezzo-soprano, she touches the lives of so many 19th-century composers. She died in 1910, aged nearly 90.

learning but a lot of emotion. Be blessed then and grant me a place in Paradise.'[171]

In December 1866, Rossini had some kind of stroke or thrombosis. Around eighteen months later, he became ill; about ten days before he died a short operation was performed on his rectum; and again two days later. Sadly, his last few days until 13 November 1868 were spent in great pain.

He was buried in the Père Lachaise cemetery. Olympe survived him by ten years: a tough woman, she at first stipulated that his body could only be exhumed and returned to Italy provided, to the outrage of Verdi, she could in due course take her place beside him. But eventually she was persuaded that he could be moved there after she had replaced him in the tomb in Père Lachaise. So his body was moved to Santa Croce in Florence in 1887.[172]

Rossini left an enormous fortune with a large fund to found a conservatoire in Pesaro and also a home for retired operatic performers, the Maison de Retraite Rossini.

For us, he left a legacy of memorable operas and gorgeous melodies. Some of his final advice was: 'Let us not forget, Italians, that musical art is all ideal and expressive … that enjoyment must be the purpose of this art. Simple melody – clear rhythm.'[173]

Simple, so sensible.

MEYERBEER, BELLINI AND DONIZETTI

CHAPTER 8

OPERA WAS BIG business and, on the whole, it was a mass-production operation. This was not new: Haydn wrote many operas, and Rossini in his early years composed at least one a year, sometimes more. By the time *Don Pasquale* was staged at the Théâtre des Italiens in January 1843, Donizetti had written almost 70 operas, most of which are never heard nowadays.[1] Unless a work was an enormous success, the composer just had to keep churning out new ones to keep the cash flowing. Speed was of the essence: Donizetti wrote *Don Pasquale* in eight days; it took him fourteen days to write *L'Elisir d'Amore*.[2] There was potential for re-packaging as well: Giovanni Pacini merged various Rossini arias into a 'pasticcio' called *Ivanhoe*, based on the novel by Sir Walter Scott.

Most of us do not remember Pacini, even though he was sufficiently handsome to be chased by Napoleon's exquisite sister, Princess Pauline Borghese, and sufficiently famous to have a street named after him.[3] So one is reminded of just how many others were involved in this colossal musical enterprise. Who now has heard of, or would want to have heard of, Anfossi, Coccia, Federici, Fioravanti, Generali, Guglielmo (father and son), Manfroce, Martini, Mosca …?[4] This list goes on and on. For us, however, three opera composers stand head and shoulders above the rest in the

Above: MEYERBEER, BELLINI AND DONIZETTI

1830s and 40s: Giacomo Meyerbeer, the leading exponent of Grand Opera, a German despite his first name; Vincenzo Bellini from Sicily; and Gaetano Donizetti, who was born almost 1,000 miles to the north. They were predecessors to Verdi.

The style of opera, Grand Opera, was new, and the world beyond was changing. Revolution was festering during the years that Bellini and Donizetti spent in Italy. When, in 1848, the insane Donizetti was moved back to Italy to die in his birthplace in Bergamo, revolutionary armies were converging on the Austrians and all the provinces of Italy were 'in a highly-wrought state of revolutionary excitement'.[5] The turmoil spread elsewhere in Europe and affected the careers of many composers described in this book, including Liszt, Wagner and Verdi. In this chapter, we shall therefore look at the upheavals and the early steps in a series which led eventually to the unification of Italy. The Risorgimento had begun.

Paris, however, was the main centre for opera production: it acted as a magnet for composers, who could earn more there; also, the high standards demanded in Paris, and the actual quality, were self-sustaining. Both Bellini and Donizetti moved there in the mid-1830s. By the end of the decade, their operas were dominating the boulevard des Italiens, and there was far less concentration on Rossini. As we have seen, nearly four out of five evenings at the Théâtre des Italiens in the early 1820s were devoted to Rossini. By 1839, the Rossini proportion had reduced and the spread was much wider: there were 33 Rossini evenings; 29 evenings were devoted to Donizetti and 17 to Bellini.[6]

Thus, to appreciate these composers, we shall look at Paris in the 1830s and 1840s and at the social pressures which were building up there as well. We shall conclude with the tragic deterioration of Donizetti. First, however, we shall consider the remarkable success of Grand Opera in the 1830s, the triumphs of Meyerbeer, and his contemporaries Daniel Auber and Fromental Halévy.

Grand Opera in the 1830s and 1840s

Grand Opera, the new fashion, was immensely successful. The public marvelled at Spontini's historic or fantastic stories, and at the spectacular pageantry. It enjoyed the epic crowd scenes and processions in which the chorus took part, instead of standing 'like rows of onions set in two straight lines on either side of the stage'.[7] The clothes were sumptuous and magnificent. The orchestra was enormous. Dramatic theatrical effects could be created which had not been technically possible before: gas lighting had replaced sooty, smoky oil lamps. Composers exploited the colourful instruments, complementing the colour on the stage. Financiers backed the big-budget ventures, putting 160,000 francs behind staging Meyerbeer's *Les Huguenots* and 150,000 francs behind Halévy's *La Juive*.[8]

There were some great shows, with long runs; the successes were no longer played just a few times and then put away. Daniel Auber's *La Muette de Portici* opened in 1828 and played 122 times up to 1830. Within three years of its première, Meyerbeer's *Robert le Diable* had reached its 100th performance in Paris and had appeared on the programmes of 77 theatres in ten countries.[9]

However, does anyone now remember Boieldieu's sensational *La Dame Blanche*? Many of these hits are now virtually forgotten. To illustrate the nature and scope of these successes, it is worth taking a brief look at some of them; this may also give us a clue as to why Rossini felt it was time to take early retirement.

La Muette, set in Naples in 1647 during the Spanish occupation, is full of local colour. Large crowds congregate outside the cathedral and in the small fishing port of Portici nearby. Amazingly, the *prima donna*, Fenella, is dumb, the part often being played by a ballerina. When a rebellion is sparked off because Fenella has been seduced by the Viceroy's son, there is a beautiful duet, 'Mieux vaut mourir que rester misérable'. To reflect both history and the requirements of the censor, the rebels are defeated; the dumb heroine, abandoned, rushes towards Vesuvius, which erupts to the crashing of cymbals; she throws herself into the crater. The pyrotechnics were specially arranged by an Italian, and stones and cinders fell as the curtain dropped.[10] It is dramatic, powerful stuff, set to attractive and tuneful music, alive, startling. It was new, very clever, and highly effective. No wonder it was such a success in its time.

Dr Véron, recently appointed director of the Opéra, capitalised on this success. He teamed up with Eugène Scribe, the prolific librettist. Véron was the businessman, manager and public relations director; Scribe contributed his sense of the theatre; Adolphe Nourrit was their star tenor, François-Antoine Habeneck their conductor. Véron recognised the commercial importance of attracting the bourgeois classes: besides producing an evening of excellent entertainment, he spread the word that going to the

Opéra was a sign of social status.[11] He provided a full evening, including, say, a three-act Grand Opera and a ballet, or a one-act opera and two ballets. He reduced the number of boxes and created more cheap seats; he also cracked down on the besetting problem of free complimentary tickets.[12] His business was totally commercial.

In 1831, this team had a phenomenal success with Meyerbeer's *Robert le Diable*, another improbable work, but with ample room for spectacular effects. The Devil has followed his son Robert, Duke of Normandy, to Palermo, where he has gone to win the hand of Isabelle. The Devil hopes to prevent the marriage and acquire the soul of Robert. He makes Robert gamble away his fortune and he convinces him that only with his assistance can Isabelle be won. Robert goes to a ruined convent and, with ghostly nuns dancing wildly around him, is given a mystic cypress branch. Isabelle persuades him to break the branch and denounce the Devil. Robert almost signs his soul away, but the clock strikes twelve; the Devil disappears and Robert marries Isabelle.*

Those who did not enjoy the nuns' ballet were appropriately outraged. Mendelssohn, ever prim and prissy, called it 'a veritable scandal'. Schumann wrote that 'the world has rarely seen such a conglomeration of monstrosities'.[14] Henry Manning, later cardinal but then a young English Protestant clergyman, had already decided, after a single visit to the Paris opera, 'never to put my foot into a theatre again'.[15]

Most of the Parisian public lapped it up, and even Berlioz was swept off his feet by it.[16] Subsequently, if a new opera failed, management would replace it with *Robert*, knowing that the losses could soon be recouped.

In 1835, there was another smash hit with Halévy's *La Juive*, again with a libretto by Scribe. Halévy himself was Jewish; yet in Eléazar, he portrays a caricature of the vengeful, usurious Jew of the 1400s. Like *La Muette*, the plot is about seduction. In the dénouement, the heroine is about to be burnt, her execution presided over by a cardinal. Just as it transpires that the heroine is actually the cardinal's own daughter, she leaps dramatically into the flames. The cast for the procession to the stake included the horses

* Many today would enjoy seeing this opera staged. Among the few recordings, we can hear Joan Sutherland performing a mixture of *bel canto* and acrobatics in 'Ah, viens Robert, idole de ma vie'. It soars beautifully over a chorus accompaniment.[13]

1 2 3 4

SOME PARIS COMPOSERS IN THE FIRST HALF OF THE 19TH CENTURY
Luigi Cherubini (1), as depicted by Ingres, was director of the Conservatoire in Berlioz' youth. Michele Carafa (2) worked in the shadow of Rossini. Fromental Halévy (3) was father-in-law of Bizet and composer of *La Juive*. The long-living and clearly highly decorated Daniel-François-Esprit Auber (4) wrote the sensational hit *La Muette de Portici.*

from the Cirque Olympique.[17] The titillating story, the splendid execution, the horses, the historical costumes, the swarming crowd ... oh, and last but not least, the music, all combined to create the recipe for success. It must have been a tremendous night out. It is not difficult to understand why Grand Opera became so discredited: opera had always involved illusion, but now the spectacle, the thrills and spills had taken over. The result is, some would say, vulgar.

In the year after Paris audiences heard *La Juive*, they saw Meyerbeer's *Les Huguenots*. Again, this had large crowd scenes: one in a tavern, another with the chorus conspiring in the massacre of St Bartholomew's Day in 1572. But the improbable has now become ludicrous. The music, although carefully and colourfully crafted, bears scant relationship to the text; there are vocal pyrotechnics seemingly purely for 'effect': the music for Queen Marguerite is not remotely regal, however gymnastic some queens may be. The heroine faints twice within 90 seconds. The whole caboodle is held together by the repetitive use of the Protestant chorale 'Ein feste Burg', usually sung by a character who might well have come from Belfast. In possibly one of the greater understatements of all opera, he announces: 'Master, you have walked into a trap.' However theatrical this may or may not be, it is very difficult to create a great work of art out of such material. But the French loved it, and Balzac thought the story of *Les Huguenots* was true as history itself. Wagner simply dismissed Meyerbeer's output as 'Effect without Cause or Reason'.[18]

Grand Opera, however, deserves credit for the impetus which it gave to ballet as the art form which we enjoy today. The regulations required that works staged at the Opéra should include at least one ballet. At the start of the century, ballet had been a feat of gymnastics and contortions, sometimes performed by families almost as a kind of circus act. With Grand Opera, ballerinas became frail, angelic, and romantic. It should be said that the public's interest in ballet was often for the wrong reasons. The rakes, such as the members of the notorious Jockey Club, came to the opera almost as a gang, late, although in time to view the ballet dancers in the customary second act. A favoured few were admitted to the dancers' greenroom, where there was 'the meeting of the lions and the gazelles'.[19]

Without the stimulus of Grand Opera, we would not have had Ferdinand Hérold's *La Fille Mal Gardée* and Adolphe Adam's *Giselle*. Hérold unfortunately died prematurely of tuberculosis when he was only 42.

Adam remained the leading composer of ballet music until Léo Delibes, the composer of *Coppélia* in the mid-1860s.[20] And French ballet also inspired the wonderful paintings of Edgar Degas, who used ballerinas as models to explore the effect of the body seen from unexpected angles (see colour plate 48).[21]

The requirement for a ballet annoyed both Wagner and Verdi. In March 1861, there was a fiasco with a performance of *Tannhäuser*. Knowing their market, the opera management asked Wagner for a ballet: the Venusberg music was not what the rakes had in mind and the three successive performances were wrecked with catcalls and dog whistles. The French disliked Wagner's style; they wanted the kind of graceful operas which Auber composed, melodies which 'smiled, chattered and hummed'.[22]

The composer who presided over all this Grand Opera was Giacomo Meyerbeer. Bizet said that he was 'the Michelangelo of Music'. George Sand called him 'the greatest poet of us all'.[23] She, however, is known for her novels rather than her poetry.

Meyerbeer

Jacob Beer came from a wealthy Jewish family. He was born near Berlin in 1791, about six months before Rossini. His father was an army contractor and his maternal grandfather owned the concession for the Prussian national lottery, and was also a government contractor and a banker. His parents' home was a cultural meeting place, attended even by royalty. He had his first music lessons from the royal music teacher, and studied composition with Carl Friedrich Zelter, who was also Mendelssohn's teacher. He then went on to complete his studies in Darmstadt, where one of his fellow students was Weber. According to the virtuoso pianist Ignaz Moscheles, the piano playing of Meyerbeer, as he became known, was 'unsurpassed'.

Salieri advised Meyerbeer to study in Italy where, as a student with substantial private means, he could afford to go. A short visit to Venice in 1816 was extended into a stay for nine years, during which he composed several operas in the style of Rossini, culminating in *Il Crociato*, premièred in Venice in 1824. He was hailed as a new Rossini. He moved to Paris in 1826. *Robert le Diable* was, as we have seen, a spectacular success, even though during the première a frame carrying a dozen lit lamps crashed to the floor and barely missed one singer as she went on stage.[24]

Meyerbeer had no financial need to churn out works; so, unlike Donizetti, he could afford to be meticulous in his composition. His output was very small, but now invariably successful. Five years after *Robert*, *Les Huguenots* was a great hit. Meyerbeer then had an interlude directing the Berlin opera, a position which did not work out, so he returned to Paris. *Le Prophète*, starring Pauline Viardot, was staged in 1849. It was produced at 40 theatres and, on 14 July 1851, it had its 100th performance at the Opéra. Meyerbeer was said to have become one of the richest men of his time in Europe,* more so than Rossini. His final opera *L'Africaine* was not put on in his lifetime.

Meyerbeer was naturally showered with honours by the aristocracy to whom he pandered. He was a consummate handler of the media, and the article on him in *New Grove* goes so far as to suggest that 'the modern press conference with refreshments was Meyerbeer's invention'.[26] His techniques for handling the press could be regarded as doubtful by modern standards. At this time, it was usual to pay journalists to secure a favourable review; it was said that a good review from the critic Jules Janin could be bought for 1,000 francs.[27] Meyerbeer was marginally more subtle: he got critics to compromise their independence by making them loans, for which there was a continual demand, and he had the resource to provide the supply.

Berlioz, a scrupulously 'ethical' critic, said that 'Meyerbeer not only had the luck to be talented, but the talent to be lucky'.[28] Today, it is difficult to appreciate the honoured position in which Meyerbeer stood. When he died in May 1864, a few years before Rossini, eulogies were declaimed as the remains were removed from the Rond Point des Champs Elysées to the Gare du Nord for despatch to Berlin. There they now lie in obscurity amidst the battered gravestones of the Jewish cemetery outside the old walls to the north-east of the city.[29] The politician Emile Ollivier said that Meyerbeer's music 'had forged a bond that linked ... the fatherland of Beethoven, Mozart and Meyerbeer with that of Hérold, Halévy and Auber'.[30] Ollivier's brother-in-law, Wagner, would not have agreed; and the bond, if any, would soon break with the Franco-Prussian War, as Offenbach and so many others would experience.

* At least he did not have the stranglehold on opera which Lully exercised two centuries earlier. Lully had obtained an extremely lucrative monopoly over the opera, which restricted the use of music in theatrical productions other than his own.[25]

Meanwhile, Bellini and Donizetti had come to Paris. Before looking at their lives, so tragic by comparison with the brash success of Meyerbeer, we should pause to remind ourselves briefly of the Italy and Sicily from which they came and where, for much of their lives, they lived.

Italy before 1848

Italy was generally very backward and poor (see pages 13–19). In looking at it, we shall start in the north and move southwards towards Bellini's birthplace. At mid-century, half the population of Piedmont, then known as the Kingdom of Sardinia, was still illiterate; its educated classes just became soldiers. Next door, in Lombardy – the area around Milan – the Austrians provided free and compulsory primary education. But since the Habsburgs did not want their subjects to think, the teaching was focused on the technical rather than the philosophical.[31] Also they did not regard easy communications as sensible. So, although they built a good infrastructure of roads and the Milan–Monza line was completed in 1842, railway development was relatively slow.[32]

Lombardy flourished compared with the rest of Italy, although even there a quarter of the population of a sizeable town like Lodi might be made up of paupers.[*33]

Elsewhere, the scene was bleaker. The seaport of Venice was in decline, giving way to Genoa and Trieste. Rome lived off the pilgrim trade; the countryside around it suffered from famine conditions. Until the Austrians insisted otherwise, the Papal government even prevented the building of railways, in case it upset the dormant peasantry. The Kingdom of Naples was still almost medieval. Naples itself had the largest poorhouse in Europe, with 6,000 paupers. Three quarters of the land was in the hands of the nobility or the Church. Corruption was rampant in the cities; as was brigandage in the countryside. Many peasants lived in animal-like conditions. At times, grass and seeds were the only food available to them. A black bread was made from very poor quality flour; its weight would be increased by adding stone dust.[35]

The problems were aggravated by chronic agricultural slumps.

* Milan had a major savings bank in 1823 and an insurance company in 1826. By 1859, Lombardy was producing as much silk as the whole of France. But its relative prosperity did not last: the silk industry was not helped by an unpopular tax on the mulberry harvest, and it was hit by competition from India; the downturn was aggravated by silkworm disease.[34]

Also cholera, which involves dehydration and circulatory failure, struck frequently: there was a major epidemic in 1831–2 and again, more severely, in 1835. In autumn 1836, cholera literally decimated the population in Sicily and took 14,000 in Naples. There was another epidemic in 1854–5. In an attempt to control the disease, even letters had to be fumigated. Those who travelled were often delayed by the quarantine requirements. On one occasion, Donizetti had an eighteen-day quarantine delay in Genoa before he could move on to Milan.[36]

Sicily, where Bellini was born, was particularly poor. At one stage there had been a glimmer of hope. The British saw its strategic potential as a Mediterranean base and contemplated unhitching it from Naples. But that idea was dropped following the fall of Napoleon.

The Young Bellini

It was during those Napoleonic times that Vincenzo Bellini was born in the seaport of Catania on 3 November 1801. He was the eldest of seven children. They were housed in an apartment on the first floor of a fine palazzo in a small square. The large cathedral and the fine town hall are only 200 yards away down the lava-cobbled streets; the moated Castello Ursino is nearby.

Behind Catania is Mount Etna, snow-covered in winter, which rises nearly to 11,000 feet and is surrounded by fertile vineyards and groves of exotic fruits, oranges, lemons, mulberries and olives. Here lived the Cyclops, the one-eyed giant. Here, Demeter sought Persephone; and here, Polyphemus mortally wounded Acis who was wooing Galatea. Less mythological is the mountain's propensity to erupt and deposit ash and black dust on Catania's streets.

Etna erupted in the year after Bellini was born, and there were slight eruptions in several of the following years. When he was eight, there was a bigger eruption, and again a couple of years later. Most of the eruptions, involving earthquakes, explosions and rifts opening in the side of the mountain, were harmless. But the little boy must have been alarmed by the jets of fire and smoke. And in the cathedral he will have seen the picture of the disastrous eruption, only 150 years earlier, in which the lava had scaled the 60-foot-high walls of Catania and poured in; nearby, the sea had boiled. An earthquake some years later destroyed much of the city and buried 18,000 inhabitants.[37]

In this threatened place, Vincenzo's father, Don Rosario, was a mediocre organist. Vincenzo's grandfather taught him composition. Doubtless, the family had a piano in their reasonably spacious apartment; the boy could also practise the organ in the baroque church of San Francesco e L'Immacolata, which was a few steps across the small square in front of the palazzo. Indeed, old Catania is full of churches, and Vincenzo was educated by priests.

Bellini was precocious, and provided his first composition, some church music, at the age of six. In his teens, his ambition may have been fuelled by hearing of the successful career of the up-and-coming opera composer Giovanni Pacini, who was also born in Catania, although his father was a travelling opera singer from Tuscany.[38]

Bellini remained in provincial Catania until he was eighteen, and by then had composed several small works. With the support of the governor, and with finance from the city of Catania, he continued his musical studies at the Conservatoire in the capital, Naples. In the year in which he left his birthplace there was another large eruption from Etna.

In Naples, Bellini mixed with some revolutionary friends. When they were arrested during some disturbances in 1821, he was lucky not to be implicated as well. A colleague introduced him to his first love, Maddelena Fumaroli. However, her father, a magistrate, did not think Bellini suitable.[39]

Bellini's graduation piece led to an invitation to compose an opera for the San Carlo opera house. Bellini asked for the hand of Maddelena, but was again rebuffed by her family, who did not want her marrying a poor 'cembalo player'.[40] He was turned down yet again, even after his opera *Bianca e Gernando* was a considerable success: it was applauded by Donizetti.

Bellini's Middle Years

The impresario Domenico Barbaja (see page 244) spotted Bellini and commissioned an opera for La Scala. This began Bellini's association with Felice Romani, a prolific librettist used by over 100 composers, including Rossini and Donizetti, for whom he provided the libretto for *L'Elisir d'Amore*.

Il Pirata was composed in Milan between May and October 1827, when it was premièred at La Scala. It made Bellini's reputation and enabled him to move in Milan's elegant salon society.[41] He visited the country estates of wealthy and influential friends. Gifted and charming, he was exceptionally attractive and took considerable trouble over his appearance: he was almost six feet tall, with golden curly hair,* a pink and white complexion, slim figure and blue eyes.[42] Although the southernmost of the composers featured in this book, he did not look or behave like a Sicilian, and showed none of the extrovert passion aroused by Catania's roasting summer heat and sharp contrasts between light and shade. His gestures were graceful, languid and often sentimental. Maddelena's family now thought he could be a suitable husband after all, but he had moved on to bigger and better things, and was no longer interested. She died, possibly of grief, aged 32, some fifteen months before him.

In 1829, Bellini's opera *La Straniera* was an even greater success than *Il Pirata*. In the following year, he had a severe attack of gastro-enteritis and convalesced beside Lake Como, with its two arms, one 'so luxuriantly beautiful, and the other so austere, a sublime and charming spectacle, which the most renowned site in the world, the Bay of Naples, equals, but does not surpass'.[43] There, he stayed with his friends, the rich Cantu and Turina families. Between 1828 and 1832, he had a passionate affair with Giuditta Cantu, who had married the silk manufacturer Ferdinando Turina. In the upper echelons of Milan society, the bonds of marriage seem to have been somewhat loose,** so Bellini could stay with Giuditta both in her house in Casalbuttano, near Cremona, and in Milan. He composed *I Capuleti e i Montecchi*, which was premièred at La Fenice in Venice in March 1830; this was a great success, as was *La Sonnambula*, a year later, in Milan. He seemed to lead a charmed life. He made a triumphant tour back home to Sicily.

Bellini's 'trade mark' was his luxuriant, lyrical *bel canto* melody, hence his popularity. But there is little substance and characterisation: the villain and the hero sing much the same music. Wagner liked playing his tunes and possibly summed him (and the tunes) up quite well when he said that 'for all the poverty of invention, there is real passion and feeling there, and the right singer has only to get up and sing it for it to win all hearts'. He added: 'I have learnt things from them which Messrs Brahms & Co have never learned, and they can be seen in my melodies.'[44]

* The fair, blond hair can be seen in a locket at the Bellini Museum in Catania.

** Stendhal's *La Chartreuse de Parme* (1839) portrays marriage in northern Italy as a very weak structure, from the sexual point of view, but woe betide a man who took another's female property without tacit 'consent'.

Not everything composed by Bellini was a success – *Zaïra*, for example. And *Beatrice di Tenda*, written for Venice, was a failure and led to him falling out with Romani. Even *Norma*, at the end of 1831, was not immediately successful, partly perhaps due to a claque financed by supporters of the professionally jealous Pacini. After the first performance of *Norma*, Bellini declared: 'Fiasco, fiasco, solenne fiasco.'*[45] Yet, which modern opera-goer would not give a fortune to attend a performance of *Norma* at La Scala, and hear Giuditta Pasta singing the famous and alarmingly difficult *Casta diva*, with Giulia Grisi starring as Adalgisa?

Generally, Bellini triumphed. The *diva* Maria Malibran moved from being a Rossini star to being a Bellini star.[46] In Italy, her performances of Norma, and Amina in *La Sonnambula*, were prolonged by curtain calls: there were sixteen after the first act of her Norma at La Scala, and 30 at the end. Not only was the stage littered with flowers, laurels and verses: people sobbed hysterically, they screamed and fainted; the police had to be called.

Around this time, Turina started separation proceedings from his wife; but Bellini may have been becoming more than professionally interested in Malibran. In February 1833, he contracted to go to London. *Il Pirata*, *Norma* and *I Capuleti e i Montecchi* with Pasta, and *La Sonnambula* with Malibran, were triumphs. Bellini then settled in Paris at the Théâtre des Italiens. He was fawned upon by the aristocracy, although he was shy and withdrawn and was uncomfortable with the French language.

At the time when he went to London, he broke off his relationship with Giuditta; although they corresponded for about a year, he had no wish to resume the affair. He wrote her a bitter and egotistical letter from Paris in March 1835, in response to certain accusations which she had made: 'Me forget you? Is that possible after all the anguish I have suffered for you? Don't you remember my tears at Casalbuttano on the eve of my departure? Are not the tears of a man the best and surest proof of his love?'[47]

Bellini Towards the End

The start of 1835 was truly a vintage moment for opera in Paris. It began with Bellini's *I Puritani* on 2 January. This was followed by the première of

* A fiasco is a bottle or flask. Bottles, often defective, were (and some are still) wrapped in woven straw with a flat underside to enable them to stand upright. This is said to be why the word was associated with failure.

Halévy's *La Juive* on 23 February. This was also the time that Donizetti arrived there.

Bellini was increasingly jealous of the competition he faced from Donizetti. He developed an obsession that Donizetti had become Rossini's protégé, and on 12 March 1835 he strongly criticised the première of Donizetti's *Mario Faliero*. It seems that Bellini was 'vain, haughty, devouringly egocentric and more than a little affected'.[48] On the other hand, Rossini said of him that 'he had a most beautiful, exquisitely humane soul'. And the conductor and composer Ferdinand Hiller wrote: 'His personality was like his melodies – it was captivating.'[49]

Paris: the Théâtre des Italiens

In June 1835, Bellini went to stay with an English friend, Colonel Samuel Levys (or Lewis) and his companion, a former dancer at the Opéra, at their small villa in Puteaux on the other side of the Seine from the Bois de Boulogne. The house had trees around it, and a wicket gate leading off the street; Bellini's room apparently looked out onto the garden. Very soon, he wrote to friends that he was in bed, ill with diarrhoea. Three months later, on 14 September, some friends went to try to see him, but they were refused entry. One eventually got in by pretending to be a doctor, and found that Levys had gone into Paris, and Bellini was at the villa alone and being attended by a doctor. In the next few days, the doctor sent several messages to Carlo Severini, the director at the Théâtre des Italiens, describing Bellini's condition. One recorded that Bellini had had a convulsion, was unconscious and dying. By the time his friends arrived, he was indeed dead, the place was closed up, and there was only a gardener around.

Among Bellini's possessions at the villa was a locket, a miniature portrait of Malibran; perhaps it was close to his heart.[50]

There was enough mystery surrounding Bellini's death for rumours soon to circulate that he might have been poisoned; he came, after all, from Italy 'where people know how to appreciate the pleasures of revenge'.[51] Rossini, who had taken a dislike to Levys, was particularly concerned about this. Reports of a normal death might have seemed too commonplace for such a prominent Romantic.* Possibly he died of cholera. People then always lived under the threat of this disease. Bellini himself was careful about it and, when writing *Norma*, took care to escape from Milan where the epidemic was raging. Others seem to have taken considerable risks: Liszt stayed in Paris throughout the appalling epidemic of 1832.**[53] In that year the prime minister died of it, and at one stage 800 people died in a single day; George Sand, soon to be Chopin's lover, who had taken her young daughter with her to Paris, caught a benign form of it. In her own apartment block, six people died on the lower floors; the disease climbed up 'floor by floor'.[54]

An autopsy, for what it was worth in those days, reported that Bellini died of an inflammation of the intestine aggravated by an abscess of the liver, and indicated that he may have suffered from this condition for a considerable time. Bellini had been chronically ill; maybe he had cancer. But he was a young man, not yet 34. His meteoric rise to fame had pointed to such a promising future.[55]

He was embalmed. Rossini, Carafa and Cherubini were among the pall-bearers at his funeral held on 2 October 1835 in Les Invalides. It was followed by a procession to Père Lachaise cemetery. Later in the century, he was returned to Catania.

* See the next chapter for some comments on Romanticism.

** The virtuoso violinist Paganini played at a benefit concert for the families of 1832 cholera victims. The epidemic gave rise to a religious revival. The Virgin appeared in Paris to Saint Catherine Labouré, then a novice with the Sisters of Charity of St Vincent de Paul, warning her of the impending disaster and instructing her to have a commemorative medal struck. By 1836, 8 million medals were in circulation.[52]

The Liberation of Italy: Early Days

Bellini was lucky not to have been arrested in Naples during the 1821 disturbances. In Paris, he was often at the salon of Princess Cristina Belgiojoso, who had emigrated there in 1831 after being involved in revolutionary activity in Italy.* She and her husband were Italian nationalists, and her Paris salon became a refuge for others with similar leanings. There was, by then, a strong movement pressing for the liberation of Italy from rule by the Habsburgs, and for the implementation of liberal reforms. Although its origins were in the previous century, when the term 'Risorgimento' had been coined, the movement gathered real momentum only in the years following the fall of Napoleon. It would eventually result in unification, but that would take until 1870 to complete.

At the edges, there were student protests and the kind of activity in which Schubert and Bellini got caught up. Young men, as a sign of protest, grew beards and moustaches, wore their hair longer than the usual fashion, and smoked cigars. The police would arrest them, march them to the barber's shop, and have them forcibly shaved. Much more sinister, however, were the revolutionary secret societies, whose influence had fanned outwards from Italy. One such, the Adelfi, was led by an Italian aristocrat, Filippo Buonarroti, a descendant of Michelangelo and friend of Robespierre.[56] The related society, the Carbonari, recruited thousands of ex-Napoleonic personnel; it also attracted that particularly lethal class, the unemployed professional, of which there were so many. It was counterbalanced by a counter-revolutionary organisation, the Sanfedisti, whose aim was to murder radicals and the members of the Carbonari. There was also a more moderate class calling for liberation – the intellectuals, the writers and the poets. They wanted to be part of an Italian community but did not have a particularly coherent idea of how an Italian nation would be constituted, especially as the Papal States divided the peninsula and provided a formidable blockage to any form of unification.[57]

'Les Trois Glorieuses', the uprising in Paris at the end of July 1830, triggered off revolts in the Central Duchies and in the Papal States including Bologna and Pesaro, Rossini's birthplace. This was at the time that Berlioz travelled to Rome and found himself in a brig full of revolutionaries on

* She was tough: in 1848, she raised a corps of volunteers to take part in the Milanese revolt, and in 1849 she cared for the wounded in the siege of Rome.

their way to join the insurrection. The captain put up too much sail, the ship heeled over and they were lucky not to be shipwrecked.[58]

More notably, the 1830 risings also involved the Bonapartes, who imagined putting Napoleon's son, the Duke of Reichstadt,* on the throne of a united Italy. A provisional government was declared in Pesaro and its troops took Ancona. The Carbonari were effectively destroyed by the suppression and executions which followed the subsequent defeat. Berlioz believed that most of his co-travellers in the brig were later executed.[59]

The torch of freedom passed to the Young Italy movement founded by Giuseppe Mazzini, a doctor's son from Genoa and the author of a pamphlet entitled *Filosofia della Musica*. Most importantly, he was a formidable political thinker who believed passionately in Italy, and was bitterly opposed to the Roman Catholic Church. He called for a world movement dedicated to the assassination of the rulers who used their subjects for their own ends: 'Sacred was the dagger of Brutus; sacred the stiletto of the Sicilian who began the Vespers; sacred the arrow of Tell.'[60] In 1833, Mazzini inspired an insurrection in the Piedmontese army, which was betrayed and led to 21 death sentences. In April 1834, Young Europe was formed in Geneva, joined by movements in many countries, apart from Ireland, where revolutionaries were less sympathetic to Mazzini's anti-Catholic doctrines.

A revolution planned for 1834 in Genoa failed to ignite. As part of this, Polish refugees living in Switzerland were to invade Sardinia; also, a young sailor, Giuseppe Garibaldi, was to lead a mutiny in the Genoese navy. Owing to the failure of the revolution, Garibaldi went on the run for the first of many times in his charmed life, and was sentenced to death in his absence; he moved on to South America, where he fought for the independence of Uruguay from Argentina.[61]

Terrorist attacks on monarchs continued: King Louis-Philippe survived an assassination attempt in 1835. The first of seven attempts to assassinate Queen Victoria took place in 1840; some were by cranks. A plot was unearthed by police in the Papal States in 1844. Also, a rebellion in Calabria in southern Italy failed; nine of the insurgents were shot. The authorities had been tipped off by the British government. Mazzini's

* The son of Napoleon I, in whose favour he abdicated in both 1814 and 1815, subsequently died at his grandfather's palace, Schönbrunn, outside Vienna, in July 1832.

correspondence was being opened at the general post office in Mount Pleasant in London, interference which he condemned as 'disgracefully un-English behaviour'.[62] The consequent furore led to enquiries by committees of both Houses of Parliament.

The 1848 Revolution in Italy

In June 1846, Pius IX was elected Pope. Although opposed to giving up his 'temporal powers' over the Papal States, which would be the consequence of Italian unification, he was, at that time, genuinely in favour of some liberal reform. He wanted to relax censorship, to abolish the discriminatory laws against the Jews and the persecution of heretics, and to allow laymen, as well as priests, to serve in the higher branches of the government and judiciary. He implemented an amnesty, as a result of which there were around 2,000 potential revolutionaries walking the streets of Rome and Bologna. In 1847, he established a legislative council for Rome, some members to be elected and some to be appointed by himself.

People all over Italy were delighted: they hailed him with the cry of 'Viva Pio Nono e la liberta'. This alarmed the Austrians. By late 1847, the octogenarian Field Marshal Count Radetzky, the military commander in northern Italy, was reporting that 'the whole social order … [is] … about to collapse … the Revolution will only be kept in check by fear'.[63] To protect their interests, the Austrians moved into Ferrara, a Papal 'Legation', without Pius' consent.

Not surprisingly, revolution broke out in the most backward area, Sicily. In January 1848 the people of Palermo rose, and soon the rebels controlled most of the island. The Pope, now furious with the Habsburgs, refused to allow them through his territory to suppress the revolt: Pius even asked God to bless Italy. Prince Metternich, the Habsburg chancellor, fled from Vienna in early March.

Soon, the Italian peninsula was in turmoil. The Milanese decided to hit the Habsburgs where it hurt, by boycotting smoking and gambling, both the source of much tax. This was followed by an uprising in Milan in mid-March, the glorious 'Cinque Giornate'. In Venice, the Republic of St Mark was proclaimed on 22 March. In Naples, Ferdinand II promised a constitution, an oath which he had no difficulty breaking when, using Swiss mercenaries, the tables were turned. The revolution spread north and across Europe. In Dresden, Wagner was seriously implicated, as we shall see.

In Piedmont, King Carlo Alberto also granted a constitution under pressure, but was conscious of the increasingly perilous position of his throne. In April, with the connivance of the shaky government in Milan, and to the horror of the Pope, Carlo Alberto took the opportunity of declaring war on Austria and marched into Lombardy. This was the first in a series of annexations that would turn the liberation of Italy into the unification of Italy under the domination of Piedmont.

Irregular armies marched from the Papal States and Naples to support the Piedmontese. Peasant armies marched on Bergamo, as Donizetti lay dying. But there was a severe blow to the cause of liberation when the Pope, who had become alarmed at the movement which he had unleashed, disassociated himself from the war against the Habsburgs. Although Pope Pius, later to be a friend of Liszt, sincerely wished to introduce a more liberal regime in the Papal States, he had never been in favour of Italian unification or the expulsion of the Habsburgs.

The stage was set for the counter-revolution. Count Radetzky, who had taken refuge in his fortified area south-east of Lake Garda, known as the 'Quadrilateral',* emerged and forced the Piedmontese to request an armistice at Custozza on 25 July. But elsewhere, uproar continued: at the end of August there was a major riot in Vienna, in which eighteen were killed. About 30,000 of those who had flocked into Vienna to take part in public works programmes were expelled, and the university was closed.[64]

Thinking that the French would come to their aid, the Piedmontese renewed the war. In a battle at Novara, on 23 March 1849, Radetzky again defeated them. The king abdicated in favour of his son Victor Emanuel II. Radetzky then shelled Venice, which surrendered on 22 August 1849. Johann Strauss the Elder was inspired to write the Radetzky March, hailing him as the hero who had slain 'communism'.

The Roman Republic

Like his fellow monarchs, the Pope had conceded a constitution of sorts in March 1848, although this stopped at granting civil rights to non-Catholics. After the defeat of the Piedmontese in July, Rome filled up with returning demobbed soldiers. The Pope's position was increasingly

* The 'Quadrilateral' had its corners at Peschiera, Verona, Mantua and Legnago (not to be confused with Legnano).

unstable. His chief minister was murdered in November. The civic guard fired on the Quirinale, the Pope's palace, and a bullet through a window killed a bishop. The Pope fled. Whether he left disguised as a housemaid or as a cleric, or whether he was or was not assisted by a beautiful countess, the escape seems to have been particularly undignified.[65]

Thus began the Roman Republic of 1849, which coincided with the première of Verdi's opera *La Battaglia di Legnano*. The Pope appealed to foreign Catholic governments, especially France, for help in overthrowing the revolutionaries, who were led by Mazzini and Garibaldi.

France was undergoing one of its periodic Catholic revivals, and its president, General Cavaignac, loathed by many for his brutal suppression of the 1848 upheaval in Paris, came to the rescue. An army was sent to Rome, ostensibly to forestall an attack by the Austrians; the Neapolitans came from the south; and the Spanish sent a small force.

Garibaldi dealt with the French and defeated the Neapolitan armies in June 1849. But time was not on his side. The French were embarrassed by their defeat and sent more troops. The fall of Rome was only a matter of time. Mazzini wanted a bloodbath to provide an inspiration to future generations; Garibaldi was more pragmatic. During a brief armistice, Mazzini left on a British passport, and Garibaldi escaped with a band of 4,000 men, offering his heroes only Churchillian 'hunger, thirst, forced marches, battles and death'.[66] Pursued as brigands, he and his little army doubled back and holed up in the tiny independent Republic of San Marino; then, driven from there, he obtained boats on the Adriatic and headed towards Venice. His South American wife Anita, pregnant and suffering from malaria, died. Astonishingly, Garibaldi himself got away.

Virtually nothing came immediately from all those months of chaos and conflagration. But two of the key men in the unification of Italy were now in position: Mazzini, the 'brains' behind the movement, the former chief minister of the Roman Republic; and Garibaldi, the heroic commander of the Roman army. Piedmont was now seen as a 'political beacon' under Victor Emmanuel, who was intent on acquiring more of northern Italy.[67] Unification was on its way.

Donizetti

A year before the collapse of the 1848–9 revolution, Donizetti had died in his birthplace, Bergamo in northern Italy. The city of Harlequin, Bergamo is a fortress which guards approaches to the Val Telline, the very important strategic route through Switzerland to the north.[68] The colourful, now quaint, old town is on a hill around 350 feet above the more modern lower town. Gaetano Donizetti died near his birthplace up there, just outside the Porto San Alessandro, which bears the Venetian winged lion on it, reminding the visitor that the town had long been an outpost of Venice. At the time of his birth, Bergamo was part of Lombardy and under Habsburg dominion. An army of occupation requisitioned food and billeted its troops in the city.

Donizetti was born on 29 November 1797 in a substantial house of four storeys. In the same street, Vincenzo Boromini, a well-known painter, was born 40 years before; in a house almost next door, Alfredo Piatti, the cellist whom Grieg would describe as being 'as boring as he is famous',[69] was born a quarter of a century later. We are always told that Donizetti was born in extreme poverty, the fifth of six children of a seamstress and the janitor of a pawnshop. The family was not musical.

Although his parents obtained a certificate that they could not afford to pay his school fees, Gaetano was taken into the music school at the basilica of Santa Maria Maggiore. The school had recently been reorganised by Simon Mayr, a distinguished composer of Bavarian origin. He was a central figure in the generation of Italian opera composers before Rossini: his works were performed as far afield as Dublin, Philadelphia and New York.[70]

It has been suggested that Mayr was the true inventor of the Rossini crescendo. Stendhal said that Mayr was to music what Dr Johnson was to English prose; he created a style which was 'heavy, turgid, and a thousand removes from the natural beauty of simple speech, but which, nevertheless, had a certain quality of its own, particularly when one had struggled and struggled and eventually got used to it'.[71] Mayr certainly is one of those composers who is rarely heard today. However, he was an important supporter of Donizetti. He sent him to study counterpoint with Padre Mattei in Bologna some 150 miles away.

Donizetti returned to Bergamo in 1817. Had a lady from Bergamo not paid for his exemption, he would have been conscripted.[72]

His debut was a failure. His first opera, *Enrico de Burgogna*, was performed at Venice in November 1818, but was repeated only twice. He stayed in Bergamo until 1821, when he got a commission to compose an opera for the Carnival at Rome. When the opera, *Zoraida di Granata*, was an overwhelming success, Donizetti was accorded the coveted title of being 'a leading claimant to the throne of Rossini'. The Neapolitan impresario Barbaja contracted with him to compose and conduct at the Teatro Nuovo in Naples. Donizetti's *La Zingara* in May 1822 was a success. This was at the time that Bellini was a pupil at the Conservatoire. But *Chiara e Serafina*, which opened at La Scala in October 1822, was a failure. Maybe this was because it coincided with the trial of Carbonari; many stayed away because the theatre was infiltrated with police spies. Donizetti was not invited to produce another opera there until 1830.[73]

In the 1820s Donizetti was based largely in Naples, where he conducted operas by other composers and continued as a hack to write his own operas, some with titles that today sound curious, such as *Emilia di Liverpool* and *Elisabetta, o il Castello di Kenilworth*. He also taught at the Naples Conservatoire. He could produce volumes of music very quickly: 50 operas in around 20 years, sometimes at a rate of five a year.[74] Nevertheless, he was careful and methodical. This can be seen from the original score of *L'Elisir d'Amore*, where, in a spindly handwriting, the main parts were written first and the orchestration filled in later, often in a different ink.

When Mendelssohn was in Naples he was unimpressed by Donizetti's work. But the quality of performance in Italy was low; and the quality of listeners was equally poor. When Berlioz saw *L'Elisir d'Amore*, he found the house 'full of people talking at the top of their voices, with their backs to the stage; the singers all the time gesticulating and shouting in eager rivalry. So at least I judged by seeing their huge open mouths, for the people made so much noise that it was impossible to hear a sound beyond the big drum. In the boxes some were gambling, and others were having supper … It appears however – so at least I am assured – that the Italians do occasionally listen.'[75] Berlioz' criticism was no exaggeration: Stendhal described a count and countess in a box at La Scala, talking 'with enjoyment … throughout the whole performance'.[76]

In 1828, Donizetti married Virginia, the daughter of a lawyer in Rome.* He had written a duet for two women's voices and piano for her. His parents were against him marrying, possibly because they thought that it might lead to a reduction in the remittances which he sent home. They never met Virginia.

* Virginia's brother Antonio assisted Verdi in later years.[77]

At the end of 1830, Donizetti suddenly hit the jackpot: *Anna Bolena*, the first of his works to be performed in Paris and London, marked the start of his international career. After *Anna Bolena*, there were 35 Donizetti operas still to come.

L'Elisir d'Amore and *Lucrezia Borgia* followed. Schumann described the latter as music for a marionette theatre.[78] *Maria Stuarda*, first produced in its original form at La Scala at the end of 1835, was a failure because Malibran as the Queen of Scots was ill and in poor form. When produced at the San Carlo in Naples, its title had to be changed to *Buondelmonte*, because the story of a queen being imprisoned and executed was unacceptable to the Neapolitan censors.[79]

Donizetti went for a short visit to Paris in 1835, at Rossini's invitation. After this he returned to Naples, where *Lucia di Lammermoor* 'aroused the highest enthusiasm'. The 'mad scene' became 'the chosen proving ground and applause-gatherer for an apparently unending succession of *prima donnas*'.[80] Bellini's death that year left Donizetti supreme in Italian opera until Verdi emerged with *Nabucco* in 1842.

Donizetti moved to Paris in 1838 with the intention of earning enough to be able to retire. But, by then, a number of things had started to go wrong. He was passed over for the directorship of the Naples Conservatoire, and his opera *Poliuto*, which included the martyrdom of a saint, was banned by the censor.

More importantly, in the previous year Virginia had died aged 29, after her third labour: they had lost their first two children. We do not know the cause of her death; it was possibly measles or scarlet fever; possibly it was cholera. Donizetti was overwhelmed and never really recovered. Even six years afterwards, he could not bring himself to mention her.[81]

France between the 1830 and 1848 Revolutions

At one stage, Donizetti had operas performing at four Paris theatres, much to the irritation of local musicians, including Berlioz. What were France and Paris like at this time, when Italy was, as we have seen, fermenting with revolution?

There was considerable economic progress. France was well known for the quality of its luxury and skilled finished goods like silk, gloves and porcelain. (Britain, by contrast, was seen as the mass producer of middle-quality items.) Railways were being built; more than 800 miles of new all-weather roads were being completed each year. The first transatlantic steamer sailed in 1840; the population of Paris and Lyon increased by a third between the years 1831 and 1846, four times the rate of growth in the country as a whole.[82]

Paris resonated with bourgeois values. In Daumier's cartoons published in *Le Charivari*, the capital was portrayed as 'fat, lecherous, ugly and self-indulgent'.* This was not untrue: élite restaurants began to open, as did department stores selling ready-to-wear clothing made by poorly-paid process workers. The clothes of the affluent women, with tight corsets and full dresses, reflected their inactivity and their husbands' wealth and prurience. The rich installed bathrooms with hot water and bidets; domestic manuals advised on how to counteract the stimulating aspects of hot water, keeping one's eyes closed being the suggested remedy. And of course, to reinforce its social legitimacy, the bourgeois would emphasise the importance of suitable marriage. There was regular harassment of homosexuals and prostitutes. Public order and moral rehabilitation were seen as the answers to social problems.[84]

The hypocritical bourgeois relish reports of sleaze. In 1847, two ministers were condemned to civic degradation and three years in prison for corruption in connection with public contracts. There was the sensational case when the Duc de Choiseul-Praslin, who was in love with the English governess, battered his wife to death. The wife had for many years been looked after by Mendelssohn's Aunt Jette.[85] The Duke sensibly committed suicide by taking arsenic before he could be tried by his peers.

Alongside this brittle affluence, there was the totally different, appalling world of the poor. 'Whatever the lot of the workers is', a trade minister opined in 1833, 'it is not the manufacturer's responsibility to improve it'.[86] By 1839, there were nearly 150,000 children aged between seven and fourteen working in the cotton industry. A report of a few years earlier

* Balzac described a bottle merchant visiting an artist's *atelier*. The face was of the type which artists colloquially describe as a melon. 'This fruit was mounted on a pumpkin, clad in blue cloth decorated with a bundle of tinkling watch-seals. The melon was puffing like a porpoise, the pumpkin was walking on turnips improperly called legs.' The wife 'looked as if her face was covered with mahogany stain; she was like a coconut with a head on top and a belt round the middle … On her podgy hands she proudly displayed enormous gloves like the gauntlets on a shop-sign. Feathers like those on horses at a first-class funeral waved on her overflowing hat … There followed a young asparagus in a green and yellow dress.' That was the daughter.[83]

described the workshops in a provincial town: 'Poor families with a lot of young children ... Among them are large numbers of thin, pale women, walking barefoot through the sludge...and a still larger number of young children, equally dirty and haggard, dressed in rags which are thick with oil that has fallen on them while working.'[87] Their life reflected their circumstances: a new-born bourgeois baby had a life expectancy of over 30 years, whereas that of a weaver was four years. Once through infancy, the weaver's child could expect to live to its late 20s or early 30s, while domestic servants and shoe-makers on average would live into their 40s and 50s.[88] The large Faubourg St-Antoine had only 46 doctors.*

Bread was the main diet. Most people lived in cramped multi-functional rooms. In Paris, 2,300 night-soil carts emptied the tenement buildings; elsewhere, the gutter sufficed. Only one building in five was connected to the Paris water supply by mid-century. Women had to cart water from fountains piped from near where the new sewerage system for wealthier neighbourhoods entered the River Seine. Thirteen per cent of babies were abandoned by distraught mothers, mainly from among the one third of children born outside marriage; often, pathetically, they left the name and the baby's birth-date, hoping one day to return. Two-thirds of the foundlings died while in the care of rural wet-nurses.[89]

This fetid atmosphere provided an increasingly fertile breeding ground for 'socialism'. At this stage, its advocates looked for a form of co-operative capitalism, with the workers themselves owning their own mechanised workplaces. The Society of the Rights of Man, most of whom were skilled wage-earners mainly under 30 – that is, young tailors, jewellers, painters, luxury goods workers, shoe-makers and joiners – formed an alliance with the republican middle class. This and other alliances led to the law of 10 April 1834 which required police authorisation of all associations of more than twenty people. In 1835, 30 republican newspapers were closed.[90]

Occasionally the pressures were too much. The July 1830 revolution was followed by anti-clericalism and the sacking of the Abbey of St Denis. A rising by Lyon silk workers in 1831 was suppressed. The 1832 cholera epidemic was followed by an uprising ignited by the funeral of General

* In the 1820s, almost half of all deaths in Paris were due to pulmonary consumption, pneumonia, pleurisy and intestinal complaints (cancer and heart diseases accounted for fewer than five per cent, though per capita tobacco consumption was 1 kilogram annually).

Lamarque, the chief of the republican opposition in the Chamber of Deputies, who died from the disease. During the two days portrayed in Victor Hugo's *Les Misérables*, 150 were killed and 500 wounded: barricades went up, mattresses were pushed against windows to stop stray bullets; cries of the dying could be heard in the night air. In May 1839, The Society of Seasons tried to seize power; in two days of fighting, there were 100 deaths. Some composers were sympathetic: Liszt wrote *Lyon* after the street fighting there in 1834. In July 1837, he gave a concert in aid of the striking silk workers from the same city.[91]

Some Parisians supported the 'legitimists' and called for the Bourbon monarchy to be restored and replace the Orléanist Louis-Philippe; others supported the much more popular Bonapartist movement, which looked nostalgically back to their founder, and his image as a populist democrat forced into war by intransigent English counter-revolutionaries. Napoleon's son and heir, the Duke of Reichstadt, by now was dead, and the leader of this faction was the improbable Louis Napoleon.* In the 1830 disturbances, he fought in the risings in the Papal States, and, with the help of his mother, made the first of his spectacular escapes. He tried in 1836 to incite the garrison in Strasbourg to rise against Louis-Philippe, and was expelled to America. He then settled in England as a bit of a dandy and a considerable womaniser. In 1840, he took the opportunity of the return of Napoleon's remains from St Helena to land with a small force in Boulogne. This was a total fiasco, and he was sentenced to life imprisonment in the fortress of Ham on the Somme, from which, disguised as a carpenter, he escaped to London to resume his social life.[92] He was regarded in French political classes as a buffoon: he was not the first successful politician to prosper under this cover. Meanwhile, his book *Des Idées Napoléoniennes* had sold half a million copies by 1848.[93]

By early 1847, more than one in every three Parisians had to apply for emergency relief.[94] There were attacks on grain carts, forced imposition of price reductions, and intimidation of hoarders and the wealthy. Thus, when in the following January the Sicilians rose, it was not long before there was revolution in Paris. Following the banning of a political meeting,

* He was born in 1808 to Hortense de Beauharnais, the daughter of Empress Josephine by her first marriage. His father was supposedly Napoleon's brother, the puppet King of Holland. If so, he was both a nephew and a step-grandson of Napoleon I.

there was a big demonstration on 22 February, and the barricades went up the next night. Two days later, King Louis-Philippe sensibly took to his heels, heading for Eastbourne before settling in Surrey. As the revolution spread northwards from Sicily, Gian-Maria Scotti, in whose palazzo Donizetti died, led the Bergamo legion forth against the Austrians.

Donizetti: the Downward Slope

We have heard that Donizetti moved to Paris with the intention of making enough money to retire. Whereas Rossini achieved this objective, and Verdi did subsequently, Donizetti's future was different.

Donizetti is visited by Andrea

With a few exceptions,* Donizetti's operas were successful. The première of the comic opera *Don Pasquale* in January 1843 was perhaps the climax of his life; overnight it was one of the glories of the Théâtre des Italiens.

By then, Donizetti had negotiated a contract by which he became

* *Linda di Chamounix*, in 1842, quickly caught on after a slow start. It was translated into French for a tour of the provinces. *Maria di Rohan* was premièred in Vienna, where *Dom Sébastien Roi de Portugal* was also a success, despite a poor reception subsequently in Paris. *Caterina Cornaro* was a particular failure, perhaps because Donizetti was not present to supervise its première.

Kapellmeister in Vienna. This allowed him six months leave each year. He divided his time, half being spent in Paris and half in Vienna, where he was a great social success with the Metternichs, something which did not endear him to the Italian revolutionaries. He offered to help Verdi with the production of *Ernani* in Vienna. He continued to compose frantically.[95]

By now, he had composed 70 operas. Suddenly, all this activity came to an abrupt stop. Friends had started to notice how he was degenerating, although he was not yet 45. During his time in Vienna in 1844–5, he suffered from worse headaches, fevers and pervasive depression. One can see the deterioration from his portraits: a picture of him a few years before he died shows that he was ill (see colour plates 26 and 27). Soon, he had to be accompanied by a domestic at all times. He was treated by a specialist in venereal disease, and given a routine of leeches, cupping, vesicants and foot-baths.[96] It is usually suggested that he caught syphilis when a student.

During his last days in Vienna, Donizetti's illness had taken a particularly dangerous course. His behaviour was 'marked by intense eroticism'. He would pick up tarts in the Prater amusement park; it seems that he preferred two at a time. He applied this routine also when he was in Paris. His letters became full of obscenities.[97]

At the end of January 1846, with subterfuge, under the pretext that he was being taken to Vienna, he was driven to a sanatorium at Ivry near Paris. His letters became increasingly incoherent. The sanatorium gave him a billiard table to relieve the boredom, but as the general paralysis of the insane took a grip upon him, he could not play. There is a print of him at Ivry, a nice square villa then in a country setting outside Paris, being led around the formal garden by two assistants.

His nephew Andrea, the son of Donizetti's older brother, came to visit him and suggested taking him to Italy. But the Paris prefect of police would not let him go. When Andrea was called back to Constantinople by his father, Donizetti was left, pathetically, alone in France. Andrea took his jewels and decorations back to Bergamo on the way.

Friends tried to get him out of Ivry, because by now he was harmless. Andrea returned after seven and a half months, by which time his uncle was no better than a vegetable. We can see from the daguerreotype on the previous page, dated 3 August 1847, that he was in a hopeless condition.

For almost seventeen months, he was incarcerated in Ivry. At the end of June 1847, he was at last taken into Paris. The prefect detained him there and put a guard on the house. But Andrea's father Giuseppe exerted pressure through the Austrian authorities to get him released.

On 19 September Donizetti set out on the nineteen-day trip to Bergamo, by train to Brussels, and then by coach over the St Gotthard. He stayed in the Palazzo Scotti just a few yards along the street from Santa Maria Maggiore church where his education had begun.

His carers made an extension to a wing chair so that he could lean forward to the left, chin on chest, hands firmly clenched. He uttered occasional monosyllables. One of the portraits (colour plate 27) shows him sitting in the chair, which can be seen in the museum in Bergamo, although the artist tactfully omitted the extension.

Gaetano Donizetti died on 8 April, aged just 50.[98]

When he was exhumed to put him in Santa Maria Maggiore, it was found that the cap of his skull was missing. A doctor had taken it, possibly because the bone could have provided a pathologist with evidence of his disease; it was recovered and not buried, but kept in an urn for 75 years. In 1951, it was buried with the remains of the composer, attached with adhesive tape.[99]

A more macabre incident took place in connection with Bellini. Over 40 years after his death, his embalmed corpse was transferred back to Sicily, first to lie in state in the cathedral and then to be buried there. The soft, young features of the death mask reputedly taken at the time of his death had now been replaced by the shrivelled, sunken cheeks as of an old man. Local officials wanted to do an autopsy. A young American woman gained admittance, and asked permission to kiss the corpse. Mrs Swift not only kissed Bellini's remains 'with a lover's kiss, long and resonant', but also took two hairs from his chest.[100]

Bellini and Donizetti epitomised the Italian Romantic spirit of the 1830s. Bellini wrote: 'Opera, through singing, must make one weep, shudder, die.'[101] Their sad lives, both so short, yet so different, do much the same.

Berlioz

CHAPTER 9

We recoil with horror when we hear of Bellini being kissed passionately on his lips so long after his death. But we should not be surprised: the Romantics were obsessed with death, disaster, horror and ghosts.

In his memoirs, Berlioz, an arch-Romantic, recalls following a cortège to a mortuary. Later, he bribed the doorkeeper and was able to gaze on the white face of the dead woman and kiss her limp hand. Years later, his first wife was exhumed when they closed the cemetery in which she had been buried: Berlioz describes how the coffin came apart; the grave-digger, as in *Hamlet*, took up the head and put it in a new coffin. Then he lifted, with some difficulty, the headless trunk and limbs. There was a 'blackish mass to which the shroud still adhered, resembling a heap of pitch in a damp sack'. He added, 'I remember the dull sound … and the odour.'[1]

After reading some other Romantic writers, one notices that these macabre descriptions become repetitive. George Sand, the novelist and lover of Chopin, recalled that her father dug up her baby brother on the night of the funeral; they kept the coffin in the house until the next night when they reburied it under a pear tree. Similarly, when her grandmother was buried, Sand climbed into the open grave – the night, of course, was clear and cold – and she kissed the skull of her father, which had come away from the body.[2]

We have already reached the time when some authors of memoirs, especially autobiography, write what they want the reader to think happened, rather than what actually happened. One begins to wonder what, if anything, is true. Maybe it does not matter. But it is in this questioning frame of mind that it is wise to approach the remarkable story of Hector Berlioz, who led an exaggerated, almost unreal, life full of feeling and emotion, rebellion, enthusiasm, disaster and disillusion; but who was also at the leading edge of change in music.[3]

Berlioz began life in a petty bourgeois family near Lyon, less than six months before Napoleon was declared emperor. He became a medical student and pursued his studies in Paris. But he preferred music to medicine. From a distance, he fell passionately in love with an actress, Harriet Smithson, who was at first unattainable. He composed the *Symphonie Fantastique*, won the coveted Prix de Rome, and returned to Paris where he eventually married Harriet. In her case, as in his career, the reality was very different from the dream. We shall look at his life as, increasingly bitter, he was left on the periphery of the musical establishment, and regarded more as an intellectual than as a proper composer who would charm the audience with melody.[4] Although rejected in Paris, he had a successful conducting career abroad. We shall also glance at the beginnings of the tawdry and meretricious Second Empire, because he died within eighteen months of its crash.

One has to be careful of pigeonholing artists, whether musicians, painters or writers.[5] But, without doubt, Berlioz was a Romantic. It is difficult to say precisely what one means by this. One writer has stated the problem succinctly: 'Everybody knows what a Romantic is, or thinks he knows, which may be why nobody is really sure.'[6] Understanding what it means is made no easier by the fact that the Romantic composers were each so different and indeed fought 'like hell' among themselves. Brahms and Wagner loathed each other personally and professionally and believed that the very fate of music depended on the outcome of their hostilities. If we are to label Berlioz as a Romantic, it seems appropriate to consider, at least in the very broadest sense, what the term might mean.

The Components of Romanticism

Stendhal, the novelist, had a very simple explanation. Romanticism is 'the art of presenting to people the literary works which ... can afford them the greatest pleasure. Classicism', he continued, 'presents them with works which gave the greatest possible pleasure to their great grand-parents.'[7] The Romantics certainly wanted change; they rebelled against the noble simplicity and calm, the Greco-Roman grandeur and conformity, of classicism.[8] In 1808, a lecturer on drama in the University of Vienna condemned the 'unlimited deference to the ancients' shown by the classicists.[9] So, Beethoven became an icon for the Romantics because he dared to breach the traditional classical rules about structure and content; his personal behaviour, overtly non-conforming, was also seen as 'Romantic'.[10]

In politics, this rebellious side of Romanticism came to the fore in the struggle for freedom. Political rebels in the first half of the 19th century saw themselves as Romantic figures, like the figure of Liberty holding high the tricolour in Delacroix' magnificent and evocative canvas depicting *Liberty Guiding the People*. Byron went so far as to take up the cause of Greek independence, but unfortunately died, relatively ingloriously, of fever while trying to assist a group of freedom fighters.

In painting, the Romantics rebelled against the restraints of classicism, for which colour was almost improper. Romantics luxuriated in colour. We can see this particularly in paintings. Look at the colours in a picture by J.M.W. Turner who was only five years younger than Beethoven (see colour plate 11). He was the first to realise that colour could be applied directly, independently of form and content.[11] In music, we can hear the luscious and lyrical colour and contrasts in Weber's Romantic opera of 1823, *Euryanthe*: it is a new and exquisite sound.

With colour came the exotic and the orient. This was not the simulated Turkey of Mozart's *Die Entführung*, but 'the orient of the scimitar, of the Albanian costume, of the latticed window looking out on azure waves'.[12] So, in Weber's *Oberon*, the escaping hero and heroine waft by magic between Baghdad and Tunis; on their route, they are shipwrecked and captured by pirates; they find themselves on a desert island, presumably one in the Mediterranean. 'This taste for imagining oneself in strange lands or remote periods, this joy in costume, is genuinely Romantic.'[13]

The Romantics liked to regard themselves as being more expressive, more emotional than their predecessors. In music, this claim is difficult to sustain. Earlier composers had also been passionate, dreamy, lyrical and chromatic in their writing: the essence of 'baroque' music was to express a single emotion, a sentiment, an 'affection'; and it has been said that 'inside every classical artist there was a Romantic trying to escape'.[14] Old papa Haydn had his moments of 'Sturm und Drang' (storm and stress). Mozart exudes emotion: listen to *Don Giovanni*. Perhaps the Romantics merely exaggerated the emotions: heightened, intense and passionate, the emotions came in volumes.

Not surprisingly, love was the emotion on which the Romantics thrived. Often that love was not sexual love, but something purer, like the 'total dedication of a great soul to another',[15] or the dreamy, melancholy longing, the yearning for the unattainable. Wagner's characters frequently yearn for something: to the ordinary listener, it is not always immediately obvious for what they yearn so passionately; but, no doubt, it was important to yearn.

The Romantics also thrived on melancholy and 'wonder'. The poet Chateaubriand tinged his love of the sea with melancholy. For some, the melancholy might develop into madness: sometimes clinical, as with Donizetti and Schumann; at other times, one might surmise, there was a degree of affectation by the person concerned, or it seemed suitable (maybe even fashionable?) to regard the individual as mad. George Sand's mother was thought to be mentally unstable,[16] yet there is little evidence that she was much more than occasionally inconsistent and irresponsible. Cosima Wagner thought her mother was insane,[17] although possibly the symptoms she noticed represented little more than an occasional attack of depression.[18]

For the Romantics, wonder was closely related to horror.*[20] In 1764, Horace Walpole dreamt he was in an ancient gothic castle and saw, at the top of the staircase, a gigantic hand in armour. When he awoke, he wrote the first horror story, *The Castle of Otranto*.[21] Romantic artists painted disasters, shipwrecks, storms and calamities, like Géricault's shipwreck scene, *The Raft of the Medusa*, displayed in 1819. They even seemed themselves

* Edmund Burke, better known as a political writer, said in the middle of the 18th century that awe, reverence, wide-eyed wonderment was the source of beauty; he called it 'fear'. 'Terror is the most distinctive quality' in Edgar Allan Poe's influential *Tales of the Grotesque and Arabesque*, published in 1845.[19] Debussy was obsessed by Poe's *The Fall of the House of Usher*, with its 'thousand conflicting sensations, in which wonder and extreme terror were predominant'.

to enact these disasters: the poet Shelley drowned when the schooner named *Don Juan* in which he was sailing off the Italian coast went down in a storm, or possibly when rammed by pirates.

There were other aspects to Romanticism. There was an emphasis on religion, although the religion need not be wholly orthodox. We see this emphasis in the showy Roman Catholicism of Liszt. Even the Protestant Schumann wrote a Mass and a Requiem.[22]

Romanticism – the Role of Music

Romanticism in music had strong links with the other arts, particularly with literature. The relatively wide dissemination of novels and poetry enabled composers, among others, to receive and contemplate Romantic ideas. The composer could disappear into the mountains or fields, like Schubert, and, in complete solitude, contemplate the poetry of Goethe, or, perhaps, the novels or *Lettres sur Jean-Jacques Rousseau* of Germaine de Staël. Some composers also became *littérateurs* in their own right. Weber started to write a novel. E.T.A. Hoffman was both a composer and the writer of *The Tales*.* Schumann was a poet and journalist. The notorious Wagner wrote volumes. Both Wagner and Berlioz tried, in different ways, to fuse the arts, Berlioz within the symphony, Wagner in his operas.

Musicians believed that their art had a special role to play: *suffused through music*, the many disparate and often nonsensical aspects to Romanticism could be communicated to ordinary people and seem almost coherent and sensible.[23] Without music, the love story, the horror, the madness, even the religion, and the orient would otherwise just be rejected as absurd. Hence, Wagner could say that music begins where language ends.**[24]

Possibly because composers were usually employed in courts rather than self-employed in garrets, they were relatively slow to adopt many of the Romantic aspirations, which are found earlier in the other arts. Horace Walpole wrote *The Castle of Otranto* in 1764. Well before Mozart was born, Piranesi was drawing horrific prisons, besides which the Prisoners'

* E.T.A. Hoffmann (1776–1822) was a prominent German Romantic writer. He was also a composer. Musicians know him largely because of Offenbach's famous opera, *The Tales of Hoffmann*, which is based on three of his tales. He also features in Schumann's collection of fantasies for the piano, entitled *Kreisleriana*. This was inspired by Clara Wieck, and Schumann's comparison of himself with Hoffmann's fictional Kappelmeister Kreisler.

** Contrast this with Voltaire's quip that what is too stupid to be said is sung.

Chorus in Beethoven's *Fidelio* seems limp. Henry Fuseli's *Lady Macbeth with the Dagger* was displayed in 1800, before Beethoven had published his First Symphony.[25] However, by the 1820s, when Berlioz went to Paris, Romantic trends in music were clearly becoming established: for example, Weber's *Der Freischütz*, with its colour and its spectral Wolf's Glen scene, was premièred in 1821;[26] shortly afterwards, Weber's Dresden colleague Heinrich Marschner wrote *Der Vampyr* based on Byron's *Lord Ruthwen*, and the following year *Der Templer und die Jüdin* based on Sir Walter Scott's *Ivanhoe*.

Several of the ingredients of Romanticism are recognisable in the life and works of earlier composers. However, nobody so far adopted them to such an extent, or took them to such an extreme, as did Berlioz.

Berlioz' Early Years

Hector Berlioz was born on 11 December 1803 at La Côte St André, almost halfway between Grenoble and Lyon, the second city in France. La Côte is a very small town, tucked away five miles off the main road, stretched along the side of a hill which overlooks a plain towards the mountains of Dauphiné. It has a 16th-century wooden market hall, a château rebuilt in the 17th century and an older church. In 1803, it had about 3,500 inhabitants.[27]

The Berlioz house, occupied by the family since 1730, is in a street below the market square; it has a courtyard and walled garden with a 'coach' entrance at the back. The rooms are fine, although they display some signs of bourgeois pretentiousness: on the walls are portraits of Hector's forebears, such as his grandfather, who died when Hector was twelve, the conseiller auditeur à la chambre des comptes du dauphiné, and his smartly turned-out wife. There are family trees tracing the family back to the 16th century, and pictures of a farmhouse they owned. But the successful and cultured doctor, one of the earliest exponents of acupuncture, and perhaps particularly the composer's mother, must have felt that, although reasonably prosperous and comfortably off, they were neither here nor there: they were in a backwater.[28]

Much is made of the prominence and respectability of Berlioz' family. His father, briefly mayor at the awkward time of the Restoration, when people's loyalties to the left, the right and Napoleon were put under the spotlight, is notorious for never once hearing a note of his son's compositions in the 45 years that he could have done so. One wonders how the Berlioz family compared with a pen-portrait by Balzac, the novelist, of a prominent provincial family of lawyers: they 'took snuff and had long ceased to bother about their snivelly noses or the little black specks which were scattered on the front of their dingy shirts with crumpled collars and yellowed creases. Their limp cravats rolled up into ropes as soon as they were put round their necks ... Their faces, as faded as their threadbare jackets, as creased as their trousers, seemed worn out, wizened, and simpering.'[29]

This portrait, seen through the eyes of a Paris dandy, is exaggerated, of course. However, it is not clear why the Berlioz family should have been significantly different, except that Berlioz implied that they were. At any rate, they were biggish people in a tiny place, and would have greater ambitions for their son than that he should become a professional musician.

In the turbulent years leading up to Hector's birth, there were advantages in living away from Grenoble or Lyon. Grenoble had figured prominently in the early days of the Revolution and royalist troops had been bombarded from the rooftops in the so-called 'Day of Tiles'.[30] But this was nothing compared to Lyon, which, being the centre of the luxury silk industry, suffered terribly: between 1789 and 1799, the number of silk workshops fell by more than a half. Only ten years before Berlioz' birth, Lyon rebelled against revolutionary Paris; it fell after a seven-week siege, whereupon the committee of public safety decreed that it, the birthplace of Roman Emperors Claudius and Germanicus, should be obliterated and its name disappear, except for a monument recording that 'Lyon made war on Liberty. Lyon is no more.'[31] In the repression which followed, the guillotine was too slow, so the Lyonnais rebels were blown into graves with gunshot. Then, about eighteen months later, after a famine, their murderers were duly hurled into the Rhône. La Côte St André, although at risk to bad harvests, was surely a safer place to be.

As a small boy, Hector will have heard much about the Napoleonic Wars which went on throughout his boyhood: his uncle was a cavalry officer serving in Spain and Russia, and many inhabitants of La Côte were on active service.[32] One wonders what Hector was doing when, aged eleven, Napoleon passed along the main road on his way back from Elba. Just before reaching Grenoble, Napoleon had encountered a roadblock, but called the soldiers' bluff, so they threw down their weapons. 'Before

Grenoble I was only an adventurer; after Grenoble, I was a Prince', he said later.[33] As there is no reference to this event in Berlioz' memoirs, one assumes that he did not wave the emperor on.

In the safe haven of La Côte, Hector's father taught him the classics, and a bit of music. Although there was no piano in the house, he found an old flute, and learnt the guitar, which was fashionable among the bourgeois for accompanying transcriptions from operas or dancing.[34] Hector's musical inclinations were also encouraged by his uncle, an amateur violinist and singer, and by two local teachers, one of whom came from the Lyon theatre orchestra. Soon, he was writing to a Paris publisher to get some compositions published. But his family destined him for his father's profession, so he studied medicine at Grenoble University and moved on to Paris, medical centre of the Western world, in October 1821. A few months before this, Napoleon had died on St Helena.

A Student in Paris

Hector shared lodgings with one of his cousins, also a medical student. One can imagine the rooms exhaling the 'boarding house smell', and the pair being dismayed that 'the atmosphere has the stuffiness of rooms which are never ventilated, and a mouldy odour of decay'. As in Balzac's description of a boarding house, they will have found that 'poverty without glamour reigns here, a narrow, concentrated, threadbare poverty. Although actual filth may be absent, everything is dirty and stained; there are no rags and tatters, but everything is falling into decay.'[35]

Hector's cousin bought a corpse for eighteen francs, and they set to work at the dissecting room. Hector describes the circumstances, in his customary way:* 'When I entered that fearful charnel house, littered with fragments of limbs, and saw the ghastly faces and cloven heads, the bloody cesspool in which we stood, with its reeking atmosphere, the swarms of sparrows fighting for scraps, and the rats in the corners gnawing bleeding vertebrae, such a feeling of horror possessed me that I leapt out of the window and fled home.' But he knew he had to make a go of it, and so became 'as callous to the revolting scene as a veteran soldier ... I even found some pleasure in rummaging in the gaping breast of an unfortunate corpse for the lungs, with which to feed the winged inhabitants of that charming place.'[36]

* By the time he wrote this, Berlioz was an experienced journalist.

He joined the claque, the hired applauders or booers, at the Opéra, and thus got in free and saw operas such as Gluck's *Iphigénie en Tauride* and Weber's *Der Freischütz*. At one stage, he found himself singing one of Salieri's tunes from *Les Danaïdes* 'while sawing away at the skull of my "subject"'.[37] His studies were disrupted when the school was closed by political disturbances. Pupils at both his school and the School of Law were highly politicised and had been involved in the demonstrations which followed the execution of the assassin of the Duc de Berri in the year before Berlioz arrived.[38]

Although Berlioz obtained his medical qualification, he really wanted to be a musician. His father wanted him to become a lawyer; his mother in particular was against him becoming a musician. She regarded musicians and actors as 'abominable creatures excommunicated by the Church and therefore predestined to eternal damnation'. She cursed Hector: 'Go and wallow in the filth of Paris, sully your name, and kill your father and me with sorrow and shame!'[39] His father relented and gave him an allowance for a trial period.

He enrolled and studied as a private pupil with the elderly director of the Chapel Royal, Le Sueur, who specialised in vocal music.[40] Le Sueur would provide Berlioz with a great deal of moral and some financial support in later years. Berlioz also studied with Antoine Reicha, a Czech colleague of Beethoven since his Bonn days. Reicha was known for being efficient and strict, but also for being sympathetic to new ideas.

Berlioz taught himself orchestration by following the score while watching the opera. The management cannot have planned on having him, a self-appointed guardian of musical integrity, in the pit, following the performance. He would roar out when there had been a change, as in a Gluck opera: 'there are no cymbals there! Who has dared to correct Gluck?'[41] One of his interventions almost caused an uproar.

The library of the Conservatoire National de Musique et de Declamation was open to the public. In an attempt to reduce carousing, its director had ordained that men and women enter the building by different entrances.* Hector took no notice and brushed past the porter, who fetched the director, the distinguished Cherubini.[42] A few minutes later,

* A similar rule, one staircase for men, one for women, reputedly applied at the Royal College of Music in London until the middle of the 20th century.

one of the most prominent figures in French musical life for half a century was chasing young Hector around the library table, as he said, 'knocking over stools and reading desks in the vain effort to catch me'.[43] However exaggerated the description, this was hardly an auspicious start for someone who had aspirations to enter the Conservatoire and justify himself to his parents by winning the coveted Prix de Rome. He competed for this in 1826, getting nowhere.

This strained his father's patience. The allowance was stopped and Hector had to scrape a living by giving flute and guitar lessons, and writing articles.*[44] He earned 50 francs a month singing in the vaudeville chorus at the Theatre des Nouveautés. He was so embarrassed about this activity that he kept it secret from his flatmate. He contrived to buy a piano on which he could experiment and crash out chords. He read trendy novels by Scott and Fenimore Cooper. He lived in a garret in the Latin Quarter and fed himself on leeks, vinegar, mustard, cheese, lard and bread, and the occasional quail trapped with a contraption devised by his flatmate. Towards the end of the month, as the money began to run out, the two of them might be reduced to eating just a few grapes.[45]

When a performance of a Mass which Berlioz had written was called off, his parents doubtless felt particularly justified in their dismissive attitude. But he was irrepressible. He got the Mass performed, even though the performance was a disaster. He failed to get an opera about tyranny, heroism and rescue performed, so he destroyed it, and used excerpts for later works, for example, his tuneful *Franc-Juges Overture*.

Harriet

Harriet Smithson, an actress, now entered his life (see colour plate 19). French theatre at the time was fossilised in its stylised classical forms and structures:** it was ripe for change. Shakespeare did not comply, at least to

* Berlioz was not poor. He expected a private income of 2,000 fr, or 1,200 fr at least. The (fictional) family of Balzac's law student Rastignac pinched and scraped to send him 1,200 fr a year: they considered that this was an investment; he would be the future of the family.

** In particular, there was an inflexible rule that a drama must take place on one day, in the same place, and have a plot in which all the events are connected by a single chain of cause and effect. These were known as the three 'unities' of time, place and action. Voltaire criticised Shakespeare's 'farces monstreuses qu'il appelle des tragedies'. In 1830, there was a riot at the première of Victor Hugo's *Hernani*, which offends the unity of time: the pro-classicists hissed; members of *Jeune France*, the revolutionary movement, turned up to frustrate them.[46]

the strict French standards, so his works were received badly when staged in Paris in 1822: Desdemona, when smothered by Othello, drew shouts of 'à bas Shakespeare: c'est un lieutenant de Wellington',[47] and there was a shower of rotten vegetables.

A turning point came, five years later, when a London theatre company, including the tragedian Charles Kemble, came to perform Shakespeare at the Odéon Theatre. The play billed was reckoned to be about good Romantic subjects, a Danish prince and a ghost. The audience that night included the cream of Paris *literati*, Victor Hugo, Alfred de Vigny, Alfred de Musset and Delacroix.[48] Sitting unknown to them in a free student seat in the pit, his hair 'falling over his face like a weeping willow',[49] was the young Hector.

The audience was overwhelmed by Ophelia's mad scene performed by the beautiful, blue-eyed Harriet Smithson. She was actually an indifferent actress who compensated for her weak voice and lack of skill by over-acting. She used her skill at mime to portray Ophelia's grief for her father: 'He is dead and gone, Lady; he is dead and gone; at his head a grass green turf, at his heels a stone.' When she made her first exit, the audience was first struck dumb, and then exploded. Miss Smithson did not know whether she was being applauded or about to be pelted with rotten fruit. But by the time she exited with Ophelia's final words, 'God be wi' you', there was hardly a dry eye in the house. The novelist Dumas said: 'It was the first time that I saw in the theatre real passions giving life to men and women of flesh and blood.'[50]

Hector was immediately in love, yearning for 'la Belle Irlandaise' from Ennis in County Clare. Now a star, Harriet was beyond his reach. A thousand people were unable to get seats at her benefit performance. The king sent her a purse of gold. Businessmen saw a different commercial opportunity: lithographs of her as the mad Ophelia appeared in the book and print shop windows. There was a 'coiffure à la Miss Smithson', a black veil with wisps of straw tastefully interwoven amongst the hair. The press ran her story, *Figaro* writing that for as long as she appeared at the Odéon, 'tout le quartier St Germain comprend ces mots anglais: I love you'.[51] She had the motto, 'My kingdom for a horse', painted on her carriage, possibly one of the earliest instances of personalised number plates.[52]

Hector was emotionally overwhelmed, that September night in 1827; he was soon at her performance in *Romeo and Juliet*. His presence was later recalled: 'I saw a young man whose appearance, once seen for three minutes, was unforgettable', wrote one spectator. 'His thick shock of light auburn hair was tossed back and hung over the collar of his appropriately threadbare coat. His magnificent, Marmorean, almost luminous forehead, a nose one might have supposed carved by Phidias' chisel, his fine and slender curved lips, his slightly, but not too convex chin, his whole delicacy of mien which seemed to spell the ascetic or the poet, create an ensemble which would have been a sculptor's delight or despair. His was the ideal profile for a medallion or a cameo. But all these details vanished at the sight of those wide eyes, a pale but intense grey, fixed upon Juliet with that expression of ecstasy which the Pre-renaissance painters gave to their saints and angels. Body and soul alike were wholly absorbed in this gaze.'[53]

Thus began what Berlioz described as 'the grand drama of my life'.[54] He wrote to Harriet; but stars only rarely have time to answer fan mail. He wandered around near the theatre, and observed her movements from the shadows. He was sleepless and could not compose. Then in May, against Cherubini's wishes, he put on a concert at the Conservatoire to show her that he too was an artist. She took no notice and set off on a tour of the provinces. On her return, she must have become aware of his interest in her. He got his *Waverley Overture* included in the programme at a fund-raising concert for the poor. By some chance, his apartment was opposite hers and he could see when she came and went. He persuaded himself that she was in love with him. But she did not reciprocate; and she told the concierge not to receive any communications. When eventually she left Paris, he watched from his window: 'No words can describe what I suffered ... my mind was paralysed as my passion grew. I could only – suffer.'[55]

He was inspired by a Beethoven concert and by reading Goethe's *Faust*. He wrote *Huit Scenes du Faust*, had them engraved at his own expense, and sent a copy to Goethe. But, as Schubert experienced, Goethe rarely answered letters from ordinary people. Goethe's adviser on music, Zelter, dismissed Berlioz' work as 'an abortion arising from loathsome incest'. He explained: 'Certain people can show their capabilities only by coughs, snorts, croaks and expectorations; Herr Hector Berlioz seems to be among them.'[56]

Berlioz was still obsessed with Harriet: 'I think I feel her all around me; all my memories revive and unite to destroy me. I hear my heart beat, and its thudding shakes me like the vibrations of a steam engine',[57] an appropriate contemporary metaphor however un-Romantic it may sound to modern ears. He earned some money from teaching the guitar, which was remunerative because 'guitaromania' was at its height.[58] He became a music critic writing weekly articles for *Le Renovateur*. In 1828, he entered the Prix de Rome and won the second prize, a laureate crown, a gold medal and a free pass to all the opera houses.

Prix de Rome

The Prix de Rome, so important in the musical life of France, was established by the government to enable promising young French artists, aged under 30, to study for five years without financial worry. Prizes were awarded in music, painting, architecture, sculpture and engraving. The competition was run by the Académie des Beaux Arts, of whose 40 various members six were, at least in their own view, the most distinguished musicians in France. The winner in music won a prize of 3,000 fr, for each of five years, on condition that the first two were spent at the French Academy in Rome and the third in Germany.

The process was tortuous. In the preliminary round, candidates were given a vocal fugue to work up. The shortlisted five or six were then allowed 22 days to write a piece for one or two voices and orchestra. For this, they were shut up in separate 'boxes' and forbidden to leave except for meals at 11 am and 6 pm, and, in the evening, to receive friends for a couple of hours. When selecting the winners, the examiners were joined by two members from the other sections of the Académie. The piece was played on the piano, which, as Berlioz complained, gave no indication of orchestration, or the colour. The award was made and confirmed or modified by the full Académie a week later.[59]

The set piece in 1829 was a composition based on Cleopatra's suicide. Berlioz records a conversation with the stuttering Adrien Boieldieu, distinguished composer of *Le Calife de Bagdad* and *La Dame Blanche*. 'My dear boy, you had the prize in your lap, and have deliberately thrown it away'; 'I assure you, Sir, I did my best', responded Berlioz. 'That is just it. You ought not to have done your best; your b-best is too good. How could I approve of such m-music, when soothing music is, above all others, the music I like?' To which Berlioz said, 'It seems to me rather difficult to write soothing music for an Egyptian Queen who has poisoned herself and is dying a most painful death in the agonies of remorse.'[60] No prize was awarded in 1829; Berlioz had only won the second prize, in the previous year, with the support of the painters and sculptors. His mistake was to try to compose, rather than sit an examination.

Berlioz became well known, even if contentious, in artistic circles. One comment was: 'that young man is a hopeless case; Beethoven has turned his brain'.[61] He continued to compose, including several compositions for the guitar.

In 1830, possibly sensing the atmosphere created by the July Revolution, the judges awarded Berlioz the first prize. He knew that he had won because he had made friends with the porter who collected the votes. The set piece was a cantata on The Last Night of Sardanapalus, as portrayed in a highly contentious painting by Delacroix which had been exhibited the previous year. Berlioz toned down his examination piece. He finished it 'to the sound of stray bullets coming over the roofs and pattering on the walls' outside his window.[62] Emerging on 29 July with his orchestral score, he crossed the courtyard of the Palais Royal, into the shopping precinct, notorious as a place of prostitution and gambling.[63] Here he heard the sound of the crowd singing one of his arrangements of Moore's *Irish Melodies*, his 'Chant Guerrier'. He joined forces with them and, later in the day, found himself leading a large crowd, hot from the barricade, in singing the 'Marseillaise'. That is, if you believe his memoirs.

The performance at the official prize-giving ceremony was a disaster. The set poem ended where Sardanapalus mounts his funeral pyre with his prettiest slaves; Berlioz only wrote this conflagration scene after he had won. But – 'A hundred thousand curses on musicians who do not count their bars! In the score, the horn gives the cue to the kettledrum, the kettledrum to the cymbals, the cymbal to the big drum, and the first sound of the big drum brings in the final explosion. But the damned horn missed the cue, the kettledrums hesitated, and the cymbals and big drums did nothing; nothing is heard! Nothing!!! And all the time the violins and basses carry on their impotent tremolo, and there is no explosion, a conflagration that goes out before it has begun; a fiasco.'[64] He hurled his score into the orchestra in a rage. He was so ashamed of the quality of the work that he destroyed it.

Symphonie Fantastique

Later that year, in December, Habeneck conducted the first performance of Berlioz' *Symphonie Fantastique* in the Salles des Concerts du Conservatoire. The *Symphonie* was inspired by de Musset's translation and adaptation of de Quincey's *Confessions of an Opium Eater*, and also by Victor Hugo's *Le Dernier Jour d'un Condamné*.[65] It seems that Berlioz had experimented with opium: in the story, the drugged composer dreams that he has killed his lover and is executed; the last movement is the nightmare of Hell's vengeance, a Witches' Sabbath.

Berlioz distributed a programme, so that the audience could read the story which the music purported to describe. Berlioz used the *idée fixe*, the technique of transforming themes to tell the story, convey a poetic idea or a mood. In the absence of a recognised structure such as sonata form, this technique also provided the 'glue' to hold the piece together.

'Programme music' was not new. Vivaldi's *Four Seasons* is an obvious earlier example of descriptive music, even if it does not go so far as to tell a story.* Mahler would subsequently say that behind *all* music there is a programme, because music is concerned with portraying human emotions. Berlioz, it has been said, simply exaggerated the expression and made explicit what was implicit.[67]

The relationship of the music and the programme is tenuous. Schumann, who met Berlioz at this time, said: 'Whether now, in the mind of one who did not know the composer's intention, this music would awaken pictures similar to those that the composer wished to sketch, I am not in a position to decide.'[68] Indeed some of Berlioz' programmes are so vague that they might be read into any composition: the overture *Le Corsaire*, although labelled 'd'après Byron', was originally called *Ouverture de la Tour de Nice*.

Nonetheless, the *Symphonie Fantastique* is a landmark Romantic work, and makes bold use of the programme. Yet, rather than reporting the first performance, a historic event, the press was more concerned with the treason trials of Polignac and other ministers of the deposed King Charles X.

Camille

Berlioz' love life had undergone a change. Mademoiselle Marie Moke, daughter of a professor from Ghent who had lost his money speculating, had a slender, graceful figure, wonderful black hair and large blue eyes

* Marin Marais (d. 1728) apparently wrote a witty description of a gallstone operation in a solo sonata for viola da gamba and continuo. More sensational, perhaps, were Poglietti's dance movements depicting the history of the Hungarian rebellion (1672), including the trial, the decapitation of the rebels and the final requiem.[66]

which at times shone 'like stars'. Also, she was an outstanding virtuoso pianist. She was a pupil of the leading pianists of the time, Herz and Moscheles, and of Kalkbrenner, whose concerto she had played in Brussels, aged fourteen. De Quincey described her as 'the celestial pianofortist. Heaven nor earth has yet heard her equal.'[69] Beside all this, Camille, as she was called, was highly sexed, with a pushy mother.

Camille

Around March 1830, Hector, his friend Ferdinand Hiller and Camille were all part-time teachers at Mme d'Aubrée's school for girls with orthopaedic difficulties.[70] Hiller was dating Camille, and told her of Hector's infatuation with Harriet. She then saw Hector as an interesting challenge. Her opening move was straightforward. She said that Hector should not look so sad. He should not worry: her affair with Hiller was just platonic and transient. Besides, Harriet was having an affair with her manager. Within days, Hector and this 'young and exasperatingly beautiful girl of eighteen'[71] were having their fill of mutual cheer and solace in Vincennes;[72] the cuckolded Hiller fled to Frankfurt.*

Camille's mother, known disrespectfully by Berlioz as 'l'Hippotame', ran

* Hiller became an important pianist, conductor and composer in the 19th century.

a shop for the sale of Dutch lingerie in Montmartre; her concern in life was to realise the full commercial value of her pretty and talented daughter in a profitable marriage. Berlioz was doing well. He had a very successful concert in December, which impressed Spontini, Meyerbeer and Liszt. He had good connections. But if, while Hector was in Rome, someone better came along, of course Camille could ditch him; so Mme Moke encouraged her daughter to play the field. She allowed the couple to become engaged, but insisted that marriage should be deferred for the moment.

Berlioz would have liked to stay in Paris, not just because of Camille, but because, there, he was on an upward path. He applied for exemption from the strict requirement that the prizewinner spend two years in Rome, but, in spite of doctors' certificates and letters of recommendation from Meyerbeer, Spontini and Le Sueur, the Interior Ministry insisted that he complied.[73]

Before going, he fell out with François-Joseph Fétis, professor of counterpoint at the Conservatoire, who was editing Beethoven's symphonies.* Fétis had once announced that he had found an inverted chord in the 'Eroica' Symphony which *le bon goût* did not permit. Berlioz took exception to his editorial corrections and threatened to expose him. The publishers had to cancel the publication, and Fétis had to deny publicly that he had been correcting Beethoven's symphonies. The memoirs note: 'On my departure for Italy, I thus left behind me in Paris the first really active and bitter enemy I had yet made.'[75]

In Rome

Wearing his engagement ring, Berlioz left on 30 December 1830, and went at first to La Côte. His family was pleased with the engagement. Hiller took some pleasure in writing to him to say that he had seen Camille, at a concert, looking very happy. Tortured with jealousy, Hector took to his bed for a few days.

Berlioz' life was never ordinary. On the way to Rome, to avoid crossing the Alps in winter, he went by sea from Marseilles round to Leghorn and was nearly shipwrecked.[76]

Once there, he stayed in the Villa Medici, the home of the French

* The influential *Revue Musicale,* which Fétis started in 1827, had about 200 subscribers, including important composers and leaders of the musical world. Sixteen of Berlioz' articles for it were issued as a 'Treatise on Orchestration'.[74]

Academy, where the prizewinners were housed. This impressive building, built in 1540, stands near the top of the Spanish Steps. Although rather forbidding from the front, the garden side of the villa is ornate with plasterwork. There is a fine Italian garden, replete with statuary, from which there is a panoramic view over Rome. The Academy's director, responsible for discipline but not for artistic matters, was Horace Vernet,* once a lover of Olympe Rossini.[78]

The prizewinners could enjoy tennis, pistol shooting and other recreations.[79] They would habituate the Café Greco, near the Spanish Steps, where they would smoke poor quality cigars and drink bad coffee.[80] On Thursdays, the Vernets would give a reception. It was not an easy time for the French in Rome: they were unpopular, so Vernet went so far as to arm them all.[81]

Shortly after Berlioz arrived in Rome, a letter arrived from 'l'Hippotame' to say that Camille was going to marry Camille Pleyel. As the son and business partner of the piano manufacturer and composer Ignaz Pleyel,** he was a much better prospect for Camille Moke than Berlioz. Besides, Pleyel was prepared for her to continue to give lessons and to be 'independent', which she certainly was.

Berlioz armed himself with two pistols and set out for Paris with, in his suitcase, the disguise of a ladies' maid.[83] As he went along, a number of things diluted his enthusiasm for his plan, which was to shoot the Mokes, Pleyel and then himself. First, he left his disguise behind during a change of coaches. Then, after ordering another outfit, his unusual behaviour caused the Piedmontese police to suspect that he was a member of the Carbonari, the revolutionary organisation. They directed him to go via Nice rather than Turin. So he spent a month in Nice wandering around, having a one-night stand with a girl on the beach, and being interrogated on suspicion of being a member of Young Italy.† He composed the overture to *King Lear* at this time. He returned to Rome, through Florence,

* Vernet came from a family of painters and specialised in military scenes. He painted the battle scenes for the Gallery of Battles at Versailles. His father was patronised by both Napoleon and Louis XVIII; his grandfather Joseph was a painter who depicted 18th-century life, and notable for his shipwrecks, sunsets and conflagrations.[77]

** Ignaz Pleyel had been a pupil of Haydn. He was the 24th son of a village schoolmaster who in two marriages had 38 children before his death aged 99. His publishing business was the first to issue miniature scores (in 1802).[82]

† See page 289.

where he saw Bellini's *I Capuleti e i Montecchi*. The escapade had cost him over 1,000 fr, a third of his annual bursary.*[85]

Berlioz tried to settle down. He met Glinka at one of Vernet's receptions. He also saw a lot of Mendelssohn, whom he had already met in Paris. Mendelssohn regarded him as 'agreeable and interesting and a great deal more sensible than his music'.[86]

But Berlioz found he could not compose. Rome failed to inspire him; indeed he regarded it as a 'musical sewer'.[87] 'Music in Italy must have suffered the fate of Carthage', he said. 'The traveller standing on the shore searches but finds it there no more.'[88] Berlioz would set off backpacking into the mountains with his gun or his guitar in his hands, strolling along shouting or singing.[89] To get out of the heat in the summer, he would spend whole days in St Peter's, 'established in a confessional', reading Byron.[90]

Berlioz was desperate to get away. Vernet agreed to Berlioz leaving six months early provided he stayed at La Côte and did not appear in Paris before the six months expired.[91] Once back in Paris, he took the rooms which had previously been occupied by Harriet. The concierge told him that Miss Smithson was in Paris. 'It was fate', he wrote in his memoirs.[92] It certainly was.

'Eh Bien, Berlioz, Je vous Aime'

Harriet's career had meanwhile taken a considerable turn for the worse. Indeed, the success of her Paris début can be attributed to timing and a lot of luck. On her return to London, her performances had been received badly. She was not helped by the economic situation in the theatre: Covent Garden had gone bust. Also, her attempts to get a permanent post were frustrated by Kemble's efforts to recover his fortune by launching his daughter, Fanny. So Harriet went on a tour of the provinces, including Dublin. 'Even the Duke of Devonshire', wrote *The Age*, 'could not make Miss Smithson an actress; she was a passable sentimental actress some years since at Drury Lane, and she is now grown too fat to be so any longer.'[93] She got permission for the English theatre to open at the Théâtre des

* Camille now goes backstage. Chopin dedicated his three 1833 *Nocturnes* to her. She reputedly had an affair with Liszt, using Chopin's apartment for the purpose. She separated from Pleyel in 1835 and resumed performing. She became piano professor at the Brussels conservatoire where the director was Fétis. Fanny Mendelssohn said of her: 'She interests me very much, both as a beautiful woman and a fine pianist', but added that 'one would not go to her house to learn proper behaviour'.[84]

Italiens in Paris and she put on *Richard III et Jeanne Shore*, a popular play by the Parisian dramatist Népomucène Lemercier. But in the meantime, stimulated by her 1827 visit, French theatre had developed its own Romantic genre with new plays by Hugo, Dumas and de Vigny.[94] Harriet's venture was a disaster.

Berlioz put on a concert on 9 December 1832 with the *Symphonie Fantastique* followed by *Le Retour à la Vie*, a mixture of music and discourse later known as *Lélio*. Organising a concert such as this was unprecedented and Berlioz had to pull strings through Cherubini and the powerful Vicomte Sosthène to do so.[95] The concert had much advance publicity and many in the audience would have had little difficulty identifying the beloved represented in the *Symphonie*: the *Revue de Paris* had carried a long article saying she was a *célèbre Irlandaise* who took the role of Ophelia.[96] Two days before the concert, Berlioz happened to be in Schlesinger's music shop and met an Englishman who knew Miss Smithson. Schlesinger persuaded Berlioz to give the Englishman a box at the concert, and persuaded the Englishman to invite Miss Smithson. Harriet was unaware that the programme at the concert was made up of Berlioz' works. When she entered, there was a buzz of excitement in the audience, which included Liszt, Chopin, Paganini, Hugo, Dumas, de Vigny, George Sand, Heine and Gautier. Only then did Harriet realise it was a concert of Berlioz' works and saw the programme notes.

Harriet cannot have missed the point in *Lélio*, when the artist declares: 'Oh if I could only find her, the Juliet, the Ophelia for whom my heart is searching. If I could only drink from the cup of joy and sorrow which true love offers, and then one autumn night, lulled by the north wind on some wild heath, lie in her arms and sleep a deep, last sleep.'[97] The concert got good reviews. Harriet sent Berlioz a letter of congratulation, her first positive gesture of recognition. She agreed to meet him.

Within ten days she said, 'Je vous aime',[98]* some of the few French words she knew. Berlioz wrote to Liszt: 'I will never leave her. She is my star. She has understood me. If it is a mistake, you must allow me to make it; she will adorn the closing days of my life, which, I hope, will not last long.'[99] Seven weeks later, Berlioz wrote to his father for the requisite permission to marry. Of course, his family were vehemently against the

* The obvious question is: why not 'Je t'aime'?

marriage. Harriet was three years older than him, an actress and, far worse, a Protestant. She was burdened with debts of 14,000 fr, which Berlioz would legally assume on marrying her. His father refused consent and sent Hector's uncle to Paris to scout around. Harriet's sister also tried to frustrate the marriage.

Berlioz was under great pressure: he was also in trouble over his Prix de Rome grant as, unless he could obtain exemption, the next instalment would only be paid if he did his stint in Germany. He began a legal process whereby a son requires his father not to disinherit him. Harriet was cool on the physical side of the relationship and anyway was immobilised because she had broken her leg falling out of a cabriolet.* To help her with her creditors, her friends held a benefit concert at which Liszt and Chopin played a piano duet.

Berlioz became increasingly hysterical and threatened to blow his brains out. In late summer, the process of civil marriage was begun, but Harriet's sister, who was against the marriage, tore up the document. Hector took an overdose of opium in her presence. But he survived.

Montmartre

Thus, on 3 October 1833, Hector and Harriet were married in the Chapel of the British Embassy. Liszt acted as witness in what Hiller described as a 'quiet somewhat sad ceremony'.[101] The couple went to Vincennes for their honeymoon, having been lent 300 fr by a friend. They then moved to a little two-storey cottage over the hill at Montmartre, which in those days was a rustic village, with fine views over Paris below. The Berlioz' friends enjoyed visiting them in the country, where they were insulated from the world and, in particular, the goings-on in Paris. The birth of their son Louis in the following August put an end to a plan to emigrate to America, which was beginning to open up as a destination for musicians, for both emigration and touring.**

* Berlioz told Liszt that Harriet was a virgin on their wedding night. This is a notion which Liszt would surely have found difficult to comprehend.[100]

** Americans were 'prodigious consumers of music'.[102] Immigrants brought music with them. Music societies sprouted up in the early 1800s. Easier rail transport helped: touring performers arrived 'in droves' in the 1840s,[103] around the time of the first steamship transatlantic crossing in 1847. There was much locally born enthusiasm and talent to be found in the USA, people such as Lowell Mason and his son. But it was not until Charles Ives, born in 1874, '*the* central figure in America's art music',[104] that the USA produced a home-born composer of international stature.

The marriage was a hopeless set-up. Berlioz' love was for the characters which Harriet played, rather than for the woman herself. They could hardly converse, since his English was as poor as her French. She did not appreciate music. When the annual income from the Prix de Rome stopped in 1836, Hector returned to journalism,*[105] writing weekly critiques, '*feuilletons*', for the *Journal des Debats* at 100 fr an article.[106] This left him little time for composing. He loathed the drudgery of journalism, which entailed writing reviews about now forgotten operas by composers such as Adam, Balfe, Cadaux, Bousquet, Catel, Kastner and Niedermeyer. At the same time, his style of journalism made him great enemies: he hated inexpressive music, parasites of the musical world, ornamented singing, overpaid singers, commercially-minded theatre managers and tune-mongers who made easy fortunes; and he went for them: 'I have sometimes used words in the course of conversation which might fairly be taken for regular sword thrusts', he said.[107] Indeed, it is now that we begin to come across an increasing amount of intolerance in the musical world; perhaps it is explained by the dictum of the Russian impresario Serge Diaghilev, many years later: 'In art you must know how to hate, otherwise your music will lose all individuality.'[108]**

Harriet too was stuck. She lost her looks and put on weight. A benefit performance organised to pay her debts just emphasised her decline, when she appeared alongside Marie Dorval, a leading actress and one of George Sand's lovers. She played the dumb girl in Auber's *La Muette*. Among others, both George Sand and Victor Hugo were asked to write a part for her. But nothing substantial came of these requests. The description of the sort of role Sand was asked to create tells all: 'an English woman who speaks French with difficulty and with an accent that must be justifiable, or who does not know sufficient French to express certain ideas and who therefore speaks in her mother tongue while at the same time having recourse to pantomime to help her occasionally'.[110]

Berlioz was frustrated in his professional aspirations. He would have liked a post at the Conservatoire, but his relationship with Cherubini,

* Other artists eked out a living by supplementing their earnings by journalism: Théophile Gautier, poet and novelist, who was also the author of the popular ballet *Giselle*, used the earnings from journalism to support his two mistresses, three children and two sisters.

** Prokofiev was concerned that this approach could lead to narrowness. Diaghilev retorted: 'The cannon shoots far because it doesn't scatter its fire.'[109]

together with his lack of expertise at the piano and organ, made such an appointment improbable. At the end of his life, he wrote: 'The principal reason for the long war waged against me lies in the antagonism existing between my musical feeling and that of the great mass of the Parisian public. Many looked upon me as a madman, because I considered them children or simpletons … the professors of the Conservatoire were against me, stirred up by Cherubini and Fétis, whose self-love and faith had alike been rudely disturbed by my heterodoxy in the matter of harmony and rhythm.'[111] However, he got a job at the Conservatoire library, which used him in a largely honorary capacity.

The 1830s

All this diverted Berlioz from composition. But he managed to compose several works during the 1830s. In 1834, Paganini commissioned him to compose a piece in which he could demonstrate his Stradivarius viola. Out of this came *Harold en Italie*, although Paganini did not like it, because the viola part was not prominent enough.

The government, which was keen to sponsor sacred music by a French composer, proposed an annual award of 3,000 fr and commissioned Berlioz, who went ahead with preparing the *Grande Messe des Morts* (the Requiem). The event at which it was to be performed was eventually cancelled, because the government had spent the money on a royal wedding.[112] Then Berlioz could not get his 3,000 fr out of the ministry. He had incurred considerable outlay on copyists and the 200 choristers who had rehearsed it. The official at the ministry tried to fob him off with an honour, the award of the Légion d'Honneur; 'A fig for the Cross!' cried Berlioz, 'Give me my money.'[113] There may have been a more sinister reason for the difficulty with getting paid: Adolphe Adam said, 'It was really shameful for the rest of us French composers to see government favours lavished on a man whose character and talents are so contemptible.'[114]

The death of a French general in Algeria gave the pretext for a performance of the Requiem at Les Invalides in December 1837. Even this performance gave Berlioz a headache. Cherubini had the right to compose for events such as this and had to be compensated for his disappointment, with the Cross. Habeneck had the right to conduct on these occasions. Berlioz relates what he says happened at the crucial moment when the Dies Irae goes into the Tuba Mirum. At this point, the conductor needs to give a clear beat. Instead, Habeneck put down his baton, took out his snuffbox and took a pinch of snuff. Berlioz (apparently) had to leap forward and continue the conducting.

A loan from a friend gave Berlioz the time to concentrate on *Benvenuto Cellini*, which was staged in 1838. The première was 'one of the greatest fiascos of the century'.[115] It had four full performances; there were three more performances of the first act followed by a ballet; thereafter it was not heard in Paris for 135 years.[116] This was the end of this opera for Berlioz. But, out of it, Berlioz derived the overture, *Le Carnaval Romain*. The public wanted Meyerbeer's type of grand opera; in future, the opera management was wary of staging Berlioz' operas.[117]

Some of Berlioz' works were novel: a 'Chant des Chemins de Fer' for the opening of the Lille–Paris railway, for example. He also wrote 'far-sighted fantasies' about the telephone and flying machines. He predicted that these devices would change the world: he would be able to say, 'Fetch me a soprano from Bombay for my concert tonight.'[118]

A few years later, Paganini gave Berlioz 20,000 fr, which enabled him to repay his and Harriet's debts, and provided some security for the future.* Berlioz then set to work on the *Roméo and Juliet Symphony*, which he dedicated to his benefactor. It was given at the Conservatoire in November 1839. Wagner heard it. It was a considerable success.[119]

In 1840, the government commissioned the *Grande Symphonie Funèbre et Triomphale* when those killed in 'Les Trois Glorieuses' of 1830 were reburied in the place de la Bastille. Berlioz was paid, but was annoyed as the sound was scarcely audible in the procession, and his work was drowned out when the National Guard decided to march off in the middle, beating their drums.[120]

Difficulties with Harriet and the Affair with Marie Recio

The relationship with Harriet was going downhill, and had become a serious distraction for Berlioz. There were problems with the family: Berlioz'

* Paganini gave him this even though he had recently lost a large sum investing in a casino which was closed for breaching the regulations. Paganini had a suitably 'Romantic' end. For about a month, he was unburied, as the Church thought he was an atheist. His corpse was on view in Nice, and, because of the stench, he was eventually pickled in olive oil. He was moved many times, usually at night, before finally resting in Parma.

sister Adèle was his lifeline and, when she got married, Harriet would not go to the wedding. There were problems with Louis, their son, of whom Adèle said, 'there was such an air of sadness about the boy':[121] when he was twelve, he was sent away to the Lycée at Rouen. There were problems with the servants, and problems with the neighbours who banged on the wall and shouted abuse. Berlioz spent most of his days in the centre of Paris, and Harriet became increasingly possessive and suspicious of what he was doing. He commented to his sister Nanci, 'Henriette never goes out, and I am hounded by her because I am always out.'[122]

It is sometimes said that Berlioz wrote the song 'La Mort d'Ophélie' on 7 May 1842.[123] He had begun an affair with a second-rate mezzo at the Opéra, which may explain his comparative musical inactivity in 1841–2.[124] The intimate songs *Les Nuits d'Eté*, using poems by Gautier, come from this period.

Marie Recio's Spanish-born mother encouraged their affair because Berlioz was a useful contact to have in the music world. The couple went off to Brussels together in 1842. Little Louis wrote to his aunt Nanci: 'Mother is very sad because she has not had any letters for a month. She cannot sleep, everyday she expects a letter that doesn't arrive; I do not know where my father is.'[125] Berlioz was now caught in the middle between two dreadful women.* Marie, 'a bossy shrew', demanded to sing in his concerts, but he thought that 'she sang like a cat'.[127] She was also extremely jealous of Harriet.

Berlioz tried to return to Harriet in 1843, but she was impossible. She fuelled herself with brandy. 'She gets up in the middle of the night when she knows I am asleep, comes into my room, shuts the doors, and starts shouting abuse at me for three hours on end, sometimes till daybreak; the next day, she asks me to forgive her, and swears she loves me.'[128] She let herself go with no care for her appearance; the lovely Ophelia became very fat.

At the time when Berlioz' parents had objected to his marriage, the sage Dr Berlioz predicted that Hector would in time abandon Harriet for someone else. Divorce was illegal, but separation could be arranged. From 1844, Hector and Harriet lived apart, and Berlioz bore the financial burden of

* Wagner wrote to Liszt: 'The Almighty would have done better to leave women out of the scheme of Creation', a curious comment from him. He continued: 'Berlioz enabled me once again to observe how an unpleasant woman can wantonly ruin an altogether exceptional man.'[126]

maintaining two houses, Harriet's in Montmartre and the house in Paris where Marie and her mother lived. Louis was at first placed in a pension in Paris, but was free to visit his mother every Sunday. Marie started signing herself Berlioz.

It is said that the last ten years of Harriet's life were 'unrelievedly desolate'.[129] They must have been awful for Louis as well. In 1848, she started suffering a series of strokes, which badly affected her speech. During April 1849, Berlioz nursed her through an illness associated with the cholera epidemic. For the last years of her life, she existed, nursed night and day, unable to move or barely to speak. She needed two full-time carers, which cost Berlioz 3,500 fr per annum; eventually, she needed three nurses. Twenty-six years after Berlioz had seen *Hamlet* for the first time, she died, in 1854. He had to organise the Protestant funeral for her. He had a watch chain made out of her hair for Louis. Seven months later, Berlioz married Marie.[130]

Foreign Travel

As well as composing, Berlioz took up conducting, and, at one stage, it seemed that he might get a permanent position as conductor at a new concert hall. But the government, beset by regulations, would not permit choral music to be included in the concert hall programmes and the idea collapsed. Berlioz became one of the first specialist orchestral conductors and put on his own concerts, around three or four a year.[131] For these, he had to do the business management, and pay the poor tax (a substantial percentage of gross receipts); players even expected him to provide strings and mutes. He did not make much profit from this activity. But he hoped eventually to get a significant appointment such as the conductorship of the Opéra. In August 1844, he was cartooned as a purveyor of noise when he put on a 'monster' concert for the Festival de l'Industrie with 1,000 performers, 24 horns, 25 harps etc. He was rarely taken seriously in France.

Much of the 1840s and 1850s were spent by Berlioz and Marie seeking their fortune abroad, where he was welcomed, particularly in Germany. He was also a great success in Prague. From there, he travelled to Vienna along the recently opened railway line. In Vienna, it was fashionable to wear jewellery with Berlioz cameos on it; pies were named after him. An arduous trip to Russia may have been worth it because, before going on to Moscow, he enjoyed the sunset on the banks of the Neva and a brief fling with a

1

2

CENTRES OF MUSIC: Canaletto's *Stonemasons' Yard* in back-street Venice (1) contrasts with the elegance of Dresden's Augustus Bridge across the Elbe, painted by his nephew Bernardo Bellotto in 1750 (2).

3

4

5

CENTRES OF MUSIC: Handel and Mahler worked in Hamburg (3), birthplace of Mendelssohn and Brahms. Vienna bombarded in 1809 (4): the French scored a hit on Schubert's school; Haydn was dying in his house away to the right. The Place de la Concorde in 1829 (5), the Paris of Berlioz, Chopin, Liszt, Rossini and others.

ROYALTY: A matronly Empress Maria Theresa, showing a suspicion of the protuberant Habsburg chin (6), faces the formidable Frederick 'the Great' (7), before whom J.S. Bach performed. Elector Augustus 'the Strong' of Saxony (8) was powerful in procreation, whereas Emperor Joseph II (9) looked at women in the way that people normally look at statues: here, the women with the fashionable high hairstyles are his sisters.

10

11

Franz Rousseau's painting (1754) of an elegant ball in Bonn (10) at the court of the Archbishop-Elector of Cologne; Beethoven's father is likely to have been among the musicians consigned to the galleries on either side. The pass over Mont Cenis (11), a route to Italy in Handel's time, painted by the Romantic master J.M.W. Turner a century later.

Women and Children: Like her children Karl and Franz Xaver (12), the fascinating Constanze Mozart (13) looks prosperous in Hans Hansen's portrait painted a decade after Wolfgang died. Beethoven's nephew Karl (14) gave his guardian more trouble, as did the young Clara Wieck her father (15) when she fell in love with Schumann.

16

17

18

FUN AND GAMES IN 1821: Schubert at the piano entertains his friends (16).
INSPIRING LADIES: Isabella Colbran (17), Rossini's Spanish wife;
Maria Malibran (18), star soprano, whose locket was close to Bellini's heart.

19

20

21

Inspiring Ladies: Harriet Smithson (19), Berlioz' stage idol who provided less inspiration as a wife; Mathilde Wesendonck (20), Wagner's Isolde; George Sand and Chopin (21): a reconstruction of Delacroix' double portrait of 1838 which was subsequently cut in half.

22 23 24 25

Wagner the family man (22): in his arms, his daughter Eva; at his feet, Russ. The dog is buried next to him, as is Cosima (23), shown here in the portrait by Franz von Lenbach, a fashionable painter of the second half of the 19th century. Daumier's 1856 picture of the *Heavy Burden* (24) says much about life for most people under monarchs at the time, such as Emperor Franz Joseph (25).

chorus girl, a seamstress whose fiancé was conveniently away.[132]

On his travels, laden with trunks full of scores and parts, Berlioz met many of the other leading composers, such as Schumann, Mendelssohn, Wagner and Brahms. Liszt championed his works at Weimar, and staged *Benvenuto Cellini*, albeit in a truncated version.

At Dresden, he met the English harpist Parish-Alvars and marvelled at how he got so much out of the harp: 'The advantage which the new harps possess of being able, by means of the double action of the pedals, to tune two strings in unison, gave him the idea of combinations which seem absolutely impractical on paper.'[133] There were also considerable technical advances in other musical instruments, the valve horn being one. The ultimate in musical instrument design was the Octobasse, an enormous double bass with three strings, played from a platform, with pedals which moved levers to provide fingers at the top of the strings. It was demonstrated at the London Exhibition of 1851 and the Paris 1855 Exhibition; it was praised by Berlioz.[134]

Berlioz felt increasingly bitter about his rejection by France, where, always anxious about money, he dearly wanted a permanent position and salary. In 1846, *La Damnation de Faust*, a concert opera, which was almost wholly written on his travels, was a failure in Paris; it played twice to half-empty houses. At the same time, Clapisson's *Gibby la Cornemuse* was playing to full houses. Gautier observed that they were in 'a flabby age' in which the fashion was 'all for the commonplace under the name of good sense'.[135] Berlioz began to write *Euphonia*, a portrayal of an ideal musical city where everything is committed to the service of art.

In autumn 1847, Berlioz took thirteen-year-old Louis for a fortnight to stay with Dr Berlioz, whom he had not seen for fifteen years. Then he went to London to take up the post of the conductor of Adolphe Julien's Grand English Opera, based at Drury Lane. He arrived at London Bridge station and lodged in the Juliens' house in Harley Street. He was there for eight months. The season started with *The Bride of Lammermoor*.[136]

Julien was a colourful high-spending impresario. He offered the mezzo-soprano Pauline Viardot £100 to perform on each of 40 nights. For Berlioz, however, the aspirations of the Grand English Opera contracted into a season of two Donizetti works and one by Balfe. Then, payday came and went. Berlioz agreed to take a third cut in salary, but actually got nothing at all. Anticipating the arrival of the bailiffs at the Juliens' house,

Berlioz removed his manuscripts.[137] When Julien was declared bankrupt, Berlioz was lucky that his clothes were not seized.*

The Coup D'Etat in Paris

Berlioz' London visit coincided with the 1848 risings all over the Continent. As a consequence, Berlioz decided to stay in London and put off a visit to Prague. As the 1848 disturbances continued, he became increasingly concerned about the situation in Paris, his future there and his job at the Conservatoire.

For Berlioz, revolution such as this meant disruption to musical and artistic life. 'All the artists are ruined; all the teachers are idle, all the pupils have fled; poor pianists play sonatas in the squares; historical painters sweep the streets; architects are mixing mortar on the public works ... Some of the first violins at the Opéra only had thirty-six livres a year, and were hard put to survive even by giving lessons in addition. They could not possibly have saved much; and now that their pupils are gone, what is to become of the poor creatures?'[138]

Berlioz was right about the disruption. The English, conscious of the events of 1793, fled back home; the bourgeois stopped spending: in some luxury businesses in Paris, 80 per cent of workers were laid off.[139] Over half the workers in Paris were unemployed. The government set up National Workshops to remedy this.

Prince Louis Napoleon, the leader of the Bonapartist faction, heard the news from Paris on the new electric telegraph. He made a brief visit to France but was asked to leave. Back in London, he acted as a special constable during the large demonstration in Kennington in April which supported the People's Charter, which had called for parliamentary reform.**[140] Berlioz observed: 'The Chartists dispersed in perfect order. Excellent creatures! About as fit to carry out an insurrection as the Italians are to write symphonies! The Irish are probably just the same, as O'Connell well knew when he used to say to them, "Agitate, agitate, but don't act."'[141]

At the end of April, elections were held in France. With all males entitled now to the vote, the Bonapartists did well. But there was increasing

* Julien, as such people always seem to do, quickly bounced back with a series of summer concerts at the Surrey Gardens.

** This led the government to call in the aged Duke of Wellington to defend parliament, where the demonstrators presented a petition, but these precautions proved unnecessary.

hysteria, especially when news came through of the suppression of the Polish rebellion.[142]

In June, the government had to close the National Workshops. There was no work for them to do, or the work was of so little value that someone said they might as well have bottled the waters of the Seine.*[143] The closure was seen as an act of treachery, so the barricades went up again in what was to be the first 'class' war. There was great violence for four days: railway lines were torn up, labour-saving agricultural machinery was destroyed, prisoners were released in various places. The Grenoble cutlers even refused to sharpen the guillotine. In this town-versus-country split, volunteers from the countryside came in to oppose the insurgents, who were suppressed by troops. The Archbishop of Paris was shot while attempting to mediate. Figures vary, but around 1,500–3,000 insurgents were killed, and up to 15,000 were arrested.**[144]

The dominant middle classes in Paris felt increasingly worried and threatened by all this, and demanded to have 'order' and strong government. Support for Louis Napoleon grew. He topped the poll in elections at the end of August, and took his seat, although the deputies thought he was a bit of a joker. One up-and-coming politician said: 'We will give him women and we will lead him.'[145]

In elections, held on 10 December, Louis Napoleon received three-quarters of the votes cast and the support of over 60 per cent of the total electorate.[146] He was president of the Second Republic. His presidency was glamorous, a distinct contrast from the reign of the boring King Louis-Philippe. Balls were held at the Elysée Palace, and the president installed his mistress, Miss Howard, nearby.

The new constitution under which Louis Napoleon was elected provided that the president could not stand for a second term. People waited for the election scheduled for May 1852, 'like people in the tenth century had waited for the year 1000 thinking that it would bring the end of the world'.[147] The president tried to get the constitution changed to allow him to stand again, but the assembly would not have it. Victor Hugo, the

* This was a procedure which, 80 years later, the distinguished economist J.M. Keynes might have recommended.

** The prisoners were held in dreadful conditions on barges on the Seine; there were many executions; 4,500 were transported, mainly to Algeria.

novelist, poet and dramatist, said: 'What! Because we have had Napoleon the Great, must we have Napoleon the Little?'[148]

The night of 1 December 1851 seemed quiet except for the sound of those dancing at the Elysée. Late that night, the president struck: police arrested key people and occupied the printing works.

When, on the next day, a proclamation invited the people to vote at a referendum on yet another constitution, there was some resistance. Louis Napoleon adopted new tactics by withdrawing, allowing barricades to be built before moving in force to destroy them. There was particular trouble in the boulevard Montmartre and the boulevard des Italiens, where the Café Anglais was ransacked. By the evening of 4 December, however, resistance had been crushed, at the cost of about 400 civilian lives.

Later in the month, a referendum was held to regularise the president's authority beyond the following May. There was then a massive purge of suspect politicians.[149]

The president enjoyed being hailed with 'Vive l'Empéreur'. It was not long before the senate passed an act to establish the empire. This was ratified in a referendum, in which nearly 8 million voted 'Yes', and only a quarter of a million voted 'No'. On the anniversary of his uncle's coronation, of Austerlitz and of his own *coup d'état*, Napoleon III signed the decree establishing the Second Empire. A fuller picture of the empire will have to await a later chapter.*[150]

Berlioz generally supported Louis Napoleon.[151] He disliked the pretentiousness of the previous regime; and he hoped that his relationship with the Emperor might be similar to the successful one between Le Sueur and Napoleon I. He wrote a cantata, 'L'Impériale'.

L'Enfance du Christ, *Les Troyens* and the Long Run In

In July 1848, Berlioz' father died. Two years later Nanci died of breast cancer, after six months' terrible suffering. 'And no doctor dared be humane enough to put an end to her sufferings by a dose of chloroform! They give it to a patient to prevent the pain of a quarter-minute surgical operation, and yet refuse to employ it for avoiding a six-months torture.'[152] Berlioz' share of his father's estate was about 130,000 fr, but it would have been

* See page 494.

injudicious to dispose of various properties, so that it was a long time before he was free from anxiety about money.

In 1851, Berlioz went to the London Great Exhibition in Hyde Park where he acted as a member of a jury charged with examining submissions by instrument manufacturers.[153] He was invited back for six concerts in 1852 and turned down an offer to do a similar season in New York for 25,000 fr. In London, he appeared on the same platform as Camille Pleyel. In 1854, he completed the oratorio *L'Enfance du Christ*, which, unusually for Berlioz, was a great success.

Princess Sayn-Wittgenstein, Liszt's mistress, persuaded Berlioz to write an epic opera based on the *Aeneid*. This led to him writing both words and music for *Les Troyens*, which was completed in 1858. When Wagner visited Paris in the following year, the Opéra could not cope with staging both *Tannhäuser* and *Les Troyens*. So, Berlioz' opera was delayed until 1863 when it was presented, at last, in the Théâtre-Lyrique. To Berlioz' horror and dismay, the opera was increasingly truncated as the première drew near.* The performance was greeted with jeers and catcalls; crowds in the gallery sang the 'Soldiers' Chorus' from *Faust* by way of protest. Berlioz' leading biographer has recorded that the treatment of *Les Troyens* then, and subsequently in 20th-century France, was 'one of the most astonishing musical scandals of all time'.[154] The opera had some supporters: Bizet, whose *Pearl Fishers* was premièred around the same time, was almost involved in a duel defending it;[155] and the painter Corot used to sing extracts from it when working at his easel.

Not surprisingly, Berlioz was increasingly disillusioned, especially when others were appointed to positions he would have liked. He wrote in 1854: 'I belong to a nation which has ceased to be interested in the nobler manifestations of intelligence, and whose only deity is the golden calf. The Parisians have become a barbarous people.' He added: 'I do not feel the least desire to add to the number of useful and agreeable works called opéra-comiques, daily turned out in Paris like tarts from the oven.'[156] Meyerbeer's influence was such as to render any serious success at the Opéra almost impossible. The Conservatoire was no longer available to give concerts. 'We do not possess a single good public concert-room and it

* Its two parts ran to over five hours, so only the second half, entitled *The Trojans at Carthage*, was staged.

would never enter the head of one of our Croesuses to build one', said Berlioz. 'One has to endure the robbery of the tax collectors for the *droits des hospices* who never take account of the expenses of the concert and aggravate one's loss by deducting their eighth from the gross proceeds.'[157] In Germany, as we have seen, he received a warmer welcome.

Berlioz began to suffer in 1856 from intestinal neuralgia, a severe nervous disorder. Three years later, Princess Sayn-Wittgenstein saw him: 'I have never seen such thinness', she told Liszt, who subsequently observed: 'Our poor friend Berlioz is really low and full of bitterness. His family life weighs on him like a nightmare, and outside he meets nothing but opposition and disasters ... the tone of Berlioz' voice has faded and his whole being seems to lean towards the grave.'[158]

Marie died in 1862, aged 48. Memories from Berlioz' youth had been revived during a visit to the family home, soon after his father died. One particular image was a girlfriend of his boyhood, Estelle. Now, Hector found out where she was living. Forty-nine years after they first met, he 'recognised the divine stateliness of her step; but, oh heavens! How changed she was! Her complexion slightly bronzed – her hair going grey. And yet at the sight of her, my heart did not feel one moment's indecision; my whole soul went out to its idol, as though she were still in her dazzling loveliness.'[159] He invited her to Lyon to a performance of *The Barber of Seville*, in which Patti was starring, but she could not come. He returned to Paris and wrote to her asking permission to correspond with her and to visit her once a year.

Mme Estelle Fornier has been described by the prominent writer on music Ernest Newman as a 'level headed old woman, in whom romance had completely died'.[160] She wrote back doubting that they had much in common any more. But she sent her son and daughter-in-law to visit Berlioz in Paris. She asked him for money, but he had to say he could not help. He wrote to her regularly for the rest of his life.

Louis by now had grown up and was intent on a naval career. He and his father had become increasingly close to each other. Berlioz paid for his training, and also the 900 fr to get him rigged out for his first trip at sea. Louis led a wild life: he gambled heavily* and had an affair which resulted

* Gambling was very popular: 'Spain has its bull-fights, Rome had its gladiators. But Paris takes its pride in the Palais Royal, whose teasing roulette wheels afford spectators in the pit the pleasure of seeing blood flow freely without running the risk of their feet slithering into it.' The tables

in a baby girl. In 1866, he was captain of a ship which evacuated French troops from Mexico and he was having a great time. At St Thomas, he wrote: 'I cannot fart without the inhabitants complimenting me on it.'[163] His father always dreaded the yellow fever that took so many lives in the Antilles. Sure enough, in June 1867, as Paris enjoyed the spectacle of the Great Exhibition, Louis died of fever in Havana. It took three weeks for Berlioz to receive the sad news: he wept helplessly.[164]

Berlioz had continued to travel abroad where he was admired so much. In 1862, he conducted *Béatrice et Bénédict* at Baden-Baden, where a former student at the Conservatoire held the gambling concession.

In December 1866, he had a great success conducting *La Damnation de Faust* in Vienna. He made another conducting tour to Russia, having been invited there by Grand Duchess Elena Pavlovna, who had been in Paris for the Exhibition. He worked out programmes for her and stayed in her magnificent Mikhailovsky Palace. The journey there took him four days by train. He went on to Moscow where Tchaikovsky proposed a toast to him at a banquet. It was the climax to his conducting career; but he was exhausted.[165]

Berlioz was cared for by his mother-in-law. At the beginning of March 1868, he went to Nice and had a fall on the rocks. He suffered from acute intestinal neuralgia, and relieved the pain by taking opium. In early 1869, he took to his bed; he died on 8 March. 'Enfin, on va jouer ma musique', were his last words.[166] How right he was.

A lock of hair taken from that once auburn mane shows it to have become completely white.[167]

were covered with 'baize cloth, worn threadbare by the raking-in of gold coins'.[161] Pauline Viardot's lover Turgenev described the punters at Baden-Baden sitting at the tables 'with the same dull, greedy, half stupefied, half exasperated, wholly rapacious expression which gambling fever lends to even the most aristocratic features'.[162]

MENDELSSOHN

CHAPTER 10

IT IS NO wonder that Berlioz and Mendelssohn never saw eye to eye. Their different personalities and styles are well illustrated in Mendelssohn's uncharacteristic outburst to his mother: 'Berlioz's instrumentation is so disgustingly filthy … that one needs a wash after merely handling one of his scores.'[1] Compared to Berlioz, Mendelssohn was sanitised to perfection, almost excessively refined and restrained, almost classical in his clarity and his structures. Thus, Sibelius could claim that 'after Bach, Mendelssohn was the greatest master of fugue'.[2] In Mendelssohn's music, as in his short life, there is little of that excessive enthusiasm or exaggeration displayed by Berlioz.

On the other hand, we are apt to associate Mendelssohn with religiosity, sentimentality and other 'unhealthy' Victorian values. The Victorians loved his oratorios, his melodious sacred music such as 'O for the Wings of a Dove', his *Songs Without Words*. They appropriated him, even to the extent that he might almost have been thought to be an English composer.

Felix Mendelssohn was born on 3 February 1809, just over five years after Berlioz. Whereas Berlioz' background was insecure and petty bourgeois, Mendelssohn's was more assured and cosmopolitan. His teacher introduced him to Goethe, whom he visited on several occasions. At the age of twenty, he conducted the revival of Bach's St Matthew Passion. Much of his life was spent relentlessly travelling: he went ten times to England. He directed the music at Düsseldorf and at Leipzig. We shall hear of his marriage, his visits to Queen Victoria and his death, less than six months after his sister Fanny died.

The Mendelssohns

Moses Mendelssohn, Felix's grandfather, was the son of an impoverished scribe from Dessau, some 40 miles north of Leipzig. Moses became a very

Moses Mendelssohn

distinguished philosopher. Even so, his name has been eclipsed by others, partly perhaps because he was a contemporary of the genius Immanuel Kant,* partly because he was Jewish. It has been said that the modern history of Jewry in its 'political and intellectual emancipation' begins with Moses Mendelssohn.[3]

Moses settled in Berlin when his teacher was appointed chief rabbi there. He became the tutor to the children of a rich silk merchant, then an

* Coincidentally, both men were minute and deformed, with a hunchback. Kant was less than five feet tall, with a concave chest. Although living in Königsberg, he was of Scottish extraction.

accountant in the merchant's office, and then a partner in his firm.[4] In 1767, *Phaedon*, his treatise on the immortality of the soul, was published; it was translated into more than 30 different languages; and it was read by Mozart.[5]

Moses Mendelssohn worked tirelessly to bridge the gap between traditional Jewish and the new secular learning.[6] Before the 1781 Edict of Tolerance of Emperor Joseph II, Jews had been outsiders; now, at least north of the Alps, there was more scope for them to become integrated. Moses encouraged this. Many 'assimilated', while retaining their religion. Others, including several members of Moses' own family, went much further: they left the Jewish faith so as to gain full acceptance in European society.*

Moses' son Abraham married Leah Salomon, who came from a family of prominent and rich Berlin Jews who inherited the right of abode and the right to mint money.** At the time Felix was born, Abraham and his brother Joseph were building their own fortune in their bank, Gebrüder Mendelssohn & Co in Hamburg. One supposes that they lent into businesses such as the thriving Hamburg shipping and calico printing concerns:†[9] at the turn of the century, there were 57 calico printing firms in Hamburg, five of which were under Jewish management; some were large, the biggest had 500 employees.

Flight from Hamburg

Until the French garrison took over in 1806, Hamburg's Jews were tightly regulated as to residence and occupation. In many Jewish communities, the arrival of the French was greatly welcomed because, as elsewhere, the French introduced their laws and procedures, and the Jews were emancipated.

* There has been virtually continuous persecution of the Jews throughout modern history. England, in 1290, was the first to expel them. Cromwell readmitted them in the 1650s.

** When, after the Thirty Years War, the Elector of Brandenburg wanted to rebuild his country, he imported 50 very rich Jewish families who had been expelled from Vienna. They were granted right of residence in Berlin and certain rights to trade in money or goods, mostly in the clothing and textile industries. Although Frederick the Great believed that 'to oppress the Jews never brought prosperity to any government',[7] he later divided the community into those who could bequeath a right of residence to one child and those who could not, but were able to support themselves. On payment of a vast sum, equivalent to around 70 times Bach's annual income, another child could be granted right of residence.

† Later in the century, the bank lent heavily into the railway construction industry. The family business was finally dissolved in the mid-1930s.[8]

Hamburg became a *département* of France, called the 'Mouths of the Elbe'. But, for Abraham's family, the occupation must have been a mixed blessing. The Napoleonic blockade, which was aimed at cutting off Britain's trade with Continental Europe, devastated Hamburg's business. However, there were profitable opportunities to be had, and blockade busting and racketeering were rampant and lucrative.

There would have been considerable uncertainty when the French were briefly kicked out by the Russians during 1813. But, by then, Abraham had fled to Berlin with his family, which included Felix and his sisters Fanny and Rebecka. Leaving Hamburg was a pity for a small boy: the city was a centre for the confectionery trade, which used sugar shipped in from the West Indies and Latin America.[10] More significantly, however, the Mendelssohns avoided the appallingly harsh defence of Hamburg under Marshal Davoût, during the five winter months starting in December 1813. And they avoided its anti-Semitic conflagrations six years later, after the French had gone and the clock was turned back.[11]

Berlin

At the start of the century, Berlin was provincial, small and stuffy: there were only two postal deliveries a week, and it took nine days' travel along roads infested with highwaymen to reach it from Frankfurt. Gaslight was only very slowly being installed; at ten o'clock at night, the city was deserted. There were fields inside and outside the walls, but the land inside was being bought up for development. In the summer, the dust and smells became intolerable, as did the dirty grass and thick mud in winter. Filth was partly responsible for a cholera outbreak in 1831 which killed many, including the leading philosopher Hegel.[12]

Berlin was about to revive. Appalled by Prussian defeats in the Napoleonic Wars, the Berliners decided to sort themselves out. The armed forces were reformed by Scharnhorst and Gneisenau. The educational system was overhauled by Wilhelm von Humboldt, a diplomat, man of letters and linguist, and brother of the world famous scientist and traveller, Alexander von Humboldt.* Wilhelm von Humboldt wanted to replace the French influence that prevailed: so he revised the curriculum for the élite

* The family bank lent 2,000 francs to Alexander von Humboldt to help him finance one of his expeditions.[13]

high schools (the Gymnasiums)[14] and created the new University of Berlin which was to become the cultural centre for the future Germany. By 1870, virtually every child went to school for eight years and came from a literate family. This created a formidably strong society: by comparison, at the time, almost 70 per cent of the population of Italy over six years of age was illiterate.[15]

The position of the Jews had been improved by legislation in 1812. There was now considerable pressure for them to 'assimilate': those who did not were unable to obtain a position in the state. Leah's brother converted to Christianity and took the name Bartholdy; and, when Felix was seven, the children were baptised as Lutherans, with the double-barrelled name Mendelssohn Bartholdy. Abraham admitted that Christianity was 'the creed of most civilised people and contains nothing that can lead you away from what is good, and much that guides you to love – obedience, tolerance and resignation – even if it offers nothing but the example of its Founder, understood by so few and followed by still fewer'.[16] Abraham's personal position, as the son of such a distinguished Jew, was almost impossible, and stressful. He preferred Felix to drop the name of Mendelssohn completely, and reprimanded him for using it during his first trip to England. 'There should not be a Christian *Mendelssohn*,' he said, 'for my father himself did not want to be a Christian.'[17] He and Leah did not convert to Christianity until some years after the children were baptised.

The Mendelssohns had considerable stature in the city. In Moses' time, many visitors, whether Jew or Gentile, sought to attend a kind of salon which he held in the afternoons. Then, during the Napoleonic Wars, Abraham financed two battalions; this earned him appointment to the city council. Bartholdy was on the staff of the reforming cabinet minister Karl August Hardenberg and accompanied him to the Congress of Vienna; later, he became Prussian commercial attaché in Tuscany.

A Pretty, Pampered Boy

Felix and Fanny, who was three years older, were infant prodigies. By the age of nine, he had played the piano in a private chamber concert. By then, Fanny was playing Bach's *Well Tempered Clavier* by heart. Aged eleven, Felix wrote an epic poem in three cantos. As a teenager, he was a more advanced composer than both Mozart and Beethoven at the same age. By seventeen, he had produced the Octet and the overture to *A Midsummer*

Night's Dream. Rebecka and the younger son Paul, born by the time the family was in Berlin, were less musically exceptional. Paul became a financier.[18]

Felix was a beautiful boy, with a slight lisp. Weber described 'his auburn hair clustering in ringlets round his shoulders, the look of his brilliant clear eyes, the smile of innocence and candour on his lips'.[19] Thackeray, the author of *Vanity Fair*, said: 'His is the most beautiful face I ever saw; I imagine our Saviour's to have been like it.'[20] As he grew up, Felix was athletic; he rode, danced and swam extremely well. Not surprisingly, he became almost obnoxiously self-assured and this manifested itself in him being prim, intolerant and dogmatic. He was highly strung, irritable and moody. Many years later, on his parents' silver wedding, he planned an operetta in which his friend Eduard Devrient, an actor and a baritone with the Berlin Royal Opera company, was to sing. When Devrient found that he could not participate, because of a competing royal engagement, Mendelssohn became hysterical, and only recovered after going to bed for twelve hours.[21]

The focus in the Mendelssohn household was the salon. As free speech was curtailed in this period, music, rather than conversation, was the essence of the entertainment. Among the most brilliant were the salons of Leah Mendelssohn and Amalia Beer, wife of the banker Herz Beer, and mother of Meyerbeer. These provided a welcome oasis in a city which Alexander von Humboldt thought displayed 'bigotry without religion, aestheticism without culture, and philosophy without common sense'.[22]

It was in this affluent, happy, cultured, yet unostentatious environment that the Mendelssohns lived. They were hard-working. Leah would ask: 'Felix, are you doing nothing?' Only on Sundays were the children allowed to get up after 5 am. The family was hierarchical.[23] Mendelssohn even consulted his father in his later years on matters of extraordinary detail, such as whether he should buy a horse.[24]

In 1816, following the Restoration, the Mendelssohns went on a trip to Paris. Abraham did some banking business related to the reparations payable by France for the war. They also saw Aunt Jette, who was a governess there.* Fanny and Felix were given lessons by Madame Bigot, 'a gifted and stimulating teacher'.[25]

When he was ten, Felix's general education was given to a teacher who

* Aunt Jette (Henriette) was governess to the daughter of General Sebastiani; 30 years later, the daughter, by then the Duchesse de Choiseul-Praslin, was murdered by her husband.

subsequently became professor of philology at Berlin University. For music theory and composition, he was taught by one of Abraham's friends, Carl Friedrich Zelter, the director of the Berlin Singakadamie. Zelter was founder of the first of the somewhat hearty male voice choral societies (*Liedertafel*) which spread throughout Germany. He was also a builder, but more importantly he was a particularly close confidant of Goethe. It has been said that Goethe particularly welcomed Zelter's settings of his poems because there was little chance that the music would compete with the poetry.[26]

Zelter was steeped in the traditions of J.S. Bach, whose sons Carl Philipp Emanuel and Wilhelm Friedemann had lived in Berlin. Zelter introduced Abraham to Goethe as he thought Abraham might be able to give the poet some useful investment advice. When Felix was twelve, he was taken to stay with Goethe in Weimar. 'Every morning I receive a kiss from the author of *Faust* and *Werther* and two kisses in the afternoon, from father and friend Goethe. Think of that! … In the afternoon I played for Goethe for more than two hours, Bach fugues and improvisations … I play far more here than I do at home, seldom for less than four hours, often for six and sometimes as many as eight hours … [Goethe] sits down beside me and when I've finished, I ask for a kiss or else give him one. You cannot imagine how kind and gracious he is.'[27]

Felix was doted on by Goethe's daughter-in-law Ottilie and her sister; and he played with Goethe's two little grandsons, Walther and Wolfgang, aged four and two. Goethe expressed some concern that the boy tended to be bumptious.[28] Mendelssohn must have ignored his father's orders 'to keep a strict watch over yourself; to sit properly and behave nicely, especially at dinner; to speak distinctly and suitably, and try as much as possible to express yourself to the point',[29] because at one stage he picked up some bellows and attacked a Weimar lady's coiffure.

In 1822, Abraham took the family, including the tutor and servants, on a long holiday in Switzerland. They visited all the fashionable sights including Voltaire's house at Ferney, and the area around Interlaken, Grindelwald and Wengen. Felix, who became a very competent painter, sketched the scenery and many of the waterfalls (see colour plate 41). On the way back, they called on Goethe. In August 1823, Abraham went to Silesia on business and took his two sons with him.

Six months later, on his fifteenth birthday, after the first rehearsal with orchestra of Felix's opera *Der Onkel aus Boston* (The Two Nephews), Zelter announced: 'from today, you are no longer an apprentice, but a fully-fledged member of the brotherhood of musicians. I proclaim you independent in the name of Mozart, Haydn and old father Bach.'[30] More works followed. But Abraham and Leah were far too worldly-wise simply to assume that a boy with Felix's outstanding ability had an assured career in music. Abraham consulted Jacob Bartholdy, the successful diplomat, who wrote to his brother-in-law sagely: 'A professional musician – I can't get that into my head. It's neither a career, nor a life, nor a goal ... Let the boy study as he should, let him read law at the university and begin a career in the government. Art will remain a friend to him and a diversion ... If he has to be a merchant, put him to work at once behind a counter.'[31]

Abraham also consulted the virtuoso pianist Ignaz Moscheles; he was a friend of Beethoven, and had given lessons to Felix and Fanny. The following year, Abraham took Felix to Paris, the musical centre of Europe at the time, to consult Cherubini, the director of the Conservatoire, whom Felix described as 'an extinct volcano, still throwing out occasional sparks and flashes, but quite covered with ashes and stones'.[32] Cherubini's supportive, although not enthusiastic, opinion must have gone a long way to calming Abraham's worries: 'Ce garçon est riche, il fera bien, il fait même déjà bien, mais il dépense trop de son argent, il met trop d'étoffe dans son habit.'*[33]

For a boy of Felix's age to consort with Meyerbeer and Rossini, as he did on this visit, must have been quite something. He expressed concern – perhaps justified, but presumptuous in one so young – that the Paris musical public did not know a note of Beethoven's *Fidelio*, and that it regarded Bach as 'a mere full-bottomed wig powdered with nothing but learning'.[34] However, back in Berlin, Felix was firmly put in his place when his opera, *The Wedding of Camacho*, was submitted to Spontini, the highly paid musical director of the Royal Opera. One critic described the opera as 'not really too bad for the work of a rich man's son', and another said that 'it had in no way enhanced the greatly overrated reputation of Herr Mendelssohn Bartholdy'.[35] So it was not repeated after the first performance, leaving Felix with a feeling of resentment and disappointment. He would only dabble at opera in future.

* 'The boy is rich, he will do well, he's already doing well, but he's too generous with his money, he puts too much cloth into his clothes.'

LEIPZIGERSTRASSE

In 1825, the Mendelssohns moved to Number 3, Leipzigerstrasse. This was located in a long street, which is intersected by the Wilhelmstrasse, later to be the centre of German government. Then, the residence was a slightly dilapidated palace, set in several acres of garden and meadow, with a small farm where a farmer kept twelve cows providing fresh milk and butter. The enclave was a haven from the bouts of anti-Semitism which flared up fairly regularly. Now, Number 3, Leipzigerstrasse no longer exists, not surprisingly, both because the city was so heavily bombed during the Second World War, and because the Berlin Wall ran within 100 yards of it. There is a plaque on the side of the Bundesrat building to indicate that, once upon a time, Mendelssohn's home was there.* The Potsdamer Platz, the new 'bright lights' district of Berlin, is now nearby.[36]

Felix's friend Devrient said that 'considering the family's reputed wealth, the furnishing of the house seemed almost affectedly austere'.[37] Indeed, the atmosphere was cultured rather than ostentatious. Abraham built his own observatory in the garden. The large room in the garden wing (the *Gartenhaus*) provided a setting for the family's Sunday Musicales or *Sonntagsmusik*, which was attended by ambassadors, princesses and the intelligentsia.[38] Fanny played the piano, Rebecka sang, Paul played the cello, and Felix played the piano, violin and viola. Famous virtuosos would perform: these included Moscheles, and also Frédéric Kalkbrenner, Franz Liszt, Joseph Joachim and Ferdinand David. The family also staged amateur dramatics, performing plays such as Shakespeare's *A Midsummer Night's Dream*. And they had fun with charades, games and fancy-dress.

In 1827, the year when the Overture to *A Midsummer Night's Dream* had its first performance, Mendelssohn went to Berlin University. He benefited from his contact with the considerable circle of intellectual friends of his parents, such as the Humboldt brothers and the poet Heinrich Heine.** The circle also included Hegel, who had revolutionised European thought by arguing, among many other things, that the world, far from being stable and static, as had generally been supposed, is actually in a

* The Bundesrat is the upper house in the German parliament and acts mainly in an advisory capacity. It is formed from members of the *Land* (state) governments.

** Heine converted to Christianity in 1826, saying: 'The baptismal certificate is the entrance ticket to European culture.'[39]

perpetual process of structured change: every phase of its development can be said to 'carry within itself the seeds of its own possible destruction'.[40]

FANNY

Felix and Fanny were passionately fond of each other and corresponded at times almost every day. Possibly Felix never loved another woman, even his wife, as greatly as he loved Fanny. He gave her the first 'Song Without Words', for her birthday. Fanny was small, rather plain and had Moses' crooked shoulder; her younger sister Rebecka was far prettier and more amusing.

Although Fanny was a virtuoso pianist and a composer, she was a woman. In this era and in this particularly patriarchal family, it was not regarded as appropriate for her to go out into the wide world like Felix. Her personal development was designed to end with adolescence. Abraham wrote to Fanny in 1820 from Paris: 'Perhaps music will be his [Felix's] profession, whereas for you, it can and must be but an ornament and never the fundamental bass-line of your existence and activity.'[41] On her birthday in 1828, he wrote: 'You can still improve! You must take yourself in hand and concentrate harder; you must school yourself more seriously and eagerly for your true profession, a young woman's only profession: being mistress of the house.' He added – this was after all the equivalent of a birthday card – 'I do not, however wish to preach at you, and I'm not yet old enough to be talking drivel. Accept in your heart my fatherly wishes for your well-being, and my well intentioned advice. Your father.'[42]

Her father and brother prohibited her from publishing her compositions. When at last she did so, just before she died, the music magazine, *Die Neue Zeitschrift*, expressed surprise that such works could be composed by a woman.

Fanny fell in love with the tone-deaf Wilhelm Hensel. The son of a poor Protestant clergyman, struggling to become a successful painter, Hensel was not at all what Leah had in mind for her eldest daughter, even though Hensel's circle included distinguished poets and authors such as Adalbert von Chamisso, Achim von Arnim and Clemens Brentano. Far more suitable for Fanny would be Felix's young friend Klingemann, the secretary at the Hanoverian legation, which rented some of the surplus space at their enormous house. So Leah stipulated that Hensel was to go away for five years to Rome; he and Fanny should not write to each other;

Leah would write regularly and give him the family news. If after five years, he and Fanny were still adamant, their engagement would be sanctioned. Fanny waited; Hensel returned; Leah tried a last time to dissuade her. The engagement had to be kept secret from an aunt who was an orthodox Jew, and who would have disapproved strongly. But the aunt died; Fanny and Wilhelm got married and lived in the Garden House. In her diary, Fanny noted, 'the ceremony took place at four o'clock', and added that the sermon was 'of no interest, the church full'.[43]

The St Matthew Passion

Mendelssohn had first heard parts of Bach's St Matthew Passion at Zelter's regular Friday music makings. There was always an undercurrent of interest in Bach.* Copies of some works were to be found, but few were printed and published. In 1799 an edition of one of the trio sonatas for organ was published in London.[44] Ten years later, Samuel Wesley began issuing the rest of the trio sonatas, and then he published the Forty-Eight Preludes and Fugues. Wesley considered the works 'a musical bible, unrivalled and inimitable'.[45] Goethe said: 'As listeners to Bach's music, we may feel as if we were present when God created the world.'[46]

On the whole, however, Bach's works were hard to come by and those who possessed manuscripts had to be cajoled into lending them or allowing them to be rented for copying. The St Matthew Passion had not been performed for nearly 100 years, and Devrient, who wanted Mendelssohn to conduct it, was intent on doing a full performance for its centenary in 1829. The two young men approached Zelter, whose co-operation was necessary in order to make the hall of the Singakademie available and also to persuade the choir to sing for them. Zelter said that the Passion was impossible to perform, the choir would drive them demented, they would find no suitable string players, and that better men than they had failed in similar enterprises. But they determinedly persuaded him to release the score and support the project.

Mendelssohn used a large orchestra and a choir of 400. He cut the score, omitting much that did not relate directly to the Passion; 22 numbers were omitted, including eleven arias, four recitatives and four chorales.[47] He filled out the instrumentation and provided sound effects

* J.N. Forkel, music director at the University of Göttingen, published his life of Bach in 1802.

such as a lightning-flash of sound when the veil of the temple was rent in two. By so doing, he started the process of alteration and truncation that was applied throughout the Bach revival.*

There was growing excitement in the cultural circles of Berlin as the day for the performance, 11 March 1829, approached. The king and his court were present; and the hall was packed out. A second performance was given about a week later. Mendelssohn remarked: 'To think that it should be an actor and a Jew that have given back to the people the greatest Christian work.'[49]

With this, Mendelssohn had undoubtedly provided the impetus to the rehabilitation of the status and works of J.S. Bach that now took place, and which had a lasting influence. The Bach-Gesellschaft was founded in 1850; the final, 46th volume of its complete edition was published in 1900. By then, Philipp Spitta had written the authoritative biography of Bach in the 1870s. But it would be a mistake to imagine that Bach's works were universally embraced at this time: Berlioz, when he heard a Bach concerto for three claviers played by Chopin, Liszt and Hiller, damned it: 'It was heart-rending, I assure you, to see three such admirable talents, full of fire, brilliant in youthful vitality, united in a bundle to reproduce this ridiculous and stupid psalmody.'[50]

To Great Britain

After the performance of the Passion, Abraham felt that his son, aged twenty, should travel abroad to broaden his outlook, and so Felix set off for Britain. The crossing from Hamburg was rough and foggy and Mendelssohn was extremely sick; something went wrong with the ship's engines so he was late when he finally steamed up the Thames estuary. In London, he was sought after by the most fashionable hostesses: he was handsome, elegant and witty; he could dance and ride; and importantly, he was rich. He drove in an open carriage to the city, attended a debate in parliament, and visited Dr Spurzheim's phrenological cabinet where he was shown sets of plaster cast heads of famous musicians and famous murderers placed side by side for comparison.[51]

If Mendelssohn had been seen as a professional musician, his reception

* For example, at a presentation of one of the Passions in Frankfurt in 1829, Bach's recitatives were replaced with those composed by the conductor.[48]

would have been different. Moscheles, who had emigrated to London, was required to enter great houses by the servants' entrance. One violinist was stopped in full flight by a bored duke, with a tap on the shoulder and 'C'est assez, mon cher'. Liszt was one of the first to break down the barriers with his famous snub to Tsar Nicholas, who began chatting while he was playing. Liszt just stopped – the atmosphere must have been electric – and the tsar asked him why. The answer was: 'When the Tsar speaks, Music must shut up.'[52]

Mendelssohn made his début at a concert of the Philharmonic Society in the Argyll rooms in Regent Street. He and Klingemann then went to Scotland. They attended a bagpipe competition. Goethe had described Sir Walter Scott's *Waverley* as one of the greatest books ever written, so Felix drove out to the novelist's home at Abbotsford. This was rather unsatisfactory, as Scott was just going out and brushed him off. Mendelssohn was fascinated by the Scottish landscape and stopped now and then to sketch. He set out from Oban and after a dreadful night on board, packed like sardines with the other passengers, he visited the fashionable tourist attraction, Fingal's Cave on the Island of Staffa. He sketched the opening bars of the *Hebrides Overture*, popularly known as 'Fingal's Cave'.

After an expedition to Loch Lomond, Mendelssohn and Klingemann flew away from Glasgow at 10 mph on top of the mail, past 'steaming meadows and smoking chimneys' to the Lake District.[53] Since the cumbersome travel arrangements of the previous century, there had been a considerable improvement in the roads, much due to the efforts of Macadam and Telford. 'From mere beds of torrents and systems of ruts they were raised universally to the condition and appearance of gravel walks in private parks.'[54]

The first 30 years of the 19th century were therefore the golden age and high noon of coaching. Cobbett wrote: 'Next to a foxhunt, the finest sight in England is the stage coach just ready to start.'[55] Coaches with evocative names like Rocket, Comet and Greyhound travelled at high speed. There was considerable competition on fares and speed. The owner of the London–Brighton coach offered a refund of the fare if he did not keep to time. While speed brought accidents, it also brought safety in that highwaymen found it more difficult to operate. The pressure led to the customary ill-mannered behaviour, and someone paid a compliment to Constable, the great painter, when they said: 'He was a gentleman, even on a coach journey.'[56]

The extent of coaching activity is shown by the fact that there were 2,500 horses stabled at Hounslow, the first and last change on the road linking London and the West Country.[57] But railways were about to change all this: the first locomotive-powered train was driven by George Stephenson in September 1825, travelling at speeds up to 15 mph.* In his travels in the 1830s and 1840s, Mendelssohn must surely have seen a lot of railway building.

When they got to Liverpool, Klingemann had to go on to London, but Mendelssohn went to Wales. From Llangollen, he wrote intemperately about 'Scotch bagpipes, Swiss cow horns, Welsh harps – all playing the Huntsmen's Chorus with hideously improvised variations … It's unspeakable. Anyone who, like myself, can't stand Beethoven's national songs ought to come to Wales and hear them bellowed by rough nasal voices to the crudest accompaniment.'**[60] But he found peace and idyllic family life at Coed Du near Mold, where he stayed with a rich mine owner and his three lovely daughters.

Back in London, he was about to leave to get back for Fanny's wedding when his leg was badly injured in a carriage accident. This kept him in bed for two months, and he recuperated at the house of Thomas Attwood, formerly a pupil of Mozart, and organist of St Paul's Cathedral. Mendelssohn had fallen for England, although his front teeth 'ached from trying to pronounce the English "th", and his back teeth from trying to chew English mutton'.[62]

The 'Grand Tour'

Mendelssohn turned down the opportunity to become professor of music at the University of Berlin early in 1830. Instead, after a short delay, while

* The Liverpool and Manchester, one of the earliest passenger-carrying railways, in its first year carried 445,000 passengers. Prince Louis Napoleon did this journey two years later, travelling at 27 mph. It was not too comfortable: 'A man was seen yesterday buying a third-class ticket for the new London and Birmingham railway. His state of mind is being enquired into.'[58] Mail coaches were taken off the road by 1841 (the year in which Thomas Cook carried out his first conducted tour from Leicester to Loughborough, price one shilling), and most of the stage-coaches had gone the following year.[59]

** Despite the fame of the Welsh bards since ancient times, and the strong Welsh musical tradition, the Welsh National Eisteddfod, originating in 1176, has only been held annually since 1880. The male voice choirs grew with the coalmining industry of the 19th century and the growth in the urban population. Their repertoire, originally hymns, expanded to include a wide variety of choral works.[61]

Rebecka had measles, he set out on a two-year journey starting with Munich and Vienna, and then going on to Italy. Venice inspired him to write a gondola 'Song Without Words'. Then he went to Florence, Rome, Naples, and back up to Switzerland, Munich, Paris and London. He only got back to Berlin in June 1832.

Improved transport enabled tourism to grow considerably. Samuel Taylor Coleridge, the poet, on holiday on the Rhine, wrote the following lines about what he saw:

Keep moving! Steam, or Gas, or Stage,
Hold, cabin, steerage, hencoop's cage –
Tour, Journey, Voyage, Lounge, Ride, Walk,
Skim, Sketch, Excursion, Travel-talk –
For move you must! 'Tis now the rage,
The law and fashion of the Age.[63]

In Munich, Mendelssohn met a sixteen year old, Delphine von Schauroth. 'We flirted dreadfully', he told Fanny, 'but there isn't any danger because I'm already in love with a young Scotch girl whose name I don't know.'[64] On the return journey, he saw Delphine again and the King of Bavaria encouraged him to marry her. Nothing came of it; perhaps he thought that marriage would be a distraction to his ambitions.

In Rome, Mendelssohn met Berlioz, and they saw some of the sights together. Like Berlioz, he was very critical of the state of music in Rome. In Naples, he was intoxicated by the sun and the sea and would gaze for hours at the Bay and Vesuvius. He went for long walks and visited Pompeii. He found time to complete the *Hebrides Overture*, to start his *Scottish Symphony*, and to compose the *Italian Symphony*. He had his picture painted by Horace Vernet, and was in Rome at the time when Pope Pius VIII, who had only reigned for a year, died. After a 64-day conclave, Pope Gregory XVI was elected. There was great pomp and ceremony surrounding both events.

Mendelssohn moved on to Paris at a time when, as we have seen, there was immense creative activity in the arts, which had blossomed after the desultory period of the revolution and the empire. In painting, there were Ingres and Delacroix; in literature, Balzac, Hugo, George Sand and Stendhal. In music, Grand Opera was at its height with Meyerbeer, another Berliner, on his way to becoming the most famous and prosperous opera composer of the time. Chopin had arrived a few months before;

Liszt, Thalberg and Paganini had extended the limits of virtuosity for the piano and violin.

It is hard to imagine the somewhat prissy Mendelssohn, whose mild flirtations with Delphine were the limit of his experience, entering this scene, personally or professionally. Being neither dandy nor womaniser, the wilder, steamy aspects disgusted him. He thought Meyerbeer's works were vulgar and, as we know, he disliked Berlioz' music.[65] Mendelssohn's musical style was refined, subtle, even magical: it was more similar to that of Weber and Schubert; he liked Chopin's music.

The première of Mendelssohn's *Reformation Symphony*, originally written to celebrate the 300th anniversary of the publication of the doctrinal standard for Lutheranism, the Augsburg Confession, was cancelled because the Paris orchestra thought there was too much counterpoint and too few tunes. After a fortunately mild dose of cholera, Mendelssohn escaped from Paris, never to return.

London must have seemed a relief and a contrast. He visited Moscheles in his house in Regent's Park. He saw much of Dr Horsley's family, including his respectable daughters, who held private musical parties in their house, 1 High Row, Kensington Gravel Pits, not far from the present Notting Hill Gate underground station.*

Düsseldorf and Problems with Orchestras

His father suddenly ordered him back to Berlin. Zelter had died and Abraham wanted his son to apply for his job at the Singakademie. Mendelssohn was reluctant. After blowing hot and cold, he applied, but, much to his disappointment and that of his family, the Singakademie, in what may have reflected the anti-Semitic views of many Berliners, appointed Zelter's assistant instead.[66]

Mendelssohn had a very successful appearance at the Lower Rhine Festival; a two-day Whitsuntide event, held successively in Düsseldorf, Aachen (Aix-la-Chapelle) and Cologne. Music had emerged from the salon and entered the bourgeois concert hall; the audience could now enjoy orchestral performances and solo recitals by virtuosos such as Liszt and his rival Thalberg, and by Clara Schumann.

* The eldest Horsley daughter eventually married Brunel, the engineer, builder of bridges and railways.

Mendelssohn's success led to his appointment in 1833 as director of music at Düsseldorf, then a city with a population of less than 20,000, quaint and old fashioned.[67] His duties were to direct the rehearsals and concerts of the Music and Theatre Society and to keep a watchful eye on the music of the local, mainly Roman Catholic churches. He did much to promote the oratorios of Handel there, sometimes in his own arrangement.[68]

Mendelssohn was determined to raise the standards of performance. But he faced difficulties. To stage *Don Giovanni*, the seat prices had to be increased, and this led to protests on the first night; one duet was completely drowned by whistling catcalls and howling. It was said that the perpetrators were 'mainly beer house proprietors and waiters, for in fact, by 4 pm, half Düsseldorf is drunk'.[69] Mendelssohn insisted on an apology and eventually the performances were resumed successfully. Mendelssohn, for his part, was very temperamental – at a rehearsal of Beethoven's *Egmont Music*, he flew into a rage and tore the score in two. He did not like the orchestra, many of whom were usually far from sober: 'I assure you that at the beat they all come in separately, not one with any decision.'[70]

As we have seen already, the quality of musical performance in the mid-19th century left much to be desired.[71] There was the frequent tampering with the composer's score: a conductor of Beethoven's 'Pastoral' Symphony in London had dry peas rattled in a box to enhance the storm effects.[72] Works such as Beethoven symphonies would be broken up by an Italian operatic aria, or some gymnastics by, say, Paganini.* The orchestral playing was very patchy and was becoming a constraint on the development of 'modern' music of the time: the Vienna Opera abandoned *Tristan* after 77 rehearsals; Liszt would even treat performances as if they were rehearsals and return to an earlier place and begin again.

The growing complexity of the orchestra and the decline of the continuo-playing composer-conductor meant that a conductor was particularly necessary. In the opera house, tapping or stamping was thought to be the only way of keeping the orchestra and soloists together. In Italy, the conductor tapped on the candleholders. Up to 1848, the leading Parisian conductor François-Antoine Habeneck conducted with violin bow in his right hand and, in his left, the violin part, or possibly the violin itself. Soon

* At the first Paris performance of Beethoven's Violin Concerto, between the first and second movements, the soloist Franz Clement played a show-piece of his own with the violin held upside down.[73]

we begin to see concerts conducted with a baton. Liszt was the first conductor to use gestures and facial expression to indicate the phrasing and dynamics. Hans von Bülow was the first to conduct without a score. Mendelssohn would sometimes stand back, put his baton down and let the orchestra play.[74]

English orchestras were at times appalling. There, a system applied whereby deputies could be sent to rehearsals, so long as the principal played in the performance. In 1877, Wagner left the Albert Hall rostrum in despair after the orchestra broke down three times during the *Flying Dutchman Overture*. A slightly different problem was illustrated in 1886 during Gounod's *Faust* at Her Majesty's Theatre: the orchestra stopped until they were paid in cash.

But, for Mendelssohn, the period in Düsseldorf was enjoyable: he took lessons in watercolour paintings on Sunday mornings from a local artist. He rode a great deal. He visited the quaint, picturesque towns on the Rhine like Bacharach. During a heat wave, he and his friends were bathing naked, when the Queen of Bavaria's boat came round a corner. 'We sprang just *a tempo* into the water as she approached.'[75] He composed *Songs Without Words*,* wrote the overture *The Fair Melusine*, and worked on his oratorio *St Paul*. This was given its première at the Lower Rhine festival in 1836. The Irish critic and playwright George Bernard Shaw said of this oratorio that he would 'as lief talk Sunday-school for two hours and a half to a beautiful woman with no brains as listen to St Paul over again'.[77] But it was an astonishing success. Within 18 months of its publication, it had been performed in 41 different German cities. It soon reached England, Holland, Switzerland, Denmark, Poland, Russia and America.

Mendelssohn's full-time appointment at Düsseldorf ended after a row with the management in which his friends and his father thought he was entirely in the wrong, blaming him for losing his temper and storming out instead of trying to discuss the situation calmly. Fortunately, he received a tentative enquiry from the Leipzig Gewandhaus to work there.

* When asked what he had in mind when writing a wordless song, Mendelssohn replied: 'The song, just as it stands. Even if, in one or other of them, I had a particular word or words in mind, I would not want to tell anyone, because the same word means different things to different people. Only the song says the same thing, arouses the same feeling, in everyone – a feeling that can't be expressed in words.'[76]

The Leipzig Gewandhaus

Clara Novello described the Gewandhaus, the new cloth hall built in 1781, as 'small and frightfully painted in yellow, the benches arranged that one sits as if in an omnibus – and no lady and gentlemen are ever allowed to sit together here or in their churches. So that the women sit in rows opposite one another staring at each other's dress.'[78]

Here, Mendelssohn had a better orchestra, more scope and no theatrical involvement. He also seems to have improved his human relations, and took a personal interest in the musicians who worked for him. He established a pension scheme for which he provided considerable sums himself, and he helped instrumentalists in need of financial assistance. He was conductor from 1835 until his death and under him, and his colleagues Ferdinand David, Niels Gade from Denmark and Ferdinand Hiller, the Leipzig Gewandhaus orchestra became one of the greatest in Germany.

From now on, Leipzig became Mendelssohn's musical centre, despite magnetic forces, particularly Leah, who tried to draw him to Berlin. Mendelssohn organised subscription concerts, chamber music quartets, cantatas and oratorios. He performed as solo pianist and organist, and attracted some of the leading virtuosos of the time, such as Liszt, Thalberg, Moscheles, Anton Rubinstein, Clara Schumann and the singer Jenny Lind.

Mendelssohn campaigned for recognition of forgotten 18th-century works and promoted the works of Mozart, Beethoven and Robert Schumann. He undertook a series of historical concerts, 'a kind of history of music in sound'.[79] On New Year's Day 1839, there took place the première of Schubert's Great C major Symphony, the manuscript of which Schumann had found in Vienna.

Marriage

Around the time of his appointment in Leipzig, Mendelssohn's father died. He was shattered by this. About six months later, he was in Frankfurt standing in for a friend who was ill. He was lodging with the 40-year-old Madame Jeanrenaud, the widow of the local minister of the French Reformed Church. As occasionally happens, at least before marriage, there was some confusion among onlookers as to whether Mendelssohn was in love with the future mother-in-law or the daughter. It transpired that the actual object of Mendelssohn's affection was Madame Jeanrenaud's daughter, Cécile.[80]

With the precedent of Fanny and Hensel no doubt clearly in mind, Mendelssohn went alone to the North Sea town of Scheveningen, which is best known because the name is unpronounceable other than by a true Dutchman. It is certainly guaranteed to test the temperature of one's feelings. Finding them unchanged, Felix returned to Frankfurt, proposed to Cécile on a picnic in the Taunus mountains, and was accepted. They duly got married at the Walloon French Reformed Church in Frankfurt in March 1837. None of Mendelssohn's family was present at the wedding other than an old aunt. Fanny was jealous; Leah fretted. Madame Jeanrenaud's family, which was quite snobbish, thought that Cécile could have done better.

Jenny Lind / Cécile Mendelssohn Bartholdy

Cécile was his only love. Although Clara Schumann said that Jenny Lind, a leading 19th-century soprano, always sang Mendelssohn's music so beautifully because 'she loves him no less as a man than as a composer',[81] there has never been any serious suggestion that he fell in love with anyone else.[82]

The newly-weds seem to have had a blissful honeymoon which went on for about five months. By the end of it, their son Karl Wolfgang Paul was on the way. Four other children followed at regular intervals: Marie in

1839, Paul in 1841, Felix in 1843; and Lilli in 1845.* But Cécile, their mother, was rather ordinary and unmemorable. It was some months before Felix even got round to introducing her to his family, and Fanny eventually had to come to Leipzig to meet her.

Soon after the honeymoon was over, Mendelssohn had to go to London. He made many trips to England during his short life, some of them by train to Birmingham, at the invitation of the elderly Joseph Moore, who had made a fortune making buttons.[84] There are many anecdotes of Mendelssohn's time in England. On one occasion, Mendelssohn played the organ in St Paul's so beautifully that nobody would leave the building until the organ blowers, in desperation, went off in the middle of a Bach fugue. It was in England that 'Hear my Prayer' (from Motets, Op. 39) was written in 1844.

Buckingham Palace

Mendelssohn was commanded to visit Buckingham Palace, then occupied by that blissfully happy couple, Victoria and Albert, who had been married for just over two years. Around this time the queen was referring to her husband as 'the most perfect being in existence'. She wrote: 'I doubt whether anybody ever did love or respect another as I do my dear Angel.'[85] Although rising at 8.30 am on the first morning of her honeymoon, causing the diarist Greville to comment that this was 'not the way to provide us with a Prince of Wales',[86] the queen's first child was born nine months later; one arrived on average every second year for the next sixteen years. The future King Edward VII was seven months old when Mendelssohn visited the palace twice, in late June and early July.

Three weeks before the first visit, the son of a stage carpenter at Covent Garden had tried to shoot the queen; and a week before the second visit another attempt had been made. Whether any reference was made to this, or the fact that, a few days later, she was going to return from Windsor to Paddington by rail for the first time, we do not know.[87]

There can have been no doubt that the three parts in this trio were going to blend extremely well. On the first occasion, the draught when the

* Karl became a professor at Heidelberg. Paul became an able scientist and the creator of the famous firm, Agfa. Marie's son became bursar of Magdalen College, Oxford; he was said to have 'permanently ruined [during the First World War] the digestion of his colleagues by his unnecessary injudicious economies'.[83]

queen swept in blew the sheet music onto the floor and the sovereign, her consort and Felix scrabbled around to pick it up. Later, when the queen saw Mendelssohn as she was just about to leave for her weekend at Windsor, they rummaged around to find some music which had already been packed to take away. This degree of informality was maintained when they had to remove a parrot that threatened to disturb their music making. A minor awkwardness was easily brushed off when the queen chose to sing a song which was actually by Fanny rather than Felix.

Mendelssohn wisely complimented the prince's playing of an organ chorale 'so charmingly, precisely and accurately that it would have done credit to a professional'.[88] Albert presented Mendelssohn with a ring engraved 'VR 1842'. Mendelssohn played 'How Lovely are the Messengers' from *St Paul* and the royal pair both began singing the chorus. The queen's problematic mother, the Duchess of Kent, came in. Mendelssohn amazed them all with his skill at improvisation, interweaving with 'Rule Britannia' many of the tunes which they had just played.[89]

Some 50 years later the queen, after singing a Gilbert and Sullivan duet with a courtier, turned to him and said: 'You know, Mr Yorke, I was taught singing by Mendelssohn.'[90]* The accuracy of this should perhaps be taken in a similar vein to her claim to Melba, the leading soprano, 'I knew Richard Wagner quite well';[92] had she known the man, she might not have claimed such friendship. At least Wagner would hardly have responded as Mendelssohn did when asked by the queen how she could reciprocate the pleasure he had given her: Felix said that he would like to see the royal nursery.

Mendelssohn's saccharine story contrasts with Clara Schumann's experience 30 years later when, during her performance, the queen 'talked incessantly, heard only the closing measure of each programme number and then applauded faintly'. Worse was to follow: during the tea interval the royal band blared a folk medley, followed by two bagpipers (in kilts!) who opened up in the next room. 'I was speechless', recorded Clara.[93]

Leipzig and Berlin, and Overwork

To give up Leipzig for Berlin was, Mendelssohn told Klingemann, 'one of

* In fact, the queen had taken lessons from the operatic bass Lablache who was famous for his breath control. At a dinner party he was reputed (improbably) to have sung a long note from forte to piano, then drunk a glass of wine, then sung a chromatic scale up the octave in trills, and finally blown out a candle. This was performed all within the same breath. He was a big man.[91]

the sourest apples a man can eat'.[94] Nevertheless, to please his mother, in 1841, he accepted the post of director of the musical side of the new Berlin Academy of Arts, a project dear to the heart of the King of Prussia, Frederick William IV. The Academy was to be divided into four sections, painting, sculpture, architecture and music. For these, there were to be four directors who would take it in turns to act as head of the whole institution. But in spite of endless discussion, Mendelssohn could never elicit precisely what his status or his duties would be, and it was only after a personal interview with the king, who offered him a new choir, that he accepted. So he arranged to have his deputy act at Leipzig during his absence. Unfortunately, Leah died suddenly in December 1842, and the rationale for being in Berlin disappeared.

In Berlin, Mendelssohn was required to direct the symphony concerts and the male voice choir at the cathedral, and he was also to provide incidental music for plays staged at the theatre. One was *Antigone*; another *A Midsummer Night's Dream*, for which he drew from his overture written seventeen years before. He moved into the family residence in Leipzigerstrasse. But he became increasingly dissatisfied with what he was supposed to do at the Academy, which was unclear.

Mendelssohn was more interested in the Leipzig Conservatoire, which he opened in April 1843. There, he would take charge of piano and ensemble, Schumann would be responsible for piano and composition, and Ferdinand David, the violin. Mendelssohn worked intensively at organising this. So he returned to live in Leipzig in August 1845. Earlier that year the first performance of his Violin Concerto had been given at the Gewandhaus with his two protégés, Ferdinand David and Niels Gade, as soloist and conductor respectively.[95]

In 1845, Joseph Moore invited Mendelssohn to write another oratorio for the Birmingham Festival to be held in the following summer. In the first half of 1846, Mendelssohn worked feverishly to produce *Elijah*. 'It was a sick man who was embarking on a suicidal venture with all the frenzy of one who knows that his time is running out.' In May, he was in Aachen for the Lower Rhine Festival, with Jenny Lind.* Then, he went to Cologne,

* After Mendelssohn's death, Jenny Lind toured the USA in 1850–52. Promoted by the impresario P.T. Barnum, 93 of her concerts grossed $712,000.[96] This was at a time when Abraham Lincoln's Illinois law practice earned him a 'comfortable' $2,000 per annum; by 1860, his personal and property assets amounted to around $17,000.[97]

Leipzig and on to London. His schedule was relentless and exhausting. He suffered from headaches; nobody knew the cause, but his doctor told him to slow down.

Soon after his return to Leipzig, in the latter part of September 1846, Mendelssohn said: 'I'm now leading a vegetable existence.'[98] Niels Gade took over the Gewandhaus, and Moscheles the Conservatoire teaching. The severe headaches continued. He confessed to Klingemann that he wanted to put an end to public music making, and just be able to sit at home with his family and play and compose and let the whole mad world go by.

But in the following year he went to London with Joachim, the violinist. In one fortnight, he conducted six performances of *Elijah*, four at Exeter Hall in London, one in Manchester and one in Birmingham. He suffered an attack of giddiness while standing on a bridge of the Thames. On 1 May he lunched at the Prussian Embassy, before engaging in two hours of piano playing with Victoria and Albert at Buckingham Palace. A week later, he paid a further farewell visit to the palace and then left for Dover. At the Prussian border, he was mistaken for a Dr Mendelssohn who reputedly had run off with evidence in a sensational divorce case. He was stopped and questioned for some considerable time.

When he arrived home there was a devastating blow. A message arrived from Berlin that Fanny was dead.* She had collapsed with a brain haemorrhage at a rehearsal of his cantata *The First Walpurgis Night*, which was to be performed at the salon that Sunday afternoon.

There was absolutely no question of Felix going to Berlin for the funeral. Cécile organised a holiday in his favourite holiday spot, Switzerland. They travelled via the spa at Baden-Baden. He painted watercolours, at Schaffhausen, Neuhausen, the Rhine Falls, Lucerne, Thun and Interlaken. He wrote the F minor String Quartet Op. 80. He seemed better, and when walking in the Alps Cécile and the children had trouble keeping up with him.

But the English critic H.F. Chorley wrote this sad account of his last meeting with him in Switzerland: 'My very last memory is the sight of him turning down the road, to wind back to Interlaken alone; while we turned

* There is a small plaque to her memory in Hamburg by the side of the ring road down by the harbour. It is very moving to come across it in such an unlikely place.

up to cross the Wengernalp to Grindelwald. I thought even then, as I followed his figure, looking none the younger for the loose dark coat and the wide brimmed straw hat bound with black crape, which he wore, that he was too much depressed and worn, and walked too heavily. But who could have dreamed that his days on earth were so rapidly drawing to a close?'[99]

On his return, he went to Fanny's room in Berlin, which had been left as it had been when she died. He was so shattered by this experience that he had to cancel a performance of *Elijah*. He returned to Leipzig. He could not conduct, only compose. Early in October, he collapsed on a sofa when visiting a friend.

On 25 October, he wrote to his brother Paul: 'God be praised I am now daily getting better, and my strength is returning more and more.'[100] But on 28 October, he collapsed with a stroke, while on a walk with Cécile.* And on 3 November, he had a further stroke. When Cécile asked how he was, he said, 'Tired – very tired'.[101] On the night of 4 November 1847, he died of a brain haemorrhage.**

He was worn out at 38.

An English student wrote home from Leipzig to say that people whispered in the streets as though a member of the royal family had died. Thousands filed past the open coffin with bared heads. After a service in St Paul's Church, the train left for Berlin. When it stopped briefly at Dessau, whence Moses had set forth, a chorus sang on the platform. In Berlin, a great crowd attended. To the accompaniment of 'Jesu meine Freude', Felix was laid to rest in the family vault beside his beloved sister.

His reputation suffered dramatically and quickly, although his oratorios and sacred music were adored in Victorian England. But, at a time when piano virtuosity was the fashion, his *Songs Without Words* were considered a relaxing contrast. 'Probably no piano music was performed more often, or more painfully, in the drawing-rooms of Victorian England than these charming and slight, but by no means insignificant, miniatures.'[103] Princess Alexandra of Wales had a musical box specially made to play them.

Elsewhere, posterity has not been particularly kind. Wagner damned Mendelssohn's reputation: for example, he described the *Hebrides Overture*

* Cécile died of consumption on 25 September 1853 in Frankfurt.

** It is not obvious what caused Mendelssohn's premature death. It is said that he suffered a series of haemorrhages.[102]

as 'so clear, so smooth, so melodious, as definite in form as a crystal, but also just as cold'. He called Mendelssohn 'a landscape painter, incapable of depicting a human being'.[104] Schumann liked to see in him the reconciliation of the classical and the Romantic; but his almost excessive elegance and refinement, the lack of conflicts, the 'cautiously held reins' are seen as limitations to his greatness.[105]

Most of us who love his works are more charitable and applaud unreservedly. If Mendelssohn had had just some of Berlioz' passion and poetry, would his reputation stand higher? It may indeed be easier for a camel to go through a needle's eye, than for a rich man to enter into the kingdom of God.[106]

Chopin

CHAPTER 11

AT AROUND TWO in the morning on 17 October 1849, Chopin died of consumption in an apartment in the Place Vendôme, that most elegant 18th-century square in Paris. It is almost exactly opposite the hotel where, about 150 years later, Diana, Princess of Wales set out to her death; today, Chopin's plaque can be seen above a very smart jeweller's shop.

The dying man was visited by many friends. Pauline Viardot, the well-known mezzo-soprano, said that 'all the grand Parisian ladies considered it *de rigueur* to faint in his room'.[1] Three ladies were more constant and stayed at his bedside: his sister Louise, the Polish Princess Marcelline Czartoryska and the wayward Solange Clésinger.[2] They represented the three periods of his life: his young years in Poland, his society life among émigré Poles in Paris, and his long affair with Solange's extraordinary mother, the notorious novelist George Sand. She was absent.

Frédéric Chopin had been born less than 40 years earlier, in a village near Warsaw.* We shall follow his tragically short life from the early years in Warsaw and Vienna, to the Paris of the 1830s, the Paris of Rossini, Berlioz, Liszt and George Sand. Chopin's notorious affair with Sand broke

* Warsaw took over from Kracow as the capital of Poland in 1611.

Above: A PENCIL DRAWING BY GEORGE SAND, 1844

up bitterly. Strangled by tuberculosis, exhausted with coughing, he undertook a short visit to England and Scotland. Soon after returning to France, he finally yielded to the disease which had been gnawing away at him for so long.

POLAND

The Poland into which Chopin was born, and for which he became a symbol, had long been an unhappy place. For centuries, its borders with Muscovy and the fiefdoms of the Ottoman Empire seem to have been permanently elastic. In seeking their disparate aims, thugs with Romantic names like Boleslaw and Casimir, and their supporters, hacked each other to bits. Some of the worst were that ferocious combination of grail and sword known euphemistically as the Teutonic Knights. Then, two centuries after the Knights ceased to be an active force, the Swedes and Russians inflicted damage on Poland as serious as that experienced by Germany in the Thirty Years War.* Much of the story of Poland is epitomised by the statue of King Sigismund III Vasa at the entrance to the Old City of Warsaw. Wearing his crown, he brandishes a sword in one hand; in the other, he bears an enormous cross.

An unusual feature of Poland was its paralysing political system whereby the nobility elected their king, whose powers were then constrained by the *liberum veto*: legislation could technically be frustrated by a single objecting noble's vote. As a consequence, the country was virtually ungovernable and it could easily be squeezed by powerful neighbours.

The king was usually someone backed by either the Russians or the Swedes. The Electors of Saxony, who were chosen to be kings in Poland during the 18th century, and to whose officials Bach sent his complaints, owed their Polish crown to the Russians. The Swedes tried to push them out by getting their puppet-ruler Stanislas Leszinski elected;** but the Russians twice ejected him and reinstated the Saxons, and Leszinski was compensated with the dukedom of Lorraine, which is found on modern

* War between Poles and Muscovites in the early 1600s underlies the story of Glinka's opera, *A Life for the Tsar*. There was a Polish-backed pretender on the Muscovite throne in 1606. But when Michael Romanov became Tsar in 1613, he started the dynasty which lasted into the 20th century.

** Leszinski was the father of King Louis XV's dull Queen Marie, before whom Mozart played in Paris (see page 141).

maps around Nancy in the north-east of France bordering with Germany. Chopin's forebears, it seems, followed King Stanislas there.

The Saxons, however, took little interest in their Polish domains. On the death of Augustus III, the Poles elected Stanislas Poniatowski, a veteran of the bedroom of the Russian Empress Catherine the Great. But his attempted reforms were too much for both his ex-lover to the east and his neighbour to the west. In 1772, the Prussian King Frederick the Great dismembered Poland: he diverted the Russians and Austrians from a war over moribund Turkey, in which victory by either would have destabilised the balance of power. He awarded each of them a slice of Poland; for himself, he took the tastiest portion, which enabled him to join up Berlin with East Prussia. This outrageous action reduced Poland's population by a fifth.[3]

Following a few years of considerable instability, there was a second 'Partition' in 1793. Poland was shorn of two thirds of its people. Around this time, the composer's father, Nicholas Chopin, returned to Poland to work as an accounts clerk in a tobacco factory. This went bust, but before he could go back to France, Nicholas got caught up in a revolt led by Thaddeus Kosciusko, who had fought in the War of Independence in the United States. Kosciusko's Polish peasants, armed with pikes and war scythes, were no match for the Russians. The Poles retreated into Warsaw and, after two months, the city was sacked with great cruelty: up to as many as 20,000 were slaughtered in a single day.[4] Nicholas must have been very fortunate to survive.

Under the final partitions of 1795–6, Poland, which had once been twice the size of France,* disappeared. The Russian Romanovs, the Austrian Habsburgs and the Prussian Hohenzollerns agreed that they should 'abolish everything which can recall the memory of the existence of the Kingdom of Poland'.[5] There was a saying at the time: 'God made a mistake when he created the Poles.'[6]

However, a few years later, when Napoleon defeated Prussia and Austria, a remnant of Poland was re-constituted as 'the Grand Duchy of Warsaw'. This entity benefited from the introduction of French administrative procedures and laws. Thus it was, when Frédéric Chopin was born, as February turned to March, in 1810. However, the Grand Duchy did not

* Just before the first partition, Poland-Lithuania's borders reached as far as the west bank of the Dnieper and almost to Kiev.

last long. After Napoleon was defeated, the Kingdom of Poland, which emerged in 1815 from the lengthy discussions at the Congress of Vienna, was a Russian fiefdom and only three quarters the size of Napoleon's Grand Duchy.[7] With the pragmatic support of the leaders of the Polish nobility, it was ruled by a viceroy, the tsar's brother, the 'ill-tempered and brutal' Grand Duke Konstantin.[8]

Chopin's Youth in Poland

Chopin's father Nicholas had ended up staying in Poland, possibly because illness kept him there. His fluency in French made him a suitable tutor for aristocratic children.* When he was working as resident tutor with the impoverished and downwardly mobile Skarbek family, he met Justyna, one of the Skarbeks' relatives, who lived in the household as a kind of companion. In 1806, they married and then had four children: Louise, Frédéric, the robust Isabelle, who lived until 1881, and the sickly and consumptive Emilia, who died aged 14.[9]

There are few places whose local guidebook is prepared to concede that the landscape is 'striking with its monotony', but Żelazowa Wola, then the seat of the Skarbeks, is one.[10] It is in the flat farmland, the fruit and vegetable garden of Warsaw. But Frédéric's birthplace has a definite charm, set as it is beside a fast-flowing stream in a luxuriant garden, the trees covered in mistletoe. He was born in a wing of a larger mansion, of which now there are only a few foundation stones to be seen. The Chopins' apartment was nicely furnished, with warm stoves to resist the bitingly cold wind as it blew from the Urals. Baby Frédéric was baptised in the church in which his parents had been married.**[11]

Someone with Nicholas' skills was ideal to be appointed professor of French at the Lyceum, one of the leading schools in Warsaw. So, when Frédéric was only seven months old, the Chopins moved the 30 miles into the capital. The school was housed in one of the fine palaces built to the south of the Old Town.

In contrast with his later sickly life, Frédéric, although delicate, appears to have been an active little boy with a considerable sense of humour.

* One of his pupils subsequently became Napoleon's mistress, the Countess Walewska (see page 196).

** The church is an unusual building, because it is built in the form of a fortress, itself indicative of the turbulence which prevailed in Poland.

He played the piano with his mother, and showed early skill at improvisation. His first teacher gave him a grounding in Bach and Mozart. He soon performed in public, and by the time he was seven, he was dedicating a polonaise to Countess Skarbek, and even being hailed as Mozart's successor.

Nicholas took in boarders for the school. Frédéric had an adolescent crush on one who was two years older than him: indeed, the correspondence might point to something more intense.[12] Other boarders were two brothers of Maria Wodzinska, with whom Frédéric was eventually to fall in love. Rents from boarders, Nicholas' salary and thrift allowed the Chopins to live very comfortably in a fashionable part of the city. And Frédéric, the boy prodigy, enabled his parents, who would normally have moved in bourgeois circles, to gain an entrée to aristocratic salons. So Frédéric, whose grandfather had been a wheelwright in Lorraine, was brought up to behave with the refined manners which his father had seen in the aristocratic Polish houses in which he taught.

In 1823, Frédéric went to his father's Lyceum. As well as receiving a good general education, he played the organ for services at the nearby Church of the Visitation Nuns, a church remarkable for its elaborate baroque pulpit in the shape of the prow of a ship. He had private music lessons with Josef Elsner, a competent teacher and composer of sorts, who was director of the musical side of the Warsaw Conservatoire. In the summers, he would go to the country estates of his friends, and hear the peasant music to which some attribute the Polish aspects of his music.

The Poles have certainly claimed Chopin as embodying the nationalism of the Polish people, although very few of his works actually contain an identifiable folk tune. Some claim that 'the Polish blood throbs with particular vigour in his warlike polonaises, whose boldly arching melodies are of bent steel',[13] and yet others have found evidence of him making political statements through his music, whatever this may mean.[14] Yet, a composer does not have to be Polish to write a polonaise or mazurka: Schumann wrote polonaises, and the Viennese were writing and playing mazurkas early in the century. Chopin wrote waltzes, yet nobody suggests that he was Austrian. Poland and its woes certainly stimulated his imagination; but it seems fair to say that 'Polish music owes to him something more and something greater than he does to Polish music'.[15] The Poles, when their national identity had been obliterated, rallied round his music;

he became a focus for their nationalism.* Chopin's music was, however, unique, polished like the most exquisite French furniture.

Less nationalistic, and indicative of the ambivalence necessary in his upbringing and life, was his performance before the Tsar of Russia in 1825 when he was opening the Polish Diet, the parliament. The Tsar presented him with a diamond ring. This was around the time that his first opus, a rondo, was published.

At the age of sixteen, he gave his first solo recital at a Silesian spa to which he was sent to recover from a cold in the chest. He then went to the Warsaw Conservatoire, where he received a thorough training in theory, composition and instrumental teaching. He was not the star pupil, but he enjoyed himself, and made many friends. He devoted his spare time to piano compositions such as the Rondo 'à la Mazur', and the *Variations on Là Ci Darem*, a popular tune from Mozart's *Don Giovanni*. In 1828, he was invited to accompany one of his father's friends who was attending a scientific conference in Berlin. He saw Mendelssohn and Spontini, although he felt too shy to introduce himself. But he found time to draw some caricatures of those attending the conference: he was a good mimic and actor, and had a refined sense of humour.[16]

Back in Warsaw, he continued his studies and frequented the popular Warsaw cafés. He did the social round and developed the taste for 'Society' which never left him. Many of the aristocrats whom Chopin met were fiercely nationalistic: the ancient families such as the Potockis were involved in Kosciusko's rising; the Czartoryskis were to be involved in the rising in 1830. These connections would be very important in his later life in Paris.

To Vienna

Warsaw was a backwater; Chopin became increasingly frustrated with it and he set off to Vienna, then still the Mecca for musicians. He had sent some works to the Viennese music publisher Haslinger, and arrived with a letter of introduction. Haslinger agreed to publish, provided Chopin played the works for free. A concert at the Kärntnertor theatre was a great

* Because Chopin did not express a form of nationalism which was associated with any particular faction, he was particularly suitable to become 'a sacred national icon'. It might be fair to make the same comment about Liszt and Verdi.

success, Chopin's delicate musical textures being a welcome contrast to the hammer and tongs works of Liszt. The Viennese were surprised that a place such as Warsaw could produce such talent. He did another concert, again for nothing, so as to avoid any implication that the first was not a success. But, when Haslinger suggested yet another, Chopin put his foot down and refused.

Back in Warsaw, Chopin fell in love with Constantia Gladowska, the daughter of one of the city's civic dignitaries and a singing student at the Conservatoire. Chopin's father packed him off to tutor Prince Radziwill's two daughters, where he wrote the Polonaise for Cello and Piano for the prince. He became absorbed in composition, so was not involved in the initial disturbances which arose when news arrived of the July 1830 Revolution in Paris: he was busy working on his Piano Concerto in E minor which he performed in October of that year.

Au revoir, Poland

Warsaw was no place to stay, even though Chopin's father was concerned that it was not a suitable time to be travelling. Frédéric exchanged rings with Constantia. At the beginning of November, he left Poland and her, for what was to be the last time. She married someone else a few years later. In her blind old age, she dismissed the suggestion that her love affair with Frédéric was serious, saying that she found him 'temperamental, full of fantasies and unreliable'.[17]

Thus, late in 1830, two years after the death of Schubert, Chopin took a leisurely journey to Vienna, stopping at Breslau and Dresden, where he played at soirées. After a day in Prague, he reached Vienna. But in contrast to his earlier visit, he was no longer an amateur performing for free: he was a professional competing with others for public favour and money. His piano playing began to attract criticism, however, because its refined and small tone lacked the vigour of the contemporary virtuosos.[18]

The Viennese were more interested in the waltz. Chopin wrote: 'During supper, Strauss or Lanner play waltzes. After each waltz, they receive tremendous applause; and if they play a quodlibet, i.e. a potpourri of opera tunes, songs and dances, the public is so pleased that it goes off its head – it just shows you how rotten the taste of Vienna is.'[19] Chopin subsequently developed the waltz into a piano piece for the refined salons of Paris, rather than Viennese beer-gardens and ballrooms.

Chopin's visit to Vienna coincided with the Polish rebellion of late 1830, which was inspired by the events we have seen in France and Belgium. Someone placed a placard on the Grand Duke Konstantin's residence saying 'House to let, after the New Year'. The Russians were loathed: they refused to treat Poland as a separate kingdom and suspected that it was a haven for revolutionaries who had participated in the uprising in St Petersburg five years earlier. A decline in the Polish economy created political circumstances favourable to rebellion. In November, there was a rising by a group of junior officers, and there was a bungled attempt to assassinate the grand duke.

At first, this rebellion was condemned by experienced nationalists such as Adam Czartoryski, a descendant of the Lithuanian royal house and Poland's spokesman at the Congress of Vienna. But, in an attempt to get the rebellion under control, Czartoryski had to assume the lead. A large Russian army advanced into Poland. The Poles won two early victories before the tide began slowly to turn against them. In August–September 1831, the Russians retook Warsaw and suppressed the Poles with a ferocity that outraged public opinion in Western Europe. Poland then became a Russian province: the army was abolished, as was the Diet, and the University of Warsaw was closed; the Russian legal system was introduced; the Orthodox Church was brought in to replace the Roman Catholic Church. Many Polish nobles were deprived of hereditary status. This 'Russianisation' fuelled the flames of nationalism.* About 10,000 Polish exiles went westwards, mostly to France.[20]

Chopin seems to have been deeply troubled by the rebellion and his own ambivalent position. On the one hand, many of his friends were rebels, on the other, he owed much to the patronage of the Russian administration; he worried about the safety of his family and about Constantia. His money, just an allowance from his father, was running out. His moods varied from deep despair to light-hearted nonchalance, as he went from one social engagement to another.[21] He had difficulty getting his Concerto in E minor performed, and, when at last he did, it was on a stage shared with several other artists.

* The patriots then stirred up the peasants. In 1846 there was a rebellion, but the peasants confused the objectives and massacred many Polish nobles. A rebellion of 1863 was repressed brutally. In May 1864, the Kingdom of Poland ceased to exist and everything became Russified.

He realised that there was no future for him in Vienna. The political situation in Italy made it unsafe to go there. Being a Pole, he had some difficulty getting a passport from the Russian embassy. But, eventually, he set off for France via Salzburg and Munich, where he was delayed, because the upheaval in Poland meant that he could not receive his allowance. When he got to Stuttgart, he heard the news of the fall of Warsaw, and he went into a frenzy of despair and fury. He arrived in Paris in mid-September.

Arrival in Paris

George Sand, in a novel, described arriving in Paris: 'Look at Paris, the beautiful Paris that you had dreamed of as being so marvellous! Look at it stretched out there, black with mud and rain, noisy, foul, and swift as a torrent of mud. There is the perpetual revelling, always brilliant and perfumed, that you had been promised; there are the intoxicating pleasures, the gripping surprises, the treasures of sight, hearing and taste … Look over there at the Parisian who had been described to you as friendly, courteous, and hospitable, rushing along, always in a hurry, always careworn. Tired out before you have mingled with this ever-moving population or entered this inextricable maze, overcome with fear, you fall back into the cheerful precincts of a furnished hotel room.' Sand also provides a description of a hotel room, the 'bought refuge which has sheltered so many travellers, so many lonely strangers, but is hospitable to none of them'. She says quite candidly that she, the novelist, is 'not sure that there's anything more horrible than staying in a furnished room in Paris … in a narrow, dark street where only a damp, murky daylight creeps reluctantly about the smoky ceiling and dirty windows'.[22]

But we may assume that Chopin, armed with letters of introduction, quickly made contact with the literary, artistic and musical world, which, at the time, was prospering.[23] Only four months before he arrived, Heinrich Heine, the distinguished poet and journalist, had moved to Paris. That year, Victor Hugo published *Notre Dame de Paris*, Balzac published *La Peau de Chagrin*, Musset his *Contes d'Espagne et d'Italie* and Stendhal *Le Rouge et le Noir*. Eugène Delacroix, almost certainly the illegitimate son of the serpentine prelate and politician Charles-Maurice de Talleyrand, was already a leading painter. As well as mingling with the literati, Chopin joined the Polish émigré community on the Ile St Louis where Czartoryski, sentenced to death, had set up as 'Poland's king in exile'. Poland's aspirations were articulated by the outspoken poet, Adam Mickiewicz.

The musical life of Paris, the Romantic Paris of Berlioz, was, as we have seen, intensely active. The Opéra was staging *Robert le Diable*, a hit by Meyerbeer. The Opéra-Comique was presenting works by the conservative Cherubini who was director of the Conservatoire, and by Weber and Auber. On the concert platform, Liszt was dazzling his audiences. Chopin was soon at home in this world.

Chopin tried to arrange lessons with Frédéric Kalkbrenner, the finest pianist of his generation, who had 'an overweening fondness for honours and a well-developed sense of his own superiority'.[24] But he would only take Chopin on for a three-year period as a minimum, so the matter dropped. On 26 February 1832, Chopin appeared at his first concert at the Pleyel rooms; Liszt and Mendelssohn were in the audience. This concert made his name. The programme included Kalkbrenner's *Grand Polonaise* played on six pianos by the composer, Chopin and several others. Monsieur Frédéric Chopin de Varsovie played one of his concertos as a piano solo, probably supported by a string quartet rather than an orchestra. The critic Fétis, in the *Revue Musicale*, praised him for creating a personal style of piano music, with great originality, the kind of composition which they had been looking for 'en vain depuis longtemps'.[25] One of his friends wrote: 'Our dear Fritz has given a concert which has brought him a great reputation and some money. He has wiped the floor with all the pianists here; all Paris was stupefied.'[26] But he had his ups and downs. Three months later, he took part in a charity concert at the Conservatoire playing the first movement of the F minor Concerto; but his refined style and delicate playing were lost in the large hall. He only appeared in concert halls sporadically thereafter, and restricted himself to playing in salons.

Chopin's 'aristocratic' style was ideally suited to the salon. His conception of musical art was one of detail, delicacy and refinement, appropriate to the Pleyel piano of his time, which had less sustaining power than a modern grand piano.* But his withdrawal from the concert platform meant that he gave up the chance of earning the big money available to Liszt. He became depressed and, like Hector Berlioz, contemplated joining

* Chopin experimented with the sustaining pedal and its possibilities. When he was playing, his foot almost seemed to vibrate as he played certain passages (see page 183).

the increasing number of musicians who were emigrating to America.[27]

Through the Polish aristocrats, the Radziwills, Chopin was put in touch with the Rothschilds, an immensely powerful family because of their wealth, and connections in Paris and internationally.* With Rothschild patronage, Chopin, with his highly polished manners, was, like his father, the ideal person for an aristocratic mother to ask to teach her daughters. He was apparently excellent at teaching, and selective about the technical exercises which he expected his pupils to perform. He earned twenty francs a lesson – cash on the mantelpiece.** Soon, he was one of the more affluent Polish émigrés in Paris, with a manservant and a carriage. He set up in a handsome apartment in the chaussée d'Antin, a district for the up-and-coming, as we have seen in connection with Rossini, who also lived there. Chopin, a bit of a dandy, wore fashionable clothes from the most exclusive shops. 'My carriage and white gloves cost more than I earn; without them I should not be *de bon ton*', he was writing at the beginning of 1833.[29] Some of his friends obviously thought all this was a bit too effete. He received a waggish scrawl from Montmartre addressed to 'Chopinetto mio', and signed 'What a joke! Too bad. HB.'[30]

In his compositions, Chopin broke new ground, although, once having done so, his style, in Schumann's view, remained static and did not progress. Under the name 'Mazurka', he created a dance fantasy out of a Polish country dance;[31] out of the technical exercise, he created the Etude. In the Préludes, he concentrated on a single motif and developed its musical and pianistic possibilities. And he evolved the Nocturne, which eventually 'sighs itself away into silence, and night'.†[33]

* The Rothschilds' network knew of the Duc de Berri's assassination in 1820 some 24 hours before overseas governments were informed by their couriers. A famous case of the network being used profitably was in 1815 when Nathan Rothschild sold successive amounts of British government stock. 'Rothschild knows', whispered the stockbrokers as the price collapsed, 'Waterloo is lost'. When the price was at the bottom, he bought up a giant parcel for a song.

** Flaubert's fictional character, Madame Bovary, living in a country town near Rouen, told her husband: '"I ought to take lessons, but …". She bit her lips and added: "Twenty francs a time: that's too dear." "It certainly is rather a lot", said Charles with a foolish giggle … "There are lots of musicians who have not made a reputation as yet but who are often worth more than the celebrities."'[28] So one wonders if the 20 fr paid to Chopin, in Paris, was so special. A male employee in a Rouen textile factory earned between 1.92 fr and 2.76 fr a day.

† The Notturno was in use in the late-18th century in the sense of a Serenade. The name and mood of the Nocturne appears to have been created by John Field, the Irish composer and salesman for Clementi pianos in Russia.[32]

Chopin had his works published simultaneously in France, England and Germany, to avoid piracy. Breitkopf, the publishers in Germany, spread his fame through their agency network throughout the world. Schumann hailed (in his journal) the *Là Ci Darem Variations* with: 'hats off, gentlemen – a genius',[34] and persuaded the young pianist Clara Wieck to perform them in Leipzig.

Chopin was a good businessman. In England, to increase sales, the Mazurka was called *Souvenir de la Pologne*; some of the Nocturnes were renamed *Murmures de la Seine*, and others as *Les Soupirs*. There was great rivalry between the publishing houses in Paris at this time. On the one side was Schlesinger, who published Chopin's works and promoted them in his publication, the *Gazette Musicale*; on the other was the virtuoso pianist, Herz who bided his time in his journal, *La France Musicale*. Herz was a colourful figure, 'a musical industrialist on a grand scale',[35] and a notorious womaniser who in later years took as his mistress the *grande horizontale*, Thérèse Lachmann, well known as 'La Païva' after the Portuguese marquis she married. In February 1838, Herz's journal included a sneering review of Chopin's A flat major Impromptu. The feud between Herz and Schlesinger actually led to a duel between Schlesinger and one of Herz's pupils; Schlesinger was sued, with Chopin being cited as a witness.[36]

Meanwhile, in 1835, Chopin met his parents, halfway, at Karlsbad, the highly fashionable spa in western Bohemia, where they were taking the waters.*[37] On the way back, he called in to Dresden and there found Maria Wodzinska, the sister of those boarders in the Chopin household almost two decades earlier. Her family were now *émigrés*. She was a good pianist, and very attractive; Chopin fell in love. But he fell ill, so seriously that it was rumoured in Warsaw that he had died. In the following year, Maria and Chopin met in Marienbad, another spa, and got engaged. As her mother did not expect her father to consent, the couple were required to wait, and the proposal was to be kept secret. The mother also required Chopin to look after his health and not have any late nights in the Paris salons (whatever this may have meant). He was very ill with 'flu over the winter of 1836–7 and was coughing blood.[38] His letters were unanswered, or answered coldly.

* A geyser propels water, naturally heated to 73°C, to a height of 12 metres (40 feet) in quick bursts, 40 to 60 per minute. The water is supposed to be good for the liver and gall bladder, and for diseases of the stomach and intestines. 'Everyone' went there.

Whether it was because the Wodzinskis did not want a delicate son-in-law, or because Maria was not that keen, the romance fizzled out and she eventually married someone else. The rupture was a bitter blow to the sensitive Chopin, who tied up the letters in a packet with a piece of pink ribbon and wrote on the outside, 'Moja Bieda' (My Misery).[39]

In May 1834, Chopin and Ferdinand Hiller, the recitalist and composer, had attended the Lower Rhine Music Festival. There, they met Mendelssohn, who had much in common with Chopin in terms of refinement, and regarded him as the perfect virtuoso. Chopin's reserved approach was certainly the opposite of that displayed by Liszt, with whom relations became strained when he made himself at home in Chopin's apartment with Camille Pleyel, who was once Berlioz' lover.[40] This probably offended Chopin's sense of delicacy rather than his morals, as he is reputed to have had an affair with Countess Delphine Potocka around this time. In summer 1837, Chopin and Madame Pleyel's husband, 'famous for his pianos and for his wife's adventures',[41] went to London for a fortnight. Chopin called himself Mr Fritz. They visited Windsor and Richmond, and they went to Blackwall, celebrated at this time for the extraordinary 'fish dinners' to be obtained there.

George Sand

Sometime towards the end of 1836, Chopin met the author George Sand, who was almost six years older than him (see colour plate 21). Their meeting was probably at Liszt's apartment, which she then shared with Liszt's mistress, the golden-haired, blue-eyed Comtesse d'Agoult. Chopin and George Sand were at first like oil and water. On the one hand, there was Chopin, frail, foppish, fair-haired, fastidious; on the other, in trousers, the dumpy, double-chinned, cigar-smoking purveyor of 'pot-boilers'.[42] Her eyes were fascinating, and maybe it was with these that this beetle-like woman seduced her lovers, whom she then consumed.* Chopin's first reaction was to say: 'What an unprepossessing woman that Sand is.'[44] But so central was she to be to Chopin's life, that we must spend a few moments on her story.

* The male insect, the mantis, is 'a slender and elegant lover'. After copulation the female devours the male 'mouthful by mouthful, leaving only the wings', wrote the early-20th-century expert on insects, J.H. Fabré. 'I have seen the same Mantis treat seven husbands in this fashion. She admitted all to her embraces and all paid for nuptial ecstasy with their lives.'[43]

Sand's proper name was Aurore, Baroness Dudevant; she was descended from kings of Poland. We have already come across her great-grandfather: Maurice, Maréchale de Saxe was one of the reputed 354 bastard children of King Augustus the Strong, with whom Bach 'corresponded'. Saxe was sired on Augustus' mistress, the beautiful Countess Aurora von Königsmarck.

Aurore Dudevant's mother was a Paris tart whose father had kept a billiards hall and sold canaries and goldfinches on the streets. She started giving birth to Aurore while dancing a quadrille which Aurore's father was accompanying on his violin. He regarded himself as quite a musician; in his own opinion, he was up to the standard of Haydn. The baby was brought up by her paternal grandmother, the Maréchale's daughter, in a delightful 18th-century country house, Nohant, about 50 miles from Bourges. This is in the middle of France, nearly 200 miles away from the centre of life, Paris. Nohant is set in a relatively dull part of France, seemingly on the only hilly area in the district. Aurore, however, described the countryside around Nohant as 'truly beautiful; in the evening perfumes waft into my room: lilac, and lily of the valley; then butterflies come: yellow ones with black stripes; nightingales sing under my window ... It is delicious.'[45]

Balzac, the novelist, called the house a château and described finding Sand 'in her dressing gown, smoking an after dinner cigar by the fire-side, in a vast lonely room'.[46] The house is actually rather small, and very intimate. Some of the antics claimed to have taken place – corridor-creeping lovers dodging the dog, the servants, children, husband, everybody – do not make much sense:[47] any creaking floorboards would have been heard throughout most of the house. Its upkeep was apparently prohibitive, twice as much as living in Paris.[48] Again, this is surprising; but many things about Sand were unreliable. Romantics were prone to exaggerate.

Aurore married Casimir, Baron Dudevant in August 1822; they had a son, another Maurice. Casimir seemingly did not arouse her, which was possibly her problem, and he was unfaithful.* An earlier sweetheart came back into her life; they had a rendezvous in Paris and nine months later her

* In Balzac's *Le Père Goriot*, Rastignac says: 'To have a mistress, and a place in this almost royal caste – that is the badge of power.'[49] The rules were clear. The seduction of a well-born unmarried woman was unusual and unacceptable. A girl could give up hope if she were not married by 25; men settled down to marriage at 35. (A woman aged 47 might be called a little old lady) On

daughter Solange was born. With three-year-old Solange, Aurore moved into a Paris garret with another lover, Jules Sandeau, and became a journalist working for *Le Figaro*. Together they produced a short story under the joint pen-name of Jules Sand. During autumn 1831, she, on her own, wrote *Indiana*, which she had published under her own name, as G. Sand.

Indiana is a clever Romantic novel, its style and sense of drama calculated to appeal to a wide readership.* It is the tale of a slender, pale and sad nineteen-year-old wife from Réunion Island in the South Seas who falls for a man who is the personification of selfishness. The novel thus explores 'the ill-organised relationship between the sexes due to the constitution of society' which prevailed at the time.[52] Critics, however, interpreted it as 'a carefully thought-out argument against marriage'.[53] That outrageous suggestion made Sand instantly successful. Thereafter, she wrote 68 novels, many plays and much correspondence;[54] the philosopher Nietzsche compared the seemingly effortless flow of her prose to that of a milk-cow.[55] She was fortunate to live at a time when book sales grew rapidly, driven by serialisation of novels, the import of cheap Belgian editions, and the growth of lending libraries and reading rooms.

In real life, Sand caught Sandeau with the laundry-maid and left him. By then, she knew that true love was rare and that, fortunately for society, 'promises of love are not binding on a man's honour'.[56] In an increasingly frustrated search for bedtime satisfaction, she had a lesbian relationship with Marie Dorval, a leading actress, who at the time was the mistress of the Romantic writer, and somewhat disconcerted, Alfred de Vigny. Then, she tried a disastrous one-night stand with Prosper Mérimée, the author of *Carmen*. 'I had Mérimée last night, it was nothing out of the ordinary', she told Dorval, 'The experiment failed completely.'[57] The story was soon around Paris, no doubt enhancing book sales. There were further scandals when one of her supporters had a duel with a literary critic over her highly contentious book dealing with sexual dissatisfaction, *Lélia*, described by one critic as a 'work of lewdness and cynicism'.[58]

Between 1833 and 1835, she had a wild affair with the golden-haired

the morning after a wedding, essentially a business deal, the couple attended church alone. For one year, the wife was accompanied by her husband or chaperoned; thereafter it was 'open season'.[50]

* Here is a typical extract: '"Die then, but die of happiness", cried Raymon, pressing his lips on Indiana's. But it was too violent a storm for so tender a plant. She turned pale, and putting her hand to her heart, she fainted.'[51]

poet and dandy, Alfred de Musset, who, like so many Romantics, had fashionable fits of madness: Berlioz' *Symphonie Fantastique* had been influenced by Musset's translation of Quincey's *Confessions of an Opium Eater*. Sand and Musset went to Venice, where both were seriously ill, and were looked after by a blond and charming doctor. Soon Musset was moved on, and George had set up with Doctor Pagello, who seems at last to have satisfied her; but, after four months with him, she was ready to return to Paris. After briefly picking up with Musset again, she had an affair with a prominent and desiccated lawyer from Bourges, Louis-Chrysostome Michel, who was regularly in and out of prison for his republican sympathies. He helped her with legal aspects of her separation* from her husband Casimir, and spent the day persuading the court of his mistress' chastity, while at night he was having her, and she him, in a hotel halfway to Bourges. They both had other lovers: she ran the heart-throbbingly handsome Charles Didier at the same time. She then moved on to the stage star, Pierre-François Bocage. To complete the circle, Sandeau became Dorval's lover. This seems to have been normal behaviour in the literary world of Paris, only about fifteen years after the chaste Jane Austen died in Winchester.[59]

Aurore's speed of movement, and the medical consequences, leave one quite breathless. In the middle of it all, she met Franz Liszt, one of the most potent sexual icons of the period, but their relationship is always said to have been platonic.[60]

Enter Chopin; frail and fragile, prudish, an 'also ran', in most senses, compared to Liszt. When Aurore returned from the country to Paris in autumn 1837, Chopin's reticence made her all the keener. He turned down an invitation to Nohant. At a performance given by him, she scribbled a note: 'On vous adore.'[61] Then: 'I was playing and she looked deep into my eyes. It was a somewhat sad music, legends of the Danube; my heart danced with hers. Her eyes held mine, dark, unusual. What were they saying? She leant over the piano and her gaze burnt me and flooded me … My heart was captured. I have seen her twice since. She loves me. Aurore, what a lovely name.'[62] Alone among all her lovers, he always called her Aurore.[63]

She, however, returned to Nohant for the winter and settled down with

* Divorce had been abolished with the Restoration in 1814.

Félicien Mallefille, her son's tutor.* In spring 1838, she was back in Paris. Chopin had a preference for a platonic rather than a physical relationship and this just made Aurore wilder. She wrote: 'I can't remember exactly what he said, but I think it was that *certain actions* could spoil the memory. Now wasn't that a stupid thing for him to say? Did he really mean it? Who is the unfortunate woman who has left him with such impressions of physical love? Did he have a mistress who was unworthy of him? Poor angel. They should do away with all women who defile in men's eyes the most respectable and holy thing in all creation, that divine mystery, the most serious act in life, the most sublime thing in the universe … It is this manner of separating the spirit from the flesh that makes convents and brothels necessary.'[64] This, as we have seen, was her style.

Chopin, quintessentially respectable, obsessed with appearances, shrinking from controversy, at ease in society drawing rooms, meticulous, a connoisseur of women's clothes. Sand, arguably the most controversial person in Paris, of all the artistic set the most outrageous, the proponent of sexual freedom of all types, flaunting herself in men's clothes and smoking cigars. They lived separately; she came to Paris periodically and called herself Mme Dupin (her maiden name). She would come round to Chopin's when he had finished giving his lessons. She wrote to the painter Delacroix, 'If God sends death to take me within the hour, I shall still not complain for I shall have had three months of intoxication without blemish.'[65]

Mallefille, the tutor, became wildly jealous. He had once challenged another person who he thought was too keen on George to a duel. In an incident which adds an element of true farce to the love story, he waited outside Chopin's apartment and, when George came out, he aimed his gun. Nobody knows quite what happened next. Either a wagon rolled down the street and crossed the line of fire, or Count Gryzmala, a go-between and friend of Chopin, leapt into the gap.**

Majorca, at First

Chopin was unwell; he had suffered from poor health, and, since his childhood, had a propensity to cough, which always got worse in the winter. A

* Julien, the frail tutor and trainee priest in Stendhal's *Le Rouge et Le Noir*, was similarly successful with the wife of his first employer and the daughter of his second.

** Gryzmala was present at Chopin's death eleven years later.

fashionable physician told George Sand that her lover was not actually tubercular, but only extremely delicate and could be saved by sunshine, rest and loving care. Ignoring the disastrous precedent of her trip to Italy with Musset, the pair decided that they needed to get away from it all and spend the winter of 1838–9 in Majorca.*

Why go there? Surely there was somewhere nearer? Possibly they were prompted by a neighbour, the Spanish consul in Paris, or his friends. Whatever, Majorca was hardly ideal or a convenient place to take a piano for Chopin, who depended on sitting at a piano when he was composing. The French had been so unpopular in the Islands during the wars less than thirty years before, that French prisoners had had to be evacuated from nearby Minorca to save them from being lynched. Also, Barcelona, through which they travelled, was in the grip of a civil war, called the Carlist Wars. Rather like in Vienna 100 years earlier, the Spanish king had died leaving only daughters, who could not inherit under Salic law; his brother claimed the throne, yet the queen, Maria-Christina, set herself up as regent for her daughter and civil war broke out.[66]

A trip to Majorca must have been some Romantic dream, engendered, one may speculate, by Delacroix, in the interests of Sand's son Maurice, who was showing great talent as an artist. The spectacular beauty of Majorca, the mountain scenery, the changes in light, make it ideal for the painter. Besides, Sand wanted to get away and concentrate on a novel. Her explanation that Maurice needed a holiday in a dry, warm climate looks weak.

So she dragged Chopin there. Fact and fiction are again confused by the instalments which Sand wrote for a periodical a year later, which were subsequently published as a travel book, *A Winter in Majorca*. This piece of journalism, which has been treated as factual by many writers on Chopin, makes good reading as a study in bile, spite, half-truth and anti-clericalism if not obvious falsehood.

Their departure was kept secret. To pay for it Chopin sold his Préludes in advance to Pleyel. In mid-October, despite his qualms about the effect the scandal might have on his family, and armed with his volumes of Bach, his own unfinished manuscripts and plenty of music paper, Chopin set off

* Majorca is the largest of the Balearic Islands off the east coast of Spain. With a range of high mountains on the northern coast reaching 4,600 feet, it is protected from the gales and is warm in winter.

in secret and met with Aurore in Perpignan. From there, they went to Barcelona with the maid and the two children. They spent some time looking around and then took a boat to Palma.

Palma was full of political refugees from Spain, so there was nowhere to stay and they had to set up in a couple of rooms above a cooper's workshop. But they were blissfully happy, as Chopin wrote: 'The sky is like turquoise, the sea like emeralds, the air as in heaven.'[67] Surprisingly, perhaps, the Moorish influences of Palma, the lemons and oranges, almonds, cactuses and palms, seem to have had no effect on his output, unlike other Romantic composers inspired by their surroundings in the orient, the Caucasus, Spain or Algeria. The sole influence seems to have been the weather, which soon wrecked their stay, but apparently inspired the 'Raindrop' Prélude.

The experience quickly palled: the idyll did not last long. If one believes Sand, they became nauseated by the food and the smell of it, always pork, whether roasted, stewed, in broth, as pancake or even as dessert. To get Chopin to eat anything, Aurore had to do the cooking. The mosquitoes were terrible. She was irritated by the fact that the typical inhabitant 'always finds some good reason why he should not hurry' and that 'if you want to allow yourself the exorbitant luxury of a chamber pot, it's necessary to write to Barcelona'.[68] They could not get an apartment. Aurore's smoking shocked the Majorcan people even more than Parisians, as did the fact that they did not go to Mass.[69] She appears to have been wholly impervious to local sensitivities.

Meanwhile, Liszt's Comtesse d'Agoult wrote delightedly to a friend: 'The trip to the Balearics amuses me. From what I know of the two of them, they should be at each other's throats after a month of living together. Their personalities are as different as night and day. But what does that matter? It's all too delicious for words.'[70] She would have relished their discomfort, had she known the truth.

They succeeded in renting a simply furnished villa in the foothills called 'House of the Wind'. The use of braziers to warm and dry the place just created noxious fumes. Chopin became very sick, and developed a chronic hacking cough. The local doctors were useless. He had to stop them bleeding him.

Then, the landlord evicted them and insisted that they paid for the house to be re-plastered and re-whitewashed; their linen was to be burned.

This was not unusual. In southern Europe, where it was believed that consumption (TB) was contagious, the law was usually harsh. Any doctor who failed to report a case would be fined and suspended from practice for a year. Paganini, another sufferer from TB, had experienced eviction as well. Further to the north, the British took a different view that TB was fundamentally inherited, but aggravated by culpable deviations from healthy living, such as sex, celibacy, masturbation and alcoholism. One British sage, seeking the cause, observed: 'We need look no further than the Catholic nunneries in France, where not more than one in ten entrants survive their period of novitiate.'*[71]

Chopin would appear to have had many of the symptoms of TB: tiredness, poor appetite, loss of weight, pallor (which often contrasted with an unhealthy flush of the cheeks), night sweats and fever, a chronically running nose, wheezing and, especially, the hacking cough. Although the disease can attack almost any organ of the body, normally a lesion in the lung spreads and may break into a blood vessel causing the patient to cough up blood. Eventually, the patient dies from asphyxiation, general toxaemia and exhaustion. Galloping consumption, as in the case of Liszt's son Daniel, Le Sueur's nineteen-year-old daughter – and Verdi's Violetta – kills very quickly. More usually, the disease was intermittent, and was fatal in 80 per cent of cases in five to fifteen years.** As a consequence of seemingly miraculous remissions, as Liszt observed on the death of his pupil Julius Reubke, composer of the massive Organ Sonata on the 94th Psalm: 'usually the patients delude themselves until the last minute, and die peacefully'.[74]

TB was prevalent among the poor. Later in the century, mortality rates were sometimes up to five times higher than among the rich. But the disease took many middle-class people: Jane Austen probably died of a form of it, as did Laurence Sterne, writer of *Tristram Shandy*. Its victims also included Purcell and Pergolesi, composer of *La Serva Padrona* and a Stabat Mater. Others claimed by it were the painter Watteau, the philosopher Spinoza, the playwright Molière and, as we have seen, Weber. In 1938–9,

* TB spreads either by the respiratory route directly from another person, or by the drinking of infected milk. In children, it can be fatal, but it can also go unnoticed and can actually provide immunity in later years. Heredity seems to make a person susceptible.

** Grieg contracted tuberculosis, but survived until his mid-60s;[72] similarly, Stravinsky, who spent five months in a sanatorium near Geneva, survived until he was almost 90.[73]

Stravinsky lost his 30-year-old daughter and his wife (who was his first cousin) to the disease within almost three months of each other.*

VALLDEMOSSA

For Chopin and Aurore, the cash began to run out. After taking temporary refuge with the French consul, they moved up the mountains to a 14th-century Carthusian monastery at Valldemossa, about ten miles from Palma. The anti-clerical government had expropriated it about three years earlier and was now trying to let it out as flats. Chopin had hired a piano while waiting for a Pleyel one, which was held up in customs; he worked on the Préludes, and wrote polonaises, mazurkas and ballades. All this was in his neat spidery handwriting, scratching out the bits he wanted to correct.[76] Aurore, when not travelling to and from Palma to sort out bankers and to get customs clearance for the piano, made progress with her latest book.

Here they were for the next 58 days. The monastery, which Sand called a 'cliff-top vantage point',**[77] is set in a valley between the mountains. It is magnificent, as Sand, as a Romantic who loved nature and the sea, declared: 'All that a poet or a painter might dream of, nature has created here … the most romantic place on earth', she wrote.[79] Chopin, whose health was getting the better of him, was less enthusiastic: 'My hair is dishevelled, I am without my white gloves, and look pale as always. My cell, which is shaped like a big coffin, has an enormous dusty vaulted ceiling.'[80]

They had quite a capacious three-room suite which had originally been occupied by a silent Carthusian monk. Before Sand and Chopin took up residence, the rooms had been hurriedly vacated by a Spanish refugee (how Romantic!). There was an entrance door off the lovely cloisters, and the suite had its own garden; exotic perfumes wafted in, and it had a fine view down across the terraces to the valley below. The children, Maurice and Solange, were in their element, romping around, gorging themselves on the fruits. Maurice painted and played around with a small model theatre.

* Between 1870 and 1880, half of all prisoners in Chatham Naval Prison developed galloping tuberculosis every winter and died; no lifer in an American prison survived for more than twelve years before 1910. But fatal diseases change: scarlet fever and rheumatic fever are no longer the killers they were; half a century ago, acute appendicitis was by far the commonest life-threatening surgical emergency.[75]

** It is not clear how she justified her claims that she used to gaze at the sea from the northern door of the monastery, and that it commanded views of the seas on both sides.[78] Modern travel writers have to be accurate as they know that their readers may visit the places they are writing about.

If Chopin had been an enthusiastic hiker like Grieg, he could have enjoyed the walks to the sea, about three or four miles away, and many feet below. As it was, he was stuck.

According to Sand's account, the inhabitants were lazy, dishonest, ignorant, garlic-smelling 'monkeys', who tended their pigs with guitar in one hand and rosary in the other.[81] The other residents of the lonely monastery were a lecherous former sacristan, a reclusive former monk who had run the monastery's pharmacy, the woman next door who helped herself to their clothes and provisions, and, occasionally, a former servant of the monks 'whose brain was often befuddled by wine and religion'.[82] To feed themselves, Chopin and Sand purchased, with difficulty from the hostile villagers, a goat and a sheep which they milked themselves. Sand, the great-great-granddaughter of a Polish king and elector of Saxony, did the cooking.

Chopin was under pressure from Paris to repay his loan, but until the Préludes were finished there was no way to do so. The Pleyel piano, an upright suitably compact to be taken on a cart, was still stuck in customs at Palma.[83] Chopin hardly ventured out of his cell. His cough got worse, and he spat up blood.

They had to return home. They left in mid-February. They then found it difficult to get rid of the piano because, of course, it might be contaminated. They had a rough crossing in a boat laden with pigs, and Chopin had a haemorrhage in the lungs. On arrival in Spain, he was transferred to a French sloop and attended by the ship's doctor. They got to Marseilles; the doctor continued to recommend sun and rest, so they stayed in the south.[84] After a brief visit to Genoa, they set off at the end of May in their carriage towards Nohant, through Provence. The children had had a great time, but, for the adults, the trip was a fiasco.

At Nohant, a doctor could find nothing wrong with Chopin's lungs, just an inflammation of the larynx. The history of medicine has been called a monument to human folly,[85] but, on this occasion, the faulty diagnosis may have helped both Chopin and posterity because treatment for TB at the time, a starvation diet and bleeding,* would have accelerated his death.

* Bleeding was the commonest treatment for TB. Blistering was thought to work, provided the treatment was 'perseveringly employed even in the face of occasional discomfort'. Cod-liver oil, an ancient remedy, was introduced at the Brompton Hospital. A doctor in Ipswich charged a guinea a time for pumping a litre of his patented gas mixtures into the patient's rectum, 'whence they were sure to reach the lungs'.[86] The monthly refill cost half a guinea.

Keats, the poet, similarly benefited when a top physician pronounced that he was suffering from a mental disease related to poetry, and so gave him a few last happy and productive months.[87]

Back in France

Back in Nohant, Chopin and Aurore led a quiet domesticated life, eating in the open and smoking. She mothered him and never allowed him to start a day without him being given some drinking chocolate or hot broth;[88] and when she suffered from rheumatism, he would look after her. At the end of the day, the family would meet for dinner. They would perhaps play charades, at which Chopin excelled because he was an excellent mimic.[89] Chopin went to bed at the same time as Maurice and Solange. Aurore would work through the night and sleep until midday.[90]

Chopin had a piano in his room upstairs and she had his door padded to absorb the sound which would otherwise have reverberated around the central stone staircase. Chopin worked slowly and meticulously, and would spend weeks working on a single passage. He never felt that a piece was finished and he delayed sending it to the publishers for as long as possible.[91]

They went to Paris in the autumn. They followed a pattern of winter in Paris and summer at Nohant. In the winter of 1839, when back in Paris, Chopin was feeble, pale and coughing a lot. He took drops of opium on sugar and gum water, and rubbed his forehead with eau de cologne. He consulted most of the leading physicians of the day.[92]

He performed at King Louis-Philippe's court, and gave a couple of concerts in 1841 and 1842 in Pleyel's rooms, which were well received. He taught, usually giving five lessons a day. Pupils were made to study Clementi's *Gradus ad Parnassum* and Cramer's studies; Bach's Preludes and Fugues were 'l'indispensable du pianiste'.[93]

In Paris, Chopin and Sand again lived separately. She was in the rue Pigalle and he was in the rue Tronchet, some distance away. Chopin's father wrote: 'We are reassured now that you are so well looked after, as you tell us; but we should be curious to learn something of this intimate friendship.'[94] They both subsequently moved to an apartment block with 50 flats, a kind of affluent artists' colony called the Place d'Orléans. Their two flats were connected with an outside staircase. In Aurore's flat there was no bed: just two mattresses on the floor, *à la turque*.

Nothing in their outward behaviour gave a clue to their relationship. It is often said that the relationship between Aurore and Chopin became maternal and platonic at this stage. It would be very dull if we knew that it did. Despite her history of numerous affairs, she wrote in 1847: 'for the last seven years I have lived with him, and with others like a virgin … I was weary of passion.'[95] She also said: 'I look after him like a child and he loves me like a mother.'[96] However, accuracy was not her strong point. Chopin himself observed that 'she does not always tell the truth – but that is the privilege of a novelist'.[97]

Just because she mothered him does not mean that they did not have sex. Let us compare her claim to 'virginity' with a quotation from the novel by her friend and admirer Gustave Flaubert, one for which he was prosecuted, but acquitted, of irreligion and immorality. Flaubert described the nature of Emma Bovary's passion: 'When she next saw [her lover] she was more on fire, more exigent, than ever. She flung off her clothes with a sort of brutal violence, tearing at her thin stay-lace so that it hissed about her hips like a slithering snake. She tiptoed across the room on her bare feet to make sure that the door was really locked, and then, with a single gesture, let her things fall to the floor. Pale, speechless, solemn, she threw herself into his arms with a long shudder.'[98]

The novel records that 'she would lean towards him, murmuring, as though choked with the rapture of her passion … She called him "child". "Child" she would say "do you love me?" And she would scarcely hear his answer in the sweet precipitancy of his kisses.'[99] Perhaps Musset found the truth when he said, after his Italian escapade with Sand: 'You thought you were my mistress, but you were none other than my mother … It was incest we committed.'[100]

Sand certainly had an affair with Louis Blanc, the socialist leader, in 1844. This affair marks the start of the real souring of her relationship with Chopin. She was having an affair with Victor Borie at the time that she finally split with Chopin.[101] Then there was a young German, and then a sculptor thirteen years younger than her with whom she had a long affair, until he died of consumption in 1864. In 1865, aged 62, she began an affair with another man.[102] Who knows, maybe someone with her appetite needs a four-year rest in the middle of her life.

Summers at Nohant

During the summer at Nohant, Chopin did most of his composing; his work was punctuated by tiresome visits from Sand's illegitimate half-brother Hippolyte, who was usually drunk and hearty. Far more congenial was the painter Delacroix, who had a studio there. Other frequent visitors who made the long journey from Paris were Pauline Viardot, the mezzo-soprano, and her husband Louis, the director of the Théâtre des Italiens. Pauline had recently made her stage début. George Sand is said to have

Pauline Viardot. Fauré fell in love with her daughter (see page 625)

done a certain amount of matchmaking to arrange their marriage.[103] In 1843, she and Chopin looked after the Viardots' baby daughter. In the hot summer, George liked lying on her back on the river floor with the water up to her chin and smoking a cigar; the fastidious Chopin, who disliked the heat and sweat, showered himself with eau de cologne.

Chopin instigated the tiny theatre for amateur dramatics.[104] Altogether, the setting must have been very pleasant. The idyll was upset, however, by his father's death in 1844. But his spirits were raised when his sister Louise and her husband came to stay, first at the Paris apartment, and then at Nohant. George gave Louise the manuscript of her latest novel and sent a valuable rosary to Madame Chopin.

Yet, the clouds were bubbling up on the horizon. The headstrong and manipulative Solange, whom Chopin taught, developed a crush on him, and he seems to have cast a blind eye at her defects. Not surprisingly, George Sand became jealous and annoyed at the behaviour of her lover and daughter.

George brought Augustine (Titine) Brault, a relative on her mother's side, to live at Nohant, largely to prevent her from becoming a kept woman. This annoyed Solange, who possibly encouraged Chopin to insinuate, foolishly, that Maurice was seducing Titine.* Maurice already resented Chopin's presence, especially when he tried to take any paternal role in the household. There were rows over the servants and Chopin had to dismiss his 'man'. Sand became furious if Chopin criticised Maurice.[105]

In 1843–4 Chopin had a permanent cough, neuralgia and considerable breathing problems. This made him bad-tempered in private, although with his pupils and in public he remained polite and charming; and he continued to compose many much-loved nocturnes, mazurkas, polonaises and waltzes.[106]

However, the tinder was dry and a small spark apparently lit the flames. At a meal in the small and elegant dining room at Nohant in July 1846, Maurice was given breast of chicken, while Chopin only got the leg. Chopin, whose temper had a short fuse, announced that he was not prepared to be treated as an object of charity; Maurice replied that he would gladly leave, as there was not room for them both in the same house. Sand stood up for Maurice.

During that summer, instalments of George's latest book were being published; she showed her nightly output of eight to ten pages to Chopin to read as she wrote them. *Lucrezia Floriani* told the tale of a small and slightly plump actress, who, although she had formerly lived with several men, was proud of her constancy: 'I have never loved two men at the same time', she said.[107] The sensitive, moody, reserved Prince Karol, some years younger, at first condemned her morals, but then fell in love with her. She nursed him back to health, but he was tormented with jealousy, and, after a few years of squabbling and bickering, she died of sorrow and disillusion.

* The source of this story seems to be Titine's father's publication, *Une Contemporaine: Biographie et Intrigues de George Sand.* He also 'exposed' Sand's relationship with Marie Dorval. Sand had the pamphlet seized for libel; she did not permit untruths to be spoken about her. It has been suggested that Maurice was having an affair with Pauline Viardot at this time; a beautiful singer, but no beauty.

This story was perhaps typical of Sand's potboilers, some of which, like *Indiana*, have a strong biographical slant; her novel *Horace* had been about Marie d'Agoult; another, *Elle et Lui*, written later, would be about her affair with Alfred de Musset.* When she read extracts from the new novel to Delacroix in Chopin's presence, Delacroix was appalled, particularly as Chopin seemed entirely to miss the point. Paris was agog, as each episode appeared in the press. Liszt was shocked, but rushed to get the latest episode. Chopin rose above all this, and praised the quality of the work.

Then Solange became engaged to a local country gentleman who George said dressed 'like a gamekeeper' and was 'as handsome as an ancient statue, and as hairy as a savage'. She added: 'You would not call him brilliant when it comes to talking.'[109] When Solange and her mother went to Paris in February 1847 to conclude the marriage contract, they visited an up-and-coming sculptor, Auguste Clésinger, who was keen to do busts of Sand's heroines. Whether the rough, debt-ridden, inebriate but handsome sculptor, fifteen years her senior, seduced Solange or vice versa, it was no time before they were coupled. It was said that Clésinger 'is the kind who would even chisel his wife's little derrière in white marble'.[110] Of course the engagement was off; George dragged Solange back to Nohant, followed impetuously by the sculptor 'with a firmness, a determination, and an obstinacy that would brook no indecision or delay'.[111] Solange thought she was pregnant and plunged herself into an icy stream.** By 16 April, there were definite plans for a marriage and, with her father's consent, the wedding took place a month later.

On returning to Nohant in July, Solange discovered that Titine was being courted by one of Maurice's friends. Wild with jealousy, Solange told the lover that Titine had been Maurice's mistress, and immediately accused George of having an affair with another of Maurice's friends, Victor Borie. The novelist described what happened: 'My son-in-law attacked Maurice with a hammer and would probably have killed him if I hadn't thrown myself between the two, slapping Clésinger in the face while he struck me on the chest. If the curé, some friends, and a servant who were there had not restrained him, Maurice who was armed with a pistol, would have

* Balzac had also published *Béatrix* in 1839, a novel based on the story of Liszt and Marie.[108]

** A step accomplished in *Indiana*, when the heroine's maid, pregnant with the child of the heroine's lover, commits suicide.

killed him on the spot. Solange fanned the flames with her vicious disdain.'[112] The Clésinger pair were ejected and took refuge in the nearby town. They had only been at Nohant for fifteen days.

The pregnant Solange did not want to use public transport to go to Blois to take the train to Paris. Chopin had usually supported her against her mother, so she wrote to ask if she could borrow his coach. He replied: 'I hasten to place my carriage at your disposal.'[113] Sand went ballistic; she was furious at what she considered Chopin's disloyalty to her.[114] Delacroix saw the scathing letter she sent to Chopin, but it is lost. Then she tried to patch things up; but it was hopeless, not least because Solange was telling Chopin that Sand was having an affair with another man. Sand wrote Chopin her final letter, which concluded: 'After nine years of unswerving devotion, I can only thank God that it has all finally come to an end in this incredible way. Let me hear from you from time to time, but it is useless to think that we can ever relive what is past.'[115]

Chopin had left Nohant, in the previous November, as it happened, for ever. He spent the next eighteen months teaching and composing, but 'was broken emotionally by the separation from Sand'.[116]

The Last Years

Chopin continued to live in Paris in the Place d'Orléans. There was no question of going back to Nohant: it was far too intimate a place for an estranged couple to coexist in. Besides, his parting from Sand had been very bitter. 'What a relief! what a relief!', she wrote. 'What a bond broken! I have constantly fought against his narrow and domineering ideas, while remaining chained to him out of pity, and fear that he would die of grief. For nine years, while full of life, I tied myself to a cadaver.'[117]

Chopin stayed in Paris throughout 1847 except for a few brief trips, for example to the Rothschilds' château at Ferrières, around 60 miles from Paris. He kept in close contact with the Clésingers, who were constantly on the move to avoid their creditors.

Soon after Chopin left Nohant, the countryside became increasingly restless as revolutionary disturbances shook Europe. These events touched the lives of so many composers: Donizetti, Berlioz, Liszt, Verdi, but most especially Wagner. There were major riots in Buzançais, near to Nohant: a château was destroyed and a landowner was murdered.[118] When the barricades finally went up in Paris in February 1848, Maurice Sand took part.[119]

But Chopin was impervious to the world around him. During the riots, he suffered from a severe attack of neuralgia. On 3 March he wrote: 'Paris is quiet, from fear. Everyone is enrolled in the National Guard. The shops are open but no buyers, the foreigners are waiting with their passports for the ruined railways to be repaired.'[120]

This was around the time when Chopin met Sand again. She had joined the ministry of information and was writing socialist propaganda. The chance meeting took place on the day of the funeral in La Madeleine* for those killed on the barricades. They passed on the staircase at a reception. Chopin was able to tell her that she was a grandmother, which she did not know. When he got to the bottom of the stairs, he turned back and told her that mother and child were doing well – actually they were not, and the child died very quickly. George asked after his own health; he replied courteously but briefly; he turned to the doorman to open the door and was away.[121]

That was it. She went to neither his funeral nor his commemoration; she destroyed their correspondence. One of her letters survived, written in 1845 enclosing a lock of her hair: in it, she said 'Aime-moi, cher Ange, mon cher bonheur, je t'aime.'[122]

London and Scotland

A few days after they met, Chopin was in London. He had a reasonable crossing and took a few hours' rest in Folkestone. For some time, his friend and pupil Jane Stirling and her sister Mrs Erskine (daughters of a wealthy Scot who had made his money through trade with India) had been urging him to visit them in Scotland. In London, Chopin met various Polish exiles, and gave lessons in a flat in Dover Street, Piccadilly. He lived a full social life: he played at the Duchess of Sutherland's before the queen, Prince Albert, the Prince of Prussia and the Duke of Wellington. He met the novelist Charles Dickens and the historian Thomas Carlyle, and all the musical notabilities. However, he was dangerously ill and frequently spitting blood.

His income did not cover his outlays and although he agreed to perform at private houses for twenty guineas a time, he could not bear the haggling that went on. Of the English, he wrote: 'They consider every-

* La Madeleine had only been completed six years before.

thing in terms of money; and would have no respect for art if it weren't considered a luxury.' He also said, 'If you say "an artist", an Englishman understands that as meaning a painter, architect or sculptor. Music is a profession, not an art.'[123]

In August, he went from Euston to Edinburgh by express train: '407 miles in twelve hours and it may have been a little too much for me', he wrote.[124] He stayed at Calder House, Midlothian, the home of Miss Stirling's brother-in-law. Of the Scots he wrote: 'they all look at their hands and play the wrong notes with much feeling. Eccentric folk, God help them.'[125]

Miss Stirling looked after his every need; she wanted to marry him and was under the misapprehension that she was showing him to her relations. She even tried to convert him to become a Presbyterian. On his side, there was no passion: 'My Scots women … want me to stay, and go on dragging round the Scottish palaces here and there and everywhere. They are kind, but so boring that the Lord preserve them!'[126]

Chopin went briefly to Manchester at the end of August and stayed with a wealthy and cultivated magnate at Crumpsall House in the suburbs away from the smoke. But his playing was too delicate and intimate for the large concert hall of 1,200 people, who missed 'the vigour of Thalberg, the dash of Herz',[127] two great virtuosos of the time.*

Chopin returned to Edinburgh to stay with a Polish doctor who was treating him and then went on to stay with Mrs Erskine in Johnstone Castle outside Glasgow. In this and other houses, most of the other guests spent their time shooting and stalking. He drew some caricatures. One had the line: 'this is a certain lord in a collar and gaiters, stuttering'; another, 'this one is a duke in high boots with spurs, deerskin breeches and a sort of dressing gown over them'.[129] But he was very weak and lonely. 'All the morning until two o'clock I am good for nothing; later, when I am dressed, everything wearies me and I gasp until dinnertime'; then he had to socialise with the men after dinner and then with the ladies in the drawing room; his man carried him upstairs and 'I am free to gasp and dream until morn-

* The USA later offered a lucrative market for such virtuosos. Herz gave around 200 concerts in 50 cities during 1846–9. Jenny Lind, Ole Bull (Grieg's supporter) and Thalberg were among many others who flocked over the Atlantic, once transportation became easier. The American-born Louis Gottschalk virtually exhausted himself to death with his tours in the 1860s: he even attempted three concerts in three different cities on the same day.[128]

ing, when the same thing begins all over again'.[130] In his diary, he drew a picture of a graveyard.

He returned to London. With what Carlyle called its smoke-tumult,[131] London was totally unsuitable for someone in Chopin's condition. He wrote to Solange: 'I am swollen up with neuralgia, can neither breathe nor sleep and have not left my room since November 1st (except on the 16th to play for an hour in the evening at the concert for the Poles). After that I relapsed; I cannot possibly breathe here; it is an inconceivable climate for persons like me, but only during these winter months. They light up at 2 o'clock.'[132] He left London at the end of November and returned to Paris.

Finally, Paris

From now on, Chopin's life was a hopeless struggle with consumption (see colour plate 28). He wrote in January: 'here we have March weather and I have to lie down ten times a day'.[133] Unable to compose or teach, he began to run out of money. The ever-solicitous Jane Stirling sent him anonymously a packet of banknotes totalling the considerable sum of 25,000 fr, but the absent-minded concièrge threw it in a drawer, unopened.

Chopin went for drives, sometimes accompanied by Delacroix. He tried several doctors; he was supplied with herbal infusions, lichen concoctions, and Pyrenees water, and was charged 10 fr a visit. In June, he wrote: 'I do not go out except sometimes to the Bois de Boulogne. I am stronger, for I am well fed and have stopped taking all the medicaments; but I gasp and cough just the same.'[134] He tried to compose. Countess Delphine Potocka sometimes sang for him. At the beginning of summer, he moved to a spacious airy abode in the rue de Chaillot. He may have moved there so as to escape the cholera which had hit central Paris in June and which killed the pianist Kalkbrenner and a star singer, Angelina Catalani.

The parcel from the Scottish ladies was found in July. Then Miss Erskine had to confess all. Chopin was uncharacteristically ungracious: 'She handled it so stupidly … that I couldn't resist telling her a thing or two. I let her know that I could never accept such a gift from anyone less than the Queen of England.'[135] But he needed 15,000 fr out of the 25,000.

Chopin's sister Louise and her husband came to see him in August. Because of the political turmoil, she only got a passport with some difficulty and some string pulling from Princess Czartoryska. His friends had written to George Sand suggesting that the former lovers should be reconciled, before it was too late. But she did not; thinking it would be too much for him. She wrote to Louise for information, but Louise did not reply.

His friends found him the splendid and sunny apartment in the Place Vendôme. Delphine Potocka was asked to sing for him on the day he received the last sacraments, 15 October. He could listen but could not speak, probably because of the accumulation of sputum in his larynx which he was too weak to cough up; this was the commonest terminal event in pulmonary turberculosis.[136] She had to force herself to sing, suppressing her sobs. After he died, Auguste Clésinger did casts of his emaciated face and hands, those small hands with the slenderest, most delicate of fingers.[137] The painter Kwiatkowski made several drawings of his head. His heart was sent in an urn to Warsaw where it was placed in the Church of the Holy Cross, just down the street from where Chopin had lived.

Chopin's funeral in La Madeleine on 30 October became a major social occasion. Miss Stirling gave Louise 5,000 fr to pay for it. Between 3,000 and 4,000 invitations were sent, and the event attracted additional publicity because of the difficulty in getting permission from the ecclesiastical authorities to have women singers for the performance of the Mozart *Requiem*. Chopin's own Funeral March from the B flat minor Sonata was also played; Léfebure-Wély, the society organist, was at the organ. Chopin was buried in Père Lachaise cemetery. Pleyel opened a subscription for a memorial, a work by Clésinger unveiled in 1850, a year after his death.

Chopin had written his last request on a sheet of paper: 'As this cough will choke me, I implore you to have my body opened, so that I may not be buried alive.'[138] A similar request, typical of the Romantics, was made by Aurore when she was dying in 1864.*[140]

Some Polish earth was placed in the grave.[141]

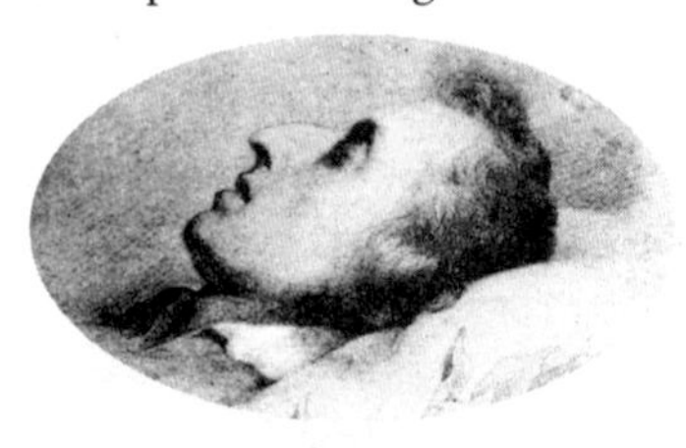

* Comtesse Marie d'Agoult, who had the same fear, would later suggest the solution: a bell should be put beside all corpses, so that they could ring for help[139]

SCHUMANN

CHAPTER 12

ROBERT SCHUMANN LONG considered his finest work to be *Paradise and the Peri*, which is now rarely heard.[1] This was based on Thomas Moore's poem about the beautiful princess Lalla Rookh who travelled from Delhi, through flower-scented valleys and exotic gardens, to her nuptials in Kashmir. 'Seldom had the eastern world seen a cavalcade so superb.'[2]

The princess fancied that the Valley of Gardens was the abode of a Peri, one of 'those beautiful creatures of the air, who live upon perfumes',[3] yet are excluded from Paradise because they are born of the union of a mortal with an angel. A minstrel sang the story of Paradise and the Peri to her. In the song, the angel at the entrance to Paradise tells the Peri that, to enter, she must bring 'the Gift that is most dear to Heaven. Go, seek it, and redeem thy sin; 'Tis sweet to let the Pardon'd in.'[4] The Peri fetches the last glorious drop of a hero's blood; but neither that, nor the precious sigh of pure self-sacrificing love, is sufficient. Only with a gift of 'the blest tears of soul-felt penitence'[5] is the Peri redeemed and Heaven won.

This fabulous story,* on which Schumann based his 'secular oratorio',

* The princess soon realised that she was irretrievably in love with the minstrel. She became progressively sadder as their inevitable parting approached. But, of course, the minstrel was her betrothed in disguise.

is Romantic in every sense. Liszt thought it was rather tedious;[6] and no doubt members of the Paris Jockey Club would have been furious, had they rolled up for the ballet during the Opéra and found Schumann's delicate work being performed. It is the antithesis of the theatricality, excess, 'effect' and commercialism of, say, the operas of Meyerbeer. For Schumann, the colour is not on the stage, but in the poetry and the music.

Listen to Schumann's 'Schlaf nun und ruhe in Träumen voll Duft':

'Sleep' said the Peri as softly she stole
The farewell sigh of that vanishing soul,
As true as e'er warm'd a woman's breast –
'Sleep on, in visions of odour rest,
In balmier airs than ever yet stirr'd
Th'enchanted pile of that holy bird,
Who sings at the last his own death lay, –
And in music and perfume dies away!'[7]

and you will get a flavour of that pure Romanticism for which Schumann and many others fought. And why Clara loved him so.

As a boy, Robert's passion for music was paralleled by an interest in literature far beyond that shown by other composers.[8] He was determined to be a successful musician, but he also became a successful journalist.

It was not easy to be married to Clara Wieck, who would have been 'the greatest living pianist, rather than merely the greatest female pianist, were the range of her physical strength not limited by her sex';[9] Chopin said that she was the only female pianist in Germany who knew how to play his music.

Robert, never a complete success, withdrew into his shell, increasingly gripped by a sense of anxiety and guilt, possibly about his wayward youth. These anxieties reached a crisis when his appointment as director of music in Düsseldorf turned into a disaster. But the Schumanns had almost thirteen years together, before he consigned himself to a lunatic asylum just outside Bonn. The release, his redemption, followed almost two and a half years later.

The Wild Youth

Schumann was born in Saxony on 8 June 1810, in a house close to the market place in Zwickau. For long, Zwickau has been known for the manufacture of that curious little Trabant car, so popular in East Germany before the fall of the Wall. The town's earlier prosperity rested on silver mines in the Erzgebirge mountains nearby. Subsidence following the mining of coal has caused much damage to the town's buildings.[10]

When Schumann was born, Zwickau was overrun by troops fighting in the Napoleonic Wars. Those returning from Moscow and the battle of Leipzig spread a deadly epidemic which decimated nearly ten per cent of the population and killed Wagner's father. The three-year-old Robert Schumann was sent away for a couple of years to escape from it all.

Robert's father, August Schumann, had prospered as a grocer and then ran a successful book selling business, Brüder Schumann. Many of the pocket-sized books which he published can now be seen at the birthplace museum. He also translated works by Walter Scott and Byron, wrote novels and published a Who's Who of 'the Most Celebrated People of all Nations and Times'. He had married a surgeon's daughter who was 'much addicted to that kind of romantic sentimentality which is only found to perfection in minds of a thoroughly commonplace type'.[11]

Robert, their youngest child, received his main schooling at the local high school of about 200 boys. He was clever: he won a prize, the works of Tacitus. One can imagine his mother proudly showing her friends a letter which the seven year old had written to her: the handwriting is perfect. One of the schoolmasters taught him the piano, and he showed a precocious ability at extemporisation and composition; aged eight, he wrote a little set of dances; four years later, he set the 150th Psalm for voices and orchestra. Around this time, he inscribed a book of a school friend: 'Everything can be bought with money, except friends and happiness; when you read these lines, think of your true friend … Robert Schumann.'[12]

He played duets with the son of the leader of the town regimental band and formed his own orchestra. His father could easily arrange for the programmes to be printed. He also took his son to concerts and to *The Magic Flute*. Robert was an active member of the school's literary society, and assisted with his father's Who's Who.

By the time he was fifteen, Robert's parents realised that he needed a more advanced music teacher. They enquired if Weber would teach him, but he was too busy.[13] Robert recognised his debt to his original teacher: when he celebrated a 50th anniversary in 1852, Robert sent him a laurel wreath and a letter of appreciation.

When Robert was sixteen, his father died. Around the same time, his sister Emilie seems to have drowned herself, driven to distraction by a persistent skin complaint.[14] His father's death left him with a fortune of 10,000 thalers,* which was held in trust for him.[16]

His mother had wanted him to become a lawyer and, after his final exam at the Lyceum, he was sent to Leipzig University. But he really wanted to be a musician, to the dismay of his family. He had hired a piano and composed several keyboard works and songs which he sent for comment to the musical director at Brunswick and got a positive reply.

Johann Paul Richter, known as Jean Paul, provided inspiration for many Romantics, including Schumann

Schumann went on a short trip with some friends in southern Germany. In Munich, they introduced themselves to the poet, songwriter and vituperative journalist Heinrich Heine, nephew of a wealthy Hamburg banker.[17] Schumann would in due course set several of his poems.

Schumann and his friends also sought out the widow of Jean Paul Richter, then Bayreuth's most famous citizen. He was an early Romantic novelist whose books were enormously popular and influential in the 19th

* This was a sizeable amount: 800 thalers was considered a good salary for a civil servant and the rent for a family apartment was twelve thalers a month. There were three thalers to the mark.[15]

century, and which Robert read avidly. They do not make easy reading.* They are witty, but also high-flown and improvisatory; and there are abrupt changes of mood. Jean Paul (as he is always known) uses exaggerated imagery; at times, he is virtually incomprehensible. 'With the main idea of a sentence he almost invariably associates a crowd of subordinate ideas; and they are often grouped in an order so capricious and so fantastic that the meaning can be made out only by the closest study.'[19] It was a style Schumann would emulate and with which he would dismay his audience.

Robert's days were full of dreamy introspection: he yearned for valleys, mountains and woods, and admired the beautiful flowers. But he punctuated this with roisterous drinking bouts and orgies. He may have practised some youthful homosexuality with his colleagues and flatmates. He had affairs with two girls, Nanni and Liddy; he fell in love with a chemist's daughter in Augsburg; he then became infatuated with the flirtatious Agnes Carus, wife of a doctor in Colditz.** Aged nineteen, Robert experienced the 'most debauched week' of his life,[20] lurching and reeling from tavern to tavern, passing out and being carried home. It was a succession of wine, women, song and cigars; the wine was often champagne.[21]

Arguably, this type of behaviour was (and is) not unusual in a well-heeled young man. Besides, some Romantic artists believed that debauchery, drinking and drugs stimulated creativity.[22] However, for an idealist, this self-indulgence may also have left a latent feeling of guilt.

Lessons with Wieck

The Carus couple moved to Leipzig, and in their house Schumann met Friedrich Wieck, a leading piano teacher, who also ran a piano factory and music lending library. Schumann started to have lessons with him. Wieck was virtually self-taught and had developed his own method, which stressed the importance of all-round musicianship. He taught the pupil to find the meaning of the music; he encouraged sensitive playing, not just

* Jean Paul's tales can be very entertaining, if the reader likes German humour: for example, his story of the 'Army-Chaplain Schmelzle's Journey to Flätz'. Others seem impenetrable, for example, 'Life of Quintus Fixlein, down to our own times, extracted from fifteen letter boxes'. The study of his works used to be compulsory in German schools. The conductor Bruno Walter records: 'For years, I read nothing but Jean Paul.'[18] Jean Paul inspired the Death March in Mahler's First Symphony and Walter's own epitaph to Mahler, quoted at the end of Chapter 24.

** This town is now best known for the secure fortress from which prisoners of war made spectacular escapes during the Second World War.

pyrotechnics. He considered it vital to cultivate and stimulate the student's mind; importantly, he regarded both physical and moral wellbeing as integral to musicianship.[23] The virtuoso pianist and conductor Hans von Bülow, son-in-law of Liszt, would later pay fulsome tribute to him: 'You were the one who first … taught my ear to hear, who impressed upon my hand the rules of correct formation, and who led my talent from the twilight of the unconscious towards the bright light of the conscious.'[24]

But Wieck was also an intolerant minister *manqué*, driven by bitter memories of a deprived childhood. He had an 'unsmiling resolution to claw his way to the top'.[25] Rather like Leopold Mozart, he recognised the commercial prospects of his prodigiously talented daughter, and her potential to provide him with an entrée to society. Clara was the best advertisement for his teaching method. When asked why he did not make the same effort for his other children as for his eldest daughter, he said that he had only one life to give away. Clara said: 'He is a very good man, and has done for me what not many fathers would readily do. But he has never known a noble and beautiful love, and cannot understand what it is like.'[26] His first wife could not stand it, and left for Berlin.

In May 1829, Schumann transferred his law studies to Heidelberg where the best jurists of the day were to be found. Or, at least, this was how he explained it to his mother who was funding him. In fact, he took the opportunity to make a trip to Switzerland and Italy, where he claimed to have heard Giuditta Pasta singing Rossini operas at La Scala.[27] He practised the piano in his spare time, and even on his journeys through Switzerland he took a dumb keyboard with him. He was obviously very talented: he played a difficult work by the piano celebrity Ignaz Moscheles at a concert.

His law professor was a keen musician; he and Schumann would sing together at weekly parties. But it became clear to Schumann that he was unlikely to have a future in the legal profession, which was fine, as he did not like 'chilly jurisprudence with its ice-cold definitions'.[28]* So, in July 1830, he wrote to his mother asking her to find out from Wieck what he thought of his prospects as a musician. Wieck wrote back to her: 'I pledge myself to turn your son Robert, by means of his talent and imagination, within three years into one of the greatest pianists now living.'[29] This was generous: Wieck did not approve of Schumann's immoral ways; besides, he

* He did, however, actually graduate from the university.

was already a mature student, and might be difficult to teach.

In the autumn of 1830, Robert became a resident pupil in Wieck's house. By the following May, he was in bed with another resident student or a servant in the house, called Christel, an affair which may have lasted for at least a year.[30] Because there is still some disagreement about the cause of Schumann's madness, much attention is paid to his private life at this time. According to his final medical records, he said that he had been dosed with mercury as a treatment for syphilis, 'and had been cured'.[31] He had another fling some years later; whether that needed a similar cure, we do not know.

Schumann was particularly fond of children. He would read bedtime stories to Clara, the infant prodigy, and her young brothers. He would play with them, sometimes dressing up as a ghost.[32] He took them to see the animals at the zoo. Clara had already performed two years earlier in a supporting role at the Leipzig Gewandhaus, the city's concert hall, and in private houses. At the age of eleven, she made her official début at the Gewandhaus.[33]

Schumann was a difficult and eccentric student. When Wieck went off on a seven-month tour, Schumann incensed him by suggesting that he would study with the large and jovial Hummel, a composer and pianist of international renown, and a pupil of Mozart. Schumann refused to study harmony and counterpoint with the distinguished, learned and conscientious cantor of St Thomas' and went instead to Heinrich Dorn, the conductor at the Opera House. But even with Dorn, also a former law student and only a few years older, Schumann objected that he was being taught that music was nothing but a collection of fugues. They fell out, and Schumann was left to analyse theory books and study Bach's *The Well Tempered Clavier*.

While Wieck was away, Schumann experimented with mechanical devices to develop his hand positioning and finger strength. These were quite common when teaching the piano at the time. Later in the century, Saint-Saëns also used such a contraption, a small electrical device which would send a current from shoulder to finger.[34]

Schumann's device was possibly a DIY version made out of one of his cigar boxes.[35] It kept his fourth finger straight while he practised with the remaining fingers. The effect was crippling.* He tried all sorts of remedies,

* Possibly the problem with his fingers was a consequence of mercury treatment. Clara attributed it to practice on a stiff dumb keyboard.[36]

including immersing his hand in the blood of a freshly killed ox, a cure tried by Clara when she hurt her wrist a third of a century later.[37] But, much to his disappointment, his injury finished his prospects as a concert pianist and he had to restrict himself to composing. His disability enabled him to avoid military service, however.[38]

Schumann's experimental compositions (the *Abegg Variations*, dedicated to a mythical Countess Abegg, and *Papillons*) were supported in the Viennese press by the famous poet Franz Grillparzer. Grillparzer observed, perhaps not surprisingly considering Schumann's unorthodox musical education, that he followed no school, but 'has created a new and ideal world for himself, in which he revels almost recklessly, and sometimes with quite original eccentricity'.[39] Indeed, Schumann wanted his music to be novel, 'something else, something new',[40] and, in particular, to convey a mood. Many of the compositions were given titles with the mood in mind.

Schumann was determined to demonstrate his credentials as a composer by writing a symphony. A first movement, performed in Zwickau, was not a success. Being a loner, he bottled up this failure and his anxiety about his increasingly precarious future. One person with whom he would share his worries was his brother Karl's wife, Rosalie. Her tiny son, Schumann's godson, died; Rosalie herself was dying of malaria; his brother Julius was dying of tuberculosis; his own career as a virtuoso was finished; and his career as a composer seemed to be in a mess. All this came to a head in October 1833 on the night that Rosalie died. He had a breakdown; he suddenly felt that he might be going mad; he nearly jumped out of the window. For some time he suffered from severe depression. After this, he was always afraid of heights, and disliked tall buildings.[41]

Journalism

With his interest in literature and his knowledge of music, Schumann was well suited to be a journalist and critic. He started in 1831 by writing the article hailing Chopin as a genius. In the Kaffeebaum coffee house, Schumann and his friends would discuss music and deplore the public's preference for the flamboyant styles of Rossini and Herz. They also clubbed together and gave Clara a watch for her sixteenth birthday.[42]

In 1834, they started their own musical newspaper, the *Neue Leipziger Zeitschrift für Musik*, of which Schumann soon became editor. Wieck was somewhat doubtful about this venture but joined the board. The paper appeared twice weekly as a four-sided folded sheet, generally printed in double columns. It was independent of the music publishers who, in their journals, were keen to serve their own interests.

In his articles, Schumann adopted a verbose, flowery style of prose, reminiscent of Jean Paul, whose writings he so admired. For example, when comparing Rossini and Beethoven, he wrote: 'The butterfly flew in the way of the eagle; he moved aside lest he should crush the insect with the beating of his wings.'[43] When describing a piece composed and played by Clara, he wrote: 'Here, white yearning roses and pearly lily calyxes inclined their heads; there, orange blossoms and myrtle nodded, while alders and weeping willows spread out their shadows. In the midst of all, a maiden's radiant countenance gently moved, seeking flowers for a garland. I often spied little boats, hovering daringly over the water. There lacked only a master's hand at the helm, a smartly spread sail, to send them cutting swiftly, triumphantly and surely through the waves.'[44]

To convey his views, he used fictitious characters, entirely of his own creation, which he collectively described as the Davidsbund. Key members of this league were Florestan, the man of action, and Eusebius, the dreamer. In Schumann's articles, these fictional characters would present differing viewpoints. They targeted the Philistines of Art, such as those who pander to popular taste 'in order to raise money and noise'.[45] They castigated Rossini and also Meyerbeer, 'a ringmaster at a circus'.[46] The travelling virtuosos, typically Liszt, were the 'Pedlars in Art'.[47] While Schumann admired Liszt's technical wizardry, he said drily that 'he must be heard and also seen; for, if he played behind the scenes, a great deal of the poetry of his playing would be lost'.[48] When reviewing Liszt's difficult arrangements of Schubert's songs, he wrote: 'a witty fellow wonders whether an easier arrangement could not be published, and also whether the result of such a one would be the original Schubert song again'.[49] Schumann also abhorred the bourgeois sentiment and reticence so prevalent at the time.* He was searching for a new style of music, much more elevated and pure.

* This became known as the Biedermeier period. Gottlieb Biedermeier, self-confident, smug and middle class, was a fictional schoolmaster who featured in a series of satirical articles published in a mid-1850s popular magazine. The term 'Biedermeier' was applied retrospectively to the outlook and art of 1815–48 Germany and Austria, although there is not any distinctive 'Biedermeyer' style. The English equivalent, if there was one, was the sentiment portrayed by Charles Dickens. His *Oliver Twist* appeared in 1837–8.[50]

Clara

In Leipzig, Schumann was at the centre of the rich musical life. Distinguished musicians passed through, and Mendelssohn was the conductor of the Gewandhaus orchestra. Wieck's house was an important meeting place for musicians. There, Schumann often saw Clara (see colour plate 15). But there was to be a prelude to his romance with her.

Schumann's doctor said that he needed a wife, presumably as a means of risk management. In summer 1834, he had a whirlwind romance with Wieck's beautiful eighteen-year-old student, Ernestine von Fricken, ostensibly the daughter of a baron. Schumann described her to his mother: 'She has a delightfully pure, childlike mind, is delicate and thoughtful, deeply attached to me and everything artistic, and uncommonly musical – in short, just such a one as I might wish to have for a wife.'[51]

Ernestine came from a little town called Asch. Schumann was fascinated by the potential for making musical themes out of words. He composed some variations using the musical letters ASCH (A, E flat, C and B natural). These were developed into *Carnaval: Scènes Mignonnes sur Quatre Notes*.

Within a few weeks, Robert and Ernestine wanted to get engaged. But the relationship fizzled out, particularly when he discovered that she was adopted, and actually the illegitimate daughter of a relation of the baron. As a consequence, her financial expectations were not so good as Schumann had anticipated. This was a surprisingly mercenary attitude for someone as romantically inclined as he; even if it was the deception which had upset him,[52] his inconstancy is unlikely to have made a good impression on the stern Friedrich Wieck.[53]

By the time the love affair with Ernestine came to an end, Schumann was captivated by the sixteen-year-old Clara. The Sonata in F sharp minor was inscribed 'To Clara from Florestan and Eusebius'. At the end of 1835, he came to say goodbye before Clara left for yet another gruelling tour with her father. They kissed on the stairs. He followed her to Zwickau, the first destination, his birthplace. There they kissed, 'deeply, passionately, memorably'.[54] To gratify his physical needs, he reverted, it seems, to Christel.

Wieck, who is now cast as one of the bogeymen of music's history, was horrified when he got wind of what was happening between his pupil and daughter, and whisked Clara away to Dresden. He prohibited all further contact between the two. He knew more than most prospective fathers-in-law about a daughter's beloved, the drinking, the irresponsibility over money, the womanising, and he probably had his own suspicions about the medical problems and their cause. He called his daughter 'an immoral girl who has been seduced by a miserable wretch'.[55] She was his priceless jewel, an incomparable virtuoso, musically streets ahead of Schumann. Robert Schumann was not going to have his daughter.

Schumann did not hear from Clara; when he did, it was only to be asked to return *her* love letters. He became despondent and suicidal, and turned again to drink. He became so disorderly that his landlady nearly threw him out.[56]

Then, through a mutual friend, Clara asked him to send back all *his* love letters, which her father had compelled her to return to him. He refused and said that she could have new ones. 'Write the simple word "yes" if you will give your father a letter from me on your birthday', he wrote to her. 'Just now he is well disposed towards me and will not reject me, if you beg for me.' She wrote 'Yes'.[57] Schumann, although warned by the intermediary that it was premature, wrote to Wieck enclosing a letter to Clara which Wieck very reluctantly handed over, although only after she became hysterical.

Schumann then had what he described as a dreadful meeting with Wieck. 'He has a new method of destruction, he drives blade and haft into one's heart … He treats me like the dirt beneath his feet.'[58] But with the help of Clara's nanny, the couple managed to exchange rings, before she left on a tour to Vienna. Her nanny also set up a correspondence route with the help of some friends in Leipzig, who re-addressed letters in a handwriting which Wieck would not recognise.

Clara's tour through Bohemia and Austria was sensational: in Prague she was recalled to the platform thirteen times. Vienna fell before her: Grillparzer wrote a poem inspired by her performance of the 'Appassionata' entitled: 'Clara Wieck and Beethoven'. The box-office results were excellent, and she played twice in Pressburg in order to raise money for victims of a recent flood disaster. Her success made Wieck dig in his heels even more.

Meister Allesgeld, as Schumann had called him in his diary, set them impossible conditions. He agreed to their marrying, provided that Schumann had a guarantee of an impossibly high income, and also provided that they would agree to leave Leipzig so that they would not be measured against the standard of living of Felix Mendelssohn or his assistant Ferdinand David. Schumann investigated the possibility of moving the *Neue Zeitschrift* to Vienna where Clara was clearly very popular and where he would earn royalties. Not surprisingly, given Austria's reputation for very tough censorship, he found it too restrictive and the bureaucracy too burdensome.* (During his stay in Vienna, Schumann went to Schubert's brother and found a pile of manuscripts including the Great C major Symphony, which, on his return, he persuaded Breitkopf and Härtel to publish.)

Wieck piled on the psychological pressure. He sent Clara off to Paris on her own, so that she would appreciate how dependent she was on him. The scheme seemed to work. She asked Robert to postpone their marriage, while he found ways of guaranteeing an annual income of 1,000 thalers.

But Robert could not let this go on; his love, and the pressures on his fragile mental health, were too great. He appealed to the High Court for permission to marry without her father's consent. There was a fruitless attempt at arbitration by a Protestant pastor. A bitter court hearing began in December 1839. Clara noted sadly in her diary: 'This day has torn to pieces the tender bond between father and child – my heart too feels as if it were torn in pieces.'[60] Wieck's outbursts resulted in a call to order by the court president. Early in January 1840, the court rejected Wieck's objections to Schumann, except that of drunkenness, which Wieck was given the opportunity to prove.

Wieck was desperate, even to the extent of championing Camille Pleyel as a rival virtuoso to Clara. Under a pseudonym, he circulated a libellous attack on Schumann's personal character. But, it was to no avail. To bolster his status, Schumann obtained an honorary doctorate from Jena University. On 1 August 1840, the court said that Clara was free to marry him, without parental consent. After ten permitted days, Wieck lodged no appeal.

The wedding was in the village church of Schönefeld, outside Leipzig, on 12 September. The bride wrote: 'There was a little dancing, no excessive gaiety, but every face shone with real satisfaction. The weather was lovely. Even the sun, which had hidden his face for many days, shed his

* Censorship was carried out by the secret police, with whom Schubert was familiar, and took between five and six months, although in the early 1820s Grillparzer took two years to get his drama *König Ottokar* cleared. One hoped for an *imprimatur* rather than *damnatur*.[59]

warm beams upon us as we drove to Church, as if to bless our union. It was a day without a jar, and I may thus enter it in this book as the fairest and most momentous of my life.'[61]

Newly Weds

Just *before* their marriage, Robert presented Clara with a volume of songs, beautifully bound in red velvet and inscribed to 'My beloved Clara on the eve of our wedding, from her Robert'. This inscription contrasts nicely with a present soon *after* their marriage of a cookery book with the dedication to 'Meiner Hausfrau' printed in gold on the cover. Soon Clara would write: 'We have been married three months today and they have been the happiest three months of my life. Every day I fall more deeply in love with my Robert.'[62] They kept a diary together in which they used a little symbol to indicate the nights on which they made love.

For a few hours each day they studied together, starting with Bach's Forty-Eight and moving on to the Mozart and Beethoven symphonies. But Paradise had some limitations. They both found the thin walls difficult: she would practise, he would try to compose. She was worried that she would have insufficient time for playing or for composition because he expected her to devote herself increasingly to domestic matters. As she was the primary breadwinner, this demand must have seemed unreasonable.[63]

Schumann continued to express his joy in song. Having previously written mainly piano music, some of his most popular pieces today, in 1840 he composed 138 vocal pieces. He worked frantically at times: the First Symphony in B flat was sketched between 23 and 26 January 1841, and completed by 20 February. On 31 March, it was performed under Mendelssohn.

A year after the wedding, Clara gave birth to her first child, Marie. Among the godparents were Mendelssohn (although absent) and Schumann's old landlady. Wieck maintained complete silence when told of the birth of his granddaughter; he was totally estranged. He turned his attentions to promoting Clara's young half-sister Marie. And it was not until just before the birth of her second child Elise in April 1843 that Wieck invited Clara to Dresden where he had moved. Only at Christmas of that year were he and Schumann grudgingly reconciled, over three years after the wedding.

Robert gave Clara a monthly allowance. He kept a meticulous record of expenses and discovered that they were spending more than their income, even though he had received a large sum when the Schumann family publishing business was sold.[64] Robert found it difficult to cope with the fact that Clara did most of the wage earning and took umbrage when she had an important engagement and he was not invited. They went on a tour to Bremen and Hamburg where his Symphony in B flat was played and she also played the piano. But she got much more applause than he did and this worried him. He refused to accompany her on a tour to Denmark, and drowned his sorrows in beer and champagne, thus giving Wieck the opportunity to spread the rumour that the couple had bust up.[65] After two years' intensive work, Schumann became ill with 'weakness of the nerves'[66] such that during the winter 1842–3 he could not compose.

Schumann joined Mendelssohn's newly founded Leipzig Conservatoire as a professor of piano, composition and score reading. At that time, he often met Berlioz as he passed through on his travels. Being impetuous in character, Schumann was more similar to Berlioz than Mendelssohn. He and Mendelssohn were very different: the adventurous and idiosyncratic Schumann compared with the polished, charming, suave Mendelssohn. One can hardly imagine Mendelssohn spending 'a night out on the town', swilling beer and champagne and ending up in a brothel.[67]

A Russian Visit

In January 1844, the Schumanns went to Russia on tour together. Having left the children in the care of Robert's brother Karl, they went first to Berlin and called in on the Mendelssohns, who by then were based there. Then they took a 48-hour journey by flying coach to Königsberg. The piano manufacturer who had been supplying pianos for Clara's concerts lent them a sleigh which took them to the border, where they changed to a flying coach to Riga. The hotel accommodation was appalling, and in one room they dared not even sit down. They reached St Petersburg after a five-day stop at Dorpat (Tartu in Estonia) en route. Of course, in early March it was very cold, with 23 degrees of frost, and Schumann got a chill. But the local dignitaries looked after them well, and provided food and better bedding. Marie got a letter from her mother saying: 'We have driven in carriages and sleighs, across the ice of three rivers, all larger than the Elbe … There are many wolves in the forests here; they often appear beside the road and watch the travellers as they pass by; so far we have not seen any, but everybody who goes from here to St Petersburg comes across them.'[68]

On arrival in St Petersburg, they were welcomed by the star mezzo-soprano Pauline Viardot, who was doing a season there. Clara performed at concerts and before the tsarina. The Schumanns went on to Moscow in mid-April, but as the season was over, they were really just tourists. Robert sketched a picture of the Kremlin. He also looked up an uncle on his mother's side of the family, a regimental doctor living in Tver, about 100 miles from Moscow.

Robert Schumann's impression of Moscow. Some might regard him as less talented than Mendelssohn

One can imagine the inns in which the Schumanns stayed, where 'the walls are always the same and they are covered with oil paint, grimy near the top from tobacco and shiny at the bottom from the backs of innumerable travellers, and more especially, from the backs of the merchants of the district, for the merchants repaired there regularly on market days with six or seven companions to drink their two cups of tea'.[69] They returned home via St Petersburg and took a ship, stopping at Helsinki, Stockholm and Copenhagen. They got back to pick up their children on 30 May. What a joyful reunion it must have been!

They returned to the routine in Leipzig. The only cloud on the horizon was Robert's worsening health. He was becoming increasingly withdrawn and silent, quietly puffing away on a cigar.[70] After he overworked on

Byron's *Corsair* and Goethe's *Faust*, his health broke down again, much more seriously. He resigned from his newspaper.

Dresden

After a holiday in the Harz mountains failed to help, they moved to Dresden, in autumn 1844. There, Schumann held no appointment and he never penetrated the 'Establishment':[71] anyway, the musical world was relatively quiet compared to Leipzig. From Dresden, Schumann wrote to Ferdinand David, head of the violin department at the Leipzig Conservatoire: 'Here one can get back the old lost longing for music; there is so little to hear.'[72] He ran a choral society, a 'Liedertafel', for men, and also a parallel one for mixed voices. The Schumanns organised concerts together with Ferdinand Hiller, Berlioz' onetime competitor for the charms of Camille Pleyel. At one such concert, the teenage violin prodigy Joseph Joachim played Mendelssohn's Violin Concerto.

The Schumanns were to be found in Engel's restaurant in the Postplatz, a meeting place for artistic people. Robert needed money and therefore composed energetically. Piano music, chamber music, symphonies poured forth. He wanted to write a 'German' opera; 1847 was mainly taken up with writing one based on the legend of Genoveva, an 8th-century countess wrongly ejected by her husband for infidelity. Eventually the opera was staged in Leipzig in June 1850, having been delayed for a performance of Meyerbeer's *Le Prophète*. The première was spoilt by stage accidents, but Clara was generally pleased with later performances. She wrote about her husband taking the applause: 'I could have wept for joy to see how he came forward so simply and unassumingly; if ever he seemed to me lovable, it was at this moment, as he stood there, true artist and man!'[73] But even many of their closest friends questioned the dramatic viability of the work. Schumann then turned to writing music for Byron's *Manfred*.

Their domestic life continued happily. They played chess and dominoes.* Clara's life was centred around concerts, composition and children. They continued to have a succession of these. Clara was pregnant nine times during the thirteen and a half years that she lived with Robert, and bore eight children. In March 1845 Julie was born, and their son Emil was born in February 1846, although he died just over a year later. While the

* In the Zwickau birthplace museum, one can see boards for chess and dominoes, and Robert's tobacco box and letter box.

earlier births were welcomed joyously, the recurring pregnancies were greeted with dismay, and described as her 'new fear', her 'frightening expectation'.[74] Schumann, however, was delighted with the children.[75] He composed many works with them in mind, sent them to the kindergarten and took a considerable interest in their progress.

His mental state gave her increasing cause for concern. To start with in Dresden, 'Robert never had a night's sleep, his imagination brought the most horrible pictures before him, and I usually found him bathed in tears in the early morning: he gave up all hope for himself'.[76] He suffered from chronic physical weakness, giddiness and headaches; he had a continuous singing in his ears; every external sound turned itself into music. Clara took him to stay at the castle of Maxen, about ten miles outside, in the beautiful wooded hills above the Elbe. Their friends, the wealthy, music-loving Major Friedrich Anton Serre and his wife, lived there.

Robert's hypochondria increased. He was neurotic about infection, especially cholera. He was an impossible patient and turned down every prescription he was given. His homeopathic doctor put his symptoms down to 'excess', as happens to those who concentrate too much on one particular activity, 'like businessmen who spent all their time adding and subtracting figures'.[77] He was ordered to take cold plunge-baths.

When they went on tour to Vienna in 1846–7, they took the tiny children with them. Schumann sent Marie and Elise out to deliver a letter, and Clara was appalled to find them wandering around the streets unaccompanied.[78]

The audience attendances were poor for this Viennese trip. Clara's programmes included less of the showy works which had appealed so much to the Viennese on her previous tour eight years before. They would have faced considerable losses had it not been for the soprano Jenny Lind who volunteered to join them in a concert. The Schumanns were very selective about the music they were prepared to play. Clara observed about Jenny that 'she should sing only good music, and discard all that stuff … of Meyerbeer's, Bellini's, Donizetti's etc., for she is too good for that'.[79] But it was that 'stuff' which drew the audiences.

One can see here early evidence of the polarised view of music which was to bedevil the second half of the 19th century.* Views about the future

* Such disputes were nothing new: in the past, there had been the Gluck-Piccinni row about the future of opera (see page 153).

of music became increasingly extreme, and individual composers were acrimoniously critical of each other's work. The bitterness was amazingly intense, as we shall see in later chapters. It was in evidence in the Schumanns' relations with the ostentatious conductor at the Dresden court theatre. Although the reclusive Schumann was interested in Wagner's work, Clara loathed it, and having seen *Tannhäuser*, she noted in her diary: 'this is no music at all to me – though I do not deny that Wagner has great dramatic power ... I do not feel one spark of sympathy for this composer.'[80] The feeling was reciprocated: some years later Wagner, having seen Schumann's *Genoveva*, expressed his 'utter dismay over the vulgarity and crudeness of this work'.[81]

Relations with Liszt, who visited occasionally, also became strained. Schumann disliked Liszt's swooning audiences, the medals and decorations, the hobnobbing with royalty. Both the Schumanns and Mendelssohn thought his character was 'a continual alternation between scandal and apotheosis'.[82] There was an ugly scene, shortly after Mendelssohn died, when Liszt arrived late for a dinner at the Schumanns' house. He proceeded, surely unwisely, to criticise Schumann's piano quintet, which is loved so much today, and to compare Meyerbeer, of all people, favourably to Mendelssohn. Schumann lost his temper and stormed out. Liszt tried to make it up and continued to be a considerable supporter of Schumann: he played his works and staged *Genoveva* in Weimar.[83] But Clara never made peace on either a personal or an artistic level: she refused to go on the same stage as Liszt at the Mozart Centenary Festival in January 1856.

The 1848 Revolution – the Schumann Experience

Dresden was about to become a very hot spot. Warned by the trouble in France, the King of Saxony appointed a new government and made various concessions, such as electoral reform, freeing the press, improving the administration of justice and introducing trial by jury for certain crimes. Schumann felt excited by these developments, and wrote three patriotic and revolutionary songs, although, at the time, they were not published. Clara was greatly alarmed. The scene in Dresden remained under control until, suddenly, the prohibition of a public demonstration on 2 May 1849 aroused the mob to seize the city and appoint a provisional government, events in which Wagner was deeply involved. Prussian troops arrived and, after two days of fierce street fighting, the rising was put down.

On 3 May 1849, the Schumanns saw dead bodies piled up in the hospital forecourt. A couple of days later, men called to demand Schumann's enrolment in their street guard. Clara escaped with him and Marie through the garden door. They got away, first by train, and then on foot, to take refuge at the Serres' castle in Maxen.

Naturally Clara was very worried about the children who had been left behind. A few days later, although seven months pregnant with her third son Ferdinand, she left at 3 am with two other women and made her way back to the house. She was brave and tough: in a Paris insurrection, she had risked the street firing in order to see what was happening. Now, 'we entered amidst the continuous thunder of the cannon, and suddenly we saw forty men with scythes coming towards us'.[84] All the houses in their street were shut; she found the children asleep, dressed them and grabbed a few necessities. An hour later, Clara, an ailing maid and the cook were in the field outside; before dinner, they were back in Maxen.[85] By the time they returned again to Dresden, it was swarming with Prussians.

Düsseldorf

In the autumn of 1849, Ferdinand Hiller suggested that Schumann should be appointed to the Düsseldorf music directorship, which he was vacating. Schumann was concerned that Düsseldorf was a long way away and that there might be little work for Clara. He was also worried that 'among the places of note in that town, I found mentioned three convents and a madhouse'.[86] Despite practical concerns, like moving the children from school and arranging their music lessons, Clara wanted to get Robert away from Dresden, where he held no appointment. Always keenly ambitious for him, she wanted him to have a position. So they moved to Düsseldorf on 1 September 1850. The ladies of the choir in Dresden gave him a carpet as a farewell gift.*

The job in Düsseldorf started well. The Schumanns were given a warm welcome, with laurel trees placed outside their hotel; they were serenaded by the choral society; two days later, the local orchestra serenaded them

* Before Schumann left Dresden, he took a leading part in founding the Bach-Gesellschaft, the Bach Society. This was a further important step in the Bach revival for which Mendelssohn's performance of the St Matthew Passion in 1829 had been such a landmark event. The Bach-Gesellschaft marked the centenary of Bach's death by issuing a complete edition of his works. Schumann always had a deep reverence for Bach.

with the *Don Giovanni Overture*, as they had their dinner. A ball was held in their honour, but new faces, unsuccessful house hunting and a long journey meant that they were exhausted.

There were domestic worries with the move: the dilatoriness of workmen, and the pert cook, whom Clara had to sack. Schumann liked and helped his assistant. But Clara, increasingly protective, and sensitive to any threat, took an immediate dislike to him.[87] Schumann began a great burst of musical activity, writing many works including the *Rhenish Symphony* and a cello concerto.

Schumann took weekly rehearsals for the regular subscription concerts, together with a few extra performances connected with the local Roman Catholic churches. He was not a good conductor. Clara's diaries had recorded disastrous performances on earlier occasions, for example, after a Berlin performance of *Paradise and the Peri*, she wrote: 'I was in agonies, and thought I would sink into the ground.'[88] Now, the Düsseldorf singers, who needed inspiration and clear direction, were confused by the musings and lack of incisiveness of 'this remote, shy, withdrawn visionary', whose own music reflected his character and who was incapable of leading them to realise the music in the way that he expected.[89]

At one rehearsal, the sopranos got lost and stopped; the other voices then stopped, but Schumann carried on conducting. When the accompanist stopped, Schumann called him over and just said, 'Look! this bar is beautiful'.[90] At times, he would stand ready with baton in hand and yet not begin to conduct, so the orchestra would start off on its own. The membership dropped as people started staying away. As his health deteriorated, Schumann's tempos got slower and slower. In March 1851, only six months after his arrival, the rumblings had begun: an anonymous article appeared in the *Düsseldorfer Zeitung* which criticised his directorship.

The Schumanns' daughter Eugénie was born in December 1851. Then Schumann was unwell. But a cure at Bad Godesburg near Bonn made him worse: he was hearing things, and had an increasing speech disorder. A concert in August reduced him nearly to breakdown. They went to Scheveningen in Holland, to bathe in the sea. The shock of the cold water gave Clara a miscarriage. He turned to religious music, an oratorio on the life of Luther, a Mass and a Requiem. Hiller came to help with most of the conducting for the spring 1853 festival, at which Joachim, increasingly a family friend, played the Beethoven Violin Concerto.

Around this time, Schumann became involved in table rapping, a form of communication with 'the other world'. This craze originated in 1848, in New York, when a family called Fox were disturbed by unexplained knockings. Kate Fox discovered that the cause of the sounds was intelligent and that the spirit, a murdered pedlar, would make raps as requested. When the Fox girls went to stay with a married sister, Mrs Fish in Rochester, communication was established with lost relatives and dead celebrities: one rap meant 'No' and three 'Yes'; by pointing to letters of the alphabet and awaiting the rap, complicated messages could be passed between this world and the next. After a medium came to Europe in 1852, the spiritualist movement took off like an epidemic; a decade later, it was estimated that possibly 40 per cent of the population of the United States were involved.[91]

The Schumanns' home life continued happily. The children's musical progress meant a great deal to Robert. When he was pleased, he would give them pennies from his writing desk as a reward. Robert had a happy birthday on 8 June 1853. But, at the end of July, he suffered a strange paralysis, which the doctor said was rheumatism; at the end of August, he suddenly lost his voice. They had a very happy wedding anniversary on 12 September. She conceived yet again. Then there was a fiasco in mid-October with an appalling performance of a Mass, in which the choir refused to sing. In one rehearsal of Joachim's difficult *Hamlet Overture*, Schumann took the players through endless repetitions of certain passages without any clear indication of what he wanted to correct.[92]

Schumann was asked to hand over some of the less important conducting to his assistant. Clara was apoplectic. To her, a wonderfully loyal, truly great lady, any thought of Robert being found wanting was inconceivable. He was supported also by Joseph Joachim and by an unknown twenty-year-old called Johannes Brahms, who had been introduced by Joachim a month earlier. Much to Clara's fury, a deputation arrived, and insisted that Schumann hand over the conducting of all but his own works to the assistant. The Schumanns escaped on a successful winter tour in Holland and Hamburg. Schumann composed and worked on a project to publish a collection of his articles.

But, in February, Schumann suffered 'so violent an affection of the hearing that he did not close his eyes all night'. Sometimes, he would hear a single note, sometimes a full orchestra. Sometimes, the music was more wonderful and played 'by more exquisite instruments than ever sounded on earth'. At other times, it was 'a cacophony of hyenas and demon voices'.[93] He begged Clara to leave him, in case he harmed her. During the night, he jumped out of bed to write down a theme which the angels had sent him.

On 26 February, he asked to be put into an asylum. Clara implored him: 'Robert, is it your wish to abandon your wife and children?' 'Yes', he said, 'It won't be for long. I will come back recovered.' Next day, he was deeply melancholy; he said: 'Ah Clara, I am not worthy of your love.'[94] He made a fair copy of the variations on the angels' theme.

The following day, for a short time, she went next door to talk to the doctor, leaving him with little Marie. Schumann got up, grabbed his overcoat, nothing else, no boots, and went out.

Bertha, the faithful housekeeper, suddenly burst in and said that he had disappeared.[95] Clara later said: 'No words can describe my feelings, only I knew that I felt as if my heart had ceased to beat.'[96]

A search party was sent out, desperate to find him. He was brought back an hour later by some fishermen: he had jumped into the Rhine and had been rescued by the captain of the steamer, *Viktoria*.*[97]

Schumann was looked after around the clock by male nurses and, so as not to excite him, Clara went to stay with her blind friend, Fräulein Leser. Family and friends rallied around. Clara's mother came from her home in Berlin; Brahms rushed over from Hanover, and Joachim came to help in the middle of his busy concert programme. Hiller and Härtel offered to help.

The Asylum

The last act began. On 4 March 1854, Dr Robert Schumann, by now at last a composer of international repute, was taken at his own request on the eight-hour journey to Dr Richarz' private asylum at Endenich near Bonn. As he got into the carriage, he hardly took any notice of Clara; she gave him a little bouquet of the flowers he loved so much;[98] the children watched from upstairs. Little did Clara know, she would not see him again for two and a half years.

Today Endenich is in a flat part of Bonn near the Poppelsorf Palace, and not far from the old cemetery where Schumann was eventually laid to rest. The institution consisted of several smallish buildings with a large

* Jüngermann, the fisherman, was awarded a silver medal.

garden, in which Schumann took his daily walks and enjoyed the flowers. He had a private room with a grand piano. He looked out onto the Siebengebirge, those seven mounds of earth left by the giants when they dug out the Rhine – there were no landfill sites in those days. One, the Drachenfels, was where Siegfried was supposed to have slain the dragon.

The asylum housed about fourteen patients and, thank goodness, was no bedlam: the physical restraints, straitjackets and handcuffs which we associate with lunacy in earlier periods, were kept to a minimum; anyway, Schumann, though excitable, was only occasionally violent. Dr Richarz was highly regarded as 'probably one of the most experienced and competent psychiatrists to be found in the Rhineland at that time'.[99] But, by modern standards, the treatment would have been 'crude and cruel', even 'barbaric', and the doctors arrogant, insensitive and unimaginative. It seems that Richarz was under pressure with expansion of the business and delegated the care of Schumann to a Dr Peters. The treatment included baths at extreme temperatures. The body systems were purged by bleeding, and by force-feeding heavy meals at one end, and encouraging excretion at the other.

There has been much speculation as to the reasons for Schumann's condition. Christel is sometimes held to blame. Dr Richarz' papers recording his view that Schumann was suffering from the final stage of cerebral neurosyphilis were only made public in 1994. Schumann died *with* syphilis;* but whether he actually died *of* it is less clear.[100]

It seems that it was some guilt-complex that drove Schumann to enter the asylum: whether it was connected with Christel or Ernestine, or even his sister-in-law Rosalie, who knows. His guilt may not have been simply about behaviour inconsistent with a person of his class; more likely, he felt guilty that his behaviour had stained his concept of pure artistic idealism; now Fate, that evil woman, was catching up with him. It seems possible that he may finally have died from self-starvation, perhaps from despair at the prospect of never being let out, perhaps because of revulsion at the treatment and the diet: it is known that there was an epidemic of suicides by self-starvation in Endenich, at one stage.

* One might wonder about the effect on Clara and the children. Once the primary sores are healed, syphilis should not transmit. All Clara's eight children were born without complications. However, one, Ludwig, spent the second half of his 46-year life in an asylum.

When Clara had the baby Felix in mid-June, she waited to baptise him, in case Schumann should be let out. Indeed, around this time, he appeared to be recovering. But every up was followed by a down.

Dr Richarz did not want Clara to see Robert. It was feared that a visit by her would remind the patient of the attempted suicide and enhance his excitability; the warders even withheld her letters. Schumann at one stage asked Brahms if Clara had died, because he never heard from her. She passed by Bonn a number of times without visiting him, but, at the turn of the year, he was allowed visits from Joachim and Brahms, who reported back to her. Brahms had to warn her against over-optimism. She was inconsolable when the news was bad. She was allowed to write to him on their wedding anniversary, also her 35th birthday. When she read Robert's reply, Brahms said that she looked as rapturous as Leonore in the finale to *Fidelio*.

Clara had to support the family of seven children. Mendelssohn's brother Paul sent a credit for 400 thalers. But she proudly refused offers of financial assistance and was able to augment Schumann's capital rather than deplete it. The fees at the asylum, 700 thalers per year, were about the equivalent of Schumann's salary as music director.*[102] She taught, and almost all her time was spent organising tours, or on tour. On one, she had nearly 30 public and private engagements, taking in Liverpool, Manchester and Dublin.

Brahms, who was nearly fourteen years younger than Clara, was a great source of strength. He looked after the children when she was away. He wrote to her about them: 'Ludwig is too stubborn, and Felix is even more stubborn …'[103] He had to smack Ferdinand on the bottom because he was lazy and would not read; he had to entertain them with gymnastics on the stair landing, doing handstands; he had to calm them during terrific thunderstorms in September 1855 when windows were blown in and panes of glass smashed.

Clara became very dependent on Brahms and loved him in a maternal way. He started writing to her as 'My dearly beloved Clara', saying: 'I can no longer exist without you … Please go on loving me as I shall go on loving you, always and for ever.'[104] Indeed her friend Fräulein Leser warned her to be careful, as Brahms' attentions might draw adverse comment. But Robert came first. On her 36th birthday, her diary records: 'Nothing

* Fritz Brahms' salary as a music teacher in a teacher training school was 125 thalers a year.[101]

was lacking that birthday celebrations should have, yet without Him, everything was wanting.'[105] She missed him desperately, especially at night.[106]

In the asylum, Schumann would suffer convulsive jerks and would sometimes hear things that made him talk wildly, pace up and down his room, or fling himself on his knees and wring his hands. He could be violent and noisy, he would bellow or curse or simply talk nonsense. For long periods, however, he could be lucid. Eight months after admission, he wrote to Brahms saying: 'Write to me again soon dear Johannes and also about our friends.'

When Brahms visited him, they discussed Clara's travels, and Brahms gave him an inkstand and some cigars. Schumann had been writing some fugues. He wanted copies of a music magazine. They played duets on his square piano, which was out of tune. 'We did not keep strictly together', Brahms reported to Clara, 'but it's ages since he played duets.' With the permission of his warders, Schumann then accompanied Brahms to the railway station, a couple of miles each way. 'The warder always walked either behind or beside us (a few paces away). Imagine my joy as I now tramped a long way and merrily with him, the precious man ... and so we went to the Cathedral, to the Beethoven Monument.' When Brahms described this to Clara, he regretted that he could only state 'quite simply and drily what we spoke about together. I cannot describe the other, lovelier things, his beautiful, tranquil eyes, his warmth when he spoke of you ... Just imagine it all as beautifully as you possibly can.'[107]

Others were quick to suggest alternative treatments, especially when Schumann seemed to improve. In marched the septuagenarian poetess and friend of Beethoven, Bettina von Arnim, the one who had said, almost half a century before, 'I have got to have a child by Goethe at all costs – why, it will be a demigod.'[108] She regarded herself as knowledgeable about lunatic asylums and did not like what she saw. So Brahms investigated an alternative place which catered for rich people including lots of young people who had 'destroyed themselves by masturbation'.[109] Nothing came of this.

It has been implied that Clara, career woman that she was, consciously and coldly deserted Robert so that she could pursue her own career, which is what she really wanted to do. She was undoubtedly spoilt, opinionated, determined and formidable, as Brahms would discover. However, the suggestion that she refused to countenance her husband returning home to die seems to rest on 'late twentieth-century hindsight rather than on mid-nineteenth-century treatment of the mentally ill'.[110]

Robert wrote his last letter to Clara on 5 May 1855, in his small handwriting. A copy of this can be seen at Endenich. 'Dear Clara', he wrote, 'I sent you a Spring message [possibly violets] on May 1st. The following days were troubled; you will learn more from the letter which you will receive the day after tomorrow. A shadow flickers across it, but the rest of its contents will please you, my darling … I have enclosed the drawing by Felix Mendelssohn, so that you may put it in the album. A priceless keepsake. Leb. wohl, Du Liebe! Dein Robert.'[111]

But it was no good. Brahms wrote to Joachim in April 1856: 'I saw Schumann. How he had changed! He welcomed me joyfully and warmly as always, but I shuddered in horror for I understood not one word he said. He spoke almost continuously, often to be sure, he merely blabbered something like bababa-dadada.'[112] He was assembling place names from an atlas, towns and rivers whose names began with Aab Ab Aba etc., gathering together the many St Juans, carefully recording the location of the city, latitude and longitude. Schumann showed Brahms sheets of paper completely covered with such writing.*

The doctors still kept Clara away. She was forewarned of the patient's rapidly deteriorating condition. Brahms subsequently described the end as it approached. 'A week before his death (Wednesday), we received a telegraphic message. I only read it; it said something like, "If you want to see your husband while he is still alive, hurry here immediately. His appearance to be sure, is horrifying." We went. He had had an attack, which the doctors thought would be followed immediately by death ... I went to him, saw him, however, just as he was in convulsions and greatly agitated, so that I too, like the doctors, dissuaded Frau Schumann from going to him and persuaded her to go home. Schumann just lay there, took nothing more than wine and jelly from a spoon. But Frau Clara's suffering during those days was so great that, on Saturday, I <u>had</u> to suggest that we go there once more to see him.'[114]

* Dr Richarz wrote his own account of Brahms' visit: '[Schumann] had visit yesterday from Herr Brahms, was pleased, almost entirely incomprehensible. [Brahms] found him very changed for the worse, since his last visit one year ago. During the visit a few words understandable.'[113]

Having been denied access to him for two and a half years, Clara described her reunion: 'Now I lay silent at your feet hardly daring to breathe. Only now and then I received a look, clouded as it were, but unspeakably gentle.' His limbs twitched. He was emaciated. He must recognise her. Speaking was a great effort; he was incomprehensible. 'He said "My". Presumably he wanted to add "Clara", for he looked at me affectionately. Then he said: "I know" – presumably "you".'[115]

'My Robert ... he smiled, and put his arm round me with a great effort, for he can no longer control his limbs. I shall never forget it. Not all the treasures in the world could equal this embrace.'[116]

Young Johannes Brahms confirms Clara's account of that most intimate occasion, adding that 'he often refused the wine that was offered him, but from her finger he sometimes sucked it up eagerly, at such length and so passionately that one knew with certainty that he recognised the finger'.[117] Brahms added: 'Surely I will never again experience anything as moving as the reunion of Robert and Clara.'[118]

Brahms wrote to Joachim, at Clara's request, telling him to come if he wanted to see Schumann again, but warning him: 'it is very, very wrenching and pitiful. Schumann is very wasted, there is no question of his talking or being conscious.'[119]

Clara too wrote to Joachim: 'I did receive a few tender glances – those I will take with me throughout my entire life! Once he even embraced me, he recognised me! Ask God for a gentle end for him – it cannot last much longer, as Richarz says. I will not leave him any more! Ah, Joachim, what pain, what suffering to see him again in this way! But that glance – not for all the world would I miss it any more. We are just on our way there again! Think of him and of your Clara Schumann.'[120]

So it was. Brahms recorded: 'Now and forever we thank God that it happened, for it is absolutely essential for her peace of mind. She was still able to see him on Sunday, Monday and Tuesday morning. That afternoon about four he died.'

Brahms had actually been out at the time: 'Tuesday noon Joachim [came] from Heidelberg; that delayed us somewhat in Bonn, otherwise he would have arrived before his passing; as it was, we came half an hour afterwards ...' Brahms recorded that Schumann 'had passed away very gently, so that it was scarcely noticed. His body looked peaceful, then; how comforting it all was. A wife could not have stood it any longer.'[121]

Maybe Schumann had finally settled the account for the excesses of a wild and uncontrollable youth.

> Farewell, ye vanishing flowers, that shone
> In my fairy wreath, so bright and brief –
> Oh! What are the brightest that e'er have blown,
> To the lote-tree, springing by Alla's Throne,
> Whose flowers have a soul in every leaf!
> Joy, Joy for ever! – my task is done –
> The Gates are pass'd, and Heaven is won!*[122]

Clara continued her spectacular career as a concert pianist. By the time of her last performance in Frankfurt aged 71, she had performed nearly 1,300 programmes, some of them jointly with her daughter Marie.[123]

She worked incredibly hard: 'make use of minutes' was her admonition to her children, whether in music, needlework or general studies. Her daughter's description of her method shows just how hard a great concert pianist has to work to achieve that greatness. Practice began with exercises for an hour: 'scales rolled and swelled like a tidal sea, legato and staccato; in octaves, thirds, sixths, tenths and double thirds; sometimes in one hand only while the other played accompanying chords. Then, arpeggios of all kinds, octaves, shakes, everything prestissimo and without the slightest break ...'[124] Then she would play Czerny's Toccata op. 92, which her father recommended as a challenging piece to be played daily to instil confidence; and then some Bach, Schumann's Toccata, and Chopin Etudes. Only after all this would she turn to the works which she specifically wanted to practise.

Friedrich Wieck, her father and teacher, lived on until 1873, when he was 88. Clara died in May 1896, almost 40 years after her husband. A telegram, indicating that she had fallen asleep peacefully, was sent to Professor Joachim, Berlin: 'Unsere Mutter sanft entschlafen** – Marie Schumann'.[125] On Whitsunday, with Brahms present at the graveside, Clara was at last

* This is the final stanza of *Paradise and the Peri*. The poet adds a footnote: 'Mahomet is described, in the 53rd chapter of the Koran, as having seen the angel Gabriel "by the lote-tree, beyond which there is no passing; near it is the Garden of Eternal Abode". This tree, say the commentators, stands in the seventh heaven, on the right hand of the Throne of God.'

** Our mother passed away peacefully.

reunited with her Robert, in that green churchyard on the way in to Bonn. The birds were singing, and the grave was bedecked with flowers.[126]

Today, some cars stop at the busy road junction. They stop for the traffic lights, unaware of where they are.

Above: ROBERT SCHUMANN (NOTE THE EYES HALF SHUT; SUFFERERS FROM SYPHILIS REPUTEDLY HAD DIFFICULTY WITH LIGHT). BENEATH IS THE VIEW OF DÜSSELDORF WHERE HE JUMPED INTO THE RHINE AND THE *VIKTORIA* WHICH PICKED HIM UP (P. 416)

LISZT

CHAPTER 13

AUDIENCES ARE USUALLY amazed when they hear and see a pianist perform the brilliant piano works of Franz Liszt. However, his contemporaries were not quite so sure about all this virtuosity and showmanship. Wagner was annoyed by Liszt's habits and disliked much of his music, despite being his protégé and son-in-law. Clara Schumann, at the opposite end of the Romantic spectrum, condemned his vast and varied output as trivial and wearisome.[1] His compositions 'will soon disappear now that he has gone', was her epitaph. 'His personal charm and brilliant execution have always turned people's heads', was her explanation.[2] Eduard Hanslick, the Viennese critic, who often reflected the views of Brahms, said trenchantly: 'After Liszt, Mozart is like a soft spring breeze penetrating a room reeking with fumes.'[3]

These people, who often fought bitterly among themselves, seemed to unite in their dislike of Liszt.* Why? Was it the showmanship, which

* Some disagreed: Hugo Wolf, the Lieder composer, thought that there was more intelligence and sensitivity in a single cymbal crash of Liszt's than in all the symphonies of Brahms.[4] Isadora Duncan, the American avant-garde dancer of the early 20th century, may have been more discerning when she said: 'Liszt reached all his life for the sky, but for Schubert the sky reached down to him.'[5]

implied a lack of concern for pure art? Or was it that they sensed that so many aspects of his colourful life reeked of hypocrisy – his nationalism, his Roman Catholicism, his notorious sex-life? These aspects, which touch on some important events of the 19th century, can easily deflect us from Liszt's excellent qualities – his charitableness, his selfless support for the avant-garde, his achievement in 'inventing' the symphonic poem and the master-class. He was an innovator: 'new wine calls for new bottles', he said.[6] For the last 50 years of his life, he never charged anyone for a lesson.[7]

To get this extraordinary man and these issues into perspective, we shall first look at Liszt's early years as a virtuoso pianist and his affair with the Comtesse d'Agoult. After that, there were years composing and teaching in Weimar, living with Princess Carolyne; then there was the long old age spent commuting between Rome and his teaching activities in Budapest* and Weimar.

Youth

Franz Liszt was born on 22 October 1811 in a modest house, slightly bigger than a cottage, in the village of Raiding some 30 miles from Vienna. Raiding was a sheep farm on the vast estates of the Esterházy family, for whom Haydn had worked. Raiding nestles in scenic, rolling hills, and was then just inside Hungary. Franz's father, Adam Liszt, had earlier worked as a clerk at the Esterházy 'headquarters' in nearby Eisenstadt. He was subsequently sent out to Raiding to be steward, responsible for a substantial proportion of the enormous flock of around 150,000 merino sheep grazing the Esterházy estate.[9]

The pale and sickly Franzi was taught by his father, who had been in the orchestra at Eisenstadt. The boy may have learnt some of his subsequent showmanship by observing the performances of gypsies based around Raiding. His concert life as an infant prodigy began at the age of nine, in the nearby town of Sopron.**

The Esterházys were stingy about financing Franz's further education. But some other noblemen who recognised his ability provided the funds. Adam gave up his job and the family moved to Vienna, where Franz studied

* The fortress citadel of Buda and the business and intellectual city of Pest, on the right and left banks of the Danube respectively, came together formally only in 1873.[8]

** Sopron chose to remain in Hungary after the Second World War. Raiding is now just inside Austria, in the attractive Burgenland wine district.

composition and harmony with Salieri. Karl Czerny, a bachelor and workaholic, taught him the piano. No doubt Liszt sailed through Czerny's excellent technical exercises, subsequently the despair and discouragement of so many ordinary pianists. Franz met Beethoven and Schubert, and had some successful public concerts. He was invited to join with the other 50 composers, including Beethoven, whom the publisher Diabelli asked to write one Variation on the same theme. Then his mother went away to live with her sister, while Adam accompanied his twelve-year-old prodigy to Paris so that he might enter the Conservatoire.

Adam was a competent business manager, rather like Leopold Mozart. When they got to Paris, they made an arrangement whereby Erard, the piano manufacturer, would provide the pianos on which Franz performed. It turned out a good deal for Erard: Liszt would eventually use their pianos as far away as Constantinople. But Cherubini, the director of the Conservatoire, would not admit him to its piano department because it was inundated with foreigners and the rules were being amended to restrict their entry. So Franz had private lessons with Reicha, the teacher of Berlioz, and also from Ferdinando Paër, a prolific composer of operas and reluctant colleague of Rossini at the Théâtre des Italiens.[10]

Although there were other prodigies around,* Franz's appearances in fashionable houses and concerts were sensational by comparison. In the first three months in Paris, he did 38 performances of his showpieces, usually Hummel's piano concertos and his own improvisation on themes submitted from the audience.[11] He played many times in London, and at Windsor before the king. His tours, on which he often shared the stage with singers who performed popular songs, included the French provinces, Ireland and Switzerland. His remuneration was considerable. In Manchester, although upstaged by a harpist, the Infant Lyra, who was not yet four years old, Franz's fee was an astronomical £100. This represented around three months' pay for a high-level professional musician.[12]

The pressure was too great. The fifteen-year-old broke down. To rest, he was taken to Boulogne, where his father died of typhoid. As he expired, he forewarned his son that women would be the bane of his life. The son, at this time, wanted to become a priest, a vocation his father had also once contemplated for himself. He prayed, fasted and read religious books.[13]

* Such as George Aspull from Manchester and Anne de Belleville. There were 'famous' virtuosos such as Arabella Goddard, and Emma Busby from Camberwell. All now also forgotten.

Recovered, and back in Paris where his mother now joined him, Liszt became a fashionable teacher. He asked his confessor about the meaning of the Commandments which prohibit adultery and the coveting of one's neighbour's wife.* Neither forbids an unmarried music teacher from falling in love with an unmarried pupil. However, the pupil's father, the minister for commerce, saw things rather differently and quickly put a stop to all that nonsense.

The Young Virtuoso in Paris

This was an ideal time for piano virtuosos in Paris. The iron-braced frame, crucial for high-tension strings, had transformed the instrument's potential. There was an increase in home music-making and piano ownership: as we have seen in connection with Rossini's move to Paris, the number of amateur musicians increased from 3,500 at the time of the Revolution to 80,000 in 1829; and a piano was to be found in around ten per cent of middle-class households.[15] Manufacturers such as Erard and Pleyel prospered, as did Broadwood and Clementi in London. There was a corresponding increase in the number of public concerts, in which Liszt performed on the same stage as celebrated virtuosos such as Hiller, Moscheles, Herz, Thalberg and Kalkbrenner.

Liszt's natural inclination to be showy received a fillip when he saw Paganini, the violinist, in action. Paganini is credited with taking the virtuoso craze to absurd levels. Fanny Mendelssohn described him 'looking like a demented murderer'; she said that he 'gesticulates like a monkey. A supernatural, wild genius'; and she added: 'He is extremely exciting and provocative.'[16] Liszt modelled himself on Paganini and made full use of his long blond hair and facial expressions. He became a supreme exhibitionist** and celebrity. This was showbiz: Felix Mendelssohn observed critically that 'Liszt is now set around by a manager and a secretary who administer his affairs so abominably that the whole audience was incensed'.[19]

* The 7th and 10th Commandments in the Anglican order; the 6th and 9th according to Roman Catholic and Lutheran enumeration.[14]

** The distinguished critic Fétis bemoaned the way that Liszt just followed the fashion for wild and crazy piano music: Liszt had been born at a time when, in his view, pianists 'ont fait de la musique une folie, et vous avez cédé au torrent'.[17] In later years, Liszt must have calmed down, because he would tell pupils who swayed from side to side: 'You metronomise, just like the great Clara.'[18] Nevertheless, the black eyebrows, long white hair and cassock were still used to full effect.

A Few 19th-Century Virtuosos

Ferdinand Ries (1) was a pupil of Beethoven; Frédéric Kalkbrenner (2) was the leading pianist around 1830. Ignaz Moscheles (3) knew Beethoven, studied with Salieri and hosted Mendelssohn in London. Henri Herz (4) was also a piano manufacturer and concert hall proprietor. Sigismond Thalberg (5) was the rival of Liszt. Ferdinand Hiller (6) and Hans von Bülow (7) were 'all-rounders'. Hiller was also Berlioz' rival for the favours of Camille Pleyel (see p. 318). Von Bülow was first husband of Cosima Wagner. Joseph Joachim (8), the brilliant violinist, was a colleague of Brahms. Arabella Goddard (9), a pupil of Kalkbrenner, married *The Times* music critic J.W. Davison.

Many of the virtuosos, such as Liszt, wrote their own compositions. Fantasies or variations on favourite opera tunes from Rossini, Meyerbeer and Donizetti were particularly popular. The virtuosos were also expected to elaborate the works of other composers to make them more showy. At the same time, composers now wanted their works to reach beyond the narrow confines of the privileged classes: art was for the people. So piano transcriptions were prepared for the wider market, frequently in the form of duets which were popular in the home: Liszt's *Reminiscences of 'Robert le Diable'* sold over 500 copies on the day it appeared, and was immediately reprinted.[20]

New techniques for printing music enabled the increased levels of demand to be met. Previously, music had been printed by using engraved copper plates, a technique which was more expensive than copying by hand.* Lithography, a cheaper process and more suitable for mass production, was invented in Germany at the end of the 18th century. It was adopted slowly in France, because the necessary limestone was cumbersome and expensive to import. However, once zinc plates were found to be a less expensive alternative to the stones, the new technology could be exploited. Also, there was an improvement in printing materials: factory-produced ink was cheaper; and paper made with vegetable fibre became available, whereas previously it had been made more expensively from hemp, linen or cotton rags.[22]

Religion Again

At the end of the 1820s, Liszt seems to have suffered another nervous breakdown: he was even reputed to have died. He returned to his 'religious' studies. He became involved with the Saint-Simonians and the thinking of the Abbé de Lamennais.

The Saint-Simonian movement peaked in 1829–32. Disciples of the Comte de Saint-Simon, a philosopher who had died a few years earlier, wanted to achieve progress through peaceful socialism rather than by revolutionary violence. They also had some modern views on the importance of industrial productivity in contributing to progress, and the need to incentivise those who, by their efforts, contribute more than others to the

* At a time when manuscript copies cost 50 centimes for twelve pages, the equivalent when printed would cost 1.75–2.25 francs. A shoemaker's daily wages were 3 fr in 1847; a labourer might earn 2 fr for ten hours' work.[21]

economic and spiritual well-being of the nation. They wore distinctive blue clothes.[23]

However, they were also 'way out' and hippy. Their ceremonies featured 'sobs, tears, embraces' and emotionally charged sermons.[24] They revered their leader Barthélemy Enfantin almost as God. They permitted all kinds of personal relationships, provided that the union resulted in progress for the individual and society, a matter to be determined by Enfantin and his wife-to-be, the Mother of Humanity, 'La Femme'. In order that Enfantin and La Femme (once she appeared) could perform their ministry, the rules allowed them to have sexual relations with their followers.[25]

Some musicians became closely involved. Liszt would perform at the ceremonies; Nourrit, the virtuoso tenor, would sing. The young composer Félicien David went to the East as a missionary for the movement and returned with exotic ideas which were influential in subsequent French music.[26] The Halévys and the Rodrigues, Bizet's relatives, were at the top of the Saint-Simonian hierarchy. Mendelssohn, however, was shocked and repelled; Berlioz took a look and kept away.[27]

The authorities were concerned that the Saint-Simonians might be linked to the rebellious weavers of Lyon and other dangerously dissident groups. In January 1832, ten days after it was announced that La Femme was about to appear, there was a crackdown. Thirteen Saint-Simonians were expelled to Turkey on a ship whose mate was called Giuseppe Garibaldi.*[29]

Importantly for Liszt, the Saint-Simonians believed that whereas scientists can only indicate the means to an end, it falls to the artist/poet to proclaim the ideals to which society should be striving. Thus an artist has a very important, almost priestly, role to play.[30] This was also a view held by the controversial and unorthodox Abbé de Lamennais,** whom Liszt visited in Brittany in 1834. Liszt put the Saint-Simonian theory into practice

* Garibaldi, the Italian freedom-fighter, became the symbol of Italian patriotism. One of those expelled was Félicien David. Enfantin later became a successful railway industrialist and secretary-general of the Paris–Lyon line.[28]

** Lamennais first advocated a strongly centralised Catholic Church under papal control (known as 'ultramontanism'). But by the 1830s he had done a U-turn, and favoured the separation of church and state, thus enabling the church to champion nationalist causes such as the Poles against the Russians, the Belgians against the Dutch, the Irish against the English. By 1834, Lamennais had been condemned in two papal encyclicals. He was refused a proper burial at his death twenty years later.[31]

throughout his life, whether publishing his compositions widely, giving master-classes in Weimar, teaching in Budapest, or simply playing to raise funds for the weavers of Lyons. At this time, in the 1830s, we see him arguing that music should be introduced into elementary schools and cheap editions should be made available for people to play.[32]

Comtesse Marie d'Agoult

It was not long before Liszt turned from religion to women. One imagines that the very tall, willowy musician with enormous blue eyes was wildly attractive as a toy-boy to the ladies of the salons. He seems to have stayed for part of the winter of 1832–3 with Comtesse Adèle Laprunarède in Switzerland.[33]

Around this time, he met the lovely, blond and highly intelligent Comtesse Marie d'Agoult. When he entered the salon she gasped, unable to work out whether his appearance provoked her 'to contradiction or to intimate assent'.[34]

Six years older than Liszt, Marie was the daughter of the Comte de Flavigny, who was an '*émigré*', as the Royalists who fled from France during the Revolution were called. Her mother came from a banking family prominent in Frankfurt, where Marie spent her early years. Marie had married Captain Charles d'Agoult, who was twenty years older than her. She was vivacious: she claimed once to have danced until five or six in the morning on 63 successive nights.[35] A scar on the right cheek,* cut when she fell during a dance, was the only blemish on the beauty of the tall, graceful heiress. Her husband admired her magnificent blonde hair, her intelligence and her gentleness.[37]

We are told that it was a year before the increasingly intimate relationship between the Comtesse and Liszt was consummated.[38] During this time, Franz visited her at her château at Croissy, six miles from Paris. They had deep intellectual discussions on Romantic subjects, including religion, and they wrote to each other frequently. In mid-1835, shortly after the death of her first child, Marie (who by then was pregnant) eloped with

* The scar may be the reason why there are so few revealing portraits of Marie. The conversation piece by Danhauser, 'Liszt at the Piano', shows her sitting at Liszt's feet, her back to the artist.[36] A plaster cast of her tiny and delicate hand can be seen in the Liszt Museum in Bayreuth.

Liszt,* first to Basle and then to Geneva. This caused a sensation similar to that caused by George Sand's fling in Venice with Alfred de Musset: one year after marriage, it was considered acceptable to have an affair, and indeed an appropriate one could 'add lustre to the salon of a wife' such as Marie.[40] But flaunting a passion, or abandoning home and daughter, as Marie was doing, was a scandal.

The immediate result, Blandine, was born in December 1835. She was handed over to a wet-nurse and then boarded with a pastor.[41] The lovers made Geneva their base for the next four years. Liszt taught music, and studied philosophy, at the university. His countess regarded herself as something of an expert on religious and philosophical subjects, so every second day was devoted to reading.[42] She also began to write articles, which at first were published in journals under Liszt's name. The *ménage* became more complex when the fifteen-year-old Hermann Cohen, a pupil of Liszt, joined them.

In summer 1836, George Sand, who had recently separated from her husband and was keen to give her son a break from the jibes of his friends about his mother's lifestyle, joined them all on a wild trip to Chamonix.[43] After this, they returned to Paris, where Sand, Liszt and Marie set up house in a *ménage à trois*. Their salon in the Hôtel de France in the Rue Laffitte was a rendezvous for literary and musical celebrities. It was here that Sand was introduced to Chopin.

Sand invited Liszt and Marie to her home at Nohant. But Liszt followed Marie there only after he had held a contest with Sigismond Thalberg, the reputedly highly-born but actually illegitimate virtuoso, the idol of Vienna. Sponsored particularly by the music critic and editor of the *Revue Musicale*, François-Joseph Fétis, Thalberg delighted his audiences with melodies from the popular operas. These were played with the thumbs in the centre of the piano, accompanied by the hands swirling arpeggios to the left and right. This gave the impression that he had three hands, and a cartoonist drew him with ten. Liszt's PR could not permit such behaviour to go unchallenged.[44]

Liszt and Thalberg were well matched: the demure Fanny Mendelssohn said that Thalberg was guilty of 'behaving like a virtuoso, showing off, and

* Almost 30 years earlier, Marie's half-sister eloped with Clemens Brentano, the poet and brother of Bettina, the friend of Beethoven and of the Schumanns.[39]

being very pleased with himself'.[45] The contest, held in March 1837 in aid of Italian refugees, took place in the salon of Princess Belgiojoso, an exile from Italy.* Both contestants were declared to have won. They co-operated, together with Pixis, Herz, Czerny and Chopin, by contributing a variation to the *Hexaméron* on a theme from Bellini's opera *I Puritani.*

At Nohant, Liszt would walk, talk and play the piano, with George Sand crouching underneath. The countess would flit in and out in her expensive outfits. 'Ah! If only I were loved', said George to Liszt.[47] One can make what one will of Marie's cryptic remark, expressed in her memoirs years later, that she was 'an unhappy barrier between two destinies made to fuse with, and complete, each other'.[48]

Liszt and his countess left Nohant to live in Italy, and on the way performed at a concert in aid of striking Lyon silk workers. Six months later, at Christmas, their daughter Cosima was born at Bellagio on the 'supremely beautiful'[49] Lake Como; she would become Cosima von Bülow, and Cosima Wagner, but she was Cosette to her father.[50]

Liszt composed and finished the *Transcendental Studies* and started various pieces from the *Années de Pèlerinage*, the Paganini studies and Rossini transcriptions. He wanted to be considered an intellectual as well as a virtuoso; so he wrote articles, for example: 'De la situation des artistes et de leur condition dans la société', and 'Lettres d'un bachelier ès musique'. In these, he attacked the circus-like antics of the kind he himself performed.[51]

Marie wanted him to be an aristocratic composer, a kind of super-Chopin. But he longed to continue his career as a virtuoso pianist; and possibly he wanted some space from his super-Romantic blue-stocking idealist. The Danube flood disaster of March 1838 gave him the opportunity to go to Vienna and raise funds in eight concerts. In the following year, Daniel was born in Rome, where Ingres, then the director of the French Academy at the Villa Medici, dedicated to Marie a drawing which he did of Liszt. The *ménage* moved on to the fishing village of San Rossore near Pisa, near where Puccini would be born twenty years later. Here Liszt heard that a mere 424 francs had been raised for the Beethoven memorial in

* Visitors to Princess Belgiojoso's bedroom were ushered in by a turbaned, bearded Negro through a gallery decorated with skull and cross bones; the bed was an altar of ebony inlaid with elephant tusk. Thalberg's tours took him to Brazil and the USA, where he lived for a time. Eventually, he retired to grow wines on his estate near Naples.[46]

Bonn, and in October 1839, pretext or not, he offered his services to raise funds.* Marie and the three children went to Paris, although for reasons of propriety the children lodged with Liszt's mother.[53]

Liszt began eight years of touring in which he appeared on well over 1,000 occasions. He covered an area stretching from Ireland to Gibraltar to the Urals; from southern British towns to Moscow and Constantinople. Sometimes he travelled 50 to 60 miles a day.[54] He no doubt experienced bad roads, mud, drunken coach-drivers, threadbare inns, and meals of 'cabbage soup with puff pasties, specially kept for travellers for weeks, brains with peas, sausages with cabbage, roast chicken, salted cucumbers and the invariable sweet pastries'.[55] The tedium in provincial towns must have been barely relieved by the occasional games of whist or billiards, played with minor dignitaries. Unlike modern concert virtuosos, Liszt was often trailed by secret police who were ubiquitous in those troubled times. Presumably he was well used to them: when Marie and Liszt were together at Lake Como, they were being watched by secret police employed by the government in Vienna.

He lapped up the adulation, the Lisztomania which swept across Europe. The audience swooned at his *Lucia di Lammermoor* fantasia and his *Galop Chromatique*. Ladies would even pick up his cigar butts, and keep his coffee dregs in glass phials. And of course, sometimes he met grandees and royalty, who dished out decorations and medals. On one occasion when in Vienna, he was unable to pay his enormous hotel bill; so he borrowed the money and, in the lobby, in full public view, paid the proprietor, having lined up the staff to whom he gave extravagant tips.[56] All that was missing was the press corps.

But the considerable stresses and strains of this lifestyle were concealed by the cognac and cigars. He would sometimes reel into a concert blind drunk, although, like Mussorgsky subsequently, he was brilliant enough to carry it off and perform magnificently.[57]

He was not universally well received. Leipzig, home of the Schumanns, did not warm to him. The English, of course, did not approve of him at all: long hair, a 'reputation', vulgar; they much preferred the reputedly aristocratic Thalberg. But in 1840, Liszt played before the queen, having

* This project raised considerable interest among Romantic composers. Schumann planned to help the fund-raising by providing copies of his Piano Fantasie in C for sale.[52]

installed Marie and the three children at Richmond. He played in Reading Town Hall and in Edinburgh. He even performed in a tiny inn at Clonmel, about 100 miles south west of Dublin.[58]

When they were apart, Liszt and Marie often wrote to each other. He continued to be possessive: the suggestion from Charles d'Agoult that she might return to him led the composer to threaten a duel.[59] During the summer months of 1841, 1842 and 1843, when the concert season was over, Liszt would meet up with her and the children on the long narrow island at Nonnenwerth, near Bonn.[60] Downstream, the island has a wonderful view of the Siebengebirge, the ruin on the Drachensfels emerging prominently above; and upstream, there is the magnificent, broad sweep of the Rhine towards Remagen. Steeped in romance and mystery, this was where Roland of Roncevaux had died of love. Liszt and his 'family' stayed in the secularised half-ruined Benedictine convent, which was run as a small hotel. A more Romantic setting could hardly be found.

But the romance between Franz and Marie was doomed. In 1840, George Sand wrote a play about a middle-class mother who fell for a Venetian nobleman; the husband made way, but the noble turned out to be no better than Casanova. The woman, called 'Cosima', committed suicide in order to save her husband from a duel with the lover. Although the play was a flop, its message was ominous.[61]

When Liszt and Marie broke up in 1844, their separation was very bitter. Marie developed a literary career under the pen name Daniel Stern.[62] In this she was perhaps more successful as a journalist and historian than novelist or dramatist. She also ran one of the most fashionable Paris salons in her residence near the Arc de Triomphe.[63] As she herself said, a salon was 'the supreme ambition of the Parisienne, the consolation of her middle age, the glory of her old age'.[64] Hers was a particular focus for left-wing views, both during the upheavals of 1848–9 and during the Second Empire. She wrote a history of 1848, a play on Joan of Arc, a dialogue between Dante and Goethe, and *Mes Souvenirs et Mémoires*.* What particularly incensed Liszt, however, was her novel *Nélida* (an anagram of Daniel) about her

* She was one of the many Romantics who suffered from chronic bouts of acute depression, and attempted suicide. She was frequently admitted to the clinic at Passy, run by the fashionable Dr Blanche. Cosima found her hard to handle when she came to stay. She died in 1876, the same year as George Sand, in Paris, where she lived with her other daughter Claire, Comtesse de Charnacé.

relationship with him. It drew attention to his low-class birth and lack of morals.*

Princess Carolyne von Sayn-Wittgenstein

When in Kiev, during his tours, Liszt met the 28-year-old Princess Carolyne, who was in the city to trade wheat.[66] Liszt went to see her to thank her for some money which she had sent him. She was Polish by birth, and was married at eighteen to a Prussian prince whose father had

Princess Carolyne, in later years, dressed for an audience with the Pope

fought against Napoleon and was aide-de-camp to the Governor of Kiev. By the time Liszt met her, she was estranged from her husband. She was small, dark and plain, and her teeth were stained with the tobacco from the cigars which she smoked. She was an efficient businesswoman, dominant and even slightly masculine. Through her inheritance from her father, she

* Views differ on Liszt's opinion of *Nélida*: Marie's biographer refers to a letter in which he congratulated her on the novel. Sand and Balzac had already written novels based on Liszt's affair with Marie.[65]

was one of the wealthiest heiresses in the Ukraine. Her father had used 30,000 serfs to work his vast estates.[67]

The princess invited Liszt to stay with her and her ten-year-old daughter Marie, who was looked after by 'Scotchy', the governess. It says much for the princess' magnetism that Liszt was prepared to travel the 150 miles to her estate in Voronovytsia, a journey that takes three and a half hours by car today.* When he arrived, he found a gem of a country house, beautifully decorated with stucco, Doric columns and niches. It is placed upon a hill with commanding views for miles over the steppe, the princess' abundant fields of rye, oats, wheat and sugar-beet, and woodland. The approach to it is an avenue of willows.

Although Liszt stayed for only ten days, he returned there after a summer recital tour to Constantinople, which was prolonged by having to go in and out of quarantine. Despite the pleasures of the flesh and the stimulation of the mind, Liszt, dedicated to art as he was, could not linger with the princess in the Ukraine forever. So the excessively serious princess was prepared to sacrifice everything for him. She sold up in April 1848, left Russia, having filed a request for the annulment of her marriage, and settled with Liszt in Weimar.

The Children – a Sequel

Before going with them to Weimar, we should digress and consider what happened to those three children of Liszt and Marie d'Agoult: Blandine, Cosima and Daniel. Because they had been born abroad and were illegitimate, their mother had no rights over them, and Liszt was their legal guardian.[69] When their parents split up, the oldest was not yet ten and the youngest five.

Liszt refused them access to their mother who, he thought, would corrupt them. Yet he himself did not see them for nine years, although he wrote to them and regularly sent money for their upkeep. They were brought up by his mother, and the girls went to a fashionable boarding

* The house, which is in very bad condition, has been a school and a memorial museum to a pioneer aviator who lived there in the early 1870s. Were it not for this, it would surely have been destroyed. Near the house, beyond a statue of Lenin, there is a small Polish church.[68] As for Scotchy, governesses were an important export from Great Britain: later, the Mahlers had an English governess, Miss Turner.

school in the rue Montparnasse. Their other grandmother, the Comtesse de Flavigny, refused to recognise them.

When they surreptitiously got their mother's address and went to see her, Liszt was furious. To supervise them in Paris, he imported from St Petersburg Madame di Fossombroni, a former governess of Princess Carolyne. This septuagenarian's response to the children's lamentations was: 'Tears are only water.'[70] They did not see their mother for a further four years, until they caught sight of her sitting in an audience. Their first reunion with their father was in October 1853, when he arrived with Berlioz, Princess Carolyne and her daughter. Also in the party was Wagner, who proceeded to read to them the closing scene of his poem about the Nibelungen.[71] After eight days, Liszt departed, although nine months later he invited the children for a few days to Brussels.

The children hoped that they might be allowed to live with their father in Weimar; but, as we shall see, their presence would have embarrassed him and the princess, so that particular idea was out of the question. Then Madame di Fossombroni disclosed to Liszt some correspondence between Blandine and her mother. He flew into a rage; when the distraught Blandine suggested that the Madame had no right to show him her private correspondence, Liszt became even more furious.[72]

The girls were sent off to Berlin, to the home on the Wilhelmstrasse of the mother of one of Liszt's pupils, Hans von Bülow, later to be the first superstar conductor.[73] After a disastrous performance of *Tannhäuser*, Cosima comforted its sensitive conductor, who was in a state of shock. Cosima subsequently wrote that Hans' gratitude on this occasion 'was the seed from which our union sprang'.[74] They married in 1857.

Daniel continued to live with his grandmother. He was a very bright boy and was sent to the Lycée Bonaparte, where he tried to live up to his father's demanding expectations of him. He was eventually sent to Vienna to study law, but he died of galloping consumption in December 1859, aged just twenty.[75] When, many years later, Cosima visited his grave, she observed bitterly that her brother had been 'the victim of my father's and mother's thoughtlessness and the cruel indifference of Princess Wittgenstein'. She added: 'At the time, I was too young and inexperienced to oppose them effectively and take firm measures.'[76]

Blandine married Emile Ollivier, who was prime minister at the time when France declared war against Prussia. Blandine died in 1862, following a botched operation to remove an abscess from her left breast following child-birth.[77] It was performed by Ollivier's brother-in-law, an obstetrician but, regrettably, also a bit of a quack.

Weimar – the Altenburg

We move to Weimar, where Liszt and his princess held court in the Altenburg, which now seems rather a nondescript, featureless and small residence for such a wealthy woman. What a contrast to the magnificence of the house and estate at Voronovytsia! But it had magnificent views down over Weimar below and, in the distance, over the broad fields and woods.*[78]

Attended by a staff of five and by Scotchy, the princess and Liszt could dedicate themselves to art. They received a procession of distinguished callers who climbed, or were driven, up the hill to the house. These included George Eliot, the English novelist, and her partner G.H. Lewes who was researching for his biography of Goethe. She was most impressed by Liszt's playing; Scotchy she found 'an amiable but insignificant person'.[79]

Why Weimar? Five years earlier, Liszt had been appointed 'Honorary Kapellmeister' there at the instigation of the heir apparent, who wanted to restore the city of Goethe and Schiller to its former elegance and glory as 'the Athens of the North'. Liszt now wanted more time to compose, his concert career having left him exhausted: he was fed up with being a kind of performing dog.** The presence and support in Weimar of Grand Duchess Maria Pavlovna, sister of the tsar, was another reason: she could influence her brother, Tsar Nicholas I, in the matter of the princess' annulment; she also provided their house.[80]

But their flamboyant presence created a difficult situation, unpleasant for many reasons. It drew the opposition of the proud descendants of the composer Hummel and of the writers Goethe, Schiller, Herder and Wieland. They, living below in the city, were incensed when the Altenburg posed pretentiously and exclusively as the centre for the 'Music of the Future', the 'New German School'. Besides, Liszt and his lady were Roman Catholics, living 'in sin' and corrupting her young daughter. As to Princess Carolyne, they disliked her appearance, her accent and her habit of smoking cigars in public places; Weimar people cut her dead.[81] The Liszt-

* The woods now contain the memorial to the tragedy at Buchenwald, during the Nazi regime.
** A dog at the time was reputed to play dominoes and be acquainted with the principles of geography and botany.

Wittgenstein cause was not helped when unmarried couples being convicted for living together shouted abuse in court about there being one law for some and another law for others.[82]

Aside from all this tittle-tattle, by the mid-1850s, Liszt, aged only around 40, had become the leader of the musical avant-garde.[83] He was responsible for a large number of first performances: in the twelve years at Weimar, he presented 44 different operas, 25 by living composers.[84] Weimar saw the first performance of *Lohengrin* and performances of Berlioz' *Benvenuto Cellini*, and works by Schumann such as *Genoveva* and *Manfred.* Liszt invited Berlioz there twice, for Berlioz weeks. But resources were thin. In an era when the quality of orchestras was notoriously bad, Liszt's standards were very high. Although he badgered the court for more support, it was not forthcoming.

His own compositions flourished.* He updated the first versions of *Années de Pèlerinage*, the Hungarian Rhapsodies, the *Transcendental* and *Paganini Studies*, partly to make them easier to play, partly to reflect the improved technology of the piano. The Sonata in B minor was finished in 1853. It was now that he prepared Bach transcriptions and wrote most of the organ music.

Being fundamentally a pianist, Liszt found writing for the orchestra difficult at first. So, to start with, he used colleagues to help him with the orchestration.[86]

He first used the description 'symphonic poem' in 1854 for *Tasso*. His aim was the 'renewal of music through its inner connection with poetry'.[87] The music, which departed from the classical sonata-form structure, was held together by recurring themes, *idées fixes* or *Leitmotive*, which were moulded through 'metamorphosis' to express his poetry. The work was not intended as a description of the Italian poet Tasso, rather as the representation of the feelings and emotions that the poet aroused in the composer.[88] This was an era when stories were being assigned to many composers' works, Beethoven's and Chopin's among others. Liszt wrote prefaces to his symphonic poems after the music was composed in order to pre-empt others from making their own story to fit.

The disciples who flocked to Liszt became well known in their time: they included Hans von Bülow, the virtuoso pianist Carl Tausig, the com-

* Liszt's *oeuvre* is colossal: there are around 770 entries (some multiple) in the catalogue of his works in *New Grove*.[85]

poser Peter Cornelius, the conductor Karl Klindworth and many others. But it was Liszt's championing of the supremely ungrateful Richard Wagner for which he is best known. We must wait until the next chapter for the story of his assistance to this notorious freedom-fighter when on the run. Liszt deserves great credit for performing and promoting Wagner's works and also for pressing, courageously but largely unsuccessfully, for him to be given an amnesty.

Liszt's advocacy for Wagner did him no good with the court at Weimar, especially after his ducal patron died in 1853. The new duke's interests were directed more towards theatre than opera. Liszt fell out with the theatre manager in Weimar, and conducted very little there after 1858. He resigned after the hissing and lengthy demonstration which took place at his performance of Peter Cornelius' opera, *The Barber of Baghdad*.[89] He gradually withdrew from musical life in the city, although it was to be two and a half years before he left. In 1859, he lost his patron when Grand Duchess Maria Pavlovna died.

Princess Carolyne's Annulment

Meanwhile, things were not going at all well for Carolyne. Some cousins, who felt cheated when left out of her father's will, schemed against her. The tsar turned down her petition for the annulment of her marriage. When she refused to return to Russia, her land and estates were sequestered and eventually were put into trust for her daughter Marie, to whom she had already passed over half of her wealth. Having been once so rich, Carolyne became financially dependent on her daughter; she was also technically an exile, which made her position in Weimar even more difficult.[90]

In return for a large donation by Marie, the Archbishop of St Petersburg eventually granted her mother an annulment, on the basis that she had been forced unwillingly into her original marriage. But this decision was not recognised by the bishop in Germany. Carolyne had to go to Rome to sort out the mess. Her visit was intended to be brief, but she never returned. She was ensnared in a very complicated situation.

The stumbling-block was that her son-in-law Konstantin Hohenlohe,* an aide-de-camp to the King of Prussia, feared that if the annulment

* The Hohenlohes were very well connected and influential: Prince Chlodwig, an older brother, was Chancellor of Germany, 1894–1900.[91]

went through, Marie might be declared illegitimate; if so, their family would lose their entitlement to the whole Sayn-Wittgenstein fortune.[92]

Carolyne had an audience with the Pope, who promised his support for her cause. But Konstantin's brother Gustav Hohenlohe, a senior prelate, had evidence that the Russian annulment had been obtained by exaggerating the extent of force which had been used to get Carolyne to marry her first husband. It was suggested that no more force was applied than the symbolic gesture which a father traditionally made to his daughter during a wedding ceremony in Russia.

In the end, Carolyne's case was upheld, and she and Liszt were free to marry at any time after January 1861. Liszt however, by then, was in no rush. In 1861, he left Weimar and it was seventeen months before he met up with Carolyne in Rome.[93] They swore an intention to marry; all that remained was for the banns to be read. Yet the night before the wedding, a note came from the Pope, prompted by Monsignor Hohenlohe, to say that, to avoid a scandal, he had withdrawn his permission.

Carolyne seems to have lost the will to fight any more. When her husband died in March 1864, the obstacle to marriage with Liszt disappeared; yet they never married. Cosima's explanation seems to tell it all: she was convinced that her father looked forward to his marriage 'as to a burial service'.[94]

Carolyne lived in Rome, so far from the Ukraine, in a smoke-filled apartment, eating chocolates, surrounded by plants and flowers. Before entering, even Liszt had to wait in an outer chamber to avoid letting in any of the fresh air which she loathed.[95] She was much disliked by the Liszt family for her influence upon him. Wagner said: 'When the witch interferes, everywhere is Hell.'[96] The sentiments were reciprocated. She disliked Cosima, whose Protestant divorce, conversion and marriage to Wagner was, in her view, blasphemous, beneath contempt, and a solution which she herself had rejected when attempting to solve her own marriage difficulties.

The princess spent her time writing a 24-volume treatise called the *Interior Causes of the Exterior Weaknesses of the Church in 1870.* Long books were the fashion: Marshal Junot's widow wrote an eighteen-volume *History of Napoleon* and Blandine Liszt's husband's defence of Napoleon III ran to seventeen volumes. But this was a bad time to be writing about the Church. Two of Carolyne's volumes, dealing with the Vatican Council and Appointments, were put on the *Index Librorum Prohibitorum*.[97] The final volume of her book was finished two weeks before her death in March 1887.

Rome, Budapest and Tivoli

In Rome, Liszt lived at first with contemplative Dominican friars in the impenetrable monastery of the Madonna del Rosario on the Monte Mario, a hill which looks over the city towards the Villa Medici. Twice a week, he would leave the monastery and take the half-hour walk down into Rome to teach or attend *soirées*. He transcribed Beethoven symphonies and wrote *St Francis of Assisi Preaching to the Birds* and *St Francis of Paola Walking on the Waters*. He was soon visited by Pope Pius and Gustav Hohenlohe, and was invited to stay in the papal summer palace, Castel Gandolfo.

Monsignor Hohenlohe, having been a supposed antagonist in the matter of the princess, metamorphosed into Liszt's champion. Although Liszt never became a priest, in 1865 Hohenlohe admitted him to minor orders (those of doorkeeper, reader, acolyte and exorcist) and he assumed the status of Abbé. It was, however, a flexible arrangement: he could not celebrate Mass, nor hear Confession, and he undertook no vows of celibacy and could at any time retract.[98] Someone described Liszt as Mephistopheles disguised as an Abbé.[99]

A few days after he took orders, he set out by train to Hungary for the first performance of his oratorio *St Elisabeth*, and to celebrate the 25th anniversary of the Pest Conservatory of Music. Hohenlohe was keen that Liszt should take the lead in developing the musical life of Hungary.

Back in Rome, Liszt moved into Hohenlohe's sumptuous private apartment for fourteen months from mid-1865. There he studied religion, and composed. On becoming a cardinal, Hohenlohe resided in the Renaissance Villa d'Este at Tivoli, about twenty miles from Rome. Liszt was welcome to stay there.[100]

When in Italy, Liszt divided his time between Tivoli, the princess, and his friends in Rome such as Giovanni Sgambati, one of the outstanding pianists of the day, with whom he enjoyed dining, cards and making music. In Tivoli, he lived a secluded life: he attended Mass at dawn, and composed. The Villa is an almost perfect setting.* Inside, it has beautiful

* A traveller a century earlier said, surprisingly: 'Tivoli is but a wretched hole, but has in all ages been celebrated for the salubrity of its air'[101]

murals on its walls. Outside, it has one of the world's most splendid water gardens, in which over 500 water jets play in fountains and cascade down the hill. Here, Liszt composed the Second *Mephisto* Waltz and many other works. He continued to arrange other composers' works, such as Saint-Saëns' *Danse Macabre* and Gounod's Waltz from *Faust*.

Liszt's mother died in 1866 in Paris. When he went there, the French were intrigued to see the Abbé in his clerical collar and cassock. A performance of his 'Gran' Mass* in Saint-Eustache was a disaster: Parisians did not take him seriously as a composer. But he dined at the Tuileries, and Napoleon III presented him with a grotesque bronze cigar holder supported at the corners by four negroes.[103] The emperor talked of the heavy burden of his office. 'There are days when I feel as if I had lived for a century' drew the response from Liszt: 'Sire, you are the century.'[104] Liszt then reduced Empress Eugénie to tears by playing Chopin's Funeral March; and a few days later he received the Légion d'Honneur. He surely shares with Mendelssohn the first prize for obsequiousness.

Weimar – the Garden House

Weimar was keen to have him back, provided the princess did not come too, and provided that the arrangements were less ostentatious than before. So he lodged on the first floor of a little house, formerly the head gardener's house, on the corner of the park. It was diametrically the other end of the city from the Altenburg where he had previously lived. From contemporary prints, one can see that the surroundings in the park were suitably Romantic, being decorated with grottoes, bridges and statuary.[105] In the house, one can see the small drawing room in which he held the master-classes: there is a Bechstein concert-grand piano and an Ibach upright; one can see Liszt's desk and his modest bedroom.[106]

The master-classes, a concept which he virtually invented, were held on Mondays, Wednesdays and Fridays in the afternoon. The housekeeper, one of Carolyne's former domestic servants at the Altenburg, would serve refreshment and cakes.[107]

The focus of these master-classes was on interpretation rather than technique. To them he attracted and created some of the greatest pianists

* He wrote the Missa Solemnis for the opening of the rebuilt cathedral in Gran (Esztergom) in 1856. This was written in an ecstatic style, in contrast to the Renaissance style known as the 'Caecilian' revival, which many other composers were adopting at the time.[102]

of the day. Almost every well-known pianist at the turn of the century had studied with Liszt: Borodin, Albéniz, Anton Rubenstein; Grieg brought his piano concerto to him. Although Liszt himself never practised now, there was so much playing of the piano in Weimar that the authorities had to regulate the practising times and require windows to be shut.[108]

More Travel

Liszt generally spent the first three months of the year in Budapest, the spring in Weimar and the rest of the year in Rome. He called this his 'vie trifurquée'. Wagner told him that these places were his three flagpoles.[109]

Cardinal Hohenlohe wanted him to be appointed official head of music in Budapest. From 1875, he was director of the Hungarian Royal Academy of Music. He was also appointed a royal Hungarian councillor, which entitled him to sit in the legislature. During these years, he must have seen considerable change in Budapest, which by the early 1900s had become the sixth largest city in Europe: it had electric lights in the streets in 1873, a telegraph in 1881, and electric trams in 1887. However, less than a third of the tiny intelligentsia of 128,000 people were book readers. Budapest was characterised by 'cultural lethargy and parochialism'.

In 1878, Liszt's relationship with Hungary was strained when there was severe press criticism of him – the usual stuff, saying that he was a virtuoso but not a lasting composer. He forbade performances of his 'Gran' Mass and withdrew from concerts.[110]

He continued his charitable concerts. In 1876, there were Danube floods reminiscent of the great flood of 1838 when half of Pest was destroyed, so Liszt arranged another charity concert. He was still doing flood relief concerts in March 1879, when a harvest failure also led him to do fund-raising at Tivoli.

He had tremendous energy and continued to travel relentlessly: he did on average 4,000 miles a year.[111] To save time he usually travelled at night, and to save money he travelled third class. But he also suffered from occasional depression and melancholia, especially as he got older. His tendency to consume large amounts of brandy cannot have helped. Although he was rich, with large deposits at the Rothschild bank in Paris, he fell into genteel poverty in the 1870s and 80s. He looked like an old organist, according to Carolyne, shuffling around in a pair of old slippers without heels.[112] The face of a once handsome young man became disfigured with warts.

The Wagners

Liszt was very disapproving when his pupil Hans von Bülow was cuckolded by Cosima having an affair with Wagner. Liszt and Wagner did not meet for five years, but were reconciled around the time of the laying of the foundation stone for the Bayreuth Festspielhaus. The Wagners, who by then had married, visited him in Weimar in September 1872 and heard a performance of *Christus* at Weimar eight months later, although they did not like what they heard, because they were very opposed to Liszt's style. Cosima's diary notes in relation to her father's Second *Mephisto* Waltz: 'We agree that silence is our only proper response to so dismal a production.'[113]

Liszt visited the Wagners frequently and continued to give them unstinting support, which, as a celebrity, was of considerable value. He appeared at a Wagner concert in Budapest in 1875, thus preventing it from being a flop. He was present at the opening ceremony at Bayreuth in 1876. Tension continued, however. As well as disliking Liszt's music, Wagner was irritated by the endless games of whist, and 'the constriction of our living space, all the disturbance arising from his visit'. Cosima put a brave gloss on it: 'It is wonderful and touching to see how these two such fundamentally different natures, who have taken such divergent paths, respect, understand and protect each other.'[114]

Last Years

In 1881, Liszt was immobilised for eight weeks after he fell down the staircase at the Garden House in Weimar. Hans von Bülow and his daughter Daniela came to look after him.[115]

His last years were pathetic. He was depressed, indeed occasionally only his religion deterred him from taking his own life. He became swollen with dropsy, his eyesight deteriorated, and he had no teeth. He had had some dentures made in 1864 by the prominent American dentist in Paris, Thomas Evans, but he never wore them. He was increasingly dependent on alcohol: he consumed a bottle of cognac daily and occasionally two bottles of wine as well; when absinthe became fashionable he took that up.[116]

In 1881, a book which the princess had edited resulted in accusations of anti-Semitism, which was especially awkward in Hungary as it had a large and growing Jewish population. Surprisingly to us, 'particularly sensitive to Jews was her view that they be given their own site in Palestine, by force of western arms if necessary'.[117] Threats to Liszt led to a performance of the *Faust* Symphony in Budapest being cancelled. His piece for the opening of the Budapest Opera was also withdrawn because it was thought excessively nationalist.

In 1882, Liszt joined the Wagners in Venice. In January 1883, he went on to Budapest and there he heard of Wagner's death. When told, he whispered: 'He today, I tomorrow.'[118] That year, Grieg did a concert tour which took in Weimar, where he found Liszt 'incredibly old'. 'It was pitiful to see him', he said.[119]

Nevertheless, Liszt kept up the master-classes. In 1885, there were 41 Weimar classes. One was attended by 40 people; and more than 180 works were played between 28 June and 9 September of that year.[120]

Liszt went on a final tour in 1886, during which he spent sixteen days in London, where he had not been for 45 years. He was received almost as royalty would be. He stopped at Penge on the way, and went to the home of the head of Novello, the publishers. He played at the Royal Academy of Music, and before the queen. She wrote to her daughter: 'We have just heard Liszt, who is such a fine old man. He came down here and played four pieces beautifully. What an exquisite touch.'[121] She gave him a bust of herself as a memento. His oratorio *St Elisabeth* was repeated by popular demand. When he went on to Paris, it was performed at the Trocadéro before 7,000 people. But he took the train from Paris and caught a chill because a pair of lovers wanted to open the window to see the dawn coming up. When he reached home, he had to be lifted from the train.[122]

He attended his granddaughter's wedding in Bayreuth, went to *Parsifal* and *Tristan*; Cosima wanted him to be there to help reinforce her fund-raising activities to pay off the deficit on the building projects at Bayreuth. But his chill developed into pneumonia. He became comatose in the early hours of 31 July; that afternoon, the doctor prescribed a cocktail of heavy wines and champagne which was forced into him and almost revived him. At night, they injected him twice in the region of the heart with either morphine or camphor; he suffered violent convulsions and died at 11.30 pm. No priest had been called and he never received the last rites.[123]

The Wagner family were keen that the Bayreuth Festival should not be disrupted, so the news of Liszt's death was played down. A contemporary said: 'Everything was made to look, as if on purpose, Franz Liszt's passing was not of sufficient importance to dim the glory of the Festival.'[124] He was buried in the general cemetery next to the Lutheran church at Bayreuth, near the grave of the writer Jean Paul. After the funeral, Cosima hurried away in order to supervise that night's performance of *Tristan.*

Why this rather muted end? Was it simply that the 74-year-old had lived beyond his time? Or was it that, by then, musicians such as Clara Schumann regarded him as 'little better than a charlatan',[125] even though, in earlier years, they had been overwhelmed by his performance and personality? To obtain some insight into these aspects, and the times in which he lived, we should look briefly at Liszt's showmanship, his nationalism, his Roman Catholicism, and his relationship with his women. These are some of the matters which caused unease.

Showmanship

Liszt was a showman, with some justification. Some say he was the greatest ever pianist; many of his piano works are recognised to be phenomenally difficult, such as the *Transcendental Studies.* He also had the ability to sight-read a work as difficult as Grieg's Piano Concerto.[126] He benefited from having unusually long fingers so that he could play tenths as easily as most performers play octaves. But, as well as having these attributes, he also worked very hard. He would, in his early years at least, often practise for ten to twelve hours a day.[127] When he was in his 60s, he slowed down. Brahms could write: 'As you know, people are used to exceptional entertainment from Liszt'; but he added: 'I'm really pleased that at last, grey hair and all, he presented an image which does not make a complete caricature of the magnificent person.'[128]

Although the bourgeois worships the celebrity who lightens up his life, a bourgeois competitor does not always see it that way. Schumann told his wife when he met Liszt for the first time: 'How extraordinary his playing is, so bold and daring, and then again so tender and delicate! I have never heard anything like it. But his world is not mine, Clärchen. Art, as we know it – you when you play, I when I compose – has an intimate charm that is worth more to me than all Liszt's splendour and tinsel.'[129]

Publicity, celebrity, scandal – all this was symptomatic of the features which the Schumanns and their circle felt corrupted the purity of proper Romantic music, and fought so bitterly: for them, the very future of music was at stake. They disliked the way Liszt ignored the classical formal structures, such as sonata form. They associated him with those composers, like Meyerbeer, who were concerned more with providing entertainment than with the quality of the art that they created.

This criticism became particularly acrimonious when Franz Brendel, Schumann's successor as editor of the *Neue Zeitschrift*, championed Liszt's New German School. Brahms weighed in, as we shall see, and attacked this. Liszt never played a single work of Brahms in public.[130] Clara Schumann refused to go on the same stage as Liszt at the Mozart Centenary Festival in January 1856.[131] The violinist Joachim, who was at first patronised by Liszt, turned against him. They did not speak to each other for nearly 25 years after 1857.

Nationalism

If Liszt's showmanship gave the impression that he was bogus, so did his association with Hungarian nationalism. His contribution to Hungarian musical education was indeed considerable; however, his nationalistic credentials are suspect. He is sometimes described as a Hungarian composer, but he never learnt to speak 'the daunting Magyar language'.[132] The Liszts were German and had only recently Magyarised their name from List.[133] His music is essentially Teutonic and the Hungarian features, usually gypsy-inspired,* are but a veneer. Indeed, Bartók – 'the greatest musician ever produced by Hungary'[135] – said that Liszt 'seldom writes in Hungarian'.[136] Yet Hungary claimed Liszt as its son, and he gloried in its adulation.

This started early on. He was given a tremendous reception when he performed in Hungary in 1839. He travelled in what he called 'toute une caravane aristocratique'. The crowds particularly enjoyed his arrangement of the Rákóczy March, music associated with a noble who led a serf rebellion in the early 1700s and thus symbolised freedom and nationalism.[137] Liszt, wearing a Hungarian costume, took part in torchlight processions, addressing the crowd in French. To his delight, they tried to unearth an aristocratic background for him. In January 1840 in Pest, he was presented with a jewelled Sword of Honour addressed 'to the great artist Ferenc Liszt

* The cafés of Paris, Berlin and St Petersburg exploited an image of the Hungarian relaxing in an alcoholic haze to the sound of a fiddle played 'in his ear' by a gypsy. Hence the international popularity of folksy, sentimental or noisy so-called Hungarian gypsy music, whose provenance and authenticity was, at best, doubtful.[134]

for his artistic merit and for his patriotism from his admiring compatriots'.[138] This caused some wry comment elsewhere in Europe.

His patriotism, Hungarian or otherwise, was not greatly in evidence when Europe exploded in 1848. This was at the time that he and Carolyne moved to Weimar, which was relatively quiet.[139] She was ill and Liszt could not leave her; apart from visiting a few barricades in Vienna, Liszt, unlike Wagner, took no part. As this was a dreadful time for Hungarian nationalists, and Liszt attracted some criticism, it is relevant to know what he managed to avoid.

Hungarian nationalism was particularly potent. The country was dominated by 50 spectacularly wealthy Roman Catholic families, such as the Esterházys and Pálffys, who lived like maharajahs.[140] Beneath, there were 40,000 Magyar gentry, predominantly Protestant, fiercely nationalistic. The Hungarians knew that it was with their backing that the Habsburgs had retained their status as a great power; they knew that they had agreed to the succession of Empress Maria Theresa back in 1740 only on condition that their constitution was granted in perpetuity.[141]

A hundred years later, politicians in Hungary and Bohemia wanted to have home rule. Following demonstrations in Vienna in March 1848, the long-serving Chancellor Prince Metternich fled, and Emperor Ferdinand conceded a constitution for Hungary under a government brokered by Count Batthyány.[142]

Even though violence continued in Vienna, and the Habsburg court had escaped to Innsbruck, the tide soon turned as support dwindled. The peasantry was mollified by the abolition of the feudal system; as in other countries, the middle classes were worried about revolutionary excess. The Habsburgs achieved counter-revolution in Italy. Soon, Prague, where extremists had taken over, was bombarded into submission, and the disturbances in Vienna were crushed.[143]

The government then dealt with Hungary, at first with some difficulty. The constitution was withdrawn and Batthyány resigned. In early October, there was a mutiny by one of the regiments in Vienna which had been ordered to attack Hungary; rioters took control of old Vienna, and a government minister was lynched. The royal family fled, this time to Olmütz; Vienna was evacuated by the middle class. The city was surrounded, and bombarded; there were 2,000 arrests and 25 executions.

The Habsburg family concern, led by a formidable array of ladies, forced Emperor Ferdinand, 'a good-natured but retarded epileptic',[144] to abdicate. They passed over his brother and appointed his nephew as emperor. He assumed the name Franz Joseph (see colour plate 25). As he was not contaminated by any compromises with revolutionaries, he had a free hand. He set about creating a unified state.

The patriot Lajos Kossuth, who had been a member of Batthyány's government, refused to recognise Franz Joseph's authority. So the Hungarian revolution continued. Franz Joseph,* in considerable desperation, turned to Tsar Nicholas I of Russia for support. He also exploited the traditional Croat hatred of Magyar. The Hungarians with 150,000 men and 450 cannon were no match for the pincer movement of Russians, Austrians and Croats who had almost double the number of men and 12,000 cannon. When the Hungarians surrendered, Kossuth got away, at first to Turkey; but thirteen generals and 114 others, including Batthyány,** were executed on the bloody morning of 6 October 1849, and 2,000 were imprisoned.[146] Hungary, an occupied country, Liszt's native land, to all intents and purposes ceased to exist.

Meanwhile, Liszt kept his head well down. He first returned to Hungary in August 1856 for the dedication of the great Basilica high above the Danube at Gran.

Franz Joseph's policy to unify Hungary with Austria was unworkable. A rapid U-turn established the union of the two sovereign states within one monarchy. This compromise (known as the Ausgleich) was solemnised with a coronation in Budapest on 8 June 1867. For this, Liszt wrote a special Mass. The empress wore clothes designed by Worth;[147] nobles were clad in bearskins or carried animal heads.[148] It must have made a colourful, even bizarre, spectacle. It is not surprising that, when the crowd applauded Liszt, a tall imposing figure in a long black cassock studded with decorations, he liked to think that they could have mistaken him for the emperor.[149] His skill at managing his personal position certainly deserved such recognition.

* The elderly Franz Joseph, then revered by many, took the world into the Great War of 1914–18.

** Franz Joseph's mother was in love with Batthyány and, because she was spurned, insisted he die, so the story goes. Batthyány's mistress smuggled a knife into the prison in a loaf of bread; as a consequence of the damage he inflicted upon himself, Batthyány could not be hanged, but was shot.[145]

Roman Catholicism

Liszt's Roman Catholicism has also caused unease, especially when considered in conjunction with his womanising. Rome was a surprising place for him to make his base at that time. The middle of the century was most turbulent for the Papacy and the Roman Catholic Church, both on the political front, which was fraught, and in relation to dogma, which was contentious.

Pius IX, Pio Nono, fled from Rome 90 miles south to Gaeta during the 1848–9 upheavals (see page 291). Although a person of warmth and charm, he had diametrically changed from his liberal and nationalist stance (in which he appeared to support the unification of Italy). He now vigorously asserted the inseparability of his temporal powers as ruler of the Papal States and his supra-national spiritual powers as head of the Church. He believed that he held the States in trust for all Roman Catholics; he knew that his status as ruler enhanced his prestige among other sovereigns; besides, a Pope could not become the subject of another sovereign. He 'would prefer the death of a martyr to the repetition of the blunder he committed in going to Gaeta'.[150] He claimed that, in implementing this policy, he was entitled to support from other Christian states. France responded, and thus the Pope was sustained in Rome by the force of a French garrison. All this so angered one young man that he murdered the Archbishop of Paris in January 1857.[151]

The good Pope delegated political matters to his secretary of state, Cardinal Antonelli, a supporter of Princess Carolyne. Antonelli has been described as an 'anachronistic reminder of the age of the Borgias':[152] his brother ran a bank. He allowed the economy of the area around Rome to become deplorable, depressed and infected with malaria. The 'Legations' were not so bad: Bologna, where silk and hemp were produced, was the only genuine industrial centre; but the Papal States were backward compared with burgeoning Lombardy. An attempt to assassinate Antonelli in 1855 was foiled. The assassin was publicly guillotined, the fifteenth person to be beheaded in the States during one month.[153] Before the execution, in the presence of the priests who had been sent to him, he sang several times Manrico's execution aria from Verdi's *Il Trovatore*.

Pius himself concentrated on theology, particularly on determining three matters about which there was no unanimity: the doctrine of the

Immaculate Conception, the Syllabus of Errors, and the matter of Papal Infallibility. The doctrine that St Anne, the grandmother of Christ, had been a virgin at the time of Mary's birth was not new. In 1830, in the rue du Bac in Paris, St Catherine Labouré saw the Virgin bearing a scroll which read: 'O Mary, conceived without sin, pray for us who have need of you.' In June 1848, when most people in Italy were preoccupied with other matters, Pius set up a commission to consider the doctrine. Six years later, with the support of a large majority of bishops, he proclaimed that: 'the most blessed Virgin Mary, in the first instant of her conception … was preserved free from all stain of original sin.'[154] The truth of this appeared to be confirmed when, in February 1858, in a grotto at Lourdes in the foothills of the Pyrenees, Bernadette Soubirous, the fourteen-year-old daughter of an impoverished miller, saw the first of several apparitions. At the sixteenth, six weeks later, Our Lady revealed to her 'Que soy era Immaculada Conceptiou' – 'I am the Immaculate Conception'.[155] By then, the crowds had arrived and the first miracle, in which a woman's dislocated arm was healed, had taken place.*

A more divisive issue was the Syllabus of Errors, which the Pope published in 1864. In this he listed 80 propositions, being the chief errors and false doctrines of the age. The 80th proposition condemned the notion that the Roman Pontiff should reconcile and harmonise himself with 'Progress, Liberalism and Modern Civilisation'.[157] This appalled many distinguished Roman Catholic scholars and, of course, Protestants.

The divisions soon emerged in Austria–Hungary, a loyally Roman Catholic realm. The Pope condemned as 'infamous laws' (*leges infandae*) legislation which wrested back from the Church such matters as education and marriage. All over the age of fourteen were to be given the choice of

* This must have seemed curious to scientists and others who, since the 1830s, had been discussing the theory of evolution. Darwin's paper 'On the Origin of Species by Means of Natural Selection' was eventually published in 1859. But to theologians such as John Henry Newman (later Cardinal), a scientific discovery which appeared to contradict a truth of revelation merely exposed a limitation in our understanding: 'Mr Darwin's theory need not be atheistical, be it true or not: it may simply be suggesting a larger idea of Divine prescience and skill.' Some composers took a similar view: for Mahler, for example, the belief in a hereafter had an 'inner truth' to which rational argument was irrelevant. The French composer Henri Duparc, whose suffering from a crippling neurosis had caused him to abandon composition, obtained considerable relief from a visit to Lourdes, although he became blind and paralysed. Marianism in France reached a peak in the 1870s, when there were nine major apparitions.[156]

whether to go to confession, and, in mixed marriages, the government in Vienna decreed that the son should follow the father's religion and the daughter the mother's. The Bishop of Linz, patron of Anton Bruckner, supported the Pope's hard-line position in a pastoral letter. When he was arrested for breach of the peace, he claimed that he was not subject to civil courts. He was dragged before the courts and condemned to fourteen days in prison, which he avoided only by receiving an imperial pardon.[158]

Yet despite this unsatisfactory situation, the Pope's prestige was at its height, and his Church was spreading its influence in the New World, in Africa and South America. The Pope's picture could be found in many Roman Catholic households. Amongst all the confusion, people yearned for a firm and authoritative papal voice. This background provided the Pope, and his assistant, Archbishop Manning of Westminster, with the confidence to press ahead with the issue of Papal Infallibility. Accordingly, the first general council of the Church for over 300 years was opened in December 1869. Almost as the Franco-Prussian War began and the French garrison withdrew, the Pope rose to say the words 'definimus et apostolica auctoritate confirmamus'. The Pope is infallible when, in discharge of the office of Pastor and Doctor of all Christians, he defines a doctrine regarding faith and morals to be held by the Universal Church.*[160]

Liszt's view on this was that 'our Church is only so strong because it exacts total obedience. We must obey, even if we hang for it.'[161] He gave his support to the Syllabus of Errors. Nevertheless, he genuinely admired the more liberal stance of his mentor, Cardinal Hohenlohe, who became so disillusioned that he left Rome.**

Liszt's opponents sarcastically drew attention to a similarity between papal pronouncements and Liszt's set-up at Weimar, at which a new phase of genius was announced at least once a month 'with solemn strokes of the tamtam'.[162] Doubts about Liszt were also intensified by a perception that he was anti-Semitic: critics to the north regarded him as 'guilty by association' with Wagner's anti-Jewish views, and also those of Princess Carolyne.

* The consequences were considerable and awkward for many. King Ludwig of Bavaria was put in such a bad humour that it affected his generosity to Wagner who, at the time, was desperate for funds to build his opera house.[159]

** Hohenlohe was seen as a candidate for the papal succession. When, in 1878, Leo XIII became Pope, Hohenlohe continued to oppose the Vatican, even to the extent that he was in fear of assassination. He died suddenly of a heart attack in October 1896.

Five of the most prominent people who opposed the style of Liszt's New German School were Jewish – Mendelssohn, Joachim, Hiller, Ferdinand David and Hanslick.[163]

Women

Possibly the most damning indictment of Liszt arises from his attitude to women. Even though he never took a vow of chastity, Liszt's views on religion and sex seemed incompatible to many. One biographer has said that Liszt 'collected princesses and countesses as other men collect rare butterflies, or Japanese prints, or first editions'.[164] Liszt had two great love-affairs,

This time, Liszt was 'seduced': in 1885, Fräulein Senkrah persuaded him to feature in her promotional literature

with Marie and Carolyne. But he was fundamentally promiscuous, enjoying many women as he toured around, some better known than others. It is somewhat sordid to recite his conquests, after the manner of Leporello in *Don Giovanni*. But it is necessary to make some reference, to complete the picture.

Liszt had a brief three-week fling with the Limerick-born dancer and adventuress Lola Montez, who was later to seduce and bring down King Ludwig I of Bavaria.[165] Liszt's affair with her caused Marie d'Agoult to say that, 'while she did not object to being Liszt's mistress, she did object to being one of his mistresses'.[166] He also reputedly had an affair with Marie Duplessis,* the Lady of the Camellias, who was to become the subject of Dumas' novel and Verdi's *La Traviata*. She was the typical Paris courtesan, a role so many women chose to perform just to survive. In 1845, according to one account, Liszt was sitting in a theatre foyer with a colleague, a music critic, when she just sat down beside him. Liszt gave her piano lessons.

While in Weimar, Liszt had an affair** with the cousin of one of his pupils, the 28-year-old, sexually experienced, Agnès Klindworth. He used many pretexts to deceive Carolyne about this, even after Agnès had left Weimar six months pregnant.[168]

Another intimate friend was Baroness Olga von Meyendorff, the widow of a Russian ambassador to Weimar. A more colourful picture was provided by one of his pupils in Rome: Olga Janina, aged nineteen, was determined to have him. She wore a jacket and trousers and smoked cigars, took drugs, cut her hair short like a man, and carried both a revolver and a dagger. Liszt conceded that 'George Sand seems faint and timid to her'.[169] She was ostensibly a cossack countess, but all Polish ladies abroad were supposed to be countesses. Her father was actually a boot polish manufacturer from Lemberg.

Olga followed Liszt to Tivoli, got in disguised as a garden boy, seduced him, and, afraid that he might repent, resolved to stab him if his first words were not of love. She then pursued him to Weimar and Hungary. She pushed into his apartment in Budapest on one occasion and threatened to kill him and poison herself. Olga was a bad pianist, and the affair came to an end after Liszt was infuriated by her lapse of memory during a disastrous concert performance.

When he was approaching 60, Liszt can hardly have been exactly 'a

* Marie's father was a tinker, the product of a prostitute and a priest. She was successively a maid at an inn, a laundress, a milliner, and a prostitute. During a canter through the peerage, she was picked up by a duke, and then by a young *vicomte* by whom she had a son. A baron set her up, provided she gave up prostitution. In 1846 she was married in Kensington Registry Office to an impecunious count, who then left her with no money. She died, aged 23, the following year.[167]

** It has been suggested that Agnès was sent by her father, previously Metternich's spymaster, to gather intelligence on the various 1848 fugitives who passed through the Altenburg.

gazelle or young stag upon rugged mountains'. On one occasion, Olga referred to the Song of Solomon* in the presence of Cardinal Hohenlohe. He rebuked her, and asked Liszt if she had ever paraphrased the Song for him. She saucily replied that 'the Abbé prefers the real thing'.[171]

Liszt was a formidably great musician and innovator. We must surely try to avoid allowing the frail humanity of his kaleidoscopic personality to be intermingled with, and cloud, his musical reputation.

Besides, during Cosima's bust-up with Hans, Liszt advised her that 'passion dies, but the pangs of conscience remain'.[172] One imagines that he was deeply concerned that there was no priest available to minister to him when he lay on his shoddy deathbed in Bayreuth.

* 'Open to me, my sister, my love, my dove, my perfect one; for my head is wet with dew, my locks with the drops of the night' (*inter alia*).[170]

WAGNER

CHAPTER 14

WHEREAS LISZT MAY have caused controversy, few composers are so lastingly controversial as his son-in-law, Richard Wagner. Bizet regarded him as the greatest living composer of his time. But for Berlioz, the Prelude to *Tristan* proceeded 'with no theme other than a sort of chromatic groaning'. Scriabin thought that there were two or three enchanting moments in *Die Walküre*, but 'all the rest is frightfully dull'. Indeed Verdi, no Wagner enthusiast, said that he dozed off during *Tannhäuser*. After watching *Das Rheingold*, Clara Schumann wrote: 'The whole evening I felt as though I were wading about in a swamp.' The 20th-century novelist Virginia Woolf disliked the 'bawling sentimentality'. Leo Tolstoy thought the opera *Siegfried* was a 'stupid Punch and Judy show, which is much too poor for children over seven years of age. Moreover', he continued, 'it is not music. And yet thousands of people sit there and pretend to like it.'[1]

There are some matters on which people do tend to agree about Wagner – this extraordinary man who was five feet five inches tall with an outsize head and a vile temper.[2] That he was utterly unscrupulous, totally self-obsessed, and rapacious. That most of his voluminous writings are not only tedious but often virulently offensive.[3] That there are stretches of his music, particularly during a description or explanation, when an ordinary listener becomes bored and the mind inevitably wanders.

Also, Wagner's poor reputation can be attributed to his anti-Semitism: Hitler was a notorious fan of his works. Yet, many Jews have admired his irrepressible energy and charm. They recognised that Wagner's genius and the beauty of his works overrode his views and character: the person whom he asked to lead the fund-raising for the enormous project to build an opera house at Bayreuth was Jewish;[4] Hermann Levi conducted the première of *Parsifal*; Bruno Walter had no reservations about performing his operas; Georg Solti issued the first recording of the complete *Ring*;[5] Daniel Barenboim conducts his works.

A mark of the great composer is to do something different. As such, Wagner was astonishingly ambitious and influential. Others before had thought of creating an amalgam of 'philosophy, politics, history and literature, as well as myth, language, poetry, drama and music'[6] – a *Gesamtkunstwerk* – but never with such imagination or such vision. In the first few bars of *Tristan*, Wagner takes us from the 19th century into the 20th, in one leap.[7] It has been claimed that 'never since Orpheus has there been a musician whose music affected so vitally the life and art of generations'.[8] His contemporaries were amazed; of course, those merely out for an evening's entertainment knew that they were in the wrong place.

We shall follow Wagner's struggle to build a career, and his part as a revolutionary in 1848. After a lucky escape, he settled in Zurich, where he wrote and read rather than composed.* When the businessman bankrolling him was about to discover that Wagner was having an affair with his wife, it was time to move on. The wanderer became increasingly desperate for his compositions to be performed. As is well known, King Ludwig II of Bavaria came to his help. But Ludwig's support was unpopular and Wagner was thrown out of Munich. He moved to Switzerland, where Cosima von Bülow joined him and became his wife. We shall look at their life together and see him achieve his dream of building an opera house suitable for his works to be performed. We shall observe his total self-centredness, born not so much from the need to satisfy his personal desires but because he was one of those artists who 'made their honey as do the bees, and in truth this honey benefited all others, but could be made only on condition of not thinking about others while they made it'.[9] The Wagners moved to

* The library at Wahnfried contains over 2,300 books and scores.

Bayreuth, but, like his Flying Dutchman, he was always on the move: his death was in Venice.

EARLY DAYS

On 22 May 1813, Richard Wagner was born in Leipzig, in Saxony. This was shortly before Napoleon's Grand Army was defeated in the battle there.* In the wake of military action there was usually an epidemic: so, typhus killed Wagner's supposed father, a policeman who enjoyed amateur dramatics. Wagner's mother then married Ludwig Geyer, an actor in the court theatre in Dresden who had comforted her while the policeman was away with one of the amateur actresses. Geyer was very attached to her son, and fulfilled the role of father. As a consequence, for a long time the boy was known as 'Geyer' rather than 'Wagner'.[10] He was a lively lad: there is a drawing of him fooling around with his sister, imitating fairground tightrope walkers, dressing in masks and ambushing passers-by.[11]

The family moved to Prague, where his sister Rosalie, one of the family's main breadwinners, had a job as an actress. When Wagner was fifteen, they moved on to Leipzig, where he went to the St Nicolas school. There, he was more interested in writing a play which he tried to set to music, than in the normal curriculum. He studied counterpoint and piano with the Cantor of St Thomas', and he made a piano transcription of Beethoven's Ninth Symphony, but he had no formal musical education as such.

As he grew up, he seems to have been boisterous, and joined his fellow-students in their gambling, swaggering and brawling.[12] He was involved in five duels.[13] These were a regular feature of Teutonic student life, and the wounds were regarded as a mark of honour.** Wagner was involved in

* Saxony, one of the more prominent German states, had a tendency to 'back the wrong horse'. After the Battle of Leipzig, the king was taken prisoner and the country was ruled as a defeated nation. The Congress of Vienna in 1815 gave well over half of its territory, including Thuringia, to the Prussians. Saxony made the further mistake of backing the Austrians in the war of 1866. After this, it lost its army; its postal service and foreign representation were given to the Prussians.

** The weapon used was a sword with a blade of three and a half feet. This was wielded by the wrist. The body was thoroughly covered, with only the face exposed; the eyes were protected by metal spectacles or a peaked cap. After honour was satisfied, the duellists usually went to the beer cellar. The mortality rate was tiny, only about half a per cent. Even in 1890, the Kaiser praised duelling clubs for 'providing the best education which a young man can get for his future life'. In the Paris of the mid-1890s, an improbable duellist, Marcel Proust, fought with pistols in a forest outside the city; even in 1908, he was challenging someone to a duel. In Hungary, those briefly imprisoned for duelling could reasonably expect butler-service from their gaolers.[14]

proper street-fighting in July 1830, in response to the revolutionary events in France. But he seems to have suffered little more than a hangover the next day. Around this time he became interested in politics, and associated with members of the pro-democratic and subversive group called Young Germany.

The Struggle to Get Going

In January 1833, Wagner left Leipzig to stay with his brother Albert at Würzburg, where he was appointed chorus master and was responsible for taking the singers through their parts in spectaculars such as Marschner's *Der Vampyr* and Meyerbeer's *Robert le Diable*. Wagner disliked these operas; he considered that the audience simply gaped at the usually absurd and crude spectacle in front of them, and were not emotionally or intellectually involved.[15] Also, he much preferred the musical style of Weber, and particularly admired his opera *Euryanthe*. The following year, Wagner wrote the music for his first opera, *Die Feen* (The Fairies). Two years later, he wrote *Das Liebesverbot* (The Ban on Love, or Measure for Measure).

Around this time, Wagner first heard the soprano Wilhelmine Schröder-Devrient, whom Beethoven had asked to perform Leonore in the revival of *Fidelio*. She had also created the role of Agathe for Weber's *Der Freischütz*.[16] She inspired Wagner so much that he eventually had her portrayed as Tragedy over the door of his house in Bayreuth; and she was even in his thoughts a few days before he died.[17] Not everyone admired her. Berlioz disliked her way of interspersing her singing 'with spoken phrases and interjections, like our vaudeville actors in their couplets, the effect of which is execrable … she never sings such words as O God; yes; no; impossible. They are always spoken or rather shouted in the loudest voice.' He dismissed her style as 'most anti-musical and trivial, and beginners ought to be warned against imitating it'.[18]

Wagner reluctantly took a job as musical director of a fleapit in tiny Lauchstädt, near Handel's birthplace of Halle. The theatre company moved on to Magdeburg, where Wagner built a reputation as a good conductor and staged *Das Liebesverbot*. Schröder-Devrient took part in a benefit concert for him; but it was not a success because many did not expect her to turn up, and so stayed away. Those who attended were deafened by the sound effects and cannon in a performance of Beethoven's 'Battle' Symphony.

In Lauchstädt, Wagner met Christine Wilhelmine Planer, known as Minna, and her daughter Natalie, who had been fathered by an officer who had deserted her. After the theatre company went bust, Wagner joined Minna in the Baltic port of Königsberg, where she was already involved with another man. Nevertheless, she and Wagner were married in November 1836 and began their quarrelsome life together. Six months later, she went off with a merchant. Wagner traced her to Dresden; they were reconciled, yet soon she was off again. He then became conductor at Riga for two seasons, and hoped that his marriage would become more stable.[19] The relationship cannot have been eased by Minna's miscarriage, caused by their escape across the border into East Prussia in order to avoid their creditors. The cart toppled over and the Wagners landed in a heap of manure. They then stowed away on a ship bound for London, a journey which gave him some ideas for *Der Fliegende Holländer* (The Flying Dutchman).[20]

In London there was no welcome, so they crossed the Channel to Boulogne where they met Meyerbeer, who gave them introductions to officials at the Paris Opéra. Wagner wanted to get his opera *Rienzi* staged in Paris, where they now spent two and a half poverty-stricken years. Some writers attribute Wagner's anti-Semitism to his perception that a clique of powerful Jews was responsible for rejecting his opera, and also to his annoyance at his dependence on money-lenders, mostly presumably Jewish, at this time. 'He knew what it was like to have no soles to his shoes, to have pawned most of his furniture, to live on bread and potatoes for six months and have cheeks sunken with hunger, to be threatened with imprisonment for debt.'[21] He borrowed off the husband of his stepsister Cécile, who lived in Paris. He did hack work doing piano arrangements of popular works by other composers such as Donizetti, and he prepared vocal scores. He also earned fees for articles in journals such as the *Revue et Gazette Musicale*.[22] In June 1840, he obsequiously sent to Meyerbeer a sketch for a one-act opera based on *Der Fliegende Holländer*. He was rebuffed; and he did not endear himself to the leaders of the Paris opera world by subsequently sending a review to Schumann's journal in which he reported that Fromental Halévy, the distinguished composer of *La Juive*, was 'not a deliberately cunning swindler like Meyerbeer'.[23]

There was no hope of getting the Paris opera community to stage *Rienzi*, but the Dresden Opera agreed to it being performed. In April

1842, the Wagners travelled across Germany for its première. Wagner subsequently wrote: 'I saw the Rhine for the first time; with tears swelling in my eyes I, a poor artist, swore eternal loyalty to my German fatherland.'[24]

The story of *Rienzi*, in which the hero brings to an end the corrupt rule of the aristocracy, struck a chord in these increasingly troubled times, and was a success in Dresden. At last, Wagner's position was beginning to improve. Schröder-Devrient, who took part in *Rienzi*, sang the role of Senta in *Der Fliegende Holländer*, which followed in January 1843. She also lent Wagner money. Persuaded by Minna and by Weber's widow, the 30-year-old Wagner accepted an appointment as one of the conductors at Dresden.

Tannhäuser, his 'first fusion of lust and piety',[25] was completed and staged in Dresden in 1845. *Lohengrin* was written in the following year, while Wagner was spending the summer in a small house just outside the city, near the royal palace of Pillnitz.

The 1848 Revolutionary

It was to be expected that Wagner, by now prominent as composer, conductor and journalist, would be drawn into the circle of intellectuals who met at a restaurant in Dresden. There they discussed political and philosophical issues of the time, such as Hegel's novel view that the world is always in a process of change. One member of the group was August Röckel, a failed musician and political activist who had been involved in Paris in 'Les Trois Glorieuses' of 1830. He was a nephew of the composer Hummel, and son of the first Florestan in Beethoven's *Fidelio*. Wagner found a position for him at the Dresden Opera. Röckel introduced Wagner to the arch-revolutionary anarchist, Michael Bakunin.[26]

In the mid-1840s, Wagner believed that soon there was bound to be an upheaval, which was not an unreasonable view to take.[27] Various forces – industrial, agricultural and religious – were contributing to the growing unrest. Germany, still a conglomeration of many antiquated states, had been experiencing the pressures and tensions arising from industrialisation. Some of the businesses which are now so familiar – Krupp and Siemens for example – began to appear. The first railway was built in 1834, and during the 1840s the length of track (if Austria is included) grew from 600 to 4,000 miles. Just as the mechanisation of the textile industry in England forced down wages, so the German textile workers' incomes were squeezed below subsistence levels.[28]

With food accounting for 80 per cent of the spending of poor families, agricultural stability was crucial.[29] But there were harvest failures in 1845–7, years which many associate with the appalling famine in Ireland when nearly 29 per cent of the population died in the province of Connaught, following the import of potato blight from North America.[30] In Continental Europe, when the price of rye and potatoes doubled, parts of the rural population had to resort to eating grass, clover and potato peelings. There were sporadic outbreaks of trouble with peasant revolts, and considerable disruption among the weavers. In parallel, there were also rumblings from Protestants who were concerned about the revival of Roman Catholicism.*

The usual sleaze at the top level of society attracted publicity. The Prussian king was known as the 'red-nosed king' because of his liking for drink; one of his brothers was embroiled in financial scandals; another's wife had an affair with a huntsman that led to a messy divorce. The 60-year-old King Ludwig I of Bavaria, creator of 19th-century Munich, went off with the 'Spanish' dancer and adventuress, Liszt's girlfriend, Lola Montez.

All this provoked considerable dissent, but the regimes cracked down on it. When the professors in Göttingen protested against the abolition of the constitution in 1837, the King of Hanover** dismissed them, and remarked that 'professors and whores can always be had for money'.[32] Austria banned 5,000 books, including works by Spinoza, Rousseau, Goethe and Schiller; censors even monitored inscriptions on gravestones, cuff-links and tobacco boxes. Because people had no right to associate together in large groups, much of the dissent was fostered in gymnastic groups and choral societies. The German choral societies soon had at least 100,000 members.

The revolutions which broke out in 1848 began, as we have seen, in Sicily. In February, King Louis-Philippe was thrown out of Paris. As in 1830, 'sympathetic' uprisings took place elsewhere – in Vienna, Prague and Budapest. In Berlin, barricades built out of carts, beams and woolsacks

* In 1844, half a million pilgrims went to see 'the Holy Coat' displayed in Trier. In Leipzig in 1845, there were shootings when the king's brother Prince John, a staunch supporter of the Jesuits, was insulted at a military review.

** The Duke of Cumberland, who succeeded his brothers George IV and William IV to the throne of Hanover, was an arch-reactionary, a born mischief-maker, and was said to have ravished his sister and murdered his valet. The birth of Princess Victoria fortunately prevented his succession to the throne of England where, unlike Hanover, women were not debarred from the succession.[31]

went up on 18 March: 300 people were killed. In Saxony, the king's initial response was to dismiss his ministry and, just like his fellow monarchs elsewhere, to agree to reform. Liberals across Europe demanded freedom of speech and association, the abolition of serfdom, and judicial reform, including trial by jury.[33]

Wagner's actions in this crisis seem to have been driven by his egocentricity and his need for cash. He welcomed the changes, but was inactive until the end of April, when he had finished writing *Lohengrin*. In May, he presented a lengthy 'Plan for the Organisation of a German National Theatre for the Kingdom of Saxony', in which he called for the administration of the orchestra and theatre to be democratised. Had this been accepted and had he been appointed sole Kapellmeister, which was possibly all he wanted, his revolutionary enthusiasm might have been dulled.[34]

As it was, when rebuffed, Wagner dug himself in deeper. On 14 July, he made a speech entitled: 'How do republican aspirations stand in relation to the Monarchy?' In this he rejected 'communism' but called for the abolition of the aristocracy; he said that the king should be the first and most genuine republican. The authorities responded by removing *Rienzi* from Dresden opera repertoire. Wagner tried to justify himself in letters addressed to the king, and then set off for Vienna, where he took part in revolutionary activity. Back in Dresden, *Lohengrin* was cancelled because of Wagner's article 'Germany and its Rulers', which appeared in Röckel's paper. Wagner's tone became increasingly radical: 'I will shatter the power of the mighty, of the law and of property', he declared.[35]

As elsewhere, the revolutionary activity was too successful too quickly, and the leaders were lulled into a false sense of security. It was only a matter of time before the counter-revolution. The peasantry lost interest in revolution once feudal privileges were abolished. The people in Saxony were not interested in deep social issues. They were a nation of hard-working, self-reliant people who just wanted a framework of stability and the rule of law in which to thrive. Besides, the army stayed loyal to the king.[36]

Meanwhile, some self-appointed liberal officials and lawyers met and planned elections. This 'Frankfurt Parliament' was just a talking-shop. It 'had a minister of the interior without police, a minister of finance without revenue'.[37] The Parliament offered the German crown to the King of Prussia, but he did not see the point of being beholden to such a gathering, so refused the offer. The parliament eventually fizzled away.

In Dresden, the authorities prohibited a public demonstration, planned for 2 May 1849, in support of the Frankfurt parliament. The prohibition ignited the disturbances which led the Schumanns to leave the city in haste. Prussian intervention was expected, so the following day the town council set up a defence committee. Wagner was involved in buying rifles and hand grenades.*

He wrote and distributed an appeal to the king – 'Are you with us against foreign troops?' – and distributed copies to the Saxon soldiers.[38]

Wilhelmine Schröder-Devrient incites the riot in Dresden.
She was arrested and exiled

Barricades went up, with one made of carts and wood with a flag on top, just next to Engel's restaurant, where the intellectuals had met. From her window, Schröder-Devrient incited the rioters to march on the Zwinger Palace, which was subsequently badly damaged. The old opera house went up in flames. Wagner got Minna out of the city, and worked indefatigably for the provisional government. He distributed leaflets; he acted as a look-out. He took up a position high on the 256 steps of the tower of the Kreuzkirche, from where he could see over the city to the curve of the Elbe and 'Saxon Switzerland' in the distance.

* A grenade is on display at Wagner's house in Bayreuth.

But within six days the uprising was crushed by the Prussians, and its leaders were on the run. Wagner escaped arrest by a double stroke of luck: he missed the coach in which several of his comrades were escaping; and by the time he caught up with them in Chemnitz, about 45 miles away, he fortunately went to a different inn, and so was not around when they were arrested.

Escape

Had Wagner been caught, the history of music might have been rather different. Röckel, who was carrying letters from Wagner, was condemned to death, although his sentence was commuted and he spent the next thirteen years in gaol. Bakunin was eventually incarcerated in St Petersburg and then sent to Siberia. There was a mass exodus of hundreds of thousands who went from Europe to the USA, Switzerland or some other safe haven.[39]

Wagner escaped to Liszt's house, the Altenburg, in Weimar. There was a certain irony in this, as Wagner had been none too polite about Liszt in his journalistic writings for the Dresden newspapers: he disliked Liszt's showmanship and materialism.[40] As we have seen, under the veneer, Liszt was a man of astonishingly disparate qualities, and he readily leapt to help a colleague in need. When Wagner reached Weimar on 13 May, Liszt was away. But on the following day, he obtained for Wagner a false identity as Professor Werder from Berlin. Nevertheless, it was only a matter of time before an arrest warrant would arrive from Dresden, upon which the authorities would have to act. With some insouciance, Wagner managed to have an intellectual conversation with Liszt's mistress Princess Carolyne, to sit at the back of the rehearsals of *Tannhäuser* which Liszt was preparing, and to see the Grand Duchess Maria Pavlovna in Eisenach where she was spending the summer. The warrant was issued on 16 May, and 'Wanted' notices bearing Wagner's name were printed. Liszt got wind of this on 18 May, when he received a letter from Minna saying that the Dresden police had raided the house. Wagner was then hidden in the home of a friend, before being despatched to the nearby village of Magdala, with money borrowed from Carolyne. This was in the nick of time: a couple of hours later, the warrant arrived.[41]

After ten days, Wagner reached Zurich. Of course, he missed the première of *Lohengrin*, conducted by Liszt in Weimar on 28 August 1850. He was now on the run, an exile. Minna and Liszt worked hard and courageously to get him an amnesty, but, despite repeated applications, it was refused. He was watched, suspected of inciting revolution, especially when he was in the Habsburg dominions, such as Venice. Even when, after eleven years, he was allowed back into Germany, he had to obtain both the permission of the individual German state which he wished to visit, and permission from Saxony as well.

Two of Wagner's female admirers provided him with an allowance. He planned to elope to Greece with Jessie Laussot, the English wife of a French wine merchant, and chased her as far as Bordeaux, but was turned back by French police. Not surprisingly, his relationship with Minna, who joined him in Zurich, became increasingly fraught. One has much sympathy for her: she had experienced the deprivations in Paris; she shared none of her husband's enthusiasm for change, whether in music or politics. Other causes of friction were her inability to have another child and the presence of her daughter Natalie, whom Wagner asked to leave. Minna had a bad heart, and had to take laudanum to help her sleep. Wagner's health was also poor, and he was irritated by skin inflammation and rashes.[42]

For several years after the escape, Wagner composed no music. Much of his income came from conducting.* Most of his time was spent reading, and writing prolifically and polemically 'on almost every subject ... except on his own method of composing'.[43] He wrote *Art and the Revolution*, *Artwork of the Future* and the infamous *Judaism in Music*, which reflected and developed the prejudices of an increasing number of people on the Continent in the 19th century. In his own writings, such as his adaptation of the *Ring* story, he used the style of old German poetry which he had been studying, a style which at times is so alliterative as to be 'devoid of sense'.[44] The *Ring* poem was read to an invited audience in 1853. Also, as we have seen in chapter 13, when visiting Paris with Liszt, Wagner took the opportunity to read the *Ring* poem to Liszt's children, including the shy sixteen-year-old Cosima. They must have been amazed.

Wagner's own reading included works by 'foggy, mystic, pessimistic'[45] metaphysical philosophers such as Ludwig Feuerbach and Arthur Schopenhauer, whose voluminous *The World as Will and Representation* (*Die Welt als Wille und Vorstellung*) Wagner read four times.[46] These

* He performed eight symphony concerts in London in 1855. He did not like foggy London or the English, and although the queen received him, he failed to kowtow to important and influential critics such as Davison of *The Times*.

philosophers explored the nature of whatever might exist beyond the world we experience, a very complex and cerebral subject which only philosophers can grasp.*

Wagner developed his own theories, and was duly gratified when he found that the great thinkers seemed to confirm his opinions. His views on the purpose of music, and on the world of his gods and heroes, generally reflected his latest notions, which tended to change as his reading and his thoughts progressed. At the time he composed *Das Rheingold* in November 1853, he believed that music's role was similar to that of the Greek chorus, and should comment on** and amplify the drama being acted on the stage. A year later, when he completed *Die Walküre*, music for him had become the dominant art, with all else subordinate to it. By the time that *Götterdämmerung*, the last opera in the *Ring* cycle, was finished 21 years after that, Wagner was completely sure of what he was trying to do: the essence of the drama is not what you see on the stage; it is what is being represented in the music.[47]

His evolving views partly account for the varied style of the operas within the *Ring* cycle. They also explain why the content of so much of Wagner's output is so incomprehensible. There is another reason for this. Notions such as Wagner's tend to have a short shelf life, if only because, if all the Ultimate Questions were answered, 'little statesmen, philosophers and divines'[48] would quickly be out of business. Whereas certain religions – for example, Christianity – have lasted for centuries, buttressed and imposed by strong institutional support, that was a luxury not enjoyed by Schopenhauer and lesser philosophers such as Wagner. The foundation stone of Wagner's whole artistic edifice began to crumble during his life; his protégé Nietzsche was instrumental in demolishing it.

Thus, it is no wonder that we are bemused by much of Wagner's work, by the characters such as the gods in the *Ring*, or Parsifal, or the yearning Tristan. Anyone who tries to understand them and their language in terms

* Immanuel Kant, the leading philosopher of the 18th century, thought that it is purely speculative to believe in the existence of anything beyond that which we can experience, see, feel or touch. There may well be something out there, but we would never know. For those who took the Bible, the soul, God, for granted, this thinking was particularly challenging. Schopenhauer developed a philosophy of considerable complexity about what might be beyond the world we experience.

** So, in *Das Rheingold*, he experimented with musicalising speech: the distinction between recitative and aria was lost.

of familiar people and behaviour – as one might expect from, say Verdi's Othello or Falstaff – rapidly becomes confused and distracted. The ordinary listener is well advised to put aside Wagner's theories and just enjoy Wagner's glorious music and the performance as a whole.*

The Wanderer

Let's return to the actual world of the early 1850s. Early in 1852, Wagner met Mathilde Wesendonck (see colour plate 20), aged 23, a writer, poet and composer of songs, whose husband Otto had made his fortune in a New York silk business. With Otto's help, Wagner made a trip to Italy and also paid off a large amount of debt. Otto agreed to provide him with a regular allowance in exchange for the receipts for future performances from his works. He also provided Wagner with a small house called Das Asyl (The Refuge) in the grounds of a substantial villa which he was having built for his own family. This was helpful, as Wagner had found it difficult to work in his apartment in Zurich, which was opposite a tinsmith and had neighbours who included five pianists and a flautist.[50]

Wagner, the ultimate egoist, seemed to regard it as his right to enjoy Otto's money, his villa and also his wife. Some believe that the affair was platonic.[51] Who knows? Wagner composed the *Wesendonck-Lieder* using Mathilde's poems, significantly 'a rare instance of Wagner's using lyrics that were not his own'.[52] The romance was both intense and hopeless, and coincided with work on *Die Walküre* and the poem about Tristan: final consummation of Tristan's hopeless love for Isolde, wife of his liege lord, could be achieved only in death.** Wagner regarded two of the Lieder as studies for the opera, and a third evokes the sounds of the first act.

Wagner was an inveterate liar, and seems to have persuaded Otto that the relationship with his wife was pure. He had less success with Minna; in April 1858, she intercepted an incriminating letter, rolled in a pencil sketch of the *Tristan* Prelude. She confronted Wagner and Mathilde with

* Wagner made particular use of '*Leitmotive*', the short musical themes which recur, and portray a person, an object or an emotion. Weber had used them in *Der Freischütz*, and Wagner used them in *Der Fliegende Holländer*. But in later works he expanded their use considerably: an expert has counted 1,003 significant uses in *Götterdämmerung*.[49]

** This was consistent with Schopenhauer's view that existence is a meaningless round of striving and yearning, that suffering is inescapable because we are doomed to die and decay, and pleasure is merely a release from pain. Wagner's own *dénouement* was deferred for a further 30 years.

the letter and threatened to show it to Otto. Mathilde somehow fixed the situation with Otto; but it was time for the Wagners to go.

Meanwhile, Wagner composed the first act of *Tristan* and generated ideas for *Parsifal.* On 9 August 1857, he stopped work on the *Ring* in Act II of *Siegfried*, when the hero rests under the trees and thinks about his parents. One should not suppose he got stuck: the rest of the opera was mainly composed eight years later. 'Nobody today can place his finger on the score ... and show the point of interruption.'[53]

Having left Zurich, Wagner took an apartment in a palace on the Grand Canal in Venice, 'the fallen Queen of the Seas'. He settled there, by 'the foul smelling lagoon' with 'the faintly rotten scent of swamp and sea', among the 'gloomy windings of many canals, beneath balconies of delicate marble traceries flanked by carved lions'. Here, wandering around 'slippery corners ... past melancholy facades with ancient business shields reflected in the rocking water',[54] he wrote the second act of *Tristan*. But the late 1850s were a particularly unstable time in northern Italy, where the slogan 'Viva Verdi' was being used to whip up war fever. The Habsburgs were desperately trying to retain their hold on Venetia. The ex-revolutionary who was already under surveillance was soon *persona non grata* in Venice. Wagner had to get out, so he finished *Tristan* in Lucerne. Otto Wesendonck still financed him,[55] and agreed to buy the copyright (but not the performing rights) of the four *Ring* scores.*

Wagner moved on to Paris, but his visit was a failure. The Prelude to *Tristan* was not understood. There was a sensational fiasco with a performance of *Tannhäuser* in March 1861. This had been sponsored by the emperor. The opera house management knew that their high-society patrons, including the rowdy members of the Jockey Club, would, in accordance with opera-house rules, expect a ballet to be included in the second act. The management asked Wagner for a ballet, and insisted that the opera be conducted by the resident conductor. Cuts were made to conserve the voice of the lead tenor. The result was disastrous. There were over 160 rehearsals. The 'Venusberg' music was not what the rakes wanted: the successive performances were wrecked with catcalls and dog whistles. Princess Pauline Metternich, who tried to lead applause, broke her fan in her rage.[56] On the other hand, Prosper Merimée, author of the novel

* This had to be re-negotiated when Schotts of Mainz offered Wagner a better deal.

Carmen, complained: 'I could write something similar tomorrow inspired by my cat walking up and down the keyboard.' He added: 'Some say that Wagner has been sent to us to force us to admire Berlioz.'[57] After three performances, the work was withdrawn. This confirmed Wagner in his hatred of Paris and everything French.

Wagner tried to get *Tristan* put on in Vienna, but the tenor could not remember the part; after 77 rehearsals, it was abandoned.[58] Still, he was well looked after by the lovely niece of a doctor, who provided him with lodgings.*

In 1862, Wagner moved to a fine villa in Biebrich, near Mainz. There, he started to compose *Die Meistersinger*. Minna joined him. She knew about his ladies, and the get-together was explosive. Wagner wrote to Peter Cornelius, the composer: 'There is no question about it; I cannot live with my wife any longer! These were ten days of hell!'[60] Minna escaped to Dresden, where he saw her for the last time later that year; they had agreed to separate.

The conductor Hans von Bülow and his wife Cosima, Liszt's second daughter, visited him in Biebrich that July.

At this time, Wagner conducted concerts in Vienna, Prague, Budapest, and as far afield as Moscow and St Petersburg. He had composed *Das Rheingold*, *Die Walküre*, *Tristan* and parts of *Die Meistersinger*; yet none had been performed. It required considerable self-motivation to keep going.

In 1863, Wagner issued his *Ring* poems with a preface in which he described the hopeless state of opera in Germany, and what he wished to achieve. He called for a prince who would provide the theatre and the resources. 'Will such a Prince be found?', he asked. He had written to Cornelius: 'My position is extremely precarious. It is most delicately balanced: a single jolt and all is over and nothing more can ever come out of me, nothing, nothing! A light must show itself; a man must arise, who will give me immense assistance now.'[61] Wagner went to a suburb of Vienna and set up in a house which he furnished luxuriously with silks and satins. But after an expensive Christmas, he had to disappear to escape his creditors.

* There were other ladies at this stage: among those sometimes mentioned are Liszt's eldest daughter Blandine Ollivier, and Mathilde Maier, a 28-year-old daughter of a notary.[59]

King Ludwig

In March 1864, Ludwig II, not yet nineteen, the grandson of the lover of Lola Montez, ascended the Bavarian throne. He was tall, handsome, athletic, and to his people in Munich, a real fairy-tale Prince Charming. Within five weeks of his accession, he sent his cabinet secretary, Franz von Pfistermeister, in search of Wagner. Having looked in Vienna and Switzerland, Pfistermeister caught up with the financial fugitive in Stuttgart.

To us, Ludwig is known as the Mad King, but he was certainly less mad than some of his relatives. His mother, a princess of Prussia, may only have been odd; she is recorded as saying: 'I never open a book; I simply can't understand how people can spend all their time reading.'[62] His aunt, however, was convinced that she had once swallowed a grand piano made of glass. His brother Otto had to be locked up after he rushed into High Mass and loudly confessed his sins in front of the archbishop. A sensible member of his family was his great uncle, whose daughter became the beautiful, tragic Elisabeth, Empress of Austria. Her epitaph to Ludwig was: 'The King was not mad; he was just an eccentric living in a world of dreams.'[63]

Ludwig was brought up in Hohenschwangau, the castle on the edge of the Alps in which, according to tradition, Lohengrin had lived. Ludwig's father renovated it and decorated the rooms with illustrations of the tales of the Holy Grail, Tannhäuser and Lohengrin, painted by second-rate artists who worked from sketches mostly by Moritz von Schwind, Schubert's friend. There were swans on the Schwanensee and swans on the walls. Ludwig had been given Wagner's 100,000-word essay *Opera and Drama* for Christmas when he was thirteen years old.[64] It was thus no wonder that the boy suffered from hallucinations. The doctors assured his mother that this phase would pass over. As for his musical skills, his piano teacher admitted that he could not tell a Strauss waltz from a Beethoven sonata.

That was some years earlier. When Pfistermeister caught up with Wagner, the composer lay low: he feared that he was yet another creditor looking for repayment. But, by that evening, Wagner was writing: 'Beloved gracious King. I send you these tears of most heavenly emotion, to tell you that now the marvels of poetry have come as a divine reality into my poor, loveless life. That life, its ultimate poetry, its finest music, belongs henceforth to you, my gracious young King; dispose of it as your own. In utmost rapture, faithful and true – Your subject, Richard Wagner.'[65] The former anti-monarchist revolutionary then borrowed enough to pay for a first-class ticket to Munich.

The bizarre meeting between the small, embittered republican and the tall, lanky descendant of the 700-year-old Wittelsbach family took place on the next day. The king recorded that Wagner 'bent low over my hand and seemed moved by what was so natural; he remained a long time thus without saying a word. I had the impression that our roles were reversed. I stooped down to him.'[66] Ludwig's ministers were content that Wagner would distract their sovereign from meddling in politics. Kings need distractions.

Wagner was established at a villa near Berg, the king's castle on the relatively dull Starnberger See, which is some fifteen miles from Munich. 'I fly to him as a lover', Wagner wrote. 'Often we sit in complete silence lost in each other's eyes.'[67] The two saw themselves as joint creators of great masterpieces: for Wagner, this requires no explanation; for Ludwig, he was not merely financing Wagner – he felt that he was an integral part of the creation of Wagner's works. Ludwig's biographer Wilfred Blunt is qualified to assess their relationship:[68] 'Wagner felt for Ludwig much as a middle aged married schoolmaster of sensibility might feel for an attractive, lonely, affectionate, well-connected pupil with an unhappy home life, who chanced to share his interests and enthusiasms.' Blunt continues: 'The King did not love him; he worshipped him and what he worshipped was the artist rather than the man, to whose faults, even at the height of his infatuation, he was never blind.'*[69]

Ludwig paid off Wagner's debts and gave him a salary of 4,000 gulden, larger than that paid to the head of a ministerial department after eighteen years of service.** He gave him a birthday present of a Bechstein piano designed to sit on the top of a desk: Wagner subsequently used this for composing parts of *Die Meistersinger*, *Götterdämmerung* and *Parsifal*. He was given a palatial house in Munich which he embellished, with the help of his Viennese furnisher, with costly fabrics: silk, tulle, lace and satins. He was also to receive 30,000 gulden for the completion of the *Ring* within three years, after which it would belong to the king. (That this was already

* Ludwig may have become a homosexual later. He befriended an actor, the son of a Hungarian provincial railway employee; together, they went in search of William Tell in Switzerland.[70]

** This type of behaviour by a monarch was not unprecedented: in the mid 1700s, Elector Karl Eugen poured money into the Italian opera headed by the composer Jomelli, making Stuttgart one of Europe's most splendid musical centres, until the money ran out.[71]

pledged to Wesendonck and others was beside the point.) He was given a carriage with an annual grant of 1,200 gulden for its upkeep.

In June 1864, Cosima von Bülow arrived in Bavaria with her two children. Her husband Hans came a few weeks later. Nine months later, Cosima gave birth to Wagner's daughter Isolde.

Hans von Bülow started work conducting the rehearsals of *Tristan*. One should not underestimate the significance of the first performance of this

In search of William Tell: King Ludwig II and his friend

opera: Richard Strauss said that it 'is the ultimate conclusion of Schiller and Goethe and the highest fulfilment of a development of the theatre stretching over 2,000 years'.[72] The performance was delayed because the Isolde, Malwina Schnorr von Carolsfeld, had lost her voice, and also because the bailiffs had arrived to collect one of Wagner's old debts. But when the opera at last took place, it was a success, particularly for King Ludwig, who wrote: 'Unique One. Holy One. How glorious. Perfect, so full of Rapture. To drown, to sink down – unconscious – supreme joy. Divine work!'[73] It was marred only by the fact that Malwina's husband Ludwig, the 29-year-old Tristan, died a few weeks later.

Far from distracting King Ludwig from politics, Wagner decided to meddle. The guest, nominally a Protestant in a predominantly Roman Catholic country, even provided the king with a memorandum of advice which was passed on to the incensed ministers led by Pfistermeister and the Minister President, Baron von der Pfordten, known as 'Pfi' and 'Pfo'. By now, the politicians had taken a dislike to Wagner and his Protestant friends such as Hans von Bülow, who was notoriously tactless: during the *Tristan* rehearsals, for example, Bülow wanted the orchestra pit enlarged, thus losing 30 stall seats; there was a fuss, whereupon Bülow said: 'What on earth does it matter whether we have plus or minus thirty *Schweinehunde* in the place?'[74] This remark got into the press. Also, Wagner was still asking for a spectacular amount of money: 200,000 gulden. The politicians arranged that when Cosima came to collect 40,000 gulden, she was handed several sacks of coin. A tough lady, arguably one of the most formidable of all the supporting actresses in the drama of music, Cosima just hailed two cabs in which to take the swag away.

Ludwig's ministers had justifiable cause for concern. Their king should have been conserving resources and taking a moderate interest in the considerable developments that were happening in Germany at the time. Two months before Pfistermeister had invited Wagner to Bavaria, yet another War of Succession provided significant opportunities for those who wished to seize them. No matter that the events were unfolding many miles to the north, in Schleswig-Holstein beyond Hamburg, where modern Germany juts northwards towards Denmark. It was not unreasonable to expect at least some degree of attention from the monarch of the second most important state in Germany, behind Prussia.

War broke out in 1866. The Prussians entered Dresden, and, with almost a quarter of a million men on either side, the Habsburgs were defeated at Königgrätz (Sadowa) in central Bohemia. On the day on which war was declared, Ludwig was found with his aide-de-camp, dressed as Barbarossa and Lohengrin, in a darkened room lit by an artificial moon.[75] A week later the Bavarians, who sided with the Austrians, were defeated at Kissingen. Had Bavaria been adjacent to Prussia, no doubt it would have been mopped up like Hanover and Saxony, which were foolish enough to back the losers. The Franco-Prussian War, five years later, would provide the pretext for annexing Bavaria.

Wagner, of course, advised the king on the 'Schleswig-Holstein crisis' as it evolved. Wagner's colleagues were rightly alarmed at his interference in these weighty political matters. Peter Cornelius wrote: 'When Bülow first told me about it, a shudder ran through me: I saw the beginning of the end.'[76] By the time of the Battle of Königgrätz, Wagner had been expelled.

Tribschen

Wagner had played his hand very badly. He wrote an anonymous article for a Munich newspaper in which he attacked the politicians. He then lied to Ludwig, denying that he was the author. When eventually the politicians pressurised the king to banish him for six months, Wagner was amazed. But, accompanied by his servant Franz and his sick old dog Pohl,* he left Munich before dawn on the morning of 10 December 1865, nearly twenty months after his first meeting with the king. After staying in Geneva, he moved to Tribschen, a villa on a promontory reaching out into Lake Lucerne.

Ludwig was so depressed that he wanted to abdicate and join Wagner in his 'landscape of sugar candy and marzipan'.[78] To the left of the villa, 30 minutes walk away, is the quaint, ancient city of Lucerne with its wooden bridges, painted houses and old walls; to the right, an incomparable view up the lake. Here, in the atmosphere of an idyll rather than Valhalla, Wagner was to spend the next six years, from mid-1866 to mid-1872. To start with, Cosima was ostensibly acting as his secretary taking dictation.

King Ludwig came to visit them at Tribschen, and liked Cosima. He continued to finance Wagner, and paid for the expensive improvements which Wagner made to the villa and its furnishings. Although they had their ups and downs, the king at first could not do without the composer. 'I love no woman, no parents, no brother, no relations, no one fervently and from the depths of my heart – as I love you', he said.[79] The king's threat to abdicate horrified Wagner, as the flow of cash would dry up.

It was not always easy-going, however. The relationship became soured when Wagner contributed articles to a newspaper on 'German Art and German Politics' in which he criticised the Church and state, and attacked France and French culture.

The Munich press kept up the attack. A report referred to 'Madame

* Wagner was fond of animals, and was invited to become a patron of the anti-vivisection society.[77] We hear of Wagner separating dogs fighting in the middle of the railway line, and rescuing one that had fallen into the water near the Lucerne ferry. One of the family dogs was run over by a train and killed.

Hans de Bülow' who in the last twelve months had 'got away in the famous two cabs with 40,000 gulden from the Treasury for her "friend"(or what?). Meanwhile the same Madame Hans ... is with her "friend" (or what?) in Lucerne where she was also to be found during the visit of an exalted person.' Bülow rushed off to consult his wife and Wagner. The three then foolishly conspired to get Ludwig to sign a document saying that there was no truth in the insinuation that Cosima was Wagner's mistress. This was at a time when she was already pregnant with Wagner's next child, Eva, who was born in February 1867. Cosima compounded the dishonesty by writing to the king: 'My Royal Lord, I have three children, and it is my duty to hand down to them their father's honourable name untarnished.'[80]

Wagner continued to work on *Die Meistersinger*, which was staged in Munich in summer 1868, even though he had wanted it put on in Nuremberg. Richard Strauss' father Franz, who regarded Wagner as a drunken ruffian, played the horn in the orchestra. Wagner attended the première on 21 June and acknowledged the applause, at Ludwig's command, from the royal box. This infuriated the aristocracy and the public. However, the opera was highly successful and Ludwig was delighted. He wrote: 'To the immortal German Master Richard Wagner.' 'Fate', he said, 'called us to a great task. We came into the world to testify to the truth ... I owe everything, everything – to you. Hail German art! In this sign will We conquer!'[81] Afterwards, however, when Wagner returned to Tribschen, the guilty couple could not any longer conceal their affair from Ludwig, who was deeply wounded by their deception. He did not meet Wagner again for eight years.

Cosima: Family Life

Siegfried Wagner was born in June 1869. Cosima mentions that she suffered 'raging pain' and had a severe haemorrhage.[82] Some weeks later, the Wagners celebrated his christening with a colossal banquet, the menu including soup, trout, filet of beef, duck and charlotte russe.[83]

It would be easy to dismiss Cosima in terms of the press campaign about her: a Berlin satirical magazine called her Cosima fan tutte. She had a large Roman nose inherited from her father, but some portraits give her a striking and distinguished beauty (see colour plate 23). She began a diary which she continued until Wagner's death. This reveals the agonies of conscience she felt about leaving Hans, especially when she heard that he was ill, or when her daughter Blandine accused her of being 'a nasty mama, who had left papa and run off with someone else'.[84]

Cosima got no support from Liszt, who was appalled at the Wagner *ménage*. And Wagner was largely concerned that a divorce should go through and that Cosima should become Protestant. She remained genuinely fond of Hans, and recorded in her diary on his birthday: 'My feelings towards him are today still the same as 12 years ago: great sympathy with his destiny, pleasure in his qualities of mind and heart, genuine respect for his character, however completely different our temperaments.'[85]

For Wagner, she had enormous respect and devotion, which almost amounted to hero worship. 'He is unutterably good to me', she wrote.[86] She expressed their relationship in Wagnerian terms as 'a reincarnation which brings me nearer to perfection, a deliverance from a previous erring existence; yet I feel, and tell him, that it is only in death that we shall be united completely, freed from the barriers of individuality'.[87] Wagner and she were married in August 1870, four years after Minna's death.

It was indeed a genuine love affair. On one occasion Wagner said to Cosima, probably for once genuinely: 'Since the world came into existence, no man of his age had loved a woman as much as he loved me.'[88] Her diary records some delightful detail. He brings her some pretty material for a negligée; he gets the hairdresser in to highlight her blonde hair; he gives her a splendid garnet-red velvet costume as a birthday present. She records a long conversation in which they talked about love: 'Feelings and thoughts pass to and fro between us, until it is just glances we are exchanging, and we go off to bed.' On an evening stroll to watch the sunset, Wagner asks her: 'But where can I grasp you?' '"Grasp me" I say to him, and we put our arms round each other as we stroll. The loveliest night, perhaps, that we have ever experienced! My whole being immersed in his.' In Florence, she awakes in his arms 'and now I hesitate to write down what he said – though I should like to show you his love for me, my children, I just cannot; such things one may scarcely even acknowledge as having been spoken!'[89]

This did not stop the rogue misbehaving with visitors. Notable ones were Judith Mendès and Augusta Holmès. Judith was the daughter of Théophile Gautier, the poet, novelist and author of *Giselle*. Judith's husband Catulle* was chasing the beautiful and vivacious, golden-haired Augusta, who was nominally the daughter** of an elderly army officer from Ireland. She was also a composer whom we shall meet in connection with César Franck and Saint-Saëns.

They all turned up, with Saint-Saëns, on the way to the première of *Das Rheingold* in Munich in September 1869. It must have been an odd occasion. One of the group was bitten by the Wagner dog, thought he had rabies, and then bored everyone with poetry readings. The conductor Hans Richter fell for Augusta. Both Cosima and Judith's 'antennae' led them to get Augusta out of the way as quickly as possible.[92]

Wagner's dalliance with Judith blossomed again some years later, starting with the first Bayreuth festival in 1876. Wagner and Judith corresponded through a go-between, the local barber. At first, Cosima did not see what was going on, but at one stage she caught Wagner in the act of burning a love-letter. She seems to have warned Judith off. When she came to stay some years later, relationships were strained.[93]

Meanwhile, domestic life was routine. The composer would work in his study, writing, inking in sketches, dealing with the copyists. He would rule the paper – on one occasion 334 pages – on which to orchestrate the music. Cosima learnt to knit. The pipes froze, the bath overflowed, the bells were out of order, cooks were bad, the servants stole coins from the master's writing desk. The family went on excursions to nearby Mount Pilatus, and on sleigh rides. She thought she was pregnant; she told him, then found she was not.

In the evenings, they often read together plays of Shakespeare, but also works of Gibbon, Carlyle and, of course, Schopenhauer. The English books were read in German translations, as Wagner never mastered

* Catulle became a leading contributor to the journal *Parnasse Contemporain*. The Parnassians wished to differentiate themselves from earlier Romantic poets: they affirmed the beauty and necessity of form, and wanted to rid the language of sentimental insipidities. With Augusta, he produced three daughters.[90]

** Augusta was said to be the daughter of her godfather, the poet Alfred de Vigny, who was also rumoured to have been her lover. At one stage, the Paris press predicted that her engagement to Wagner would be announced. Her works were influenced by the military bands she heard in Versailles, where she lived. It was said that all of them were like the last scenes of *Götterdämmerung*. Her *Ode Triomphale*, which celebrated the 100th anniversary of the Revolution, was performed in 1889 by 1,200 musicians in the Palace of Industry. She was a supporter of Home Rule in Ireland and of Garibaldi; she wrote the symphonic poems *Irlande* and *Pologne*.[91]

English. The philosopher Nietzsche was often present, and was treated almost as a grown-up son and sent on shopping errands; at this stage, he had a high regard for Wagner.[94] Wagner was irritated that he was a vegetarian. When Liszt came to stay, which was quite often, they would play whist. Or Wagner would play the piano, perhaps the tarantella from Auber's *La Muette de Portici*, which was one of the most popular operas of the century.[95]

The children misbehaved, fought and bickered. They caught coughs, colds and more worrying diseases such as scarlet fever and typhoid fever. They had children's parties in fancy dress, with puppet shows and dancing; they put on *tableaux vivants*; Christmas Day, which was also Cosima's birthday, was a particularly special occasion. They had a Christmas tree and presents, and all the festivities which we would now expect.

The most wonderful present of all, probably ever, was the birthday present in 1869, the *Siegfried Idyll.* Cosima had arranged some months earlier for Wagner's conductor Hans Richter and the Paris quartet to come and play on his birthday. A few days before Christmas, when having coffee, Wagner chided her for having organised that surprise for him: 'In a love like ours it is surely almost unbearable having to conceal things from each other.' So, they planned to have no presents for each other. But on her birthday, she woke up to a sound, the sound of the *Idyll* played on the landing outside her room. 'It grew ever louder, I could no longer imagine myself in a dream, music was sounding and what music!'[96]

For Wagner's birthday, the children stuck candles on his bathtub and surrounded it with wreaths and bunches of flowers. There was 'merry laughter about it all'.[97] For another birthday, they assembled flower pots containing roses which had been wrapped in paper, on which their youngest daughter Isolde had drawn pictures depicting some event in his life. Wagner was delighted.

Wagner by now was a celebrity. A doctor whom he visited for treatment asked: 'Are you *the* Richard Wagner, I mean the particular Richard Wagner?'; to which he got the reply: 'If you mean the one who has written such pretty things – yes I am he.' And when an enormous silver brooch arrived, the Order of Iftekhar sent by the Bey of Tunis, Wagner and Nietzsche immediately used it to decorate the roof of the children's puppet theatre. Cosima commented delightedly: 'He does not intend to acknowledge its receipt since it is too ridiculous to be refused.'[98]

The children and stepchildren continued to give great pleasure as they grew up. Fidi (Siegfried) gave his mother a birthday present of a table which he had made in his carpentry lessons. There were tears when the elder girls, Wagner's stepchildren, were sent off to boarding school and wrote sorrowful letters back home. 'It was necessary – but necessity is hard', wrote their mother. They returned with bad reports, and were difficult adolescents. Daniella's behaviour was 'down-right alarming'. Fidi's tutor, the handsome fair-haired Herr von Stein, was too severe on him. Then there were the first dances for the girls, and then weddings: the prospective son-in-law, although an Italian count, had no money and needed a job. 'It will be a hard task to find the right occupation for our future son-in-law; his education has not equipped him for anything.'[99]

At the time when Wagner was working on *Götterdämmerung*, their horse, Grane, took fright when some drunken peasants ran into them. Grane headed off across the fields with the carriage behind: Wagner might have thought of the dung heap in Riga many years before. 'The children in extreme fear, but R and I calm enough to stop their screaming and make them sit still', Cosima's diary records. 'No mishaps, apart from Grane's injury. The cantonal magistrate makes a record of it, we continue the long journey on foot. R heads for Tribschen while I take the children to the confectioner's.' Then the magistrate did not make any charge, because the farmer was a conservative and he was a conservative: 'We have resigned ourselves to the prospect of having to pay the court costs on top of all the damage.' On another occasion, Grane took fright in town and knocked down a child, badly injuring it.[100]

There was local news to be digested: the entire family of an inoffensive smith was murdered by a thief; a boat was sucked into the paddle of the steamer on the lake, and the man and child in it were killed; the man who supplied their fish was drowned in the lake just in front of the house. There was international news to be discussed: 'R expresses his annoyance with the Queen (Victoria), the silly old frump, for not abdicating, for she thereby condemns the Prince of Wales to an absurd life; in earlier times, he says, sons became their mother's guardians when they came of age.'[101]

News now travelled quickly by telegraph, so they could read about the events in Paris in 1870–71 – the Franco-Prussian War and the Commune – very soon after they had happened (see pages 505, 590, 598). The Wagners had relatives in France: Cosima's sister Blandine had been married to the French prime minister; her stepsister Claire, Comtesse de Charnacé, lived in Versailles, and her son was called up into the French navy. But this did not prevent the Wagners from being passionately pro-German and pro-Bismarck.* After his rough time in Paris, we can perhaps understand the diary entry in which Cosima noted that 'R says that the burning of Paris would be a symbol of the world's liberation at last from the pressure of all that is bad'. On the other hand, when Paris went up in flames following the Commune, they were very worried about what might happen to the Louvre and its treasures. 'I let out a cry of anguish which, R observes, hardly 20 people in France would echo', wrote Cosima.[103]

Bayreuth: Foundation

Wagner longed for security, for somewhere where he could settle with his family after so many years of wandering. He also wanted a temple fitting to stage his great operas, which he sincerely – that is, if he were ever capable of sincerity – believed would supplant the Church as the chief means of revealing the deepest truths.[104] Earlier, the king had agreed to build him one in Munich, and to set up an opera school. But Munich, where *Das Rheingold* and *Die Walküre* were premièred, was not a feasible location for a complete *Ring*, despite the King's wishes.

In April 1871, the Wagners visited the elegant city of Bayreuth to consider the splendidly ornate opera house of the sister of Frederick the Great, which had the largest stage in Germany. But the Margrave's opera house was too small: it took only 450 people. It was also too magnificently baroque. There were tempting proposals from other cities, such as Darmstadt, whose theatre had recently burnt down, and from the watering-hole of Baden-Baden. Although locations such as these were falling over each other to attract the project, pleasure-seeking tourists and commerce did not fit easily with the artistic importance of Wagner's venture. He determined to create a new purpose-built opera house at Bayreuth. Thus began the enormous project to finance and construct the theatre and the Wagners' own villa.[105]

The Wagners moved to Bayreuth, where, on the composer's 59th birthday, various notables trudged through the mud to lay the foundation stone

* The French took exception to Wagner's insensitivity, and particularly disliked a farce he wrote called *The Capitulation*.[102]

for a new opera house, up on a hill overlooking the town. The event was marked with a performance of Beethoven's Ninth Symphony in the Margrave's opera house.

Wagner, single-handed, provided the inspiration and the drive for the Bayreuth project. Much of his time was now taken up in the design and business dealings. He had to deal with bankers who said that credit facilities must be available for the whole operation before any work could begin; and bankers who said that work must stop because the money was running out. He was involved in sending circulars to his patrons. The workers threatened to strike unless they were paid. At one stage, Wagner was so exasperated that he suggested abandoning the project and just proclaiming to the world that it would only hear the *Ring* once enough money was raised. He also had to spend time conducting performances intended to raise finance.

With his well-known anti-Semitic views, raising funds was not the ideal role for Wagner, and in the middle of it all, to avoid the effects of adverse publicity, he and Cosima had to buy in Wagner's correspondence with Minna from the 1860s. The first Isolde, Malwina Schnorr, ever jealous of Wagner's love for Cosima, had threatened to publish this. Malwina was a depressive, having never quite recovered from her husband's premature death.[106]

The opera house building was provisional, with a much larger edifice intended for the future. It was therefore made of wood covered with plaster. One of the plans included ornaments. 'The ornaments must go', wrote Wagner on it. The house was to be totally functional. It was designed so that the audience of 1,900, mainly sitting on hard seats, deep-raked as in the Greek amphitheatre, could peer undistracted across the concealed orchestra and conductor to the gas-lit music drama, the world of the gods, beyond. With half the orchestra, including the brass, under the stage and with virtually no drapery, the acoustics were excellent.

Bayreuth: Finance

The cost at first was estimated at 300,000 thalers,* which was planned to be raised by the issue of 1,000 'patrons certificates' at 300 thalers

* Wagner's figure included rehearsing and staging the first performances of the *Ring*. A temporary opera house built in Dresden cost 70,000 thalers. The 300,000 thalers (900,000 marks) can be compared with the 100,000 marks which Senator Buddenbrook paid to build a grand residence in Lübeck, assuming Thomas Mann's figures in his novel[107] make sense.

each.* Although Liszt subscribed for three, the Sultan of Turkey ten, and the Khedive of Egypt sent £500, it soon became clear that the certificates would raise only around 40 per cent of the appeal, and also that the cost was going to exceed the estimate.**

There were various plans to bridge the deficit, none of which was too promising. A lottery had been used to finance the completion of Cologne Cathedral, but this idea was dropped.[109] Wagner's new fund-raiser, a music dealer from Mannheim, devised a scheme for setting up Wagner-Vereine, associations around the world which would enable lesser mortals to contribute to this important cause. This scheme would be time-consuming because it necessitated Wagner's involvement, and did not yield a significant amount. A manifesto drafted by Nietzsche was intended to shame the German nation into stumping up, but its publication in 4,000 bookshops yielded only a handful of marks. This was more, however, than was forthcoming from an attempt to stimulate theatres into giving benefit concerts.[110]

The imperial government in Berlin was reluctant to interfere in what they saw as a Bavarian matter. If only King Ludwig himself would give a guarantee, the Coburg bankers would come up with a substantial amount immediately. In the end, after protracted negotiations, the king came to the rescue with a loan of 100,000 thalers and lent Wagner money for the completion of his small villa in the park behind the New Palace (see colour plate 52). The Wagners occupied the villa in April 1874. When Wagner was having trouble with the builders, he called it Ärgersheim, House of Annoyance, but it was actually to be Wahnfried. *Wahn* means illusion; *Friede*, peace. On the façade, a painting over the main entrance depicts Schröder-Devrient as Tragedy, Schnorr as the Wanderer, Cosima as Music and young Siegfried as Art of the Future. On either side is an inscription: 'Here where my illusion found peace, be this house named by me Peace from Illusion.' Schopenhauer would have understood, perhaps.

* To obtain some feel for the context, one might compare a 300-thaler certificate with the annual income of three average Germans at the time, and the annual rent paid by two separate residents of Berlin. Two certificates approximated the annual remuneration of a factory manager. In 1851, Paul Mendelssohn sold 3 Leipzigerstrasse to the government for 100,000 thalers.[108]

**By midsummer 1873, only 130,000 thalers had been subscribed. Rehearsal costs were 2,000 marks daily.

Bayreuth: Opening

Despite all the continuing difficulties, and despite some accidents during the construction, and with the banker reporting that cash would run out in three weeks, rehearsals of the *Ring* began in summer 1876. The first performance of *Das Rheingold* at Bayreuth took place on Sunday 13 August 1876. There were disasters: the ring itself was lost; and when the backdrop was raised too soon, all the stage-hands could be seen standing around in their shirt-sleeves. Wagner luckily caught the Kaiser as he tripped and fell. Rather nicely, at the banquet after a week which saw the first *Siegfried* and *Götterdämmerung*, Wagner proposed a toast to his father-in-law, Liszt, without whom, he said, no one would have known anything about him.[111]

Describing the world première of the *Ring*, Nietzsche said: 'the whole riff-raff of Europe had been brought together, and any prince who pleased could go in and out of Wagner's house as if it was a sporting event'.[112] For Nietzsche, this acceptance of the false values of existing society betrayed everything he stood for; but for Wagner it was a necessary means of raising the funds to pay off the deficit on the cost of the theatre. Nietzsche by now had become disillusioned with Wagner – not with the music, so much as Wagner's thinking.*

Late Years

Although the opera house was up, the financing was incomplete because, according to the agreement, the king's loan was repayable after eighteen months of its granting.[113] Worse still, the first season had run at a colossal deficit of nearly 150,000 marks, and creditors were clamouring for payment.[114] The theatre stood as a white elephant for six years. The pressure on Wagner was relentless while he worked on his next project, *Parsifal*.[115]

The fund-raising ventures took the Wagners to England, which Wagner regarded as Alberich's dream** come true: world domination, activity, work, everywhere the oppressive feeling of steam and fog. They met Liszt's friend, the novelist George Eliot, and Cosima sat for the painter Burne-

* Nietzsche virulently attacked Wagner. At the age of 44 he went mad with syphilis, and lived on for another eleven tragic years.

** Alberich, the leader of the Nibelungen, hobgoblins who lived in caverns, longed for world power. This, the Rhine's gold – once forged into a ring – would provide. In *Das Rheingold*, Alberich forswore love to acquire the gold.

Jones. They both had a session with a photographer. The tour was not a financial success. The managing agents went bankrupt, and the concerts at the Royal Albert Hall were not as profitable as had been estimated because so many boxes were owned by the founders, who did not have to pay for their use: the Wagners cleared only about £700. But Wagner took the opportunity to buy a toy construction set for Fidi's birthday.[116]

The Wagners' personal financial problems were a continual source of worry throughout their life together. Persistent rumours reached them that the king, their crucial source of finance, would be certified insane – if any doctor had sufficient nerve to sign the certificate. The Wagners' financial insecurity shows through in Cosima's diary. She hoped to put aside her money for the children, but it was frequently being called upon – for example, for payments on the house at Wahnfried. 'Are things so bad?', she had once asked; 'God knows they are', he sighed. It must have been truly alarming, as 'life was harsh' and business dealings ruthlessly unsentimental.[117] When Schotts paid a large sum for *Götterdämmerung*, Cosima summed up their position: 'This is probably our last large piece of income, and our growing expenses fill me with worry. R has an unquenchable confidence in himself, and I an all-absorbing mistrust in Fate.' Appearances mattered, so despite the financial pressures they acquired a new carriage.[118]

The underlying financial position at Bayreuth was desperate. After Cosima's inheritance from her mother was absorbed, and the *Idyll* was sold,[119] there was still a hardcore liability of around 100,000 marks, together with the original loan. Wagner thought of throwing everything up and moving to America. He also contemplated setting up a conservatoire in Bayreuth.[120] It did not help when more incriminating correspondence, this time with his furnisher from Vienna, was published.[121] But there was considerable good-will on the part of King Ludwig's financial advisers. Eventually, a further loan was raised and the debt due to King Ludwig was deferred.[122] The Bavarians were given the right to produce all the works in the Munich Court theatre without payment and, crucially, it was agreed that ten per cent of the gross receipts would go towards the discharge of the aggregate liabilities. It took until 1906 to do this.

Wagner became even more testy, and obsessed with the wickedness and mendacity of the world: 'So well do I know, when he gets so angry and violent and tries to hurt someone or other, that his malaise takes complete possession of him', wrote Cosima. 'Any reply, however conciliatory, only pours more oil on the flames.'[123] Racked by chest spasms and other pains, troubled by insomnia, he began to drink brandy quite heavily. On 8 December 1881, there was a fire at the Vienna opera house just as the curtain was about to rise on Offenbach's *The Tales of Hoffmann*; 400 people were killed. When Wagner heard this, instead of expressing regret, he went into a fury and said that the most useless people frequented such an opera house: 'If poor workers are buried in a coal mine, that both moves and angers him, but a case like this scarcely affects him at all.'[124]

Wagner completed the full score of *Parsifal* in January 1882, in Sicily, and it was first performed in July of that year. He was concerned by the fact that the audience did not know whether or not to applaud, and was afraid that the artists would be displeased by the lack of applause. But his life's work was now done. The Wagners went off to Venice, where they occupied an apartment in the Palazzo Vendramin. Wagner enjoyed watching the gondolas, and was particularly amused by a man who, accompanied by a barrel organ, imitated opera singers and conductors.[125]

There was the Sirocco and fog; and then glorious weather. At one moment, near the Doge's Palace, 'I hear amid all the crush and noise "Psst" and I know at once that it is R. ... True enough, there he is sitting on the bench beside the Doge's Palace and in very good spirits; the air is splendid, and he has been happily watching two lovely boys of five and seven playing with sand on the bench; he put some money in the sand pit for them.' They strolled around Venice and looked at 'some blue fabric which has caught R's eye. He says he hates himself because he is such a nuisance to me. As I go to sleep, I hear him say: "I am like Othello, the long day's task is done."'[126]

Two days before he died, Wagner dreamt of the soprano of his youth, Schröder-Devrient: 'All my women are now passing before my eyes', he said.[127] He was in fact working on his essay 'On the Feminine in Mankind' at the time. On the day of his death, Tuesday 13 February 1883, Cosima was furious because an English soprano, one of the Flower Maidens to whom he had taken a fancy, was due to come and visit them. Wagner was at his desk and had told them to go ahead with lunch. He collapsed; Cosima led him to the sofa, where he died in her arms. It was 3.30 pm. Cosima was prostrate. Even Hans, one person whose integrity consistently shines in the Wagner story, telegraphed her: 'Soeur, il faut vivre.'[128]

Wagner was buried in the small garden at Wahnfried where, after 47 years, the 92-year-old Cosima joined him in the *Liebestod* which they had anticipated for so long. For half a century, clad in black, known in the business as 'the Mistress', the regal Frau Wagner*[129] was a considerable force in German music. Russ, their dog, is buried nearby.

Three years after Wagner's death, on Whit Sunday, it seems that Ludwig took revenge on the doctor who had reported him insane. He went out for a walk with the distinguished specialist in mental diseases. About three hours later, they both were found floating in the Starnberger See, in shallow water about twenty yards from the bank.

Cosima had confided to her diary, just a few days before Richard died: 'As I go to sleep I hear him speaking divine words to me, words which I may not repeat, words which wrap me round like guardian angels and settle deep, deep in my heart like the most sacred of my treasures. "Good night my angel" I said to him yesterday. "Good night, my dear wife – that means much more."'[130]

Perhaps this astonishing composer was a real person, capable of affection and of being loved. Unlike his awful gods.

Richard and Cosima Wagner

* There was a strict rule at Bayreuth that Verdi could not be mentioned. When the conductor Bruno Walter did so, 'Frau Wagner's face became icily frigid'. He spluttered something about Verdi's development from his early *Ernani* to the final opera, *Falstaff*. She merely remarked: 'Development? I can see no difference between *Ernani* and *Falstaff*.' Walter never saw her again.

OFFENBACH AND JOHANN STRAUSS

CHAPTER 15

AN OPERA BY Wagner leaves the listener almost breathless, if not emotionally exhausted. So it is appropriate, before turning to his rival Giuseppe Verdi, to have a break, and to meet some lighter composers such as Offenbach and the Strausses. It is easy to be snobbish about light music, which is 'sophisticated and elegant, yet simple and accessible',[1] and also about music which is composed purely for commercial reasons, perhaps to accompany a film or television programme. Yet, secular music of all varieties has always been intended to give pleasure, to stir the emotions, to entertain. Fiddlers accompanying dancers on a Mayday village green, folksongs, operetta and musicals, jazz and pop are arguably as important and interesting as what is conventionally called 'classical' music.

Demand-driven entertainment music is thought to be distinguishable from creative 'art music'. The operettas of Jacques Offenbach can be distinguished from the operas of, say, Verdi. Baroque dance suites, Weber's *Invitation to the Dance* and the waltzes of Chopin can be distinguished from the dance music of Johann Strauss. This book will not dare to try to identify the distinguishing features. It is sometimes suggested that art music has mind-provoking qualities; it is perhaps inspiring, or disturbing, or even mystical. Yet, much of the success of a modern musical, *Les*

Above: OFFENBACH AND JOHANN STRAUSS

Misérables for example, can be attributed to its ability to stir the emotions.

There is an assumed superiority about art music: its composers and their audience believe that they operate on a higher plane. So Brahms was content to be photographed with Johann Strauss, because Strauss had different objectives and was not a competitor (see colour plate 42). One cannot imagine Brahms consenting to be photographed with adversaries like Wagner, Bruckner or Hugo Wolf. Similarly, Wagner, who enjoyed playing Strauss waltzes,[2] could condescend to say that Offenbach wrote music like Mozart:[3] it was idle talk, piffle; anyway, nobody would dream of formally comparing the two.

Rather than aiming for the immortal and unattainable, Offenbach and Johann Strauss were deliberately attempting to complement the glitzy aspects of the world in which they lived. Offenbach satirised the Second Empire of Napoleon III. His shows also provided a way for the more affluent classes to escape for a brief moment from the awful reality behind 'the fair imperial harlot of civilised humanity'.[4] His decline in popularity followed the collapse of the empire, in 1870, when the emperor was taken prisoner by the Prussians.*

Strauss provided a counterpoint to the death march of the doom-laden Habsburg dynasty. The waltzes and the operettas, with their attractive tunes, their happy endings, their dance and chorus numbers, and comic antics, provided a means of escape.[6] Austria might be consistently defeated on battlefields, its stock market might crash, but it could still produce Strauss; just as Great Britain, increasingly overshadowed by the United States, could a century later contribute a galaxy of film, pop and sporting celebrities.

Offenbach's Early Years

Offenbach was born in Cologne on 20 June 1819. His grandfather came from a place called Offenbach, about five miles from Frankfurt. Isaac, his father, married the daughter of a moneychanger and lottery-office keeper who worked in an area of Cologne which was full of dance halls and gambling joints. Jacob, as Jacques was then called, and his elder brother and

* Balzac had a premonition of this, in 1834, when his character Rastignac 'saw Paris spread out below ... His gaze fixed almost avidly upon the space that lay between the column of the Place Vendôme and the dome of the Invalides ... He eyed that humming hive with a look that foretold its despoliation.'[5]

sister played opera selections and dance music at the restaurants and wine bars, sometimes in both the afternoon and the evening.

When he was fourteen, his father realised that if he and his elder brother Julius were to progress, they should go to the Paris Conservatoire. Paris was attractive, because there Jews were relatively favourably treated. So, in November 1833, the Offenbachs set off on the four-day journey. Cherubini, the director of the Conservatoire, allowed the boys an audition and they were admitted. After getting them some remunerative work singing in a synagogue choir, Isaac returned to Cologne.[7]

Jacques left the Conservatoire a year later and worked in theatre orchestras and then as a cellist at the Opéra-Comique. When *La Juive* was a sensational success, he approached its composer Fromental Halévy, obtained a free ticket and also persuaded him to give him some lessons in composition. He and some others from Cologne set up in a garret in the rue des Martyrs on the way to Montmartre.

With no access to courts, palaces or churches, Offenbach had to compose with an alternative market in mind. He found this in the lively centre of Paris, with its ostentatious wealth, its dandies,* its gambling, its cafés and restaurants, such as the Café de Paris and Tortoni's. The boulevard du Temple, where several theatres were situated, was almost a fairground with its sword eaters, human skeletons, dwarfs and giantesses. Here, waltzes were the rage.

Offenbach succeeded in getting some of his waltz suites played in the fashionable Jardin Turc. Meanwhile, he earned his living by playing the cello in the salons and by giving lessons. He churned out the waltzes and sentimental ballads which were just what his salon audiences wanted. In 1839, he was commissioned to compose a number of items for a vaudeville piece, *Pascal et Chambord*, but it was not a success. In a laborious way, he made a reputation as a cello virtuoso.[9]

Offenbach frequented the salon of Mme Mitchell, a Spanish lady married to an English concert agent. He fell in love with Herminie, her daughter by her first husband. The Mitchells agreed to their marriage provided that Offenbach had a successful English tour and changed his religion. He

* The novelist Emile Zola describes the dandy, who had 'adopted a weary, swaying form of locomotion and spoke in a gently, drawling tone of voice, using slang expressions and sentences which he couldn't be bothered to complete'.[8]

went to England and played before Queen Victoria. And after becoming a Roman Catholic, Jacques married Herminie in 1844. They had four daughters and a son.

We have seen Berlioz commenting on the way work opportunities for musicians evaporated in the difficult revolutionary days, in early 1848. Offenbach's audience disappeared. He took Herminie and their little daughter back to Cologne, with virtually no money. When he returned after about a year, he resumed the same round of salons and concerts, and tried to get works played at the Opéra-Comique. Then the director of the Comédie-Française needed someone to conduct the orchestra in the interval, and lit upon Offenbach. He became conductor for 6,000 francs a year. The 'Second Empire' was just beginning.[10]

The Second Empire

The reign of Napoleon III lasted almost twenty years, nearly twice as long as that of his illustrious forebear. Emperors have to wed suitably. So, having provided for his long-time mistress, who had formerly belonged to the jockey who won the first Grand National,[11] the emperor married 'the Spanish Beauty', Eugénie de Montijo (see colour plate 31). Although the daughter of a grandee, her Scottish grandfather was a wholesale fruit and wine merchant in Malaga,[12] where he also served as US consul. To start with, the French people's reaction to the royal wedding was bad: it was considered a poor match, she being a bit of a parvenue. After the engagement was announced, gilts on the Stock Exchange fell by 2.5 per cent, and railway shares by 15 per cent.[13]

One could get the impression that the reign was one long steamy orgy of men in black suits and women in crinolines, typified by the imperial couple. This aspect was portrayed, fictionally, by Emile Zola in the person of the eighteen-year-old Nana.* The truth eventually dawns on her lover, the empress' deeply religious chamberlain, that 'as he was taking his frock-coat off in the company of that slut, his wife was stripping in her lover's bedroom'.[15] Nana surveys the grandstand at the races at Longchamp race-

* Published in 1880, *Nana* went through more than 50 editions in a few weeks. Some of the descriptions used by Zola would make even Lady Chatterley blush. Nana had used 'a tiny object, a little thing that people made jokes about, a dainty, naked titbit, a tiny slit, unmentionable and yet possessing the power to shift worlds, so that by its unaided efforts … she had sent Paris tottering and built up a fortune on buried corpses'.[14]

course through her binoculars: 'That lot up there does not impress me any more; I know them all too well; You ought to see them when they take their wrappings off; there's no respect any more! It's all gone. Filth at the top, filth down below, there's nothing but filth and more filth.'[16]

Zola describes a lesbian restaurant where a 'herd of fat women' were competing with each other for the prostitutes' favours 'like anxious old bachelors, by offering them tasty titbits'.[17] The madame had a country house with seven bedrooms. Of the heterosexuals, 'the most prim and proper were the dirtiest; all their veneer vanished, they became like animals, insisting on the most revolting practices and every possible refinement of perversion'.[18]

However, behind all this nonsense, much was being achieved. Paris was being rebuilt, and there was considerable industrial progress. Baron Haussmann, the prefect of the Seine, transformed 'the windings of the Paris labyrinth'[19] into the glorious city we now know.* Around 20,000 houses in the centre, including the Offenbach family apartment in the rue Laffitte, were demolished and around 40,000 new ones were built.[20] With the help of a huge aqueduct, the number of buildings with running water increased nearly fivefold.

It was boom time for businessmen and nouveaux riches, for whom the railway opened up the Riviera as a holiday resort. Banks sprang up, such as the Crédit Lyonnais and the Société Generale.[21] Stores like Bon Marché and the Louvre appeared. There was even a form of telecommunication: Napoleon III, when on manoeuvres in Boulogne, could communicate daily by telegraph with Eugénie in Biarritz,[22] one extremity of France to another, in one and a half hours. The bureaucracy mushroomed too: by 1870, there were 700,000 employees at departmental and municipal levels.[23]

There were considerable technical developments. The Exhibition of 1867 was visited by about 10 million people, including 57 ruling monarchs and royal princes. It included displays of the new featherweight wonder metal called 'aluminium' and petroleum. Technical developments also influenced living patterns: with steam-powered mechanisation, work was transferred from the home to the factory.[24]

The population became more educated: the number of libraries outside

* Haussmann's wide boulevards facilitated troop movements; and he replaced the paving stones, so useful to rioters, with macadam.

Paris more than doubled between 1851 and 1878 to over 5,000. One household in four or five was buying a newspaper. Jules Verne's travel novels (*Around the World in 80 Days* and *20,000 Leagues Under the Sea*) came off the presses in editions of 30,000, whereas the average print-run during the Restoration had been 1,500.[25]

The bourgeois supported the empire: they had never been so prosperous or hypocritical. Flaubert was prosecuted, but acquitted, in 1857 for his novel *Madame Bovary* on the grounds of irreligion and immorality. The effete Goncourt Brothers* were arrested in 1852 for 'outrage against public morality':[26] they had quoted mildly erotic Renaissance verses in one of their articles. Baudelaire was convicted and fined for publishing *Les Fleurs du Mal* because six of the poems, those which contained descriptions of feminine beauty and love-making, were thought immoral.[27] Following tighter laws against paedophilia in 1863, 3,300 men were arrested.[28]

The Other Side of the Coin

Beneath the bourgeoisie, there were very serious problems. Haussmann, a Lutheran who was addicted to figures and detail, estimated that almost three-quarters of Parisians lived in poverty.[29] Its population more than doubled between 1851 and 1881, while the population of the country as a whole only grew by 5 per cent.[30] Whereas rich and poor had tended to live in the same areas of Paris, the rich now lived in one part and the poor were ominously polarised in another. The affluent continued westwards towards the Bois de Boulogne; in the east, some areas like Belleville were virtually squatter camps.[31] Adulterous wives were still subject to prosecution, so it was easier not to get married. The working classes therefore commonly lived together, marrying only when children arrived.[32]

The fear of poverty and destitution was intense. In another novel, *Germinal*, Zola portrays almost too graphically, and from some distance, the coal fields in Northern France, their bleakness and their blackness. Around the clock, shifts of men, women and young children sweated a third of a mile down, relentlessly hacking out the coal. They were desperate for work: there was no choice, if they wanted to avoid starvation. Their

* The Goncourts kept a diary of social life, and although Jules was killed early on by syphilis, Edmond survived until 1896. His estate provided funds to award a prize to the author of an outstanding work of French literature. The hypocritical aspects of society are vividly portrayed by Guy de Maupassant in his short stories.

main solace was sex, both below ground, and above in the numerous dancehalls, bars and pubs. In Zola's story, the miners who degenerate into animals below ground behave like starved animals above, when they protest with a horrific, hopeless and ultimately disastrous strike. To make ends meet for a family of wanted and unwanted children, a mother pleads for five francs from the comfortable bourgeois owners who acquired their mining shares in opportunistic speculation during the Revolution. They do not give her money, because it was a known fact that, as soon as the poor had two sous, they 'drank them'. The bourgeois, whose dividends had tripled during the empire, whereas miners' wages had increased by a third, emphatically agree when the destitute woman admits that it is best 'to try to do your job properly in the place God has put you'. 'Yes', say the bourgeois, 'with such sentiments, my good woman, one is proof against misfortune.'[33]

The great majority of female industrial workers were employed in the textile and clothing industries. Fifteen-year-old country girls were recruited on four-year contracts to the Lyons silk industry, working seventeen hours a day in unhealthy workshops, where there was never a ray of sunshine.[34] Half of the girls got chest illnesses before the end of their contract. On average, weavers and spinners, who had survived the most vulnerable years of infancy, could expect to live to the age of 27–36.[35] In Paris, as a domestic servant, a woman could expect to survive into her 40s or 50s.

So, why begrudge La Païva, the mistress of the piano virtuoso and composer Henri Herz,* for climbing her way from the Moscow ghetto to a house in Paris with an alabaster staircase worth a million francs, and a bed for business said to have cost 100,000 fr?[37] She was lucky. Outside, for the average wage of 3.81 fr, the Parisian worker had to work an eleven-hour day; a shoemaker received 3 fr.[38] The lot of the 17,000 women earning only between 50 centimes and 1.25 fr a day was particularly bad. Poverty usually drove women to ordinary prostitution in the gutter, where the charge was 50 centimes.[39]

The Glitz at the Top

The imperial couple and their set insulated themselves from the awful reality by holding receptions and balls, lavishly decorated and lit. The empress wore a new dress on every occasion.[40] The imminent arrival of the prince

* Herz, who had joined with Chopin, Liszt and others in composing the *Hexaméron*, was professor at the Conservatoire; he also founded a piano factory, and owned a concert hall.[36]

imperial, born in March 1856, led her to introduce the crinoline,* which was to become almost the symbol of her reign.

The crinoline was constantly, and alluringly, in motion, allowing, if lucky, a thrilling glimpse of the ankle or even the long white linen pantaloons, trimmed with lace, which came down to it. The feet and ankles were then as seductive as the anatomy further up has been for later generations. No wonder the lustful King of Italy, having asked the French Empress whether it was true that the ballet dancers did not wear pants, said that, if so, 'it would be absolute heaven for me'.[42]

And this indeed was the tone set by the empire and its hangers on. For example, Napoleon was 'caught' making love to Comtesse Walewska, the wife of his foreign minister.[43] On a train journey, the swaying of the carriage caused the door to open; his cousin Princesse Mathilde** (and the minister) observed him 'astride on Marianne's knees, kissing her on the mouth and thrusting his hand down her bosom'.

His regal and requisite hypocrisy was exemplified by his reaction to Manet's picture, *Déjeuner sur l'Herbe*, which portrayed a naked model picnicking on the grass with two dandies (see colour plate 32). It was excluded from the official salon in 1863, although it could be seen nearby at the *Salon des Refusés*, where the rejected works were allowed to be displayed. The emperor declared that the painting was an offence against modesty, and it was reported that he and the empress averted their gaze from it. The picture of the year, which he bought, was the *Birth of Venus* by Alexandre Cabanel, a Prix de Rome winner of 1845 and a recently elected member of the Academy; it embodies all that the Impressionists were trying to avoid; a highly finished, classical nude (see colour plate 33).

* There was an important architectural improvement in 1828, when the invention of the metal eyelet enabled tighter lacing. Beneath, skirts were filled out with, say, seven petticoats enhanced with small pads, often made of horsehair, 'crin'. This became cumbersome, so a further engineering solution was necessary. Hoops were sewn into the underskirt giving the impression of wearing a great number of petticoats without wearing any at all. Crinolines had their disadvantages: 2,000 women were burnt to death in the cathedral of Santiago in 1863 when candles ignited their light flimsy dresses.[41]

** Princess Mathilde, the handsome and vaguely intellectual daughter of Jérome, King of Westphalia, was cousin of both the emperor and the tsar. She was candid about her background: 'If it were not for the French Revolution', she said, 'I would be selling oranges on the streets of Ajaccio.'[44] Her salon was a most fashionable place for intelligentsia. She was surrounded by pug dogs and literati. Rossini attended her salon, and Saint-Saëns played the organ for her.

The imperial couple's *mores* extended to their family and coterie. The emperor's 'brains', the Duc de Morny, a bastard son of the emperor's mother (and a bastard grandson of Talleyrand), had as his mistress the red-haired Cora Pearl. Emma Crouch, as she was born, was the daughter of the Plymouth music teacher who wrote the Irish song 'Kathleen Mavourneen'.[45] Emma's lover from Covent Garden took her to Paris where she stayed with a succession of aristocratic lovers. It was said that 'every man of any note for the last fifteen years has passed a few hours with Cora'.[46] She kept a register in three columns: names, dates and gifts, with a space for observations. At one of her dinner parties, she had herself served up by four men who carried her on a huge silver salver, naked, with a sprinkling of parsley.[47] When, in 1866, she appeared as Eve at a fancy dress ball, an English journalist noted that 'her form and figure were not concealed by any more garments than were worn by the original apple eater'.[48] As her breasts were said to be 'as beautiful as if they had been sculpted in marble',[49] she must have been quite something.*[50]

Sex was not the sole component of the sleaze, however. Morny combined *le chic et le chèque*.[51] When in March 1865 he was dying, officially 'of bronchitis', but possibly from using an arsenic-based rejuvenator, a friend put his love letters down the lavatory. It was a 'smart permissive society dedicated purely to pleasure, full of people whom a society hostess would pick up in the course of some short lived intimacy, where a duke rubbed shoulders with a crook ... People wanted one thing only: to have fun.'[52]

Offenbach in the Second Empire

The empire which has just been described was a setting in which Offenbach could thrive. 'The operetta would never have been born had the society of the time not itself been operetta-like; had it not been living in a dream world, obstinately refusing to wake up and face reality.'[53] The age demanded banquets and feasts and intoxicating revels, thrills that lifted the moment from the commonplace and drowned the agitation of the socialists, the republicans and the students.

Offenbach believed that there was a market for light, witty, cheerful

* In the end, one lover shot himself in her presence. Cora died of cancer aged 51, in more straitened circumstances, having tried to revive her fortunes as Cupid in a revival of Offenbach's *Orpheus*. Dr Véron, the director of the Opéra, once served up a ballerina on a salver, decorated with green trimmings; this seems to have been a trendy thing to do, if you could afford it.

music. But his success was slow in coming, and at one stage he planned to emigrate. He got his break, however, with the Great Exhibition of 1855. The organist at St Eustache, under the *nom-de-plume* Hervé, had opened a small theatre, the Folies-Nouvelles. There, Offenbach staged *Oyayaye*, about a man who escapes from a cannibal queen by rowing away on his double bass. This success, and financial backing from the founder of *Le Figaro*, enabled Offenbach to set up on his own. He opened in a tiny wooden theatre, formerly used by a conjuror, on the Champs Elysées, near the Exhibition site. Thus began Les Bouffes-Parisiens.[54]

The licence only allowed for one-act shows comprising comic plays with words and music for two or three characters. Offenbach turned these restrictions to his advantage: the show could gradually be refreshed as each one-act play was replaced. Only two months after the Bouffes was founded, it had become a recognised institution. *Les Deux Aveugles*, a skit on Paris beggars, ran to 400 performances.*

The Bouffes became one of the sights of Paris: Meyerbeer attended frequently; the novelist Thackeray went there, as did Tolstoy. The company soon moved to another building, the 'Théâtre des Bouffes-Parisiens'. The support of Morny, who helped Offenbach get French citizenship and contributed to the libretto for *Monsieur Choufleuri*, gave this theatre royal warrant status.[55]

From novels of the period, we get an impression of what the theatre might have been like. With its flaring gas jets, it would have been stiflingly hot and stuffy. Backstage, 'the gas man was at his post beside a complicated array of taps; a fireman was leaning against a flat, craning his neck to watch; and at the very top, the curtain raiser was sitting resignedly on his bench knowing nothing about the performance, just waiting for the bell before operating his ropes'.[56]

The atmosphere was most unpleasant, 'with its strong underlying stench of gas, stage-set glue, squalid dark corners, and the smell of the female extras' unwashed underwear. The passage way was even more suffocating; from time to time the sharp scent of toilet water and soap drifting down from the dressing-rooms blended with the pestilential odour of human breath.' Accompanying this was 'a sound of washbasins, laughter, shouts, and banging doors releasing female smells in which the musky odour of make-up mingled with the harsh animal scent of hair'.[57]

* Sullivan's *Cox and Box* was inspired by *Les Deux Aveugles*.

There was not much respect for the music. While 'the leader of the orchestra was raising his bow and the musicians launched into the overture, people were still coming in, and the din and general commotion were increasing'.[58]

Nevertheless, people flocked to Offenbach's operettas, a term which he invented for *La Rose de Saint-Flour* in 1856. People laughed, clapped and wanted to dance; Offenbach's music was sung everywhere. Without knowing it, people laughed at themselves, and some later complained that his satire weakened the fabric of the empire. For librettist, he joined up with Fromental Halévy's nephew, Ludovic, a civil servant. *Ba-ta-clan*, a *chinoiserie musicale*, was their first collaboration. In 1857, Offenbach's father-in-law was persuaded to bring the Bouffes to London where it did an eight-week season at the St James' theatre, with Jules playing in the orchestra.[59]

Between 1858 and 1870, Offenbach would visit Bad Ems,* one of the oldest spas, with thermal springs, set in wooded hills by a tributary to the Rhine, not far from Coblenz.[60] Here, on a stage in the Marble Hall, with its sixteen magnificent pillars, Offenbach was theatre manager, composer, director of music. The room was small and hence only small-scale works were composed and staged.[61]

Offenbach was not good at managing his own affairs. He was regularly on the run from his creditors, Bad Ems being a good place to which to escape. There he wrote *Orpheus in the Underworld*, which was premièred on 21 October 1858, the first full-length work to be done at the Bouffes. It was not an immediate success, but audiences picked up after some amendments were made. The enthusiasm was fuelled after the critics Théophile Gautier and Jules Janin said it was profane; everyone had to go and look for themselves. The waltzes and gallops became the rage, and the cancan gave an opportunity to see some pretty legs. After the 228th performance, the players were so exhausted that the operetta had to be taken off, although a special performance was staged for the emperor.[62]

Offenbach at his Peak

Offenbach was now a star in his own right. The successful composer's Paris residence was close to the palace of the Rothschilds. He was to be seen

* Bad Ems, Wiesbaden, Baden-Baden and Homburg were the major European spas: in France, casinos had been banned by Louis-Philippe by a decree in 1837. Bad Ems was a regular haunt of King Wilhelm I, and others such as Dostoyevsky and Gogol.

strolling in yellow trousers and waistcoat, a light blue velvet coat, grey gloves and grey hat, 'looking like a grotesque character escaped from one of his own operettas'.[63] He was an unmistakable figure, 'a cross between a cock and a grass-hopper'.[64] He was very thin and never weighed more than 50 kilos (7 st 12 lbs). He had a hawk-like nose, side-whiskers and long, blond, wavy hair about which he was very vain. He had a daily coiffure.

He was also a workaholic: he wrote operettas at a rate of about four a year; of these over 50 were in one act only. Between 1855 and his death, he wrote at a rate of one act every six and a half weeks. Often his trick was to quote well-known tunes. Thus we hear tones of Gluck's 'Che farò' in Offenbach's *Orpheus in the Underworld*.

The Offenbach household only woke up in the evening. Then, Renoir, the impressionist, would often drop in and have a cigarette while Offenbach was having his breakfast coffee and croissant.[65]

Offenbach was now rich enough to build himself a summer residence at Etretat, a small seaside village, to the north of Le Havre. Fashionable Parisians, in search of scarce fresh air, then flocked to the Normandy coast: the empress might be seen at Trouville, the Duc de Morny at Deauville. It would have been rather difficult to promenade at Etretat, if the beach was as pebbly then as now. But, framed at either end by dramatic white cliffs, Etretat in the 19th century attracted artists, including Courbet and Monet.[66] The novelist Guy de Maupassant spent his childhood there.

Offenbach peaked in the mid-1860s, with two operettas using librettos by Henri Meilhac and Ludovic Halévy. *La Belle Hélène* was premièred in December 1864, *La Vie Parisienne* in October 1866. The star in these was his mistress Zulma Bouffar, by whom Offenbach had two children.

For the 1867 Exhibition, Offenbach wrote a Ruritanian farce, *La Grande Duchesse de Gerolstein*. While reviewing her troops the Grand Duchess falls for a soldier, Fritz, and sings a charming aria, 'dîtes-lui qu'on l'a remarqué'. She promotes Fritz over her Commander-in-Chief, General Boum. When it transpires that Fritz wants to marry the peasant girl who really loves him, the Grand Duchess has him demoted; she then has a dalliance with Baron Grog who turns out to be married. The censors were somewhat concerned by the story, and they thought that the tsar might think it a parody on Catherine the Great and her lover Potemkin. But when the tsar's train stopped on its way to Paris, he sent a cable to the Russian embassy ordering them to reserve a seat for him for that evening's performance.[67]

The part of the Grand Duchess was performed by Hortense Schneider who had sung in Offenbach's early operettas, including *La Belle Hélène*. She had a son by Duke Ludovic de Gramont-Caderousse, a horse racing enthusiast, who had already lost a million francs at cards, killed someone in a duel, and was coughing blood from consumption. His wild escapades were extravagant: on one occasion, he filled the grand piano at the Café Anglais with champagne to see if it could serve as an aquarium; he also gave Hortense an Easter egg containing a coach and horses.[68]

As the 1870s approached, Offenbach was becoming less popular: his music was considered repetitive, and the public wanted something new. Hervé was preferred to Offenbach, and Blanche d'Antigny, another courtesan, to Schneider. But, worse, General Boum was about to take his revenge on the whole society which Offenbach ridiculed.

The Fall of Babylon

The disruption caused by Haussmann's rebuilding and the general discontent made the regime very unpopular. There had been an attempt on the emperor's life in April 1855. In January 1858, there was the assassination attempt by Count Felice Orsini, an Italian patriot.[69] The assassins attacked as the emperor and empress arrived at the opera for a benefit concert for Eugène Massol, the very distinguished baritone.[70] They threw three bombs made in Birmingham; eight people were killed and 156 were wounded.

The political situation was becoming increasingly unstable. After each of the three revolutions, 1789, the July days in 1830, and the uprisings of 1848, the French worker felt in retrospect that he had been swindled.[71] The bourgeoisie had somehow always won. A cholera plague in 1853–4 added to the discontent: it killed 143,000 people and there were further epidemics in 1865 and 1866.[72] The blockade of the southern states during the American Civil War prevented cotton reaching the textile centres such as Lyon, and caused unemployment and distress.[73]

The opposition, including republicans such as the Jacobins, Blanquists, Proudhonists, Anarchists and later Internationalists, gathered momentum. This was facilitated by the relaxation of press censorship and by permitting the right to strike. The emperor, such a mass of contradictions, had, after all, fought as a revolutionary in Italy in the 1830s. Ironically, as he loosened the reins, France became one of the more democratic parliamentary monarchies among the major powers. But it was to be overwhelmed.

The first issue of Rochefort's *La Lanterne*, a satirical magazine like the modern *Private Eye*, sold 100,000 copies instead of an estimated 4,000. In January 1870, one of the emperor's relatives, Prince Pierre Bonaparte, was visited by a republican journalist, who struck the prince after he called him a scoundrel. The prince grabbed a revolver and shot the journalist.[74] He was acquitted of murder, but Rochefort, who had been vituperative in his criticism of the regime, was imprisoned for six months.*

Although 70 per cent of France supported the emperor in a referendum held at the time, ominously, in Paris, almost 60 per cent were against him. The results, however, caused Emile Ollivier, the prime minister and Liszt's son-in-law, to declare on 30 June 1870 that 'at no epoch was the peace of Europe more assured'.[75]

As often happens, something out of the blue brought down the regime. Two days after the prime minister's remark, the Spanish government offered the vacant Spanish throne to Prince Leopold of Hohenzollern. The French government, which did not want France to be surrounded by Germans, and which was concerned at the growing strength of Prussia, demanded that he should refuse to accept it (see page 20).

After the protests from France, the prince's candidature was withdrawn. But the foreign minister, instead of allowing the Prussians to withdraw gracefully, cabled to his ambassador in Prussia, to demand a guarantee that Prussia would not seek to appoint its candidate to the Spanish throne. On 13 July the King of Prussia received the ambassador in Bad Ems, where Offenbach was performing: the King refused to give the guarantee and sent a telegram to his chancellor, Bismarck. Bismarck had been waiting for such an opportunity and, having strengthened the wording, gave the provocative document to the press, which was outraged by the French arrogance. Two days later, France declared war. *A Berlin*, they cried.

There was hysteria in Paris, where the French still regarded Germany with the kind of amused contempt that Prussians reserved for Austrians. *Le Figaro* opened a subscription fund to present every soldier in the army with a glass of brandy and a cigar. Prime Minister Ollivier said that he entered the war 'with a light heart',[76] a phrase for which he was never forgiven.

* Marquis Henri de Rochefort also wrote musical comedies. Prince Pierre, Lucien Bonaparte's son, married a working-class girl, and was *persona non grata* at the Tuileries. *La Marseillaise* had published an article critical of the Bonapartes. Prince Pierre challenged the journalist to a duel; hence the fatal visit.

At what was to be the last of the Tuileries masked balls, Eugénie, arguably the single most disastrous influence upon the emperor in his later years, had appeared magnificently dressed as Marie Antoinette.

The War

The French were complacent about their military strength. We shall read in connection with Verdi how they had come out on top in the often bloody battles to remove the Habsburgs from Italy; they had achieved their objective of annexing Savoy and Nice. But against the Prussians, the balance of advantage was different. Whereas the Germans could mobilise 1.2 million men within eighteen days, in France, the élite could avoid the draft by purchasing a substitute for around 1,500 fr. On 28 July, the emperor left Paris to command his armies in the field. He was suffering from such pain from the stone in his kidneys that he could hardly ride and certainly could not think clearly. Eugénie told him: 'Louis, fais bien ton devoir.' His plan was to bring the South German states and Austria into the war on his side.[77]

The Prussians struck hard as soon as the French had captured Saarbrücken. The emperor handed over command to Marshal Bazaine, who was defeated and penned in at Metz. The progress of the war became so bad for France that the empress, who had been left behind to run the government in Paris, was afraid that, if her husband returned to Paris, he would be lynched. She sent an army under General MacMahon towards the Belgian and Luxembourg frontier to join the emperor and relieve Metz. That army was duly penned in at Sedan in the Ardennes. There were rations only for a few days. At 3.15 pm on 1 September, the white flag went up, and an army of 84,000 men, 2,700 officers and 39 generals capitulated.[*78] The emperor and MacMahon were taken prisoner. Sedan, once an important textile centre in France, no longer figures prominently on its maps.[79]

On the outbreak of war, Offenbach returned from Bad Ems to Etretat. He was in a difficult position, being a German who had become naturalised as a Frenchman. The Republicans were now hostile towards him. He fled to Bordeaux, Milan and then San Sebastian, where Herminie had gone with the children. So Offenbach was out of Paris during both the Siege and the Commune.

* The empress fled on 4 September and hid in the house of the American dentist, Dr Evans; from there she went to Deauville and the Isle of Wight. She settled with her husband, when he was released, at Camden Place in Chislehurst, Kent.

We must await the chapter on Bizet, who remained in Paris for the Siege, for a fuller story. But, briefly, events unfolded as follows. Trainloads of treasures from the Louvre were sent off to Brest. Refugees poured in and there was no attempt to move non-combatants out. The capital held out against the besieging Germans through one of the coldest of winters. But it capitulated on 28 January 1871. The people of Paris no longer had to fend off the Germans; but, following an incident at Montmartre, they set about fighting themselves. The government escaped and set up in Versailles. The Commune began and Paris was besieged again, this time by compatriots. A couple of months later, government troops got through an unguarded gate. Barricades went up. As the Versailles forces passed inwards, the Communards set the city on fire. The Archbishop of Paris was murdered with other hostages. The retribution was severe: anyone with a gun was shot. In the 'semaine sanglante', 20,000 citizens were killed.* The London *Times* wrote: 'So far as we can recollect, there has been nothing like it in history.'[81]

Later Years

Offenbach tried to resume his old life in Paris. But, without the empire behind him, nothing was ever the same again. He had a series of a few successes but many failures. He was seen as a symbol of the bad old days. Also, his show had simply run its course. By 1875, Halévy wrote in his diary: 'Offenbach, Meilhac and I are exhausted; that is the truth; we have done too much. We have said all that there is to say about choruses, entrances, exits, processions, partings, verses for bridesmaids and rondos for pages.'[82]

In July 1873, Offenbach took over the Théâtre de la Gaîeté. This opened with a play for which he supplied the music, but it was a failure. He decided to produce *Orpheus* as a pantomime, and this ran to full houses for months. But this was followed by *La Haine*, which was another failure. The Gaîeté seemed to be collapsing, in spite of the fact that audiences in London were enthusiastic about Offenbach's ballet for the pantomime *Dick Whittington and his Cat*.

To avoid penury, Offenbach went to seek his fortune in New York. His visit coincided with the last real gold rush, in South Dakota, and the

* In the Terror of 1793–4, around 2,500 were executed in Paris over a period of fifteen months. During the Terror, 'the national body count ran to several hundreds of thousands', however.[80]

United States was still characterised as the land of the cowboy, Buffalo Bill and the Wild West. As we shall see in connection with Tchaikovsky's visit twenty years later, this was a time when fortunes could also be made without enduring the coach robberies, lawlessness, drunkenness and sudden hangings which would later be depicted by Puccini in *La Fanciulla del West*.[83]

Offenbach set out for America in April 1876 in the *Canada*, a ship of the French Line which was on its maiden voyage; it developed propellor problems and then ran into a storm. Once he got there, he conducted selections from *Orpheus* or the *Grand Duchess* in Gilmore Garden, a huge pleasure ground, which featured an artificial waterfall which was intended to look like Niagara Falls. It was the predecessor to Madison Square Garden; it could hold more than 8,000 people, and had recently been used for the religious revivalist meetings of the hymn-writers Moody and Sankey. Offenbach went on to Philadelphia.

He sailed for home on 8 July after a final concert in New York. On his return, there was a revival of *La Belle Hélène*; there was also an adverse article about a conversation onboard ship, in which he had seemed to be disloyal to France.[84]

He continued to compose; he needed the money. He also wanted to create something with more *artistic* quality.* He started negotiating for the production of *The Tales of Hoffmann*, but the Théâtre-Lyrique, which wanted to produce it, went bankrupt. When his opera was well advanced, Offenbach wanted a quick decision about its fate and arranged a concert at his home; the audience were enthusiastic. During the summer, he took a trip to Germany and then went to Etretat, where he was bedridden with gout. He wrote *La Fille du Tambour Major*, his 100th operetta, which was a success. Shortly before the middle of September, he returned to Paris. The thought of the first night of *The Tales of Hoffmann*, for which he had written the piano arrangement, was all that kept him alive. But he died on 5 October 1880. His funeral service was held in La Madeleine. The hearse, followed by Hortense Schneider, did a tour of the theatres before going to Montmartre, where he was buried.

The first night of *The Tales of Hoffmann* took place four months later. Ernest Guiraud orchestrated it and completed the final act.

* Later, Sir Arthur Sullivan would have the same ambition.

Imperial Habsburg Splendour

While the remnants of the Second Empire in France quite suddenly went up in smoke, in Vienna, the gradual but relentless asphyxiation of the Habsburg monarchy continued. This was accompanied by the tunes of the waltzes and operettas of Johann Strauss the Younger.

On the surface, all seemed prosperous and well. Like Paris, Vienna became an enormous construction site.[85] The old fortifications round the inner city were pulled down. The large empty space, the Glacis, which in the past had been so useful for the military to intimidate the populace into submission, was filled with buildings linked by the Ringstrasse, two miles long. Many of Vienna's superficially elegant buildings sprang up, the large and gothic Rathaus, the new Burg theatre, the Palace of Justice, the Houses of Parliament, a church to commemorate the emperor's escape from assassination.[*86] In May 1863, the first stone of the Imperial Opera House was laid.

The court maintained a splendid appearance. The royal family and aristocracy continued to be portrayed by Franz Winterhalter. Balls were held for the emperor wherever he went. The most resplendent was the annual court ball held each February: the knights of the different Habsburg orders would crowd into the Redoutensaal, the largest room in the Hofburg, lit by 10,000 candles. The orchestra was under the direction of Johann Strauss or Carl Ziehrer. A more select 'ball at court' took place a few days later, to which only 700 guests were invited.

Behind this scenery, the Habsburg family was in deep trouble, and the structure of their empire was disintegrating. Bismarck, who in September 1862 became head of the Prussian government, only needed to win a few tricks, and there would be a new united Germany. The states which had formerly looked to Vienna would become controlled from Berlin. Austria would become just a pawn in Europe.

The Family: Elisabeth, Rudolf and Maximilian

Emperor Franz Joseph's mother found him one of her nieces to marry. But when they were introduced, he fell instantly in love with Princess Elisabeth, the fifteen-year-old sister of his intended bride, and married her

* A young Hungarian patriot attempted to assassinate Franz Joseph in 1853. A woman shouted, so the emperor turned just in time to miss the strike of the dagger, which caught the collar of his coat and the edge of his cap.

instead. There was a splendid state wedding, and afterwards the mother put the imperial and nuptial pair to bed, accompanied them on their honeymoon, and provided the empress with a lady in waiting, Countess Sophie Esterházy.*[87]

Elisabeth, known to her family as Sisi, was now far from her parents' remote and beautiful home in Bavaria, and deeply unhappy. She hated her mother-in-law, who took control of the daughter born the following year. Elisabeth insisted on taking her child with her on her travels, and unfortunately the two year old died. Elisabeth wilted under the pressure and when the next two children, Rudolf and Gisela,** were born, she took little interest in them. She became self-centred and obsessed about her weight. She installed a gymnasium, and exercised, walked and rode;[89] she took a cold shower each morning and bathed in olive oil at night; she slept in a mask of raw veal or strawberries. Although five feet eight inches tall, she weighed usually around 110 pounds; she had a waist of twenty inches.

Much of the empress' time was spent travelling, escaping from the rigid and suffocating protocol in Vienna.† When the political situation in Hungary improved, she found every excuse to go there, and to surround herself with Hungarians. Her favourite was the Hungarian prime minister, the dashing Count Andrássy, known in Paris as 'le beau pendu', because he had been sentenced to death in the aftermath of the 1848 troubles.[91] He used her influence to exert pressure on Vienna. During the festivities for the Great Exhibition which was held in Vienna in 1873, she got bored and went off, pleading health reasons. She spent much time hunting in England and Ireland, but this lost its appeal when another beau, Captain Bay Middleton, got married.[92] Eventually, in 1898, an Italian anarchist, out to kill someone prominent, plunged a sharpened file into her breast as she walked from the Beau Rivage hotel in Geneva to a boat on the Lake.

Her son's tragedy has been told in the ballet *Mayerling*, created by

* The family which Haydn served continued to be prominent, so much so that a seven-year-old Esterházy, when attending a retainer's funeral, asked: 'Do the upper classes die too?'

** Before the First World War, Gisela used to attend concerts in Munich (she married a Bavarian cousin). Sitting in the front row, 'her head, adorned by a tall feather, would droop to one side, and she was awakened only by the applause, in which she joined with a friendly smile'.[88] The conductor found this disconcerting.

† The dining arrangements were indicative of this. As soon as the emperor had finished a dish, all the plates were cleared. Since he ate very quickly, many of the 60 archdukes, who attended the weekly glittering family dinner, left unfed.[90]

Kenneth MacMillan and John Lanchbery, using music written by Liszt. In early February 1889, it was announced that Crown Prince Rudolf, by then in his 30s, had died of apoplexy. A few days later, newspaper readers would have been surprised to hear that he had actually committed suicide with his mind deranged, a formula which was possibly more accurate, and which enabled the church to give the heir to the Habsburg throne a Christian burial.

Rudolf did not get on with his father. He was 'alarmingly' liberal, and had secretly contributed articles to a liberal newspaper, which even the editor had to tone down. He was bored; he complained that 'the most minor court adviser has more to do with government than I do'.[93] Even after he married and had a daughter, he kept his bachelor quarters, where, as an alcoholic, and riddled with venereal disease, he compensated the enthusiastic ladies with a souvenir, a cigarette box engraved suitably according to their rank. One was Mary Vetsera, aged seventeen. A few years before, Rudolf had enjoyed her mother, who now arranged for her compliant daughter to take her turn. By then, the depressive prince wanted to commit suicide, but felt he needed a partner to ensure that he carried it through. So, a fortnight after giving her the requisite gold cigarette case, he took Mary to Mayerling, a hunting lodge in the beautiful Vienna Woods above Baden. There, he seems to have murdered her and then shot himself.*

Another family tragedy arose from the French Emperor's attempt, in the mid-1860s, to set up a Latin American empire, despite US policy not to tolerate foreign powers interfering in adjacent countries. Franz Joseph's brother Maximilian was selected as a puppet Emperor of Mexico, a country chaotic with civil war. The appointment pleased Maximilian's ambitious Belgian wife, Charlotte, and suited Franz Joseph, who wanted his colourful and attractive younger brother out of the way. Once the US Civil War was over, and the going became too hot, the French pulled out, and offered to bring Maximilian back. Seemingly, Charlotte would not let him leave and went around Europe trying to gather support, without any

* Some say that the unwanted crown prince was picked off by army sharpshooters. They were under orders from his uncle, on behalf of the conservative faction, which was worried that he would not have the guts to complete his own transaction. It could not be said that the heir to the throne had died in bed with his mistress; so they had to get Mary out 'alive'. Dressed again, and jammed upright between her two uncles, she was driven, lurching, to a grave in the nearby Heiligenstadt Abbey. The ballet begins and ends with this macabre scene.[94]

success. Maximilian was captured by rebels, and was shot, as depicted in Manet's famous painting.*[95]

The Dynasty Crumbles

Meanwhile, the hard-working emperor struggled to hold his diverse empire together. He lived in plain rooms, and slept on a simple iron bedstead: there was no bathroom; he used a washbasin, and a bucket for a chamber pot. His consolation was his supposedly platonic relationship with a 30-year-old actress, Kati Schratt.

He had to contend with Italy, the growing power of Prussia and growing and strident nationalism in Bohemia and Hungary. The 1860s were particularly difficult. A flashpoint came in an unlikely place, Denmark. Just to the north of Hamburg, German and Danish culture and language interfaced and clashed in the duchies of Schleswig and Holstein. Bismarck regarded the duchies, next door to him in Prussia, but at the far end of Europe from Vienna, as a useful source of friction. A war of succession in Denmark generated circumstances in which the Prussians could attack Austria.** In summer 1866, the Austrians and Saxons were defeated at Königgrätz (Sadowa), in central Bohemia. The defeated armies had nearly 25,000 killed and 20,000 taken prisoner; the Prussians lost less than 10,000. Ex-Emperor Ferdinand, from his retirement in Prague Castle, observed pathetically, 'Even I could have done as well as that.'[96] The Pope's secretary of state is reputed to have said that the world was coming to an end.†[98]

Germany was now well on the way to unification. Hanover and Saxony, which had backed the wrong side, were absorbed by Prussia. The Austrians

* Berlioz' son Louis captained a ship involved in evacuating the French troops. Empress Charlotte went mad, but lived another 60 years.

** When the last Oldenburg King of Denmark died in autumn 1863, a German duke contested the right of the new Danish King, Christian IX, to rule in the duchies of Schleswig and Holstein. Prussian and Austrian armies overran Denmark. The king, whose daughter Alexandra later married the Prince of Wales, had to renounce all claims to the duchies. The Austrians wanted the duchies created into a separate state, but the Prussians were not having that.

†Momentous events were also taking place elsewhere in the 1860s, the decade of the American Civil War, and the assassination of Abraham Lincoln. More prosaic was the appearance in 1860 in Birkenhead, Cheshire, of the first street railway, pulled by two horses, and, fifteen months later, the opening of the metropolitan steam railway between Paddington and Holborn Hill. Passengers welcomed the smoothness of the rails.[97] We forget the jolts and judders that must have been a part of everyday life in a city.

consented to the formation of the North German Confederation, and Venetia, the last Habsburg foothold in Italy, was lost. The Franco-Prussian War later brought the southern German states into the Prussian fold: the risk of not backing the Prussians was too great. Early in 1871, the King of Prussia was hailed as Kaiser in the Hall of Mirrors in Versailles.

By this stage, anyway, economic growth in Austria was falling far behind Prussia. Prussian development was phenomenal,* with all the advantages of the latecomer over the industrial pioneer.

Fiddling While Rome Burns: Johann Strauss

The Austrian decline, thinly papered over with imperial glory, created the environment in which Johann Strauss the Younger could thrive. The Viennese could be proud of his international success. His waltzes could distract them from the disasters that were taking place.

Theatres boomed. With the destruction of the city walls in 1857, the theatres beyond, such as the Theater an der Wien, the theatre of *The Magic Flute*, were absorbed into the central life of the capital. Previously, they had been frequented by domestic servants; now, all classes went to them and the servants made a bit on the side by touting tickets.[101]

Offenbach's works, in pirated versions, had found their way to Vienna, but their small casts reduced their attraction to the Viennese, who required a different product. They wanted humour rather than subtle satire; waltzes, polkas, folk-singing and yodelling rather than gallops and cancans; more romance and sentimentality, and some cross-dressing, as well, to titillate the men.** Franz von Suppé started doing this with some very successful operettas composed for Vienna in the 1860s; Johann Strauss the Younger would eclipse him in the 1870s and 1880s.

Strauss' father, Johann Strauss the Elder, was the leading performer and composer in the waltz craze which was underway by the time of the Congress of Vienna. He had started in a band which played in the coffee houses, which were frequented by Schubert, and also in the Prater amuse-

* In 1865, Prussia possessed 15,000 steam engines with a total horsepower of 800,000; Austria had just 3,400 engines with a horsepower of 100,000.[99] In the third quarter of the century, the German rail network grew by 500 per cent, to 24,000 miles.[100] The decades in mid-century saw the foundation of Bayer, BASF, Hoechst, and the Deutsche and Dresdner banks.

** By contrast, Gilbert and Sullivan prohibited cross-dressing and stipulated that women should wear no dress that could not be worn at a private fancy dress ball.[102]

ment park, where the lower orders could hear excerpts from the operas being played to the aristocracy elsewhere. He travelled with his own orchestra to France and England, where he took part in Queen Victoria's coronation celebrations.[103]

Johann the Younger was born in Vienna on 25 October 1825. He was educated at one of Vienna's most prestigious schools, because his father wanted him to be a banker.[104] The leader of his father's band gave him lessons on the side. In 1842, once his father left to live with a seamstress, with whom he had seven more children, Johann could take proper instruction, and study with the choirmaster of the cathedral. Although still a minor, he was granted a licence to give public concerts and formed his own band, which made its first appearance at a casino near Vienna. For a time, the son's band became a serious competitor to the father's, until Johann Strauss the Elder died in 1849.

Strauss took part in the 1848 troubles, during which he was to be heard playing the 'Marseillaise' on student barricades.[105] This did not endear him to the authorities. During the 1850s he played in private homes, sometimes attending three or four events in a night, so that he could appear at each in person. Between 1856 and 1886, as the King of the Waltz, he toured throughout Europe; he would conduct, fiddle in hand. His brothers, the melancholy Joseph and Eduard, shared in leading the orchestra. The audience was captivated by his music, which was easy to the ear, with a 'diatonic' sound,[106] a standard rhythm, and predictable eight-bar phrases. He used a standard format: five waltzes, prefaced by a slow introduction, and followed by a coda which repeated the catchy tunes which had gone before. This had been his father's formula.[107]

His international stature was assured in 1867 when the 'Blue Danube' Waltz was performed during the Paris Exhibition at a ball given by Princess Pauline Metternich, the socialite wife of the Austrian ambassador. But his revolutionary reputation delayed his appointment to the post of Imperial Royal Director of Music for Balls, a title that had been created specially for his father. It was only granted after he undertook not to play in dubious taverns and casinos. Eduard then took over running the orchestra, which he continued to do until the turn of the century.[108]

Johann Strauss resigned from the court post in 1871 because of a chronic ailment. In 1872, he went to Boston for the 'World Peace Jubilee', a well-intentioned, but clearly ineffective, event which followed the end of the Franco-Prussian War. Monster concerts were the fashion at the time.*[109] Strauss conducted 100 sub-conductors, who managed the 20,000 singers and 10,000 orchestral players. The conservative musical population of Boston disapproved of these shows, and this one was a financial disaster for its promoter, the Irishman, Patrick Gilmore. Four years later, Strauss dedicated the Centennial waltzes to the Citizens of the United States on the anniversary of the Declaration of Independence.

Strauss' first wife Henriette was a singer. It was she who suggested that he turn to operetta, which would be far less demanding on his time, and more remunerative. He would be paid a royalty per performance, and receive the profit from benefit performances (such as anniversaries); on top of this, the highlights could be sold separately as sheet music, for home performance. So, whereas he was paid 250 fl for the 'Blue Danube', from his first operetta, he made 16,000 fl for the stage work and 10,000 fl selling the dances to his publisher.[110]

His market was already assured. The audiences already knew his dance tunes. Those who could not afford piano reductions of his dances could participate in the performance and, after the happy ending, 'leave with one of his tunes humming in their ears'.[111] The gallery had almost certainly hummed or clapped the tunes along during the performance. For a few hours the audience were entertained and could escape from reality.

Indigo was premièred in February 1871. In this, the enrichment of Ali Baba the mule trader mirrored the Viennese prosperity of the time; there was a harem, guarded by two eunuchs called Falsetto and Soprano. The oriental theme was topical: fifteen months earlier the Suez Canal had been opened, with great pomp, jointly by Franz Joseph and Empress Eugénie in a gesture of Austro-French solidarity.[112]

In 1874, *Die Fledermaus* was a sensational success. Its launch was helped by the stock market crash which took place in the previous year and which badly hit the entertainment industry. Attendance levels at masked balls had fallen dramatically: at one of the main ballrooms, Schwenders, attendance was down by over 60 per cent.[113] In December 1872, average

* They had begun in the 1850s under Louis Antoine Jullien, who conducted Beethoven with a jewelled baton and white gloves brought to him on a silver salver. Gilmore was Jullien's successor. His Peace Jubilee in 1869, with Ole Bull (Grieg's supporter), as concertmaster, was a success. The performance included Verdi's 'Anvil Chorus' with 100 local firemen in uniform, and helmets, playing the anvils.

champagne consumption in a prominent city restaurant was 40 bottles a night; a year later, two. Those who could no longer afford to go to a ball could now take 'vicarious pleasure' in Prince Orlofsky's ball on the stage.

Strauss' success continued. *The Gipsy Baron*, first performed in 1885, was performed on German-speaking stages 7,420 times between 1896 and 1921.[114]

After his first wife died, Strauss married an actress, but she left him after nine years. He then married a banker's widow, Adele, who was Jewish. The law in Austria did not permit divorce or inter-faith marriages. To get around this, the Strausses went to an area of modern Romania (the Siebenbürgen) where they converted to the Evangelical church and then wed.[115] Strauss was obliged to give up his Austrian citizenship, and became a citizen of Saxe-Coburg-Gotha.

Whereas Offenbach never satirised the Jews, some of Strauss' works reflect the increasingly anti-Semitic attitudes which we shall see building up, particularly in Vienna. Anti-Semitism brewed among former rural workers now living in urban squalor, and among the craftsmen, small shopkeepers, office workers and minor civil servants. They felt oppressed by the strongly Jewish middle class above them and those whose wealth was on display in the Ringstrasse, known then as the 'street of Zion in the new Jerusalem'.[116] In 1861 over 60 per cent of the Viennese medical profession was Jewish; in 1890, half of the journalists and as many as two-thirds of lawyers in Vienna were Jewish. Strauss' audience will have enjoyed the overtly Jewish lawyer Dr Blind, in *Die Fledermaus.*[117]

Composers of light music often yearn to write something more 'serious', as did Offenbach in *The Tales of Hoffmann*. Strauss tried to do the same thing with *Ritter Pásmán*, premièred in the Court Opera. But who has heard of that? It was a glittering social occasion, a sell out and a flop.[118]

Strauss died on 3 June 1899. The turn of the century also saw the death of Arthur Sullivan,* who had worked with W.S. Gilbert to produce the operettas which gave such special pleasure and amusement to English audiences. Yet the concept of operetta, something musical but lighter than

* Sullivan, the son of the bandmaster at the Sandhurst Military Academy, studied at the Royal Academy of Music and Leipzig, where he was a contemporary of Grieg. He then became an organist in London. His partnership with W.S. Gilbert followed the successful London performance of Offenbach's *La Périchole*. *Trial by Jury* led to the collaboration with the impresario Richard D'Oyly Carte, and eventually to the Savoy operas, such as *HMS Pinafore* and *The Pirates*

opera, was far from dead, as anyone who visited Broadway or the West End at the turn of the following century will be well aware. The product is perhaps not to everybody's taste. When Tchaikovsky saw *The Mikado* performed in Vienna, he could barely endure two-thirds of an act and walked out.[120]

Others, we must remember, feel the same about opera, whether by Wagner or Verdi.

of Penzance. The Mikado (1885) ran for 672 successive performances. The partners became embroiled in litigation over the production expenses for *The Gondoliers* (1889). Anyway, their relationship was uneasy, in part because Sullivan's ambition was to be a 'serious' composer. He used a different librettist for *Ivanhoe* (1891). When he died, he was given an enormous funeral in St Paul's Cathedral.[119]

VERDI

CHAPTER 16

AROUND 10 OCTOBER 1813, less than six months after Wagner was born in Leipzig, Giuseppe Verdi was born near Busseto close to Parma. This was then part of Napoleon's puppet Kingdom of Italy, so the boy was registered as Joseph rather than Giuseppe. When he died on 27 January 1901, Queen Victoria was lying in state in Osborne. Their demise was celebrated with comparable state funerals. Just as the Queen dominated 19th-century Britain, Verdi stands astride the music of 19th-century Italy.

Verdi knew exactly how to convey emotion and drama in beautiful melody. The arias which we love, such as 'La Donna è Mobile' from *Rigoletto*, have a naturalness and simplicity. His operas therefore provide a contrast to the complex, 'orchestral' operas of Wagner. They are essential items in the opera house and elsewhere: how many brides have walked down the aisle to the strains of the Grand March from *Aïda*! No matter that theatrical productions of the March often include elephants and giraffes.

With a canny sense of timing and some genuine sympathy, Verdi espoused the cause of Italian nationalism. The combination of his music and his stories conveyed an emotional message to his compatriots, who yearned for delivery from despotic monarchs. This was an aspect which the check-list used by the strict but pedantic censors was not designed to identify.

Thus, Verdi could emulate the work of the poet Alessandro Manzoni, whose tragedy *Adelchi*, about Charlemagne's overthrow of the Lombard domination in Italy, contained many veiled allusions to the burden of Habsburg rule. In Verdi's *La Battaglia di Legnano*, the knights swear to repel Italy's tyrants beyond the Alps. No wonder that, on the eve of their revolution, the citizens of Rome were delirious about it. No wonder that the chorus in *Nabucco*, 'Va, pensiero', in which the captive Hebrews long for their homeland, launched Verdi's career.

Verdi's direct contribution to the revolutionary cause was, however, limited to setting rousing words to beautiful and memorable tunes. During the upheavals of 1848, he was actually based in Paris pursuing his career and his mistress, the former *prima donna* Giuseppina Strepponi. However, the story of the unification of Italy is such important background to Verdi's life that, having considered his early years, we must return again to it and to the achievements of Giuseppe Garibaldi, the colourful freedom-fighter, who led the battle for it.

The 1850s saw the three important and very popular operas by Verdi – *Rigoletto*, *Il Trovatore* and *La Traviata* – which were less obviously political. Thereafter, the rate of composition decelerated and came to a halt with *Aïda*, which was produced in Cairo on Christmas Eve 1871, and the Requiem of 1874, written in honour of Manzoni. There was a long pause before Verdi emerged from retirement to write the two last operas, *Otello*, produced in February 1887, and finally *Falstaff*, which was premièred in 1893, just before he was 80.

Verdi kept away from, and was not asked to join, the titanic struggle that rent the musical world to the north: he is not to be found on either side of the fissure which divided Brahms and his adherents from the New Music of Berlioz, Liszt and Wagner. This irritated Verdi, who was annoyed that the new generation did not regard his work as modern art. But with *Otello* and *Falstaff*, one an *opera seria*, the other an *opera buffa*, both unarguably great works of art, Verdi brought the development of Italian opera to its ultimate conclusion. Italian operas composed afterwards, even those of Puccini, are at best but an imitation of what Verdi achieved.

Verdi's Early Life

Verdi's story was by no means the rags to riches one that legend (and particularly he) would have it be: his family, small-holders, were among the less than ten per cent of the population who could read and write.[1] Carlo, his father, was an innkeeper who got into trouble for failing to pay his rent and for various irregularities such as permitting unlicensed gambling to take place on his premises; his mother was the daughter of another innkeeper from a few miles away.

Giuseppe Verdi was born in a small two-storey house* in Le Roncole, a small village a few miles from Busseto. We can imagine that, outside Carlo's inn, 'there hung a grey dishcloth attached to a stick; on the cloth was inscribed the word *Trattoria*'. Perhaps 'a tattered bedsheet, supported on two very slender wooden hoops and hanging down to within three feet of the ground, protected the door from the direct rays of the sun'. Perhaps the bedroom was very large and fine; perhaps it had 'grey canvas instead of glass in its two windows' and 'four beds, each six feet wide and five feet high'.[2]

As he grew up, solemn young Peppino helped in the inn and played the organ in the little church which was about a hundred yards from where he was born. One day, the priest, whom he was assisting at Mass, angrily swore at him, saying 'May God strike you down'. Shortly afterwards, the cleric and two choristers, but fortunately not Verdi, were struck by lightning. This episode did not endear Verdi to religion.[3]

Verdi was keen to progress, so the local organist persuaded Carlo to buy him an old spinet, hardly a normal item of furniture for such people. A friend repaired it for free. When the organist died, Verdi took over, and on high days and holidays he had to return to Le Roncole from Busseto, where he went to school, and lodged with a cobbler.

When he was twelve, Verdi had lessons in counterpoint and composition from a Busseto organist. He was sponsored by Antonio Barezzi, a prosperous, flute-playing grocer and distiller who started the local Philharmonic Society. Barezzi became a second father to him; on Barezzi's death many years later, Verdi said: 'I owe him absolutely everything.'[4] The Philharmonic Society of around 70 amateur musicians no doubt played marches, overtures and variations, and the latest hit by Rossini. It also played compositions written by the young Verdi, who soon fell in love with Barezzi's elder daughter Margherita, and wanted to be in a position to marry her.

* There is some question about the actual location; the original birthplace may have been burnt by soldiers fighting in the Napoleonic wars.

When he was nearly nineteen, Verdi applied to enter the Milan Conservatoire, but he was turned down on several grounds: he was too old, there was no room, he had learnt an inappropriate piano method, and his counterpoint needed discipline. Also, he was a foreigner: his home state of Parma, although a puppet of Austria, was a separate country from Austrian Lombardy.*

Having been rejected, Verdi was advised to go to Milan and study privately. Apart from the Napoleonic interlude, the walled city of Milan had long been one of the most important and lucrative possessions of the Habsburgs. It had a correspondingly impressive musical tradition, employing Giovanni Battista Sammartini, and, for a time, Bach's son Johann Christian, who later moved to London. The Ducal Theatre, which had been burnt down in 1776, had been replaced by La Scala on the site of the church of Santa Maria della Scala. With financial support from Barezzi, Verdi studied privately with Vincenzo Lavigna, a minor composer who had had some success at La Scala. He gave Verdi an excellent grounding in counterpoint and fugue.

Verdi, who seems to have led the high life, lodged with his former headmaster's nephew and chased his daughter.[6] There were complaints about his 'boorish manners'. He was described as 'ill-educated in his manners, arrogant and … something of a scoundrel'.[7] Barezzi ticked him off. But Verdi was learning works by Rossini, Donizetti and Bellini, and hearing performances by *prima donnas* such as Malibran and Pasta. He was progressing: he accompanied a rehearsal of Haydn's *Creation* on the piano, but soon had taken over the baton; in the end, it was agreed that he should conduct the performance.

Although apparently Verdi could have been appointed to the well-remunerated post of organist in Monza Cathedral, he chose to return to Busseto as local director of music. Verdi's behaviour in Milan, and his free-thinking religious views, may have led the residents of Busseto to suspect him of being a liberal; indeed, had he worn his distinctive black beard at this time, they would have been sure that he was a member of that 'most insolent set of people'. The novelist Stendhal, who knew Italy well, wrote

* Parma was ruled by a duchess, Napoleon's Empress Marie-Louise, who had obtained it by virtue of the Congress of Vienna. She lived there with her lover, the one-eyed Austrian General Count Neipperg, whom she married in 1821 after Napoleon's death. When the first count died, she took up with another, René de Bombelles. The Lord Chamberlain responsible for the Vienna Opera when Mahler was in charge was a grandson of Marie-Louise.[5]

in 1839 that 'the deepest dungeons were reserved for the blackest Liberals'.[8] We should not therefore be surprised that the residents of Busseto did not want Verdi as organist of their principal church. They put forward their own candidate, one Giovanni Ferrari, for that job. What may seem petty to us was important to them: the violence between Ferrari's and Verdi's supporters reached such a pitch that the dragoons were called in, and at one stage the duchess felt obliged to forbid music in the Busseto churches.

Eventually, Ferrari was appointed organist and Verdi took the municipal duties, which entailed giving lessons at the music school and conducting concerts of the Philharmonic Society. Verdi entered into a three-year contract with the municipality for 657 lire per annum, rising to 1,000 lire.* Although embittered, this gave him security and a position. He could marry Ghita Barezzi and settle down for three years to the life of a provincial music master in this insignificant town, which is set in flat countryside relieved only by the view of the Apennines in the far distance.

A daughter was born nine months after the wedding, and then a son. They were called Virginia and Icilio, both names with liberal overtones. Virginia lived only for seventeen months. It must have been a difficult time for the restless and ambitious Verdi, who had started work on an opera, *Oberto, Conte di San Bonifacio*. He did not renew his three-year contract in 1839, but moved back to Milan. There he could try to get *Oberto* staged. He could also attend the salons, where aristocracy and artists could mingle well away from the government, whose officials were usually kept out.[10]

La Scala was run by the impresario Bartolomeo Merelli, who also ran the Kärntnertor theatre in Vienna. *Oberto* was premièred at La Scala in November 1839, after Verdi had made various adaptations as requested. It was sufficiently successful that the publisher Giovanni Ricordi** bought the rights for 2,000 lire. Merelli commissioned three further operas to be given at intervals of eight months.[12]

Although Verdi seemed to be starting to make his way, this was a diffi-

* Around this time, a travelling actor was regarded as well remunerated with 32 lire a month; members of the lesser nobility had an income of 3–4,000 lire per annum.[9]

** Ricordi started a copying business, and after study with Breitkopf & Härtel in Leipzig, set up his publishing business in Milan. During the first half of the 19th century, he absorbed Artaria's business, and entered into exclusive publishing contracts with many of the opera houses in Italy. By 1837, he was able to advertise more than 10,000 publications, and by his death in 1853 had issued 25,000.[11]

cult and tragic time. After deducting the 50 per cent payable to Merelli, the proceeds from *Oberto* were equivalent to Verdi's previous annual salary; but money was short and Ghita had to pawn her jewellery in order to pay the rent. Then Ghita and Icilio died quite suddenly; Verdi himself suffered throat trouble.[13] Disaster struck professionally as well: the first of the commissioned operas, *Un Giorno di Regno*, was taken off after the first performance. Verdi never forgave Milan for this, just as he nurtured his dislike of the citizens of Busseto, and kept in his desk a reminder of his rejection by the Conservatoire.

Nabucco and Success

According to one account, Merelli found Verdi a libretto which had been turned down by a leading composer based in Vienna, Otto Nicolai. Verdi was particularly attracted by its Hebrew chorus 'Va, pensiero', with its yearning for freedom. *Nabucco* was produced at La Scala in Spring 1842.

The lead role of Abigaille, the unpleasant eldest child of King Nabucco, was sung by Giuseppina Strepponi, a star *prima donna* of the 1830s. (Verdi had nearly succeeded her father as organist of Monza Cathedral.) Verdi was apprehensive about the première. Exhausted by overwork and the stress of giving birth to a succession of abandoned children,[14] Strepponi's voice had deteriorated to such an extent that it was unusual for her to perform well for three successive days. Fortunately, she was in good voice on the night, and the première was a success.

Indeed, it was a triumph. When it was revived in the following autumn, it ran for 57 performances, 'a figure unmatched before or since' in the annals of La Scala.[15] Verdi visited Vienna and toured Italy. Old Carlo was able to witness his son's success during the run at Parma in the spring of 1844. *Nabucco* was put on in all the major centres in Europe, in New York, and in such less likely places as Algiers, Constantinople, Havana and Buenos Aires.

The censors seem to have overlooked the political message in *Nabucco*, as they did for Verdi's next opera, *I Lombardi*, which was premièred at La Scala in November 1843. This was about crusaders who express much the same emotions as the Hebrews in *Nabucco*. When the censors reviewed *I Lombardi*, they were primarily concerned with changing an aria beginning with 'Ave Maria' and having the baptism of an infidel removed. They seem to have had no premonition of the effect that Verdi's melodies and 'strong, slow-surging rhythms' would have.[16] Verdi asked Count de Bombelles if he could dedicate it to the Duchess of Parma; she received him and presented him with a diamond pin.

After Verdi's initial success, he thought about writing operas based on *King Lear* and Byron's *The Corsair*. Occasionally, he returned to the idea of an opera about *King Lear*, but he never created it: perhaps the story was too like *Nabucco*, the mad king with a nasty child. For Venice, he thought about *The Two Foscari*, also by Byron: but he was worried, at this stage, that the story might offend some of the Venetian nobility. Then Verdi was introduced to Francesco Maria Piave, the son of a glass manufacturer from Murano. Verdi was not motivated by Piave's suggestion of an opera about Cromwell, and instead they worked together on Victor Hugo's *Ernani*, the drama which had caused such a sensation in Paris on its first night in 1830. The opera was produced in Venice's La Fenice in March 1844. '*Ernani* was more than a success; it became a fashion, keeping Verdi's name before the public.'[17] It represented the start of the partnership with Piave, who wrote the librettos for *Rigoletto*, *La Traviata* and *La Forza del Destino*.

Verdi was soon recognised as the leading opera composer in Italy. Bellini was dead, Rossini had retired, Donizetti was in an asylum; the only other contender was Saverio Mercadante, the director of the Naples Conservatoire. Verdi was accepted in Milan society: a salon which he frequented was that of Countess Clarina Maffei, whose husband, an improbable combination of government official and poet, was involved with the librettos of *Macbeth* and *I Masnadieri*. At this salon, Verdi met members of Young Italy, a conspiratorial and anti-clerical society of under-40s which the journalist Mazzini had founded.[18] Its aim was a united republic of Italy. However, Verdi did not join it.

He planned to work himself hard, spending 'years in the galleys', and then retire, as Rossini had done.[19] So he composed, he travelled, almost to exhaustion and certainly to depression. Between *Ernani* in March 1844 and *Rigoletto* in March 1851, he composed or arranged eleven operas: *I Due Foscari*, *Giovanna d'Arco*, *Alzira*, *Attila*, *Macbeth*, *I Masnadieri*, *Jérusalem* (the French version of *I Lombardi*), *Il Corsaro*, *La Battaglia di Legnano*, *Luisa Miller*, and *Stiffelio*.

Verdi's appeal to patriotic emotions, as expressed in *Nabucco* and *I Lombardi*, was the secret of much of his success at this time. In 1846, around the time of the accession of Pope Pius IX, seen then as a great liberator, the Bolognese audience at Verdi's *Ernani* chanted 'A Pio Nono sia gloria ed onor'* to the music that accompanied the king's granting of a general pardon.[20] Verdi's opera with the title *Giovanna d'Arco* obviously had patriotic overtones.

Verdi was demanding on his librettists and specified in meticulous detail what he wanted musically and in the staging. 'Study closely the dramatic situation, and the words', he said; 'the music comes of itself.'[21] From several preliminary sketches he would prepare a skeleton, with the vocal lines, the bass and a few instrumental cues. Then he wrote the singers' parts. He left the orchestration until the piano rehearsals, at which he moulded the composition, even giving the specific singers alternatives from which to choose. For the Act 1 duet in *Macbeth* he had over 150 rehearsals, holding up the dress rehearsal for more, so much so that Macbeth seemed to be about to murder Verdi rather than King Duncan. His effort was rewarded: on the first night, there were over 30 curtain calls.[22]

At this time, Verdi's operas were by no means always successful. And he was not always well-regarded, especially beyond the Alps. Nicolai, who composed *The Merry Wives of Windsor* (*Die lustigen Weiber von Windsor*) in 1849, wrote in his diary: 'the Italian opera composer of today is Verdi ... But his operas are truly dreadful and utterly degrading for Italy. He scores like a madman, is quite without technique and he must have the heart of a donkey and in my view is truly a pitiful contemptible composer.'[23] There were complaints that he forced singers' voices: Hans von Bülow called him Attila to the throat. Queen Victoria observed in her diary that his music was 'very noisy and trivial';[24] but maybe she was annoyed that he had refused to be presented to her.

Unlike so many great artists, Verdi was a good businessman. If a theatre would not pay him his advance, he suspended rehearsals. He commanded big money. However, the English would not stump up the equivalent of the 90,000 lire, the country house and carriage which he required as compensation for becoming the musical director at Her Majesty's Theatre.[25] By the time of *La Battaglia di Legnano* and *Luisa Miller*, he had earned enough to retire, and he indicated in his letters to friends that he shortly would.

Verdi now applied his business acumen to his farming enterprise. He

* 'Honour and glory to Pope Pius IX.' *Giovanna d'Arco* was about Ste Jeanne d'Arc, who fought against English rule in France; St Joan had not been canonised in Verdi's time.

had bought himself a palazzo in Busseto in 1845. Three years later, he bought the country house and farm at Sant'Agata, which is a couple of miles the other side of Busseto from Le Roncole. His family had originally come from there, but his choice of location was surprising, given his aversion for the people in his home town.

At first, Verdi spent most of his time in Paris, and he established his parents at Sant'Agata. Carlo managed the property incompetently and there was a dispute, even to the extent that father and son had to correspond through lawyers. His relations with his father may well have been soured by his own irregular domestic arrangements with Strepponi (see colour plate 44), which very possibly began with the Parma performance of *Nabucco* in 1844.[26]

Peppina Strepponi had been trained at the Milan Conservatoire, and Verdi came across her when she was cast in the first performance of *Oberto* and then, of course, in *Nabucco*. She had a 'lovely figure and, to Nature's liberal endowments, she adds an excellent technique'.[27] As was so frequently the case when singers needed money, she had strained her voice by singing too much too young. By the time she was 31, she was exhausted and had to retire. Verdi had provided her with a letter of introduction to the Escudier brothers, publishers in Paris, and she set up there, running a singing school for young gentlewomen. At this time, Verdi wrote her a love letter, sealed and never opened;[28] thus, we shall see, it remains. He joined her in Paris, where they lived together. They were resident there during the Italian upheavals of 1848–9, which now demand our attention.

The Liberation of Italy: 1848–9

Verdi was in sympathy with the momentum to remove the Habsburgs from Italy.* In 1847, a performance of *Nabucco* almost caused a riot in Milan, and the conductor Angelo Mariani was threatened with imprisonment for fomenting rebellion. Although Verdi took no active part in politics, he was perceived as 'a prophet of the people, of the forces of nationalism that were carrying Italy in its tide'.[29] In this, he was consistent with writers such as Alfieri** (who coined the word '*Risorgimento*' to denote the

* Events leading up to and during the 1848 revolution are described on page 288 et seq.

** Schumann read works of Alfieri before visiting Italy, aged nineteen. Verdi's two children were named after characters in Alfieri's dramas.

resurgence of Italian national consciousness)[30] and Manzoni; and with the recent moderate writers and journalists who advocated an end to Habsburg rule but did not necessarily go so far as calling for a united Italy.[31] There appeared to be insuperable barriers to unification, not least the existence of the Papal States, which divided the peninsula geographically.

The upheavals of 1848–9 started in Sicily. Encouraged by the fall of Metternich in early March, Milan rose with the 'Cinque Giornate', the five days, and Venice proclaimed a Republic. Verdi returned to Italy very briefly during this time, and was in Rome for the première of *La Battaglia di Legnano*, which took place ten days before Rome was declared a Republic early in the following year; the opening chorus 'Long live Italy, a sacred pact unites its children' drove the audience into a frenzy, and the last act had to be repeated completely. But Verdi's principal preoccupation at the time was the purchase of the farm at Sant'Agata.[32]

The revolutions eventually were crushed by the authorities. At the battles of Custozza and Novara,[33] the Habsburg army put down the insurrection in northern Italy, including Milan, by defeating the Piedmontese.* The Habsburg armies then bombarded Venice, which, starved and suffering from cholera, capitulated. Largely through the intervention of the French, the Roman Republic was destroyed. Pope Pius IX returned to his throne. By this stage, Verdi, safely back in Paris, was wringing his hands about the wretched times in which they lived.[34]

But despite the setbacks, two important 'players' had survived: Mazzini and Garibaldi, the 'brains' and the 'brawn' respectively. There was also a king committed to the cause: the new King of Sardinia, Victor Emmanuel II, the ruler of Piedmont, which retained its 'liberal' constitution. The territory ruled by this dashing *Re Galantuomo* – whose main interests were women, hunting and eating peasant food cooked in garlic – became a haven for liberals. They formed the Italian National Society, pledged to support the cause for independence. The prime minister's 'Nous recommençerons' expressed the determination of the Italians in the north to oust the Habsburgs and their allies in Rome and Naples. Victor Emmanuel would eventually become the first King of Italy.** However, his success was

* The King of Sardinia, whose main sphere of operations was Piedmont, ruled from his capital in Turin. He had found himself in an improbable role as a champion of independence. After his defeats, he abdicated in favour of his son Victor Emmanuel II.

** His tomb, bearing the inscription Padre della Patria, is in the Pantheon in Rome. Cavour, who

derived not so much from his own efforts as those of the irregular forces led by Garibaldi, and most particularly because of events abroad.[36]

The Liberation of Italy: the 1850s and the Battle of Solferino

Although the revolutions of 1848–9 had failed, Italy was unstable and the violence continued. The Kingdom of the Two Sicilies, with its capital in Naples, was regarded as an outrage by liberal-thinking people elsewhere. One former minister, who was sentenced to 24 years in irons, in a dungeon, was visited by the English politician William Gladstone. In foetid darkness, occasionally being given a portion of stinking soup, the prisoners were allowed to emerge, as in Beethoven's *Fidelio*, for half an hour on Thursdays to see their friends. In an exaggerated 'polemical publication of vast impact',[37] Gladstone reported that there were 20,000 political prisoners in the Kingdom.* Not surprisingly, there was an assassination attempt in 1857 on the King of Naples. By this time, assassins had succeeded in killing Carlo III of Parma, and his successor could rule only with the aid of an Austrian garrison.

Camillo di Cavour, who became prime minister of Piedmont, realised that one consequence of the failed revolutions of 1848–9 was that the ejection of the Habsburgs and eventual unification would require external assistance.[39] He stepped out onto the European stage and brought Piedmont into the Crimean War behind the French and British. He sought the help of Napoleon III, knowing that he had supported the Italian cause in the 1830s. The future of Italy was important to Napoleon because, paradoxically, in these decadent years of the Second Empire, Roman Catholics comprised an important and growing part of the emperor's power base.**

became prime minister in 1853, wanted the king to marry a Russian princess, so he insinuated that the king's mistress Rosina had been unfaithful to him. Rosina countered by saying that the attentions paid to her were 'so constant and insatiable that they left her with no appetite or stamina for other men'.[35]

* Gladstone's findings were published in 'A Letter to the Earl of Aberdeen'. The correct number was more like 2,000. His intervention earns his portrait a place in the Museo del Risorgimento in Milan.[38]

** The extent of the religious revival can be seen by the number of priests and nuns. In 1875, there was one priest to 639 people in the French countryside, whereas in 1821 there had been one in 814, an increase of over twenty per cent. The number of nuns had increased more than ten times since earlier in the century.[40]

To influence the Emperor's attitude, Cavour supplied him, shortly after he married Eugénie, with the beautiful Countess Virginia di Castiglione, his own cousin and the mistress of his king. Cavour told her: 'Succeed, cousin, by any means you like, but succeed.'[41] In one respect, she did: Napoleon reputedly gave her a pearl necklace costing more than 400,000 francs, and an allowance of 50,000 francs a month at a time when a woman worker might expect to be paid one and a half to two francs a day.[42] Whether or not Virginia had any political influence, in 1858 Cavour met the Emperor secretly at Plombières (in the Vosges). They agreed that the Habsburgs should be provoked into war and defeated. Afterwards, Piedmont would get northern Italy, while central and southern Italy would become French satellites all under the nominal presidency of the Pope. There was a price attached to the deal: Piedmont would transfer Nice and Savoy to France.

On New Year's Day 1859, Napoleon III publicly provoked the Habsburg ambassador by saying that relations between their countries had deteriorated, while adding that he should tell his emperor that 'my personal feelings for him have not changed'. War fever grew, with the slogan 'Viva Verdi' being widely used. 'Verdi' was actually an acronym for 'Vittorio Emanuele Re d'Italia', although the police could be persuaded that it meant something to do with the composer.[43]

The British, as might be expected, launched a diplomatic initiative to make peace. The Emperor of France, whom the Habsburg Emperor described as a 'scoundrel',[44] then proposed a conference to discuss Italy. Vienna, who had nothing to gain from this, said that it would not participate unless Victor Emmanuel moved his troops away from their border. On 22 April, Vienna gave Piedmont an ultimatum to disarm; when they did not, Vienna declared war and Habsburg troops advanced on Turin.

Verdi's house at Sant'Agata was only fifteen miles from the Habsburg positions at Piacenza. He professed that he would have liked to join up, 'but what could I do who couldn't even undertake a march of three miles? My head won't stand five minutes of sun, and a breath of wind or a touch of damp sends me to bed for weeks on end.'[45] He clearly did not regard himself as suitable military material. But he did get involved in fund-raising for the families of those killed.

The Habsburgs were not well prepared for the war. Their star general, Count Radetzky, had died and been succeeded by a far less resolute commander. Modern communication systems enabled France to get 200,000 soldiers to Piedmont in 25 days, some by sea, some by railway. On 4 June 1859 the Habsburgs were defeated by the French at the battle of Magenta. The Piedmontese stood and watched; the French lost 4,600 men; the Habsburg armies lost 10,200, but retreated in good order into their fortified area known as the Quadrilateral.[46] Napoleon III and Victor Emmanuel entered Milan. The Parma royal family fled.

The Habsburg Emperor, who also had his wife's antics on his mind – 'Sort yourself out for love of me', the desperate man wrote on 15 June; 'get enough sleep and eat enough so you don't get too thin'[47] – took personal command. He hoped that the Prussians might come to his assistance, but they did not. On 24 June, Franz Joseph was again defeated, despite considerable Piedmontese inefficiency, at Solferino to the south of Lake Garda. This battle, with each side led by an emperor, saw the largest number of troops engaged since the Napoleonic battle of Leipzig over 45 years earlier. The French lost nearly 12,000 men, the Piedmontese around 5,500 and the Habsburg armies around 22,500.[48] The bloodshed and sufferings were appalling: ladies went from French châteaux to serve as nurses at the headquarters at Solferino.*

Napoleon III was shocked by the carnage, fed up with the ineffective Piedmontese, concerned about the attitude of his Catholic supporters behind in France, and worried that the Prussians might attack him on the Rhine. He knew that it would be virtually impossible to get the Habsburg troops out of their fortresses in the Quadrilateral. So, much to Cavour's annoyance, the two emperors met alone at Villafranca and negotiated an armistice.[50] By this, the Habsburgs would lose Lombardy but would retain Venetia; and the Habsburg puppet rulers in the Central Duchies of Tuscany, Parma, Modena and Lucca, who had been thrown out, would be restored.

The Piedmontese paid for this by surrendering Savoy, their original family heirloom, and Nice, the birthplace of Garibaldi, to France. Verdi's somewhat misplaced comment, considering the lamentable military performance by the Italians, was: 'What an outcome after so many victories! How much blood shed for no purpose!'[51]

* The horrors were related in a book by a young Swiss stretcher bearer, Henri Dunant, and this led to the formation of the International Red Cross at Geneva five years later.[49]

Verdi the Politician

For Verdi, the immediately relevant part of the armistice was the imminent restoration of the Habsburg puppet regime in Parma. Verdi became an important figurehead in the process by which the people of Parma and the other Central Duchies rejected the restoration and instead voted for annexation by Victor Emmanuel. Plebiscites were held in which all males over 21 had the vote. But they were 'a triumph of creative electioneering … Hitler and Stalin, in their heyday, never achieved results like this'.[52] There was intimidation and, since most of the voters were illiterate, the ballot papers often had 'Sí' (Yes) already written on them. Fewer than 756 votes in all, 0.2 per cent of those voting, were cast against. Still, it was a colourful occasion, with bands playing, solemn processions and free wine flowing.

Verdi was elected the representative of Busseto, and in mid-September led the delegation that waited on King Victor Emmanuel and requested annexation. When this was implemented, Verdi was asked by Cavour and the British ambassador to become a member of the parliament which sat in Turin. As Cavour put it, Verdi's presence 'will contribute to the dignity of Parliament in and beyond Italy … it will convince our colourful colleagues from the south of Italy, who are very much more susceptible to the influence of your artistic genius than we denizens of the cold Po valley are.'[53]

While the proposed annexation was being considered, there was unrest. The mob took its revenge: the chief of police was recognised on the steps of Parma station and decapitated. Verdi was drawn into discussions about the deteriorating situation, but he tried to keep his direct involvement to a minimum. Shy and withdrawn as he was, he remained totally aloof from his constituency. He took his seat but rarely appeared, especially after Cavour died later in 1861. 'I'm still a deputy against every wish and every desire, without having the slightest inclination nor aptitude nor talent', he said.[54] He resigned his seat four years later; his real interests, wisely if not heroically, were shooting, collecting autographs, gardening and developing his estates. He was not interested in politics.[55]

Towards the Kingdom of Italy

Italy at this stage consisted of an enlarged Piedmont in the north, the Papal States in the middle, and the appalling Kingdom of Naples in the south. And the Habsburgs still ruled Venetia. Progress towards unification seemed slow, but the momentum continued.

Insurrection soon broke out in Sicily, which Garibaldi determined to support.

In early May 1860, he sailed from Quarto with 1,089 volunteers, ranging from a boy of twelve to a man of 60. After about eight weeks, in a brilliant and colourful campaign, he had expelled the Neapolitans from Sicily and was preparing to invade the mainland from the south. In September, he swept up through Calabria and entered Naples, accompanied by some

Giuseppe Garibaldi

English visitors who included the public orator of Cambridge University. The English were considerable supporters of Garibaldi: red blouses and round, kepi-shaped Garibaldi hats became fashionable in London at the time.[56]

At a service in the cathedral, the blood of St Januarius, the patron saint of Naples, beheaded in 304 AD, liquefied in Garibaldi's honour.[57] For 62 days, until early November 1860, Garibaldi ruled all but a small area of the Kingdom as its dictator.

Verdi and Giuseppina were delighted: 'Hurrah for Garibaldi!', Verdi wrote. 'God, he is a man before whom we truly should kneel.'[58] But the Neapolitans did not like the boisterousness of his supporters, who swaggered around the streets and interrupted performances at the opera. The orchestra was required to play the 'Garibaldi Hymn' written by Verdi's

Neapolitan rival Mercadante,* a demand enforced at the point of the bayonet when the Garibaldini leapt into the pit.[60]

Cavour realised that the Piedmontese needed to seize back the initiative from Garibaldi, who, despite his effectiveness, was dangerously 'red' as far as they were concerned. Garibaldi's determination to march on Rome would have brought international intervention, thereby putting at risk many of the achievements so far. The Piedmontese invaded the Papal States from the north, dispossessed Pius IX of the Marches and Umbria, and helped Garibaldi finally to defeat the Neapolitan army.

Plebiscites were held which approved Piedmont's annexation of the various territories. Garibaldi met the king. 'I salute you the first King of Italy', said Garibaldi, and doffed his hat.[61] Meanwhile, Emperor Franz Joseph fulminated against 'Garibaldi's banditry, Victor Emmanuel's thievery and the fraudulent practices of the Parisian scoundrel'.[62]

Garibaldi retired to Caprera, his island off the north coast of Sardinia, with his four donkeys which he named Pius IX, Napoleon III, Oudinot (the French general who defeated the Roman Republic) and the Immaculate Conception. This was much to the indignation of French Roman Catholics, but to the delight of English Protestants.[63]

Finally, Venetia and then Rome

Thus, by the end of 1860, the whole Italian peninsula had been absorbed into Piedmont, except for Austrian Venetia and a few remnants of the Papal States around Rome. On 14 March 1861, Victor Emmanuel declared the birth of the Kingdom of Italy, of which Florence became the capital. There had been no justification for conquering the Papal possessions, but the Piedmontese got away with it.

To the concern of northern liberals such as Verdi, the political scene remained disturbed. Garibaldi was still determined to take Rome, declaring 'Rome or death', a call to which Empress Eugénie responded: 'Death if they like, but Rome never.'[64] French troops were sent to defend Rome. In 1862, Garibaldi invaded Sicily and crossed to the mainland, but had no will to fight the Italian army and retreated into the mountains. When he was attacked, he refused to fire on Italians and was wounded and taken prisoner. When this news was received in Vienna, the value of shares on

* A couple of years before, Mercadante had written a hymn for the accession of King Francis II.[59]

the stock exchange immediately rose by 10 per cent. But there was uproar elsewhere: there were demonstrations in support of Garibaldi all over Italy. The government in Turin fell. 100,000 people demonstrated in Hyde Park in London. In October, Garibaldi was released from prison and carried out on a special bed which Lady Palmerston, wife of the British prime minister, had sent him. Garibaldi visited England, where he was feted. The queen was not pleased, and noted in her diary: 'Honest, disinterested & brave, Garribaldi certainly is, but a revolutionist leader.'[65]

It took two external events, the Austro-Prussian and the Franco-Prussian wars, to complete the unification of Italy. Neither was glorious for the Italians, but they resulted in Venetia being lost by the Habsburgs and then Rome being lost by the Pope.

At the time of the Austro-Prussian war in 1866 (see page 477), the Piedmont government agreed with the Prussians to open a second front against the Habsburgs, in return for being given Venetia. Franz Joseph was anyway prepared to give up Venetia in return for Italian and French neutrality. So, either way, Piedmont could obtain Venetia. But since Piedmont distrusted Vienna, war rather than neutrality was the preferred option. Italian troops gathered along the Po. In Sant'Agata, while focusing on writing *Don Carlos*, Verdi wrote: 'I'm so near the field of battle that I wouldn't be surprised to find a cannon ball rolling into my room one fine morning.'[66] The Italians were duly defeated at the second battle of Custozza and in a naval battle at Lissa. But to the Habsburgs their victories were to no avail: after the Prussians defeated the Austrians at Königgratz in Bohemia, the Habsburgs were at last expelled from Italy. Meanwhile, La Fenice, the opera house in Venice, was kept closed.[67]

During this campaign, to keep him out of mischief, Garibaldi was invited to run a guerrilla campaign into the Alpine Tyrol.* His little army included Giulio Ricordi** and Arrigo Boito. Verdi had set a hymn by Boito for the London Exhibition four years earlier. Twenty years on, Boito, by then

* Garibaldi was then told to withdraw from the Tyrol. He became increasingly outspoken, and a liability for the Italian government. He was imprisoned and returned to Caprera, where the Italians placed a naval patrol to blockade him. He escaped through a fog and, in yet another amazing flight, got to Florence. The French intervened again in support of the Papacy, and Garibaldi was defeated and arrested and confined to Caprera. Thereafter, he retired to write novels and re-marry. He died, in his bed, in 1882.

** Giulio Ricordi was the grandson of the founder of the Ricordi business.

one of Verdi's greatest friends, would write the librettos for *Otello* and *Falstaff*.*

After 1866, Rome was still outside the Kingdom of Italy. As we have seen from Liszt's sojourn there, the 1860s saw some turbulent and, for some, surprising developments in the Roman Catholic Church. Verdi's antipathy to them was exemplified in *Don Carlos*, performed two years after the Pope published the Syllabus of Errors (see page 454). There is a central scene in that opera in which King Philip of Spain struggles to reconcile his duty to the Church with his personal feelings. Verdi required the Grand Inquisitor, representing the Church, to be 'exceedingly old, and blind (for reasons which I won't put down on paper)'.[69]

It took the Franco-Prussian War finally to dislodge the French garrison and leave the Pope exposed and unprotected. The French troops were needed at home, and the garrison withdrew. Pius IX was allowed to retain the Vatican with its dependencies, the church of Santa Maria Maggiore and Castel Gandolfo on the Alban Hill. Unification of Italy was at last complete. But Verdi, the unbeliever, was not entirely happy. 'It's a great event', he wrote to Countess Maffei, 'but it leaves me cold ... I cannot reconcile Parliament and the College of Cardinals, freedom of the press and Inquisition, the civil code and the Syllabus ... *Pope* and *King of Italy* – I can't see them together even on the paper of this letter.'[70]

In November 1874, in recognition more of his wealth than anything else, Verdi was nominated a senator, 'an honour which no more required his attendance in the Italian Parliament than does a peerage in the British House of Lords'.[71] It allowed him free tickets for travel on the railways, although it is said that he always insisted on paying.[72]

The momentous events of the unification of Italy are important in the life of Verdi, if only because he played a relatively small *direct* part in them. He knew how to be politically correct: 'You talk to me of music', he said in 1848. 'What are you thinking of? Do you think I want to concern myself

*Meanwhile, their friendship was interrupted by Boito's ode which compared 'the defiled altars of Italian music to the splattered walls of a brothel'. Boito, the son of a destitute Polish countess, had just completed his studies at the Milan Conservatoire. He frequented the salon of Clarina Maffei and became prominent in the *scapigliatura*, a radical artistic movement reflecting the disillusionment that followed the initial enthusiasm for Italian unification. Despite its aims, its members were better known for their disorderly behaviour, holding forth in cafés, drinking absinthe and duelling. Boito's attempts at opera composition ended when his *Mefistofele* lasted until well past midnight at La Scala.[68]

now with notes and sounds? There should be only one kind of music pleasing to the ears of Italians of 1848 – the music of the guns.'[73] But, apart from providing inspiration, he personally remained on the sidelines.

Sant'Agata and the People of Busseto

In recording these political events, we have jumped ahead in time and must now return to the late 1840s and early 1850s. Around the time of the collapse of the revolutionary movement in 1849, Verdi and his mistress Giuseppina Strepponi returned to Italy from Paris. They moved their base to Sant'Agata, even though they returned to Paris for long periods. At Sant'Agata, Giuseppina occupied one bedroom on the ground floor leading out into the garden, while Verdi worked late into the night next door. He liked his estates. Giuseppina described how 'his love for the country has become a mania, madness, rage, fury, everything exaggerated that you can say. He gets up almost at dawn to look at the wheat, the corn, the grapevines etc. He comes back dropping with fatigue.'[74] His gun cupboard* can be seen in his bedroom.

A frequent shooting companion was Angelo Mariani, a leading conductor and a patriot in Milan in 1847–8. The two would spend hours at the piano or hunting in the woods by the banks of the Po. In later years, Mariani also helped the Verdis find the flat which they used in Genoa during the winter, and he occupied the flat next door.[75]

Verdi fell out with his father who, as we have seen, may have objected to the *ménage* with Giuseppina. Father and son separated 'in residence and in business',[76] and Verdi provided his parents with a horse and an allowance. In this era, a person's concern for their parents was regarded as a measure of their character, and Verdi's treatment of his parents displeased the residents of Busseto nearby.

But, worse. The residents were 'shocked' by the Verdi *ménage*. They cut Giuseppina in the street and cold-shouldered her in church, much to Verdi's fury. This confirmed him in his dislike of the local people, their clerical tendencies, hypocrisy and gossip. The upheavals over his appointment back in 1833 continued to rankle with him.

Verdi was rich enough to be able to ignore his neighbours. When his patron Barezzi expressed concern about the relationship between the

* The cupboard also contains some duelling pistols and an ordinary pistol.

celebrity and the town, he retorted: 'Neither I nor she owes anyone an account of our actions.'[77]

The antipathy between Verdi and Busseto rumbled on. Verdi put his secretary and amanuensis Muzio* forward for the post of municipal musical director at Busseto, but he was turned down. Verdi refused to be named as the patron for the town's Philharmonic Society. In the early 1860s, there was a row about the theatre, to be named Teatro Giuseppe Verdi. He felt that public money was being wasted at a time of national crisis. The local people felt that Verdi should pay towards its upkeep and activities. In the end, Verdi offered a large contribution, which also led to a misunderstanding when he claimed to offset it against some money owed him by the town. A box was reserved for his use but he never went inside the theatre.[78]

Giuseppina seems to have provided a stabilising influence on the tactless, humourless and unforgiving workaholic. Verdi and Giuseppina did not get married for eleven years; it is not clear why. It has been suggested that she thought herself unworthy of him, whatever that may mean. Alternatively, it has been suggested that, had they married, Verdi would have been obliged to accept responsibility for her surviving and abandoned children, so long as they were minors. Possibly to avoid embarrassment, when Verdi became politically prominent, at the time of the slogan 'Viva Verdi', they eventually did get married. The ceremony took place quietly at Collonges-sur-Salève in the diocese of Annecy.[79] This was on 29 August 1859, around the time that the attention of the nation was focused on the battle of Solferino. They adopted the orphaned child of one of Verdi's cousins, Maria Filomena, from whom Verdi's heirs are descended.

Rigoletto, *Il Trovatore* and *La Traviata*

The 1850s saw three very important operas, *Rigoletto*, *Il Trovatore* and *La Traviata*. With *Rigoletto* (*La Maledizione*,** as it was called at the time), Verdi had great difficulty with the censors. The Venetians totally rejected Piave's libretto, its 'repellent morality and obscene triviality', and no doubt the picture of royal profligacy. Verdi reacted violently: 'Putting on the stage a character who is grossly deformed and absurd but inwardly passionate and full of love is precisely what I feel to be so fine. I chose this subject

* Verdi had employed Emanuele Muzio, one of his pupils who, like him, had failed to get into the Conservatoire; he was also from Busseto.

** The curse; the story was based on Victor Hugo's *Le Roi s'amuse*.

precisely for those qualities, those original traits, and, if they are taken away, I can no longer write music for it.'[80] The location was changed, the rape toned down, and King François of France became the Duke of Mantua whom we know. Premièred in March 1851, the opera was sensationally successful. Rossini said that *Rigoletto* was the first opera which made him aware of Verdi's greatness. The sixteen operas which he wrote before *Rigoletto* are certainly less well known today.

Verdi then worked on *Il Trovatore*, but the poet who was writing the libretto died when it was unfinished. The management in Venice were keen to follow upon the success of *Rigoletto*, and became restive. So, with deadlines looming, Piave prepared a libretto based on Dumas' *La Dame aux Caméllias*. Verdi worked on both operas at the same time.

Il Trovatore was first performed in Rome, very successfully. If the Venetian management had taken Verdi's advice, it would have staged *Il Trovatore*. But the management insisted on pressing ahead with *La Traviata*, even though Verdi was not totally happy with it or the proposed cast. So the first night was a disaster: the sight of a healthily robust soprano dying of consumption seemed absurd. It was only after it was revived and Verdi made some changes that *La Traviata* became the success that we recognise today. Verdi was able to exclaim: 'then it was a fiasco; now it is creating an uproar.'[81]

Frustrations

After *La Traviata*, Verdi slowed down the intense pace of composition. The list of his compositions, dominated by opera, is considerably skewed towards his early years. Twenty-four operas were composed before he was 50; only four, *Don Carlos*, *Aïda*, *Otello* and *Falstaff*, were composed in the last 38 years. Meanwhile, the frustrations with productions and performances continued to occupy a considerable amount of his time.

He moved to Paris for a couple of years and adapted many of his operas for the Paris stage. He had an apartment in the Champs Elysées, but he disliked the social and operatic conventions of Paris. In 1855, he fell out with the star librettist Scribe, who wrote the libretto of *Les Vêpres Siciliennes*, because he was reluctant to make various changes which Verdi wanted. He tried to have its première stopped because of casting difficulties: the *prima donna* had eloped with a baron. Berlioz observed: 'Verdi is having to wrestle with all the Opéra people. Yesterday he made a terrible scene at the dress rehearsal. I feel sorry for the poor man; I put myself in his position. Verdi is a worthy and honourable artist.'[82]

Simon Boccanegra, produced in Venice in March 1857, was not particularly successful. Verdi then considered writing a 'King Lear', but could not find the right singer to perform the part of Cordelia. He then had great difficulty with the Neapolitan censors over Scribe's libretto about the assassination of Gustavus III of Sweden, which he used for *Un Ballo in Maschera*. He stormed out of Naples, and put on an altered version in Rome. But by then, Gustavus, who had already been changed to a fictional duke in Pomerania, had become Riccardo in colonial Boston.

As if these frustrations were not enough, Verdi also had difficulties with his publishers and with copyright. His operas were appearing in pirated forms. He complained to Ricordi about the conditions under which his foreign rights were being sold, and the practice of making available the plates rather than the original score, thus depriving him of his percentage. It did not help that both Ricordi and the French publishers suffered from what at best may be described as accounting and financial weaknesses; at worst, the publishers were just fraudulent.

Verdi was incurring considerable expenses on developing the property at Sant'Agata, even though it remained just a large country house built around a courtyard; there is nothing flashy or particularly grand about it. He was offered an attractive fee by a Russian for *La Forza del Destino*. Verdi and Giuseppina went to St Petersburg, but the production of *La Forza* was called off because some of the cast became ill. They returned to St Petersburg for the first performance in the following year, after a visit to London for the International Exhibition of 1862.

The production of *Don Carlos* commissioned for the Paris Exhibition of 1867 was not a success. Bizet found it full of good intentions and nothing else. The rehearsals had been disrupted by rows. The bass engaged for the role of Emperor Charles V complained that his part was not that of a principal; there was a fight between the *prima donnas*. Verdi preferred to miss a day's rehearsal rather than 'watch the grimaces of one soprano' when the other was singing.[83]

January 1869 was a significant month because Verdi made his peace and returned to La Scala for the first time for twenty years. Performing in *Don Carlos* was a young soprano from Prague, Teresa Stolz. Verdi agreed to conduct a production of *La Forza del Destino* at La Scala in the following month.

Aïda

In November 1869, when the Suez Canal was opened, the Khedive of Egypt planned also to open a new opera house in Cairo, as part of the celebrations. The opera season began with *Rigoletto*, and Verdi was asked to write a new work, *Aïda*, for the subsequent season. The idea of Verdi writing it was promoted by a French Egyptologist in the vice-regal service. Verdi was very reluctant.

Then, in July 1870, the Franco-Prussian War intervened. Despite the fact that a French garrison was propping up the Pope in Rome, Verdi was pro-French: 'France gave freedom and civilisation to the modern world. And if she falls, don't let us delude ourselves, all our liberties and civilisation will fall with her.' He added: 'Ah the North! It is a country, a people that terrify me.'[84] He set aside 2,000 francs for the wounded from his *Aïda* commissioning fee. When Paris was under siege, so were the *Aïda* costumes. Thus *Aïda*'s première was postponed until the end of 1871.

In 1870, following the death of Mercadante, Verdi was offered the directorship of the Naples Conservatoire, but he turned it down. He did not want to move his home, and he wanted his independence to compose. He also said that to give effect to his ideas about musical education would require constant surveillance on his part: he expected students to be given a basic grounding, constant exercise in fugue and counterpoint, and a broad study of literature. He said: 'Let us return to the past; it will be a step forward.'[85] But he did agree to serve on a committee for the reform of music education which sat in the capital, Florence, in 1871.

The Requiem

In 1873 the death took place, aged 88, of Alessandro Manzoni, a fervent Roman Catholic and virtually the sole exponent of the Romantic school in Italian literature. His works belong to the second and third decades of the century, when he wrote the tragedy *Il Conte di Carmagnola* and the historical novel *I Promessi Sposi*, which was described by Sir Walter Scott as the finest novel ever written, and by Verdi as 'one of the greatest books ever to come from the human brain'.[86] By the 1870s, he was regarded as the patriarch of Italian letters, and he was 'one of the few human beings whom Verdi revered'.[87] He was buried with great pomp at a state funeral in Milan.

Verdi's Requiem Mass in honour of Manzoni was performed in May

1874 in Milan. Hans von Bülow launched an attack on Verdi's 'latest opera, though in ecclesiastical robes', whereupon Brahms riposted: 'Bülow has made an almighty fool of himself. Only a genius could have written such a work.'[88] Wagner was far less enthusiastic: he said that the Requiem is 'a work of which it is better not to speak'.[89]

A Long Pause

After the Requiem, Verdi stopped composition for a long time. Although he wintered in his apartment in Genoa and frequently visited Milan, his main base was in Sant'Agata, where he enjoyed developing the formal gardens and running his 1,500-acre farm.

He created an ornamental lake with bridge and statuary, and a tree-lined drive from the house through the fields to the Ospedale which he had founded. He imported trees from as far away as Japan and South America. Both Verdi and Giuseppina were very fond of dogs; in the garden one can see a monument over the tomb of their dog, inscribed with the legend: 'D'un vero amico', 'To the memory of a real friend'.

However, there are less unanimous stories about his care for his 200 workers. Some tell tales of Verdi being a harsh landlord whose land agent gave his tenants flour and meal which made even the pigs vomit. Others paint a different picture. Apparently, when times were hard, he raised wages and invested the farming profits in charitable projects such as the Ospedale and in a musician's rest home in Milan, the Casa di Riposa. Although the more affluent classes benefited from unification, the lower classes did not: Verdi and Giuseppina made substantial gifts to relieve their abject poverty and hunger, which was aggravated by a tax on flour.

Whatever, to many people Verdi seemed unforgiving and dislikeable; descriptions like 'testy', 'sly' and 'proud' abound. Many years later, one commentator remembered Verdi as 'very taciturn for an Italian'.[90] Giuseppina, on the other hand, was apparently an endearing person.

Teresa Stolz

Given the self-centred nature of Verdi's character, his marriage was bound to be a rocky one, and it became increasingly strained as the years went by. He gave Giuseppina a very hard time; he was sometimes 'so abrasive, so difficult'. 'This evening there was an uproar about an open window … He flew into a rage saying that he would sack all the servants.' He complained that she stood up for them 'even when he makes perfectly justified complaints'. His attitude was perhaps summed up in his own statement: 'Horses are like women; they have to please the man who owns them.'*

By the early 1870s, Giuseppina was in her matronly middle-50s. In September 1871, Teresa Stolz, who had sung many of Verdi's heroines, and was nearly twenty years younger, paid her first visit to Sant'Agata to study *Aïda* under Verdi's guidance; he had probably seen her first on the occasion of his return to La Scala. Teresa was 'the Verdian dramatic soprano, par excellence, powerful, passionate in utterance, but dignified and disciplined in manner'.[92] She had an instinctive feeling for the interpretation of Verdi's music and an impeccable vocal technique.[93]

At the time, Stolz was engaged to the 50-year-old Angelo Mariani, once Verdi's great friend and hunting companion. Although Mariani was totally devoted to Verdi, their friendship suffered when Verdi hatched a plan to mark the first anniversary of Rossini's death: Verdi wanted a Requiem, to which all the leading composers would contribute. It would be given once only in San Petronio in Bologna, and then would be sealed up and deposited at the Liceo Musicale. Verdi's controversial idea was not enthusiastically received. This annoyed him. When Mariani offered to provide the Pesaro chorus** to sing at it, Verdi wrote him a stinging letter: 'Do you mean to say that we have to beg *you* to be allowed the chorus that you have at Pesaro?', he asked.[94]

Teresa broke off her engagement to Mariani,† and Verdi took up with her. On Saturdays, Verdi would have an assignation with her in a hotel in Cremona. The press got hold of this, and published a series of lurid and defamatory articles during 1875. On one occasion, it was said that Verdi thought he had lost his wallet containing 50,000 lire. Obviously, his first reaction was to blame the servants, but then the wallet was found on Teresa's sofa, having slipped out during some activity thereon. Another paper deplored the fact that, at a time of great economic hardship, Verdi should have such a large amount of money in his wallet.

* Verdi's misogyny was not unique. In 1910, an article was published by Max Funke entitled 'Are Women Human Beings?' ('Sind Weiber Menschen?'). It concluded that women are a missing link between *Homo sapiens* and less advanced species. In this context, Verdi's comment may seem less extreme.[91]

** Pesaro was Rossini's birthplace.

† Mariani died in lonely circumstances a couple of years later, after Verdi had tried to have him evicted from his apartment in Genoa.

Whatever the truth of the stories, the relationship caused Giuseppina bitter anguish, which was compounded by his 'psychological and verbal violence'.[95] She was reduced to pleading with him not to be abandoned. Somehow, however, Giuseppina, Teresa and Verdi managed to develop a successful *ménage à trois*.

THE LAST YEARS, *OTELLO* AND *FALSTAFF*

Verdi emerged occasionally. In 1879, following devastating spring floods, there was a charity performance of the Requiem. The following evening, the Verdis had dinner with the Ricordis. Giulio Ricordi steered the conversation round to the subject of Shakespeare, a dramatist who had always enthralled Verdi. Ricordi had identified Arrigo Boito as a librettist who could get Verdi to start composing again.*[96]

Verdi was gradually persuaded to compose an opera based on *Othello*. But first he revised *Simon Boccanegra* and abridged *Don Carlos*. He set to work on *Otello* in 1884–5. But when he heard a rumour that Boito wished that he himself were composing the opera, Verdi stopped writing and offered to return the libretto. Boito had to calm him down and persuade him that he alone could compose it. It was a slow process: *Otello* was eventually performed at La Scala in February 1887. Two years later, Boito sent Verdi a sketch for *Falstaff*, which was first performed in February 1893, Verdi's 80th year.

Otello and *Falstaff*, the one tragic and the other comic, were Verdi's crowning achievement. They were both received deliriously at La Scala. After *Otello*, according to Boito, the pandemonium was 'insane: the crowd tried to shoulder Verdi's carriage and carry it from La Scala to the Grand Hotel up the street'.[97] The ovations for *Falstaff* lasted almost half an hour. For Verdi they were tinged with the sadness of knowing that they marked the end of his artistic career.[98]

Were it not for these last two operas, we might place Verdi on the same level as Donizetti and Bellini. Writing about *Otello*, one expert says that 'the vocal lines display at its highest pitch of development Verdi's genius for

* One may be mildly surprised when one hears that, in 1893, Cambridge awarded Boito an honorary doctorate as a substitute for Verdi. At the time when Boito was working on *Otello*, a young composer was introduced to him with the name of Giacomo Puccini. Boito 'represented the foremost arbiter of Milan's intellectual and artistic taste. Poet, writer, critic and composer in one person and the leader of Italy's *avant-garde*, his influence was immense.'[96]

revealing character by the curve of a phrase. Subtle passing harmonies add their inflection to individual words while, on a larger scale, harmonic structures define and help to organise the musical structure. The orchestration is adventurous but unobtrusively so.' *Falstaff* is full of 'melodic abundance'.[99]

After *Otello* and *Falstaff*, Boito tried to tempt Verdi with *Antony and Cleopatra*, and he thought again about an opera based on *King Lear*. But Verdi was too old and tired; he had already had a stroke in 1883. On one occasion, Giuseppina, herself crippled with arthritis, found him lying in bed, seemingly paralysed and unable to speak. He scribbled on a piece of paper: 'Coffee.' This revived him.[100]

Giuseppina was operated on for an abdominal cyst in the 1880s. As she aged, she suffered from nausea which kept her from eating. She died in November 1897 at Sant'Agata, after an attack of bronchitis. She had requested that with her should be buried the love letter which Verdi sent her before she set up in Paris; but it could not be found. Eventually it was, but has remained sealed. The following year, Verdi published *Quattro Pezzi Sacri*, which were compiled at the time she was failing. To *Laudi alla Vergine*, written some years before, he added three other sacred works: *Ave Maria*, *Stabat Mater* and *Te Deum*. He himself was not religious; but Giuseppina's bedroom has a crucifix above the bed, and a little shrine.

Verdi now lived most of the time in his suite in the Grand Hotel et de Milan, just down the Via Manzoni from La Scala. His good looks in old age drew compliments. Stolz was his companion. There is little doubt that there was a 'passionate bond' between them, even when he was 87 and she 66.[101] Around them, the Italian political scene was chaotic. There were riots in Milan in 1897–8, and the king was assassinated in July 1900. The queen wrote a prayer for her dead husband; Verdi had tactfully to avoid her request to set it to music.

In January 1901, Verdi had another stroke. He collapsed when trying to button his vest. He had been living well: his menu for the day before included julienne en croûte, followed by truite grillée, boeuf à la jardinière, game and turkey, and asparagus; the meal concluded with raspberry ice cream and desserts. He lingered for a few more days.* Traffic was diverted,

* A room at Sant'Agata has been furnished to look like the room in which he died. In it can be seen a plaster cast of his right hand, in which the third and fourth fingers are unusually the same length.

tram-drivers were told not to sound their bells outside; all was quiet. He died on 27 January.

Three days after his death, he was taken to join Giuseppina in Milan's Cimitero Monumentale; it was estimated that 200,000 people filled the streets. A month later, they were both removed to the Casa di Riposo. More than 300,000 mourners accompanied the cortège. The crowd broke softly into 'Va, pensiero', the moving chorus from *Nabucco*. It had launched his career, and also signified the Italian liberation movement with which he has been so much associated.

Brahms

CHAPTER 17

'SUDDENLY I SAW a man unknown to me, rather stout, of middle height with long hair and a full beard, coming towards me. In a very deep and hoarse voice, he introduced himself as "Musikdirektor Müller", making a very stiff and formal bow, which I was on the point of returning with equal gravity, when, an instant later, we all found ourselves laughing heartily at the perfect success of Brahms' disguise.'[1] Thus it was that an English friend saw the transformed Brahms. Formerly 'a golden youth with piercing blue eyes and with a lower lip apt to be pressed forward in moments of emotion', he was now, although aged only 45, the ultimate bourgeois, the German traditionalist.[2]

The bourgeois Musikdirektor Müller is the image we have of Brahms: 'one of quiet, inward happiness, contentment and ease',[3] the carpet slippers and open collarless shirt, in an atmosphere reeking of smoke and the odour of beer and coffee. His beloved Clara Schumann's last words with him were: 'What are you going to do with all that tobacco?' His response, quite normal, given his propensity to ask others to do the same, was 'Smuggle it'. A table was reserved for him and his bachelor friends at Gause's beer-hall in Vienna. Tchaikovsky wrote: 'I have been on the booze with Brahms.' Grieg found him 'jovial and friendly', having taverned with him.[4] Another described how Brahms 'did ample justice to the excellent Munich beer, of which he consumed an astounding quantity before we parted, long after midnight'.[5] He also drank lots of coffee, and would brew his own in the morning.

It comes as a surprise that this was the man who moulded his music on the example of Robert Schumann, whose focus was on the unsentimental, unshowy beauty of Romanticism. This was the man who brought 'the classical and romantic technique of expression to complete and fruitful union; it was an amazing marriage'.[6] This was the man who showed that something new can be created with classical forms, that it was still possible to write sonatas, trios, quartets and even fugues.

Beware of the cosy, stolid image. Although he helped those he admired, such as Dvořák, he was capable of exploding into colossal rows with many of his best friends, including Clara Schumann and the celebrity violinist Joseph Joachim; he was objectionable to many others. He could be contentious and undiplomatic. He created a major controversy about the 'New German School' of music: he disliked Wagner, for whom it did not matter, and he hated Bruckner, for whom it did. But all of that is for later. First we must chronicle his early life in Hamburg, his help for Clara Schumann when Robert was in the lunatic asylum, his autumns teaching in Detmold, his passing loves. He would enjoy idyllic summers in Baden-Baden near Clara. A tentative move to Vienna became permanent. The success of the Requiem provided financial security and enabled him to live comfortably, to be 'Doktor Müller' and to spend summers in the mountains around Bad Ischl. He had many friends in Vienna, but also made enemies, such as Bruckner. Time moved on: in his last years, he made a recording using Edison's phonograph.

Hamburg Years

Johannes Brahms was born on 7 May 1833 in anything but bourgeois circumstances, in a cramped tenement building in part of old Hamburg known as Gängeviertel. The streams traversing it were flooded with the tide. As the water crept up, the residents would escape with their belongings, returning later 'like rats to their oozy and dripping abodes'.[7] Later in the century, a warning telegram would be sent from Cuxhaven, nearly 100 miles down the Elbe at the North Sea; three shots would then be fired at the harbour entrance, with a further three shots being fired if the progress of the tide indicated danger.

The botanist Linnaeus compared Hamburg to an open sewer.[8] In the year before Brahms was born, more than 1,650 people had died in a cholera epidemic and, when he was seventeen, another 1,765 people died similarly. It was not much better at the end of the 19th century: in 1892, when Mahler was there, some 17,000 people fell ill with cholera and 8,600 died. Robert Koch, the bacteriologist who 'discovered' the causes of cholera, visited the squalid quarters in the Gängeviertel. He noted: 'I have never so far seen such unhealthy living quarters, dens of pestilence and breeding grounds for all kinds of infection.'[9] Disease was not the only threat: when Johannes was nine, had it not been for a change in the direction of the wind, he would have been among the 20,000 made homeless when a catastrophic fire destroyed over 4,000 buildings.

Instead of joining the family business, a combination of grocery and pawnbroking, Brahms' father Jakob played the double-bass and wind instruments* in the dance halls and dives of Hamburg.[10] He married his impoverished landlady, who was seventeen years older than him; she was formerly a seamstress, and then a housemaid. Marriage did not stop him carrying on with the daughter of the previous house where he had been lodging. He was an old rogue, whom Brahms adored. When, many years later, Brahms was honoured with the Freedom of the City of Hamburg, he wrote: 'My first thought in such a situation is my father, and the wish that he had lived to see it; fortunately, he didn't depart dissatisfied with me, even without this.'[11]

From his mother, Brahms, his brother and sister heard the horror stories of the Napoleonic occupation under the ruthless and taciturn Marshal Davoût,[12] the occupation which the Mendelssohns managed to avoid. The suburbs were destroyed to improve the line of fire, forced labour was used on the fortifications, 25,000 useless mouths were expelled into the winter cold. It was not surprising that Brahms had no love for the French.[13]

In the 19th century, Hamburg was the 'first of all the seats of commerce on the Continent',[14] an accurate description given that, if one looked across the Channel, the ports of London, Liverpool and Glasgow were larger. Hamburg's imports and exports were more than those of Holland, of Belgium or of Spain. It was also an important banking and insurance

* His trumpet (along with his son's toothbrush and coffee- and tea-making equipment) can be seen in the museum at Gmunden.

centre. It saw phenomenal growth in Brahms' life: just before he was born, it possessed 146 ships totalling 25,722 tons; by 50 years later, it had grown almost 800 per cent. Accordingly, in mid-century, its prosperous burghers rebuilt the church of St Nicholas to the design of Sir Gilbert Scott: the spire was the second highest building in the world, after the cathedral at Rouen, until Cologne supplanted it.[15]

We can doubt the stories about the pretty, sensitive, fair-haired boy being sent out to play the piano among the coarse sailors and their painted whores in the dockside taverns and bars. The Brahms were good Lutherans, living among the respectable working poor: they gave their children a sound education at the best schools and sent them to the leading music teachers. It is preferable perhaps to picture Johannes sentimentally looking out to sea at the old ships mooring to piles in the open water, and the lighters taking the cargo ashore.[16]

But times were hard. When Brahms' parents bought his aunt's shop, Jakob used the stock to barter for music, for instruments, and to enjoy himself. The business failed.[17] They thought of leaving for America. Hamburg was a point of departure for emigrants:* an average of 30,000 left through its port every year, part of the five million outflow who left Germany between 1816 and 1914.[19]

The Brahms had a piano in their home, but with thin walls it was probably difficult for the children to use it. From the age of seven, Johannes learnt the piano from Otto Cossel, a pupil of the distinguished piano teacher and composer Eduard Marxsen, to whom Cossel later passed him on. Brahms remained loyal to Cossel and was still in touch with his family in the year that he died.[20]

After a successful performance at a public concert, an American tried to lure the ten-year-old Johannes to the USA for a tour as a child prodigy. But this was resisted. He continued to take the steamboat to have lessons with Marxsen at Altona, one of the suburbs of Hamburg. There he studied Bach, Beethoven and the showy works of Thalberg and Herz. He had a pleasant holiday when, aged thirteen, a friend of his father's invited him to the country to teach his daughter Lischen the piano. He romped with Lischen through the countryside and conducted the choir. Again, one can

* In 1847, the Hamburg Amerikanische Pakettfahrt A. G. (Hapag) was founded. Its first ship, the *Deutschland*, sailed to New York with over 200 passengers in very cramped conditions on a crossing lasting over six weeks.[18]

see Brahms' loyalty to his roots: many years later he paid the tuition fees for Lischen's daughter, then an aspiring singer.[21]

Brahms played in concerts in Hamburg in the winter of 1847 and in 1848. Then, in September 1848, he had his own concert and, six months later, one at which he played Beethoven's Waldstein Sonata. Maybe he caught his first glimpse of Clara Schumann, who, around this time, performed in Hamburg together with Jenny Lind, the lovely soprano whom Mendelssohn admired. At Marxsen's suggestion, Brahms sent Robert Schumann some of his compositions, but the package was returned unopened.[22]

The port of Hamburg was an obvious place for Hungarian refugees to congregate following the severe suppression of the revolutions in 1849. There had been night searches, rapes and thefts by the victorious soldiers, especially by the wild troops from the Balkans; there had been executions and imprisonments.[23] This led to an exodus; among those who had capitulated to the Russians at Vilagós (see page 452) was the flamboyant violinist Ede Reményi, whose original name was Eduard Hoffmann.[24] He now passed through Hamburg. Reményi is said to have had 'a bad press in Brahms' biographies, emerging as an opportunist musical charlatan of poor taste and wayward morals'.[25] Reményi performed in Hamburg in 1850 and then went on to the USA, as one of the many virtuosos flocking there now that transport was becoming so much easier.[26] In 1852, he returned to Hamburg and went with Brahms on a short tour of nearby towns. Probably it was on these tours that Reményi introduced Brahms to the 'gypsy' music that was played so frequently in Hungary.[27]

Brahms and Reményi played before Queen Victoria's cousin, the blind King of Hanover. The household staff at Hanover included Joseph Joachim, the violin prodigy and pupil of Mendelssohn, who was two years older than Brahms. He took Brahms and Reményi to visit Liszt at Weimar, where he had worked a few years before.

Liszt and Brahms were temperamentally unsuited to each other. When attending Liszt's rarefied court, Brahms is said to have dozed off while the Master played his own B minor Sonata. Liszt stopped playing immediately and walked out. Following this, or possibly because of it, Brahms and the ambitious Reményi parted and their paths did not cross again.*

* Reményi went on to a brilliant career as a virtuoso, especially in Paris, London and the USA. He died while playing at a concert in San Francisco.[28]

The Schumanns

Brahms went to Göttingen to join Joachim, who was attending lectures at the university. Later, in 1853, through Joachim, he met Robert Schumann, and stayed at his house in Düsseldorf that autumn. Schumann recognised Brahms' abilities and inclinations. 'This is he that should come', he declared in a letter to Joachim.[29] Schumann then went even further by publishing a verbose eulogy in the journal *Neue Zeitschrift für Musik*.*

As is often the case with compliments which appear 'over the top', Schumann's eulogy did Brahms more harm than good. Contemporaries were jealous; Brahms could not possibly live up to the reputation created for him. But for the moment he was on a high: he performed at the Leipzig Gewandhaus before Liszt and Berlioz. After what had been an astonishing nine months, he returned to Hamburg for Christmas 1853 as the accepted associate of the great musicians of the day. In the New Year, he returned to Hanover to stay with Joachim.

At the end of February, Robert Schumann was fished out of the Rhine. With his lifelong friend, the pianist and composer Julius Otto Grimm, Brahms rushed to Clara Schumann and comforted her. Throughout 1854, Brahms became her general factotum: he kept the household accounts, taught the older boys to read, and dealt with correspondence. This behaviour alarmed his parents, who saw a brilliant career going off the rails.[31]

Thus began the truly wonderful, surely platonic, romance with Clara; it would last, with occasional ups and downs, throughout their lives. In June, Brahms wrote to Joachim saying that he loved Clara and 'am under

* Under the title 'Neue Bahnen' (New Ways Forward) and mixing his classical analogies, he wrote: 'Years have passed – almost as many as those I dedicated to the early editorship of this journal, namely ten – since I appeared on this scene so rich to me in memories. Often, despite pressing creative activity, I have felt tempted; many new and considerable talents have appeared, a fresh musical energy has appeared to thrust itself forward in the work of many gifted artists of the present time, even though their works are, for the most part, known only to a restricted circle. I have thought, watching the progress of these chosen ones with the greatest sympathy, that, after such a beginning, One must inevitably appear destined to give the highest and most enlightened expression to the ideals of our time, One who would not reveal his mastery by slow development but spring armed like Minerva from the head of Jupiter. And now He has come, a young blood whose cradle was watched over by the Graces and Heroes. His name is Johannes Brahms.' Schumann concluded: 'There is in all periods a secret union of kindred spirits. Bind close the circle, ye who belong to it, that the truth of Art may shine ever brighter, spreading joy and blessing throughout the world.'[30]

her spell. I often must restrain myself forcibly from just quietly putting my arms around her and even ... I do not know, it seems to me so natural that she could not misunderstand. I think I can no longer love an unmarried girl – at least, I have quite forgotten about them. They but promise heaven, while Clara shows it revealed to us.'[32] In November 1854, she agreed to use the familiar 'Du' form of address, confiding to her diary that she 'could not refuse, for indeed I love him as a son, so tenderly'.[33]

After Robert's death, Clara and two of the children went with Johannes and his sister Elise to stay near Lucerne in Switzerland; but there was

Clara Schumann

always a chaperone. Then there was a rapid cooling off in the romance, and in October 1856 there appears to have been some bust-up. Brahms returned to Hamburg, leaving Clara desperately sad: she wrote in her diary that she returned from the railway station as if from a funeral.[34]

Brahms came and went, but when Clara moved to her mother's house in Berlin in 1857, Brahms settled in Hamburg. He took part in social life and concerts, and educated himself in art and literature. He formed and conducted a women's choir of about 40 who met weekly, sang and serenaded in the moonlight whenever possible, and went on excursions and picnics. He wrote a humorous set of rules for them in mock legalese in order to regulate rehearsals. The ladies loved him. They presented him with a silver inkwell, 'In memory of the summer of '59 from the Frauenchor'.[35]

Detmold and Passing Loves

For three years, 1857–9, Brahms spent the autumns at Detmold, where he taught the family of Prince Leopold III. Detmold was the capital of Lippe, a tiny principality with a population of 120,000 people. Its territory of about 450 square miles was surrounded by the Electorate of Hanover and by lands ruled by the Bishops of Paderborn and Fulda. Lippe was shortly to throw in its lot with the Prussians, whereupon its army formed but a battalion of the 6th Westphalian infantry. For Brahms, Lippe's wooded hills, fields, forests and its horses provided a welcome contrast to the city of Hamburg.[36]

He was lodged in the best inn, with meals and wine included. His work took him into the castle's great rooms, which were hung with damask and Gobelins tapestries and lit by Murano glass chandeliers. Occasionally, he could get out to hike in the surrounding country, the Lippische Schweiz – so called as it is reminiscent of the lowlands of Switzerland. Surprisingly, given his later portly appearance, Brahms was athletic: even in his late 40s, he enjoyed swimming naked in the early morning, in water he called 'warm', around 19°C (66°F). He enjoyed himself thoroughly – so much that, when he was offered a teaching job by Ferdinand Hiller at Cologne Conservatoire, he turned it down because he preferred to be in Detmold.[37]

Brahms' duties included conducting the orchestra and the amateur choral society which met weekly at the castle to perform works such as *Messiah* and a variety of songs and folksongs. He found the choir work useful for developing his choral technique. A few years earlier, he had decided that his technique at counterpoint needed improving, and he exchanged exercises regularly with Joachim. Even in his 40s, he told Clara: 'All winter long I have been doing counterpoint exercises very assiduously.'[38] He seems to have used the rehearsals at Detmold to try to lower his high-pitched voice. As a consequence, he made a sort of rasping sound when he spoke.

He fell in love with a beautiful soprano, Agathe von Siebold, the daughter of a medical professor, for whom he composed some songs. Grimm, whose wife and Agathe were best friends, warned him that if he continued to carry on with Agathe, he would have to marry her; whereupon 'the answer came "I love you", I must see you again, but bound I cannot be', according to Agathe's account of events in later years.[39] She felt jilted, and that was the end of it. Many decades later, Agathe, by then rather less romantically called 'Frau Dr Sanitation Commissioner Schütte',* took an interest in Brahms' folksongs.[41]

Another love was Louise Meyer-Dustmann, *prima donna* at the Imperial Opera in Vienna. Brahms met her at the Lower Rhine Festival in 1862. She was the only person ever known to get away with calling him 'Hansi'.[42]

Dame Ethel Smyth

Clara became very jealous of Brahms' piano pupil, the beautiful, golden-haired Elisabeth von Stockhausen, daughter of the Hanoverian ambassador to Vienna. Men would be transfixed by the beauty of Elisabeth's perfectly white neck and shoulders. The English composer Ethel Smyth found her dazzling and bewitching, one 'whose modesty was of the type that used to be called maidenly'.[43] After Elisabeth married an indifferent composer and teacher, Heinrich Herzogenberg, Brahms was able to

* Titles like Sanitary Commissioner were prized, just as Herr Doktor, Professor, 'and countless other handles became an inseparable part of one's name'. It has been said that 'what businessmen mostly angled for was not a noble title or the Order of the Eagle, but the title Commercial Councillor'.[40]

have a distant and safe relationship with her. He sent her many of his works for criticism and comment before they were published.

The formidable Ethel Smyth, later a colleague of the suffragette Mrs Pankhurst, took a dim view of Brahms' attitude to women: 'If they did not appeal to him, he was incredibly awkward and ungracious; if they were pretty, he had an unpleasant way of leaning back in his chair, pouting out his lips, stroking his moustache, and staring at them as a greedy boy stares at jam tartlets.'[44] One can guess into which category Smyth fell.*

Brahms also fell in love with Bertha Porubsky, a girl from Vienna who sang in his Hamburg choir, and for whom he would subsequently write the *Lullaby* when her second son was born. Brahms was on the verge of proposing to Ottilie Hauer, who was in the Vienna ladies' choir. When he got around to it, she had just agreed to marry someone else. She remained a great friend, a kind of favourite sister.[46]

Clara was not beyond a bit of match-making. One of Brahms' publishers, supportive during lean times in the 1860s, was the Swiss Melchior Rieter-Biedermann, who ran a predecessor firm to Peters Edition. Clara suggested his daughter Ida as a wife for Brahms, having first ascertained that Ida would marry him. But nothing came of it.[47]

The Controversy about the 'New German School'

We return to 1858, the year of Brahms' romance with Agathe. Brahms completed his Piano Concerto in D minor, on which he had been working for four years. When he performed it in Leipzig in January of the following year, it was a disaster, and was savaged by the critics: in his own words, it was 'a brilliant and decisive flop'.[48] Breitkopf and Härtel refused to publish it, allowing Simrock to step in, at first reluctantly, as Brahms' publisher at this time.

The disaster with the Piano Concerto coincided with Brahms falling

* Smyth, about whom it has been said that 'virility is a strongly marked characteristic of her genius', later composed *The Wreckers*, *The Boatswain's Mate* and *The Prison*. When she was 72, Smyth seduced the 48-year-old novelist Virginia Woolf. 'She has descended upon me like a wolf on the fold', wrote Virginia, 'a bluff, military old woman … in a three cornered hat and tailor made suit'. Smyth was imperious, demanding, egotistical. The affair was 'like being a snail and having your brain cracked by a thrush'. She was also the lover of the Princesse de Polignac, the prominent patron of the arts in Paris, who supported Fauré and *avant garde* composers such as Stravinsky and Ravel.[45]

out with the musical establishment, including Karl Brendel, editor of the *Neue Zeitschrift*, professor of music history and aesthetics at Leipzig Conservatoire, and friend of Robert Schumann. Brendel, whose journal had written encouragingly of Brahms' Piano Concerto, had coined the name 'New German School' for the 'progressive' school of music represented by Liszt, Wagner and Berlioz. Brahms was persuaded by Joachim and Grimm – together with Bernard Scholz, a teacher – to object publicly to the claim that everyone who mattered in music had accepted the principles adopted by this 'progressive' school. And so began one of the most serious and enduring rows in the history of music.[49]

Much effort and correspondence went into drafting the formal Declaration, writing around to collect signatures. In the event, there were only the four signatures of Brahms, Grimm, Joachim and Scholz. It was leaked prematurely to the press as follows:[50] 'The undersigned have for long followed with regret the proceedings of a certain party whose organ is Brendel's *Zeitschrift für Musik*. The said *Zeitschrift* continually argues the theory that the most serious minded and talented musicians are in sympathy with the aims it represents, that they recognise, in the compositions of the new school, works of artistic value, and that the arguments for and against the Music of the Future, especially in North Germany, have been fought out and finally decided in its favour.'

This turgid statement continued, appallingly: 'The undersigned regard it as their duty to make a public protest against such a distortion of fact, and declare that, so far as they are concerned anyway, they do not acknowledge the principles advanced by Brendel's journal, and that they can only regret and condemn the productions of the leaders and followers of the so-called New German school, which in part apply those principles in practice, and in part require the promotion of new and unheard of theories which are contrary to the very nature of music.'[51] Brahms was aged 26; his Piano Concerto had recently been hissed off the platform. From him and his pals, this outburst about something being 'contrary to the very nature of music' was laughable.[52]

One might well wonder what the real controversy was all about. It cut so deep that we must spend a moment on it. First of all, there was a stuffy aspect to it. Brahms hated the showy and anything that appeared to be showbiz. For Brahms, Liszt's music was 'ein Schwindel'; to Joachim, Liszt was 'a cunning contriver of effects'.[53] Clara and Joachim consistently refused to play virtuoso potboilers merely to please audiences, and, with Brahms' support, Joachim gave up a lucrative concert tour in England so as not to prostitute his art. The feeling was reciprocated: Liszt never once performed or conducted a work of Brahms throughout his influential career.[54]

The more technical explanation was this. Beethoven's predecessors believed that music was based on agreed rules and structures, timeless and 'true', such as sonata form, or variations on a theme. Using these as a foundation, Beethoven began to create new structures, and he provided a lead for subsequent generations to follow. While Brahms adhered to recognisable classical forms, the progressives, particularly Berlioz, Liszt and Wagner, virtually jettisoned them: their music was determined by their feeling, their 'inner experience'. For Brahms, these radical composers had the effrontery to decide for themselves what was and was not musically acceptable. In the symphonic poems, for example, the music was at the whim of the composer, who made up his own rules, thereby opening the flood-gates with uncontrolled and uncontrollable consequences. (Those who dislike certain aspects of 20th-century music might, perhaps, agree.)

Brahms versus Wagner

Brahms' attitude manifested itself in his relationship with Wagner. He met Wagner in Vienna four years after the Declaration and had a sociable evening with him, and yet eventually Wagner became Brahms' implacable enemy. Wagner attacked Brahms in his article 'On Conducting', published in 1869. It has also been suggested that their antipathy arose because Wagner was jealous that Mathilde Wesendonck became infatuated with Brahms after her affair with Wagner came to an end.[55] Her tryst with Brahms was itself terminated when she asked him to set to music her poem entitled 'Ode for the Ceremony of Cremation'.

There was some correspondence, two frosty letters each way, between Wagner and Brahms in 1875. Brahms was a keen collector of manuscripts, and possessed the one for the second scene of *Tannhäuser*, which Wagner wanted back. Wagner acknowledged receipt, while observing that it had been defaced while being copied in Paris. He sent Brahms in return the special first edition of *Rheingold*, inscribing it: 'To Herr Johannes Brahms as a well-conditioned substitute for an ugly manuscript. Bayreuth, 27 June 1875. Richard Wagner.'[56]

The Wagner view can be sensed when one hears Cosima Wagner

describing one of Brahms' letters as being 'as artificial and unedifying as his compositions'. They refer to Herr Brahms, 'that silly boy', and his damaging and bigoted influence on the educated middle classes. She records: 'I make the acquaintance of Herr Brahms, who plays a piano quartet of his own making, a red, crude-looking man, his opus very dry and stilted.' When sent a copy of the Second Symphony of Brahms, she commented that they were utterly shocked at 'all its triviality blown up by orchestral effects, its tremolando theme which might have come from the introduction to a Strauss waltz'.[57]

The gloves by then were off. Clara refused to go to or to perform in any concert in which Wagner's music was being played.[58] She wrote about '*Tannhäuser*, in which Wagner goes through the whole gamut of abominations. They told me in Prague about the music of *Tristan and Isolde*. Apparently it is even worse than what has gone before, if that were possible.'[59]

The conductor Bruno Walter describes the consequences in his description of Berlin in the 1890s. Wagner's name was never mentioned within the precincts of the Stern Conservatoire in Berlin. While the opera houses were filled with people enjoying Wagner, 'a considerable part of the public – and by no means the worst part – stood aloof, lined up on the side of the Conservatoires in an attitude of quiet but determined repudiation. I repeat: by no means its worst part. It consisted of those who felt that the purity of music was threatened by the "Art of the Future" and who were backed by the infinitely valuable and truly music loving circles in whose houses altars to classical music had been erected.' He adds: 'Even the opposition of these serious circles would have been powerless if it had restricted itself to a purely negative attitude towards the works of Wagner. They drew vital strength, however, from a positive attitude towards Brahms, around whom they gathered and whom they had raised up as Wagner's counter-idol.'[60]

Walter continued: 'Brahms was considered the man to carry on the traditions of great music, and Wagner was the destroyer and corrupter from whom to guard the ear and the soul ... I had to listen to scornful references to "Wagala weia" and "Hojotoho".* Besides, the corrupter of the language had also corrupted the music, had abandoned all moderation and form,

* This refers to Wagner language used in the *Ring*. 'Hojotoho! Heiaha!' is a call used by Brünnhilde and the Valkyries in the 'Ride'.

and had vitiated the sound of the orchestra by the augmentation of brass and percussion instruments. Such noise could not be borne by any cultivated ear and, more than that – it was added in a low voice – there was another wicked and impure element in Wagner's music, one that was still beyond me. I knew quite well that they were referring to sensuality, which I found rather interesting and by no means wicked.'[61]

The values that the German bourgeoisie held dear were 'seriousness, respect, rectitude' and were epitomised by Brahms, the Musikdirektor Müller.[62] 'Life's musical enrichment was a thing to be worked for. The raising of the cultural level through the ennobling influence of music was part of the educational programme of almost every middle class family. Musical appreciation was thus not only a general possession, but also a very personal and highly valued one because it had been gained by years of individual endeavour.'[63] This attitude was typified by Brahms when he wrote to an aspiring composer about a piece he was writing: 'Let it rest, let it rest, and keep going back to it and working at it over and over again, until it is completed as a finished work of art, until there is not a note too much or too little, not a bar you could improve upon. Whether it is *beautiful* also, is entirely a different matter, but perfect it *must* be.'*[64]

This was a theory which had a practical effect. Sometimes Brahms' own music became constrained by the very forms and structures he was so keen to defend. But, at the same time, one has only to listen to the last movement of his Fourth Symphony to appreciate what could be done with an old dance form such as the passacaglia or chaconne. The classical approach suited Brahms, who temperamentally was introverted and serious, and who was comfortable expressing his feelings using the well-hallowed rules. Not for him histrionics, the frivolity of Rossini. Brahms thought of writing an opera but never did; one doubts if he could have.[65]

The hatred of some of these composers, one towards another, is astonishing. Hugo Wolf, one of the greatest composers of Lieder, considered Brahms a mere copyist, and would admit that he had one virtue – 'that of artful workmanship … Herr Brahms knows how to vary a given theme as no one else does. His entire creative output, however, is only a great variation on the work of Beethoven, Mendelssohn, Schumann.'[66]

The flames were fanned by the eminent Viennese musical critic and friend

* The emphasis has been added.

of Brahms, Eduard Hanslick, who was despised by Wagner and lampooned as Beckmesser in *Die Meistersinger*. Hanslick believed that music was an end in itself, never a means to an end of poetic or dramatic expression. To him, Wagner subordinated the music to the words. Reviewing the Tchaikovsky Violin Concerto, Hanslick wrote: 'As I listened to Mr Tchaikovsky's music it occurred to me that there is such a thing as stinking music.' At least Tchaikovsky could give as good as he could take. Writing of Brahms' Violin Concerto, he said: 'he has more mastery than inspiration. There are all sorts of preparations for something, a lot of hints at something which is about to appear and delight everyone, but nothing ever comes of it, apart from boredom. His music is not fired by genuine feeling, he has no poetry, but on the other hand he has great pretensions to depth.'[67] The rumblings carried on; one of the most notable victims, as we shall see, was Bruckner.

Family Rows

Brahms' family had hardly set him an example of concord. His parents were frequently at loggerheads. His 73-year-old mother was rapidly going blind; his sister Elise was suffering from migraines. They were living in a pitiable state, with no food and no money. His father had deserted them, and he pocketed the money which Brahms sent home for them. Just before his mother died, she wrote a bitter ten-page letter to Brahms about her past, describing how her husband gambled, idled about and spent whatever money there was. At the end of January 1865, she had a stroke while returning from a concert. On the following night, she died. Brahms rushed back to Hamburg. He commemorated his mother in the sombre *Adagio mesto* of the Horn Trio; and her death provided him with the stimulus to finish the Requiem which he had begun over ten years before.[68]

Despite all this, Brahms was loyal to his father. He paid his rent. He was supportive when his father announced he was marrying Karoline, a widow eighteen years younger. He sent a photograph of himself to give to his stepmother, and was very fond of her. Brahms took his father to the Austrian mountains; until then, his father had never seen a mountain. He helped him with the travel arrangements, to make the long journey from Hamburg to Vienna: it took 23 hours, with two stops, to get to Prague, where Brahms recommended a day's rest before taking the twelve-hour night train on to Vienna. He advised him about the best ticket to get – 'the ticket must be valid for 5–8 days' – and told him on which side to sit to get the best view on the scenic stretch between Dresden and Prague. They then did all the things tourists do: in Vienna, they saw the emperor with the Turkish Pasha; and in Salzburg they saw two emperors, Franz Joseph and Napoleon III, together.[69]

In February 1872, his father died of liver cancer. From Vienna, Brahms wrote a loving letter to his stepmother and sent her more money.

Clara and Baden-Baden

Alongside all the contention between the Romantics, it is hard to picture the happy and productive, almost idyllic decade that Brahms spent just outside Baden-Baden. In 1863, Clara had moved to a modest house in Lichtental, next to this popular, fashionable spa on the edge of the Black Forest. Baden-Baden provided the cosmopolitan middle class with remedial waters for bathing and drinking, and also with legally authorised roulette at the Casino, which was known euphemistically as the Conversation House. There was lively music-making at the Kurhaus and abundant shooting and hunting in the forest. The French felt at home because the grand duchess was from the Napoleonic Beauharnais family. The English went there because the Prince of Wales enjoyed the horse races and the gambling, and found Baden a good place to buy jewellery for his lady friends.[70]

There was a strong Russian connection at Baden-Baden because one of the duke's daughters married into the Russian royal family. Thus, Clara's friend Pauline Viardot lived there in a *ménage à trois*, in grand circumstances. This comprised Pauline, her husband Louis Viardot, formerly director of the Théâtre des Italiens, and the prominent Russian novelist, poet and playwright Ivan Turgenev, the author of the novel known as *Fathers and Sons*.[71]

Clara's far more modest house was on the edge of the town. It had a small garden with a burbling stream running at the bottom of it. Brahms visited her there in 1863, and also in 1864 when he was staying in the Russian composer Anton Rubinstein's villa. In the following year, he took a couple of attic rooms in a little house up on a rocky slope, about a mile beyond Clara's. He stayed there for ten summers from 1865 to 1874. His rooms had magnificent views up the valley; he would go for walks in the fields behind. Here he worked on parts of the Requiem, the Alto Rhapsody, the *Schicksalslied*, the first two String Quartets and his First Symphony.

Brahms would join Clara for tea on her little balcony and return later for dinner. Hermann Levi, one of the leading conductors of the century, was a regular visitor. He amused the children with his pranks, once startling Brahms by leaping from one of Clara's travelling trunks exclaiming 'O Freunde', as from the Beethoven Ninth Symphony; on another occasion, he made the St Bernard dog tipsy on champagne. Anton Rubinstein, in 1863 still only 33, and shortly to return to Russia, came and went.[72]

When, in 1878, Clara took a staff appointment at Frankfurt's Hochconservatoire, Brahms would visit her:* then, 'life became gayer, less formal, and it was impossible to keep to strict discipline'. But it was not always a lark, and there were moments of great seriousness. When her son Felix became incurably ill, Brahms wrote: 'God grant that you may be spared any further cares, for you have surely had enough for one life … let this deep love of mine be a comfort to you for I love you more than myself and more than anybody or anything on earth.'[74] Felix, Brahms' godson, died aged 25 in February 1879.

Many have speculated on the nature of the relationship between Brahms and Clara, who was nearly fourteen years older than him. Because of the partial implementation of their decision to burn their letters, only Brahms' letters to her during the early, most intense, period have survived. At that awful time, when Schumann was in the asylum, it is unlikely that she, fertile and strait-laced as she was, would have risked or wanted an affair. Also, she needed to support her family by playing and touring, and could not afford the disruption caused by a pregnancy. One would also imagine that Brahms, like all 19th-century men, would be particularly careful of cohabiting, had he even remotely suspected that she might be the wife of a syphilitic.** [76]

Clara's love for Brahms, according to her diary, was maternal, and on meeting his elderly mother she confided: 'Perhaps I am destined to be a mother to him in her place.'[77] She was equally fond of both Brahms and

* Another visitor, in 1895, was the thirteen-year-old Stravinsky, whose family used to travel outside Russia in the summer.[73]

** His correspondence does not indicate that he suspected that Schumann suffered from syphilis. Brahms was not ignorant about matters of health: six months after Schumann's death, he was recommending to Joachim that he read 'Personal Protection – from the English – by Dr Laurentius in Leipzig', a manual of sexual anatomy, disease and behaviour, already in its 17th edition.[75]

Joachim.* It seems likely that she enjoyed being their unattainable model of female propriety: 'If ever you are in doubt as to how to behave, think of what Frau Schumann would do', Brahms said.[78] Possibly he was afraid of marrying her: his own parents had exemplified the problems that can arise when a very much older woman marries a younger man. But one of her granddaughters believed that if asked, she would have married him.

Possibly, their passion failed to coincide. Clara was miserable whenever he appeared to be falling in love with someone else. And in 1861, he chided her: 'In everything which concerns me, you have been and you will be as if I am yours entirely, and in everything which concerns you, I am not permitted to be anything to you.'[79] Whatever, he had the deepest reverence for one of the leading pianists of the 19th century. The magic of their relationship would surely immediately evaporate, once we knew that it were consummated.

Of course they had their tiffs, and those recorded in their correspondence show that they could be bitter. There was a row over whether or not Brahms should contribute a new composition to the first Schumann memorial festival in Bonn, organised by Joachim. There was the question of whether Brahms' Requiem should be performed at the festival; Brahms was annoyed, because the first he knew that it would not be performed was when he picked up a newspaper and read about it.[80]

In the late 1870s, there was to be a concert in Leipzig to celebrate the 50th anniversary of Clara's debut at the Leipzig Gewandhaus. She wrote to say that unless he could combine the journey with some useful objective, she had rather he did not come just on her account. She then became offended when he took her at her word, as he was totally absorbed in his Violin Concerto at the time.[81]

There was a row in autumn 1891, when Brahms got Schumann's Fourth Symphony published without her permission. Clara was suffering from an ear ailment which prevented her from hearing pitches correctly. This may be why she was irritated, for there is no other obvious reason. This breach lasted nearly two years, ending in January 1893.[82]

They argued over the complete Schumann Edition on which they

* In the museum at the asylum in Endenich, there is a piano cover which Clara embroidered for Joachim, with his initials, staves and notes. It lies over the square piano on which Liszt played at the opening of the Beethoven memorial in 1845 in Bonn, and which was apparently in Endenich during Schumann's time.

worked together, and Brahms helped her with the business arrangements. This was an arduous exercise, especially when she started inserting metronome marks; she bought a watch with a second hand.[83]

Yet, in the middle of this, Brahms wrote to Clara: 'you and your husband constitute the most beautiful experience of my life, and represent all that is richest and most noble in it.'[84] Brahms and Clara must have been equally difficult. In 1893, she wrote: 'Brahms comes today. How anxious I feel at heart! If only we could frankly discuss all that has happened during the past year, and that has distressed me so much, but with him this is impossible, he gets so violent that one is reduced to silence.' And: 'Brahms left. It was a release, but a melancholy one. The last eight days have been like a nightmare.'[85]

At one stage, it seemed that Brahms was falling in love with Clara's daughter Julie. When she became engaged to an Italian count, Brahms was upset. Clara described him as 'quite altered … he seldom comes to the house and speaks in monosyllables when he does come … And he treats Julie in the same manner, though he always used to be so specially nice to her. Did he really love her?'[86] He expressed his emotions about her in the Alto Rhapsody, which he told Julie was a bridal song for her wedding. Brahms apparently so loved the Rhapsody that he kept the score of it under his pillow.

Vienna: the City

Meanwhile, Brahms had moved his base to Vienna in September 1862, although he continued his peripatetic existence, and stayed with friends or lived in temporary lodgings. He did not settle finally in Vienna until 1869; it was only in 1871 that he moved into Karlsgasse 4, near the baroque Karlskirche with its Greek portico and highly decorated columns. There, Brahms had a picture of Bach above his bed, and a bust of Beethoven, a head of Bismarck and a print of the Mona Lisa.[87]

With introductions from Clara and excellent connections, Brahms quickly made contact with the most important musicians in Vienna. One of his supporters, Julius Epstein, paid for a hall in which he could give a solo appearance.[88] It was a great success. Hanslick invited him to illustrate an important lecture series.

This was the new Vienna of Emperor Franz Joseph. It was the city of the beautiful Empress Elisabeth, the city with the vast pleasure park called the Prater, the city of the waltzes of Strauss and Lanner and the light opera.* Just before Brahms' arrival, there was a period of feverish industrial activity accompanied by a mixture of suppression and reform. The medical services were reorganised, the roads were classified, regulations were introduced prohibiting cruelty to animals, and so on. It was a 'Josephinist fantasy come to life'.[90] In the 1860s, at the time when the emperor changed his policy towards Hungary, a liberal regime replaced the autocratic government of earlier years. Once wars in Italy and Germany no longer had to be financed,[91] the middle class thrived, and there was a boom, the 'Austrian miracle'.**

At the time when Brahms moved to Vienna, the walls were being dismantled, and much of the city was, as we have seen in connection with Strauss, an enormous building site, an opportunity for development, investment and profit. Buildings were erected commemorating the enduring importance of the Habsburgs and, at the same time, the contribution from the liberals.[93] Bankers and industry chiefs built their own sumptuous houses along the new street which replaced the old walls, the Ringstrasse.

The boom culminated in the International Exhibition of 1873, which was five times the size of the Paris exhibition of 1867. It was held in the Prater; the central dome was entered through a triumphal arch, which the Viennese called a giant cake. There were 50,000 exhibitors from 40 countries, including Japan, which participated for the first time. Brahms' piano (formerly Schumann's, collected specially from Hamburg) was on display, together with Beethoven's and Mozart's.[94] But the exhibition attracted only seven million admissions against the twenty million expected, possibly owing to an outbreak of cholera.[95]

Eight days after the opening of the exhibition, the boom hit the buffers and there was the first 'Black Friday' crash on the Stock Exchange. On 8 May, 110 companies were bankrupted, the number growing to 230 on the next day.† There were over 150 suicides.[97]

* There was a contrary view: Debussy later described it as 'an old city covered in make-up, overstuffed with the music of Brahms and Puccini, the officers with chests like women, and the women with chests like officers'.[89]

** Between 1840 and 1870, the population of Vienna doubled. The economy benefited from free trade, and the abolition of the forced labour system (robot; see page 101) helped agriculture; there were good harvests. Exports of sugar grew by 130 per cent in one year; the corn trade grew by 20 per cent. In the 1860s, 70 banks were founded in Vienna and 65 in the provinces; 376 joint stock companies were formed.[92]

The resultant slump lasted into the 1880s, and did no good for the reputation of capitalism. Work on the great buildings on the Ringstrasse came to a halt. With poor harvests, there was famine in many places, more than half a million dying in Hungary alone.[98]

Also, despite all their good intentions, the Viennese liberals 'unwittingly summoned from the social deeps the forces of a general disintegration'.[99] They alienated the Roman Catholics by their educational reforms, by their attitude to the Church and by their lack of support for the Pope. They could not control forces such as Pan-Germanism and Czech nationalism, which we see evoked in music by Wagner, Smetana and Dvořák. As a consequence of these forces, by the end of Brahms' life, the Habsburg government was paralysed. This manifested itself in a particularly nasty way, in anti-Semitism, which Brahms, a liberal, called 'madness'.[100] He had several good friends who were Jewish: Joachim, Levi, Hanslick, Henschel, Hiller, Tausig and Marxsen, to name but a few. Brahms' death coincided with the appointment of a flagrantly anti-Semitic mayor of Vienna, Karl Lueger, and with this 'the era of classical Liberal ascendancy in Austria reached its formal close'.[101]

Brahms kept abreast with politics and world events, and commented in his correspondence about the battle between Prussia and Austria at Königgrätz, and other major events of the time. He much enjoyed reading the political satirical weekly *Kladderadatsch*, published in Berlin.[102]

He took a keen interest in the Franco-Prussian War. Its outbreak caused him to cancel a visit to the Passion Play at Oberammergau. Clara was alarmed when her son Ferdinand was called up.[103] Because Baden-Baden was so near the border, the gunfire around Strasbourg, less than 40 miles away, was audible. But she decorated her house with flags, and made bandages and comforts for the wounded. Brahms took a patriotic attitude to it: he was a fan of Bismarck, and anyway he disliked the French for their flippant attitude towards artistic matters.[104] He dedicated the *Triumphlied* to the German Kaiser. He also defended an outspoken speech by the Kaiser in which he expressed his determination to hold on to Alsace: the Kaiser said that every stone would remain German, even if it took the slaughter

† The number of banks in Vienna reduced to eight over the subsequent ten years. Two thirds of the provincial banks disappeared. Also, in 1880, less than 50 miles of railway track were completed, compared to the earlier boom years when a fifth of state expenditure was going into railway construction and an average of almost 1,000 miles of track was being laid each year.[96]

of eighteen army corps and 42 million Germans laid out in a row like animals killed in the hunt.[105]

Vienna: the Musician

When he was first living in Vienna, Brahms longed to be in Hamburg and regarded his life in Vienna as temporary. In the autumn of 1862, he thought he had been head-hunted for the directorship of the Hamburg Philharmonic, and that the job was in the bag. But the appointment went to Julius Stockhausen, a distinguished singer, fluent in several languages, and a champion of public concerts and cheap seats for the people. Stockhausen wrote Brahms an appropriate letter and was subsequently helpful to Brahms' family. For Brahms, the rejection 'was a blow which he never forgot, never forgave, and in some personal sense never overcame'. Clara commiserated: 'It does happen so often in life that what seemed so harsh, leads to good fortune later on.'[106] The experience still rankled with him 22 years later, when he was invited to take over as director of concerts and head of the Conservatoire in Cologne. In his letter turning down the invitation, Brahms referred to the fact that such a permanent post like the one he hankered after in Hamburg used to be something he really wanted.

Brahms played at concerts and gave piano lessons. He also accepted an appointment as director of the Vienna Singakademie. But as the position was not well paid, and he disliked the chores that were involved, he gave up the post at the end of the first year. Brahms was then almost wholly self-employed and freelance. To earn a living, he had to sell his work to the publisher, who in turn sold it to the public. To stimulate demand, and to make ends meet, he had to promote concerts of his works, and arrange the larger works in piano reductions for four hands. He still would have liked to have a permanent post, however, as it went with his notion of the decent middle-class citizen. But he was passed over for the Hamburg job again, in 1867.[107]

In 1872, after several offers and much shilly-shallying, Brahms took the conductorship of the performing arm of the Gesellschaft für Musikfreunde, the Vienna Philharmonic Society, a top job. The Society was made up of amateurs, supplemented by professionals. Levi had warned him: 'You are not the man to drive yourself to victory over the thousand petty obstacles which are inseparable from every public post. I am afraid you would succumb to them in a short time, and then, embittered and damaged, you would retreat into apathy.'[108] However, Brahms introduced the Viennese to some of the great baroque music, including works by Bach and Handel. This appointment stimulated the flow of his own orchestral music, including the Violin Concerto (1878), the Second Piano Concerto, first performed in 1881, and the Double Concerto (1887). Eventually he resigned from this post, partly to devote more time to composition.

The Requiem and Subsequent Compositions

It was with the German Requiem, however, that Brahms had made his name throughout Europe. Although some of the movements had been performed earlier in Vienna, the first performance was in Bremen Cathedral on Good Friday 1868. The Bremen clergy were concerned about doctrinal aspects; there was nothing in the Requiem about redemption through Christ. To placate them, half-way through, Joachim's wife Amalie performed Handel's 'I know that my Redeemer liveth'. Clara wrote: 'As I saw Johannes standing there, baton in hand, I could not help thinking of my dear Robert's prophecy, "let him but once grasp the magic wand and work with orchestra and chorus" which is fulfilled today … It was a joy such as I have not felt for a long time.'[109] The first full performance of all seven movements was at the Leipzig Gewandhaus on 18 February 1869.

The Requiem resolved Brahms' financial difficulties: he could now demand five times as much for the Requiem as for any other work he had sold before. For financial advice, he turned first to Hermann Levi's brother, formerly a professional bass and now a successful banker. After Hermann Levi moved closer to Wagner, his friendship with Brahms cooled. Then Brahms handed his financial affairs over to Fritz Simrock, his publisher. Meanwhile, Levi's brother invested Brahms' money, clipped his coupons, and sent large donations back to the Brahms family in Hamburg. It is clear that Brahms enjoyed his wealth and kept an eye on it. In 1895, Simrock managed to lose 20,000 marks of Brahms' money in a speculative investment. Brahms brushed it off: 'You must know that, for now, I still have enough to live on, in spite of the bankruptcy. I have obviously not given the matter a moment's thought – except when writing to you.' He added a pungent, indeed model, observation from a client to his broker: 'Only one thing about it could have annoyed me: if it had been my own fault, namely, if I myself had requested the purchase of those shares.'[110]

Brahms issued a steady stream of compositions. He would send his drafts to both Clara and Joachim for their comments, and also to Elisabeth von

Herzogenberg. Brahms found Elisabeth the more fluent score reader, as well as a younger and more broad-minded critic. He tended to send a piece first to Elisabeth, asking her to forward a text as soon as possible to Clara. 'You know Frau Schumann is very touchy', he added on one occasion.[111]

In 1873, on the Starnberger See near Munich, Brahms completed the Variations on a Theme by Haydn. We get a picture of him in 1876, working on the First Symphony on the island of Rügen, off Stralsund in the Baltic, a well-known place for Germans to take their summer holidays.* He went with Henschel, a Lieder singer who was subsequently the first conductor of the Boston Symphony Orchestra, and who founded the London Symphony Orchestra. They kept out of each other's way in the working hours, coming together to relax, sometimes even getting into the same hammock together.[113] Henschel wrote: 'His whole appearance vividly recalls some of the portraits of Beethoven … He eats with great gusto and in the evening regularly drinks his three glasses of beer, never failing, however, to finish off with his beloved Kaffee.'[114]**

The First Symphony came to fruition after twenty years. Its first performance was not a success. Brahms envisaged the work as a unified whole, which was inconsistent with the audience's habit of applauding each movement and even requesting encores of individual movements. Within a few months, he wrote the Second Symphony.

Celebrity

Brahms began to collect honours. When the University of Breslau (Wroclaw) offered him an honorary doctorate, he wrote a composition which, a year later, developed into the Academic Festival Overture (1881). He was delighted to be awarded the Freedom of Hamburg in 1889, although the commander-in-chief of the German army, General Moltke, and Chancellor Bismarck got there first. Brahms had, with Joachim, been offered an honorary doctorate at Cambridge in 1876, but he turned this down. 'The English pester me terribly. I must have the doctor's hat placed

* The Nazis later built a vast holiday resort on Rügen, for the faithful to enjoy a reward for political acquiescence and 'their toil in the service of the Fatherland'.[112]

** Was Brahms' image contrived to make it appear that, although he hailed from north Germany, he was now a true southerner by adoption? In Vienna, the Brahms' northern traits would have distinguished him. Northern Germans considered their southern compatriots to be somewhat comical beer-swilling characters who spoke an incomprehensible dialect.[115]

on my head in C[ambridge], that entails concerts and more of the same in London. But I have absolutely no desire to go to England. Absolutely not! It is dreadful how I am being plagued by this business, and by Englishmen generally.'[116] The English universities seem to have been desperate to confer honorary degrees on foreigners who were not always too polite.* When Saint-Saëns received his Cambridge doctorate, he told the provost of King's: 'Vous savez que je ne parle pas anglais, sauf avec les cabmen et les waiters.'[118]

For some reason, Brahms did not take to England, a country Clara toured nineteen times; the explanation that he was afraid of getting seasick seems unlikely. Given his influence on the so-called English renaissance, on Stanford and Parry, there is a considerable irony in his reluctance to visit the country.[119] He turned down an offer to conduct the Royal Philharmonic Society concerts in 1880. The offer of a degree came yet again from Cambridge in the following year, but Brahms rejected it again. Later, he wrote to Simrock: 'The English Doctorate is getting to be more and more dubious! Bruch will get it in the company of Boito.' And then, in a disparaging comment about the composers whom he despised, he added: 'Who knows how many more there will be before and between us; Rubinstein, Mascagni, Gounod, Massenet for sure!'[120]

In 1877, Brahms was appointed to a committee which was asked to advise the Austrian government on the award of grants to assist composers: the successful candidate for the year was Dvořák. Brahms also did a considerable amount of editing of works by Schubert, Schumann, Mozart, Chopin and Couperin. When the editor of the monumental Bach Gesellschaft edition suddenly died, he was asked to take over, but did not.

We can picture Brahms in those days, dealing with endless correspondence and going to the theatre which he enjoyed so much. He wrote more than 800 letters to his publisher Fritz Simrock. There was so much correspondence that he used to send a pre-paid acknowledgement card, or alternatively a photograph as a temporary thanks; but then he received thank-you letters for the photograph![121]

* Some years later, in response to a request to nominate someone for a doctorate at Oxford, an elderly don suggested (perhaps remembering Cambridge) Tchaikovsky; it had to be pointed out that he had been dead for fourteen years.[117]

Maturity: Vienna, Bad Ischl and Elsewhere

In 1878, Brahms grew the patriarchal beard. Clara demanded that he shave it off, but he took no notice.[122] Beards and gold-rimmed spectacles were very fashionable at the time, as an outward manifestation of inward learning; newspapers advertised products which hastened the beard's growth.[123] But Brahms was generally very careless about his appearance: once, some friend thought that the caller at the door was an old tramp to whom she sometimes gave scraps; she rang for a maid to take him to the kitchen.

Brahms settled down to a routine. He based himself in Vienna in the winter, and for the summer, between mid-May and the last week in September, he would go to the mountains and compose. A favourite summer spot was Bad Ischl, about 35 miles from Salzburg. With its mineral springs and brine baths, casino and theatre, it was a fashionable watering-place for the Viennese, and Franz Joseph had his magnificent hunting lodge there. Brahms would meet his friends such as Johann Strauss* at the Café Ramsauer, and eat and drink at Café Walter on the Esplanade. Sometimes, he went to Lake Thun in Switzerland instead. But he stopped going there when a new riverside promenade was built, allowing English sightseers to get too close to his house.

Brahms enjoyed visiting his friends the Herzogenbergs, although he hesitated to invite himself to stay with them rather than in a hotel. In 1878, he wrote: 'I'll rely on my good luck – if necessary, even on the stars, – with which Baedeker designates so many houses in Leipzig.'[124]

In that year, Brahms began making visits, eight in all, to Italy: he loved his 'magic days' in Venice, Florence and Rome.[125] On the first trip, he was accompanied by Theodor Billroth, a founder of modern abdominal surgery.

Brahms stayed with the Duke and Duchess of Meiningen** on the beautiful Lake Como. The duke ruled a small principality located about 40 miles south of Eisenach, Bach's birthplace. Although in 1880, Meiningen

* Bad Ischl is particularly associated with Franz Léhar, the composer of *The Merry Widow*, who was Strauss' successor as Waltz King. This was after Brahms' time, however. At the time when Brahms visited Ischl, Léhar was a conductor of military bands.

** Queen Adelaide, who married King William IV of England, was a princess of Saxe-Meiningen. Her two daughters would have taken precedence over Queen Victoria, but they died. Greville the diarist described her as 'very ugly with a horrid complexion'. She became a model stepmother to her FitzClarence children, whom her husband had fathered before he and his brother had desperately sought to sire an heir to the throne. Elgar's father used to tune her pianos.[126]

had only about 11,000 inhabitants, it was a magnet for culture.[127] It is a place where the modern pedestrian crossing the street is continually confronted by a plaque noting a birth or residence of some distinguished person, such as Jean Paul Richter, Schiller, or Max Reger. Its Duke Georg II, who lived in the unusually shaped and coloured castle, the Elisabethenburg, loved the theatre so much that he married an actress, Ellen Franz. The theatre went on tour, and was known for its elaborate set and costume design and the co-ordination of its crowd scenes;[128] also, the Meiningen orchestra, conducted by Hans von Bülow (and later briefly Richard Strauss) was one of the only touring orchestras. Brahms' Fourth Symphony had its first performance in Meiningen.

Friends in Vienna

Brahms always took an interest in young women. In 1883, in Wiesbaden, he met the young contralto Hermine Spies, for whom he wrote many songs. Later, he was captivated by Alice Barbi, an international mezzo-soprano, aged 28. She married a baron, and Brahms was the accompanist at her farewell concert.

Brahms also enjoyed meeting his friends in Vienna, many of whom were rich Ringstrasse businessmen. There was Bertha Faber, whom – as Bertha Porubsky – he had known and loved since the days of the Hamburg ladies' choir. There were the Fellingers: Richard Fellinger was the head of Siemens in Austria, and arranged for Brahms' apartment to have electricity installed – one of the first in Austria; his wife Maria was a sculptor and photographer. There were the Wittgensteins: Karl Wittgenstein was Austria's leading steel magnate and father of the philosopher Ludwig Wittgenstein; the Wittgensteins 'continued the noble tradition of those leading Vienna groups who considered it incumbent on them to further Art and the artists'.[129]* But Brahms could enjoy an ordinary life as well: on Sundays, he might go to the Vienna Woods, or to Klosterneuburg for afternoon coffee.

One of Brahms' early biographers records arriving when Brahms was working at the piano: there was a growling sound, a whining and moaning

* The music room in the Wittgensteins' house was decorated with sculptures by Max Klinger, who created the Brahms-fantasy, 'a series of forty-one engravings, etchings and lithographs, semi-surrealist responses to Brahms' texts as well as his music'.[130]

that became a kind of howling. He thought Brahms had got himself a dog. After about half an hour, the music stopped, the visitor entered the room and found that only Brahms was there.[131]

The Joachim Row

Aside from this, there was another, obstreperous, unattractive side to Brahms' character. His manners were never polished. There was an unfortunate incident, in 1892, when Hanslick carelessly forwarded a letter from Billroth, which attributed Brahms' bad manners to deficiencies in his upbringing. At a subsequent soirée at Billroth's house, 'Brahms displayed his churlish side to the utmost'.[132] Sadly, this was the last such gathering, because Billroth died shortly afterwards.

Brahms had also fallen out with Joachim, with whom he went on a very successful concert tour of Transylvania in 1879. Joachim, who was a particularly jealous person, became convinced that his wife, Amalie, nine years younger than him, was having an affair with Brahms' publisher, Fritz Simrock. Close friends believed that Joachim's attitude was totally unjustified. Brahms visited the Joachims' house in Berlin to see for himself what was happening, but ostensibly to discuss some performances of the Requiem. Then Brahms wrote a letter backing Amalie, who used it in her divorce case.[133]

Brahms' letter was forthright: 'He has done you and Simrock the greatest injustice', he said, and referred to lies and deceit, and a web of imaginings, inventions and hasty conclusions. 'Despite a thirty-year friendship, despite all my love and admiration for Joachim, despite all the artistic interests that should have bound me to him, I am none the less very careful in my dealings with him. So, I rarely socialise with him for long or intimately. I wouldn't even think of wanting to live in the same town and join him in a common undertaking.'[134] Of course, Brahms' friendship with Joseph Joachim, who was arguably the greatest violinist of the century, could not survive words such as these. When the Joachims separated, Brahms gave Amalie moral support and helped her to obtain concert engagements.

When, three years later, Brahms set about healing the breach, he still referred to the 'events which I regret but for which I cannot ask forgiveness … Writing that letter is something I cannot repent. It was for me also a solace, a liberation to be able to tell your tormented wife the same things I had told you often enough.'[135]

It took the Herzogenbergs a further two years to rebuild Brahms' friendship with Joachim. But while Brahms' row with Joachim was possibly well-intentioned, his attitude to Bruckner shows just how spiteful he could be.

Bruckner, Wolf and Mahler

We have already seen that, because of the friction among leading composers, Mount Olympus was not a happy place to be. One most unfortunate side-effect was that Brahms took his hatred out on Bruckner. From a musical and moral point of view, this was unforgivable.

By the time Bruckner was in Vienna, Brahms was successful and prosperous. But Bruckner was a sorry figure with a Charlie Chaplin moustache. Dressed in old and grotesquely ill-fitting clothes, he was struggling to make ends meet.[136] Nobody paid for or published his compositions, and he had to pay the copying fees out of his meagre earnings. Yet, partly because Bruckner had the support of the Wagner enthusiasts, Brahms obstructed him, and was rude to him. 'Everything has its limits', he wrote to Elisabeth von Herzogenberg. 'Bruckner lies beyond them, one cannot make head or tail of his things, one cannot even discuss them. Nor him as a person. He is a poor deranged man.'[137] It is suggested that their antipathy reflected the unstable Viennese politics of the time: Brahms was supported by the liberal pro-Jewish faction, and Bruckner by the conservative Roman Catholics.

In particular, Brahms despised Bruckner as a Wagner supporter, which no doubt he was. Indeed, Brahms was so concerned about Bruckner's (in his view) disastrous influence as a teacher of the next generation of musicians that he tried unsuccessfully to persuade Dvořák to come to Vienna as a counter-weight.

Anton Bruckner was an improbable person who suffered nervous breakdowns and extraordinary obsessions. That he was obsessed with qualifications and examinations may not be unusual for a musician; however, most would concede that nine major examinations, celebrating every one as a major event, was a bit over the top. He was also obsessed with religion and women: he would fall on his knees at the sound of the Angelus bell; Ave Marias and Pater Nosters ran side by side with dance hall visits, polkas, waltzes and quadrilles with young ladies, in and out of fancy dress. While this too may be acceptable, his proposals of marriage to a succession of astonished teenagers, whom he hardly knew, were not. He was also obsessed with numbers: he would count everything in sight, 'whether windows, weathercocks, church crosses, dots, buttons or ornamental figures'.[138] And he was obsessed with dead bodies, whether it was the exhumed corpse of Beethoven or Schubert, or Emperor Maximilian's body returned from Mexico, or just those burnt to death when the Imperial Opera House in Vienna went on fire in December 1881.

Thankfully, Bruckner's most valuable characteristic was his self-confidence in his own ability: when his friends tried to persuade him to make

Anton Bruckner

his works easier and shorter, he dug his heels in. 'They want me to write in a different way. I could, but I must not', he said. 'Out of thousands, God gave talent to me … One day, I shall have to give an account of myself. How would the Father in Heaven judge me if I followed others and not him.' He destroyed many compositions because he was not completely satisfied with their quality.[139]

Bruckner was the first of a family of eleven, five of whom died in infancy. Son of a schoolmaster, he was born eleven years before Brahms, on 4 September 1824, in the schoolhouse just beside the church in Ansfelden. This small hamlet, which looks towards Linz in the distance on the far side of the Danube, was peopled by simple, hard-working peasants, proficient in local dance and music, and devoutly Roman Catholic. Anton eventually went as pupil and chorister five miles over the rolling hills to the magnificent baroque monastery of St Florian, where there was one of the greatest organs on the Continent.[140]

Having qualified as an assistant in elementary schools, Bruckner had a series of miserable teaching jobs, one of which also involved muck-spreading in the fields. In 1845, he was appointed organ teacher at St Florian with a salary of 36 florins. Here he remained, teaching the two lowest forms, for a decade. However, he became chief organist ten years later. He was then appointed first organist at Linz cathedral in 1856 and also obtained the backing of its bishop, Dr Rüdigier. His income now enabled him to study in Vienna with Sechter, with whom Schubert had sought lessons in the year he died.[141]

At the age of 44, Bruckner moved to Vienna. His life settled down to a rigid routine of academic and scholastic duties: he was professor of through-bass, counterpoint and organ at the Conservatoire. He also taught the piano at a seminary for women teachers, St Anna, where he became involved in a disciplinary action when two women said that he had insulted them. Bruckner became lecturer in harmony and counterpoint at Vienna University in April 1876.

Bruckner's works tend to attract adverse comment, their length being a particular problem. Sir Thomas Beecham, the conductor, described his reactions to a Bruckner movement: 'I counted six pregnancies and five miscarriages.' To one writer in the middle of the 20th century, he was 'not merely long-winded and platitudinous ... The stumbling block is, of course, the long extent of Bruckner's movements, portentous and discursive, the whole passing slowly and monumentally. Even in an opening allegro, Bruckner is unhurried, static.'[142]

His First Symphony was rejected by Vienna Philharmonic orchestra because of 'its wildness and daring'. The Second was dismissed as 'nonsense and unplayable', and the Third as 'unperformable'.[143] When the Third was eventually performed two years later, there was whistling and catcalling; the audience walked out so that, at the end, only 25 young musicians, including the seventeen-year-old Gustav Mahler, remained to applaud. The 'Romantic' Symphony, number Four, had a better hearing; the Fifth had to wait from 1876 to 1894, two years before Bruckner's death, to be performed. Of the Sixth, only two movements were performed in his lifetime.

After the success of the Seventh Symphony in Leipzig, things looked up; there, the applause lasted for a quarter of an hour, even though Hanslick recorded that 'in between the flashes of lightning are interminable stretches of darkness, leaden boredom, and feverish overexcitement'.[144]

Brahms also picked on Bruckner's followers who studied at the Conservatoire. One such was Hugo Wolf, with whom 'the modern song reached its limits'.* Gustav Mahler, too, was made to feel 'the icy blast of Brahms' spite'.[146] These aspiring composers were virtually destitute at the time, and could ill afford Brahms' abuse. One, who was told by Brahms that he should give up music altogether, was literally driven insane: he warned a passenger on a train against lighting up a cigar, on the grounds that Brahms had filled the train with dynamite; shortly afterwards he died in a lunatic asylum.[147]

Brahms' Final Years

The world was moving on. Brahms played the piano for a recording of his Hungarian Dance No. 1. A letter to Clara in November 1889 refers to the phonograph: 'it's as though one were living a fairy tale', he wrote.[148] In the previous year, the machine had been used to record a performance in England at the Crystal Palace, where it was said to have 'reported with perfect accuracy the sublime strains, vocal and instrumental' of a performance of Handel's *Israel in Egypt*.[149] Thomas Edison had invented the machine, which used cylinders of solid-cast waxes, as a by-product of telegraphy. Edison had astonished himself in August 1877, when he said 'Mary had a little lamb', and played the words back.**

After writing the Double Concerto, Brahms began to feel that, aged 57, he had run his course as a composer. Yet he wrote to Clara about a trip to Italy: 'I myself don't notice my 60 years ... I was definitely the sturdiest

* There was only one further step possible, to replace the piano with the orchestra, as did Mahler and Strauss.[145]

** Edison turned to developing the phonograph commercially only in the mid 1880s. Mass production of cylinders was difficult, other than by re-recording. Just before the turn of the century, Emile Berliner, a German working in Washington, invented the wax disk, which could easily be copied. Fundamentally a dictating machine, the equipment was better at recording voice than instruments. The first decade of the 20th century heard records made by leading singers such as Melba and Patti. A Caruso record for RCA Victor in 1902 was the first to sell a million copies.[150]

one with the greatest perseverance, always the last to bed and the first one out. And my companions were much younger.'[151] His friends and acquaintances started dying. Elisabeth von Herzogenberg died in January 1892. He wrote to her husband: 'You know how unutterably I myself suffer by the loss of your beloved wife.'[152] His sister Elise died in June 1892; then Billroth and Bülow.

Then Spitta, the leading musicologist, died at his desk at a time when Brahms was corresponding with him about folksong.[153] Brahms had been incensed by a recent publication of folksongs, the Erk-Böhme *Deutscher Liederhort*, which he regarded as excessively sanitised, with everything in the major mode and nothing unusual. As a retort against this, Brahms published his own settings of *Forty-nine German Folksongs.**

There was a short blossoming in 1891, with the Clarinet Trio and Clarinet Quintet. But Brahms had lost the creative urge. Around 1895, he wrote no music at all for a year. Simrock noted: 'he sent me his last will.'[155]

It was not all gloomy, however. Gmunden, that beautiful town on the Traunsee, which could inspire such disparate composers as Schubert and Schoenberg, became a favourite. In his last two years, Brahms stayed for a considerable time with some Viennese friends, Victor von Miller zu Aicholz and his wife, at their villa there.** He was also a guest at the villa of Queen Marie of Hanover. The ex-queen, her son the Duke of Cumberland and Princess Mary of Hanover became friends.

Then Clara Schumann died on 20 May 1896, nearly 40 years after Robert. She was aged 76, and in March had had a slight stroke. She had sent Brahms birthday greetings. Joachim had written to Brahms earlier that year: 'I cannot bear the thought of losing her, and yet we shall have to get used to it'; Brahms' response was: 'The idea of losing her cannot frighten us any more, not even my lonely self, for whom there are far too few living in this world. And when she has gone from us, will not our faces light up with joy at the remembrance of her, of this glorious woman, whose great qualities we have been permitted to enjoy through a long life, only to

* Songs comprise nearly a third of Brahms' overall output. He published nearly 200 solo songs in 31 volumes, six volumes of duets, and five volumes of solo quartets with piano accompaniment. His first songs in the 1850s were inspired by one of his favourite books, *Des Knaben Wunderhorn*, the anthology of folk poems collected by Achim von Arnim and Clemens Brentano, which influenced so many in the 19th century, including Mahler.[154]

** After Brahms' death, Miller purchased the contents of Brahms' house at Ischl.

love and admire her more and more? In this way only shall we grieve for her.'[156]

Brahms wrote the *Four Serious Songs*, the last of his compositions to be published in his lifetime. To Marie Schumann he said: 'I wrote them in the first week of May. Some such words as these have long been in my mind, and I did not think that worse news about your mother was to be expected – but deep in the heart of man something often whispers and stirs, quite unconsciously perhaps, which in time may ring out in the form of poetry or music. You will not be able to play the songs yet, because the words would affect you too much, but I beg you to regard them and to lay them aside merely as a death offering to the memory of your dear mother.'[157] The words taken from the Book of Ecclesiastes are desperately depressing: 'Man has no pre-eminence above the beasts: for all is vanity. All go unto one place; all are of the dust and all turn to dust again.' The fourth song must surely be the saddest ever rendering in music of St Paul's famous words about love and charity,* which today we conventionally expect to hear at weddings.

After this, Brahms completed the Eleven Chorale Preludes for organ, which are so symbolic of his loyalty to classicism and reflective of his love and reverence for Clara. But despite the gloom, he could be cheerful. He wrote to Simrock, sending him the *Serious Songs*: 'You might be surprised that a man of my age is still having a new coat made for himself.' He said he needed some money to pay the tailor, and concluded: 'Is the gleeful mood growing? I sincerely hope so. Your J. Br.'[158]

On 14 June 1896, he went to the Fellingers' silver wedding celebrations in Vienna and then returned to Ischl. He had caught a chill at Clara's funeral. Friends noticed a yellowing of his usually ruddy face and, at their suggestion, he eventually saw the doctor. Bruno Walter says that Mahler visited him in Ischl and described 'how the old man's dark and morose mood had corresponded to that of the first of his group of *Four Serious Songs*'. He continued: 'Mahler reported that he had left Brahms toward evening. As he walked through the dark corridor towards the door, he took a backward look and saw the sick man go to an iron stove and take from inside it a piece of sausage and some bread. Mahler described the grotesque and sad impression that the ill man's frugal, solitary supper had made on

* 1 Corinthians, chapter 13.

him. Deeply moved, he kept murmuring to himself: "for all things are but vanity".'*[159]

Brahms went to Karlsbad for a cure in early September. In October, he wrote about his jaundice, saying: 'it is a quite commonplace jaundice, which unfortunately has taken a notion not to leave me … I have not had one day of pain or anything – nor lost my appetite for even one meal.' But by the end of the year he was talking about 'its very uncomfortable aspects'.[160] The physicians reassured him that there was nothing serious. In fact, like his father, he had cancer of the liver. He continued to dine with his friends and attend concerts and interest himself in musical matters. The Duchess of Meiningen sent him slipper socks made by the orphanage which she sponsored.[161]

By mid-February, he was not feeling any better, but was irritable and despondent. His last public appearance was at the première of a Johann Strauss operetta on 13 March. On 27 March he put himself to bed. He sent Karoline Brahms a postcard written in pencil. On the night of 2 April he drained a glass of hock in two gulps, saying: 'That tastes good.' The next day, he was dead.[162]

Far to the north, on the Elbe, the ships lowered their flags to half-mast.[163]

* 'Denn es ist alles eitel', from the first of the *Four Serious Songs* – see above. Also, 'Denn alles Fleisch es ist wie Gras' is the second section of the German Requiem.

Bizet

CHAPTER 18

On 3 March 1875, the Opéra-Comique saw the première of a new opera. Exactly three months later, its composer was dead. The opera had played to half-empty houses. The critics had said that it lacked drama, it was vulgar, it was dull and obscure.[1] Besides, this type of show, with murders and harlots, was not what the market wanted: the Opéra-Comique derived a significant amount of its income from bridal couples who met there to discuss their wedding arrangements. Each night, half a dozen boxes were taken for this purpose.[2]

The opera was, of course, *Carmen*, 'one of the greatest creations of the musical stage'. Doubtless, it was a considerable disappointment for those who looked for something 'joli, clair, bien ordonné'.[3] Yet, even at the time, *Carmen* had its supporters. Brahms, improbably, was so enthusiastic that he went to twenty performances.[4] He asked his publisher to obtain the full score for him, 'for in fact I love it more than all of the things you publish [i.e. his own works], which isn't saying much and not enough'.[5] Bismarck, the Prussian chancellor, went to see it 27 times.[6] Tchaikovsky, who saw one of the last performances of the run in Paris, described it as 'one of those few works which are destined to reflect in the highest degree the musical aspirations of an entire epoch'.[7] Nietzsche suggested that it should be used as an antidote to the poison of Wagner's operas.[8]

For most of us, *Carmen* provides some of the most powerful music and memorable tunes in the repertoire. We can also admire how effectively Bizet presents the disintegration of Don José's character, and applaud his portrayal of the Toreador, the conceited, successful sportsman, whom 'neither bull nor woman can resist'.[9] The dénouement, when the Toreador's triumphal music breaks in over music depicting the personal tragedy of Carmen and Don José, gives us one of the most dramatic moments in all opera.

Six months after the Paris première, *Carmen* was performed in Vienna. Then it swept Europe and America. The opera has been a success ever since. But the adverse Paris reaction precipitated Bizet into a depression which contributed to his premature death, aged only 36.[10]

Behind the coffin, as it was taken to Père Lachaise cemetery, walked his old father, Adolphe, the Rouen hairdresser, wigmaker and singing teacher. Georges was his only child, born in Paris on 25 October 1838. He and his wife Aimée had registered him pretentiously as Alexandre-César-Léopold Bizet but, by the time he was baptised at Notre-Dame-de-Lorette, the boy was simply Georges. Aimée had been perhaps a bit more genteel and bourgeois than her husband: her father had been a lawyer, wine merchant and café proprietor.[11] She was an excellent pianist, and started Georges on his career.[12] Adolphe had lost her, too, fifteen years ago. They had both been so proud of Georges: everyone had been astonished by his talent. Like his teacher Gounod, he won the Prix de Rome. But when Georges returned to Paris, he was continually frustrated, even put down, by the 'system': there was no room for him as a composer; even *The Pearl Fishers* got bad reviews. He could have become a virtuoso pianist, but he did not want to be one. He had an affair with a maid and a child followed. Then he married Geneviève, who, as an heiress, gave him some financial security, but also much anxiety, because she was so unstable. He lived through the Siege of Paris and the even more horrifying Commune. Then there was *Carmen*, soon to be followed by his death.

The Prodigy

As a boy, Georges quickly showed great promise and was given much encouragement by his parents. Through the influence of his maternal uncle, who was a prominent singer and teacher, and whose wife had held a position at the Conservatoire, he was admitted there while still only nine; this was a year before the official age for admission. He excelled, especially at the piano, and won many prizes.[13]

It was not a propitious time at the Conservatoire. Its director was the diminutive Daniel Auber (see page 277), whose successful opera *La Muette de Portici* had been first staged a decade before Bizet was born. But Auber, the very epitome of Parisian wit, charm, delicacy and success, was now almost 70. He himself admitted that his happiest ideas were created between yawns.[14]

Charles Gounod

Eventually, death in his 90th year, during the Commune, forced him to vacate the Directorship. Ludovic Halévy, the librettist, described Auber as 'never deeply affected by anything', adding that he 'never has any passions, but simply preferences, and those never very strong. He is a ladies' man, but never in love; he has women, but no mistresses; acquaintances but no friends.'[15]

One of Bizet's teachers was Ludovic's uncle, the eminent and sociable Fromental Halévy, composer of the highly successful Grand Opera, *La Juive*, which appeared in the mid-1830s. Halévy too was 'past it': sometimes he did not even turn up for his classes, but left the pupils to teach each other. Bizet's professor, Zimmerman, passed him on to his son-in-law Charles Gounod who gave him the opportunity to earn some money by arranging many of his works.

Gounod

Gounod had a profound influence on Bizet and later on Massenet and Puccini. The well-known duet from Bizet's *The Pearl Fishers*, 'Au fond du Temple Saint', is in the style of Gounod, as is the duet between Micaela and Don José in the first act of *Carmen*.[16]

Gounod composed melody so charming that it became the fashion for ladies to swoon during the second crescendo of his Ave Maria. Berlioz and Saint-Saëns were enthusiastic supporters of him. It has been claimed that Gounod put poetry back into music, and Ravel said that Gounod was 'the true founder of song in France'.[17] Wagner, on the other hand, thought his *Faust*, the opera which made Gounod's reputation, was 'a sugary, vulgar, nauseating, bungling piece of work'.[18] Gounod's choral music was much loved by the English, although there were differing views about it: the conductor Charles Hallé said that he would refuse to rise from the dead if the Last Judgement were accompanied by the strains of Gounod's music.[19]

When a prizewinner in Rome, Gounod came under the influence of a Dominican preacher; later, he even dressed and described himself as an *abbé*, and signed his name preceded by a cross.[20] But, quite rightly, he doubted his own ability to uphold the vow of chastity.[21] Just as well. Bizet said of Gounod, at a time when it was suggested that he might be appointed director of the Conservatoire, 'his private life is not sufficiently pure to permit their thinking of trusting him with a school for young girls'.[22]

Prix de Rome

Bizet followed Halévy and Gounod as a Prix de Rome winner, winning the second prize in 1856 and the first in the following year. Gounod said when Bizet won the first prize: 'Your real life as an artist is about to begin – a secure and serious life because you will now be able to struggle with your problems at ease, without any worries.'[23]

Meanwhile, in 1856, Bizet entered a competition for a one-act operetta, the prize being offered by Offenbach, who wanted to promote his Bouffes-Parisiens. The set work was called *Le Docteur Miracle* and Bizet won, jointly with Charles Lecocq, who later became a popular composer in Paris. Bizet frequently attended Offenbach's Friday evenings. The star performance at one of them, given to celebrate 'the imminent end of the world', as foretold by some, was a solo polka danced by Léo Delibes.* A week or so later, the postponement of the Day of Judgement was celebrated, with Bizet playing the piano.

Bizet's stay as a prizewinner at the Villa Medici in Rome was a happy time in his life. He was popular with the other laureates; there was much tomfoolery, making of apple-pie beds and so forth. Sometimes it was not so harmless. Bizet had a violent temper and was apt to rush into challenging to a duel someone with whom he disagreed; in Venice, he picked a quarrel with an unsuspecting gondolier, and went for his throat.

Bizet loved the Italian climate, the opportunity to travel into the hills, and to see the antiquities. He also enjoyed the bordellos and the women. In his journal, during the return journey to Paris, he recorded: 'In the train we met two sweeties. I would almost have **** one.'[24]

Bizet had a good sense of humour. When he went to Rome, Rossini's crony Carafa gave him a letter of introduction to Saverio Mercadante, the director of the Naples Conservatoire, and an important composer. Bizet opened it. In it, Carafa had written some extremely uncomplimentary remarks about him and his professional ability. When Carafa subsequently asked Bizet whether he had passed the letter to Mercadante, Bizet answered: 'When one has the good luck to own the autograph of a man like you, Monsieur Carafa, one keeps it.'[25]

The position of a Frenchman in Rome was difficult: on the one hand, the French were propping up Papal rule in the Papal States; on the other, in the north, they were fighting on behalf of Italian liberation from Habsburg rule. Bizet's mother felt that her son should be taking more interest in the political scene. He was on holiday when the French defeated the Habsburg army at Magenta in June 1859 (see page 529). He and his friends named their dog Magenta: 'When we call him in the street, the priests thumb their noses at us in fine fashion.'[26] He also complained that the French seemed to be doing all the fighting and the Italians very little.

Bizet occasionally thought that he was beginning to develop into the natural creative genius that he aimed to be. 'I am beginning to think of myself as an artist', he felt, 'but what howlers, what failures.'[27] The prizewinners were supposed to send back a work each year; he sent back an opera, *Don Procopio*, instead of the prescribed Mass. He was reprimanded

* Delibes was not considered a serious composer until *Coppélia* in 1870.

for this. He had thought of writing something religious, but the religion would have been pagan.

Paris

Bizet returned to Paris, with two years of his pension from the Prix de Rome left. His life in Paris coincided with the Second Empire. Offenbach's operetta was in its heyday. In the boulevards could be found people such as the Goncourt brothers and Nestor Roqueplan, the director of the Opéra, an Oscar Wilde-like dandy, who said, 'my dream is to die insolvent and in style':[28] he lined the walls of his room with bed-warmers. However, behind the opera house curtain, the finance director was in charge; the *prima donna* reigned; the composer, at the bottom of the pecking order, just had to fit in with stage manager, ballet master and librettist.

The Opéra was musically static and exclusive, as Berlioz found. Only eight of the 54 Prix de Rome laureates between 1830 and 1860 had a work performed at the Opéra. Ambroise Thomas' *Hamlet*, rarely heard now, was typical of the repertoire; and Gounod had difficulty getting his *Sapho* produced there, even though he had the support of the star mezzo-soprano Pauline Viardot.

The other theatres were not much better. The octogenarian Auber was still writing operas for the Opéra-Comique, where about half the Prix de Rome winners managed to have their operas performed.[29] The Théâtre des Italiens frequently staged second-rate Italian operas. The one glimmer was the Théâtre-Lyrique, founded in the early 1850s and directed by the tough and demanding Mauritius-born Leon Carvalho.[30] Its finances were precarious and it thus preferred to stage potboilers, a typical one being Victor Massé's *La Reine Topaze*: years later, Proust would cite, as evidence of the vulgarity of Swann's mistress, her thrill at the prospect of going to that show.[31] However, the Théâtre-Lyrique did also sponsor works by young composers, and also staged a truncated version of Berlioz' *Les Troyens*.

The only openings were in the salons, where, as a piano virtuoso, Bizet could have had a successful career. At a dinner in 1861 at the Halévys', Liszt played an exceptionally difficult piece, and claimed that only he and Hans von Bülow were capable of playing it properly; Bizet then amazed Liszt by playing a large amount of it from memory and by sight-reading the rest. Gounod introduced Bizet to the salon of Princess Mathilde, the emperor's cousin. 'But social success never served to mitigate his sense of persecution.'[32] Bizet wanted to compose and did not want his compositions labelled 'musique de pianiste'.

The Pearl Fishers and Mogador

In 1862, the arts minister, Count Walewski,* granted the Théâtre-Lyrique a subsidy of 100,000 francs on condition that, every year, it should produce a three-act opera by a winner of the Prix de Rome. Bizet was commissioned, an exceptional opportunity, given the difficulty of getting an opera performed. He worked intensively to compose *The Pearl Fishers*; it got a bad press, with only Berlioz giving it a good review. A critic in *Le Figaro* said: 'There were neither fishermen in the libretto nor pearls in the music.'[33] There was criticism of Bizet for taking an ovation, and for the unconventional clothes which he wore when he did. After eighteen performances, the opera was dropped; he regarded it as a failure.

Meanwhile, Bizet had enjoyed his parents' maid, Marie Reiter, by whom he had a son, born in June 1862. Then in October 1863, some land came up for sale at Le Vésinet, a few miles from Paris. It was cheap because the railway out to St-Germain-en-Laye (where Debussy was born in the previous year) was being built very close by. Adolphe bought enough land to build two small bungalows, one for himself and one for his son.[34] Bizet would enjoy walking along the banks of the Seine with his large dog, living off home-grown vegetables, eating food cooked by his father and drinking the wine sent him by a pupil, whom he taught by a kind of correspondence course. In one communication to his pupil, Bizet made a telling remark so relevant to all musicians: 'I don't believe that you *felt* this work. It is a lesson; it is not music.'[35]

Bizet also befriended one of his neighbours, the celebrated *grande horizontale* Elisabeth-Céleste Venard, known by her stage name Céleste Mogador. She was 41 and he was 27. One of her many lovers had been Alfred de Musset, who took her on after he ended his affair with George Sand. Mogador later claimed that her relationship with Bizet was platonic.[36] Whatever, it has been suggested that she must have provided some ideas for *Carmen*.[37] Bizet seems to have fallen out with Céleste's mother, who would empty the chamber pot on him from an upstairs window when he visited the house.

* The illegitimate son of Napoleon I.

Brought up in the Paris slums, Céleste had fended off her mother's lover, escaped and spent time in the St Lazare prison before registering as a prostitute, aged sixteen. One of the clients of the brothel 'took pity on her', and took her to his apartment. She became a circus performer and a dancer, specialising in the new dance, the polka. When men clamoured to dance with her, her boss said that 'it would be easier to defend Mogador [a Moroccan city recently bombarded by the French], than to fend them off'.[38] She picked up the Comte de Morton de Chabrillan in the Café Anglais; he had her name deleted from the list of registered prostitutes and they married in London in 1854. They went to Australia where he was French consul in Melbourne. He died, and she returned to Paris to act, publish memoirs and novels, and direct the Bouffes-Parisiens recently abandoned by Offenbach, and a theatre in Belleville, a slum.[39]

By the time Bizet took up with Céleste, his Prix de Rome pension had run out. He undertook laborious hackwork, preparing the two- and four-hand piano transcriptions of popular opera numbers. In the days before records, this was the way in which music was generally disseminated. He also arranged vocal scores and composed third-rate dance music. He worked at the Opéra and the Théâtre-Lyrique, playing scores submitted for performance. And he taught. Sometimes he worked sixteen hours a day. He began to suffer from the chronic and painful throat abscess, quinsy, which he had earlier experienced in Rome. This health problem cannot have been helped by his smoking: he regularly smoked cigars, and later seldom was without his pipe.[40]

Bizet was determined to write successfully for the stage. But getting works accepted seemed almost impossible. He wrote *Ivan IV* for Carvalho, but this was postponed: the Théâtre-Lyrique was already recycling costumes from other operas in the repertoire in order to save money, and had moved away from the boulevards to cheaper premises.[41] Carvalho gave him the libretto of *La Jolie Fille de Perth*, but that opera was also postponed. When eventually it was put on at Christmas time in 1867, it was preceded by considerable PR, and a big picture of Bizet appeared on the cover of a popular magazine.[42] It got a good press, but it only had eighteen performances.

Bizet had been very hopeful for *La Jolie Fille*. He wrote to Choudens, the publisher: 'more and more rebuffs and disappointments surround me, and I can't understand why'.[43] Its failure knocked his self-confidence and he became very depressed; this seemed to coincide with a recurrence of the throat trouble, which he treated with a gargle. But he pressed on with his *Roma Symphony*, and some other operas, now forgotten. It was around this time (1865–8) that he wrote most of his music for piano and his solo songs and other vocal music. Then, in 1869 and 1870, he began, or at least planned, eight operas.

Bizet became music critic to *La Revue Nationale et Etrangère*, but when the editor tried to censor his article, he resigned. He entered for a prize offered by the organisers of the Great Exhibition in 1867, the highpoint in the reign of Napoleon III. A cantata by Saint-Saëns was the winning entry, but even that was eclipsed by Rossini's 'Hymn to the Emperor and his Valiant People' which included military effects such as gunfire. Bizet, who had entered almost anonymously, did not figure. Something similar happened when he hesitated to enter his opera *La Coupe du Roi de Thulé* for a competition the Opéra had offered. The prize was won by one Diaz, with a work which was mainly that of Diaz' teacher, who was a member of the jury. Bizet became very dejected. 'This so called artistic milieu is no better than the gutter', he said.[44] But in February 1869, three movements of the *Roma Symphony* were performed successfully, conducted by Jules Etienne Pasdeloup.*

The Great Exhibition of 1867 had a negative effect on the developing theatre. The promoters wanted safe works, such as Offenbach's *Grande-Duchesse* and Gounod's *Romeo and Juliette*, both of which were very successful. Ludovic Halévy said: '*Romeo* is not an opera, it is a perpetual love duet.'[45] Perhaps not surprisingly, Verdi's *Don Carlos* closed after only fifteen performances.

Geneviève

Bizet, who was 'a cheerful, clubbable fellow',[46] had become engaged to Fromental Halévy's daughter, Geneviève, in October 1867: 'No more parties! No more sprees! No more mistresses! I have met an adorable girl whom I adore. In two years, she will be my wife', he wrote.[47] But her family at first objected, so his engagement was called off after a month. Possibly the Halévys regarded him as 'a penniless, left-wing, anti-religious,

* Pasdeloup conducted the Société des Jeunes Artistes du Conservatoire, and then the Concerts Populaires.

Bohemian type of character'.[48] He certainly could be considered an intellectual: at this time, he prepared 'a summary of the history of philosophy from Thales of Miletus to the present day'. His rejection by the Halévys caused him more despair and, in 1868, he seems to have had a breakdown accompanied by very severe attacks of throat trouble.

Geneviève's distinguished father (see page 277) had died in 1862; 15,000 mourners marched in his funeral procession. Her mother, born Léonie Rodrigues,* came from a rich and prominent Jewish banking family, who claimed to have migrated from Palestine to Portugal in AD 133; they then settled in Spain, until ejected by the Inquisition, whereupon they moved to Bordeaux. Madame Halévy's brother, Hyppolite, a retired stockbroker, helped bring about Bizet's wedding, which took place in mid-1869, in a civil ceremony. Bizet's marriage, at least, solved some of his financial problems: Geneviève's dowry was 150,000 fr plus 500,000 fr later.[50] He also now had a beautiful wife with a 'svelte figure, flawless olive complexioned skin and magnificent black eyes'.[51]

Like many scions of old families, Léonie was very eccentric: periodically she went into a sanatorium to sort herself out. The painter Delacroix observed, a decade earlier: 'At the Halévys': suffocating heat. His poor wife fills the house with old pots and pans and old furniture; this new folly will send her to the hospital';[52] however, this did not stop Delacroix asking her for the recipe of her tomato hors-d'oeuvre.

Léonie was convinced that Bébé, as Geneviève was known, had caused the death of her elder sister Esther, who had died quite suddenly in 1864, aged twenty. As a consequence, Geneviève also became unhinged; whereupon mother and daughter had to be kept apart. **

The Siege

About a year after Bizet's marriage, there occurred the series of events which were to bring down the political pack of cards with astonishing speed. 'Certainly no nation in modern times, so replete with apparent grandeur and opulent in material achievement has ever been subjected to a worse humiliation in so short a time.'[53] At the time, the outlook had

* Her cousin was Olinde Rodrigues, who was one of the two pères leading the Saint-Simonian movement in which Liszt was caught up during the 1830s. Olinde's father was a friend of Abraham Mendelssohn; Felix took great exception to Olinde when he met him.[49]

** Esther was the fiancée of the librettist Ludovic Halévy.

seemed 'set fair': we recall that the French prime minister, Liszt's son-in-law, said: 'at no epoch was the peace of Europe more assured'.[54]* But the offer of the Spanish throne to a German led France, which was increasingly neurotic about the strength of Prussia, to declare war on 15 July 1870 (see page 504). There was the customary jingoism whipped up on these occasions: *A Berlin*, the mob cried. Albert Fauré, who was in the navy, wrote enviously to his brother Gabriel regretting that the war would be land-based: 'in your militia regiment you will soon be engaged in driving out this pack of northern savages', he said.[56]

Bizet, as a Prix de Rome winner, was exempt from conscription. When the emperor went forth in command of his armies, Bizet observed the monarch's relative inadequacy compared to his forebear: 'The uncle at least knew where to find the enemy', he wrote.[57] Soon enough, however, the nephew did. The Prussians struck hard: Napoleon III was penned in at Sedan in the Ardennes where he capitulated on 1 September, ironically, on the day Albert Fauré wrote the letter to Gabriel. There was nothing to stop the German armies reaching Paris.

When the appalling news of Sedan came through two days later, Edmond Goncourt wrote: 'Who can describe the consternation written on every face, the sound of aimless steps pacing the streets at random, the anxious conversations of shopkeepers and concièrges on their doorsteps, the crowds collecting at street corners and outside town halls, the siege of the newspaper kiosks, the triple line of readers gathering around every gas-lamp? ... Then there is the menacing roar of the crowd, in which stupefaction has begun to give place to anger. Next there are great crowds moving along the boulevards and shouting "Down with the Empire! Long live Trochu!"'[58]** On 17 September, the Prussians began to encircle Paris; it was only eleven weeks since the prime minister had made his fateful statement.

At the outbreak of war, Gounod was at the seaside with his family. Although he wrote a patriotic cantata, *A la frontière*, he escaped to England. Once there, he wrote to the German crown prince, asking for protection for his property in St Cloud; he also claimed that his artistic

* Sixty-eight years later, the British prime minister Neville Chamberlain made a similar statement: 'I believe it is Peace for our Time.'[55]

** General Trochu was the governor of Paris who had assumed the position of president.

development stemmed from the German spirit and German art. In London, he conducted the Royal Albert Hall Choral Society: his style suited the English taste and the queen was particularly fond of *Faust*.*[59]

Offenbach took his family to Spain.[60] But some musicians stayed behind. Ambroise Thomas, aged 60, volunteered. Marmontel, the aged pianist who, twenty years before, had taught Bizet at the Conservatoire, served in the same regiment as his son. César Franck had the task of assisting with food and fuel supplies. Saint-Saëns, Massenet and Widor enlisted, as did young composers such as Duparc, Guiraud and Fauré. Augusta Holmès, friend of Wagner and much loved in the salons, served in the ambulance service; La Mogador set up a women's corps.[61] Some gave concerts of patriotic music, as did Saint-Saëns and Pasdeloup, the conductor. Opera stars sang the previously banned 'Marseillaise' at the end of performances, one dressing up in the tricolour. More prosaically, during the bombardment, the composer Vincent d'Indy, who had been rejected for active service, would pace the boulevards in search of any news from the front; bored, he would 'pick up a tart in a brasserie off the Boulevard Montparnasse'.[62]

There were artistic losses: the painter Henri Regnault, who had won the art section of the Prix de Rome with a painting of Augusta Holmès dressed as Thetis, was killed in action at Buzenval. The foyer of the Théâtre-Lyrique became a casualty station. The church of St Sulpice was damaged by gunfire. There was hardship and disruption: opera employees were dismissed and had no visible means of support. Aristide Cavaillé-Coll, the outstanding organ builder, found his firm's stock of 32 foot pipes useful in propping up his workshop during the bombardment.**

However, the war had an important consequential effect in reviving French music. When there was an attempt to ban German music at concerts, it was found that there was nothing much to put in its place. French composers realised that French music had long been too dependent on

* Birmingham paid Gounod £4,000 for *La Rédemption*, which was almost as popular in England as Mendelssohn's *Elijah*; he was paid 100,000 fr for *Mors et Vita* which was given at the Birmingham Festival of 1885. The one-time abbé also picked up and had an affair with Georgina Weldon, who ran the National Training School of Music in Bloomsbury.

** It seems improbable that the war cost Cavaillé-Coll the contract to build the organ at The Royal Albert Hall, as is sometimes suggested. There was a 'done deal' with Willis, the English builder.[63]

foreign music. Thus, after the war, Saint-Saëns founded the Société Nationale de Musique which aimed to make known 'published and unpublished works of French composers forming part of the Society, and to aid the production and popularisation of all serious musical works'.[64] Soon, in the 1870s, the Société was giving nine or ten concerts a year. Compositions were selected by a voting committee. Many of the composers of the period, such as Fauré, who was its secretary, Duparc, Chabrier and even Debussy, owed their first hearings to this initiative.

Concert life, which Pasdeloup had done much to foster during the Second Empire, received a further boost from Edouard Colonne, the former principal violinist at the Opéra, and also from the talented, but touchy, Charles Lamoureux. They both founded concert societies. Colonne subsequently promoted works by composers such as Debussy and Ravel. He was also a supporter of Berlioz' works, and performed *La Damnation de Faust* 172 times before the First World War. Lamoureux also did much to raise the standards of concert music in Paris and promote new works.[65]

Bizet in the War

When war suddenly broke out, Bizet was staying in Barbizon, a village on the edge of the forest of Fontainebleau.[66] This was a retreat for a group of painters such as Francois Millet and Gustave Courbet, who had pioneered 'realism' in the 1850s. Millet was a painter of rustic and working-class subjects, such as *The Gleaners*, a picture of peasant women harvesting.[67] Courbet wanted to shock the bourgeoisie out of its complacency: there were no graceful poses, no flowing lines, no impressive colours, none of the prettiness preferred by the bourgeoisie. One of his best-known works is his picture of himself walking in the fields, called *Bonjour, Monsieur Courbet.*

Bizet and Geneviève left Barbizon for Paris, where they stayed throughout the Siege. He wrote to Hyppolite: 'Geneviève says that she is in no state of mind to endure one day separated.' Bizet joined the National Guard of 360,000 men, and started drilling. At first, it was very heavy work: he stood sentry duty on the fortifications; he loaded heavy guns onto the gun-carriages: 'Our guns weigh fourteen pounds – that's heavy for musicians', he wrote. 'The weapons recoil, spit, do everything possible to be more disagreeable to those who use them than to the enemy.'[68] But as things settled down, he had more time to himself; he also helped the wounded in the hospitals.[69] Others in Paris at the time were the

Impressionist painters Degas, Manet and Berthe Morisot; Monet and Pisarro were in England.

Paris was still a fortified city, surrounded by a wall, 30 feet high, and by a moat ten feet wide. Beyond the moat, at a distance of 1–3 miles, lay a chain of sixteen powerful forts, including the mighty Mont Valérien. The line of forts filled out a circumference of 40 miles which meant that an investing army would have to have a front of around 50 miles for a siege to be watertight. The government was reasonably confident, and anyway was optimistic that it would be rescued by the provinces within 80 days. It had no contingency plans for a long siege.[70]

Bismarck demanded to be given Alsace and part of Lorraine. Negotiations held at the Rothschild palace at Ferrières, north of Paris, collapsed. Within two days of their beginning to encircle Paris, the Prussians had obtained a commanding view across the city from the Châtillon plateau.

Bismarck had scornfully predicted that 'eight days without *café au lait* will be too much for the bourgeois Parisians to endure'.[71] A phoney war began. Life in Paris became dull, only enlivened by rumour, the publication of obscene caricatures of a virtuous and frigid Empress Eugénie, and by bizarre suggestions for what should be done. One idea was to 'use *mitrailleuses* as Sirens who would lure the Kultur-lovers forward by playing music of Wagner and Schubert, whereupon they would be mowed down'.[72] Although at first all theatres were closed, musical events were revived to help sustain morale and raise money. On 5 November, the Opéra reopened.

There was an occasional sortie, such as an attack on Le Bourget, just under four miles outside the city walls, where the French sustained considerable losses; fortunately Fauré, who took part in it, survived. The government was rightly scared of revolution. At the end of October, the left wing tried a putsch at the Hôtel de Ville but was outmanoeuvred by government forces, who entered through a tunnel; the government reneged on an agreement that there would be no reprisals, causing great bitterness on the Left.

Gambetta, a leading Republican, planned to organise the relief of Paris from the south. On 7 October, he left by balloon, made of varnished cotton and filled with coal gas, to head south to Tours, where a relieving army was to congregate. During the Siege, 65 balloons left Paris: they carried

164 passengers, 381 pigeons, 5 dogs and nearly 11 tons of official despatches, including around 2.5 million letters.[73] They were a great morale booster. Wagner, sitting in comfortable Tribschen, observed to Cosima that the French government in balloons would be a suitable subject for a comedy in the style of Aristophanes.*[77]

Ballooning was a risky business. The crew were liable to be shot as spies. The course of the balloon was tracked by the Prussian telegraphy system; Krupp's anti-balloon cannon were used to try to shoot them down. Only five fell into enemy hands, but many simply were blown off-course.**[78]

The carrier pigeon was the only means of penetrating the blockade, which balloons, even with experimental propellers, never succeeded in doing. A pigeon could carry 40,000 despatches in the form of microphotographs, which were projected by magic lantern, on arrival. Three hundred and two birds were sent off, of which 59 reached Paris. For long, there was a myth that the front page of the London *Times* was pigeon-posted into Paris.[79]

There was enormous confusion as a result of the difficulty of communication. Originally, it was intended that Paris would be re-victualled by opening a line through to the coast. When the decision was taken to adopt Gambetta's plan to relieve Paris from the south, 400 guns, 54 pontoons and 80,000 men had to be transferred from one side of the city to the other. The Germans got wind of all this and were ready for the Great Sortie when it took place. The circumstances were unpropitious, because the River Marne was in flood, but the government was so afraid of the Paris mob that it did not dare risk delay. In three days, the Great Sortie cost 12,000 officers and men. The wounded were brought into Paris in horse-drawn buses and bâteaux-mouches; they were deposited on the banks of the Seine.[80]

Richard Wallace, heir to a great art collection, organised an ambulance

* The first hydrogen-filled balloon had ascended from the Tuileries in 1783. Robespierre established an 'Ecole Aérostatique'.[74] Mozart stayed away from an ascent from the Prater amusement park in 1791, because he thought it would fail.[75] The military use of balloons was not successful until the mid-19th century. They were used in the American Civil War. Wagner's reference may be to *The Birds* (in which 'Cloud-cuckoo land' first appeared) or to *The Clouds*, both written around 420 BC.[76]

** One balloon carrying crucial military despatches was blown out to sea. The crew later saw pine trees; they were in the centre of Norway, having travelled 900 miles in 15 hours.

service at his own expense. The Conservatoire building was converted into a hospital. Fashionable ladies tended the wounded, many of whom died from septicaemia. Most hospitals had a 'death shed' into which any who contracted septicaemia were quickly transferred. Epidemic became a serious problem. During one week in November, smallpox claimed 500 victims, one of which was the seventeen-year-old ballerina who, in the previous May, had starred in the première of Delibes' *Coppélia*.[81]

The rich survived reasonably well, because food was rationed by price. Goncourt found the writer Théophile Gautier lamenting 'that he has to wear braces for the first time, his abdomen no longer supporting his trousers'.[82] It has been said that 'for those with even a little money, the situation was rarely worse than it was for the average Briton during the direst moments of the U-boat blockade in the First World War'.[83] That type of situation, presumably, would have been the Bizets' experience.

Infant mortality soared through lack of milk, but very few adults actually died of starvation:* the main food, to begin with, was horsemeat, which had been introduced in Paris four years earlier as a cheap food for the poor. By mid-November, signs had gone up: 'Feline and Canine butchers'. An American observed that cat 'tastes something like the American grey squirrel, but is even tenderer and sweeter'.[85] It has been calculated that, during the entire Siege, 65,000 horses, 5,000 cats and 1,200 dogs were eaten, but only 300 rats.[86] The horses of Auber, the director of the Conservatoire, went to the butcher.

Brewery rats were more expensive than sewer rats. Fewer rats were eaten than is generally believed, because the sauces to make them palatable were only available to the rich. A British journalist said 'salmi de rat' was 'excellent – something between frog and rabbit'; a month later he reported, 'I had a slice of spaniel the other day'.[87] The elephants at the zoo, Castor and Pollux, were also eaten. But there was never any shortage of alcohol.

When Orléans fell in early December, there was no hope of relief, but the government, terrified of the mob, still did not dare to surrender. The Prussian King was very reluctant to sanction a bombardment. But this

* The French losses during the Siege were relatively low. Deaths from all causes amounted to 6,251, of these only six are listed as having died apparently from starvation, though there were a further 4,800 infants, infirm and aged whose deaths may be said to have been hastened by food shortages. It was far worse 70 years later in the 900-day siege of Leningrad (now St Petersburg), in which Shostakovich took part.[84]

eventually began on 5 January. At night time, after 10 pm for four or five hours, 300–400 shells would rain down, mainly on the Left Bank, the domes of the Panthéon and Les Invalides being favourite targets. Around 12,000 shells fell on Paris, but, as a result, only 97 people were killed and 278 wounded. There was another failed sortie on 22 January. Paris capitulated on January 28th. The siege had lasted 130 days.[88]

Then, there was a great exodus, with considerable touting for rail tickets. Although the Bizets at first thought of staying, by 7 February, they got safe passes and left, at Bizet's mother-in-law's invitation, for Bordeaux. 'As soon as the officials of the Orléans railway can give passengers more reliable encouragement than "we shall resume operations somehow or other", we shall leave', he said.[89] The visit was short. The last time mother and daughter had met was at the asylum in Ivry; again, they had an explosive row. In two days, Geneviève begged to be taken away; she had a breakdown and began to show a facial tic which lasted the rest of her life.[90]

In elections held on 8 February, the left wing was defeated; the 73-year-old veteran Adolphe Thiers, once a protégé of Talleyrand, was overwhelmingly elected. Bizet supported Thiers and disliked the movement that was growing for a restoration of the monarchy. Under the peace terms, which were ratified by the assembly sitting in Bordeaux, France fatefully lost Alsace and most of Lorraine including Metz and Strasbourg; and there was a war indemnity payable of 2 billion francs, with German occupation continuing until it was paid off. To seal the victory, there was to be a triumphal march by the Prussians through Paris on 1 March, and the city would be occupied for two days. While at Versailles, Bismarck had arranged for the Prussian King to be proclaimed Kaiser: the German Empire had begun.

On 3 March, Bizet wrote that the Prussians had gone. 'We did our duty on this sad occasion. At the first beat of the drum we took our guns and went to establish a *cordon sanitaire* around our enemies.' A few days later, he was able to say: 'Paris is regaining her ordinary appearance. Peace has been restored to us. There is no longer any problem about food and we remember vaguely having sustained ourselves on horsemeat, rice and chocolate.'[91]

Little did he know what was to come.

The Commune

Two hundred cannon had been taken by the National Guard up to Montmartre, possibly to prevent them falling into German hands, possibly to threaten the city. The regular army was ordered to recover the guns just before dawn on 18 March, but they foolishly failed to bring along the horses necessary to remove them. When they went to fetch horses, the mob collected, drummed up by the anarchist schoolteacher and amateur poet, the 'Red Virgin' Louise Michel. The troops left behind began to defect. Their general, and another who was foolish enough to show interest in what was going on, were seized and butchered; the corpses were flung into a house once occupied by Scribe, who had supplied so many librettos earlier in the century.[92] Women began to urinate on one of the corpses, which was still warm.[93]

Bizet wrote to Rodrigues explaining that the assassination of the generals 'is a horrible infamous act, but isolated'.[94]* He went to support the government forces in the city. 'They kept us waiting eighteen hours; we didn't see a superior officer and we were not given an order. Our battalion chiefs did not deign to come and find out about us. Mine appeared briefly around two o'clock and never came back. At midnight, some sort of staff officer came to advise us to go home.'[96] Fortunately, Bizet resisted pressure from some of the Montmartre men to join their forces.

Thiers moved the government from Paris to Versailles. On 28 March, the day on which Queen Victoria opened the Albert Hall in London, a municipal council, which called itself the Commune de Paris, installed itself. It was controlled by 'Reds' in proportions of four to one, but it was not communist; it had no ideology, no programme. The Reds comprised a motley collection of Jacobins, old socialists, anarchists, intellectuals and Bohemians.[97]

The press office was run by the poet, Paul Verlaine. There was no real leader. However, the Commune took some immediate steps: they repealed the Rent Act and banned gambling. But they failed to get a grip on the Bank of France, which leaked out funds to Versailles.[98]

* Readers interested in how a mob of French women might be expected to behave at this time should turn to Zola's novel *Germinal*.[95] In this, shrieking women parade a lump of hairy, bleeding flesh formerly belonging to the local grocer and gombeen man. The terrified bourgeois watching the riot think that the object is rabbit skin. Louise Michel, for all her extremism, was found playing the organ in a deserted church, during a lull in the fighting.

There was spy mania. Pierre Auguste Renoir, who had recently returned to Paris, was quietly painting by the Seine and was suspected as a spy sketching the river defences. An amiable old lady recommended drowning him, on the grounds that 'unwanted kittens, who do far less damage than spies, are normally drowned'.[99] However, Renoir was hauled off to the nearest *mairie*, where there was a permanent firing squad on duty. Fortunately for art, the Commune's chief prosecutor, who happened to be there, recognised Renoir as someone who had helped him when he had been on the run, and had him released.[100]

Bizet, with Geneviève, decided to run for it, especially when universal conscription was announced. 'I was liable to confinement at home as a suspect or to be forced to join one of the "right-thinking" batallions', he wrote.[101] The Prussians were still encamped around the eastern perimeter, and it was quite easy to get out of Paris through their lines. Zola got out on a Prussian passport. On 29 March, Bizet wrote from the Hôtel de Fleurs in Compiègne about 45 miles from Paris: 'When the gentlemen of the Commune were about to cancel all communication with the rest of the country, I flung myself with Geneviève on the first train I could catch, and here we are at Compiègne ... what will happen to our books, our belongings, and Madame Halévy's? What will happen to Paris?' he despaired. 'Here we are, deep in Germany. Four thousand Prussians are stationed in Compiègne.'[102] He became very despondent about the future: 'the clericals will wreak vengeance ... Between the wrath of the Whites and the wrath of the Reds there will no longer be any place for decent people. Music will have no future here.'[103]

On 30 March, the Marquis of Gallifet, a hero of Sedan, led an attack on Paris from Neuilly. There was a cannonade on Palm Sunday, 2 April. Next day, a mob set out from Paris. Half of it retreated when a gun was fired from Mont Valérien. The rest pressed on, whereupon the Versailles cavalry destroyed them and killed their leaders. The response of the Commune was to pass the Law of Hostages: the execution of any Commune prisoner-of-war would lead to the shooting of three hostages who would be drawn by lot. One who suffered this fate was a journalist and good friend of Bizet.[104]

In early May, the important fortress at Issy fell. On 8 May, Thiers issued a proclamation warning Paris that it would be attacked. Four days later, Bizet reported hearing the distant noise. He wrote to his mother-in-law, with whom he maintained cordial relations, 'the cannons are rumbling with unbelievable violence. I didn't close my eyes all night.' Also, he said: 'Geneviève is getting fat … she is rosy, gay, happy and not much affected by the events going on around us.'[105]

To divert attention from the impending collapse, the Communards held a series of concerts in the Tuileries Palace to collect funds for the wounded. The audience was supplied with brioches and beer. A vast open-air concert was held in the gardens, during which 1,500 musicians performed. In order to expel 'the musical obscenities of the Empire',[106] they played works by Mozart and Meyerbeer.

Priests were arrested, including the Archbishop of Paris. There was looting and random destruction. The mob, including Courbet the painter, who was normally 'sodden with drink',[107] pulled down the 155-foot-high column in the place Vendôme. Shortly after the column fell, the arsenal near the champ de Mars blew up. Verlaine fought off a proposal to destroy Notre-Dame. The *Venus de Milo* fortunately survived under a pile of dossiers at the Préfecture de Police.

Thiers had been responsible for the construction of Paris' defences during the reign of Louis-Philippe and knew of a weak point at the Pont-du-Jour at the south-west of the city. This area had been so heavily bombarded that its defenders had withdrawn. An engineer walking in the area on Sunday 21 May saw that there was nobody defending it, and let the Versailles troops in. Verlaine and his wife were woken by their pretty maid saying that the Versaillais had entered.*

The Communards took to the barricades and fought to the death. As they retreated, Paris was set alight in a scorched earth policy. There had been dry weather and there was a strong wind. The Théâtre-Lyrique was destroyed. The smart shops and cafés of the rue Royale went up in flames. The Tuileries was fired, barrels of gunpowder having been placed in the Salle des Maréchaux where, so recently, the last of the concerts had taken

* 'Mme Verlaine at once packed to take refuge with her parents, leaving her husband contemplating the means of seducing the maid.'[108] Verlaine subsequently abandoned his wife and child and was imprisoned for trying to shoot the man he ran off with. He became a Trappist, and then taught drawing and French in England, before totally degenerating into alcoholism and debauchery. Debussy composed many songs using his poems (see page 795).

place. The Hôtel de Ville was destroyed. Notre-Dame would also have been fired, were it not that there was a hospital for Communard wounded next door. The organist Widor (whose Toccata is often played at weddings) wrote that everything around him was on fire and he expected to be roasted alive.[109]

The situation for the Communards was hopeless, as the Germans cut off any retreat in the rear. During 24 May, Versailles troops under Marshal MacMahon captured the Gare du Nord, the Porte St Denis, the Conservatoire, the Bank and the Bourse. A few days later, Bizet wrote to Mme Halévy: 'the last cannon shot was fired on Sunday at half past two'. He became very concerned about the hostages: he wrote to Mme Halévy: 'there is no news of the hostages. Has the Archbishop of Paris been shot?'[110] Archbishop Darboy had indeed already shared the same fate as his predecessor Monsignor Affre, who had been killed attempting to mediate at the barricades in 1848. Shot with the archbishop was Abbé Duguerry, Saint-Saëns' priest at La Madeleine, who had used his pulpit to denounce the insurrection and the vandalism. Bizet's journalist friend was one of the first to be shot on 23 May.

By the time Bizet was writing, the terrible vengeance had indeed started. On Whitsunday, the corpse of the archbishop was found: 147 men were then taken to Père Lachaise cemetery and shot. This was only the beginning. Anyone with blackened hands was assumed to have been involved in incendiary operations, and was shot on sight; an unfortunate chimneysweep was shot for this reason in the rue Saint-Honoré. At the Opéra, soldiers dressed up in skulls, masks and costumes from the recent productions of *Der Freischütz* and *Coppélia*, in order to watch the executions taking place in the courtyard.[111] The new director of the Conservatoire, Salvador Daniel, an expert on Arab music and a friend of Courbet, was shot after only ten days in the job.[112]

Prisoners' convoys were marched to Versailles; stragglers were of course shot. Gallifet set up his own sifting process at the Porte de la Muette on the edge of the Bois de Boulogne. 'I am Gallifet', he said, 'you people of Montmartre may think me cruel, but I am even crueller than you can imagine.' One woman who begged him for mercy received the frosty response: 'Madame, I have frequented every theatre in Paris; your acting will have no effect on me.'[113] She was shot. Grey-haired men were presumed also to have been involved in the events of 1848. So they were called out and shot. Those with watches had presumably been officials of the Commune, so they were shot.*

Back to Normal

The municipality of Paris, then a city regarded possibly as *the* centre of civilisation, paid for the burial or disposal of 17,000 corpses. Probably between 20,000 and 25,000 people were killed. The work of the 26 courts martial continued until 1875. The judges were relatively lenient: only 23 death sentences were carried out. But 20,000 prisoners were stored in hulks on the Seine during the long cold winter. Captain de Bussy was sent to prison. Many, including Louise Michel, were sent off to the penal colony in New Caledonia in the South Pacific. Courbet received six months' imprisonment and was ordered to pay 250,000 fr towards the rebuilding of the Vendôme column. He fled to Switzerland rather than pay this.[115]

The English were fascinated: Thomas Cook organised special excursions to see the 'ruins'. Worth, the fashion designer, bought up part of the ruins of the Tuileries to make sham ruins in his garden. Gautier returned, and saw the street where Mérimée had lived: 'it seemed to be deserted throughout its length, like a street of Pompeii'.[116] There was enormous administrative chaos because nothing done during the Commune was recognised by law. But in general, things quickly returned to normal, as Bizet had envisaged. On 8 June, Bizet and Geneviève returned for a couple of days to find that their apartment was intact. From Le Vésinet, twelve days later, he wrote: 'Paris is trying hard to resume its ordinary way of life. The playhouses are open. The lyric theatres are trying to reopen but that is more difficult … I never go to Versailles and very rarely to Paris since transportation is very difficult because of the destruction of the bridges.'[117]

In July 1873, the National Assembly voted to build the Basilica of Sacré Coeur at the place where the Commune had started, 'in witness of repentance and as a symbol of hope'.[118] By the following September, the indemnity

* The blood flowing in the Seine flowed on into the 20th century: Lenin studied all this and concluded that in Soviet politics, there should be no half measures, utter ruthlessness being essential. The first Russian spacemen in 1964 took with them three relics: a picture of Marx, a picture of Lenin and a ribbon off a Communard flag.[114]

to Germany had been paid off and the last German soldier left. Despite the peaceful intentions at Sacré Coeur, the determination for revenge against Germany simmered away.

Geneviève gave birth to a son, Jacques, in 1872.*[119] His grandmother Léonie moved to Versailles; she would waylay her grandson on his walks in the park and force sweets upon him. All this launched Geneviève into another breakdown.

Not surprisingly, the Bizets' marriage was hardly normal or happy: for some months early in 1874, they lived separately. Meanwhile, Bizet tried to help Mme Halévy in her business affairs. The family owned a development property in the boulevard Malesherbes, and now its value was worth less than the mortgage. The strain of sorting this out affected his health, and he had yet another attack of his recurrent throat trouble. He wrote to Hyppolite: 'the circumstances that give Geneviève her strange terror of me are distressing and painful enough without my having to take the least responsibility for Mme Halévy's affairs ... outside of family politics, I have the warmest affection for Mme Halévy.' He added: 'I shall never hesitate to put Geneviève and her health above every other interest.'[120]

Around this time, Bizet wrote the overture, *Patrie*, of which Winton Dean, his biographer, says: 'it is an awful warning of the danger of confusing art with patriotism', adding that it 'should be consigned to that limbo which houses Beethoven's Battle Symphony, Tchaikovsky's 1812 Overture and other aberrations of the loftiest public spirit'.[121]

Mme Halévy wanted to pull strings to get Bizet a job as chorus master at the Opéra. But Bizet would have none of it: he had 'a horror of being dependent, supported, recommended'.[122] When the job came up, Mme Halévy started to lobby for his appointment, much to his fury.

Bizet worked on a number of operas, *Grisélidis, Clarissa Harlowe* and *Djamileh*. But he had trouble getting them staged. *Djamileh* was eventually performed in May 1872; it ran for eleven performances and disappeared until 1938. It did not help that the leading *prima donna*, at one moment, jumped forward 32 bars, and 'the orchestra had to race to catch up with her'.[123]

* Subsequently, Jacques, together with his cousin Ludovic Halévy's son Daniel and the pampered, asthmatic Marcel Proust, formed a trio of rather undisciplined literary intellectuals at their upper-class school in Paris. Proust proposed adolescent sex to Jacques, but was rebuffed.

In an attempt to revive the *mélodrame*,* Bizet wrote music for Daudet's play, *L'Arlésienne*. The overture and entre-actes, the only time the composer is really heard, were drowned by people coming in and out and talking. When he re-scored four extracts as a suite for full orchestra, it was a success. He also wrote *Dom Rodrigue*, about the Cid, the Spanish hero. But its production was deferred partly because the Opéra building, the Salle Le Peletier, was burnt down on 28 October 1873.[124]

Carmen

As well as composing, Bizet continued to study. He even attended incognito César Franck's organ class at the Conservatoire. In 1872, he had requested a list of Spanish songs from the library at the Conservatoire.[125]

He finished the score of *Carmen* in summer 1874. Rehearsals began in October and lasted nearly five months. The management at the Opéra-Comique was very nervous about the content and wanted it toned down. The orchestra found it too difficult to play; the chorus found it too difficult to sing. Although Bizet continually revised the text and score, the librettists of *Carmen*, Meilhac and Ludovic Halévy, Geneviève's cousin, had other works running in Paris at the same time, and did not give it their full attention. In mid-January, Bizet sold the score to the publishers Choudens for 25,000 fr; foreign royalties were to be divided equally between the two librettists, the composer and the publisher.[126]

While this was going on, the new opera building, which we know today, was opened. It had been started in 1860, and was now a reminder of the imperialism so recently destroyed. It was the largest theatre in the world in terms of acreage, if not seating capacity. Charles Garnier apparently used more than twenty miles of drawing paper designing it. The opening was attended by the King and Queen of Spain, the King of Hanover and the Lord Mayor of London in the state coach. Appropriately, the programme at the gala event included excerpts from Auber's *La Muette*, Rossini's *William Tell*, Halévy's *La Juive*, Meyerbeer's *Les Huguenots*. Renoir loathed the building. 'To think that the Germans missed it with their Big Berthas!' he would exclaim.[127]

The first performance of *Carmen* took place at the Opéra-Comique on 3 March 1875, the same day as the announcement of Bizet's appointment

* This is a play where music is interspersed with, and provides background to, dialogue.

as a chevalier de la Légion d'Honneur. *Carmen* was too long: Act One lasted for 58 minutes and the whole opera for four and a half hours including intervals; the fourth act began after midnight. One of the only enthusiasts in the audience was Shilovsky, a friend of Tchaikovsky. Others were highly critical of its content. They objected to the clamorous roar of the orchestra. The proponents of the Auber tradition accused it of being Wagnerian; the proponents of Wagner did not see it as a music drama.[128]

What made the audience particularly uncomfortable was not so much the music as the dramatic power of the opera. The audience was used to heroines being 'spotless sopranos',[129] like the sweet country girl Micaela who was so shockingly jilted for the coarse Carmen. But in this opera the heroine was also the villain, *and* she seduced Don José on the stage. Of course, Verdi's *La Traviata*, which had appeared over twenty years earlier, was also about a whore, but Violetta was a respectable whore, who certainly did not seduce someone on the stage; besides, she died tragically of tuberculosis, whereas *Carmen* was brutally murdered. Some also felt that portraying Spaniards as brigands could damage the new friendship between France and Spain.[130]

After the hostile reception, a dejected Bizet wandered round Paris for half the night with a colleague. Late in that month, the severe chronic throat abscess recurred and he suffered from acute depression. He talked about noises in his ears, the sound of a double A flat-E flat going through his head continuously. On 27 May, he left for Bougival, and foolishly indulged his passion for swimming by bathing in the Seine. Although on 1 June he had a severe heart attack, the doctor did not seem too worried. Bizet had a second heart attack on the next night and, by the time the doctor arrived, he was dead.[131]

Marie Reiter, the housemaid, attended him on his deathbed, and remained in the service of the family until she died in 1913.[132] Their son Jean was brought up in the household as a sort of cousin. He was tacitly regarded as the son of Bizet's father; he became a director of the newspaper *Le Temps* and was honoured with the Légion d'Honneur; he died in 1939.[133] Jacques, Bizet's son with Geneviève,*[134] later founded one of the

* After Bizet's death, the beautiful, witty Geneviève seems to have become more normal, although she remained dependent on drugs. She married Emile Straus, a rich lawyer connected to the Rothschild family, who had disconcertingly half-closed eyes. Her Sunday salon at 134 boulevard Haussmann became 'one of the most brilliant in Paris', and was attended by the *gratin* (the upper

first car-hire businesses in France. Like his mother, who was addicted to veronal, he took morphine and alcohol to ward off acute depression, partly brought on by the failure of his second marriage. He shot himself, aged 50, about a fortnight before the death from pneumonia of his childhood friend, Marcel Proust.[135]

In 1938, on the centenary of Bizet's birth, *Carmen* was played for the 2,271st time at the Opéra-Comique.[136]

crust of Paris society, such as Princesse Mathilde) and by Fauré, Maupassant, Degas and Sarah Bernhardt among others. Goncourt observed the 'coquettishness' of her posturing as an invalid, while holding in her lap the latest in a line of black poodles. She was a patron of the novelist Marcel Proust, who worshipped her and took her advice on drugs. She provided inspiration for his character, the Duchesse de Guermantes. She died in 1926, aged 77.

Late-19th-century France: Franck, Saint-Saëns and Fauré

CHAPTER 19

SHORTLY AFTER the centenary of his death, a visitor to César Franck's memorial, in the garden in front of his basilica of Sainte-Clotilde, was not surprised to see a notice pinned to the plinth saying that it had been knocked down by a tree and its restoration had still to be decided upon by Paris City Council. Franck was always down on his luck.

His father's ambitions for him to be a virtuoso came to a halt. He had no luck with his compositions. Gounod condemned the *Symphony* as 'the affirmation of incompetence pushed to dogmatic lengths'.[1] After the audience shuffled out at the close of the first, and only, performance of the oratorio, *Les Béatitudes*, Franck confided to his wife: 'Of one thing I am certain; it is a very fine work.'[2] He did not have much luck with his wife: she became a shrew.

Why bother with this quaint figure, a kind of Bruckner,* with his tall black stovepipe hat and ill-fitting clothes? First, because we remember him for 'Panis Angelicus', the *Symphony in D minor* and his fine organ music; surprisingly, he is said to have been 'possibly the most highly-rated French composer among the concert going public in England in the middle of the

* The analogy with Bruckner is often contested. Franck was not as naïve and unworldly as Bruckner. Certainly, both were misunderstood, misinterpreted and underrated.[3]

Above: FRANCK, SAINT-SAËNS AND FAURÉ

twentieth century'.[4] Second, and more importantly, as professor at the Paris Conservatoire, he taught a small but talented group of devoted pupils. Thus, he has been called 'the father of modern French music', even though one critic has drily commented that 'he would need unusual wisdom to recognize his own children'.[5] Franck provides a bridge between late Romanticism and the 20th century movement in France.

In the late 19th century, audiences much preferred the phenomenally successful and rich Camille Saint-Saëns, 'one of the most talented all-round musicians ever, a brilliant pianist, sight-reader, improvisor'.[6]* He is now remembered largely for a few excerpts from *Samson et Dalila*, some concertos, the *Organ Symphony*, his *Danse Macabre* and his 'Dying Swan'.** They also preferred Jules Massenet, who created the brand exemplified in his popular opera *Manon*. We shall come across him in connection with Puccini.

Saint-Saëns committed the cardinal sin of presenting himself as a reactionary, of fighting the school of Franck on the one hand, and Debussy on the other. Although, occasionally, Saint-Saëns could be innovative, a recent biographer criticises him for being 'a latter day Luigi Cherubini, frozen in retrograde classicism, prophesying the doom of serious music'. Much more contentiously, the biographer adds: 'In certain respects, his opinions have been proved correct and much of twentieth-century composition represents a wasteland, which the average listener shrinks from absorbing.'[9]

The music of Franck and his pupils may seem 'specialist', perhaps a bit dull, except to 'enthusiasts'. And Saint-Saëns' music may, on reflection, seem relatively lightweight. We have to await Claude Debussy before we find a composer who begins to match up to the quality of the artists in other fields. From the ashes of Paris after the Commune there emerged an astonishing array of talent; in literature, Zola, Maupassant, Verlaine, Mallarmé, Sardou and Proust; in sculpture, Rodin. In painting, the list is long: familiar names include Manet, Monet, Renoir and Degas; then Cézanne, Van Gogh, Gauguin and Matisse. In the sciences, we should

* Sibelius said that in the history of music there were only three child prodigies – Mozart, Mendelssohn and Saint-Saëns – 'of whom the last never in the end attained the status of the other two'.[7]

** Saint-Saëns was particularly successful in the days of the silent cinema. Then, he accounted for twenty per cent of the background scores, whatever the nature of the film. He was the first composer to write film music, in 1908, for *L'Assassination du Duc de Guise*.[8]

remember Louis Pasteur, whose Institute was founded in 1888, and the Curies, who discovered radium in 1898.*

Meanwhile, this chapter will look at the lives of Franck and Saint-Saëns, two so very different composers. It will also look at Saint-Saëns' protégé, Gabriel Fauré, who is both loved and derided as the composer of the Requiem, a work composed during a very insecure time for religion in France. As people, Saint-Saëns and Fauré were also different, Saint-Saëns being a loner and probably homosexual, whereas Fauré, whom Debussy condemned as 'the Master of Charms',[11] was most at home in the salons of the rich such as the Princesse de Polignac, and with other women. Curiously, it was Fauré who ended his career as a pedagogue, as director of the Conservatoire, a position Franck craved to fill. Fauré's appointment followed a turbulent period in musical politics, which came to a head when Maurice Ravel was turned down, after several attempts, for the award of the Prix de Rome.

In this chapter, we cover a very wide spectrum, leaping from the first half of the 19th century to the first half of the 20th. Franck was born on the day that Beethoven completed the *Missa Solemnis*; Saint-Saëns died about a week after the Anglo-Irish treaty was signed dividing the Ireland we know; Fauré died around nine months after the death of Lenin. So, in this chapter, we must ration the background information provided. We shall look briefly at some aspects of Franck's Belgium in the 1830s, at France after the Franco-Prussian War, and at the lead-up to the First World War.[12]

Franck's Early Life

Franck was born on 10 December 1822 in Liège. Although Belgium has rarely produced great composers, Orlando di Lasso being an exception, places like Brabant, Hainault and Flanders, and names such as the Count of Egmont, who was executed in Brussels in 1568, ring out in the annals of music. The region was ruled cruelly and severely by the Spanish Habsburgs who inherited it from the Dukes of Burgundy. In the time of Louis XIV, bits of it were chipped away and became French. By the time of Franck's birth, Belgium was part of the Kingdom of the Netherlands. This arrangement did not work: the Belgians were pro-French and predominantly Roman Catholic, whereas the Dutch had noticeably different national characteristics and were Protestant. The Dutch ruled very efficiently

* The Curies' daughter was a childhood friend of Poulenc. He found that images of her, and of his wire-haired terrier Mickey, provided inspiration.[10]

and economically, but not so effectively. Surprisingly, they showed considerable insensitivity, especially in matters like education. As a consequence, the Roman Catholics entered into an unlikely alliance with the French liberals, in an attempt to get rid of the Dutch. Brussels became a refuge for conspirators from almost every country in Europe.[13]

When César was eight, a few months before he was enrolled at the Liège Conservatoire, the July 1830 revolution took place in Paris. The news of this coincided with the Brussels première of Daniel Auber's highly successful opera, *La Muette de Portici*, which was about an uprising against Spanish rule in Naples in 1647 (see page 277). Although the Spanish win in the end, the work 'abounds in passages well calculated to inflame the populace in their then excited state'.[14] Having heard the duet, 'Amour sacré de la patrie', the Brussels audience rushed onto the street, shouting 'Imitons les Parisiens'.[15] Thus, in a sense, tiny little Auber may be said to have caused a big revolution, an achievement that even Verdi could not rightfully claim.

For the next couple of years, there was considerable violence as the Dutch sought to retain control. The excessively serious Leopold of Saxe-Coburg was placed on the throne;[16] he was the widower of Princess Charlotte, once heir to the British throne; he was also Queen Victoria's uncle. The violence and destruction continued, and Leopold was nearly defeated. But, with French and British protection, he became more secure. The 'final and irrevocable' separation of Holland and Belgium was agreed.[17] But it was only at the end of the 1830s that the country stabilised; the Dutch had to be evicted from Antwerp by the French; and there was a dispute about the status of Luxembourg.

Such was the Belgium of César's youth. The Franck family background did not place them in either camp, Dutch or Belgian. His father's family lived near the German border and his mother was wholly German; to the end of his life, he said his daily prayers in German.[18]

Franck's father was a typical example of the over-ambitious parent with whom we are now quite familiar. He reckoned that, in César and his brother Joseph, he had two musical prodigies whose value he could exploit. Little attention was paid to their general education. At Liège, César was a great success, and won prizes, one of which was the full score of Meyerbeer's *Robert le Diable*, a treasured possession for the rest of his life.[19] After a series of concerts in Liège, Brussels and Aachen, César's father wanted him to take by storm the salons of Paris. So, there they moved in May 1835.

The plan did not work. Liszt saw the gauche young César Auguste perform and concluded that he lacked the necessary social attributes to succeed in the salons. Liszt also drew attention to the pretentiousness of his name.[20] A concert promoted by César's father attracted little attention.

Franck could not go straight into the Conservatoire because of his foreign nationality. But when, a year later, he was enrolled, he won prizes for piano and counterpoint. His father withdrew him, just as he was about to enter the Prix de Rome, and they returned to Belgium to take part in the concert circuit. After a couple of years, they went back to Paris; his father then had his early compositions published in a special edition to which Meyerbeer, Halévy, Chopin and Liszt all subscribed.

But the virtuoso career did not take off: César wilted under the strain and had a nervous breakdown. *Ruth*, an oratorio which he composed in 1846, was not a success, and the failure did much to destroy his self-confidence.[21]

Not completely, however. César broke loose. When the rest of the family were out, he packed his bags and left. This followed a row with his father, who had torn up a song dedicated to Félicité, a pupil whose parents were mere actors in the Comédie Française. César married Félicité. It was February 1848: the bridal couple used a grille from the church floor to climb over a barricade and get to the church.[22]

To make ends meet, César took pupils and was organist at Notre-Dame-de-Lorette, a new church, where the organ was built by Aristide Cavaillé-Coll, who became France's most distinguished organ builder in the 19th century. Franck's family would have liked him to write an opera and 'make money'.[23] In the early 1850s, he quietly worked away at a small opera, *Le Valet de Ferme*. But it came to nothing. He then composed very little until the mid-1870s. He withdrew into the shelter of his home: he became a hack music teacher; he gave occasional recitals, which often featured sentimental items and popular transcriptions.[24]

Franck also became artistic adviser to Cavaillé-Coll. Then, after five years as organist at another church, Franck was appointed to Sainte Clotilde.* This was yet another new church which was being built on the

* In around 500 AD, Queen Clotilde persuaded her husband Clovis, King of the Franks, to embrace Christianity. Her church, which has two 69-metre steeples, was officially opened on 30 November 1857. Franck, assisted by the aging society organist Lefébure-Wély, inaugurated the organ, which was built by Cavaillé-Coll. Charles Tournemire and Jean Langlais were subsequently organists at the church.[25]

Left Bank, and which may be found just behind the Assemblée Nationale.

At Sainte Clotilde, Franck composed organ works, music which Liszt thought worthy of a 'place beside the masterpieces of Bach'.[26] There, visitors would flock to hear him improvising. Around this time, in 1859–60, he also wrote a *Mass for Three Voices* to which, several years later, he added the ever-popular 'Panis Angelicus'.

Unlike many other composers who got away from Paris at the time of the Siege,* Franck, as perhaps might be expected, was among those such as Bizet who remained behind. He was assigned the task of assisting with the distribution of food and fuel in his district, despite the looting. His two surviving sons, Georges and Germain, enlisted. He himself would stumble from street to street with buckets of coal to warm the aged.[27] It was a hard task: fuel ran out and, at night, the temperature sometimes fell to minus 14°C (7°F). The Francks themselves seem to have survived by drinking hot chocolate.

By the end of the Siege and Commune, Franck was in his 50th year. He then blossomed. But before considering this fruitful period, we should first take a look at what France, at first humiliated and on her knees, was like at that time.

France after the War

France recovered quickly. Loans raised to pay off the war indemnity were oversubscribed thirteen times over. Monsieur Thiers, now in his 70s, led a conservative administration, with some success. He was followed by Marshal MacMahon, the Duc de Magenta, who had little to talk about other than the weather, food and hunting. MacMahon was a devout Roman Catholic, and his government sought at first to maintain the authority of the Church and the upper classes.**

At one stage, the monarchy was almost reinstated, but the royalist cause was divided. Half supported the childless Henri, Comte de Chambord, a grandson of Charles X, and the son of the Duc de Berri, who was assassinated outside the Opéra in 1820. Chambord was the last in the direct line

* See page 590.

** The desire for a moral 'clean-up' was reflected in the growth in the numbers of nuns and monks, many of whom provided important educational, medical and social care. Between 1850 and 1880, the number of nuns doubled to around 135,000 and the number of monks increased to 30,000.[28]

from Louis XIV. The other half supported Louis-Philippe's grandson, the Comte de Paris, a descendant of Louis XIV's brother Monsieur. The comte's father, the popular Duc d'Orléans, had been killed in the summer of 1842: he was thrown from his calèche when driving to have lunch with his parents.[29]

Chambord, the senior claimant, played his cards appallingly: he insisted that he had to have the flag of the Bourbons rather than the tricolour. 'Henri V cannot abandon the white flag of Henri IV', he declared.[30] This was ludicrous considering that it was Henri IV who nearly 300 years before had renounced his Protestant religion, saying: 'Paris vaut bien une Messe.' Pope Pius IX commented wryly about Chambord: 'All that, over a napkin.'[31]

In late summer 1873, flags and bunting were prepared for the Restoration. But then Chambord repeated his demands and refused to give way in favour of the Comte de Paris, so that was that. A resolution on the powers of the senate, which described the role of the President *of the Republic*, was passed by 353 votes to 352. Thus, by a single vote, 'the Republic crept in furtively and as though by a side door'.[32] By the time Chambord died in exile in 1883, support for a Restoration had dwindled. The family of the Comte de Paris have been the forlorn pretenders to the 'French throne', thus qualifying for an occasional appearance in a glossy magazine.

The European power play had changed as a consequence of the war. There was a unified Germany, a unified Italy and a revived Russia. France was intent on revenge, *revanche*, for its defeat. It was determined to recover the surrendered provinces of Lorraine, in the north-east near Luxembourg, and Alsace, the country west of the Black Forest around Strasbourg. In case anyone should forget, until 1918, the statue representing Strasbourg in the Place de la Concorde was draped in black.[33]

Five-year conscription was introduced, even though there were several ways in which a young man could claim exemption. There was a war scare in 1875, when it seemed that the Germans might make a pre-emptive strike. Anti-French feelings were whipped up in the German press. The British and Russian governments used diplomacy to restore calm.[34]

The possibility of Bonapartist restoration was eliminated by the death of Louis Napoleon's son, the prince imperial, while fighting in the British army against the Zulus in 1879. Then in the late 1880s, a Bonaparte-alternative emerged in the form of the war minister, the charming, handsome, half-Breton, half-Welsh General Boulanger. His every move, reducing conscription, improving conditions, was accompanied by maximum publicity, and even Bismarck was rattled by the build-up of his image as the man who could recover those lost provinces. Boulanger's popularity was increased by a war scare, when a French official was arrested by the Germans. When the government decided to get Boulanger out of the way by posting him away from Paris, 3,000 people occupied the track at the Gare de Lyon in order to stop the train from departing.

A scandal brought down MacMahon's successor, the austere and drab Jules Grévy, whose son-in-law had trafficked in honours and abused the presidential facilities.* Memories of Louis Napoleon's coup in 1851 were revived when Boulanger was successful in a number of by-elections. The crowd roared: 'A l'Elysée'. But the government held its nerve, and Boulanger did not have the determination to capitalise on his success.**[36]

Just before the height of the Boulanger crisis, there was a devastating fire at the Opéra-Comique, which cost over 70 lives. The gauze scenery caught fire during a performance of the ever-popular *Mignon*,† an opera by Ambroise Thomas, director of the Conservatoire. When the doors were opened there was a rush of air, which fanned the flames. The chief gas controller turned off the gas for fear of an explosion. As a consequence, people could not see where they were going and were trapped in the dark passages; employees in the dressing rooms and workshops were also trapped: to reach the exits they had to cross two wooden bridges which were destroyed. The director, Carvalho, was sentenced to three months in prison, as a consequence of the disaster.††[39]

* The son-in-law's sister, Mme Pelouze, gave work to the young Debussy and helped to found the *Revue Wagnérienne.*

** Boulanger fled with his mistress to Belgium, where, a couple of years later, he committed suicide.[35]

† *Mignon* received 1,000 performances in under 30 years. Mahler's wife-to-be wrote in her diary in 1899: 'It is a major step forward that I now realise how awful this opera really is. Thomas' graceful ditties and sentimental dirges leave me unmoved. I hear nothing but appalling capriciousness, a lack of proficiency and a loused-up text.'[37]

†† Fire was always a terrible hazard. In 1897, a tent in which Paris socialites were running a charity bazaar caught fire, trapping and killing 140 people. Various men were accused of using their canes to beat a path to safety. Bizet's widow escaped by the only exit, which entailed rushing through the blaze.[38]

On a happier note, celebrations for the centenary of 1789 included a banquet for all the mayors of France at which 15,000 people sat down to table, and 45,000 bottles of wine were uncorked.[40] The Exhibition attracted 25 million visitors, and endowed Paris with the Eiffel Tower. In January 1889, the Tower was already higher than the Great Pyramid and its builders were 'enjoying sunshine when all beneath them was an ocean of fog'.[41]

A Good Autumn

Such was some of the background to the final, more productive, years of Franck's life. We return now to the early 1870s when he became professor of organ at the Conservatoire. Franck began to make an impact. His classes, although officially called 'organ classes', became lessons in composition and extemporisation. As the organ was a compulsory subject in the curriculum, all students at the Conservatoire came under his influence, including Debussy.

His own compositions got a weak reception: he continued to be out of luck. On Maundy Thursday 1873, there was a disastrous première for his 'poème symphonie', *Redémption*. The orchestra disliked it; it had been badly copied and was badly conducted. Also, on the following day, Good Friday, there was the première of Jules Massenet's emotional *Marie Magdaleine*. There was 'no contest'; one might try to ask the general public to compare, say, Birtwistle and Lloyd Webber. Indeed, Franck's works of this period are hardly known: they include the symphonic poems, *Les Eolides*, *Le Chasseur Maudit* and *Les Djinns*; and the operas *Hulda* and *Ghiselle*, which failed to get to the stage. The *Symphony*, a work we do recognise, was first performed at the Conservatoire in 1889.

Franck's wife was hardly supportive. Félicité sensed that he was a failure. When he was experimenting, she would sit in the next room and occasionally roar: 'César! I really dislike that.'[42]

In his teaching, Franck was receptive to new ideas and his circle of young pupils worshipped him. Many of them were Wagner supporters. Rather like Liszt's disciples, their names are not always as familiar as that of their teacher, although their influence on subsequent 20th-century composers was considerable: Chabrier, Duparc, Magnard, Lekeu and the prosperous, militaristic and anti-Semitic Vincent d'Indy.[43] There was also

Ernest Chausson, the wealthy son of one of Haussmann's building contractors.*[45]

In 1886, Franck was elected as president of the Société Nationale following a 'palace revolution'.[46] The Société had been founded by Saint-Saëns specifically to promote French music: works composed by foreigners were banned at its concerts. When a decision was taken to allow foreign music to be performed, Saint-Saëns promptly resigned, asking: 'what will become of us, the day that Wagner is played in Paris?'[47] Franck's election was a significant step. Without his work to internationalise the programmes, the Russian and Spanish influences, which were to be important in the development of 20th-century music, would not have come to Paris.

Franck died on 8 November 1890 from pleurisy, having caught a chill a few weeks earlier. His health had deteriorated following an accident six months previously. Franck had been unlucky: he got in the path of a horse omnibus when crossing the Pont Royal and received a severe blow on the chest.[48]

At the time, Franck was part way through a series of pieces for the harmonium, seven pieces for each of the chromatic keys. During the summer months, he had finished the *Trois Chorals* for the organ. The first was dedicated to the organist Eugène Gigout, the second to the publisher Durand, the third, and arguably the greatest, 'à mon élève Augusta Holmès'.

Rimsky-Korsakov regarded Augusta's appearance as 'très decolletée'. Saint-Saëns wrote poetry to her and went on her frolicking picnics in the forest of Fontainebleau, and proposed to her. 'We were all in love with her', he said, 'and any one of us would have been proud to have made her his wife.'[49] Franck did not stand a chance.**[52]

* Some came to unfortunate ends: Lekeu died on his 24th birthday, after getting typhoid from some contaminated sherbet. Chabrier, composer of the comic opera *Le Roi Malgré Lui*, died from syphilis. Chausson died after fracturing his skull in a bicycle accident. Cycling gripped Europe in the 1890s; Zola was a keen cyclist, as was Mahler. The first time Mahler encountered Alma, his future wife, they were both on bicycles.[44]

** There was an unfortunate incident in 1880 when Saint-Saëns stormed off the platform at the end of the Société Nationale performance of Franck's Piano Quintet, which had been dedicated to him. It has been suggested that he was jealous about Franck's crush on Augusta, or that the scene was related to his recent bereavement, or difficulties with his wife. Augusta was another with a sad end, aged only 56. When her admirers drifted away, she took to drink.[50] When she died, Saint-Saëns wrote: 'My rusty autumn leaves flutter at the memory of those green days of spring.'[51]

The Prodigy Saint-Saëns

When Franck died, the ministry of fine arts did not bother to send a representative to the funeral; Delibes represented the Conservatoire. We can contrast this with Saint-Saëns' state funeral, his coffin accompanied to the port of Algiers by the governor-general with a full military escort; the subsequent magnificent service in La Madeleine; the endless speeches from dignitaries, on a bitterly cold Christmas Eve, as he was buried. 'It may safely be said that no composer has ever been laid to rest with greater pomp or solemnity.'[53]

Camille Saint-Saëns was born in the Latin Quarter on 9 October 1835, nearly thirteen years after Franck. His father, whose family originally came from Saint-Saëns in Normandy, was an accounts clerk, sufficiently reliable to be in charge of the secret accounts ledger at the ministry of the interior. He died very shortly after Camille's birth.

The boy was frail and tubercular; so, for a couple of years, he was looked after by a foster mother in the fresh country air of a village on the road to Fontainebleau. After this, he lived with his mother, a carpenter's daughter, in an unsuccessful bookshop run by her genteel but impoverished aunt and uncle. Great Aunt Charlotte gave Camille piano lessons.

Camille's childhood appears to have been particularly precocious, in general education as well as music. Apparently, he composed his first piano piece shortly after his third birthday.[54] At five, he was closely studying Mozart's *Don Giovanni*. At seven, he had already mastered all the Latin grammar needed to read authors such as Virgil, Horace and Cicero.[55] He was soon breeding caterpillars, studying geology, astronomy and mathematics, and could be found in quarries looking for fossils.[56] When he was older, aged seven and a half, he was having keyboard and composition lessons with leading teachers. And later, he had singing classes with Bizet's uncle.*[58]

Unlike Monsieur Franck, Madame Saint-Saëns at this stage was wise enough not to push her son too hard, even though one teacher wanted to capitalise on the success of his sensational pupil. Aged ten, Camille made his début at the Salle Pleyel; in this, he offered as an encore to play any one

* Some of these events are actually corroborated by contemporary journals and newspapers. Paris was full of prodigies at this time, most of them now totally forgotten, such as Emile Paladilhe, Francis Plante, Paul Julien, Alphonse Duvernoy and Alexis Fissot.[57]

of Beethoven's piano concertos from memory. Théodore Gautier said that 'the whole Conservatoire was desperate with envy'.[59]

In this unreal world, Camille had few contacts with children of his own age. He was dominated by his formidable mother and equally formidable great aunt. In later life, he was almost certainly homosexual, even though his voluminous correspondence is full of comments on pretty girls, and he proposed to two women and married one. He is known to have attended soirées where youths appeared in tableaux, and to have visited a bathing place on the Seine, a meeting place for homosexuals. It does not appear, however, that Saint-Saëns was a highly active homosexual, like Tchaikovsky or Poulenc.*[61]

Saint-Saëns, this meteor, entered the Paris Conservatoire in 1848. He won prizes, but he failed to win the Prix de Rome in 1852. Indeed he created quite a stir when he had another attempt many years later, aged 29; then he suffered a humiliating defeat when the prize was won by Sieg, a name few of us would recognise today. Saint-Saëns' talent, however, was prodigious. His ever-popular Second Piano Concerto took him seventeen days to write. He could orchestrate happily for twelve hours at a time, and talk while doing it. He was very much an all-rounder: Fauré described him as 'the most complete musician France had ever possessed'.[62]

Unlike Franck, he was completely at ease socially, and exuded charm. Gounod took a fatherly interest in him. Pauline Viardot, the mezzo-soprano, introduced him to the Rossini evenings and to Berlioz. He was soon meeting the literary set, people such as Flaubert, the Goncourts and the Dumas. Meanwhile, he gained exemption from military service either for health reasons or through the influence of the emperor's cousin, Princess Mathilde.[63]

Because religion had a high profile, the top organist appointments were eagerly sought after. Camille was briefly organist at St Severin; then, after Madame Saint-Saëns had cultivated the curé, he moved to St Merri, a parish of 26,000 people. The post was well remunerated: well over 200 wedding services would be held there each year.[64] At the age of only 22, Saint-Saëns was then appointed to La Madeleine, a plum appointment with a very 'fashionable' congregation. Recognised as one of the leading

* As we shall see, Saint-Saëns had a lifelong friendship with Fauré, a kind of father–son relationship, but 'Fauré's sexual proclivities were strongly in the opposite direction'.[60]

instrumentalists of France, he dazzled the congregation with his improvisations:[65] Liszt said he was the greatest organist in the world. Naturally, he was chosen to join seven others to perform at the inauguration of the organ at Notre-Dame by Archbishop Darboy.[66] In 1859, he helped Berlioz edit the text of Gluck's *Orphée* for the Théâtre-Lyrique.

Saint-Saëns' Middle Years

After Saint-Saëns' failure to win the Prix de Rome – his membership of the Viardot circle, which included left-wing people, cannot have worked in his favour – he settled down to a career as a virtuoso pianist. He continued to be one for the whole of his life. He practised for two hours every day; when travelling, he would use a silent piano of two octaves with an adjustable touch, light or heavy. He even practised the piano on the last day of his life.[67]

He cut a curious figure: he was thin, pale and short, with an enormous hooked nose: photographs usually show him from an angle which flatters his profile. He had staccato gestures, he spoke with a pronounced lisp, and switched topic suddenly. Compared to Liszt, his manner on the platform was frigid: 'surtout pas d'émotion', he would say to his pupils.[68] Certainly his music, for all its lyricism, can be slightly clinical; hence, perhaps, the failure of his operas.[69]

'Madame Clemence Saint-Saëns, Mère' attended all his concerts. Every morning, she opened his post and read it aloud to him.[70] With Great Aunt Charlotte, she instilled a work ethic into him which made him feel, throughout his life, that he ought to be composing. Madame Clemence was ruthless in her criticism. After everybody had applauded a cello sonata, she proclaimed that it was 'exécrable'.[71] He, aged nearly 40, tore it up and worked on it for eight days, emerging from his study only for meals. On one occasion, she wrote to her adult son: 'I thought I had brought up a man. I have raised only a girl of degenerative stock … Either you will play well, or I will renounce you as my child.'[72] He adored both mother and great aunt.

In 1861–5, Saint-Saëns taught at the new Ecole de Musique Classique et Religieuse. This was founded by Louis Niedermeyer to remedy low standards in church music. It gave a particular emphasis to plainsong and renaissance polyphonic works. 'We were not allowed to play Schumann or Chopin: Niedermeyer did not consider this music suitable for young people', said Gabriel Fauré, one of Saint-Saëns' pupils there.[73] After

Niedermeyer died and Saint-Saëns took over the piano class, the curriculum was widened to include contemporary music, including works by Schumann and Liszt.

In 1867, Saint-Saëns started sketching *Samson et Dalila*, and at one of his regular Monday evening salons that year, he played excerpts including 'Amour, viens aider ma faiblesse' and 'Mon coeur s'ouvre à ta voix'. However, it was difficult to get a biblical subject staged, so the first performance was delayed until 1877, when Liszt performed it in Weimar; only fifteen years after that, was *Samson et Dalila* staged in Paris. It represented an antidote to Wagner and reached back to the days of grand opera. By 1922, six months after the composer's death, it had been performed 500 times.[74]

At the time of the Exhibition of 1867, Saint-Saëns and Wagner were involved in what must be one of the earliest examples of commercial endorsement: they endorsed one of the exhibits, a salon organ manufactured by the Estey Company of Vermont. Saint-Saëns also won a competition for a cantata to mark the Exhibition, but, on the day, it was replaced by a hymn to the emperor composed by the aged Rossini.[75]

When the Franco-Prussian war broke out, Saint-Saëns joined the National Guard. He diverted himself by noting the key in which the shells whined overhead; and he played appropriately patriotic music when performing at La Madeleine. At the time of the Commune (see page 598), he got out of Paris on one of the last trains to leave for the Channel before the exits of the city were blocked.[76]

In 1871, Saint-Saëns visited England, where he played before Queen Victoria. He studied Handel manuscripts in the library of Buckingham Palace; there he found a melody which he used for the principal theme in his opera, *Henry VIII*.[77] He made a lot of contacts in London, and he opened the Albert Hall organ jointly with Bruckner. He admired Gilbert and Sullivan's operettas and wrote his own, *La Princesse Jaune*, which was dropped after fifteen performances.[78]

In 1872, he started work as a critic on *La Renaissance*. Four years later, he received a large bequest from a rich postal official, primarily to enable him to write a Requiem; this also enabled him to leave his position at La Madeleine and concentrate on composition.

Saint-Saëns was deeply upset when Aunt Charlotte died, aged 92: at first, he went into a round of concerts, but after about a year, his health gave way and he went to Algeria to recover. Algeria had only just become a safe place to go to. Two years earlier, while the French army was tied up in suppressing the Commune, the colonists had been blockaded in their ports in the latest of a series of insurrections. By the time of Saint-Saëns' first visit, it was being colonised by residents of Alsace and Lorraine, now part of Germany, who wanted to retain their French nationality.*

A Tragic Marriage

In 1875, aged nearly 40, Saint-Saëns, somewhat impulsively, married the nineteen-year-old Marie Truffot, the sister of one of his pupils. They did not go on honeymoon; the poor girl just moved into the house in rue Faubourg St Honoré, where she had to cope with her mother-in-law. Saint-Saëns meanwhile went off on a tour to Russia, during which, on the stage of the Moscow Conservatoire, he and Tchaikovsky danced a ballet to music played by Nikolai Rubinstein.[80]

The marriage ended in tragedy. They had two sons. André, aged two and a half, was killed falling out of a fourth-floor window, which had been left open by the maid. Within six weeks, the other son, Jean, died of pneumonia. These sad events scarred Saint-Saëns for life. The marriage struggled on for another three years. He behaved very badly: he called Marie his 'Diablesse from Rheims',[81] and he did not bother to answer any of her letters to him when away on tour. Then, in 1881, while on holiday with her at a health spa, he suddenly disappeared.

She never saw him again. A fellow guest at the hotel, Henri Duparc accompanied the distraught lady back to Paris. Surprisingly, Saint-Saëns' music from this period shows no signs of strain or depression. He seems to have been quite heartless: ten years later, he compared Marie's condition to that of a redundant organ blower from La Madeleine: 'They are both alike, unemployed and miserable', he said.[82] She, however, was always supportive of him; she died only in 1950, aged 95.

* Algeria had been unstable since 1830, when, fed up with the attacks from Algiers on their shipping, the French seized it from the ruling Turkish janissaries. The intervening years had seen battles and atrocities, as the French tried to repress the Arabs. In the 1860s, cholera, drought, locusts and famine added to the misery of the place. Later, French attention turned to Tunisia: in May 1881, the Bey of Tunis accepted the status of a French protectorate; after a year of punitive expeditions, virtually the whole of the country came under French control. There were also colonial ventures in Madagascar, the Congo and Tonkin.[79]

The Carnival of the Animals

Saint-Saëns had objected to Wagner's *Capitulation*, which celebrated the defeat of France. He also had said that French military bands should be prohibited from playing Wagner's music. As a consequence, when he performed in Berlin in 1886, he got a bad reception. The Leipzig press urged all theatre directors to blackball him. It was in this atmosphere that he wrote *The Carnival of the Animals*, parodying Offenbach, Berlioz, Mendelssohn, Rossini, his own *Danse Macabre* and several popular tunes. As he was afraid that the publication of *The Carnival* would harm his reputation as a serious composer, he forbade its performance during his lifetime. The Swan, which the ballerina Anna Pavlova immortalised, even though it was Dying, was the only part of it that he allowed to be published.[83]

The *Organ Symphony* was first played in June 1889 on the vast instrument constructed by Cavaillé-Coll for the Salle des Fêtes in the Trocadéro Palace. This building, similar in concept to the Royal Albert Hall, was on the other side of the Seine from the Eiffel Tower. It was opened at the time of the 1878 Exhibition and destroyed in 1935 to make way for the 1937 Exhibition. The organ recitals given at the Trocadéro provided the first opportunity to hear organ recitals outside a church in Paris.[84]

A Cantankerous Nomad

The loss of his mother in 1888 left a gap in Saint-Saëns' life. She died aged 80, having caught pneumonia in the cold December weather. He travelled to Algeria, then came back to sort out his mother's affairs. He contemplated suicide, and went so far as to hand over all his family treasures to the museum in Dieppe where they are displayed. Then he disappeared. In Paris, there was a furore because his opera, *Ascanio*, was about to be staged. He had in fact gone to the Canary Islands incognito. There, his solitariness attracted attention. After he was seen sketching the coastline, it was thought that he might be a spy; besides, through the keyhole of his room, he could be seen jotting down masses of little signs on lined paper. After he realised that he was being followed, he moved hotel. His cover was blown when he helped a little girl who had fallen in the mud: another person who had rushed to help recognised him from his picture in newspaper reports about the success of *Ascanio*. By the evening, many residents of Las Palmas were besieging him for auditions.[85]

Saint-Saëns continued a lonely nomadic life, with only his dogs and his manservant Gabriel to keep him company. He travelled the Atlantic, the Mediterranean, the Indian Oceans; he went to Uruguay and Scandinavia and spent three months in Ceylon. In 1894 he set off for Saigon, looking up French officials he knew there. He also frequently visited England.

Throughout his life he maintained his interest in science and astronomy. He even recommended to the Academy of Sciences that there should be a government-approved metronome,[86] a proposal which the European Commission, at some stage, will perhaps take forward. He arranged his tours to suit his other interests. One was arranged so that he could see Etna erupting. Aged 70, he travelled to Burgos to see a total eclipse of the sun.[87]

Saint-Saëns became increasingly cantankerous. He thoroughly disapproved of orchestral trade unions. He wrote: 'Art is a cult, not a form of merchandise', and declared that the musicians had turned themselves into workers.[88] On one occasion, the musicians refused to continue playing until he had withdrawn some remarks which they considered offensive.[89]

It is regrettable that Saint-Saëns was not more tolerant, especially for posterity. He pursued Debussy relentlessly and ensured that he was not elected to 'the Institute', the prestigious musical section of the Académie des Beaux Arts. 'Debussy did not create a style', he said. 'On the contrary, he cultivated the absence of style and the absence of logic and commonsense.'[90] He also disliked Richard Strauss' music, then, by his standards, at the forefront of the *avant-garde*. He described Strauss' *Salomé* as 'this horror … a pathetic comment on the times we live in'. He continued: 'the public no longer creates success; it has success imposed upon it'.[91] Compare this with Debussy's verdict on *Salomé*: 'I don't see how anyone can be other than enthusiastic about this work – an absolute masterpiece … almost as rare a phenomenon as the appearance of a comet.'[92]

Saint-Saëns himself was often under attack: Mussorgsky said to him, 'You'll deceive no-one with your pretty tunes. You're just about as important as a pretty woman politely handing round bags of jujubes to her friends.'[93] But, on the whole, Saint-Saëns was highly regarded, although as the years wore on, he was overtaken by Massenet as the acknowledged leader of French composers.[94]

In 1915, he did a tour of the USA where, despite poor health, he gave performances in New York, Philadelphia and Chicago. He also played before President Roosevelt in Washington. He liked feeding nuts to the squirrels in Central Park and was impressed by the city lit up by electric light. He liked the ensuite bathrooms, private telephones and efficient railway system. 'I was continually coming across people whom I had seen the previous week six hundred miles away', he said.[95]

Aged 85, he went on a long recital tour of Belgium and Switzerland and then went to Algiers. He played dominoes with his secretary. He suffered from congestion; 'this time I think it's really the end', he said.[96] About this, he was right.

The Young Fauré

One composer of whom Saint-Saëns did approve was Gabriel Fauré. He was born on 12 May 1845, in Pamiers, a small town to be found where the foothills of the Pyrenees begin, some 40 miles south of Toulouse on the way to the mountain principality of Andorra. This part of southern France is sprinkled with romantic castles, where, in the age of chivalry, songs sung by the high-born and lovesick troubadours were interrupted by a barbaric, bloody crusade waged against heretics. 'Song should express joy, but sorrow oppresses me, and I have come into the world too late', wrote one troubadour.[97]

Almost 600 years later, sponsored by the local parliamentary deputy and the bishop, the nine-year-old Gabriel was sent to Paris from the town where his father had become the head of the Ecole Normale. His harmonium playing in the school chapel had apparently been noticed by a blind lady, who alerted his father to his youngest son's talent.[98] The journey was long: 500 miles in three days.

For eleven years, Gabriel was a boarder at the Ecole Niedermeyer. There, Saint-Saëns developed a paternal, if not romantic, relationship with him. The Fauré parents would send gifts of country produce to the Saint-Saëns' house in the rue St Honoré. During summer 1862, Saint-Saëns stayed with them at Tarbes, near Lourdes, where they had moved.

Gabriel graduated from the Ecole Niedermeyer with first prize in composition for his *Cantique de Jean Racine*. He was then, for four years, organist at Rennes in Brittany, until he was sacked. He had been ticked off for smoking in the porch during sermons, and for arriving for an early service in evening dress, straight 'from the night before'.[99] Also, the local priest did not approve of his accompanying the church scene in Gounod's *Faust* at the local theatre.[100]

In 1870, Saint-Saëns got him a job as assistant organist at Notre-Dame-de-Clignancourt, beyond Montmartre. But Fauré continued to push his luck: he missed a service in order to go and hear *Les Huguenots*, for example. In his own words, he was 'an incorrigible religious defaulter'.[101] A year later, he was appointed assistant organist at Saint-Sulpice in the Latin Quarter. The composer of the Organ Toccata, Charles-Marie Widor, who was four months older than Fauré, had just begun his 64-year tenure there.[102]

In the Franco-Prussian War, Fauré joined the Imperial Guard; during the Siege, he was placed at the advance posts and served as a liaison officer. He took part in the abortive sorties aimed at relieving Paris, at Champigny, Le Bourget and finally Creteuil. He gave improvised recitals at abandoned houses in the suburbs.[103]

After the Siege, Fauré escaped on a forged passport to Rambouillet, outside Paris. He first went to London, where Pauline Viardot's lodgings had become a centre for French musical émigrés. He then spent the summer in Switzerland teaching composition at the Ecole Niedermeyer which had taken refuge near Lausanne.

In January 1874, Saint-Saëns, who was becoming increasingly exasperated by his duties at La Madeleine, appointed Fauré as his deputy and, a few years later, he became choirmaster. Fauré was laid-back, without any ambition or sense of self-importance and, at this stage, his life was mainly centred on the daily service at La Madeleine and giving lessons. This left only the summer holidays as a time for composition, a cause of some frustration and depression. He wrote piano music and songs, but as he had sold the copyright in his songs to his publisher for a nominal amount, he earned very little from this source.

He frequently visited the Viardots, who bought a country house in Bougival, just up the hill from where Bizet had recently died.[104] Pauline Viardot, famous singer and the owner of the manuscript of *Don Giovanni*, also had a literary salon at her Paris residence at 28, rue de Douai on Thursdays and a musical one on Sundays. 'We performed charades with Turgenev and Saint-Saëns as actors and Flaubert, George Sand, Ernest Renan and Louis Blanc as spectators',* Fauré recorded.[105] George Sand was by then a grand old lady; these evenings represented quite a gathering of talent.

Fauré became engaged to Pauline's daughter Marianne, with whom he

* Ernest Renan was a former priest and professor at the University of Paris, whose *Life of Christ*, in which Christ's divinity was denied, caused an uproar; Louis Blanc was a veteran socialist who played no part in the Commune.

was deeply in love: during a period of three weeks when they were apart, he wrote her 35 letters.[106] She broke off the engagement, however;* the letters were returned and he kept them until the end of his life. As a distraction, Saint-Saëns took him to Weimar for the first performance of *Samson et Dalila*. Fauré became particularly interested in Wagner's works, and would travel far to hear them. He wrote: 'If one has not heard Wagner at Bayreuth, one has heard nothing! Take lots of handkerchiefs because you will cry a great deal! Also take a sedative because you will be exalted to the point of delirium!'[108]

In March 1883, Fauré married Marie Fremiet, the daughter of a well-known sculptor. From some correspondence with the composer Henri Duparc one can see that Fauré had been a typical bachelor. 'Farewell, you delightful chap', wrote Duparc. 'To think that I shall find in you a man who is staid, wedded, respectable, the proprietor of a charming home! … I just cannot get used to the idea.'[109] Massenet and César Franck wrote to congratulate him: 'I know that your "intended" is a woman of accomplishment and that her family is charming', wrote Franck.[110]

This was the time of the colourful, delightful Paris as portrayed by the Impressionists; the man in a tall hat, with a monocle 'beneath the groined arch of his eyebrow',[111] the lady wearing 'a ravishing hat and holding atilt a sunshade redolent with summer fragrance'.[112] But Fauré just had to plod on. He had to spend about three hours a day commuting to work in the centre of Paris. He said he had a 'real need to see other places than the eternal Gare St-Lazare'.[113] To supplement the meagre family income, Marie painted fans.

Nine months after the wedding, Emmanuel was born. Madame Clemence Saint-Saëns, Mère duly sent a letter of congratulations.[114] Philippe was born five and a half years later. However, this was not a happy marriage: Marie, somewhat sandwiched between her father and her husband, was difficult; and Fauré had many affairs. Whenever Fauré went travelling, Marie stayed at home. Although they wrote to each other often, she became embittered and priest-ridden.[115] Fauré found it best to take his holidays separately in order to compose in peace.

Fauré's charm and slightly swarthy appearance were seemingly irresistible, particularly in the London drawing rooms and Paris salons. He

* She later married Alphonse Duvernoy, the pianist and composer.[107]

had an affair* with Emma Bardac, the future Madame Debussy.[117] When he came to London for his first English all-Fauré concert in 1896, he stayed with the Earl and Countess de Grey.[118] Lady de Grey was 'tall and dark, a proud black swan who according to a contemporary made any woman near her look pale'.[119] She held musical parties at her house in Kingston. It was said that she 'could not live without a love affair'; her husband, one of the best shots in England (he never wounded a bird), was happy just at sport. Fauré made other conquests in England and Wales. One was the wife of his publisher, Adela Maddison, who moved to Paris to be near to him.[120]

Religious Problems in France, the Fauré Requiem

Fauré had composed incidental music for plays, such as *Caligula*, a tragedy by Dumas Père. He said in his self-effacing way that this was the only form 'which suits my limited abilities'.[121] But, in the long period from 1877 to 1890, he also composed the Requiem, his widely known work from the period before the turn of the century; its orchestration was only finally completed in 1900.

The Requiem was written against a highly charged religious background. We have seen that the number of priests and nuns had grown enormously, and Franck's early career had coincided with a considerable programme of church building in Paris. By 1880, 40 per cent of children were being taught at schools which were mainly run by Roman Catholic clergy.[122] While this had its educational advantages, it was a matter of increasing concern to those who perceived the church as reactionary, led by a royalist, a foreigner, a pope tarnished by his promulgation of the Syllabus of Errors and the Decree of Infallibility (see page 454).

* It was normal for prosperous Parisians to keep mistresses, who were just about tolerated by the wives. A rich noble might support his with 100,000 fr a year, and buy her a necklace costing 30,000 fr. A prostitute in a brothel might cost 20 fr (but, of course, for a single visit).The music 'industry' was perceived as a source of supply for courtesans, according to the novelist Colette (1873–1954), a 20th-century George Sand, at least in the literary sense. In *Gigi*, set in 1899, the heroine is the fifteen-year-old daughter of a singer whose name appears in small print on playbills of the Opéra-Comique. Gigi is groomed by her relatives, veteran ladies of the profession, to become the mistress of an heir to a fortune in the sugar trade. In *Chéri*, the hero is the son of a rich *demi-mondaine* who, between the ages of ten and sixteen, was a ballet dancer.[116]

The government, despite considerable protest, was determined to secularise education. It mandated the disbanding of the Jesuits, and of all other congregations who failed to obtain specific authorisation. Teaching congregations were deprived of the right to teach in state primary schools, and Roman Catholic universities were no longer empowered to confer degrees. Words such as God, Soul, Hope and Prayer were not allowed to be used during teaching in schools.[123] There was a relentless, but gradual, purge of clergy from charities, hospitals and the armed forces.

There was another purge in 1900, when the powerful Order of Assumptionists, who organised pilgrimages to Lourdes and elsewhere, were convicted of subsidising nationalist candidates in the elections; the Order was dissolved.*[125] In 1905, further legislation stopped all subsidies to religions and required church revenues to be handed over to lay *associations cultuelles* for the purpose of maintaining local religious services. The Church became an outlaw and many of the clergy were very badly affected. Right-wing activists blockaded Franck's Sainte-Clotilde when government officials arrived to schedule the church's possessions.[126]

The Church fought back. The enlightened Leo XIII, who died in 1903 in his 90s, had refused to condemn the Republic, calling France 'the eldest daughter of Rome'. But Pius X, his successor, disciplined bishops for holding republican sympathies; there was a row over the appointment of bishops, and Pope Pius protested against the visit of the President of France to the Italian government in Rome, a government which he still refused to recognise. Diplomatic relations between France and the Vatican were severed.[127]

The calm, languid tone of Fauré's Requiem seems out of place, when set against this turbulence, anti-clericalism, even religious persecution. It has also been accused of failing to portray Christian hope. Fauré had a simple explanation: 'Perhaps I have instinctively sought to escape from what is thought right and proper, after all the years accompanying burial services on the organ', he wrote. 'I know it all by heart. I wanted to write something different.'[128]

* By the end of 1902, 12,000 schools, all those run by unauthorised congregations, had been closed. Fifty-four male congregations were dissolved, comprising 20,000 friars and monks in 1,500 houses. Eighty-one applications for authorisation from female congregations were rejected *en bloc* and all congregations were compelled to give up teaching, with a transitional period of ten years.[124]

The style is considered almost too charming by some. Poulenc, who claimed he had 'always been allergic' to Fauré's music, said that 'his Requiem makes me lose faith, and it is a real penance for me to hear it. It is one of the few things I hate in music.'[129] The Requiem is often criticised for its weak orchestration. It is said that Fauré often delegated orchestration to fellow pupils or musicians, and maybe he did so when writing the Requiem.*

THE PRINCESSE DE POLIGNAC

During the time he was composing the Requiem, Fauré also wrote much else besides. 'Clair de Lune', in which he used a poem by Verlaine, comes from this period. In 1894, Fauré wrote *La Bonne Chanson*, which he dedicated to Emma Bardac, Debussy's second wife. It is a setting of 9 of the 21 poems which Verlaine wrote for his fiancée in 1870.** It 'can stand as an equal beside any nineteenth-century song cycle, German or French'.[132]

Verlaine and Fauré were brought together by Winnarette Singer, whose father Isaac had patented a sewing machine, around 1850, and mass-marketed it using the hire-purchase finance scheme used to sell pianos.[133] In the 1890s, she divorced her first husband and married the witty Prince Edmond de Polignac, grandson of Marie Antoinette's favourite, and the son of the minister who was largely responsible for precipitating the 1830 July Revolution against King Charles X. As the Princesse de Polignac, Winnarette became a noted collector of Impressionist pictures and the leading Parisian patroness of *avant-garde* music and art in the first half of the 20th century.† She brought Diaghilev and the Russian ballet to Paris; she supported Stravinsky, Ravel, Picasso and many others; she commissioned Poulenc's *Organ Concerto*.[136]

The prince, of whom Proust said, 'he was always youthful, but, from his youth, he had the face of an old man',[137] had studied at the Conservatoire. His opera, *La Coupe du Roi de Thulé*, had been placed two

* The continuous use of the organ is criticised; also, the flute and clarinet players sit for 40 minutes in order to play a mere eleven bars of relatively unimportant music.[130]

** The alcoholic Verlaine, by now resident in Hospital Broussais, Lasègne ward, bed 30, was desperate for money: 'because of some poetry set to music by you, a music publisher owes us some money ... see that what is due to me gets to me absolutely as soon as possible', he wrote.[131]

† Her mother, by then the Duchesse de Camposelice, is thought to have provided the inspiration for the sculptor F.A. Bartholdi, when he created the head of the Statue of Liberty, presented by the French to New York.[134] Several of Stravinsky's works were given their first (private) perfor-

places higher than one by Bizet in a competition held at the time of the Great Exhibition in 1867. Polignac was homosexual, but, as Winnarette was a lesbian, this did not matter much. Goncourt said after the wedding, which was blessed by the Pope, that it 'was concluded on the basis that the husband does not enter his wife's room provided that she pays him enough to enable him to stage his music which the opera houses do not want'.[138]

The princesse was quite discreet about her relationships, although female homosexuality was less risky than male. Following the Oscar Wilde case in London, the turn of the century saw a crackdown on male homosexuality. Friedrich Krupp committed suicide after being accused of paedophilia; the Kaiser's favourite, Prince Philipp zu Eulenburg, was prosecuted on flimsy evidence.*[140]

Although the princesse held court in her palatial residence on what is now the avenue Georges-Mandel, 'the salon' was gradually becoming a thing of the past. Hostesses were now mainly interested in furthering their husbands' careers. Towards the end of the century, it became increasingly the practice for musicians and painters to meet in cafés, bistros and absinthe dens.[141]

France Approaching the First World War

In 1892, a slightly reluctant Fauré applied to succeed Guiraud, who had died, as professor of composition at the Conservatoire. This provoked Ambroise Thomas, the highly distinguished, rigidly conservative director to say: 'Fauré, never, if he is nominated, I resign.'[142] Instead, Fauré became inspector of the conservatoires in the provinces. This meant that he had to travel throughout France.

The France through which Fauré travelled was increasingly industrialised. Electricity, one of the wonders of the 1889 Paris Exhibition, was soon replacing gas. By 1890, the mileage of railway track had doubled since 1870, and the telephone was being increasingly used. The Paris Metro began operations in 1900. By 1914 there were almost 100,000

mance in the princesse's house, for example, *Mavra, Les Noces*, the Piano Concerto and *Oedipus Rex*.[135] The princesse's many lovers included Brahms' acquaintance, Ethel Smyth (see page 553).

* Parisians called Berlin Sodome-sur-Spree. Eulenburg's alleged activities had been revealed to the press by a disgruntled politician who hounded him. The prosecution was adjourned when the prince's health collapsed; he retired to his estates and never saw his boss, the Kaiser, again.[139]

motor vehicles in the country; Michelin had already started producing their green Guides in 1900.*

But France was still predominantly an agricultural country. Over half the population lived in the countryside farming smallholdings, two-thirds of which were less than 25 acres. Despite this, the land was less densely populated than England. Although the traveller would often come across deserted villages, the peasant was better clothed, fed and housed, and more independent of the curé and the château than ever before.[144]

The Music Profession

In February 1896, Ambroise Thomas died, aged 85. As a result of the jockeying for jobs, and much lobbying, Fauré succeeded Dubois at La Madeleine, and Massenet as professor of composition. Fauré seems to have done little active teaching: he usually arrived late or left early, or both. But he had a considerable capacity to inspire his pupils.[145]

Fauré's own style of writing now became bolder and more forceful than that familiar to listeners of the Requiem. In the first years of the new century, he was very definitely a '20th-century' composer. This caused his mentor Saint-Saëns some surprise and considerable regret.

Fauré was commissioned to write a work for the festival held in Béziers in the Languedoc. Saint-Saëns was its patron, and encouraged Fauré to write a large-scale work. The result was the lyric tragedy *Prométhée*, which was written for an enormous orchestra and choir, totalling nearly 800 performers.[146] Its première in 1900 was a great success.

For long, Fauré had suffered from migraines, sometimes 'absolutely unremitting'.[147] Around 1901, he noticed the first signs of deafness.[148] In August 1903, he wrote: 'Now there are areas of music, sonorities, where I can hear nothing, nothing.'[149] This got progressively worse. When listening to Verdi's *Falstaff* in 1919, he told Marie that intervals between notes became increasingly distorted, as the music went up or down the scale: 'It is sheer hell', he said.[150] But he kept going, and the last twenty years of his life were a time of great activity, teaching, composing. He was also active as a music critic for *Le Figaro*.

* France was falling behind in world terms. By 1913, its output of coal was only 41 million tons compared with 279 million in Germany and 292 million in Great Britain. Although its population had increased to 40 million, it was smaller than Britain's population of 43 million and Germany's 70 million.[143]

Director at the Conservatoire

One of Fauré's pupils was another who had his roots in the very far south of France, Maurice Ravel, the son of an engineer of Swiss origin and a Basque mother. Ravel had a reputation for moving in fashionable circles, wearing smart clothes* and chain smoking strong cigarettes, which he often lit from the butt of the previous one. He tried several times to win the Prix de Rome. He entered in 1900, and also in the three following years when the winners were Caplet, Kunc and Laparra, musicians whose names we do not now recognise. Ravel tried again in 1905, by which time he was aged 30 and an established composer, having already written the *Pavane pour une Infante Défunte* and several other works. As his entry broke many of the academic rules, he may have intended it as a challenge. He was again passed over, and there was an enormous rumpus; meanwhile Ravel went cruising on the French rivers with a rich friend and the painter Pierre Bonnard. The row led to the resignation of the director of the Conservatoire, the authoritarian Dubois. Much to everybody's surprise, but at the instigation of the minister for the arts, Fauré was appointed director.[151]

Fauré immediately wrote to Saint-Saëns: 'As it is you who brought me up and it is to you that I owe what I am, it is only fit and proper that the first words I write at the Directorial table should be addressed to you.'[152] He proceeded to lead a major reorganisation of the Conservatoire, and his determination and toughness led to him being nicknamed 'Robespierre'.[153] His reforms attracted some interest overseas, including England. In 1908, he wrote: 'The awful thing is: the Queen wants to visit our Conservatoire and go to some of the classes! Moreover she is deaf, but not blind, and will no doubt be taken aback by our miserable conditions.'[154]

In the following year, Fauré accepted the presidency of the Société Musicale Indépendante, which was founded by Ravel. This aimed to give modern music, whether 'French or foreign … published or unpublished, without exceptions of genre or style', an opportunity to be heard.[155] It was a breakaway movement from the Société Nationale, which had become bogged down in an attempt to encourage music towards a more contrapuntal style, like that of the composers of the 16th century.**

* He travelled with 50 pastel shirts and 20 pairs of pyjamas, when he toured the USA in 1927.

** The Schola Cantorum was formed in 1894 by Vincent d'Indy, Charles Bordes and Alexandre Guilmant, in direct opposition to the Conservatoire, in order to further music of the 16th century.

Over five summers, with much of the time spent in Lugano, Fauré wrote the lyric drama *Pénélope*. In August 1912, he set about orchestrating it, 1,000 pages. 'Now it's just a matter of physical work,' he said.[156] It was a great success at its first performance in Monte Carlo in 1913. But it was submerged when the First World War broke out in 1914.

The First World War

The apparent ease and elegance of what we call the Edwardian period concealed many of the factors which were leading the European nations to attempt to annihilate each other. The flashpoint was in the Balkans, where the Serbs were opposed to the Habsburgs. In the last days of June 1914, Archduke Franz Ferdinand, the heir to the Habsburg throne, was assassinated, together with his wife, in Sarajevo by a Serb. Following this, the government in Vienna issued an ultimatum demanding, among other things, that Serbia allow Austro-Hungarian monitoring of specific steps to ensure that hostilities ceased. The ultimatum expired; Austro-Hungary declared war on Serbia; the Russians came to the aid of their fellow Slavs. Alliances were triggered; on 3 August, Germany declared war on France, which was allied to Russia. The whole of Europe was suddenly engulfed.

Fauré unfortunately was at Bad Ems, Offenbach's old haunt in Germany, when war was declared. A few days before, he had written to Marie: 'Here one lives in the midst of people – the Germans – who are always serious minded and solemn. So one is unable to judge whether they are more serious minded and solemn than usual, and whether the news worries them.'[157] But, by the following evening, he had decided that he had better get out. When he left for Paris on the next day, the French frontier was closed. The elderly composer, aged almost 70, got to Basle partly on foot and partly by car. He was then stuck in Geneva with his luggage.[158]

During the war, Fauré remained in Paris as head of the Conservatoire, with an occasional holiday in the south of France. He performed concerts in aid of the Red Cross and other charities.[159] His younger son Philippe was on active service throughout the war, and this was a continual worry.[160]

Ravel also enlisted. He was too small and underweight for the army, so he tried to get into the air force, but without success. Instead, he became a driver in the motor transport corps.*

Fauré's compositions of this period have been described as being 'among the most powerful in French music having unusual force and even violence'.[162] He also edited the complete piano works of Schumann and the organ works of Bach.

Fauré's deafness and infirmity got worse. In October 1920, at the prompting of the ministry of fine arts, he resigned from the Conservatoire. There was a difficulty over his pension arrangements, because he had only served 28 rather than 30 years. This left him somewhat insecure financially, but he now had more time to compose.[163] His final years saw a wealth of fine works: the Second Cello Sonata, the Second Piano Quintet, the song cycle, *L'Horizon Chimérique*. Gradually, however, declining health, including the consequences of his heavy smoking, took over, with deafness and increasing symptoms of sclerosis. He died on 4 November 1924 in his 80th year.

What should we say of Franck, Saint-Saëns and Fauré today? Their lives, but particularly their reputations, have one thing in common: 'Fortune is full of fresh variety: constant in nothing but inconstancy.'[164]

* A minute man who looked rather like a jockey (see page 799), Ravel was invalided out with dysentery. In 1916, his mother, a source of considerable inspiration and support, died. This, the effect of the war, and poor health, slowed his creative process. He wrote *Le Tombeau de Couperin* in 1917. In 1921, he moved from Paris to live at Montfort-l'Amaury near Rambouillet. He wrote the opera, *L'Enfant et les Sortilèges*, in 1925, to a text by Colette, the author of *Gigi, Chéri and Claudine.* His career came to an end with the onset of a progressive disease, in which his muscular responses became confused. Possibly, this illness was precipitated by concussion suffered in a car crash involving a taxi in which he was travelling. He died in December 1937, having never really come round from a brain operation. One of his last compositions was the *Boléro* (1928). At its première, a lady shouted out that its composer was mad. When told that, Ravel said that she obviously understood the piece.[161]

RUSSIAN COMPOSERS: GLINKA AND THE FIVE

CHAPTER 20

IN RUSSIA, AS in most countries, the Church wielded enormous power and its requirements greatly influenced the national heritage. The sound of the Russian Orthodox chant permeates much 'Russian' music. That sound remained substantially unchanged when, during the 16th and early 17th centuries, art music in the west of Europe gradually coalesced around rhythms based on two or three beats, and major or minor keys.* Because it does not conform to our rules, the chant, 'the awful howling of the deacons',[2] can seem to us fascinating, almost oriental, perhaps medieval.**

The bells of the Russian Church are also an important ingredient in the

* The Russian church did not adopt the grammar of Western classical music, which used as its first building blocks the major and minor 'diatonic' keys, equivalent to the keyboard octave of eight white notes starting on notes C and A respectively. The flavour of the music changes where the composer uses a different series of tones and semitones (intervals) between the notes: for example, the chromatic scale, which is a succession of all twelve semitones, and the whole-tone scale, which comprises the six notes each a whole tone apart.[1]

** The rulebook in the West did not permit the key to be ambiguous (as when fifths are played without the third), thus such music can sound foreign, 'oriental'. In common with the Russians, the chants originating in the earlier Western liturgy also adopted other 'modes', that is melody based on the seven consecutive white notes starting on notes other than C and A.[3]

Above: GLINKA, MUSSORGSKY AND RIMSKY-KORSAKOV

exotic flavour of Russian music.* It is no coincidence that Moscow was said to have 1,600 belfries, usually onion-shaped.[4] Or that Glinka, who led the 19th-century flowering of classical music in Russia, came from the area of Smolensk, an ancient city with strident bells, 250 miles to the west.

Bells are prominent in the music of Borodin's *Prince Igor* and Mussorgsky's *Boris Godunov*, and in works of Rimsky-Korsakov. Scriabin was a devotee of the mystical aspect of bells,[5] and they can be heard in many works by well-known composers of the 20th century, Stravinsky, Prokofiev and Shostakovich.

There is another, less exotic, and more Western-orientated, aspect to Russian music. This is exemplified by the dancing of the classical Russian ballet, by the works of Tchaikovsky – arguably the least Russian of the Russian composers,[6] yet possibly responsible for more 'best-loved work' than any other composer. We think also of the tuneful piano concertos of Rachmaninov (whose music also resonates with the sound of bells, and who even wrote a choral work, *The Bells*). Indeed, Russian composers faced an identity crisis: should their musical idiom derive from the West, like St Petersburg, which 'differed from other European cities by being like them all'?[7] Or should they reorientate themselves eastwards towards Moscow and beyond, to the Urals, the Caucasus and the Asiatic steppes?

In this chapter, we shall look at Glinka, and the galaxy of talent, including the 'Mighty Five', who followed him, and who aimed to reorientate and evolve a truly 'Russian' style. We will dwell particularly on Modeste Mussorgsky, the composer of much extraordinary, yet so sensitive music, and on whose life the Emancipation of the Serfs had a particular impact. Tchaikovsky and the later composers must await later chapters.

First let us attempt to conjure up the vast distances, the snow and ice, the violence and vodka, the poverty and the mystical qualities that are so peculiarly Russian.

Vast Distances, Vodka and Serfs

In Handel's time, a British emissary took four months to struggle from Vienna to Smolensk.[8] Liszt's lover Princess Carolyne took over a fortnight to get to St Petersburg from her home in the Ukraine; at one stage, her

* Apart from summoning, warning, tolling and festive use, bells are used, for example, to ward off evil spirits, avert pestilence and protect the souls of the dead. Their shape is also significant.

carriage had to be floated across a swollen river on a raft.[9] Berlioz described the four weary days and nights spent travelling from the Russian frontier to St Petersburg: the sledge was a 'hermetically sealed metal box, into which however the snow dust succeeds in penetrating and powdering your face; you are ceaselessly and violently shaken, like shot in a bottle, the result of which is a great many contusions on the head and limbs, caused by perpetual shocks from the sides of the sledge'. Berlioz also wrote about the unbearable cold: 'towards the middle of the night, notwithstanding all one's fur bags, cloaks, and pelisses, and the hay stuffed into the sledge, it becomes quite unbearable'. He described suffering 'from an unspeakable discomfort and nausea that may fairly be called snow-sickness on account of its likeness to that produced by the sea'.[10]

A story written by Alexander Pushkin portrays the tedious bureaucracy: at each change of horses, the stationmaster laboriously copied the travel warrants into his ledger, creating a useless record of useless information. The traveller's frustration was only slightly relieved by tea, occasionally laced with liquor, taken from the ubiquitous samovar.[11]

Yet Western composers went to Russia; and Berlioz even went back when he was an old man. Whatever the attraction, it was not the weather. Paintings of St Petersburg show the recently built St Isaac's Cathedral, a fine backdrop for elegant people riding in phaetons. But the same site also provided a freezing wintry setting for horse-drawn sledges. For five months of the year, the broad River Neva became a highway, and the barges were stuck in ice. Snow covered the peasants' shacks made of wood and thatch, and huddled figures struggled forward against the driving blizzard.

The minimum temperature for the year was around minus 29°C and the maximum 28°, with Moscow slightly more extreme.[12] In St Petersburg, frosts, exacerbated by the wind-chill factor, began in mid-September and went through to mid-May. In June, there were the eerie white nights, about which Tchaikovsky said: 'one cannot sleep with this peculiar combination of daylight and nocturnal silence'.[13] In spring and autumn, peasant carts were bogged down in the impassable mud. Then, in December, there was what Tchaikovsky called the 'abominable slush'.[14]

Russia was also the scene of crude violence and formal duels, heavy drinking and reckless gaming, and much suffering.[15] When Handel was in London promoting Italian opera, Bach in Weimar and Vivaldi in Venice, Tsar Peter the Great, ostensibly the civilised creator of St Petersburg, had his son and heir flogged and racked to death in his presence.[16] A predecessor, Tsar Boris Godunov, the wicked anti-hero of Mussorgsky's opera, died having left the dinner table with blood bursting from his orifices. Shortly thereafter, his wife was strangled, a fate which also befell his son, but only after he had had his genitals ripped off.[17]

Peter's grandson married a cultured German princess, who became the formidable Catherine the Great. To her credit, she insisted that operas should be short;[18] to her debit, she had her husband strangled. Her son Paul fared no better: at the instigation of Paul's son, drunken guards strangled him with his sash, one of his decorations, not normally intended for this purpose. It was arguably an appropriate end for a tsar who had ordered 1,000 strokes of the knout for an army officer who had criticised an order of knighthood which he had named after his mistress.[19]

The son was Alexander I. He said that ruling his country was beyond the powers of a genius,[20] and, like so many who strut on the world stage, found refuge in foreign affairs. He entered Paris in 1814, dazzled the ladies of London, started a fashion in Europe for trousers, and inspired the Holy Alliance which kept order in Europe.

Nobility and Serfs

The Russian nobility, who were only one per cent of the population,[21] provided the tsar's entourage, and were rigidly structured according to their rank in his service.[22] Nobles were exempt from tax and enjoyed the sole right to own serfs. Liszt's Princess Carolyne inherited her father's 30,000 serfs who worked on his fourteen estates.*[24] The master could sell them, beat them and send them for military service: in the middle of the 19th century, the writer Turgenev, who, by any measure, was relatively enlightened, bought a pretty one from a cousin and made her his mistress.[25] There had been some attempts at liberalisation: at the start of the century, the tsar allowed serfs to buy their land and freedom, but, of course, there was nowhere for them to get the money to make the purchase.

* Most serfs lived on the vast estates of a few nobles. Half belonged to the nobles and half were state peasants controlled by the Ministry of State Properties, the Church or members of the imperial family. Some were assigned to factories. Serfs lived in communes controlled by elders, who shared out the allotments among households so that all could meet their obligations. Thus there was little sense of property ownership. The village also included the poorly educated clergy.[23]

The government knew that education could disturb the stability of the country and 'would do more harm than good'. So, secondary schools and universities were forbidden to educate serfs. Indeed, it was suggested that it would be much safer to educate women than men. Although the number of people receiving education went up by 75 per cent in the first three decades of the century, in around 1830, only 1 in 208 inhabitants was being educated, and 20 years later the figure was still only 1 in 143. Even in 1920, only 40 per cent of adults were literate.[26]

Russia was noticeably backward in industrial production. In the first six decades of the 19th century, the production of pig iron in Russia barely doubled, whereas in Great Britain it increased 24-fold. Coal production in Russia just before the outbreak of the First World War was seven per cent of that in the United States.[27]

As the century wore on, the middle class had an infusion of intelligentsia, doctors, lawyers, teachers and journalists. They were the people who would eventually bring the pack of cards down; it was to this group that most of the composers adhered.[28]

The West or the East?

Was this extraordinary nation Byzantine, Tartar, Asian? Or European? In 1820, the French ambassador to St Petersburg described the Russians as 'half-savage'. Queen Victoria, when contemplating the Romanovs as potential spouses for her family, thought them 'half oriental', 'false' and 'unfriendly'.*[29]

By the early 19th century, the Russian educated classes were divided into two. There were those who preferred the traditions of the Slavs, the Orthodox Church and the countryside; for them, Moscow arising from the ashes of 1812 represented an emblem.[30] On the other hand, there was a privileged French-speaking élite, the product of the massive social engineering project of the early 1700s when Peter the Great founded St Petersburg in order to modernise Russia and face it westwards. This division was to be found not only in the great houses of St Petersburg and Moscow; next-door neighbours in the remote provinces might also be French-speaking and pro-West, or Russian-speaking and pro-Slav.[31]

* The Russian royal family was, by ancestry, hardly more Russian than Queen Victoria was English.

Russian music also experienced this 'schizophrenia'.[32] The music had deep roots: a simply decorated, 13th-century stringed instrument from Novgorod can be seen in the Glinka Museum in Moscow, and there is evidence from wall paintings in St Sophia's Cathedral in Kiev of jolly people playing wind and stringed instruments, similar to flutes, shawms and the bandura.[33] But the development of a distinctive Russian musical culture was hampered by the prohibition of instrumental accompaniment for the Russian Orthodox sung liturgy.[34] So, for secular music, Western influences filled the vacuum. Peter the Great brought in German musicians to train his military bands. His daughter Anna invited Venetian musicians to Russia. Even the Russian folksong, especially where sung in towns, became infected with more regular rhythms and structures, and the harmonies and melodic patterns familiar in the West.[*35]

This influx of Western musicians and music coincided with the time that the Italian Francesco Rastrelli was designing, in the ornate and colourful 'baroque' style, churches with golden, onion-shaped domes, and elaborate palaces.[36] The impact of the influx was considerable. From around 1730, instrumental music and opera got going, as did music printing. A musical journal was circulating in 1774 and Catherine the Great wrote a libretto, *Oleg's Early Rule*, around seventeen years later.[37] The Italian Giovanni Paisiello took a position at court, as did Domenico Cimarosa, whose *Il Matrimonio Segreto* of 1792 was an enormous success. In the first years of the 19th century, Clementi visited Russia on a performing and piano-selling visit. He was accompanied by John Field, the Dublin-born piano virtuoso and father of the Nocturne. Field lived in either St Petersburg or Moscow for over half of his life.[38]

Glinka

Not surprisingly, some Russians resented this Westernisation and felt that it was time for a Russian to take a leading position. Michael Glinka, who was born on 1 June 1804, stepped in. The bells in Smolensk accustomed him to dissonance; he was introduced to the unusual harmonies of Russian folk music by his nanny, and to church music by the Russian orthodox clergy, who chanted before the icons; and he rehearsed his uncle's serf orchestra. Intended for the diplomatic service, Glinka went to St Petersburg.

* A collection of 100 of these made a considerable impact after it was published in 1790.

There, he studied music with Field,* and frequented the salons, where he heard works by Rossini, Haydn, Mozart and Beethoven. He put aside the career which his family had planned for him.

Glinka fraternised with Pushkin and the other members of the literary 'set'.[40] In 1830, he visited Italy, where he became well known as a pianist, and met Bellini, Donizetti, Mendelssohn and Berlioz. But he decided that he 'could not sincerely be an Italian ... A longing for my own country led me gradually to the idea of writing in the Russian style.'[41]

Both Pushkin and Glinka got caught up in some of the sporadic and ineffective political protest that began to bubble when officers returned from the Napoleonic Wars.[42] The soldiers brought with them more liberated Western ideas. A group met quietly at the Davidov family home in Kamenka, deep in the southern Ukrainian countryside. Pushkin, in the interests of art, was kept outside the circle of conspirators; but he visited Kamenka and was inspired by its scenery and granite cliffs.[43] Nearly half a century later, Tchaikovsky would be similarly inspired, during his frequent visits to Kamenka to stay with his beloved sister, Sasha, who was married to Colonel Davidov's son.**

Tsar Alexander died suddenly in 1825. His brother and successor Konstantin, before whom Chopin had played, had entered into a morganatic marriage with a Roman Catholic Polish aristocrat. Because the marriage was kept secret, there was some confusion about who was the heir to the throne. Nicholas, the third brother, forced the pace by insisting that an oath supporting him was sworn on 26 December of that year.†

Some of the frustrated and disaffected, who were subsequently immortalised as 'Decembrists', met with a view to forming an interim government and arranging elections; but they were unco-ordinated and were quickly routed by Nicholas' troops. Five were executed, 31 exiled to Siberia for life and 85 for less.[46] Three of those executed were from the group which met in Kamenka; one of the exiles was Colonel Davidov.[47] Years

* Rachmaninov's grandfather, a soldier, also had lessons from Field.[39]

** Colonel Davidov's mother, Catherine, had been given the estate by her uncle, Prince Potemkin, the lover of Catherine the Great. Davidov's wife may have been a serf: his mother strongly disapproved of the marriage.[44]

† In Russia, dates lagged behind western Europe by eleven days in the 18th century, twelve in the 19th, and thirteen in the 20th. In February 1918, the Russians finally replaced the Julian calendar with the Gregorian.[45]

later, Tchaikovsky greatly respected the colonel's wife, who, like many others,[48] accompanied her husband to the penal settlement in Siberia. There, several of her children, including Tchaikovsky's brother-in-law, were born.*

Glinka was suspected of sheltering his former tutor who had taken part in the Decembrist revolt, and had to disappear back to his family property in the country. He subsequently went to Berlin where he studied composition. He then wrote an opera in the Italian style, *A Life for the Tsar*. This was based on the story of Ivan Susanin, a serf who in the early 1600s saved the life of the first Romanov tsar by diverting a detachment of Poles who were out to kill him. This story had already been set in the previous decade, with great success, by a Venetian composer based in St Petersburg, Catterino Cavos. It was now even more topical as, only five years before, the Russians had retaken Warsaw after the Polish uprising.

Although Glinka's music is Western in style, the story is highly nationalistic and the text is in Russian. At its central climax, Susanin exclaims: 'I fear neither fear nor death. For the Tsar, for Rus, I will die.' Thus, the première in December 1836 was a considerable success, and thereafter its performance on all national occasions became part of the ritual.[50] Today, however, the nationalistic sentiment verges on the tedious as it recurs regularly throughout the three and a half hours of this work. Glinka uses orchestral colour to evoke the spirit of Russia and, as the novelist Gogol rightly observed, one can indeed recognise whether a Russian or a Pole is singing.[51] Delightful jolly music accompanies the Poles whenever they appear. The contrast with the nobility of the serf, who duly knows his place, is distinct, and can sound faintly absurd. Yet, the music is fine and moving, and the Russian élite of course loved the jingoism, an ingredient which also justified the opera to the Soviet regime in later years.

With *A Life for the Tsar*, Glinka was acknowledged as Russia's leading composer, and a role model.[52] Tchaikovsky commented on the opera: 'What mastery! And how did he accomplish it all? Incomprehensible, that from such an extremely limited and commonplace dilletante … there should develop such a colossus??!!'[53]

Glinka hoped that Pushkin would write a libretto for him based on his *Ruslan and Ludmila*,[54] but Pushkin was killed in a duel with his brother-in-

* She had six children before and seven during the exile; her husband died very shortly before an amnesty, and she returned to Kamenka, where she died aged 93, two years after Tchaikovsky.[49]

law, whom he accused of seducing his wife.* When eventually Glinka's *Ruslan* was produced in 1842, it was a failure; however, its music had a considerable influence on Russian composers, as did its use of the whole tone scale, its rhythms, its colourful melody and harmonies.[55]

Glinka started to search for further ways of merging Russian influences with the structures and forms of Western music, its counterpoint and harmonies. He travelled to Spain and to Paris, which he had to leave when France and Russia went to war in the Crimea. He went to Berlin in 1856 to study further. The following January, after a concert at which Meyerbeer conducted an excerpt from *A Life for the Tsar*, he caught a cold. Within a fortnight, he was dead.

Russia in Mid-century: the Crimean War

Before moving on to the other composers who followed Glinka's lead, we should briefly look at the dissent which continued to foment in Russia, and at the Crimean War, which was also a consequence of the tension between East and West. War exposed Russia's fundamental weaknesses and provided the catalyst for much change, including the Emancipation of the Serfs, such as those on the Mussorgsky family estate.

At the time that the 1848 revolutions rocked the capitals of Europe, Russia was relatively quiet. But there was some disturbance. In 1849, the regime cracked down on a network of radical discussion circles, civil servants, junior officers, teachers and students. This group was called the Petrashevtsy after its leading figure. Among those sentenced to be shot was Fyodor Dostoyevsky, a military engineer. At the last minute, when the condemned were already clothed in their shrouds, the sentences were commuted. Dostoyevsky's was reduced to four years' hard labour at Omsk, and then four years' service as a soldier in the ranks.[56]

At this time, as a precaution, admission visas and exit passports were restricted, censorship was tightened, and the intake to Moscow University was cut by nearly two-thirds. One of the more foolish measures was to summon home those Russians living abroad; around 80,000 came back and spread information about the interesting developments taking place elsewhere.[57]

Russia then experienced the Crimean War. We usually remember this for Florence Nightingale, and for the heroic charge of the British Light

* The pistols used may possibly be those in the Pushkin and Tchaikovsky museum at Kamenka.

Brigade on 25 October 1854, which was immortalised in Tennyson's poem. After riding for twenty minutes in the 'Valley of Death', fewer than 200 of the 670 returned.

As always, the background to this war was complex. Until Vladivostok became available following the annexation of the Asiatic territories in the 1860s, the Black Sea provided Russia's only outlet to unfrozen sea. So Russia had an important strategic and commercial interest in the ailing Ottoman (Turkish) Empire and its territories in the Balkans. By mid-century, the Great Powers such as Britain, France and Austria suspected that Russia was bent on acquisition in the Balkans and were concerned that the balance of power should not be upset.[58]

When Napoleon III, whose regime depended on Church support, revived Roman Catholic claims to control various holy places in Jerusalem and Bethlehem, he was in effect issuing a challenge to the Orthodox Church. The Tsar, who anyway disliked Napoleon intensely, was bound to respond. Despite diplomacy by the other powers, his interference provoked the Turks into declaring war on Russia. After the Russian destruction of the Turkish Black Sea fleet was portrayed as a 'massacre', Britain and France joined in to support the Turks. Anglo-French forces landed in the Crimea in September 1854.

The vast armies of Britain and France got bogged down, far from home, with no real chance of penetrating Russia. Equally, Russia lacked the roads and railways to get troops to the front. It spent the equivalent of three years' income on the war, and covered the deficit with paper money, thus accelerating the rate of inflation.[59]

There could be no real victory for anyone, just lasting resentment. The terms of the peace which concluded the Crimean War were extremely harsh to Russia. A later minister for foreign affairs said: 'Russia is not sulking. Russia is thinking',[60] and used the opportunity of the Franco-Prussian War to repudiate the clauses which prevented her from constructing a Black Sea fleet.[61]

Meanwhile, Tsar Nicholas died in March 1855. He had insisted on inspecting troops in 23 degrees of frost, caught a cold, and got pneumonia.[62] Alexander Herzen, who was devoted to continuing the struggle of the Decembrists, danced for joy in the street when he heard of the Tsar's death.*

* Herzen's periodicals, such as *The Bell*, published by the Free Russian Press in London, were smuggled into Russia. When looking at Ghe's painting of *The Last Supper*, exhibited at the St Petersburg Academy of Arts in 1863, visitors recognised Herzen in the figure of one of the Apostles. Herzen was also well known in artistic and musical circles in Paris.[63]

East–West Struggle in Music: the Rubinsteins and the Mighty Five

The mounting East–West tension in the musical world was illustrated when it was suggested that one of Liszt's concerts in St Petersburg in the early 1840s should be disrupted by a demonstration against pro-Western influences. The bitterness became magnified when the pro-Western forces led by Anton Rubinstein joined battle with the so-called 'Mighty Five', a group of largely self-taught composers, led by Mily Balakirev. In 1855, Rubinstein wrote an article in which he dared to criticise Glinka and to question the possibility of writing 'Russian' operas.[64]

Rubinstein was a virtuoso pianist comparable to Liszt, who used to call him Ludwig II because he looked so like Beethoven.[65] As a composer, however, he has suffered from a 'bad press'. He has been accused of not having 'the necessary concentration of patience' and never allowing himself to mature.[66] Tchaikovsky said of him: 'the liberties taken by the composer merit astonishment but not imitation'.[67] Rubinstein's much-loved Melody in F is virtually the only composition, of the countless ones he dashed off, to have survived. 'Rubinstein bestrewed us all with his spring-buds, but never brought forth fruit.'[68]

Rubinstein had, however, a colossal influence on musical life in Russia. He was born on 28 November 1829 near Moscow, and studied in Berlin. Suave and polished, he obtained the patronage of Grand Duchess Elena Pavlovna, the German-born widow of Grand Duke Michael, who was the younger brother of the Tsars Alexander and Nicholas. Rubinstein played at her soirées, and stayed with her in Nice in the late 1850s. He had an apartment in one of her palaces. In 1859, Rubinstein and the grand duchess formed the Russian Musical Society, a concert-giving organisation which also provided teaching. One of the earlier pupils was Tchaikovsky. The Society evolved into the St Petersburg Conservatoire which, with the help of a subsidy from the tsar,* was opened in 1862 with exclusively German instructors.

Anton's younger brother Nicholas, also a piano virtuoso, was sent to Moscow where he set up the Moscow Conservatoire in his house. Nicholas was a great *bon viveur*, hard drinker, womaniser and gambler. He is reputed to have eaten a dozen oysters on his deathbed.[70]

* Rubinstein was so determined to get money to finance the Conservatoire that he is said to have even performed as a street musician in order to raise funds.[69]

Portraits and statues of the Rubinsteins rightly pervade the Conservatoires of St Petersburg and Moscow. However there is little now to record the support provided for them by the formidably influential and effective grand duchess. There is not much sign of her in her magnificent Mikhailovsky Palace, now the Russian Museum in St Petersburg.

It was remarkable that the grand duchess should associate herself with two Jews, although, in mid-century, the government wanted the country's myriad of ethnic groups to be assimilated and become Russianised. Laws still existed, from earlier in the century, which prescribed the areas in which Jews could live; they were restricted to jobs which historically can cause resentment to other ethnic groups, such as small traders, shopkeepers, moneylenders and urban professionals.*[71]

The Mighty Five

In contrast to the Westernised Rubinsteins, a leading 'pro-Russian' composer was Alexander Dargomijsky, a disciple of Glinka. He was the illegitimate son of a nobleman who eloped with a princess who was also a poetess. He disliked Italian opera with its 'melodies flattering to the ear. I want the note to express the word directly', he said, 'I want truth.'[72] While all leading composers have taken music forward, Dargomijsky and his successors such as Mussorgsky deserve particular credit for the degree to which they were prepared to experiment. Dargomijsky developed a new type of speech song, full of Russian character. His opera *The Stone Guest* did not appeal to Tchaikovsky, who described his music as 'the pitiful fruit of a dry, utterly rational process of invention, being capable only of inflicting a sense of mortal tedium on the audience'.[73]

Mily Balakirev, however, became the conscience of the pro-Russian composers, and dominated the 'Mighty Five', who dedicated themselves to creating distinctively Russian music, and often met in Dargomijsky's house.[74] The Five included Balakirev, César Cui, who was an authority on building fortifications,[75] Alexander Borodin, who was a leading scientist, and the young naval officer, Nicholas Rimsky-Korsakov. The greatest of

* In 1827, compulsory military service was applied to Jews from the age of twelve instead of the normal age of twenty. The extent of persecution fluctuated. It surged after the assassination of the tsar in 1881, and with the expulsion of those living illegally in Moscow in 1891. There were fearsome pogroms in 1905–6 when, for example, in Odessa, which had a large Jewish population, above 800 were killed and 5,000 wounded in just three months.

them was surely the civil, or not so civil, servant Modeste Mussorgsky. His music seems to penetrate the Russian soul:[76] to experience this, just listen to his opera, *Boris Godunov.* We shall now look briefly at each of these.

Balakirev and Cui

Balakirev was very close to Glinka, whose sister asked him to organise the publication of her brother's works, after his death. Balakirev was an inveterate interferer, forcing subject matter, folk themes and keys of compositions on the others and supervising their progress.* In his own works, he

Alexander Borodin / Mily Balakirev / César Cui

merged the style of the oriental music which he encountered when travelling in the Caucasus with Glinka's more Western idiom.

To counter Rubinstein's educational initiatives, Balakirev set up the Free School of Music. Although he became conductor of the Russian Musical Society, he lacked the personal skills necessary to handle the grand duchess. At first, she was unsuccessful in having him removed, but he was eventually obliged to resign. Over-stressed mentally, musically and financially, Balakirev turned to religion and to a soothsayer. He withdrew to become a supervisor in the goods department of the Warsaw railway and

* To Balakirev's persistence we also owe the preservation of Chopin's birthplace in Żelazowa Wola in Poland. He was a great admirer of Chopin.[77]

to teach. His colleagues even thought he had gone mad. But he returned in the 1880s, and through his church connections became director of the Imperial Court Chapel with Rimsky-Korsakov as his assistant, and worked on harmonisation of the liturgy.[78]

Cui's father was a Frenchman who remained in Russia after the Retreat from Moscow in 1812. He married a Lithuanian and lived at Vilnius where he taught French at the Gymnasium. In 1851, Cui entered the Engineering School at St Petersburg, and then the Academy of Military Engineering, where he subsequently became a professor. His opera *William Ratcliff* was given, with a mixed reception, at the Maryinsky (later Kirov) Theatre at the end of the 1860s; Rimsky-Korsakov described its orchestration as clumsy. Cui became a prominent music critic, with a strong bias in favour of the nationalist composers.[79]

Borodin

Far better known to us is Alexander Porfiryevich Borodin, whose family background was rather similar to Dargomijsky's. He was born on 12 November 1833, the illegitimate son of an elderly prince. He was registered at birth by the name of one of his father's serfs, Porfiry Borodin. As well as music, his early interests were in chemistry and making fireworks. He became a surgeon. In 1858, he received his doctorate for an essay 'on the Analogy of Arsenical with Phosphoric Acid'.

In 1859, Borodin went to Heidelberg, to continue chemistry studies for three years. There, he met his future wife, Catherine, a brilliant pianist, who suffered from tuberculosis. She introduced him to the works of Chopin, Liszt, Schumann and Mendelssohn. She also inspired his much-loved String Quartet in D, which he dedicated to her, and which evokes their happy days in Heidelberg together.

Because of his wife's health, the Borodins lived until 1862 in Viareggio, a town very close to where Puccini was to live. Then Borodin returned to St Petersburg to become professor of chemistry in the Medical Academy, where he had the unenviable task of competing with well-resourced German research. There, ten years later, he started running medical courses for women.*

* In the previous year, women had been given the right to work in telegraph, railway, postal and business offices, and to teach and become midwives. Official university-led courses for women, the first of their kind in Europe, opened in Russia in 1878.[80]

26 27 28 29

ILLNESS: Donizetti's deterioration (26 and 27) is evident from these portraits now in the Museum at Bergamo. Chopin (28) knows that his tuberculosis is terminal. Did Tchaikovsky (29) die of cholera, or commit suicide? He is shown here with his wife of short duration, Antonina.

30

31

32

33

34

35

36

37

BOURGEOIS DOMESTICITY: Josefina Čermáková and her sister Anna (34), who married Dvořák, play the piano at home, a scene typical of 1870. Dvořák, who originally preferred Josefina, is seen feeding the doves (35) in his yard at Vysoká. Janáček and his wife Zdeňka (36); Smetana and his second wife Bettina (37).

OPPOSITE: THE SECOND EMPIRE: Napoleon III (30) and Empress Eugénie (31) averted their gaze from Manet's *Le Déjeuner sur l'Herbe* (32), but bought the prize-winning *La Naissance de Vénus* by Alexandre Cabanel (33).

38

39

40

Sibelius (38), shortly before his marriage, painted by his future brother-in-law Eero Järnefelt. English honorary degrees: Grieg (39) walks with the grandee Lord Derby to receive an award at Oxford in 1906. The picture shows how slight a man Grieg was. Grieg was inspired by Norway's scenic fjords, here shown in the *Bridal Procession in Hardanger* (1848) by Adolph Tidemand and Hans Frederik Gude (40).

41

42

43

Mendelssohn the skilled watercolourist: the Rheinfall at Schaffhausen (41). Johann Strauss with Brahms (42); Hugo von Hofmannsthal and Richard Strauss (43).

44 45 46 47

Giuseppina Strepponi (44), Verdi's mistress, later his wife. Debussy on his trike (45). Enigma rather than Pomp and Circumstance (46): Talbot Hughes' portrait of Elgar in 1905. The maestro at the wheel: Puccini (47) goes for a jaunt in his De Dion Bouton (1901).

OPPOSITE: CHANGING STYLES AND HABITS: Backstage at the Paris Opéra (48): Edgar Degas' ballerinas; (49) Oskar Kokoschka's *Die Windsbraut* (also called *The Tempest*) (1914), said to portray the painter with Alma Mahler.

48

49

50

51

52

53

TWENTIETH-CENTURY SCENES: Shostakovich the firefighter (50) defends the Conservatoire during the Siege of Leningrad. The site of the Mendelssohn family home today (51); in the foreground a watch tower from the Berlin Wall. An American soldier (53) poses as a pianist in the drawing room of Wahnfried, now restored (52).

Borodin's First Symphony, which was conducted by Balakirev at the Russian Music Society in March 1868, made a poor impression. He was given the text for *Prince Igor*, on which he worked off and on for the rest of his life. Although Borodin's performances of his First Symphony and parts of *Prince Igor* spread his reputation abroad, it was increasingly hard for him to combine his professional responsibilities with music. He told his wife about the 'difficulty of being at one and the same time a Glinka and a civil servant, scientist, commissioner, artist, government official, philanthropist, father of other people's children, doctor and invalid ... You end by becoming only the last.'[81] His wife's health required her to spend more time in warmer Moscow and this also took up time.

On the morning of 27 February 1887, he worked at the piano on his Third Symphony. That evening, he dropped dead while attending a fancy dress ball organised by the professors of the Medical Academy. He was only 53. His wife survived him by only five months. He had recently returned to *Prince Igor* and composed several numbers including the overture and the chorus of Russian prisoners. *Prince Igor* and the Third Symphony were completed by Alexander Glazunov, posthumously. Indeed one British critic in the early 20th century commented on Borodin that 'no musician has ever claimed immortality with so slender an offering'.[82]

Mussorgsky: Early Life

If Borodin left a few works unfinished, Modeste Mussorgsky left many in that condition, although, in his case, alcohol was to blame. In one respect, the two had a similar ancestry. Mussorgsky's grandmother, who was still alive when he was a boy, had been a serf. Her son, the composer's father, was eventually recognised as a noble. He owned an estate of 27,000 acres and 18 villages at Karevo (later renamed Mussorgsky), 250 miles southwest of St Petersburg.[83] The quality of the land was poor, and it is unlikely that the family could be counted among the more affluent nobility, those who squandered their possessions and held elaborate parties for half the province in their mansions, which comprised 'white stone buildings with their multitudes of belvederes, chimneys and weather-vanes, surrounded on all sides by numerous wings and buildings for the guests ... Through the night the gardens are brilliantly lit by lights and lampions and resound to the thunder of music.'[84]

Nicholas Gogol, in his novel *Dead Souls*, paints a vivid picture of the less affluent form of life in the Russian countryside in the decades before Emancipation. The boorish, and usually lonely, 'nobles' munch their 'famous dish which is served with cabbage soup and consists of a sheep's stomach stuffed with buckwheat, brains and sheep's trotters'.[85] The dreary, deprived serfs plough, drink heavily, drive the troika and cheat their master. Gogol pictures the 'red roof and white chimneys of the manor house, the tall, narrow, wooden belfry, and the dark, vast old wooden church'[86] and wonders whether the landowner is a 'jovial fellow himself or as gloomy as the last days of September, looking perpetually at the calendar and talking everlastingly about his rye and wheat'.[87] One suspects that this may represent a reasonable portrait of the rather down-at-heel Mussorgskys.

Modeste, who was born on 21 March 1839, learnt Russian folksongs from his nurse and could be found improvising on the piano before he had any lessons. Taught by his mother, he progressed quickly, and at nine years old he performed a John Field concerto before a large audience in his parents' house. When he was thirteen, he was sent to the cadet school in St Petersburg and then joined the crack regiment, the Preobrazhensky Guards. Immaculately turned out and with 'lisping French and exquisite manners',[88] he had the reputation for being something of a fop. He may have picked up his habit for heavy drinking when in the regiment.

At one stage, he was on guard duty at the hospital where Borodin worked. This led to his introduction to the circle around Balakirev. At the age of 21, Mussorgsky's Scherzo in B flat was performed at a concert of the Russian Music Society. But the Emancipation of the Serfs in 1861 required him to return home for two years, in order to help his elder brother Filaret manage the estate at Karevo. The events leading to Emancipation had been under way for some time.

The 'Emancipation' of the Serfs

At the end of the Crimean War, the hundreds of thousands of demobilised soldier-serfs could not simply be returned to the countryside.[89] Wars usually have considerable ramifications. Anyway, the structure of serfdom was chaotic: it had been abolished in the Baltic provinces by 1820 and, when Finland and Poland were acquired, serfdom was not introduced there.[90] Thus the regime was liberal at the periphery, but not at the centre, in Russia itself. Russian institutions were in a mess: even at the end of the century, Russia was still a centralised autocracy, trailing behind other leading countries in political development.

Shortly after Tsar Nicholas I died, the new Tsar Alexander II was taking the waters in Bad Kissingen, a popular spa in Bavaria, reputedly good for one's eyes and ears, and for catarrh, rheumatism, scrofula and bowel problems. Grand Duchess Elena Pavlovna was also there. She spoke forcefully to her nephew on the subject of the serfs, about which she was knowledgeable. She had set up a 'think-tank' to advise her on how to free her Ukrainian serfs. The key issues were identified: the serfs had to own their land, and be given enough to prosper, otherwise Emancipation would fail. The government would have to provide finance to enable them to buy out the landowners; the finance would have to be redeemed over several years.[91]

One can only surmise what the meeting between the Tsar and his intelligent aunt was like: the new Tsar was neither bright nor decisive, and his experience was largely confined to attending committee meetings, such as those of the board which supervised the construction of the St Petersburg–Moscow Railway. 'When the Tsar talks to an intellectual', said a poet, 'he has the appearance of someone with rheumatism who is standing in a draught.'[92]

The tsar initiated a consultation process, which started slowly and conservatively, with the government more concerned about aristocratic resistance than peasant revolt. In late 1857, local governors were encouraged to submit views on implementation. In the following year, press restrictions were relaxed. The legislation was developed and signed by the tsar on 3 March 1861. The publication of it was accompanied by an extensive security operation; troops were quartered in the villages.

The legislation was so complex that most serfs thought that they had been cheated and were not yet free. There were disturbances in almost all of the provinces to which the legislation applied; 647 incidents took place between April and July 1861.[93] The worst disturbance was near Kazan, where one peasant naively proclaimed that the serfs had been granted wholesale freedom. There was a riot, troops fired on the crowd, dozens were killed and the deluded peasant was executed.

There was to be a two-year period in which the serfs would use government finance to buy out the landowners. The serf was responsible for the redemption of the finance plus interest. The landowners were appeased by being allowed to base the price on the value of the serfs' production, rather than on the land value, which was much lower.[94]

These arrangements were disastrous. The peasants were encumbered with redemption obligations; they were dependent on landowners for pasture, forest and water supplies; in the fertile south, they had surrendered almost a quarter of their allotments. With the population growing at 1.5 per cent per annum,[95] the increased demand for land drove up rents. To survive, the peasants found themselves having to work for the gentry at pitiful wages. A long agrarian depression between 1875 and 1895,[96] and a harvest failure in 1891, resulted in terrible rural poverty. A repressive government ensured that, for the moment, the sense of injustice and resentment did not manifest itself in major outbreaks of violence and arson.

This would have immense consequences politically. For us, the direct experience of the implementation of Emancipation in 1861 enhanced Mussorgsky's 'Russianness' and intensified his sympathy with the Russian peasant. The process also left him and his brother considerably and increasingly impoverished.

Mussorgsky: the Second Half

Back in St Petersburg, Mussorgsky worked in the Central Engineering Authority: working in government service, civil, naval or military, was virtually the only available occupation for members of Mussorgsky's class, such as younger sons who were not landowners. He lived, at first, with five other men obsessed with art, religion, philosophy and politics. He transferred to his brother Filaret's St Petersburg household, when, following his mother's death in 1865, he had his first bout of dipsomania. Financial circumstances, however, soon forced Filaret to sell up and move entirely to the country.

Mussorgsky experimented with song and conversation, trying out his ideas on his nephew and niece, in the *Nursery Songs*. 'My music must be an artistic representation of human speech in all its finest shades', Mussorgsky wrote in a letter to Glinka's sister.[97] He also composed *St John's Night on the Bare Mountain*, partly based on some writings of Gogol. Another member of the Big Five, either Balakirev or Rimsky-Korsakov, it is not clear which, scribbled on the completed manuscript in pencil: 'A load of rubbish.'[98]

Mussorgsky tried making an opera out of another story from Gogol, but this proved too experimental. He rejoined the civil service as assistant head clerk in the third section of the forestry department of the Ministry of State Property, but was made redundant in 1867, in a downsizing. He lived with friends and started working on *Boris Godunov*, a Russian opera about a Russian subject.*[100]

The only means of getting an opera performed was to send it to the Director of Imperial Theatres. The opera committee of the Maryinsky Theatre, the theatre devoted to Russian works, rejected his unconventional score, so he recast the work, making drastic changes.** He did this while sharing an apartment with Rimsky-Korsakov. Three scenes from *Boris* were subsequently performed successfully, and, at the end of January 1874, the full première was sold out. Mussorgsky's fee was 125 roubles per performance; Verdi had recently been paid over 100 times this for the première of *La Forza del Destino*, which took place in St Petersburg.

In *Boris Godunov*, Mussorgsky aimed to represent in music not just feelings but human speech. He wrote: 'I explore human speech … thus I arrive at the embodiment of recitative in melody.'[101] Hardly anyone at first understood what he was trying to do. Tchaikovsky described it in a letter to his brother Modeste as 'the most banal base parody of music':[102] he had gone to sleep when excerpts were played through at a soirée held by Cui. Cui himself issued a stinging criticism of it, following the full performance.[103]

It is possible that, following the success of *Boris*, Mussorgsky could have made 'the break'. His friend and adviser Vladimir Stasov, a critic, and the 'self-appointed champion of the national school in all the Russian arts',[104] urged him to visit Liszt, who was enthusiastic about Mussorgsky's music. But he failed to grasp the opportunity, possibly because drink was getting the better of him: on most days, he was to be seen in a restaurant with a bottle;[105] occasionally, there was also trouble with the police.

Mussorgsky wrote the piano suite, *Pictures at an Exhibition*, in memory of his friend, the artist and architect Victor Hartmann, who died in 1873. The work was written within twenty days;†[106] but, as with the death of any

* Thirty years before, the tsar had decreed that no member of the Romanov royal family could be portrayed on the stage. It made sense to choose a subject from a period before the Romanovs.[99]

**A manuscript in the Demidov autograph book in the St Petersburg Conservatoire shows extraordinarily neat handwriting (in 1863), considering his personal habits; but Mussorgsky was devoted to precision and accuracy.

† It was subsequently orchestrated by Ravel. The original version, for the piano, demonstrates a wonderful variety of colour and contrast.

person close to him, the loss sent him into another bout of dipsomania.

He moved into a flat with a young poet, Count Kutuzov, and wrote some songs using his poems. But when the count moved out in order to get married, Mussorgsky degenerated further, sleeping rough, and in rags. His friends gave him up as a lost cause.[107] Glinka's sister, a close friend, had to turn him away from her door. On one occasion, Rimsky-Korsakov turned up to invite Mussorgsky to stay at his dacha, only to find him in bed vomiting.

Mussorgsky's drinking habits did not enhance his prospects in the civil service. He was eventually transferred to a department whose director was a folksong enthusiast, and who allowed him leave to accompany a 50-year-old contralto who was undertaking a concert tour of the Ukraine, the Crimea and towns along the Don and Volga rivers. Mussorgsky enjoyed this tour considerably, even though it brought in less money than he had expected.[108]

His friends rallied round. In 1880, they guaranteed him a monthly pension of 100 roubles provided he completed *Khovanshchina*, another opera about the troubled times at the beginning of the reign of Peter the Great. Other friends promised him 80 roubles a month, provided he completed *Sorochintsy Fair* within a year. He did not complete either work. He made further appearances as the contralto's accompanist, and she employed him at a music school which she set up in St Petersburg. His friends thought that he was demeaning himself by this, as she was not very highly regarded. But the money from accompanying was necessary, because, for subsistence, he only had meagre royalties and possibly some residual income from the Karevo estates.[109]

In February 1881, he acknowledged the applause at a concert in which his *Destruction of Sennacherib* was conducted by Rimsky-Korsakov. Eight days later, in a state of agitation, he told the contralto that he would have to go and beg on the streets; later that evening, he had a fit of alcoholic epilepsy. He had three more fits the next day. He was removed to the military hospital, which he found a comfortable contrast to his previous existence. There was a temporary improvement in mid-March, during which his portrait was painted by another protégé of Stasov, Ilya Repin. Mussorgsky's brother brought him some money, and according to one account he used this to buy brandy, which he consumed in one go. He died on 28 March 1881. It was his 42nd birthday.[110]

Shortly before his death, Mussorgsky wrote an autobiographical sketch, in which he said that 'neither in the character of his compositions nor in his ideas about music does Mussorgsky belong to any of the prevailing musical trends. A formulation of his artistic creed can be derived from his ideas about the duties of Art: "Art is a means towards communication with human beings, not an end in itself."'[111] The sentiment is one which some of his modern successors appear often to overlook.

Glinka's sister probably provided the most apt epitaph, when Mussorgsky died: 'this is an irreplaceable loss for Art and for his friends', she said. 'But, for his own future, there was nothing better in view.'[112]

Rimsky-Korsakov

When Mussorgsky died, many of his works were incomplete. César Cui finished a performing version of *Sorochintsy Fair*. Rimsky-Korsakov set about tidying up some of the other works and sanitising them. The *Bare Mountain* music was virtually rewritten. He re-scored much of *Boris Godunov*, inserting some of his own music. He also completed a version of *Khovanshchina*, which was first performed in 1886.*

Like many of the other Russian composers, Rimsky-Korsakov, who was born on 18 March 1844, came from a prosperous family. When he was twelve, he went to the naval cadet school in St Petersburg, and he passed out six years later. His elder brother, a senior naval officer, encouraged him to continue his naval career: he sailed in a clipper which took him to Gravesend, the Baltic, New York, Rio and the Mediterranean. This lasted about two and a half years.

From an early age, he liked to pick out tunes on the piano, particularly tunes from *A Life for the Tsar*. Towards the end of his cadet training, his piano and harmony teacher introduced him to Balakirev, who encouraged him to compose a symphony; he finished the slow movement on his ship at Gravesend. When he returned at the beginning of 1865, Balakirev made him complete the work.

Back in St Petersburg his naval duties were undemanding; this enabled him to lead an active social life and he became known as a bit of a

* Later, Shostakovich also completed editions of *Boris Godunov* and *Khovanshchina*. He said: 'Rimsky-Korsakov groomed, waved, and sluiced Mussorgsky with eau de cologne. My orchestration is crude, in keeping with Mussorgsky.'[113]

dilettante. But he also composed. In 1871–2, he worked at *The Maid of Pskov*, which was produced at the Maryinsky Theatre in 1873. At this time, he shared a room with Mussorgsky, who worked at the table and piano in the morning, Rimsky-Korsakov taking his turn in the afternoon. In July 1871, although he had virtually no experience or training, he was appointed to the St Petersburg Conservatoire to become professor of composition, and to direct the orchestral class. When, shortly after his marriage, he resigned his naval commission, his friend, the Minister of Marine, appointed him to a new and well-paid post, as Inspector of Naval Bands.[114]

Rimsky-Korsakov composed, inspected bands enthusiastically,[115] and in 1875 succeeded Balakirev as conductor of the Free School. His work there included giving the first performances in Russian of excerpts from Bach's St Matthew Passion. He worked on folksong and wrote an opera, *May Night*, based on Gogol's short stories about peasant life in the Ukraine.

His opera on Ostrovsky's play, *The Snow Maiden*, was produced in 1882. The first half of that year was mainly taken up with sorting out Mussorgsky's chaotic legacy. At first, he tackled *Khovanshchina*; he found *The Night on a Bare Mountain* more difficult, and he only completed this four years later.

He was one of a group of composers who met regularly at the house of Mitrofan Belaiev, an amateur viola player and chamber music enthusiast. He was rich because his father had a successful timber business.[116] Belaiev was very enthusiastic about the works of Glazunov, who was one of Rimsky-Korsakov's pupils, but those works, including eight symphonies, have generally not stood the test of time.*[117]

In the second half of the 1880s, Rimsky-Korsakov returned to composing his own original pieces, works such the *Spanish Capriccio*, with its brilliant instrumental colouring, and *Shéhérazade*. However, he became depressed, partly through poor health – he was an asthmatic – and partly as a result of deaths in his family. He felt that his creative powers had gone. He wrote in May 1891: 'No music that I hear pleases me … it all seems to

*Glazunov, apart from being an important teacher, kept the St Petersburg Conservatoire, where he was Director, on an even keel during the period of the Revolution and afterwards. Also in this group was Sergey Taneyev, the first gold medallist at the Moscow Conservatoire, whose vocal works include settings in Esperanto. He was a friend of Tolstoy and more particularly of Tolstoy's wife. He is highly regarded in Russian circles, but has little following in the UK. His pupils included Rachmaninov and Scriabin. Neither Glazunov nor Taneyev are well known in the West;

me dry and cold.'[118] This included his own opera *Mlada*, produced in 1892, which he described as 'cold – like ice'.[119] He took self-criticism to a point 'dangerously near creative annihilation'.[120] He loathed being called a genius.

Rimsky-Korsakov hardly touched a piano for a year, resigned his posts, and worked on musical aesthetics. Tchaikovsky's death in 1893 aroused him to conduct a concert of his friend's works. From this time come works such as *Christmas Eve*, *Sadko* and *The Barber of Baghdad*. According to one commentator, his operas can be regarded as musico-scenic fairy tales;[121] they lack dramatic power and the capacity to create characters in sound.[122] His one-act *Mozart and Salieri*, based on Pushkin's story, dates from 1897.

The imperial family did not like Rimsky-Korsakov. Tsar Nicholas II himself, on hearing that *Sadko* was to be similar to *Mlada* and *Christmas Eve*, personally crossed it off the list of compositions for the Imperial Theatre. Fortunately, the wealthy merchant class of Moscow was keen to support the arts, and the railway magnate Savva Mamontov came to the rescue and financed a performance of *Sadko* by the Private Russian Opera.*[123]

Meanwhile, Tsar Nicholas II was not doing too well. Rival ambitions in Manchuria and Korea led Japan to attack in January 1904.[124] The complacent Russians suffered a series of devastating defeats. Although the disasters aroused little interest at home, where the war was regarded as a matter for court and capitalists, there was a sense that the government was incompetent. Thus the Japanese War provided a catalyst for smouldering discontent to burst into flame. There were peasant uprisings in the countryside; there were lootings and burnings.[125] Much more serious was the first Bloody Sunday, in St Petersburg on 22 January 1905: troops outside the Winter Palace opened fire on a procession of unarmed petitioners who were merely bearing a very simple message to their deified ruler: 'Destroy

equally, Russians might not immediately recognise many English composers from the same period. Belaiev's offer to finance Glazunov's works led him to form a publishing firm in Leipzig, which eventually became part of C.F. Peters. It was established in Leipzig so as to secure the international copyright, which at that stage did not extend to Russia. Belaiev relied on Rimsky-Korsakov for advice on publishing and concert promotion. He became an important supporter of Scriabin.

* Shortly after the state monopoly of the theatre was lifted, Mamontov, who had set up an arts and crafts colony at his home, founded his private opera. He unfortunately came unstuck fifteen years later, when he went bankrupt after being accused of embezzling company funds to support the opera.

the wall between thyself and thy people', was all they asked.[126] This tragedy was followed by a general collapse and a stoppage throughout the empire: there were peasant riots; the first Soviet, a spontaneous organisation of factory labour delegates, was formed; and, notoriously, there was a mutiny on the battleship Potemkin.

Less famously, there was a strike by the workers in the sugar refinery in Kamenka: one of the local farms, in which Tchaikovsky used to stroll a few decades earlier, was burnt to the ground. When it seemed that the harvest would be disrupted, the dragoons were brought in to restore order, and some of the rioters were exiled.[127]

Not surprisingly, the students of the Conservatoire got caught up in the events of Bloody Sunday. The apolitical Igor Stravinsky, who had recently left university, was somehow involved in a minor student disturbance and was detained for seven hours.[128] At a more junior level, the fourteen-year-old Prokofiev, to his father's horror, signed a piece of paper threatening to leave the Conservatoire.[129] In February Rimsky-Korsakov together with Rachmaninov and other leading musicians sent a letter to the press in which they demanded political reforms. Six weeks later, the building was surrounded by police. Rimsky-Korsakov published an open letter to the director, his former pupil, supporting the student strikers, and made a stinging attack on those who controlled the Conservatoire. The director resigned; Rimsky-Korsakov was dismissed from his professorship. A week later, a student performance of Rimsky-Korsakov's *Kashchey*, conducted by Glazunov, was followed by a wild political demonstration of homage to the composer.[130] Although performance of Rimsky-Korsakov's music was temporarily forbidden by the police, at the end of the year, the Conservatoire was reopened with the professors reinstated and Glazunov appointed as director.

Peace with Japan brought some, but little, respite, and was followed by a succession of strikes and further mutinies. On the day the tsar announced concessions, including the calling of a parliament (the Duma), the St Petersburg Soviet of workers was formed under the chairmanship of Trotsky, and this inspired the formation of more Soviets elsewhere. The members of the Soviets were arrested, the Revolution was repressed, but it was all 'too little, too late': the tsar repeated the ancient formula, redolent of Ivan the Terrible and Peter the Great: 'Obedience to his authority, not only for wrath but also for conscience sake, is ordained by God himself.'[131] This left no outlet for popular disaffection apart from further revolution.

Rimsky-Korsakov wrote *The Golden Cockerel*, based on Pushkin's tale about the stupidity of the autocracy, a particularly apt topic at the time. The hassle which he experienced with the censors clouded the last months of his life, and probably aggravated the heart trouble from which he died in 1908.

It is regrettable, perhaps, that many today know Rimsky-Korsakov mainly for the 'Flight of the Bumble Bee', an orchestral interlude from the opera *The Tale of Tsar Saltan*, which was written as the century turned.[132] Yet, Rimsky-Korsakov had achieved much: not only did he compose his own works and sort out much of the shambles left behind by Mussorgsky, he taught Prokofiev. He took Stravinsky, who was a friend of his son, under his wing after his father died. He also had a considerable influence upon composers such as Ravel, Debussy and Dukas.

Rimsky-Korsakov was the last of the Five. Before we consider his pupils, we must look at the career of one Russian composer, Tchaikovsky, who also had a considerable influence on Stravinsky. As we have seen, Tchaikovsky disliked the compositions of his fellow Russian composers, such as Mussorgsky. 'Mussorgsky's music is utterly and damnably awful', he said. 'It is the most vulgar and squalid parody of music.'[133] And later, Tchaikovsky said that Mussorgsky 'is spoilt by the coarseness of his methods and his leaning towards musical ugliness'.[134] Tchaikovsky had much more sympathy with the life and art of the West. This may be the reason why today he is the most popular of all the Russian composers.

TCHAIKOVSKY

CHAPTER 21

OF ALL COMPOSERS, Tchaikovsky must provide one of the more interesting studies for an armchair psychologist. The disastrous marriage, the mysterious relationship with his patroness, the alcoholism, the taste for young boys, which he was desperate to conceal, all make for a colourful life. Even his death, at only 53, provides one of the most absorbing 'whodunits' since the senile Salieri claimed to have murdered Mozart.

His outward appearance, tall, distinguished and elegant, with grey hair and blue eyes, concealed the tempestuous personality reflected in his compositions. This 'exhibitionism' has been regarded as decadent, a last outpouring of 19th-century Romanticism. He 'intensified everything to the extreme', said one commentator.[1] Experts, while acknowledging his skill at orchestration,[2] have referred to his 'unbearable vulgarities', his 'cheap chains of sequences', his 'naked feelings'.[3]

Yet, Tchaikovsky's popularity provides an interesting example of the gulf between people's taste and the experts' opinion. So often, the general public love the music which the experts disdain, and dislike the music of which the experts approve.

We will start with Tchaikovsky's early life, and then turn to the Moscow years. We need to consider three important women in his life; his sister

Sasha, his patroness Madame von Meck, and his far from normal wife, Antonina. For a long time, he was a rolling stone. He eventually settled near Klin, a small town not far from Moscow. However, his work as a conductor took him abroad to London and the USA. He deteriorated and died suddenly. Why? We shall probably never know.

The Young Tchaikovsky

If one uses the Julian calendar, which applied in Russia until 1918, Peter Ilich Tchaikovsky was born on 25 April 1840, although for us that would have been 7 May. His father ran the mining and ironworks at Votkinsk, near the Urals. This was an important industrial complex which provided iron with which to build the Trans-Siberian Railway and ships for the Caspian Sea.[4] Tchaikovsky's father had the rank of major-general. Many civilian jobs were carried out by people with military rank.[5]

The family name came from Tchaikovsky's Kazakh great-grandfather, who apparently could imitate the call of a seagull (a *tchaika*). More importantly perhaps, he had fought for Peter the Great when he defeated the Swedes in the Battle of Poltava in 1709; his son was given the noble suffix '-sky' for services as a military doctor.[6]

As the crow flies, the Tchaikovsky home was about 600 miles east of Moscow, on the edge of European Russia. The major-general was a big noise in a small and distant place, a place which Gogol might have described as a 'dull provincial hole'. The kindred spirits could typically have been the governor, the vice-governor, the president of the court, the chief of police and the liquor tax contractor. The tedium could have been broken by games of whist or the regular 'governor's balls', because 'where there is a governor, there is a ball, for otherwise he would not enjoy the respect and love of the nobility'.[7] The place was sufficiently remote that, only a few years before, a suitable sentence for Alexander Herzen, the socialist, revolutionary and journalist, was six years' exile working in the provincial bureaucracy.*

Peter (or Pyotr, but we shall call the boy Petya) had an older brother, Nicholas and a younger sister, Sasha. Ten years after he was born, twin brothers arrived, Anatole and Modeste. When Petya was four, his mother, who was said to have been descended from a French Huguenot family,

* In recent years, the town had a factory manufacturing nuclear missiles.[8]

employed a young Swiss governess to teach Nicholas and a cousin. The nanny, or governess, was a central pillar of the prosperous Russian household,[9] so, not surprisingly, Petya became very attached to her: she knew how to handle the difficult child, who was prone to tantrums.

The family enjoyed music. They had a piano and a large musical box called an 'orchestrion' which played excerpts from operas by Mozart, Rossini, Bellini and Donizetti. Petya was given piano lessons by a freed serf, and he used to make up songs for the family to sing. However, he wrote later: 'It was my good fortune that fate brought me up in a not very musical family and, in consequence, I did not suffer in childhood from that poison in which music is steeped after Beethoven.'[10]

When he was eight, this happy life was disrupted. The family moved to Moscow where the major-general thought he had a new job lined up. By the time they arrived there, the job had gone to someone else, and an epidemic of cholera was raging. So they went on to St Petersburg. Petya must have been impressed by the city, every bit an imperial capital, with its ornate buildings, its boulevards, its canals and the broad River Neva. But it cannot have been much fun being teased as country bumpkins at the fashionable Schmelling school, where the boys were sent.[11]

His father then found himself a job in a town beyond the Urals, almost 1,000 miles to the east of Moscow, virtually in Siberia. The governess had left and Petya's unlovable stepsister, his mother's daughter from an earlier marriage, was now responsible for his education. In these bleak surroundings, Petya consoled himself by playing the piano and writing letters to the governess.

In planning the boy's schooling, Petya's parents had an eye on his future career. The civil service was the only choice for upper-middle-class boys not destined for a profession such as medicine for Borodin, or for the forces, like Mussorgsky in the Guards and Rimsky-Korsakov in the Navy. The prospects were good: the vast country needed administration, so the bureaucracy had mushroomed: there was one official per 2,250 people at the beginning of the century, and one official to less than 1,000 people by mid-century.[12] In the 1840s, 165,000 sheets of official papers headed 'urgent' were prepared annually in the Ministry of the Interior; a decade later, 1,351 separate documents were needed to notify all relevant authorities of the sale of a piece of land. A Finance Ministry official described how 'everyone's perpetual concern to safeguard himself against having to take legal responsibility requires an enormous effort, and a massive consumption of paper, ink and time. It slows down the transaction of business, removes from the provincial and district agencies all feelings of independence, and teaches them to act surreptitiously if at all.'[13] One only needs to read Gogol's play, *The Government Inspector*, to sense the softly sleazy small-mindedness that characterised this bureaucracy.

The élite schools for the upper middle classes, ambitious for the future of their sons, were the Imperial Law School in St Petersburg and the Academy at Tsarskoe Selo nearby. Nobles' sons were also sent to these schools, so the upper-middle-class boy could develop a useful old-boy network for the future. Thus it was not long before Petya went back to St Petersburg to start at a preparatory school which would lead on to the Law School. When his mother, of whom he was obsessively fond, left him there, they had to be forcibly separated. The boy was of course very homesick; yet he seems to have been reasonably content, and even quite liked the school food, the borsch and the gruel. He survived a scarlet fever epidemic at the school. The son of the friends who were acting *in loco parentis* died of it, and Petya seems to have developed a deep sense of guilt that he was somehow responsible for the child's death.[14]

But things at first looked up. In 1852, Petya's father retired, so the family moved back to St Petersburg. Petya did well in the entry examination for the Law School; and he spent a delightful summer holiday on a country estate. Then, in 1854, his parents got cholera, and although his father recovered, his mother died very suddenly. Twenty-five years later, he would write: 'Every moment of that appalling day is as vivid to me as though it were yesterday.'[15] However, losing one's mother was sadly not unusual for a Russian child in the 19th century.[16]

Despite its name, the Law School encouraged music. Its alumni included eminent musicians such as the critic Vladimir Stasov and the composer Alexander Serov.* Tchaikovsky took extra-curricular lessons from a German, who soon became professor at the Conservatoire. But the professor advised the major-general that there was no sense in his son becoming a musician: he lacked talent, and, besides, it was a hard life.

* In the 1860s, Serov's two operas, *Judith* and *Rogneda*, were popular and highly lucrative. Despite this, he wore the same hat for twenty years.[17]

The Civil Service

Tchaikovsky left school in 1859 after nine years and, in his words, 'as one of the best pupils of my year'.[18] He became first class clerk in the Ministry of Justice. This was headed by a reactionary, who liked keeping parrots because they said what he told them to say.[19]

The Ministry would have been very busy preparing the detailed policy and legislation necessary to 'emancipate' the serfs and to implement other changes such as the reform of the legal system and of local government. Giving effect to Emancipation was complex: for example, it necessitated a redefinition of all the legal relationships between landlord and serf. Also, the legal system itself was archaic and greatly in need of reform: defendants were guilty until proved innocent; there were no juries or lawyers; judges sat behind closed doors; only written evidence was taken. Alexander Herzen declared: 'A man of the humble class who falls into the hands of the law is more afraid of the process of law itself than of any punishment. He looks forward with impatience to the time when he will be sent to Siberia; his martyrdom ends with the beginning of his punishment.'[20] A new structure, more Western, was introduced: this involved the creation of an independent and properly remunerated judiciary, and the introduction of public trials and juries.*[21]

So, much was being changed. Leo Tolstoy said: 'he who was not alive in the Russia of 1856 does not know what life is'.[22] Fyodor Dostoyevsky, in one of his novels, gives an impression of the extent to which even the provincial towns were buzzing with the changes: 'They talked about the abolition of the censorship and spelling reform, of the substitution of the Roman alphabet for the Russian one, of the exile of someone the day before, of some public disturbance in the shopping arcade, of the advisability of a federal constitution for the different nationalities in Russia, of the abolition of the army and the navy, of the restoration of Poland as far as the Dnieper, of the agrarian reform and of the political pamphlets, of the abolition of inheritance, the family, children, and the priesthood, of the rights of women … and so on and so forth.'[23] Another writer has written about this period: 'Not even bureaucrats could wholly ignore the prevailing atmosphere of intellectual excitement.'[24]

Yet, it seems that Tchaikovsky did. During this period of bureaucratic

* As the pressures on the administration increased, much of this was watered down.

hyperactivity, Tchaikovsky could write to his sister: 'In my work at the Ministry, I hope soon to obtain a post with responsibility for special duties; the salary is twenty roubles* more *and there isn't much to do.*'[26] He cannot have been oblivious of what was going on around him; his sister had married a landowner from the Ukraine who must have been deeply involved in the practical aspects of the Emancipation. Besides, the reforms were advantageous for Tchaikovsky: after Tsar Nicholas' death, passports for foreign travel became freely available. So, he could set off on a trip to Paris and Western Europe as an aide of a friend of his father's, hearing operas.

Apart from this, Tchaikovsky was enjoying the rich cultural life of St Petersburg. He went to the ballet and opera and took part in amateur plays. Musical life in St Petersburg was very active: Verdi's *La Forza del Destino* had its first performance at the Maryinsky (later Kirov) Theatre in 1862. Tchaikovsky saw Mozart's *Don Giovanni*, Glinka's *A Life for the Tsar* and Weber's *Der Freischütz.* He also heard Anton Rubinstein performing: 'Like everybody else I was carried away by him', Tchaikovsky said.[27] He composed a romance based on Italian opera. Although he now wanted to turn to a musical career, his father could not afford him an allowance: he had handed his fortune over to a female swindler, who lost it within twelve months.[28]

Tchaikovsky made several friendships at this time. One was with the up-and-coming, flagrantly homosexual poet Alexei Apukhtin whom he had known at school. He seems also to have had a relationship with a middle-aged singing teacher, who dyed his hair and wore rouge.

At the Conservatoires

It comes as little surprise to hear that in 1863, aged 23, Tchaikovsky was passed over for promotion and left the Ministry. He had been studying at the Russian Musical Society and was part of the initial intake into the new Conservatoire. As well as learning the organ, he studied the flute, so that he could play in the orchestra. He gave piano lessons to eke out a living. The three and a half years he spent at the Conservatoire gave him a training which had not been available to the earlier Russian composers.

* In Gogol's novel *Dead Souls*, a landowner sells two serf girls to a priest for 100 roubles each; a lady's attire for a party could cost around 1,000 roubles; a superintendent of factories could be paid 5,000 roubles.[25]

However, neither Anton Rubinstein nor César Cui thought his graduation work, a cantata on Schiller's 'Ode to Joy', was any good.

Tchaikovsky then moved to Moscow, where Nicholas Rubinstein founded the Conservatoire. He moved in with Rubinstein, who was, like him, a heavy drinker. Moscow, a city where food and drink consumption was prodigious,[29] was an intellectual backwater and relatively provincial compared to St Petersburg. Its literary evenings consisted of 'a whole crowd of deep thinkers who, having arrived at the age of twenty, had managed to experience everything, feel everything, and bore everyone'.[30]

When the highly successful Serov turned down the professorship of harmony, the post was offered to Tchaikovsky. 'Gradually I am beginning even to look like a professor', he wrote.[31] He worked very hard; he composed, taught and started conducting. He helped draw up a lengthy memorandum on the organisation of the Conservatoire.* He worked on his First Symphony, day and night, until he virtually had a nervous breakdown. He showed it to Anton Rubinstein and to his professor in St Petersburg, but they rejected it, although when it was first performed in 1868, it was well received.

Tchaikovsky then wrote a festival overture on the Danish National Anthem for Princess Dagmar's marriage to the Tsarevitch; he revised the First Symphony and wrote the folk opera, *The Voyevoda*, which he later described as 'beyond doubt, a very bad opera'.[32] Mily Balakirev suggested he should write an overture on Romeo and Juliet; but on the whole, Tchaikovsky kept a distance from Balakirev and the other members of the Five, while remaining on fairly good terms with them.

Kamenka

Although Tchaikovsky lived with Rubinstein, he had no fixed base of his own. He would go on extended visits to friends, such as his louche school friend Prince Galitzine, who had an estate near Kharkov, about 460 miles from Moscow. Nicholas Kondratyev, another friend with whom Tchaikovsky stayed, also lived in the Kharkov area. He often stayed near Kiev with his pupil Vladimir Shilovsky, the stepson of the repertory director of the Moscow Imperial Theatres. Soon, however, his preference for the

* Eventually, the Conservatoire moved into its impressive building just up from the Kremlin, nowadays near the Tass Press Agency building.

summer months would be to stay at the home of his sister Sasha Davidova in Kamenka, a beautiful village in the Ukraine.*[34] (See page 641.)

Sasha had met Lev Davidov in Kiev and they were married in November 1860. For Major-General Tchaikovsky, this was a good connection for his daughter, even though Lev was actually only an employee of the family: Lev was regarded in law as illegitimate, having been born in Siberia when his father was in exile there, following the Decembrist uprising of 1825.

Kamenka is about 150 miles to the south of Kiev, a journey which takes about three hours by car today. Although Tchaikovsky could take the train, the journey must have been tedious and tiresome: Kiev itself is over 550 miles from Moscow and 800 miles from St Petersburg. Once there, however, Tchaikovsky would meander in the woods and fields; he would wander along the gently flowing Tyasmin river, with its granite cliffs which inspired Pushkin who stayed there when the Decembrists were hatching their plot. Tchaikovsky would pick violets and lily-of-the-valley; he would join the family in boating parties to Pushkin's Rock, go to the house in the woods to play games, or drive into the nearby town in the family landau.** He visited a village fair, and was inspired by the folksong on which the Andante Cantabile in the first string quartet is based, and which moved Tolstoy to tears when he heard it for the first time. He wrote an early version of *Swan Lake* for the children.[36]

The Davidovs' house, in the woods above the river, is elegant but not large. So they built another two-roomed cottage where Tchaikovsky could be alone and play his upright piano in peace. He would go up to the big house for certain meals, to take tea, and to play party games, especially a form of whist. He improved his English with Miss Eastwood, the family governess.[37]

Although there was continuing unrest in the countryside after the Emancipation of the Serfs, and major outbreaks of disorder in Kiev province between 1875 and 1878, the Davidovs were one of the very few

* Liszt's last public recital for money was in nearby Elisavetgrad, when he was aged 35.[33]

** The Davidov estate is largely flat arable land, part of the bread-basket of Russia, so murderously plundered by Stalin in the 1930s, and fought over by the Germans in the Second World War. In 1844, Kamenka had a sugar refinery, and later a cloth mill and brick factory. In 1880, it had 482 homesteads, 2 Orthodox churches, 1 synagogue, 3 schools, 8 post stations, 32 small shops and 2 windmills. It also seems to have had a factory making matches.[35]

enlightened families, and one does not hear of any trouble on their estate.

Although enlightened, Sasha's family were by no means straightforward. Tchaikovsky was horrified when his niece Tanya and the music teacher got up to all sorts of hanky-panky under a rug in the carriage. 'I have always lived exclusively among women who were beyond reproach', he wrote somewhat sententiously.[38] The girl then started taking morphine. She was rushed off to Paris by her uncle Modeste on the pretext of getting a cure for her drug taking, but actually to have a baby. The child Georges was fetched back from Paris by Tchaikovsky, and was adopted by his brother Nicholas and his wife Olga. All this was kept secret, and it would appear that Sasha knew nothing about the baby.[39] Tanya, still on drugs, soon afterwards dropped dead at a masked ball in St Petersburg.[40]

That was all later. In the mid-60s, Tchaikovsky's family tried unsuccessfully to marry him off to Sasha's sister-in-law, Vera. In 1868, he told his father that he was engaged to the virtuoso singer Desirée Artôt, who was a pupil of the international mezzo-soprano Pauline Viardot.[41] But this came to nothing, because Desirée's mother thought him too young, and she herself wanted to continue her career; she went off and married a Spanish baritone. Vera, however, Tchaikovsky could not avoid at Kamenka, where he found himself fending off her advances on many occasions. On one day, he wrote cruelly in his diary: 'all that she recalls is to me personally repulsive'.[42]

Tchaikovsky preferred boys.[43] Sometimes he sought rent-boys in the back streets of cities, a boy singer in Florence, a black youth in Paris,* or Nazar, the valet of his homosexual brother Modeste. He also had his regulars, particularly his own valet Alexei (Alyosha), who accompanied him on his travels. Alexei was drafted into the army when universal conscription was introduced.[45] Tchaikovsky would hang around the barracks in the vain hope of an hour or two when Alexei came off duty; and he even agreed to take part in the musical soirées of the commanding officer's wife in order to see him.

His greatest and most enduring love, however, was Sasha's son, his nephew, Vladimir Lvovich Davidov, who was called 'Bob'. Tchaikovsky fell in love with 'my marvellous incomparable Bob' when staying at Kamenka, at a time when Bob was aged thirteen.[46] 'A strange thing: I am terribly

* At the turn of the century Le Cuziat's male brothel, to be found at 11 rue de l'Arcade, was frequented by Proust, the novelist.[44]

reluctant to go away from here', he wrote in his diary, 'I think it's all on account of Bob.'[47]

Tchaikovsky's affairs sometimes ended tragically. His fifteen-year-old pupil Eduard Zak committed suicide;[48] and a young artillery officer Vanya Verinovsky, whom he met in Tiflis, Georgia in 1886, also committed suicide soon after Tchaikovsky departed.[49] Bob, 'a hundred times divine',[50] committed suicide in the early 20th century.

Tchaikovsky himself had some deep sense of guilt.[51] He is neither the first nor the last to note his sexual urges in his diaries with a symbol: in his case, 'Z' seems to have been used for that purpose.* Gladstone, the British Prime Minister, who had an interest in 'rescuing' prostitutes, used a symbol, a whip, in his diaries to signify, one presumes, his activities.[53]

In 1876, Tchaikovsky wrote to Modeste that he thought that Sasha 'guessed everything and that she forgives everything'.[54] However, it seems unlikely that, in that era, a woman who married at eighteen would really have been so worldly-wise. In England, for example, until women worked alongside men in the services during the First World War, homosexuality was rarely mentioned in mixed society. Most women would not recognise it for what it was. Oscar Wilde's wife did not suspect her husband until the year he was brought down, when she returned home unexpectedly.[55] In Tchaikovsky's time, no one thought it 'odd' if a 'toff' took an 'interest' in some working-class man or lad.[56]

Homosexuality was quite common at the time, and it was rife in the tsar's entourage. The story of Oscar Wilde illustrates the extent of it in London. After Wilde was jailed, the aristocratic and leisured classes seemed to prefer Paris, or even Nice out of season, to London where the police might act with such unexpected vigour: 'Never was Paris so crowded with members of the English governing classes; here was to be seen a famous ex-Minister; there the fine face of the president of a Royal Society; at one table at the Café de la Paix, a millionaire recently ennobled and celebrated for his exquisite taste in art; opposite to him, a famous general.'**[57]

* It has been suggested that Z was a sign of misanthropic anger about those around him.[52]

** In the 20th century, there was less need for discretion. Francis Poulenc (1899–1963) overtly enjoyed a series of lovers from varied backgrounds, a painter, a chauffeur, a travelling salesman, a junior executive at Citroën, a colonial infantryman. These were apart from nocturnal adventures in the Paris pissoirs, picking up 'peasants' from the countryside and a young clergyman in Boston. He also sired a daughter on a relative of one of his lovers and proposed 'marriage' to a

The Rolling Stone

In 1871 Tchaikovsky moved from Nicholas Rubinstein's house into a small flat of his own. His domestic life continued to be lonely, so he was usually on the move. He went gambling with Rubinstein in Wiesbaden. He went several times to Paris. In 1870, he went on an exhausting journey, St Petersburg to Paris non-stop, in order to visit his friend Shilovsky, who was ill. After three days, they left together for a sanatorium town near Wiesbaden, but were driven out of there by the onset of the Franco-Prussian War; they went to Interlaken in Switzerland for six weeks and then on to Vienna via Munich.

He continued to compose. His Second Symphony was a great success in Moscow in early 1873. Then he wrote the incidental music for the *Snow Maiden*. Grand Duchess Elena Pavlovna offered prizes for the best two settings of an opera based on Gogol's *Christmas Eve*. So, Tchaikovsky wrote *Vakula the Smith*. He confused the entry dates, and submitted it a year too soon; he then caused annoyance when he wanted it performed early. He eventually won the prize.

The First Piano Concerto, one of 'the most popular and frequently-heard pieces of music ever written',[59] was dedicated to Hans von Bülow, who had written a very complimentary article about Tchaikovsky in an Augsburg newspaper. Bülow gave its first performance in Boston. Tchaikovsky got the news of its success by a cablegram, thought to be the first ever between Boston and Moscow.[60] He revised it and the later version, not the earlier, contains the familiar big chords. He received a commission to write a ballet from the Directorate of Imperial Ballet. *Swan Lake* was first performed in 1877, but it was not a success and no new production was ever mounted in his lifetime.

In Paris, he got to know Saint-Saëns. He heard *Carmen*, an event which he said changed his life. In his capacity as a music critic, he visited the 1876 first full performance of *The Ring* at Bayreuth. He remarked to his brother Modeste: 'as music, it is unbelievable chaos, through which there flash from time to time remarkably beautiful and striking details'. He also said: 'It may be that the Nibelungen is a great masterpiece, but there surely was not anything more boring or long winded than this interminable thing.'[61]

childhood girlfriend of whom he was deeply fond. He found time to write much light, charming music and graceful melodies, and more serious works besides (see page 799).[58]

He did eventually concede that *The Ring* was 'one of the most significant events in the history of Art'.[62] In Bayreuth, he met Liszt and Wagner, and read Dante's *Divine Comedy*, which inspired him to write the symphonic fantasy *Francesca di Rimini.*

Around him, events involving Russia and Turkey were unfolding, which even Tchaikovsky could not miss. In mid-1876, when Turkish irregulars destroyed 60 villages in Bulgaria, 1,200 people were burnt alive in their village church. There was outrage in Europe; and in England, Gladstone wrote a pamphlet in which he advocated expulsion of the Turks, 'bag and baggage from the continent they have too long profaned'.[63] Serbia and Montenegro declared war on Turkey. 'Everything that the idle crowd usually does to kill time was now being done for the benefit of the Slavs. Balls, concerts, dinners, matches, ladies' gowns, beer, inns – everything bore evidence of the public sympathy for the Slavs.' Thus wrote Tolstoy, who sent Vronsky, the hero of his novel *Anna Karenina*, away to fight in Serbia.[64] Russia even experienced her first 'commercial newspaper boom'.

Tchaikovsky's contribution to the war effort was to write the 'Slavonic March', for a charity concert in aid of Serb soldiers. An equivalent of 'Land of Hope and Glory', it was written in five days in the first week of October. It was so well received at the performance in November 1876 that there had to be a complete encore. In his correspondence Tchaikovsky had written: 'It is frightening but also pleasing that our beloved country is ready at last to give proof of her character.'[65]

Tchaikovsky saw the less attractive aspects of war when travelling on a train full of young soldiers: there were emotional scenes at every station, as the soldiers parted from their mothers and wives. He was distressed by seeing military trains with soldiers conveyed like sheep, for days on end: a reserve regiment had been travelling for nine days, with nothing to eat but bread. There was a train crash involving a military and a goods train. And he came across a hospital train full of typhoid victims. In Venice, he was annoyed by the newspaper vendors shouting out 'Turkish Victory'.[66]

The Russians eventually defeated the Turks, but the resulting treaty was felt by the British to upset the balance of power in Europe. The attitude was expressed in the music hall ditty, 'We don't want to fight, but, by Jingo, if we do, we've got the men, we've got the ships and we've got the money too'.[67] The treaty was then referred to a European Congress at Berlin, at which Russia was forced to give up many of the fruits of its victory, a severe blow to the prestige of the regime. The British were content: Disraeli, the Prime Minister, returned from Berlin with 'Peace with Honour'.*

Madame von Meck

A number of women had a considerable influence on Tchaikovsky's life: his mother, his nurse, his sister and Desirée Artôt. Now, around May 1877, about the time when he was working on the Fourth Symphony, two ladies hit him like bolts from the blue: his patroness and source of regular financial support, Nadezhda von Meck, and his wife Antonina Ivanovna Milyukova.

Madame von Meck was nine years older than Tchaikovsky. Her husband had died in the previous year, leaving her with a large family of more than ten surviving children. He had started as an engineer on the Moscow–Warsaw railway and then set up his own railway construction business, which benefited from large subsidies from the government. There had been a considerable railway boom: in the years between 1866 and 1875, almost four times as much track had been constructed as in all previous years.[69] Madame von Meck was extremely rich.[70]

She had heard Tchaikovsky's symphonic fantasia *The Tempest*. At the suggestion of one of his pupils, who had a job accompanying her on the violin, she wrote to Tchaikovsky to ask him to write a piece for her which would convey the impression of a broken heart. He replied that she would have to wait, adding, testily: 'I trust you would never imagine that I would undertake any musical work purely for the sake of the 100 rouble note at the end of it.'[71] At the same time, he asked her for money, and told her that he was working on a symphony. When she sent money, he sent her his photograph. For the next fourteen years, she provided him with financial independence and some crucial moral support. There was an odd condition: she did not want to meet him in person. 'The more fascinating you are to me,' she said, 'the more afraid I am of making your acquaintance.'[72] Perhaps she feared that the image might shatter.

Five times, Tchaikovsky enjoyed 'unforgettable marvellous days' on her estate, Brailov in the Ukraine.[73] The vast, modern, somewhat featureless

* The Peace lasted nearly 50 years. This phrase was also used by Neville Chamberlain when returning from Munich just before the outbreak of the Second World War: 'This is the second time that there has come back from Germany to Downing Street peace with honour. I believe it is peace for our time.'[68]

house, with around 150 rooms, stands on a slight hill above a river, on the other side of which is a nunnery; below the house is also an attractive lake with ducks and geese. Itineraries were arranged so that Tchaikovsky and Madame von Meck did not meet, although, on one unfortunate occasion, much to their confusion, they bumped into each other when walking in the woods: nothing was said; he just raised his hat.*[74]

On another occasion, she provided accommodation for him in Florence; he was supplied with a new grand piano, books, Russian newspapers and his favourite cigarettes. She stayed nearby. They wrote to each other daily, and, on her walks, she would stop outside his window: 'on the dot of eleven-thirty, she walks past and peers into my window, trying to catch sight of me … not succeeding because of her short-sightedness. But I can see her perfectly. Apart from this, we saw each other once at the theatre.'[75]

Their families met. Indeed Sasha's daughter Anne married Madame von Meck's second son in 1884. Tchaikovsky attended the wedding, but Madame von Meck did not.

In an improbable conjunction of stars, in summer 1880, Debussy came to join the von Meck household, but near Moscow, and not at Brailov. Nadezhda von Meck and Debussy played piano arrangements of Tchaikovsky's Fourth Symphony together.[76]

Marriage

In the first few months of 1877, Tchaikovsky worked on the highly emotional Fourth Symphony. He offered to dedicate it to Madame von Meck, and asked her for a loan of 3,000 roubles. Then, in April, another lady suddenly appeared on the scene.

Tchaikovsky knew that it might be sensible to get married: 'I seek marriage or some sort of public involvement with a woman so as to shut the mouths of assorted contemptible creatures whose opinion means nothing to me, but who are in a position to cause distress to those near to me.'[77] But his letter to Modeste continued: 'I won't do anything suddenly or without careful thought … if I do in fact get involved with a woman, I will be very circumspect about it.' This he signally failed to be.[78]

* Brailov is nowhere near Kamenka. However, it is less than 40 miles from Liszt's mistress' (Princess Carolyne) charming house at Voronovytsia. By the time Mme von Meck lived there, Brailov was accessible by train (over 700 miles from Moscow); Voronovytsia, in Liszt's time, was not.

Out of the blue, he received a love letter from one Antonina Milyukova. She said that she had met him at the Conservatoire, although up to then she had been content to love him from afar. She was 28, and had been a seamstress before becoming a music student. Two years before this, she had dropped out of the Conservatoire, probably from lack of both talent and money.[79]

Tchaikovsky took no notice. He then got another letter from her threatening suicide.[80] He visited Milyukova on 20 May, and said that he could never love her.

At the time, he was also working on *Eugene Onegin*, an opera based on the poem by Pushkin. In this story, the young Tatiana writes at night to the Byronic Onegin, pouring out her feelings for him; the following day, he callously tells her to forget him. There is a country house dance, with the famous waltz, which is followed by a duel. Many years later, the tables are turned. Tatiana is by then the wife of a retired general. In her residence, there is a magnificent ball, at which the well-known Polonaise is played. Onegin falls in love with Tatiana; but she rejects him.

Tchaikovsky had become totally involved with these characters: 'I am in love with the character of Tatiana', he wrote.[81] Mixing fact with fiction, he feared that, in rejecting Milyukova, he had acted rather like Onegin did in callously rejecting Tatiana. Events in the real world then moved ahead with astonishing speed. He went back to Milyukova; he seems to have told her about his irritability, moodiness, anti-social nature and uncertain financial circumstances. Then, amazingly, he asked her whether she wanted to be his wife. She immediately accepted the offer.

He told nobody. At the end of May, he went on a brief holiday and, a week later, had finished the part of the opera which deals with Tatiana's impassioned letter. Around three weeks later, having sketched out the greater part of the opera, he wrote to his father and his brother Anatole to tell them about his forthcoming marriage. His father was delighted. Tchaikovsky did not write to Modeste or Sasha, whom he only told once he was married. Also, after the marriage, he wrote to Madame von Meck explaining that 'No man can escape his destiny', as he was to discover.[82]

On 18 July, only eight weeks after they had first met, the ill-matched couple were married at St George's Church by the Professor of the History of Church Music at the Conservatoire (see colour plate 29). After the service, Tchaikovsky went straight back to his bachelor apartment, having left his brother Anatole to welcome his bride to the reception at the Hermitage Hotel.

The happy couple met at 7 pm at the railway station in order to take the train to St Petersburg. Tchaikovsky felt obliged to talk to Antonina for the 60 miles to Klin. At the second stop, a prince, who was later to attract the sobriquet 'Prince of Sodom and citizen of Gomorrah',[83] got into the train. He managed to calm Tchaikovsky down such that, having returned to his wife, he slept like a log.

In St Petersburg, they spent the first evening at a concert and then went back to the Europa Hotel. Antonina became very upset about something; again he had to calm her down, take his draught of valerian and go to sleep. But first, he had to make clear the nature of their relationship, which was to be platonic. Five days after the wedding, he wrote to Anatole: 'Physically my wife has become totally repugnant to me ... yesterday morning, while she was taking a bath, I went to mass at St Isaac's Cathedral. I had an urgent need to pray.'[84] The bridal couple then returned to Moscow where Tchaikovsky sought refuge in the bottle.

Three weeks after their marriage, he fled to Kiev on his way to Kamenka, having told everyone that he had gone to take the cure in the Caucasus. He wrote to Madame von Meck in late August that his wife was 'repellent' to him.[85] It seems that Antonina was a great talker and she particularly upset him by telling stories about her previous lovers.

In September, at the start of term, he had to return to Moscow and his wife. He found it impossible to work. On one of his evening walks wandering through the back streets, he waded into the Moskva river hoping to die: he wrote on the score of the Fourth Symphony: 'In the event of my death. Deliver this to Madame von Meck.'[86] However, he did not drown or die of pneumonia. He cabled Anatole asking him to telegram as if from the conductor of the St Petersburg Opera summoning him to St Petersburg. When Tchaikovsky got there, he collapsed for 48 hours. The doctor advised him never to see his wife. When Anatole and Nicholas Rubinstein broke the news to Antonina, she was very calm, and said that for Tchaikovsky she would 'endure anything'; after Rubinstein left, she blithely told Anatole: 'I never expected I'd have Rubinstein drinking tea with me today.'[87]

Sasha subsequently invited Antonina to stay; but then she would not leave and Anatole had to come and take her away. Antonina agreed to a divorce, which would have to be on the grounds of adultery, but then changed her mind. She wanted an allowance of 100 roubles a month. She settled for a lump sum of 10,000 roubles, provided Tchaikovsky would also pay off her debts.[88] Fortunately, Madame von Meck provided the cash.*

Tchaikovsky wrote to Madame von Meck, hardly a disinterested party, about his wife: 'her head and her heart are both completely empty', he said, 'never once did she show the least interest in my work'.[90] Madame von Meck told him not to take any notice of her. Anatole whisked Tchaikovsky off to Switzerland, where he was joined by her protégé, the handsome young Kotek, a pupil of the violin virtuoso Joachim. Tchaikovsky wrote the Violin Concerto.**

Tchaikovsky resigned from the Moscow Conservatoire: 'My goodness! What bliss it is to be free and not to have to correct sixty harmony and orchestration exercises every day!'[92] He refused an appointment in St Petersburg. He was, however, deeply unhappy: 'I seem to sail between the devil and the deep blue sea, having at the same time an indescribable repugnance toward making acquaintances, and yet a feeling of depression in solitude.'[93] But there was an occasional glimmer. At New Year 1880, he looked back at the previous year and said: 'I can honestly say that throughout the year I have enjoyed a sense of unclouded well being and have been happy', adding, however, 'in so far as happiness is possible.'[94]

Increasing Political Unrest

The political situation in Russia was gradually cooking up. The countryside was relatively quiet, although peasants were still being flogged and sent to Siberia for minor protests, even for questioning the activities of some bureaucrats. In the middle of the 1870s, students, teachers, lawyers, physicians, officers and some conscience-stricken noblemen 'went to the people' in order to enlighten the peasants about the possibility of change.[95] But the few peasants who understood what these missionaries were about suspected their motives, and the police arrested them.[96]

The main political activity developed in the towns. The urban population

* Antonina reneged on the deal: she took a lover and had a child, the first of several; she continued to pester Tchaikovsky for money; he bequeathed her an annual pension of 1,200 roubles; she spent her last two decades in a lunatic asylum, and died in 1917.[89]

** Although finished in March 1878, the Violin Concerto was not actually performed until 1881. Its dedicatee, Leopold Auer, thought it too difficult.[91]

was growing fast: Moscow roughly tripled in size between 1846 and 1897. In May 1870, there was a strike of textile workers in St Petersburg. Six and a half years later, there was the first overtly political demonstration there, with the red flag appearing. The governor-general, who had ordered the flogging of a demonstrator for failing to be deferential, was nearly assassinated in early 1878, a fate which befell the security chief seven months later. Fifty-three strikes took place in 1878, 60 in 1879. The first relatively stable underground organisation, Land and Liberty, was formed; out of this came the People's Will, which was dedicated to assassinating the Tsar.[97]

Tchaikovsky described the situation in one of his many letters to Madame von Meck: 'We are living through dreadful times and when you start to think about what is going on it becomes frightening ... Happy is the man for whom the world of Art is a refuge from the contemplation of this melancholy scene.'[98] He said that people felt 'as if they were all walking on top of a volcano which was about to burst open and erupt ... We are ruled by a kind agreeable man whom nature has endowed with little in the way of brains, who is badly educated, and is, in short, ill fitted to take into his feeble hands the shattered mechanism of government.'[99]

Tsar Alexander was keen to make concessions, and favoured the progressives, partly because they were prepared to tolerate his long affair with his mistress, whom he married after the tsarina died in 1880. Equally, he was capable of profligate extravagance: he sent a special train to the Russian border to meet Offenbach's *prima donna* Hortense Schneider when she visited St Petersburg.[100]

There had been several attempts to assassinate the Tsar.* Terrorists attempted to blow up the imperial train, and the dining room in the Winter Palace. The People's Will, led by a governor's daughter, eventually got the tsar on 13 March 1881. Ironically, this happened on the day that he signed Acts implementing some financial and local government reforms. After taking exercise in the Riding School, he made his way back to the Winter Palace. The first bomb missed, but, as he stepped out of his carriage to inspect the damage, he was killed by another one. The terrorists were publicly hanged a month later.[102]

At the time of the assassination, Tchaikovsky was in Italy with the dead tsar's nephew, Grand Duke Konstantin Romanov, a poet who used the *nom*

* In the mid-1860s, Shostakovich's grandfather was implicated in one and was exiled to Siberia.[101]

de plume KR, and who was almost certainly a homosexual. Tchaikovsky had earlier turned down the young grand duke's wild scheme for them to go together on a three-year world tour. But they did meet up in Rome at this time; Tchaikovsky accompanied him to Naples. Once the bad news came through, the grand duke had to rush back to St Petersburg.[103]

The new tsar, Alexander III, guided by his tutor, the Procurator of the Holy Synod, wanted to turn the clock back. There were tough emergency measures: the universities were disciplined, censorship was tightened, land captains were sent to control the peasantry. The limited arrangements which had been introduced for local government were phased out. For a time, these measures kept the revolutionaries at bay. As tension increased, the minister of the interior drew attention to the presence of alien forces. There were periodic pogroms of Jews in the south and west; ten years later, Jews resident illegally in Moscow were expelled.[104]

Tchaikovsky's creativity had tailed off, following his marriage. He was still a troubled spirit, still constantly on the move, still travelling far afield. He went several times to Tiflis to see Anatole. He wrote *Capriccio Italien* in Italy in 1880. He rushed to Paris where Nicholas Rubinstein was dying, but failed to get there in time. He travelled around with Modeste, who was a bit of a drifter.

In Paris and Berlin, he enjoyed going to the theatre or cruising the homosexual meeting places. 'Society put up with a great deal that was illegal, and sometimes did so knowingly. Countenancing illegality did not amount to sanctioning it, however, and the atmosphere could change at any time.'[105] Unlike Wilde, Tchaikovsky did not have 'to pick his way among blackmailing boys and furious fathers',[106] although he seems to have been indiscreet and taken considerable risks. On one occasion in Paris, he recorded: 'Could not sleep. Went out. The incident at the coiffeurs, my rage. Terrible drunkenness in various places.'[107]

Tchaikovsky did not enjoy travel. He wrote: 'I suffer from a disease which the Germans call railway fever. For several days before the journey, I always fuss about and get bothered, and all because I hate travelling in a crowded train with people who either stare at you or talk to you.'[108] He had some typical travelling experiences: he stayed in flea-ridden hotel bedrooms; he was shunted in a snowstorm into a railway siding at Dijon where the carriage was forgotten. 'Crowded train. Pullman car. A fat repulsive lady, an attractive officer landowner; an old Greek, etc. Slept', he recorded in his diary.[109]

To get to Tiflis, on one occasion, he travelled down the Volga to Astrakhan, then by sea to Baku, and onwards by train. In Baku, he visited the oil sites which by the end of the century would raise Russia to second place in world petroleum production.[110] No doubt, as he travelled down the Volga in his steamboat, he saw the barge haulers struggling to pull along the barges.[111]

Between 1878 and 1884, he composed few important pieces. The Piano Trio, stimulated by Rubinstein's death, and *Manfred* were the only exceptions. The *Serenade for Strings* and the *1812 Overture* were written at much the same time. Of the *1812*, written for the Moscow Exhibition, he said, 'The overture will be very loud and noisy, but I wrote it without warmth or love, and so it will probably not have any artistic merit.'[112]

Settling in Klin

In 1885, he decided at last that he had to settle down: 'Somehow or other I must have a home; it is becoming odd and barbaric to live like a planet in orbit. Where is my home to be?'[113] He needed calm and quiet surroundings in which he could work. He first rented a house in Maidanovo, a mile from Klin, which is about 60 miles from Moscow. Apart from its silver birch trees and its stream, it is hardly an inspiring place, but Tchaikovsky was not surrounded by the concrete blocks of flats and factories which oppress the modern visitor.*

At Maidanovo, Tchaikovsky would take an afternoon walk down by the river or into the forest; then he would jot down ideas in notebooks. Unlike in Kamenka, where he was miles from anywhere, here he was distracted by Muscovites coming to their dachas for their summer holidays, and also by the beggar boys and 'a painter; a clerk; a man whose children were burnt; women; old men etc. etc.'[115] In the winter, he was concerned for the local people and their circumstances. 'The cottages in the local village are wretched, small and dark', he wrote. 'They have to live in there, cramped and gloomy, for eight months.' He added: 'It is pitiful to see the children, who are condemned to live both mentally and physically in constant, stifling gloom.'[116] He contacted the village elder and started a local school for which he provided funds.

* Maidanovo is now a cluster of very run-down blocks of flats, separated by a mud road. Klin is now graced by a US-branded fast-food outlet and a statue of Karl Marx.[114]

After three years, Tchaikovsky moved to another place a couple of miles away, Frolovskoe. Set in the pleasant wooded valley of the Sestra river, this was more like Kamenka; it was insulated from the interruptions at Klin. However, he was horrified when he found that 'all the woods, literally all, have been cut down, and they are now busy cutting down what is left. There is nowhere to go for a walk.'[117] He returned to Maidanovo in 1891 for a year, before moving finally to his last home, which was conveniently close to the town, its railway station and amenities.

This last house was a two-storey, grey, wooden building set in its own grounds, close to the Klin–Moscow road.* Here, in an atmosphere scented with burning perfume, he would play piano reductions of big works and compose. He would travel into Moscow by express train, be taken around Moscow in a phaeton, visit his publisher Jurgenson, have lunch or go on binges with his friends. He once raged at a man in the train who had the temerity to point out that he was in a no-smoking compartment. Sensibly, he took a flat in Moscow for the winter.[118]

In these years, he wrote a succession of works with which we are so familiar, such as the Fifth Symphony, *Sleeping Beauty*, *The Queen of Spades*, the *Nutcracker* (which includes the 'Dance of the Sugar Plum Fairy') and the Third Piano Concerto.

He was by now recognised internationally: his works were played all over Europe and America. But all was not well: he was stung by the Tsar's lukewarm 'Very nice' when he attended the première of *Sleeping Beauty*: Tchaikovsky's reaction uses five exclamation marks where today we might use asterisks: '!!!!!. His Majesty treated me very haughtily. God bless him.'[119]

Another disappointment arose in 1890, when he was in Tiflis staying with Anatole. He had a letter from Madame von Meck saying that she could not afford to continue the annuity which she had paid him for many years. Some years earlier, she had indicated that her finances were giving her trouble; but, then, when he offered to relieve her of the burden of his annuity, she had replied: 'The sum involved is so paltry beside my million rouble ruin that it really doesn't tip the scales either way.'[120] Even though railway construction was at a low level, it seems that tuberculosis and the

* The house, now a museum, was lived in after his death by Alexei and Modeste. They made substantial alterations. Modeste's room is tastefully decorated with a couple of statutes of nude males.

behaviour of her children, including the one who had married Tchaikovsky's niece, were at the root of her problems.*

At this time, Tchaikovsky was sufficiently successful that the withdrawal of her financial support did not matter much: the annuity represented only about a third of his income.[122] But he was very upset by the rupture, because he had thought that the friendship with Madame von Meck transcended finance. He wrote to his publisher: 'What distresses and troubles me, and, to be frank, is deeply insulting, is not the fact that she doesn't write, but that she has completely stopped taking an interest in me.'[123]

The International Conductor in the USA

Soon after settling in the Klin area, Tchaikovsky took up conducting seriously. 'I had never imagined what a profound, powerful, indescribable pleasure a conductor feels when he stands at the head of a fine orchestra', he said.[124] So his life at Klin became punctuated with conducting tours. He travelled relentlessly, although he always wanted to get home as quickly as possible.

His tours took him to London and New York. He had some difficulty with the English language and customs, even though, in the early 1880s, he had started learning English so that he could read Shakespeare, Dickens and Thackeray in the original. The foreigner banging on the doors to get into St James' Hall in London, saying 'Tchaikovsky', was told several times to go away because all the seats were sold. When rehearsing the finale of the Fourth Symphony, he wanted more brio and could only shout, 'Vodka, more Vodka'.[125]

Tchaikovsky's visit to New York was marred by hearing suddenly and unexpectedly about the death of Sasha shortly before he left to cross the Atlantic. But, even for the depressed composer, there would have been something thrilling about going to the New World in that period of immense change which followed the end of the Civil War.** Twenty million immigrants poured in during the last three decades of the century.

* Railway construction, an important indicator of prosperity and economic activity, dropped down to just over 2,000 miles in 1881–5 and to just below 1,900 miles in 1886–90. But then it picked up; in the final decade of the century over 14,100 miles of track were constructed.[121]

** The Civil War in the US, principally about slavery, took place at the time that the serfs were being 'emancipated' in Russia. After the Civil War, the reconstruction of the defeated Southern States was complex and unsatisfactory. Carpetbaggers (with a few spare clothes in their carpet-

The length of railtrack increased sevenfold.[127] The country was spanned in May 1869, once Irish labourers building from the East had met up in Utah with Chinese coolies building from California. Cowboys drove their longhorns to the railheads. These were the years of Sitting Bull, Crazy Horse, the Lone Ranger, Hopalong Cassidy and Roy Rogers. The last Gold Rush, to the Black Hills of South Dakota, took place only fifteen years before Tchaikovsky arrived in the USA.[128]

In the cities, this was what Mark Twain, the author of *Tom Sawyer* and *Huckleberry Finn*, called the Gilded Age.* It was the heyday of the boss and the party machine, of votes being delivered in return for fees, of political patronage of grotesque proportions. Vast fortunes were made by industrialists, Vanderbilt, Stanford and Gould in railroading, McCormick in farm machinery, Frick and Morgan in steel, Guggenheim in copper and Rockefeller in oil. It has been said that the cheque which Andrew Carnegie received for the sale of his share in US Steel totalled more than the entire value of the USA in George Washington's day. The rich were ostentatious and 'a brassy vulgarity permeated American life'.[131]

In among all this, Walt Whitman wrote beautiful poetry. And there was a phenomenally rich musical life. The railways had opened up 'a vast land of wonders and virgin audiences' for touring musicians.[132] The Theodore Thomas orchestra of around 50 musicians travelled extensively in the 1870s and 1880s and reached remote places such as Poughkeepsie, New York and Zainesville, Ohio. Wagner's works were particularly popular, and 'a city such as San Francisco took to Verdi with an enthusiasm reserved today for blockbuster movies'.[133] High standards were demanded: the residents of both St Joseph's, Michigan and Burlington, Indiana telegraphed Thomas asking for Beethoven symphonies to replace some of the lighter pieces scheduled. A concert by Anton Rubinstein in New York comprised all the last five sonatas of Beethoven.

There were two aspects of the American musical scene which would have considerable consequences for the future. First of all, it was

bags) rushed south to line their pockets. Alcoholism increased. Evangelists, such as the hymn-writers Dwight Moody, 'the most successful evangelist in the second half of the nineteenth century', and Ira D. Sankey, thrived.[126]

* Ulysses Grant's presidency was a 'carnival of corruption' and scandal.[129] Around 125,000 people controlled at least half the USA's wealth.[130] With the Depression of 1893–4, the Gilded Age came to an abrupt halt.

dominated by immigrant German* influences which were conservative in taste and tradition: thus a view took root that the old 'classical' music of German origin was superior. The other notable feature, which would affect Dvořák and more especially Mahler, was the fact that the musical world was heavily influenced by well-intentioned, but very determined, women. Practically every town of any size had a music club, whose membership was exclusively female. Women called the shots; there was no court or church patronage, so their rich husbands footed the bill.[134]

This was the stage onto which Tchaikovsky stepped. He conducted at the opening festival concerts at the building which became the Carnegie Hall. He was overwhelmed, as modern visitors still can be, by the unalloyed kindness and the hospitality proffered by residents of New York. He enjoyed the food, the dinners at Delmonico's, the impressive mansions on Fifth Avenue and the company of the mega-rich, including of course Carnegie himself. Looking down on the Broadway pavement made him feel dizzy. He visited the music store run by the enormously wealthy Gustav Schirmer. He was shown the Wall Street gold vaults and the Stock Exchange.

'Central Park is magnificent', Tchaikovsky wrote. 'It is remarkable that people of my generation can remember very well when it was nothing but cows grazing in the fields.'**[135] Later he wrote, 'I am besieged by visitors: reporters, composers, librettists, and, above all, absolute mountains of letters from all corners of America asking for autographs, to which I reply very conscientiously.'[136] When given a model of the Statue of Liberty, recently presented to New York by the French, he wondered whether he would be allowed to take it into Russia.

He also performed in Washington, a city 'literally drowned in the luxuriant foliage of chestnut, acacia, oak and maple trees'.[137] He toured Philadelphia and Baltimore. During his travels, he went under the Niagara Falls, 'an awe-inspiring sight',[138] although he was disappointed to see that the picking of wild flowers was prohibited.

He travelled back on a new liner, the *Fürst Bismarck*.† He arrived back in St Petersburg eleven days after he left New York.[139]

* In the second half of the century, German immigration rivalled that from Ireland. Twenty-two of the 53 founding members of the New York Philharmonic Society, founded in 1842, were Germans.

** Cows were finally expelled from St James' Park in London in 1885, when the last Milk Fair was held.

† It was on the return leg of its maiden voyage: it had taken only six days and fourteen hours to do the Hamburg–New York run.

Gloom and Death

Tchaikovsky's London visit in summer 1893 preceded his award of an honorary degree from Cambridge University, along with Saint-Saëns. He was surprised at the 'colleges resembling monasteries and the peculiar customs and traditions which retain much from medieval times'.[140] Among those receiving a degree was a maharajah whose clothes delighted Saint-Saëns: 'being the enemy of the commonplace, and of the neuter-tints of our modern garb, I was enchanted', he wrote.[141] But Tchaikovsky got away as soon as he could. London depressed him. 'I have discovered at last what a London fog is', he wrote. 'I could not have imagined one such as we had today at 12.30 in the afternoon: it was absolutely dark, like 8 o'clock in the autumn on a moonless evening in St Petersburg … I feel deep down as if I were sitting in a dark underground prison.'[142]

Following Sasha's death, he had become increasingly gloomy, and aged far beyond his years. He started work on the orchestration of the Sixth Symphony, of which the final movement expresses such deep despair. The first performance was conducted by him in St Petersburg on Saturday 28 October 1893;* on the following day, he named it the *Pathétique Symphony*. The autograph can be seen in the Glinka Museum in Moscow: it is dedicated to Bob; there is a scribble on the top-left-hand corner: 'make sure the publishers note all my alterations'; and the word 'Pathétique' has been added at a different time.

The events of the next few days leading up to his death are very controversial. After the performance, he dined in the Grand Hotel. On the Monday, he wrote a letter to his publisher saying that he would be in Moscow on the following Saturday. It is not certain what he did on the Tuesday. On the morning of Wednesday 1 November, a lawyer, one of his school colleagues, visited him; he went for a walk and then lunched with Vera, Bob's aunt, whom he had so many years earlier refused to marry. He then went to the theatre and afterwards dined in Leiner's restaurant. He ate macaroni, washed down with white wine and mineral water. It seems that he then asked for ordinary water, whereupon the waiter said that there was none boiled. Modeste, with whom he was lodging, arrived just as the

* A few days earlier he had attended a gala performance of Glinka's *Ruslan* in which Stravinsky's father, a bass, sang. Young Igor saw Tchaikovsky in the foyer, a memory which remained with him for ever. Stravinsky was a great admirer of Tchaikovsky's music.[143]

waiter came with the water on the tray. He forbade him to drink it, but Tchaikovsky grabbed the glass and sank the contents.[144]

He would have been well aware of the need for caution. An epidemic of cholera had begun eighteen months earlier: by the time it ran its course in early 1896, about half a million had caught the disease, of which half that number died.[145] But cholera was rarely found among the affluent, precisely because they took the necessary steps to avoid it.

The following day, at lunch, Tchaikovsky left the table complaining of nausea and vomiting. That evening, Dr Lev Bertenson, the royal doctor, was sent for, although he only arrived after 10 pm. His brother Vasily had got there earlier, but Tchaikovsky's case was beyond his expertise.*

The next morning, Friday, Tchaikovsky appeared to be recovering and, by Saturday, his only apparent remaining symptom was insatiable thirst. But, that afternoon, he deteriorated. The doctors persuaded him to undergo a hot bath treatment in order to get the kidneys working. He went into a coma. They called a priest from St Isaac's Cathedral. In the early hours of Monday 6, he died. Fifteen people had gathered round the bedside of the dying man, not counting the priest.

People stood on the stairs and around the entrance to the house. Among those who held requiems beside the open coffin were pupils of the Law School and the choir of the Imperial Russian Opera. One person, emotionally, kissed his head and face. The funeral, on the following Friday, was a state occasion, said to be the biggest funeral St Petersburg has ever seen. He was buried in the Alexander Nevsky cemetery where now lie the remains of the great Russian composers, Cavos, Glinka, all the Five, Serov, Anton Rubinstein and Dargomijsky; and nearby is Dostoyevsky. On the other side of the wall from this necropolis containing the earthly remains of so much talent, busy traffic now roars round a thoroughfare in front of a vast tourist hotel dating from the Soviet era.[146]

Tchaikovsky's last days have been chronicled in some detail, because there are many surprising things about them. There was a complete failure to apply standard cholera sanitary regulations: sheets which had been borrowed for the dying man were returned unwashed. Quickly, there were rumours that Tchaikovsky's death was not simply due to cholera. Two days

* The Bertensons might not have been too familiar with cholera, because it was not prevalent among the class from which they drew their patients.

later, Dr Lev Bertenson felt it necessary to publish an article about his death; this was followed by one by Modeste five days afterwards. The articles go into surprising detail, what Tchaikovsky's stools were like, how his kidneys were functioning. But they are inconsistent about the date of the theatrical scene with the unboiled water.[147]

There has therefore been much speculation about what actually happened, and the sleuths have focused on the events of Tuesday 31 October, which are unaccounted for. This is because, according to one tradition,* there was at some stage a 'Court of Honour' attended by eight alumni of the Law School, convened by an eminent lawyer called Jacobi. The meeting took five hours, after which Tchaikovsky was observed by Mrs Jacobi rushing out of the room, unsteadily, without saying a word. Around this is spun a yarn: Jacobi had been approached by a count, who said that he was about to complain to the tsar that Tchaikovsky had seduced his nephew. Jacobi convened a group of old boys of the school who happened to be in St Petersburg, and they told Tchaikovsky that if he did not commit suicide, they would pass the count's complaint to the tsar. It is then surmised that, on the following day, Jacobi visited Tchaikovsky and gave him some arsenic. This would have resulted in symptoms similar to cholera. The drama in Leiner's restaurant with the glass of water was staged to give the lie.[148]

The death was certainly mysterious. There is such a discrepancy between the stories as written by Bertenson and Modeste that it has even been suggested that Tchaikovsky died 24 hours before the death was announced, and Modeste and Bertenson spent the time clearing up the evidence.[149]

There are alternatives. It is suggested that Tchaikovsky committed suicide because the tsar had now decreed that he should leave the capital.** This followed the discovery that Tchaikovsky had seduced the son of the caretaker of Modeste's apartment block. No, it was the tsar's nephew Konstantin, even his son, who had been seduced. No, he caught cholera from his sexual partners in St Petersburg.[150]

One writer has suggested, surely rightly, that too much attention has been focused on the cause of death: 'let's dig him up, and then perhaps we

* Jacobi's wife told the story to another alumnus, who handed it on.

** The tsar had generally enjoyed Tchaikovsky's music, especially *Onegin*, and had granted the composer a pension for life of 3,000 roubles.

can all rest in peace'.[151] Whichever story the sleuth believes, these events took place just two years before Oscar Wilde read the misspelt card left by the Marquess of Queensberry at the porter's lodge at the Albemarle Club; it was addressed to 'Oscar Wilde, ponce and Somdomite'. Before Wilde was prosecuted, Queensberry informed him: 'I will not prevent your flight, but if you take my son with you, I will shoot you like a dog.'[152]

Although Tchaikovsky was desperately keen to hide his homosexuality, who knows whether potential exposure would have driven him, who seems to have had a particular horror of death,[153] to suicide. After all, even though he was passionately keen on his native Russia, he could have done as Queensberry suggested to Wilde, and escaped abroad, perhaps to Paris; or, perhaps, he could have lain low at Kamenka. Several of the tsar's own relatives and his highest officials were believed to be homosexual, the tsar's brother Grand Duke Sergei, for example.[154]

Tchaikovsky was always exhausted, suffering from back pain, and fearful of old age. Could it be that this lonely, rootless, irascible insomniac and alcoholic committed suicide for no special motive?[155] Perhaps such a tawdry end would seem inconsistent with the beauty and the drama of his music.

Bob

Central-European Nationalists:

Smetana, Dvořák, Janáček and Bartók

CHAPTER 22

When we talk of Italian opera in the 17th and early 18th centuries, and German church music in the 18th, the national label indicates a particular style and genre, that of the country which was culturally dominant at the time. So, there was nothing unusual in Handel, Saxon in origin and English by adoption, being a prolific composer of 'Italian' operas.[1]

But, in the 19th century, we find that individual composers and their music are assigned a specific national identity. Sometimes this is relatively straightforward: certain Russians, as we have seen, purported to compose music which was identifiably Russian. Occasionally, the situation is more complex. Liszt was claimed by the Hungarians, and Chopin was appropriated by the Poles; no matter that Liszt's family was not Magyar and Chopin's was more French than Polish. Precision, after all, never seems too important in politics.

We shall now look at some composers whose nationalist credentials are not in question. Smetana, from Eastern Bohemia, is often called the 'father of Czech music'. Dvořák, whose travels famously took him to the New World, was, according to Janáček, the 'sole representative of Czech music'.[2] It is sometimes suggested that you only have to hear a bar of a work by

Above: SMETANA AND DVOŘÁK

Grieg to know that you are in Norway;[3] and the same applies to Sibelius, except that the terrain is Finnish.

In this chapter, we shall consider the Slavs, the Czech composers, and conclude with Bartók, their neighbour from Hungary, where the people had different and very complex ethnic roots. In the next chapter, we go north, to Scandinavia. First, however, we should consider briefly whether there really is any such thing as Czech music, or Hungarian, Norwegian or Finnish music, other than in the sense of local folk music. And with Smetana, we will soon encounter the emotive issue of spoken language itself, as a manifestation of national culture. Bartók was against his family speaking German,[4] and Janáček was so aggressively Czech that he would not travel on trams where the destination was indicated in German rather than in Czech.[5]

Nationalist Music?

Why is Smetana's opera *The Bartered Bride* regarded as Czech? Is it because the words are in Czech? Or because it describes Bohemian swains and damsels? Or is there some quality in Smetana's music that makes it descriptively Czech? He seems to have thought so. In his suite of symphonic poems called *Má Vlast*, Smetana invites us to follow the Vltava river that flows through Prague, starting at its two small sources, the cold and the warm; he takes us to meet defeated Hussite heroes taking refuge in the mountains.*[7] One of the movements is said to breathe the valleys and streams of Bohemia. Yet what is meant by this? If it were not for the music, the Hussite stronghold at Tábor would today be disappointingly unexceptional. And large tracts of the central Bohemia in which Smetana lived, when he was not in Sweden, are noticeably flat and dull. Even though the modern visitor to Prague may feel worn by the repetition of *Má Vlast* by street musicians (redeemed by excerpts from *Don Giovanni*), nobody could say that any part of a competent performance of it is flat or dull.

We may well wonder whether music can express anything pictorial, let

* Jan Hus, an advocate of Church reform, although lured with the promise of a safe conduct, was burnt as a heretic by the Council of Constance in 1415. This ignited twenty years of religious and rebellious 'Hussite' wars in Bohemia and Moravia. Radical Hussites, centred on Tábor, were eventually defeated in 1434. A prominent opponent of Hus was the Bishop of Litomyšl, Smetana's birthplace. Almost a century after Hus' death, Luther maintained that the Pope, by condemning Hus' views, had thereby condemned the Gospel. The Hussites soon began to represent a symbol of freedom for Czech people.[6]

alone political or nationalist. What did Grieg mean when, excited by the odour of the trawlers berthed in Bergen harbour, he exclaimed: 'in fact, I am sure my music has a taste of codfish in it'?[8] Constant Lambert, the composer and pungent critic in the 1930s, conceded that Richard Strauss, 'the most accomplished master of photographic suggestion in music, can, it is true, suggest a flock of sheep by a bleating on muted trombones, a couple of monks by a modal passage on two bassoons, and a boat on the water by the usual aqueous devices'. 'But', Lambert continued, 'it is highly improbable that, by a combination of the three, he could bring before our eyes a picture of two monks in a barge with a lot of sheep.'[9]

Once one puts aside the few occasions when a composition imitates a specific noise, such as the sound of a lion roaring, birds twittering, a farmyard, the weather or hammering in a forge, what, if anything, can music portray?

Stravinsky took a simple, although extreme, position: 'I consider that music is, by its very nature, powerless to express anything at all, whether a feeling, an attitude of mind, a psychological mood, a phenomenon of nature, etc … if, as is nearly always the case, music appears to express something, this is only an illusion, and not a reality.'[10]

Some might respond, 'speak for yourself, Igor'. Most of us would probably think that, at the very least, the minor key can, with considerable effect, be used to express pain or sadness, the major key to express pleasure, especially where the composer's intention is known in advance, or by means of the words accompanying the music. Some of Bach's music, much of the St Matthew Passion, for example, succeeds in being pictorial. Music can even convey a light sense of humour, as does Haydn in *The Creation*, Strauss when describing Till Eulenspiegel's merry pranks,[11] and Poulenc, many of whose works are often described as 'witty'. When forewarned, we can associate sounds with pictures and ideas: gently flowing music can seem consistent with a pastoral scene. However, it is unlikely that we would think of a pastoral scene every time we hear gently flowing music. We might think of love instead?

Most of us, on reflection, accept that musical expression has its limitations. So, we can understand Beethoven's annotation on the score of his Sixth Symphony: 'Pastoral Symphony, or recollection of country life. *More expression of feeling than painting.*'[12] But even Beethoven's seemingly undemanding claim is not free of contention. Debussy said that music is not the expression of a feeling, *it is the feeling itself*: it 'is a dream from which the veils have been lifted'. He added caustically: 'They want to use it to tell lurid anecdotes, when the newspapers do that perfectly well.'[13]

Given the limitations, and aside from martial music and national anthems, how can we expect the language of music to express as complex a subject as nationalism? One answer might be: by the use of folk music or rhythms associated with folk music and the language. That will not do: *The Bartered Bride* does not contain a single folksong.[14] Sibelius never consciously made use of folksong.[15] Dvořák's dances may sound rustic rather than courtly or ecclesiastical, but it would be a brave person who assigned specific rhythms exclusively to any one European nation state. Accelerate 'Greensleeves' and you might easily imagine you were hearing a Central European gypsy dance, the kind of sound often to be heard in cafés in Paris, Berlin and St Petersburg in the 19th century.[16]

Several great composers, Grieg and Ravel for example, had a deep respect for their local heritage and made explicit use of material drawn from authentic folk tunes.[17] Rimsky-Korsakov composed a string quartet using Russian folk tunes, and Stravinsky quotes some in *The Firebird*.[18] Janáček compiled anthologies of folk music, and Bartók made a systematic study of folk music and its origins.[19]

However, none of the eminent composers would wish their *primary* works to be considered as glorified compilations of folk tunes, making their creators equivalent to handicraft workers weaving baskets and providing delicious cream teas, say, in the Malvern Hills. So, in searching for musical nationalism, we should not place too much emphasis on folk music.

A more probable explanation of musical nationalism is that composers can draw inspiration from their people and the beauty of their beloved country and use that inspiration to develop a personal style.*[20] The beauty and peace of Worcestershire inspired Elgar.[21] Mussorgsky drew on turbulent Russian history for *Boris Godunov* and *Khovanschina*. Grieg looked for inspiration from the spectacularly grand and beautiful Hardanger Fjord (see colour plate 40), which runs into remote country up behind Bergen.**

* The magnetic attraction of a home country is illustrated by Prokofiev, who returned to live permanently in the USSR in 1936 at the height of the purges, a couple of months after the Soviet newspaper *Pravda* had condemned Shostakovich.

** Scenery seemingly can be evocative of music. Here is Grieg's widow walking in the Norwegian countryside of fjord, snow-clad mountains and waterfalls: 'There, in the grass, flowers smile,

The beauty of the changing light, or the full moon, over the lake and trees at Hämeenlinna or Tuusula could easily have inspired Sibelius.

Yet we should not get carried away by this explanation. One expert has said that 'it is the customary confusion, or some might call it the customary trick, of nationalistic art history to designate as national what is purely personal style'.[24] This argument is particularly compelling when we look below the surface: Grieg's best-known works, the Piano Concerto and the *Peer Gynt* music, were written mainly in Copenhagen, Oslo or Bergen. His inspiration derived from the Hardanger landscape died away as quickly as it had arisen: 'The serenity of nature is too cold for me', he wrote. 'It finally occurs to me that the mountains have nothing more to express. I was getting empty-headed by looking at them, and found that it was time to leave.'[25]

Vaughan Williams, having discovered how a film director seemed to be able to manipulate his music to fit any scene, warned: 'You must not be horrified if you find that a passage which you intended to portray the villain's mad revenge has been used by the musical director to illustrate the cats being driven out of the dairy.'[26] As we turn to the lives of Smetana, Dvořák, Janáček, Bartók and the Scandinavian nationalist composers, we should recognise that, whereas music is infinitely expressive, on its own it is not too good at describing concrete, earthly objects or concepts. We should treat the remarks so often made about a piece's national characteristics with an appropriate degree of scepticism. Aside from folk music, the characteristics and the emotions they evoke are often in the ear of the listener, or even just the presenter, little more. A work can affect different audiences in different ways at different times: much depends on what the listener wants, or is conditioned, to hear.

Smetana – Early Years

Bedřich Smetana, known to his family as Fritz, was born on 2 March 1824, a few months after Weber had conducted the 50th performance of *Der Freischütz* in Prague. He was the eleventh child and first surviving son of a reasonably prosperous German-speaking family: the servants would

more numerous and with brighter colours than are seen anywhere else, and with every step Edvard's music sounds in my heart and in my ears.'[22] One expert suggests that Prokofiev's *Classical Symphony* reflects the virginal purity of the Siberian landscape;[23] we may wonder if that occurred to Prokofiev's wife Lina when she was languishing in a labour camp there.

have spoken Czech, which was regarded as low class. Smetana's grandfather was a cooper, a barrel-maker; his father František sold beer to Napoleon's troops, and moved from being a brewer for one member of the nobility to another. At the time of Bedřich's birth, he was working for Count Waldstein in Litomyšl, a colourful town in a relatively colourless part of eastern Bohemia. The Smetanas lived in the ground floor of the brewery opposite the castle, up above the town.[27]

The castle dates from the late 1500s, and was designed in the Spanish style by Italian artists for a noble who wished to please his Spanish wife by providing surroundings that would be familiar to her. The walls are ornately decorated with white pictures etched on black, a process known as *sgraffito.* The castle is particularly notable, however, for its tiny and almost unique baroque theatre built in 1797, which seats, at most, 100 people.[28] There, the count's family held their amateur dramatics; and there, Smetana performed as a boy. He also appeared in the staterooms upstairs, where his father reputedly enjoyed a game of billiards with the count. Smetana learnt music from his father, a keen violinist. He played a piano arrangement of Auber's *La Muette* overture at a concert when only six and a half.[29]

In 1831, the family moved further south into a part of the country in which, some 30 years later, Mahler would be brought up. Later, František bought himself a fine country house, a small château, to which he retired to farm and hunt. There was some friction when Bedřich, intent on his musical career, refused to return and help his father run the estate. František could not afford the cost and eventually had to sell up.*[31]

Smetana's Prague

Bedřich went to a succession of schools including one in Iglau, one in Prague and the Pilsen** high school, where his cousin was a teacher. When he was nineteen, he settled in Prague. The city had recently undergone considerable modernisation: streets had been widened and cobbled, wooden water pipes had been replaced by cast iron ones, tree-lined parks had been laid out. A suspension bridge was built over the river, enabling new areas

* Růžkovy Lhotice is very much the 'big house'. The large village, Čechtice, is over half a mile away. Deep in the countryside, its residents have magnificent views and enjoy farmyard sounds. Smetana's father must have been very disappointed that he was not prepared to help him run it.[30]

** Modern names for the major cities to which reference is made in this chapter are Praha (Prague), Brno (Brünn), Jihlava (Iglau), Olomouc (Olmütz), Plzeň (Pilsen).

to be opened up. The two-horse cabs in the Old Town Square were replaced by lightweight hackney carriages and omnibuses. Stagecoach gave way to paddle steamer and railway. A railway line to Olmütz, the ancient capital of Moravia, was about to be built and, over the following 40 years, Prague became the hub for ten railways, each with many tunnels and viaducts.[32]

There was further progress as the years went by. Between 1863 and 1872, nineteen banks opened. In 1874, the walls of Prague were pulled down, like those in Vienna. The following year, the foundation stone for the completion of St Vitus Cathedral was laid. Wenceslas Square, formerly the Horse Market, was changed into a city boulevard. New schools, hospitals and churches were built. By the 1880s, electricity was installed, as was the telephone. The extent of change in Smetana's lifetime was substantial.

At the time Smetana arrived, there was a vigorous musical life in the city which had seen the first performances of *Don Giovanni* and *La Clemenza di Tito*. The Prague Conservatoire had been founded in 1811. Music was centred on church and theatre. In 1826, the Society for the Perfection of Church Music in Bohemia was formed. Four years later, this was followed by the founding of the Organ School, whose alumni would include Dvořák and Janáček. The focus of Prague's theatrical and operatic life was the small Theatre of the Nobility, the 'Estates Theatre', where *Don Giovanni* was first performed, and where Weber was director between 1813 and 1816. There were high-quality concerts: Liszt, Berlioz, Paganini, Mendelssohn and Clara Schumann performed in Prague in the middle of the century. There was a piano school run by Joseph Proksch, whose teaching methods were among the most modern in Europe.[33]

Smetana took full part in the artists' life in the capital: on one occasion he dressed up as Gluck for the artists' carnival. He attended Proksch's school, with financial assistance from his eventual mother-in-law. At first, Smetana was penniless: his father's financial position precluded him giving his son any support. But he got a job teaching the family of Count Thun, and he composed. His studies with Proksch finished in mid-1847, whereupon he toured as a concert performer.

In August 1848, Smetana set up his own music school on the corner of the Old Town Square, close to the theatre. He had asked Liszt for a loan to help him finance this, but, although Liszt accepted the dedication of Smetana's Opus 1, the loan was not forthcoming. Concerts put on at Smetana's school were highly acclaimed by Prague music lovers. Smetana supplemented his earnings by whiling away the time for the deposed Emperor Ferdinand, who was lodged in Prague Castle.[34]

In the next year, Smetana married Katerina, the daughter of family friends. He had known her since the time when he was at school in Pilsen. Katerina was not robust and showed symptoms of tuberculosis. Three of the Smetanas' four daughters died in infancy. Only Sofie survived.

To Sweden

Prague's 1848 Revolution was preceded by increasing unrest: for example, 1,000 cotton workers demonstrated in the city centre, machines were broken, and there were attacks by railway construction workers on shops belonging to Jewish merchants.[35] The revolution then followed a broadly similar pattern to that in other capital cities. In early June 1848, the liberal democrats met and issued a petition and a manifesto attacking political and national oppression; they proposed constitutional changes. But the participants were divided and there was soon confrontation with the army. Smetana helped to man the barricades and wrote the 'Song of Freedom' and two marches, the 'Marsch der Prager Studenten Legion' and the 'Nationalgarde-Marsch'. But the Habsburg general, Prince Alfred von Windischgrätz, bombarded the city until it capitulated. Martial law was imposed and the defeated residents began ten bleak years.

Around this difficult time, Smetana seems to have become disillusioned with Prague. It is not clear whether he had to leave because the authorities suspected that he was too nationalistic: they would not accept the dedication of the *Triumph-Symphonie*, which he wrote to celebrate the marriage of the Emperor Franz Joseph.[36] In 1856, Smetana went to Sweden for a five-year stay, at first without Katerina. He was recruited as piano teacher by the wife of a rich merchant in Gothenburg, where he also gave recitals and concerts and entered into social life. So many ladies wished to take lessons from him that he found it difficult to cope with the demand.[37] He went back and forth a few times. On the way back to Prague in spring 1859, Katerina died.

Just over a year later, Smetana remarried (see colour plate 37). He took his wife, Bettina, back to Gothenburg, but he did not stay there long: there were nationalistic developments in Prague which attracted him back. At about this time, he started learning to speak Czech. To appreciate the significance of this step, it is necessary briefly to consider the rise of Czech nationalism and the importance of the Czech language. We can then understand why seemingly peripheral matters, such as the building of a National Theatre,* and an interim or 'provisional' theatre, where plays and operas in Czech could be performed, became such an important visible symbol of national emancipation and were so significant for Smetana.

BOHEMIAN NATIONALISM AND THE CZECH LANGUAGE

Bohemian, that is Czech, culture had once been magnificent: Prague University, founded in 1348, had for some time been the only university in central Europe. But, as described in the Prelude to this book, the country was crushed in November 1620 when, following a vacancy in the Habsburg direct line of succession, there was a power struggle in which the Protestants were defeated at the Battle of the White Mountain, just outside Prague (see pages 21–3). The Protestant nominee, Elector Frederick of the Palatinate, fled; the gates of Prague were closed and troops allowed to loot.[38] 'Better a desert than a land full of heretics', the new Habsburg emperor declared.[39] Lands were confiscated and concentrated in the hands of a few powerful nobles: over half of the manorial estates changed hands.[40] By the end of the Thirty Years War, Prague had lost 40 per cent of its pre-war population.

In the following century, Bohemia fared little better. It was the theatre for the wars of Frederick the Great. Subsequently, under the centralisation policies of Empress Maria Theresa and Emperor Joseph II, it became a mere province of the empire, administered from Vienna.** Czech culture was eclipsed by German culture. The German language was made compulsory in schools; all lectures in the University of Prague were required to be delivered in German, except for those conducted in Latin.[42] Talented musicians, such as Stamitz, creator of Mannheim's famous orchestra, and Dussek, celebrated for his piano concertos, went abroad. Reicha went to Paris, where he taught Berlioz, Liszt, Gounod and Franck.

In the 19th century, throughout Europe, the inexorable and growing tide of nationalism† accompanied the pressure for change, then called

* The small Estates Theatre, meanwhile, remained the centre of Prague's theatrical life and *Tannhäuser*, *Lohengrin* and *The Flying Dutchman* were performed there in the 1850s.

**Some writers allude to an analogy in the relationship between England and Ireland.[41]

† Nationalism grew despite pressures towards globalisation similar to those which we experience today. Modern air transport and telecoms had their equivalents in the railways and the telegraph. A leading Czech nationalist sought to explain away the conflict by saying that 'the greater the nations' contacts the more they see, feel and become aware of their national differences'.[43]

'reform'. German nationalism was manifested in a complacent and arrogant sense of cultural dominance. There was a traditional saying that a German will as soon do a good deed to a Slav 'as a snake will warm itself upon ice'.[44] In response, partly as a defence, the Slavs, including the people of Bohemia, created their own forms of nationalism.

The Czech language was a crucial element of Czech nationalism and essential to the survival of Bohemian identity. The language itself became a rallying point, rather like a flag. It was also a means of communicating the traditional values of the nation. In the attempt to mould and uplift the language to reflect modern needs, Smetana's operas had an important part to play.

The language revival developed like one of Rossini's magnificent crescendos. At the start of the 19th century, although the German language was deeply entrenched, Czech was by no means dead. Towards the end of the previous century, some poems in Czech were published, the first Czech newspaper was inaugurated and the professorship of Czech language and literature at Prague University was founded. Major operas were performed in Czech, such as *Don Giovanni*, *The Barber of Seville*, *Der Freischütz* and *La Muette de Portici*. The first opera known for certain to have been composed specifically to a Czech text was in 1826, a simple Singspiel called *The Tinker*; it was composed by a conductor at the Estates Theatre, František Škroup.[45] In 1834, his comic opera, *The Fiddlers' Festival*, had its first performance; one of its songs was used for the Czech national anthem.[46]

It was, however, in the second half of the century that the nationalist movement really took off. It was given a considerable boost in 1860 when the Habsburg emperor issued the so-called October Diploma, which, although primarily directed at Hungary, signalled a U-turn in the repressive policies adopted since the revolutionary time some twelve years earlier: the attempt to impose absolutist rule had failed.[47] Certain of the restrictions imposed after the 1848 Revolution were now removed. Prague civic authorities started doing business in Czech in 1860. From 1862, education in Czech started in all primary schools in Prague. From 1863, the Prague polytechnic was teaching in both Czech and German.

A temporary 'national theatre', called the Provisional Theatre, with a small stage, which could seat 800 but hold almost 1,000 people,[48] was hurriedly constructed in six months, and was opened in 1862. Smetana became conductor of the Czech Choral Society and the first head of the music section of the Artists' Club, both of which were founded at this time;[49] the newly formed Czech physical education society was, to us, of lesser interest.

The German-speaking residents, many of whom were in powerful positions in Vienna, became nervous of being marginalised, and with good cause. Whereas by the end of the 1840s, more than half the people of inner Prague were German-speaking, by the 1880s, the number was less than fourteen per cent. The fact that the language issue would eventually paralyse the Habsburg government was something the nationalists cannot have foreseen. Meanwhile, a German Choir was formed to counterbalance the Czech Choral Society.[50]

There was a hiccup in the mid-1860s. In 1866, Bohemia again became a theatre of war, a reminder, if one was necessary, that it constituted strategically important middle ground dividing the rising Prussian Empire from the declining Habsburg Empire. The Prussians caught the Austrians in a pincer movement at Königgratz, some 40 miles north of Smetana's birthplace. For a time, Prussians occupied Prague, and their departure was followed by considerable economic hardship and unemployment. There was then an outbreak of cholera because the drinking fountains were supplied with untreated water from the river, into which the sewers poured.[51]

When Franz Joseph was crowned emperor of Hungary in 1867, the expectations of the people of Bohemia were raised. This colourful and seemingly great event, in which Liszt played an ostentatious part, was actually a milestone in the dénouement of the Habsburg dynasty: the other provinces within the empire, such as Bohemia, felt that they were entitled to 'a similar deal'.[52] Of course, to prevent the disintegration of the Empire, the authorities in Vienna had to resist demands for this. So, there was no likelihood that the Czechs would be given similar status to Hungary.

But the momentum was relentless. The Czechs held demonstrations. Large numbers of people marched to the White Mountain. Smetana hammered in the foundation stone at the ceremony for the National Theatre. His opera, *Dalibor*, was performed to celebrate this national occasion. But this was followed by a crackdown; martial law was imposed for a time. Although the coronation jewels had been returned from Vienna, the government reneged on a promise to stage a Czech coronation for Franz Joseph, and various constitutional freedoms were not implemented. For the coronation, Smetana had written *Libuše*, an opera about medieval Bohemia; its performance had to be withdrawn.[53]

The tension continued to build up. The Germans in Bohemia became particularly incensed when the government sought to require civil servants to speak both Czech and German. Then, in 1880, the government tried a different tack. German was pronounced the official internal administrative language, but, in their dealings with the public, the authorities were required to make use of the specific language of the peoples they were addressing. Prague University was divided into two universities, the Czech and the German, providing an ideal structure for the student violence which rocked the decade. At the end of the 1880s, the anniversary of the French Revolution incited demonstrations. There was a colossal row when the names of great Czechs carved in the foyer of the new National Museum deliberately omitted the name of Jan Hus; a Habsburg magnate further raised the temperature by declaring that the Hussites were not so much freedom fighters as terrorists. The Germans of course boycotted the colourful National Jubilee Exhibition of 1891, in which Janáček's *Scenes from Moravian Slovakia* were performed. Protest and violence continued, often provoked by seemingly innocuous events: there was a rumpus when the government would not permit street names to be in Czech, and an article in a journal, criticising a nationalist poet, provoked demonstrations which peaked with a massive one on the emperor's birthday in 1893; a state of emergency was declared.

There was another attempt in 1897 at offering equality of status for Czech and German and obliging civil servants throughout Bohemia to master both languages within four years. This proved to be explosive.* The Vienna parliament, the Reichsrat, degenerated into chaos; then when the legislation was suspended, there was chaos in Prague. In less than three years, there were four changes in government, and not a single law was passed. As one would expect, the government eventually tried to solve the problem by pouring in money: it launched a very expensive programme of railway and canal construction.**[56]

* Occasionally, at the micro level, the situation seems to have degenerated into a farce. Janáček was fanatically pro-Czech, and his daughter did not speak German. She thus could not converse with her cousins. Her uncle described family meetings as 'a Babel-like confusion of tongues'.[54]

** The status of the 3 million 'Sudeten' Germans in Czechoslovakia was a significant component of the crisis which preceded Neville Chamberlain's appeasement of Hitler at Munich in 1938.[55]

Both Smetana and Dvořák identified themselves and their compositions with this nationalist movement. By the time Janáček went to study in Vienna for a short time, the movement was rampant.

The Bartered Bride

We go back to the time when Smetana returned from Sweden to Prague. Over the next few years he spent much of his time on concert tours, teaching and doing critiques. He won a prize with a patriotic opera, *The Brandenburgers in Bohemia*, which he conducted at the Provisional Theatre, with considerable success.

He was passed over for the directorship of the Prague Conservatoire in 1865, but in autumn 1866 he became conductor of the Provisional Theatre, where he conducted a wide repertoire and put on subscription concerts.

In that year, he had a breakthrough with *The Bartered Bride*. On 30 May 1866, this was premièred in a two-act version, with spoken narrative. The story of the opera is about jolly village life in Bohemia, with a maiden, a farm lad, a village idiot, a fair, circus troupes and even choruses in praise of beer. There is much local colour. The première was not wholly successful, because it unfortunately coincided with the war between the Prussians and Austrians.[57]

Smetana was instrumental in setting up an opera school in the Theatre. But he encountered considerable opposition. The Prague musical world was divided between those who supported him, and perceived him as a modernist and a Wagnerian, and those who did not. His opponents were those who wanted a Czech opera developed on the lines of Italian opera with the sung voice predominating. One adversary was Jan Nepomuk Mayr, whom Smetana had supplanted as conductor of the Provisional Theatre; another was the music critic Pivoda, the founder of the Prague School of Singing.

Pivoda hoped that his School of Singing would supply the Provisional Theatre with its singers. But when Smetana started looking for soloists outside Prague, Pivoda began a public row, which grew angrier with the years. Pivoda accused Smetana of being an extreme Wagnerian. Mayr joined in the bickering. There was an attempt to oust Smetana, without success.[58]

Poor Health

While this argument was raging, Smetana recorded on 30 April 1874 in his diary that he had an ulcer, although he did not note where it was located; then he recorded that his throat was troubling him. This was followed by a rash in mid-July. Almost certainly, he had caught syphilis.[59]

In late July 1874, Smetana was feeling deaf and giddy. In September, he had to write to his chairman about the 'cruel fate' that had overtaken him. He heard notes at different pitches and said that he had 'a buzzing and tingling in my ears, as if I were standing by a huge waterfall'.[60] Meanwhile, the feud with Pivoda continued. Smetana was accused of accepting an annual salary of 600 florins for only two hours' teaching a week. In fact, he was in increasing financial straits. His former pupil, Eliza Thun, by now married into the aristocratic Kaunitz family, got his pupils together to raise funds with a concert, and an old flame arranged a concert in Gothenburg. Pivoda denounced the fundraising as unnecessary. It was very unpleasant.

As he could not afford to pay his rent, Smetana moved into the forester's lodge at Jabkenice in central Bohemia. The husband of his daughter Sofie was forester to the local landowner, Count Thun.

Smetana did not like the loneliness of the country. Jabkenice is a village deep in the forest, with nothing much else around other than trees. Smetana would have preferred to be in busy Prague. But he kept in touch with developments there, and started a highly productive period of his life, despite recording that 'deafness would be a relatively tolerable condition if only all was quiet in my head'.[61] Most of his masterpieces, operas, string quartets, piano and vocal compositions come from this time. One is particularly popular: *Má Vlast* was given its first performance in 1882. Other works in the last decade were the String Quartet in E minor, the comedy *The Kiss* and *The Secret*.

Smetana had completed the opera *Libuše* just before he began to go deaf. It was performed at the opening of the Czech National Theatre, nine years later, in June 1881. Its first performance was a great personal success, although, by the time of that historic occasion, Smetana was almost stone deaf. Sadly, less than three months later, the new theatre was burnt down. Dvořák took part in the considerable movement to raise the funds to rebuild it.[62] Smetana's *Libuše* was performed at the reopening in 1883.

But, by this time, Smetana was near the ghastly end which Donizetti and so many others had met. He died in the Prague lunatic asylum on 12 May 1884.

Dvořák

In the orchestra of the Provisional Theatre, working under Smetana, and just over seventeen years younger than him, was the viola player, Antonín Dvořák. He was born on 8 September 1841.

Dvořák was the eldest son of an innkeeper and butcher who, from the year of his son's birth, rented an inn called the Engelhardt in Nelahozeves. Located some twenty miles north of Prague, the village had between 400 and 450 inhabitants. Dvořák's birthplace is just below the large square castle, Schloss Mühlhausen an der Moldau.* Next to the dwelling is a tiny church; the railway line is next to that, and then the River Vltava (which, in German, is called the Moldau). The construction of the railway, part of the Prague–Dresden line, provided the basis for Dvořák's lifelong passion, trains. The first trains came through in spring 1850; the line was formally opened by Archduke Albrecht in 1851. One can imagine the thrill for the small boy.

Nelahozeves was reputedly a lively place, like a scene out of *The Bartered Bride*. Furiants and polkas were danced in gaily coloured costumes on the village green after church.[63] The Dvořák family played the fiddle and the zither. Antonín was a clever child; he won a prayer book as a prize for diligence.[64] His father wanted him to become a butcher and, crucial for the upwardly mobile, to learn German. He was sent to Zlonice, some fifteen miles away, where he studied music with the local organist in the impressive church. His father moved his business there in 1855. But, although Antonín began his apprenticeship as a butcher, his real interest was music, and he composed some early works, a polka for the piano and a symphony.

In autumn 1857, Dvořák went to study at the Organ School in Prague. He lodged at first with his cousin, who seems to have regarded him as a bit of a country bumpkin, and then with his aunt. His work was solid and by no means outstanding.

* The castle belonged to the wealthy Lobkowitz family, members of which did much to support Beethoven. But it was not a main residence and was, at the time, in a state of considerable decay with its *sgraffito* ornamentation falling to bits.

In 1859, Dvořák joined a dance band as a viola player. This band formed the nucleus of the orchestra of the new Provisional Theatre. Thus it was that Dvořák came to spend nine years working under Smetana's conductorship. Dvořák moved into the rooms of a fellow member of the orchestra where, as well as a square piano, there were to be found a medical student, two other students and a tour guide.[65]

Much time elapsed between Dvořák's leaving the Organ School in 1859 at the age of eighteen and his emergence before the public as a composer, in March 1873. His first big public success was the Hymnus, *The Heirs to Bílá Hora* (the White Mountain). A year later, about a month before Smetana observed his deafness starting, he conducted Dvořák's Third Symphony at a Philharmonic concert.

In 1874, Dvořák gave up his orchestral work and became organist of St Adalbert's Church in Prague, for three years. He worked on symphonies and chamber music. A perfectionist, he would study, particularly the works of Beethoven; he would then compose and burn what he had written.

Dvořák also gave lessons to the families of prosperous burghers. He fell in love with a sixteen-year-old pupil, Josefína Čermákova (see colour plate 34), one of the daughters of a goldsmith,[66] who lived in the Prague suburb of Florenci, in a house sandwiched between a railway station and a brewery. Josefína was at the start of a prominent career acting in soubrette roles, at first at the Provisional Theatre. She was not in love with Dvořák, and the words of his songs written at this time, 'Oh, what a beautiful dream', 'My heart dwells in painful memories', reflect his circumstances. He recovered from the rebuff: in November 1873, following the success with the Hymnus, he married Josefína's sister, Anna, who by then was three months pregnant.[67] Some years later, Tchaikovsky, after dining with the Dvořák's, observed: 'His wife is a simply charming woman and an excellent hostess.'[68] She was also a good contralto.

Dvořák wanted to write an opera. *The King and the Charcoal Burner*, about Alfred the Great, was staged in November 1874. But it was with his Third and Fourth Symphonies that the 33-year-old Dvořák was awarded an Austrian state grant for 'young, talented and impecunious writers, artists and musicians'.[69] This was his lucky break. The prize was 400 fl but, more importantly, the judges included Brahms and the influential critic Eduard Hanslick. Brahms recommended Dvořák's *Moravian Piano Duets* to his publisher, Simrock, who then commissioned him to write some

Slavonic dances. Knowing on which side his bread was buttered, Dvořák wrote to Brahms: 'As I did not know how to set about these, I have tried to obtain your famous Hungarian Dances, and I shall take the liberty of making them serve as my model in adapting the Slavonic dances. Once more I ask you, Master, to accept my most sincere gratitude for everything.'*[70]

Dvořák was awarded prizes again in 1876 and 1877. Brahms continued to encourage him (see page 569). Dvořák was much touched by Brahms' compliment: 'I merely wish to say that to occupy myself with your things gives me the greatest pleasure.' To this he responded: 'I cannot find word enough to express to you, Master, all that I feel. I can only say that I shall be indebted to you all my life.'[71]

The first concert devoted exclusively to Dvořák's works was in 1878, by which time he was aged 37. He conducted it. This was followed by a spectacular increase in his fortunes resulting in commissions and numerous performances abroad. Simrock paid him ten times as much for the second set of *Slavonic Dances* as for the first set. Dvořák felt confident enough to give up his job as organist and devote himself to being a composer.

For Dvořák, however, the late 1870s were a tragic period. His daughter Josefa died in September 1875; two years later, his first son died, a month after the death of another daughter. Only Otilie, born in 1878, survived childhood. She married the composer Josef Suk, and sadly died in her 20s. After the deaths of the young children, Dvořák composed the Stabat Mater. Its performance was delayed until three years after its completion.

Meanwhile Josefína married 'extremely well',** Count Wenzel von

* Brahms, a German from Hamburg, living in Austria, wrote some Hungarian dances. Dvořák, a Czech, wrote Moravian piano duets and Slavonic dances. Style was still as relevant as nationalism.

** It is bizarre that the nationalist Dvořák should be closely related to a scion of the family of which the most distinguished member was chancellor to Maria Theresa and Joseph II. After her death, Josefína Čermákova's husband became the penultimate occupant of the great château at Austerlitz, twelve miles from Brünn, also associated with Napoleon I who, after the battle there, declared an armistice from its balcony. However, Count Dr Václav Kounic, as he became known, was a rebel against his family tradition: he was a signatory to the 1868 Declaration calling for Czech autonomy and became deeply involved in politics, supporting the Young Czechs, in the difficult 1880s. He was to be seen at workers' meetings. He advocated an eight-hour day and women's rights, and took a particular interest in the social conditions of the workers in the Przibram silver and lead mines.[72]

Kaunitz. Her husband gave her a wedding present of a small château at Vysoká near Przibram (now Příbram), close to Pilsen and around 40 miles from Prague.* The Dvořáks stayed there, at first in the yard, a conglomeration of estate workers' cottages. Soon Dvořák's growing wealth enabled him to buy from his brother-in-law a granary at the other end of the village. He developed this into his own country house, Villa Rusalka. Within the walls of his own miniature estate, Dvořák planted trees, created an English garden and built a summerhouse. He could wander out and roam the muddy paths in his brother-in-law's forest and search for Rusalka, the water nymph, in her lake.[74] Less romantically, perhaps, Dvořák would go for drinks in the pub, and reared his doves and pigeons, his great interest other than trains (see colour plate 35). Understandably, he would never eat pigeon for dinner.[75]

Both Brahms and his colleague Hanslick exerted considerable pressure on Dvořák to move his sphere of interest to Vienna, particularly because they wanted a younger composer to resist the influence of Bruckner and Wagner. Hanslick, a German-speaking native of Prague who had made Vienna his home, wrote to suggest that 'it would be advantageous for your things to become known beyond your narrow Czech fatherland, which in any case does not do much for you',[76] and recommended that his works be translated into German. In 1882, the paternalistic, almost patronising, critic wrote: 'If as a sincere friend and warm admirer I may dare to put forward a suggestion, it is as follows: you should seriously and painstakingly make yourself acquainted with good German poetry and also set some German poems to music.' He also said: 'After such a great initial success, your art requires a wider horizon, a German environment, a bigger non-Czech public.' He added, surely disingenuously, considering the tumultuous politics of the 1880s, in which Dvořák's brother-in-law took a prominent role: 'These are just casual hints; sort them out in accordance with your own views, but don't disregard them.'[77]

Hanslick was keen to find and promote a new German opera composer. He arranged for Dvořák to be offered the chance to write an opera, 'partly lively, partly sentimental, and including some folk elements',[78] which

* Przibram was a significant mining town. Slag heaps are still to be seen as one enters the town, which extends to Birkenberg (now Březové Hory) nearby. The complex then included one of the deepest mineshafts in the world, 3,350 feet. Recently, it was notorious because political prisoners were used there to mine uranium.[73]

would be performed at the Imperial Opera House in Vienna. Dvořák's conscience, however, told him that he had to remain true to his Czech roots. Had he not, his reputation as a nationalist might have been severely dented. Hanslick nevertheless remained a great supporter; and his advice was not wholly unreasonable or untypical at the time, even if he was insensitive to the political upheavals in Prague. Despite the progress of Czech culture, German culture opened up broader vistas and was predominant in high places. For the ambitious, it would be career-enhancing to pay due respect to this: for composers, one has only to see the 'richly moulded opera houses'[79] around the Empire to appreciate its significance.

The tension between German and Czech was illustrated by the reception of Dvořák's works. *The Cunning Peasant* was a success in Prague but a failure in Vienna. An altercation with Simrock about whether his first name should appear on publications as Antonín (Czech) or Anton (German) resulted in Dvořák providing a neat solution: 'Ant.'[80]

England and the USA

In the mid-1880s, Dvořák began a series of visits to England, where the Stabat Mater and his choral music were particularly successful. He wrote *The Spectre's Bride* and a Seventh Symphony for the London Philharmonic Society in 1885. The oratorio *St Ludmila* was written for Leeds, and the Requiem for Birmingham, where the authorities had suggested that he set *The Dream of Gerontius*, although he turned this suggestion down.

Dvořák stayed with the Novello publishing family in 'the beautiful seacoast town of Brighton, where the richest class of Londoners go in the summer'. He added: 'The beautiful view of the sea from my lodgings, the spectacle of the thousands of people swarming everywhere, the beautiful English women bathing here (and in public), the men and the children, the vast quantity of great and small ships, then again the music playing Scottish national songs, and all kinds of other things: all this is so enchanting and fascinating that whoever has seen it will never forget it.'[81] His native Bohemia is, of course, landlocked.

Cambridge University gave him an honorary degree in 1891; he sat next to Stanford, the composer and professor, at the banquet. He was showered with other honours. In Vienna, he was received by the emperor, a difficult experience no doubt: Franz Joseph was interested in rifle shooting and amassing his collection of 55,000 trophies,[82] but he never so much as read a book for pleasure. The extent of his musical interests was well illustrated in a misspelt communication to his wife from Paris: 'I went to the Théâtre-Lyrique where they were performing Gounaud's new opera Romeo and Juliet and I slept very well once again.'[83]

Dvořák was in Vienna for the International Exhibition when, on 31 May, Przibram experienced what was, at the time, the world's worst ever mining disaster, with 319 men killed in the Mary mineshaft. Fourteen of the casualties came from the Vysoká area, some of whom Dvořák knew from the village pub; their dependants included 34 children. But Dvořák had to press on: he conducted the opera *Dimitrij* on 2 June, and later that month composed the Te Deum for the start of his visit to the USA.[84]

In September 1892, Dvořák crossed the Atlantic. He arrived just as the USA was celebrating the fourth centenary of the discovery of America. As we have seen, the promotion of music in the USA was dominated by women, largely because music clubs, 'the most potent force' in American music, were exclusively female. So it was Mrs Jeanette M. Thurber, wife of a wholesale grocer in New York, who invited Dvořák.*[85] She wanted a 'big name' for the National Conservatory, which she had founded a few years before. A Viennese friend suggested Dvořák or Sibelius. The offer was cabled to Vysoká in spring 1891, around the time that Tchaikovsky was making his successful visit to New York. Dvořák at first declined, but Mrs Thurber was not the kind of lady to take no for an answer: she just sent him a draft contract, and he accepted.[86] He took up the two-year post as director, with a salary of $15,000 a year. Official duties were to take up eight months in each year; he would conduct ten concerts of his own works.

From his house at 327 East 17th Street, Dvořák wrote to Brahms: 'I have left five children in Prague [with Granny Čermákova and Josefína] and my boy Otákar and my wife are here quite alone [with me], so we frequently feel nostalgic.'[87] But, nine months later, the children came across and joined him for an excellent holiday at Spillville, a Czech settlement in Iowa, Massachusetts.[88] There, the father of a friend from Prague was choirmaster of St Wenceslas' Church; Dvořák played in the church for services. He also took an interest in the Native Americans, and enjoyed hearing

* Mrs Thurber, a very enlightened lady, also founded the American Opera Company (to perform operas in English, at reasonable prices). Its coast-to-coast tours over-extended it financially, so it ran out of money.

their music and watching their dancing, just as in New York he took an interest in black music. He took the opportunity to visit the Chicago World Fair; he went on to Omaha to see a wealthy compatriot and to St Paul to see a Moravian priest. His travels included the Niagara Falls on the way back to New York. Doubtless a subject of conversation was the stunt that had taken place, about seven years before, when two brothers navigated the Falls in a ten-foot barrel.[89]

Dvořák's colleagues in Vienna continued to provide much support and encouragement. As soon as he arrived in New York, he received a letter from Hanslick: 'If I can be useful to you in any way in Vienna, I am at your disposal.' Because of the delays in communicating over the Atlantic, Brahms undertook to correct proofs of Dvořák's works. Still pressing him to come to Vienna, Brahms offered to support him financially there: 'If you need anything, my fortune is at your disposal', he said.[90]

Dvořák composed his Ninth Symphony, 'From the New World', which was first performed in the Carnegie Hall on 16 December 1893. As might be expected, it was an enormous success, and provided 'a wake-up call' to American music.[91]

Meanwhile, Dvořák was able to indulge his interest in trainspotting.* He would sometimes drive out of New York in order to see the Chicago Express go roaring past. Because access to the New York Central Station was limited for non-passengers, Dvořák also extended his interest to ships, and, twice a week, he would go down to the docks to view the liners. Twice a week, he visited a railway station and, on the other weekdays, he went for a walk in Central Park.[92] On one occasion his son-in-law Josef Suk, the composer of the much-loved Serenade for Strings, got into trouble for returning with the number of the coal tender instead of the engine.

When Dvořák's two-year contract came to an end, Mrs Thurber wanted him to renew it. But she was having difficulty paying his remuneration, because her husband's fortune had been depleted by the financial crash of 1893.** Indeed, just after the 'New World' première, Dvořák's

* Brahms was also interested in trains, such a conspicuous example of recent technology.

** By 1894, 169 railroads were in bankruptcy; 600 banks collapsed.[93] At one stage, around this time, it was more economic to burn corn as fuel than to sell it. There was also increasing resentment at a system (typified by monopolies and trusts) which could 'clothe rascals in robes and honesty in rags'.[94] It was in this relatively sombre context that the première of the 'New World' Symphony was held.

pay-cheque was delayed, and a $7,500 cheque deposited in Prague bounced. By April, Dvořák was so concerned about his own financial position that he wrote to Mrs Thurber threatening to publicise what was happening, if the money did not come through. He paid $215 for the ticket for himself and his family to sail to Europe in May 1894. But he returned to New York in October.

After spending the winter in New York, Dvořák went back to Prague in April. Although pressed to return to the USA, he wrote to Mrs Thurber and told her that, for 'family reasons', he could not do so. He resumed his duties as director of the Conservatoire. He completed the Cello Concerto, which he had started when in America, and which included a variation of the favourite song of Josefína Kaunitz, who was dying at the time.[95] It was at this stage that Brahms, just before his death, tried yet again to encourage Dvořák to become a professor at the Vienna Conservatoire.

When Dvořák returned to Prague, a city reeling from student demonstrations and mass prosecutions, he immersed himself in Bohemian folklore. He composed four symphonic poems based on folklore from Erben's *Kytice*, something he would never have dared to do in Brahms' lifetime. His last years were devoted to opera: he revised *The Jacobin* and composed *The Devil and Kate* and *Rusalka*.

The première of *Rusalka* in March 1901 was marked by a couple of 'disasters'. First of all, as a consequence of management changes at the National Theatre, there was a strike and a new orchestra and chorus had to be rehearsed. Secondly, the prince with whom Rusalka has fallen in love when she sings the aria 'O Silver Moon' was in no state to emerge from the pub. A stand-in had to be found urgently; there was no time for a rehearsal; besides, the stand-in had been working in a recording studio all day and his voice needed to be conserved. Fortunately, he knew the part, because he had originally hoped that he would be assigned it. The première was a great success.[96]

Dvořák seems to have become increasingly eccentric, irritable and stubborn, as he puffed away on his legendary cigar. He could also consume a liberal amount of beer. 'There was something bold and impetuous about his being, which might seem offensive to those who did not know him', wrote Grieg.[97] Some years before, Brahms had excused him: 'He is strange', he said, 'But his heart is in the right place.'[98] A few years later, in 1903, Grieg wrote that 'it was amusing to meet Dvořák; he is quite original, to say the least, but very likeable all the same'.[99] In early 1904, his beer consumption seems to have been considerable. He had to leave the first performance of his opera *Armida* because of a pain in his side.[100] He died very suddenly in Prague on 1 May.

The young Janáček

Meanwhile, Janáček, disillusioned by the failure to get his opera *Jenůfa* performed in Prague, was working away in the large city of Brünn, where he

Leoš Janáček / Bartók

did much to promote Dvořák's music. The composers were friends and they sometimes shared holidays together. But the establishment in Prague regarded Janáček as an outsider, and he was, at this time, hardly recognised in the Czech lands and not at all beyond.

Leoš Janáček was born on 3 July 1854 in the schoolhouse of a remote village in Austrian Silesia now known as Hukvaldy.* The village occupies a spectacular position, where the foothills of the Carpathians suddenly sprout up from the flat plain of modern Poland.[101] Hukvaldy, perhaps rather larger

* It was then very close to the border with Prussia. Hukvaldy is now to be found in the eastern end of the modern Czech Republic near the border with Poland. The castle where Beethoven visited his patron Prince Lichnowsky is only around 30 miles away. Frederick the Great had seized his slice of Silesia, the area so rich in minerals, on the accession of Maria Theresa, at the time Haydn went to Vienna (see page 106).

than a village, contained a mill and a brewery, and it boasted a mayor. It existed because, near the school and the attractive little church, there was the summer residence of the Archbishop of Olmütz, a title once enjoyed by Beethoven's patron Archduke Rudolf. The city of Olmütz (now Olomouc) is about 60 miles away; Brünn is a further 40 miles on the road south to Vienna.

The archbishop owned the park full of deer and wild sheep, and the impressive ruined castle, one of the largest in those parts, now hidden at the top of the steep hill covered in beech trees, above. More significant for the future of mankind, Sigmund Freud, the founder of psychoanalysis, was born two years after Janáček, in the small town of Freiberg (now Příbor), only five miles away. The coincidence of stars in such an out of the way place is surely extraordinary.*

Leoš was the tenth of fourteen children, five of whom died in infancy. His father and grandfather were teachers in the area, which had been impoverished by the appalling famine years of 1847–8. Leoš used to go round the village and collect the dues for his father, who enjoyed music and keeping bees.[102]

When he was eleven, Leoš was sent away to be a chorister in the Augustinian monastery in Brünn Old Town, at the foot of the hill on which stands the Spielberg fortress, then an army barracks,[103] but, until shortly beforehand, a formidable prison for political detainees (see page 247). Leoš' move there relieved the domestic strain in Hukvaldy's tiny schoolhouse. However, the scholarship only provided board and lodging, leaving fees and books to be paid for by the pupils, who were known as 'blue boys', on account of their uniforms.[104]

Since the 17th century, the monastery had its own music school and was 'a significant centre of musical life for the whole of Moravia'.[105] The choirmaster, a highly respected composer,[106] had been a pupil of Leoš' father; he was particularly involved in the promotion of social and cultural activities for Czech people in what was still a predominantly German city: only in Prague was the level of German-speaking people down to below twenty per cent.**

* František Palacký the Czech nationalist, was born fourteen miles away.

** The monastery, dating back to 1350, was very wealthy and had been lucky to survive the reforms of Joseph II. Its library had 27,000 books. One of the Augustinians when Janáček first went there was J. G. Mendel, an important geneticist. He kept his beehive on the slope above.[107]

Years later, Janáček recorded that the separation from his family, aggravated by the death of his father a year later, was an 'unthinkable cruelty'.[108] When he left school at the age of fifteen, he obtained a scholarship at the teacher training college to qualify to be a teacher in general, rather than musical, studies. During the time he was undergoing his compulsory practical experience, he acted as deputy choirmaster at the monastery, and became conductor of the weavers' working men's choir. Thus his first compositions were for unaccompanied male choir.* He was demanding in his standards, and his singers were soon made aware of what one student described as his 'fiery temper' and 'uncontrollable anger'.[109] His temperament had, it seems, been inherited from his grandfather.

After qualifying to teach in Czech-speaking schools, Janáček was granted a year's leave to study at the Organ School in Prague. He was remitted the first year, but the penniless twenty-year-old crammed the remaining two years' work into one. Indeed, he is said to have been so poor that he could not hire a piano and had to resort to a table on which he had marked the keys with a piece of chalk. He was recognised as a star pupil although he got into very deep water for writing a scathingly critical review of a work by one of his professors.[110] He was present at the first performance of Smetana's *Vltava* and met Dvořák.

The Turbulent Marriage

When Janáček returned to Brünn, he introduced Dvořák's music to the choirs he conducted. But his interpersonal relationships with his singers remained fraught and it was probably just as well that, when he was 25, he went off to study in Leipzig and Vienna. Before he left, he had fallen in love with a pupil, Zdeňka, the daughter of the principal of the teacher training college. Although only fourteen she was already tall and slim, and had beautiful blue eyes.[111] He sent her love letters when he was away, and married her when she was not quite sixteen (see colour plate 36).

Sadly, the marriage was no romance. Janáček seems to have returned from Vienna a rabid Czech nationalist: he refused to speak German and insisted that she spoke Czech. Although her father spoke Czech, Zdeňka's family was strongly pro-German, and her grandmother was one of those

* On the outbreak of the First World War, when the men went off to fight, the situation was reversed and Janáček composed for all-female choirs.

who typically regarded Czech as a language fit only for servants.[112] Although Zdeňka's father provided them with considerable support (and a magnificent grand piano), Janáček became increasingly resentful and surly towards her family. It is not clear whether the language issue, or jealousy at their relative affluence, or at the birth of her brother, an after-thought, was the cause of his insensitive, rude, ungrateful attitude. The marriage began to come unstuck even before it was consecrated, and it only went ahead because Zdeňka had not the will to resist the momentum that led her inexorably towards it.

'Apart from violent outbursts of my husband's passion, there was no tenderness and warmth between us … he never had time for me', Zdeňka recorded.[113] He would not allow her to see her parents. When, a year after the wedding, their daughter Olga was born, Janáček was disappointed that the baby was not a boy. He asked his mother to come and live with them, whereupon Zdeňka departed with Olga, and they were formally divorced. Janáček and Zdeňka continued to meet, for example, when he was seeing Olga, and her love for him surged up again. After they reunited two years later, Vladimir was born; but he died suddenly of meningitis, following scarlet fever caught off Olga.

The resumed marriage became a roller coaster. The couple did not live as man and wife.[114] It was not long before Janáček was having affairs with women such as the daughter of the Hukvaldy brewer;[115] when he was away in places such as Luhačovice, the spa town which he would visit to cure his poor health, he would enjoy what he called the 'annual congress of beautiful women'.[116] After Vladimir's death, Zdeňka begged him to give her another child. According to her, he responded: 'That may be what you want, but I don't.'[117] She was stuck, with nowhere to go,[118] so they continued ostensibly together, unhappily and with increasing bitterness between them.

Brünn's Leading Musician

Meanwhile, Janáček was indefatigable in promoting music in Brünn. His commitments left him with very little time to compose. He taught choral singing, violin and organ at the training college. He set up an Organ School on the lines of the one in Prague, and started a school for violinists, he conducted the choral society, was choirmaster at the monastery, and did a considerable amount of journalism.

In February 1887, he started work on the first of his nine operas, *Šárka*. For this, he used a play drawn from an old Czech legend, set around the time of Queen Libuše. He showed the opera to Dvořák, who suggested some changes.[119] But the playwright refused permission for it to be performed, so it fell by the wayside.

His Czech nationalism was presumably fed by the provincial and straitened circumstances in which he struggled. But he was also strongly pro-Russian: he learnt to speak Russian, he called his children by Russian names, and he became chairman of the Russian circle in Brünn.[120] Fundamentally, he was probably mainly anti-Habsburg: it is said that 'his strong reaction to the long Austrian domination of his country is evident from the Czech, Moravian or Russian background of all his operas'.[121]

At this time, Janáček became deeply involved in Moravian folk music.[122] He used to return to Hukvaldy, where his sister was now the schoolteacher. With a group of locals, including the brewer,* he would make music, and he dedicated some songs to their 'Little Circle under the Acacia Tree'. He travelled with the headmaster of the Brünn junior high school to collect and analyse folksongs and dances. Together they published *Folksongs of Moravia Newly Collected*, a two-volume edition of over 2,000 songs. On the footing that all folksong had developed from speech sounds, Janáček would scribble down snatches of speech melody, if necessary, writing them on his shirtcuffs. He would note down the speech melodies of the children in the cottage in which he stayed when he was in Hukvaldy. Many years later, when he was in London, he noted down the sounds of the monkeys in London Zoo and the messenger boys in the hotel in which he was staying.[123]

Jenůfa

An amazing example of him writing down speech melody is found in the scribbles which he made while his daughter Olga was in the throes of death. In March 1902, the nineteen year old, a considerable beauty, was sent to St Petersburg to stay with her uncle, perhaps to cool her ardour for a German-speaking suitor of whom Janáček disapproved. Olga had never been healthy: the rheumatic fever from which she had suffered as a child

* The brewer was capable (he supplied the court of Emperor Franz Joseph with beer), and a character (he fathered twelve illegitimate children). Janáček had an affair with his married sister.

left her with heart disease. Although a lively girl, she was not allowed to join in the energetic things that other children do. In St Petersburg, she fell ill with typhoid. Both parents went to visit her and she was brought back to Brünn in a very weak condition. The heart disease gradually took its grip, and the poor girl suffered a protracted, agonising death, disfigured and swollen up with dropsy. Janáček wrote down the speech sound of Olga's last sigh, 'Aja'.

At the time of Olga's death, Janáček was completing *Jenůfa*, the opera on which he had been working for at least nine years. This is a searing story in which an illegitimate baby is drowned in the frozen river. Not only was Janáček noting down his daughter's dying sighs: we also have an extraordinary, 'heart-rending image of the composer finishing his opera – whose central tragedy is the death of a child – whilst in the adjoining room his own daughter lay dying'.[124] He played the opera through to Olga, at her request, a few days before she died in February 1903. He later said that her death felt as though someone was tearing his heart out.[125]

After Janáček composed *Jenůfa*, he found that he could not get it staged. His undiplomatic personality had already been proved a stumbling block; now it proved to be disastrous. Just before *Jenůfa* was ready, he had written a scathingly critical article about a work written by the conductor and director of the National Theatre in Prague, who, until then, had been a friend and considerable supporter.* So, Janáček could not get *Jenůfa* performed in Prague, where he was dismissed as a folklorist and was not even regarded as a serious composer: none of his music was played at the Prague festival of Czech music in 1904. However, *Jenůfa* was performed in Brünn, although the orchestral resources were not up to an adequate production.

The breach between the composer and the Prague conductor/director was healed only almost thirteen years later. In May 1916, following the intervention of some long-suffering but loyal friends, *Jenůfa*, in an amended version, was staged in Prague. After the performance, Janáček said: 'I feel as though I am living in a fairy tale.'[126] Soon, *Jenůfa* was being performed in Vienna and elsewhere. However, it was not received with universal acclaim: a distinguished English critic ripped into the New York production of 1920: 'A more complete collection of undesirables and

* The director probably could not take too many risks. As we have seen in connection with *Rusalka*, he had only recently been appointed and was facing industrial action from his employees.

incredibles has never previously appeared in any one opera.'[127] Although the prominent writer Max Brod did much to promote Janáček's work, particularly by translating his operas into German,[128] Janáček's reputation only became assured after the Second World War. When the President of Czechoslovakia* visited Brno (as Brünn had by then become) in the mid-1920s, not a single piece by Janáček was performed.

Although well into his 60s, Janáček now underwent an 'amazing creative upsurge'.[129] He was spurred on by the success of *Jenůfa*, and by patriotic pride in the newly independent country: 'a new epoch is coming, springtime for the nation', he said.[130] After completing the comic opera, *The Excursions of Mr Brouček*, Janáček composed, in the last decade of his life, three of his best-known operas, *Káťa Kabanová*, *The Makropulos Case* and *The Cunning Little Vixen* – for the last he did a considerable amount of research with friends in Hukvaldy and even joined in their foxhunting. He also wrote *From the House of the Dead*, based on Dostoyevsky's novel, in the year before he died. His enormous level of activity may also have been inspired by his love for Kamila** Stösslová, who was 38 years younger than him. He was bewitched by her black hair as it fell loosely around her shoulders and, less understandably perhaps, by her tendency to walk around the house with no shoes on.[131]

Kamila

For a long time, Janáček and Zdeňka had lived under the same roof, in a strained relationship. When the Organ School was rehoused up nearer the centre of Brünn, they established themselves, together with their housekeeper and poodle, in a new house which had the luxury of electric lighting. They were close to the Botanical Gardens and the Janáčeks created their own tiny, scented garden, full of lilacs, in which he would enjoy tending the cucumbers and going up a ladder to pick the pears, plums, apricots and cherries. During the First World War, Janáček also looked after the hens.[132]

* At the end of the First World War, there was a general strike, and then on 28 October 1918, Czechoslovakia was formed as a unitary state. The birth pangs were considerable: there were anti-Jewish riots in 1920; a minister was assassinated in Prague in 1923.

** This was not the first Kamila. There had been another in Luhačovice around the time of the *Jenůfa* première.

Zdeňka cosseted and supported Janáček through years of self-doubt and considerable ill health; yet he could publicly describe her as his 'stupid wife'.[133] The tiny house into which they now moved provided little space for tension to be relieved, although he could escape to his study in the Organ School next door. Occasionally, there was a crisis and Janáček and Zdeňka fell apart; occasionally they came together. 'What a strange person!', Zdeňka wrote about her husband. 'How rich in feeling, yet sympathy and forgiveness were things he didn't know. He could love so much, he knew how to be so full of love! ... And yet the same person who could take supper in a friendly fashion with the hens, could cruelly and without feeling kick aside someone that he knew loved him above her own life. He knew how to inflict wounds that wouldn't heal.'[134]

At the time of the Prague production of *Jenůfa*, Janáček had an affair with Madame Horvátová, the leading soprano who sang the role of the Kostelnička, the stepmother, who drowns Jenůfa's unwanted child. Janáček was keen to have a child by Horvátová, but although the affair went on for a considerable time, it came to nothing. The affair led Zdeňka to attempt suicide by taking an overdose. The Janáčeks again underwent divorce proceedings, although they were less formal, and permitted both of them to live under the same roof.

In summer 1917, when, for Janáček, the soprano's extra-mural attractions were fading, he met Kamila Stösslová and her husband David, an antique dealer. Zdeňka described Kamila, in contemporary language, as 'this clever, cheerful, nice little Jewess'.[135] Kamila was not remotely interested in music: at the time when Janáček met her, she had not even heard of Wagner. Over the next eleven years, to Zdeňka's chagrin, Janáček wrote to Kamila nearly every day; she rarely responded and, when she did, she insisted that he destroyed her letters. Janáček wore an engagement ring with Kamila's name on it and often visited her at her house in Pisek in southern Bohemia. In his last year, he kept a special diary about her; in the last sixteen months of his life, he sent her around 300 letters and postcards,[136] which soon joined a collection whose pecuniary value David Stössel sought to maximise.[137]

Although the relationship with Kamila was 'entirely platonic',[138] it is sometimes suggested that Janáček's strongest creative impulse was erotic.[139] 'It is possible to see in the succession of female heroines a commentary on his attitude to Kamila Stösslová.'[140] Wishful thinking about her perhaps was part of the inspiration for *Káťa Kabanová*, his opera about the neglected wife who takes a lover. *The Cunning Little Vixen* perhaps represents the fulfilled wife and mother. Janáček then comes down to earth with *The Makropulos Case*, which is about the fascinating, but icy, Emilia Marty. The Second String Quartet was also an expression of his love for Kamila.

The visits of the Stössels put a strain on the Janáčeks' domestic arrangements in their tiny house, in more senses than one. They already had to cope with the food shortages caused by the First World War. Relatives of their loyal and long-serving housekeeper Mářa would send in food from the countryside. The deprivations were considerable: clothes were made from nettle fibre or paper; in Hukvaldy, bells were taken from the church, farm animals were sequestered and a field hospital was set up. The state subsidies to the Organ School were stopped, and the teachers became entirely dependent on the fees paid by the students; one paid with a loaf of sugar, which was possibly quite welcome.

At the start of the war, Janáček's strongly pro-Russian stance proved particularly awkward, because the Russians now were enemies. Zdeňka had quickly to train ivy to grow over the Russian inscription on Olga's grave and Janáček disbanded his Russian Circle, but not before he had organised the shredding of minutes and their replacement by sanitised ones.

After the war, the food shortages continued, and there was terrible misery in Hukvaldy. This was compounded by the outbreak of Spanish influenza. Travel was well-nigh impossible, and when Zdeňka's father came to Brünn after her mother died, his cases were ransacked on the train.[141]

As well as working tirelessly at composing the operas, the Czech independence which followed the war encouraged Janáček to turn the Organ School into a Conservatoire. Although he was no longer the director, he was allowed to continue to live in the tiny house next door. In 1926, he briefly visited London. He arrived at the end of April, was put up at the Langham Hotel, and there was a concert of his works at the Wigmore Hall on 6 May. Janáček's difficult temperament was in evidence in the rehearsal: he blew up, because he did not approve of the way the pianist, a distinguished virtuoso, interpreted his Concertino.

The concert was held three days after the General Strike had begun,* so

* The coal industry was by far the largest single industry in Britain, employing more than a million workers. Imported Polish and German coal resulted in the mines running at a loss. 'Nowt

the audience was small; nevertheless, it was enthusiastic. While Janáček was in London, the strike manifested itself in what has been called 'class war, in polite form'.[144] The propertied classes volunteered to drive the trains and lorries; the police and strikers played football against each other. Janáček will not have been too perturbed: there had been a general strike in Czechoslovakia a few years earlier. He left London on 8 May, four days before the national strike was called off.

Janáček's obsession with Stösslová continued: if one believes Zdeňka, Kamila gained Janáček's favour 'through her cheerfulness, laughter, temperament, Gypsy-like appearance and buxom body'. Zdeňka also thought that she reminded him of the soprano from *Jenůfa*, 'although she had none of that woman's demonic qualities or artfulness'.[145] The eternal youth, which the good-looking, grey-haired septuagenarian craved, could not last, however.

Now that he was successful, Janáček could afford to buy his sister-in-law's small cottage and adjoining lands in Hukvaldy. He was also to be seen back in Luhačovice taking the mineral waters for his rheumatism. In July 1928, he invited Kamila, her husband and her eleven-year-old son for a holiday at Hukvaldy, which now had the comfort of electric light instead of the old oil lamps. The innuendo in his correspondence was increasingly outspoken. Kamila, even though she was annoyed by his banging away on the harmonium,[146] at last began to reciprocate his advances. Zdeňka suspected that the Stössels were sponging off Janáček, as it was known that they were now short of money.

Janáček's health had been poor. In the summer of 1927, he wrote to Kamila: 'I've been done in, even for me these last days in Hukvaldy have been stifling.'[147] Walks in the steep woods, although they provided the joy of hearing the birds and wonderful glimpses through the beech trees towards the Beskydys hills and the Polish plain, demanded someone with

doing'[142] was the miners' response to the suggestion that their wages should be cut, so the government provided a subsidy for nine months, and set up a Royal Commission. When the Commission later recommended a reduction in wages, the coal miners were intransigent: 'Not a penny off the pay, not a minute on the day.'[143] The national strike only lasted a few days and was good hearted; but the miners held out for six months and were driven back to work by starvation. They had to settle for longer hours and lower wages, and there was no implementation of the improvements which the Commission had also recommended.

strong heart and lungs.* Janáček is said to have caught a chill when Kamila's son had to be retrieved, having apparently got lost in the woods. The chill developed into pneumonia, and Janáček died in hospital in nearby Ostrava on 12 August 1928.**

Béla Bartók

Whatever reservations we may have about Janáček's personality, there can be no question about the sincerity of his nationalism, even if it may have been too pro-Russian for some people's taste. We shall conclude this chapter with the life of Béla Bartók. He is often hailed as Hungary's greatest composer,[149] however awkward this may be for the reputation of Liszt, whose 'national' music is perceived as new 'Gypsy-Hungarian' in style, artificial rather than authentic.

Bartók, like Janáček, carried out a considerable amount of research into folk music. He would travel into the countryside with his camera and his Edison wax disks to record Hungarian, Romanian and Slovakian folk music and customs. He went to Turkey and to north Africa to pursue the origins of these. 'We must isolate the very ancient, for this is the only way of identifying the really new', he said.[150] This painstaking work, which was often undertaken in conjunction with the composer Zoltán Kodály, led to works such as *Twenty Hungarian Arrangements of Folksongs*, the *Romanian Folk Dances from Hungary* and *Improvisations on Hungarian Peasant Songs*. Folk idiom is detected in Bartók's own works, such as the *Allegro Barbaro* and the String Quartets.†

Bartók was born on 25 March 1881, in Nagyszentmiklós (now Sânnicolau Mare). His birthplace, although only around 140 miles from Budapest as the crow flies, is just inside modern Romania. None of the places where he spent his youth is in modern Hungary.[151] His father, who

* The road into Hukvaldy has a twelve per cent gradient. 'Medium demanding hiking', says the tourist notice.

** The telegram to Zdeňka arrived too late for her to come. Janáček had amended his will to favour Kamila, who outlived him by seven years, dying of cancer; Zdeňka died three years after that. The relationship between the two women was particularly acrimonious before Janáček was buried. Then there was litigation about the will, in which David Stössel took a prominent part.[148]

†Despite the protestations, it is debatable how pure the folk influences in the works of Bartók and Kodály are. Kodály's *Háry János* opera makes use of some recent material.

taught in an agricultural college, died when he was young. The sickly boy was brought up by his mother, who eventually found a living in Pressburg (now Bratislava*) where she was a piano teacher. He was a brilliant virtuoso pianist. Although he won a scholarship to study in Vienna, he chose to go to the Budapest Conservatoire. His time there was interrupted by the ill health which dogged him throughout his life.[152]

Bartók associated himself with the Hungarian nationalists. The 'Compromise' (*Ausgleich*) granted to Hungary in 1867 had created Austro-Hungary, known as 'the dual monarchy'. Despite the considerable progress and prosperity which followed this,** many Hungarians believed that the constitutional compromise was wrong, and that there should be complete separation from the Habsburgs. Of course, there was also the usual question of the language. It comes as no surprise that Bartók wore national dress and gave up speaking German.[154] One of his earlier works was *Kossuth*, a symphonic poem about Hungary's hero of the 1848 Revolution, who had recently died. At this stage, Richard Strauss' symphonic poems provided a considerable influence; later it would be the works of Debussy.

When Bartók competed for the Rubinstein prize, in Paris in 1905, he entered for both piano and composition sections. Wilhelm Backhaus, who became one of the 20th century's most distinguished pianists, won the piano section, and no prize was awarded for composition. Two years later, Bartók was appointed professor of piano at the Budapest Conservatoire, where he settled and married a sixteen-year-old pupil, Márta. In the 1920s he divorced her, and married another pupil, Ditta.

The professorship gave him a base from which he could develop his other activities. But 'he was a reluctant teacher and would have preferred a research post'.[155]

The rejection of his own compositions did not help Bartók's painful shyness.[156] *Duke Bluebeard's Castle* was rejected by a jury in an opera competition, and publishers were keener to get him to prepare teaching editions of classical composers than to publish his own works. He immersed himself in his studies of folk music.

As a consequence of the First World War, Hungary lost two-thirds of its territory. There were 133 days during the middle of 1919 when it was run

* Bartók would have called it Pozsony, the Hungarian name for it.

** Literacy levels doubled.[153]

by a rigid and unpragmatic disciple of the Russian Communists, Béla Kun, 'a cross between a Social Insurance clerk and a journalist'.[157] His repressive regime was embroiled in battles for territory with Hungary's neighbours, and it collapsed, partly because of food shortages caused by the attempt to nationalise the farmers. Márta kept house, for example, by bartering 60 eggs for a shirt, and 30 litres of milk for a pair of stockings.[158] Meanwhile, Bartók participated in a group asked to reform music education, and there was a plan to appoint him director of a folk music department of the National Museum.[159] Bartók's ballet *The Miraculous Mandarin* was written at this time.

But the Béla Kun government was kicked out. After three turbulent days in early August, power was seized by 'Whites' led by Miklós Horthy, a former aide-de-camp to Emperor Franz Joseph, and a distinguished admiral in the war. White terror then exceeded Red terror many times over 'both in cruelty and in the number of its victims'.[160] Three months later, Horthy entered Budapest proclaiming, 'We shall forgive this criminal city.'[161] The Habsburg monarchy was officially restored in Hungary, although Horthy refused to allow Franz Joseph's great-nephew and successor, 'King' Karl, to return, and dethroned him after a failed coup in 1921. The authoritarian Horthy ruled Hungary as 'Regent' until the Second World War.[162]

After the end of the Béla Kun regime, Bartók returned to his previous work. He found living in a village was preferable to a 'palace on the shores of the Danube'.[163] Between the wars, he toured widely as a concert pianist. His own compositions were often received very badly by the critics. This did nothing to help his reticence.

The 1930s heard the *Cantata Profana* and *Music for Strings, Percussion and Celesta*. When Admiral Horthy's regime leant towards Nazi Germany, Bartók would not perform there; later he refused to allow his works to be broadcast there.[164] So he was attacked in the Hungarian and Romanian press, and, in an attempt to persecute him, his racial origins were investigated. He sent his manuscripts to London for safety reasons, saying that 'the political situation in Hungary becomes more and more crooked ... at least my manuscripts should be somewhere safe'.[165]

Despite Bartók's strictures, Horthy's policies seemed successful: the economy prospered and, in 1938 and subsequently, Hungary was given back some of its territory which had been ceded to its neighbours, notably

Czechoslovakia. At the start of the Second World War, Horthy attempted to sit on the fence, at first expecting an Axis victory.* But, once Hitler invaded Yugoslavia in 1941, Hungary, positioned where it was, could not maintain this ambivalent stance. It allowed the Germans to cross its territory and sent a small force to help Germany in its attack on Russia. It continued to vacillate between the Nazis and the Allies. By then, however, Bartók had gone. He emigrated, via Geneva and Lisbon, to the USA.

Bartók at first worked on Serbo-Croatian folk music at Columbia University.[167] He was desperately homesick for Hungary: 'I would like to go home, for ever', he said.[168] On one occasion, he spent three hours lost in the New York subway,[169] an experience perhaps not unfamiliar to many a traveller in a foreign subway system.

Bartók lived on disguised charity. Serge Koussevitsky, the Russian-born publisher and conductor of the Boston Symphony Orchestra, commissioned the Concerto for Orchestra, and Yehudi Menuhin commissioned the Violin Sonata.

Bartók's health was never good, even though there was no obvious diagnosis. He died in New York on 26 September 1945. It was a sad, somewhat penurious and pathetic end.[170]

Today, the fierce and committed nationalism of these composers may seem like something from a bygone age. After all, it is more politically correct today to be 'European', or even 'global', rather than Czech or Hungarian. Only twenty years after Bartók's death, the astronaut Buzz Aldrin took Dvořák's 'New World' Symphony in his personal flight kit when he went to the moon in the Apollo 11 spaceship.[171] Dvořák, fervent nationalist that he was, can never in his wildest dreams have thought that his symphony would apparently be the first music to be played beyond the confines of our globe.

Maybe it will be some time before a work by Janáček or Bartók is played on the moon.

* The phrase 'Rome–Berlin Axis' was coined by one of Horthy's premiers (Count Bethlen) in 1934.[166]

Scandinavian Nationalists: Grieg and Sibelius

CHAPTER 23

'Even if Sibelius had written nothing else, this one work would entitle him to a place among the greatest masters of all time.'[1] So wrote an English critic in the 1930s. Today, the ordinary listener, albeit taken aback, might assume that the critic was talking about *Finlandia*, the *Karelia Suite* or the 'Valse Triste'. No, the comment related to Sibelius' culminating work, perhaps less well known today, the tone poem *Tapiola*. It has also been implied that some of his symphonies gave him a stature equal to, or perhaps even in advance of, that of Haydn and Mozart.[2]

No such extravagant claims have been made for the diminutive Edvard Grieg, who, 22 years older, is sometimes described disparagingly as a salon composer and a miniaturist.[3] It is conceded grudgingly that although Grieg 'certainly does not belong among the great of music … the charming national colour of his work has had international success'.[4] Like it or not, the two *Peer Gynt* suites, together with his A minor Piano Concerto – one of the most popular of all – assure him a place in this book, and, more significantly, immortality.

These two composers were both Scandinavian, but very different in background, career and indeed appearance. Grieg, whose soprano wife was more at home in Denmark than Norway, became directly involved in the

Above: GRIEG AND SIBELIUS

national music of the Hardanger region of Norway; surprisingly, he also became entangled in French politics, the Dreyfus case, which will require some explanation. Sibelius married into a family deeply involved with Finnish culture and nationalism. Gaunt and ten inches taller than Grieg, he withdrew into Ainola, his villa, and hardly emerged. They apparently shared a considerable difficulty in generating the necessary inspiration to compose.

Grieg's Youth

Grieg was born on 15 June 1843 in the seaport of Bergen on the south-west coast of Norway.

Like Bohemia, Norway was, in the 19th century, yearning for independence from its dominant power, in its case, Sweden. It had experienced a turbulent ride over the centuries. The crowns of Norway, Sweden and Denmark came together in 1397 under the remarkable Queen Margaret, daughter of the King of Denmark, and wife of the King of Norway. At a meeting held in that year in Calmar, the countries agreed to be ruled by a single sovereign, while retaining their local laws and customs. At the beginning of the 1500s, Sweden was taken out of this 'permanent' union by Gustavus Vasa, the son of one of 90 nobles who had just been massacred. For almost 300 years, Norway and Denmark, however, stayed together and thus developed very strong and lasting cultural links. After 1814, Norway was united uncomfortably with Sweden under the same king, even though, strictly speaking, it was a separate and independent kingdom.* In the late 19th century, with fisheries, principally cod and herring, its most important source of national wealth, Norway was the most sparsely populated country in Europe.**[5]

Grieg's great-grandfather Alexander came from Rathen, a few miles from Fraserburgh in Aberdeenshire. He emigrated from Scotland to Bergen in the 1760s and started an export business in dried fish and lobster.[6] When Edvard was twelve, Bergen was almost destroyed by fire and considerable trading disruption arose from the side-effects of the Crimean

* Verdi's *Ballo in Maschera* is based on the story of the Francophile King Gustavus III of Sweden who had been shot at a masked ball in 1792; he was about to launch a war to save King Louis XVI.
**In 1882, Norway had a growing population of just under 2 million, of which around 80 per cent lived in the countryside. Bergen was about a third of the size of the capital, Christiania, which, since 1924, has been called Oslo. Trondheim and Stavanger were half the size of Bergen.

War.[7] The family business fortunately avoided the bankruptcies which toppled 88 major businesses.[8]

Edvard's parents were models of respectability and took an active part in the Harmonien, Bergen's musical society and orchestra, one of the oldest in the world. His mother, Gesina, was the daughter of a provincial governor, and was a very competent pianist who had studied music in Hamburg; she also wrote poems and plays.[9] Other than in winter, the prosperous family lived in the elegant country house which she had inherited.[10] This was located a few miles outside the port, up on a hill, where it had beautiful views over a lake to the fjords beyond.

Edvard showed an early interest and talent in music and was taught to play the piano by his mother. When he was fifteen, he was sent to study in Leipzig. This followed advice from a relative, the famous and colourful violinist Ole Bull who, among other things, had founded the National Theatre in Bergen and had tried to set up a colony for Norwegian emigrants in North America.* Edvard found Leipzig claustrophobic and was unhappy with the teaching there. His mother had to fetch him home in the middle of his course, when he suffered a bad attack of pleurisy.[13] The consequence of his illness was one collapsed lung, and he remained very frail with lopsided shoulders. But he returned and completed the course, and apparently saw Wagner's *Tannhäuser* fourteen times during a stay in Dresden.

The Young Composer

Grieg first established himself in Bergen, where he taught and gave concerts, and performed his own compositions. But the real focus of Norwegian intellectual and artistic life was still in Denmark, in Copenhagen. There, the influential Scandinavian musicians, especially Niels Gade, a friend of Schumann and Mendelssohn, were to be found. Grieg went there in spring 1863.

* The eccentric, charming, utopian socialist Ole Bull, known as the Norwegian Paganini, travelled more than 100,000 miles and gave more than 200 concerts during his first tour of the USA in 1843–5, a time when several virtuosos visited the country. Bull married an American and for a time lived in Boston. When he returned to Norway, he lived in an elaborately decorated house, crowned with an onion dome, on an island a few miles south of Bergen.[11] The motto of his National Theatre was: 'Norwegian plays, Norwegian actors, Norwegian music, and Norwegian ballet.'[12]

But Ole Bull told Grieg to 'throw off the yoke of Gade. Create your own style',[14] and Grieg determined to devote his life to Romantic nationalism. He made friends with a Norwegian composer and enthusiast of around his own age, the composer of the Norwegian national anthem, Rikard Nordraak, who had recently returned from study in Berlin. The two of them took part in forming an organisation, intended to promote contemporary Scandinavian music and act as a counterweight to the conservative Musical Association which was controlled by Gade. Grieg and Nordraak planned to spend the autumn and winter of 1865 in Rome. Sadly, Nordraak did not reach Rome: he contracted galloping pulmonary consumption. His sudden death seems to have intensified Grieg's sense of responsibility for promoting Scandinavian music.

After seeing the sights of Rome, and after being surprised by Liszt's antics with the ladies and Ibsen's drinking,*[16] Grieg decided to settle in Christiania (now Oslo). With a view to an appointment, he took organ lessons. Although he failed to get appointed music director at Christiania Theatre, an all-Norwegian concert in October 1866 made his name. Still, he felt very isolated in petty bourgeois, philistine Christiania, where the orchestral resources were lamentable and the press unenthusiastic.[17] An attempt to establish a Norwegian Academy of Music failed because of lack of public funding. Bergen was not much better, and when, in later years, Grieg became conductor of the Bergen Harmonien, he complained: 'I am up to the neck in stupidity, anonymous abuse and all the rest of it.'[18] His solace in Christiania was his friendship with Bjørnstjerne Bjørnson, the Norwegian poet, playwright, orator and leading patriot, whom Grieg would later describe as 'Norway's grandest waterfall, roaring and raging, fuming and foaming'.[19]

In Copenhagen, Grieg had become secretly engaged to his cousin Nina Hagerup, who was two years younger than him. She sang his songs, and he regarded her as his finest interpreter. They were both unusually small, and when they performed together, it was said that they looked like two little goblins.[20] Nina's family were not pleased with the engagement; her mother

* Ibsen, a Norwegian, was then possibly the greatest international playwright. He had settled in Rome, because he was disillusioned with his country for failing to support Denmark in resisting German encroachment in Schleswig and Holstein. In his later plays, such as *The Doll's House*, *Ghosts* and *An Enemy of the People*, he expressed some of the social problems of the time; many found the plays shocking.[15]

said that Grieg 'is nothing, he cannot do anything, and he writes music which nobody wants to listen to'.[21] When eventually they got married, none of the family was present.

The year immediately following their marriage was blissful. Their daughter Alexandra was born. They rented a cottage in Denmark and Grieg wrote what is possibly his most popular work, the Piano Concerto in A minor. This has been described as 'the most complete musical embodiment of Norwegian national romanticism'.*[22] Concert performances of this work provided an important source of income for him and he continued to revise it right up to his death.[24]

The idyll was not to last. The death of Alexandra aged thirteen months left the happy couple bereft. They reverted to being a pair of artists who functioned in their own right on the concert platform. Grieg supplemented his income from this by teaching.[25]

When establishing the Norwegian Theatre, Ole Bull had put on plays interspersed with songs and dance. It was quite usual at the time to stage plays accompanied by incidental music. Thus, Grieg accepted Ibsen's request to compose incidental music for *Peer Gynt*. This was first performed in Christiania in February 1876, although Grieg was not present at the première, either because he was mourning the death of his parents, or because he was thoroughly disillusioned with the quality of orchestral performance in Christiania, and by the degree of audience attentiveness. As the play lasted five hours, perhaps one can have some sympathy for the audience.

In August 1876, Grieg was in Bayreuth for the first performance of the complete *Ring*. He was keen to compose an opera himself, but could not find a suitable libretto. An attempt to write a Norwegian national opera with Bjørnson foundered. Bjørnson, like Ibsen, wanted to evoke social issues.[26] It was only in the 20th century that composers found a musical vocabulary to handle topics such as factories, barracks and telegraphs.

* One biographer finds national colouring in the Piano Concerto, citing the 'tonic-leading note-dominant motive in the soloist's opening bars, the dotted rhythm of the theme that follows … the augmented fourths of the next melodic idea, with its short sequential phrases, the folk-fiddler type of figuration in the animato section, the song-like theme of the slow movement enriched harmonically and colouristically in the manner of the later folk-song arrangements, and the *halling* and *springdans* rhythms of the finale'.[23] (The *halling* is a men's solo dance; the *springar* is a fast couple dance.)

Grieg had no wish to write something badly, so he dropped the idea. This caused a considerable rift between him and Bjørnson.[27]

The Hardanger and Grieg's Middle Years

Grieg sought to find inspiration in the Norwegian folk idioms. He told Bjørnson that he aimed 'to write music depicting the Norwegian scenery, the life of the Norwegian folk, the country's history and folk poetry'.[28] He would visit the Norwegian countryside, and, in later years, he was sometimes accompanied on his hikes by Frederick Delius, who was in Sweden as a representative for his father's Bradford-based woollen business.*[29]

The Griegs had no home of their own in Bergen once his parents had died. Grieg decided to settle in the wild and desolate, but supremely beautiful country at the top of the Hardanger fjord (see colour plate 40). The winter of 1877–8 was spent on a farm by the Sørfjord, a narrow branch off the Hardanger, looking across towards one of the largest glaciers in Norway. The main means of transport was by boat. The local people fished, and grew apples, plums and cherries.

No doubt this existence had its attractions, but spending the winter in a tiny hut in such a lonely place would put any marriage under strain, even if the boredom was relieved by listening to the fascinating folk music played on the Hardanger fiddle.** Grieg was testy when his musical inspiration was slow in coming. For Nina, who had been brought up in the metropolis of Copenhagen, all this was too much. Not surprisingly, the Griegs parted company at one stage. Grieg even contemplated going off with a lady-friend to live in Paris.[31]

A hiking companion, Frants Beyer, intervened. He reconciled the Griegs and persuaded them to build their own small wooden villa near to his own on Lake Nordås, below the house where Grieg had spent his summers as a child. The Griegs called their villa Troldhaugen, the hill of the trolls, the forest goblins who were said to live in the valley below. It was

* Grieg subsequently persuaded Delius' father to let him be a composer. Delius borrowed a Norwegian melody for his piece, 'On hearing the first cuckoo in spring'. Another colleague was the Australian-American folksong enthusiast and composer, Percy Grainger.

** The Hardanger fiddle, often beautifully crafted with inlay, has four playing strings, and between three and eight understrings which resonate sympathetically. The effect of the understrings is to provide a resonance which gives a tone almost sounding like a wind instrument. Bartók, who was interested in Norwegian folk music, bought his own Hardanger fiddle. There is a collection of fiddles in the museum at Utne.[30]

completed in 1885. From the verandah, the Griegs had a beautiful view out onto the lake and the serene and gentle scenery beyond, a total contrast to the drama of the fjords. Grieg could go fishing with Frants Beyer.[32] Nina kept a small vegetable garden on the tower which tops the roof. To get away from the domestic activity, and to seek inspiration, Grieg would lock himself away in a hut down by the lake.[33] He kept his toy troll on his desk, he relaxed on the rocking chair, and he experimented at the upright piano. Being only five feet tall, he would sit on a copy of Beethoven's sonatas placed on top of the stool.[34] The hut was chilly, so after the first year he had a stove installed.[*36]

The Griegs had to find the money to pay for Troldhaugen, and their autumns and winters were spent on lengthy concert tours, ranging from Warsaw to Cheltenham and Liverpool. He was much in demand, and had to turn down many invitations. In his pocket, as he went onto the platform, Grieg would fondle a little stone frog which he kept there. In an era when the use of the domestic piano was at its height, his ten books of *Lyric Pieces for the Piano* added to his popularity.[37] When Atlanta offered him $25,000 to conduct, he declined because he felt that he was not strong enough to undertake the journey; in his place, Richard Strauss was hired for $6,000.[38]

Grieg picked up a lot of honours on the way, including, as might be expected, doctorates from Oxford and Cambridge (see colour plate 39). In Bergen, he was of course greatly revered, and there were considerable celebrations for the 25th anniversary of his début as a conductor and recitalist, for his 60th birthday, and, perhaps somewhat ironically, for his silver wedding.

Grieg had fair hair and an almost boyish beard and moustache.[39] Tchaikovsky described him in his early 40s as 'small, middle-aged, and of sickly appearance'.[40] Tchaikovsky also said that his 'sky-blue eyes were irresistibly charming and reminded me of the gaze of an innocent child'.[41] But this appearance concealed a forceful and even controversial personality. He caused a stir when he engaged the Amsterdam Concertgebouw Orchestra, rather than a local orchestra, to play at the Bergen Festival in 1898, which coincided with the International Fisheries Congress and Arts and Crafts Exhibition.[42] The organising committee resigned *en bloc*.

* Carl Nielsen wrote the first movement of his Violin Concerto in the hut in 1911.[35]

The Dreyfus Case

Grieg was also insensitive to the prominence that his international success gave him. He got involved when it looked as if there might be war between Norway and Sweden, and wrote to the Kaiser and King Edward VII asking them to intervene.*[44] But the biggest and most unlikely rumpus in which Grieg became embroiled was the scandalous, anti-Semitic Dreyfus affair in far-off France.[45] In 1894, French intelligence services sensed that military information had been leaking to the Germans. Alfred Dreyfus, a young Jewish staff officer, was tried at a secret court martial, condemned to public degradation and sent to solitary confinement on Devil's Island, slightly north of the mouth of the Amazon.

Subsequently, an intelligence officer** came across evidence that the document essential to the conviction had not been written by Dreyfus but by another officer called Esterhazy. When the intelligence officer raised this with his superiors, he was posted off to north Africa. His successor, Colonel Henry, duly fixed the file with a forgery. But the intelligence officer's lawyer raised the matter with the vice-president of the Senate.

Dreyfus' brother and the vice-president then brought a formal charge against Esterhazy, who was acquitted by secret court martial and hailed as a hero by enthusiastic crowds. Emile Zola issued an open letter, 'J'accuse', to the president of France, in which he claimed that the army had procured the Dreyfus conviction on the basis of a document not shown to the defence, and that Esterhazy had been acquitted on instructions from a superior officer. Zola was twice tried and condemned for slander, verdicts hailed with delight by the crowds shouting 'Death to Zola' and 'Death to the Jews'. He appealed, and his conviction was quashed, but he fled to England before the retrial.

Bourgeois France was split on whether or not Dreyfus was guilty. The league of the 'Patrie Française' argued that the whole affair was a plot to undermine France and discredit the army: it was better that the innocent man should perish, than the whole nation. The Dreyfusards argued that

* Sweden threatened to suspend the constitution just before the final separation in 1905. To get full independence, the Norwegians had to agree to give up her fortifications along the eastern frontier and to the creation of a neutral zone. They elected a new king, Haakon VII, a Danish prince and naval officer, married to the youngest and liveliest daughter of England, Princess Maud, who thereby escaped the clutches of her possessive mother, Queen Alexandra.[43]

** Colonel Picquart; he was later a friend of Mahler.[46]

the affair represented arbitrary justice. Families were divided; people were so hostile to each other that organising salons and parties became extremely difficult. The salon of Bizet's widow became a centre for Dreyfusard activity (see page 605 fn);[47] the painter Degas refused to attend it, and departed for ever from the Halévy circle where he had previously been welcomed almost as a family member. Saint-Saëns was regarded as a Dreyfusard; Sardou, the author of *Tosca*, as anti-Dreyfus: so, to be even-handed, the French government made both grand officers of the Légion d'Honneur.[48]

In summer 1898, when the new minister of war, a member of the League of the 'Patrie Française', attempted to lay proof of Dreyfus' guilt before the parlement, a review of the Dreyfus trial became inevitable. Colonel Henry was questioned by the minister and committed suicide; Esterhazy, the real villain, slipped away to England, where he lived quietly as a count under an assumed name. In the middle of this shabby affair, the president of France, Félix Faure, had a cerebral haemorrhage one afternoon when in bed with his mistress; she had to be hurried out of a side door, wrapped in a blanket; he died later in the evening. The new president was then struck with a cane by an anti-Dreyfusard baron at Auteuil races, and the minister had to resign for having not given the president adequate protection.[*49]

Into this massive French embroglio waded the diminutive Edvard Grieg from Norway. Around the same time as the news about the Dreyfus conviction, he received an invitation from Edouard Colonne to conduct his orchestra in Paris. Grieg was staying with the Bjørnsons, with a large household, who were scathing about the case. He replied to the invitation, saying that he would not appear in a country where such a miscarriage of justice could occur. Bjørnson's son-in-law, a journalist, who had helped translate the letter into French, asked Grieg's permission for it to be published. It appeared in the *Frankfurter Zeitung*, at a time when Franco-German relations were still highly strained: *revanchistes* were determined to avenge the loss of Alsace and Lorraine.

* There were plots against the government. The leader of an anti-Dreyfusard *coup d'état* was acquitted, showing the partiality of French justice. In August 1899, the retrial of Dreyfus began at Rennes: two out of the seven judges acquitted Dreyfus, the majority found him 'guilty of intelligence with the enemy with attenuating circumstances'. The president of France pardoned Dreyfus; but that was not enough, and, in 1906, the Rennes verdict was also quashed. Parlement passed a special resolution for Dreyfus' rehabilitation.

The letter was publicised internationally. The reaction in France is illustrated by a French journal, which addressed itself to the 'compositeur de musique juive, E. G.' and threatened, if he were to appear in Paris, 'de le recevoir dans notre ville par coups de pied dans la partie le moins noble de son individu'.[50] For some time, concert promoters were afraid to advertise Grieg's works for fear of demonstrations.[51] When, in 1903, Grieg eventually went to Paris, demonstrators tried to wreck his concert: he had to be escorted back to his hotel by a police guard.

By this stage, the quality of Grieg's art was under the spotlight. The concert had ended with the closing scene from *Götterdämmerung* preceded by Grieg's works. Debussy, who had described Grieg's *Elegiac Melodies* as like having in one's mouth 'le goût bizarre et charmant d'un bonbon rose qui serait fourré de neige', left before the Wagner saying: 'on ne mange pas de rosbif après les petit fours'.[52]

Nevertheless, Grieg continued to be a celebrity and moved in royal circles. He was asked to play before Edward VII, but had twice to stop as the king was talking so loudly. When Grieg complained to King Haakon, he was told that 'the King of England can talk and listen at the same time'.[53] Edward VII's cousin, the Kaiser, used to visit the Hardanger,* and once invited Grieg on board his yacht. The Kaiser kept his private orchestra on board, for he was a keen amateur musician, with ambitions as a composer and conductor. The orchestra played before Grieg and the Kaiser. Grieg was invited back the next evening and described the Kaiser as 'a very unusual man, a strange mixture of great energy, great self confidence and great kindness of heart'.[54]

Grieg's Later Years

Grieg did not live long enough to experience the catastrophe when the countries ruled by these imperial cousins went to war against each other. Between concerts, he would attempt to restore his fragile health in sanatoriums in Norway and abroad.** After 1900, his life 'became one long

* One town on the Sørfjord was so concerned for the Kaiser's welfare that the municipality bought a Ceres patent lavatory for his use. It can be seen in the Folk Museum at Utne.

** Grieg had a great sense of humour. He wrote from Karlsbad in 1887: 'I have chronic gastritis, a swollen intestine, enlarged liver ... I have always had a penchant for the augmented – in terms of intervals. N.B. – But now I think that I want to switch over to the diminished, that is for a short while.'[55]

illness', 'a catalogue of asthma, bronchitis, the coughing up of mucous, and difficulty in breathing'.[56] He kept going on drugs such as quinine and aspirin, and the usual sedatives bromide and chloral. Probably the mountain trips which he still took were the best medicine.

Spring 1907 was spent in Copenhagen. In late August, he was recuperating in Voss in the mountains about 60 miles from Bergen. He intended to leave Troldhaugen on 2 September to catch the boat which would take him to England, where he was to conduct a performance of the Piano Concerto, with Percy Grainger as soloist. But his doctor called it off. Grieg died in hospital in Bergen on 4 September. His nurse described how he had dozed off, and then sat up in bed, and seemed almost to give a bow to an audience before lying back and expiring. Nina outlived her husband by 28 years; she died in Copenhagen when she had just turned 90. Her remains are buried next to his in the cliff face at Troldhaugen, on the other side of the promontory from his hut, in the place where the sun is last seen at sunset.

Although we mainly remember Grieg for his war-horse, the Piano Concerto in A minor, and the *Peer Gynt Suites*, his other works, such as his songs, had a considerable influence on Jean Sibelius, and also on composers such as Delius, Grainger, Nielsen, Peter Warlock and John Ireland. Of these, the best remembered is undoubtedly Sibelius, who is remarkable, among other things, for his longevity. He was nearly 92 when he died. At the time of his birth, the average life expectancy in Finland, for a male, was around 35 and a half years.[57]

Sibelius' Youth

Jean Sibelius was born on 8 December 1865 in Tavastehus (Hämeenlinna, in Finnish), an important town of around 3,000 people, some 50 miles north of Helsingfors (now Helsinki). Sibelius' father, who was from a musical family, was the town physician. His practice included the Russian garrison which was stationed next to the medieval fortress, originally built by the Swedes, but by then a prison. The town was built of wood and had recently been ravaged by fire. The doctor and his wife Maria, the daughter of a Lutheran pastor, rented one of the new one-storey houses from the apothecary.

Finland was then a small but autonomous grand duchy belonging to the Russian tsar. It had long been involved in a tug of war between Sweden and Russia. Peter the Great and his successors had progressively seized parts of Finland from the Swedes, who fought to recover the areas they had lost. However, it was finally annexed by Russia in 1809. Swedish, the language of the Sibelius family, was the official language, although Russian was made compulsory in state schools from 1872. Finnish, a language in the 'Finno-Ugric' group, which also includes Estonian and Hungarian Magyar, was encouraged by the authorities. The complex heritage is apparent today from the road signs, many of which are bilingual in Swedish and Finnish; the elegant central area of Helsinki is graced by statues commemorating a tsar and tsarina.[58]

Finland, which is just larger than Norway, was an inhospitable place in which to live: the average temperature in Helsingfors at the time Sibelius was born was just below 4°C; on the day of Sibelius' birth, it was minus 17°C;[59] but large wood-burning porcelain stoves in each room would have kept the house relatively warm.

The country was covered with vast forests. Lakes and marsh constituted a third of it, so that Finland was more abundantly supplied with water than any other country in the world at the time.[60] Food was a different matter: even as late as 1848 whole villages died of starvation. And the quality of the water was poor: Sibelius' father died in a typhoid epidemic of 1867.

The family was left with a bankrupt estate. It must have been a time of great strain for Maria, who was aged only 27. All the family possessions were seized and she had to petition the administrators to obtain clothing.[61] She was pregnant with Christian, and had five-year-old Linda and tiny Janne, as he was known, to bring up.

Fortunately, Maria could shelter with her widowed but prosperous mother, who already accommodated her unmarried son and two daughters. After a few years, they all moved to a considerably larger residence which had originally been built for a wine merchant. So, Janne was brought up by his imperious grandmother, his mother and his two aunts, one of whom taught the piano. The ladies must have seemed formidable in their black dresses.

In the summer, the family, with Aunt Julia's miniature harmonium usually in the baggage,[62] would visit Granny Sibelius. She lived in a small wooden house by the church in Lovisa, a town situated on an inlet of the Gulf of Finland, about 55 miles east of Helsingfors. One might imagine Janne and his siblings running down the pretty market square to the sea.

But the water was reedy and murky, and probably they did not swim, but instead went sailing in the bracing sea air.*

At home in Tavastehus, the children would skate on the lake in winter and throw stones into it when the ice melted.[64] The dreamy Janne would enjoy letting his imagination roam as he looked across to the wooded, gently rolling hills, where later he would walk and hunt.[65]

Janne's schooldays coincided with a period of about ten years, starting in 1873, when the Finnish Language School decamped from Helsingfors to Tavastehus. With it came an influx of teachers and pupils. Janne went to the school, and it was there that he started to develop the 'fervent nationalist and patriotic spirit that was so integral a part of his personality and a source of inspiration for many of his compositions'.[66] But the family continued to speak Swedish among themselves. They also mixed with the considerable number of Russian families.

Janne was taught the violin by the garrison conductor, and no doubt enjoyed watching him conduct the parades on the large town square. Although he was no child prodigy, a friend recalled that 'while the other boys were doing their homework, Janne was playing the violin or piano. The family were always having to urge him to study.'[67] The family enjoyed chamber music and held musical soirées, with Linda at the piano, Janne on the violin and Christian on the cello. They could also visit the theatre restaurant, which was an important centre of cultural life in the town, where musicians performed regularly.

Maria's mother disapproved of her grandson becoming a musician, although he wanted to be a violin virtuoso. So, when he went to the University of Helsingfors, it was to study law. But he spent most of his time on music, having enrolled as a part-time student at the Conservatoire. After leaving university, he went to Berlin where he heard much new music; he lived life, which for him meant wine, women and song, to the full.

Sibelius returned to Finland in 1891. As well as teaching, he composed *Kullervo*, a choral work based on the *Kalevala*. This was the Finnish national epic, 'equalling the Iliad in length and completeness',[68] which had been assembled in the 1830s. In the last decades of the 19th century, the *Kalevala* inspired many artists with whom Sibelius associated.

By his late 20s, Sibelius was no longer wholly dependent on his grand-

* There is now a nuclear power station nearby.[63]

mother and friends for finance, although his lifestyle meant that he was usually in debt. He was then tall, with bushy chocolate-coloured hair and a moustache. He himself said that he could subdue a lion with the glance of his piercing, blue, falcon-like eyes. But this image is a long way from the picture we have of him as portrayed in his mid-80s in those (literally) awful, bald, unsmiling, but much-acclaimed photographs by Karsh of Ottawa.[69]

Marriage into the Järnefelt Family

In June 1892, a couple of months after *Kullervo*, Sibelius married Aino,* the youngest surviving daughter of Major-General Järnefelt, a military topographer in the Russian army, and later a provincial governor in Finland. Aino's mother was also a general's daughter, from an Estonian aristocratic family based in St Petersburg. She had an artistic background as well: she had close relatives who were sculptors and painters. And she was a strong supporter of the new nationalistic ideas which got going in the 1880s. Both parents spoke Finnish to their children and Aino and her many brothers and sisters were educated at the Finnish-speaking school in Helsinki, as Finnish nationalists called their capital.

By the time Aino got engaged, her brother Eero was already an up-and-coming artist who was winning the prizes which prefaced a remarkably distinguished career as a very versatile painter. Another brother, Arvid, was a prominent writer for whom Sibelius would set the incidental music to the play *Kuolema*. Armas, two years older than Aino, was abroad studying to become a conductor and composer. Thus, Sibelius was absorbed into one of the more prominent Finnish-speaking families which was very closely involved with the nationalist movement and the arts in Finland.[70]

The turn of the century was a time of political unrest, as the Russians sought to counter the growing Finnish nationalism: Tsar Nicholas II issued a decree known as the 'February Manifesto' which deprived Finland of her autonomy; it also curtailed the freedom of speech and assembly that the Finns had hitherto enjoyed. This served to boost Sibelius' sense of nationalism. He wrote *En Saga* and the *Karelia Suite*,** with its popular march.

* Aino is the name of a beautiful maiden in the *Kalevala*.

** Karelia is the area overlapping Finland and the Russian border. The 1890s have been called the 'Age of Karelianism' in the art world: inspired by French realist art, young Finnish artists (together with Sibelius) sought inspiration in their own people and landscapes.[71]

He also wrote the *Four Legends about Lemminkäinen*, which drew on the *Kalevala*. He became interested in folksong, although he did not absorb folk melodies consciously into his major works. His nationalism had not, however, precluded him from writing a cantata for the Coronation of Tsar Nicholas II in 1896.[72]

He would meet other Finnish musicians for long discussions and heavy drinking sessions. Despite being awarded a state pension in recognition of his prominence as Finland's leading composer, his big spending meant that he was always short of cash.

Sibelius had intended to write an opera, but, like Grieg, he gave up that idea after a visit to Bayreuth indicated to him how difficult it would be to write one successfully. His First Symphony, composed in 1899, was a great success, and his reputation was spread internationally by his friend, the conductor Robert Kajanus, who founded the Helsinki Philharmonic Orchestra. Sibelius continued to write works with a national theme, including four tableaux, one of which was *Finlandia*. He was surprised at the popularity of this work, because he regarded it as a 'pretty insignificant piece in relation to the rest'.[73]

A similarly popular work was the famous 'Valse Triste' which came from the incidental music for *Kuolema*. Sibelius subsequently regretted selling the rights to this to Breitkopf & Härtel for 300 marks. Although his debts were mounting like his alcohol consumption, he bought a plot of land a few hundred yards from Lake Tuusula near Järvenpää, about 25 miles north-east of Helsinki. There, he built Ainola, a tall wooden villa secluded in a clump of pine and birch trees. The location was then relatively isolated, although it had already become a kind of artists' colony: Sibelius' brother-in-law Eero Järnefelt had built a villa there some three years before.

Settling in Ainola

Sibelius lived in Ainola for virtually the whole of the rest of his life. Aino, a talented lady who translated French and English literature into Finnish, created the garden and managed the domestic and practical side of life. They had five daughters.[74]

In spring 1908, Sibelius was troubled by throat pains and a tumour was diagnosed. He had thirteen operations before it was cured.[75] For long, he lived in fear of the cancer returning. He gave up alcohol and cigars for the best part of a decade.[76]

In the early 1900s, Sibelius wrote the Second and Third Symphonies and the Violin Concerto. A trip with Eero Järnefelt to Koli, a beauty spot in Karelia, is said to have inspired the unusual Fourth Symphony which was completed two years later in 1911, much of it composed in a room which looks over the trees across Lake Tuusula.[77] This is strange, austere music; it is sometimes considered to be a reaction to his illness, or to the large and richly coloured works of Mahler and Strauss. It is called the 'Barkbrod' Symphony, because it recalls the grim times when starving Finns were forced to eat the bark of trees. When it was first performed in New York, many people walked out.[78]

In the first decade of the century, Sibelius was already a celebrity. His reputation grew, aided by the spread of gramophone records. He travelled to England, America and Continental Europe. On his tours, he lived the high life: when one Copenhagen restaurant went bankrupt, the newspaper attributed it to Sibelius' departure.[79] During his last visit to London, he was accompanied by the composer Ferruccio Busoni: the conductor Sir Henry Wood said that 'they were like a couple of irresponsible schoolboys'.[80]

Sibelius' music was particularly applauded in England and in the USA, where his style of romantic nationalism has always been particularly popular. In England, one reputable critic in the 1930s went so far as to claim that Sibelius was 'the most important symphonic writer since Beethoven'.[81] Just before the First World War, Sibelius had a very successful tour in the USA. Yale gave him a doctorate. He never returned to the USA after his 1914 visit, despite being offered the position of director of the Eastman School in Rochester, New York, one of the leading American schools of music.* By the mid-1930s, a poll of US radio listeners indicated that he was the most popular composer in the world.[82]

Meanwhile, Finland had continued to be turbulent. To forestall left-wing risings at the time of the Russian Revolution in 1917, the middle classes in Finland organised themselves into military cadres, known as the White Guard. The communist Red Guards attempted a coup and civil war began. Ainola was occupied by Red troops and Sibelius had to move temporarily to his brother's house. After the Whites, with German aid, liberated the country from the Reds, Finland became an independent republic.

* Others include the Juilliard in New York City, the Curtis Institute in Philadelphia, the New England Conservatory in Boston and Northwestern University in Chicago.

In the 1920s, Sibelius returned to writing a considerable amount of lighter music: he was trying to repeat his success with the 'Valse Triste'. His precarious financial situation had been made worse by the First World War, when he stopped receiving his royalties from Breitkopfs. He also wrote some major works, the Sixth and Seventh Symphonies, and the incidental music to *The Tempest*.

Virtual Silence

Apart from a few unimportant works for the piano and violin, the tone poem *Tapiola*, written in 1926, was his last work of importance. There was suddenly a Rossini-like silence (see page 263). Sibelius retired to the seclusion of Ainola and its woods, and almost never emerged for the remaining years of his life. Although drink may have affected his creativity, it is easy to forget that he was already in his 60s, when many retire anyway. There was also something to be said for keeping one's head down at the time: outside, there was a considerable amount of disruption in Finland as the Second World War approached. Finland, mainly as a response to the Russian threat to the east, aligned itself with Germany. Indeed Sibelius' music was appropriated for propaganda purposes by Nazi Germany. After the Molotov Pact allied Germany with Russia, the Russians could attack and defeat Finland. When Germany reneged and launched Operation Barbarossa against Russia in 1941, Finland launched a punitive assault on Russia.

In his seclusion, Sibelius kept in touch with musical developments by listening to the radio and to records, sometimes late into the night.[83] There was enormous pressure, in the press and elsewhere, to publish an Eighth Symphony, but somehow it did not come forth. Or, whatever did, he burnt. The Royal Philharmonic Society, which had secured the rights to the world première of the symphony, invited him to compose a work to mark the Festival of Britain in 1951.[84] But that was not forthcoming either.

Those who knew him at this time found Sibelius full of charm, courtesy and wit, despite the granite-like image. He enjoyed his walks in the countryside, and even kept a matchbox with him full of moss so that he could get the smell of the woods.[85] He also enjoyed his sauna, where he would chat to Heiki, his attendant.[86] He took pleasure in his valuable collection of Finnish art which lined his walls. He received countless gifts of cigars. 'Churchill and Sibelius were the two most famous cigar-smokers in the world.'[87] During the Second World War, when tobacco was rationed, he was supplied with a special issue from the factories.

He had become an institution in his own right. Few great composers have received such public recognition and inspired such devotion during their own lifetime. VIPs would go out from Helsinki to visit him. On his birthdays, tributes, gifts and telegrams were showered on him. On his 85th birthday, the president of Finland motored out to his villa to pay the nation's respects. On his 90th, there were even more plaudits, including a gift of cigars from Churchill and 12,000 telegrams.

As he approached his 90s, Sibelius would hardly go out of the house. He began to lose interest in the world and seemed depressed. On 20 September 1957, he woke up feeling a bit giddy, and collapsed at lunchtime. In mid-afternoon, he lost consciousness and he died just before 9 pm.[88]

This was now the second half of the 20th century, so we should not be surprised that politicians such as the chairman of the UN General Assembly made memorial speeches. And of course, the US ambassador conveyed the condolences of the American people. After a state funeral in the cathedral in Helsinki, which has some of the steepest steps in the world for a guard of honour to lift a coffin up, Jean Sibelius was laid to rest at Ainola, where Aino joined him some twelve years later.[89]

Perhaps the common factor between the composers described in this and the previous chapter is that they came from 'nations' which saw themselves as oppressed. Maybe the oppression provided a source of inspiration; maybe, like Chopin, these composers and their music provided something relatively uncontentious round which their compatriots could rally. Sibelius' personal secretary conceded that 'when a small nation of four million people produces an artist whose acclaim is truly universal, it is easy to understand that in his own country his importance is unreasonably exaggerated'.[90] Does this astonishingly candid remark perhaps give us an insight into what nationalism in music is really about?

Mahler

CHAPTER 24

Bridging the 19th and 20th centuries, there were two composers, one from Moravia, the other from Bavaria, who, each in their own way, took forward the Wagnerian Romantic tradition. Both often used a very large canvas, and a very large orchestra: the title of Mahler's Eighth Symphony, the 'Symphony of a Thousand', speaks for itself; and, in the tone poem *Ein Heldenleben*, Strauss requires eight horns, five trumpets and quadruple woodwind. Both composers could also produce music of exquisite delicacy. In this chapter, we shall describe the turbulent life of Mahler, and in the next, that of Richard Strauss.[1]

After a hard childhood, Mahler went to study in Vienna. Despite the disadvantage of his Jewish birth, he eventually secured top conducting positions, first in Hamburg, then in Vienna and New York. 'In the spare time of the career of a conductor as great and extensive as Toscanini himself', he succeeded in composing ten symphonies 'of immense range and reach'.[2] He also seems to have had an exceptional number of successful love affairs, although his marriage to Alma Schindler, 'the most beautiful girl in Vienna',[3] and nearly twenty years younger than him, did not work out well. His struggles during the great years at the Imperial Opera, the climax of his conducting achievement, were compounded by the anti-Semitism prevalent in the prosperous, but superficial, *fin-de-siècle* Vienna.

Mahler died before his 51st birthday, after an unsatisfactory period in both his professional life in New York and his marriage. However, just over eight months before his death in May 1911, he experienced the thrill of hearing the first performance of his Eighth Symphony. This was only a very short time after Arnold Schoenberg began to compose music of a very different order. Just before Mahler returned to New York for the last time, he attended an exhibition of Schoenberg's experimental paintings.[4] It was now, after all, the 20th century.

Mahler's Early Years

Gustav Mahler was born on 7 July 1860, in the village of Kaliště on the Bohemian side of the Moravian border, not too far from the farm where, five years before, Smetana's father had decided to settle. The word kaliště means a trap for hunting wild animals;[5] the village is in the middle of the countryside, and is tiny. It is over twenty miles from the large market town of Jihlava, which was then called Iglau.

Mahler's father, Bernard, was the sole German in the village. He went from door to door in a barouche, selling mainly liquor. His market can only have comprised the 500 inhabitants of Kaliště, a few other villages and the larger Humpolec, over four miles away. It was a tough life; and discrimination against the Jews made it particularly difficult. Perhaps as a result of this hardship, Bernard was violent. He would beat up and abuse his frail and limping wife,* the daughter of a prosperous soap manufacturer.

However, there was reason to be hopeful about the future. Recently, there had been a considerable easing of the restrictions on the Jews, which had been severe. Since the early 17th century, Jews could only enter Iglau for the market through one gate, on payment of a poll tax; they could not spend the night there. Since the early 18th century, the number of Jews allowed to live in the whole of Moravia was restricted, by decree, to 5,106 families. A father could bequeath his right of residence to his eldest son, who alone was allowed to get married. The rest of the males had to leave the country, and many left for Poland and Hungary. When a family had only daughters, the line was considered extinct. This law applied until 1848, when Bernard was 21.

* Gustav inherited his mother's weak heart; possibly as a consequence of her limp, he also developed an odd way of walking, with a change of pace after every three or four steps.[6]

Empress Maria Theresa had wanted to expel the Jews from her domains, but was persuaded of the wisdom of letting them stay, so long as they paid a hefty tax. Her son Joseph, with a mixture of despotism and humanitarianism, attempted to integrate the Jews, and issued an Edict of Tolerance in 1781.* But anti-Semitism continued: Jews were burdened with heavy taxes. And there was a spy scandal implicating the mistress of a privy counsellor: the girl was a rabbi's daughter.[7] Perhaps, therefore, it is not surprising that when Bernard was ten, there were only seventeen Jews resident in Iglau, out of a population of 16,000; a few years later, some were deported for illegal residence.[8]

Even after many of the restrictions were lightened, the situation remained difficult. In May 1850, by which time the number of Jews in Iglau had increased to around 100, there were anti-Jewish riots. But the future was brighter. After the Italian military disasters of 1859, Emperor Franz Joseph realised that he had to take steps to prevent the collapse of the rest of his empire. Very shortly after the emperor decreed far-reaching changes and improvements in late October 1860,** the enterprising and determined Bernard Mahler was in Iglau with his wife and three-month-old son. A week later, he was given permission to open up a grocery business, which was soon extended to include the sale of liquor. Before long, at the Mahlers' store, one could buy Bordeaux wine, Jamaican rum, kümmel, maraschino, chartreuse and fine Russian and Chinese teas; or, if one preferred, one could simply drink a glass of hot punch.[9]

The domestic side of life was troubled and became terribly sad. Gustav's mother had fourteen children,† of whom eight died in infancy. Gustav never knew his older brother. Karl died aged two in December 1865; Rudolf died aged one in December 1866. When Gustav was eleven, both the two-year-old Arnold and the eight-month-old Friedrich died. Alfred, aged one, died eighteen months later, and so it went on. When Gustav was thirteen, the death of twelve-year-old Ernst must have been a particular

* Joseph repealed a law which required Jews to wear a yellow badge. But he required them to adopt German names from a prescribed list, and they were required to stop using Hebrew and Yiddish.

** This 'October Diploma' began a period of constitutional rule in the Habsburg monarchy. Equal rights for Jews only came in December 1867; two years later, the number of Jews in Iglau had jumped to nearly 1,100.

† Earlier in the century, Schubert's brother married twice and had 28 children, of whom twelve survived.

blow. By the time he was 21, the death of two-year-old Konrad might have appeared almost routine.[10]

On Gustav's sixth birthday, 1,600 wounded were brought in from the Battle of Königgrätz (now Sadowa), which had taken place four days before, about 60 miles to the north (see page 511).[11] There had been great jubilation as the Habsburg army went north to meet the Prussians; but now, just a few days later, the victorious Prussians took occupation, and billeted their officers all over the town. Bernard's shop must have experienced their depredations, but the worst legacy of the two-month occupation was a cholera epidemic which carried away over 80 Prussian soldiers and over 300 inhabitants.[12] After the Prussians had gone, there was a visit from Emperor Franz Joseph who was keen to revive morale. The royal visit was, of course, accompanied by appropriate festivities.[13]

Because Iglau continued to be a military depot, there were regular parades. As Gustav walked to school, he would have heard the bands playing, and also the folk groups which frequented the town's enormous market square. He was a conscientious schoolboy, and it is recorded that he handed in a purse which he found with a lot of money in it.[14] His musical studies were begun on an old piano in his grandparents' attic. The deaths of Karl and Rudolf were marked by an early composition: 'Polka with an introductory funeral march'.[15] More happily, when he was ten, Gustav gave a recital.

The Mahlers' business must have prospered considerably because, when Gustav was eleven, he was sent to a prestigious school in Prague. Earlier that year, the railway line had opened, and the journey must have been a novel and exciting experience.[16] But, away from home, Gustav was very unhappy. He did very badly in his schoolwork and came bottom of the class. He learnt something, however: he apparently saw one of the sons of the house where he was lodging having the maidservant.[17]

Bernard retrieved Gustav back to Iglau to continue his education. To obtain an opinion on Gustav's musical ability, he consulted a friend, a keen musician. The boy should become a professional musician, he was told; so, when he was hardly fifteen, Bernard took Gustav to Vienna to see Professor Julius Epstein at the Conservatoire. Epstein immediately accepted him for that autumn, and paid half his fees.

Mahler arrived in the city of Brahms. As he looked at the brand new Imperial and Royal Opera House, opened only five years previously, a boy with Mahler's ambition might well have dreamt, or determined, that he would some day be its musical director. He will have heard of the Opera's magnificent performances of Wagner's works, before the stock market crash of December 1873 depleted its audiences overnight. By the time of Mahler's arrival in Vienna, the Opera was recovering, and works like *Carmen*, recently rejected by Paris, were being well received.[18] Verdi came there to conduct *Aïda* and his Requiem; and Wagner stayed there to supervise performances of *Tannhäuser* and *Lohengrin*. But there was much more than music, because Vienna was above all a centre for art. Art provided the illusion which enabled the people of the capital to escape from the reality of the relentless deterioration of the Habsburg regime.

Mahler returned periodically to Iglau to complete his general education and to perform in concerts. Despite the distractions of music, he scraped through his exams sufficiently to matriculate at the philosophical faculty of Vienna University, which he attended between 1877 and 1880. Alongside the study of history and philosophy, he heard some of Bruckner's lectures.[19] Somehow he managed to keep reasonably clear of Brahms, who was so virulently opposed to the influence Bruckner was having on the younger generation.

Mahler led a bohemian life, and was close to members of the radical student movements, where he made several lasting friendships. One of his musical friends was Hugo Wolf who was about four months older than him. Wolf would make a major contribution to the Lied (song), before, in his mid-30s, he became insane with syphilis. Mahler and Wolf shared lodgings and at times one bed; they often lived on cheese-parings, and slept rough.[20]

At the Conservatoire, Mahler excelled, and won piano and composition prizes. After he graduated there, he had to complete his university studies. To keep going, he earned a little on the side, by teaching. For a time, he was piano tutor to a family in Hungary.

Mahler came under the spell of an anthology of old popular legends and songs, *Des Knaben Wunderhorn*, which had been collected by the German writers Clemens Brentano and Ludwig Achim von Arnim, on their travels through parts of Germany, in the first decade of the century. This collection, named after the opening poem, which tells of a youth who brings the empress a magic horn, was highly influential in the Romantic movement. The poems express a wide variety of moods: the cuckoo and the nightingale have a song contest which the donkey judges; dead soldiers answer the reveille, the sentry sings a night-song, a prisoner sings a song with his sweetheart, St Anthony preaches to the fishes.[21] These songs were to influence many of Mahler's compositions. He used *Wunderhorn* poems in 'Das Klagende Lied' and the *Lieder Eines Fahrenden Gesellen*, and in the Second, Third and Fourth Symphonies. In the 1890s, he wrote settings of twelve *Wunderhorn* poems for voice and piano.

'Das Klagende Lied' was completed on 1 November 1880, when Mahler was aged twenty. He entered it for the 1880 Beethoven Prize sponsored by the Vienna Philharmonic Society. It probably did not help Mahler's cause that the jury was headed by Brahms and his colleague, the critic Eduard Hanslick. Mahler's composition was rejected. Bruckner was more supportive and asked him and another student to make a piano duet arrangement of his disastrous Third Symphony.[22]

Conductor

Mahler was still only twenty but impoverished: one way to earn a living was to become a conductor. This was a time when even small towns like Rostock, Oldenburg and Trier had opera houses, and concert life flourished. 'Regular performances were given in almost all towns, large or small, and smaller still.'[23] Besides, 'neither courts nor cities ever expected their theatres to show a profit or even to be self-supporting'.[24]

Mahler began his meteoric career as a conductor in summer 1880 in a tiny wooden theatre seating about 200 people at Bad Hall, a small spa set in rolling agricultural countryside near Linz. Its waters, strong in iodine, were recommended for heart and vascular complaints; in earlier years, the poet Franz Grillparzer had frequented it. Mahler conducted musical farces and comedies, and was general factotum: he tidied up after performances, and during the intervals he pushed the musical director's child around in its pram.[25]

Mahler conducted at Laibach (now Ljubljana) during the following year. His first significant appointment, however, was when he became conductor to the theatre at Olmütz (now Olomouc) in Moravia, in January 1883. There, he conducted a repertoire including Bizet's *Carmen* and works by, among others, Meyerbeer and Verdi. No Mozart or Wagner was performed there, but Mahler had a considerable success with Méhul's *Joseph* and Flotow's *Martha*. His achievement led to his appointment later that year as second conductor in Kassel. Although Kassel, destroyed in the

Second World War, may to us sound somewhat uninspiring, it was the city of Grimm's fairytales and the centre of German folklore. *Des Knaben Wunderhorn* was first published there.

By now, Mahler was on his way. He developed an immense grasp of the technical problems of an opera house. His ability to get good results out of poor material was spotted. Bruno Walter, a leading conductor in the first half of the 20th century, later recalled Mahler's skill at getting 'singers to the point of almost instrumental musical exactitude and at the same time to achieve a full measure of dramatic expression'. Mahler 'demanded the utmost of himself and others'; he 'renewed himself every minute' and 'did not know the meaning of slackening either in his work or his vital principles'.[26] And he had the power to inspire enthusiasm for spiritual values. Walter continued: 'he knew no trivial moment, he thought no thought and spoke no word that might have meant a betrayal of his soul'.[27] The practical implications of this were that orchestral players did not enjoy working under Mahler, 'they learned to fear him';[28] this had already been noticed at Laibach.

In Kassel, Mahler made a great impact. Even though his repertoire was confined, from there he could travel to hear Wagner performed at Dresden and at Bayreuth. He also succeeded in having a passionate love affair which inspired him to compose the song cycle *Lieder Eines Fahrenden Gesellen*.*

He concluded at Kassel with a musical festival at which he conducted Beethoven's Ninth and Mendelssohn's *St Paul*. He then became conductor at the new German Theatre in Prague. There, he held his own against the Czech Nationalist Theatre, the home of Smetana (who had died the year before) and Dvořák. He also had an affair with a singer.[29] He then moved on to Leipzig, where, to great acclaim, he began to conduct Wagner's operas.

In December 1886, he met Captain von Weber, whose more celebrated grandfather had sketched a comic opera which Mahler proceeded to complete, *Die Drei Pintos*. This was successful; it spread his reputation and provided him with a useful source of income. He also took the opportunity to have an affair with the captain's wife.[30]

In October 1888, Mahler began a ten-year contract as artistic director of the Royal Opera in Budapest, with a salary of 10,000 fl.**[32] There, in three years, he created a Hungarian opera with local artists, and conducted

* He had had a romance with a postman's daughter, in Vienna, when he was nineteen.

** A junior civil servant would earn around 500 fl per annum at this time.[31]

his First Symphony. Mahler should have felt relatively comfortable in Budapest, which had a large Jewish community, the number of Jews in the city approaching almost a quarter of its residents.[33] However, he fell out with the Hungarians, not least because his vision extended wider than Hungarian nationalism. But he departed with 25,000 fl compensation. This move has a slightly modern twist to it: no compensation was strictly necessary, as he had already been appointed to Hamburg.

Hamburg, with its dark skies, rain and fog, was then considered the second city in Germany although, in the opinion of Hamburgers, it ranked first. It, says Bruno Walter, 'had a personality, which was more than could be said of Berlin.'[34]

Hans von Bülow, Liszt's son-in-law and by far the most famous musician resident in Hamburg at the time, wrote to his daughter: 'Hamburg has now acquired a simply first rate opera conductor in Mr Gustav Mahler.'[35] In Hamburg, Mahler had an international cast of singers, and could perform the major works. He made a colossal impact, despite his small size and unusual appearance: he was not much over five feet tall,* 'lean, fidgety … with an unusually high, steep forehead, long dark hair, deeply penetrating bespectacled eyes, and a characteristically spiritual mouth'.[37] To start with, he undertook nineteen operas a month.[38] Later, he was conducting nearly every night of the week for long stretches of time. He introduced Puccini's *Manon*, Verdi's *Falstaff* and Humperdinck's *Hänsel und Gretel*. Tchaikovsky, who was in Hamburg in 1892, wrote: 'The conductor here isn't just some middling character: he's a positive genius, and dying to conduct the first performance [of *Onegin*]. I heard him conduct the most astounding performance of *Tannhäuser* … they call him Mahler.'[39] By now, even Brahms was pleased.

Mahler's Method

Wherever he worked, Mahler was utterly determined to raise standards and to create a blending of music and stage. This was at a time when stage directors and conductors were not expected to weld groups of artists into a harmonious whole. The public 'demanded voice, voice, and again voice. They were quite ready to overlook a lack of acting ability, an unfavourable stage appearance, and even the absence of musical talent.'[40] As late as 1901,

* 'I know of only one Mime and that is me', he said on one occasion.[36] Mime is the dwarf in Wagner's *Das Rheingold* and *Siegfried*.

the programmes of the Vienna Imperial Opera stated the names of the singers in any given performance, but not the name of the conductor.

Although Mahler had 'the gift of transmitting his energy to the entire cast',[41] he was not a warm person. He regularly fell out with his superiors. To say that his handling of people was insensitive would be an understatement: he would scream 'Idiot!', he would curse – two singers went so far as to challenge him to a duel. Bruno Walter attributes this to the 'matter-of-fact ego-centricity of the exalted creative man whose task makes him lose sight of his fellow-man, and whose absorption in music often blots out his feelings for humanity ... he knew the meaning of friendship; he was a friend in his own way. But there was not within him a steadily flowing source of warmth.'[42]

Mahler lived on his nerves. 'Basically, all that Mahler thought, spoke, read or composed was concerned with the questions of whence, to what purpose, whither ... The atmosphere of his soul was stormy and unpredictable. Cheerful childlike laughter would suddenly, and without outward cause, give way to an inward spasm, the rising of fierce and desperate suffering.'[43] Mahler's wife, when she first met him some years later, observed his hands disfigured by nail biting:[44] 'he's dreadfully restless. He stormed about the room like a savage. The fellow is made entirely of oxygen. When you go near him, you get burnt.'[45] Not surprisingly, Mahler had chronic breakdowns.

When his father, mother and another sister died in the same year, Mahler felt himself responsible for the remnants of his family. Any remaining ties with Iglau were severed.*[46] His sister Justine ('Justi'), who was then aged around nineteen, became his housekeeper, later to be joined by the much younger sister Emma. Justine was 'a charming high-spirited woman, passionately devoted to her brother'.[47] They were assisted by Natalie Bauer-Lechner, a slightly spinsterish divorcee, whom Mahler had met when he was at the Conservatoire.**[50]

* He continued to write to his music teacher Heinrich Fischer. He sent him a postcard from New York in April 1908.

** At this stage, Mahler had two brothers left: one subsequently committed suicide; the other escaped to America to avoid creditors. Emma married Eduard Rosé, a cellist, in 1898;[48] Justina married Eduard's brother, the leader of the Vienna Philharmonic, Arnold Rosé. She died in 1902. Her daughter became director of the women's orchestra in Auschwitz, where she perished. The Rosé Quartet pioneered several of Schoenberg's early works, in difficult circumstances: 'You really would have thought you were in on a cats' concert',[49] was a typical comment from a critic in 1908.

However intense the Mahler household may have been, there was still scope for relaxation and fun. Gustav enjoyed playing duet arrangements of works by Schubert, Mozart, Schumann and Dvořák, and he would invent his own Viennese dialect texts to sing with them. He disliked hearing jokes cracked, and his response was deadpan. But he had his own brand of humour, which Bruno Walter called the Austrian type 'uttered in the Viennese dialect'.[51] For example, he much enjoyed Austrian food, and would announce that anybody who disliked a particular dish must be an absolute fool; he would then get a kick from asking his guests whether or not they liked it.

In Hamburg, he had yet another affair. This time it was with one of his 'discoveries', the brilliant soprano Anna von Mildenburg from Klagenfurt, 'the mighty Isolde of later days'.[52]* She was then but a beginner.

Mahler's only opportunity to compose was during the summer; he could then use the opera season to orchestrate and to make corrections. In his early years, he would spend his summers composing, cycling, swimming and walking at Steinbach on the Attersee, a breathtakingly beautiful lake in the Alps, very close to Lake Traun, which Schubert had loved so much. Tended by Natalie and Justine, he would work in a little hut by the lakeside, looking over the lake towards the green hills and the snow-capped mountains, and with the sheer cliffs of the Steinbach behind him. There, he completed his Second 'Resurrection' Symphony in July 1894. As he had grown tired of his status as a composer, 'remaining undiscovered like the South Pole',[54] he decided to engage the Berlin Philharmonic, at his own expense; and he secured the assistance of the chorus of the Berlin Singakademie. Bruno Walter records how, at the first performance, 'the work, masterfully conducted by Mahler in spite of an almost unbearable attack of migraine, had the effect of an elemental event. I shall never forget my own deep emotion and the ecstasy of the audience as well as of the performers.'[55]

Mahler was by now also a conductor of international repute. He conducted as far afield as London and Moscow. But trouble was brewing in Hamburg. The despotic director's 'gloomy reserve and Mahler's fiery

* He ended his affair with Mildenburg when she joined the Vienna company, as he knew how the Viennese would make the most of any hint of scandal. However, she 'hung around' – in due course, much to the anguish of Alma, Mahler's wife.[53]

impetuosity were bound to lead to an eventual parting of the ways'.[56] Mahler also had difficulty with the chief stage director whose means of livening up the chorus was to snap his fingers, even during performances. Mahler had his eye on Vienna, one of the most powerful and influential positions in the musical life of the Continent. As a Jew, an appointment there was bound to be controversial, because anti-Semitism was ever-increasing in Vienna.

Anti-Semitism in Vienna

There was also a growth in the notion of Pan-Germanism, fuelled by the disillusionment caused by the Habsburg defeat at Königgrätz in 1866, and by admiration for the formation of the German Empire five years later. The supporters of Pan-Germanism took the view that the German *Volk* should disassociate themselves *en bloc* from the rest of the Habsburg rag-bag, and join a customs union with the German Reich to the north.

The failure of the liberal government to deal satisfactorily with the issues such as Pan-Germanism and Czech nationalism, together with the economic depression of the 1870s and 1880s, bred a general unease which translated itself into an increased level of anti-Semitism. This was against the background of a noticeable increase in the Jewish population.[57] In Vienna, this increased from under two per cent in 1857 to almost nine per cent some 50 years later. In the Inner City and Leopoldstadt, Jews made up a third of the population; many were immigrants from Eastern Europe 'who attracted attention by their strange appearance'.[58] According to Alma Schindler, writing at the turn of the century, 'the opera public is mostly Jewish', a perception which reflects pervasive attitudes rather than reliable statistics.[59]

In the early 1880s, the flamboyant politician Georg von Schönerer, who had considerable support from the students of the universities of Vienna, Graz and Prague, was saying that the 'Jews were a sucking vampire that knocks on the narrow-windowed house of the German farmer and craftsman',[60] and that the mixing of Jews and Germans was unacceptable. He advocated 'the removal of Jewish influence from all areas of public life'.[61]* Schönerer disappeared from view after he was prosecuted for a raid against the Jewish-owned newspaper, the *Neues Wiener Tagesblatt*.[63]

* Schönerer's wealth was inherited from his father, who built Austria's first railway, ironically with backing from bankers such as Rothschild. His sister Alexandrine owned and ran the Theater an der Wien.[62]

His mantle was, to a great extent, assumed by Karl Lueger, a 'Christian Socialist', whose power base was built on the artisan class. By drawing attention to the strong presence of Jews in the professional classes – at least half of Vienna's doctors, lawyers and journalists were Jews – Lueger was able to whip up support using the theme that the Christian people of Vienna were no longer masters in their own house;[64] in the face of anti-Christian Jewish exploitation, he said, the 'little man' faced economic disaster.*[65] Lueger eventually became Mayor of Vienna.**

The anti-Semitism spread to the educated classes and did not augur well for Mahler, even though many successful musicians in Vienna were Jewish, and Lueger took a pragmatic attitude: 'I decide who is a Jew', he said.[67] Eventually, in October 1897, after becoming a Roman Catholic, Mahler took over as artistic director at the Imperial and Royal Opera at a salary of 24,000 fl, plus gratuities and a pension.[68] The appointment followed a trial performance of *Lohengrin*, which was a sensation. At the age of 38, he was now 'dictator of music of Central Europe in the Imperial Opera of Vienna at the high noon of its splendour'.[69] Somewhere in the backstreets of Vienna, another Jew, Arnold Schoenberg was just starting to compose.[70]

At the Vienna Imperial Opera

The *fin-de-siècle* imperial Vienna into which Mahler returned with his two sisters showed superficial signs of considerable prosperity. Vienna claimed to have the best parks and public buildings, the cleanest streets and the purest water in Europe. Electric lights had been installed on the streets. Mayor Lueger provided a public transport system, gas works and power stations.†

The imperial success story was reinforced when, eighteen months after

* Although heavy industry was concentrated in a few firms, in the Vienna of 1902, 86 per cent of the 105,000 industrial and commercial businesses employed fewer than five people; a third of all wage earners were employed in these tiny workshops.

** Lueger was elected in 1895 but the emperor refused to ratify the election. The Viennese reaffirmed their choice in the polls, and Lueger was appointed on Good Friday 1897; this was around the time that Brahms died. At the same time, the Austrian government faced a crisis over language ordinances in the Czech lands. The emperor had to dissolve government and govern by decree.[66]

† In 1899, the first international automobile race was held there; ten years later, there were 3,000 cars on its streets. Mahler was an enthusiastic motorist. The city railway system was constructed in 1894–1901; its stations were built by Otto Wagner, whose work throughout Vienna was distinguished by the attempt 'to dignify the technological, and to celebrate it as "culture"'.[71]

Mahler arrived, Franz Joseph celebrated his 50th jubilee. The assassination of the empress in Geneva in 1898 seemed shocking, but an aberration (see page 509). As the novelist Stefan Zweig said: 'The possibility of a relapse into a new barbarity, such as for instance war between nations of Europe, seemed as remote as demons or witches ... Everything about our thousand-year-old Austrian monarchy appeared grounded upon eternity.'[72]

Yet Alma Schindler, even though just turned nineteen, was perhaps more perceptive when she noted in her diary on the night before the jubilee: 'The Viennese are quite right to illuminate the streets: it's their way of thanking the Emperor for all the stupid things he's done for them. His entire term of office has been nothing but a series of blunders, which he attempted to put right and, in the process, only made worse. Austria is not far from collapse.'[73]

Beneath the imperial veneer, the workers were the worst housed in Europe: of the dwellings built in the lead up to 1914, over 90 per cent had no individual water supply or individual lavatory. Rents absorbed up to a third of income.[74]

Vienna was in fact experiencing the 'tremors of social and political disintegration'.[75] The liberalism of the 1860s had been paralysed by the uncontrollable forces such as Czech nationalism, Pan-Germanism and Zionism. Now there was socialist class warfare and anarchist terror. The *Neue Freie Presse* wrote: 'Instead of the gay waltz, one hears only the cries of an excited brawling mob, and the shouts of police trying to disperse antagonists.'[76]

Culture and learning continued to provide an escape route from these unpleasant aspects, from the decadence and the corruption. Vienna blossomed with the poetry of Hugo von Hofmannsthal, among others. But the underlying tensions were illustrated by the Viennese Establishment's rejection of Sigmund Freud, the founder of psychoanalysis, and of Gustav Klimt, the Secessionist painter, both of whom were labelled Jews, Freud correctly, Klimt incorrectly.* Gustav Mahler was unlikely to have an easy ride.

* Freud's promotion to a medical professorship was delayed in 1897. This was also the year in which the Secession was formed with Klimt as President. The Secessionists disliked the stranglehold which the official institutions exercised on art in Vienna, and they attracted a considerable following. They organised their own exhibition in March 1898 which was attended by 57,000 visitors. The battle raged on. Eighty-seven faculty members of Vienna University signed a petition protesting against Klimt's 'Philosophy', one of three panels commissioned to adorn the University Great Hall. In 1902, Mahler conducted his own arrangement of Beethoven's Ninth Symphony when Max Klinger's sculpture of Beethoven was displayed, controversially, in the Secession Building.[77]

The opera house in which Mahler worked was part of the escapist illusion. It was magnificent and traditional. It provided Mahler with a handsome, modern apartment, designed by Otto Wagner, the prominent architect. A court carriage service was made available to the female artistes, who were called for at their homes and driven back after the performance.

Hans Richter, Mahler's distinguished predecessor, had not exercised a tight grip on the Vienna Opera. Mahler started producing Mozart's operas 'properly', restoring recitatives and the harpsichords, and staging Wagner's operas without cuts. He was not impressed by theatrical tradition, which he identified with 'self-satisfaction and slovenliness'.[78] He stood no nonsense, and he supervised every aspect of the work in hand. There were strict rehearsal disciplines: no deputies were allowed to stand in for orchestral members. At the performance, the house lights were dimmed before the curtain rose; latecomers were excluded.

To start with, the Viennese gave Mahler the benefit of the doubt and, despite his gaucheness, he entered into the social life of the upper echelons of the capital. His first new production was Smetana's *Dalibor* (see page 699). With Czech nationalism being such a hot political issue at the time, the production was performed in German. But what a risk to take! *Dalibor* had been used to celebrate the opening of the Czech National Theatre. It was not long before the Viennese started expressing their displeasure. One critic, following a performance of Mozart's 'Jupiter' Symphony, reported that 'the unsuspecting listener experienced several surprises, not all of which were agreeable'.[79]

Vienna has had a long tradition of humiliating great men. For Mahler, this started in 1901. While he was convalescing from a major haemorrhage, the critics pointedly praised two Philharmonic Society concerts performed in his absence; on his return, he withdrew his candidacy for re-election to the conductorship of the Society.

Mahler concentrated on the Opera. Together with the designer Alfred Roller, who shared his disregard for the naturalistic conventions of the contemporary theatre, Mahler was responsible for some remarkable productions. Roller believed that 'the whole of modern art has to serve the stage ... Traditional methods are simply worn out ... Modern art must embrace costume, accessories, the whole revitalization of the work.' Everything on the stage should *mean something* rather than *represent something.*[80] 'The stage is not a picture; the stage is a space', he said, 'a space which is divided up, made meaningful by the movements of the actors. It means one thing when the actor smiles and another when the actor cries. For me, the set must be constructed only out of essentials, which do not represent the setting, but which must above all be conditioned by the purpose, like the words or the tempo.'[81]

'The stage is not a picture; the stage is a space': the audience must have been amazed at the *mise-en-scène* when the curtain went up for *Tristan* in 1903. Then, in one season in 1905–6, Mahler and Roller staged five entirely new Mozart productions to mark the 150th anniversary of the composer's birth.

Mahler described his decade in Vienna as ten war years. Bruno Walter said: 'It must be admitted that Mahler's violent actions, his peremptory manner in questions of art, his engagements and dismissals, and his fight against tradition and time-honoured customs had helped to swell the ranks of his enemies among the artistic personnel, especially among the members of the orchestra, but also among the theatre officials, the public and the newspapermen.'[82]

Mahler was fortunate to enjoy the support of the Lord Chamberlain who was responsible for the Imperial Opera, Prince Montenuovo, who was a grandson of Napoleon's wife Empress Marie-Louise. For a time, Montenuovo was a defence against 'men and women of high society', some of whom, 'even in the entourage of archdukes, were trying to gain his ear in their efforts to dethrone Mahler'.[83] Mahler soon longed to work somewhere less political and traditional. 'As a man I am willing to make every possible concession,' he said, 'but as a musician I make none.'[84]

To get away from the pressure, Mahler would go to the countryside to compose. After 1896, Attersee had become crowded with trippers and the hotel owners put their prices up, so he went to Bad Aussee nearby. Four years later, he went further south, to the Wörthersee near Klagenfurt. He had a lakeside villa built there, with, in the grounds, a hut in which he could compose. His output was considerable. During his ten years in Vienna, five symphonies were composed, published and performed; he also composed several songs and revised some of his earlier works.

Marriage to Alma

In November 1901, Mahler met Alma, the 22-year-old daughter of the Viennese landscapist, Anton Schindler. She was beautiful, bewitching, a brilliant pianist and talented composer, and a bit of a rebel. She had been to Mahler's performances and admired his conducting, although she did not particularly like his compositions. Mahler and Alma had met each other on a cycling outing, but they had never been formally introduced.[85]

Alma's widowed mother had married Karl Moll, one of the founders of the Secessionist group of artists. Many of these wooed Alma, who flirted with them, especially with Klimt.* At one stage, Klimt asked the nineteen year old, 'have you ever thought of visiting me in my studio ... just you, on your own?' Alma observed: 'even if he's hitched up with his sister-in-law, it's me that he loves'.[86]

Alma's candid diary records, for July 1901, that the former director of the Burg theatre had stroked her legs 'from under my skirt down to the knees',[87] and she suffered dreadful pangs of conscience afterwards.** She was quite mixed up: for all the eroticism expressed in her jottings, she seems to have had a confused understanding of what was actually involved in sex. Certain physical aspects of it shocked her, as one would expect of a well-brought-up girl at the time. But she was of an age when there was indirect pressure on her to marry and to leave the family nest; besides, it had recently been invaded by the birth of a stepsister. 'I long for rape – Whoever it might be', she wrote.[89] She then became consumed with desire for the composer, and her teacher, Alex von Zemlinsky: 'Alex, my Alex, let me be your font. Fill me with your holy fluid ... we two whose bodies had coiled in love's wildest embrace.'[90]† Her mother and friends were, however, adamant that she should not marry Alex: he was penniless, and she had no money of her own.

* Moll introduced Mahler to Roller.

** This was a time when, as Zweig said, 'The lines of the female figure were so completely disguised that even the bridegroom at the wedding feast had not the remotest chance of guessing whether his future companion was straight or crooked, plump or thin, long in the leg or short in the thigh.'[88]

†Zemlinsky's sister married his pupil Arnold Schoenberg. Born in 1874 in Vienna, son of a cobbler, Schoenberg was a string player. At first, he worked in a bank. In 1899, he wrote the string sextet *Verklärte Nacht*. With Richard Strauss' help, he obtained a post at the Stern Conservatoire in Berlin. He was possibly one of the greatest music teachers ever, and his *Treatise on Harmony* was published in 1911; his pupils included Berg and Webern. In Vienna, in 1904–5, with Zemlinsky, he formed a society of contemporary musicians of which Mahler became honorary president. *Erwartung* (1909) was one of his early atonal works. His opera *Moses und Aron* (1930–32) preceded his return to the Jewish religion, partly as a protest against Nazism. He then emigrated to the University of California. He died in 1951; his last word was 'Harmony'.[91]

On Thursday 7 November, Alma's diary records: 'Met Mahler.'[92] She did not fall for him immediately, and a couple of days later she wrote about Zemlinsky: 'I shall never forget the touch of his hand on my most intimate parts … Everything about him is holy to me. I would like to kneel before him and kiss his loins – kiss everything, everything. Amen!'[93] But suddenly it all changed: four days later, she was writing: 'I can't even think of writing to Alex, I feel absolutely nothing for him.'[94] Alma, immature and impressionable, was emotionally torn between the two composers.

By early December, she and Gustav were on first name terms. Alma asked herself: 'Do I really love him? I have no idea. Sometimes I actually think not. So much irritates me: his smell; the way he sings; the way he speaks (can't roll his rrr's) … He is a stranger to me. Our tastes differ ... and his art leaves me cold, so dreadfully cold.'[95] Mahler went off to Berlin to conduct the Fourth Symphony. His sister Justi was against the relationship, and Alma continued to flirt with others. When Mahler wrote to her saying that he expected his wife to abandon her ambitions as a composer, there was almost a crisis; it was an indication of what was to come.

However, on Monday 23 December, they got engaged: 'If my relationship with AZ was wild and carnal, then with Mahler I feel imbued with the holiest feelings.'[96] She had lots of fun from the engagement. Her appearance at the Opera was a 'veritable début. Every opera-glass was focused on me – every single one.' She added an understandably feline comment: 'Mildenburg came down to meet me – awfully sweet.'[97]

The diaries are surprisingly frank. On New Year's Day 1902, she and Gustav attempted to consummate their love, but 'just as I felt him penetrate, he lost all strength. He laid his head on my breast, shattered – and almost wept for shame.'[98] However, within 48 hours this difficulty, which left her extremely frustrated, seems to have been resolved to her satisfaction.

When they married in the Karlskirche in March, Alma was pregnant with their first daughter, Putzi. Another daughter, Gucki, was born two years later. This whirlwind romance, in which she had put aside her concerns that 'he's a sick man, his position is insecure, he's a Jew, no longer young …',[99] was hardly likely to be stable. During the Zemlinsky affair, she had already been repelled by the thought of having 'little, degenerate Jew-kids'.[100] During her engagement to Mahler, she had difficulty with his friends, 'all conspicuously Jewish. I could find no bond.'[101] She loathed the Wörthersee villa, where they did not fit comfortably with the local residents;* she was lonely when Mahler was composing; she was embarrassed by his awkwardness in social circles. Mahler's emotions were even more complex. On the one hand, he, almost twice her age, worshipped her as a kind of 'redeemer' or saviour; on the other, his writings to her indicate that he expected her to subordinate herself and her considerable musical talents entirely to him. He had no notion of, or interest in, 'what gave a girl pleasure'.[103]

Meanwhile, the campaign against Mahler by the anti-Semitic press in Vienna gained momentum as he promoted more and more of his own music. There were protests at his handling of a trade dispute with the opera house employees, and a demonstration was addressed by a socialist member of parliament. 'I am hunted like a stag, hounds in full cry … what is the good of being pelted with mud, time after time. The curs obviously take me for a lamp-post', he wrote, following the savaging of his Third Symphony by the Berlin critics.[104]** He handed in his resignation to the Vienna authorities on 31 March 1907. In his departing letter to the Opera staff, he summed up his aspirations and problems: 'I meant well and aimed high … I have always given my all, have subordinated my person to the cause, my inclinations to my duty. I did not spare myself and was therefore justified in demanding that others, too, should exert their strength to the utmost. In the crush of the struggle, in the heat of the moment, wounds were sustained, errors committed, by you as well as by me.'[106] He was well treated, given a large pension and a promise that Alma, as a widow, would be entitled to a substantial state pension.

That year, in which he composed nothing, was particularly traumatic, for other reasons as well as his problems in the opera house. Putzi, 'a lovely grave-faced girl of four',[107] died of scarlet fever and diphtheria when the family were on their summer holiday. In a harrowing scene, when Putzi's coffin was removed from the villa, both Alma and her mother collapsed. The doctor was called and, to lighten the tension, Mahler suggested that he too should be examined. The doctor discovered that he was suffering

* During one summer, women on the Wörthersee protested against Gucki playing naked in Mahler's private garden. They remarked that 'nudity is not pleasing in the sight of God'.[102]

** The first complete performance of the Third Symphony was at the annual festival in Krefeld in 1902. Richard Strauss was president of the festival and led the applause. It was, according to Bruno Walter, 'a prodigious success. This marked an epoch in his life. It stamped him as a great composer and assured him of a proper place in the foreground of contemporary interest.'[105]

from a bad heart, and would have to give up his walking, cycling and swimming. He had a heart lesion, the tell-tale sign of the inexorable progress of bacterial endocarditis, caused by rheumatic fever, syphilis or streptococcal infection of the throat. His chronic sore throats indicated that they were the likely cause.[108]

He was determined to earn enough to retire after his 50th birthday and devote his life to composition. But his time was running out.

New York

Mahler had secured an appointment for a four-month winter opera season at the Metropolitan Opera in New York in 1907–8.* His last opera performance in Vienna was *Fidelio* on 15 October 1907; his first performance in New York was *Tristan* on 1 January 1908.

The Met, desperate to head off competition from the Hammerstein Manhattan Opera which opened in the beginning of November, also persuaded the distinguished director of La Scala, Giulio Gatti-Casazza, to come to New York. With him came Toscanini. After two successful seasons, there was no room for Mahler at the Met.** Mahler then accepted the conductorship of the New York Philharmonic, with which he performed 46 concerts in the 1909–10 season.

For the summer of 1908, there was no question of returning to the villa in Wörthersee, with its painful memories. So, Alma found them a farmhouse in the Salzburg Dolomites, and a little hut was constructed to enable Mahler to compose in his customary way. Although he would stop to feel his pulse on walks, his work composing and conducting did not decelerate.

Das Lied von der Erde, a song cycle, and the Ninth Symphony were completed in summer 1909. The Tenth was completed the following year, but not performed in full until 1964. The Eighth Symphony, known to Mahler's displeasure as the 'Symphony of a Thousand',[110] had been

* The New York Metropolitan Opera Society was formed in 1883 with the assistance of several millionaires.

** Mahler went to New York just at the end of the second term of Theodore Roosevelt who regarded 'Americanizing the world' as the nation's destiny. The decade saw the construction of the Panama Canal, Ford's Model T automobile, the Wright brothers' successful flight and the formation of big businesses such as General Electric and Westinghouse. President Wilson said in his Inaugural following the 1912 election: 'There has been something crude and heartless and unfeeling in our haste to succeed and be great.'[109]

completed in summer 1906, although it was not performed until four years later.

Das Lied von der Erde reflected a fashion for orientalism in the arts as exemplified in Busoni's *Turandot* and Puccini's *Madame Butterfly*. Mahler was entranced by *Die Chinesische Flöte*, a collection of Chinese poems, and used extracts from it in *Das Lied*. So in *Das Lied*, which uses poetry which is originally Chinese, Mahler uses 'the most refined and sparest of orchestral textures',[111] rather than the massive sound which we hear in the symphonies.

Back in New York, relationships between conductor and management reached breaking point. The players disliked him; he drove them very hard, and lost his temper with them; they found his beat hard to follow, as he sought flexibility and constant subtle variations of tempo; and they objected to his changes to the scores. Apart from his appalling human relations, he also ran up against 'that fearful matriarchy which has blighted so much of New York's musical life'.[112] He would not do their bidding or attend their social functions; in this, he compared badly with Toscanini. Alma told an American journalist: 'In New York, to his amazement, he had ten women ordering him about like a puppet.'[113] Thus it was that 'New York, with its notoriously shallow and sensation-seeking approach to music, added him to its roll of sacrificial victims'.[114]

A crisis point was reached in early 1911. Mahler was summoned to a full committee meeting, there were bitter recriminations and he was informed of a considerable limitation of his powers, which a lawyer was called in to define.

The Breakdown with Alma

Mahler's last years were blighted by the breakdown of his marriage. The strain of her marriage drove the highly sexed and energetic Alma, who was still in her 20s, to the brink of breakdown. His idea of a cosy evening was for her to read to him Eschenbach's *Parsifal* or Lange's *Geschichte des Materialismus*, and report back on the lectures on astronomy which he had asked her to attend. 'You have an abstraction for a husband', a helpful friend told her.[115]

She went on a rest cure to a sanatorium. There, her doctor prescribed dancing. She soon met a handsome architect, Walter Gropius, who was four years younger than her. Gropius wrote to her saying that he could not live without her and asked her to leave Mahler and live with him. By accident or design, he addressed the letter to Herr Direktor Mahler. At a meeting of the three, Mahler insisted that she should choose between him and Gropius. 'Almschili, if you had left me at that time, I should simply have gone out like a torch deprived of air', he wrote to her some weeks later.[116] Desperate, he sought advice from Freud, who was then based in Holland; Freud apparently told him that he was expecting too much from his wife.[117] He became more caring for her and even played songs composed by her; he sent her passionate love letters; he scribbled on the manuscript of the Tenth Symphony: 'farewell my lyre … you alone know the meaning of this … Almschili, to live for you, to die for you … have mercy O Lord why hast thou forsaken me?'[118]

She wrote later, 'I knew that my marriage was no marriage and that my own life was utterly unfulfilled. I concealed all this from him, and although he knew it as well as I did, we played out the comedy to the end.'[119]

Freud

The End

Meanwhile, Mahler was extraordinarily busy: he conducted in Paris, Rome and Cologne; he sketched the Tenth and prepared for the first performance of the 'Symphony of a Thousand', in Munich. Bruno Walter, who had selected the soloists and studied their parts with them, wrote that the première at the Munich Exhibition Hall in September 1910 marked a culminating point in Mahler's life and that none of the listeners or participants would ever forget the occasion. '"Accende lumen sensibus, infunde amorem cordibus" [Inflame the senses with light, instil love into the hearts]. That he was permitted to release to the world through the voices of a mighty host of singers this leitmotif of his greatly agitated soul, that he was able to pronounce the message of life and faith while the seeds of death were already in his heart, was a thrill beyond anything he had ever experienced.'[120] It was also ironic.

Mahler's decline was very fast indeed. A few days before the Munich première, he had developed a septic throat and this returned when he and Alma were in New York in February. Alma's mother rushed across the Atlantic to assist them. His last concert in New York was on 21 February 1911. He sailed for Europe in April.* He went to a sanatorium in Neuilly, a suburb of Paris. Bruno Walter saw him there, and spoke to him of his works, 'but he replied with bitterness, and I thought it best just to entertain him which I partly succeeded in doing'.[122] Alma took him, at his request, to Vienna. His journey there was fully covered by press reporters eager for the latest news. 'Alma's account puts it quite simply: "his last journey was like that of a dying king".'[123] On 18 May 1911, he died, six weeks short of his 51st birthday. He was buried beside Putzi in Grinzing.

Sequel

Alma then became the mistress of Oskar Kokoschka, another of the Secessionist painters.[124] One of his pictures, *The Tempest*, portrayed him and Alma in 1914 united in a swirling vortex of cloud and wind (see colour plate 49). She then married Gropius in 1915, and had a daughter, Muzi. Gropius was a cavalry officer on the western front during the First World War, and this did not leave much time for Alma.**

The marriage with Gropius came asunder in 1919. It had been

* The murderer Dr Crippen had been arrested on board a liner eight months earlier, with the assistance of the newly invented wireless. The sinking of the *Titanic* in April 1912 was after Mahler's death.[121]

** Gropius had an important influence on modern architecture. After the war, he was director at Weimar Staatliches Bauhaus, which moved to Dessau with the promise of better financial support and to escape the growing antagonism of the Weimar community. The Bauhaus school advocated that design should take into account a systematic study of needs and problems, having regard to modern construction materials and techniques. In 1934, Gropius emigrated at first to England and then to America where he became professor of architecture at Harvard.

complicated by Alma's affair with a prominent German author, Verdi enthusiast and conversationalist, Franz Werfel, whom she married in 1929.* Their salon in the 1930s included Alban Berg, the composer of *Wozzeck*, and his wife.** Alma's daughter Muzi, an 'angelic being',[127] died from polio in 1935 and is commemorated in Alban Berg's Violin Concerto. Alma herself died in 1964, having written books about Mahler and herself. Their daughter, Gucki (Anna), became a distinguished sculptress.

All this seems an inappropriate sequel to the tempestuous, but so elevated, life of the great composer and conductor, who predeceased his young, lovely and so frustrated wife by more than half a century. He had asked that his headstone should record, simply, 'Gustav Mahler'. 'Any who come to look for me will know who I was, and the rest do not need to know.'[128]

As his coffin was lowered, an immense crowd stood in reverential silence. Bruno Walter was reminded of some words of Jean Paul, whose works Mahler had so much admired: 'Thou soughtest behind, beneath, and beyond life something higher than life; not thy self, thy I – no mortal, not an immortal, but the All-First, God! … Now thou art reposing in real being. Death has swept away from the dark heart the whole sultry cloud of life, and the eternal light stands uncovered which thou didst so long seek; and thou, its beam, dwellest again in the fire.'[129]

Like so much of Jean Paul, these words are not easy to absorb. Yet, think of them when listening to Mahler's symphonies and songs.

* At the beginning of the Second World War, they fled from France to Beverley Hills, via the Pyrenees and Spain, Alma carrying the manuscript of Bruckner's Third Symphony under her arm.[125]

** Berg's wife was the natural daughter of Emperor Franz Joseph.[126]

Richard Strauss

CHAPTER 25

Richard Strauss and Gustav Mahler were born within four years of each other, so it is tempting to compare them. Here, we must resist the temptation to do so, at least in relation to their greatness as artists: unique composers are not susceptible to comparison in a brief description of their lives such as this.

There is one point of comparison to which reference has to be made, if only to record that it will not here be resolved. Strauss' music is sometimes accused of being relatively superficial. Stravinsky thought that Strauss could charm and delight, but could never move listeners: 'because he was never committed. He didn't give a damn.'[1] Much the same point was put by the world-famous conductor Bruno Walter, no lover of Strauss, when he spoke of Strauss' tone poem *Tod und Verklärung*: 'I felt perplexingly overwhelmed by it; but in spite of the intoxicating splendour of the orchestration and the dramatic force of the conception, I was excited and disturbed rather than deeply moved and uplifted.'[2] Strauss himself perhaps identified the issue: 'Mahler is always seeking Redemption', he said; 'I don't know what I am supposed to be redeemed from.'[3]

Walter, victim of Strauss' relationship with the Nazis, had an axe to grind. And, despite the dismissive criticisms, Strauss' music can be profoundly moving. Listen to some of the Marshallin's music in *Der Rosenkavalier* or, if you are still unmoved, listen to his *Four Last Songs*.

Like Mahler, Strauss spent his early years in several conducting jobs, as well as composing; but whereas Mahler's large compositions were symphonic, Strauss' were operatic. Strauss reached his peak, in the ten years before the First World War, with *Salomé*, *Elektra* and *Der Rosenkavalier*. At that time, Strauss was regarded as *avant-garde*; but that reputation did not last long, as he struggled, like Saint-Saëns and Elgar, to preserve some of the tonality and style of the previous century.

Strauss lived for a further 35 years after the outbreak of a war which shook the world as never before. Those long years are perhaps best summarised in the comment by a leading biographer: 'In many cases, after the death of a composer there is a dip in his reputation for about twenty years. This did not occur with Strauss, for it had occurred during his lifetime.'[4] Only 21 months after Strauss' death, Schoenberg, the pioneer of atonality and serialism, died in Los Angeles. By then, Strauss, at least in a historical perspective, was an anachronism.

The Young Richard Strauss

Richard Strauss was born in Munich on 11 June 1864, almost exactly three months after King Ludwig, Wagner's patron, succeeded to the Bavarian throne. King Ludwig's grandfather had transformed Munich so that it was 'unrivalled for architectural magnificence among the smaller capitals of Europe'.[5]

Richard's father, Franz-Joseph, was the principal horn player in the court orchestra. Previously, he had been in the service of Duke Max, the father of Empress Elisabeth of Austria. Franz-Joseph Strauss was sufficiently talented and prominent that Wagner felt that he had to tolerate him, even though he was an impossibly difficult player to manage.[6]

Franz-Joseph Strauss' first family was wiped out by tuberculosis and the 1854 cholera epidemic. His second wife, Josepha Pschorr, came from a prosperous family who ran a brewery near the Frauenkirche in the centre of Munich. 'Beer was big business',[7] even though the large beer halls run by the big breweries only arrived in Germany a few decades later. But her wealth was little solace to Josepha, who was a manic depressive. For treatment, she went to the eminent, but possibly flawed, psychologist who subsequently drowned with the king.[8]

Richard was brought up in the city centre above the brewery, in a small, modest apartment with no electric light or running water. Despite his parents' affluence, hard work and economy were instilled in him: he was told to walk rather than take the horse-tram; chocolate was only allowed at Christmas; and there were no fancy clothes, except for special occasions, such as having a formal photograph taken.

There was much music. Aged six, the beautiful boy with curly hair composed his first work, the 'Schneider-polka': he wrote out the notation with a neat hand, and his mother added the tempo and dynamics.[9]

Around this time, Richard will have seen the celebrations in the streets after the defeat of France in the Franco-Prussian War, but the small boy cannot have appreciated their significance.[10] The Bavaria into which he had been born was about to be swallowed up by mighty Prussia: as king of the second most important kingdom in Germany, King Ludwig was prevailed upon to invite his Uncle Wilhelm to become emperor. In July 1871, there was a large victory parade at which the crown prince of Germany distributed iron crosses; the day ended with a gala performance at the Opera, where no doubt Richard's father was playing the horn.

Richard went to the grammar school (known as the Gymnasium). When he went to the university, he read philosophy, aesthetics and history of art. He learnt his music from colleagues of his father, but had no formal musical education. He took part in a small orchestra run by his father. He attended rehearsals at the court orchestra which, from 1872, was conducted by Hermann Levi, a friend of Wagner and Brahms, and regarded as one of the leading conductors of his time.[11]

Strauss' progress at music was meteoric, and he found composition very easy. As well as Levi, two other important Wagnerian conductors recognised his talent, Hans von Bülow,* 'the undisputed ruler of German orchestral music',[13] and Franz Wüllner, who had conducted the first performances of *Das Rheingold* and *Die Walküre*. Before Strauss was nineteen, Wüllner had conducted Strauss' *Serenade for Wind Instruments* in Dresden, and his Violin Concerto had been performed in Vienna.

Strauss spent some time in Berlin, which was formerly the dull capital of Prussia. It was like the country around it, 'flat and dreary, although the

* Bülow demanded that 'a conductor must not have his head in the score, but the score in his head'.[12]

lakes of the Havel and the scrubby pine woods on their sandy soil had a peculiar charm, especially at sunset'.[14] Mendelssohn had regarded it as a bit of a backwater.

Later in the century, one could enjoy sitting in the Kroll Garden restaurant, 'especially toward evening, when the gas lamps were burning and the wind was rustling the leaves so excitingly and romantically'.[15] There was the sound of the horse trams, the ringing of the milk carts, the cries of the vendors as they pushed their vegetable and potato carts through the streets, and the junk dealers shouting 'rags, bones, paper, old boots'.[16] There were the massive boats loading and unloading their cargoes, which had to be carried down the Spree and through the canals. Berlin was vibrant and prosperous. It was now the proud capital of an empire which was experiencing a tremendous rate of economic growth.* It must have been an exciting place to be.

Strauss, from a brewing family, settled in well, even though the North Germans ridiculed beer-swilling Bavarians,** and had difficulty understanding their 'perfectly unintelligible Munich phrases'.[19] He lived the high life; he went to dances and developed a craze for playing cards, particularly skat, a three-handed card game which was popular in Germany. Skat remained an obsession throughout his life, and it was said that he could even compose when playing it.[20]

The Conductor

Hans von Bülow commissioned a work from Strauss, who conducted it with the Meiningen touring orchestra of which Bülow was then both mind and spirit. Bülow appointed Strauss as his assistant. Strauss played the piano solo in a Mozart concerto and conducted his own Symphony.

Bülow, Cosima Wagner's first husband, looked like a small version of Don Quixote (see picture on page 429), and was similarly eccentric and

* Between 1850 and 1910, Berlin's population multiplied by five. Germany was growing into the economic power which we recognise today. In 1880, the empire's merchant navy possessed less steam tonnage than Spain; 30 years later, Germany's steam tonnage was three times greater than France's, four times greater than America's; only the British merchant marine was larger. Even the telecoms figures are impressive. Germans made 155 million phone calls in 1888; by 1904, the number had reached one billion and by 1913 it was two and a half billion.[17]

** Bavarians were 'lazy and frivolous', and Munich was regarded as 'a place where they eat cake with a knife, and the very princes speak bad grammar'.[18]

chivalrous. Once, when playing the Funeral March in Beethoven's 'Eroica', Bülow had 'the utterly mad idea of putting on black gloves'. After a performance in Berlin, he declared that, while Beethoven had crossed out the Symphony's dedication to Napoleon, 'We ourselves will dedicate it to Bismarck, the greatest living German.' The audience disapproved of a political statement and began to hiss; whereupon Bülow took out his handkerchief and dusted his shoes, saying: 'See how I shake the dust of Berlin off my feet!' On another occasion, he played Beethoven's Ninth Symphony twice in succession, a rebuke perhaps to 'a certain narrow-minded part of the public, which still resented the daring features of the work'.[21]

A few months after Strauss' appointment, Bülow suddenly resigned. He was incensed when, without first clearing it with him, Brahms agreed to take his place as conductor of his Fourth Symphony in Frankfurt. The Duke of Meiningen appointed the 21-year-old Strauss to succeed him. But, without the distinguished Bülow, it was planned to scale back the orchestra, so, after six months, Strauss moved to Munich as third conductor. However, during his stay in Meiningen, he worked with Alexander Ritter, who was one of Bülow's assistants and was married to a niece of Wagner. Ritter introduced Strauss to the symphonic poems of Liszt and Berlioz, and to Schopenhauer's philosophy.[22]

By 1892, a critic was calling Strauss 'the outstanding living composer'.[23] He overworked and needed a break. He went on holiday to Italy. This led to his fantasy, *Aus Italien*. The booing and applauding at its first performance provided Strauss with a helpful *succès de scandale*. This was followed by *Don Juan* and *Macbeth*; then he composed *Tod und Verklärung*, a tone poem about the agony of a dying artist.

During the 1890s, Strauss composed several other tone poems. There was the humorous *Till Eulenspiegel*, about a buffoon who, despite execution, still lives on. He also wrote the symphonic fantasy *Also sprach Zarathustra* and *Don Quixote*. Strauss was writing for a vast orchestra. The massive *Ein Heldenleben*, which, at one stage, he was tempted to call 'a new tone poem "Eroica"',[24] resulted in accusations of megalomania.

Strauss preferred to call these works 'tone poems' rather than symphonic poems, because they were 'less "symphonic" in design', there being 'no special emphasis on thematic or tonal contrast'.[25] They were not universally admired. Alma Schindler, having been to a concert at which *Till Eulenspiegel* and *Ein Heldenleben* were performed, described them as 'programme-music in the worst sense of the word. In both works you have to wade through endless pages of prose, just to gain some vague idea of the composer's intentions.'[26] They had been played in a different order to the order in which they had been advertised and she listened to the whole of *Till* under the impression that it was *Ein Heldenleben*. 'I realized afterwards that they might just as well have swapped the titles! We laughed heartily at our [and Strauss'] mistake.'[27] However, the primary aim of Strauss' tone poems was to develop a poetic idea, rather than tell a story.

Marriage

When he was nineteen, Strauss had a passion for Dora Wihan, a flirtatious divorcee, who was formerly married to a well-known cellist. Strauss' father wrote to him in Meiningen warning him that the gossip would do his reputation no good. Eventually Dora went to live abroad, but they continued to correspond, even long after Strauss got married.

After three years in Munich, Strauss moved to Weimar. Many of the leading soprano parts, such as Pamina in *The Magic Flute*, Isolde and the lead in his own opera *Guntram*, were sung by Pauline de Ahna. He had met and fallen in love with Pauline several years before. Her father had a villa next to Strauss' aunt's villa on Lake Starnberg, just south of Munich. He was a general in the Bavarian army, and he was also a Wagner enthusiast and enjoyed singing;[28] his wife was rather snobbish.

Richard and Pauline married in 1894; two and a half years later, Franz (Bubi) was born. As a wedding present, the bridegroom gave the bride *Four Songs*. Indeed, most of Strauss' songs were composed in the years up to 1906, after which Pauline retired from the concert platform.

The critic Hanslick described Pauline as Strauss' better and more beautiful half.[29] But she also had the forceful, formidable characteristics of the *prima donna*. Their marriage was stormy, but was held together by their mutual love of music. When Strauss died, his daughter-in-law said about Pauline: 'I never realised anyone could weep so much.'[30]

Whereas Strauss enjoyed travelling, Pauline did not, and tended to stay at home. She would easily lose her temper: on one occasion, in 1902, she opened some correspondence from a woman who asked for complimentary tickets. Strauss was in England; Pauline jumped to a conclusion, wrote a letter demanding a divorce, and put it in hand. Around this episode, Strauss based *Intermezzo*, a comedy about a quick-tempered wife who opened a mis-addressed love letter to her husband; she seeks a divorce, but they are reconciled. After the first performance of *Intermezzo*, the chauffeur who drove the composer and his wife home said that the thunderstorm in the car was worse than the one outside.[31]

Elgar told a story of his visit to Strauss. When Strauss wanted to show him some score or paper of interest, he applied to 'Frau Strauss', who produced a bunch of keys, provided the item and duly locked it all up again when they had finished.[32] Apparently she also required tradesmen who visited the Strausses' villa to pull slippers over their shoes before walking on the parquet floor.*[33]

Meanwhile, Strauss' career continued its spectacular progression. In 1896, he succeeded Hermann Levi at the Munich Opera; two years later, he moved to Berlin, which, with Vienna, was one of the most prestigious appointments in the world. He was conductor there until 1919.

The Berlin Opera was headed by the tall and effeminate Count Hochberg who was responsible to the Kaiser for the 'Department-Muses'.[34] It was highly bureaucratic: 'the harsh voice of command mingled disharmoniously with the chorus of the Muses ... If the orders were not of a downright military character, they were at any rate "official instructions" to do so and so.'[35] Strauss worked hard; in his first eight months, he conducted 71 performances of 25 operas, including two first performances and a *Ring* Cycle.**[36]

Composers' Rights

Strauss had an obsession about the future prosperity of his family, should he or his works become unfashionable. This was surprising, because he had less to worry about than most composers in terms of his finances. Throughout his life, Strauss crusaded on behalf of composers' rights and copyright. In this he was supported by Friedrich Rösch, a friend and composer, and by Hans Sommer, a professor of physics, who, in his mid-40s, gave up science to become a composer.[37]

Although the German copyright laws of 1870 extended rights for 30

* Needless to say, when Strauss' sister suggested a family reunion with Dora Wihan, Pauline exploded; this was around the time of the first performance of *Der Rosenkavalier*, and marked the end of Dora's connection with Strauss.

** In the late 1890s, with Mahler directing the Opera in Vienna and Strauss in Berlin, the mind boggles at the display of talent.

years after death, there was the usual question as to whether the composer or the publisher owned the performance rights, specifically the rights to the musical content.[38] In 1898, the Triumvirate, as Strauss and the other two were known, wrote to 160 composers, formed a Composers' Association and submitted proposals to the Reichstag, the Berlin parliament. Strauss fought off opposition from entrenched interests in the publishing industry and the theatre. In 1901, he succeeded in getting legislation passed which improved the position. He also formed a performing rights society.*

In 1902, the University of Heidelberg gave Strauss a doctorate, after which he always called himself Doktor Richard Strauss. At a time when 'seriousness, respect, rectitude' were the prized virtues,[40] designations such as this mattered enormously.

In 1904, Strauss toured the USA. In New York, a whole floor of the Wanamaker department store was cleared and converted into a concert hall for him. He worked incredibly hard: 'twenty-one concerts with about twenty orchestras got through in four weeks, together with travelling day and night, dinners in my honour and other damned nonsense';[41] not to mention many Lieder recitals with Pauline. We can easily forget that, even two decades later, a journey from, say, Chicago to Los Angeles, took three nights and two days, in compartments without air-conditioning.[42]

High Noon

After 1900, Strauss concentrated on opera. His first opera, *Guntram*, had been a failure: there was a virtual strike by the orchestra, and the opera only had one performance. In 1901, he wrote the comic one-act opera, *Feuersnot*, which was premièred in Dresden. The audience there much enjoyed this satire about the Munich public who had angered Strauss by rejecting *Guntram*. His breakthrough, however, was with *Salomé*, based on Oscar Wilde's play about John the Baptist and King Herod's daughter, a '*femme fatale*, the sexually aware woman'.[43] The furore which arose when it was premièred in Dresden, in December 1905, resulted in it being performed by 50 opera houses within two years.[44] It has been said that it changed the whole nature of opera.

* Strauss' relationship with publishers could be stormy. Angry that his publishers had an option on his songs, he set a scurrilous poem; the publishers got the court to order him to provide proper songs. He complied by composing songs which were deliberately unmarketable.[39]

Salomé was entirely consistent with the decadence of the *fin de siècle*. Cosima Wagner, not exactly a prude herself, described the work as an obscenity.[45] The first Salomé objected: 'I am a decent woman.'[46] The censor in Vienna regarded it as salacious and blasphemous, and would not give Mahler permission to stage it.[47] The Prussian royal family objected to it, and J. Pierpoint Morgan's daughter got the New York production withdrawn after one performance.

Salomé: Aïno Ackté, star soprano from Helsinki, performed the Dance of the Seven Veils at the London première in 1910

The success of *Salomé* enabled Strauss to buy a plot of land in the woods at Garmisch, 50 miles from Munich, just in the embrace of the Bavarian Alps. This was already a holiday retreat for the wealthy and successful: the extension of the railway line had opened it up.

The villa at Garmisch would be Richard Strauss' main base for the rest of his life. He decorated it with the pictures and baroque church carvings which he enjoyed collecting. Its interior design gives a feeling of coolness, light and air. In his study, the furniture is made of light cherrywood; even the case for the Ibach piano is specially designed, as is the chest of drawers in which he kept his scores. Here, he could relax on a sofa and read a book taken from the bookshelves, perhaps by Goethe, whose complete works he read three times; or he could contemplate the bust of Gluck, representing opera, and the statuette of Beethoven, the master of instrumentation.

He would compose at his curved desk, again designed specially for this purpose, with the surface broad enough to place side by side the short and full scores. He could look up and see the Zugspitze, Germany's highest mountain. Next door was the living room, the setting for *Intermezzo*. Pauline would interrupt and order him to take his daily afternoon walk. Friends would come in, and they would play skat.*[48]

One of his friends wrote: 'Strauss knows how to relax. There is a touch of Bavarian indolence about him. I am sure that after hours of intensive life, when his energy is strained to the utmost, he spends hours of empty nothingness.'[49]

Elektra and *Der Rosenkavalier*

Around the turn of the century, Strauss met the distinguished writer and poet Hugo von Hofmannsthal (see colour plate 43). The son of a banker, 'a Viennese patrician of the purest dye, a true aristocrat of the spirit',[50] Hofmannsthal was a product of the liberal era of the second half of the 19th century. He came from the class of well-to-do children who were reared in the museums, theatres and concert halls of the new Ringstrasse,[51] 'a virtual hothouse for the development of aesthetic talent'.[52]

Hugo von Hofmannsthal told Strauss about a ballet he was writing. But Strauss said that he had enough work to keep him occupied for three years. They subsequently worked together by creating *Elektra*, based on Hofmannsthal's version of Sophocles' drama. Strauss was concerned that the subject was too like *Salomé* because it involved a *femme fatale*, the daughter of Agamemnon. When first performed, in Dresden in January 1909, it was described as 'barbaric dissonance',[53] but it enjoyed considerable *succès de scandale*.

Dresden also saw the first performance, on 26 January 1911, of *Der Rosenkavalier*, the first work which Hofmannsthal wrote specifically for Strauss. It was 'one of the great operatic evenings of the sunset period before the First World War'.[54] When the news leaked that it was to be a comedy set in 18th-century Vienna, special trains were run from Berlin to

* In his study at Garmisch can be seen a presentation from the skat circle of Ammergau, nearby.

Dresden. Opera houses queued to include it in their repertoire. This was the peak of Strauss' operatic success.

Curiously, despite their co-operation, there was very little personal rapport between Hugo von Hofmannsthal and Richard Strauss. They met rarely, and mostly communicated by post. Hofmannsthal did not get on at all with Pauline.

It was difficult to repeat the success of *Der Rosenkavalier*. Strauss' next work was a challenge to the market, *Ariadne auf Naxos*. In this, Molière's play *Le Bourgeois Gentilhomme*, accompanied by incidental music, preceded 'the leaden weight of a mythological opera'. It has been said that 'the project was doomed from the start'.[55] An opera audience does not go to see a play; and a theatre audience does not go to see an opera. It was revised in 1916 and subsequently. Today, we can appreciate how very clever it is, and how glorious is the colour of Strauss' music.

Strauss started work on *Die Frau ohne Schatten*, in which Hofmannsthal spins a fable about motherhood. An empress, a demi-goddess from the Far East, visits a dyer and his shrewish wife in order to seize the wife's shadow, a precondition of a woman's fertility. This is surely an excellent example of an opera in which the complexity can distract the audience's attention from the beauty of the music – even if Strauss could not understand why.*

In April 1913, Strauss travelled in Italy with Hofmannsthal and they discussed the opera. It was a sign of the times that they went in a Mercedes-Knight. 'There was nothing now but motor-cars driven each by a moustached mechanic, with a tall footman towering by his side ... Can anyone find these motor-cars as elegant as the old carriage-and-pair?', asked one novelist wistfully looking back at lost times.[56] Strauss valued the motorcar as a means of transport and also as a way of getting out into the countryside. But he was not interested in technology except for its utility, whether it was telephone, electric light, central heating, radio or cinema. The only film which interested him was the film for the Olympics in 1936 for which he wrote an overture.

* The shadow was used for various symbolic purposes in 19th-century Romantic literature, and may therefore have had more relevance to Strauss' audience than it does now. A straightforward story contributes to the popular success of many operas from Mozart to Verdi. Puccini's operas benefit from a recognition of the principle that the audience does not arrive in time to undertake extensive 'pre-course reading'. Others, including Wagner, have risked ignoring this.

The First World War and After

The First World War now intervened in Strauss' life. His investments, which were banked in London, were sequestrated. The Meiningen orchestra was closed down. Theatre staff were called up; works requiring a large orchestra had to be abandoned. As the war progressed, deprivation and malnutrition took its toll.

Hugo von Hofmannsthal, who was a reservist, was called up, although he was subsequently released because of his poor eyesight. Strauss' son Bubi volunteered, but was not accepted. Strauss, the patriotic but sincere father, wrote: 'It is a quite unexpected stroke of luck for you and for us that ... you will be spared from risking life and limb in this dreadful war.'[57]

As the war progressed, Strauss' patriotism turned to disillusionment. He shut himself up; he worked on *Die Frau ohne Schatten* and *Intermezzo*, and he revised *Ariadne*. He took the view, in a letter to Hofmannsthal, that 'in the midst of all the unpleasantness ... hard work is the only salvation'.[58]

The production of *Die Frau ohne Schatten* was delayed until after the war. It was produced in 1919 at the Vienna State Opera, where Strauss was appointed on a five-year contract. His remuneration and extravagance – 'I am here to lose money', he said – caused some fuss.[59] Strauss had that fatal insensitivity to the world around him from which so many successful people suffer. In his case, this trait would cost him dearly.[60]

It has been said that no country suffered more than Austria as a result of its defeat in the First World War. In one block of 62 one-roomed flats in Vienna, 34 of the tenants were war-widows. An empire of 50 million people crumbled into a republic of six and a half million, with more than a third of the population concentrated in Vienna, which 'became overnight a huge city of starving and freezing beggars'. Children were said to have swallowed coal dust in order to stifle hunger pains, and, in the soup kitchens, sawdust and wood shavings were mixed with gruel. There was galloping inflation, and disruption by communists.[61]

Strauss, who was never too sensitive to events around him,[62] built himself an impressive house in Vienna, having borrowed funds from a card-playing friend and financier, Emanuel von Grab. Strauss' son Bubi and Grab's daughter Alice were married in 1924.

Still insecure about his own financial position, Strauss continued conducting, when he really might have preferred to spend his time composing.

His conducting style had changed. As a young man on the rostrum, he had thrown himself around; now he adopted that style which we saw in late performances of Otto Klemperer: a tiny movement could produce the most exciting effect, a mere raising of the left hand could create the final pages of *Tristan*. For those who go to orchestral concerts expecting to admire the ballet, the performance must have been dull.

Together with the distinguished Max Reinhardt – whose productions of the dramas *Salomé* and *Elektra* had exercised a considerable influence on the operatic versions – Hofmannsthal and Strauss were responsible for the foundation of the regular Salzburg festival that began in the 1920s.[63] In an attempt to capture the *Der Rosenkavalier* market again, Strauss started working on *Arabella*. In July 1929, Hofmannsthal, who had just finalised the libretto, collapsed and died, as he was leaving for the funeral of his son, who had committed suicide. Strauss did not finish *Arabella* until 1932. Its première in Dresden was to have been conducted by Fritz Busch, with Lotte Lehmann as the lead soprano. However, political pressure led to the withdrawal of both. This reflected the dark times, the background to which it is now appropriate briefly to mention.

Nazism

The German political scene was becoming very disturbed indeed. Germany reeled from its sudden and surprising defeat in the First World War, a defeat suffered only a few months after it had been about to capture Paris. During the Weimar Republic,* in the decade between 1920 and 1930, there were twenty coalition governments.[64] Inflation was rampant. By 1922, the mark had fallen to a tenth of its 1920 value; during 1923, it ceased to have any value at all: on 1 July a dollar was worth 160,000 marks, a month later, 1 million. Three months after that, it took a 'million million' marks to equal the purchasing power of one 1914 mark.[65]

One conductor has described how rehearsals had to be interrupted to enable the musicians to protect their earnings: 'During the intermission, the representatives of the orchestra informed me that the musicians were just then being paid their salaries, and they asked me to understand that they would at once have to make some kind of purchase: if they waited to

* The Assembly chose to meet in Weimar, where the constitution was drawn up. It was distanced from Berlin both geographically and politically, and it had the merit of being the residence of Goethe. The Bach and Liszt connections seem to have featured less prominently.

do so two hours later, the purchasing power of their money would in the meantime have shrunk ... I no longer know in what queer merchandise the money was invested, though I believe a musician told me that he had bought bags of salt.'[66]

In this environment, dodgy characters thrived, sleaze and perversion were widespread. In the early 1930s, just before Hitler seized power, the atmosphere in Berlin was 'heavy with dust and perspiration and cheap scent'.[67] Some dangerous ideas easily took root on this compost heap. There was the anti-Semitism which had evidenced itself earlier. There was also the curious notion, spread through the German streamlined education system, that German *Kultur* was a superior concept, particularly in comparison with the French equivalent. Oswald Spengler, in *Decline of the West,* maintained that *Kultur* has a soul, whereas civilisation is a French concept representing the 'most artificial and external state of which humanity is capable'.[68] Intellectual nonsense like this provided a base upon which National Socialism could build.

In the 1930 election, with a considerably increased turnout, and defections from the bourgeois parties, the Nazi party had received 18.6 per cent of the vote;[69] Hitler was then at the head of the second strongest party in Germany. There was considerable violence as the Communists and the Nazis fought each other: 'Knives were whipped out, blows were dealt with spiked rings, beer-mugs, chair-legs or leaded clubs; bullets slashed the advertisements on the poster-columns, rebounded from the iron roofs of latrines. In the middle of a crowded street a young man would be attacked, stripped, thrashed, and left bleeding on the pavement.'[70]

A couple of years later, the Nazis had pushed up their share of the vote to well over a third and, as the largest democratically elected party, it was only a matter of time and negotiation before Hitler became Chancellor.[71] This happened in January 1933. Then, through a combination of constitutional manipulation and terror, Hitler ensured that, by the middle of that year, there was a one-party state. Hitler had promised to protect the small tradesmen, and good times were coming. The small businessmen of Berlin were 'suddenly proud of being blond ... the Jews, their business rivals, and the Marxists, a vaguely defined minority of people who didn't concern them, had been satisfactorily found guilty of the defeat and the inflation, and they were going to catch it. The town was full of whispers. They told of illegal midnight arrests, of prisoners tortured in the barracks, made to spit on Lenin's picture, swallow castor oil, eat old socks.'[72]

Strauss found himself, a very prominent person, living at the most unenviable time in extremely complex circumstances. He was aged nearly 70. His son was married to the daughter of a Jew, and he had many Jewish friends. At the time, he was working on *Die Schweigsame Frau*, whose librettist was the novelist Stefan Zweig, who was Jewish. One of Strauss' apologists has written: 'It requires an immense exercise of the historical imagination to understand the national and international climate of 1933.'[73] Many prominent people left Germany at this time. Some, such as Otto Klemperer, acidly suggested that Strauss did not leave because there were 56 opera houses in Germany in which to perform his works, but only two in the USA.

There are varying views about how culpable Strauss was for the action which he now took. The political reality was that the regime needed the support of its prominent citizens, a form of mutual reinforcement which is quite usual in almost all political structures. Strauss was important in providing just such support. For that he carries the blame, and shame.

His support became noticeably visible. At a concert in the Leipzig Gewandhaus, Strauss stood in for the world-famous conductor Bruno Walter, who had fled. Thus the concert, which otherwise would have been cancelled, went ahead. Strauss also stood in for Toscanini, who refused to conduct the 1933 *Parsifal* at Bayreuth. He also signed an ill-considered condemnation of the writer Thomas Mann who appeared to criticise Wagner, the Nazis' idol, in a lecture marking the fiftieth anniversary of his death.[74]

The significance of standing in for the performance at Leipzig emerges when one reads Bruno Walter's side of the story. Walter, who was Jewish, had been told by an official: 'we don't wish to prohibit the concert, for we are not interested in getting you out of an awkward predicament or in relieving you of your obligation to pay the orchestra. But if you insist on giving the concert you may be sure that everything in the hall will be smashed to pieces.'[75] Walter escaped that evening. His commentary on Strauss' action speaks for itself: 'the composer of *Ein Heldenleben* actually declared himself ready to conduct in the place of a colleague who had been forcibly removed. This made him especially popular with the upper ranks of Nazism. Later, to be sure, for reasons unknown to me, Strauss was said to have fallen out with the government.'[76]

Walter's economical but masterly comments on Strauss in his memoirs published in 1947 indicate how Strauss' reputation stood after the Second World War. In 380 pages of text, Walter limits references to Strauss to less than twenty pages. Six are purely factual, four are brief and withering. In the remaining pages, he tells the story of the Leipzig concert, and he condemns *Elektra*, *Der Rosenkavalier* and *Ariadne*. He is, however, complimentary about *Don Quixote*, mischievously perhaps, because it has sometimes been considered not to be one of Strauss' finest works.

Bruno Walter relates how Strauss, back in 1914, when there was a shortage of players, was unconcerned about the extent to which a score was ripped apart, so long as the opera, in some form or another, went ahead. 'When I pointed out to him that the score called for eight clarinets, and that I had not got that number, nor seven, nor six, or even five, he replied: "Four will do!"'[77] There was an important production of *Der Rosenkavalier* at Covent Garden, to which Walter attributed the world-success of that opera. He implies that the London success was due to the quality of the performers, rather than the work.

Perhaps Walter's most damning story relates a visit to Garmisch to discuss *Ariadne*. 'I am still conscious of the pleasure the composer's cool and perfect piano performance of the rather artificial but masterly work gave me. His playing was as lucid and objective as his written music on the desk before us, but in spite of its uniform coolness, it still left the impression of latent agitation. True, the storm and heat of the dramatically moving scenes impressed me as being ordained by the enthroned power of a weather god rather than by the upsurging of a human emotion. I was strangely affected when I found at the end of the neatly written manuscript the words in his handwriting: "Finished on Bubi's birthday".' He added, 'My chilled soul thawed slightly at this indication of a friendly family feeling.'[78]

Of course, Bruno Walter's damning indictment of Strauss was written too soon after the Second World War to be anything other than subjective. One wonders how differently his views would have been expressed, had his book been written fifteen or more years earlier or later.

Strauss' cardinal error arose when he became president of the music section of the Reich chamber of culture. In May 1933, Goebbels said that the new regime 'would link up all of cultural life with conscious political-ideological propaganda', and would wrench it out of the 'Jewish-liberalistic' course it had followed in the Weimar period.[79] Anyone involved in the art world was compelled to join one of the chambers for music, literature, theatre, the fine arts and films, press and broadcasting. Strauss may have thought that he could use his considerable influence beneficially in the very difficult circumstances; and he indeed used his position to get the copyright laws extended from 30 to 50 years. But he was in an indefensible position. These sections of the Reich chamber were self-regulatory, and, by accepting the presidency, Strauss supplied respectability.

Stefan Zweig wrote to him: 'Sometimes I have the feeling that you are not fully aware ... of the historical greatness of your position ... everything you do is destined to be of historical significance.'[80] Possibly the only possible decision Strauss could sensibly have taken was to get out; but the emigration of him alone would not have been enough. The whole family would have had to go as well. That was a step he would not take.

The Nazi interference with the arts gathered pace. In December 1934, a musical crisis arose over Paul Hindemith. The Nazis disliked Hindemith's atonal* music, his work with the Jewish Kulturbund and his anti-Nazi views. In November 1934, a boycott of his works was announced. Wilhelm Furtwängler, who had recently conducted the first performance of Hindemith's symphony *Mathis der Maler*, came to his defence. A couple of months later, Hindemith was given six months' leave of absence from his job.

In June 1935, the first performance of Strauss' *Die Schweigsame Frau* took place at Dresden. The National Socialist Cultural Unit had taken steps to distance itself from this work, because the libretto was by Zweig: works by Jews were not allowed to be performed.** Zweig's name was deleted from the poster advertisements and programmes. After Strauss protested, it was reinstated, but neither Hitler nor Goebbels attended the première; and, after four performances, the opera was banned. Meanwhile,

* The use of the word 'atonal' at that time was usually pejorative. This prompted Berg to observe that, although atonal music had rhythm and melody, its harmony did not 'conform to laws of tonality familiar until then', which was based on the familiar triad. He observed caustically that 'so long as a certain kind of music contains enough triads, it causes no offence, even if in other ways it clashes violently with the sacred laws of tonality.'[81]

** The Nazis, had they been consistent, should presumably have been equally concerned about the librettos of Hofmannsthal, because he was the great-grandson of Isaak Löw, a successful merchant and one of the founders of Vienna's Jewish community early in the 19th century. (His services to the state won him the title Edler von Hofmannsthal. His son became a Christian and married an Italian Catholic.)[82] The Nazis tied themselves in knots over Johann Strauss, whose father was one quarter Jewish. Because the Nazis liked his 'healthy native music grown from the depths of the Volk',[83] they falsified records of his birth.

an indiscreet letter from Strauss to Zweig had been intercepted; in it, Strauss said that he was going through the charade of being president of the Reich music chamber. As a consequence, Strauss was obliged to resign, ostensibly on the grounds of ill health.[84]

As his position became increasingly insecure, Strauss became more and more worried about the position of his daughter-in-law Alice, who was Jewish, and the grandchildren, who were classified as 'Mischlinge 1 Klasse' (half-breeds, first class). He grovelled to Hitler and asked for an interview, but his request was ignored. His grandson Richard was beaten up in school. After Strauss complained to Hitler about the treatment Richard had received, it was decreed that his grandchildren should be regarded as Aryans, but not be eligible for party membership, military service or public office. But the Nazis still had uses for Strauss, and he acquiesced. He wrote the 'Olympische Hymne' for the 1936 Olympics.*[85]

His one-act opera *Friedenstag* was performed in Munich in July 1938, and *Daphne* in Dresden in October of that year. *Friedenstag* achieved 100 performances in two years.[86]

On 9 November 1938, there was a pogrom in Germany in which 200 synagogues were burnt down, 7,500 Jewish shops and businesses were looted and 91 Jews were murdered. This was known as Crystal Night, from the broken glass littering the streets. The Garmisch Nazis planned to arrest Alice, but she had escaped; her boys were made to spit on Jews rounded up in the central square.[87]

Twenty-six members of Alice's family were murdered in the Nazi extermination camps. On one occasion, Strauss was travelling past the camp in which Alice's grandmother was apparently incarcerated; he drove up and announced: 'My name is Richard Strauss, I want to see Frau Neumann.'[88] The prison guards thought he was an idiot and told him to push off. He had an extraordinary strain of naivety – or was it insensitivity, or was it that he felt he was somehow above it all?

Strauss in the Second World War

During the war, Strauss settled in Vienna, where Governor von Schirach saw him as a useful component in his attempt to restore Vienna to its place

* The adjacent villages Garmisch and Partenkirchen came together at the time the Winter Olympics were staged there. Strauss also celebrated the jubilee of Japan with 'Festmusik zur Feier des 2600 jährigen Bestehens des Kaiserreichs Japan, 1940'.

as the European cultural centre. In Vienna, he wrote the Second Horn Concerto. With Clemens Krauss conducting, he produced *Capriccio* at Munich in October 1942.

Strauss, who needed to travel around, had to circumvent endless bureaucratic restrictions in order to obtain petrol and to defer the conscription of his chauffeur. As things got worse, he was told that the chauffeur would have to be called up, and evacuees and homeless people would be boarded in the Strauss family home. He objected; and there was a row with the Kreisleiter of Garmisch who said threateningly: 'Es sind schon andere Kopfe gerollt als die Ihre, Herr Dr Strauss.'*[89] The issue was dealt with 'at the highest level' and the eventual decision is summarised in Martin Bormann's edict: 'The personal association of our leading men with Dr Richard Strauss shall cease. However, the Führer, to whom Reichsminister Dr Goebbels referred the question, decided today that no obstacles should be put in the way of the performances of his works.'[90]

Gradually the places with which Strauss was associated collapsed: he was particularly distressed by the bombing in October 1943 of the National Theatre in Munich, where *Tristan* and *Die Meistersinger* were first performed, and where his father had worked. And, in February 1945, the Dresden opera house was destroyed: it had staged the premières of so many of his works. The Vienna State Opera House was destroyed too.

The première of *Die Liebe der Danae* was to have been at the Salzburg Festival in 1944, but this was cancelled, following the bomb plot on 20 July, in which an oak table had absorbed a bomb explosion and protected Hitler from assassination. All festivals were cancelled, but the Gauleiter of Salzburg got permission for a dress rehearsal and a concert by the Berlin Philharmonic under Furtwängler, which was held in mid-August.

Soon, as the state of the country got worse, all theatres and opera houses were closed. Strauss became increasingly concerned that the Nazis would move against Alice and the grandchildren. One evening, Bubi and Alice were arrested, after the house had been searched. Their release was only obtained two days later. The situation became increasingly alarming. Strauss' grandson Richard fled on a bike from Vienna to Garmisch.

* 'Other heads than yours have already rolled, Dr Strauss.'

Post-war

When the American troops arrived in Garmisch, they tried to commandeer the Strausses' villa. Strauss announced: 'I am Richard Strauss, the composer of *Rosenkavalier* and *Salomé*. Leave me alone',[91] so the officer asked his men to show respect.

In the following weeks, many American soldiers were welcomed to the villa, shown round and given autographs. Alice got fed up with them pointing to the bronze of Beethoven and asking 'Who's that guy?' 'If they ask once more', Strauss told her, 'tell them it's Hitler's father.'[92] The atmosphere was by no means wholly philistine: musicians are indebted to an American soldier, John Lancie, an oboist in the Pittsburg Symphony Orchestra, who inspired Strauss to start writing the oboe concerto.

One journalist who came to visit was Thomas Mann's son Klaus.* He was annoyed at the way the Strauss family expected special treatment; he wrote a very adverse report. He was hardly objective: his father had been vehemently anti-Nazi in the 1930s.[93]

The sequel was inevitable. Strauss' past was examined by a denazification tribunal and his royalties were appropriated by Allied Property Control, so he had no income.**

In October 1945, Richard and Pauline Strauss had to go into voluntary exile in Switzerland. He took with him various newly copied manuscripts which were put in the safe as security for their hotel bill. He described himself and his wife as 'two sad Germans, who have lived only for Art'.[95] He visited England, at Sir Thomas Beecham's invitation. In a pathetic understatement, for a composer responsible for at least seven operas which are essential items in the opera house repertoire, Strauss said: 'I may not be a first-rate composer, but I am a first-class second-rate composer.'[96]

The denazification tribunal's report on 7 June 1948 found that Strauss was not incriminated. After an operation in Lausanne for a gallstone, he returned to Garmisch in May 1949, taking with him the *Four Last Songs.*

* Thomas Mann's children Klaus and Erika were great friends of Bruno Walter's children, so Klaus cannot be said to have been independent in his opinions.

** Furtwängler, who was against the Nazi regime but 'stayed behind', was denazified in December 1946 and could only resume conducting the following April. Even then, he was excluded from the Chicago Symphony Orchestra. But he had not been particularly popular in the USA where a combination of his very personal style of interpretation and his disregard for the orchestral management did not help his reputation.[94]

The calendar on his desk in his study stops at 8 September. He said to Alice that dying seemed 'just as I composed it in *Tod und Verklärung*'.[97] In this, the dying and suffering artist 'recalls his youth and unfulfilled idealism'.[98]

The artist died and his soul was transfigured. Ariadne sang, when leaving Naxos: 'In the land where you are taking me, we forget what *here* has brought us pain.'[99]

DEBUSSY

CHAPTER 26

IN ONE WAY, Debussy seems unique. The musical origins of most composers, Mahler and Strauss, or Bach, Beethoven and Brahms, are generally fairly clear, but Debussy's music almost seems to have come from nowhere. Indeed, one mid-20th-century critic was so bold as to claim that 'in all music extant to 1870, there is not a hint of his advent'.[1] A composer who gave this impression inevitably caused passions to run high among his contemporaries. Saint-Saëns wrote to his friend Fauré: 'I advise you to look at the pieces for two pianos ... which M. Debussy has just published. It is really unbelievable, and we must at all costs bar the door of the Institut against a man capable of such atrocities; they should be put next to the cubist pictures.'[2]

In a limited sense, Saint-Saëns was right. An institute which was dedicated to maintaining the classical harmonies and structures was not a suitable abode for a composer for whom sonority, tone colour and mood were the all-important ingredients of composition. Augmented fifths, chains of ninth chords, parallel seconds were not the usual musical language sanctioned by the Institut at the time.[3]

Debussy's musical style has been likened to that of the Impressionist painters. But he disliked this comparison, and was irritated at being called

'Le Whistler de la Musique'.[4] The pictures which he preferred were not by the Impressionists, but were those of the Pre-Raphaelites, of Turner, Botticelli, Gustave Moreau and Hokusai.

Although we have already leapt far forward with many composers, Debussy's childhood takes us back again as far as the Paris Commune. He came to the attention of the public in 1894 with the *Prélude à l'Après-Midi d'un Faune*. This was new ground. He was almost 40 when his opera *Pelléas et Mélisande* was staged. By that time, he had had several unfortunate love affairs and an unsatisfactory marriage. He then settled down happily with the relatively prosperous Emma Bardac; their daughter Chouchou became the apple of his eye. But Debussy became ill with rectal cancer, and at the time Paris was about to be taken by the Germans in March 1918, he died.

Youth

Claude-Achille Debussy was born on 22 August 1862 in St-Germain-en-Laye, at the top of an escarpment on the left bank of the Seine, thirteen miles west of Paris. St-Germain then had a healthy and bracing air which made it a favourite summer residence for Parisians. Chopin's Scottish pupil Jane Stirling had lived there with her sister.[5] The church contains a memorial erected by Queen Victoria in memory of King James II, who died at the palace in 1701, and whose intestines were buried there.[6] In Debussy's childhood years, the palace was being restored.

Debussy's parents, who do not seem to have been at all musical,[7] ran a crockery shop. It was unsuccessful, something that is difficult to imagine in what today is a chic suburb, bustling with well-dressed people. The composer's father, Manuel-Achille, was subsequently a travelling salesman and a printer's assistant. In the late 1880s, he became an assistant book-keeper, but he was suddenly dismissed, the reasons unknown.

The start of the Franco-Prussian War provided an ideal opening for a chancer such as Manuel-Achille. He quickly found work in the commissariat at the Hôtel de Ville. He joined the National Guard and then was swept up by the Communards (see pages 598–602). On 8 May 1871, at two in the morning, we find Captain de Bussy at the head of his company, on the way to the fort of Issy, a scene of particularly fierce fighting. Soon, he was in overall command of his battalion, because the commanding officer, having been kicked by a horse, was invalided out. Once the Versailles troops opened fire, de Bussy's men ran for it; unfortunately, there was nobody left for the captain to command. He was on his own: he could only surrender. He was very lucky not to be shot, there and then.[8]

The subsequent days and months must have been a very alarming time for his wife and family, at least as bad, if not worse, than the Rossini family had experienced a hundred years before, when Giuseppe Rossini had backed the wrong side in northern Italy. Mme de Bussy, in a letter of 8 June 1871, pleaded with the military authorities that her husband had only joined the National Guard so as to support his wife and children. Fortune again favoured the captain: on the grounds that he was a person of weak character, he was sentenced to just four years. As it transpired, after a year of imprisonment, he was released, although his civil rights were suspended for four years.[9]

Throughout this difficult period, it seems that the family was supported by Manuel-Achille's sister Clémentine. She had run a business, 'Madame Debussy Couture'; in 1864, she became the mistress of a broker, and settled in Cannes where she ran a guesthouse. Claude-Achille's sister had been parked with her, and the little boy eventually went to stay with her as well (see colour plate 45). She gave him some piano lessons, when he was eight or nine.[10]

With such a disrupted family life, it is not surprising that Claude-Achille became noticeably self-centred, while being shy and unsociable.[11] He and his siblings went their own way. His sister Adèle, who lived until 1952, was a trimmer in millinery establishments and later became an outfitter. His brother Emmanuel was a bad sort, who often had to be fetched from the police station, and ended up as a farm hand. Alfred, on the other hand, had a comfortable life, and became a buyer in Cardiff for a Paris firm.[12]

While idling away his time in the prison, the captain had a chat with another prisoner whose mother purported to have been a pupil of Chopin, although it seems more likely that she had merely heard Chopin play.* She gave Claude-Achille piano lessons and suggested that he should train to become a virtuoso. This must have seemed like manna from heaven to the captain. He and his wife were soon imagining the riches that would come their way. In October 1872, Claude-Achille was accepted at the Conservatoire.[13]

It must have been a considerable blow to the ambitious parents when their son failed to win the first prize in the piano class. Claude-Achille was more interested in composition. Even in that subject, one of his teachers

* Mme de Mauté was the wife of a grocer. The Mautés' main claim to fame was that their daughter Mathilde had recently married, aged sixteen, Verlaine, the poet of 'Clair de Lune'.

described him as 'a pupil with a considerable gift for harmony, but desperately careless'.[14]

Around this time, Debussy travelled abroad several times. He went to Italy and Vienna. He also went to Russia where he saw a more affluent way of life, and worked for Mme von Meck, Tchaikovsky's supporter. Back at home, he developed a friendship with Mme Vasnier, aged 32, wife of a building contractor. She sang his songs.

Debussy was already showing signs of the egocentricity that was such a major feature of his character. At the time of Debussy's relationship with Mme Vasnier, Paul Vidal, who won the Prix de Rome in 1883, wrote of him: 'I don't know whether his egoism will ever be subdued. He is incapable of any sacrifice whatever ... he is nothing but a pleasure seeker.'[15] Debussy seems to have found it normal that those of his friends and relatives who were comfortably off would 'lend' him money without any hope of ever getting it back.

Debussy came second in the Prix de Rome competition in which Vidal won the first prize. In the following year, Debussy himself won with a cantata, 'L'Enfant Prodigue'. But he did not like his time at the Villa Medici, which he described, in a letter to M. Vasnier,* as 'this abominable villa'.[16] He missed Mme Vasnier, and he disliked the requirement to send the series of *envois* back to the Académie des Beaux Arts. Nor did he enter into the spirit of the place: 'Luckily I've found a way to get myself out of boring social occasions. I told [the director] I'd sold my evening dress and that my financial resources did not permit me to have another suit made. He thought I was mad, but who cares? I got what I wanted, because he's too much of a decorum-worshipper to allow a mere lounge suit to appear amid the splendour of décolleté gowns and tail-coats.'[17] He returned to his parents' home in Paris in February 1887, after staying in Rome for the minimum two years.

France at the Time

The France to which Debussy returned was in poor shape. The country was led by a 'set of largely grey mediocrities',[18] and, between the Commune

* This is another example of a *ménage à trois* in which the husband seems to have tolerated his wife's infidelities, whether apparent or real. Other examples include the Viardots (and Turgenev) and the Seligmans (and Puccini).

and the First World War, there were 60 governments.[19] Phylloxera had wrought havoc in the vineyards, and French wine production fell by more than two-thirds between 1875 and 1889. The depression in the countryside was compounded by the crash of the Union Générale Bank into which a large number of farmers had put their savings. People migrated to the towns, thus transferring the economic problems there. By the mid-1880s, there was much distress and simmering discontent.[20]

This provided an ideal background for the antics of General Boulanger, who, as we have seen, looked as if he might stage a 'Napoleonic' coup, a prospect which rattled the Germans.* Early in 1887, at the time Debussy returned to Paris, there was a war scare, with Bismarck running a press campaign against the French 'warmongers'.

But it was not all doom and gloom. Shocked by the Boulangist upheavals, the republicans and their opponents, the conservatives and clerics, made a genuine attempt at conciliation, and tried to make the Republic work. The 1889 government lasted for a year, and the next one for two years. There was also a considerable amount of economic growth. For this became the *belle époque*, and the public found a new kind of refuge from materialism, in a new craze for mass entertainment. Hundreds of thousands flocked to the Eiffel Tower, the crowning glory of the 1889 International Exhibition, which marked the centenary of the French Revolution.[21] This was also the year that the Moulin Rouge opened in Montmartre, to be followed by other haunts of the demi-monde, the Folies Bergères. Public phone booths began to appear in the 1880s, trams in the 1890s, and the Paris métro in 1900.

Yet, alongside this, there was an insidious growth in public scandals, culminating in the Dreyfus case, in which we have seen Grieg becoming embroiled.** This took place in the 1890s, and ripped the country apart. First, however, the government became enmeshed in a scandal about the Panama Canal which was constructed by the French during the 1880s. The costs and difficulties were considerably underestimated, and a third of the billion francs raised in loans was dissipated in charges from banks and publicity agents. Lottery bonds issued to raise the rest of the finance were under-subscribed, and the canal company went into liquidation. Ferdinand de Lesseps, the engineer for the Suez Canal,[22] and various offi-

* See page 614.
** See pages 732–4.

cials were condemned for fraud, although the charges were later quashed. Then, in September 1892, an anti-Semitic paper, the *Libre Parole*, accused the canal company of paying bribes to parliamentarians through a Jewish financier, who was found dead. The events unfolded in a familiar way. After a commission of inquiry, five deputies and five senators including two former ministers, a former prefect of police and a former governor-general of Algeria were charged. In the case of all, except for the former minister of works, who had received 375,000 fr, the charges were eventually dropped. But many were tainted with the stigma of having been *chequards*.

The affair had created an atmosphere which, in the words of an eminent British historian, 'lasted for years, like the smoke that continues to hang over the spot where a high-explosive shell has struck the ground'.[23] It drove the anti-Semitism which characterised the Dreyfus Affair.

'Anarchists' began to appear: the apartment of a friend of Saint-Saëns, a salon hostess and painter, was robbed and set on fire. The composer Vincent d'Indy found a note pinned to the rostrum saying: 'Death to the aristocrats. Next time we will finish you off, you and your kind.'[24] In 1893, a bomb exploded close to La Madeleine and damaged the offices of the music publishers Durand & Cie. In mid-1894, President Carnot was assassinated, stabbed with a six-inch knife.

There was trouble abroad as well. France was building its north-African empire, taking in places such as Dahomey, the Ivory Coast and Timbuctoo. It was only a matter of time before the French would encroach on British colonial interests. The relationship with Britain was steadily deteriorating: in 1893, the British ambassador in Paris described the attitude towards Great Britain as one of 'animosity and bitter dislike'.[25] A crisis broke in 1898, when the British demanded the withdrawal of a French expeditionary force at Fashoda in the Sudan, territory which the British regarded as being within their sphere of influence. The French government sensibly decided that their real enemy should be Germany and not Britain, and withdrew.*

French society at this time was marked by 'an acute caste snobbery':[27] the old nobility regarded themselves as superior to, and might even be deliberately rude to, the empire nobility, who in turn stuck their noses up at the world of finance and 'big business'. Way beneath these strata, the

* When King Edward arrived for a state visit in 1903, he was greeted with: 'Vive Fashoda, Vivent les Boers, Vive Jeanne d'Arc'. Fortunately his visit was a success and relations then improved considerably and became the entente cordiale.[26]

impecunious Debussy, who was living with Gabrielle Dupont, a pretty green-eyed girl from Normandy, led a bohemian way of life. On the boulevards, he would meet his friends, mainly poets and writers such as Henri de Regnier, Catulle Mendès, Paul Valéry, Pierre Louÿs and André Gide, who subsequently won the Nobel Prize. Debussy would go to the circus, to the Chat Noir, to pantomimes, or just listen and dream at Mallarmé's salon. It was difficult to take Gaby to the middle-class salons; but he might end the day with her in the Auberge du Clou or the Café Wéber. At other times, he would browse in the tiny bookshop in the Chaussée d'Antin run by Edmond Bailly, his wife and their cat. Bailly was an expert on magic and the occult, and would only sell to customers he liked; he preferred to spend the time talking to friends.[28]

Debussy became a close friend of Ernest Chausson, a wealthy composer who was also a member of Franck's circle. The Chaussons had a grand residence in the boulevard de Courcelles, in which they hung their fine art collection which included paintings by Renoir and Gauguin. There, they would entertain leading writers, painters and musicians. Chausson, who provided Debussy with funds, was one of the most active committee members of the Société Nationale de Musique. But Chausson was extremely angry with Debussy when, early in 1894, and with Gaby still 'around', he became engaged to a salon singer, and then abruptly broke off the engagement.[29]

Debussy's artistic contacts broadened his experience. Another important influence on him was the Javanese gamelan, an Indonesian orchestra comprising bells, gongs and many percussion instruments. He heard this during its performances in Paris at the time of the 1889 Exhibition. Both Debussy and Ravel* took a considerable interest in Javanese music.[30]

Debussy was still under pressure from his family. His mother, according to Paul Vidal, 'turned his stomach by always wanting him to be with her and to make sure he was working hard'.[31] Debussy observed: 'My mother decided that I was not providing what a son ought to, no fame was accruing … It is clear that those castles in the air built on the anticipation of my fame have fallen horribly to the earth.'[32]

He completed *Fêtes Galantes*, using poems by Verlaine. It was not until the performance of *La Damoiselle Elue* at the Société Nationale in April 1893 that Debussy's music came to the notice of the public. Then, with the *Prélude à l'Après-Midi d'un Faune*, as Pierre Boulez has said, 'the art of

* See page 634.

music began to beat with a new pulse'.[33] *L'Après-Midi* was first performed in December 1894.

It was about this time that, having seen a performance of Maeterlinck's play *Pelléas et Mélisande*, Debussy started sketching the opera. But it took until 1902 to reach the stage. As one later critic put it, 'Monet in search of suitable material, went to the fogs of London, and Debussy went to the poetic prose of Maeterlinck.'[34] Meanwhile, in December 1893, his String Quartet in G minor was performed.

His relationship with Gaby Dupont was stormy and, at one stage, she tried to commit suicide. On New Year's Day 1899, Debussy wrote to Georges Hartmann, the publisher and his financier, saying that 'Mlle Dupont, my secretary, has resigned her position. Altogether it's extremely disturbing, and even if one's a composer, one is none the less a man.'[35]

When Debussy wrote: 'Too well my mouth remembers yours, your caresses have left an indelible mark, as hot as fire, as gentle as a flower ... I yearn for the blush of your red lips', it was not Gaby he was addressing.[36] Rather, he was writing to her friend Rosalie (Lilly) Texier, a mannequin, whom he described as being as 'pretty as someone out of a story book'.[37] On 19 October 1899, they were married and began an impecunious existence, particularly when Hartmann died in the following year and that source of funds dried up.

In 1901, Debussy became music critic of *La Revue Blanche*, an important, lively periodical closely associated with the modern literary movements; writers such as André Gide and Marcel Proust contributed to its pages, and its covers were often designed by prominent artists such as Toulouse-Lautrec. But, for Debussy, money was still short. Lilly was tubercular and needed an operation. During the rehearsals of *Pelléas*, he was prosecuted for non-payment of debts.

Pelléas et Mélisande

The first performance of *Pelléas et Mélisande*, on 30 April 1902, was a landmark in French music. The opera had experienced a stormy gestation. The playwright Maeterlinck was upset that his mistress had been turned down for the part of Mélisande. There was a noisy public dress rehearsal; the première was quieter, perhaps because the audience found the opera incomprehensible. The Establishment was irate: the director of the Conservatoire, Theodore Dubois, forbade his students to go to it. Others were just puzzled by the opera's formlessness, the unusual harmonies, the absence of arias and dance. Those used to operas by Verdi, Wagner and Richard Strauss found it difficult to appreciate that 'passion need not be measured in decibels', that Debussy's reticence is 'a concentration of feeling, not a lack of it'.[38]

Of course, this was exactly the style of music that Debussy wanted to create. 'How much one first has to find, and then suppress, to reach the naked flesh of emotion', he wrote.[39] He explained his reasons for choosing *Pelléas*: 'I wanted from music a freedom which it possesses perhaps to a greater extent than any other art, not being tied to a more or less exact reproduction of Nature, but to the mysterious correspondences between Nature and Imagination.'[40] He also said: 'In Art, there can be no obligatory respect; that is the sort of nonsense that has been offloaded on to a number of people who have become respectable only through having lived long ago ... Love of Art does not depend on explanations or come from experience, as in the case of those who say of a new work "I need to hear that several times". Utter rubbish! When we really listen to music, we hear immediately what we need to hear.'[41] The production of *Pelléas* launched Debussy into a very prolific period, and it was in the following years that he wrote the second set of *Fêtes Galantes*, the *Images* and *L'Isle Joyeuse*. In the two years starting with summer 1903, he wrote the work which is so enduringly popular, *La Mer*.

One enthusiast for *Pelléas* was Marcel Proust, whose enjoyment of it was a result of hearing it several times. He had paid little attention to the opera when it was first produced. But in 1911, he installed a 'theatrophone', a new gadget to which he listened in the bed in which he chose to spend much of his time. For the payment of 60 fr a month, he was provided with a large black ear-trumpet connected through telephone lines to eight Paris theatres and concert halls including the Opéra, the Opéra-Comique, the Concerts Colonne and the Comédie-Française. The quality was poor.[42] On one occasion, Proust said that he thought the rumblings he heard were 'agreeable, if a trifle amorphous'[43] until he suddenly realised that it was the interval.*

* Technology was changing fast. It was not long before Proust wanted his grand piano adapted with a pianola 'player piano'. Much to the exasperation of the supplier, the Aeolian Company, Proust demanded rolls that had never been requested before, such as a piano transcription of Beethoven's late quartets.[44]

EMMA

Lilly was kind, naïve, and remote from her husband in cultural taste and experience. Debussy was already drifting away from her when, in autumn 1903, he met Emma Bardac. Like Debussy, she was also aged 42; she was the wife of a banker, Sigismund Bardac, by whom she had a son, Raoul, and a daughter, Dolly. She had also, it seems, had an affair with Fauré, who had dedicated his song cycle, *La Bonne Chanson,* to her. In July 1904, she and Debussy went off to Jersey together and then to Dieppe, only returning to Paris at the end of September. Lilly tried to commit suicide, and the news of this led many of Debussy's friends to desert him.[45]

Debussy moved with Emma into a house, bought with her money, in the avenue du Bois de Boulogne. There, he lived for the rest of his life. It was a comfortable, well-appointed town house with a small garden, away from the noise of the city, except for the railway which passed nearby. They had two servants, an English governess, and their own telephone.*

Debussy found difficulty in coping with Emma's poor health: 'Struggling on one's own is nothing! But struggling "en famille" is terrible!'[47] However, on the whole, the relationship was very happy. Debussy could talk to Emma about his music: she understood his language and aims. This would have been impossible with Lilly. For many years, Debussy would write Emma musical messages, particularly at Christmas.[48]

In October 1905, they had a daughter, Claude-Emma, whom they soon called Chouchou. Although both parents secured divorces at this time, they did not marry until January 1908. In 1907, Emma's uncle, a rich financier, disinherited her. So, to pay for their extravagant lifestyle, Debussy had to perform on the piano and conduct his works. This took him to England, Belgium, Holland, Austria, Hungary, Italy and Russia.

Debussy said of his divorce from Lilly: 'I intend to live according to my wishes, and without bothering myself with the below-stairs gossip that will be made up around my life … which, by the way, is of child-like simplicity.'[49] This lack of sensitivity lost him many friends. Divorce was greatly frowned upon.[50] Ravel seems to have contributed to a fund to help Lilly.

Indeed Ravel and Debussy quarrelled, partly because of the divorce, but

* Proust's response to telecommunication was not unusual. He wrote: 'Like all of us nowadays, I found too slow for my liking, in its abrupt changes, the admirable sorcery whereby a few moments are enough to bring before us, invisible but present, the person to whom we wish to speak.'[46]

also because Ravel was irritated that Debussy was being credited with the development of *avant-garde* music, whereas Ravel felt that Debussy had to a great extent plagiarised his *Habanera*.[51] Nevertheless, Ravel always had great respect for Debussy. He said of *L'Après-Midi*: 'It was hearing this work, so many years ago, that I first understood what real music was.'[52]

Debussy's tendency to depression was relieved by Chouchou, a lively and amusing little girl. He completed *Children's Corner* in 1908 for her. He wrote letters to her on his trips abroad, written in his very small and flat

Maurice Ravel / Francis Poulenc

handwriting. There is one from the Grand Hôtel d'Europe in St Petersburg in 1913 asking her (aged eight) for news about their dog Xantho.[53]

As we have seen, the arrival of Diaghilev's *Ballets Russes* in Paris in 1909 influenced many leading composers.* One of the best-known roles of the famous dancer Vaslav Nijinsky was in *L'Après-Midi*, in which his erotic dancing scandalised the first-night audience. When Diaghilev suggested

* The impresario Sergei Diaghilev had organised five concerts at the Paris Opéra in 1907, in which Rachmaninov took part. Diaghilev staged *Boris Godunov* in the following year. In 1909, his Russian ballet programme included excerpts from Borodin's *Prince Igor* and, in the following year, Rimsky-Korsakov's *Shéhérazade*. Diaghilev commissioned several ballets for Paris: from Ravel, *Daphnis et Chloë*, from Debussy, *Jeux*, and from Stravinsky, *The Firebird* and then *The Rite of Spring*.[54]

that Debussy should write a ballet, Debussy observed, 'Naturally, I can't suggest a ballet subject at the drop of a hat; and they are talking to me about 18th-century Italy! … which, for Russian dancers, strikes me as a bit contradictory.'[55] In the event, he wrote the ballet *Jeux*. However, Stravinsky's *Le Sacre du Printemps* (*The Rite of Spring*), which was performed by Diaghilev's company a few days earlier, eclipsed it.

Stravinsky and Debussy had met in 1910 at the time of the very successful first performance of Stravinsky's *The Firebird*. They had played a piano duet of *The Rite* in June 1912, with Debussy playing the bass and Stravinsky the treble, and in the following year Debussy presented him with a copy of the second book of his *Préludes*. At that time, Debussy was very excited about Stravinsky. 'There's a young Russian composer who has an instinctive genius for colour and rhythm … I still think of the performance of *The Rite of Spring* ... It haunts me like a beautiful nightmare and I try in vain to recall the terrifying impression it made.'[56] He also said that it is 'an extraordinarily savage affair, primitive music with every modern convenience'.[57]

Debussy and Stravinsky both admired each other although, after Stravinsky became successful, Debussy felt some pangs of professional jealousy. However, when he was near his end, he wrote to Stravinsky: 'It is a special satisfaction to tell you how much you have enlarged the boundaries of the permissible in the empire of sound.'[58]* Stravinsky himself said, 'The musicians of my generation and I myself owe the most to Debussy',[60] and composed a chorale, which he used as the final part of *Symphonies of Wind Instruments* in 1920.

Cancer

Early in 1909, Debussy had begun to suffer from rectal cancer, and needed to take drugs to alleviate the pain. But he continued to be very active. The first French biography of him was published, and he began five of the first book of *Préludes* for the piano. He was in London for the British première

* The frontiers of music were being pushed out. The poet Jean Cocteau, who has been described as 'a publicist for everyone from a transvestite tight-rope walker … to a black American boxer, his lover' wrote *Parade*, a ballet for the *Ballets Russes*, in 1917.[59] In the score, the witty Erik Satie (1866–1925) experimented with typewriters, sirens and other modern sources of sound. Picasso did the set and costume design. It was not a success, but it was at this time that the word 'Surrealist' was coined.

of *Pelléas*, which was a success. He wrote to his parents describing the curtain calls: 'The singers were recalled a dozen times and, for a quarter of an hour, there were calls for the composer … Received opinion states that such a reaction is extremely rare in England, where the temperature of the public tends to remain below zero.'[61]

Debussy was appointed a member of the advisory board of the Paris Conservatoire. He was on the examining staff, doubtless because he needed money. He observed wryly on one occasion that 'the jury included some odd musicians who'd have been more at home, I fancy, judging livestock'.[62] 'Think of me with sympathy this Sunday. I shall be listening to eleven performances of the Rhapsody for B flat Clarinet; I'll tell you all, if I survive.'[63] This was at the old Conservatoire building in the rue du Faubourg Poissonière, 'the same gloomy, dirty place we remember'.[64]

In 1915, Debussy's publisher Durand asked him to produce an edition of the works of Chopin; he himself composed his two books of Études for the piano. Several of his projects were failures or were abandoned or left incomplete. His incidental music to *Le Martyre de St Sebastien* was a flop; the Archbishop of Paris forbade Roman Catholics to attend. A long-standing project to write an opera on *The Fall of the House of Usher* was, among others, never completed, even though Debussy was totally absorbed by the story written by the Boston-born writer Edgar Allan Poe. Indeed Debussy said that Poe exerted 'an almost agonising tyranny' over him.[65]

We can see why. Debussy and Poe were masters of atmosphere. In less than twenty pages, Poe evokes the house and its proprietor, Roderick Usher, with his 'cadaverously wan' countenance.[66] In the house, next to its lake with its 'pestilent and mystic vapour, dull, sluggish, faintly discernible, and leaden-hued, … an air of stern, deep, and irredeemable gloom hung over and pervaded all'.[67] The narrator says Usher's 'long improvised dirges will ring forever in my ears'.[68] His 'morbid condition of the auditory nerve … rendered all music intolerable to the sufferer, with the exception of certain stringed instruments'; and he played on his guitar 'a certain singular perversion and amplification of the wild air of the last waltz of Von Weber'.[69] The 'sulphureous lustre' of a performance of Debussy's opera, almost a sequel to *Pelléas*, would have been fascinating; as it was, although started in 1908, he only wrote two scenes.

Debussy said: 'We must agree that the beauty of a work of Art will always remain a mystery; in other words, we can never be absolutely sure "how it's made". We must at all costs preserve this magic which is peculiar to music and to which, by its nature, music is of all arts the most receptive.'[70] For him, this mysterious world was changing fast and was shattered, first by the First World War, then by his death.

The First World War

Events in Paris had followed the usual round. In January 1910, there were considerable floods in Paris, and the boulevard Haussmann was a rushing river. Two years before, there was an attempt to rig the stock price of De Beers, by an employee of the company, who used his claim to have found a way of manufacturing diamonds to force down De Beers' stock with a view to buying at the bottom. In August 1911, the *Mona Lisa* was stolen, although it turned up in Florence two years later.[71]

The main worry, however, was the threatening war on the horizon. There was another scare in 1911. German colonial and militaristic aims were frustrated when the French sent an expeditionary force to rescue France's citizens blockaded in Fez, in central Morocco. The Germans responded by sending a gunboat to the seaport of Agadir. Fortunately the crisis was defused by negotiation. But the omens were not good, and so there was an attempt to reintroduce three-year military conscription.[72]

The First World War began in 1914 as a result of numerous factors, many of which lay deep in the history of Europe. As we have already seen, the flashpoint was in the Balkans, where the pro-Slav Serbs were opposed to the Habsburgs. When, in the last days of June, the heir to the Habsburg throne attended troop manoeuvres in Bosnia close to the Serbian border, the Serbs saw this as an act of provocation. The archduke and his wife were assassinated in Sarajevo by a Serb on 28 June 1914. The first attempt to blow him up failed; it was only when the royal couple returned to visit two injured officers that a change in the route resulted in his carriage being stationary for a moment. Then an assassin got them.

Following the assassination, the Austrians gave an ultimatum to Serbia. It was to make amends and take drastic measures to eliminate conspiracy and terrorism directed against Austro-Hungary. These measures were to be taken under the Habsburg monarchy's supervision. It only took this ultimatum to begin the slide into war, even if there was still some room for an element of bluff and counter-bluff.

So, the powers 'slithered into war'.[73] After the expiry of the Austrian ultimatum, Austro-Hungary declared war on Serbia; the Russians, who wanted to stop Austro-Hungarian expansion into the Balkans, mobilised to help their fellow Slavs. Germany was allied to Austro-Hungary and Italy, so Germany gave Russia an ultimatum to withdraw. France and Great Britain were allied to Russia. 'The dice were tumbling', in the German chancellor's words.[74]

The German declaration of war against Russia on 1 August meant that a European war was inevitable. That day France mobilised. Events moved astonishingly quickly: on 2 August, German troops entered Luxembourg and demanded free passage through Belgium. One can understand the expostulation of Saint-Saëns: 'Do they possibly imagine that the Germans will have the effrontery, the incredible wickedness, to invade Belgian territory? It would bring down all Europe on them. It would mean a World War – they cannot be so mad! ... Don't let us worry over this scare.'[75] On the pretext that French aeroplanes had bombed Nuremberg, Germany declared war on France; on 4 August, the Germans marched through Belgium, and Great Britain could wait no longer.

Germany expected to be able to destroy the French armies within six weeks and then deal with Great Britain and Russia.* By the beginning of September, most of Belgium was in German hands, the Belgian army was blockaded in Antwerp and the Germans had penetrated almost to Paris. The French government evacuated to Bordeaux. But the German lines were too extended and the French hit the German right flank at the Battle of the Marne. By the end of the year, the opposing armies were dug in on a front extending from the Channel to the Vosges and the Swiss frontier.

Despite the lead up to the war, its outbreak caught many by surprise; Fauré was in Germany, as we have seen; Ravel, in Saint-Jean-de-Luz, had 'not had the slightest inkling of its imminence'.[77] The French president and prime minister were in Russia on a visit when the crisis began.[78] At the time, the attempt by the French government to reintroduce three-year conscription was about to be thrown out.

The war created considerable anxiety in the Debussy household. There

* A similar view was held in France, where Proust wrote: 'With the terrible advance of artillery, the wars of the future, if there are to be any more wars, will be so short that, before we have had time to think of putting our lessons into practice, peace will have been signed ... You have only to think what a cosmic thing a war would be today. It'd be a bigger catastrophe than the Flood and the *Götterdämmerung* rolled into one. Only it wouldn't last so long.'[76] How wrong he was.

was enormous pressure to join up, and Emma had both a son and a son-in-law in the army. In the first five months, 300,000 French were killed and 600,000 wounded, captured or missing. 'My life is one of intensity and disquiet. I am nothing more than a wretched atom hurled around in this terrible cataclysm', said Debussy.[79] 'The side effects of the war are more distressing than they seem.'[80] Some of his comments are particularly perceptive: 'When will the practice cease of entrusting the destiny of nations to people who see humanity as a way of furthering their careers?'[81]

Many composers immediately expressed their nationalism, others wrote funeral marches. Saint-Saëns demanded the suppression of all German music. Ravel was threatened with a boycott of his music when he refused to toe the line.* Vincent d'Indy proposed the impeachment of the Paris municipal authorities for allowing the name of Meyerbeer to appear on opera posters. 'As for Beethoven, someone's just made the fortunate discovery he was a Fleming', Debussy observed.[83] 'I think of the youth of France, wantonly mown down by those *Kultur* merchants, and of its contribution to our heritage, now for ever lost to us.'[84]

Fortunately for music, the supreme sacrifice chosen by Albéric Magnard was exeptional among composers. Following the invasion of September 1914, this affluent composer was killed in his house in Baron-sur-Oise, a house full of first editions by Diderot and paintings by Boucher and Corot. Seeing some German cavalry approaching, Magnard decided to fight his own war. He took up a position at the top of the house, and managed to pick off two Germans, before he was killed. The house was burnt down and its contents, including many of his musical manuscripts, were lost. Such is heroism.[85]

As a practical matter, the war had an adverse effect on performance: in particular, the enormous orchestras needed for the works of Richard Strauss and Gustav Mahler, and for Stravinsky's *The Rite of Spring* were no longer available. Debussy faced practical problems of a different kind: 'For some days I've been in the same condition as Russia! That's to say, no supplies; no more of the manuscript paper "Quarto Papale" which I've recently become so attached to.'[86]

Debussy's health did not permit him to become directly involved. It

* This led him to suggest that Saint-Saëns, rather than composing second-rate music, would have spent his time better by servicing howitzers.[82]

simply deteriorated relentlessly. In December 1915, he had an operation. On the day before, he wrote a touching letter to Emma, to be taken to her bedroom, which was just above his study: 'As one never knows the outcome of even the simplest event, I want to tell you one last time how much I love you and how sad I should be if any sort of accident were to prevent me ensuring our happiness, either now or in the future. And you, my darling, love me in the person of our little Chouchou … you are the only two for whose sake I do not want to leave this earth altogether.'[87]

He had a rubber ring to sit on and was heavily dosed with medicine. Of course, it was hopeless. 'I've just started a new treatment. It's all shrouded in mystery and I'm asked to be patient … Good God! Where am I to find patience?'[88] After 60 days of various tortures, he wrote: 'Without realising it, I've spent a full six months now contemplating my misery; it's too long for someone who hasn't the time to lose any more. Will I ever again know what it is to be well? I don't dare to think so and I'd much rather have a sudden end than this pursuit of health, in which, so far, the disease is always one step ahead of me.'[89] There was bound, in the circumstances, to be a considerable amount of tension. 'This house has some curious points of resemblance with the House of Usher … we share a certain hypersensitivity.'[90]

In December 1916, he wrote: 'Naturally I don't take this poor tattered body* for walks any more, in case I frighten little children and tram conductors. But if they could see inside my head!'[91] Stravinsky thought Debussy's 'subtle, grave smile had disappeared, and his skin was yellow and sunken; it was hard not to see the future cadaver in him'.[92]

To enable him to recuperate, the Debussys went to Cap Ferrat near Nice and to Saint-Jean-de-Luz near Biarritz. Debussy still had enough strength to sack Chouchou's piano teacher, because he was worried that his daughter was making no progress. So far as he himself was concerned, he wrote: 'Music's completely abandoned me.'[93]

Meanwhile, the war pounded on. Had the Germans not been tied up on the Russian front, it is doubtful whether the western front would have held out. In February 1916, the Germans launched an attack against Verdun, believing that French attempts to save it would lead to such heavy losses that France would be bled white. The calculation underlying this

* In a photograph of him on his deathbed, he looks completely wasted.

attack assumed that the ratio of Allied to German losses would be 5:2.[94] In the following July, on the Somme, there perished 'the zest and idealism with which nearly three million Englishmen had marched forth to war'.[95]

The 1917 Revolution in Russia made inevitable a Russian withdrawal from the war. The outlook in France must have been grim. Writing to the publisher Jacques Durand, Debussy said: 'If you understand anything of what's happening in Russia, it would be very kind of you to let me know.'[96]

Death

During 1917, there was no end in sight to the war. The Germans had new bombers called Gothas, which carried thirteen bombs and were much more effective than the Zeppelins. Cocteau, hearing the sirens, observed: 'there goes the Eiffel Tower again, complaining because someone has trodden on her toe'.[97] Marcel Proust, in the Ritz hotel, watched the 'wonderful Apocalypse in which the aeroplanes climbing and swooping seemed to complement and eclipse the constellations'. He continued: 'The unbelievable thing was that, as in the Greco painting in which there is the celestial scene above and the terrestrial below, while we watched this sublime mid-air spectacle from the balcony, below us the Hotel Ritz ... appeared to have turned into Feydeau's *Hôtel du libre échange*. Ladies in night-dresses or bathrobes roamed the vaulted hall clutching their pearl necklaces to their bosoms.'[98]

Food became increasingly scarce, and sugar rationing started in January of that year. Fortunately, the first US troops started arriving in June 1917, but it was not clear whether the Allies would be strong enough to defeat the German offensive expected for 1918.

January 1918 was particularly grim.*[99] It was unusually cold, with snow and ice. On 30 January, the Germans dropped 267 bombs on Paris, killing 259 people. Thereafter, Paris was shelled or bombed nightly. 'The air was

* In this month, the insouciant bon-viveur Francis Poulenc (1899–1963) was called up, as a driver. His flippancy was consistent with the 1920s' reaction against the horrors of the First World War. His ballet, *Les Biches*, in which three rowers court sixteen women, was written for Diaghilev; it was described as 'musical lemonade' by Satie. An article in January 1920 entitled 'Les Cinq Russes, les Six Français et M. Satie' implied that Poulenc, Honegger and Milhaud together with Auric, Durey and Germaine Tailleferre comprised a Six comparable to the great Russian Five. Being the son of one of the founders of the chemical combine Rhône-Poulenc, Poulenc was well-heeled. He lived in Noizay among the châteaux of the Loire, and the wine from Vouvray. His dramatic opera, *Dialogues des Carmélites*, premièred at La Scala in 1957, was an immediate success. His songs, many irreverent, are much enjoyed, as are his many ballets, his organ concerto and much piano music.

perpetually buzzing with the vibration, vigilant and sonorous, of French aeroplanes', wrote Proust. 'But, at intervals, the siren rang out like the heart-rending scream of a Valkyrie – the only German music to have been heard since the war – until the moment when the fire-engines announced that the alert was over, while beside them, like an invisible street-urchin, the all clear at regular intervals commented on the good news and hurled its cry of joy into the air.'[100]

On 21 March, just before Debussy died, the Germans, commanded by General Ludendorff, struck and threw in all their weight before large contingents of Americans could get to Europe. The terrifying bombardment was described by Churchill shortly afterwards as 'the greatest onslaught in the history of the world'.[101] On a front of 40 miles, the Germans launched simultaneously 37 divisions of infantry, covered by nearly 6,000 guns. As Debussy declined, it looked as if Paris would have to be evacuated again.

The notorious Big Bertha long-range gun claimed many lives and caused considerable damage. Shrapnel from an exploding shell landed on Widor's table at the Institut. Fauré's wife was obliged, along with many others, to flee from Paris. Debussy died three days after the bombardment began. On it went: Fauré, in Paris on 22 May, wrote: 'last night, quite a long raid – from 10.30 pm till one in the morning ... The cannon bombarded us heavily, particularly between 11.30 pm and 12.30 am.'[102] Saint-Saëns complained at the time: 'how can you not understand the anomaly of a Schumann Festival at the moment when the Germans are bombarding Paris and, in a frightful battle, are making superhuman efforts to crush us ... France first; music afterwards.'[103] On 2 June 1918, the Germans got through to Château Thierry only 50 miles from Paris. Prime Minister Clemenceau used words echoed twenty years later: 'We will fight on the Loire, we will fight on the Garonne, we will fight even on the Pyrenees. And if at last we are driven off the Pyrenees, we will continue the war at sea.'[104]

But the Germans' offensive failed, and weakened them irretrievably. The slaughter was horrific. Churchill himself sums it up neatly: 'The British had actually killed and wounded or captured nearly four hundred thousand Germans ... while all their own losses in men and material had by the activities of their Government been more than replaced.'*[106] The

* Churchill was minister for munitions. Following the 21 March offensive, he calculated that the British had lost over 300,000 officers and men. The French losses subsequently were also enormous.[105]

Allied counter-offensive began at the end of June. By 1 August, 1,145,000 men of the Allied forces had landed in France and nineteen divisions were ready to be sent to the front. Reinforcements were arriving at the rate of 250,000 a month. It even became conceivable that the Germans could be defeated in 1918. A favourite remark of Marshal Foch, supreme commander of the Allied forces, was: 'L'édifice commence à craquer. Tout le monde à la bataille!'[107]

By September, the Germans were in full retreat. On 11 November, the Armistice was signed and France's long ordeal was over. The statistics speak for themselves: 1.3 million French were dead, three quarters of a million were maimed, 289,000 houses destroyed and 3 million acres of good land left unfit for cultivation.[108] The economy was in ruins. Saint-Saëns wrote: 'The War is over. But, never were difficulties more difficult.' He continued: 'I am not able, as many others, to give myself up to joy … thinking of a future so disturbing and of all the bereavements and ruins which surround us.'[109] By then, Debussy was dead.

Debussy's last almost indecipherable effort at writing was a New Year's note to Emma. 'According to a tradition dear to us, it was yesterday evening that I sent you my New Year's greetings. On this occasion, I am sadly [bound to my bed] and I have nothing but these sadly restricted means to tell you of my love. But it is acknowledged that love …' Mais il est admis que l'amour …[110]

The note was dated 1 January 1918, and was unfinished. It is no wonder that the twelve-and-a-half-year-old Chouchou said to her stepbrother that when her father died: 'struggling with Mama's indescribable grief is truly terrible'.[111]

He died on Monday 25 March, when Paris was almost about to fall. 'The Allies were not only retreating. They were falling apart.'[112] In the musical press, it was noted that Debussy's death 'will arouse emotions in the little world of musicians only, for the general public cares less than ever at the present time for any art except for the art of war'.[113]

One of the more wonderful things is the poise and maturity of Chouchou at this terrible time. The little girl tells the end of the sad story in a letter to her half-brother Raoul, written in large handwriting, on black-edged paper: 'Thursday arrived, the Thursday when he was to be taken from us for ever! I saw him one last time in that horrible box – lying on the ground. He looked happy, so happy and then I could not control my tears. I almost collapsed but I couldn't embrace him. At the cemetery Mama, naturally, couldn't have behaved better and as for me, all I could think of was, "I mustn't cry because of Mama". I summoned up all my courage. Where did it come from? I don't know. I didn't shed a single tear. Tears restrained are worth as much as tears shed, and now it is night for ever. Papa is dead. Those three words. I don't understand them or rather I understand them too well.'[114]

Sixteen months later, Chouchou died. She had been given the wrong treatment for diphtheria.[115]

Debussy and fellow Prix de Rome laureates on the steps of the Villa Medici

PUCCINI

CHAPTER 27

ONE OF THE first musical 'events' of the 20th century was the première of *Tosca* in Rome on 14 January 1900. It was magnificent theatre, and a great 19th-century opera. Organisers of events to mark the turning of centuries and similar jubilees would be hard pressed to find anything better to stage: a simple, straightforward drama, with a big spectacle. It provided an opportunity for Puccini to write some of his best and most memorable songs, such as 'Vissi d'Arte' and 'E Lucevan le Stelle'. Anyone hearing it would surely agree that 'where erotic passion, sensuality, tenderness, pathos and despair meet and fuse, he was an unrivalled master'.[1] Yet, Puccini's name does not appear in the index of Alfred Einstein's leading work on *Music in the Romantic Era* written just after the Second World War.

So where does he fit in? Although traces of *Tristan*, Debussy and the whole-tone scale are detected in some of his works, Puccini is hardly a 20th-century composer: Stravinsky's *The Rite of Spring* was premièred in May 1913, over a decade before *Turandot*.

Most composers have damned him. Stravinsky dismissed *Madame Butterfly* as 'treacly violin music'.[2]* Fauré labelled *La Bohème* a 'dreadful

* On the other hand, *Madame Butterfly* is said to have provided inspiration for Janáček's *Káťa Kabanová*.[3]

Italian work'[4] and Richard Strauss said that he could not distinguish between it and *Butterfly*.[5] The leading Italian conductor Arturo Toscanini put his finger on the problem: 'In many Puccini operas you could change the words, and any other set would do.'[6] Of the Paris première of *Tosca* in 1903, Fauré wrote to his wife: 'At the very beginning of September there will be an important première at the Opéra-Comique; important because of the personality of Sardou, the librettist, and the bizarre school of music to which the composer of the music belongs, Puccini. They consist of three or four fellows who have conjured up a neo-Italian art which is easily the most miserable thing in existence; a kind of soup, where every style from every country gets all mixed up. And everywhere, alas! they are welcomed with open arms.'[7]

Nevertheless, there is no doubt that, as far as Broadway and the West End was concerned, Puccini was 20th-century in his skill with the voice and with melody, in his soft harmony and gentle orchestration, and most particularly in his remuneration. A Decca recording presenting the great moments in opera performed by the world's leading artists includes six items by Puccini, far ahead of the others. There are only two each from Wagner, Donizetti and Verdi. Trailing behind are Rossini, Mozart, Bellini, Bizet and Offenbach, each with one item to represent them.[8] The composer of 'Your tiny hand is frozen' from *La Bohème* and 'One fine day' from *Madame Butterfly* looks well placed to survive the test of time. 'Nessun dorma' from *Turandot* was the theme music for the 1990 Football World Cup. Few could deny that Puccini wrote very effective and tremendously enjoyable music.

As a person, however, apart from Janáček, Puccini is possibly the least likable of all the composers described in this book. But, as a loyal supporter said of Janáček, 'his contribution to the arts is so great that it outweighs any flaws in his character'.[9] Puccini's self-centred personality benefited from an attractive raffishness absent in Janáček's. Success, measured by prodigious remuneration, went to Puccini's head. His 'melancholia demanded relief in violent sex, slaughtering birds and driving high-powered cars at reckless speed'.[10] Perhaps he summed himself up quite well when he said: 'I am a mighty hunter of wildfowl, beautiful women and good libretti.'[11]

Puccini was not initially as successful as his contemporaries Leoncavallo and Mascagni, but he quickly outshone them and took his place alongside Massenet, who inspired his style. We shall look briefly at Massenet before observing Puccini create the operas which brought him such fame. We shall also look at the sordid tragedy of Doria Manfredi, a real-life story to equal that told in any of his operas.

Early Years

Giacomo Puccini was born around 22 December 1858, in Lucca, the birthplace of Boccherini. About thirteen miles from Pisa, Lucca is an old walled town, with narrow streets, and boasts a Roman amphitheatre.

Giacomo's birth brought to five the number of generations of musicians in Puccini's family. One biographer has gone so far as to say that the Puccinis rank only after the Bachs in the order of families 'in which a creative gift for music was hereditary'.[12] Puccini's great-grandfather was a member of the Accademia Filarmonica of Bologna and may well have been present when Mozart was admitted in 1772. Puccini's grandfather, Domenico, had written *Il Trionfo di Quinto Fabio*, an opera which had been commended by Haydn's contemporary, Giovanni Paisiello.[13]

The family effectively possessed the hereditary right to the post of organist and choirmaster of Lucca's cathedral of San Martino, with its altarpiece by Tintoretto and a relic, the Sacred Countenance, said to be carved by Nicodemus.[14] Giacomo's father died when he was five. His mother, who was eighteen years younger than her husband, had once been his father's pupil. She was now left to bring up Giacomo, his younger brother and five sisters on a tiny pension from the city council.[15]

Puccini studied with his uncle, who was keeping the organ seat warm until he came 'of musical age'. He gained a broad experience: he sang in the choir, worked part-time at a casino, and provided music for both a convent and a bordello.[16] He smoked from an early age and began his waterfowling career on the Lago Massaciuccoli, which is a few miles over the hills from Lucca. When he needed money, he stole and sold the organ pipes from a village church in which he accompanied the services: he could easily alter the harmonies so as to conceal his theft. A walk to Pisa to see Verdi's *Aïda* inspired him to go to the Milan Conservatoire,[17] which he eventually did, in September 1880, financed by a bursary, augmented by a loan from a great-uncle, who was a prosperous bachelor.[18]

In Milan, he survived on thin minestrone, tobacco and the occasional visit to the cafés in the Galleria Vittorio Emanuele. One of his teachers at this time was Amilcare Ponchielli who had composed *I Promessi Sposi* and the very popular *La Gioconda*.

Puccini's brother joined him in Milan as did Pietro Mascagni, who was some five years younger. Mascagni, the son of a Livorno baker, was expelled from the Conservatoire after two years for lack of application; he had to turn to playing the double bass and conducting third-rate operetta companies.[19] Puccini graduated with an exercise, the *Capriccio Sinfonica*, which showed his talent for melody and colourful orchestration.

The poor quality of musical performance in Italy at the time is indicated by Tchaikovsky: 'A scoundrel conductor. Despicable choruses. In general everything is provincial. Left after the second act.'[20] He described 'the ludicrously stout singer with a voice like a huckster's', adding that 'this time the orchestration of *Aïda* seemed vilely coarse to me in places'.[21] Then for *I Puritani*: 'the singing not bad, but the orchestra and production awful'.[22]

A crucially important person in Milan musical circles was Giulio Ricordi, who ran his family's publishing house, which owned the copyright in virtually every opera produced in Italy. The Ricordi business had branches throughout Europe, the USA and Latin America. His grandfather, a copyist at La Scala, had started the business and had acquired the copyright in the works of Rossini, Bellini and Donizetti and then Verdi.[23] A wealthy industrialist and newspaper magnate, Edoardo Sonzogno, decided to challenge Ricordi's monopoly, so he sponsored a competition for a one-act opera.[24] The prize was 2,000 lire.* Puccini entered with *Le Villi* (the witches), but did not win, possibly because his entry, like so many of his later compositions, was almost illegible.

Another person with great influence was Arrigo Boito, soon to be celebrated as the librettist of Verdi's *Otello* and *Falstaff*. Puccini played *Le Villi* on the piano at a salon at which Giulio Ricordi and Boito were present. They were so impressed that they decided to stage it. Ricordi suggested some changes,[26] and it was a great success. Boito, who was working on *Otello*, introduced Puccini to Verdi.

Ricordi then commissioned another opera using Fontana, the librettist of *Le Villi*. The newspaper *Corriere della Sera* was ecstatic: 'In a word, we believe sincerely that in Puccini we may have the composer for whom Italy has long been waiting.'[27]

* This was the equivalent of £80 at the time. Puccini's rent for the single room in the lodgings he shared with Mascagni was 30 lire per month.[25]

Puccini was frequently invited to dine at the house of a former schoolmate, a prosperous merchant in olive oil, coffee, spices, wines and spirits. There, he would play duets with Elvira, his school friend's wife. She was tall, majestic and had a very slim waist.[28] Puccini, for whom 'conquests were easy and numerous',[29] quickly cuckolded his friend, and Elvira joined him, abandoning her baby, but bringing her daughter Fosca with her. Their son Antonio was born on 23 December 1886, when Puccini was just 28.[30]

It was a difficult time for him: the people of Lucca were scandalised by his behaviour; he was greatly in debt to Ricordi; and he was hounded by landlords. His great-uncle observed that, if he could afford to keep a mistress, he could afford to pay back the money which he had given him. *Edgar*, the opera which Ricordi had commissioned, was not a success.* After this, Puccini thought of emigrating to Argentina, but his brother put him off: he himself had gone there and was finding it impossible to make ends meet. But the experience with *Edgar* taught Puccini an important lesson: the composer must be absolutely ruthless about the quality of his libretto.

Mascagni and Leoncavallo

Then Mascagni was suddenly propelled to fame. After years of hardship, and having been rejected by Ricordi, he entered for Sonzogno's second contest for one-act operas in 1888. He intended to submit an opera called *Guglielmo Ratcliff*, but his wife entered the recently completed *Cavalleria Rusticana*, without his knowledge. When it was put on in 1890, it was 'a hit if there ever was one',[31] and Mascagni was instantaneously world famous. In Belgrade, the whole work had to be repeated before a hysterical audience would leave the theatre.**[32]

Puccini, meanwhile, worked slowly and laboriously on *Manon Lescaut*. The libretto was being written by Ruggiero Leoncavallo, a café pianist and would-be composer, who had fallen on hard times.† But Puccini was not at all happy with Leoncavallo's draft, and turned instead to a couple who

* It was produced in 1889, conducted by Franco Faccio, the conductor at La Scala and a friend of Verdi and Boito. Faccio died of syphilis, in an asylum.

** With *Cavalleria Rusticana*, Mascagni established a musical fashion for *verismo* subjects that dominated operatic style for a decade. This was consistent with developments in the theatre: Ibsen's exalted works, like *Peer Gynt*, were being superseded by his 'realistic' down-to-earth plays such as *A Doll's House* and *An Enemy of the People*.

† Leoncavallo had invested his savings with an impresario, with a view to staging his own opera *Chatterton*, but the impresario went off with the cash.

would serve him well in the future: Luigi Illica, an author of light comedies, and Giuseppe Giacosa, a prominent playwright, who lectured on drama at the Conservatoire. Leoncavallo stormed off in a huff. In what must have been a particularly galling experience for Puccini, Leoncavallo then composed *I Pagliacci*, which was inspired by a murder trial over which his father had once presided as a police magistrate.[33] When Ricordi rejected *Pagliacci*, Sonzogno scooped it up. When premièred under the young Toscanini in May 1892, it was a colossal success.

Jules Massenet / Pietro Mascagni / Ruggiero Leoncavallo

With Puccini seeming to be unsuccessful and having difficulty making ends meet, Elvira became jealous of Mascagni's and Leoncavallo's success and their purchasing power. She became increasingly difficult, and went off to live in Florence with her sister. Puccini returned to Torre del Lago, a small village of fishermen and bohemian painters, located between the sea and the shallow reedy Lake Massaciuccoli, where he had poached as a boy. There, he took one of the hunting lodges rented by weekend sportsmen to shoot wild duck and moorhen. Elvira eventually returned to join him there. Their difficult relationship was well expressed in the comment: 'Theirs was the almost classic dilemma of an abnormally sensual and egocentric couple, who could not live in harmony for long periods, but found it even more intolerable to stay apart.'[34] One of Puccini's last words on his deathbed was to tell his step-daughter: 'Remember your mother is a remarkable woman.'[35]

Puccini, by now aged 34, had his break when *Manon Lescaut* opened on 1 February 1893. It was staged in Turin so as to avoid competing with Verdi's *Falstaff*, which was produced at La Scala about a week later. The conductor was Toscanini. With 30 curtain calls, *Manon Lescaut* was phenomenally successful, and immediately made Puccini's reputation outside Italy. No doubt Elvira's attitude towards him immediately improved.[36]

Puccini had achieved at least the same degree of success as Leoncavallo and Mascagni. The difference between Puccini and his contemporaries was that Puccini had further successes, whereas the other two had none. Mascagni's subsequent operas failed; he conducted around the world, his great warhorse being Tchaikovsky's Sixth Symphony. In 1929, he assumed the duties of Toscanini at La Scala, after Toscanini, a supporter of Mussolini* until he swung to the right, fell out with the regime. Mascagni died, discredited for his fascist associations, in a seedy Roman hotel in August 1945.[38] Similarly, Leoncavallo wrote several more operas, and began a trilogy intended to rival Wagner's *Ring*. There is no need to record the history of that.[39]

Puccini's success enabled him to buy back the family home in Lucca and to repay the accumulated advances of 18,000 lire which he had received from Ricordi, who had been making monthly payments of around 300 lire for nine years.** Certain of the shareholders in Ricordi's publishing house had wanted to drop Puccini after the failure of *Edgar*. It was only the determined support of Giulio Ricordi which kept him going, an astonishing example of a publisher's judgement paying off.[41]

The Influence of Massenet

Puccini drew a considerable amount of his inspiration from Jules Massenet, best known for his *Manon*, so we should spend a moment looking at him. Both composers made colossal fortunes.

* Benito Mussolini once told Stravinsky that he played the violin. 'I quickly suppressed a remark about Nero', wrote the composer.[37] The dictator, a one-time socialist and supremely gifted orator, came to power in October 1922 in the aftermath of the First World War, and following a general strike. His blackshirted followers were called Fasci di Combattimento, because they believed that their ties were as secure as the bundle of rods with an axe in the middle (*fascis*) which was the symbol of authority in ancient Rome. Mussolini's steps to bring law and order were widely admired at the time.

** A Humber bicycle, bought to help him keep trim, cost Puccini 220 lire in July 1893.[40]

Massenet found the recipe for commercial success.* On Good Friday 1873, a couple of years after the terrible experience of the Franco-Prussian War and the Commune, Paris heard the première of *Marie Magdaleine*, a work about the reformed courtesan. A great mezzo-soprano of the century, Pauline Viardot, came out of retirement to sing the Magdalen. Even the discerning were bowled over:[43] Bizet exclaimed: 'never has our modern school produced anything comparable'.[44] Massenet's reputation was made. After the lavishly expensive production of a subsequent work, *Le Roi de Lahore*, the absurd Gounod embraced him: 'Dans mes bras, mon fils, embrasse Papa.'[45]

Massenet created a brand which reflected the ideas, prejudices, anxieties and preoccupations of his contemporaries. 'The melodies go straight to the heart ... Dazzled by the constantly refreshed brilliance of youthfulness and love, we never dream of probing the depth of an idea. His lightness is enough, for it consists of smiles, tenderness, and grace.'[46] His 'historic encyclopaedia' of operas are all of a single type, 'a sort of amorous epic poem' with 'much sentimentalism, an atmosphere of sighs, caresses, spasms and tears'.[47] The moment in history is always different, but the music is always similar. The composer Vincent d'Indy condemned it as 'discreet and pseudo-religious eroticism'.[48]

When *Manon*,** a story about another beautiful sinner, was premièred in 1884, Massenet became France's most popular composer. He mass-produced twenty further operas after that – 'always on the look-out for ways to add a bit of spice to what remained fundamentally the same musical recipe'.[49] He himself said: 'The public likes it and we must always agree with the public.'[50] He seldom attempted any subject that lay outside the scope of his talent. This recipe ensured that he was greatly honoured in his time.

Massenet had been appointed professor of composition at the Conservatoire in 1878, a time when the middle-aged César Franck was still

* Massenet's first piano lesson was interrupted by street disturbances during the 1848 rebellion. He was born on 12 May 1842. After winning the Prix de Rome, he returned to play the piano in a café in Belleville, a shanty town in the east of Paris. He was in the National Guard for the Franco-Prussian War and Commune. Many of his works have now disappeared; others, such as *Werther*, are sometimes staged. Many were written specifically for Sibyl Sanderson, an American, who had played a leading part in his life, as well as in a number of his operas, including *Manon*.[42]

** The title of Puccini's opera deliberately distinguished it from Massenet's work.

struggling for recognition. This appointment had the effect of polarising French musicians: almost every French composer either followed Massenet's style or loathed it. In this respect, he had a considerable influence on the development of music in France. Debussy expressed one point of view, witheringly: 'His brethren could not easily forgive this power of pleasing which, strictly speaking, is a gift. His is a delightful kind of fame, the secret envy of many of those artists who can only warm their hands at the somewhat pallid flame provided by the approbation of the elect.'[51] Massenet and his adherents were no more than charlatans, talentless mountebanks: 'For them and their tawdry products one or two booths at a fair would be enough.'[52]

La Bohème

Puccini, however, modelled himself on Massenet. He had no pretensions to high art; that did not interest him. His interest in literature was utilitarian: a play or story was worth looking at if it could be made the basis of a libretto. He had a sure eye for this, and *Tosca*, *Madame Butterfly*, *La Fanciulla* and *Il Tabarro* are based on plays which had been clearly successful in the market place. 'He conceived an opera above all as a spoken drama to which music was to lend a third dimension.'[53] In this sense, he was the forerunner of the composers of musicals in the 20th century.

Constantly chain-smoking, and relieving his sore throat with cups of coffee, he worked away at *La Bohème*. He was painstaking and meticulous, and it took three years and nine months to complete. He relied on Ricordi for a free supply of score paper and Stephen's blue-black ink.[54] He shaped the libretto, while Illica elaborated the scenario and invented picturesque incidents, and Giacosa did the versification and provided the literary polish. All three constantly quarrelled.

Ricordi, possibly aware that Leoncavallo was also writing an opera using the Bohème theme, was afraid that Puccini would give unguarded interviews to the press; so he wrote to him: 'Remember please that it is imperative that you keep your mouth shut and do not talk to anyone about your plans.'[55] Unfortunately this letter was found on Puccini when he was apprehended during a visit to Malta: he was arrested when photographing the fortifications.* It took him some time to explain the true circumstances.

* A similar difficulty with military authorities arose when Stravinsky tried to take Picasso's portrait of him over the Swiss–Italian border. They insisted it was not a portrait but a plan.[56]

There was an element of the bohemian about his own lifestyle. He enjoyed holding wild parties with his friends. At one stage, he was even prosecuted for poaching. He would drink and play cards in an inn at Torre, which was renamed Club La Bohème. The group drew up a constitution, the fourth rule of which empowered the treasurer to abscond with the money; the sixth rule prohibited the playing of games permitted by law.[57] After a booze-up, they would go back to Puccini's house, where the jollifications would continue in the background, while he would work away deep into the night.

La Bohème was completed at Torre just before midnight on 10 December 1895. Puccini recalled completing the last notes of Mimi's death scene: 'I had to get up, and standing in the middle of the study, alone in the silence of the night, I wept like a child. It was like seeing my child die.'[58] He then joined his mates for a binge.

To his great disappointment the opera was not immediately successful when it was first produced at Turin on 1 February 1896, under Toscanini.* This began an almost standard routine whereby his premières were panned by the critics, but then the operas immediately enjoyed enormous public acclaim. After an outstanding success in Palermo, Puccini did not look back: by the time he was in Manchester** for the Carlo Rosa performance of *The Bohemians*, the opera was sensationally popular and even babies were being called Mimi.[60] The cash flowed in: he had a yacht called *Mimi I*; he built a larger villa for himself at Torre. This two-storey villa is surprisingly modest, considering the character of its owner. But it has a fine view, out over the lake to the Luccan hills in the distance.

Tosca and *Madame Butterfly*

Although his work was interrupted by the activities of architects and builders, Puccini worked on Sardou's play *La Tosca* which had been staged a decade earlier. His opera opened in Rome in January 1900.

This was at a time of much unrest, largely because of the poor economic conditions. Also, it was now apparent that the unification of Italy had been achieved through 'conquest' by the Piedmontese. To the south, this entailed the imposition of northern, 'foreign' administrative practices and

* The première of Leoncavallo's opera, using the Bohème story, was eighteen months later.

** Puccini did not like the 'land of black smoke, darkness, cold, rain, cotton (but woe to anyone who does not wear wool!) and fog. A veritable inferno! A horrible place to stay!'[59]

procedures. There was much resentment, and by the late 19th century, 'Italy had one of the strongest and most violent anarchist movements in Europe'.[61] By the time of the *Tosca* première, parliament had been dissolved by royal decree, there had been two attempts on the life of King Umberto and there were reports from Milan of 80 people being killed in street riots. It was rumoured that a bomb would be thrown during the performance, although it was not unknown in Italy for such terrorism to be 'artistically' rather than politically inspired. The opera must have seemed quite topical: it was set in Rome during the chaotic French revolutionary wars, at a time when a Roman republic was proclaimed and the Pope was deported.* The performance of *Tosca* went ahead. As with *La Bohème*, the critics disliked it at first.[63]

Six months later, *Tosca* was very well received in London. Puccini was lionised in London 'Society'. Escoffier had created *pêche melba* in honour of the Australian soprano Nellie Melba; so the head chef at the Savoy, where Puccini usually stayed, offered to create a special Tuscan dish named after him. The composer took the opportunity to attend a performance of *Madame Butterfly*, a one-act play being performed in a double bill at the Duke of York's theatre.[64]

Back in Torre, Puccini sketched his opera, *Madame Butterfly*. He would work in breeches and riding boots at the piano, before a huge log fire. His gun was loaded, his dogs ready, and he merely awaited a whistle from his friend to go hunting.[65]

He bought himself a new car, a Clement, a plaything of rich, successful playboys like him.** But for Puccini, it almost led to disaster.[69] On the Quiesa Pass, four miles from Lucca, the car, driven by his chauffeur, skidded off the road and plunged down a fifteen-foot embankment before hitting a tree and overturning. Puccini was trapped underneath. Elvira and

*For a while, an army from Naples seized back control, but it was soon expelled by the French. Nelson, the British admiral, whose fleet had supported the Neapolitan army, reported: 'The Neapolitan Officers have not lost much honour, for God knows, they had but little to lose; but they lost all they had.'[62]

** There had been earlier steam-powered vehicles, but, despite Ravel's father patenting a petrol engine in 1868,[66] the first cars had only become technically possible in the mid-1870s when the four-stroke gasoline engine was built by Niklaus August Otto. Within ten years, Carl Benz's three-wheeler powered by a two-cycle, one-cylinder engine went into commercial production. Almost immediately, this was followed by Gottfried Daimler's four-wheeler.[67] A mile a minute was reached in France in 1893.[68] In 1898, there were 50 automobile companies in the USA, and,

their son Tonio were slightly bruised, but Puccini was lucky to escape being gassed by the fumes.* He had a compound fracture of the right leg. It was badly set, and he had a permanent limp thereafter. His convalescence took eight months. During this medical treatment he was found to be a diabetic.

The accident delayed the completion of *Madame Butterfly*, which took three years to finish. The first night, in February 1904, was the usual disaster. One critic dismissed it as 'a diabetic opera, the result of an automobile accident'.[71] The first act was received quietly. In the second act, when Butterfly's kimono was blown by a gust of wind from the wings, there was a shout, 'Butterfly is pregnant' – the *prima donna* was Toscanini's mistress.[72] There was increasing pandemonium, and the audience particularly derided a concert of twittering birds which Tito Ricordi had arranged to signal the break of dawn.[73] By the time the opera was performed in Brescia and Buenos Aires, Puccini had revised and shortened the score. It was a sensational success. It enabled him to buy himself a new motorboat which he called *Butterfly*.[74] He replaced the Clement with a Lancia. He then attended the summer season in South America for a fee of 50,000 francs plus expenses.[75]

Puccini was invited to New York for a festival of his operas. Four of his operas, including *Butterfly*, were being staged there in the 1906–7 season. This was part of an attempt by the Metropolitan Opera Company to revive its fortunes which had come under serious threat. Unfortunately, the company had been on tour in San Francisco when the earthquake struck just after 5 am on the morning of 19 April 1906. The quake and fire destroyed vast areas of the city: 'the streets could be seen to bulge and wave as if about to crack open and let the populace down into caverns'.[76] The tour was wrecked and valuable scenery and costumes were destroyed. As well as financial difficulty, the Metropolitan Opera faced stiff competition from Oscar Hammerstein's** new Manhattan Opera on West 34th Street.

ten years later, 241. British technology was held back by the public's negative, anti-machinery attitude: a 2 mph speed limit in cities (4 mph in rural areas) was repealed in 1896; there had also been a requirement for someone to go behind the steam engine with a red flag. Only after Henry Ford, creator of the Model-T, had implemented assembly line production did the car become generally available to those with a modest income.

* Prokofiev was another enthusiast for, and crasher of, cars. Once, the wheel came off while he was travelling at full speed, 40–50 mph. In 1937, he imported to Russia a blue Ford, which was conspicuously out of place in Moscow.[70]

** He was grandfather of the Oscar Hammerstein who with Richard Rodgers wrote *Showboat*,

During his stay in New York, Puccini visited Broadway. He had been searching long and hard for his next libretto.* He was attracted by a performance of *The Girl of the Golden West*, a play by Belasco, who had written the play on which *Madame Butterfly* was based. Belasco was a flamboyant author and impresario, not unlike some impresarios later in the century: visitors were led along a corridor lined with flunkies, and entered a room to find the great man at an enormous desk, and surrounded by oriental bric-à-brac.[79] Not surprisingly, Belasco's new play was showbiz stuff: the performance started with a cinematograph screen portrayal of the setting in the Cloudy Mountains of California; there was a band of 'authentic' Californian minstrels; 32 players operated wind and snow machines in order to create the appropriate effect. To Puccini, it seemed ideal. But personal circumstances intervened before *La Fanciulla del West* could be brought to fruition. Indeed, seven years elapsed between *Madame Butterfly* and *La Fanciulla*.

Doria Manfredi

Elvira and Puccini had been living together for twenty years. They were married in January 1904, after her husband died. Elvira was now middle aged, increasingly uncomfortable in the international fast set in which Puccini moved, and she suffered from coughing fits. Puccini made no attempt to involve her in his creative life. She became increasingly possessive and started spying on her husband, sometimes ludicrously dressed in his clothes.[80] To discourage competition, she would put camphor in his pockets and, whenever an attractive woman was invited to dinner, she would lace his wine with an aphrodisiac antidote.[81]

Shortly after the car accident, the Puccinis engaged as a maid a quiet, rather plain, shy girl from the village, the sixteen-year-old Doria Manfredi, 'a rare domestic pearl'.[82] Puccini's reputation as a rampant womaniser was well known, and Doria's parents had been reluctant to let their daughter work at his house. Elvira soon began to suspect Puccini and Doria of having

Oklahoma!, *Carmen Jones*, *South Pacific*, *The King and I* and *The Sound of Music*. Another casualty of the earthquake was the Cantonese opera theatre in San Francisco. By now, Chinese music performed in public was anyway only barely surviving, even though at one stage the railway employees had supported four theatres.[77]

* He considered using *Oliver Twist* as the basis for a libretto. It would have been interesting, and even appropriate, had Puccini composed the first *Oliver*.[78]

an affair. One night, late in 1908, Elvira woke with her coughing, heard talking, and went down and found Puccini and Doria chatting together: Doria would often do the ironing after dinner. Elvira shrieked abuse, and accused Doria of being her husband's mistress. When Doria escaped to her room, Elvira hammered on the door for several hours. Next day, Doria fled to her parents. Elvira then hounded the wretched Doria around the village, denouncing her as a slut, a tart and a whore.

Puccini escaped to Milan and Paris, where he received the King of Greece at a performance of *Tosca*. Doria remained holed up in her cottage, and refused to eat. Three weeks later, she swallowed a corrosive poison and died after five days of agony. She left an illiterate note declaring her innocence. An autopsy showed that she had died a virgin.[83]

Doria's brother swore vengeance. Her family prosecuted Elvira for defamation, libel and menace to life and limb. There was sensational publicity in Italy. Although Puccini tried to persuade Elvira to settle, the case went to court. Elvira was found guilty and sentenced to five months and five days' imprisonment, and a fine of 700 lire. Elvira appealed, but before the appeal was heard, the Manfredis were bought off with 12,000 lire, which enabled them to put up a monument to little Doria and buy a house for themselves near the lake.[84]

The whole incident left its mark on Puccini. He fell out with Tonio who took his mother's part. He nearly separated from Elvira, and indeed their relationship only recovered towards the end of his life. His creativity was adversely affected, hence possibly the delay in the composition of *La Fanciulla*. Fifteen years after the incident, Puccini created Liù, the faithful slave girl who, even when threatened with torture, refuses to disclose to Turandot the secret of her master's name; rather, she stabs herself to death, thus revealing to Turandot, one of the more heartless characters in opera, the meaning of love.

London

Puccini regularly visited London. This was the London of the Edwardian period, before the traumatic events of the First World War. Like the king, the beauties of the late 19th century, such as Gladys de Grey and Daisy Warwick, were now older and plumper, but still sovereign.[85] For this was still the world of the Honourable Harry Cust, not himself a lord, but from whom many of the members of the hereditary peerage, particularly those who have large sapphire-blue eyes, are said to be descended.[86] The Honourable George Keppel allowed the king to enjoy his wife's 'lovely face and fashionably curved figure'.[87] For the rich, like Margot Asquith, whether dancing a nymph to Mendelssohn's 'Spring Song', or dancing in grey draperies to Chopin's Funeral March,* it was an idyll.

When in London, Puccini moved in the pretentious circle slightly below this aristocratic one: he was patronised and captivated by Sybil Seligman, the wife of a merchant banker, David Seligman. The Seligmans had made their fortune in trade, at first in San Francisco where their store, the only brick building in town, survived the series of fires which engulfed the wooden city in May, June and September 1850. Then, after they had profited from providing uniforms for the Union army in the Civil War, they went into merchant banking. The New York bank of J. & W. Seligman was founded in 1862. David Seligman now lived in Upper Grosvenor Street in London. Sybil, with a similar background, although from Montego Bay, presided over a drawing room for artistic people. Although not a beauty, she looked good when wearing her expensive Worth designs. David consoled himself with a succession of mistresses,[89] because Sybil, who had endured a painful forceps delivery of her son Esmond, apparently wanted no more children.[90]

The Seligmans and Puccinis became very friendly, and they went on holiday to Nice together.[91] Sybil was ornamental, and pleasant to look at, even though her presence served to highlight the dowdiness of the matronly Elvira. Puccini and Sybil had a passionate love affair, which developed into a genuine friendship which lasted for the rest of his life.[92]

La Fanciulla

With all this diversion, it took until December 1910 before *La Fanciulla del West* opened at the Metropolitan Opera House.** Tickets were sold on the black market for 30 times their face value, which was anyway double the normal ticket price. 'The production of *La Fanciulla* was one of the most spectacular events in the annals of the Metropolitan Opera.'[93] With Caruso as Johnson and Emmy Destinn as Minnie, the opera was an immediate

* It was said that her toes were wonderfully able to express sorrow.[88]

** Two months later, in February 1911, Mahler had his confrontation with the committee of the New York Philharmonic (see page 762).

success: there were over 50 curtain calls;[94] and cash poured into the box office. Puccini celebrated by buying a new 15-metre yacht, *Minnie*, with a very powerful engine. But the normal trend was reversed. Whereas his other operas had poor beginnings and then established themselves as great successes, *La Fanciulla* was the opposite: possibly because it lacked a 'memorable tune', it has never been one of his popular operas.

Puccini and the First World War

Puccini did not read much, except, as we have seen, when there was the basis of a possible libretto. He mainly read newspapers to look at the advertisements for boating equipment. Politics passed him by, and he failed to understand the implications for him when the First World War began. Italy joined the war in 1915, tempted by the promise of territorial pickings in the Tyrol and the Adriatic when the Austro-Hungarian Empire was defeated.[95]

Puccini did not appreciate that war in the 20th century called for unconditional, unquestioning patriotism. The lighthearted playboy made the unfortunate mistake of saying: 'As far as I am concerned, the Germans can't capture Paris too soon.'[96] He became associated with the pro-Germans, then Italy's enemies, somewhat unfairly, as Puccini was not really interested in anyone apart from himself. The Opéra-Comique banned his operas.

During the war, he complained about the discomforts for himself, the lack of petrol for his cars. He took the opportunity to have an affair with the wife of a German officer, who lived across the Swiss border: the border guards were concerned that he might be a spy, because his visits were so frequent.[97] The lady then moved to Bologna, and Puccini had considerable difficulty extricating himself from her financial demands.

By contrast, Toscanini came back from the USA and organised concerts for war relief, and conducted military bands at the front. The testy little Toscanini, who crusaded to raise the low behavioural standards in Italian opera houses, for example by requiring ladies to remove the large hats which prevented others from seeing the performance properly, now also looked for ways to economise: he had the house lights dimmed, and he stopped the practice of ending an opera with a ballet. This did not make him popular, and, on one occasion when he was hissed at La Scala, he snapped his baton on the desk and tossed the pieces into the stalls. He then stormed out, swearing never to conduct there again.[98]

Puccini's very different attitude to the war annoyed Toscanini, and opened up a rift between them. Puccini also rowed with Tito Ricordi, who became head of the firm after his father's death in 1912. Giulio had been Puccini's mentor, impresario and banker; the relationship with the son was different. Their falling-out led Puccini to accept a lucrative offer from a Vienna theatre to write an operetta. The result, *La Rondine*, was well received at Monte Carlo in March 1917. Tito Ricordi dismissed it as 'bad Léhar';[99] and Puccini offered it to Sonzogno.

Puccini's next work was a triptych, *Il Trittico*, made up of three one-act operas: a horrific episode in *Il Tabarro*, a sentimental tragedy in *Suor Angelica* and a comedy in *Gianni Schicchi*. It must have been bizarre when the famous composer and notorious lecher went in search of ideas for *Suor Angelica*: he did his research in the convent at which his sister was by then Mother Superior.[100] *Il Trittico* opened in New York in December 1918. At the time, New York was the only place with the resources to stage it.

By now Puccini was aging and ill. Reading the date of his birth on programmes reminded him that soon they would record the date of his death. He suffered from insomnia; he took sleeping tablets. White patches in his hair showed plainly through the dye. He investigated the possibility of having an operation carried out which would rejuvenate him and consulted a specialist 'famed for his experiments in restoring the aged to youthful vigour by grafting on to their reproductive glands those of apes'.[101] But for his diabetes, he might have undergone the operation.

Puccini was irritated by a noisy and smelly peat factory which had been set up nearby by the wartime administration. Early in 1921, he started building a bungalow-type villa at Viareggio; Torre would remain as a shooting lodge. In the new villa, he had all his gadgets, electric clocks, even a switch which opened the front gate at a touch. He also had a watering system with camouflaged pipes, which he used to give guests a shower when they strolled in the pines.[102] This was possibly a vulgar throwback to the pranks of rich men in the baroque era.

Turandot and the End

As so often happens when composers of his stature grow older, Puccini became concerned about his artistic reputation: he was being vilified by the younger generation for being bourgeois, for lacking ideals and for being purely commercial. He started to work on *Turandot*, the libretto being based on a drama by the 18th-century Venetian playwright, Gozzi. He hoped that this opera would improve his reputation. Always so careful about his libretti, he groaned when presented with the first act: 'This isn't an Act, it's a conference', he said. 'How can I possibly set a conference to music?'[103] Always a slow worker, he found composing *Turandot* particularly difficult; at the same time, he was desperate to get it completed. He began to work so fast on it that he overtook his librettists.

Towards the end of 1923, he suffered more acute pain in his throat. By the time his doctors diagnosed cancer in October of the following year, it was too late for surgery. He started spitting blood. He was recommended six weeks' radium treatment at the Ledoux Clinic in Brussels. As he got into the train to go there, he asked Toscanini, with whom he had patched up his quarrel, not to forget his *Turandot*. He had left three sketches for the final two scenes.[104]

On 24 November 1924, radioactive crystal needles were inserted into the tumour. The operation, with a local anaesthetic, took nearly four hours. This unpleasant treatment lasted several days, during which he breathed through a tube above the Adam's apple and was fed through the nose. At first, the treatment seemed to be going very well. Then, suddenly, two days before the needles were due to be removed, he had a heart attack in his chair and collapsed. Ledoux quickly removed the needles, but Puccini died in the early hours of the morning of 29 November.[105]

The coffin was returned to Milan. It was covered with the Italian flag, and with wreaths from the King of Italy and Mussolini, whose Fascist party Puccini had joined. Italy went into mourning. Toscanini directed the La Scala orchestra and chorus at the service in the Duomo; Mussolini gave the funeral oration.

Toscanini asked Franco Alfano, a Neapolitan composer, to complete *Turandot*. For the first performance on 25 April 1926, Toscanini ended the performance where Puccini had stopped, at the death of Liù.[106]

Puccini was later placed in the mausoleum which his son Tonio created on the ground floor of the villa in Torre. This creates a difficulty for pilgrims. Emotions suitable for the maestro's gunroom and study are hardly appropriate to the grave that is located just behind the piano. The overall effect is profoundly disturbing. However, the pilgrim is quickly returned to the important world of commerce, by the ice-cream vendors and restaurants outside.

The Russian Sequel

CHAPTER 28

BORIS PASTERNAK, THE author of *Dr Zhivago*, whose family had a dacha close to Scriabin's, considered him to be 'a personified festival and triumph of Russian culture'; and Pasternak said that he himself loved 'music more than anything and Scriabin more than anyone else'.[1] The beard and military mustachios, perfectly trimmed and waxed, belied the eccentricity of this tiny composer, who, like Grieg and Mahler, was only just over five feet tall.[2] Some of those described in this book might reasonably be regarded as odd, but none quite so much as Scriabin. His obsession with the pronoun 'I' might even surpass that of a modern politician, although it is difficult to think of a recent one who has gone so far as to write: 'I am God. I raise you up and I am resurrected and then I kiss you and lacerate you.'[3] Scriabin once tried imitating Christ by trying to walk on the waters of Lake Geneva, and when he found that somewhat difficult, he climbed into a boat and started preaching.[4]

It therefore comes as no surprise that Scriabin has been called 'the most mysterious and complex musical personality of the twentieth century'.[5] His reputation is stronger in Russia, where Soviet Radio played his orchestral *Poem of Ecstasy* as Yuri Gagarin made his first flight into space. For us, he is best known for his piano music, where his sonatas 'move without a break

Above: SCRIABIN, PROKOFIEV AND SHOSTAKOVICH

from conventionality into modernity'.[6] He wrote only a handful of pieces for the orchestra – he began one which incorporated an aeroplane propeller in the orchestra.[7]

We will round off our earlier survey of Russia and Tchaikovsky with a few words on Scriabin and his contemporary Rachmaninov, who was about fifteen months Scriabin's junior, a complete contrast and certainly no modernist. We shall then stretch forward and look briefly at Stravinsky and Prokofiev, fruit of that rich cultural harvest yielded by the Russian Empire as the 19th century drew to an end: in literature, there was Anton Chekhov, the author of *The Cherry Orchard* and the short stories; in painting, there were the experimental painters such as Vassily Kandinsky, whose abstract pictures often had titles reminiscent of a musical composition,[8] and Marc Chagall, whose two large murals adorn the home of the New York Metropolitan Opera at the Lincoln Center.[9]

Stravinsky and Prokofiev take us far into the 20th century, even out of bounds perhaps? No; they were already important composers at the time of the First World War, the time when this book begins to draw to a close. But once we even glimpse them, we are bound to go on and consider in some detail the disturbing life of Dmitry Shostakovich, because his enigmatic quest for survival in Stalinist Russia provides a counterpoint without which the story of Stravinsky and Prokofiev would be incomplete.

The Soviet regime repelled Rachmaninov and Stravinsky. Yet Prokofiev, surprisingly, chose to return to this lions' den, even though, a couple of months before he irrevocably did, Shostakovich's opera *Lady Macbeth of Mzensk* had been ripped apart by Stalin's intrusive and horrifying regime. Shostakovich doggedly determined to remain behind.[10]

Pussy

First, Scriabin. Alexander Scriabin was born into an aristocratic military family on 6 January 1872, which, in the old style, was Christmas Day 1871. His father was usually away on consular duty, and his mother, a pupil of Anton Rubinstein, died of tuberculosis when he was very young. So, rather like Saint-Saëns, Sasha was brought up by doting female relatives; and he was almost as precocious: at the age of eight, he wrote an opera to be called after his playmate, Lisa.[11]

Scriabin was at first educated at a school for military cadets. Then, aged sixteen, he went to the Moscow Conservatoire, where he studied with

Taneyev and with Zveryev, who besides being Russia's star piano teacher was its 'most talked about homosexual, except perhaps for Tchaikovsky'.[12] Known by his contemporaries as Pussy, Scriabin's own brand of effeminacy was far from straightforward. He liked very young girls and much older, taller men. One of his first loves was the fifteen-year-old Natalia to whom he wrote over 50 letters. When he later settled in Switzerland, his closest friend was a burly, uneducated fisherman, Otto.[13]

Scriabin had a similar experience to Robert Schumann, at this stage: he damaged his right hand, probably through excessive practice on the piano. Thereafter, this disability constrained his career as a virtuoso. He also suffered from the difficulty, being very small, of having a hand which stretched hardly more than an octave.[14]

The Conservatoire awarded him the second gold medal, Rachmaninov winning the first that year. After graduating, Scriabin spent some time socialising and drinking heavily. A couple of years later, he began his very great friendship with the much older and taller Mitrofan Belaiev, the patron of Rimsky-Korsakov. Until Belaiev died in 1903, he gave Scriabin an allowance, and his firm published his works. They travelled abroad together and Belaiev sent him to a psychiatrist to help him with his nervous problems, and his severe migraine.[15]

Against Belaiev's advice, Scriabin married Vera Isaakovich, another gold medallist. From the outset, the marriage was disastrous, although it lasted seven years. Before Scriabin abandoned Vera and their four children, he had already seduced a fifteen-year-old student at a girls' school where he was a part-time teacher, and had begun a long affair with Tatiana Schloezer, with whom he had three further children.[16]

Shortly after his first marriage, Scriabin became a professor at the Moscow Conservatoire, where he was considered to be an exceptional teacher. But when the marriage broke up, he left this position and went abroad. His divorce from Vera was not recognised in Russia and was only legalised on his deathbed.[17]

Theosophy

During the years 1904–9, when he was outside Russia, Scriabin became interested in the Theosophical Society founded in 1875 by a Ukrainian, Helena Blavatskaya. This provides a mystical approach to religion: God must be experienced directly to be known at all.[18]

Scriabin went rather further, 'over the top'. Having been born on Christmas Day (under the old calendar), he concocted the notion that the world would be regenerated through a cataclysm which would spring from his own creativity.[19] Unfortunately, he could not bring this to a conclusion. His plans for the *Mysterium*, which would be premièred in an Indian temple, were terminated by his premature death.

More tangible and audible was Scriabin's wonderful *Poem of Ecstasy* which he composed between 1905 and 1907. He said that, when you listen to it, you look straight into the eye of the Sun. One biographer has written: 'Its musical tension produces the resounding "I am", the orgiastic climax.'[20] A later work, *Prometheus: The Poem of Fire*, is said to be 'the most densely Theosophical piece of music ever written. Its symbolism is endless.'[21] Of the Tenth Sonata (1913) Scriabin said: 'Here is blinding light as if the sun has come close. Here is the suffocation one feels in the moment of ecstasy.'[22]

Scriabin viewed the First World War as part of the cosmic regeneration. But, shortly before its outbreak, he contracted a painful lump on his upper lip. This appeared during a concert series in London in 1914. During the visit, he had hoped to meet Annie Besant, then the guiding light for the Theosophical movement, but she was away in India where Scriabin was preparing to go: in anticipation, he was immersing himself in its language and yoga, and he bought some tropical clothes.[23]

First, Scriabin returned to Russia to write the *Mysterium*. But in April 1915, the pimple reappeared. It quickly became septic, and by 27 April he was dead.

Rachmaninov, Early Years

Rachmaninov, who was one of the pallbearers at Scriabin's funeral, then played Scriabin's works at a series of concerts for the benefit of the family. His performance was so different from Scriabin's rendering that there was considerable criticism from the composers who attended. Prokofiev said: 'When Scriabin had played, everything seemed to be flying upward; with Rachmaninov, all the notes stood firmly planted on earth.'[24] Rachmaninov's Romantic style was rapidly being overtaken by more 'modern' approaches.

Born on 1 April 1873, Sergei Rachmaninov was only nine years older than Stravinsky and eighteen years older than Prokofiev; he was aged twenty when Tchaikovsky died.

Rachmaninov's father dissipated the family fortune, and the family estate near Novgorod had to be sold to pay his debts. The family moved to St Petersburg in 1882, where Rachmaninov entered the Conservatoire. Because he did not take his studies seriously enough, he was sent three years later, through the influence of his cousin Alexander Siloti, to the Moscow Conservatoire. There his prodigious talents were developed, and he won the Great Gold Medal in 1892.

For several years, Rachmaninov boarded with Scriabin's teacher, Zveryev. But he was thrown out, following a complaint that the single practice room in the lodgings did not allow him sufficient scope to compose. He moved in with a Conservatoire friend, and then for a time with some of his own relatives, the Satins.

He received considerable encouragement from Tchaikovsky.[25] He completed his First Piano Concerto and, shortly after graduation, his well-known composition, the Prelude in C sharp Minor. His First Symphony, which was performed in 1896, was a disaster: César Cui said that it was like 'a programme Symphony on the Seven Plagues of Egypt'.[26] This adverse criticism sent Rachmaninov into a deep depression. But, thanks to the support of the railway industrialist Mamontov, he was engaged for the 1897–8 Moscow Private Russian Opera season. He had a successful début at Queen's Hall in London in 1899.

Rachmaninov's depression and inertia were chronic, and he had hypnosis to provide relief. It cannot have helped when Tolstoy, the novelist, asked him whether anyone really wanted his sort of music.[27] Despite his lassitude, and fortified by the inhalation of twenty cigarettes a day,[28] he completed his Second Piano Concerto, which is one of the most popular of all piano works, and which brought him international recognition.

Although the Orthodox Church prohibits first cousins to marry, Rachmaninov married his first cousin: his aunt fortunately had the necessary influence with the clergy and the quiet wedding was held on the outskirts of Moscow. Some four years later, a similar problem was resolved by Stravinsky and his first wife, who were also first cousins: they used the services of a village priest who was not too rigorous in his enquiries.[29]

Following a long honeymoon in Europe and the birth of their first daughter, Rachmaninov became conductor at the Bolshoi, and opened the season with Dargomijsky's *Rusalka*. But, after the political upheavals in 1905, he went to live in Dresden. In May 1907, he took part in Diaghilev's

Saison Russe in Paris; then the Rachmaninovs returned to Ivanovka, his wife's family estate about 300 miles south-east of Moscow. There, their second daughter was born.[30]

In 1909, Rachmaninov went on his first American tour. This was at the time that he wrote the Third Piano Concerto, which he performed in New York under Mahler. As well as being a virtuoso pianist he became, with Sergei Koussevitsky, one of the leading conductors in Russia. The strain of composing and performing eventually exhausted him, so that, in 1912–13, he cancelled his final appearance and took the family off to Switzerland, and then to Rome, before returning to Russia. Ivanovka was a place where he could relax, enjoy the farm and the horses, and go for rides in his new motorcar.

The Fall of the Romanov Tsars

At this time, the Romanov dynasty was heading towards its doom, despite its 300-year anniversary being celebrated with appropriate pomp and circumstance in 1913.*[31] Attempts at land reform had been made by the tough and uncompromising Prime Minister Peter Stolypin, but he was assassinated at a gala performance at the Kiev Opera House on 14 September 1911. A few months later, troops fired on strikers in the Siberian goldfields, and the protests culminated in an enormous strike in the summer of 1914. By then, 'the strike movement reached alarming proportions'.[32] The First World War was about to begin.

The stresses and strains caused by the war, particularly the food shortages, brought down the dynasty four years later. With the tsar at the front, the tsarina was in charge; she came increasingly under the spell of the Siberian peasant, Rasputin. Bolsheviks,** partly financed by Germany and led by Lenin, fomented dissent, particularly with the slogan, 'Land to the Peasants'. There was a massive strike of metal and textile workers in early March 1917; three days later, the troops fired on demonstrators. The army gradually deserted, the final blow to the regime being the desertion of the Cossacks. In early March, the tsar abdicated, at first in favour of his son, but, when he was informed that he would have to part from him, he withdrew his abdication. He then abdicated in favour of his brother, who

* The haemophiliac Tsarevich had to be carried in the procession by a Cossack.

** 'Bolsheviks' meant 'the majority', who supported Lenin's rules for the Communist Party, at a conference in Brussels in 1903.[33]

refused to accept the crown unless the Duma, the parliament, appointed him, which it did not. Around the time that the tsar abdicated Rachmaninov gave a recital in Moscow in aid of those wounded in the war.[34]

For a few months, there was a 'government' supported by the ruling classes, whereas actual power resided with the 'Soviets', the workers' and soldiers' councils, which ostensibly had mass support. On 16 April, Lenin returned to Petrograd* (prior to the war, St Petersburg), with a view to scotching this dual arrangement, which many dogmatic Marxists accepted as a necessary stage in the evolution towards socialism. Lenin was determined to accelerate the seizure of power: 'All power to the Soviets' became the slogan. In any case, co-operation within the dual government was bound to collapse because the cabinet, tempted by the prospect of juicy pickings, such as the Dardanelles and the Bosphorus,[36] supported the continuation of war, which was going very badly; on the other hand, the Soviets offered 'bread, peace and freedom'.

The commander-in-chief of the army led an abortive right-wing coup, which indicated that the officer corps was a spent force. Lenin seized the opportunity to deal a deathblow to the government. During the night of 6 November, Bolshevik forces seized strong points in Petrograd. Lenin announced: 'We shall now proceed to construct the socialist order.'[37] So it was that, in a short period of eight months, 'a tiny band of underground revolutionaries, numbering less than 25,000 around the time of the February revolution, had catapulted themselves into a governing authority for nearly 150 million people'.[38]

Rachmaninov during the First World War and Afterwards

During the war, Rachmaninov and Koussevitsky toured southern Russia giving concerts for the war effort. But the deteriorating political scene persuaded Rachmaninov that he should get out: he said that he would not take political instructions from his houseboy.[39] His family left, for ever as it happened, on a concert tour to Scandinavia. From there, they went to the USA. Like so many Russian émigrés, they longed to return to Russia

* Shostakovich, at the time he wrote the Twelfth 'Lenin' Symphony, claimed that he was at the Finland station when Lenin's armoured train arrived. A recent biographer suggests that it is unlikely that a ten-year-old would have been allowed out until after 11 pm, the time when Lenin arrived.[35]

and hoped that the old times would return; in their home, the Rachmaninovs tried to recreate the atmosphere of Ivanovka, and employed Russian servants and customs.[40]

During the 1920s, Rachmaninov spent a considerable time in Europe, undertaking a relentless round of concerts and recitals. He formed a publishing firm in Paris to publish works by Russian composers, and called it 'Tair' after his two daughters, Tatiana and Irina. In 1925, he worked on his

Sergei Rachmaninov / Igor Stravinsky

Fourth Piano Concerto, but it was not a success. Around the time at which he wrote the *Variations on a Theme by Corelli* and the *Rhapsody on a Theme of Paganini*, he wrote a letter to the *New York Times* in which he criticised the Soviet regime. As a consequence, the performance and study of his works was banned in the Soviet Union; but he was restored to favour in 1933 once the USA and the Soviet Union resumed diplomatic relations.

In 1939, with the threat of world war looming, Rachmaninov returned to the USA with his family. He decided that his 1942–3 season should be his last. He had undertaken exhausting tours and was suffering from lumbago, arthritis and extreme fatigue. On tour in January 1943, he was unwell; his doctor diagnosed pleurisy, but Rachmaninov insisted that the tour should go ahead. A concert at Knoxville on 17 February was his last. He went back to Los Angeles, where he died of cancer on 28 March.[41]

STRAVINSKY AND *THE RITE OF SPRING*

During Rachmaninov's life, music in a totally different style was being composed by Stravinsky, and even more so by the *enfant terrible*, Sergei Prokofiev. We will now consider them, before looking at some background to Shostakovich's life.

Of Polish aristocratic extraction, Igor Stravinsky was born near St Petersburg on 17 June 1882. His grandfather was a senior official in the Russian government, and his father a bass singer at Kiev and at the Maryinsky Theatre in St Petersburg, to which, as a boy, Igor received a free pass.

Stravinsky was a frequent visitor to the regular weekly salons which Rimsky-Korsakov held for his pupils. He performed his work there, made friends with Rimsky-Korsakov's sons, Andrei and Vladimir, and composed the orchestral fantasy *Fireworks* in celebration of the marriage of their sister Nadezhda. Yet, although Rimsky-Korsakov became a kind of father figure to Stravinsky, he does not seem to have singled him out for any special praise. Nor did Glazunov, the other doyen of the St Petersburg musical scene, think that Stravinsky showed much promise.[42]

Stravinsky's break came when Diaghilev heard *Fireworks* and the *Scherzo Fantastique* and invited him to orchestrate some Chopin music for the Paris 1909 performance of *Les Sylphides*. *The Firebird*, performed at Paris in 1910, was a great and lasting success. It was followed by *Petrushka* and *The Rite of Spring*. Indeed it is said that whereas Diaghilev created the *Ballets Russes*, their success 'was in large measure due to Stravinsky'.[43]

The first performance of *The Rite*, at the inauguration of the Théâtre des Champs-Elysées on 29 May 1913, rivalled Wagner's sensational performance of *Tannhäuser* in Paris over 50 years before (see page 472). The rumpus started almost as soon as the performance began and the uproar was magnified by the objections of those demanding quiet. Diaghilev, who 'in his frockcoat and top hat, his monocle and white gloves was a sight worth seeing',[44] had anticipated trouble and had told the conductor, Pierre Monteux, to ensure that the orchestra kept playing until the end, which it did, although nobody could hear it. About 50 'combatants' stripped naked and were arrested by the police. Despite all this, the dancers kept going, directed by Nijinsky, the famous dancer and choreographer, who was standing on a chair in the wings.[45] The work itself had a considerable effect: 'We were dumbfounded, flattened as though by a hurricane', wrote one critic.[46] Fortunately it had a less rowdy reception in London in July; and then, in Paris in the following April, Stravinsky was carried shoulder-high through the streets.

By 1914, Stravinsky had made his name as one of the most exciting and talented of the up-and-coming generation of composers. At the outbreak of war, he remained in Switzerland, where he had been a regular visitor; in 1920 he moved to France and then to Hollywood, USA. After *Pulcinella* and *Les Noces*, he wrote no further works for Diaghilev. His style at first became more neo-classical, as in the *Symphony of Psalms* and *Oedipus Rex* and culminating in *The Rake's Progress*. Then, under the influence of his friend Robert Craft, he adopted serialism.* Reflecting this, in later years, Stravinsky calculated that sales of records for his new works in the US were a tenth of the level for a new performance of *The Firebird*.[48]

When he was 80, Stravinsky returned to Russia for a short visit of a few weeks. Until then, he had refused to visit Russia, for reasons which will become even more obvious when we hear the story of Shostakovich later in this chapter. Stravinsky's official explanation for his refusal was that he regarded Soviet orchestras as being insufficiently familiar with his style of music, and that of Schoenberg, Berg and Webern, so it would take too long to rehearse a professional performance. The real reason was that Russia during those years was such a ghastly place in which to be.

Bolshevik Russia

The November revolution in 1917 had been followed by three years of civil war, as the Bolsheviks, the 'Reds', fought to consolidate power and resist those 'Whites' who fought for a restoration of the old regime. A harsh peace treaty with Germany deprived Russia of vast areas of territory, including Finland and the Baltic States. It was an appallingly difficult time. Within a few months of the revolution, the Cheka, a Bolshevik secret police, was mandated to eliminate counter-revolution.[49] It was designed initially on the lines of the tsar's secret police, and was equally, if not more, imaginative in its use of torture. To enforce discipline, the Communist

* Serialism, in which the twelve notes of the chromatic scale are arranged in a fixed order, gave a coherent, even if to most listeners unidentifiable, structure to the atonal music of Schoenberg, Berg and Webern.[47]

Party announced a ban on factionalism, that is, any opposition whatsoever. Yet, for a brief period, an element of capitalism had to be reintroduced, just to keep the show on the road.

During this chaos, land cultivation dropped by 40 per cent, and there were considerable shortages of food.[50] The government was faced with the difficulty of feeding the urban population. It suspected that the root of its troubles was the group of élite farmers, the tenth of farms which accounted for over half of the grain produced,[51] who had objected to low farm prices. So it instituted a policy of enforced collectivisation of farms, creating units such as the model pig farm run by one of the characters in Prokofiev's politically correct opera, *Semyon Kotko*.[52] In the real world, 7 million people, the more prosperous peasant farmers and their families, were evicted and exiled, in many cases, to labour camps.[53] Consequently, over 3 million people died of starvation in 1933.[54]

Lenin had died in January 1924, having been out of action for some time. He had never fully recovered from an operation to extract from his neck a bullet fired at point-blank range during an assassination attempt.[55] Meanwhile, Joseph Stalin had become the chairman of the Central Committee of the Communist Party, and during the rest of the 1920s, he tightened his grip. By 1930, his major opponent, Trotsky, was banished; the remaining opposition was cowed and repentant.

Those swept away at this time included Anatoly Lunarcharsky, Lenin's first commissar for education, a long-serving communist intellectual whose tastes, according to Prokofiev, were those of 'an aesthete and theatre-lover'.[56] He protected the heritage during the civil war years, and liked Shostakovich, Prokofiev, futurist poets and women. Because his focus was cultural rather than technical, his star waned once attacks on the intelligentsia gathered momentum at the end of the 1920s, and technicians were being rounded up, accused of sabotage and espionage.[57] He was sent off to be an ambassador overseas and died there at the early age of 58.

The political purges of the 1930s followed. As we shall see, musicians such as Shostakovich and other artists were drawn into the vortex. There was death or, at best, humiliation for many. In 1933, there was an appalling example of the regime's ruthless cruelty and lack of concern for its artistic heritage: the itinerant, mostly blind, musicians, the bards of the Ukraine, 'a living museum, the country's living history',[58] were invited to a congress; they were all taken out and shot.

After the Great Patriotic War of 1941–5, as the tyrant aged, he flailed around even more wildly. In February 1948, it was again the musicians' turn to be targeted. Some close colleagues of Stalin heard him muttering to himself: 'I trust no one, not even myself.'[59] Unfortunately, he survived until 1953, when he died aged 73. More of this later.

Stravinsky, Last Years

The General Secretary of the Composers' Union was, we may assume, wise to denounce Stravinsky, then living safely in Hollywood, as 'an apostle of reaction in bourgeois music'.[60] And Stravinsky's reluctance to have anything to do with his home country during these years is understandable. After Stalin's death there was a thaw, of sorts. Eventually, Stravinsky agreed to return for a short visit, the pretext being a desire to help the younger generation of Russian musicians. The visit was made up of concert performances, sightseeing and receptions, where he met leading composers including Shostakovich and Khatchaturian. He failed at first to recognise the elderly Vladimir Rimsky-Korsakov who had been best man at his wedding 56 years earlier. He stepped even further back into history when one event took place in a hall where, 69 years earlier, he had been at a concert held to mourn the death of Tchaikovsky. He called on Nikita Krushchev, the premier, who attended a performance of *Petrushka*, *Orpheus* and *The Firebird*.

It was an exhausting schedule, and Stravinsky buckled. Doctors called to treat him when he felt ill during a concert were amazed to discover that, beforehand, he had swallowed ten drops of opium washed down with two tumblers of whisky; Stravinsky recovered after a brandy and a coffee.

Stravinsky lived to a grand old age: after all, his great-grandfather is said to have died aged 111, after a fall climbing over a gate when returning home after a night out against doctors' orders.[61] Into his 80s, Stravinsky travelled around the world, conducting and performing. At the very end of his long life, he moved to New York, for medical reasons. He died there on 6 April 1971, and was buried in Venice, close to Diaghilev.

One composer whom Stravinsky could not meet during his return visit to Russia in 1962 was Prokofiev, who had died nearly ten years before. In earlier times, Stravinsky and Prokofiev, who was nine years younger, had had a distant and uneasy relationship. However, during the Moscow visit, Stravinsky attended a performance of Prokofiev's controversial opera, *War and Peace*. Prokofiev had conceived this as a small, intimate opera. Even after he had amended it, on advice from the committee of arts, into an 'epic and heroic work'[62] and enlarged the war scenes and increased the patriotic elements, the first night for 1943 was cancelled. It was eventually premièred posthumously, some five years before Stravinsky's visit.

Prokofiev, Before the Return to the USSR

Sergei Prokofiev was born on 23 April 1891 in the Ukraine, where his father managed a large estate. He was an only child, and grew up to be particularly self-centred. As we saw in chapter 20, he was at the Conservatoire when the 1905 disturbances took place. He would attend evenings of contemporary music, attended by the St Petersburg musical avant-garde, where works of Schoenberg, Strauss and Stravinsky were played. His own piano pieces were described as 'ultra modern', 'unintelligible'.[63] So, when he graduated aged 23, it was only with great reluctance that Glazunov, the head of the Conservatoire, was persuaded to preside at the ceremony when Prokofiev was awarded the prestigious Rubinstein Prize.

He avoided conscription during the First World War, either because he was exempt, because he was the only son of a widow, or because he enrolled again as a student.

A visit to Rome to see Diaghilev led to the ballet, *The Tale of the Buffoon*, but the hostilities entailed the postponement of its first performance. The opera, *The Gambler*, was also postponed, because its performance coincided with the March revolution in 1917. That may have been fortuitous because by then the singers, orchestra and director were already up in arms about it. In the troubled months of mid-1917, when the bourgeois government was struggling with the Bolsheviks, Prokofiev was to be found in the countryside outside Petrograd, composing his *Classical Symphony* and reading Kant.[64] 'It seemed to me that, had Haydn lived to our day, he would have retained his own style while accepting something of the new as well', Prokofiev later wrote.[65] He also composed the First Violin Concerto at this time.

When Lenin seized power in November, Prokofiev was with his mother, who was taking a cure in the Caucasus. He sent his manuscripts to be put in his publisher's safe in Moscow.[66] He heard conflicting reports about what was happening in Petrograd and Moscow; occasionally a train would arrive and its load of 'panic-stricken bourgeois' pour out.[67] With

Russia in a state of civil war, Prokofiev considered that the outlook for a composer was unpropitious, and he decided to leave for America. He had met the farm machinery magnate Cyrus McCormick, who had told him to look him up if he ever came to America. McCormick helped him when eventually he got to Chicago.

The Love for Three Oranges was composed for Chicago in 1919, although Prokofiev was very seriously ill with scarlet fever and its associated throat problems. But the death of the conductor led to its postponement and a row about compensation. Putting aside the justification for this claim, there is no question that Prokofiev was a forceful character. A director who lost his temper with him and asked, 'Who is in charge here, you or I?' was told, 'You are; but you are here to carry out my wishes.'[68] His abrasive, arrogant, abrupt and often tactless personality would not serve him well in the future.[69] And he did not make friends with his acid quips. 'Stravinsky's music is like Bach with the wrong notes' and 'Diaghilev has better taste in boys than in music' are just two examples.[70]

Prokofiev was disillusioned with the American reception for his music, and in March 1922, he went to live for a short period near Oberammergau, in southern Germany. 'Why did I not return to my native land?', he asks in his autobiography written twenty years later. He gave a suitably politically correct explanation: 'I had not yet fully grasped the significance of what was happening in the USSR. I did not realize that the events there demanded the co-operation of all citizens, not only men of politics, as I had thought, but men of art as well.'[71] Around this time, Prokofiev married the attractive Spanish-born Lina, and soon after moved to Paris.

In the early 1920s, he wrote a ballet for Diaghilev, which was aimed not merely to entertain, but also to show the new life that had come to the Soviet Union. *The Age of Steel* (Le Pas d'Acier) was to be a ballet 'of construction, with hammers big and small being wielded, transmission belts and flywheels revolving, light signals flashing, all leading to a general creative upsurge'.[72] Ironically, the Bolshoi had to take it off after it was criticised by the Association of Proletarian Musicians, who regarded it as a 'mockery of a revolution'.[73] It was first staged some years later at the New York Metropolitan Opera, which Prokofiev condemned as the 'most bourgeois of bourgeois theatres'.[74]

Meanwhile, in 1927, Prokofiev was welcomed back to the USSR for a recital tour. He was given VIP treatment. The celebrity skated nimbly and cockily over the surface of the drab society beneath. He could command 3,500 roubles for a solo recital, whereas the boyhood friend, now veterinary surgeon, with whom he used to play chess, was lucky if his whole family brought in 400 roubles a month.[75] But the vet's fate was preferable to that of Prokofiev's first cousin, once an aristocrat, now a political suspect, who shared a prison with common criminals;[76] or the fate of Nina, with whom Prokofiev had once enjoyed dancing lessons as a small boy, who had been shot as a White.[77] All the time there was the suspicion that someone might be listening, and there were signs that the telephone was bugged.[78] Prokofiev's genuine attempts to secure the release of his cousin met with continual procrastination.

Prokofiev located Glazunov's flat in the old family mansion;[79] the front was boarded up and, to get to it, he had to go in through the back and ascend the filthy communal staircase. At least the Glazunov mansion seemed preferable to those houses now turned over to eighteen families, all using the same kitchen.*[81] How far we have moved from Scriabin, less than fifteen years earlier! Scriabin, for health reasons, as well as distaste, would put on gloves before taking or giving money to a tradesman at his apartment door![82]

Prokofiev's diary describes the son of Jurgenson, Tchaikovsky's once-powerful publisher, who was now a minor clerk in the music section, working in the building where his firm, now nationalised, had once been.[83]

The Soviet Union continued to woo Prokofiev: he received an increasing number of commissions, and performed various concert tours. This lulled the prodigal son into feeling that he wanted to return permanently. Prokofiev had never held very strong political views, but returning to Stalinist Russia was an unwise step. Once home, the prodigal could be treated differently. At the time, Shostakovich was already being denounced. 'Quite simply he wanted to go home' is the most plausible explanation for Prokofiev's virtually incomprehensible move.[84]

On his return, in response to the considerable demand for children's music, Prokofiev wrote *Peter and the Wolf.* He had also composed *Romeo and Juliet* for the Kirov (formerly Maryinsky) Theatre in Leningrad,

* Even in 1935, only six per cent of families in Moscow had more than one room. Although the shortage of space arose partly from circumstances, the government also forced people to live communally, with a view to destroying their individualistic, bourgeois mindset.[80]

although it was not put on. The tennis- and chess-playing, car-loving bon-viveur and gourmet would quickly realise how awful were the circumstances to which he had returned.[85]

Life and Death under Stalin

Opponents of dictators have to be eliminated, otherwise they may be silently biding their time. Whether or not the assassination in December 1934 of Sergei Kirov, head of the Leningrad Communist Party, was at the instigation of Stalin, this event inaugurated a 'saturnalia of blood and violence over the next four years'.[86] Immediately, more than 100 'counter-revolutionaries' were shot. In the spring of 1935, the deportations to Siberia, and executions, began. Thousands, more like tens of thousands, of Leningrad (formerly Petrograd and St Petersburg) inhabitants suspected of deviationist tendencies were liquidated. The extent and reach of the purge is indicated by the fact that in early 1936, a quarter of the 3 million members of the Communist Party had gone. As they were cast as 'wreckers, spies, diversionists, and murderers sheltering behind the Party card and disguised as Bolsheviks',[87] we can guess their fate. One commentator has written: 'the list of the eliminated was a *Who's Who* of Soviet celebrities'.[88]

The purge was extended and 'no sphere of Soviet life, however lofty, was left untouched'.[89] The onslaught on musicians, when it came, was focused on Shostakovich, as we shall see. The writer Maxim Gorky, who interceded on behalf of Shostakovich, and who, like Prokofiev, had been lured back from abroad, 'died'. The first of the great show trials took place in August 1936, when sixteen prominent party leaders were tried and shot. In the following January, the Trial of the Seventeen took place; thirteen 'Trotskyists' were shot and four received long prison sentences. In June 1937, Marshal Tukhachevsky was first withdrawn from representing the USSR at the coronation in London, and then, a month later, together with seven other generals, was summarily executed without trial.*[90] The terror, the denunciations, the eliminations and liquidations continued. In March 1938, the trial took place of the Twenty-One, for treason, espionage, terrorism and wrecking. In that year, the poet Osip Mandelstam died in transit

* Tukhachevsky was a distinguished soldier from the civil war. With Trotsky, he bloodily suppressed a mutiny by the sailors at Kronstadt in March 1921. They foolishly demanded political freedom and civil rights, and 'Soviets without Bolsheviks'. Tukhachevsky's hobby was to make violins.

to a labour camp; the writer Isaak Babel was shot a year later; the top avant-garde theatre director, V.E. Meyerhold, who had worked closely with both Prokofiev and Shostakovich, was shot in 1940, the year in which Trotsky was felled with an axe in Mexico.[91]

The Great Patriotic War

The Second World War eventually intervened and provided a form of respite. Russian entry into the war had been deferred until 1941, as a consequence of a non-aggression treaty, known as the Molotov Pact, which involved yet another tasty partition of Chopin's Poland. This was stitched up between Hitler and Stalin just days before the British declared war on Hitler. But it was a temporary relationship on both sides. Two years later, Hitler was convinced that he could secure a quick three, or at the most five, months' Blitzkrieg campaign to pre-empt an attack on him from Russia.

Hitler was confident that the Soviet leadership had been so weakened by the purges that resistance to his Operation Barbarossa would collapse; this assessment was not totally daft, as it now seems, because London and Washington, presumably expert in such matters, assumed the Russian resistance would only last six to eight weeks.[92] On 22 June 1941, Hitler totally surprised the Soviet leadership by launching against Russia the largest army ever mobilised for a single campaign.* At first the Germans were completely successful. Leningrad was encircled by 8 September, leaving Lake Ladoga, to the immediate north-east of the city, as the only means of communication with the rest of the Soviet Union. Hitler would starve it into submission; meanwhile, being a more successful leader than Napoleon, he would move on to Moscow, which he would raze and replace with an artificial lake with central lighting.[94] The name of Moscow would disappear for ever. But by mid-October, the Germans stopped outside Moscow.[95]

Prokofiev was evacuated, at first to the southern states of the Soviet Union. He subsequently spent a year in the east of Kazakhstan, almost on the Chinese border, where he worked with the distinguished film-maker Sergei Eisenstein on his *Ivan the Terrible*.[96]

* It comprised 3.2 million men, including 17 panzer and 13 motorised divisions, 3,350 tanks, 600 motor vehicles and 600 horses. The Japanese attack on Pearl Harbor, Hawaii, on 7 December 1941, which Roosevelt called a 'date which will live in infamy', brought the USA into the war, on the following day.[93]

After the War

When peace came, Stalin was still alive. Severe psychological pressure was once again exerted on composers. The aging Soviet dictator believed that discipline should be reasserted, the superiority of the Marxist-Leninist state should be re-emphasised, and all contact with the West and imitation of its subversive individualism should be banned. Art was not to be exempt; indeed, it would provide a means of reinforcing the Stalinist message.

In August 1946, Zhdanov, Stalin's latest henchman, began an attack on artistic and intellectual life by denouncing two literary journals for publishing 'apolitical' and 'ideologically harmful' material by a satirist who 'oozed anti-Soviet poison'.[97] Anna Akhmatova, a poet who was greatly respected in literary circles, was condemned for corrupting Soviet youth with her self-obsessed love poems, and called a 'mixture of a nun and a whore'.[98] Art, Zhdanov had insisted over twelve years before, was expected to be a servant of the Party and the state. It was to reinforce ideological orthodoxy, the 'Soviet realism' in which the New Soviet Man and Woman, 'perfect imbeciles with good teeth and fair hair', were portrayed as 'striding steadily and unthinkingly onward and upward, smashing down every obstacle to material progress' and denouncing anyone who failed to conform.[99]

Early in September, the cinema, which Stalin regarded as a crucial part of his propaganda machine, was singled out for correction.[100] Eisenstein, with whom Prokofiev had worked on the film *Alexander Nevsky* as well as *Ivan the Terrible*, was denounced. In June 1947, it was the turn of the philosophers.

By the end of 1947, officials, the *apparatchiki*, were circulating briefs denouncing shortcomings in Soviet music.[101] In early January 1948, Stalin saw an opera to commemorate the anniversary of the revolution and was displeased. It was written by V.I. Muradeli, a fellow Georgian. There was a post-mortem the following day; Zhdanov thought it was a cacophony and there was not a single memorable melody.[102] A conference of over 70 musicians was immediately summoned for Zhdanov to denounce the opera and require the musicians to expose the unhealthy elements in their midst. This worked perfectly: the composers imploded with mutual self-criticism.

Individualism, cosmopolitanism, 'formalism'* were to be rooted out.[104]

* The term 'formalism', the opposite of 'socialist realism', was applied to an artwork in which form and structure were given more emphasis than artistic feeling, as defined in Marxist terms.[103] The atonal works of Schoenberg and Berg were possibly the 'worst' examples.

Prokofiev, Shostakovich and other composers were denounced for their 'formalistic perversions and anti-democratic tendencies that are alien to the Soviet people and its artistic tastes':[105] they wrote '*avant-garde* compositions for a limited audience, instead of appealing to the masses with tuneful music in celebration of Soviet achievements'.[106] Prokofiev's *War and Peace* was singled out. Also, Shostakovich's Ninth Symphony was accused of showing 'the unwholesome influence of Igor Stravinsky, an artist without a fatherland and without confidence in advanced ideas'.[107]

The scene was dire. Prokofiev's wife Lina, who was Spanish-born, was arrested in late February and, 'suspected' of being a spy, interrogated in the Lubyanka prison and then sent for eight years to a labour camp. So much for the VIP treatment which she had been accorded during the recital tour in the mid-1920s, when she had worn her distinctive leopard-skin coat: she had been received by ministers and officials in the Kremlin, and gone shopping for blue-fox and squirrel fur reserved for export. Her consolation, one supposes, was that she had avoided the far worse fate of so many of those whom she had met at that time.*[108]

For the whole of the 1940s Prokofiev and Lina had been estranged. In 1941, he left her to live with the 27-year-old Mira Mendelson, who had become his assistant. She is said to have had good connections in political circles, however fragile or counter-productive such links might be.** They finally married less than six weeks before Lina's arrest.[109]

The Prokofiev sons turned for help to Shostakovich, who had recently been re-elected to the Russian Supreme Soviet, but he was hardly in a position to assist. Besides, it would appear that Prokofiev himself, possibly wisely, had not been prepared to risk his neck to save Lina.

After Zhdanov, once seen as Stalin's successor, 'died' at the end of August 1948, there were 'homicidal goings on' in Leningrad, while his clique was being purged. The heirs were now jockeying for position; the aging Stalin began a ruthless anti-Semitic campaign.[110] In the summer of 1952, 25 Jewish writers were executed for being agents of American imperialism; a

* Lina was released in 1956 during an amnesty by Krushchev. She died in 1989. She fared better than the wife of the Soviet official head of state, Kalinin, who was sent to a labour camp having first been beaten senseless in the presence of the chief of the secret police (Beria). The wife of Molotov, the anti-West foreign minister and provider of the cocktail, also went to jail.

** This is denied by some commentators. Her Jewish parentage would throw doubt on her power to exercise any meaningful influence.

prominent Jewish actor was mysteriously killed in a car crash. And Stalin turned on his nine doctors, seven of whom were Jewish. 'Only Stalin's fatal illness averted a bloodbath in the very highest Kremlin circles.'[111] Fortunately, Stalin died on 5 March 1953; Prokofiev died on the same day.

Although aged only 50, Prokofiev had experienced the first of a series of heart attacks back in 1941. His health continued to be bad, and several months in 1945 were spent in a sanatorium near Moscow. In spring 1946, he moved with Mira to a village west of the city, and this became his home.

As we shall now see, Shostakovich managed to ride the roller coaster; however, Prokofiev, it seems, could do no good. When in December 1948 officials from the Party and the Union of Composers had a preview of a proposed opera about a Second World War pilot, they gave it the thumbs down. It was withdrawn. Prokofiev's health deteriorated. His last appearance was the première of the Seventh Symphony, five months before his death.[112]

Shostakovich, Early Years

Prokofiev, despite being an important composer, was not at the eye of the storm. It was Shostakovich who bore the main brunt. His career illustrates vividly how difficult and terrifying, if survivable, life could be, even for one who chose, willingly or unwillingly, to stay in his homeland. As a young man, he ignored his mother's plans for him to move to the USA;[113] after that, he probably had little room for choice.

Dmitry Shostakovich was only eleven when the revolution broke out in 1917. He was born in St Petersburg on 25 September 1906. His father and mother had both come from Siberia. Dmitry at first attended the same school as sons of other 'well-to-do liberal intelligensia',[114] such as Kerensky, who would lead the government in mid-1917, Kamenev, who would criticise the speed at which Lenin was pressing forward, and Trotsky. The Shostakovich family supported the aims of the revolution and were among the million mourners at the funeral for those killed in March 1917.[115]

Through this turbulent time, the Conservatoire, still directed by the highly regarded Glazunov, managed to continue its tradition and teaching. But during the civil war which followed the November revolution and lasted until 1921, nobody in the cities could avoid the cold and hunger.[116] The infrastructure had collapsed; industrial production was halved. There was little food and fuel for the likes of Shostakovich: the amount of grain reaching Petrograd was half the pre-war level because everything was being diverted to the Red Army.

So, by the time Dmitry enrolled in 1919, he had to make his own way to the Conservatoire, because there was no public transport. He endured considerable hardship. He developed tuberculosis. When his father died, his mother had to get a job in order to provide for the family. Shostakovich supported himself by playing the piano in cinemas, occasionally to the surprise, if not shock, of the audience.[117]

In May 1926, Shostakovich's First Symphony established him. Five months later, he underwent an examination in Marxist theory, compulsory for students at the Conservatoire. At least there was some humour in the midst of the gloom. They were asked what was the difference, from a sociological and economic point of view, between the work of Chopin and Liszt. When he and his colleagues fell about laughing, the examination had to be adjourned until the next day.[118]

Shostakovich's opera, *The Nose*, was performed in a concert performance in 1929, when some criticised it for 'its avoidance of a Soviet theme, its musical complexity, and its inaccessibility to the masses'.[119] This was but an appetiser; the main course and other courses were to follow later.

Meanwhile, in March 1930, Shostakovich condemned gypsy music, and called for censorship, the expulsion of the erring from composers' societies, and the issue of propaganda.[120] In the following year, he issued a 'Declaration of a Composer's Duties'. He denounced all his own theatrical and film music and said: 'the situation on the musical front is catastrophic'.[121] From August 1932, the year in which he got married, he was elected to the board of the Union of Soviet Composers.

Katerina, Lady Macbeth

Big Brother descended on the successful Shostakovich in the mid-30s at the time of the Great Purge, which followed the assassination of Kirov, the Leningrad chief. Shostakovich had started to work on *Lady Macbeth of Mzensk* (*Katerina Izmailova*) in 1930; it was cleared by the appropriate commissar* in May 1933, and premièred in January 1934, ten months before Kirov's assassination. It was initially a great success in Shostakovich's home city of Leningrad, in Moscow and internationally. That year

* This commissar was shot a few years later.

Shostakovich was a true celebrity: he was elected the equivalent of an MP, and had an affair; he divorced his wife Nina, but remarried her when he found she was pregnant.[122] In November 1935, he could record: 'today is the happiest day of my life: I saw and heard Stalin'.[123]

But Shostakovich's fame was too much: in those uncertain times, he cannot have been totally surprised when his turn came in January 1936. Stalin attended a performance of *Lady Macbeth*, but ominously left before the end; two days later, 'the deliberately dissonant, muddled stream of sounds ... the din, the grinding, the squealing' were condemned in an article in *Pravda*, the state newspaper, under the headline, 'Muddle instead of Music'.[124] The opera, which at first had been deemed consistent with Party requirements, was now accused of the 'leftish deformity' that tainted so much modern music and art.[125] Meetings were held at which Shostakovich's faults were condemned and held up as a warning to others. Shostakovich applied to meet Stalin, but was refused.

Stalin's scheme was to make everybody, right up to his closest and most senior henchman, feel completely and permanently insecure; and anyone who constituted a real threat, or did not play the part, was simply eliminated. Yet, somehow, in this atmosphere, the chain-smoking, poker-playing soccer fan continued to work on his Fourth Symphony.[126] Sensibly, but petrified, he 'withdrew it' almost on the day scheduled for its first performance.

With his disgrace, Shostakovich's income dropped to around a fifth of its previous level.[127] He was reminded that a dictator's tentacles have an extensive reach: his sister and her husband were arrested; his mother-in-law was sent to a labour camp. In June 1937, he must have been horrified at the summary execution of his friend Marshal Tukhachevsky. Tukhachevsky had tried to intercede with Stalin on Shostakovich's behalf, but to no avail.[128] Now it was the marshal's turn. Shostakovich was hauled off to the sinister Interior Ministry and interrogated.*[129]

Shostakovich's fortunes recovered, even as the purge deepened. The Fifth Symphony was alarmingly well received at its première in November 1937, and ominous comments were made about the unhealthy nature of the adulation, the 'psychosis'.[130] But this marked his rehabilitation, for the

* Fortunately, his interrogator was arrested before further harm could be done.

moment. Although the tyrant was sent a memo denouncing the Piano Quintet for having created an atmosphere of unhealthy sensation and for its Western orientation, Shostakovich received a Stalin Prize for it. In that year, 1940, Shostakovich took the opportunity to describe Scriabin as 'our bitterest enemy'.[131]

SHOSTAKOVICH: THE WAR AND AFTERWARDS

When the Germans began their 900-day siege of Leningrad, in September 1941,[132] Shostakovich volunteered to join up, he dug ditches and acted as a firefighter (see colour plate 50); he also began his Seventh Symphony. The image of the composer on the roof of the Conservatoire, defending the beleaguered city with both physical and artistic endeavour, caught the public imagination, both at home and abroad, and made excellent propaganda.

Shostakovich remained in Leningrad until 1 October when he was evacuated with his wife and small children, including the three-year-old Maxim, at first to Moscow. They then went on a seven-day train journey eastwards to Samara (then Kuybyshev) on the Volga, where the government had established itself. There, Shostakovich completed the Symphony, having resisted pressure to conclude it with a hymn in praise of Stalin. It was a sensational success when premièred the following March and when it was played in Leningrad (by musicians revived with special food rations) in August.[133] It was accorded a similar reception in England and in the USA.

By then, Shostakovich was safely away from the hostilities, which in the case of his country were so particularly cruel. During the Second World War, the Soviet Union suffered over 20 million deaths as combatants, or from the consequences of war, such as air raids and famine.*[134]

Shostakovich continued to ride the lethal roller coaster. There was a minor blip in 1944 when Stalin ordered him to work with the Armenian composer Khatchaturian** to partake in a competition for a new national anthem, but then awarded the prize to the director of the Red Army

* The USSR figures are estimated at 10 million killed in action, 3.3 million as prisoners of war and 7 million civilians. The British and Commonwealth overall figure was 484,000; the USA suffered 363,000 military deaths. The Jewish death toll was 6 million, of which half were Polish. Forty to fifty million were killed in the Hitler-Stalin period: half or even more of these died from brutal treatment, or extermination.

** Aram Khatchaturian (1903–78) is best known for the Piano Concerto, the *Sabre Dance* and *Spartacus*.

Chorus. Shostakovich said that the director choked with 'the delight and the saliva of a faithful retainer' when he heard of his award.[135]

There was the particularly worrying time in early 1948, when Zhdanov attacked the composers. The hors-d'oeuvre course was served with suitable subtlety, psychologically at least. Everything seemed to be going nicely for the composer, despite the fact that the satirical writer with whose denunciation Zhdanov began his cultural attack was a member of Shostakovich's poker-playing circle.[136] Shostakovich was appointed chairman of the Leningrad branch of the Composers' Union, awarded the Order of Lenin and appointed to the Russian Supreme Soviet. He was also nominated People's Artist of Russia.[137]

Then Shostakovich hit the buffers. In February 1948, the Central Committee issued its resolution condemning his and others' music as formalistic and anti-democratic.

As Krushchev put it so pragmatically, 'When Stalin says dance, a wise man dances'.[138] For Shostakovich, this meant humbling himself. Fortunately, he recanted, and admitted that he had begun to 'speak in a language incomprehensible to the people'.[139] Sensibly, he confirmed that he was deeply grateful for the criticism.

Although subjected to public humiliation and ostracism, luckily the accused composers did not suffer arrest and death; a theatre director was, however, arrested and tortured. But, for Shostakovich, it was nasty. In mid-February, a list was published of works whose performance was prohibited. He was stripped of his position in the Composers' Union. The press stoked the flames. He received poison letters.[140] Maxim was required to denounce his father in a music school exam.*[141] Not surprisingly, Shostakovich was almost driven to suicide.

Yet, in March 1949, Stalin rang up the composer and told him to join a delegation attending a conference in the USA. The proscription of most of his works was lifted. Shostakovich's visit took place shortly before Joseph McCarthy accused the US State Department of being infiltrated by over 200 communists. US officials required Shostakovich to get out as soon as the formal proceedings were concluded. On his return to the USSR, he was put through a refresher course in Marxist-Leninism.[142]

Also in 1949, Shostakovich served with 74 other leading figures on the

* Maxim Shostakovich subsequently became a well-known pianist and conductor.

committee which organised the celebration of Stalin's 70th birthday. At this, the Soviet Academy of Sciences pragmatically hailed Stalin as 'the greatest genius of mankind'.[143] The celebrations culminated with a gala at the Bolshoi Theatre and a giant portrait of the paranoiac dictator was suspended from a balloon and picked out by searchlights.

At this difficult time, Shostakovich wrote many film scores. He organised his compositions so that those published were politically correct and conformed with Soviet requirements; others, which he withheld, were in accordance with his artistic conscience. As we have seen, the period before Stalin's death was very tense. With Stalin viciously attacking Jews, Shostakovich was surely wise to withhold his song cycle, *From Jewish Folk Poetry*.[144]

The signals were never clear. Although he was re-elected an 'MP' to the Russian Supreme Soviet in 1951, his Twenty-Four Preludes and Fugues were criticised for failing to revive the Russian polyphonic tradition by infusing it with contemporary vitality.

After Stalin's Death

Soon after Stalin died, an article in *Pravda* in November 1953 signalled an improved atmosphere. But that did not stop the Union of Composers ripping into Shostakovich's Tenth Symphony in the following spring. The composers' system of peer review, and of choosing winners for the Stalin Prize, facilitated cannibalism.[145]

In 1956, at the time when Krushchev was denouncing Stalin and his era, a committee from the Ministry of Culture still decided that *Lady Macbeth* should remain proscribed.[146]

It was a difficult and sad time for Shostakovich. Nina, who worked on research into cosmic radiation, died of cancer in her mid-40s. Shostakovich's mother died a year later. But it would be wrong to think that Shostakovich felt relentlessly oppressed. He welcomed an environment in which he could work without worrying about mundane matters such as money. In 1954, we find him claiming that an artist in Russia 'has more freedom than the artist in the West'.[147]

Honours soon flowed in his direction from abroad and at home. In 1962, the year when Stravinsky had made the triumphant return to his homeland, Shostakovich was elected to represent Leningrad on the Council of Nationalities of the Supreme Soviet. He also married his third wife, the 27-year-old Irina. She had earlier been an inmate of an orphanage for children of enemies of the people.[148]

In 1961, he took the brave step to set to music some poems which condemned anti-Semitism, written by Yevtushenko, a controversial poet. Shostakovich absorbed these into his Thirteenth Symphony. The cultural atmosphere surrounding its première in December 1962 was tense, not least because its first performance took place less than three weeks after Krushchev had gone to an art exhibition and denounced various paintings for looking like 'daubs made with a donkey's tail'.[149] Although the Symphony was well received, it was cold-shouldered by the authorities. It had to be withdrawn and some of the poetry amended.

So, Shostakovich's current immunity from state criticism was by no means assured. But he continued outwardly to profess total loyalty to the regime. Rostropovich, for whom he wrote the Cello Concertos, protested about a press campaign against Alexander Solzhenitsyn, who had recently won the Nobel Prize for Literature. Shostakovich forcefully denounced Rostropovich for his efforts.[150] Almost three years later, Shostakovich's name was included on a list of those denouncing the nuclear physicist Andrei Sakharov. A writer said that the composer's action 'demonstrated irrefutably that the Pushkinian question has been resolved for ever: genius and villainy are compatible'.[151]

For many years Shostakovich's health had been poor, and he suffered a series of heart attacks. In early 1973 lung cancer was diagnosed, and his incurable condition was confirmed by the doctors whom he consulted surreptitiously during a visit to the USA.[152]

'Genius and villainy are compatible.' Whether or not this judgement is harsh, Shostakovich's adroitness in very difficult circumstances enabled him to die, 'in his bed', on 9 August 1975. Was he just a puppet swinging on a string, whose limbs had to be supple, or else he would be put in the rubbish bin? Or was he a member of the cast, a supporting actor who knew that his survival required him to play to perfection the part to which he was assigned? Those who might suspect that he was an active participant in a charade can still be confident that, had he died earlier, or had his work been more constrained, posterity would have been deprived of much valuable music.

England: Elgar, Vaughan Williams and Britten

CHAPTER 29

English composers have been conspicuously absent from this book. For the two centuries after Purcell, there were countless English musicians, and much talent, but nobody truly exceptional,[1] when measured against the standard of the Viennese classical composers or the European Romantics. England obtained a reputation as 'Das Land ohne Musik', the land without music.[2] The taunt was incorrect and unjust. Much music was composed and made, not least by foreigners attracted to the country. Also, England was a significant centre for the manufacture of musical instruments, such as harpsichords in the 18th century and pianos in the 19th.[3] However, the 'great' composers came from the Continent, not from England.

England was certainly not a land without art. Just taking 18th-century painters alone, we think of Reynolds, Gainsborough and Stubbs, to name but a few. We can also enjoy the works of the English novelists, playwrights and poets. The artistic heritage is immense.

Before turning to look at Elgar and, much more briefly, Holst, Delius and Vaughan Williams, and finally Britten, we should consider a few reasons why England seemed not to be able to produce indigenous composers of the same quality as those from Germany, France and Italy. We should also quickly survey the scene before Elgar appeared.

Above: ELGAR, VAUGHAN WILLIAMS AND BRITTEN

English Music in the 18th and 19th Centuries

England was not alone. Spain had a magnificent flowering in the 16th century. For three centuries thereafter, despite considerable patronage by the king and leading nobles, exceptional local talent was rarely to be found in Spain. Many talented musicians went to Italy for work; those who remained were less prominent. The dearth is sometimes attributed to consequences arising from the accession of the French Bourbon family to the Spanish throne, at the time of the War of the Spanish Succession, the war in the early 1700s in which the Duke of Marlborough won battles such as Blenheim.* Whatever, Spanish music had to await Albéniz and Granados in the 20th century, to revive.[5]

Germany had a notable advantage: it was a disunited empire rather than a united kingdom; each aristocratic court, however tiny or absurd, had its own centre of culture. By the middle of the 19th century, there were in Germany around 70 travelling opera companies, 23 court operas and 100 municipal and other permanent institutions performing opera. Small cities had opera houses. Music was spread over the country, and there were opportunities for many to develop their talent.[6]

The stolid, worthy, mercantile middle classes predominant in the United Kingdom preferred their roast beef and mutton to their music. Mutton and music do not mix well, unless the music comprises the solid, strong oratorios of Handel and Mendelssohn sung in local choral societies. The oratorios were also consonant with the religious revival of the time, and with national aspirations. Handel and Mendelssohn, surprisingly for foreigners, seemed to share the national objective to build the Kingdom of God on Earth in the model of the British empire.

Luxuries and fripperies like fancy food, fashion and other kinds of music were best imported, bought with hard-earned British sterling.** Joseph Addison, the journalist at the start of the 18th century, observed

* King Philip V of Spain, formerly Duc d'Anjou, and his Italian wife, Elizabeth Farnese, were not particularly interested in a Spanish national culture, and 'began a systematic reduction of national art, a process faithfully continued by the Spanish Bourbons'.[4] Philip and his successor Ferdinand VI were besotted with the Italian castrato Farinelli.

**The desire for musicians to be foreign was not just a British phenomenon: Mozart's father never stood a chance of being promoted: the Archbishop of Salzburg wanted his top musicians to be Italian; Mozart himself found much the same situation when he looked for a job in Munich.[7]

that the English do not know what music they like, but if it is foreign, 'let it be *Italian*, *French*, or *High-Dutch*', they will assume it must be good.[8] Thus, as well as Handel and Mendelssohn, London welcomed Johann Christian Bach, Haydn, Rossini, Clementi, Cramer and many others.

Some have detected a British prejudice against musicians. At the start of the 19th century, their pay was on the same level as that of a shop-keeper.[9] Elgar, before he became established, tried to avoid being seen carrying his violin case, because he did not want people to think that he was a professional musician.[10] The authorities at Harrow school for a long time 'refused to acknowledge that music could be of the slightest possible relevance in the grooming of an English gentleman'.[11] Even as recently as the middle of the 20th century, an Eton College housemaster admonished a boy who preferred to spend the afternoon at the piano instead of playing football. Any playing, said the master, should be 'for the House'; the boy replied that he thought music was 'for the Whole World'.[12] The master's reaction is not recorded.

It is not surprising therefore that the annals of English music read like the contents pages of a cathedral chant and service book.* 'Organ-loft composers' predominated and poured out their oratorios, service settings and chants. Anglican church music is often very beautiful. And one cannot doubt the scholarship or sincerity of the distinguished musicians who, within the precincts, rediscovered so much early music, both sacred and secular.[14] The cathedral tradition, 'the choral service, embracing words, music, ceremonial and (in the broadest sense) architecture, represented the pinnacle of religious art'[15] and is an important part of the English cultural heritage; but, except in achieving uplifting ecclesiastical objectives, its scope is surely somewhat limited. Names like Elvey (brothers), Smart (uncle and nephew) and Wesley (father, sons and grandson) do not appear in modern concert programmes or at the opera house.

Yet, even if these English musicians were less interesting as composers, they were often interesting for their connections. Samuel and Charles

* For example, the Georgians, such as Cooke, Battishill, Arnold, Callcott and the infant prodigy Crotch. And the Victorians: Pearsall, Goss, Walmisley and S.S. Wesley, 'a towering figure, touched at times by genius'.[13] Apart from a few hymns, the works of Sir Joseph Barnby, Sir John Bacchus Dykes and the Jamaican-born Sir Frederic Hymen Cowen have faded from memory. Outside the chancel, Sir John Stainer's *Crucifixion* may sometimes be heard: the exception which proves the rule.

Wesley were the talented nephews of the founder of Methodism. Stephen Storace, who composed *The Haunted Tower* and *No Song, No Supper*, was the brother of Nancy, the first Susanna in Mozart's *Marriage of Figaro*; Thomas Augustus Arne, brother of the leading actress Mrs Cibber, wrote 'Rule Britannia' and much more besides. Thomas Attwood was a pupil, and Thomas Linley a friend, of Mozart. The Duke of Wellington's father was professor of music in Dublin.

British Prime Ministers sometimes conduct orchestras: here the Duke of Wellington (Prime Minister 1828–30) rehearses the Concerts of Ancient Music. Edward Heath (Prime Minister 1970–74) showed similar talent

Sir Henry Bishop, composer of 'Home, Sweet Home', *The Brazen Bust* and *The Royal Nuptials, or The Masque of Hymen*, can nowadays be said to have 'made history' by being the first English musician to have a knighthood conferred upon him by the sovereign.*[17] Who, outside the choir stall

* Sir George Smart, called 'the mountebank knight' by Samuel Wesley, had bought himself his knighthood on a trip to Dublin in 1811. It became normal in the 19th century to give musicians knighthoods, just as in later centuries it has been normal to award them to sportsmen. Britten was appointed a life baron, the first composer so to be. This enabled a recent edition of *The Dictionary of National Biography* (a useful source of information on British composers' honorary degrees) to refer to the young Britten as 'Benjamin (later Baron) Britten'. Unusually, maybe uniquely, his reputation long outlived the life.[16]

or academe, now remembers him, or the infant prodigy and founder of St Michael's College, Tenbury, Sir Frederick Ouseley, Baronet? Sir Frederick's work is said to be 'massive and sincere, but it is usually very dull'.[18]

All these were honoured in their generation. Both Mendelssohn and Schumann pinned their hopes for England on Sir William Sterndale Bennett, who was later principal of the Royal Academy of Music. But his oratorio, *The Woman of Samaria*, has been condemned as 'decorously dead'.[19] In *The May Queen*, Robin Hood's bass solo ''Tis jolly to hunt' is said to bring 'a whiff of fresh air from the woods' into the 'atmosphere of a boarding school prize-giving'.[20]

The Promenade Concerts have kept alive the name of Sir Hubert Parry, director of the Royal College of Music, who wrote the music to 'Jerusalem' and 'Blest Pair of Sirens' and the coronation anthem 'I was Glad'. He, with Sir Charles Stanford, was an exceptional teacher, administrator and publicist.[21] Both were important contributors to the English musical 'renaissance' that took place at the end of the 19th century.* The playwright Bernard Shaw summed Parry up caustically: 'P. was a d—d nice chap; and if he had been a little less nice, he would also have been a little less d—d.'[23]

All sorts of explanations have been forthcoming for the relative dearth in England. Janáček blamed the sea, which shaped the 'northern' character.[24] A more likely explanation was given by Dame Ethel Smyth, the composer and suffragette: 'Year in year out, composers of the Inner Circle, generally University men attached to our musical institutions,** produced one choral work after another – not infrequently deadly dull affairs – which, helped by the impetus of official approval, automatically went the rounds of our Festivals and Choral Societies, having paid the publisher's expenses and brought in something for the composers, before they disappeared for ever.'[25]

Ralph Vaughan Williams made much the same point more diplomatically: 'The truth is that the young Englishman is too musicianly. The "musicianly" composer has studied the whole anatomy of inspiration, and has found out all the mechanical means by which beautiful music is

* The renaissance is sometimes attributed to the amateur choral and folksong movements and the 'rediscovery' of earlier music, whether by Tudor composers or J.S. Bach.[22]

** Around 1950, in some desperation, the editor of *The Oxford Companion to Music* (ninth edition) listed over 50 qualifications obtainable by British organists and teachers; the list fills more than eight lines of text.

produced. Equipped with this knowledge, he proceeds to build up compositions with yard-measure and plumb-line, quite forgetting that no man can make a living body out of dead clay, unless he has first stolen some of the heavenly fire.'[26]

There was also a more straightforward cause. The quality of performance was bad and this could have been contagious. In 1877, Wagner left the Albert Hall rostrum in despair, after the orchestra broke down three times during the *Flying Dutchman Overture*. Poor quality is sometimes attributed to the procedure whereby deputies, often students, could be sent to orchestral rehearsals, provided that the orchestra member turned up for the performance; but, as Prokofiev observed, this procedure was adopted in Paris in the 1920s as well. Sometimes, the reason was very simple: on one occasion, the orchestra just stopped playing during Gounod's *Faust* at Her Majesty's Theatre, until paid in cash.*[27]

What about the Celtic Fringe where bards once occupied such an important position in daily life? It has been claimed that, in the Middle Ages, the Scottish Chapel Royal, which had close links with the Continent, was the 'rival of Rome'.[28] Eighteenth-century Edinburgh, like London, attracted foreign musicians.[29] Some might be tempted to attribute the lack of indigenous Celtic art music to the bagpipes: yet 18th-century French musicians showed how the equivalent, the Musette, could be used most artistically for delightful pastoral music. Ireland's sons emigrated: Field went to Russia; Stanford and Balfe** to England. It has been said that 'Wales is still waiting for its own great composer'.[31] But one would be wise to avoid the politics of devolution.

However, those among us who do not get beyond the first crotchet or quaver must approach these benighted doctors and their works with respect and humility. Besides, the British Isles were not a musical desert. The Three Choirs Festival at Gloucester, Worcester and Hereford was started in 1724. Music's history was written by Burney and Hawkins in the 18th century and Grove compiled his masterly *Dictionary* in the 19th. The Philharmonic Society, which had the charity and wisdom to send Beethoven £100 on his deathbed, was founded in 1813. The Royal

* A conductor of Beethoven's 'Pastoral' Symphony had dry peas rattled in a box during the storm sequence. This, on that occasion, may well have enhanced the quality.

** Michael Balfe composed 'Come into the Garden, Maud'. His 21 operas include *The Bohemian Girl*, which contains 'I dreamt that I dwelt in marble halls'.[30]

Academy of Music was founded in 1823. In 1859, Birmingham started its school of music. It has been estimated that 10,000 glees, that is part-songs suitable to be heard in mixed company, were composed between 1760 and 1830. The madrigal was central to the repertoire of the active mixed voice amateur choirs which blossomed in Victorian England. And, in the early 20th century, even impoverished miners and farmers 'learned songs together from tonic solfa,* singing in a circle around the fire', accompanied on a high rosewood piano.[33]

Yet, none of this provided an English equivalent of Brahms or Wagner. It is no wonder that it was thought that England had at last found a great musician in Sir Edward Elgar. One critic, looking back after 50 years, wrote of the occasion in 1908 when Elgar's A flat Symphony was first performed: 'I cannot hope, at this time of day, to describe the pride taken in Elgar by young English students of that far away epoch.'[34] But Elgar still fails to get much support outside Great Britain. He merits less than twenty lines in the memoirs of a world-class German conductor of the first part of the 20th century.[35] In France, where he is perceived as a 'late-born, elegiac and depressive offspring of Brahms',[36] the standard dictionary of music only devotes four lines to him. Between the beginning of 1965 and May 1999, Elgar featured in concerts broadcast in France 'only twenty-three times, an average of less than once a year and a phenomenally small number compared to the English musicians best known in France, Purcell and Britten'.[37] This, sadly, is the rather dismal background, as we turn now to the life of Elgar.

Elgar's Early Years

Elgar had the benefit of not having had the academic training of the kind condemned by Vaughan Williams. As a composer, he was a late developer. Over a period of only fifteen years, he produced his most memorable works: the 'Enigma' Variations, *The Dream of Gerontius*, the two symphonies, the Introduction and Allegro for Strings, the Violin Concerto, the Cello Concerto and *Falstaff*. He could write 'a damned fine popular tune':[38] 'the people simply rose and yelled' when Sir Henry Wood conducted the

* Tonic sol-fa is a method evolved in the 19th century by John Curwen for teaching sight-singing. The degrees of any major scale are given the syllables Doh, ray, me, fah, soh, lah, te, doh. It was widely used in the British empire and missions. Early in the 20th century, it was being used by Sioux Indians in South Dakota, and considered by experts as 'the natural way of learning music'.[32]

first London performance of the *Pomp and Circumstance Marches*.[39] However, as a Roman Catholic, and with no university degree to his name, he gave the Great and the Good a considerable problem.

He was only grudgingly accepted in his time. Comments such as 'there are parts of Gerontius's confession of faith which, though sincere, nevertheless suggest an atmosphere of artificial flowers'[40] and phrases like 'the heavy millstone of aristocratic fashionableness hanging round his neck'[41] can titillate us now. But it was no fun for him, loner, neurotic, dreamer and deeply sensitive man that he was. All this, together with his lower-middle-class origin, gave him an 'outsize chip on his shoulder'.[42] Subsequent generations have taken exception to his association with British imperialism, not something modern people seem proud about. Elgar's amalgam of Wagner, Tchaikovsky and Franck irritated and annoyed Benjamin Britten. Was Elgar too cautious when he put in a little frame on his desk the words of Mozart to his father: 'Passions whether violent or otherwise must never be expressed to disgust. Music, even in the most terrific situation, never gives offence to the ear, but ever delights it'?[43]

Edward Elgar was born on 2 June 1857, in a tiny redbrick cottage known as The Firs, at Broadheath, outside Worcester, the distinguished cathedral city located around 130 miles from London. The cottage looks towards the beautiful Malvern Hills, with their springs, the Holy Well with water of perfect purity and the Benedictine Abbey, dating from before the Norman Conquest. When he was very young, the family moved into Worcester, where Elgar's father, whose family came from Dover, was organist at St George's Roman Catholic Church and ran a music shop, Elgar Brothers, at No 10, High Street. His father had followed his mother and had become a Roman Catholic.[44]

Elgar's happy childhood with his brothers and sisters must have been severely disrupted when his younger brother died aged seven. Elgar was educated locally, at first at the primary school known as a 'dame' school, which the dictionary defines as 'a primary school of the kind formerly kept by old women'.[45] Edward described himself later as a 'dreamy child who used to be found in the reeds by the Severn side'.[46] He learnt the piano and the violin at an early age, and came across works of Bach. His father tuned the pianos for a country house clientele, whom he would visit on a thoroughbred horse. Young Edward used to roam around the parks while his father was inside the stately homes attending to the instruments. The widow of

William IV had been a client: Mr Elgar's stationery proudly proclaimed him as 'By Special Appointment to Her late Majesty Queen Adelaide'.[47] She had died several years before Edward was born.

Edward learnt German with a view to going to Leipzig to study, but the family could not afford to send him there. In 1872, Elgar was articled to a solicitor, who was in the congregation at St George's. At this time, Elgar's song, 'The Language of Flowers', and piano piece, 'Chantant', were composed. The legal job did not last long, and soon he was back, helping his father in the shop, and working locally. He taught the violin and played it in the orchestra at the Three Choirs Festival. He became conductor of the Worcester Glee Club, and played bassoon in a wind quintet, in which brother Frank played the oboe. He was appointed band instructor of the lunatic asylum at Powick, a mile or so south of Worcester.[48]

He studied diligently. He wrote part of a symphony bar by bar against the template of Mozart's G minor Symphony. After saving hard, he visited Paris, where he heard Saint-Saëns playing in La Madeleine, and went on to Leipzig for a couple of weeks.[49] He benefited also from the active concert life in England. August Manns, an immigrant from Poland, had introduced the works of Schubert and Schumann and many others at the concerts in the Crystal Palace at Sydenham.[*50]

To hear these concerts, Elgar commuted to London: he rose at six, walked a mile to the station, and took the seven o'clock train which steamed into Paddington at 11 am; then he took the underground to Victoria, and the train to Crystal Palace; after the concert, at around 5 pm, he rushed to Victoria and did the journey in reverse, reaching Worcester at around 10.30 pm.[51] This may be a routine not unfamiliar to a modern commuter, but it was less usual at a time when the radius of a lady's activities 'extended no further than the eight or ten miles which she could cover in a four-wheeled dogcart driven by the groom'.[52]

Elgar joined William Stockley's orchestra in Birmingham in 1882. Some of his own compositions were performed in Birmingham and Worcester. He was in the orchestra which Dvořák conducted at the Worcester Three Choirs Festival in 1884, which marked the 800th anniversary of the cathedral.

* Manns asked Sir George Grove to write the programme notes. Charles Hallé had founded his orchestra in Manchester in the year of Elgar's birth; from 1873, William Stockley ran a series of orchestral concerts in Birmingham, the location of the first performance of Mendelssohn's *Elijah*.

He seems to have fallen for the daughter of a Worcester shoe shop owner; but she went off to New Zealand.[53] In 1886, he started giving piano lessons to Miss Caroline Alice Roberts. She was descended from the founder of Sunday Schools, Robert Raikes; her father had been an Indian army Major General, Sir Henry Gee Roberts.[54] Elgar won £5 in a competition in which he set a song by her. She had already published a novel.[55]

Alice Roberts looked after her mother, Lady Roberts, until she died in 1887. To the consternation of her family, Alice and her music teacher then got engaged. He was an unknown, impecunious musician earning two guineas for a violin recital, and teaching at Worcester College for the Blind; his family were in trade; his health was thought to be poor. But worse, he was Roman Catholic. The Raikes relatives acted decisively: one aunt cut Alice out of her will and another stipulated that income paid to Alice for life should not pass to her children. In later years, this increased Elgar's sense of insecurity about money, because he realised that his daughter would inherit nothing from the 'awful aunts'.[56]

In fairness to the aunts, this was a time of rigid class distinction. Sir Siegfried Sassoon wrote of the period before the First World War: 'I was strictly forbidden to "associate" with the village boys. And even the sons of the neighbouring farmers were considered "unsuitable".'[57]

When Alice and Edward married in Brompton Oratory, she was aged 40 and he almost 32; thus began one of the few truly happy and supportive marriages of the composers given a chapter in this book. For a wedding present, the priest at Worcester gave them a copy of Cardinal Newman's poem, *The Dream of Gerontius*.[58] It was annotated with marks and underlinings copied from the book belonging to General Gordon, the imperial hero.* The Elgars honeymooned in a guesthouse in Ventnor on the Isle of Wight. Then they went to London.

* General 'Chinese' Gordon, who had crushed the Taiping rebellion in 1864, was sent to Khartoum to withdraw British troops from the Sudan. He decided instead to crush the rebels led by the Mahdi, but was besieged. He held out for 317 days; he was killed in January 1885, two days before the arrival of the expeditionary force sent to relieve him. This had been delayed through the vacillation of Gladstone, the Prime Minister. But Gordon had disobeyed orders by not evacuating; and he could have got away, had he wanted to. The Queen sent a telegram *en clair*: 'These news from Khartoum are frightful', she wrote, 'and to think that all this might have been prevented and many precious lives saved by earlier action is too frightful.'[59] Gordon was admired for his bravery and saintliness, a combination of qualities popular with imperialists.

A Struggle to Make a Career

Mr Edward Elgar, Violinist, taught music. References on his suitability could be obtained from the Countess of Radnor, Lady Alwyne Compton, Canon Claughton and Adolphe Pollitzer of the London Academy of Music, of whom Elgar described himself as 'pupil'.[60] He hawked his music around publishers. Schotts bought 'Salut d'Amour' for virtually nothing, and made a fortune from it.[61] From this work is perhaps derived Elgar's reputation for composing 'smart society music – the kind of production that seeks and finds its reward in the West End drawing-room, clever and shallow and artistically quite unpromising'.[62]

In 51 Avonmore Road, West Kensington, the Elgars were miserable: 'All day & today until two o'clock we have been in a sort of yellow darkness', he wrote. 'I groped my way to church this morning & returned in an hour's time a weird and blackened thing.'[63] Alice, pregnant with their daughter Carice, cried with the cold. Elgar suffered from an eye or throat complaint.

They fled back to Malvern. He returned to teaching, which he found 'like turning a grindstone with a dislocated shoulder'.*[65] He did the round of choral societies and played the violin in the Worcester Festival. He continued to travel to London to hear concerts, including some conducted by the Frenchman Charles Lamoureux, and by the German conductor Hans Richter, a protégé of Wagner and Mahler's predecessor in Vienna. This was the time when Elgar avoided being seen in the street with his violin case; he was depressed and insecure. But Alice, 'Braut', as he called her,[66] with her small private income and her determination, kept them going.[67] She ruled the bar lines on his manuscript paper to save him time.[68] She wrote poems for him. And they managed to get away for the occasional holiday in Sussex and in Germany, where a friend of Alice's took them.[69]

Alice sustained him throughout her life with him. We hear of 'Mrs Elgar, with her array of rugs, shawls and cushions, extra body-belts and knitted bed-socks for Edward's comfort'. On one occasion, seven hot-water bottles were filled for his bed 'on the occasion of Elgar's complaining of a slight chill'.[70]

It seems that she may have advised him that, in order to make his name, he should compose works for festivals: the Leeds, Birmingham and Three Choirs Festivals were the best platform for English composers. Worcester

* This may be compared with Puccini's comment that the classroom gave him claustrophobia.[64]

performed Elgar's *The Black Knight* in 1893 and *The Light of Life* in 1896. The *Musical Times* conceded that he was 'no wayside musician whom we can afford to pass and forget'.[71]

In 1896, Elgar wrote to Stanford, professor of music at Cambridge, to see whether one of his works could be performed by the Bach Choir. Stanford replied that the moment was financially inopportune; but Elgar need not be concerned at the slowness of societies to take up his works, because 'to succeed one needed a surname which ended in -vitch or -owski'.[72] We should forgive Stanford, who was perhaps busy with his opera *Shamus O'Brien* and his choral ballad *Phaudrig Crohoore*, or tied up sending invitations to foreign musicians on whom he wanted to bestow an honorary degree.

Success at Last

Elgar was commissioned by the Leeds Festival to write a cantata and wrote 'Caractacus'. He formed the Worcestershire Philharmonic with himself as conductor (see colour plate 46 for a portrait of Elgar around this time).

The turning point for Elgar came with Queen Victoria's diamond jubilee in 1897. In England, royal events can make a musician's career. The *Imperial March* and *The Banner of St George* made his name in London.

But it was with the success of the Variations on an Original Theme, the 'Enigma' Variations, first performed in June 1899, that Elgar finally reached the top. Each variation he called by the nickname of a friend: 'To my friends pictured within.' The first few bars of Variation XI were suggested by a bulldog falling down a steep bank into the River Wye. The dog belonged to Elgar's friend, G.W. Sinclair, the organist of Hereford Cathedral; the dog's name, Dan, is actually written on the score.[73] The first performance of the Variations was conducted by Hans Richter, who had moved from Vienna to Manchester where he was conductor of the Hallé Orchestra; he was also director of the triennial Birmingham Music Festival.[74]

Elgar added the word 'Enigma' to the autograph, in pencil, and it is by this name that the Variations are universally known. The significance of this, the secret of the Enigma, died with Elgar and the conundrum it created has occupied many and annoyed others, particularly critics who thought that they were kept in the dark.[75] Apart from Elgar, the only others who knew it are thought to be Alice and Arthur Jaeger, Elgar's excellent contact at the publisher Novello. Jaeger, an immigrant from Düsseldorf, appeared on the scene in 1897. He was a considerable source of inspiration and friendship for Elgar, perhaps because he also had a chippy view about the cathedral tradition and the Establishment dominated by the professors at the universities and academies, and the directors of music at the public schools.[76]

In 1899, the Elgars moved into a larger house at Craig Lea at Malvern Wells and during the summers they rented a cottage, Birchwood Lodge, in a lovely setting on the side of the Malvern Hills, among narrow, winding lanes. Elgar went cycling and would sometimes pedal around 50 miles a day, strenuous work in the hilly countryside around Worcester and Malvern.*[78] He had many interests: he would go with a lady-friend to watch Wolverhampton Wanderers playing football; he enjoyed kite-flying, beagling, fox-hunting and golf. He was a habitual doodler, and enjoyed drawing caricatures. He also did the crossword puzzle in the newspaper.

The Dream, the First Symphony and *Pomp and Circumstance*

The Sea Pictures and *The Dream of Gerontius* came after the 'Enigma' Variations. *The Dream* was written for the Birmingham Triennial Festival, whose organisers had asked for a work to follow *Caractacus*. The poem had been written many years earlier in 1865 by John Henry Newman, poet, and writer of 'Lead, kindly Light, amid the encircling gloom'. Newman was 'a dreamer whose secret spirit dwelt apart in delectable mountains, an artist whose subtle senses caught, like a shower in the sunshine, the impalpable rainbow of the immaterial world'.[79]

According to a recent biographer, Newman's poem is 'a flawless masterpiece. If he had written nothing else it earns him a place in the history of literature.'[80] Newman seems so different from his fellow Anglican convert and cardinal, Archbishop Manning, who, in Lytton Strachey's trenchant prose, 'displayed a superior faculty for gliding adroitly to the front rank'.[81] The modern biographer has put it more softly: 'Newman was a thinker of deep perception and a writer of genius; Manning, for all his gifts, was

* In the 1870s, there was a craze for roller skating, cycling and lawn tennis. About 1890, the bicycle, in spite of its clumsy and primitive form, its solid tyres and lack of gearing, was very popular. In London, people would drive in their carriages to Battersea Park where they would mount their bicycles, which had been taken there by the servants. Elgar indicated in red his cycling routes on the maps to be seen today in the museum at Broadheath. On the Continent, at the end of the century, Alma Mahler would go cycling in the mountains at Bad Ischl; her mother would accompany her in the buggy.[77]

neither.'[82] Besides, Newman could play the violin, whereas Manning was tone-deaf.

Elgar's *Dream* is very moving, although some find the intensity of the music almost oppressive.[83] When Elgar finished it, he wrote on it: 'Birchwood. In summer'. He quoted the Victorian *littérateur* and art critic, John Ruskin: 'This is the best of me; for the rest, I ate, and drank, and slept, loved and hated, like another: my life was as the vapour and is not; but this I saw and knew; this, if anything of mine, is worth your memory.'[84]

However, the Anglican Establishment was hardly enamoured of an oratorio using text written by Newman. Newman had rocked Oxford University and the Anglican Establishment earlier in the century when, returning to the ideals of the pre-Reformation church, he found himself drawn inexorably into the arms of the Roman Catholic church. Elgar wrote to Jaeger about his own work: 'Of course, it will frighten the Low Church party, but the poem must on no account be touched! ... Them as don't like it can be damned in their own way – not ours.'[85] Stanford, the Irish Protestant, (while confiding that he would have given his head to have written Part I of *The Dream*) said that 'it stinks of incense'.[86] The Bishop of Worcester, probably prompted by the Archbishop of Canterbury, tried to forbid its performance in his cathedral. Fortunately, once the bishop wrote to the dean, the dean had to take a contrary position, so its performance went ahead; however, the poem was de-romanised in certain places, for example, the word 'Masses' was replaced by 'Prayers'.*

The Dream of Gerontius is an example of how excellent literary work and music can be brought together. Nevertheless, the first performance on 3 October 1900, under Hans Richter, was a disaster.[87] There was a delay in producing the music for the choir. The rehearsals went badly, with everyone getting more agitated. In the performance, the chorus lost pitch and the soloists did not perform well. Elgar was very disappointed, and deeply wounded. But just over a year later, *The Dream* was performed at Düsseldorf with considerable success. Elgar's mother died in 1902 and within ten days he conducted *The Dream* at Worcester Three Choirs Festival. It did not reach London, however, until the Westminster Cathedral performance of 1903.

* Stanford's communication was to the composer and teacher Herbert Howells. For the relationship of bishops to deans, see the novels of Anthony Trollope, such as *The Warden* and *Barchester Towers*.

Of course, Alice went along to give him support. Jaeger wrote after the first full practice of *Gerontius* at Düsseldorf: 'As for dear Mrs E, you can imagine her state of seventh-heaven-beatitude, with eyebrow lifting, neck twisting, forget-me-not glances towards the invisible Heavens! Don't think I am making fun of her! I am not; but you know her signs of deep emotion over the Dr's music, don't you?'[88]

Reference has already been made to Elgar's First Symphony which, as England's first symphony, was received rapturously. There were nearly 100 performances of it in the first year. The Symphony actually dates from 1898 when Elgar had in mind a kind of 'Eroica' in honour of General Gordon.[89] Not everybody approved; the conductor Sir Thomas Beecham did not like it. It was 'neo Gothic, the equivalent of the towers of St Pancras Station', he said.[90] In the first years of the new century, Elgar also wrote the *Pomp and Circumstance Marches* and *Cockaigne: In London Town* and *The Apostles*.

The trio from the *First Pomp and Circumstance March* became 'Land of Hope and Glory'. Although those words were fitted later, the *Pomp and Circumstance Marches* coincided with the peak of British imperialism.* Neville Cardus, cricketer and critic, summed up this era before the First World War: 'It was high noon over the seven seas; not a cloud was to be seen on the clear sky of Britain's splendour ... the flag is unfurled, waving possession not belligerence; the trumpet and drum of satisfied conquest are alternated with the cathedral's thanksgiving for all the good things vouchsafed to His chosen people by the Lord. The terrace and the country house and the major-general and the gaitered bishop and the group of noble dames.' Cardus continued: 'So the pageant of Elgar's music passes: Oxford movement and Church militant, the trooping of the colour and evensong, children in Kensington Gardens and Phil May's cockneys; the ripening pippin in Gloucestershire, and the tumult of the Spithead review.'[91]

The First World War made 'Land of Hope and Glory' Elgar's most popular composition.[92] When the conductor of the Last Night of the Proms, Sir Malcolm Sargent, died almost 50 years afterwards, there was a considerable protest when the BBC tried to remove it and 'Rule Britannia' from the programme.[93] But, by then, the underlying sentiment had changed considerably. The protest probably represented an objection to a change in tradition rather than support for empire.

* Cecil Rhodes died in South Africa in March 1902, saying: 'So little done, so much to do.'

In 1900, Cambridge conferred an honorary doctorate on Elgar. Four years further on, he was knighted, which, as Carice, then aged 14, said to the parlour-maid, 'puts Mother back where she was before they married'.[94]

Despite his success, Elgar, ever insecure, was still concerned about his financial situation. In autumn 1900, he was talking of having to take up a trade, and, in 1904, he wrote to Jaeger saying that he was 'woefully short of money. I really think I must take some violin pupils again.' A week later: 'It's all very well to talk about doing all the things I want to do, but tell me what & who is going to keep a roof over our heads?'[95] For his honorary doctorate at Cambridge, colleagues organised a whip-round to pay the necessary £45 to acquire his robes. Not surprisingly, Elgar was jealous at the wealth and position achieved by authors and painters. Sir John Millais, painter of *Bubbles* and the *Little Princes in the Tower*, at the peak of his career, earned over £25,000 a year, a colossal sum at that time.[96]

Elgar's insecurity led to an intemperate streak in his character. When, in the 1920s, Queen Mary, so charmingly acquisitive,[97] was assembling her Doll's House,* Elgar was among the Great and the Good 'asked' to contribute. He responded angrily: 'We all know that the King and Queen are incapable of appreciating anything artistic; they have never asked for the full score of my Second Symphony to be added to the Library at Windsor. But as the crown of my career I am asked to contribute to – a Doll's House for the Queen! I've been a monkey-on-a-stick for you people long enough. Now I'm getting off the stick.' He asked the private secretary not to have the impertinence to press the matter on him any further: 'I consider it an insult for an artist to be asked to mix himself up in such nonsense.'[98] He was not alone, however: his friend, the Irishman, Bernard Shaw, also refused 'in a very rude manner'[99] to contribute to a 'library' for the Doll's House.

In response to a journalist's question about the best way for a professional musician to enjoy his summer holiday, Elgar said that 'the ordinary professor might study music, if not too violent a change'.[100] Not surprisingly, he fell out with Stanford, and they did not speak to each other for twenty years. In December 1904, Elgar received what Alice described as an 'odious' letter from Stanford.[101] It seems that this row was related to the

* This can be seen at Windsor Castle.

Birmingham professorship endowed specifically for Elgar by a rich industrialist. In a lecture, Elgar launched an attack against conductors, singers, critics and 'specifically, English music written since 1880 and the composers of Rhapsodies such as Stanford'. He said: 'Our art has no hold on the affections of the people and is held in no respect abroad.'[102] When he in turn was criticised for this, he became ill.[103] At Alice's suggestion, he stopped lecturing and merely took the chair while others gave the lecture.

The Reluctant Member of the Establishment

Sir Edward was now part of the very Establishment he derided so much. There was a three-day Elgar Festival in March 1904 at Covent Garden. He received further honorary degrees from many universities including Oxford and Yale. In 1911, he received the Order of Merit, and twenty years later a baronetcy. He became Master of the King's Musick on the death of Sir Walter Parratt in 1924. Elgar liked to regard the honours bestowed on him as a recognition for music as an art.[104]

Elgar enjoyed the company of the rich and cosmopolitan, the layer of society below the landed aristocracy. Although birth was still important in the new century, wealth and fashion went a long way towards compensating for lack of pedigree.[105] So Elgar made friends with patrons of the arts, many of them with German connections, such as the Speyers and the Schusters. The Speyers lived at Ridgehurst in Hertfordshire; Lady Speyer was a professional violinist. Frank Schuster, also a friend of Fauré,[106] was a homosexual who lived with his sister at 'The Hut' at Bray; he invited Elgar to join his party for a month's cruise in the Mediterranean in 1905.[107] Another friend was Alfred Rodewald, a Liverpool textile magnate, who owned a house at Betws-y-Coed in Wales, where Elgar wrote *The Apostles*.[108]

Elgar had some close, but presumably platonic, friendships with women, which Alice seems to have tolerated. There was Dora Penny, the lady he took to see Wolverhampton Wanderers. There was Millais' daughter, Lady Stuart-Wortley, wife of the Conservative MP for Sheffield. She became his musical confidante, and possibly is the soul enshrined in the Violin Concerto, which he composed in 1909–10.[109]

Elgar enjoyed horseracing. No doubt, despite his reservations about the Establishment, he shared the enthusiasm when King Edward's horse

Minoru won the 1909 Derby.* The king had won it twice as Prince of Wales, but 'that he should, as King of England, achieve the highest ambition of every sportsman, marks a red-letter day in the annals of the Turf'.[111]

In 1912, the Elgars moved to Severn House in Hampstead, which had belonged to the painter Edwin Long. Friends rallied round to help Elgar to furnish it. But when Sir Edgar Speyer sent him a cheque, the result of 'speculation in shares undertaken for Elgar',[112] he refused to accept it. Elgar painted the staircase and he and Alice both planted the bulbs in the garden. The house eventually proved to be beyond their means. Also, the fuel rations during the war were insufficient to heat it adequately. Besides, *The Apostles* and *The Kingdom* were not as successful or remunerative as *The Dream of Gerontius* had been. They are difficult, and they were costly to perform, because, for many years, Novello levied every performance.

In Severn House, Elgar did his carpentry and practised his chemistry experiments.[113] On display in the museum at Broadheath is a 'sulphuretted hydrogen machine' which Elgar invented. For this was a time of exciting advances in science: Wilbur Wright achieved a record flight of 40 miles in 1908, and Signor Marconi's wireless telegraphy spanned the ocean. Some attempts at progress were less successful. When, in 1912, the *Titanic* went down when trying to set a record for sailing the Atlantic, Elgar said: 'I have felt this terrible Titanic disaster acutely and I have been lonely.'[114] And then ten months after that, the news came through of the tragedy of the explorer Captain Scott who, having reached the South Pole, perished on the return journey.[115]

During the First World War, Elgar became a special constable and later joined the Hampstead Volunteer Reserve. It was a tricky time for some of his cosmopolitan friends. Speyer was attacked in the press for his alleged pro-German sympathies and even accused of signalling to German submarines from his Norfolk home.[116]

Elgar withdrew to Brinkwells, a tiny and isolated cottage on the edge of woods near Petworth in West Sussex. There, he wrote chamber music, works such as the Violin Sonata, the String Quartet, the Piano Quintet. There, he also started composing the Cello Concerto, which was first

* When he was made a baronet in 1931, the director of the Royal College of Music and professor of music at Oxford wrote to him: 'This is splendid news and the proper way to celebrate Derby Day. The money is put on the right horse, and it is a bad day for the bookies, Yours ever H P Allen.'[110]

performed in 1919. He could enjoy the wonderful view and he could fell trees and saw up wood, activities which gave him much pleasure.[117]

After Alice

Alice was aging and became unwell. Elgar was stunned when she died on 7 April 1920, aged 71. Thereafter, his 'last fourteen years are a long and slow diminuendo'. 'I am so desperately lonely', he wrote pathetically to one friend.[118]

The Cello Concerto was the last of his works to receive 'immediate and uninhibited public acclaim'.[119] Elgar was by now an anachronism. Looking around him, he must have felt it. Even before the First World War, ladies wore the narrow skirt and even V-necks. Gone were the high-necked bodices, the ferocious lacing and corseting; gone was the bustle of Edward and Alice's youth, which, by the mid-70s, stood out eighteen inches or even two feet, held by 'old wire fencing', as the satirical magazine *Punch* put it.[120]

Ways of life and attitudes had changed. Just before the turn of the century, the middle classes found that they sometimes had to queue for service, rather than be served immediately; a novel concept then.[121] The Bloomsbury Group started meeting in 1905.*[123] This was a world about as remote from Elgar's as one can imagine: 'Sex permeated our conversation', wrote Virginia Woolf, the novelist, 'We discussed copulation with the same excitement and openness that we discussed the nature of Good.'[124] Her sister Vanessa Bell had a lover, Duncan Grant, and Duncan Grant had a lover, David 'Bunny' Garnett. Both men were pacifists, exempted from service on condition that they work as farm labourers for the duration of the war.[125]

In music, there were considerable changes: Stravinsky's *The Firebird*, *Petrushka* and *The Rite of Spring* all preceded the First World War. As we have already seen, Diaghilev's ballet arrived in Paris in 1909 and caused a sensation among those solely familiar with ballerinas of the type painted by Degas.

Elgar moved to a London flat and frequented Brooks Club. In 1923, he went on the Booth Steamship Company's cruise 'A 1000 Miles up the Amazon'.[126] In that year, he also returned to his roots and took houses near

* One of the group was Lady Ottoline Morrell, chatelaine of Garsington, the location of the opera festival.[122]

Worcester and in Stratford. In 1929, he settled into his final home, Marl Bank in Worcester. At one stage, he was fortunate when the motorcar he was driving mounted the pavement in Bromsgrove High Street and crashed into Messrs Halford's shop.[127] Although he broke the downspout and the wooden frame, the car was only slightly damaged and he was able to proceed. The crash was reported in the newspapers. He seems to have been luckier than Prokofiev, who around the same time seriously damaged his hands when his car turned over.[128]

Elgar kept up his interest in horseracing, in his dogs, in the good life. He loved animals, especially dogs; he would telephone Worcestershire just to hear his dogs and, when at home, the dogs would sit beside his chair at mealtimes. He enjoyed listening to the gramophone: he pioneered recording his own music for His Master's Voice.[129] With Menuhin, in 1932, he recorded his Violin Concerto. In the last days of his life, he supervised, by post office circuit, a final recording session in London.[130]

He wrote a *Nursery Suite* in June 1931 for the daughters of the Duke and Duchess of York. In October 1933, Elgar was diagnosed with a malignant tumour pressing on his sciatic nerve. This gave him periods of intense pain. He was no longer a religious person and he refused to see a priest. He objected to the church's mumbo jumbo, he said. He died on 23 February 1934, and was buried beside Alice in Little Malvern.[131]

Vaughan Williams

That year, 1934, was a sad one for British music. Three months after Elgar died, Gustav Holst suffered 'an untimely death following an operation',[132] and, just over two weeks after that, Frederick Delius finally succumbed to the syphilis from which he had suffered for fourteen years. Holst is particularly remembered for *The Planets*, whose popularity has 'tended to obscure its utter originality'.[133] He was from Cheltenham, an Englishman despite his name. His career started as a trombonist.[134] He was for 30 years the director of music at St Paul's Girls' School, Hammersmith. He also directed music at Morley College for Working Men and Women, and was a professor of composition at the Royal College of Music.

Frederick Delius died, blind and paralysed, in France, where he had lived for the last 45 years. In the first years of the century, he had composed *A Village Romeo and Juliet*, *Brigg Fair* and a *Mass of Life*. He has been described as 'on the whole a water-colourist of music, not a filler of big canvases with oils',[135] a description which could have suited his friend and sponsor Edvard Grieg. 'There are no State Occasions in the music of Delius, no emotion that is not personal and intimate, no beauty that is not thin-spun and touched with the sense of brevity ... Even in *Brigg Fair*, for example, the flesh-and-blood jollity of countryside revels is left out.'[136]

Ralph Vaughan Williams, who now carried the British torch onwards, found Delius' music always reminded him of 'a curate improvising'.[137] He was born on 12 October 1872, and like Holst was a late developer.

Frederick Delius / Gustav Holst

Vaughan Williams was solidly English upper middle class in background. His father, who died when he was very young, was the vicar of Down Ampney, which is signposted on the Swindon–Cirencester road; his mother was a niece of Charles Darwin and the daughter of Josiah Wedgwood. The family moved to a house set in a 400-acre estate on the side of Leith Hill, just south of Dorking, Surrey. Wedgwood had acquired it when he resigned his partnership in the family pottery business. It is the highest point in south-east England, and enjoys exceptional panoramic views and colourful rhododendrons.[138] Ralph went to a preparatory school in Rottingdean and then to Charterhouse, the boys' public school near his home. When he left, he was over six feet tall, a large man in every sense.

Having written some works for the toy theatre and for his school concerts, Vaughan Williams went to the Royal College of Music, where Holst also studied, with a view to becoming a church musician. He then went to Cambridge where he met his first wife, Adeline Fisher. He studied with Parry and Stanford, and with Max Bruch in Berlin. Bruch is particularly known for the sensuous slow movement in his Violin Concerto in G minor.

Vaughan Williams then became organist of St Barnabas, South Lambeth and compiled the English Hymnal. He made a particular study of English folksong. This enabled him to invent his own tunes, which sounded just like folksongs, as in the orchestral piece, *In the Fen Country*.

Even though he became established as a figure in English music, Vaughan Williams was extremely self-critical. He became concerned that he was in a rut, and so, presumably to obtain a different perspective, he went to study with Ravel in Paris. To his consternation, Ravel looked at his music and said that he should write 'a little minuet in the style of Mozart'.[139] On his return, he wrote *On Wenlock Edge*, *A Sea Symphony* and the *Fantasia on a Theme by Thomas Tallis*, scored for two string orchestras and a string quartet. A *London Symphony* followed just before the First World War.

That war, as we have seen, changed everything. Holst, who until then had called himself Gustav von Holst, dropped the von. Vaughan Williams, who was by then aged 42, volunteered. He joined the Royal Army Medical Corps (RAMC) in France.

The author Sir Siegfried Sassoon has described this ghastly time. There was the last, desperately forced smile at Victoria Station as the soldier left for the front.[140] Then the trench, 'loathsome to live in as it is hateful to remember. The air was dank and musty.'[141] There was the mud; there were gas masks; there was pneumonia. 'The machine guns rattled out their mirthless laughter.'[142] The whiz-bangs were followed by the death of a friend:[143] at one moment, 'the chaplain's words were obliterated by the prolonged burst of machine-gun fire; when he had finished, a trench-mortar "canister" fell a few hundred yards away, spouting up the earth with a crash … A sack was lowered into a hole in the ground. The sack was Dick. I knew Death then.'[144]

Nobody can sufficiently describe the horror, the hearts 'going pit-a-pat', ducking from five in the morning until six in the evening with the only thing to keep the spirits up being 'an odd song and a smoke from a

Woodbine*'.[145] Stretcher-bearers were constantly being sniped at. One RAMC officer from Dublin, who was awarded a medal for gallantry,[146] wrote home: 'Thank God have got over nerves. Felt a bit jumpy before the flag fell, but now feel as if I am in the middle of a good hunting run ... I must admit I will be very glad when it is all over, as if one waits long enough one must be "kilt".'[147]

The war decimated the artistic intelligentsia, as it decimated everything else. Vaughan Williams wrote to Holst in August 1916: 'out of those seven who joined up together in August 1914, only three are left'.[148] George Butterworth, composer of the idyll, *The Banks of Green Willow*, and *A Shropshire Lad*, was killed in the Battle of the Somme; others killed were the poets Rupert Brooke and Wilfred Owen, whose poems Benjamin Britten would use for his *War Requiem*. Others were very lucky to survive: Arthur Bliss was twice wounded, gassed and mentioned in despatches.[149]

But people have to remain cheerful and retain a sense of humour in wartime. To avoid the censors and to let his wife know where he was, Vaughan Williams headed a postcard with a scale, beginning on D, but using just the white notes of the piano, and no sharps. This scale is called the 'Dorian mode'. From this, she could deduce that her husband was somewhere in Greece, of which Doria had been a district in ancient times.[150]

Vaughan Williams became Director of Music, First Army, BEF** France. By February 1919, he had founded nine choral societies, three music classes, an orchestra and a military band.[151]

Vaughan Williams' 'Pastoral' Symphony was a result of his wartime experience. It is a song of a soldier far from home, who thinks of a landscape he loves. As we have seen so many times, musicians have an extraordinary capacity for spite: Peter Warlock, the pen name of Philip Heseltine, saw in the 'Pastoral' Symphony just 'a cow looking over a gate'.[152]

The Royal College of Music gave the first performance of *Hugh the Drover*, the ballad opera which Vaughan Williams wrote before the First World War. *Riders to the Sea* was first performed in 1937. According to some, it ranks 'as one of the great masterpieces of English Opera'.[153] Works which are especially memorable include the *Fantasia on Greensleeves*, his setting of the Old Hundredth psalm tune, his songs, his hymns, and *The*

* An inexpensive cigarette.

** British Expeditionary Force.

Pilgrim's Progress. Vaughan Williams seems to have developed as the years went on. It has been suggested that only Verdi shows a similar rising graph of achievement over a long life.[154]

In 1935, he accepted the Order of Merit, but did not want any grand titles. He turned down the offer to be appointed Master of the King's Musick.

In his later years, he wrote a considerable amount of film music. He was 68 when he tackled his first film score, *The 49th Parallel*. 'It is extraordinary how, under the pressure of necessity, a dozen or so bars in the middle of a movement are discovered to be redundant, how a fortissimo climax really ought to be a pianissimo fade-out', he wrote. 'The truth is that within certain limits any music can be made to fit any situation.'[155] The *Sinfonia Antartica*, drawing from the music he wrote for the 1948 film *Scott of the Antarctic*, was his seventh symphony out of his total of nine.

Vaughan Williams lived at a smaller house in Dorking, near Leith Hill Place, which he handed over to the National Trust in 1945. In 1951, his wife Adeline died, aged 80. Two years later, he married a widow, Ursula Wood, and they lived in Hanover Terrace in Regent's Park. He died on 26 August 1958 in his 86th year.

Britten

Vaughan Williams spent much of his life teaching at the Royal College of Music. He was on the examining board when a young man from East Anglia submitted his entry for the annual composition scholarship in 1930. One member of the board reputedly asked what an English public schoolboy was doing 'writing music of this kind'.[156] Benjamin Britten, like Vaughan Williams, came from an upper-middle-class background, although one suspects that, in the early years of the 20th century, the Vaughan Williams family would have endeavoured to distinguish itself from the Brittens by pointing to its Wedgwood lineage and Church of England connections. Britten, born on 22 November 1913, was the son of a dentist in Lowestoft, on the East Anglian coast, some 120 miles from London. He was educated at Gresham's School, Holt, but his early musical talent was nurtured through having lessons, largely during holidays and weekends, from the composer Frank Bridge, whose reputation today largely rests on the skills which he taught to the young Benji.

Britten was somewhat frustrated by his three years at the Royal College of Music. On the one hand, he already knew most of what he was being taught. On the other, he seems to have felt constricted by the determination of his composition professor, John Ireland,* to provide him with a traditional academic grounding in composition in the style of Palestrina, counterpoint and fugue.

Britten was by now a very talented pianist and accompanist. After leaving the College, he returned to Lowestoft for two years, and then earned his living largely from editing film unit music. His first major work was *Our Hunting Fathers* in which he used words from the poet W.H. Auden, who also worked at the film unit. The first performance of this song-cycle at the 1936 Norwich Festival caused considerable surprise, both by its music and by its anti-blood-sport content.[158]

After his mother died in 1937, Britten used his inheritance to buy the Old Mill at Snape near Aldeburgh, a town on the sea to the south of Lowestoft. He lived there, to start with, with Lennox Berkeley, another composer.

Around 1936–7, Britten met Peter Pears, who was about three and a half years older than him. Pears would in due course share his life and provide so much inspiration. He would also perform many of Britten's operatic parts and songs, in his unique and unusual tenor voice with its 'clear, reedy almost instrumental quality'.[159] Pears was from a similar upper-middle-class background. The two men performed a recital together in aid of the Republican side in the Spanish Civil War.

With the approach of the Second World War, a planned visit to the USA developed into a longer stay. Britten and Pears set out in April 1939, and it was on the journey there, through Canada, that their relationship seems to have been consummated.** At first, they stayed with friends on Long Island. In the following year, they moved into a sort of commune where, among others, W.H. Auden and the painter Salvador Dalí resided. It was around this time that Britten wrote *Paul Bunyan*, and also discovered the poetry of George Crabbe, a poet from his home country of East Anglia.

Britten wanted to return home. But England was at war. Auden was criticised for avoiding the call-up, and Britten was also attacked in news-

* John Ireland described himself, unassumingly, as 'England's slowest and most laborious composer'.[157] He is possibly best known today for his lovely tune to the hymn, 'My song is love unknown'.

** Male homosexuality was illegal in England at this time. Britten's style and behaviour were discreet, in contrast, for example, to the overt homosexuality of Poulenc.

papers, including the *Musical Times*. There was talk of a boycott of his works.[160]

In March 1942, Britten and Pears sailed in a Swedish merchant ship which was part of a convoy from the USA to England. On board, Britten completed *A Ceremony of Carols*. When they disembarked, they registered as conscientious objectors. At first, Britten, like the conscientious objectors in the previous war, was destined to work in non-combatant essential activities, such as agriculture and firefighting. But this stipulation was withdrawn, and for much of the rest of the war, he and Pears toured giving recitals.

At the start of 1944, Britten began composing *Peter Grimes*, which was first staged to mark the reopening of Sadlers Wells Theatre. The story was set in East Anglia. The outsider, Grimes, was a character with whom Britten could identify. The work was 'welcomed as the first important opera' since Purcell's *Dido and Aeneas*.[161]

Peter Grimes also exudes Britten's sense of compassion and his concern for the young. Many of his works had the young in mind, *The Young Person's Guide to the Orchestra*, *The Little Sweep*, *Noye's Fludde*, for example. For Britten the adult, the paradise of childhood was irretrievably lost.[162]

Britten formed the English Opera Group. This led to the foundation, in June 1948, of the Festival at Aldeburgh, where he lived with Pears. Britten composed for the festival, performed at it, and undertook the demanding role of festival manager. His musical output was immense. Gustav Holst's daughter Imogen was there to assist him. Compositions poured forth, such as *The Rape of Lucretia*, *Albert Herring*, *Billy Budd*, *The Turn of the Screw*, *A Midsummer Night's Dream*. *Gloriana* was written to mark the queen's coronation in 1953. One of his most significant works was the *War Requiem* written for the consecration of the new Coventry Cathedral, replacing the one bombed in the Second World War.

Britten's strenuous work took a toll on his life. In the early 1970s, his health began to deteriorate noticeably. He had trouble raising his left hand to conduct, and found it hard to get up stairs. His doctors advised that he needed a heart-valve replacement, but he was determined first to finish composing *Death in Venice*. The operation in May 1972 was not a success. A stroke suffered in the operating theatre left his right hand partly paralysed, and he could no longer play the piano. He was not strong enough to undergo another operation. He continued composing but he continued to go downhill. He died in Peter Pears' arms on 4 December 1976.[163]

It takes us beyond the scope of this book to consider the lives of many other distinguished British composers. Maybe that is just as well. Das Land ohne Musik is today renowned for the success of its pop music. And who can say if composers such as Walton and Tippett, and the many others, will qualify to be regarded as Great Composers? As one eminent historian of English music has written: 'It will be for the historian of the future to determine what in their work is merely talented and what can be accounted evidence of genius.'[164]

Postlude

THE LIVES OF these great composers were so different as they strode upon the world's stage. Despite this diversity, their works, in their own very individual way, adhere to a principle applied around Purcell's time, that 'Music hath 2 ends, first to pleas the sence, … & secondly to move ye affections or excite passion'.[1] This rule, this advice, has arguably commanded less respect in recent years. By the middle of the 20th century, a distinguished critic could regret that 'today, the composer chooses to remove himself from the mass of reasonably intelligent listeners ... he would perish rather than write music easy to understand and remember'.[2]

To a younger generation, this type of remark can seem idiotic, like that of the Berlin music critic who having heard Schoenberg's *Pierrot Lunaire* in 1912, wrote: 'If that is the music of the future, then I have a prayer to my maker: please never make me endure another performance.'[3] We should be careful of taking too negative an attitude to 'modern' works. Prokofiev said: 'To write only according to the rules laid down by classical composers of the past means to be only a pupil and not a master. Such a composer is easily understood by his contemporaries but he has no chance of outliving his generation.'[4]

The notion, which now pervades all the arts and their production, that the true artist is 'above it all' and can be impervious to public opinion, is not new. It constitutes part of the scenery described by this book. It was expressed by the novelist George Sand, who figures so prominently in Chopin's life: 'The artist is an explorer', she said, 'who should be deterred by nothing and who commits neither good nor evil, walking to the right or the left: his aim sanctifies everything.'[5]

The opposite view, Massenet's simplistic dictum that 'the public likes it and we must always agree with the public',[6] is clearly equally misconceived, at least for those who aspire to immortality. Who now remembers those hits in Paris during the 1820s and 1830s, Daniel Auber's sensational *La Muette de Portici*, which triggered a revolution in Brussels,[7] or Giacomo Meyerbeer's even more successful *Robert Le Diable*? And the kind of music that 'the moronic blonds of the New Soviet Society could sing in unison in the fields' will never be regarded as great art.[8]

For the present, there surely has to be a halfway house. Was it encapsulated in those eight words of Benjamin Britten who said that composers should aim at 'pleasing people today as seriously as we can'?[9]

The public of the future will decide which composers, ancient and modern, are great. The public will be ruthless. We, after all, have rejected all but a few of the 16,558 symphonies known to have been written between 1720 and 1810. And we rightly reject some works by great composers: Beethoven's 'Battle' Symphony immediately comes to mind. Besides, 'every composer now and again lapses into formulae or mere habit, when inspiration burns feebly, the machine creaks and obtrudes – Wagner and his sequences; dotted crotchet and quaver and two-bar phrases in Elgar; the thrum-thrum of Sibelius' strings with the wood-wind and brass's sharp ejaculation in the background; major and minor modulations in Schubert; the block harmony of Schumann – they show the tricks of the trade overmuch at times, the greatest as well as the smallest'.[10]

Although individual works have not been examined here, one is bound to wonder what was, and is, the secret of the success of the great composers. Their compositions often seem to be uplifting, spiritual and timeless. Maybe the novelist Thomas Mann, who was so concerned with the role of the artist, came as close as anyone can to identifying the truly special ingredient when he wrote: 'For an intellectual product of any value to exert an immediate influence which shall also be deep and lasting, it must rest on an inner harmony, yes, an affinity, between the personal destiny of its author and that of his contemporaries in general.'[11] Mann's explanation may assist us to appreciate the value of the priceless inheritance which these great composers have bequeathed to us and, not least, it reminds us why the scenery behind them is indeed important.

NOTES

Preface

1 Walpole, *Anecdotes of Painting*, ch. 12, in *Oxford Dictionary of Quotations* (Oxford: Oxford University Press, 1979).
2 W. Blunt, *On the Wings of Song: a biography of Felix Mendelssohn*, (London: Hamish Hamilton, 1970). Blunt is quoting Alfred Bacharach, who is echoing E.C. Bentley.
3 S. Levas (trans. P.M. Young), *Sibelius: a personal portrait* (London: J.M. Dent, 1972), p. 80.
4 A. Einstein, *Music in the Romantic Era* (London: J.M. Dent, 1947), p. 13.
5 R. King, *Henry Purcell*, (London: Thames and Hudson, 1994), p. 42.
6 K. Bailey, *The Life of Webern* (Cambridge: Cambridge University Press, 1998), p. 186.
7 M. Bukofzer, *Music in the Baroque Era*, (London: J.M. Dent, 1947), pp. 219, 220.
8 B. Rees, *Camille Saint-Saëns, a life* (London: Chatto and Windus, 1999), p. 374.
9 M. Bukofzer, op. cit., p. 218.
10 R. King, op. cit., p. 234.
11 M. Proust, *In Search of Lost Time: Swann's Way*, trans. S. Moncrieff and T. Kilmartin, rev Enright (London: Chatto and Windus, 1992), p. 372.
12 M. Bukofzer, op. cit., p. 152.
13 H. Acton, *The Last Medici* (London: Macmillan, 1980).
14 *New Oxford Companion to Music* (ed. D. Arnold) (Oxford: Oxford University Press, 1983), p. 1092.
15 C. Harman, *Fanny Burney* (London: HarperCollins, 2000), p. xix.
16 Stendhal, *Life of Rossini*, trans. Richard N. Coe (London: Collins, 1956), p. 478.
17 F. Bowers, *The New Scriabin* (Exeter: David and Charles, 1974), p. 57.
18 Information from the Troldhaugen Museum.
19 D. Cairns, in Bloom (ed.) *Music in Paris in the Eighteen Thirties* (New York, NY: Pendragon Press, 1987), p. 95.
20 B. Walter, *Theme and Variations*, trans. J. Galston (London: Hamish Hamilton, 1947), p. 297.
21 R. Okey, *The Habsburg Monarchy*, (London: Macmillan, 2001), p. 47.
22 Lady Mary Wortley Montagu, *The Letters of Lady Mary Wortley Montagu, ed. by her grandson Lord Wharncliffe* (London: Richard Bentley, 1837), vol. 3, p. 73 (letter of 23 July 1753).

Prelude

1 J.N. Forkel (1802, trans. 1820), quoted in H.T. David and A. Mendel, *The Bach Reader* (New York, NY: W.W. Norton and co., 1972; original edition 1945), p. 317.
2 *New Oxford Companion to Music* (ed. D. Arnold) (Oxford: Oxford University Press, 1983), p. 173.
3 E. Gombrich, *The Story of Art* (London: Phaidon Press, 1963), p. 341.
4 J. Addison, *Remarks on Several Parts of Italy in the Years 1701, 1702, 1703* (London, 1761), Preface.
5 Ibid.
6 M. Bukofzer, *Music in the Baroque Era* (London: J.M. Dent, 1947), p. 223.
7 *Oxford Companion*, op cit., p. 1413.
8 Pope Pius VII, quoted in H. Hearder, *Italy in the Age of Risorgimento 1790–1870* (London: Longman, 1983), p. 101.
9 National Gallery, Room 39.
10 J.G. Keysler, *Travels Through Germany, Bohemia, Hungary, Switzerland, Italy and Lorraine* (London: A. Linde and F. Field, 1756), vol. 3, pp. 254–5.
11 J. Addison, op. cit., p. 59.
12 *Oxford Companion*, op. cit., pp. 1704, 462.
13 M. Bukofzer, op. cit., p. 58.
14 *Oxford Companion*, op. cit., p. 1196; and *New Grove Dictionary of Music and Musicians* (ed. S. Sadie) (London: Macmillan, 1980), vol. 12, p. 1514 and vol. 1, p. 646.
15 *New Grove*, op. cit., vol. 15, p. 265.
16 Ibid., vol. 20, p. 36.
17 K. Heller (trans. D. Marinelli), *Antonio Vivaldi: The Red Priest of Venice* (Portland, OR: Amadeus Press, 1991), p. 97.
18 Ibid., p. 29.
19 J. Addison, op. cit., p. 62.
20 Shakespeare, *Othello*, Act 1 Scene 3 and Act 2 Scene 1.
21 *Encyclopaedia Britannica*, ninth edition, 1875–89.
22 E. Crankshaw, *Maria Theresa* (London: Longman, 1969), p. 122.

23 Ibid., p. 121.
24 C. Ingrao, *The Habsburg Monarchy 1618–1815* (Cambridge: Cambridge University Press, 1994), p. 15.
25 C. Pick, *Embassy to Constantinople (Lady Mary Wortley Montagu)* (London: Century, 1988), p. 80; and D. Beales, *Joseph II: In the Shadow of Maria Theresa 1741–1780* (Cambridge: Cambridge University Press, 1987), p. 23.
26 K. Heller, op. cit., p. 54.
27 N. Stone, 'The Last Sultans', *Times Literary Supplement*, 8 December 2000.
28 *Encyclopaedia Britannica*, ninth edition, op. cit., vol. 5, p. 121.
29 J. Addison, op. cit., p. 65.
30 J.G. Keysler, op. cit., vol. 2, p. 8.
31 Ibid., pp. 328, 317.
32 Ibid., p. 311.
33 Ibid., p. 27.
34 Ibid., p. 32.
35 *Encyclopaedia Britannica*, ninth edition, op. cit.
36 H. Acton, *The Last Medici* (London: Macmillan, 1980), p. 46.
37 M. Brion (trans. G. and H. Cremonesi), *The Medici* (London: Elek, 1969), p. 203.
38 Ibid.
39 H. Acton, op. cit., p. 160.
40 Ibid., p. 259.
41 J. Addison, op. cit., p. 123.
42 Ibid.
43 J.G. Keysler, op. cit., p. 371.
44 J. Addison, op. cit., p. 124.
45 Ibid., p. 250.
46 Ibid., p. 112.
47 Ibid., p. 113.
48 Ibid.
49 C.V. Wedgwood, *The Thirty Years War* (London: Jonathan Cape, 1938), p. 34.
50 Ibid.
51 R. Okey, *The Habsburg Monarchy* (London: Macmillan, 2001), p. 8.
52 C. Schorske, *Fin-de-Siècle Vienna* (New York, NY: Vintage Books, 1980), p. 146.
53 *Encyclopaedia Britannica*, ninth edition, op. cit.
54 C. Ingrao, op. cit., p. 38.
55 G. Parker, *The Thirty Years War* (London: Routledge, 1984), pp. 244–5.
56 C.V. Wedgwood, op. cit., p. 120.
57 A. Fraser, *Cromwell Our Chief of Men* (London: Weidenfeld and Nicolson, 1973), pp. 346, 338.
58 C.V. Wedgwood, op. cit., pp. 291, 350, 410.
59 Ibid., p. 479.
60 P. Young, in *Of German Music: A Symposium* (London: Oswald Wolff Publishers, 1976), p. 23.
61 C.V. Wedgwood, op. cit., p. 59.
62 M. Bukofzer, op. cit., p. 103.
63 Ibid., p. 97.
64 J.G. Keysler, op. cit., vol. 4, p. 28.
65 M. Bukofzer, op. cit., pp. 10–12, 222.
66 Ibid., p. 20.
67 R. Holmes, *Darker Reflections* (London: HarperCollins, 1998), p. 361.
68 P.H. Lang, *Music in Western Civilisation* (London: J.M. Dent, 1963), p. 440.
69 *Oxford Companion*, op. cit., p. 306.
70 M. Bukofzer, op. cit., p. 368.
71 Ibid., p. 167; and *Oxford Companion*, op. cit., p. 1770.
72 K. Heller, op. cit., p. 74.
73 Ibid., p. 279.
74 J. Harding, *Saint-Saëns and his Circle* (London: Chapman and Hall, 1965), p. 101.
75 M. Kennedy, *Richard Strauss: Man Musician, Enigma* (Cambridge: Cambridge University Press, 1999), p. 128.
76 Information from *The Travel Diaries of William Beckford of Fonthill*, quoted in D. Libby, in N. Zaslaw (ed.), *The Classical Era* (London: Macmillan, 1989), pp. 24, 34.
77 K. Heller, op. cit., p. 33.
78 Ibid., p. 26.
79 Ibid., p. 34.
80 C. Vitali, in D. Burrows, *The Cambridge Companion to Handel* (Cambridge: Cambridge University Press, 1997), p. 37.
81 K. Heller, op. cit., p. 269.
82 D. Libby, in N. Zaslaw, op. cit., p. 45.
83 M. Bukofzer, op. cit., p. 395.
84 K. Heller, op. cit., p. 124.
85 A. Einstein (trans. E. Blom), *Gluck* (London: J.M. Dent, 1964), pp. 12–13.
86 Addison, quoted in W. Thompson, *Handel* (London: Omnibus Press, 1994), p. 44.
87 P.H. Lang, op. cit., p. 449.
88 J. Keysler, op. cit., vol. 3, pp. 263–4.
89 P.H. Lang, op. cit., p. 449.
90 D. Burrows, *Handel* (Master Musicians) (Oxford: Oxford University Press, 1994), p. 223.

91 A. Heriot, *The Castrati in Opera* (London: Secker and Warburg, 1956), p. 14.
92 M. Bukofzer, op. cit., p. 373.
93 P. Giles, *The History and Techniques of the Counter Tenor* (Aldershot: Scolar Press, 1994), p. 393.
94 P. Barbier, *The World of the Castrati* (London: Souvenir Press, 1989), p. 11.
95 P. Giles, op. cit., pp. 391, 392; and A. Milner, 'The Sacred Capons', *Musical Times*, vol. 114, 1973, p. 250.
96 M. Bukofzer, op. cit., p. 398.
97 1 Corinthians Chapter 14: 34.
98 T. Beeson, *Window on Westminster* (London: SCM Press, 1998), p. 198.
99 Deuteronomy Chapter 23: 1.
100 P. Giles, op. cit., p. 392.
101 R. Halliwell, *The Mozart Family: Four Lives in a Social Context* (Oxford: Clarendon Press, 1998), p. 404.
102 *New Grove*, op. cit., vol. 3, p. 875.
103 A. Hedley, *Chopin* (London: J.M. Dent, 1947), p. 117.
104 P. H. Lang, op. cit., p. 1009.
105 Ibid., p. 459.
106 Shakespeare, *Macbeth,* Act 5, Scene 5, ll. 23–7.

Chapter 1

1 W. Thompson, *Handel* (London: Omnibus Press, 1994), p. 125.
2 E. Walker (revised J.A. Westrup), *A History of Music in England* (Oxford: Clarendon Press, 1952), p. 223.
3 Joseph Addison, quoted in P. H. Lang, *Music in Western Civilization* (London: J.M. Dent, 1963), p. 521.
4 M. Bukofzer, *Music in the Baroque Era* (London: J.M. Dent, 1947), p. 105.
5 J. Butt, in D. Burrows (ed.), *The Cambridge Companion to Handel* (Cambridge: Cambridge University Press, 1997), pp. 17–18.
6 D. Burrows, *Handel* (Master Musicians) (Oxford: Oxford University Press, 1994), p. 7.
7 D. Blackbourn, *Germany 1780–1918* (London: HarperCollins, 1997), p. 20.
8 *Encyclopaedia Britannica*, ninth edition, 1875–89, vol. 11, p. 395.
9 J. Butt, in D. Burrows, 1997, op. cit., p. 22.
10 W. Thompson, op. cit., p. 29.
11 M. Bukofzer, op. cit., p. 308.
12 *New Grove Dictionary of Music and Musicians* (ed. S. Sadie) (London: Macmillan, 1980) vol. 8, p. 63.
13 Information from permanent exhibition at the Museum für Hamburgische Geschichte, room 230.
14 I. Keys, *Johannes Brahms* (London: Christopher Helm, 1989), p. 90.
15 D. Burrows, 1994, op. cit., p. 16.
16 M. Bukofzer, op. cit., p. 87.
17 H. Acton, *The Last Medici*, (London: Macmillan, 1980), p. 209.
18 *New Grove*, op. cit., vol. 11, p. 832; and *New Oxford Companion to Music* (ed. D. Arnold) (Oxford: Oxford University Press, 1983), p. 1813; and P. H. Lang, op. cit., p. 508.
19 *New Grove*, op. cit.
20 M. Bukofzer, op. cit., p. 318.
21 Ibid., p. 321.
22 D. Burrows, 1994, op. cit., p. 34.
23 *Encyclopaedia Britannica*, ninth edition, vol. 10, p. 772 and vol. 6, p. 577.
24 C. Vitali, in D. Burrows, 1997, op. cit., p. 28.
25 A. Hicks, 'Fantasia on a Theme', *Times Literary Supplement*, 31 May 2002; and C. Vitali, in D. Burrows, 1997, op. cit., pp. 30–31.
26 *New Grove*, op. cit., vol. 8, p 86.
27 *Oxford Companion*, op. cit., p. 354.
28 *Encyclopaedia Britannica*, ninth edition, op. cit., vol. 24, p. 689.
29 M.S. Anderson, *Europe in the Eighteenth Century 1713–83* (London: Longman, 1961), p. 72.
30 G. Rudé, *Revolutionary Europe 1783–1815* (London: Fontana, 1964), p. 9.
31 V. Glendinning, *Jonathan Swift* (London: Hutchinson, 1998), p. 245.
32 B. Weinreb and C. Hibbert, *London Encyclopaedia* (London: Macmillan, 1993), p. 642.
33 J. Ellis, 'Women in Augustan England', *History Today*, vol. 45 (12), December 1995, pp. 20–26.
34 S. Richardson, *Pamela; or, virtue rewarded* (Oxford: Oxford University Press 2001; first published 1740), p. 262.
35 I. Gilmour, *Riot, Risings and Revolution* (London: Hutchinson, 1992), p. 42.
36 Ibid., p. 77.
37 Ibid., p. 155.
38 Ibid., pp. 153, 149, 150.
39 Ibid., p. 168.

40 Lord Macaulay, *History of England* (London: Longman, Green and co., 1880), vol. 4, p. 530.
41 M.S. Anderson, op. cit., p. 26.
42 C. Harman, *Fanny Burney* (London: HarperCollins, 2000), p. 28.
43 M. D. George, *London Life in the Eighteenth Century* (London: Kegan Paul, Trench, Trubner, 1925), pp. 32, 56.
44 Wroth, *London Pleasure Gardens of the Eighteenth Century* (London: Macmillan, 1896), pp. 294, 299.
45 Ibid., p. 293.
46 D. Johnstone, in D. Burrows, 1997, op. cit., p. 72.
47 *Englands Gazetteer*, 1751, quoted in Wroth, op. cit., p. 303.
48 Wroth, op. cit., p. 304.
49 C. Harman, op. cit., p. 60.
50 A. Ribeiro, *Dress and Morality* (London: Batsford, 1986), p. 106.
51 W. Weber, in D. Burrows, 1997, op. cit., p. 45.
52 J. Johnston, *The Lord Chamberlain's Blue Pencil* (London: Hodder and Stoughton, 1990), p. 23.
53 R. Mander and J. Mitchenson, *The Theatres of London* (London: Hart-Davis, 1961), p. 109.
54 Ibid., passim; and J. Roose-Evans, *London Theatres* (London: Phaidon, 1977). Information about the theatres differs: J. Milhous and R.D. Hume, in D. Burrows, 1997, op. cit., p. 55, state that Vanbrugh's was one of the two patent theatres.
55 D. Burrows, 1994, op. cit., p. 460, quoting W. Dean, 'A French view of Handel's operas', *Music and Letters*, 1974, p.172, quoting Fougeroux, a French traveller.
56 J. Milhous and R.D. Hume, in D. Burrows, 1997, op. cit., p. 56; and K. Vlaardingerbroek, 'A Dutch Music Lover in Italy and France 1723–4', *Music and Letters*, vol. 72, 1991, p. 547; and E. Walker, op. cit., p. 219.
57 *Evelina*, quoted in C. Harman, op. cit., p. 35.
58 E. Walker, op. cit., p. 219.
59 Ibid., p. 220.
60 G. Rudé, op. cit., p. 13.
61 V. Glendinning, op. cit., p. 110.
62 J. Milhous and R.D. Hume, in D. Burrows, 1997, op. cit., pp. 58–9.
63 M. Bukofzer, op. cit., p. 324.
64 R. Hayden, *Mrs Delany, her Life and her Flowers* (London: British Museum Publications, 1980), p. 28.
65 W. Weber, in D. Burrows, 1997, op. cit., p. 51.
66 I. Gilmour, op. cit., p. 69.
67 R. Hatton, *George I: Elector and King* (London: Thames and Hudson, 1978), p. 59.
68 R. Halsband, *The Life of Lady Mary Wortley Montagu* (Oxford: Clarendon Press, 1956), p. 20.
69 W. Thompson, op. cit., p. 77.
70 M. Bukofzer, op. cit., p. 333.
71 D. Burrows, 1994, op. cit., p. 103.
72 D. Burrows, 1994, op. cit., p. 59.
73 J. Milhous and R.D. Hume, in D. Burrows, 1997, op. cit., p. 58.
74 L. Lindgren, in D. Burrows, 1997, op. cit., p. 89.
75 *New Grove*, op. cit.
76 D. Burrows, 1994, op. cit., p. 113.
77 E. Walker, op. cit., p. 241.
78 D. Burrows, 1994, op. cit., p. 7.
79 E. Walker, op. cit., p. 218.
80 Ibid., p. 249.
81 C. Steven La Rue, in D. Burrows, 1997, op. cit., p. 115, quoting P. Nettl, *Forgotten Musicians* (New York: Greenwood Press, 1969), quoting J.J. Quantz.
82 *New Grove*, op. cit.
83 E. Walker, op. cit., p. 218.
84 D. Burrows, 1994, op. cit., p. 115.
85 D. Johnstone, in D. Wyn Jones (ed.), *Music in Eighteenth-Century Britain* (Aldershot: Ashgate Publishing, 2000), p. 261.
86 C. Harman, op. cit., p. 13.
87 W. Lawson, *The History of Banking* (London: R. Bentley, 1855), p. 489.
88 Ibid. p. 208.
89 Ibid. p. 209.
90 D. Burrows, 1994, op. cit., p. 460, quoting Fougeroux, as above.
91 M.D. George, op. cit., p. 83.
92 Brühl Exhibition Guide, 'The split in Heaven', 2000, item 263.
93 L. Stone, *The Family, Sex and Marriage* (London: Weidenfeld and Nicolson, 1977), p. 537.
94 C. Harman, op. cit., p. 10.
95 P. Olleson, in C. Bashford and L. Langley (eds) *Music and British Culture* (Oxford: Oxford University Press, 2000), p. 26.
96 L. Stone, op. cit., p. 378.
97 Ibid., p. 537.
98 M.D. George, op. cit., p. 53.
99 B. Weinreb and C. Hibbert, op. cit., p. 860; and W. H. Irving, *John Gay's London* (Cambridge, MA: Harvard University Press, 1928), p. 177; and R. Hayden, op. cit., pp. 121,122.

100 J. Riding et al., *Handel House Museum Companion* (London: The Handel House Trust, 2001), pp. 23–4.
101 R. Hayden, op. cit., p. 131.
102 B. Weinreb and C. Hibbert, op. cit., pp. 955, 642.
103 Information from the Geffrye Museum in London.
104 J. Hecht, *The Domestic Servant Class in the Eighteenth Century* (London: Routledge, 1956).
105 J. Stead, *Food and Cooking in Eighteenth Century Britain* (London: English Heritage, 1985), p. 21.
106 S. Richardson, op. cit., pp. 534, 535.
107 Quoted in notes to S. Richardson, op. cit., p. 369.
108 J. Stead, op. cit.
109 I. Brooke and J. Laver, *English Costumes in the Eighteenth Century* (London: A. and C. Black, 1931), pp. 12, 22; and N. Bradfield, *Historical Costumes of England* (Edinburgh: Harrap, 1970), pp. 113, 118.
110 R. Hayden, op. cit., p. 27.
111 A. Ribeiro, op. cit., p. 93.
112 Congreve's *The Way of the World* (1700), quoted in A. Ribeiro, op. cit., p. 93.
113 I. Brooke and J. Laver, op. cit., p. 38.
114 A. Ribeiro, op. cit., p. 100.
115 R. Hayden, op. cit., p. 125.
116 I. Brooke and J. Laver, op. cit., p. 18.
117 A. Ribeiro, op. cit., p. 106.
118 Ibid., p. 96; and I. Brooke and J. Laver, op. cit., pp. 26, 28.
119 S. Richardson, op. cit., p. 486.
120 R. Hayden, op. cit., p. 28.
121 W.H. Irving, op. cit., p. 165.
122 D. Johnstone, in D. Burrows, 1997, op. cit., p. 69; and E. Walker, op. cit., p. 222.
123 E. Walker, op. cit., p. 247.
124 D. Johnstone, in D. Burrows, 1997, op. cit., p. 69.
125 J. Caldwell, *The Oxford History of English Music* (Oxford: Oxford University Press, 1999), p. 12.
126 E. Walker, op. cit., p. 247.
127 There is a copy in Handel's birthplace museum in Halle.
128 T. Burke, *Travel in England from Pilgrim and Pack-Horse to Light Car and Plane* (London: Batsford, 1942), p. 57; and J. Plumb, *England in the Eighteenth Century* (Harmondsworth: Penguin, 1950), p. 27.
129 R. Halsband, op. cit., p. 178, quoting Lady Mary Wortley Montagu.
130 Dr C. Burney, *An Eighteenth-Century Musical Tour in France and Italy* (Oxford: Oxford University Press, 1959; first published 1771), p. 50.
131 W. Brockedon, *Illustrations of the Passes of the Alps* (London, 1838), vol. 1, p. 33.
132 J.G. Keysler, *Travels Through Germany, Bohemia, Hungary, Switzerland, Italy and Lorrain* (London: A. Linde and F. Field, 1756), vol. 1, p. 188.
133 T. Burke, op. cit., p. 340.
134 Dr C. Burney, 1959, op. cit.
135 W. Thompson, op. cit., p. 117.
136 C. Hibbert, *George III* (London: Viking, 1998), p. 10.
137 P. Langford, *A Polite and Commercial People* (Oxford: Guild Publishing, 1989), p. 35.
138 Hogarth, quoted in W. Gaunt, *The Great Century of British Painting: Hogarth to Turner* (London: Phaidon, 1971), p. 14.
139 J. Plumb, op. cit., p. 92.
140 M. Bukofzer, op. cit., p. 331.
141 J. Mainwaring, quoted in D. Burrows, 1994, op. cit., p. 195.
142 M. Bukofzer, op. cit., p 336.
143 Ibid., pp. 123, 124, 127; and *Oxford Companion*, op. cit., p. 1323; and A. Einstein, *Music in the Romantic Era* (London: J.M. Dent, 1947), p. 177; and J. Caldwell, op. cit., p. 108; and D. Burrows, 1994, op. cit., p. 5.
144 T. Burke, op. cit., p. 58.
145 *Oxford Dictionary of Quotations* (Oxford: Oxford University Press, 1979).
146 R. Hayden, op. cit., pp. 48, 62.
147 Ibid., p. 79.
148 Ibid., p. 48.
149 W. Thompson, op. cit., p. 150.
150 D. Burrows, 1994, op. cit., p. 272.
151 J. Caldwell, op. cit., p. 40.
152 D. Chandler (ed.), *A Guide to the Battlefields of Europe* (London: Evelyn, 1965), p. 164.
153 D. Burrows, 1994, op. cit., p. 286.
154 Quoted in F. Maclean, *Bonnie Prince Charlie* (London: Weidenfeld and Nicolson, 1988), p. 125.
155 F. Maclean, op. cit., p. 125.
156 Ibid., p. 128.
157 A. Einstein (trans. E. Blom), *Gluck* (Master Musicians) (London: J.M. Dent, 1964), p. 23.
158 Ibid., pp. 25, 26.
159 *New Grove*, op. cit., vol. 7, p. 456.
160 F. Maclean, op. cit., p. 289.

161 J. Prebble, *Culloden* (London: Secker and Warburg, 1961), p. 278.
162 F. Maclean, op. cit., p. 291.
163 D. Burrows, 1994, op. cit., p. 292.
164 J. Milhous and R.D. Hume, in D. Burrows, 1997, op. cit., pp. 62, 58.
165 W. Thompson, op. cit., p. 165.
166 A contemporary report on Tunbridge, quoted in P. Langford, op. cit., p. 102.
167 B. Weinreb and C. Hibbert, op. cit., p. 287.
168 M.D. George, op. cit., p. 43.
169 W. Thompson, op. cit., p. 9.
170 D. Burrows, 1994, op. cit., p. 360.
171 Ibid., p. 349.
172 D. Burrows, 1994, op. cit., p. 349.
173 Ibid., p. 359.
174 C. Tomalin, *Samuel Pepys* (London: Penguin, 2002), p. 64.
175 C. Harman, op. cit., p. 307.
176 D. Burrows, 1994, op. cit., p. 363
177 D. Johnstone, in D. Burrows, 1997, op. cit., pp. 72, 73.
178 W. Thompson, op. cit., p. 8.
179 Ibid., p. 12.

CHAPTER 2

1 C. Wolff, *Johann Sebastian Bach* (Oxford: Oxford University Press, 2000), p. 23.
2 P.H. Lang, *Music in Western Civilisation* (London: J.M. Dent), p. 526.
3 E. Devrient, in W. Blunt, *On Wings of Song: a biography of Felix Mendelssohn* (London: Hamish Hamilton, 1974), p. 52.
4 J.J. Quantz, in A. Einstein *Music in the Romantic Era* (London: J.M. Dent, 1947), p. 48.
5 R. Orledge, *Gabriel Fauré* (London: Eulenberg, 1979), p. 231.
6 G. Jacob, in G. Dyson (ed.), *Musicianship for Students* (London: Novello, 1940).
7 A. Einstein, 1947, op. cit., p. 339.
8 F. Lesure (ed.) and R. Nichols (trans.), *Debussy: Selected Letters* (London: Faber and Faber, 1987), p. 323.
9 P.H. Lang, op. cit., p. 492.
10 Ibid., p. 512; and M. Bukofzer, *Music in the Baroque Era* (London: J.M. Dent, 1947), p. 260.
11 O. Chadwick, *The Reformation* (London: Pelican, 1964), p. 57.
12 G. Reese, *Music in the Middle Ages* (London: J.M. Dent, 1968; original edition 1940), p. 233.
13 D. Maland, *Europe in the Seventeenth Century* (London: Macmillan, 1966), p. 7.
14 *New Oxford Companion to Music* (ed. D. Arnold) (Oxford: Oxford University Press, 1983), p. 1553.
15 *New Grove Dictionary of Music and Musicians* (ed. S. Sadie) (London: Macmillan, 1980), vol. 14, p. 46.
16 M.S. Anderson, *Europe in the Eighteenth Century 1713–83* (London: Longman, 1961), pp. 83, 85.
17 C.V. Wedgwood, *The Thirty Years War* (London: Jonathan Cape, 1938), p. 475.
18 *Oxford Dictionary of Quotations* (Oxford: Oxford University Press, 1979).
19 Novello Edition (Organ Works Bk 15).
20 C. Wolff, op. cit., p. 26.
21 P. Langford, *A Polite and Commercial People* (Oxford: Guild Publishing, 1989), p. 91.
22 D. Blackbourn, *Germany 1780–1918* (London: HarperCollins, 1997), p. 2.
23 K. van Winkle Keller, in D. Nicholls, *The Cambridge History of American Music* (Cambridge: Cambridge University Press, 1998), pp. 53, 56.
24 C. Sanford Terry, *Bach: a biography* (Oxford: Oxford University Press, 1928), p. 26.
25 The author visited Harz in March 2000 and 2001.
26 C. Wolff, op. cit., p.56.
27 R. Hatton, *George I: Elector and King* (London: Thames and Hudson, 1978), pp. 55–9.
28 C. Sanford Terry, op. cit., p. 49.
29 C. Wolff, op. cit., p. 66, 68.
30 Ibid., p. 78.
31 Information from the Arnstadt museum.
32 W. and T. Lewis, *Modern Organ Building* (London: William Reeves, 1939), p. 228.
33 H.T. David and A. Mendel, *The Bach Reader* (New York, NY: W.W. Norton and co., 1972; original edition 1945), p. 52.
34 C. Wolff, op. cit., p. 84–5.
35 C. Sanford Terry, op. cit., p. 69.
36 *Baedeker's Germany* (London: AA, 1993), p. 69.
37 H.T. David and A. Mendel, op. cit., p. 53.
38 Information found locally.
39 C. Wolff, op. cit., p. 540.
40 D. Blackbourn, op. cit., p. 2.
41 O. Chadwick, op. cit., p. 188, 189.
42 P.H. Lang, op. cit., p. 471; and M. Bukofzer, op. cit., p. 268.
43 M. Bukofzer, op. cit., pp. 79, 279.

44 P. H. Lang, op. cit., pp. 478, 470.
45 A. Bullock, *Hitler and Stalin: parallel lives* (London: HarperCollins, 1991), p. 95.
46 C. Sanford Terry, op. cit., p. 85.
47 C. Wolff, op. cit., p. 123.
48 *Encyclopaedia Britannica*, ninth edition, 1875–89, vol. 21, p. 353.
49 A. Fauchier-Magnan, *The Small German Courts in the Eighteenth Century* (London: Methuen, 1958), p. 24.
50 M.S. Anderson, op. cit., p. 284.
51 A. Fauchier-Magnan, op. cit., pp. 90, 24.
52 R. Halsband, *The Life of Mary Wortley Montagu* (Oxford: Clarendon Press, 1956), p. 73.
53 A. Fauchier-Magnan, op. cit., pp. 27, 32.
54 Ibid.
55 N. Boyle, *Goethe: the poet and the age* (Oxford: Oxford University Press, 1991), p. 238.
56 Ibid., pp. 233–40; and M.S. Anderson, op. cit., pp. 283, 284.
57 C. Wolff, op. cit., p. 175.
58 R. Friedenthal, *Goethe, his Life and Times* (London: Weidenfeld and Nicolson, 1963), p. 199.
59 C. Wolff, op. cit., p. 175.
60 R. Friedenthal, op. cit., p. 185.
61 C. Wolff, op. cit., p. 151.
62 Ibid., p. 170.
63 M. Boyd, *Bach* (Oxford: Oxford University Press, 2000), p. 120.
64 C. Sanford Terry, op. cit., p. 111.
65 Ibid.
66 J.N. Forkel (trans. A.C.F. Kollmann), 'On Johann Sebastian Bach's Life, Genius and Works', in H.T. David and A. Mendel, *The Bach Reader* (New York, NY: W.W. Norton and co., 1972; original edition 1945), p. 304.
67 C. Wolff, op. cit., p. 179.
68 Ibid., pp. 154, 165.
69 *New Grove*, op. cit.; and J. Warrack, *Carl Maria von Weber* (Cambridge: Cambridge University Press, 1976), p. 67; Weber, Baron M.M. von (trans. J. Palgrave Simpson), *Carl Maria von Weber* (London: Chapman and Hall, 1865), vol. 1, ch. 7.
70 D. Cairns, *Berlioz 1832–1869: Servitude and Greatness* (London: Allen Lane, 1999), p. 223.
71 E. White, *Stravinsky: The Composer and his Works* (London: Faber and Faber, 1979), p. 28.
72 B. Ivry, *Francis Poulenc* (London: Phaidon, 1996), p. 26.
73 H.T. David and A. Mendel, *The Bach Reader* (New York: W.W. Norton and co., 1972; original edition 1945), p. 75.
74 Information obtained locally in Cöthen.
75 M. Bukofzer, op. cit., p. 287.
76 C. Sanford Terry, op. cit., p. 135.
77 C. Wolff, op. cit., p. 211.
78 *New Grove*, op. cit., vol. 1, p. 793.
79 C. Wolff, op. cit., p. 219.
80 H.T. David and A. Mendel, op. cit., p. 82.
81 C. Wolff, op. cit., p. 136.
82 M. Bukofzer, op. cit., p. 114.
83 *New Grove*, op. cit.
84 G. Rudé, *Revolutionary Europe 1783–1815* (London: Fontana, 1964), p. 19.
85 O. Chadwick, op. cit., p. 55.
86 D. Blackbourn, op. cit., p. 7.
87 C. Wolff, op. cit., p. 239.
88 B.A. Brown, *Gluck and the French Theatre in Vienna* (Oxford: Clarendon Press, 1991), pp. 43–44.
89 H.T. David and A. Mendel, op. cit., p. 87.
90 Ibid., p. 88.
91 Ibid., p 90.
92 Ibid., p. 91.
93 Ibid., p. 92
94 Ibid., p. 94.
95 A. Einstein, op. cit., p. 25.
96 C. Wolff, op. cit., p. 394.
97 Lady Mary Wortley Montagu, *The Letters of Lady Mary Wortley Montagu, ed. by her grandson Lord Wharncliffe* (London: Richard Bentley, 1837), vol. 1, p. 309 (letter of 21 November 1716).
98 B.A. Brown, op. cit., p. 43.
99 T. Blanning, *Joseph II* (London: Longman, 1994), p. 32.
100 Lord Chesterfield, *Letters to his Son* (London: Folio Society, 1973; first published 1774), pp. 44, 54, 60.
101 J. Warrack, *Carl Maria von Weber* (Cambridge: Cambridge University Press, 1976), p. 181.
102 Ibid.
103 Brühl Exhibition Guide, 'The Split in Heaven', 2000, item 270.
104 N. Mitford, *Frederick the Great* (London: Hamish Hamilton, 1970), p. 33.
105 C. Duffy, *Frederick the Great: a military life* (London: Routledge and Kegan Paul, 1985), p. 6.
106 N. Mitford, op. cit., p. 66.

107 M. Boyd, op. cit., pp. 106, 104, 120, 121; and C. Sandford Terry, op. cit., p. 161.
108 H.T. David and A. Mendel, op. cit., p. 121.
109 For the structure of the Gymnasium, see J.-P. Richter (trans. R. Nichols), *Life of Quintus Fixlein* (Columbia, SC: Camden House, 1991).
110 M. Boyd, op. cit., p. 107.
111 C. Wolff, op. cit., p. 352.
122 David and Mendel, p. 335, quoting Forkel.
113 C. Wolff, op. cit., p. 365.
114 M. Bukofzer, op. cit., p. 406.
115 *Encyclopaedia Britannica*, fifteenth edition, 1974.
116 C. Wolff, op. cit., pp. 406, 408.
117 C. Sandford Terry, op. cit., p. 269; and C. Wolff, op. cit., p. 335; and H.T. David and A. Mendel, op. cit., p. 193.
118 C. Wolff, pp. 411, 412, 382, 383, 394, 395.
119 D. Blackbourn, op. cit., p. 2.
120 V. Glendinning, *Jonathan Swift* (London: Hutchinson, 1998), p. 222.
121 *New Grove*, op. cit., vol. 1, p. 877.
122 H.T. David and A. Mendel, op. cit., p. 98 et seq.
123 Ibid., p. 112.
124 Ibid., p. 113.
125 Ibid., p. 120.
126 Ibid., p. 123.
127 Ibid., p. 125.
128 C. Wolff, op. cit., pp. 349, 323.
129 C. Sandford Terry, op. cit., p. 221.
130 H.T. David and A. Mendel, op. cit., p. 137 et seq.
131 Ibid., p. 158.
132 C. Wolff, op. cit., pp. 392, 400, 401.
133 *New Grove*, op. cit., vol. 14, p. 600.
134 A. Einstein (trans. E. Blom), *Gluck* (Master Musicians) (London: J.M. Dent, 1964), p. 29.
135 P.H. Lang, op. cit., p. 494.
136 A. Einstein, 1964, op. cit., p. 29.
137 C. Wolff, op. cit., p. 379.
138 C. Sandford Terry, op. cit., p. 249.
139 N. Mitford, op. cit., p. 100.
140 C. Duffy, op. cit., p. 2.
141 R. Browning, *The War of the Austrian Succession* (Stroud: Alec Sutton, 1994), pp. 247, 249.
142 A. Bullock, op. cit., pp. 743, 955, 968.
143 Information from private communication with D. Maw.
144 C. Wolff, op. cit., p. 448.
145 H.T. David and A. Mendel, op. cit., p. 189.
146 Hiller, *Choir and Organ* vol. 14, no. 6, p. 19.
147 Comments from 1752, in A. Einstein, 1947, op. cit., p. 48.
148 The travel writer was J.G. Keysler, in *Travels Through Germany, Bohemia, Hungary, Switzerland, Italy and Lorrain* (London: A. Linde and F. Field, 1756), p. 48.
149 *New Grove*, op. cit., vol. 1, p. 803.

Chapter 3

1 M. Holdroyd, *Bernard Shaw* (London: Chatto and Windus, 1988), p. 241.
2 William Jones, in the *Treatise of Music* (1784), quoted in G. Pestelli (trans. E. Cross), *The Age of Mozart and Beethoven* (Cambridge: Cambridge University Press, 1984), p. 106.
3 G. Pestelli, op. cit., pp. 111, 112.
4 P.H. Lang, *Music in Western Civilisation* (London: J.M. Dent, 1963), p. 586; and *New Oxford Companion to Music* (ed. D. Arnold) (Oxford: Oxford University Press, 1983), p. 1780.
5 Information on Harrachs taken from the guidebook of Schlossmuseum Rohrau (Graf Harrach'sche Gemäldegalerie, 2000), p. 9.
6 K. Geiringer, *Haydn: A Creative Life in Music* (Berkeley, CA: University of California Press, revised. 1968); and R. Hughes, *Haydn* (Master Musicians) (London: J.M. Dent, 1978).
7 T. Blanning, *Joseph II* (London: Longman, 1994), p. 104.
8 R. Okey, *The Habsburg Monarchy* (London: Macmillan, 2001), p. 14; D. Beales, *Joseph II: Against the World 1780–1790* (Cambridge: Cambridge University Press, 2009), vol. 2. p. 249.
9 K. Geiringer, op. cit., pp. 7–10; and R. Hughes, op. cit., p. 4.
10 R. Okey, op. cit., p. 14.
11 C. Ingrao, *The Habsburg Monarchy 1618–1815* (Cambridge: Cambridge University Press, 1994), p. 147.
12 K. Geiringer, op. cit., p. 15.
13 D. Heartz, *Haydn, Mozart and the Viennese School 1740–80* (London: W.W. Norton, 1995), p. 13.
14 Ibid., p. 80.
15 B.A. Brown, in N. Zaslaw (ed.), *The Classical Era* (London: Macmillan, 1989), p. 108; and D. Heartz, op. cit., pp. 80–82; and *New Grove*

Dictionary of Music and Musicians (ed. S. Sadie) (London: Macmillan, 1980), vol. 15, p. 773, vol. 5, p. 747; and K. Geiringer, op. cit., p. 20.
16 D. Beales, *Joseph II, In the Shadow of Maria Theresa 1741–1780* (Cambridge: Cambridge University Press, 1987), p. 45.
17 Ibid., p. 36.
18 K. Geiringer, op. cit., p. 23.
19 The figures vary; the English traveller was J.G. Keysler (*Travels though Germany, Bohemia, Hungary, Switzerland, Italy and Lorrain* (London: A. Linde and F. Field, 1756), vol. 4, p. 11); however, C. Ingrao (op. cit., p. 124) suggests 80,000 people in 1,000 residential buildings.
20 H.C. Robbins Landon, *Mozart and Vienna* (London: Thames and Hudson, 1991), p. 55.
21 Lady Mary Wortley Montagu, *The Letters of Lady Mary Wortley Montagu, ed. by her grandson Lord Wharncliffe* (London: Richard Bentley, 1837), vol. 1, p. 273 (letter of 8 September 1716).
22 C. Ingrao, op. cit., p. 164.
23 J.G. Keysler, op. cit., vol. 4, p. 11.
24 C. Ingrao, op. cit., p. 134.
25 Ibid., p. 125.
26 Dr C. Burney (ed. P. Scholes), *An Eighteenth-Century Musical Tour in France and Italy* (Oxford: Oxford University Press, 1959), p. 72.
27 Ibid., p. 112; and E. Crankshaw, *Maria Theresa* (London: Longman, 1969), p. 148.
28 D. Beales, op. cit., p. 13.
29 C. Ingrao, op. cit., p. 125; and T. Blanning, op. cit., p. 28.
30 C. Pick, *Embassy to Constantinople (Lady Mary Wortley Montagu)* (London: Century, 1988), p. 63.
31 Lady Mary Wortley Montagu, op. cit., vol. 1, p. 286 (letter of 14 September 1716), and p. 293 (letter of 20 September 1716), and p. 323 (letter of 16 January 1717).
32 J.G. Keysler, op. cit., vol. 4, p. 29.
33 C. Ingrao, op. cit., pp. 149, 128.
34 Ibid., p. 128.
35 D. Beales, op. cit., pp. 17, 23, 25.
36 E. Crankshaw, op. cit., pp. 33, 30.
37 D. Blackbourn, *Germany 1780–1918* (London: HarperCollins, 1997), p. 3; and T. Blanning, op. cit., p. 29.
38 A. Wheatcroft, *The Habsburgs* (London: Viking, 1995), p. 219.
39 N. Mitford, *Frederick the Great* (London: Hamish Hamilton, 1970), p. 56.
40 Ibid., p. 155.
41 G. MacDonogh, *Frederick the Great* (London: Weidenfeld and Nicolson, 1999).
42 *Oxford Companion*, op. cit., p. 1423.
43 K. Geiringer, op. cit., p. 25.
44 P.H. Lang, op. cit., p. 616, quoting *Vienna Theatre Almanack*, 1794.
45 C. Ingrao, op. cit., p. 169.
46 B.A. Brown, *Gluck and the French Theatre in Vienna* (Oxford: Clarendon Press, 1991), p. 31.
47 Ibid., pp. 30, 31.
48 Ibid., p. 3.
49 D. Heartz, op. cit., p. 33; and B.A. Brown, op. cit., 1991, p. 106.
50 D. Heartz, op. cit., pp. 41, 45.
51 K. Geiringer, op. cit., p. 32.
52 Ibid., p. 4; and information from Haydn birthplace museum.
53 D. Heartz, op. cit., p. 60.
54 K. Geiringer, op. cit., p. 36; and *Oxford Companion*, op. cit., p. 1478; and P.H. Lang, op. cit., p. 626.
55 K. Geiringer, op. cit., p. 36.
56 D. Heartz, op. cit., pp. 49, 50, 47; and B.A. Brown, op. cit., 1991, p. 21.
57 K. Geiringer, op. cit., p. 36.
58 Morzin's palace is at Dolní Lukavice near Přeštice.
59 R. Okey, op. cit., p. 62.
60 B.A. Brown, op. cit., 1991, p. 82.
61 K. Geiringer, op. cit., pp. 38, 41, amended by author.
62 D. Beales, op. cit., p. 77.
63 L. Somfai, in N. Zaslaw, op. cit., p. 271.
64 Information from Eisenstadt Castle leaflet.
65 G. Rudé, *Revolutionary Europe 1783–1815* (London: Fontana, 1964), p. 16.
66 G. St Aubyn, *Queen Victoria, a Portrait* (London: Sinclair-Stevenson, 1991), p. 94.
67 E. Crankshaw, op. cit., p. 131; D. Beales, op. cit., vol. 2, p. 438.
68 L. Somfai, in N. Zaslaw, op. cit., p. 273.
69 *New Grove*, op. cit., vol. 8, p. 333.
70 K. Geiringer, op. cit., p. 56.
71 D. Beales, op. cit., p. 324; and B.A. Brown, op. cit., 1991, p. 15.
72 K. Geiringer, op. cit., p. 247. Although rare, the baryton can be seen in various museums, for example the Paris Musée de la Musique, the Berlin Musikinstrumenten Museum and (less obviously) the Moravian National Museum in Brno.
73 Ibid., p. 57.

74 N. Mitford, op. cit., p. 182.
75 K. Geiringer, op. cit., pp. 58, 41.
76 L. Somfai, in N. Zaslaw, op. cit., p. 286.
77 *New Grove*, op. cit., vol. 8, p. 339.
78 K. Geiringer, op. cit., p. 41.
79 There is a plaque on the church at Hainburg, dated 1756–7.
80 Information on Esterháza from the Hungarian National Tourism Service guidebook.
81 G. Pestelli, op. cit., pp. 101–5; and *Oxford Companion*, op. cit., p. 846.
82 E. Crankshaw, op. cit., pp. 135, 150.
83 C. Ingrao, op. cit., p. 182.
84 D. Beales, op. cit., p. 141; and R. Okey, op. cit., p. 31.
85 P.H. Lang, op. cit., p. 430.
86 C. Gowan, *France from the Regent to the Romantics* (Edinburgh: Harrap, 1961), p. 104.
87 P.H. Lang, op. cit., pp. 432–4, 440.
88 K. Clark, *The Romantic Rebellion* (London: John Murray, Sotheby Parke Bernet, 1975), p. 45.
89 C. Ingrao, op. cit., p. 197; and T. Blanning, op. cit., p. 58; D. Beales, op. cit., vol. 2, p. 662.
90 T. Blanning, op. cit., p. 61.
91 C. Ingrao, op. cit., p. 197; and T. Blanning, op. cit., p. 65.
92 T. Blanning, op. cit., p. 70; D. Beales, op. cit., vol. 2, p. 438.
93 T. Blanning, op. cit., p. 67.
94 D. Beales, op. cit., p. 236.
95 E. Crankshaw, op. cit., p. 310.
96 T. Blanning, op. cit., pp. 61, 80; D. Beales, op. cit., vol. 2, p. 116.
97 T. Blanning, op. cit., p. 59.
98 D. Beales, op. cit., pp. 242, 435.
99 For plough print, see D. Beales, op. cit., plate 14; and R. Okey, op. cit., p. 62.
100 C. Ingrao, op. cit., p. 199; D. Beales, op. cit., vol. 2, pp. 220, 230, 237, 603.
101 C. Ingrao, op. cit., p. 209.
102 D. Beales, op. cit., pp. 374, 78. For sexual misunderstanding, see also A. Mahler-Werfel (trans. A. Beaumont), *Diaries 1898–1902* (London: Faber and Faber, 1998), p. 324.
103 A. Einstein (trans. E. Blom), *Gluck* (London: J.M. Dent, 1964), p. 83.
104 *New Grove*, op. cit.
105 A. Einstein, op. cit., pp. 98, 99.
106 D. Beales, op. cit., p. 233.
107 *New Grove*, op. cit.
108 S. Williams, in R. Erickson (ed.), *Schubert's Vienna* (New Haven, CT: Yale University Press, 1997) p. 228; and D. Heartz, op. cit., pp. 41, 43.
109 G. Pestelli, op. cit., p. 114.
110 L. Somfai, in N. Zaslaw, op. cit., p. 286; and *New Grove*, op. cit., vol. 8, p. 338.
111 G. Pestelli, op. cit., p. 114, 116.
112 D. Beales, op. cit., pp. 340, 350.
113 See the concert bills for 1785 in the Mozart house, Vienna.
114 K. Geiringer, op. cit., p. 74.
115 D. Heartz, op. cit., p. 70.
116 K. Geiringer, op. cit., pp. 82, 95.
117 J. Girdham, *English Opera in Late Eighteenth Century London* (Oxford: Oxford University Press, 1997), p. 9.
118 J. Girdham, 'A Note on Stephen Storace and Michael Kelly', in *Music and Letters*, vol. 76, 1995, pp. 64–76 (p. 64).
119 B.A. Brown, op. cit., 1991, p. 10; and T. Scull, 'More Light on Haydn's English Widow', in *Music and Letters*, vol. 78, 1997, pp. 45–55 (p. 45).
120 *New Grove*, op. cit., vol. 1, p. 640; and D. Heartz, op. cit., p. 75.
121 K. Geiringer, op. cit., pp. 91, 85.
122 Ibid., p. 87.
123 P.H. Lang, op. cit., p. 721.
124 Ibid., p. 694.
125 J. Girdham, 1997, op. cit., p. 88 ff; and D. Saunders, *Authorship and Copyright* (London: Routledge, 1992), p. 130.
126 D. Saunders, op. cit., p. 126. The case about *La Sonnambula* was Boosey v. Purday.
127 The two cases were Millar v. Taylor 1769 and Donaldson v. Beckett 1774.
128 For copyright, see J. Sachs, 'Hummel and the Pirates: the Struggle for Musical Copyright', in *Musical Quarterly*, vol. 59, 1973, pp. 31–60 (p. 31); and B. Brown, op. cit., 1991, p. 40; and J. Girdham, 1997, op. cit., p. 88; and D. Heartz, op. cit., p. 70; and M. Bukofzer, *Music in the Baroque Era* (London: J.M. Dent, 1947), p. 410; and J. Samson, *Chopin* (Master Musicians) (Oxford: Oxford University Press, 1996), p. 89; and D. Saunders, op. cit., pp. 69, 70, 109, 107; and E. White, *Stravinsky, the Composer and his Works* (London: Faber and Faber, 1979), pp. 65, 125.
129 K. Geiringer, op. cit., p. 101.
130 *New Grove*, op. cit., vol. 8, p. 342.
131 C. Harman, *Fanny Burney* (London: HarperCollins, 2000), p. 24; and J. Girdham, 1997, op. cit., pp. 65, 67; and R. Porter, *English*

Society in the Eighteenth Century (London: Penguin, 1982), p. 13.
132 J. Plumb, *England in the Eighteenth Century* (Harmondsworth: Penguin, 1950), pp. 78, 100, 104.
133 K. Geiringer, op. cit., p. 105.
134 T. Smollett, *Travels Through France and Italy* (London: Folio Society, 1979; first published 1766), p. 21 (letter of 15 July 1763).
135 Ibid., pp. 18, 17, 16.
136 K. Geiringer, op. cit., pp. 105, 111.
137 W. Weber, in N. Zaslaw, op. cit., p. 312.
138 C. Harman, op. cit., pp. 22, 60.
139 J. Girdham, 1997, op. cit., p. 67; and W. Weber, in N. Zaslaw, op. cit., p. 310; and J. Caldwell, *The Oxford History of English Music* (Oxford: Oxford University Press, 1999), p. 124.
140 *New Grove*, op. cit., vol. 8, p. 344.
141 K. Geiringer, op. cit., p. 114.
142 C. Harman, op. cit., pp. 31, 108, 157.
143 Lord Macaulay (ed. H. Trevor-Roper), *Essays* (London: Fontana, 1965), p. 113.
144 *Encyclopaedia Britannica*, ninth edition, 1875–89.
145 J. Plumb, op. cit., p. 171.
146 The description of Old Sarum was by Lord John Russell. See W. Edwards, *Notes on British History* (London: Rivingtons, 1962).
147 Lord Macaulay, op. cit., p. 407.
148 I. Woodfield, in C. Bashford and L. Langley (eds), *Music and British Culture* (Oxford: Oxford University Press, 2000), pp. 1–16.
149 W. Weber, in N. Zaslaw, op. cit., p. 301.
150 C. Chinn, *Better Betting with a Decent Feller: Bookmaking, Betting and the British Working Class, 1750–1990* (London and New York: Harvester Wheatsheaf, 1991), p. 8.
151 R. Mander and J. Mitchenson, *The Theatres of London* (London: Hart-Davis, 1961), pp. 66, 110; and *New Grove*, op. cit.
152 J. Girdham, 1997, op. cit., p. 25
153 Ibid., p. 201.
154 L. Somfai, in N. Zaslaw, op. cit., p. 274.
155 N. Bradfield, *Historical Costumes of England* (Edinburgh: Harrap, 1970), p. 130; and I. Brooke and J. Laver, *English Costume in the Eighteenth Century* (London: A. and C. Black, 1931), pp. 74–86.
156 I. Gilmour, *Riot, Risings and Revolution* (London: Hutchinson, 1992), pp. 343, 372.
157 T. Scull, op. cit., p. 45.
158 K. van Winkle Keller, in D. Nicholls (ed.), *The Cambridge History of American Music* (Cambridge: Cambridge University Press, 1998), p. 65; and *New Grove*, op. cit., vol. 15, p. 6.
159 A. Einstein, *Music in the Romantic Era* (London: J.M. Dent, 1947), p. 40.
160 I. Evans, *A Short History of English Literature* (London: Penguin, 1963), p. 251; and *Encyclopaedia Britannica*, op. cit., vol. 15, p. 166.
161 D. Beales, op. cit., pp. 310, 311; B.A. Brown, op. cit., 1991, p. 48.
162 *New Grove*, op. cit., vol. 8, p. 347.
163 H. Hearder, *Italy in the Age of the Risorgimento 1790–1870* (London: Longman, 1983), p. 140.
164 *New Grove*, op. cit., vol. 4, p. 399.
165 R. Hattersley, *Nelson* (London: Weidenfeld and Nicolson, 1974), p. 74.
166 C. Hibbert, *Nelson, a Personal History* (London: Viking, 1994), pp. 214, 215.
167 K. Geiringer, op. cit., p. 204.
168 D. Matthews, *Beethoven* (Master Musicians) (London: Dent, 1985), p. 45.
169 K. Geiringer, op. cit., p. 198.
170 Ibid., p. 207.
171 Ibid., p. 399.
172 R. Hayden, *Mrs Delany: her Life and her Flowers* (London: British Museum Publications, 1980), p. 11.

Chapter 4

1 A. Mahler-Werfel (trans. A. Beaumont), *Diaries 1898–1902* (London: Faber and Faber, 1998), p. 204.
2 P.H. Lang, *Music in Western Civilisation* (London: J.M. Dent, 1963), p. 636.
3 E. Gombrich, *The Story of Art* (London: Phaidon, 1963), p. 315.
4 B. Walter (trans. J. Galston), *Theme and Variations* (London: Hamish Hamilton, 1947), p. 239.
5 P.H. Lang, op. cit., p. 659.
6 J.G. Keysler, *Travels Through Germany, Bohemia, Hungary, Switzerland, Italy and Lorrain* (London: A. Linde and F. Field, 1756), vol. 1, p. 50.
7 Ibid.
8 Information from the Mozart Museum, Salzburg.
9 D. Beales, *Joseph II: In the Shadow of Maria Theresa 1741–1780* (Cambridge: Cambridge University Press, 1987), p. 61; and C. Ingrao,

The Habsburg Monarchy 1618–1815 (Cambridge: Cambridge University Press, 1994), p. 136.
10 R. Halliwell, *The Mozart Family: Four Lives in a Social Context* (Oxford: Clarendon Press, 1998), pp. 473, 29.
11 *New Oxford Companion to Music* (ed. D. Arnold) (Oxford: Oxford University Press, 1983).
12 P.H. Lang, op. cit., p. 637.
13 R. Halliwell, op. cit., pp. 525, 256, 211, 248.
14 Ibid., p.446.
15 *New Grove Dictionary of Music and Musicians* (ed. S. Sadie) (London: Macmillan, 1980).
16 C. Harman, *Fanny Burney* (London: HarperCollins, 2000), pp. 22, 65.
17 Goethe in conversation with Eckermann, quoted in J. Harding, *Saint-Saëns and his Circle* (London: Chapman and Hall, 1965), p. 1.
18 For details of Mozart's early journeys, see I. and P. Zaluski, *Mozart's Europe: The Early Journeys* (Lewes: The Book Guild, 1993).
19 R. Halliwell, op. cit., p. 30.
20 Ibid., p. 36.
21 Lady Mary Wortley Montagu, *The Letters of Lady Mary Wortley Montagu, ed. by her grandson Lord Wharncliffe* (London: Richard Bentley, 1837), vol. 1, p. 273 (letter of 8 September 1716).
22 G. Pestelli (trans. E. Cross), *The Age of Mozart and Beethoven* (Cambridge: Cambridge University Press, 1984), p. 94.
23 E. Anderson (ed.), *The Letters of Mozart and his Family* (London: Macmillan, 1966), p. 5.
24 E. Crankshaw, *Maria Theresa* (London: Longman, 1969), p. 19.
25 D. Beales, op. cit., p. 66.
26 D. Heartz, *Haydn, Mozart and the Viennese School 1740–80* (London: W.W. Norton and co., 1995), p. 113.
27 H.C. Robbins Landon (ed.), *The Mozart Compendium: A Guide to Mozart's Life and Music* (London: Thames and Hudson, 1990), p. 167.
28 I. and P. Zaluski, op. cit.
29 Ibid., p. 31.
30 Ibid., p. 71.
31 N. Mitford, *Frederick the Great* (London: Hamish Hamilton, 1970), pp. 98, 151; and C. Ingrao, op. cit., p. 176.
32 A. Walker, *Franz Lizst: Volume 2, The Weimar Years* (London: Faber and Faber, 1989), p. 5.
33 I. and P. Zaluski, op. cit., p. 93.
34 E. Anderson, op. cit., p. 28.
35 I. and P. Zaluski, op. cit., p. 92.
36 A. Cobban, *A History of Modern France: Volume 1 1715–1799* (London: Pelican, 1957), p. 110.
37 T. Smollett, *Travels Through France and Italy* (London: The Folio Society, 1979), p. 53.
38 E. Anderson, op. cit., p. 34, amended by the author.
39 M.S. Anderson, *Europe in the Eighteenth Century 1713–83* (London: Longman, 1961), p. 83.
40 J. Mongrédien, in N. Zaslaw (ed.), *The Classical Era* (London: Macmillan, 1989), p. 66.
41 G. Pestelli, op. cit., p. 167.
42 I. and P. Zaluski, op. cit., p. 114.
43 A. Cobban, op. cit., p. 54.
44 G. Gooch, *Louis XV: The Monarchy in Decline* (London: Longman, 1956), p. 157.
45 Ibid., p. 121.
46 I. and P. Zaluski, op. cit., p. 108.
47 A. Cobban, op. cit., p. 54.
48 P.H. Lang, op. cit., p. 536.
49 R. Halliwell, op. cit., p. 76.
50 W.W. Wroth, *London Pleasure Gardens of the Eighteenth Century* (London: Macmillan, 1896), pp. 200, 206.
51 I. Woodfield, 'New Light on the Mozarts' London Visit', *Music and Letters*, 1995, p. 187; and W.W. Wroth, op. cit., pp. 200, 206.
52 C. Hibbert, *George III* (London: Viking, 1994), p. 48.
53 Ibid., p. 42.
54 Ibid., p. 97.
55 C. Harman, op. cit., p. 194.
56 Ibid., p. 199.
57 Joseph Yorke to his brother Lord Hardwicke in 1765, in W. Stafford, *Mozart's Death* (London: Macmillan, 1991), p. 79.
58 I. and P. Zaluski, op. cit., p. 163.
59 Dr Burney (ed. P. Scholes), *An Eighteenth-Century Musical Tour in France and Italy* (Oxford: Oxford University Press, 1959; first published 1770), p. 42.
60 D. Beales, op. cit., p. 88; and R. Halliwell, op. cit., p. 123.
61 B.A. Brown, *Gluck and the French Theatre in Vienna* (Oxford: Clarendon Press, 1991), p. 432.
62 D. Heartz, op. cit., p. 35; and B.A. Brown, op. cit., p. 432.
63 R. Spaethling, *Mozart's Letters, Mozart's Life* (London: Faber and Faber, 2000), pp. 41, 45.
64 Ibid., p. 5.
65 W. Brockedon, *Illustrations of the Passes of the Alps* (London, 1838), vol. 2, p. 53.

66 W. Stafford, op. cit., p. 145.
67 F. Carr, *Mozart and Constance* (London: John Murray, 1983), p. 6.
68 R. Spaethling, op. cit., p. 8.
69 J. Keysler, op. cit., vol. 2, p. 340.
70 M.S. Anderson, op. cit., p. 68.
71 M. Bukofzer, *Music in the Baroque Era* (London: J.M. Dent, 1947), p. 136.
72 The newspaper was *The London Times*.
73 B.A. Brown, op. cit., pp. 49, 52.
74 R. Halliwell, op. cit., pp. 167, 193, 172, 173, 136; and H.C. Robbins Landon, 1990, op. cit., p. 167; and R. Spaethling, op. cit., pp. 28, 35, 29, 43.
75 C. Eisen, in N. Zaslaw, op. cit., pp. 167, 177 and R. Halliwell, op. cit., pp. 177, 178.
76 D. Beales, op. cit., p. 369.
77 *Encyclopaedia Britannica*, ninth edition, 1875–89.
78 C. Eisen, in N. Zaslaw, op. cit., p. 179.
79 Ibid., p. 177; and R. Halliwell, op. cit., p. 514.
80 G. Pestelli, op. cit., p. 29.
81 R. Halliwell, op. cit., p. 244.
82 Ibid., pp. 177, 214, 224.
83 C. Eisen, in N. Zaslaw, op. cit., p. 179.
84 R. Halliwell, op. cit., pp. 190, 202, 473, 30, 250, 339.
85 The shooting target can be seen at the Mozart Museum.
86 G. Pestelli, op. cit., p. 141.
87 C. Eisen, in N. Zaslaw, op. cit., p. 182; and R. Halliwell, op. cit., pp. 196, 206, 211.
88 R. Halliwell, op. cit., p. 225.
89 E. Anderson, op. cit., p. 475.
90 A. Hanson, *Musical Life in Biedermeyer Vienna* (Cambridge: Cambridge University Press, 1985), p. 18.
91 R. Halliwell, op. cit., p. 241.
92 Ibid., pp. 247, 261, 267, 272, 268.
93 Ibid., p. 261; and R. Spaethling, op. cit., p. 109.
94 W. Stafford, op. cit., p. 92.
95 R. Halliwell, op. cit., pp. 471, 475.
96 J. Warrack, *Carl Maria von Weber* (Cambridge: Cambridge University Press, 1976), p. 26.
97 *New Grove*, op. cit.
98 C. Duffy, *Frederick the Great: A Military Life* (London: Routledge and Kegan Paul, 1985), pp. 263 ff, 272; and E. Crankshaw, op. cit., pp. 286 ff; and R. Halliwell, op. cit., pp. 279, 320; and D. Beales, op. cit., p. 386; and E. Anderson, op. cit., p. 470.
99 R. Halliwell, op. cit., p. 288.
100 Ibid., p. 283; and R. Spaethling, op. cit., p. 128.
101 A. Einstein (trans. E. Blom), *Gluck* (Master Musicians) (London: J.M. Dent, 1964), pp. 135, 138.
102 Ibid., p. 150.
103 E. Anderson, op. cit., p. 561.
104 Michael Kelly the singer, quoted in H.C. Robbins Landon, 1990, op. cit., p. 136.
105 R. Halliwell, op. cit., pp. 301, 316.
106 Ibid., p. 338.
107 F. Carr, op. cit., p. 32.
108 E. Anderson, op. cit., p. 1102.
109 P. Olleson, in C. Bashford and L. Langley (eds), *Music and British Culture* (Oxford: Oxford University Press, 2000), p. 30.
110 E Anderson, op. cit., p. 468, amended by the author.
111 J. Rice, in N. Zaslaw, op. cit., p. 126.
112 E. Anderson, op. cit., p. 739.
113 R. Halliwell, op. cit., p. 371.
114 B.A. Brown, op. cit., p. 64; and D. Beales, op. cit., pp. 232, 233.
115 I. Keys, *Mozart: His Music in his Life* (London: Elek, 1980), p. 143; D. Beales, op. cit., vol. 2, pp. 455–9, 579.
116 R. Spaethling, op. cit., p. 318.
117 Brühl Exhibition Guide, 'The Split in Heaven', 2000, pp. 271, 272.
118 T. Blanning, *Joseph II* (London: Longman, 1994), p. 80.
119 R. Halliwell, op. cit., p. 381; and D. Beales, op. cit., p. 444; and R. Okey, *The Habsburg Monarchy* (London: Macmillan, 2001), p. 34; and E. Anderson, op. cit., p. 736.
120 F. Carr, op. cit., p. 35.
121 E. Anderson, op. cit., p. 1166.
122 Ibid., p. 1197.
123 A. Hanson, op. cit., p. 18.
124 R. Halliwell, op. cit., p. 383; and F. Carr, op. cit., p. 35.
125 R. Spaethling, op. cit., p. 301.
126 A. Einstein, op. cit., p. 34.
127 F. Carr, op. cit., p. 47.
128 J.G. Keysler, op. cit., vol. 4, p. 26.
129 E. Anderson, op. cit., p. 933.
130 F. Carr, op. cit., pp. 97, 146.
131 R. Halliwell, op. cit., p. 389.
132 Ibid., pp. 365, 411 ff, 434, 543.
133 Ibid., p. 425.
134 C. Ingrao, op. cit., p. 217.

135 T. Blanning, op. cit., pp. 167, 170.
136 B.A. Brown, op. cit., p. 33.
137 W. Doyle, *The Oxford History of the French Revolution* (Oxford: Oxford University Press, 1989), p. 168.
138 O.E. Deutsch (trans. E. Blom, P. Branscombe and J. Noble), *Mozart: A Documentary Biography*, second edition (London: Black, 1966), p. 530.
139 H.C. Robbins Landon, *Mozart's Last Year* (London: Thames and Hudson, 1988), p. 61; and R. Halliwell, op. cit., pp. 501, 473, 476; and R. Spaethling, op. cit., p. 340.
140 H.C. Robbins Landon, 1988, op. cit., p. 61.
141 Information from Mozarthouse in Domgasse.
142 R. Halliwell, op. cit., pp. 477, 570; and R. Spaethling, op. cit., pp. 400, 412, 392; and D. Heartz, op. cit., p. 64; and H.C. Robbins Landon, 1988, op. cit., p. 57.
143 R. Halliwell, op. cit., pp. 556, 564, 575, 568.
144 Ibid., pp. 521, 527, 537; and R. Spaethling, op. cit., p. 327.
145 D. Beales, op. cit., vol. 2, pp. 474, 564.
146 G. Rudé, *Revolutionary Europe 1783–1815* (London: Fontana, 1964), p. 46.
147 C. Hogwood and J. Smaczny, in N. Zaslaw, op. cit., p. 188.
148 G. Pestelli, op. cit., p. 146.
149 R. Cowgill, in C. Bashford and L. Langley, op. cit., pp. 45, 46.
150 D. Beales, op. cit., vol. 2, p. 471.
151 Schikandeder, Preface to *Der Grandprofoss* (1787), quoted in K. Honolka (trans. J.M. Wilde), *Papageno: Emanuel Schikaneder in Mozart's Time* (Portland, OR: Amadeus Press, 1990).
152 S. Williams, in R. Erickson (ed.), *Schubert's Vienna* (New Haven, CT: Yale University Press, 1997), p. 218.
153 D. Beales, op. cit., vol. 2, pp. 587, 593, 596.
154 D. Beales, op. cit., vol. 2, p. 459.
155 T. Blanning, op. cit., p. 200; and R. Okey, op. cit., pp. 52, 54.
156 R. Spaethling, op. cit., pp. 412, 423.
157 H.C. Robbins Landon, 1988, op. cit., p. 76.
158 D. Beales, op. cit., vol. 2, p. 473.
159 Ibid., p. 149.
160 Ibid., pp. 142, 144.
161 R. Spaethling, op. cit., p. 442.
162 H.C. Robbins Landon, 1988, op. cit., p. 169.
163 W. Stafford, op. cit., p. 50; and F. Carr, op. cit., p. 141; D. Beales, op. cit., vol. 2, p. 325.
164 O.E. Deutsch, op. cit., p. 446.
165 R. Halliwell, op. cit., p. 572.
166 R. King, *Henry Purcell* (London: Thames and Hudson, 1994), p. 230.
167 H.C. Robbins Landon, 1988, op. cit., p. 193.
168 R. Halliwell, op. cit., p. 581.
169 Ibid., p. 599.
170 Ibid., pp. 620, 622; and H.C. Robbins Landon, 1988, op. cit., p. 152.
171 J. Reed, *Schubert* (Oxford: Oxford University Press, 1997; first edition 1987), p. 8; and G. Pestelli, op. cit.; and A. Walker, *Franz Lizst: Volume 1, The Virtuoso Years, 1811–47*, p. 74; and P.H. Lang, op. cit., p. 669.
172 D. Beales, op. cit., vol. 2, p. 473.
173 *New Grove*, op. cit.
174 Ibid.
175 F. Carr, op. cit., p. 113.
176 W. Stafford, op. cit., p. 9.
177 Brühl Exhibition Guide, op. cit., p. 362.
178 W. Stafford, op. cit., p. 268.
179 F. Carr, op. cit., p. 167.
180 R. Halliwell, op. cit., pp. xxiii, 614.
181 H.C. Robbins Landon, 1990, op. cit., p. 49.

Chapter 5

1 W. Blunt, *On Wings of Song: A Biography of Felix Mendelssohn* (London: Hamish Hamilton, 1974), p. 38.
2 R. Friedenthal, *Goethe: His Life and Times* (London: Weidenfeld and Nicolson, 1963), p. 412.
3 For royal protocol at the time see also C. Hibbert, *George III* (London: Viking, 1998), p. 204.
4 G. Pestelli (trans. E. Cross), *The Age of Mozart and Beethoven* (Cambridge: Cambridge University Press, 1984), pp. 167, 226.
5 I. Keys, *Mozart: His Music in his Life* (London: Elek, 1980), pp. 222, 143.
6 F. Routh, *Stravinsky* (Master Musicians) (London: J.M. Dent, 1975), pp. 34, 180; and E. White, *Stravinsky: The Composer and his Works* (London: Faber and Faber, 1979), p. 92.
7 J.W. von Goethe (trans. M. Hulse), *The Sorrows of Young Werther* (London: Penguin, 1989; first published 1774), p. 32.

8 *New Grove Dictionary of Music and Musicians* (ed. S. Sadie) (London: Macmillan, 1980).
9 B. Cooper, *Beethoven* (Master Musicians) (Oxford: Oxford University Press, 2000), p. 107.
10 P.H. Lang, *Music in Western Civilisation* (London: J.M. Dent, 1963), p. 752.
11 H. Weinstock, *Rossini: A Biography* (London: Oxford University Press, 1968), p. 122.
12 A. Einstein, *Music in the Romantic Era* (London: J.M. Dent, 1947), p. 91.
13 Brühl Exhibition Guide, 'The Split in Heaven', 2000, pp. 140, 150, 243, 270.
14 D. Blackbourn, *Germany 1780–1918* (London: HarperCollins, 1997), pp. 50, 327.
15 D. Matthews, *Beethoven* (Master Musicians) (London: J.M. Dent, 1985), p. 6.
16 Information from model of Bonn in Bonn City Museum.
17 *New Grove*, op. cit.
18 D. Matthews, op. cit., p. 7.
19 T. Blanning, *Joseph II* (London: Longman, 1994), p. 148.
20 B. Cooper, op. cit., p. 27.
21 D. Matthews, op. cit., p. 13.
22 G.R. Marek, *Beethoven: Biography of a Genius* (London: William Kimber, 1970), p. 99.
23 D. Matthews, op. cit., p. 11; and G. Pestelli, op. cit., p. 222.
24 *Beethoven's Letters* (ed. E. Hull) (London: HarperCollins, 1997), p. 377.
25 D. Matthews, op. cit., p. 11.
26 G.R. Marek, op. cit., p. 81.
27 J. Hardman, *Louis XVI* (New Haven, CT: Yale University Press, 1993), p. 25.
28 G. Rudé, *Revolutionary Europe 1783–1815* (London: Fontana, 1964), pp. 26, 73; *Financial Times*, 17 August 2002.
29 W. Doyle, *The Oxford History of the French Revolution* (Oxford: Oxford University Press, 1989), p. 43.
30 G. Rudé, op. cit., p. 96.
31 A. de Tocqueville, quoted in G. Rudé, op. cit., p. 69.
32 J. Hardman, op. cit., p. 194. A good chronology may be found in W. Doyle, op. cit., p. 434.
33 W. Doyle, op. cit., p. 191.
34 D. Blackbourn, op. cit., p. 65.
35 B. Cooper, op. cit., p. 40.
36 D. Blackbourn, op. cit., p. 67; and Brühl Exhibition Guide, op. cit., p.83.
37 C. Ingrao, *The Habsburg Monarchy 1618–1815* (Cambridge: Cambridge University Press, 1994), p. 225.
38 Translation by the author of letter to Simrock, 2 August 1794.
39 B. Cooper, op. cit., p. 41.
40 D. Matthews, op. cit., p. 15; and G. Pestelli, op. cit., p. 170.
41 D. Matthews, op. cit., p. 18; and B. Cooper, op. cit., pp. 48, 58.
42 B. Cooper, op. cit., p. 44.
43 G. Dyson, *Musicianship for Students* (London: Novello, 1940), p. 45.
44 B. Cooper, op. cit., pp. 50, 79.
45 *New Grove*, op. cit.
46 *New Oxford Companion to Music* (ed. D. Arnold) (Oxford: Oxford University Press, 1983), p. 1427; and *New Grove*, op. cit.; and G. Pestelli, op. cit., p. 12.
47 A. Hanson, *Musical Life in Biedermeyer Vienna* (Cambridge: Cambridge University Press, 1985), p. 14.
48 D. Matthews, op. cit., p. 20; and B. Cooper, op. cit., pp. 55, 73.
49 D. Matthews, op. cit., p. 30; and B. Cooper, op. cit., pp. 113, 194, 124, 166.
50 R. Halliwell, *The Mozart Family: Four Lives in a Social Context* (Oxford: Clarendon Press, 1998), p. 36.
51 B. Cooper, op. cit., p. 88.
52 *Beethoven Letters*, op. cit., p. 52.
53 B. Cooper, op. cit., p. 159; and W. Blunt, op. cit., p. 20.
54 F. Knight, *Beethoven and the Age of Revolution* (London: Lawrence and Wishart, 1973), p. 66.
55 O. Sonneck, *Beethoven: Impressions by his Contemporaries*, quoted in D. Matthews, op. cit., p. 25.
56 M.S. Anderson, *Europe in the Eighteenth Century 1713–83* (London: Longman, 1961), p. 31.
57 L. Stone, *The Family, Sex and Marriage* (London: Weidenfeld and Nicolson, 1977), p. 536.
58 G.R. Marek, op. cit., p. 224.
59 D. Matthews, op. cit., p. 26.
60 B. Cooper, op. cit., p. 148.
61 Ibid., p. 110.
62 *New Grove*, op. cit.; and B. Cooper, op. cit., pp. 202, 192.
63 *Encyclopaedia Britannica*, ninth edition, 1875–89; and A. Walker, *Franz Liszt, Volume 1:*

The Virtuoso Years, 1811–47 (London: Faber and Faber, 1983), p. 190.
64 R. Friedenthal, op. cit., p. 410.
65 D. Matthews, op. cit., pp. 48, 47.
66 *Beethoven's Letters*, op. cit., p. 33.
67 *New Grove*, op. cit.
68 *Beethoven's Letters*, op. cit., p. 82.
69 C. Ingrao, op. cit., p. 232; and B. Cooper, op. cit., p. 178.
70 F. Knight, op. cit., pp. 112, 139, 146.
71 C. Barnett, *Napoleon* (London: George Allen and Unwin, 1978), p. 53; and H. Hearder, *Italy in the Age of the Risorgimento 1790–1870* (London: Longman, 1983), pp. 21, 24.
72 *Encyclopaedia Britannica*, fifteenth edition, 1974.
73 B. Cooper, op. cit., p. 129.
74 R. Halliwell, op. cit., p. 614.
75 D. Matthews, op. cit., p. 30.
76 *Beethoven's Letters*, op. cit., p. 17.
77 Ibid., pp. 20, 23.
78 K. Clark, *The Romantic Rebellion* (London: John Murray, 1975), p. 75.
79 D. Matthews, op. cit., pp. 20, 52.
80 *Beethoven's Letters*, op. cit., p. 9.
81 Information provided by Dr R. Aubrey.
82 G. Pestelli, op. cit., p. 221.
83 Author's translation.
84 D. Matthews, op. cit., p. 34; and B. Cooper, op. cit., p 121.
85 W. Schweisheimer, 'Beethoven's Physicians', *Musical Quarterly*, vol. 31 (3), 1945, p 289.
86 O. Sonneck, *Beethoven: Impressions by his Contemporaries*, quoted in D. Matthews, op. cit., p. 25.
87 P.H. Lang, op. cit., p. 760.
88 F. Knight, op. cit., p. 68; and B. Cooper, op. cit., p. 160.
89 D. Matthews, op. cit., p. 37.
90 P.H. Lang, op. cit., p. 763.
91 A. Einstein, op. cit., p. 66.
92 B. Cooper, op. cit., p. 141.
93 *New Grove*, op. cit.; and D. Matthews, op. cit., pp. 36, 39; and B. Cooper, op. cit., pp. 137, 171, 150.
94 *Beethoven's Letters*, op. cit., p. 57.
95 C. Barnett, op. cit., p. 116.
96 Ibid., p. 117.
97 E. Bruce, *Napoleon and Josephine* (London: Weidenfeld and Nicolson, 1995), p. 188.
98 C. Ingrao, op. cit., p. 237.
99 D. Blackbourn, op. cit., p. 79.
100 B. Cooper, op. cit., p. 152.
101 D. Matthews, op. cit., p. 43; and C. Ingrao, op. cit., p. 233.
102 *Beethoven's Letters*, op. cit., p. 62.
103 B. Cooper, op. cit., pp. 181, 193, 192.
104 G. Pestelli, op. cit., p. 220.
105 D. Matthews, op. cit., p. 43.
106 Ibid., p. 42.
107 R. Okey, *The Habsburg Monarchy* (London: Macmillan, 2001), p. 73.
108 C. Ingrao, op. cit., p. 234.
109 A. Palmer, *Metternich* (London: Weidenfeld and Nicolson, 1972), pp. 54, 55.
110 D. Matthews, op. cit., p. 45.
111 C. Ingrao, op. cit., p. 236.
112 K. Geiringer, *Haydn: A Creative Life in Music* (Berkeley, CA: University of California Press, 1968; original edition 1946), p. 206.
113 C. Barnett, op. cit., pp. 152, 155.
114 C. Barnett, p. 131.
115 A. Palmer, op. cit., pp. 54, 55.
116 C. Barnett, op. cit., p. 131.
117 C. Ingrao, op. cit., p. 233; and F. Knight, op. cit., p. 76.
118 B. Cooper, op. cit., p. 201; and O.E. Deutsch (trans. E. Blom), *Schubert: A Documentary Biography* (London: J.M. Dent, 1946), p. 19.
119 A. Hanson, op. cit., p. 15, 84.
120 B. Cooper, op. cit., p. 238.
121 N. Nicolson, *Napoleon 1812* (London: Weidenfeld and Nicolson, 1985), p. 161; and E. Bruce, op. cit., p. 471; and H. Hearder, op. cit., p. 170.
122 B. Cooper, op. cit., p. 225; and A. Hanson, op. cit., p. 84.
123 H. Nicolson, *The Congress of Vienna* (London: Constable, 1946), p. 9.
124 Ibid.
125 *Encyclopaedia Britannica*, ninth edition, op. cit.
126 H. Nicolson, op. cit., p. 132.
127 Ibid., pp. 204, 205, 163.
128 A. Palmer, op. cit., p. 131.
129 Ibid., p. 132.
130 H. Nicolson, op. cit., p. 127.
131 F. Knight, op. cit., p. 94.
132 M. Solomon, *Beethoven* (New York: Schirmer, 1998) p. 288; B. Cooper, op. cit., p. 236.
133 H. Nicolson, op. cit., pp. 127, 292.
134 A. Palmer, op. cit., p. 20.
135 H. Nicolson, op. cit., p. 36.

136 H. Nicolson, op. cit., pp. 226, 148; and A. Palmer, op. cit., p. 90.
137 *La Garde Chambonnas*, quoted in H. Nicolson, op. cit., p. 230.
138 Lord Clancarty, quoted in H. Nicolson, op. cit., p. 230.
139 F. Knight, op. cit., p. 78.
140 D. Matthews, op. cit., p. 51.
141 E. Aldrich, in R. Erickson (ed.), *Schubert's Vienna* (New Haven, CT: Yale University Press, 1997).
142 A. Hanson, op. cit., p. 156.
143 O.E. Deutsch, op. cit., p. 64.
144 D. Matthews, op. cit., p. 52. ('Deplorable' was the Streichers' word.)
145 B. Cooper, op. cit., pp. 212, 246, 155.
146 *Beethoven's Letters*, op. cit., p. 217.
147 Ibid., p. 210.
148 *New Grove*, op. cit.; and D. Matthews, op. cit., p. 3.
149 B. Cooper, op. cit., pp. 268, 273, 246.
150 Ibid., pp. 274–6.
151 *Beethoven's Letters*, op. cit., p. 236.
152 R. Spaethling, *Mozart's Letters, Mozart's Life* (London: Faber and Faber, 2000), p. 81.
153 *New Grove*, op. cit.
154 *Beethoven's Letters*, op. cit., pp. 205, 206, 360, 238.
155 Ibid., pp. 239, 242, 243.
156 Ibid., p. 247.
157 *New Grove*, op. cit., vol. 2, p. 409.
158 *Beethoven's Letters*, op. cit., p. 340.
159 B. Cooper, op. cit., pp. 260 ff, 297; and *Beethoven's Letters*, op. cit., p. 290.
160 B. Cooper, op. cit., p. 285.
161 Ibid., pp. 285, 291.
162 D. Matthews, op. cit., p. 69.
163 *Beethoven's Letters*, op. cit., p. 289.
164 Ibid., p. 356.
165 B. Cooper, op. cit., p. 343; and *New Grove*, op. cit.
166 G. Pestelli, op. cit., p. 252.
167 Ibid., p. 253.
168 *New Grove*, op. cit., vol. 16, p. 232.
169 J. Warrack, *Carl Maria von Weber* (Cambridge: Cambridge University Press, 1976), pp. 307, 199.
170 A. Einstein, op. cit., p. 108; and J. Warrack, op. cit., pp. 154, 205, 185, 67, 80, 154, 160.
171 P.H. Lang, op. cit., p. 716; and B.A. Brown, *Gluck and the French Theatre in Vienna* (Oxford: Clarendon Press, 1991), p. 112.
172 *New Grove*, op. cit.; and J. Warrack, op. cit., p. 54; and P.H. Lang, op. cit., p. 715.
173 Stendhal (trans. R.N. Coe), *Life of Rossini* (London: John Calder, 1956; published 1824), p. 118.
174 Weber, Baron M.M. von (trans. J. Palgrave Simpson), *Carl Maria von Weber* (London: Chapman and Hall, 1865), vol. 2, ch. 7.
175 P. Cornelius, in A. Einstein, *Music in the Romantic Era* (London: J.M. Dent, 1947) p. 262; P. Lang, *Music in Western Civilisation* (London: J.M. Dent, 1963) p. 798.
176 J. Warrack, op. cit., pp. 253, 369, 227; and *New Grove*, op. cit., vol. 18, p. 254.
177 J. Warrack, op. cit., p. 222.
178 Ibid., p. 229.
179 Rochlitz, quoted in D. Matthews, op. cit., p. 65.
180 *Beethoven's Letters*, op. cit., p. 383.
181 A. Hanson, op. cit., pp. 32, 45.
182 *Beethoven's Letters*, op. cit., p. 392.
183 D. Matthews, op. cit., p. 75; and B. Cooper, op. cit., p. 347.
184 W. Schweisheimer, op. cit., p. 289.
185 O.E. Deutsch, op. cit., pp. 620–24.
186 D. Matthews, op. cit., p. 75.

Chapter 6

1 P.H. Lang, *Music in Western Civilisation* (London: J.M. Dent, 1963), p. 778.
2 *New Oxford Companion to Music* (ed. D. Arnold) (Oxford: Oxford University Press, 1983), p. 1720.
3 G. Pestelli (trans. E. Cross), *The Age of Mozart and Beethoven* (Cambridge: Cambridge University Press, 1984), p. 100.
4 N. Cardus, *A Composers Eleven* (London: Jonathan Cape, 1958), p 24.
5 A. Einstein, *Music in the Romantic Era* (London: J.M. Dent, 1947), p. 91.
6 *New Grove Dictionary of Music and Musicians* (ed. S. Sadie) (London: Macmillan 1980).
7 S. Williams, in R. Erickson (ed.), *Schubert's Vienna* (New Haven, CT: Yale University Press, 1997), p. 237.
8 O.E. Deutsch (trans. R. Ley and J. Nowell), *Schubert: Memoirs by his Friends* (London: A. and C. Black, 1958), p. 135.
9 Ibid., p. 179.
10 Information from leaflet from birthplace

museum; and O.E. Deutsch, 1946, op. cit., pp. xxx, 83.
11 O.E. Deutsch, 1946, op. cit., p. 2.
12 Ibid.
13 E. Bruce, *Napoleon and Josephine* (London: Weidenfeld and Nicolson, 1995), p. 188.
14 *New Grove*, op. cit., vol. 16, p. 752.
15 R. Spaethling, *Mozart's Letters, Mozart's Life* (London: Faber and Faber, 2000), p. 442.
16 O.E. Deutsch, 1946, op. cit., pp. 7, 10; and J. Reed, *Schubert* (Oxford: Oxford University Press, 1997; [original edition, London: J.M. Dent, 1987]), p. 3.
17 B. Cooper, *Beethoven* (Master Musicians) (Oxford: Oxford University Press, 1959), p. 267.
18 J. Reed, 1987, op. cit., p. 9.
19 O.E. Deutsch, 1946, op. cit., p. 12; and J. Reed, 1997, op. cit., p. 11.
20 W. Heindl, in R. Erickson, op. cit., p. 41.
21 O.E. Deutsch, 1958, op. cit., p. 50, quoted in J. Reed, 1997, op. cit., p. 4.
22 *New Grove*, op. cit.; and J. Reed, 1987, op. cit., p. 9.
23 J. Reed, 1997, op. cit., p. 8.
24 R. Okey, *The Habsburg Monarchy* (London: Macmillan, 2001), p. 76.
25 C. Ingrao, *The Habsburg Monarchy 1618–1815* (Cambridge: Cambridge University Press, 1994), p. 232.
26 O.E. Deutsch, 1946, op. cit., p. 37.
27 A. Hanson, *Musical Life in Biedermeyer Vienna* (Cambridge: Cambridge University Press, 1985), pp. 19, 20, 28.
28 J. Reed, 1997, op. cit., p. 248.
29 O.E. Deutsch, 1946, op. cit., p. 63.
30 *New Grove*, op. cit., vol. 16, p. 753.
31 Ibid., p. 754.
32 J. Reed, 1997, op. cit., pp. 14, 186.
33 O.E. Deutsch, 1958, op. cit., p. 131.
34 J. Chissell, *Clara Schumann: A Dedicated Spirit* (London: Hamish Hamilton, 1983), p. 105.
35 O.E. Deutsch, 1946, op. cit., p. 76, amended by the author.
36 J. Warrack, *Carl Maria von Weber* (Cambridge: Cambridge University Press, 1976), p. 317.
37 O.E. Deutsch, 1946, op. cit., pp. 420, 422.
38 Ibid., p. 46.
39 J. Reed, 1997, op. cit., p. 14.
40 O.E. Deutsch, 1946, op. cit., p. 65.
41 Ibid., p. 82.
42 J. Reed, 1987, op. cit., p. 273; and O.E. Deutsch, 1946, op. cit., p. 260; and J. Reed, 1997, op. cit., p. 19.
43 J. Reed, 1997, op. cit., p. 237.
44 Ibid, p. 145, 53, 15, 70; and B. Cooper, op. cit., p. 155; and A. Hanson, op. cit., p. 122.
45 J. Reed, 1997, op. cit., p. 60; and R. Steblin, Review of B. Newbould, *Schubert, The Music and the Man,* in *Music and Letters*, vol. 79, 1998, p. 128.
46 O.E. Deutsch, 1946, op. cit., p. 49.
47 Ibid., p. 76.
48 Ibid., p. 729.
49 D. Heartz, *Haydn, Mozart and the Viennese School 1740–80* (London: W.W. Norton and co., 1995), p. 69.
50 O.E. Deutsch, 1946, op. cit., p. 685.
51 O.E. Deutsch, 1946, op. cit., p. 305, quoted in J. Reed, 1987, op. cit., p. 98.
52 A. Hanson, op. cit., pp. 150, 151, 152, 155, 162, 168, 169, 171, 172.
53 Ibid., pp. 1, 76, 77.
54 M. Brion (trans. J. Stewart), *Daily Life in the Vienna of Mozart and Schubert* (London: Weidenfeld and Nicolson, 1961), p. 122; and O.E. Deutsch, 1946, op. cit., p. xxviii.
55 A. Hanson, op. cit., pp. 129, 130.
56 R. Okey, op. cit., p. 80.
57 Stendhal (trans. M. Shaw), *The Charterhouse of Parma* (London: Penguin, 1958; first published 1839), p. 248.
58 H. Nicolson, *The Congress of Vienna* (London: Constable, 1946), p. 267.
59 J. Reed, 1997, op. cit., p.57.
60 A. Palmer, *Metternich* (London: Weidenfeld and Nicolson, 1972), p. 170.
61 Ibid., p. 181.
62 N. Gogol (trans. D. Magarshack), *Dead Souls* (London: Penguin, 1989; first published 1842), p. 22.
63 H. Nicolson, op. cit., p. 268.
64 Count Kolowrat, quoted in R. Okey, op. cit., p. 76.
65 J.-P. Bled (trans. T. Bridgeman), *Franz Joseph* (Oxford: Blackwell, 1992), p. 12.
66 J. Ridley, *Napoléon III and Eugénie* (London: Constable, 1979), p. 60.
67 A. Hanson, op. cit., p. 35.
68 O.E. Deutsch, 1946, op. cit., p. 128, amended by the author.
69 J. Reed, 1997, op. cit., p. 69.
70 A. Einstein, 1947, op. cit., p. 57.
71 Information from the author's visit to Zseliz.

72 O.E. Deutsch, 1946, op. cit., p. 92.
73 *Encyclopaedia Britannica*, ninth edition, 1875–89.
74 O.E. Deutsch, 1946, op. cit., p. 92.
75 A. Hanson, op. cit., p. 30.
76 O.E. Deutsch, 1946, op. cit., p. 100.
77 Ibid.
78 Ibid., p. 102.
79 *New Grove*, op. cit., vol. 16, p. 757.
80 O.E. Deutsch, 1946, op. cit., p. 99, amended by the author.
81 J. Brown, in R. Erickson, op. cit., p. 186.
82 O.E. Deutsch, 1946, op. cit., p. 121.
83 Information from Baedeker and author's visit.
84 O.E. Deutsch, 1946, op. cit., pp. 121, 126; and J. Reed, 1987, op. cit., p. 75.
85 *New Grove*, op. cit.; and R. Osborne, *Rossini* (Master Musicians) (London: J.M. Dent, 1986), p. 24.
86 O.E. Deutsch, 1946, op. cit., p. 135.
87 A. Einstein, 1947, op. cit., p. 102.
88 O.E. Deutsch, 1946, op. cit., p. 149.
89 J. Reed, 1997, op. cit., p. 203.
90 *New Grove*, op. cit., vol. 16, p. 769; and O.E. Deutsch, 1946, op. cit., p. 754; and A. Hanson, op. cit., pp. 32, 108, 62, 107.
91 R. Steblin, op. cit., p. 128.
92 J. Reed, 1997, op. cit., pp. 80, 93, 179, 101, 192.
93 A. Einstein, 1947, op. cit., p. 87.
94 O.E. Deutsch, 1946, op. cit., p. 551.
95 Ibid., p. 550.
96 J. Reed, 1987, op. cit., p. 83.
97 Ibid., pp. 102, 105; and *New Grove*, op. cit., vol. 16, p. 761.
98 E. Sams, 'Schubert's Illness Re-examined', *Musical Times*, vol. 121, 1980, p. 15.
99 O. Friedrich, *Olympia: Paris in the Age of Manet* (London: Aurum Press, 1992), p. 282.
100 Ibid., p. 281.
101 A. Einstein (trans. E. Blom), *Gluck* (Master Musicians) (London: J.M. Dent, 1964), p. 32; and S. Avins, *Johannes Brahms: Life and Letters* (Oxford: Oxford University Press, 1997), p. 623; and A. Hanson, op. cit., p. 13.
102 *Encyclopaedia Britannica*, fifteenth edition, 1974; and E. Sams, op. cit.
103 *Encyclopaedia Britannica*, fifteenth edition, op. cit.; and E. Sams, op. cit.
104 J. Reed, 1987, op. cit., p. 106.
105 O.E. Deutsch, 1946, op. cit., p. 279.
106 Ibid., p. 286.
107 Ibid., p. 288; see also J. Reed, 1997, op. cit., p. 205.
108 O.E. Deutsch, 1946, op. cit., p. 314.
109 Ibid., p. 339, quoted in J. Reed, 1997, op. cit., p. 100.
110 C. Harman, *Fanny Burney* (London: HarperCollins, 2000), p. 82.
111 J. Reed, 1987, op. cit., p. 119; and O.E. Deutsch, 1946, op. cit., pp. 364, 369; and R. Steblin, op. cit., p. 129.
112 *New Grove*, op. cit., vol. 16, p. 763.
113 O.E. Deutsch, 1946, op. cit., p. 380.
114 Ibid., p. 383, amended by the author.
115 Information from the author's visit to Gmunden; and J. Reed, 1987, op. cit., p. 139; and J. Reed, 1997, op. cit., p. 124; and O.E. Deutsch, 1946, op. cit., p. 454.
116 *New Grove*, op. cit., vol. 16, p. 765.
117 Ibid., p. 765; and O.E. Deutsch, 1946, op. cit., p. 478; and J. Reed, 1987, op. cit., p. 150.
118 O.E. Deutsch, 1946, op. cit., p. 538.
119 J. Reed, 1997, op. cit., pp. 126, 130, 132.
120 Ibid., p. 142.
121 O.E. Deutsch, 1946, op. cit., p. 222.
122 Ibid., p. 659; and J. Reed, 1997, op. cit., p. 138.
123 O.E. Deutsch, 1946, op. cit., pp. 668, 679.
124 S. Williams, in R. Erickson, op. cit., p. 236.
125 J. Reed, 1997, op. cit., p. 130.
126 O.E. Deutsch, 1946, op. cit., p. 635.
127 Ibid., pp. 806, 807; and J. Reed, 1987, op. cit., p. 205.
128 J. Reed, 1997, op. cit., p. 40.
129 O.E. Deutsch, 1946, op. cit., p. 820.
130 V.L. Levine, in D. Nicholls (ed.), *The Cambridge History of American Music* (Cambridge: Cambridge University Press, 1998), p. 3.
131 J. Fenimore Cooper, *The Last of the Mohicans* (London: Penguin, 1986), pp. 67, 69, 70, 167, 177, 219, 231, 254, 277; and *Encyclopaedia Britannica*, ninth edition, op. cit.
132 Information from leaflet from Franz Schubert Memorial Rooms, Historishes Museum der Stadt Wien.
133 O.E. Deutsch, 1946, op. cit., p. 819; and J. Reed, 1987, op. cit., pp. 210, 212.
134 O.E. Deutsch, 1946, op. cit., p. 825.
135 Information from Kettenbrückengasse 6.
136 A. Einstein, 1947, op. cit., p. 86.
137 *New Grove*, op. cit., vol. 16, p. 772; and J. Reed, 1987, op. cit., p. 51.

138 A. Hanson, op. cit., p. 10.
139 J. Reed, 1997, op. cit., p. 180.
140 R. Sams, op. cit.
141 R. Rhodes James, *Lord Randolph Churchill* (London: Weidenfeld and Nicolson, 1959), p. 360.
142 Ibid., p. 361.
143 R.F. Foster, *Lord Randolph Churchill* (Oxford: Clarendon Press, 1981), pp. 59, 96.
144 For 'ergot', see *Encyclopaedia Britannica*, ninth edition, op. cit.
145 O. Friedrich, op. cit., p. 281.

Chapter 7

1 *La Casa di Rossini: Catalogo del Museo* (Fondazione Scavolini, 1989), p. 159.
2 B. Rees, *Camille Saint-Saëns: A Life* (London: Chatto and Windus, 1999), p. 1.
3 Stendhal (trans. R.N. Coe), *Life of Rossini* (London: Collins, 1956; first published 1824), p. 1.
4 H. Hearder, *Italy in the Age of the Risorgimento 1790–1870* (London: Longman, 1983), p. 156.
5 B.A. Haddock, in B. Waller (ed.), *Themes in Modern European History 1830–90* (London: Unwin Hyman, 1990), p. 70.
6 R. Price, in B. Waller, op. cit., p. 16.
7 M. Clark, *The Italian Risorgimento* (London: Addison-Wesley, 1998), p. 21.
8 Ibid., p. 63.
9 H. Hearder, op. cit., p. 96; footnote: M. Clark, op. cit., pp. 21, 63.
10 H. Hearder, op. cit., p. 125; and C. Headlam, *The Story of Naples* (London: J.M. Dent, 1927).
11 H. Hearder, op. cit., p. 53; and J. Ridley, *Garibaldi* (London: Constable, 1974), p. 1.
12 M. Clark, op. cit., p. 17.
13 *New Grove Dictionary of Music and Musicians* (ed. S. Sadie) (London: Macmillan, 1980).
14 J.G. Keysler, *Travels Through Germany, Bohemia, Hungary, Switzerland, Italy and Lorrain* (London: A. Linde and F. Field, 1956), vol. III, p. 56, and information obtained locally.
15 *New Grove*, op. cit.
16 H. Hearder, op. cit., p. 43.
17 R. Osborne, *Rossini* (Master Musicians) (London: J.M. Dent, 1986), p. 11.
18 H. Weinstock, *Rossini: A Biography* (London: Oxford University Press, 1968), p. 27.
19 H. Hearder, op. cit., p. 28.
20 H. Weinstock, op. cit., p. 32.
21 *Encyclopaedia Britannica*, fifteenth edition, 1974.
22 H. Weinstock, op. cit., pp. 45, 53.
23 *New Grove*, op. cit., p. 228.
24 H. Weinstock, op. cit., p. 118.
25 Ibid., pp. 61, 37.
26 *New Grove*, op. cit.
27 H. Weinstock, op. cit., p. 58.
28 C. Gowan, *France from the Regent to the Romantics* (Edinburgh: Harrap, 1961), pp. 90–103.
29 G. Kobbé, *The Complete Opera Book* (London: G.P. Putnam's Sons, 1930), p. 303; *New Grove*, op. cit., vol. 16, p. 232.
30 H. Weinstock, op. cit., pp. 59, 75, 82, 84.
31 *New Grove*, op. cit., p. 235.
32 Stendhal, quoted in R. Osborne, op. cit., p. 25.
33 N. Cardus, *A Composers Eleven* (London: Jonathan Cape, 1958), p. 25.
34 E. Newman, *Memoirs of Hector Berlioz* (New York, NY: Dover Publications, 1932), p. 50.
35 C. Hibbert, *George III* (London: Viking 1998), p. 356.
36 Ibid., p. 355.
37 F. Fraser, *The Unruly Queen* (London: Macmillan, 1996), p. 294 et seq.
38 Ibid., p. 54.
39 H. Weinstock, op. cit., p. 95.
40 C. Headlam, op. cit., p. 360; and H. Hearder, op. cit., p. 138.
41 Stendhal (trans. M. Shaw), *The Charterhouse of Parma* (London: Penguin, 1958; first published 1839), pp. 197, 199.
42 *Encyclopaedia Britannica*, ninth edition, 1875–89.
43 R. Osborne, op. cit., p. 56.
44 Stendhal, 1956, op. cit., pp. 150, 165.
45 R. Osborne, op. cit., pp. 59, 54.
46 H. Hearder, op. cit., p. 103; and M. Clark, op. cit., p. 12.
47 P. Barbier (trans. R. Luoma), *Opera in Paris 1800–1850* (Portland, OR: Amadeus Press, 1995), p. 185; the figures are 8 out of 16 operas in the repertoire, and 119 out of 154 evenings.
48 H. Weinstock, op. cit., p. 125.
49 R. Osborne, op. cit., p. 61.
50 Stendhal, 1956, op. cit., pp. 403, 404, 405, 407.

51 H. Weinstock, op. cit., p. 135.
52 A. Palmer, *The Life and Times of George IV* (London: Weidenfeld and Nicolson, 1972), pp. 203, 206.
53 W. Blunt, *On Wings of Song: A Biography of Felix Mendelssohn* (London: Hamish Hamilton, 1974), p. 223.
54 R. Cowgill, in C. Bashford and L. Langley (eds), *Music and British Culture* (Oxford: Oxford University Press, 2000), p. 50.
55 P. Barbier, op. cit., p. 63.
56 C. Tomalin, *Jane Austen* (London: Viking, 1997), p. 220.
57 R. Osborne, op. cit., p. 65; and *Encyclopaedia Britannica*, ninth edition, op. cit.; and I. Evans, *A Short History of English Literature* (London: Penguin, 1963), p. 62; and P. Olleson, in C. Bashford and L. Langley, op. cit., p. 35; and H. de Balzac (trans. S. Raphael), *Eugénie Grandet* (Oxford: Oxford University Press, 1990; first published 1833), p. 25.
58 W. Cobbett, quoted in D. Thomson, *England in the Ninteenth Century* (London: Penguin, 1950), p. 12.
59 D. Thomson, op. cit., pp. 16, 17.
60 *Encyclopaedia Britannica*, ninth edition, op. cit.
61 S. O'Faoláin, *Newman's Way* (1952), quoted in D. Newsome, *The Convert Cardinals: Newman and Manning* (London: John Murray, 1993), p. 24.
62 D. Newsome, op. cit., p. 45.
63 P. Barbier, op. cit., p. 196.
64 The figures come from Balzac's short story, 'Facino Cane', in H. de Balzac (selected S. Raphael), *Short Stories* (London: Penguin, 1977).
65 H. Weinstock, op. cit., pp. 439, 440; and *New Grove*, op. cit.
66 H. de Balzac (trans. M. Crawford), *Le Père Goriot* (London: Penguin, 1951; first published 1834–5), p. 27.
67 Ibid., p. 62.
68 J. Harding, *Saint-Saëns and his Circle* (London: Chapman and Hall, 1965), pp. 7, 8, 9; and J. Barzun, in P. Bloom (ed.), *Music in Paris in the Eighteen Thirties* (New York, NY: Pendragon Press, 1987), pp. 1–4.
69 Mme Cherubini speaking to Hiller, quoted in P.H. Lang, *Music in Western Civilisation* (London: J.M. Dent, 1963), p. 788.
70 M. Root-Bernstein, 'Popular theatre in the French Revolution', *History Today*, February 1993, p. 25.
71 P. Barbier, op. cit., pp. 12, 72.
72 R. Wangermée, in P. Bloom, op. cit., p. 555; and *New Grove*, op. cit.; and J.-M. Nectoux, in P. Bloom, op. cit., p. 483; and D. Cairns, *Berlioz 1803–1832: The Making of an Artist* (London: André Deutsch, 1989), p. 245; and D. Kern Holoman, in P. Bloom, op. cit., pp. 389, 395.
73 P. Barbier, op. cit., pp. 63, 67, 71; and D. Cairns, 1989, op. cit., p. 181; and D. Cairns, *Berlioz 1832–1869: Servitude and Greatness* (London: Allen Lane, 1999), pp. 389, 239; and H. Lacombe (trans. E. Schneider), *The Keys to French Opera in the Nineteenth Century* (Berkeley, CA: University of California Press, 2001), pp. 20–24, 42.
74 D. Beales, *Joseph II: In the Shadow of Maria Theresa 1741–1780* (Cambridge: Cambridge University Press, 1987), p. 316; and E. Newman, *Memoirs of Hector Berlioz* (New York, NY: Dover Publications, 1932), p. 183; and J.L. Hall-Witt, in C. Bashford and L. Langley, op. cit., pp. 122, 141.
75 M. Proust (trans. S. Moncrieff and T. Kilmartin, revised D.J. Enright), *In Search of Lost Time: The Guermantes Way* (London: Chatto and Windus, 1992; first published 1920), p. 36.
76 Stendhal (trans. M. Shaw), *Scarlet and Black* (London: Penguin, 1953), p. 285.
77 H. de Balzac (trans. H.J. Hunt) *La Peau de Chagrin* (London: Penguin, 1977; first published 1831), p. 209.
78 Ibid., p. 156.
79 H. Nicolson, *The Congress of Vienna* (London: Constable, 1946), p. 67; and A. Palmer, *Metternich* (London: Weidenfeld and Nicolson, 1972), p. 102.
80 P. Mansel, *Paris Between the Empires, 1814–1852* (London: John Murray, 2001), p. 69.
81 R. Bolster, *Marie d'Agoult: The Rebel Countess* (New Haven, CT: Yale University Press, 2000), p. 25.
82 R. Magraw, *France 1815–1915*, p. 113; and *Encyclopaedia Britannica*, ninth edition, op. cit.
83 P. Mansel, op. cit., pp. 166, 167; and A. Cobban, *A History of Modern France: Volume 2 1799–1871* (London: Penguin, 1961), p. 82; and P. McPhee, *A Social History of France 1780–1880* (London: Routledge, 1992), p. 115.
84 Stendhal, 1953, op. cit., p. 266.

85 N. Simeone, *Paris: A Musical Gazetteer* (New Haven, CT: Yale University Press, 2000), pp. 173–6.
86 For French opera, see P. Barbier, op. cit.; A. Faris, *Jacques Offenbach* (London: Faber and Faber, 1980), p. 39; D. Cairns, 1999, op. cit., p. 209; and H. Lacombe, op. cit.
87 P. Barbier, op. cit., p. 72.
88 A. Einstein, *Music in the Romantic Era* (London: J.M. Dent, 1947), p. 122.
89 P.H. Lang, op. cit., p. 832.
90 R. Spaethling, *Mozart's Letters, Mozart's Life* (London: Faber and Faber, 2000), p. 415.
91 H. de Balzac, *Eugénie Grandet*, 1990, op. cit., p. 70.
92 A. Fitzlyon, *Maria Malibran: Diva of the Romantic Age* (London: Souvenir Press, 1987), pp. 126, 153; and P. Barbier, op. cit., p. 185.
93 A. Fitzlyon, op. cit., p. 19.
94 P. Barbier, op. cit., p. 154.
95 *New Grove*, op. cit., vol. 17, p. 528.
96 J.-M. Nectoux, in P. Bloom, op. cit., pp. 474, 506; and J.L. Hall-Witt, in C. Bashford and L. Langley, op. cit., p. 140; and A. Fitzlyon, op. cit., pp. 105, 74n; and *New Grove*, op. cit.; and K. Preston in D. Nicholls (ed.) *The Cambridge History of American Music* (Cambridge: Cambridge University Press, 1998), p. 194; and P. Barbier, op. cit., p. 154.
97 A. Fitzlyon, op. cit., p. 248.
98 *New Grove*, op. cit.
99 A. Fitzlyon, op. cit., p. 18.
100 Quoted in P. Barbier, op. cit., p. 158.
101 *Encyclopaedia Britannica*, fifteenth edition, op. cit.; and H. Lacombe, op. cit., p. 51.
102 E. Zola (trans. D. Parmée), *Nana* (Oxford: Oxford University Press, 1998; first published 1880), p. 12.
103 P. Barbier, op. cit., p. 184.
104 *New Grove*, op. cit.
105 P. Barbier, op. cit., p. 192.
106 Ibid., p. 193.
107 Lady Holland, quoted in H. Nicolson, op. cit., p. 290.
108 C. Jones, *The Cambridge History of France* (Cambridge: Cambridge University Press, 1994), p. 63.
109 P. McPhee, op. cit., p. 115.
110 P. Mansel, op. cit., p. 191; and P. Barbier, op. cit., pp. 18, 23, 17.
111 C. Jones, op. cit., p. 200; and A. Cobban, op. cit., pp. 82, 161.
112 J. Hardman, *Louis XVI* (New Haven, CT: Yale University Press, 1993), pp. 55, 78.
113 See P. McPhee, op. cit.; A. Cobban, op. cit.
114 R. Price, in B. Waller (ed.), *Themes in Modern History 1830–90* (London: Unwin Hyman, 1990), p. 9.
115 D. Newsome, op. cit., p. 30.
116 P. Mansel, op. cit., p. 301.
117 Ibid., p. 118.
118 H. Weinstock, op. cit., p. 177.
119 S. Kracauer, *Offenbach and the Paris of his Time* (London: Constable, 1937), p. 5.
120 P. Barbier, op. cit., p. 38.
121 H. de Balzac, *La Peau de Chagrin*, 1977, op. cit., p. 57.
122 H. de Balzac, *Le Père Goriot*, 1951, op. cit., p. 159.
123 H. de Balzac, *Eugénie Grandet*, 1990, op. cit., p. 31.
124 H. de Balzac, *Le Peau de Chagrin*, 1997, op. cit., p. 255.
125 R. Osborne, op. cit., p. 79.
126 H. Weinstock, op. cit., p. 227.
127 Quoted in R. Harrington, 'The Neuroses of the Railway', *History Today*, vol. 44 (7), July 1994.
128 R. Osborne, op. cit., p. 90.
129 H. Weinstock, op. cit., p. 476.
130 Ibid., p. 184.
131 R. Osborne, op. cit., p. 94.
132 S. Richardson, *Pamela: Or, Virtue Rewarded* (Oxford: Oxford University Press, 2001; first published 1740), p. 1.
133 E. Zola, *Nana*, 1998, op. cit., p. 245.
134 P. McPhee, op. cit., pp. 123, 142, 143.
135 H. de Balzac, *La Peau de Chagrin*, 1977, op. cit., p. 152.
136 H. de Balzac, *Le Père Goriot*, 1951, op. cit., p. 36.
137 W. Atwood, *The Lioness and the Little One: The Liaison of George Sand and Frederic Chopin* (New York, NY: Columbia University Press, 1980), p. 50.
138 G. Robb, *Balzac* (London: Picador, 1994), p. 182; and H. de Balzac, *La Peau de Chagrin*, 1977, op. cit., p. 157.
139 H. de Balzac, *La Peau de Chagrin*, 1977, op. cit., pp. 161, 163.
140 G. Robb, op. cit., p. 182.
141 H. Weinstock, op. cit., p. 451.
142 P. Mansel, op. cit., p. 331.
143 M. Phillips-Matz, *Verdi: A Biography*

(Oxford: Oxford University Press, 1993), pp. 508, 853.
144 H. de Balzac, *La Peau de Chagrin*, 1977, op. cit., pp. 135, 125, 151.
145 R. Osborne, op. cit., p. 84.
146 Much of the information in this and the next few paragraphs is found in H. Weinstock, op. cit.
147 *New Grove*, op. cit., vol. 16, p. 241.
148 P. Barbier, op. cit., p. 169.
149 H. de Balzac, *Le Père Goriot*, 1951, op. cit., p. 58.
150 P. Mansel, op. cit., p. 134.
151 H. Noel Williams, *Mme Recamier and her Friends* (London: Harper Brothers, 1901), p. 200.
152 M. Proust (trans. C.K. Scott Moncrieff and T. Kilmartin, revised D.J. Enright), *Sodom and Gomorrah* (London: Vintage 1996), p. 622; J. Barzun, in P. Bloom, op. cit., p. 12.
153 M. Proust (trans. S. Moncrieff and T. Kilmartin, revised D.J. Enright), *In Search of Lost Time: Swann's Way* (London: Chatto and Windus, 1992, first published 1913), part 2, p. 346.
154 Ibid., p. 344.
155 M. Proust, *In Search of Lost Time: The Guermantes Way*, 1992, op. cit., p. 618.
156 M. Curtiss, 'Bizet, Offenbach and Rossini', *Musical Quarterly*, vol. 40, 1954, p. 357.
157 Ibid., p. 358.
158 Ibid., p. 357.
159 *New Grove*, op. cit., vol. 3, p. 768.
160 M. Curtiss, 'Unpublished Letters by Georges Bizet', *Musical Quarterly*, vol. 36, 1950, p. 350.
161 J. Warrack, *Carl Maria von Weber* (Cambridge: Cambridge University Press, 1976), p. 303.
162 M. Curtiss, 1954, op. cit., p. 355.
163 A. Walker, *Franz Liszt, Volume 2: The Weimar Years, 1848–60* (London: Faber and Faber, 1989), p. 538.
164 H. Weinstock, op. cit., p. 347.
165 Ibid.
166 R. Obsorne, op. cit., p. 109.
167 M. Curtiss, 1954, op. cit., p. 356.
168 H. Weinstock, op. cit., p. 284.
169 Ibid., p. 346.
170 *New Grove*, op. cit; and B. Rees, op. cit., p. 135.
171 *New Grove*, op. cit., vol. 16, p. 243, amended by the author.
172 H. Weinstock, op. cit., pp. 371, 373.
173 *New Grove*, op. cit., vol. 16, p. 243.

CHAPTER 8

1 H. Weinstock, *Donizetti and the World of Opera* (London: Methuen, 1964), pp. 194, 37.
2 A. Einstein, *Music in the Romantic Era* (London: J.M. Dent, 1947), p. 268.
3 *New Oxford Companion to Music* (ed. D. Arnold) (Oxford: Oxford University Press, 1983), p. 1382.
4 Stendhal (trans. R.N. Coe), *Life of Rossini* (London: Collins, 1956; first published 1824), p. 26.
5 *Encyclopaedia Britannica*, ninth edition, 1875–89, vol. 5, p. 275.
6 *New Grove Dictionary of Music and Musicians* (ed. S. Sadie) (London: Macmillan, 1980); and P. Barbier (trans. R. Luoma), *Opera in Paris 1800–1850* (Portland, OR: Amadeus Press, 1995), p. 185.
7 P. Barbier, op. cit., p. 39.
8 Ibid., p. 83.
9 Ibid., pp. 76, 81; and J. Warrack, in P. Bloom (ed.), *Music in Paris in the Eighteen Thirties* (New York, NY: Pendragon Press, 1987), p. 577; and D. Cairns, *Berlioz 1803–1832: The Making of an Artist* (London: André Deutsch, 1989), p. 135.
10 J. Warrack, in P. Bloom, op. cit., p. 575.
11 A. Fitzlyon, *Maria Malibran: Diva of the Romantic Age* (London: Souvenir Press, 1987), p. 150; and P. Barbier, op. cit., p. 114.
12 P. Barbier, op. cit., pp. 39, 119.
13 See *The Golden Years of Ezio Pinza* (Pavilion records); and P. Findlay, sleeve notes to Sutherland/Bonynge, *L'Orchestre de la Suisse Romande* (Decca, 1970).
14 P.H. Lang, *Music in Western Civilisation* (London: J.M. Dent, 1963), p. 832.
15 D. Newsome, *The Convert Cardinals: Newman and Manning* (London: John Murray, 1993), p. 43.
16 L. Davies, *Cesar Franck and his Circle* (London: Barrie and Jenkins, 1970), p. 23.
17 J. Warrack, in P. Bloom, op. cit., pp. 577, 583.
18 P.H. Lang, op. cit., pp. 830, 832.
19 P. Barbier, op. cit., pp. 42, 110, 55.
20 *New Grove*, op. cit.

21 E. Gombrich, *The Story of Art* (London: Phaidon, 1963), pp. 397–9.
22 V. Massé, quoted in H. Lacombe (trans. E. Schneider), *The Keys to French Opera in the Nineteenth Century* (Berkeley, CA: University of California Press, 2001), p. 289.
23 L. Davies, op. cit., p. 23.
24 *New Grove*, op. cit.; and P. Barbier, op. cit., p. 48.
25 M. Bukofzer, *Music in the Baroque Era* (London: J.M. Dent, 1947), pp. 147, 152.
26 *New Grove*, op. cit., vol. 12, p. 253.
27 D. Cairns, *Berlioz 1832–1869: Servitude and Greatness* (London: Allen Lane, 1999), p. 72.
28 M. Curtiss, *Bizet and his World* (London: Secker and Warburg, 1959), p. 147.
29 Information from author's visit to Berlin.
30 H. and G. Becker (trans. M. Violette), *Giacomo Meyerbeer: A Life in Letters* (London: Christopher Helm, 1983), p. 14.
31 H. Hearder, *Italy in the Age of the Risorgimento 1790–1870* (London: Longman, 1983), p. 31.
32 D. Webb, 'Italy by Rail', in *History Today*, June 1996.
33 M. Clark, *The Italian Risorgimento* (London: Addison-Wesley, 1998), p. 29.
34 R. Okey, *The Habsburg Monarchy* (London: Macmillan, 2001), p. 114.
35 H. Hearder, op. cit., pp. 152, 125–52.
36 Ibid., pp. 36, 39, 141; and H. Weinstock, op. cit., pp. 79, 123.
37 *Encyclopaedia Britannica*, op. cit.; and from information in Catania Museum Guide (Catania: C. Neri, 1998).
38 *New Grove*, op. cit.
39 Catania Museum Guide, op. cit., p. 28; much of the information about Bellini can be found in this Guide.
40 Ibid., pp. 28, 30; 'cymbale' might mean cembalo, i.e. a clavier – see ibid., p. 53; it might also mean a cymbal-player.
41 M. Clark, op. cit., p. 19.
42 A. Fitzlyon, op. cit., pp. 175, 176.
43 Stendhal (trans. M. Shaw), *The Charterhouse of Parma* (London: Penguin, 1958; first published 1839), pp. 24, 39.
44 G. Skelton (ed.), *Cosima Wagner's Diaries (an abridgement)* (London: Pimlico, 1994), p. 301.
45 *New Grove*, op. cit.
46 A. Fitzlyon, op. cit., p. 182.
47 Catania Museum Guide, op. cit., p. 127.
48 H. Weinstock, op. cit., p. 87.
49 *New Grove*, op. cit., vol. 2, p. 448.
50 Catania Museum Guide, op. cit., pp. 37, 68, 105, 107.
51 Stendhal, 1839, op. cit., p. 393.
52 P. McPhee, *A Social History of France 1780–1880* (London: Routledge, 1992), p. 150; and *The Book of Saints*, compiled by the Benedictine Monks of St Augustine's Abbey, Ramsgate, sixth edition (London: A. and C. Black, 1989), p. 116.
53 A. Walker, *Franz Liszt, Volume I: The Virtuoso Years, 1811–47* (London: Faber and Faber, 1983), p. 173.
54 B. Jack, *George Sand* (London: Chatto and Windus, 1999), pp. 196, 205; and P. Mansel, *Paris Between the Empires, 1814–1852* (London: John Murray, 2001), p. 284.
55 Catania Museum Guide, op. cit., p. 37; and H. Weinstock, op. cit., p. 113.
56 H. Hearder, op. cit., p. 177.
57 M. Clark, op. cit., pp. 32, 36, 44, 45, 46.
58 E. Newman (ed.), *Memoirs of Hector Berlioz* (New York, NY: Dover Publications, 1932), pp. 119, 120.
59 H. Hearder, op. cit., pp. 80, 107; and *Encyclopaedia Britannica*, op. cit; and H. Macdonald, *Berlioz* (Master Musicians) (London: J.M. Dent, 1982), p. 23; and E. Newman, op. cit., p. 120.
60 J. Ridley, *Garibaldi* (London: Constable, 1974), p. 20.
61 Ibid., pp. 29, 224; much of the information about political developments can be found in Ridley's *Garibaldi*.
62 D. Mack Smith, *Mazzini* (New Haven: Yale University Press, 1994), p. 42.
63 R. Price, in B. Waller (ed.), *Themes in Modern History 1830–90* (London: Unwin Hyman, 1990), p. 8.
64 J.-P. Bled (trans. T. Bridgeman), *Franz Joseph* (Oxford: Blackwell, 1992), pp. 41, 43.
65 J. Ridley, op. cit., p. 264; and M. Phillips-Matz, *Verdi, A Biography* (Oxford: Oxford University Press, 1993), p. 238; and H. Hearder, op. cit., p. 116. Hearder says that the Pope was accompanied by Countess Spaur, who was married to an English archaeologist.
66 H. Hearder, op. cit., p. 207.
67 M. Clark, op. cit., p. 5.
68 C.V. Wedgwood, *The Thirty Years War* (London: Jonathan Cape, 1938), p. 32.

69 R. Layton, *Grieg* (London: Omnibus Press, 1998), p. 121.
70 *New Grove*, op. cit.
71 Stendhal, 1824, op. cit., p. 23. See also Lord Macaulay (ed. H. Trevor-Roper), *Essays* (London: Fontana Press, 1965), p. 113.
72 *New Grove*, op. cit., vol. 5, p. 553.
73 H. Weinstock, op. cit., pp. 21, 27, 34, 35.
74 Ibid., p. 106; and *New Grove*, op. cit., vol. 5, p. 554.
75 E. Newman, op. cit., p. 183.
76 Stendhal, 1839, op. cit., p. 105.
77 M. Phillips-Matz, op. cit., p. 489.
78 H. Weinstock, op. cit., p. 145.
79 A. Fitzlyon, op. cit., p. 206.
80 H. Weinstock, op. cit., p. 111.
81 Ibid., pp. 116, 126.
82 P. McPhee, op. cit., p. 120; and J. Bury, *France 1814–1940* (London: Methuen, 1969), p. 69.
83 H. de Balzac (selected S. Raphael), 'Pierre Grassou', in *Short Stories* (London: Penguin, 1977), p. 262.
84 P. McPhee, op. cit., pp. 148, 126, 127, 125.
85 A. Cobban, *A History of Modern France 1799–1871: Volume 2* (London: Penguin, 1961), p. 128; and B. Rees, *Camille Saint-Saëns: A Life* (London: Chatto and Windus, 1999), p. 48; and H. Kupferberg, *The Mendelssohns* (London: W.H. Allen, 1972), passim.
86 C. Jones, *The Cambridge History of France* (Cambridge: Cambridge University Press, 1994), p. 207.
87 P. McPhee, op. cit., p. 145.
88 Ibid., p. 146.
89 Ibid., pp. 145, 146, 148, 147.
90 Ibid., pp. 136, 139.
91 Ibid., pp. 149, 139; and A. Cobban, op. cit., p 102; and *Grand Larousse Encyclopédique*, 1960; and P. Mansel, op. cit, p. 285; and A. Walker, op. cit., pp. 151, 157, 244.
92 J. Ridley, *Napoléon III and Eugénie* (London: Constable, 1979), passim.
93 P. McPhee, op. cit., p. 151.
94 Ibid., p. 174. A more precise figure is one in every 2.4.
95 Much of the information in the following paragraphs comes from H. Weinstock, op. cit.
96 Ibid., p. 234.
97 Ibid., pp. 146, 171, 224, 226.
98 Information from plaque on Palazzo Scotti; and museum in Bergamo.
99 H. Weinstock, op. cit., p. 271.
100 A. Fitzlyon, op. cit., p. 259.
101 Ibid., p. 188.

Chapter 9

1 E. Newman, *Memoirs of Hector Berlioz* (New York, NY: Dover Publications, 1932), p. 507.
2 B. Jack, *George Sand* (London: Chatto and Windus, 1999), pp. 45, 99.
3 A. Walker, *Franz Liszt, Volume 2: The Weimar Years, 1848–60* (London: Faber and Faber, 1989), p. 339.
4 H. Lacombe (trans. E. Schneider), *The Keys to French Opera in the Nineteenth Century* (Berkeley, CA: University of California Press, 2001), p. 273.
5 K. Clark, *The Romantic Rebellion* (London: John Murray, 1975), p. 19.
6 J. Barzun, in P. Bloom (ed.), *Music in Paris in the Eighteen Thirties* (New York, NY: Pendragon Press, 1987), p. 4.
7 Stendhal (*Racine et Shakespeare*, ed. H. Martineau), quoted in P. Raby, *Fair Ophelia: A Life of Harriet Smithson Berlioz* (Cambridge: Cambridge University Press, 1982), p. 47.
8 K. Clark, op. cit., p. 20. (Greco-Roman grandeur is a term of Winckelmann.)
9 Schlegel, quoted in L. Plantinga, in R. Erickson (ed.), *Schubert's Vienna* (New Haven, CT: Yale University Press, 1997), p. 83.
10 D. Cairns, *Berlioz 1832–1869: Servitude and Greatness* (London: Allen Lane, 1999), p. 200.
11 K. Clark, op. cit., p. 245.
12 Flaubert, quoted in A. Einstein, *Music in the Romantic Era* (London: J.M. Dent, 1947), p. 59.
13 Ibid., p. 57.
14 Ingres, quoted in K. Clark, op. cit., p. 179.
15 J. Barzun, in P. Bloom, op. cit., p. 7.
16 B. Jack, op. cit., pp. 24, 156, 180.
17 G. Skelton (ed.), *Cosima Wagner's Diaries (an abridgement)* (London: Pimlico, 1994), pp. 40, 107.
18 R. Bolster, *Marie d'Agoult: The Rebel Countess* (New Haven, CT: Yale University Press, 2000), pp. 245, 251.
19 D. Galloway, introduction to E. Allan Poe, *The Fall of the House of Usher and Other Writings* (London: Penguin, 1986), pp. 9, 11.
20 E. Allan Poe (ed. D. Galloway), *The Fall of the House of Usher and Other Writings* (London: Penguin, 1986), p. 155.

21 K. Clark, op. cit., p. 45.
22 A. Einstein, op. cit., p. 172.
23 Ibid., p. 21.
24 P.H. Lang, *Music in Western Civilisation* (London: J.M. Dent, 1963), p. 744.
25 K. Clark, op. cit., p. 62.
26 A. Einstein, op. cit., p. 113.
27 D. Cairns, *Berlioz 1803–1832: The Making of an Artist* (London: André Deutsch, 1989), p. 41.
28 *Guide du Musée Hector Berlioz* (La Côte St André: Association Nationale Hector Berlioz, 1991), p. 17.
29 H. de Balzac (trans. S. Raphael), *Eugénie Grandet* (Oxford: Oxford University Press, 1990; first published 1833), p. 37; see also Stendhal (trans. M. Shaw) *Scarlet and Black* (London: Penguin, 1953), p. 27.
30 W. Doyle, *The Oxford History of the French Revolution* (Oxford: Oxford University Press, 1989), pp. 83, 89.
31 *Encyclopaedia Britannica*, fifteenth edition, 1974.
32 D. Cairns, 1989, op. cit., p. 44.
33 D. Chandler (ed.), *Waterloo: The Hundred Days* (London: Osprey, 1987), p. 18.
34 Information from Cité de la Musique, Paris.
35 H. de Balzac (trans. M. Crawford) *Le Père Goriot* (London: Penguin, 1951; first published 1834–5), pp. 30, 31; and picture at La Côte, nondescript courtyard with stone staircase.
36 E. Newman, op. cit., p. 19.
37 Ibid., p. 21.
38 P. Mansel, *Paris Between the Empires, 1814–1852* (London: John Murray, 2001), p. 174.
39 E. Newman, op. cit., p. 37.
40 *New Grove Dictionary of Music and Musicians* (ed. S. Sadie) (London: Macmillan, 1980).
41 E. Newman, op. cit., p. 54.
42 *New Grove*, op. cit.
43 E. Newman, op. cit., pp. 34, 33.
44 D. Cairns, 1989, op. cit.; and H. de Balzac, *Le Père Goriot*, 1951, op. cit., p. 34.
45 D. Cairns, 1989, op. cit., p. 123; and E. Newman, op. cit., pp. 37, 45.
46 *Encyclopaedia Britannica*, ninth edition, 1875–89.
47 P. Raby, op. cit., p. 46.
48 Ibid., pp. 58, 75.
49 D. Cairns, 1999, op. cit., p. 17.
50 Dumas, Mémoires, quoted in P. Raby, op. cit., p. 68.
51 *Le Figaro* 15 September 1827, quoted in P. Raby, op. cit., p. 75.
52 P. Raby, op. cit., p. 90.
53 Ferrand de Pontmartin, *Nouveau Samedi*, p. 101, quoted in P. Raby, op. cit., p. 77.
54 E. Newman, op. cit., p. 66.
55 Ibid., p. 93.
56 H. Macdonald, *Berlioz* (Master Musicians) (London: J.M. Dent, 1982), p. 15.
57 Correspondence with Ferrand, 6 February 1830, quoted in P. Raby, op. cit., p. 111.
58 Information from Cité de la Musique, Paris.
59 E. Newman, op. cit., p. 82; and J. Harding, *Saint-Saëns and his Circle* (London: Chapman and Hall, 1965), p. 46.
60 E. Newman, op. cit., p. 95, amended by the author.
61 This is attributed to Henri Berton; quoted in D. Cairns, 1989, op. cit., p. 332.
62 E. Newman, op. cit., p. 108, amended by the author.
63 H. de Balzac (trans. H.J. Hunt) *La Peau de Chagrin* (London: Penguin, 1977; first published 1831), p. 21.
64 E. Newman, op. cit., p. 113, amended by the author.
65 D. Cairns, in P. Bloom (ed.), *Music in Paris in the Eighteen Thirties* (New York, NY: Pendragon Press, 1987), p. 86.
66 M. Bukofzer, *Music in the Baroque Era* (London: J.M. Dent, 1985), pp. 111, 248.
67 D. Cairns, in P. Bloom, op. cit., pp. 88, 89.
68 A. Einstein, op. cit., p. 134.
69 *New Grove*, op. cit., vol. 15, p. 11.
70 D. Cairns, 1989, op. cit., pp. 348, 349.
71 E. Newman, op. cit., p. 102.
72 P. Raby, op. cit., p. 123. ('Mutual cheer and solace' is a phrase found in Boccaccio's Decameron.)
73 H. Macdonald, op. cit., p. 21.
74 P. Bloom, op. cit., pp. 56, 72.
75 E. Newman, op. cit., p. 195.
76 H. Macdonald, op. cit., p. 23.
77 *Encyclopaedia Britannica*, fifteenth edition.
78 R. Osborne, *Rossini* (Master Musicians) (London: J.M. Dent, 1986), p. 87.
79 D. Cairns, 1989, op. cit., p. 410.
80 E. Newman, op. cit., p. 124.
81 D. Cairns, 1989, op. cit., p. 410.
82 J. Harding, op. cit., p. 26; and *New Grove*, op. cit.
83 P. Raby, op. cit., pp. 121, 123.

84 F. Tillard (trans. C. Naish), *Fanny Mendelssohn* (Portland, OR: Amadeus Press, 1996), p. 254.
85 D. Cairns, 1989, op. cit., p. 442.
86 F. Tillard, op. cit., p. 254.
87 H. Macdonald, op. cit., p. 23.
88 D. Cairns, 1989, op. cit., pp. 473, 475.
89 E. Newman, op. cit., p. 145.
90 Ibid., p. 139.
91 D. Cairns, 1989, op. cit., p. 472.
92 P. Raby, op. cit., p. 123.
93 *The Age*, 16 June 1832, quoted in P. Raby, op. cit., p. 125.
94 P. Raby, op. cit., p. 127.
95 D. Cairns, 1989, op. cit., p. 242.
96 P. Raby, op. cit., p. 132.
97 Ibid., p. 133.
98 D. Cairns, 1999, op. cit., p. 2.
99 P. Raby, op. cit., p. 136.
100 D. Cairns, 1999, op. cit. pp. 1, 22.
101 P. Raby, op. cit., p. 150.
102 K. Preston, in D. Nicholls (ed.), *The Cambridge History of American Music* (Cambridge: Cambridge University Press, 1998), p. 189.
103 Ibid., p. 200.
104 W. Brooks, in D. Nicholls (ed.), *The Cambridge History of American Music* (Cambridge: Cambridge University Press, 1998), p. 43.
105 *Encyclopaedia Britannica*, fifteenth edition.
106 D. Cairns, 1999, op. cit., pp. 52, 85.
107 E. Newman, op. cit., p. 485.
108 S. Prokofiev (trans. O. Prokofiev), *Soviet Diary 1927 and Other Writings* (London: Faber and Faber, 1991), p. 252.
109 Ibid.
110 P. Raby, op. cit., p. 158.
111 E. Newman, op. cit., p. 484.
112 D. Cairns, 1999, op. cit., p. 40.
113 E. Newman, op. cit., p. 212.
114 D. Cairns, 1999, op. cit., p. 207.
115 P. Barbier (trans. R. Luoma), *Opera in Paris 1800–1850* (Portland, OR: Amadeus Press, 1995), p. 86.
116 D. Cairns, 1999, op. cit., p. 163.
117 Ibid., p. 118.
118 H. Macdonald, op. cit., p. 47.
119 A. Walker, *Franz Liszt, Volume 1: The Virtuoso Years, 1811–47* (London: Faber and Faber, 1983), p. 176.
120 E. Newman, op. cit., p. 232.
121 D. Cairns, 1999, op. cit., p. 317.
122 P. Raby, op. cit., p. 165.
123 D. Cairns, 1999, op. cit., pp. 230, 231.
124 P. Raby, op. cit., p. 165.
125 Ibid., p. 167.
126 D. Cairns, 1999, op. cit., p. 233.
127 E. Newman, op. cit., p. 167.
128 P. Raby, op. cit., p. 168.
129 Ibid., p. 169.
130 D. Cairns, 1999, op. cit., pp. 507, 532, 439.
131 H. Macdonald, op. cit., p. 29.
132 E. Newman, op. cit., p. 444.
133 Ibid., p. 291.
134 There is a picture of an octobasse in the *Guide du Musée de la Musique*, Cité de la Musique (Paris, 1997), p. 223.
135 D. Cairns, 1999, op. cit., p. 364.
136 Ibid., p. 393.
137 Ibid., p. 412.
138 E. Newman, op. cit., p. 18, amended by the author.
139 P. McPhee, *A Social History of France 1780–1880* (London: Routledge, 1992), p. 177.
140 J. Ridley, *Napoléon III and Eugénie* (London: Constable, 1979), pp. 204, 206.
141 E. Newman, op. cit., p. 17.
142 B. Jack, op. cit., p. 311.
143 J. Bury, *France 1814–1940* (London: Methuen, 1969), p. 79.
144 Ibid., p. 79.
145 Thiers, quoted in J. Ridley, op. cit., p. 224.
146 J. Ridley, op. cit., p. 231.
147 Ibid., p. 286.
148 Ibid., p. 289.
149 Ibid., pp. 298, 299.
150 Ibid., p. 319. The figures in the referendum were 7.8 million 'Yes' and 253,000 'No'.
151 D. Cairns, 1999, op. cit., p. 543.
152 E. Newman, op. cit., pp. 467, 457.
153 H. Macdonald, op. cit., pp. 53, 55.
154 Claude Rostand, quoted in D. Cairns, 1999, op. cit., p. 778.
155 M. Curtiss, *Bizet and his World* (London: Secker and Warburg, 1959), p. 143.
156 E. Newman, op. cit., pp. 472, 473.
157 Ibid., pp. 476, 477.
158 A. Walker, 1989, op. cit., pp. 518, 538.
159 E. Newman, op. cit., p. 514.
160 Ibid., p. 530.
161 H. de Balzac, *La Peau de Chagrin*, 1977, op. cit., p. 23.
162 D. Cairns, 1999, op. cit., p. 514.
163 Ibid., p. 738.
164 Ibid., p. 751.

165 Ibid., p. 765.
166 Ibid., p. 775.
167 On view at the La Côte Museum.

Chapter 10

1 W. Blunt, *On Wings of Song: A Biography of Felix Mendelssohn* (London: Hamish Hamilton, 1974), p. 127.
2 S. Levas (trans. P.M. Young), *Sibelius: A Personal Portrait* (London: J.M. Dent, 1972), p. 68.
3 *Encyclopaedia Britannica*, ninth edition, 1875–89, vol. 13, p. 679.
4 F. Tillard (trans. C. Naish), *Fanny Mendelssohn* (Portland, OR: Amadeus Press, 1996), pp. 22, 30, 31.
5 R. Spaethling, *Mozart's Letters, Mozart's Life* (London: Faber and Faber, 2000), p. 115.
6 J. Israel, *European Jewry in the Age of Mercantilism* (Oxford: Clarendon Press, 1985), p. 253.
7 *Encyclopaedia Britannica*, ninth edition, op. cit., vol. 13, p. 680.
8 C. Wolff, *Johann Sebastian Bach* (Oxford: Oxford University Press, 2000), p. 540.
9 Museum für Hamburgische Geschichte, room 230; and Mendelssohn-Archivs, Staatsbibliothek zu Berlin, Exhibition 2002.
10 Museum für Hamburgische Geschichte, room 230.
11 D. Blackbourn, *Germany 1780–1918* (London: HarperCollins, 1997), p. 68.
12 Ibid., p. 33; and F. Tillard, op. cit., pp. 186, 185.
13 Mendelssohn-Archivs, Staatsbibliothek zu Berlin, Exhibition 2002.
14 B. Waller (ed.), *Themes in Modern European History 1830–90* (London: Unwin Hyman, 1990), pp. 118, 119.
15 B.A. Haddock, in B. Waller (ed.), op. cit., p. 70; the figure was 69 per cent.
16 W. Blunt, op. cit., p. 29.
17 P. Jourdan, in C. Bashford and L. Langley (eds), *Music and British Culture* (Oxford: Oxford University Press, 2000), pp. 103–4.
18 *Times Literary Supplement*, 19 March 2004; F. Tillard, op. cit., pp. 53, 55; and *New Grove Dictionary of Music and Musicians* (ed. S. Sadie) (London: Macmillan, 1980).
19 W. Blunt, op. cit., p. 31.
20 Ibid., p. 59.
21 P. Radcliffe, *Mendelssohn* (Master Musicians) (London: J.M. Dent, 1954), p. 20.
22 *Encyclopaedia Britannica*, ninth edition, op. cit., vol. 12, p. 344.
23 F. Tillard, op. cit., pp. 70, 55.
24 W. Blunt, op. cit., p. 171.
25 H. Kupferberg, *The Mendelssohns* (London: W.H. Allen, 1972), pp. 76 ff. Mme Bigot sight-read Beethoven's 'Appasionata' Sonata (see p. 185).
26 R. Friedenthal, *Goethe: His Life and Times* (London: Weidenfeld and Nicolson, 1973), pp. 517, 408; and *New Grove*, op. cit.
27 F. Tillard, op. cit., pp. 100–101.
28 P. Radcliffe, op. cit., p. 8.
29 W. Blunt, op. cit., p. 39.
30 Ibid., p. 53.
31 F. Tillard, op. cit., p. 72.
32 W. Blunt, op. cit., p. 59.
33 F. Tillard, op. cit., p. 120.
34 P. Radcliffe, op. cit., p. 11.
35 W. Blunt, op. cit., p. 75.
36 F. Tillard, op. cit., pp. 123, 172, 190, 74.
37 W. Blunt, op. cit., p. 41.
38 F. Tillard, op. cit., pp. 198, 312.
39 Ibid., p. 136.
40 B. Magee, *Wagner and Philosophy* (London: Allen Lane The Penguin Press, 2000), p. 43.
41 F. Tillard, op. cit., p. 68.
42 Ibid., p. 139.
43 Ibid., p. 173.
44 P. Olleson, in C. Bashford and L. Langley, op. cit., p. 28.
45 A. Einstein, *Music in the Romantic Era* (London: J.M. Dent, 1947), p. 48.
46 Ibid., p. 49.
47 F. Tillard, op. cit., p. 148.
48 A. Einstein, op. cit., p. 75.
49 P. Radcliffe, op. cit., p. 16.
50 H.T. David and A. Mendel, *The Bach Reader* (New York, NY: W.W. Norton and co., 1972; original edition 1945), p. 373.
51 W. Blunt, op. cit., p. 97; and P. Jourdan, in C. Bashford and L. Langley, op. cit., pp. 99 ff.
52 W. Blunt, op. cit., p. 98.
53 Mendelssohn, quoted in W. Blunt, op. cit., p. 108.
54 De Quincey, quoted in T. Burke, *Travel in England from Pilgrim and Pack-Horse to Light Car and Plane* (London: Batsford, 1942), p. 93.
55 T. Burke, op. cit., p. 90.
56 Ibid., p. 95.
57 Ibid., p. 98; and *Encyclopaedia Britannica*, fifteenth edition, 1974.
58 T. Burke, op. cit., p. 117.

59 J. Ridley, *Napoléon III and Eugénie* (London: Constable, 1979), p. 94.
60 W. Blunt, op. cit., p. 109.
61 *New Grove*, op. cit., vol. 20, p. 164.
62 W. Blunt, op. cit., p. 95, amended by the author.
63 Coleridge, quoted in R. Holmes, *Coleridge: Darker Reflections* (London: HarperCollins, 1998), p. 553.
64 W. Blunt, op. cit., p. 121.
65 J.-M. Bailbé, in P. Bloom, *Music in Paris in the Eighteen Thirties* (New York, NY: Pendragon Press, 1987), pp. 30, 31.
66 F. Tillard, op. cit., p. 210.
67 B. Waller, op. cit., pp. 100, 102.
68 *New Grove*, op. cit.
69 W. Blunt, op. cit., p. 168.
70 Ibid., p. 169.
71 P.H. Lang, *Music in Western Civilisation* (London: J.M. Dent, 1963), pp. 964, 968.
72 A. Walker, *Franz Liszt, Volume 2: The Weimar Years, 1848–60* (London: Faber and Faber, 1989), p. 273.
73 Ibid.
74 D. Kern Holoman, in P. Bloom, op. cit., pp. 389, 395; and P.H. Lang, op. cit., pp. 961, 966; and A. Walker, op. cit., pp. 271, 273.
75 W. Blunt, op. cit., p. 171.
76 Ibid., p. 84.
77 Ibid., p. 183.
78 Quoted in W. Blunt, op. cit., p. 176.
79 *New Grove*, op. cit.
80 Ibid.; and W. Blunt, op. cit., p. 190.
81 J. Chissell, *Clara Schumann: A Dedicated Spirit* (London: Hamish Hamilton, 1983), p. 99.
82 W. Blunt, op. cit., p. 247.
83 Ibid., p. 276.
84 Ibid., p. 193.
85 G. St Aubyn, *Queen Victoria: A Portrait* (London: Sinclair-Stevenson, 1991), p. 148.
86 Ibid., p. 147.
87 Ibid., pp. 160, 210.
88 W. Blunt, op. cit., p. 224.
89 For Mendelssohn's visit to Buckingham Palace, the parrot, etc., see also H.E. Jacob (trans. R. and C. Winston), *Felix Mendelssohn and his Times* (London: Barrie Books Ltd., 1963), p. 262.
90 G. St Aubyn, op. cit., p. 498.
91 W. Blunt, op. cit., p. 223.
92 Ibid., p. 499.
93 J. Chissell, op. cit., p. 167.
94 W. Blunt, op. cit., p. 218.
95 *New Grove*, op. cit.
96 M. Broyles, in D. Nicholls (ed.), *The Cambridge History of American Music* (Cambridge: Cambridge University Press, 1998), p. 218.
97 G.R. Marek, *Gentle Genius: The Story of Felix Mendelssohn* (London: Robert Hale Ltd., 1972), p. 311; and D. Donald, *Lincoln* (London: Cape, 1995), pp. 151, 152.
98 W. Blunt, op. cit., p. 252.
99 W. Blunt, op. cit., p. 266, amended by the author.
100 P. Radcliffe, op. cit., p. 50.
101 W. Blunt, op. cit., p. 268.
102 G.R. Marek, op. cit., p. 316.
103 W. Blunt, op. cit., p. 83.
104 G. Skelton (ed.), *Cosima Wagner's Diaries (an abridgement)* (London: Pimlico, 1994), p. 44.
105 P.H. Lang, op. cit., p. 811; see also P. Jourdan, in C. Bashford and L. Langley, op. cit., p. 99.
106 St Matthew, Chapter 19, Verse 24.

Chapter 11

1 J. Samson, *Chopin* (Oxford: Oxford University Press, 1996), p. 260.
2 A. Hedley (revised M.E.J. Brown), *Chopin* (Master Musicians) (London: J.M. Dent, 1974; original edition 1947), p. 116. Hedley is explicit on those present, although Solange is noticeably absent in the oil painting by T. Kwiatkowski.
3 J. Lukowski and H. Zawadzki, *A Concise History of Poland* (Cambridge: Cambridge University Press, 2001), Part 1.
4 W. Doyle, *The Oxford History of the French Revolution* (Oxford: Oxford University Press, 1989), p. 258.
5 J. Lukowski and H. Zawadzki, op. cit., p. 105.
6 A. Hedley, op. cit., p. 37.
7 H. Nicolson, *The Congress of Vienna* (London: Constable, 1946), p. 148.
8 J. Lukowski and H. Zawadzki, op. cit., p. 125.
9 J. Samson, op. cit., p. 6.
10 Żelazowa Wola Guide, *Żelazowa Wola: The Place of his Birth* (2001), p. 1.
11 A 19th-century print shows his birthdate as 2 March 1809; his birth certificate is dated 22 February 1810; he was baptised on 4 May 1810. Source: Chopin Museum in Warsaw.
12 H. Opie'nski (trans. E. Voynich), *Chopin's Letters* (New York, NY: Dover Publications, 1988), p. 67; and W. Atwood, *The Lion and the*

Little One: The Liaison of George Sand and Frederic Chopin (New York, NY: Columbia University Press, 1980), p. 35; and B. Jack, *George Sand* (London: Chatto and Windus, 1999), p. 279.
13 P.H. Lang, *Music in Western Civilisation* (London: J.M. Dent, 1963), p. 816.
14 Jeffrey Kallberg, discussed in J. Samson, op. cit., p. 102.
15 A. Einstein, *Music in the Romantic Era* (London: J.M. Dent, 1947), p. 60.
16 A. Hedley, op. cit., pp. 11, 15, 38.
17 Ibid., p. 31.
18 J. Samson, op. cit., pp. 28, 29.
19 A. Hedley, op. cit., p. 150, amended by the author.
20 D. Saunders, *Russia in the Age of Reaction and Reform* (London: Longman, 1992), pp. 177, 178; and A. Hedley, op. cit., p. 32; and H. Acton, *The Last Medici* (London: Macmillan, 1980), p. 162; and J. Lukowski and H. Zawadzki, op. cit., p. 136.
21 J. Samson, op. cit., p. 79.
22 G. Sand (trans. S. Raphael), *Indiana* (Oxford: Oxford University Press, 1994; first published 1832), p. 234.
23 W. Atwood, op. cit., p. 65.
24 *New Grove Dictionary of Music and Musicians* (ed. S. Sadie) (London: Macmillan, 1980), vol. 9, p. 778.
25 P. Bloom (ed.), *Music in Paris in the Eighteen Thirties* (New York, NY: Pendragon Press, 1987), p. 67.
26 A. Orlowski, quoted in A. Hedley, op. cit., p. 48.
27 A. Hedley, op. cit., p. 52.
28 G. Flaubert (trans. G. Hopkins), *Madame Bovary* (Oxford: Oxford University Press, 1981; first published 1856), Part 3, Chapter 4, p. 251.
29 A. Hedley, op. cit., p. 53, amended by the author.
30 In the Chopin Museum, Warsaw (item 151 in catalogue).
31 A. Hedley, op. cit., p. 164.
32 Ibid., p. 152.
33 E. Walker (revised J.A. Westrup), *A History of Music in England* (Oxford: Clarendon Press, 1952), p. 270.
34 J. Chissell, *Schumann* (Master Musicians) (London: J.M. Dent, 1948), p. 201, amended by the author.
35 S. Kracauer, *Offenbach and the Paris of his Time* (London: Constable, 1937), p. 76.
36 A. Hedley, op. cit., p. 56.
37 *Baedeker's Czech Republic* (London: AA, 1994).
38 J. Samson, op. cit., p. 127.
39 The packet is in the Chopin Museum, Warsaw.
40 A. Hedley, op. cit., p. 50.
41 J. Samson, op. cit., p. 135.
42 A. Hedley, op. cit., p. 71.
43 J.H. Fabré, *Social Life in the Insect World* (London: Pelican, 1937), p. 70.
44 R. Jordan, *George Sand* (London: Constable, 1976), p. 168.
45 B. Jack, op. cit., p. 179.
46 Ibid., p. 277.
47 Ibid., p. 186.
48 Ibid., p. 289.
49 H. de Balzac (trans. M. Crawford), *Le Père Goriot* (London: Penguin, 1951; first published 1834–5), p. 146 ff.
50 J. Barzun, in P. Bloom, op. cit., pp. 17, 20.
51 G. Sand, 1994, op. cit., p. 58.
52 Ibid., p. 10.
53 Introduction to G. Sand, 1994, op. cit., p. 3.
54 Introduction to G. Sand, 1994, op. cit., p. viii.
55 B. Jack, op. cit., p. 359.
56 G. Sand, 1994, op. cit., p. 101.
57 B. Jack, op. cit., p. 221.
58 Ibid., p. 226.
59 Ibid., pp. 234, 241, 255, 273, 221; and R. Jordan, op. cit., pp. 116, 132.
60 B. Jack, op. cit., p. 245.
61 R. Jordan, op. cit., p. 171.
62 Ibid.
63 Ibid., p. 193.
64 W. Atwood, op. cit., p. 51.
65 R. Jordan, op. cit., p. 179.
66 *Encyclopaedia Britannica*, ninth edition, 1875–89.
67 A. Hedley, op. cit., p. 76.
68 W. Atwood, op. cit., pp. 91, 87.
69 R. Jordan, op. cit., pp. 187, 185.
70 W. Atwood, op. cit., p. 95.
71 T. Dormandy, *The White Death: A History of Tuberculosis* (London: The Hambleton Press, 1999), p. 54; The information on TB in this chapter is largely taken from T. Dormandy and the *Encyclopaedia Britannica*, fifteenth edition, 1974.
72 E. Dahl and M. Jangaard (eds), *Edvard Grieg*

(Troldhaugen: Edvard Grieg Museum, 2000), p. 85.
73 E. White, *Stravinsky: The Composer and his Works* (London: Faber and Faber, 1979), p. 113; and F. Routh, *Stravinsky* (Master Musicians) (London: J.M. Dent, 1975), p. 44.
74 A. Walker, *Franz Liszt, Volume 2: The Weimar Years, 1848–60* (London: Faber and Faber, 1989), p. 488.
75 T. Dormandy, op. cit., pp. 22–5, 44, 46, 48, 79.
76 *Valldemossa Monastery Guide* (Barcelona: Escudo de Oro, SA).
77 B. Jack, op. cit., p. 283.
78 G. Sand, *A Winter in Majorca* (Palma: Edicions Cort, 1998; first published 1842), pp. 129, 193, 159.
79 Ibid., pp. 130, 143.
80 W. Atwood, op. cit., p. 111.
81 G. Sand, 1998, op. cit., pp. 150, 183, 185.
82 Ibid., p. 145.
83 W. Atwood, op. cit., p. 120.
84 B. Jack, op. cit., p. 285.
85 Oxford Regius Professor Sir George Pickering, quoted in T. Dormandy, op. cit., p. 15.
86 T. Dormandy, op. cit., pp. 46, 48.
87 Ibid., pp. 13–21.
88 R. Jordan, op. cit., p. 192.
89 Ibid., p. 267.
90 Ibid., p. 192.
91 W. Atwood, op. cit., p. 136; and J. Samson, op. cit., p. 269.
92 T. Dormandy, op. cit., pp. 106 ff.
93 A. Hedley, op. cit., p. 128.
94 Ibid., p. 85.
95 R. Jordan, op. cit., p. 217.
96 J. Samson, op. cit., p. 247.
97 W. Atwood, op. cit., p. 224.
98 G. Flaubert, op. cit., Part 2, Chapter 6, p. 274.
99 Ibid., p. 257.
100 Quoted in W. Atwood, op. cit., p. 23.
101 J. Samson, op. cit., p. 241.
102 For Sand's affairs, see B. Jack, op. cit., and R. Jordan, op. cit.
103 R. Jordan, op. cit., p. 217.
104 J. Samson, op. cit., p. 194.
105 B. Jack, op. cit., pp. 296, 315, 314.
106 J. Samson, op. cit., pp. 202–4; and A. Hedley, op. cit., p. 213.
107 W. Atwood, op. cit., p. 204.
108 R. Bolster, *Marie d'Agoult: The Rebel Countess* (New Haven, CT: Yale University Press, 2000), p. 182.
109 W. Atwood, op. cit., p. 214.
110 Ibid., p. 224.
111 Ibid., p. 216.
112 Ibid., p. 224.
113 Ibid., p. 230.
114 J. Samson, op. cit., pp. 249–50.
115 W. Atwood, op. cit., p. 234.
116 J. Samson, op. cit., p. 251.
117 B. Jack, op. cit., p. 301.
118 P. McPhee, *A Social History of France 1780–1880* (London: Routledge, 1992), p. 174.
119 B. Jack, op. cit., p. 306.
120 H. Opie'nski, op. cit., p. 345.
121 B. Jack, op. cit., p. 307.
122 R. Jordan, op. cit., p. 248.
123 H. Opie'nski, op. cit., p. 394.
124 Ibid., p. 395.
125 Ibid., p. 379.
126 Ibid., p. 397.
127 A. Hedley, op. cit., p. 111.
128 K. Preston, in D. Nicholls (ed.), *The Cambridge History of American Music* (Cambridge: Cambridge University Press, 1998), pp. 200, 201, 219.
129 H. Opie'nski, op. cit., p. 395.
130 Ibid., p. 387, amended by the author.
131 R. Holmes, *Coleridge: Darker Reflections* (London: HarperCollins, 1998).
132 H. Opie'nski, op. cit., p. 400.
133 J. Samson, op. cit., p. 259.
134 H. Opie'nski, op. cit., p. 405.
135 W. Atwood, op. cit., p. 279.
136 T. Dormandy, op. cit., p. 110.
137 There is a plaster cast at Valldemossa.
138 R. Jordan, op. cit., p. 331.
139 R. Bolster, op. cit., p. 251.
140 See also Edgar Allan Poe (*Ligeia*, *The Fall of the House of Usher*, etc.).
141 W. Atwood, op. cit., p. 289.

Chapter 12

1 P.H. Lang, *Music in Western Civilisation* (London: J.M. Dent, 1963), p. 804.
2 *Lalla Rookh*, p. 336, in T. Moore, *The Poetical Works* (London: Frederick Warne, 1892).
3 *Lalla Rookh*, p. 391, ibid.
4 *Lalla Rookh*, p. 392, ibid.
5 *Lalla Rookh*, p. 399, ibid.
6 A. Walker, *Franz Liszt, Volume 2: The Weimar*

Years, 1848–60 (London: Faber and Faber, 1989), p. 259.
7 *Lalla Rookh*, p. 396, in T. Moore, op. cit.
8 E. Jensen, *Schumann* (Master Musicians) (Oxford: Oxford University Press, 2001), p. 40.
9 Hanslick, quoted in J. Chissell, *Clara Schumann: A Dedicated Spirit* (London: Hamish Hamilton, 1983), p. 141.
10 Zwickau Museum Guide, *Robert-Schumann-Haus Zwickau* (Berlin, 2000), p.116; further information from Zwickau Hauptkirche.
11 J. Chissell, *Schumann* (Master Musicians) (London: J.M. Dent, 1948), p. 2.
12 R. Taylor, *Robert Schumann: His Life and Work* (London: Granada Publishing, 1982), p. 27.
13 J. Chissell, 1948, op. cit., p. 6.
14 R. Taylor, op. cit., p. 33.
15 Ibid., p. 19; and T. Mann (trans. H.T. Lowe-Porter), *Buddenbrooks* (London: Vintage, 1999; first published 1902), Part 9, Chapter 4, p. 479.
16 R. Taylor, op. cit., p. 34.
17 J. Chissell, 1948, op. cit., p. 10.
18 B. Walter (trans. J. Galston), *Theme and Variations* (London: Hamish Hamilton, 1947), p. 114.
19 *Encyclopaedia Britannica*, ninth edition, 1875–89, vol. 20, p. 547.
20 P. Ostwald, *Music and Madness* (London: Gollancz, 1985), p. 42.
21 R. Taylor, op. cit., pp. 48, 58.
22 P. Ostwald, op. cit., p. 191.
23 J. Chissell, 1983, op. cit., p. 15; and *New Grove Dictionary of Music and Musicians* (ed. S. Sadie) (London: Macmillan, 1980); and R. Taylor, op. cit., p. 51.
24 A. Walker, op. cit., p. 169.
25 R. Taylor, op. cit., p. 49.
26 Ibid., p. 176.
27 E. Jensen, 2001, op. cit., p. 30.
28 J. Chissell, 1948, op. cit., p. 12.
29 Ibid., p. 22.
30 E. Jensen, 2001, op. cit., p. 66.
31 S. Avins, *Johannes Brahms: Life and Letters* (Oxford: Oxford University Press, 1997), p. 747.
32 J. Chissell, 1983, op. cit., p. 20.
33 Ibid., pp. 11, 35.
34 J. Harding, *Saint-Saëns and his Circle* (London: Chapman and Hall, 1965), p. 22; and B. Rees, *Camille Saint-Saëns: A Life* (London: Chatto and Windus, 1999), p. 35.
35 P. Ostwald, op. cit., p. 88.
36 Ibid., p. 93.
37 J. Chissell, 1983, op. cit., pp. 29, 162, 58.
38 R. Taylor, op. cit., p. 67.
39 J. Chissell, 1948, op. cit., p. 29.
40 E. Jensen, 2001, op. cit., p. 297.
41 Ibid., p. 74.
42 Zwickau Museum Guide, op. cit., p. 77.
43 J. Chissell, 1948, op. cit., p. 195.
44 J. Chissell, 1983, op. cit., p. 39.
45 J. Chissell, 1948, op. cit., p. 199.
46 Ibid., p. 203.
47 Ibid., p. 199.
48 Ibid., p. 202.
49 Ibid., p. 195.
50 G. Frodl, in R. Erickson (ed.), *Schubert's Vienna* (New Haven, CT: Yale University Press, 1997), p. 174; and A. Hanson, *Musical Life in Biedermeyer Vienna* (Cambridge: Cambridge University Press, 1985), pp. 1, 2; and P.H. Lang, op. cit., pp. 805–7.
51 J. Chissell, 1948, op. cit., p. 35.
52 E. Jensen, 2001, op. cit., p. 120.
53 R. Taylor, op. cit., p. 135.
54 J. Chissell, 1983, op. cit., p. 39.
55 R. Taylor, op. cit., p. 176.
56 *New Grove*, op. cit.
57 J. Chissell, 1983, op. cit., p. 48.
58 Ibid., p. 49.
59 E. Jensen, 2001, op. cit., p. 130; and A. Hanson, op. cit., pp. 42, 47, 49.
60 J. Chissell, 1983, op. cit., p. 69.
61 J. Chissell, 1948, op. cit., p. 48.
62 J. Chissell, 1983, op. cit., p. 74.
63 E. Jensen, 2001, op. cit., p. 178.
64 R. Taylor, op. cit., p. 185.
65 *New Grove*, op. cit.
66 J. Chissell, 1983, op. cit., p. 84.
67 P.H. Lang, op. cit., p. 807.
68 J. Chissell, 1983, op. cit., p. 89.
69 N. Gogol (trans. D. Magarshack), *Dead Souls* (London: Penguin, 1961; first published 1842), p. 19.
70 R. Taylor, op. cit., p. 141.
71 E. Jensen, 2001, op. cit., p. 223.
72 J. Chissell, 1948, op. cit., p. 58.
73 J. Chissell, 1983, op. cit., p. 110.
74 S. Avins, op. cit., p. 759.
75 E. Jensen, 2001, op. cit., pp. 230, 338, 339.
76 J. Chissell, 1983, op. cit., p. 91.
77 R. Taylor, op. cit., p. 236.
78 J. Chissell, 1983, op. cit., p. 100.
79 Ibid., p. 109.

80 Ibid., p. 94.
81 G. Skelton (ed.), *Cosima Wagner's Diaries (an abridgement)* (London: Pimlico, 1994), p. 232.
82 A. Walker, op. cit., p. 341.
83 E. Jensen, 2001, op. cit., pp. 129, 317.
84 J. Chissell, 1983, op. cit., p. 105.
85 *New Grove*, op. cit., vol. 16, p. 844.
86 J. Chissell, 1948, op. cit., p. 68.
87 E. Jensen, 2001, op. cit., pp. 265, 273.
88 J. Chissell, 1983, op. cit., p. 100.
89 J. Chissell, 1983, op. cit., p. 114.
90 J. Chissell, 1948, op. cit., p. 71.
91 *Encyclopaedia Britannica*, ninth edition, op. cit. The 40 per cent of the US population was measured in 1867.
92 J. Chissell, 1983, op. cit., pp. 119, 120; and E. Jensen, 2001, op. cit., pp. 272, 274.
93 J. Chissell, 1983, op. cit., p. 122.
94 P. Ostwald, op. cit., p. 7.
95 J. Chissell, 1983, op. cit., p. 130.
96 Ibid., p. 123.
97 I. Keys, *Johannes Brahms* (London: Christopher Helm, 1989), p. 18; and Zwickau Museum Guide, op. cit., p. 106.
98 P. Ostwald, op. cit., p. 7.
99 Ibid., p. 276.
100 J. Chernaik, 'Guilt Alone Brings Forth Nemesis', *Times Literary Supplement*, 31 August 2001.
101 S. Avins, op. cit., p. 107.
102 P. Ostwald, op. cit., p. 276.
103 S. Avins, op. cit., p. 119.
104 J. Chissell, 1983, op. cit., p. 132.
105 Ibid., p. 133.
106 P. Ostwald, op. cit., p. 278.
107 S. Avins, op. cit., pp. 77, 96, 95.
108 R. Friedenthal, *Goethe: His Life and Times* (London: Weidenfeld and Nicolson, 1963), p. 410.
109 S. Avins, op. cit., p. 126, amended by the author.
110 A. Clark, 'The Reluctant Romantic', *Financial Times*, 18 August 2001. There is much literature on this point, including R. Taylor, op. cit., p. 70; J. Chissell, 1983, op. cit., p. 139; P. Ostwald, op. cit., pp. xii, 278, 292; E. Jensen, 'Buried Alive: Schumann at Endenich', *Musical Times*, vol. 139, no. 1861, March 1998, pp. 10–18; E. Jensen, 2001, op. cit., pp. 67, 314 ff, 175; and J. Chernaik, op. cit.
111 B. Berenbuch and H. Hellberg (trans. C. Spencer), *Robert Schumann and Bonn*, p. 14.
112 S. Avins, op. cit., pp. 125–6, amended by the author.
113 Ibid., p. 127.
114 S. Avins, op. cit., p. 142.
115 J. Chissell, 1983, op. cit., p. 138.
116 Ibid.
117 S. Avins, op. cit., p. 142.
118 Ibid.
119 Ibid., p. 140.
120 Ibid., p. 141.
121 Ibid., p. 142.
122 T. Moore, *Lalla Rookh*, p. 399, in T. Moore, op. cit.
123 J. Chissell, 1983, op. cit., p. xi.
124 Ibid., p. 152.
125 On display in the Endenich Museum.
126 R. Taylor, op. cit., p. 134; and J. Chissell, 1983, op. cit., pp. 208, 209.

Chapter 13

1 G. Skelton (ed.), *Cosima Wagner's Diaries (an abridgement)* (London: Pimlico, 1994), pp. 506, 140, 463.
2 J. Chissell, *Clara Schumann: A Dedicated Spirit* (London: Hamish Hamilton, 1983), p. 192.
3 A. Walker, *Franz Liszt, Volume 3: The Final Years, 1861–86* (London: Faber and Faber, 1997), p. 14.
4 A. Walker, *Franz Liszt, Volume 2: The Weimar Years, 1848–60* (London: Faber and Faber, 1989), p. 353.
5 S. Prokofiev (trans. O. Prokofiev), *Soviet Diary 1927 and Other Writings* (London: Faber and Faber, 1991), p. 142.
6 A. Walker, 1989, op. cit., p. 357.
7 Ibid., pp. 13, 390, 6; and A. Walker, 1997, op. cit., p. 253.
8 P. Ignotus, *Hungary* (London: Ernest Benn Ltd., 1972), p. 103.
9 A. Walker, *Franz Liszt, Volume 1: The Virtuoso Years, 1811–47* (London: Faber and Faber, 1983), p. 55; and R. Okey, *The Habsburg Monarchy* (London: Macmillan, 2001), p. 90.
10 A. Walker, 1983, op. cit., p. 90.
11 Ibid., pp. 96, 98.
12 P. Olleson, in C. Bashford and L. Langley (eds), *Music and British Culture* (Oxford: Oxford University Press, 2000), p. 35.
13 W. Beckett, *Liszt* (Master Musicians) (London: J.M. Dent, 1963), p. 9.
14 The Rev. Anthony Chambers enlightened

me regarding the enumeration of the Ten Commandments.
15 *New Grove Dictionary of Music and Musicians* (ed. S. Sadie) (London: Macmillan, 1980). The actual figures for piano ownership were thirteen per cent of traders, eleven per cent of officials, nine per cent of professional people and two per cent of boutiquiers, based on death statistics; for this and amateur statistics, see R. Wangermée, in P. Bloom (ed.), *Music in Paris in the Eighteen Thirties* (New York, NY: Pendragon Press, 1987), pp. 555, 572.
16 F. Tillard (trans. C. Naish), *Fanny Mendelssohn* (Portland, OR: Amadeus Press, 1996), p. 152.
17 P. Bloom, op. cit., p. 67.
18 A. Walker, 1997, op. cit., p. 298.
19 R. Taylor, *Robert Schumann: His Life and Work* (London: Granada Publishing, 1982), p. 152.
20 A. Walker, 1983, op. cit., p. 167.
21 P. McPhee, *A Social History of France 1780–1880* (London: Routledge, 1992), pp. 141, 145.
22 A. Devriès, in P. Bloom, op. cit., pp. 234, 237–40, 248.
23 R. Locke, *Music, Musicians and the Saint Simonians* (Chicago, IL: University of Chicago Press, 1986), pp. 10, 71, 227; and J. Ridley, *Garibaldi* (London: Constable, 1974), p. 23.
24 R. Locke, op. cit., p. 77.
25 Ibid., pp. 89, 90.
26 H. Lacombe (trans. E. Schneider), *The Keys to French Opera in the Nineteenth Century* (Berkeley, CA: University of California Press, 2001), pp. 183, 198.
27 R. Locke, op. cit., pp. 82, 109, 94, 108.
28 J. Ridley, op. cit., pp. 26, 25.
29 R. Locke, op. cit., p. 213.
30 Ibid., p. 230; and A. Walker, 1983, op. cit., p. 157.
31 *Encyclopaedia Britannica*, fifteenth edition, 1974; and H. Hearder, *Italy in the Age of the Risorgimento 1790–1870* (London: Longman, 1983), pp. 285, 286.
32 A. Einstein, *Music in the Romantic Era* (London: J.M. Dent, 1947), p. 347.
33 A. Walker, 1983, op. cit., p. 149.
34 Ibid., pp. 190, 191.
35 P. Barbier (trans. R. Luoma), *Opera in Paris 1800–1850* (Portland, OR: Amadeus Press, 1995), p. 128.
36 R. Bolster, *Marie d'Agoult: The Rebel Countess* (New Haven, CT: Yale University Press, 2000), p. 17.
37 Ibid., pp. 4, 5, 17, 67.
38 Ibid., p. 120.
39 Ibid., p. 36 et seq.
40 J. Barzun, in P. Bloom, op. cit., p. 17; see also H. de Balzac (trans. M. Crawford), *Le Père Goriot* (London: Penguin, 1951), passim.
41 A. Walker, 1983, op. cit., p. 214.
42 W. Beckett, op. cit., p. 16.
43 A. Walker, 1983, op. cit., p. 220.
44 *New Grove*, op. cit.; and A. Walker, 1983, op. cit., p. 226; and J. Chissell, op. cit., p. 52.
45 F. Tillard, op. cit., p. 255.
46 A. Walker, 1983, op. cit., pp. 238, 239.
47 W. Atwood, *The Lioness and the Little One: The Liaison of George Sand and Frédéric Chopin* (New York, NY: Columbia University Press, 1980), p. 39.
48 B. Jack, *George Sand* (London: Chatto and Windus, 1999), p. 273.
49 Stendhal (trans. M. Shaw), *The Charterhouse of Parma* (London: Penguin, 1958; first published 1839), p. 24.
50 A. Walker, 1983, op. cit., p. 247.
51 R. Wangermée, in P. Bloom, op. cit., p. 572.
52 E. Jensen, *Schumann* (Oxford: Oxford University Press, 2001), p. 162.
53 R. Bolster, op. cit., p. 171.
54 Liszt's journeys are shown on a map in the Raiding museum.
55 N. Gogol (trans. D. Magarshack), *Dead Souls* (London: Penguin, 1961), pp. 17–27.
56 A. Walker, 1989, op. cit., p. 4.
57 A. Walker, 1983, op. cit., p. 428; and C. Emerson, *The Life of Musorgsky* (Cambridge: Cambridge University Press, 1999), p. 137.
58 W. Beckett, op. cit., p. 30.
59 R. Bolster, op. cit., p. 170.
60 Liszt and Marie's visits are commemorated by a plaque on the bank of the Rhine at Rolandswerth.
61 R. Jordan, *George Sand* (London: Constable, 1976), p. 204.
62 W. Beckett, op. cit., p. 34.
63 J. Barzun, in P. Bloom, op. cit., p. 5.
64 P. Mansel, *Paris Between the Empires, 1814–1852* (London: John Murray, 2001), p. 122.
65 G. Skelton, op. cit., pp. 40, 95, 108, 143; and R. Bolster, op. cit., p. 236.
66 A. Walker, 1989, op. cit., p. 31.
67 Ibid., p. 26.

68 Information from author's visit, 2001.
69 A. Walker, 1983, op. cit., p. 404.
70 A. Walker, 1989, op. cit., pp. 434, 448. Mme Patersi di (or de) Fossombroni was her full name.
71 Ibid., p. 438.
72 A. Walker, 1989, op. cit., p. 430.
73 S. Avins, *Johannes Brahms: Life and Letters* (Oxford: Oxford University Press, 1997), p. 421.
74 G. Skelton, op. cit., p. 167.
75 A. Walker, 1989, op. cit., p. 477.
76 G. Skelton, op. cit., p. 101.
77 A. Walker, 1997, op. cit., p. 50.
78 Information from author's visits.
79 A. Walker, 1989, op. cit., p. 247.
80 Ibid., p. 52.
81 Ibid., p. 83.
82 Ibid., p. 82.
83 Ibid., p. 336.
84 Ibid., p. 284.
85 *New Grove*, op. cit.
86 A. Walker, 1989, op. cit., pp. 199, 205.
87 A. Einstein, op. cit., p. 140.
88 A. Walker, 1989, op. cit., p. 304.
89 A. Einstein, op. cit., p. 257.
90 A. Walker, 1989, op. cit., p. 82.
91 Ibid., p. 515. It was Prince Chlodwig Hohenlohe-Schillingfürst who became chancellor of Germany.
92 Ibid., p. 515.
93 A. Walker, 1997, op. cit., p. 26.
94 Ibid., p. 24.
95 W. Beckett, op. cit., pp. 53, 75.
96 G. Skelton, op. cit., p. 458.
97 A. Walker, 1997, op. cit., p. 323.
98 W. Beckett, op. cit., p. 53.
99 A. Walker, 1997, op. cit., p. 88.
100 Ibid., p. 166.
101 J.G. Keysler, *Travels Though Germany, Bohemia, Hungary, Switzerland, Italy and Lorrain* (London: A. Linde and F. Field, 1756), vol. II, p. 307.
102 A. Einstein, op. cit., p. 164.
103 The cigar holder is in the Liszt house, Weimar.
104 A. Walker, 1989, op. cit., p. 541.
105 See pictures by Georg Kraus in the museum at the Goethe Haus in Weimar.
106 Information from author's visit to the Liszt-Haus, Weimar.
107 A. Walker, 1997, op. cit., p. 228.
108 Ibid., p. 253.
109 G. Skelton, op. cit., p. 389.
110 A. Walker, 1983, op. cit., p. 375.
111 A. Walker, 1997, op. cit., p. 377.
112 Ibid., p. 13.
113 G. Skelton, op. cit., p. 463.
114 Ibid., pp. 506, 305.
115 W. Beckett, op. cit., p. 77.
116 A. Walker, 1997, op. cit., p. 5.
117 Ibid., p. 405.
118 W. Beckett, op. cit., p. 77.
119 J. Horton, *Grieg* (Master Musicians) (London: J.M. Dent, 1974), p. 63.
120 A. Walker, 1997, op. cit., p. 470.
121 Ibid., p. 486 (from Royal Archives, 7 April 1886).
122 W. Beckett, op. cit., p. 79.
123 A. Walker, 1997, op. cit., pp. 515, 519.
124 Ibid., pp. 520, 521. The quote is that of Felix Weingartner, the Austrian composer and conductor, amended by author.
125 J. Chissell, op. cit., p. 57.
126 J. Horton, op. cit., p. 34.
127 A. Walker, 1983, op. cit., p. 308; and W. Beckett, op. cit., p. 33.
128 S. Avins, op. cit., p. 466.
129 J. Chissell, op. cit., p. 71.
130 A. Walker, 1989, op. cit., p. 353.
131 S. Avins, p. 758.
132 A. Einstein, op. cit., p. 141; and A. Walker, 1983, op. cit., p. 48; and R. Okey, op. cit., p. 311.
133 D. Watson, *Liszt* (Master Musicians) (London: J.M. Dent, 1989), p. 2.
134 P. Ignotus, op. cit., p. 85.
135 *New Oxford Companion to Music* (ed. D. Arnold) (Oxford: Oxford University Press, 1983), p. 177.
136 H. Stevens (ed. M. Gillies), *The Life and Music of Béla Bartók* (Oxford: Clarendon Press, 1993), pp. 31, 16.
137 P. Ignotus, op. cit., p. 39.
138 A. Walker, 1983, op. cit., p. 323.
139 A. Walker, 1989, op. cit., pp. 71, 73.
140 P. Ignotus, op. cit., pp. 79, 89.
141 T. Blanning, *Joseph II* (London: Longman, 1994), p. 112.
142 J.-P. Bled (trans. T. Bridgeman), *Franz Joseph* (Oxford: Blackwell, 1992), p. 36.
143 Ibid., pp. 41, 43.
144 R. Okey, p. 94.
145 P. Ignotus, op. cit., p. 63.
146 J.-P. Bled, op. cit., p. 60.
147 Ibid., p. 153.
148 R. Okey, p. 213.

149 A. Walker, 1997, op. cit., p. 150.
150 D. Newsome, *The Convert Cardinals: Newman and Manning* (London: John Murray, 1993), pp. 226, 227.
151 J. Ridley, *Napoléon III and Eugénie* (London: Constable, 1979), p. 406.
152 H. Hearder, op. cit., p. 119.
153 Ibid., p. 120.
154 Ibid., p. 287.
155 Information taken from the guidebook of Sanctuaires Nôtre Dame de Lourdes, pp. 7, 14.
156 D. Newsome, op. cit., p. 271; and P. Franklin, *The Life of Mahler* (Cambridge: Cambridge University Press, 1997), p. 102; and *New Grove*, op. cit.; and P. McPhee, op. cit., p. 262.
157 H. Hearder, op. cit., p. 289.
158 J.-P. Bled, op. cit., p. 161.
159 E. Newman, *The Life of Richard Wagner: Volume IV 1866–1883* (London: Cambridge University Press, 1976), p. 308.
160 D. Newsome, op. cit., pp. 261, 281.
161 A. Walker, 1997, op. cit., p. 335.
162 I. Keys, *Johannes Brahms* (London: Christopher Helm, 1989), p. 9.
163 A. Walker, 1989, op. cit., p. 356.
164 Ernest Newman, quoted in W. Beckett, op. cit., p. 57.
165 A. Walker, 1983, op. cit., pp. 394, 392, 390; and W. Blunt, *The Dream King: Ludwig II of Bavaria* (London: Hamish Hamilton, 1970), pp. 12, 53.
166 A. Walker, 1989, op. cit., p. 51.
167 J. Richardson, *The Courtesans: The Demi-monde in 19th-Century France* (London: Weidenfeld and Nicolson, 1967), p. 166.
168 A. Walker, 1989, op. cit., p. 209.
169 A. Walker, 1997, op. cit., pp. 176, 172.
170 Song of Solomon, II, v. 17; V, v. 2.
171 W. Beckett, op. cit., p 59.
172 G. Skelton, op. cit., p. 13.

Chapter 14

1 M. Curtiss, 'Bizet, Offenbach and Rossini', in *Musical Quarterly*, vol. 40, 1954, pp. 375–409; and H. Lacombe (trans. E. Schneider), *The Keys to French Opera in the Nineteenth Century* (Berkeley, CA: University of California Press, 2001), p. 76; and F. Bowers, *The New Scriabin* (Newton Abbot: David and Charles, 1974), p. 77; and *New Grove Dictionary of Music and Musicians* (ed. S. Sadie) (London: Macmillan, 1980), vol. 19, p. 657; and I. Keys, *Johannes Brahms* (London: Christopher Helm, 1989), p. 108; and M. Leaska, *Granite and Rainbow: The Hidden Life of Virginia Woolf* (London: Picador, 1998), p. 179; and A. Einstein, *Music in the Romantic Era* (London: J.M. Dent, 1947), p. 254.
2 M. Eger and S. Friedrich (trans. T. Reimers and G. Shepherd), *The Richard Wagner Museum Bayreuth* (The Richard-Wagner-Foundation, 2000); and B. Millington, *Wagner* (Master Musicians) (London: J.M. Dent, 1984), p. 40.
3 N. Cardus, *A Composers Eleven* (London: Jonathan Cape, 1958), p. 40.
4 B. Magee, *Wagner and Philosophy* (London: Allen Lane The Penguin Press, 2000), p. 355.
5 *New Grove*, op. cit.
6 B. Magee, op. cit., p. 258.
7 C. Dahlhaus, 'Wagner's Place in the History of Music', in U. Müller and P. Wapnewski (eds) (trans. J. Deathridge), *The Wagner Handbook* (Cambridge, MA: Harvard University Press, 1992).
8 P.H. Lang, *Music in Western Civilisation* (London: J.M. Dent, 1963), p. 878.
9 M. Proust, quoted in W. Carter, *Marcel Proust: a Life* (New Haven, CT: Yale University Press, 2000), p. 663.
10 *New Grove*, op. cit., vol. 20, p. 104.
11 M. Eger and S. Friedrich, op. cit.
12 V. Kiernan, *The Duel in European History* (Oxford: Oxford University Press, 1988), pp. 272, 274.
13 M. Eger and S. Friedrich, op. cit.
14 R. Baldick, *The Duel* (London: Chapman and Hall, 1965), p. 150; and W. Carter, op. cit., pp. 235, 455; and P. Ignotus, *Hungary* (London: Ernest Benn Ltd., 1972), p. 83.
15 A. Einstein, op. cit., p. 232.
16 *New Grove*, op. cit.
17 G. Skelton (ed.), *Cosima Wagner's Diaries (an abridgement)* (London: Pimlico, 1994), p. 514.
18 E. Newman, *Memoirs of Hector Berlioz* (New York, NY: Dover Publications, 1932), pp. 311, 317.
19 S. Avins, *Johannes Brahms: Life and Letters* (Oxford: Oxford University Press, 1997), p. 292.
20 B. Millington, op. cit., pp. 14, 20.
21 B. Magee, op. cit., p. 66.
22 U. Müller and P. Wapnewski, op. cit., p. 568.
23 B. Magee, op. cit., p. 347.
24 B. Millington, op. cit., p. 27.
25 A. Einstein, op. cit., p. 231.

26 B. Magee, op. cit., pp. 38, 35.
27 U. Müller and P. Wapnewski, op. cit., p. 159.
28 D. Blackbourn, *Germany 1780–1918* (London: HarperCollins, 1997), p. 116, 117, 106.
29 Ibid., p. 139.
30 C. Woodham Smith, *The Great Hunger: Ireland 1845–9* (London: Hamish Hamilton, 1962), p. 409.
31 G. St Aubyn, *Queen Victoria: A Portrait* (London: Sinclair-Stevenson, 1991), pp. 23, 62.
32 D. Blackbourn, op. cit., p. 127.
33 R. Okey, *The Habsburg Monarchy* (London: Macmillan, 2001), p. 130.
34 U. Müller and P. Wapnewski, op. cit., p. 161.
35 B. Millington, op. cit., p. 37.
36 D. Blackbourn, op. cit., p. 170.
37 Ibid., pp. 148, 150.
38 U. Müller and P. Wapnewski, op. cit., p. 163.
39 D. Blackbourn, op. cit., p. 164.
40 U. Müller and P. Wapnewski, op. cit., p. 573.
41 A. Walker, *Franz Liszt, Volume 2: The Weimar Years, 1848–60* (London: Faber and Faber, 1989), pp. 114–19.
42 M. Eger and S. Friedrich, op. cit.; and B. Millington, op. cit., p. 44.
43 N. Cardus, op. cit., p. 50.
44 P.H. Lang, op. cit., p. 883.
45 Ibid., p. 938.
46 U. Müller and P. Wapnewski, op. cit., p. 287.
47 B. Magee, op. cit., passim.
48 R.W. Emerson, quoted in *Oxford Dictionary of Quotations* (Oxford: Oxford University Press, 1979).
49 *New Oxford Companion to Music* (ed. D. Arnold) (Oxford: Oxford University Press, 1983), p. 1056. The *Götterdämmerung* figures are from Jack Stein, quoted in B. Magee, op. cit., p. 260.
50 B. Millington, op. cit., pp. 52–4.
51 See I. Parrott, *Elgar* (Master Musicians) (London: J.M. Dent, 1971), p. 23.
52 P. Wapnewski, in U. Müller and P. Wapnewski, op. cit., p. 66.
53 N. Cardus, op. cit., p. 42.
54 T. Mann (trans. H.T. Lowe-Porter), *Death in Venice* (London: Penguin, 1955; first published 1911), pp. 41, 43.
55 B. Millington, op. cit., p. 67.
56 B. Walter (trans. J. Galston), *Theme and Variations* (London: Hamish Hamilton, 1947), p. 168.
57 B. Rees, *Camille Saint-Saëns: A Life* (London: Chatto and Windus, 1999), p. 111.
58 C. Crittenden, *Johann Strauss and Vienna* (Cambridge: Cambridge University Press, 2000), p. 215.
59 B. Millington, op. cit., p. 71.
60 M. Eger and S. Friedrich, op. cit., p. 9.
61 W. Blunt, *The Dream King: Ludwig II of Bavaria* (London: Hamish Hamilton, 1970), pp. 18, 22.
62 Ibid., p. 15.
63 Ibid., p. 228.
64 Ibid., p. 17.
65 Ibid., p. 23.
66 Ibid., p. 24.
67 Ibid., p. 26.
68 See W. Blunt, *Slow on the Feather* (Salisbury: Michael Russell, 1986), p. 63.
69 W. Blunt, 1970, op. cit., p. 29.
70 Ibid., p. 190.
71 B. Brown, *Gluck and the French Theatre in Vienna* (Oxford: Clarendon Press, 1991), p. 12.
72 M. Kennedy, *Richard Strauss: Man, Musician, Enigma* (Cambridge: Cambridge University Press, 1999), p. 68.
73 W. Blunt, 1970, op. cit., p. 54.
74 Ibid., p. 50.
75 Ibid., pp. 81, 79.
76 Ibid., p. 64.
77 G. Skelton, op. cit., p. 40.
78 Ibid., p. 50.
79 W. Blunt, 1970, op. cit., p. 77.
80 Ibid., p. 78.
81 Ibid., p. 113.
82 G. Skelton, op. cit., p. 24.
83 Information taken from menu in the museum at Tribschen.
84 G. Skelton, op. cit., p. 116.
85 Ibid., p. 5.
86 Ibid., p. 8.
87 Ibid., p. 72.
88 Ibid., p. 11.
89 Ibid., pp. 468, 381, 392, 394.
90 *Encyclopaedia Britannica*, fifteenth edition, 1974.
91 *New Grove*, op. cit.; and L. Davies, *Cesar Franck and his Circle* (London: Barrie and Jenkins, 1970), p. 257; and B. Rees, op. cit., pp. 129, 148.
92 J. Harding, *Saint-Saëns and his Circle* (London: Chapman and Hall, 1965), p. 107.
93 G. Skelton, op. cit., pp. 368, 441.

94 B. Magee, op. cit., p. 295.
95 G. Skelton, op. cit., p. 40; and passim.
96 Ibid., pp. 83, 84. A similar birthday present had been given to Mathilde Wesendonck. Under her window, a small orchestra played Wagner's setting of one of her poems, using themes from the *Tristan* love music. (E. Newman, *The Life of Richard Wagner* (London: Cassell, 1976), vol. 2, p. 532.)
97 Ibid., p. 209.
98 Ibid., pp. 97, 45.
99 Ibid., pp. 232, 247, 467.
100 Ibid., pp. 104, 105.
101 Ibid., pp. 67, 60, 377.
102 J. Harding, op. cit., p. 144.
103 G. Skelton, op. cit., pp. 70, 103.
104 B. Magee, op. cit., p. 285.
105 M. Eger and S. Friedrich, op. cit.; and E. Newman, *The Life of Richard Wagner: Volume IV 1866–1883* (London: Cambridge University Press, 1976), p. 309.
106 G. Skelton, op. cit., passim; and *New Grove*, op. cit., vol. 16, p. 695.
107 T. Mann (trans. H.T. Lowe-Porter), *Buddenbrooks* (London: Vintage, 1999; first published 1902), Part 7, Chapter 7, p. 357. The Buddenbrook house was built around the mid-1860s.
108 Such comparisons must be used with great care. A thaler was the equivalent of three marks; national income per capita in the German Empire was 314 marks; rents in relatively crowded and high-cost Berlin were 451 marks per capita; the annual income of an average managerial employee in a machine works near Stuttgart was 1,969 marks. See E. Newman, 1976, op. cit., pp. 418, 419, 398; J. Sheehan, *German History 1770–1866* (Oxford: Clarendon Press, 1989), pp. 737, 768; F. Tillard (trans. C. Naish), *Fanny Mendelssohn* (Portland, OR: Amadeus Press, 1996), p. 335.
109 Ibid., p. 127.
110 *Bayreuth Festspiele* (Bayreuth Festspiele GmbH, 1999), p. 13; and E. Newman, 1976, op. cit., pp. 306–19, 354, 400, 404.
111 G. Skelton, op. cit., pp. 261, 270, 266.
112 B. Magee, op. cit., p. 310.
113 E. Newman, 1976, op. cit., p. 409.
114 *Bayreuth Festspiele*, op. cit., p. 13; and E. Newman, 1976, op. cit., p. 567. The 1876 deficit was 147,851 marks.
115 *Bayreuth Festspiele*, op. cit., p. 21; and E. Newman, 1976, op. cit., p. 569.
116 G. Skelton, op. cit., pp. 281–3.
117 T. Mann, op. cit., Part 8, Chapter 4, p. 386.
118 G. Skelton, op. cit., pp. 302, 92, 188, 308. The Schott payment was 10,000 francs.
119 E. Newman, 1976, op. cit., p. 567; and G. Skelton, op. cit., p. 292.
120 E. Newman, 1976, op. cit., pp. 566, 570.
121 G. Skelton, op. cit., p. 285.
122 E. Newman, 1976, op. cit., p. 577. The agreement was dated 31 March 1878.
123 G. Skelton, op. cit., p. 453.
124 Ibid., p. 450.
125 Ibid., pp. 483, 490.
126 Ibid., pp. 512, 513.
127 Ibid., p. 514.
128 E. Newman, 1976, op. cit., p. 714; and B. Millington, op. cit., p. 118; and M. Eger and S. Friedrich, op. cit.; and *New Grove*, op. cit.
129 B. Walter, op. cit., p. 139.
130 G. Skelton, op. cit., p. 512.

Chapter 15

1 C. Crittenden, *Johann Strauss and Vienna* (Cambridge: Cambridge University Press, 2000), p. 4.
2 G. Skelton (ed.), *Cosima Wagner's Diaries (an abridgement)* (London: Pimlico, 1994), p. 197.
3 A. Faris, *Jacques Offenbach* (London: Faber and Faber, 1980), p. 27.
4 Wilfred Scawen Blunt, quoted in J. Ridley, *Napoléon III and Eugénie* (London: Constable, 1979), p. 529.
5 H. de Balzac (trans. M. Crawford), *Le Père Goriot* (London: Penguin, 1951; first published 1834–5), p. 304.
6 C. Crittenden, op. cit., p. 37.
7 A. Faris, op. cit., p. 20.
8 E. Zola (trans. D. Parmée), *Nana* (Oxford: Oxford University Press, 1998; first published 1880), p. 313.
9 S. Kracauer, *Offenbach and the Paris of his Time* (London: Constable, 1937), p. 55.
10 A. Faris, op. cit., pp. 38, 40.
11 J. Ridley, op. cit., p. 199.
12 Ibid., p. 139.
13 Ibid., p. 331.
14 E. Zola, *Nana*, 1998, op. cit., p. 405.
15 Ibid., p. 199.
16 Ibid., p. 318.

17 Ibid., p. 236.
18 Ibid., p. 238.
19 H. de Balzac, *Le Père Goriot*, op. cit., p. 55.
20 A. Faris, op. cit., p. 132; and A. Horne, op. cit., p. 23.
21 C. Jones, op. cit., p. 213.
22 J. Ridley, op. cit., p. 370.
23 P. McPhee, *A Social History of France 1780–1880* (London: Routledge, 1992), p. 200.
24 A. Horne, op. cit., p. 4.
25 P. McPhee, op. cit., p. 245.
26 *Encyclopaedia Britannica*, fifteenth edition, 1974, vol. 5, p. 357.
27 J. Ridley, op. cit., p. 405.
28 P. McPhee, op. cit., p. 209.
29 J. Rykwert, 'The Man who Made Paris', Review of Haussmann's *Mémoires*, *Times Literary Supplement*, 27 April 2001, p. 11.
30 P. McPhee, op. cit., p. 197. (The population grew from 1,053,000 to 2,269,000.)
31 O. Friedrich, *Olympia: Paris in the Age of Manet* (London: Aurum Press, 1992), p. 138.
32 P. McPhee, op. cit., p. 205.
33 E. Zola (trans. L. Tancock), *Germinal* (London: Penguin, 1954; first published 1885), p. 101.
34 P. McPhee, op. cit., p. 203.
35 P. McPhee, op. cit., p. 144. (Figures are for Mulhouse and the Haut-Rhin departement.)
36 *New Grove Dictionary of Music and Musicians* (ed. S. Sadie) (London: Macmillan, 1980), vol. 8, p. 527.
37 J. Richardson, *The Courtesans: The Demi-Monde in 19th-Century France* (London: Weidenfeld and Nicolson, 1967), p. 82.
38 P. McPhee, op. cit., p. 145.
39 O. Friedrich, op. cit., p. 222.
40 J. Ridley, op. cit., p. 391.
41 J. Laver, *Taste and Fashion* (Edinburgh: Harrap, 1945), pp. 49–53, 130; and A. Ribeiro, *Dress and Morality* (London: Batsford, 1986), p. 129.
42 J. Ridley, op. cit., pp. 407, 408.
43 Ibid., p. 404.
44 W. Carter, *Marcel Proust: A Life* (New Haven, CT: Yale University Press, 2000), p. 128.
45 J. Richardson, op. cit., p. 33.
46 *Pretty Women of Paris* (1883) quoted in J. Richardson, op. cit., p. 62.
47 J. Richardson, op. cit., pp. 58, 54.
48 Ibid., p. 55.
49 S. Kracauer, op. cit., p. 17.
50 A. Faris, op. cit., pp. 132, 142; and B. Rees, *Camille Saint-Saëns: A Life* (London: Chatto and Windus, 1999), p. 130; and J. Richardson, op. cit., p. 54; and A. Horne, op. cit., p. 7; and O. Friedrich, op. cit., p. 191.
51 S. Kracauer, op. cit., p. 191.
52 E. Zola, *Nana*, 1998, op. cit., p. 360.
53 A. Faris, op. cit., p. 174.
54 *New Grove*, op. cit.; and A. Faris, op. cit., pp. 48–50.
55 A. Faris, op. cit., pp. 52, 58, 132.
56 E. Zola, *Nana*, 1998, op. cit., p. 133.
57 Ibid., p. 121.
58 Ibid., p. 9.
59 *New Grove*, op. cit.
60 Information from visit to Bad Ems.
61 A. Faris, op. cit., p. 151.
62 S. Kracauer, op. cit., pp. 161, 171–3; and A. Faris, op. cit., pp. 62, 126.
63 S. Kracauer, op. cit., p. 278.
64 M. Nadar, the photographer, quoted in S. Kracauer, op. cit., p. 80.
65 J. Renoir, *Renoir my father* (London: The Reprint Society, 1964), p. 171.
66 See Courbet's *Falaise d'Etretat Après l'Orage* (1870), in the Louvre, and Monet's *Etretat* (1884), in Musée Eugène-Boudin, Honfleur.
67 A. Faris, op. cit., p. 143.
68 S. Kracauer, op. cit., p. 210; and J. Richardson, op. cit.
69 J. Ridley, op. cit., pp. 349, 420–23.
70 *New Grove*, op. cit.
71 A. Horne, op. cit., p. 27.
72 P. McPhee, op. cit., p. 227.
73 J. Ridley, op. cit., p. 503.
74 *Illustrated London News*, 13 January 1870.
75 J. Ridley, op. cit., p. 557.
76 J. Bury, *France 1814–1940* (London: Methuen, 1969), p. 113.
77 A. Horne, op. cit., pp. 40, 43, 38. J. Ridley, op. cit., p. 563, says that he went by train.
78 J. Bury, op. cit., p. 114.
79 J. Ridley, op. cit., pp. 565 ff.
80 C. Jones, *The Cambridge History of France* (Cambridge: Cambridge University Press, 1994), p. 191.
81 A. Horne, op. cit., p. 417.
82 A. Faris, op. cit., p. 173.
83 R. Nye and J. Morpurgo, *The Growth of the USA* (Harmondsworth: Pelican, 1965), p. 546.
84 *New Grove*, op. cit.
85 J.-P. Bled (trans. T. Bridgeman), *Franz Joseph* (Oxford: Blackwell, 1992), p. 158.

86 Ibid., p. 84.
87 R. Okey, *The Habsburg Monarchy* (London: Macmillan, 2001), p. 254.
88 B. Walter (trans. J. Galston), *Theme and Variations* (London: Hamish Hamilton, 1947), p. 225.
89 J.-P. Bled, op. cit., p. 112.
90 R. Okey, op. cit., p. 251.
91 P. Ignotus, *Hungary* (London: Ernest Benn Ltd., 1972), p. 74.
92 J.-P. Bled, op. cit., p. 241.
93 Ibid., p. 247.
94 J. Listowel, *A Habsburg Tragedy* (London: Ascent Books, 1978), pp. 122, 239.
95 J.-P. Bled, op. cit., pp. 168–71.
96 R. Okey, op. cit., p. 189.
97 *Illustrated London News*, 1 September 1860 and 10 January 1863.
98 C. Schorske, *Fin-de-Siècle Vienna* (New York, NY: Vintage Books, 1980), p. 140.
99 D. Blackbourn, *Germany 1780–1918* (London: HarperCollins, 1997), p. 245.
100 Ibid., p. 178: the 24,000 figure is for 1873.
101 C. Crittenden, op. cit., p. 2.
102 Ibid., p. 23.
103 *New Grove*, op. cit., vol. 18, p. 205.
104 R. Okey, op. cit., p. 254.
105 C. Crittenden, op. cit., p. 87.
106 Ibid., p. 110.
107 *New Grove*, op. cit., vol. 18, p. 208.
108 C. Crittenden, op. cit., pp. 92, 88.
109 M. Broyles, in D. Nicholls (ed.), *The Cambridge History of American Music* (Cambridge: Cambridge University Press, 1998), p. 233.
110 C. Crittenden, op. cit., pp. 117, 118.
111 Ibid., p. 37.
112 *Illustrated London News*, 18 November 1869.
113 C. Crittenden, op. cit., p. 137; attendance levels dropped from 8,000 on a good night to 3,000.
114 Ibid., p. 208.
115 Ibid., p. 194.
116 J.-P. Bled, op. cit., p. 158.
117 J.-P. Bled, op. cit., p. 237. (Bled's figures are 62 per cent of barristers in 1888 (i.e. 394 out of 631), 50 per cent of journalists and 61 per cent of the medical profession); see also C. Crittenden, op. cit., p. 143.
118 C. Crittenden, op. cit., p. 250.
119 *New Grove*, op. cit.
120 W. Lakond (trans. and ed.), *The Diaries of Tchaikovsky* (Westport, CT: Greenwood Press, 1973), p. 243.

Chapter 16

1 M. Phillips-Matz, *Verdi: A Biography* (Oxford: Oxford University Press, 1993), p. 10.
2 Stendhal (trans. M. Shaw), *The Charterhouse of Parma* (London: Penguin, 1958; first published 1839), pp. 199, 202.
3 *New Grove Dictionary of Music and Musicians* (ed. S. Sadie) (London: Macmillan, 1980), vol. 19, p. 652.
4 J. Budden, *Verdi* (Master Musicians) (London: J.M. Dent, 1985), p. 96.
5 H. Hearder, *Italy in the Age of the Risorgimento 1790–1870* (London: Longman, 1983), pp. 74, 75; and B. Walter (trans. J. Galston), *Theme and Variations* (London: Hamish Hamilton, 1947), p. 152.
6 M. Phillips-Matz, op. cit., p. 48.
7 J. Budden, op. cit., p. 5.
8 Stendhal, op. cit., pp. 359, 335. Stendhal's Parma was fictional, but he knew Italy from his time as consul in Civita Vecchia.
9 Incomes are from Stendhal, op. cit., pp. 157, 474.
10 M. Clark, *The Italian Risorgimento* (London: Addison-Wesley, 1998), p. 19.
11 *New Grove*, op. cit.
12 Ibid.
13 M. Phillips-Matz, op. cit., pp. 95, 101.
14 H. Weinstock, *Donizetti and the World of Opera* (London: Methuen, 1964), p. 172.
15 *New Grove*, op. cit., vol. 19, p. 637.
16 Ibid., p. 638.
17 M. Phillips-Matz, op. cit., p. 163, quoting M. Conati.
18 M. Clark, op. cit., p. 38.
19 *New Oxford Companion to Music* (ed. D. Arnold) (Oxford: Oxford University Press, 1983), p. 1905.
20 J. Budden, op. cit., p. 37.
21 *New Grove*, op. cit., vol. 19, p. 647.
22 M. Phillips-Matz, op. cit., p. 205.
23 J. Budden, op. cit., p. 26.
24 Ibid., p. 44.
25 *New Grove*, op. cit.
26 M. Phillips-Matz, op. cit., p. 150; and J. Budden, op. cit., p. 59.
27 *New Grove*, op. cit., vol. 18, p. 269.
28 M. Phillips-Matz, op. cit., p. 196.

29 Ibid., p. 230.
30 H. Hearder, op. cit., p. 161.
31 M. Clark, op. cit., pp. 45, 46.
32 M. Phillips-Matz, op. cit., pp. 240, 232.
33 M. Clark, op. cit., pp. 53, 54.
34 M. Phillips-Matz, op. cit., p. 236.
35 D. Mack Smith, *Cavour* (London: Weidenfeld and Nicolson, 1985), p. 151.
36 J. Ridley, *Garibaldi* (London: Constable, 1974), p. 400 and passim.
37 R. Jenkins, *Gladstone* (London: Macmillan, 1995), p. 125.
38 Ibid., p. 126.
39 M. Clark, op. cit., pp. 61, 70.
40 P. McPhee, *A Social History of France 1780–1880* (London: Routledge, 1992), pp. 228, 277. (There were 130,000 nuns compared with 12,000 early in the century.)
41 J. Ridley, *Napoléon III and Eugénie* (London: Constable, 1979), p. 403.
42 A. Horne, *The Fall of Paris* (London: Macmillan, 1965), p. 18; and P. McPhee, op. cit., p. 277.
43 J. Ridley, 1974, op. cit., p. 399.
44 J.-P. Bled (trans. T. Bridgeman), *Franz Joseph* (Oxford: Blackwell, 1992), p. 125.
45 J. Budden, op. cit., p. 83; and M. Phillips-Matz, op. cit., p. 392.
46 J. Ridley, 1979, op. cit., pp. 447, 448.
47 J.-P. Bled, op. cit., p. 106.
48 J. Ridley, 1979, op. cit., p. 450.
49 Ibid., p. 451.
50 Ibid., p. 454.
51 J. Budden, op. cit., p. 83.
52 M. Clark, op. cit., p. 79.
53 M. Phillips-Matz, op. cit., p. 429.
54 J. Budden, op. cit., p. 84.
55 M. Phillips-Matz, op. cit., pp. 394, 404, 481.
56 J. Ridley, 1974, op. cit., pp. 443, 484, 458; and J. Ridley, 1979, op. cit., p. 461.
57 *The Book of Saints*, compiled by the Benedictine Monks of St Augustine's Abbey, Ramsgate, sixth edition (London: A. and C. Black, 1989), p. 295; and Ridley, 1974, op. cit., p. 485.
58 M. Phillips-Matz, op. cit., p. 423.
59 *New Grove*, op. cit.
60 J. Ridley, 1974, op. cit., pp. 491, 499.
61 Ibid., p. 506.
62 J.-P. Bled, op. cit., p. 125.
63 J. Ridley, 1974, op. cit., p. 513.
64 Ibid., pp. 534, 538, 541, 542, 550.
65 Ibid., p. 551.
66 J. Budden, op. cit., p. 94.
67 H. Hearder, op. cit., p. 242.
68 *New Grove*, op. cit., vol. 2, p. 864.
69 Ibid., vol. 19, p. 652.
70 Ibid., vol. 19, p. 651.
71 J. Budden, op. cit., p. 116.
72 Information from guide at Sant'Agata.
73 J. Budden, op. cit., p. 49.
74 M. Phillips-Matz, op. cit., p. 358.
75 J. Budden, op. cit., p. 75.
76 M. Phillips-Matz, op. cit., p. 280.
77 J. Budden, op. cit., p. 59.
78 Ibid., p. 93.
79 M. Phillips-Matz, op. cit., p. 394.
80 J. Budden, op. cit., p. 57.
81 M. Phillips-Matz, op. cit., p. 329.
82 J. Budden, op. cit., p. 69.
83 Ibid., p. 95.
84 Ibid., p. 107 (letter to Clarina Maffei).
85 Ibid., pp. 107, 108.
86 M. Phillips-Matz, op. cit., p. 31.
87 *New Grove*, op. cit., vol. 19, p. 652.
88 J. Budden, op. cit., p. 115.
89 G. Skelton (ed.), *Cosima Wagner's Diaries (an abridgement)* (London: Pimlico, 1994), p. 244.
90 J. Budden, op. cit., pp. 122, 97 (quoting Henschel).
91 M. Phillips-Matz, op. cit., pp. 528, 541, 481, 540.
92 Ibid., p. 528.
93 *New Grove*, op. cit.
94 J. Budden, op. cit., p. 101.
95 M. Phillips-Matz, op. cit., p. 621.
96 M. Carner, *Puccini* (London: Gerald Duckworth and Co., 1974), p. 39.
97 M. Phillips-Matz, op. cit., p. 689.
98 Ibid., p. 719.
99 *New Grove*, op. cit., vol. 19, pp. 657, 658.
100 J. Budden, op. cit., p. 142.
101 M. Phillips-Matz, op. cit., p. 756.

Chapter 17

1 I. Keys, *Johannes Brahms* (London: Christopher Helm, 1989), p. 92, amended by author.
2 Ibid., p. 10.
3 Ibid., p. 147.
4 S. Avins, *Johannes Brahms: Life and Letters* (Oxford: Oxford University Press, 1997), p. 459; and A. Orlova, *Tchaikovsky: A Self-Portrait* (Oxford: Oxford University Press, 1990), p. 321;

and R. Layton, *Grieg* (London: Omnibus Press, 1998), p. 133.
5 I. Keys, op. cit., p. 152, amended by author.
6 N. Cardus, *A Composers Eleven* (London: Jonathan Cape, 1958), p. 78.
7 *Encyclopaedia Britannica*, ninth edition, 1875–89, vol. 11, p. 405.
8 D. Blackbourn, *Germany 1780–1918* (London: HarperCollins, 1997), p. 3.
9 Information taken from Museum für Hamburgische Geschichte, room 230.
10 I. Keys, op. cit., p. 3.
11 S. Avins, op. cit., p. 665.
12 D. Chandler (ed.), *Napoleon's Marshals* (London: Weidenfeld and Nicolson, 1987), pp. 94, 108.
13 I. Keys, op. cit., p. 3.
14 *Encyclopaedia Britannica*, ninth edition, op. cit., vol. 11, p. 404.
15 Ibid., vol. 11, p. 405; and vol. 21, p. 12.
16 I. Keys, op. cit., p. 4; and B. James, *Brahms: A Critical Study* (London: J.M. Dent, 1972), pp. 22, 23; and S. Avins, op. cit., pp. 3, 140.
17 S. Avins, op. cit., pp. 311–17.
18 Information taken from Museum für Hamburgische Geschichte, room 230.
19 *Encyclopaedia Britannica*, ninth edition, op. cit.
20 B. James, op. cit., p. 20; and S. Avins, op. cit., pp. 313, 569, 740.
21 B. James, op. cit., p. 30.
22 I. Keys, op. cit., p. 7.
23 A. Wheatcroft, *The Habsburgs* (London: Viking, 1995), p. 267; and R. Price, in B. Waller (ed.), *Themes in Modern History 1830–90* (London: Unwin Hyman, 1990), p. 19.
24 A. Walker, *Franz Liszt, Volume 2: The Weimar Years, 1848–60* (London: Faber and Faber, 1989), p. 65.
25 I. Keys, op. cit., p. 9.
26 K. Preston, in D. Nicholls (ed.), *The Cambridge History of American Music* (Cambridge: Cambridge University Press, 1998), p. 203.
27 S. Avins, op. cit., p. 362.
28 *New Grove Dictionary of Music and Musicians* (ed. S. Sadie) (London: Macmillan, 1980).
29 B. James, op. cit., p. 55.
30 Ibid., p. 185. Translation from Schumann's 'Neue Bahnen', in *Neue Zeitschrift*. I. Keys, op. cit., p. 11.
31 I. Keys, op. cit., p. 18; and B. James, op. cit., p. 67; and S. Avins, op. cit., p. 81.
32 I. Keys, op. cit., p. 21 (quoting from A. Holde, 'Suppressed Passages in Brahms Joachim Correspondence', in *Musical Quarterly*, vol. 45, 1959, p. 314).
33 S. Avins, op. cit., p. 69.
34 Ibid., pp. 760, 761.
35 Ibid., p. 200.
36 *Encyclopaedia Britannica*, ninth edition, op. cit.; and B. James, op. cit., p. 28.
37 S. Avins, op. cit., pp. 514, 182.
38 Ibid., p. 439.
39 Ibid., p. 188.
40 D. Blackbourn, op. cit., pp. 367, 368.
41 S. Avins, op. cit., p. 718.
42 Ibid., p. 779.
43 I. Keys, op. cit., p. 83.
44 Ibid., p. 103.
45 E. Walker (revised J.A. Westrup), *A History of Music in England* (Oxford: Clarendon Press, 1952), p. 340; and M. Leaska, *Granite and Rainbow: The Hidden Life of Virginia Woolf* (London: Picador, 1998), pp. 298, 340; and M. de Cossart, *The Food of Love: Princesse Edmond de Polignac and her Salon* (London: Hamish Hamilton, 1978), p. 109.
46 S. Avins, op. cit., pp. 187, 779.
47 Ibid., pp. 796, 229, 236.
48 Ibid., p. 189.
49 Ibid., p. 190; and C. Dahlhaus, 'Wagner's Place in the History of Music', in U. Müller and P. Wapnewski (eds) (trans. J. Deathridge), *The Wagner Handbook* (Cambridge, MA: Harvard University Press, 1992), p. 114; and E. Jensen, *Schumann* (Master Musicians) (Oxford: Oxford University Press, 2001), p. 184.
50 S. Avins, op. cit., pp. 221, 211.
51 B. James, op. cit., p. 187.
52 I. Keys, op. cit., p. 37.
53 A. Walker, op. cit., pp. 352, 346.
54 S. Avins, op. cit., p. 758.
55 Ibid., pp. 371, 373.
56 Ibid., p. 478.
57 G. Skelton (ed.), *Cosima Wagner's Diaries (an abridgement)* (London: Pimlico, 1994), pp. 237, 197, 214, 245, 299.
58 S. Avins, op. cit., p. 759.
59 J. Chissell, *Clara Schumann: A Dedicated Spirit* (London: Hamish Hamilton, 1983), p. 145.
60 B. Walter (trans. J. Galston), *Theme and Variations* (London: Hamish Hamilton, 1947), p. 26.
61 Ibid., pp. 41, 42.

62 D. Blackbourn, op. cit., p. 368.
63 B. Walter, op. cit., p. 27.
64 I. Keys, op. cit., p. 82.
65 C. Dahlhaus, op. cit., p. 115; and I. Keys, op. cit., p. 159; and B. James, op. cit., pp. 84, 88, 92, 94; and S. Avins, op. cit., p. 446.
66 A. Einstein, *Music in the Romantic Era* (London: J.M. Dent, 1947), p. 153.
67 A. Orlova, op. cit., pp. 230, 191.
68 I. Keys, op. cit., p. 47; and S. Avins, op. cit., pp. 304, 311, 318, 320.
69 S. Avins, op. cit., pp. 349, 350.
70 M. Curtiss, *Bizet and his World* (London: Secker and Warburg, 1959), p. 120; and G. Battiscombe, *Queen Alexandra* (London: Constable, 1969), p. 89.
71 H. Troyat, *Turgenev* (London: W.H. Allen, 1989), p. 79.
72 J. Chissell, op. cit., pp. 157, 158.
73 E. White, *Stravinsky: The Composer and his Works* (London: Faber and Faber, 1979), p. 23.
74 Ibid., p. 174.
75 S. Avins, op. cit., p. 150.
76 Ibid., p. 747.
77 I. Keys, op. cit., p. 22.
78 S. Avins, p. 767.
79 Ibid., pp. 239, 173.
80 I. Keys, op. cit., p. 71; and S. Avins, op. cit., pp. 448, 454.
81 J. Chissell, op. cit., p. 182.
82 S. Avins, op. cit., p. 688.
83 J. Chissell, op. cit., p. 185.
84 B. James, op. cit., p. 202.
85 I. Keys, op. cit., pp. 143, 138.
86 J. Chissell, op. cit., pp. 153, 156.
87 S. Avins, op. cit., pp. 339, 398; and I. Keys, op. cit., p. 68.
88 S. Avins, op. cit., p. 280.
89 F. Lesure (ed.) and R. Nichols (trans.), *Debussy: Selected Letters* (London: Faber and Faber, 1987), p. 234.
90 R. Okey, *The Habsburg Monarchy* (London: Macmillan, 2001), p. 166. For the reforms of Emperor Joseph II, see chapters 3 and 4.
91 J.-P. Bled (trans. T. Bridgeman), *Franz Joseph* (Oxford: Blackwell, 1992), pp. 91, 92.
92 C. Schorske, *Fin-de-Siècle Vienna* (New York: Vintage Books, 1980), p. 27; and J.-P. Bled, op. cit., pp. 182, 183.
93 C. Schorske, op. cit., pp. 54, 296.
94 S. Avins, op. cit., pp. 447, 458.
95 J.-P. Bled, op. cit., pp. 182–4.
96 Ibid., p. 184; the amount of railway track laid was less than 80 km.
97 R. Okey, op. cit., p. 230.
98 Ibid., p. 221; and J.-P. Bled, op. cit., pp. 184, 157.
99 C. Schorske, op. cit., p. 118.
100 S. Avins, op. cit., p. 556.
101 C. Schorske, op. cit., p. 134.
102 S. Avins, op. cit., pp. 726, 556.
103 J. Chissell, op. cit., p. 160.
104 I. Keys, op. cit., p. 66.
105 S. Avins, op. cit., pp. 660, 755.
106 Ibid., pp. 257, 259.
107 Ibid., pp. 287, 330; and I. Keys, op. cit., p. 156.
108 I. Keys, op. cit., p. 65.
109 J. Chissell, op. cit., p. 157.
110 S. Avins, op. cit., p. 726.
111 J. Chissell, op. cit., p. 194.
112 P. Monteath, 'Swastikas by the Seaside', in *History Today*, May 2000, pp. 31–5.
113 B. Walter, op. cit., p. 37.
114 I. Keys, op. cit., p. 82, amended by author.
115 For northern/southern divide in Germany, see T. Mann (trans. H.T. Lowe-Porter), *Buddenbrooks* (London: Vintage, 1999; first published 1902), Part 6, including pp. 271, 299.
116 S. Avins, op. cit., p. 494.
117 B. Rees, *Camille Saint-Saëns: A Life* (London: Chatto and Windus, 1999), p. 375.
118 Ibid., p. 304.
119 J. Caldwell, *The Oxford History of English Music* (Oxford: Oxford University Press, 1999), p. 259.
120 S. Avins, op. cit., p. 702.
121 Ibid., pp. 805, 721, xxvi.
122 I. Keys, op. cit., p. 54.
123 P. Franklin, *The Life of Mahler* (Cambridge: Cambridge University Press, 1997), p. 50.
124 S. Avins, op. cit., p. 528.
125 I. Keys, op. cit., p. 103.
126 C. Hibbert, *George III* (London: Viking, 1998), p. 372; and C. Tomalin, *Mrs Jordan's Profession* (London: Penguin, 1994), p. 309; and M. Kennedy, *Portrait of Elgar* (London: Oxford University Press, 1982), p. 18.
127 *Encyclopaedia Britannica*, ninth edition, op. cit.
128 C. Crittenden, *Johann Strauss and Vienna* (Cambridge: Cambridge University Press, 2000), p. 202.
129 B. Walter, op. cit., p. 168.

130 S. Avins, op. cit., p. 789.
131 I. Keys, op. cit., p. 100. The visitor was Max Kalbeck.
132 S. Avins, op. cit., p. 701.
133 Ibid., pp. 569–74.
134 S. Avins, op. cit., pp. 573, 572.
135 Ibid., p. 605.
136 H.F. Redlich, *Bruckner and Mahler* (Master Musicians) (London: J.M. Dent, 1963), pp. 26, 22.
137 S. Avins, op. cit., p. 619.
138 H.F. Redlich, op. cit., pp. 30, 32.
139 *New Grove*, op. cit., vol. 3, pp. 360, 359; and P. Franklin, op. cit., p. 36.
140 H.F. Redlich, op. cit., p. 5.
141 *New Grove*, op. cit., vol. 3, p. 354; and H.F. Redlich, op. cit., p. 8.
142 N. Cardus, op. cit., pp. 96, 93.
143 *New Grove*, op. cit., vol. 3, p. 356.
144 Ibid., p. 358, amended by author.
145 P.H. Lang, *Music in Western Civilisation* (London: J.M. Dent, 1963), p. 1013.
146 M. Kennedy, *Mahler* (Master Musicians) (London: J.M. Dent, 1974), p. 114.
147 P. Franklin, op. cit., p. 52. The unfortunate individual was Hans Rott.
148 S. Avins, op. cit., p. 671.
149 *Illustrated London News*, 1888, referred to in *New Grove*, op. cit., vol. 17, p. 574.
150 *New Grove*, op. cit., vol. 8, p. 620; and vol. 17, p. 574.
151 S. Avins, op. cit., p. 704.
152 I. Keys, op. cit., p. 140.
153 S. Avins, op. cit., p. 717.
154 *New Grove*, op. cit., vol. 3, p. 172.
155 S. Avins, op. cit., p. 682.
156 J. Chissell, op. cit., p. 208.
157 I. Keys, op. cit., p. 153.
158 S. Avins, op. cit., p. 733.
159 B. Walter, op. cit., p. 98.
160 S. Avins, op. cit., p. 740.
161 'Johannes Brahms und die Familie Miller-Aicholz' (Gmunden museum, 1997), p. 186.
162 I. Keys, op. cit., p. 155.
163 *New Grove*, op. cit., vol. 3, p. 161.

Chapter 18

1 W. Dean, *Bizet* (Master Musicians) (London: J.M. Dent, 1948), pp. 118, 119.
2 M. Curtiss, *Bizet and his World* (London: Secker and Warburg, 1959), pp. 351, 383.
3 P.H. Lang, *Music in Western Civilisation* (London: J.M. Dent, 1963), p. 908.
4 M. Curtiss, 1959, op. cit., p. 426.
5 S. Avins, *Johannes Brahms: Life and Letters* (Oxford: Oxford University Press, 1997), p. 591.
6 M. Curtiss, 1959, op. cit., p. 430.
7 A. Orlova, *Tchaikovsky: A Self-Portrait* (Oxford: Oxford University Press, 1990), p. 201.
8 A. Einstein, *Music in the Romantic Era* (London: J.M. Dent, 1947), p. 260.
9 W. Dean, op. cit., p. 222.
10 Ibid., p. 129.
11 M. Curtiss, 1959, op. cit., p. 4.
12 W. Dean, op. cit., p. 3.
13 M. Curtiss, 1959, op. cit., p. 14.
14 Ibid., p. 19.
15 Ibid.
16 *New Grove Dictionary of Music and Musicians* (ed. S. Sadie) (London: Macmillan, 1980), vol. 7, p. 586.
17 Ibid.
18 L. Davies, *Cesar Franck and his Circle* (London: Barrie and Jenkins, 1970), p. 29.
19 B. Rees, *Camille Saint-Saëns: A Life* (London: Chatto and Windus, 1999), p. 299.
20 W. Dean, op. cit., p. 6.
21 L. Davies, op. cit., p. 28.
22 M. Curtiss, 'Unpublished Letters by Georges Bizet', *Musical Quarterly*, vol. 36, 1950, p. 395.
23 M. Curtiss, 'Bizet, Offenbach and Rossini', *Musical Quarterly*, vol. 40, 1954, p. 350.
24 M. Curtiss, 1959, op. cit., p. 98.
25 Ibid., p. 50.
26 Ibid., p. 87.
27 W. Dean, op. cit., p. 27, amended by the author.
28 Quoted in M. Curtiss, 1959, op. cit., p. 32.
29 H. Lacombe (trans. E. Schneider), *The Keys to French Opera in the Nineteenth Century* (Berkeley, CA: University of California Press, 2001), p. 214.
30 M. Curtiss, 1959, op. cit., p. 136.
31 M. Proust (trans. S. Moncrieff and T. Kilmartin, revised D.J. Enright), *In Search of Lost Time: Swann's Way* (London: Chatto and Windus, 1992; first published 1913), p. 295.
32 M. Curtiss, 1959, op. cit., p. 162.
33 Jouvin, quoted in M. Curtiss, 1959, op. cit., p. 139.
34 W. Dean, op. cit., p. 54.
35 M. Curtiss, 1959, op. cit., p. 187.
36 M. Curtiss, 1950, op. cit.

37 M. Curtiss, 1959, op. cit., p. 171.
38 Ibid., p. 167.
39 J. Richardson, *The Courtesans: The Demi-Monde in 19th-Century France* (London: Weidenfeld and Nicolson, 1967).
40 W. Dean, op. cit., pp. 150, 55, 95.
41 M. Curtiss, 1959, op. cit., p. 185.
42 Ibid., p. 203.
43 W. Dean. op. cit., p. 58.
44 Ibid., p. 80.
45 M. Curtiss, 1959, op. cit., p. 206.
46 H. Macdonald, Review of Lacombe, *Bizet*, *Times Literary Supplement*, 20 July 2001.
47 M. Curtiss, 1959, op. cit., p. 206.
48 W. Dean, op. cit., p. 75.
49 R. Locke, *Music, Musicians and the Saint Simonians* (Chicago, IL: University of Chicago Press, 1986), pp. 94, 107.
50 M. Curtiss, 1959, op. cit., pp. 244, 237, 249; and M. Curtiss, 1950, op. cit.
51 W. Carter, *Marcel Proust: A Life* (New Haven, CT: Yale University Press, 2000), p. 94.
52 M. Curtiss, 1950, op. cit.
53 A. Horne, *The Fall of Paris* (London: Macmillan, 1965), p. 14.
54 J. Ridley, *Napoléon III and Eugénie* (London: Constable, 1979), p. 557.
55 A. Taylor, *English History 1914–1945* (Oxford: Oxford University Press, 1975), p. 430.
56 J. Barrie Jones (trans. and ed.), *Gabriel Fauré: A Life in Letters* (London: Batsford, 1988), p. 26.
57 W. Dean, op. cit., p. 86.
58 A. Horne, op. cit., p. 54.
59 *New Grove*, op. cit.; and W. Dean, op. cit., p. 89; and M. Curtiss, 1959, op. cit., p. 293.
60 B. Rees, op. cit., pp. 158–60.
61 J. Richardson, op. cit.
62 L. Davies, op. cit., p. 308.
63 I. Bell, 'Questions and Answers', in *Choir and Organ*, January/February 2002, p. 8.
64 R. Orledge, *Gabriel Fauré* (London: Eulenburg, 1979), p. 9.
65 L. Davies, op. cit., p. 34.
66 K. Clark, *The Romantic Rebellion* (London: John Murray, 1975), pp. 285, 300.
67 E. Gombrich, *The Story of Art*, (London: Phaidon, 1963), p. 382.
68 M. Curtiss, 1950, op. cit., p. 380.
69 M. Curtiss, 1959, op. cit., pp. 265–7.
70 A. Horne, op. cit., pp. 63, 66.
71 Ibid., p. 177, amended by the author.
72 Ibid., p. 131, amended by the author.
73 Ibid., p. 130.
74 A. Horne, op. cit., p. 126.
75 R. Spaethling, *Mozart's Letters, Mozart's Life* (London: Faber and Faber, 2000), p. 436.
76 *Encyclopaedia Britannica*, ninth edition, 1875–89, vol. 2, p. 509.
77 G. Skelton (ed.), *Cosima Wagner's Diaries (an abridgement)* (London: Pimlico, 1994), p. 79.
78 A. Horne, op. cit., p. 130.
79 Ibid., p. 128.
80 Ibid., pp. 143, 146, 160, 158.
81 Ibid., p. 136.
82 Ibid., p. 183.
83 Ibid., p. 185.
84 Ibid., p. 244.
85 Sheppard, quoted in A. Horne, op. cit., p. 180.
86 A. Horne, op. cit., p. 178.
87 Labouchère, quoted in A. Horne, op. cit., p. 178.
88 A. Horne, op. cit., pp. 213, 217.
89 M. Curtiss, 1959, op. cit., p. 272.
90 W. Dean, op. cit., p. 87.
91 M. Curtiss, 1950, op. cit.
92 B. Rees, op. cit., p. 163.
93 O. Friedrich, *Olympia: Paris in the Age of Manet* (London: Aurum Press, 1992), p. 219.
94 M. Curtiss, 1950, op. cit., p. 389.
95 E. Zola (trans. L. Tancock), *Germinal* (London: Penguin 1954; first published 1885), Part V, Chapter 6.
96 M. Curtiss, 1950, op. cit., p. 389.
97 A. Horne, op. cit., pp. 275, 289.
98 Ibid., pp. 288, 302, 357.
99 Ibid., p. 356, amended by the author.
100 Ibid., pp. 336, 267.
101 M. Curtiss, 1950, op. cit., p. 390.
102 Ibid., pp. 390–91.
103 Ibid., p. 392, amended by the author.
104 A. Horne, op. cit., pp. 310, 313.
105 M. Curtiss, 1950, op. cit., p. 394.
106 A. Horne, op. cit., p. 361.
107 Ibid., p. 299.
108 Ibid., p. 366.
109 B. Rees, op. cit., p. 163.
110 M. Curtiss, 1950, op. cit., p. 396.
111 M. Curtiss, 1959, op. cit., p. 290.
112 *New Grove*, op. cit.
113 A. Horne, op. cit., p. 406.
114 Ibid., p. 432.
115 Ibid., pp. 418, 422.
116 Ibid., p. 420.
117 M. Curtiss, 1950, op. cit., pp. 397–8.

118 A. Horne, op. cit., p. 421.
119 W. Carter, op. cit., pp. 66, 68, 69, 89.
120 M. Curtiss, 1950, op. cit., pp. 399–400.
121 W. Dean, op. cit., pp. 143, 145.
122 Ibid., p. 92.
123 W. Dean, op. cit., p. 97.
124 N. Simeone, *Paris: A Musical Gazetteer* (New Haven, CT: Yale University Press, 2000), p. 174.
125 W. Dean, op. cit., pp. 212, 213, 230.
126 Ibid., pp. 215, 114.
127 L. Davies, op. cit., p. 17; J. Renoir, *Renoir my father* (London: The Reprint Society, 1964), p. 45.
128 M. Curtiss, 1954, op. cit.; and W. Dean, op. cit., pp. 215, 118.
129 W. Dean, op. cit., p. 226.
130 B. Rees, op. cit., p. 186.
131 W. Dean, op. cit., p. 116.
132 W. Dean, op. cit., pp. 126, 101.
133 M. Curtiss, 1959, op. cit., p. 121.
134 W. Carter, op. cit., pp. 745, 799, 804.
135 W. Dean, op. cit., p. 101.
136 M. Curtiss, 1959, op. cit., p. 436.

Chapter 19

1 L. Davies, *Cesar Franck and his Circle* (London: Barrie and Jenkins, 1970), p. 236.
2 Ibid., p. 105.
3 Ibid., p. 110.
4 Martin Cooper, quoted in B. Rees, *Camille Saint-Saëns: A Life* (London: Chatto and Windus, 1999), p. 12.
5 N. Cardus, *A Composers Eleven* (London: Jonathan Cape, 1958), p. 159.
6 R. Orledge, *Gabriel Fauré* (London: Eulenburg, 1979), p. 232, amended by the author.
7 S. Levas (trans. P.M. Young), *Sibelius: A Personal Portrait* (London: J.M. Dent, 1972), p. 68.
8 B. Rees, op. cit., p. 17.
9 Ibid., pp. 10, 11.
10 B. Ivry, *Francis Poulenc* (London: Phaidon, 1996), p. 87.
11 *New Oxford Companion to Music* (ed. D. Arnold) (Oxford: Oxford University Press, 1983), p. 664.
12 *Illustrated London News*, 7 December 1921 and 23 January 1924.
13 *Encyclopaedia Britannica*, ninth edition, 1875–89.
14 Ibid, vol. 3, p. 527.
15 Ibid.
16 G. St Aubyn, *Queen Victoria: A Portrait* (London: Sinclair-Stevenson, 1991), p. 34.
17 *Encyclopaedia Britannica*, ninth edition, op. cit.
18 J. Harding, *Saint-Saëns and his Circle* (London: Chapman and Hall, 1965), p. 111.
19 L. Davies, op. cit., p. 43.
20 Ibid.
21 Ibid., pp. 58, 63.
22 Ibid., p. 68.
23 J. Harding, op. cit., p. 111.
24 L. Davies, op. cit., p. 78.
25 *The Book of Saints*, compiled by the Benedictine Monks of St Augustine's Abbey, Ramsgate, sixth edition (London: A. and C. Black, 1989); further information obtained at Sainte Clotilde.
26 A. Walker, *Franz Liszt Volume 3: The Final Years 1861–86* (London: Faber and Faber, 1997), p. 103, amended by the author.
27 L. Davies, op. cit., pp. 116, 115.
28 P. McPhee, *A Social History of France 1780–1880* (London: Routledge, 1992), pp. 209, 277; and J. Bury, *France 1814–1940* (London: Methuen, 1969), p. 161.
29 P. Mansel, *Paris Between the Empires, 1814–1852* (London: John Murray, 2001), p. 378.
30 J. Bury, op. cit., p. 142.
31 B. Rees, op. cit., p. 175.
32 J. Bury, op. cit., p. 148.
33 Ibid., p. 131.
34 Ibid., p. 141.
35 B. Rees, op. cit., p. 267.
36 J. Bury, op. cit., pp. 155, 177–80.
37 A. Mahler-Werfel (trans. A. Beaumont), *Diaries 1898–1902* (London: Faber and Faber, 1998), p. 200.
38 W. Carter, *Marcel Proust: A Life* (New Haven, CT: Yale University Press, 2000), p. 241.
39 B. Rees, op. cit., p. 268.
40 J. Bury, op. cit., p. 181.
41 *Illustrated London News*, 9 January 1899.
42 J. Harding, op. cit., p. 112, amended by the author.
43 L. Davies, op. cit., p. 143.
44 Ibid., pp. 269, 178; and A. Mahler-Werfel, op. cit., pp. 55, 57, 163.
45 L. Davies, op. cit., p. 178.
46 J. Harding, op. cit., p. 174, 220.
47 B. Rees, op. cit., p. 265, amended by the author.
48 L. Davies, op. cit., p. 242.

49 J. Harding, op. cit., p. 76.
50 B. Rees, op. cit., p. 231; and J. Harding, op. cit., p. 174; and *New Grove Dictionary of Music and Musicians* (ed. S. Sadie) (London: Macmillan, 1980).
51 B. Rees, op. cit., p. 356.
52 Ibid., passim.; and J. Harding, op. cit., pp. 73–5.
53 B. Rees, op. cit., p. 1.
54 J. Harding, op. cit., p. 15.
55 Ibid., passim.
56 Ibid., pp. 21, 22.
57 B. Rees, op. cit., pp. 22, 33, 37.
58 J. Harding, op. cit., p. 32.
59 Ibid., p. 27.
60 R. Orledge, op. cit., p. 8.
61 B. Rees, op. cit., pp. 190, 191.
62 R. Orledge, op. cit., p. 232.
63 B. Rees, op. cit., pp. 84, 104; and J. Harding, op. cit., pp. 43, 88.
64 B. Rees, op. cit., p. 64. (The actual figure is 232 from a census in 1863.)
65 Ibid., p. 90.
66 Ibid., p. 145.
67 Ibid., pp. 124, 35; and J. Harding, op. cit., p. 225.
68 J. Harding, op. cit., p. xiii.
69 Ibid., p. 147.
70 B. Rees, op. cit., p. 92.
71 Ibid., p. 167.
72 Ibid., p. 153.
73 R. Orledge, op. cit., p. 7.
74 J. Harding, op. cit., pp. 102, 149, 182.
75 B. Rees, op. cit., pp. 135, 136.
76 J. Harding, op. cit., p. 108; and B. Rees, op. cit., p. 162.
77 J. Harding, op. cit., p. 162.
78 B. Rees, op. cit., p. 168.
79 *Encyclopaedia Britannica*, ninth edition, op. cit., vol. 1, p. 566.
80 J. Harding, op. cit., pp. 134, 142; and A. Holden, *Tchaikovsky* (London: Bantam Press, 1995), p. 102.
81 B. Rees, op. cit., p. 230.
82 Ibid., p. 241.
83 J. Harding, op. cit., pp. 144, 170; and B. Rees, op. cit., pp. 375, 260.
84 B. Rees, op. cit., p. 218; further information from the Musée de la Musique, Cité de la Musique, Paris.
85 J. Harding, op. cit., p. 177; and B. Rees, op. cit., pp. 281–3.
86 J. Harding, op. cit., p. 166.
87 B. Rees, op. cit., p. 366.
88 Letter to Charpentier, quoted in B. Rees, op. cit., p. 354.
89 J. Harding, op. cit., p. 214.
90 Ibid., p. 215.
91 B. Rees, op. cit., p. 377.
92 F. Lesure and R. Nicholls (selected and trans.), *Debussy: Letters* (London: Faber and Faber, 1987), p. 179.
93 J. Harding, op. cit., p. 142.
94 Ibid., p. 158.
95 B. Rees, op. cit., p. 371.
96 J. Harding, op. cit., p. 225.
97 G. Reese, *Music in the Middle Ages* (London: J.M. Dent, 1968; original edition, 1940), p. 212.
98 *New Grove*, op. cit.
99 B. Rees, op. cit., p. 143.
100 *New Grove*, op. cit., vol. 6, p. 417.
101 B. Rees, op. cit., p. 150.
102 N. Simeone, *Paris: A Musical Gazetteer* (New Haven, CT: Yale University Press, 200), p. 167.
103 R. Orledge, op. cit., p. 9.
104 Ibid., p. 10.
105 Ibid.
106 J. Barrie Jones (trans. and ed.), *Gabriel Fauré: A Life in Letters* (London: Batsford, 1988), p. 33.
107 R. Orledge, op. cit., p. 11.
108 Ibid., p. 12.
109 J. Barrie Jones, op. cit., p. 54.
110 Ibid., p. 54.
111 M. Proust (trans. S. Moncrieff and T. Kilmartin, revised D.J. Enright), *In Search of Lost Time: The Guermantes Way* (London: Chatto and Windus, 1992; first published 1920), p. 496.
112 Ibid., p. 534.
113 R. Orledge, op. cit., p. 13.
114 J. Barrie Jones, op. cit., p. 55.
115 J. Barrie Jones, op. cit., pp. 72, 74.
116 M. Proust, op. cit., pp. 569, 175, 181; and Colette (trans. R. Senhouse), *Gigi* (London: Vintage, 2001; first published 1944); and Colette (trans. R. Senhouse), *Chéri* (London: Penguin, 1954; first published 1920), p. 24; and Colette (trans. A. White), *Claudine in Paris* (London: Penguin, 1963; first published 1901), p 113.
117 J. Barrie Jones, op. cit., p. 171; and R. Orledge, op. cit., p. 15.
118 R. Orledge, op. cit., p. 32, 11.

119 A. Leslie, *Edwardians in Love* (London: Hutchinson, 1972), p. 132.
120 J. Barrie Jones, op. cit., p. 84.
121 R. Orledge, op. cit., p. 188.
122 J. Bury, op. cit., p. 161.
123 Ibid., p. 163.
124 Ibid., pp. 200, 201.
125 Ibid., p. 199.
126 B. Rees, op. cit., p. 372.
127 J. Bury, op. cit., pp. 201, 202.
128 R. Orledge, op. cit., p. 113.
129 Ibid., p. 43.
130 M. Boyd, 'Fauré's Requiem: A Reappraisal', *Musical Times*, 1963, p. 408.
131 J. Barrie Jones, op. cit., p. 68.
132 R. Orledge, op. cit., p. 84.
133 J. Perkin, 'Sewing Machines: Liberation or Drudgery for Women', *History Today*, December 2002, p. 37.
134 M. de Cossart, *The Food of Love: Princesse Edmond de Polignac and her Salon* (London: Hamish Hamilton, 1978), p. 11.
135 F. Routh, *Stravinsky* (Master Musicians) (London: J.M. Dent, 1975), pp. 28, 30.
136 B. Ivry, op. cit., p. 110.
137 M. de Cossart, op. cit., p. 41.
138 Ibid., p. 43.
139 W. Carter, op. cit., p. 439; and R. Massie, *Dreadnought* (London: Jonathan Cape, 1992), p. 675.
140 M. de Cossart, op. cit., pp. 51, 83.
141 L. Davies, op. cit., p. 35.
142 J. Barrie Jones, op. cit., p. 69.
143 J. Bury, op. cit., pp. 221, 222.
144 Ibid., pp. 224, 225, 227; and *Encyclopaedia Britannica*, fifteenth edition, 1974; and W. Carter, op. cit., pp. 227, 289.
145 R. Orledge, op. cit., p. 38.
146 It was written for 200 singers, 400 instrumentalists, including military band, and 20 harpists. (R. Orledge, op. cit., p. 18.)
147 J. Barrie Jones, op. cit., p. 114.
148 Ibid., p. 108.
149 Ibid., p. 111.
150 Ibid., p. 180.
151 R. Orledge, op. cit., p. 21; and *New Grove*, op. cit; and J. Barrie Jones, op. cit., p. 118; and H. Stuckenschmidt (trans. R. Rosenbaum), *Maurice Ravel* (London: Calder and Boyars, 1969), pp. 222, 254, 19, 71.
152 B. Rees, op. cit., p. 368.
153 R. Orledge, op. cit., p. 21.
154 J. Barrie Jones, op. cit., p. 131.
155 R. Orledge, op. cit., p. 23.
156 J. Barrie Jones, op. cit., p. 147.
157 Ibid., p. 159.
158 Ibid., p. 161.
159 Ibid., p. 167.
160 Ibid., p. 173, 174.
161 *New Grove*, op. cit.; and H. Stuckenschmidt, op. cit., pp. 241, 239, 235.
162 *New Grove*, op. cit., vol. 6, p. 420.
163 R. Orledge, op. cit., p. 27.
164 The English pastoral poet Richard Barnfield (1574–1627), quoted in *Oxford Dictionary of Quotations* (Oxford: Oxford University Press, 1979), p. 34, no. 3.

Chapter 20

1 *New Oxford Companion to Music* (ed. D. Arnold) (Oxford: Oxford University Press, 1983), p. 1620.
2 O. Figes, *Natasha's Dance: A Cultural History of Russia* (London: Allen Lane The Penguin Press, 2002), p. 310, quoting Gogol.
3 *Oxford Companion*, op. cit., p. 1183.
4 R. Coughlan, *Elizabeth and Catherine* (London: Millington, 1974), p. 28.
5 F. Bowers, *The New Scriabin* (Newton Abbot: David and Charles, 1974), p. 111.
6 P.H. Lang, *Music in Western Civilisation* (London: J.M. Dent, 1963), p. 958.
7 A. Herzen, quoted in O. Figes, op. cit., p. 9.
8 J. Hartley, 'Charles Whitworth, First British Ambassador to Russia', *History Today*, vol. 50, June 2000, p. 40.
9 A. Walker, *Franz Liszt, Volume 2: The Weimar Years, 1848-60* (London: Faber and Faber, 1989), p. 38.
10 E. Newman, *Memoirs of Hector Berlioz* (New York, NY: Dover Publications, 1932), p. 425.
11 A. Pushkin, 'The Stationmaster', in 'Belkin', pp. 41, 44, in A. Pushkin (trans. and ed. A. Myers and A. Kahn), *The Queen of Spades and Other Stories* (Oxford: Oxford University Press, 1997; first published 1834); see also N. Gogol (trans. D. Magarshack), *Dead Souls* (London: Penguin, 1961; first published 1842), p. 181.
12 *Encyclopaedia Britannica*, ninth edition, 1875-89.
13 A. Orlova, *Tchaikovsky: A Self-Portrait* (Oxford: Oxford University Press, 1990), p. 297.

14 W. Lakond, *The Diaries of Tchaikovsky* (Westport, CT: Greenwood Press, 1973), p. 140.
15 For duels, see Pushkin, 'The Shot', for gaming, 'Belkin' and 'The Queen of Spades', in A. Pushkin, op. cit.
16 R. Coughlan, op. cit., p. 47.
17 I. Grey, *Boris Godunov* (London: Hodder and Stoughton, 1973), pp. 173, 175.
18 *Oxford Companion*, op. cit., p. 1384.
19 D. Saunders, *Russia in the Age of Reaction and Reform* (London: Longman, 1992), pp. 8, 9.
20 Ibid., p. 4.
21 Ibid., p. 16.
22 O. Figes, op. cit., p. 18.
23 D. Saunders, op. cit., pp. 16, 17, 24; and H. Acton, *The Last Medici* (London: Macmillan, 1980), pp. 165, 164.
24 A. Walker, 1989, op. cit., p. 26.
25 H. Troyat, *Turgenev* (London: W.H. Allen, 1989), p. 41.
26 D. Saunders, op. cit., pp. 152, 153; and O. Figes, *Natasha's Dance: A Cultural History of Russia* (London: Allen Lane The Penguin Press, 2002), p. 451.
27 M. Fainsod, *How Russia is Ruled* (Cambridge, MA: Harvard University Press, 1963), pp. 21, 24. (Coal production in 1913 was 36 million tons compared with the USA's 517 million.)
28 Ibid., p. 8.
29 G. St Aubyn, *Queen Victoria: A Portrait* (London: Sinclair-Stevenson, 1991), p. 411.
30 O. Figes, op. cit., p. 155.
31 See 'The Lady Peasant', in 'Belkin', in A. Pushkin, op. cit., p. 44.
32 P.H. Lang, op. cit., p. 939; and *New Grove Dictionary of Music and Musicians* (ed. S. Sadie) (London: Macmillan, 1980).
33 On the second floor of St Sophia, Kiev.
34 *Oxford Companion*, op. cit., p. 1598.
35 F. Routh, *Stravinsky* (Master Musicians) (London: J.M. Dent, 1975), p. 51; and *New Grove*, op. cit., vol. 15, p. 204; and O. Figes, op. cit., p. 114.
36 Information from plaque in St Andrew's Church, Kiev.
37 Information from the Glinka Museum, Moscow.
38 *Oxford Companion*, op. cit., pp. 1598, 677.
39 R. Walker, *Rachmaninoff: His Life and Times* (Tunbridge Wells: Midas, 1980), p. 3.
40 *New Grove*, op. cit., vol. 7, p. 435.
41 Ibid., amended by the author.
42 M. Fainsod, op. cit., pp. 6, 9.
43 Information at Kamenka.
44 Information at Kamenka.
45 M. Fainsod, op. cit., p. 9.
46 D. Saunders, op. cit., p. 111.
47 M. Kary, *Kamenka Tchaikovsky and Pushkin Museum Guide* (1988), p. 51.
48 O. Figes, op. cit., p. 92.
49 Information at Kamenka; and *Kamenka Tchaikovsky and Pushkin Museum Guide*, op. cit., p. 50.
50 O. Figes, op. cit., p. 116.
51 D. Brown, *Mikhail Glinka* (London: Oxford University Press, 1974), p. 88.
52 *New Grove*, op. cit.
53 W. Lakond, op. cit., p. 165.
54 *New Grove*, op. cit., vol. 7, p. 437.
55 Ibid., vol. 7, p. 442.
56 H. Acton, op. cit., p. 162.
57 D. Saunders, op. cit., pp. 189, 192.
58 Ibid., p. 188; and R. Hingley, *Russia: A Concise History* (London: Thames and Hudson, 1991), p. 128; and Encyclopaedia Britannica, fifteenth edition, 1974; and H. Acton, op. cit., p. 168.
59 D. Saunders, op. cit., p. 207.
60 Ibid., p. 279.
61 Ibid., p. 298.
62 Ibid., p. 200.
63 Guide to the State Russian Museum, p. 105; and H. Troyat, op. cit.
64 D. Saunders, op. cit., p. 166.
65 A. Walker, *Franz Liszt Volume 1: The Virtuoso Years, 1811-47* (London: Faber and Faber, 1983), p. 222.
66 Paderewski, quoted in *New Grove*, op. cit., vol. 16, p. 297.
67 W. Lakond, op. cit., p. 52.
68 Josef Labor, Alma's teacher, quoted in A. Mahler-Werfel (trans. A. Beaumont), *Diaries 1898–1902* (London: Faber and Faber, 1998), p. 98.
69 Information from staff at the Conservatoire.
70 *New Grove*, op. cit., vol. 16, p. 301.
71 D. Saunders, op. cit., p. 181; and G. Hoskings, *Russia: People and Empire* (London: HarperCollins, 1997), pp. 390-97.
72 *New Grove*, op. cit., vol. 5, p. 243.
73 A. Orlova, op. cit., p. 42.
74 A. Einstein, *Music in the Romantic Era* (London: J.M. Dent, 1947), p. 307.

75 Ibid., p. 308.
76 P.H. Lang, op. cit., p. 953.
77 Żelazowa Wola Guidebook, *Żelazowa Wola: The Place of his Birth* (2001).
78 *New Grove*, op. cit.
79 Ibid.
80 D. Saunders, op. cit., p. 314.
81 *New Grove*,, op. cit., vol. 3, pp. 56, 57.
82 Sir Henry Hadow, quoted in *New Grove*, op. cit., vol. 3, p. 57.
83 M.D. Calvocoressi (revised G. Abraham), *Mussorgsky* (Master Musicians) (London: J.M. Dent, 1974), p. 2; and C. Emerson, *The Life of Musorgsky* (Cambridge: Cambridge University Press, 1999), p. 1.
84 N. Gogol, *Dead Souls*, op. cit., p. 129, amended by the author.
85 Ibid., p. 107, amended by the author.
86 Ibid., amended by the author.
87 Ibid., p. 120.
88 C. Emerson, op. cit., p. 11.
89 H. Acton, op. cit., p. 169.
90 D. Saunders, op. cit., p. 82.
91 Ibid., p. 366.
92 Fedor Tiutchev, quoted in D. Saunders, op. cit., p. 205.
93 Ibid., p. 240.
94 Ibid., p. 233.
95 E. Acton, referred to in R. Price, in B. Waller (ed.), *Themes in Modern European History 1830–90* (London: Unwin Hyman, 1990), p. 178.
96 M. Fainsod, op. cit., p. 16.
97 C. Emerson, op. cit., p. 79.
98 The manuscript is to be found in St Petersburg Conservatoire.
99 C. Emerson, op. cit., p. 90.
100 *New Grove*, op. cit.
101 A. Einstein, op. cit., p. 313.
102 E. Garden, *Tchaikovsky* (Master Musicians) (London: J.M. Dent, 1973), p. 49.
103 C. Emerson, op. cit., p. 89.
104 O. Figes, op. cit., p. 177.
105 C. Emerson, op. cit., p. 95.
106 Ibid., p. 123.
107 Ibid., p. 138.
108 Ibid., p. 146.
109 Ibid., p. 140.
110 *New Grove*, op. cit., vol. 12, p. 869.
111 A. Einstein, op. cit., pp. 313, 314.
112 C. Emerson, op. cit., p. 154.
113 L. Fay, *Shostakovich: A Life* (Oxford: Oxford University Press, 2000), p. 120.
114 *New Grove*, op. cit., vol. 16, p. 28.
115 Ibid., p. 29.
116 Ibid., passim.
117 E. Garden, op. cit., p. 180; and *New Grove*, op. cit.
118 *New Grove*, op. cit., vol. 16, p. 31.
119 Ibid., p. 30.
120 Ibid., p. 34.
121 Ibid., passim.
122 Ibid., p. 33.
123 O. Figes, op. cit., pp. 198, 203, 204.
124 R. Hingley, op. cit., p. 142.
125 M. Fainsod, op. cit., p. 18.
126 Ibid., p. 9.
127 *Kamenka Tchaikovsky and Pushkin Museum Guide*, op. cit., p. 56.
128 E. White, *Stravinsky: The Composer and his Works* (London: Faber and Faber, 1979), p. 28; and F. Routh, op. cit., p. 4.
129 S. Prokofiev (trans. O. Prokofiev), *Soviet Diary 1927 and Other Writings* (London: Faber and Faber, 1991), p. 235.
130 *New Grove*, op. cit., vol. 16, p. 32.
131 M. Fainsod, op. cit., p. 4.
132 *Oxford Companion*, op. cit., p. 686.
133 A. Orlova, op. cit., p. 38.
134 Ibid., p. 182.

Chapter 21

1 A. Einstein, *Music in the Romantic Era* (London: J.M. Dent, 1947), p. 317.
2 P.H. Lang, *Music in Western Civilisation* (London: J.M. Dent, 1963), p. 949.
3 A. Einstein, op. cit., p. 317.
4 *Encyclopaedia Britannica*, ninth edition, 1875–89.
5 D. Saunders, *Russia in the Age of Reaction and Reform* (London: Longman, 1992), pp. 186, 187.
6 Information obtained at the museum in Klin.
7 N. Gogol (trans. D. Magarshack), *Dead Souls* (London: Penguin, 1961; first published 1842), p. 171.
8 A. Holden, *Tchaikovsky* (London: Bantam Press, 1995), p. 3; and D. Saunders, op. cit., p. 158.
9 O. Figes, *Natasha's Dance: A Cultural History of Russia* (London: Allen Lane The Penguin Press, 2002), p. 126.
10 A. Orlova, *Tchaikovsky: A Self-Portrait* (Oxford: Oxford University Press, 1990), p. 6.

11 E. Garden, *Tchaikovsky* (Master Musicians) (London: J.M. Dent, 1973), p. 3.
12 D. Saunders, op. cit., p. 125.
13 F. Pogrebinskii, Istoricheskii Archiv IA, 1956, p. 120, quoted in D. Saunders, op. cit., p. 209, amended by the author.
14 A. Orlova, 1973, op. cit., pp. 5, 6.
15 Ibid., p. 6.
16 A. Pushkin, 'Belkin', in A. Pushkin (trans. and ed. A. Myers and A. Kahn), *The Queen of Spades and Other Stories* (Oxford: Oxford University Press, 1997; first published 1834), p. 50 et passim.
17 *New Grove Dictionary of Music and Musicians* (ed. S. Sadie) (London: Macmillan, 1980).
18 A. Orlova, 1973, op. cit., p. 8.
19 D. Saunders, op. cit., p. 231.
20 A. Herzen, *My Past Thoughts*, quoted in D. Saunders, op. cit., p. 259.
21 H. Acton, *The Last Medici* (London: Macmillan, 1980), pp. 171–3; and M. Fainsod, *How Russia is Ruled* (Cambridge, MA: Harvard University Press, 1963), p. 9.
22 Eidelmann, *Tainye korrespondenty poliarnoi zvezdy*, 1966, quoted in D. Saunders, op. cit., p. 221.
23 F. Dostoyevsky (trans. D. Magarshack), *The Possessed* (London: Penguin Classics, 1971), p. 38.
24 D. Saunders, op. cit., p. 221.
25 N. Gogol, *Dead Souls*, op. cit., pp. 61, 184, 165.
26 A. Orlova, 1973, op. cit., p. 10 (italics are the author's addition).
27 Ibid., p. 7.
28 Ibid.
29 O. Figes, op. cit.
30 M. Zagoskin, quoted in D. Saunders, op. cit., p. 158.
31 A. Orlova, 1973, op. cit., p. 15.
32 Ibid., p. 21.
33 *New Grove*, op. cit., vol. 11, p. 31; and A. Walker, *Franz Liszt, Volume 1: The Virtuoso Years, 1811–47* (London: Faber and Faber, 1983), p. 431.
34 *New Grove*, op. cit., vol. 18, p. 611.
35 *Kamenka Tchaikovsky and Pushkin Museum Guide*, M. Kary, 1988, p. 53. Information about the match factory is from the guide to the museum in Sasha's house, where a model of it can be seen.
36 W. Lakond (trans. and ed.), *The Diaries of Tchaikovsky* (Westport, CT: Greenwood Press, 1973), pp. 26, 33, 32, 36, 37, 246; and *New Grove*, op. cit.; and *Kamenka Tchaikovsky and Pushkin Museum Guide*, op. cit., p. 48.
37 W. Lakond, op. cit., pp. 23–6, 36, 38–40, 41, 43.
38 A. Orlova, 1973, op. cit., p. 242.
39 W. Lakond, op. cit., p. 76.
40 Ibid., p. 149.
41 E. Garden, op. cit., pp. 17, 19.
42 W. Lakond, op. cit., p. 37.
43 Ibid., pp. 295, 293, 268, 59; and A. Holden, op. cit., pp. 80, 207.
44 W. Carter, *Marcel Proust: A Life* (New Haven, CT: Yale University Press, 2000), pp. 705, 609.
45 D. Saunders, op. cit., p. 298.
46 W. Lakond, op. cit., p. 41.
47 Ibid., p. 43.
48 A. Holden, op. cit., p. 72.
49 W. Lakond, op. cit., p. 66.
50 Ibid., p. 43.
51 E. Garden, op. cit., p. 45.
52 A. Poznansky, *Tchaikovsky: The Quest for the Inner Man* (London: Lime Tree (Macmillan), 1993), p. 438.
53 R. Jenkins, *Gladstone* (London: Macmillan, 1995), p. 103.
54 A. Orlova, 1973, op. cit., p. 58.
55 R. Ellmann, *Oscar Wilde* (London: Hamish Hamilton, 1987), p. 262.
56 H. Montgomerie Hyde, *The Other Love* (London: Heinemann, 1970), pp. 197, 198.
57 Frank Harris, quoted in H. Montgomerie Hyde, op. cit., p. 152.
58 B. Ivry, *Francis Poulenc* (London: Phaidon, 1996), pp. 65, 86, 170, 186, 194, 152, 153, 138, 63.
59 A. Holden, op. cit., p. 98.
60 E. Garden, op. cit., p. 69.
61 Ibid., p. 67.
62 A. Orlova, 1973, op. cit., p. 56.
63 R. Jenkins, op. cit., p. 410.
64 L. Tolstoy (trans. R.S. Townsend), *Anna Karenina*, (London: J.M. Dent, 1912; first published 1875–7), Part 8, Chapter 1; and D. Saunders, op. cit., p. 302.
65 A. Holden, op. cit., p. 115.
66 A. Orlova, 1973, op. cit., pp. 123, 127.
67 R. Jenkins, op. cit., p. 411.
68 A. Taylor, *English History 1914–1945* (Oxford: Oxford University Press, 1975), p. 430.
69 The figures were: until 1866, less than 2,400

miles of track had been constructed; between 1866 and 1875, 9,300 miles were constructed. (M. Fainsod, *How Russia is Ruled* (Cambridge, MA: Harvard University Press, 1963), p. 23.)
70 E. Garden, op. cit., p. 70; and A. Holden, op. cit., p. 135.
71 A. Holden, op. cit., p. 142, amended by the author.
72 Ibid., p. 139, amended by the author; see also E. Garden, op. cit., p. 70.
73 A. Orlova, 1973, op. cit., p. 125.
74 E. Garden, op. cit., p. 94.
75 A. Orlova, 1973, op. cit., pp. 150, 151.
76 A. Holden, op. cit., p. 203; further information from author's visit to Brailov, and oral information from guide.
77 A. Orlova, 1973, op. cit., p. 58.
78 Ibid., p. 59.
79 A. Holden, op. cit., p. 125.
80 E. Garden, op. cit., p. 72.
81 A. Orlova, 1973, op. cit., p. 67, amended by the author.
82 A. Holden, op. cit., p. 125, amended by the author.
83 Ibid., p. 23.
84 Ibid., p. 132.
85 E. Garden, op. cit., p. 73.
86 A. Holden, op. cit., p. 149.
87 E. Garden, op. cit., pp. 78.
88 A. Holden, op. cit., p. 176.
89 E. Garden, op. cit., pp. 78, 91.
90 A. Holden, op. cit., p. 154.
91 E. Garden, op. cit., p. 90.
92 A. Orlova, 1973, op. cit., p. 141.
93 W. Lakond, op. cit., p. 189.
94 A. Orlova, 1973, op. cit., p. 186.
95 O. Figes, op. cit., p. 220.
96 D. Saunders, op. cit., p. 331; and M. Fainsod, op. cit., p. 14.
97 D. Saunders, op. cit., pp. 313, 315, 333, 334; and M. Fainsod, op. cit., p. 9.
98 A. Orlova, 1973, op. cit., pp. 140, 141.
99 Ibid., p. 232.
100 A. Faris, *Jacques Offenbach* (London: Faber and Faber, 1980), p. 172.
101 L. Fay, *Shostakovich: A Life* (Oxford: Oxford University Press, 2000), p. 7.
102 R. Hingley, *Russia: A Concise History* (London: Thames and Hudson, 1991), pp. 125–30; and D. Saunders, op. cit., pp. 338, 311.
103 A. Holden, op. cit., pp. 201, 208, 259.
104 D. Saunders, op. cit., p. 183; and G. Hoskings, *Russia: People and Empire* (London: HarperCollins, 1997), pp. 390–97; and G. Hoskings, *Russia and the Russians* (London: Penguin, 2001), p. 318; and H. Acton, op. cit., pp. 94, 95.
105 R. Ellmann, op. cit., pp. 426, 427.
106 Ibid., p. 426.
107 W. Lakond, op. cit., p. 235.
108 A. Orlova, 1973, op. cit., p. 153.
109 W. Lakond, op. cit., p. 58.
110 M. Fainsod, op. cit., p. 23.
111 Picture by Repin at the Russian Museum, St Petersburg.
112 A. Orlova, 1973, op. cit., p. 210, amended by the author.
113 Ibid., p. 273.
114 Information obtained during author's visit.
115 W. Lakond, op. cit., p. 126.
116 A. Orlova, 1973, op. cit., pp. 284, 287.
117 Ibid., p. 367.
118 Information from *Guide to Tchaikovsky House-Museum in Klin* (Moscow Region's Committee for Culture and Tourism, 1994); see also W. Lakond, op. cit., pp. 126, 125, 161, 164, 99, 55, 162.
119 W. Lakond, op. cit., p. 286.
120 A. Holden, op. cit., p. 209.
121 M. Fainsod, op. cit., pp. 23, 24.
122 E. Garden, op. cit., p. 129.
123 A. Orlova, 1973, op. cit., p. 375.
124 Ibid., p. 310.
125 B. Rees, *Camille Saint-Saëns: A Life* (London: Chatto and Windus, 1999), p. 302; and A. Holden, op. cit., p. 337.
126 M. Broyles, in D. Nicholls (ed.), *The Cambridge History of American Music* (Cambridge: Cambridge University Press, 1998), pp. 218, 155.
127 Railtrack grew from an aggregate 35,000 miles in 1865 to 243,000 miles in 1897.
128 R. Nye and J. Morpurgo, *The Growth of the USA* (Harmondsworth: Pelican, 1965), pp. 581, 534 ff.
129 Ibid., p. 556.
130 Ibid., p. 563.
131 Ibid., p. 581.
132 M. Broyles, in D. Nicholls, op. cit., p. 218.
133 Ibid., p. 233.
134 Ibid., pp. 205, 206, 216, 146.
135 A. Orlova, 1973, op. cit., p. 382.
136 Ibid., p. 383.
137 W. Lakond, op. cit., p. 330.
138 A. Orlova, 1973, op. cit., p. 384, amended by the author.

139 E. Garden, op. cit., p. 131.
140 Ibid., p. 141.
141 A. Holden, op. cit., p. 342; and B. Rees, op. cit., p. 302.
142 A. Orlova, 1973, op. cit., p. 351.
143 E. White, *Stravinsky: The Composer and his Works* (London: Faber and Faber, 1979), p. 23.
144 Excellent descriptions of Tchaikovsky's last days can be found in A. Orlova, 1973, op. cit., and A. Holden, op. cit.
145 A. Holden, op. cit., p. 359.
146 Ibid., p. 363; and A. Orlova, 1973, op. cit., p. 410.
147 A. Orlova, 1973, op. cit., p. 410; and A. Orlova, 'Tchaikovsky: The Last Chapter', *Music and Letters*, vol. 62, 1981, pp. 125–45.
148 A. Orlova, 1981, op. cit.; and A. Holden, op. cit., pp. 356, 380.
149 A. Holden, op. cit., p. 388.
150 A. Orlova, 1973, op. cit., pp. 262, 328; and A. Holden, op. cit., p. 373.
151 D. Brown, 'How did Tchaikovsky Come to Die: And Does it Really Matter', *Music and Letters*, vol. 63, 1997, p. 581.
152 R. Ellmann, op. cit., pp. 412, 428. (Queensberry could not spell 'sodomite' correctly.)
153 O. Figes, op. cit., p. 334.
154 A. Holden, op. cit., p. 397; and A. Orlova, op. cit., 1973, p. 414.
155 Examples supporting this description of Tchaikovsky can be found in W. Lakond, op. cit., pp. 315, 63, 67, 74, 100, 120, 138, 246, 98, 100, 101, 93, 133, 321, 331, 333.

CHAPTER 22

1 A. Einstein, *Music in the Romantic Era* (London: J.M. Dent, 1947), p. 18.
2 I. Horsbrugh, *Leoš Janáček* (Newton Abbot: David and Charles, 1981), p. 33.
3 R. Layton, *Grieg* (London: Omnibus Press, 1998), p. 8.
4 *New Grove Dictionary of Music and Musicians* (ed. S. Sadie) (London: Macmillan, 1980), vol. 2, pp. 199, 203.
5 I. Horsbrugh, op. cit., p. 204.
6 O. Chadwick, *The Reformation* (London: Pelican, 1964), pp. 50, 55, 56; and *Encyclopaedia Britannica*, ninth edition, 1975–89.
7 J. Clapham, *Smetana* (Master Musicians) (London: J.M. Dent, 1972), p. 77.
8 J. Horton, *Grieg* (Master Musicians) (London: J.M. Dent, 1974), p. 3.
9 C. Lambert, *Music Ho! A Study of Music in Decline* (London: Faber and Faber, 1966), p. 83.
10 D. Cooke, *The Language of Music* (Oxford: Oxford University Press, 1959), p. 11.
11 M. Kennedy, *Richard Strauss: Man, Musician, Enigma* (Cambridge: Cambridge University Press, 1999), p. 110.
12 B. Cooper, *Beethoven* (Master Musicians) (Oxford: Oxford University Press, 2000), p. 175.
13 F. Lesure and R. Nicholls (selected and trans.), *Debussy: Letters* (London: Faber and Faber, 1987), p. 41.
14 A. Einstein, op. cit., p. 299.
15 S. Levas (trans. P.M. Young), *Sibelius: A Personal Portrait* (London: J.M. Dent, 1972), p. 84; and E. Dahl and M. Jangaard (eds), *Edvard Grieg* (Troldhaugen: Edvard Grieg Museum, 2000), p. 62.
16 P. Ignotus, *Hungary* (London: Ernest Benn Ltd., 1972), p. 85.
17 H. Stuckenschmidt (trans. R. Rosenbaum), *Maurice Ravel* (London: Calder and Boyars, 1969), p. 184.
18 *New Grove*, op. cit., vol. 16, p. 29; and F. Routh, *Stravinsky* (Master Musicians) (London: J.M. Dent, 1975), p. 72.
19 H. Stevens (ed. M. Gillies), *The Life and Music of Béla Bartók* (Oxford: Clarendon Press, 1993), pp. 25, 50, 79.
20 J. Horton, op. cit., p. 199.
21 M. Kennedy, *Portrait of Elgar* (London: Oxford University Press, 1982), p. 82.
22 J. Horton, op. cit., p. 118.
23 H. Robinson, *Sergei Prokofiev* (London: Robert Hale, 1987), p. 130.
24 A. Einstein, op. cit., p. 113.
25 E. Dahl and M. Jangaard, op. cit., p. 21.
26 Quoted in M. Hurd, *Vaughan Williams* (London: Faber and Faber, 1970), p. 56.
27 *New Grove*, op. cit.
28 Information from local visit by the author.
29 R. Habánová, in Smetana Museum Guide, *Bedřich Smetana: Time, Life, Work* (Prague, 1998), p. 81.
30 Information from local visit; and R. Habánová, in Smetana Museum Guide, op. cit., p. 81.
31 J. Clapham, 1972, op. cit., p. 17.
32 Z. Hojda, in Smetana Museum Guide, op. cit., p. 15.

33 M. Freemanová, in Smetana Museum Guide, op. cit., p. 52.
34 Ibid., p. 52; and R. Habánová, in Smetana Museum Guide, op. cit., p. 86.
35 R. Okey, *The Habsburg Monarchy* (London: Macmillan, 2001), p. 88.
36 A. Einstein, op. cit., p. 298.
37 J. Clapham, 1972, op. cit., p. 24.
38 C.V. Wedgwood, *The Thirty Years War* (London: Jonathan Cape, 1938), p. 100 ff.
39 A. Robertson, *Dvořák* (Master Musicians) (London: J.M. Dent, 1964), p. 4.
40 C. Ingrao, *The Habsburg Monarchy 1618–1815* (Cambridge: Cambridge University Press, 1994), p. 38.
41 R. Okey, op. cit., p. 15.
42 C. Hogwood and J. Smaczny, in N. Zaslaw (ed.), *The Classical Era* (London: Macmillan, 1989), p. 188.
43 František Palacký, quoted in R. Okey, op. cit., p. 183.
44 R. Okey, op. cit., p. 292.
45 J. Clapham, 1972, op. cit., pp. 6, 7.
46 *New Oxford Companion to Music* (ed. D. Arnold) (Oxford: Oxford University Press, 1983), p. 1692.
47 J.-P. Bled (trans. T. Bridgeman), *Franz Joseph* (Oxford: Blackwell, 1992), p. 116; and Z. Hojda, in Smetana Museum Guide, op. cit., pp. 23, 25.
48 O. Klobas, *Václav hrabě Kounic Šlechtic Nejen Rodem* (Brno, 1993), p. 36.
49 Z. Hojda, in Smetana Museum Guide, op. cit., p. 26.
50 Ibid., p. 23.
51 Ibid., p. 10.
52 R. Okey, op. cit., pp. 181, 190; and J.-P. Bled, op. cit., p. 165.
53 M. Freemanová, in Smetana Museum Guide, op. cit., p. 42; and Z. Hojda, in Smetana Museum Guide, op. cit., p. 23.
54 J. Procházková and B. Volný, *Born in Hukvaldy*, Moravian Museum (Brno, 1995), p. 48.
55 A. Taylor, *English History 1914–1945* (Oxford: Oxford University Press, 1975), p. 425.
56 J.-P. Bled, op. cit., pp. 181, 227, 271; and O. Klobas, op. cit., pp. 46, 50, 52, 54; and M. Zemanová, *Janáček* (London: John Murray, 2002), pp. 63, 69.
57 A. Robertson, op. cit., p. 24.
58 J. Clapham, 1972, op. cit., pp. 34, 41; and J. Clapham, 'The Smetana Pivoda Controversy', *Music and Letters*, vol. 52, 1971, p. 353.
59 J. Clapham, 1972, op. cit., p. 151.
60 Ibid., p. 43.
61 Ibid., p. 50.
62 O. Klobas, op. cit., p. 47.
63 A. Robertson, op. cit., pp. 11, 12, 14.
64 Information from Dvořák Museum, Nelahozeves.
65 A. Robertson, op. cit., p. 20.
66 O. Klobas, op. cit., pp. 36, 37.
67 Ibid., p. 40.
68 W. Lakond (trans. and ed.), *The Diaries of Tchaikovsky* (Westport, CT: Greenwood Press, 1973), p. 230.
69 J. Clapham, 'Dvořák's Relations with Brahms and Hanslick', *Musical Quarterly*, vol. 57 (2), 1971, p. 241.
70 Ibid., p. 243.
71 Ibid., p. 244.
72 O. Klobas, op. cit.; and F. Bartoš, *Bedřich Smetana: Letters and Reminiscences* (Prague: Artia, 1955), p. 78.
73 Information obtained at Přibrami-Hornické Museum, Příbram.
74 Information from visit to Vysoká and Rusalka lake.
75 A. Robertson, op. cit., p. 49.
76 J. Clapham, 1971, op. cit., p. 242.
77 Ibid., p. 249.
78 Ibid.
79 R. Okey, op. cit., p. 195.
80 *New Grove*, op. cit., vol. 5, p. 768.
81 V. Fischl, *Antonin Dvořák, his Achievement* (1942), quoted in A. Robertston, op. cit., p. 52.
82 J.-P. Bled, op. cit., p. 208.
83 Ibid., p. 206.
84 Information obtained at Přibrami-Hornické Museum, Příbram; and J. Clapham, 1971, op. cit., pp. 191, 112.
85 M. Broyles, in D. Nicholls, op. cit., pp. 222, 232.
86 A. Robertson, op. cit., pp. 64, 70.
87 J. Clapham, 1971, op. cit., p. 253.
88 A. Robertson, op. cit., pp. 69, 63; and O. Klobas, op. cit., p. 56.
89 *Illustrated London News*, 10 August 1886.
90 J. Clapham, 1971, op. cit., p. 252.
91 M. Broyles, in D. Nicholls, op. cit., p. 250.
92 A. Robertson, op. cit., p. 60.

93 R. Nye and J. Morpurgo, *The Growth of the USA* (Harmondsworth: Pelican, 1965), p. 602.
94 Ibid., p. 598.
95 *New Grove*, op. cit.; and O. Klobas, op. cit., p. 62.
96 Information from exhibition at Vysoká.
97 E. Dahl and M. Jangaard, op. cit., p. 81.
98 Ibid.
99 Ibid., p. 73.
100 J. Clapham, 1971, op. cit., pp. 171, 179.
101 J. Procházková and B. Volný, op. cit., p. 65; further information from author's visit.
102 J. Procházková and B. Volný, op. cit., p. 26.
103 Information from Špilberk Museum.
104 S. Přibáňová, 'Leoš Janáček's Memorial', Moravian Museum (Brno, 1999), p. 9.
105 *New Grove*, op. cit., vol. 10, p. 272.
106 *New Grove*, op. cit.
107 B. Samek, *The Monastery of Augustinians in Brno* (Brno: Augustinian Monastery, 1993), pp. 43, 47, 57.
108 J. Procházková and B. Volný, op. cit., p. 29.
109 I. Horsbrugh, op. cit., p. 30.
110 M. Zemanová, op. cit., p. 26.
111 Ibid., pp. 34, 78.
112 I. Horsbrugh, op. cit., p. 38.
113 Z. Janáčková (ed. and trans. J. Tyrrell), *My Life With Janáček* (London: Faber and Faber, 1998), p. 34.
114 M. Zemanová, op. cit., p. 4.
115 Ibid., p. 63.
116 Ibid., p. 107.
117 Z. Janáčková, op. cit., p. 56, amended by the author.
118 M. Zemanová, op. cit., p. 4.
119 I. Horsbrugh, op. cit., p. 42.
120 Ibid., p. 144.
121 *New Grove*, op. cit., vol. 9, p. 479.
122 I. Horsbrugh, op. cit., pp. 46–51.
123 Ibid., p. 50.
124 Ibid., p. 80.
125 Ibid.
126 Ibid., p. 120.
127 Ernest Newman, quoted in I. Horsbrugh, op. cit., p. 193.
128 M. Zemanová, op. cit., p. 3.
129 *New Grove*, op. cit., vol. 9, p. 477.
130 M. Zemanová, op. cit., p. 152.
131 Ibid., p. 182.
132 S. Přibáňová, op. cit., p. 21.
133 M. Zemanová, op. cit., p. 219.
134 Z. Janáčková, op. cit., p. 163.
135 Ibid., p. 161.
136 M. Zemanová, op. cit., p. 220.
137 Ibid., p. 263.
138 I. Horsbrugh, op. cit., p. 139.
139 M. Zemanová, op. cit., pp. 168, 224.
140 *New Grove*, op. cit., vol. 9, p. 479.
141 Z. Janáčková, op. cit., pp. 121, 123, 124, 170, 172, 179; and M. Zemanová, op. cit., p. 116; and J. Procházková and B. Volný, op. cit., p. 64.
142 Herbert Smith, quoted in A. Taylor, op. cit., p. 240.
143 A.J. Cook, quoted in A. Taylor, op. cit., p. 243.
144 A. Taylor, op. cit., pp. 245, 239.
145 Z. Janáčková, op. cit., pp. 162, 186.
146 M. Zemanová, op. cit., p. 253.
147 J. Procházková and B. Volný, op. cit., p. 77.
148 M. Zemanová, op. cit., pp. 255, 263.
149 *Oxford Companion*, op. cit., p. 177, goes so far as to call him the greatest musician ever produced by Hungary.
150 P. Ignotus, op. cit., p. 124.
151 H. Stevens, op. cit., p. 3.
152 Ibid., p. 12.
153 One third of the population could read and write in 1869; in 1910 the figure was 68.7 per cent (P. Ignotus, op. cit., p. 91); see also P. Ignotus, op. cit., pp. 72, 90.
154 For further information on national dress, see *New Grove*, op. cit., vol. 2, p. 199.
155 *New Grove*, op. cit., vol. 2, p. 203.
156 H. Stevens, op. cit., p. 60.
157 P. Ignotus, op. cit., p. 147.
158 H. Stevens, op. cit., p. 56.
159 *New Grove*, op. cit., vol. 2, p. 202.
160 P. Ignotus, op. cit., p. 150.
161 Ibid., p. 151.
162 *Encyclopaedia Britannica*, fifteenth edition, 1974.
163 H. Stevens, op. cit., p. 55.
164 Ibid., p. 82.
165 *New Grove*, op. cit, vol. 2, p. 203.
166 P. Ignotus, op. cit., p. 185.
167 H. Stevens, op. cit., p. 93.
168 *New Grove*, op. cit., vol. 2, p. 205.
169 H. Stevens, op. cit., p. 93.
170 Ibid., p. 102.
171 Information from Nelahozeves Museum.

Chapter 23

1 Cecil Gray, quoted in *New Grove Dictionary of Music and Musicians* (ed. S. Sadie) (London: Macmillan, 1980), vol. 17, p. 285.
2 Gerald Abraham, referred to in *New Grove*, op. cit., vol. 17, p. 282.
3 E. Dahl, in E. Dahl and M. Jangaard (eds), *Edvard Grieg* (Troldhaugen, Edvard Grieg Museum, 2000), p. 61.
4 A. Einstein, *Music in the Romantic Era* (London: J.M. Dent, 1947), p. 62.
5 *Encyclopaedia Britannica*, ninth edition, 1875–89.
6 E. Dahl, in E. Dahl and M. Jangaard, op. cit., p. 11, 12.
7 G.H. Hartvedt, in E. Dahl and M. Jangaard, op. cit., p. 34.
8 Ibid., p. 35.
9 *New Grove*, op. cit.
10 Information from visit to Bergen.
11 K. Preston, in D. Nicholls (ed.), *The Cambridge History of American Music* (Cambridge: Cambridge University Press, 1998), p. 200; and M. Broyles, in D. Nicholls, op. cit., p. 218.
12 E. Dahl and M. Jangaard, op. cit., p. 13.
13 J. Horton, *Grieg* (Master Musicians) (London: J.M. Dent, 1974), p. 10.
14 E. Dahl, in E. Dahl and M. Jangaard, op. cit., p. 61.
15 I. Evans, *A Short History of English Literature* (London: Penguin, 1963), p. 132.
16 J. Horton, op. cit., p. 24.
17 Ibid., pp. 29, 39.
18 Ibid., p. 60.
19 M. Jangaard, in E. Dahl and M. Jangaard, op. cit., p. 51.
20 G. Danbolt, in E. Dahl and M. Jangaard, op. cit., p. 103.
21 E. Dahl, in E. Dahl and M. Jangaard, op. cit., p. 16.
22 J. Horton, op. cit., p. 31.
23 Ibid., p. 152.
24 Ibid.
25 E. Dahl, in E. Dahl and M. Jangaard, op. cit., p. 18.
26 J. Horton, op. cit., p. 80.
27 E. Dahl, in E. Dahl and M. Jangaard, op. cit., p. 22.
28 Ibid., p. 28.
29 J. Horton, op. cit., p. 72.
30 E. Dahl, in E. Dahl and M. Jangaard, op. cit., p. 63.
31 Information from visit to Hardanger and Utne Folk Museum.
32 E. Dahl, in E. Dahl and M. Jangaard, op. cit., p. 112.
33 E. Dahl and M. Jangaard, op. cit., p. 123.
34 E. Dahl, in E. Dahl and M. Jangaard, op. cit., p. 64.
35 Ibid., p. 121.
36 Information from visit to Troldhaugen.
37 J. Horton, op. cit., p. 63.
38 E. Dahl, in E. Dahl and M. Jangaard, op. cit., p. 65.
39 J. Horton, op. cit., p. 72.
40 O.D. Laerum, in E. Dahl and M. Jangaard, op. cit., p. 85.
41 G. Danbolt, in E. Dahl and M. Jangaard, op. cit., p. 95.
42 J. Horton, op. cit., pp. 100, 99.
43 *Encyclopaedia Britannica*, fifteenth edition, 1974; and G. Battiscombe, *Queen Alexandra* (London: Constable, 1969), pp. 200, 255.
44 M. Jangaard, in E. Dahl and M. Jangaard, op. cit., p. 55.
45 J. Bury, *France 1814–1940* (London: Methuen, 1969), pp. 189 ff.
46 P. Franklin, *The Life of Mahler* (Cambridge: Cambridge University Press, 1997), p. 123.
47 W. Carter, *Marcel Proust: A Life* (New Haven, CT: Yale University Press, 2000), pp. 244, 254, 263.
48 B. Rees, *Camille Saint-Saëns: A Life* (London: Chatto and Windus, 1999), p. 344.
49 J. Bury, op. cit., pp. 189–95.
50 J. Horton, op. cit., p. 103.
51 B. Rees, op. cit., p. 330.
52 J. Horton, op. cit., p. 106.
53 Ibid., p. 113.
54 Ibid., p. 112.
55 E. Dahl, in E. Dahl and M. Jangaard, op. cit., p. 26.
56 O.D. Laerum, in E. Dahl and M. Jangaard, op. cit., p. 87.
57 *Encyclopaedia Britannica*, ninth edition, op. cit.
58 Ibid.
59 *Birthplace of Sibelius* (Hämeenlinna Historical Museum, 1999), p. 4.
60 *Encyclopaedia Britannica*, ninth edition, op. cit.
61 *Birthplace of Sibelius*, op. cit., p. 12.

62 Ibid., p. 16.
63 *Lonely Planet Guide to Finland*, J. Brewer and M. Lehtipuu (Victoria, Australia: Lonely Planet Publications, 1999).
64 *Birthplace of Sibelius*, op. cit., p. 76.
65 S. Levas, op. cit., p. xi.
66 *Birthplace of Sibelius*, op. cit., p. 81.
67 Ibid.
68 Prof Max Müller, in *Encyclopaedia Britannica*, ninth edition, op. cit., vol. 9, p. 220.
69 See portraits by Eero Järnefelt; and S. Levas, op. cit., pp. 51, 53, 4, 19, 110.
70 Järnefelt Ateneum Art Museum Exhibition Guide, *Järnefelt, Eero, 1863–1937* (Helsinki, 2001), pp. 8, 16, 74; and S. Levas, op. cit., p. 110.
71 Järnefelt Ateneum Art Museum Exhibition Guide, op. cit., p. 83.
72 *New Grove*, op. cit.; and S. Levas, op. cit., pp. 84, 146.
73 S. Levas, op. cit., p. xvii.
74 Ibid., pp. 6, 7, 10, 13, 14, 15, 44; and Järnefelt Ateneum Art Museum Exhibition Guide, op. cit., pp. 31, 33.
75 S. Levas, op. cit., p. xix.
76 *New Grove*, op. cit.; and R. Layton, *Sibelius* (Master Musicians) (London: J.M. Dent, 1978), pp. 15, 13.
77 S. Levas, op. cit., p. 8.
78 Ibid., p. xx.
79 Ibid., pp. 52, 106.
80 R. Layton, op. cit., p. 20.
81 C. Lambert, *Music Ho! A Study of Music in Decline* (London: Faber and Faber, 1966), p. 264.
82 *New Grove*, op. cit; the population polled comprised listeners to the New York Philharmonic Society's broadcasts.
83 S. Levas, op. cit., p. 73.
84 Ibid., p. 96.
85 Ibid., p. 47.
86 Ibid., p. 30.
87 Ibid., p. 117.
88 R. Layton, op. cit., p. 22; and S. Levas, op. cit., pp. 124–7; and *New Grove*, op. cit., vol. 17, p. 283.
89 S. Levas, op. cit., p. 128.
90 Ibid., p. 131.

Chapter 24

1 *New Grove Dictionary of Music and Musicians* (ed. S. Sadie) (London: Macmillan, 1980), vol. 18, p. 227; and M. Kennedy, *Mahler* (Master Musicians) (London: J.M. Dent, 1974), p. 78.
2 N. Cardus, *A Composers Eleven* (London: Jonathan Cape, 1958), p. 119.
3 B. Walter (trans. J. Galston), *Theme and Variations* (London: Hamish Hamilton, 1947), p. 174.
4 W. Reich (trans. L. Black), *Schoenberg* (London: Longman, 1971), p. 42.
5 Information from enquiries made locally.
6 M. Kennedy, op. cit., p. 3.
7 The spy scandal features in Mozart's letter to his father on 11 September 1782; see R. Spaethling, *Mozart's Letters, Mozart's Life* (London: Faber and Faber, 2000), p. 329.
8 The background on Jihlava and the Jews is taken from Z. Jaroš, *The Young Gustav Mahler and Jihlava* (Jihlava: Museum of Highlands, 1994), pp. 62–7.
9 Ibid., pp. 12, 13, 62–7; and information from Mahler Museum in Jihlava.
10 Z.Jaroš, op. cit., p. 14.
11 Ibid., p. 48.
12 Ibid., p. 48.
13 Ibid., p. 49.
14 Ibid., p. 15.
15 Ibid., p. 16.
16 Ibid., p. 38.
17 M. Kennedy, op. cit., p. 6.
18 *New Grove*, op. cit.
19 M. Kennedy, op. cit., p. 9.
20 H.F. Redlich, *Bruckner and Mahler* (Master Musicians) (London: J.M. Dent, 1963), p. 114.
21 M. Kennedy, op. cit., p. 5.
22 Ibid., pp. 9, 13; and H.F. Redlich, op. cit., p. 117.
23 B. Walter, op. cit., p. 61.
24 Ibid., p. 63.
25 M. Kennedy, op. cit., pp. 15, 120; a plaque in Bad Hall refers to Grillparzer.
26 B. Walter, op. cit., p. 84.
27 Ibid., p. 85.
28 P. Franklin, *The Life of Mahler* (Cambridge: Cambridge University Press, 1997), p. 55.
29 M. Kennedy, op. cit., p. 17.
30 *New Grove*, op. cit., vol. 11, p. 508.
31 A crown was half a florin (R. Okey, *The Habsburg Monarchy* (London: Macmillan, 2001), p. 228), and the bottom rung of the civil service earned 1000 crowns (ibid., p. 278).
32 H.F. Redlich, op. cit., p. 124; and P. Franklin, op. cit., p. 70.

33 R. Okey, op. cit., p. 316. In 1910, 23 per cent of Budapest residents, nearly half of Hungary's professional classes and 85 per cent of its finance executives were Jewish.
34 B. Walter, op. cit., p. 81.
35 M. Kennedy, op. cit., p. 21.
36 Ibid., p. 56.
37 B. Walter, op. cit., p. 83.
38 *New Grove*, op. cit., vol. 11, p. 509.
39 A. Orlova, *Tchaikovsky: A Self-Portrait* (Oxford: Oxford University Press, 1990), p. 390.
40 B. Walter, op. cit., p. 65.
41 P. Franklin, op. cit., p. 80, amended by the author.
42 B. Walter, op. cit., p. 165.
43 Ibid., p. 92.
44 A. Mahler-Werfel (trans. A. Beaumont), *Diaries 1898–1902* (London: Faber and Faber, 1998), p. 451.
45 Ibid., p. 443.
46 Information obtained at Jihlava Museum.
47 B. Walter, op. cit., p. 167.
48 A. Mahler-Werfel, op. cit., p. 76.
49 W. Reich, op. cit., p. 35.
50 P. Franklin, op. cit., p. 94.
51 B. Walter, op. cit., p. 94.
52 Ibid., p. 95.
53 M. Kennedy, op. cit., p. 42.
54 B. Walter, op. cit., p. 96.
55 Ibid., p. 96.
56 Ibid., p. 97.
57 A. Bullock, *Hitler and Stalin: Parallel Lives* (London: HarperCollins, 1991), p. 23.
58 Ibid., p. 23.
59 A. Mahler-Werfel, op. cit., p. 216; further deprecatory remarks by Alma Mahler can be found on pp. 273, 275, 421, 440.
60 R. Wistrich, *The Jews in Vienna in the Age of Franz-Joseph* (Oxford: Oxford University Press, 1990), p. 214.
61 Ibid.
62 C. Schorske, *Fin-de-Siècle Vienna* (New York, NY: Vintage Books, 1980), pp. 121–3.
63 J.-P. Bled (trans. T. Bridgeman), *Franz Joseph* (Oxford: Blackwell, 1992), p. 239; and R. Okey, op. cit., p. 230.
64 R. Okey, op. cit., p. 281. (See also p. 515 of this book.)
65 R. Wistrich, op. cit., p. 227; and B. Walter, op. cit., p. 6.
66 C. Schorske, op. cit., pp. 144, 145.
67 ('Wer Jude ist bestimme ich.') C. Schorske, op. cit., p. 145; and R. Okey, op. cit., p. 276.
68 M. Kennedy, op. cit., p. 28.
69 N. Cardus, op. cit., p. 105.
70 W. Reich, op. cit., p. 6. Schoenberg's String Quartet in D was composed in the autumn of 1897.
71 C. Schorske, op. cit., p. 81.
72 In *Die Welt von Gestern*, Frankfurt (Fischer Verlag), p. 14, quoted in P. Vergo, *Art in Vienna 1898–1918* (London: Phaidon, 1993), p. 10.
73 A. Mahler-Werfel, op. cit., p. 75.
74 W. Murray, 'Living in Vienna 1890–1939', *History Today*, May 1996, pp. 50–55. The figures were: over 95 per cent had no individual water supply; 92 per cent had no individual lavatory.
75 C. Schorske, op. cit., p. xviii.
76 Ibid., p. 6.
77 Ibid., passim.
78 P. Vergo, op. cit., p. 158.
79 Max Kalbeck, quoted in A. Mahler-Werfel, op. cit., p. 204n.
80 Interview given to *Illustriertes Extrablatt*, September 1903, quoted in K. Blaukopf, *G. Mahler oder der Zeitgenosse der Zukunft* (Vienna, 1969), p 208, quoted in P. Vergo, op. cit., p. 158.
81 'Theater und Kunst', *Neues Wiener Tagblatt*, 3 October 1934, quoted in P. Vergo, op. cit., p. 158.
82 B. Walter, op. cit., p. 173.
83 Ibid., p. 153.
84 M. Kennedy, op. cit., pp. 32, 33.
85 P. Vergo, op. cit., p. 198; and A. Mahler-Werfel, op. cit., p. 163.
86 A. Mahler-Werfel, op. cit., p. 95.
87 Ibid., pp. 419, 420.
88 P. Vergo, op. cit., p. 15.
89 A. Mahler-Werfel, op. cit., p. 421.
90 Ibid., p. 434.
91 W. Reich, op. cit.; and *New Grove*, op. cit.
92 A. Mahler-Werfel, op. cit., p. 442.
93 Ibid., p. 444.
94 Ibid., p. 445.
95 Ibid., p. 449.
96 Ibid., p. 464.
97 Ibid., p. 466.
98 Ibid., p. 467.
99 Ibid., p. 461.
100 Ibid., p. 421.
101 Ibid., p. 467.
102 B. Walter, op. cit., p. 105.

103 P. Franklin, op. cit., p. 193.
104 M. Kennedy, op. cit., p. 52.
105 B. Walter, op. cit., p. 185.
106 Ibid., p. 194.
107 Ibid., p. 193.
108 M. Kennedy, op. cit., pp. 54, 74; and *New Grove*, op. cit., vol. 11, p. 513; and P. Franklin, op. cit., p. 164.
109 R. Nye and J. Morpurgo, *The Growth of the USA* (Harmondsworth: Pelican, 1965), p. 625.
110 P. Franklin, op. cit., p. 188.
111 *New Grove*, op. cit., vol. 11, p. 524.
112 M. Kennedy, op. cit., p. 64.
113 Ibid., p. 65.
114 Ibid., p. 66.
115 Ibid., p. 71.
116 Ibid., p. 72.
117 P. Franklin, op. cit., p. 191.
118 M. Kennedy, op. cit., p. 73.
119 Ibid., p. 72.
120 B. Walter, op. cit., p. 206.
121 *Illustrated London News.*
122 B. Walter, op. cit., p. 207.
123 P. Franklin, op. cit., p. 202.
124 M. Kennedy, op. cit., p. 43.
125 *Encyclopaedia Britannica*, fifteenth edition, 1974; and E. Gombrich, *The Story of Art* (London: Phaidon, 1963), p. 420.
126 B. Walter, op. cit., p. 348.
127 Ibid., p. 349.
128 M. Kennedy, op. cit., p. 75.
129 B. Walter, op. cit., p. 207; see also P. Franklin, op. cit., p. 101.

CHAPTER 25

1 R. Craft, *Chronicle of a Friendship* (New York, NY, 1973), quoted in M. Kennedy, *Richard Strauss: Man, Musician, Enigma* (Cambridge: Cambridge University Press, 1999), p. 148.
2 B. Walter (trans. J. Galston), *Theme and Variations* (London: Hamish Hamilton, 1947), p. 53.
3 M. Kennedy, 1999, op. cit., p. 148.
4 Ibid., p. 395.
5 *Encyclopaedia Britannica*, ninth edition, 1875–89, vol. 17, p. 24.
6 W. Blunt, *The Dream King: Ludwig II of Bavaria* (London: Hamish Hamilton, 1970), p. 113.
7 D. Blackbourn, *Germany 1780–1918* (London: HarperCollins, 1997), p. 321.
8 K. Wilhelm, *Richard Strauss Persönlich: Eine Bildbiographie* (Berlin: Henschel, 1999), p. 15.
9 M. Kennedy, 1999, op. cit., pp. 10, 26; and information in the Strauss villa.
10 W. Blunt, op. cit., p. 130.
11 *New Grove Dictionary of Music and Musicians* (ed. S. Sadie) (London: Macmillan, 1980), vol. 18, p. 218.
12 B. Walter, op. cit., p. 222.
13 Ibid., p. 49.
14 Ibid., p. 37.
15 Ibid., p. 30.
16 Ibid., p. 1.
17 D. Blackbourn, op. cit., pp. 200, 332, 354. Berlin's population was 412,000 in 1850 and 2,071,000 in 1910.
18 T. Mann (trans. H.T. Lowe-Porter), *Buddenbrooks* (London: Vintage, 1999; first published 1902), p. 316.
19 Ibid., p. 273.
20 M. Kennedy, 1999, pp. 34, 234, 149.
21 B. Walter, op. cit., p. 50.
22 *New Grove*, op. cit., vol. 18, p. 219.
23 M. Kennedy, op. cit., p. 69.
24 E. Krause (trans. J. Coombs), *Richard Strauss* (London: Collet's (Publishers) Ltd., 1964), p. 249.
25 *New Oxford Companion to Music* (ed. D. Arnold) (Oxford: Oxford University Press, 1983), p. 1778.
26 A. Mahler-Werfel (trans. A. Beaumont), *Diaries 1898–1902* (London: Faber and Faber, 1998), p. 366.
27 Ibid., p. 367.
28 K. Wilhelm, op. cit., p. 70.
29 M. Kennedy, 1999, op. cit., p. 89.
30 Ibid., p. 395.
31 Ibid., pp. 86, 113, 95.
32 M. Kennedy, *Portrait of Elgar* (London: Oxford University Press, 1982), p. 229.
33 M. Kennedy, 1999, op. cit., p. 93. The story about the overshoes was denied when the author asked the Strauss housekeeper about it; besides, overshoes are a standard feature of visits to parquet-floored buildings in Germany.
34 B. Walter, op. cit., p. 133.
35 Ibid., p. 132.
36 *New Grove*, op. cit., vol. 18, p. 220.
37 M. Kennedy, 1999, op. cit., pp. 108, 218; and E. Krause, op. cit., p. 46; and *New Grove*, op. cit.
38 M. Kennedy, 1999, op. cit., pp. 107, 108.
39 Ibid., p. 200.

40 D. Blackbourn, op. cit., p. 368.
41 E. Krause, op. cit., p. 114.
42 B. Walter, op. cit., p. 308.
43 M. Kennedy, 1999, op. cit., p. 147.
44 *New Grove*, op. cit., vol. 18, p. 220.
45 M. Kennedy, op. cit., p. 276.
46 Ibid., p. 142.
47 Ibid., pp. 140–43.
48 Information from the Strauss villa.
49 Romain Rolland, quoted in E. Krause, op. cit., p. 206.
50 C. Schorske, *Fin-de-Siècle Vienna* (New York, NY: Vintage Books, 1980), p. 15.
51 Ibid., p. 298.
52 Ibid., p. 15.
53 M. Kennedy, 1999, op. cit., p. 160.
54 Ibid., p. 162.
55 E. Krause, op. cit., p. 357.
56 M. Proust (trans. S. Moncrieff and T. Kilmartin, revised D.J. Enright), *In Search of Lost Time: Swann's Way* (London: Chatto and Windus, 1992; first published 1913), pp. 510–11.
57 M. Kennedy, 1999, op. cit., p. 191.
58 E. Krause, op. cit., p. 61.
59 M. Kennedy, 1999, op. cit., p. 211.
60 *New Grove*, op. cit., vol. 18, p. 222.
61 W. Murray, 'Living in Vienna 1890–1939', *History Today*, May 1996, pp. 50–55.
62 M. Kennedy, 1999, op. cit., p. 215.
63 *New Grove*, op. cit.; and M. Kennedy, 1999, op. cit., p. 208.
64 A. Bullock, *Hitler and Stalin: Parallel Lives* (London: HarperCollins, 1991), p. 74.
65 Ibid., p. 95.
66 B. Walter, op. cit., p. 277.
67 C. Isherwood, *Mr Norris Changes Trains* (London: Penguin, 1942; first published 1935), p. 30.
68 A. Bullock, op. cit., p. 76.
69 Ibid., p. 241.
70 C. Isherwood, op. cit., p. 89.
71 A. Bullock, op. cit., p. 274.
72 C. Isherwood, op. cit., p. 181.
73 M. Kennedy, 1999, op. cit., p. 269.
74 Ibid., p. 278.
75 B. Walter, op. cit., p. 329.
76 Ibid., p. 329.
77 Ibid., p. 244.
78 Ibid., p. 238.
79 A. Bullock, op. cit., p. 451.
80 M. Kennedy, 1999, op. cit., p. 292.
81 W. Reich (trans. L. Black), *Schoenberg* (London: Longman, 1971), pp. 32, 34.
82 C. Schorske, op. cit., p. 305.
83 C. Crittenden, *Johann Strauss and Vienna* (Cambridge: Cambridge University Press, 2000), p. 104.
84 M. Kennedy, 1999, op. cit., p. 298.
85 Ibid., p. 316.
86 *New Grove*, op. cit.
87 A. Bullock, op. cit., p. 655; and M. Kennedy, 1999, op. cit., p. 316.
88 M. Kennedy, 1999, op. cit., p. 339.
89 Ibid., p. 345.
90 Ibid., p. 346.
91 Ibid., p. 363.
92 Ibid.
93 B. Walter, op. cit., p. 232.
94 *New Grove*, op. cit.
95 M. Kennedy, 1999, op. cit., p. 368.
96 *New Grove*, op. cit., vol. 18, p. 234.
97 Ibid., p. 223.
98 *New Grove*, op. cit., vol. 18, p. 227.
99 *Ariadne auf Naxos*: 'dort wohin du mich führest … er hat vergessen, was ihn schmerzen sollte'.

Chapter 26

1 N. Cardus, *A Composers Eleven* (London: Jonathan Cape, 1958), p. 172.
2 R. Orledge, 'Debussy's Musical Gifts to Emma Bardac', *Musical Quarterly*, vol. 60, 1974, p. 166.
3 P.H. Lang, *Music in Western Civilisation* (London: J.M. Dent, 1963), pp. 1018, 1020; and F. Lesure (trans. D. Stevens), 'Claude Debussy after his Centenary', *Musical Quarterly*, vol. 49 (3), 1963, p. 277.
4 *Daily Mail*, 28 May 1909.
5 J. Samson, *Chopin* (Oxford: Oxford University Press, 1996), p. 253.
6 *Encyclopaedia Britannica*, ninth edition, 1875–89; and P. Mansel, *Paris Between the Empires, 1814–1852* (London: John Murray, 2001), p. 163.
7 F. Lesure and R. Nicholls (selected and trans.), *Debussy: Letters* (London: Faber and Faber, 1987), p. 1.
8 M. Dietschy, 'The Family and Childhood of Debussy', *Musical Quarterly*, vol. 46, 1960, p. 310.
9 F. Lesure and R. Nicholls, op. cit., pp. xii, 291.
10 M. Dietschy, op. cit., p. 308.

11 F. Lesure and R. Nicholls, op. cit., p. xiii.
12 M. Dietschy, op. cit., p. 307.
13 F. Lesure and R. Nicholls, op. cit., p. 1; and M. Dietschy, op. cit.
14 E. Durand, quoted in *New Grove Dictionary of Music and Musicians* (ed. S. Sadie) (London: Macmillan, 1980), vol. 5, p. 307.
15 F. Lesure, op. cit., p. 285.
16 F. Lesure and R. Nicholls, op. cit., p. 5.
17 Ibid., p. 16.
18 C. Jones, *The Cambridge History of France* (Cambridge: Cambridge University Press, 1994), p. 221.
19 Ibid., p. 221.
20 J. Bury, *France 1814–1940* (London: Methuen, 1969), p. 170.
21 C. Jones, op. cit., pp. 225, 228; and J. Bury, op. cit., p. 181.
22 J. Bury, op. cit., pp. 177, 185.
23 Lord Bryce, quoted in J. Bury, op. cit., p. 187.
24 B. Rees, *Camille Saint-Saëns: A Life* (London: Chatto and Windus, 1999), p. 267.
25 Lord Dufferin, quoted in J. Bury, op. cit., p. 206.
26 C. Hibbert, *Edward VII* (London: Allen Lane, 1976), p. 256.
27 M. Proust, (trans. S. Moncrieff and T. Kilmartin, revised D.J. Enright), *In Search of Lost Time: The Guermantes Way* (London: Chatto and Windus, 1992; first published 1920), p. 465.
28 F. Lesure and R. Nicholls, op. cit., p. 43.
29 L. Davies, *Cesar Franck and his Circle* (London: Barrie and Jenkins, 1970), pp. 188, 182; and F. Lesure and R. Nicholls, op. cit., pp. 66, 68.
30 F. Lesure and R. Nicholls, op. cit., p. 76; a gamelan can be seen in the Musée de la Musique, Cité de la Musique, Paris.
31 Ibid., p. xiv.
32 Ibid., p. 40.
33 Ibid., p. 50.
34 C. Lambert, *Music Ho! A Study of Music in Decline* (London: Faber and Faber, 1966), p. 36.
35 F. Lesure and R. Nicholls, op. cit., p. 103.
36 Ibid., p. 106.
37 Ibid., p. 109.
38 *New Grove*, op. cit., vol. 5, p. 307.
39 Ibid., p. 309.
40 Ibid., p. 307.
41 Ibid.
42 W. Carter, *Marcel Proust: A Life* (New Haven, CT: Yale University Press, 2000), p. 497.
43 Ibid., p. 498.
44 Ibid., pp. 411, 547.
45 F. Lesure and R. Nicholls, op. cit., pp. xvi, 145.
46 M. Proust, op. cit., p. 147.
47 F. Lesure and R. Nicholls, op. cit., p. 276.
48 R. Orledge, op. cit.
49 F. Lesure, op. cit., p. 277.
50 M. Proust, op. cit., p. 169.
51 F. Lesure, op. cit., p. 282.
52 *New Grove*, op. cit., vol. 5, p. 310.
53 There is a facsimile in the museum in St Germain-en-Laye.
54 *New Grove*, op. cit., vol. 5, p. 38.
55 F. Lesure and R. Nicholls, op. cit., p. 206.
56 Ibid., pp. 250, 265, amended by the author.
57 E. White, *Stravinsky: The Composer and his Works* (London: Faber and Faber, 1979), p. 72.
58 *New Grove*, op. cit., vol. 5, p. 310.
59 B. Ivry, *Francis Poulenc* (London: Phaidon, 1996), p. 36.
60 *New Grove*, op. cit., vol. 5, p. 310.
61 F. Lesure and R. Nicholls, op. cit., p. 200.
62 Ibid., p. 216.
63 Ibid., p. 221.
64 Ibid., p. 217.
65 D. Galloway, in introduction to E. Allan Poe (ed. D. Galloway), *The Fall of the House of Usher and Other Writings* (London: Penguin, 1986), p. 11.
66 E. Allan Poe, op. cit., p. 152.
67 Ibid., pp. 140, 142.
68 Ibid., p. 145.
69 Ibid., p. 146.
70 *New Grove*, op. cit., vol. 5, p. 310.
71 W. Carter, op. cit., pp. 443, 488, 509.
72 J. Bury, op. cit., p. 217.
73 David Lloyd George, quoted in D. Blackbourn, *Germany 1780–1918* (London: HarperCollins, 1997), p. 456.
74 Bethmann Hollweg, quoted in D. Blackbourn, op. cit., p. 456.
75 B. Rees, op. cit., p. 410.
76 M. Proust, op. cit., pp. 127, 476.
77 H. Stuckenschmidt (trans. R. Rosenbaum), *Maurice Ravel* (London: Calder and Boyars, 1969), p. 158.
78 J. Bury, op. cit., p. 234.
79 F. Lesure and R. Nicholls, op. cit., p. 291.
80 Ibid., p. 292.
81 Ibid., p. 314.
82 H. Stuckenschmidt, op. cit., pp. 166, 169.
83 F. Lesure and R. Nicholls, op. cit., p. 292.

84 Ibid., p. 298.
85 L. Davies, op. cit., p. 339.
86 F. Lesure and R. Nicholls, op. cit., p. 299.
87 Ibid., p. 310. The letter was written on 6 December 1915: a facsimile is in the museum in St Germain-en-Laye.
88 Ibid., p. 314.
89 Ibid., p. 315.
90 Ibid., p. 317.
91 Ibid., p. 320. A facsimile is in the museum in St Germain-en-Laye.
92 E. White, op. cit., p. 73.
93 F. Lesure and R. Nicholls, op. cit., p. 333.
94 J. Bury, op. cit., p. 244.
95 A. Taylor, *English History 1914–1945* (Oxford: Oxford University Press, 1975), p. 61.
96 F. Lesure and R. Nicholls, op. cit., p. 331.
97 Quoted in W. Carter, op. cit., p. 644.
98 Ibid.
99 B. Ivry, op. cit.
100 Quoted in W. Carter, op. cit., p. 658.
101 W. Churchill, *The World Crisis 1916–1918 Part 2* (London: Thornton Butterworth, 1927), vol. 4, p. 412.
102 J. Barrie Jones (trans. and ed.), *Gabriel Fauré: A Life in Letters* (London: Batsford, 1988), p. 173.
103 B. Rees, op. cit., p. 427.
104 J. Bury, op. cit., p. 251.
105 W. Churchill, op. cit., vol. 4, p. 446.
106 Ibid., vol. 4, p. 459.
107 Ibid., vol. 4, p. 504.
108 J. Bury, op. cit., p. 252.
109 B. Rees, op. cit., p. 430.
110 R. Orledge, op. cit., p. 556.
111 F. Lesure and R. Nicholls, op. cit., p. 335.
112 A. Taylor, op. cit., p. 101.
113 J.G. Prod'homme, 'C.A. Debussy', *Musical Quarterly*, vol. 4 (4), 1918, pp. 555–71.
114 F. Lesure and R. Nicholls, op. cit., p. 335. A facsimile of the letter is in the museum in St Germain-en-Laye.
115 Ibid., p. 336.

Chapter 27

1 *New Grove Dictionary of Music and Musicians* (ed. S. Sadie) (London: Macmillan, 1980), vol. 15, p. 435. M. Carner, *Puccini* (London: Gerald Duckworth and co., 1974), p. 335, says that Mimi is 'romanticised almost beyond recognition'.
2 S. Jackson, *Monsieur Butterfly: The Story of Puccini* (London: W.H. Allen, 1994), p. 204.
3 M. Zemanová, *Janáček* (London: John Murray, 2002), p. 164.
4 J. Barrie Jones (trans. and ed.), *Gabriel Fauré: A Life in Letters* (London: Batsford, 1988), p. 103.
5 S. Jackson, op. cit., p. 204.
6 Ibid., p. 211.
7 J. Barrie Jones, op. cit., p. 111.
8 *Opera Gala!* Decca, 1992.
9 The Czech singer, Marie Calma-Veselá, quoted in M. Zemanová, op. cit., p. 133.
10 S. Jackson, op. cit., p. 150.
11 S. Jackson, op. cit., Foreword.
12 M. Carner, op. cit., p. 7.
13 Ibid., p. 14.
14 *Encyclopaedia Britannica*, ninth edition, 1875–89.
15 S. Jackson, op. cit., p. 5.
16 Ibid., p. 8.
17 *New Grove*, op. cit., vol. 15, p. 431.
18 M. Carner, op. cit., p. 21.
19 *New Grove*, op. cit.
20 W. Lakond (trans. and ed.), *The Diaries of Tchaikovsky* (Westport, CT: Greenwood Press, 1973), p. 28.
21 Ibid., p. 289.
22 Ibid., p. 293.
23 *New Grove*, op. cit.
24 S. Jackson, op. cit., p. 19.
25 M. Carner, op. cit., pp. 38, 27.
26 *New Grove*, op. cit., vol. 15, p. 431.
27 S. Jackson, op. cit., p. 25.
28 Ibid., p. 20.
29 M. Carner, op. cit., p. 45.
30 S. Jackson, op. cit., p. 35.
31 B. Walter (trans. J. Galston), *Theme and Variations* (London: Hamish Hamilton, 1947), p. 54.
32 S. Jackson, op. cit., pp. 43, 44.
33 *New Grove*, op. cit.
34 S. Jackson, op. cit., p. 50.
35 M. Carner, op. cit., p. 187.
36 S. Jackson, op. cit., p. 53; and *New Grove*, op. cit., vol. 15, p. 432.
37 F. Routh, *Stravinsky* (Master Musicians) (London: J.M. Dent, 1975), p. 104; further information from *Encyclopaedia Britannica*, fifteenth edition, 1974.
38 *New Oxford Companion to Music* (ed. D. Arnold) (Oxford: Oxford University Press, 1983), p. 1133; and *New Grove*, op. cit.

39 *New Grove*, op. cit.
40 M. Carner, op. cit., p. 70.
41 Ibid., pp. 49, 64.
42 *New Grove*, op. cit.
43 W. Dean, *Bizet* (Master Musicians) (London: J.M. Dent, 1948), p. 107.
44 M. Curtiss, *Bizet and his World* (London: Secker and Warburg, 1959), p. 349.
45 B. Rees, *Camille Saint-Saëns: A Life* (London: Chatto and Windus, 1999), p. 223.
46 L. de Romain, quoted in H. Lacombe (trans. E. Schneider), *The Keys to French Opera in the Nineteenth Century* (Berkeley, CA: University of California Press, 2001), p. 284.
47 P.H. Lang, *Music in Western Civilisation* (London: J.M. Dent, 1963), p. 923.
48 *New Grove*, op. cit., vol. 11, p. 801.
49 Ibid., p. 802, amended by the author.
50 Massenet said to Vincent d'Indy, 'I don't believe in all that creeping-Jesus stuff, but the public likes it and we must always agree with the public.' (*New Grove*, op. cit., vol. 11, p. 801).
51 Ibid., p. 802, amended by the author.
52 F. Lesure and R. Nicholls (selected and trans.), *Debussy: Letters* (London: Faber and Faber, 1987), p. 56.
53 M. Carner, op. cit., p. 73.
54 S. Jackson, op. cit., p. 54.
55 Ibid., p. 59.
56 E. White, *Stravinsky: The Composer and his Works* (London: Faber and Faber, 1979), p. 63.
57 M. Carner, op. cit., p. 69.
58 M. Carner, op. cit., p. 90.
59 M. Carner, op. cit., p. 97.
60 S. Jackson, op. cit., pp. 74, 75.
61 M. Clark, *The Italian Risorgimento* (London: Addison-Wesley, 1998), p. 99.
62 C. Hibbert, *Nelson: A Personal History* (London: Viking, 1994), p. 165.
63 *New Grove*, op. cit., vol. 15, p. 432.
64 S. Jackson, op. cit., p. 96.
65 Ibid., p. 106.
66 H. Stuckenschmidt (trans. R. Rosenbaum), *Maurice Ravel* (London: Calder and Boyars, 1969), p. 3.
67 *Encyclopaedia Britannica*, fifteenth edition, op. cit., vol. 1 and vol. 28 (*Encyclopaedia Britannica Macropaedia*, 1997).
68 A. Findlater, *Findlaters: The Story of a Dublin Merchant Family* (Dublin: A. and A. Farmer, 2001), p. 244.
69 S. Jackson, op. cit., pp. 114, 112; and M. Carner, op. cit., p. 133.
70 H. Robinson, *Sergei Prokofiev* (London: Robert Hale, 1987), pp. 217, 236, 333.
71 S. Jackson, op. cit., p. 121.
72 M. Carner, op. cit., p. 139; and S. Jackson, op. cit., p. 120.
73 M. Carner, op. cit., p. 140.
74 S. Jackson, op. cit., p. 133.
75 M. Carner, op. cit., p. 148.
76 *Illustrated London News.*
77 *Oxford Companion*, op. cit., p. 801; and M. Broyles, in D. Nicholls (ed.), *The Cambridge History of American Music* (Cambridge: Cambridge University Press, 1998), p. 152.
78 M. Carner, op. cit., p. 223.
79 Ibid., pp. 127, 128, 129, 146, 162.
80 S. Jackson, op. cit., p. 116.
81 M. Carner, op. cit., pp. 178, 183.
82 Ibid., p. 181.
83 S. Jackson, op. cit., pp. 176, 177, 184.
84 Ibid., p. 183; and M. Carner, op. cit., pp. 184, 185; and *New Grove*, op. cit., vol. 15, p. 432.
85 A. Leslie, *Edwardians in Love* (London: Hutchinson, 1972), p. 252.
86 Ibid., p. 279.
87 Ibid., p. 230.
88 Ibid., p. 249.
89 S. Jackson, op. cit., p. 140.
90 Ibid., p. 149; and *Encyclopaedia Britannica*, ninth edition, op. cit.
91 S. Jackson, op. cit., pp. 129, 130.
92 M. Carner, op. cit., p. 148.
93 Ibid., p. 190.
94 Ibid., p. 191.
95 S. Jackson, op. cit., p. 212.
96 Ibid.
97 Ibid., pp. 217, 221, 218.
98 *New Grove*, op. cit., vol. 19, p. 86; and S. Jackson, op. cit., p. 117.
99 S. Jackson, op. cit., p. 214.
100 Ibid., p. 220.
101 M. Carner, op. cit., p. 169.
102 S. Jackson, op. cit., p. 245.
103 Ibid., p. 240.
104 *New Grove*, op. cit., vol. 15, p. 434.
105 S. Jackson, op. cit., p. 253; and M. Carner, op. cit., p. 239.
106 *New Grove*, op. cit., vol. 15, p. 435; and S. Jackson, op. cit., p. 254.

Chapter 28

1 F. Bowers, *The New Scriabin* (Newton Abbot: David and Charles, 1974), p. 51.
2 Ibid., p. 24.
3 Ibid., p. 116.
4 Ibid., p. 58.
5 Ibid., p. xiv.
6 Ibid., p. 174.
7 Ibid., pp. 9, 101, 107.
8 E. Gombrich, *The Story of Art* (London: Phaidon, 1963), p. 428.
9 *Encyclopaedia Britannica*, fifteenth edition, 1974.
10 L. Fay, *Shostakovich: A Life* (Oxford: Oxford University Press, 2000), p. 41.
11 *New Grove Dictionary of Music and Musicians* (ed. S. Sadie) (London: Macmillan, 1980); and F. Bowers, op. cit., p. 90.
12 F. Bowers, op. cit., p. 26.
13 Ibid., pp. 25, 33, 58.
14 Ibid., p. 32.
15 *New Grove*, op. cit.; and F. Bowers, op. cit., pp. 36, 39.
16 F. Bowers, op. cit., p. 57.
17 Ibid., pp. 44, 56.
18 *Encyclopaedia Britannica*, fifteenth edition, op. cit.
19 F. Bowers, op. cit., p. 122.
20 Ibid., p. 190.
21 Ibid., p. 192.
22 Ibid., p. 179.
23 Ibid., p. 92.
24 S. Prokofiev (trans. O. Prokofiev), *Soviet Diary 1927 and Other Writings* (London: Faber and Faber, 1991), p. 253.
25 R. Walker, *Rachmaninoff: His Life and Times* (Tunbridge Wells: Midas, 1980), p. 29.
26 *New Oxford Companion to Music* (ed. D. Arnold) (Oxford: Oxford University Press, 1983), p. 1522.
27 R. Walker, op. cit., p. 43.
28 Ibid., p. 27.
29 E. White, *Stravinsky: The Composer and his Works* (London: Faber and Faber, 1979), p. 28.
30 R. Walker, op. cit., pp. 67, 73, 69.
31 R. Hingley, *Russia: A Concise History* (London: Thames and Hudson, 1991), p. 149; and M. McCauley, *The Soviet Union 1917–1991* (London: Longman, 1993), pp. 1–3, 5.
32 H. Acton, *The Last Medici* (London: Macmillan, 1980), p. 140.
33 M. Fainsod, *How Russia is Ruled* (Cambridge, MA: Harvard University Press, 1963), pp. 42, 50.
34 R. Walker, op. cit., p. 82.
35 L. Fay, op. cit., pp. 13, 222.
36 M. McCauley, op. cit., p. 3.
37 M. Fainsod, op. cit., p. 84.
38 Ibid.
39 F. Bowers, op. cit., p. 15.
40 O. Figes, *Natasha's Dance: A Cultural History of Russia* (London: Allen Lane The Penguin Press, 2002), p. 544.
41 *New Grove*, op. cit.; and R. Walker, op. cit., p. 99.
42 *New Grove*, op. cit.
43 F. Routh, *Stravinsky* (Master Musicians) (London: J.M. Dent, 1975), p. 36.
44 S. Prokofiev, op. cit., p. 249.
45 F. Routh, op. cit., pp. 11, 12; and E. White, op. cit., pp. 45, 46.
46 Laloy, quoted in F. Lesure (trans. D. Stevens), 'Claude Debussy after his Centenary', *Musical Quarterly*, vol. 49 (3), 1963, p. 265.
47 *Oxford Companion*, op. cit., p. 1668.
48 F. Routh, op. cit., p. 135. The calculation was done in the 1960s.
49 M. Fainsod, op. cit., pp. 90, 425, 426, 529.
50 M. McCauley, op. cit., pp. 25, 33.
51 In 1926–7, 11 per cent of farms accounted for 56 per cent of the grain produced in European Russia (M. McCauley, op. cit., p. 57).
52 H. Robinson, *Sergei Prokofiev* (London: Robert Hale, 1987), p. 361.
53 M. McCauley, op. cit., p. 82.
54 Ibid., p. 84.
55 Ibid., p. 25.
56 S. Prokofiev, op. cit., p. 91.
57 D. Saunders, *Russia in the Age of Reaction and Reform* (London: Longman, 1992), pp. 73, 93; and *Encyclopaedia Britannica*, fifteenth edition, op. cit.
58 Shostakovich, quoted in A. Bullock, *Hitler and Stalin: Parallel Lives* (London: HarperCollins, 1991), p. 306.
59 A. Bullock, op. cit., p. 1061.
60 E. White, op. cit., p. 146.
61 Ibid., p. 151.
62 *New Grove*, op. cit., vol. 15, p. 297.
63 Ibid., p. 289.
64 H. Robinson, op. cit., p. 131.
65 S. Prokofiev, op. cit., p. 258.
66 Ibid., p. 260.

67 Ibid., p. 261.
68 Ibid., p. 272.
69 H. Robinson, op. cit., p. 254.
70 Ibid., pp. 173, 174.
71 S. Prokofiev, op. cit., p. 274.
72 Ibid., p. 278.
73 Ibid., p. 289.
74 Ibid., p. 290.
75 Ibid., pp. 65, 49.
76 Ibid., p. xiii; and H. Robinson, op. cit., p. 47.
77 S. Prokofiev, op. cit., p. 114.
78 Ibid., p. 24.
79 Ibid., p. 75.
80 O. Figes, op. cit., p. 446.
81 S. Prokofiev, op. cit., p. 38.
82 F. Bowers, op. cit., p. 84.
83 S. Prokofiev, op. cit., p. 35.
84 *New Grove*, op. cit., vol. 15, p. 295.
85 H. Robinson, op. cit., pp. 85, 168, 217, 241.
86 M. Fainsod, op. cit., p. 158.
87 Ibid., p. 435.
88 Ibid., p. 159.
89 Ibid., p. 439.
90 A. Bullock, op. cit., p. 545.
91 L. Fay, op. cit., p. 114; and S. Prokofiev, op. cit., p. 170.
92 A. Bullock, op. cit., p. 768.
93 M. McCauley, op. cit., p. 145.
94 A. Bullock, op. cit., p. 810.
95 M. McCauley, op. cit., p. 148.
96 *New Grove*, op. cit., vol. 15, p. 297.
97 A. Bullock, op. cit., pp. 1008, 1007.
98 Ibid., p. 1008.
99 E. Crankshaw, *Krushchev's Russia* (London: Penguin, 1959), p 100.
100 O. Figes, op. cit., p. 451.
101 L. Fay, op. cit., p. 155.
102 M. McCauley, op. cit., p. 194.
103 *Oxford Companion*, op. cit., pp. 708, 1699.
104 A. Bullock, op. cit., p. 1008.
105 L. Fay, op. cit., p. 158.
106 A. Bullock, op. cit., p. 1008.
107 E. White, op. cit., p. 146.
108 H. Robinson, op. cit., p. 474, 477; and M. McCauley, op. cit., p. 184; and *Encyclopaedia Britannica*, fifteenth edition, 1974.
109 H. Robinson, op. cit., p. 365.
110 A. Bullock, op. cit., pp. 1053, 1054; and M. McCauley, op. cit., p. 199.
111 M. Fainsod, op. cit., p. 447.
112 *New Grove*, op. cit.
113 L. Fay, op. cit., p. 41.
114 Ibid., p. 10.
115 Ibid., p. 12.
116 In February–October 1917 Petrograd received 44 per cent of the 1913 level (M. Fainsod, op. cit., p. 95; and M. McCauley, op. cit., p. 9). In September 1918 industrial production was 50 per cent of the 1913 level (M. McCauley, op. cit., p. 16).
117 L. Fay, op. cit., p. 29.
118 Ibid., pp. 32, 36.
119 Ibid., p. 55.
120 Ibid., p. 59.
121 Ibid., p. 64.
122 Ibid., pp. 79, 80.
123 Ibid., p. 83.
124 Ibid., p. 91.
125 A. Bullock, op. cit., p. 454.
126 L. Fay, op. cit., pp. 110, 214.
127 Ibid., p. 94.
128 Ibid., p. 92.
129 Ibid., pp. 98, 99.
130 Ibid., p. 104.
131 F. Bowers, op. cit., p. 14.
132 L. Fay, op. cit., p. 124.
133 Ibid., p. 132.
134 Figures for the death toll for the war may be found in M. Gilbert, *Second World War* (London: Weidenfeld and Nicolson, 1989), p. 746.
135 Quoted in A. Bullock, op. cit., p. 998.
136 L. Fay, op. cit., pp. 110, 386, 151.
137 Ibid., p. 153.
138 A. Bullock, op. cit., p. 1061.
139 *New Grove*, op. cit., vol. 17, p. 265.
140 L. Fay, op. cit., p. 161.
141 Ibid., p. 162.
142 Ibid., p. 173.
143 A. Bullock, op. cit., p. 1056.
144 *New Grove*, op. cit.; and L. Fay, op. cit., p. 179.
145 L. Fay, op. cit., p. 190.
146 Ibid., p. 197.
147 Ibid., p. 193.
148 Ibid., p. 227.
149 M. Frankland, *Krushchev* (London: Penguin, 1966), p. 198.
150 L. Fay, op. cit., p. 269.
151 Chukovskaya, quoted in L. Fay, op. cit., p. 278.
152 L. Fay, op. cit., p. 276.

CHAPTER 29

1 J. Caldwell, *The Oxford History of English Music* (Oxford: Oxford University Press, 1999), p. 94.
2 N. Cardus, *A Composers Eleven* (London: Jonathan Cape, 1958), p. 196.
3 D. Wyn Jones (ed.), *Music in Eighteenth-Century Britain* (Aldershot: Ashgate Publishing, 2000), p. 13; and J. Caldwell, op. cit., p. 94.
4 P.H. Lang, *Music in Western Civilisation* (London: J.M. Dent, 1963), p. 675.
5 Ibid.; and C. Russell, in N. Zaslaw (ed.), *The Classical Era* (London: Macmillan, 1989), pp. 350–64.
6 B. Walter (trans. J. Galston), *Theme and Variations* (London: Hamish Hamilton, 1947), p. 61.
7 R. Halliwell, *The Mozart Family: Four Lives in a Social Context* (Oxford: Clarendon Press, 1956), pp. 214, 242.
8 Quoted in P.H. Lang, op. cit., p. 518.
9 P. Olleson, in C. Bashford and L. Langley (eds), *Music and British Culture* (Oxford: Oxford University Press, 2000), p. 34.
10 M. Kennedy, *Portrait of Elgar* (London: Oxford University Press, 1982), p. 51.
11 A. Walker, *Franz Liszt, Volume 2: The Weimar Years, 1848–60* (London: Faber and Faber, 1989), p. 276.
12 W. Blunt, *Slow on the Feather* (Salisbury: Michael Russell, 1986), p. 124.
13 J. Horton, *Grieg* (Master Musicians) (London: J.M. Dent, 1974), p. 74.
14 N. Kenyon, *Musical Lives* (Oxford: Oxford University Press, 2002), p. 79.
15 P. Horton, 'The Natural Romantic', *Choir and Organ*, March/April 2001, pp. 71–5. (The article is about S.S. Wesley.)
16 P. Olleson, in C. Bashford and L. Langley, op. cit., p. 36; N. Kenyon, op. cit., pp. 279, 268.
17 E. Walker (revised J.A. Westrup), *A History of Music in England* (Oxford: Clarendon Press, 1952), p. 268.
18 Ibid., p. 301.
19 Ibid.
20 Ibid., p. 305.
21 M. Kennedy, op. cit., p. 37.
22 *Oxford Companion to Music*, ninth edition (ed. P.A. Scholes) (London: Oxford University Press, 1955), p. xviii.
23 M. Kennedy, op. cit., p. 157.
24 M. Zemanová, *Janáček* (London: John Murray, 2002), p. 212.
25 A. Einstein, *Music in the Romantic Era* (London: J.M. Dent, 1947), p. 174.
26 Vaughan Williams' essay on 'Good Taste' in *The Vocalist*, 1902, quoted in M. Hurd, *Vaughan Williams* (London: Faber and Faber, 1970), p. 67.
27 A. Walker, op. cit., p. 273; and S. Prokofiev (trans. O Prokofiev), *Soviet Diary 1927 and Other Writings* (London: Faber and Faber, 1991), p. 270.
28 G. Reese, *Music in the Middle Ages* (London: J.M. Dent, 1968; original edition, 1940), p. 393.
29 J. Caldwell, op. cit., p. 542.
30 Ibid., p. 195; and *New Oxford Companion to Music* (ed. D. Arnold) (Oxford: Oxford University Press, 1983), p. 143.
31 D. Matthews, 'Enriching Influence', *Times Literary Supplement*, 24 August 2001.
32 C. Harris, 'The War Between the Fixed and Movable Doh', *Musical Quarterly*, vol. 4 (2), 1918, p. 194; and *New Oxford Companion*, op. cit., p. 1701.
33 D.H. Lawrence, *Sons and Lovers* (London: Penguin, 1948; first published 1913), p. 278.
34 N. Cardus, op. cit., p. 197.
35 B. Walter, op. cit., pp. 289, 333.
36 A. Suter, 'Nimrod in the Metro', *The Elgar Society Journal*, vol. 12 (2), p. 64.
37 Ibid.
38 Elgar, quoted in N. Cardus, op. cit., p. 193.
39 M. Kennedy, op. cit., p. 169.
40 A. Walker, op. cit., p. 339.
41 Ibid., p. 337.
42 M. Kennedy, op. cit., p. 16.
43 To be found in the Elgar Museum, Broadheath; the letter from Mozart to his father is dated 26 September 1781.
44 M. Kennedy, op. cit., p. 21; and *New Grove Dictionary of Music and Musicians* (ed. S. Sadie) (London: Macmillan, 1980), vol. 6, p. 114.
45 *Oxford Dictionary, The Concise*, fifth edition, 1964.
46 M. Kennedy, op. cit., p. 22.
47 Elgar Museum, Broadheath.
48 M. Kennedy, op. cit., pp. 21, 19; and I. Parrott, *Elgar* (Master Musicians) (London: J.M. Dent, 1971), p. 3.
49 I. Parrott, op. cit., p. 4; and M. Kennedy, op. cit., p. 30.
50 M. Musgrave, in C. Bashford and L. Langley, op. cit., p. 187; and A. Walker, op. cit., p. 319.

51 M. Kennedy, op. cit., p. 32.
52 S. Sassoon, *Memoirs of a Fox-Hunting Man* (London: Faber and Faber, 1918), p. 7.
53 M. Kennedy, op. cit., p. 31.
54 Ibid., p. 41.
55 *New Grove*, op. cit., vol. 6, p. 115.
56 I. Parrott, op. cit., p. 23.
57 S. Sassoon, op. cit., p. 9.
58 M. Kennedy, op. cit., p. 44.
59 G. St Aubyn, *Queen Victoria: A Portrait* (London: Sinclair-Stevenson, 1991), p. 456.
60 Elgar Museum, Broadheath.
61 M. Kennedy, op. cit., p. 50.
62 A. Walker, op. cit., p. 337.
63 M. Kennedy, op. cit., p. 50.
64 N. Carner, op. cit., p. 35.
65 M. Kennedy, op. cit., p. 51.
66 *New Grove*, op. cit., vol. 5, p. 115.
67 M. Kennedy, op. cit., p. 60.
68 Ibid., p. 45.
69 Ibid., p. 55.
70 Ibid., p. 146.
71 Ibid., p. 59.
72 Ibid., p. 61, amended by the author.
73 Ibid., p. 94.
74 *New Grove*, op. cit.
75 *New Grove*, op. cit., vol. 6, p. 116.
76 M. Kennedy, op. cit., pp. 83, 147.
77 J. Laver, *Taste and Fashion* (Edinburgh: Harrap, 1945), p. 73; and A. Mahler-Werfel (trans. A. Beaumont), *Diaries 1878–1902* (London: Faber and Faber, 1998), p. 156.
78 I. Parrott, op. cit., p. 7; and information from the Elgar Museum, Broadheath.
79 L. Strachey, *Eminent Victorians* (London: Penguin, 1918), p. 23.
80 D. Newsome, *The Convert Cardinals: Newman and Manning* (London: John Murray, 1993), p. 292.
81 L. Strachey, op. cit., p. 14.
82 D. Newsome, op. cit., p. 290.
83 *New Grove*, op. cit., vol. 5, p. 122.
84 M. Kennedy, op. cit., p. 113.
85 Ibid., p. 109.
86 Ibid., p. 151.
87 *New Grove*, op. cit., vol. 5, p. 117.
88 M. Kennedy, op. cit., p. 143.
89 Ibid., pp. 213, 214.
90 Ibid., p. 228.
91 N. Cardus, op. cit., p. 201.
92 I. Parrott, op. cit., p. 11.
93 M. Kennedy, op. cit., p. 66.
94 Ibid., p. 173.
95 Ibid., p. 198.
96 Ibid., p. 167.
97 K. Rose, *King George V* (London: Weidenfeld and Nicolson, 1983), p. 284.
98 M. Kennedy, op. cit., p. 305.
99 Princess Marie Louise, quoted in K. Rose, op. cit., p. 286. Rose implies that Shaw was the sole refuser.
100 M. Kennedy, op. cit., p. 64.
101 Ibid., p. 154.
102 Ibid., p. 175.
103 Ibid., p. 177.
104 Ibid., pp. 198, 172; and I. Parrott, op. cit., pp. 26, 13.
105 J. Laver, op. cit., p. 79.
106 R. Orledge, *Gabriel Fauré* (London: Eulenberg, 1979), p. 17.
107 M. Kennedy, op. cit., p. 102.
108 I. Parrott, op. cit., p. 123.
109 *New Grove*, op. cit., vol. 5, p. 118; and I. Parrott, op. cit., p. 14.
110 Letter from Sir Hugh Allen, at Elgar Museum, Broadheath.
111 *Illustrated London News*, 27 May 1909.
112 M. Kennedy, op. cit., p. 242, amended by the author.
113 I. Parrott, op. cit., p. 11; further information from Elgar Museum, Broadheath.
114 M. Kennedy, op. cit., p. 252.
115 *Illustrated London News*.
116 M. Kennedy, op. cit., p. 266.
117 Ibid., p. 233; and Elgar Museum, Broadheath.
118 M. Kennedy, op. cit., p. 288.
119 Ibid., p. 233.
120 Quoted in J. Laver, op. cit., p. 64.
121 A. Findlater, *Findlaters: The Story of a Dublin Merchant Family* (Dublin: A. and A. Farmer, 2001), p. 238.
122 M. Leaska, *Granite and Rainbow: The Hidden Life of Virginia Woolf* (London: Picador, 1998), p. 198.
123 Ibid., p. 115.
124 Ibid., p. 129.
125 M. Leaska, op. cit., pp. 193, 196.
126 I. Parrott, op. cit., p. 25.
127 Elgar Museum, Broadheath.
128 S. Prokofiev. op. cit., p. 289.
129 I. Parrott, op. cit., pp. 28, 29.
130 *New Grove*, op. cit., vol. 5, p. 119.
131 I. Parrott, op. cit., p. 30.

132 *New Oxford Companion*, op. cit., p. 871.
133 J. Caldwell, op. cit., p. 556.
134 N. Kenyon, op. cit., p. 89.
135 N. Cardus, op. cit., p. 224.
136 Ibid., p. 215.
137 M. Hurd, op. cit., p. 66.
138 Information on Leith Hill Place from Miss S. Chessum at The National Trust, and *The National Trust Handbook*, 2001.
139 M. Hurd, op. cit., p. 33.
140 S. Sassoon, op. cit., p. 297.
141 Ibid., p. 331.
142 Ibid., p. 322.
143 Ibid., p. 327.
144 Ibid., p. 334.
145 A. Findlater, op. cit., p. 259.
146 The Distinguished Service Order.
147 A. Findlater, op. cit., p. 264.
148 M. Hurd, op. cit., p. 37.
149 N. Kenyon, op. cit., p. 175.
150 M. Hurd, op. cit., p. 39.
151 Ibid., p. 39.
152 Ibid., p. 65.
153 Ibid., p. 43.
154 Ibid., p. 65.
155 Ibid., p. 56.
156 M. Oliver, *Benjamin Britten* (London: Phaidon, 1996), p. 28.
157 N. Kenyon, op. cit., p. 125.
158 M. Oliver, op. cit., pp. 38, 54; *New Grove*, op. cit., vol. 3, p. 293; and *New Oxford Companion*, op. cit., p. 265.
159 *New Grove*, op. cit., vol. 14, p. 319.
160 M. Oliver, op. cit., pp. 90, 91.
161 Ibid., p. 108.
162 Ibid., p. 213.
163 Ibid., p. 211.
164 A. Walker, op. cit., p. 360.

Postlude

1 Roger North (c. 1728) (ed. H. Andrews), *The Musicall Grammarian* (London, 1925), quoted in P.H. Lang, *Music in Western Civilisation* (London: J.M. Dent, 1963), p. 436.
2 N. Cardus, *A Composers Eleven* (London: Jonathan Cape, 1958), p. 193.
3 W. Reich (trans. L. Black), *Schoenberg* (London: Longman, 1971), p. 78.
4 S. Prokofiev (trans. O. Prokofiev), *Soviet Diary 1927 and Other Writings* (London: Faber and Faber, 1991), p. 282.
5 B. Jack, *George Sand* (London: Chatto and Windus, 1999), p. 344.
6 *New Grove Dictionary of Music and Musicians* (ed. S. Sadie) (London: Macmillan, 1980), vol. 11, p. 801.
7 H. McDonald, in P. Bloom (ed.), *Music in Paris in the Eighteen Thirties* (New York, NY: Pendragon Press, 1987), p. 457.
8 E. Crankshaw, *Krushchev's Russia* (London: Penguin, 1959).
9 M. Oliver, *Benjamin Britten* (London: Phaidon, 1996), p. 213.
10 N. Cardus, op. cit., p. 224.
11 T. Mann, (trans. H.T. Lowe-Porter), *Death in Venice* (London: Penguin, 1955; first published, 1911), p. 15.

SOURCES AND FURTHER READING

Important note

Information in the text has been taken from, and is almost wholly reliant upon, the sources set out below. The literature is vast; the fact that a particular book is absent merely implies that it was not directly used. It does not mean that the book was not consulted, least of all, that it was not respected.

The section entitled 'Notes' is intended to identify the specific source from which an item of information has been extracted, or sometimes just verified. A cursory glance will indicate the considerable extent to which reliance has been placed on individual publications and authors.

Particularly for factual information, certain sources have been relied upon extensively and generally, such as *The New Grove Dictionary of Music and Musicians*, the *New Oxford Companion to Music*, and the *Encyclopaedia Britannica* (including the ninth edition of 1875–89). Where reliance on these has been specific, rather than just general, it has been identified in the Notes.

Acton, H., *The Last Medici* (London: Macmillan, 1980).

Addison, J., *Remarks on several Parts of Italy in the Years 1701, 1702, 1703* (London, 1761).

Aldrich, in R. Erickson (ed.), *Schubert's Vienna* (New Haven, CT: Yale University Press, 1997).

Anderson, E. (trans. and ed.), *The Letters of Beethoven* (London: Macmillan, 1961).

Anderson, E. (trans. and ed.), *The Letters of Mozart and his Family* (London: Macmillan, 1966).

Anderson, M.S., *Europe in the Eighteenth Century 1713–83* (London: Longman, 1961).

Anderson, R., *Elgar* (Master Musicians) (London: J.M. Dent, 1993).

Atwood, W., *The Lioness and the Little One: The Liaison of George Sand and Frederic Chopin* (New York, NY: Columbia University Press, 1980).

Avins, S., *Johannes Brahms: Life and Letters* (Oxford: Oxford University Press, 1997).

Baedeker's Germany (London: AA, 1993).

Baedeker's Czech Republic (London: AA, 1994).

Bailbé, J.-M., in P. Bloom, *Music in Paris in the Eighteen Thirties* (New York, NY: Pendragon Press, 1987).

Bailey, K., *The Life of Webern* (Cambridge: Cambridge University Press, 1998).

Baldick, R., *The Duel* (London: Chapman and Hall, 1965).

Balzac, H. de (trans. M. Crawford), *Le Père Goriot* (London: Penguin, 1951; first published 1834–5).

Balzac, H. de (trans. H.J. Hunt), *La Peau de Chagrin* (London: Penguin, 1977; first published 1831).

Balzac, H. de (selected S. Raphael), *Short Stories* (London: Penguin, 1977).

Balzac, H. de (trans. S. Raphael), *Eugénie Grandet* (Oxford: Oxford University Press, 1990; first published 1833).

Barbier, P., *The World of the Castrati* (London: Souvenir Press, 1989).

Barbier, P. (trans. R. Luoma), *Opera in Paris 1800–1850* (Portland, OR: Amadeus Press, 1995).

Barnett, C., *Napoleon* (London: George Allen and Unwin, 1978).

Barraclough, B., *The Origins of Modern Germany* (Oxford: Blackwell, 1946).

Barrie Jones, J. (trans. and ed.), *Gabriel Fauré: A Life in Letters* (London: Batsford, 1988).

Bartoš, F., *Bedřich Smetana: Letters and Reminiscences* (Prague: Artia, 1955).

Barzun, J., in P. Bloom (ed.), *Music in Paris in the Eighteen Thirties* (New York, NY: Pendragon Press, 1987).

Bashford, C. and Langley, L. (eds), *Music and British Culture* (Oxford: Oxford University Press, 2000).

Battiscombe, G., *Queen Alexandra* (London: Constable, 1969).

Beales, D., *Joseph II: In the Shadow of Maria Theresa 1741–1780* (Cambridge: Cambridge University Press, 1987).

Beales, D., *Joseph II: Against the World 1780–1790* (Cambridge: Cambridge University Press, 2009).

Beattie, J., *The English Court in the Reign of George I* (Cambridge: Cambridge University Press, 1967).

Becker, H., and Becker, G. (trans. M. Violette), *Giacomo Meyerbeer: A Life in Letters* (London: Christopher Helm, 1983).

Beckett, W., *Liszt* (Master Musicians) (London: J.M. Dent, 1963).
Beeson,T., *Window on Westminster* (London: SCM Press, 1998).
Beethoven's Letters (ed. E. Hull) (London: J.M. Dent, 1926).
Bell, I., 'Questions and Answers', in *Choir and Organ*, January/February 2002, p. 8.
Birthplace of Sibelius (Hämeenlinna Historical Museum, 1999).
Blackbourn, D., *Germany 1780–1918* (London: HarperCollins, 1997).
Blanning, T., *Joseph II* (London: Longman, 1994).
Bled, J.-P. (trans. T. Bridgeman), *Franz Joseph* (Oxford: Blackwell, 1992).
Bloom, P. (ed.), *Music in Paris in the Eighteen Thirties* (New York, NY: Pendragon Press, 1987).
Blunt, W., *The Dream King: Ludwig II of Bavaria* (London: Hamish Hamilton, 1970).
Blunt, W., *On Wings of Song: A Biography of Felix Mendelssohn* (London: Hamish Hamilton, 1974).
Blunt, W., *Slow on the Feather* (Salisbury: Michael Russell, 1986).
Bolster, R., *Marie d'Agoult: The Rebel Countess* (New Haven, CT: Yale University Press, 2000).
Borowitz, A., 'Salieri and the "Murder" of Mozart', *Musical Quarterly*, vol. 59 (2), 1973, pp. 263–84.
Bowers, F., *The New Scriabin* (Newton Abbot: David and Charles, 1974).
Boyd, M., 'Fauré's Requiem: A Reappraisal', *Musical Times*, 1963, pp. 408–9.
Boyd, M., *Bach* (Oxford: Oxford University Press, 2000).
Boyle, N., *Goethe: The Poet and the Age* (Oxford: Oxford University Press, 1991).
Bradfield, N., *Historical Costumes of England* (Edinburgh: Harrap, 1970).
Brion, M. (trans. J. Stewart), *Daily Life in the Vienna of Mozart and Schubert* (London: Weidenfeld and Nicolson, 1961).
Brion, M. (trans. G. and H. Cremonesi), *The Medici* (London: Elek, 1969).
British History, Notes on (London: Rivingtons, 1962).
Brockedon, W., *Illustrations of the Passes of the Alps* (London, 1838).
Brooke, I. and Laver, J., *English Costume in the Eighteenth Century* (London: A. and C. Black, 1931).
Brooks, W., in D. Nicholls (ed.), *The Cambridge History of American Music* (Cambridge: Cambridge University Press, 1998).
Brown, B.A., in N. Zaslaw (ed.), *The Classical Era* (London: Macmillan, 1989).
Brown, B.A., *Gluck and the French Theatre in Vienna* (Oxford: Clarendon Press, 1991).
Brown, D., *Mikhail Glinka* (London: Oxford University Press, 1974).
Brown, D., 'How did Tchaikovsky Come to Die: And Does it Really Matter', *Music and Letters*, vol. 63, 1997, p. 581–8.
Brown, J., in R. Erickson (ed.), *Schubert's Vienna* (New Haven, CT: Yale University Press, 1997).
Browning, R., *The War of the Austrian Succession* (Stroud: Alec Sutton, 1994).
Broyles, M., in D. Nicholls (ed.), *The Cambridge History of American Music* (Cambridge: Cambridge University Press, 1998).
Bruce, E., *Napoleon and Josephine* (London: Weidenfeld and Nicolson, 1995).
Brühl Exhibition Guide, 'The Split in Heaven', 2000.
Budden, J., *Verdi* (Master Musicians) (London: J.M. Dent, 1985).
Bukofzer, M., *Music in the Baroque Era* (London: J.M. Dent, 1947).
Bullock, A., *Hitler and Stalin: Parallel Lives* (London: HarperCollins, 1991).
Burke, T., *Travel in England from Pilgrim and Pack-Horse to Light Car and Plane* (London: Batsford, 1942).
Burney, Dr C. (ed. P. Scholes), *An Eighteenth-Century Musical Tour in France and Italy* (Oxford: Oxford University Press, 1959; first published 1770).
Burney, Dr C., *General History of Music* (London, 1776–89).
Burrows, D., *Handel* (Master Musicians) (Oxford: Oxford University Press, 1994).
Burrows, D., *The Cambridge Companion to Handel* (Cambridge: Cambridge University Press, 1997).
Bury, J., *France 1814–1940* (London: Methuen, 1969).
Butt, J., in D. Burrows (ed.), *The Cambridge Companion to Handel* (Cambridge: Cambridge University Press, 1997).

Caldwell, J., *The Oxford History of English Music* (Oxford: Oxford University Press, 1999).
Cairns, D., in P. Bloom (ed.), *Music in Paris in the Eighteen Thirties* (New York, NY: Pendragon Press, 1987).
Cairns, D., *Berlioz 1803–1832: The Making of an Artist* (London: André Deutsch, 1989).
Cairns, D., *Berlioz 1832–1869: Servitude and Greatness* (London: Allen Lane, 1999).
Calvocoressi, M.D. (revised G. Abraham), *Mussorgsky* (Master Musicians) (London: J.M. Dent, 1974).
Cardus, N., *A Composers Eleven* (London: Jonathan Cape, 1958).
Carner, M., *Puccini* (London: Gerald Duckworth and co., 1974).
Carr, F., *Mozart and Constanze* (London: John Murray, 1983).
Carr, W., *A History of Germany 1815–1990* (London: Hodder and Stoughton, 1969).
Carter, W., *Marcel Proust: A Life* (New Haven, CT: Yale University Press, 2000).
Catania Bellini Museum Guide (Catania 1998).
Chadwick, O., *The Reformation* (London: Pelican, 1964).
Chandler, D. (ed.), *A Guide to the Battlefields of Europe* (London: Evelyn, 1965).
Chandler, D. (ed.), *Napoleon's Marshals* (London: Weidenfeld and Nicolson, 1987).
Chandler, D., *Waterloo: The Hundred Days* (London: Osprey, 1987).
Chernaik, J., 'Guilt Alone Brings Forth Nemesis', *Times Literary Supplement*, 31 August 2001.
Chesterfield, Lord, *Letters to his Son, 1774* (London: The Folio Society, 1973).
Chissell, J., *Schumann* (Master Musicians) (London: J.M. Dent, 1948).
Chinn, C., *Better Betting with a Decent Feller: Bookmaking, Betting and the British Working Class, 1750–1990* (London and New York: Harvester Wheatsheaf, 1991).
Chissell, J., *Clara Schumann: A Dedicated Spirit* (London: Hamish Hamilton, 1983).
Churchill, W., *The World Crisis 1916–1918 Part 2* (London: Thornton Butterworth, 1927).
Clapham, J., 'Dvořák's Relations with Brahms and Hanslick', *Musical Quarterly*, vol. 57 (2), 1971, pp. 241–54.
Clapham, J., 'The Smetana Pivoda Controversy', *Music and Letters*, vol. 52, 1971, pp. 353–64.
Clapham, J., *Smetana* (Master Musicians) (London: J.M. Dent, 1972).
Clapham, J., *Dvořák* (Newton Abbot: David and Charles, 1979).
Clark, A., 'The Reluctant Romantic', *Financial Times*, 18 August 2001.
Clark, K., *The Romantic Rebellion* (London: John Murray, 1975).
Clark, M., *The Italian Risorgimento* (London: Addison-Wesley, 1998).
Cobban, A., *A History of Modern France: Volume 1 1715–1799:* (London: Pelican, 1957).
Cobban, A., *A History of Modern France: Volume 2 1799–1871* (London: Penguin, 1961).
Colette (trans. R. Senhouse), *Gigi* (London: Vintage, 2001; first published 1944).
Colette (trans. R. Senhouse), *Chéri* (London: Penguin, 1954; first published 1920).
Colette (trans. A. White), *Claudine in Paris* (London: Penguin, 1963; first published 1901).
Cooke, D., *The Language of Music* (Oxford: Oxford University Press, 1959).
Cooper, B., *Beethoven* (Master Musicians) (Oxford: Oxford University Press, 2000).
Cooper, J. Fenimore, *The Last of the Mohicans* (London: Penguin, 1986).
Corfield, P., 'Georgian England: one state many faiths', *History Today*, vol. 45 (4), April 1995, pp. 14–21.
Cossart, M. de, *The Food of Love: Princesse Edmond de Polignac and her Salon* (London: Hamish Hamilton, 1978).
Coughlan, R., *Elizabeth and Catherine* (London: Millington, 1974). Cowgill, R., in C. Bashford and L. Langley (eds), *Music and British Culture* (Oxford: Oxford University Press, 2000).
Crankshaw, E., *Krushchev's Russia* (London: Penguin, 1959).
Crankshaw, E., *Maria Theresa* (London: Longman, 1969).
Crittenden, C., *Johann Strauss and Vienna* (Cambridge: Cambridge University Press, 2000).
Curtiss, M., 'Unpublished Letters by Georges Bizet', *Musical Quarterly*, vol. 36, 1950, pp. 375–409.
Curtiss, M., 'Bizet, Offenbach and Rossini', *Musical Quarterly*, vol. 40, 1954, pp. 350–59.
Curtiss, M., *Bizet and his World* (London: Secker and Warburg, 1959).
Dahl, E. and Jangaard, M. (eds), *Edvard Grieg* (Troldhaugen: Edvard Grieg Museum, 2000).

Dahlhaus, C., 'Wagner's Place in the History of Music', in U. Müller and P. Wapnewski (eds) (trans. J. Deathridge), *The Wagner Handbook* (Cambridge, MA: Harvard University Press, 1992).
Danbolt, G., in E. Dahl and M. Jangaard (eds), *Edvard Grieg* (Troldhaugen: Edvard Grieg Museum, 2000).
David, H.T. and Mendel, A., *The Bach Reader* (New York, NY: W.W. Norton and co., 1972; original edition 1945).
Davies, L., *Cesar Franck and his Circle* (London: Barrie and Jenkins, 1970).
Dean, W., *Bizet* (Master Musicians) (London: J.M. Dent, 1948).
Debussy's letters, see Lesure, F. and Nicholls, R.
Deutsch, O.E. (trans. E. Blom), *Schubert: A Documentary Biography* (London: J.M. Dent, 1946).
Deutsch, O.E. (ed.) (trans. R. Ley and J. Nowell), *Schubert: Memoirs by his Friends* (London: A. and C. Black, 1958).
Deutsch, O.E. (trans. E. Blom, P. Branscombe and J. Noble), *Mozart: A Documentary Biography*, second edition (London: Black, 1966).
Devrient, E., in W. Blunt, *On Wings of Song: a biography of Felix Mendelssohn* (London: Hamish Hamilton, 1974).
Devriès, A., in P. Bloom (ed.), *Music in Paris in the Eighteen Thirties* (New York: Pendragon Press, 1987).
Dietschy, M., 'The Family and Childhood of Debussy', *Musical Quarterly*, vol. 46, 1960, pp. 303–14.
Donald, D., *Lincoln* (London: Cape, 1995).
Dormandy, T., *The White Death: A History of Tuberculosis* (London: The Hambledon Press, 1999).
Dostoyevsky, F. (trans. D. Magarshack), *The Possessed* (London: Penguin Classics, 1971).
Doyle, W., *The Oxford History of the French Revolution* (Oxford: Oxford University Press, 1989).
Duffy, C., *Frederick the Great: A Military Life* (London: Routledge and Kegan Paul, 1985).
Dyson, G. (ed.), *Musicianship for Students* (London: Novello, 1940).
Eger, M., and Friedrich, S. (trans. T. Reimers and G. Shepherd), *The Richard Wagner Museum Bayreuth* (The Richard-Wagner-Foundation, 2000).
Einstein, A., *Music in the Romantic Era* (London: J.M. Dent, 1947).
Einstein, A. (trans. E. Blom), *Gluck* (Master Musicians) (London: J.M. Dent, 1964).
Eisen, C., in N. Zaslaw (ed.), *The Classical Era* (London: Macmillan, 1989).
Ellis, J., 'Women in Augustan England', *History Today*, vol. 45 (12), December 1995, pp. 20–26.
Ellmann, R., *Oscar Wilde* (London: Hamish Hamilton, 1987).
Emerson, C., *The Life of Musorgsky* (Cambridge: Cambridge University Press, 1999).
Encyclopaedia Britannica, ninth edition, 1875–89.
Encyclopaedia Britannica, fifteenth edition, 1974.
Endenich Guide, *Briefe und Dokumente in Schumannhaus Bonn-Endenich* (Bonn, 1993).
Berenbuch, B., and Hellberg, H. (trans. C. Spencer), *Robert Schumann and Bonn.*
Erickson, R. (ed.), *Schubert's Vienna* (New Haven, CT: Yale University Press, 1997).
Esterházy Castle Guide Book (Hungarian National Tourism Service, Budapest).
Evans, I., *A Short History of English Literature* (London: Penguin, 1963).
Fabré, J.H., *Social Life in the Insect World* (London: Pelican, 1937).
Fainsod, M., *How Russia is Ruled* (Cambridge, MA: Harvard University Press, 1963).
Faris, A., *Jacques Offenbach* (London: Faber and Faber, 1980).
Fauchier-Magnan, A., *The Small German Courts in the Eighteenth Century* (London: Methuen, 1958).
Fay, L., *Shostakovich: A Life* (Oxford: Oxford University Press, 2000).
Figes, O., *Natasha's Dance: A Cultural History of Russia* (London: Allen Lane The Penguin Press, 2002).
Findlater, A., *Findlaters: The Story of a Dublin Merchant Family* (Dublin: A. and A. Farmar, 2001).
Findlay, P., sleeve notes to Sutherland/Bonynge, *L'Orchestre de la Suisse Romande* (Decca, 1970).
Fitzlyon, A., *Maria Malibran: Diva of the Romantic Age* (London: Souvenir Press, 1987).
Flaubert, G. (trans. G. Hopkins), *Madame Bovary* (Oxford: Oxford University Press, 1981; first published 1856).
Ford, B. (ed.), *The Pelican Guide to English Literature, from Dryden to Johnson* (London: Penguin 1957).

Forkel, J.N. (trans. A.C.F. Kollmann), 'On Johann Sebastian Bach's Life, Genius and Works', in H.T. David and A. Mendel, *The Bach Reader* (New York, NY: W.W. Norton and co., 1972; original edition 1945).
Foster, R.F., *Lord Randolph Churchill* (Oxford: Clarendon Press, 1981).
Frankland, M., *Krushchev* (London: Penguin, 1966).
Franklin, P., *The Life of Mahler* (Cambridge: Cambridge University Press, 1997).
Fraser, A., *Cromwell Our Chief of Men* (London: Weidenfeld and Nicolson, 1973).
Fraser, F., *The Unruly Queen* (London: Macmillan, 1996).
Friedenthal, R., *Goethe: His Life and Times* (London: Weidenfeld and Nicolson, 1963).
Friedrich. O., *Olympia: Paris in the Age of Manet* (London: Aurum Press, 1992).
Frodl, G., in R. Erickson (ed.) *Schubert's Vienna* (New Haven, CT: Yale University Press, 1997).
Garden, E., *Tchaikovsky* (Master Musicians) (London: J.M. Dent, 1973).
Gaunt, W., *The Impressionists* (London: Thames and Hudson, 1970).
Gaunt, W., *The Great Century of British Painting: Hogarth to Turner* (London: Phaidon, 1971).
Geiringer, K., *Haydn: A Creative Life in Music* (Berkeley, CA: University of California Press, 1968; original edition, 1946).
George, M.D., *London Life in the Eighteenth Century* (London: Kegan Paul, Trench, Trubner, 1925).
Gilbert, M., *Second World War* (London: Weidenfeld and Nicolson, 1989).
Giles, P., *The History and Technique of the Counter Tenor* (Aldershot: Scolar Press, 1994).
Gilmour, I., *Riot, Risings and Revolution* (London: Hutchinson, 1992).
Girdham, J., 'A Note on Stephen Storace and Michael Kelly', *Music and Letters*, vol. 76, February 1995, pp. 64–7.
Girdham, J., *English Opera in Late Eighteenth Century London* (Oxford: Oxford University Press, 1997).
Glendinning, V., *Jonathan Swift* (London: Hutchinson, 1998).
Gmunden museum, 'Johannes Brahms und die Familie Miller-Aicholz', 1997.
Goethe, J.W. von (trans. M. Hulse), *The Sorrows of Young Werther* (London: Penguin, 1989; first published 1774).
Gogol, N. (trans. D. Magarshack), *Dead Souls* (London: Penguin, 1961; first published 1842).
Gombrich, E., *The Story of Art* (London: Phaidon, 1963).
Gooch, G., *Louis XV: The Monarchy in Decline* (London: Longman, 1956).
Gowan, C., *France from the Regent to the Romantics* (Edinburgh: Harrap, 1961).
Grace, H., *The Organ Works of Bach* (London: Novello, 1922).
Grey, I., *Boris Godunov* (London: Hodder and Stoughton, 1973).
Grizell, R., *The Rhone Valley and Savoy* (London: A. and C. Black, 1991).
Grove Dictionary of Music and Musicians, see S. Sadie (ed.).
Haddock, B.A., in B. Waller (ed.), *Themes in Modern European History 1830–90* (London: Unwin Hyman, 1990).
Hale, M. (trans.), *J.-P. Richter's School for Aesthetics* (Detroit: Wayne State University, 1973).
Halliwell, R., *The Mozart Family: Four Lives in a Social Context* (Oxford: Clarendon Press, 1998).
Hall-Witt, J.L., in C. Bashford and L. Langley (eds), *Music and British Culture* (Oxford: Oxford University Press, 2000).
Halsband, R., *The Life of Lady Mary Wortley Montagu* (Oxford: Clarendon Press, 1956).
Hämeenlinna Historical Museum Guide (Hämeenlinna, 1999).
Handel House Museum Companion, see J. Riding et al.
Hanson, A., *Musical Life in Biedermeyer Vienna* (Cambridge: Cambridge University Press, 1985).
Harding, J., *Saint-Saëns and his Circle* (London: Chapman and Hall, 1965).
Hardman, J., *Louis XVI* (New Haven, CT: Yale University Press, 1993).
Harman, C., *Fanny Burney* (London: HarperCollins, 2000).
Harrington, R., 'The Neuroses of the Railway', *History Today*, vol. 44 (7), July 1994, pp. 15–21.
Harris, C., 'The War Between the Fixed and Movable Doh', *Musical Quarterly*, vol. 4 (2), 1918, pp. 184–95.

Harrison, M., Introduction to disc, 'The Rubinstein Collection' (RCA, 1987).
Hartley, J., 'Charles Whitworth, First British Ambassador to Russia', *History Today*, vol. 50, June 2000, pp. 40–46.
Hartvedt, G.H., in E. Dahl and M. Jangaard (eds), *Edvard Grieg* (Troldhaugen: Edvard Grieg Museum, 2000).
Hattersley, R., *Nelson* (London: Weidenfeld and Nicolson, 1974).
Hatton, R., *George I: Elector and King* (London: Thames and Hudson, 1978).
Hayden, R., *Mrs Delany: her Life and her Flowers* (London: British Museum Publications, 1980).
Headlam, C., *The Story of Naples* (London: J.M. Dent, 1927).
Hearder, H., *Italy in the Age of the Risorgimento 1790–1870* (London: Longman, 1983).
Heartz, D., *Haydn, Mozart and the Viennese School 1740–80* (London: W.W. Norton and co., 1995).
Hecht, J., *The Domestic Servant Class in the Eighteenth Century* (London: Routledge, 1956).
Hedley, A. (revised M.E.J. Brown), *Chopin* (Master Musicians) (London: J.M. Dent, 1974; original edition 1947).
Heindl, W., in R. Erickson (ed.), *Schubert's Vienna* (New Haven, CT: Yale University Press, 1997).
Heller, K. (trans. D. Marinelli), *Antonio Vivaldi: The Red Priest of Venice* (Portland, OR: Amadeus Press, 1991).
Heriot, A., *The Castrati in Opera* (London: Secker and Warburg, 1956).
Hibbert, C., *Edward VII* (London: Allen Lane, 1976).
Hibbert, C., *Nelson: A Personal History* (London: Viking, 1994).
Hibbert, C., *George III* (London: Viking, 1998).
Hicks, A., 'Fantasia on a Theme', *Times Literary Supplement*, 31 May 2002.
Hingley, R., *Russia: A Concise History* (London: Thames and Hudson, 1991).
Hogwood, C. and Smaczny, J., in N. Zaslaw, *The Classical Era* (London: Macmillan, 1989).
Holden, A., *Tchaikovsky* (London: Bantam Press, 1995).
Holdroyd, M., *Bernard Shaw* (London: Chatto and Windus, 1988).
Holmes, R., *Coleridge: Darker Reflections* (London: HarperCollins, 1998).
Holoman, D. Kern, in P. Bloom (ed.), *Music in Paris in the Eighteen Thirties* (New York, NY: Pendragon Press, 1987).
Honolka, K. (trans. J.M. Wilde), *Papageno: Emanuel Schikaneder in Mozart's Time* (Portland, OR: Amadeus Press, 1990).
Horne, A., *The Fall of Paris* (London: Macmillan, 1965).
Horsbrugh, I., *Leoš Janáček* (Newton Abbot: David and Charles, 1981).
Horton, J., *Grieg* (Master Musicians) (London: J.M. Dent, 1974).
Horton, P., 'The Natural Romantic', *Choir and Organ*, March/April 2001, pp. 71–5.
Hoskings, G., *Russia: People and Empire* (London: HarperCollins, 1997).
Hoskings, G., *Russia and the Russians* (London: Penguin, 2001).
Hughes, R., *Haydn* (Master Musicians) (London: J.M. Dent, 1978).
Hurd, M., *Vaughan Williams* (London: Faber and Faber, 1970).
Hyde, H. Montgomerie, *The Other Love* (London: Heinemann, 1970).
Ignotus, P., *Hungary* (London: Ernest Benn Ltd., 1972).
Ingrao, C., *The Habsburg Monarchy 1618–1815* (Cambridge: Cambridge University Press, 1994).
Irving, W.H., *John Gay's London* (Cambridge, MA: Harvard University Press, 1928).
Isherwood, C., *Mr Norris Changes Trains* (London: Penguin, 1942; first published 1935).
Israel, J., *European Jewry in the Age of Mercantilism* (Oxford: Clarendon Press, 1985).
Ivry, B., *Francis Poulenc* (London: Phaidon, 1996).
Jack, B., *George Sand* (London: Chatto and Windus, 1999).
Jackson, S., *Monsieur Butterfly: The Story of Puccini* (London: W.H. Allen, 1994).
Jacob, G., in G. Dyson (ed.), *Musicianship for Students* (London: Novello, 1940).
Jacob, H.E. (trans. R. and C. Winston), *Felix Mendelssohn and his Times* (London: Barrie Books Ltd., 1963).

James, B., *Brahms: A Critical Study* (London: J.M. Dent, 1972).
James, R. Rhodes, *Lord Randolph Churchill* (London: Weidenfeld and Nicolson, 1959).
Janáčková, Z. (ed. and trans. J. Tyrrell), *My Life With Janáček* (London: Faber and Faber, 1998).
Järnefelt Ateneum Art Museum Exhibition Guide, *Järnefelt, Eero, 1863–1937* (Helsinki, 2001).
Jaroš, Z., *The Young Gustav Mahler and Jihlava* (Jihlava: Museum of Highlands, 1994).
Jenkins, R., *Gladstone* (London: Macmillan, 1995).
Jensen, E., 'Buried Alive: Schumann at Endenich', *Musical Times*, vol. 139, no. 1861, March 1998, pp. 10–18.
Jensen, E., *Schumann* (Master Musicians) (Oxford: Oxford University Press, 2001).
Johnston, J., *The Lord Chamberlain's Blue Pencil* (London: Hodder and Stoughton, 1990).
Johnstone, D., in D. Burrows (ed.), *The Cambridge Companion to Handel* (Cambridge: Cambridge University Press, 1997).
Johnstone, D., in D. Wyn Jones (ed.), *Music in Eighteenth-Century Britain* (Aldershot: Ashgate Publishing, 2000).
Jones, C., *The Cambridge History of France* (Cambridge: Cambridge University Press, 1994).
Jordan, R., *George Sand* (London: Constable, 1976).
Jourdan, P., in C. Bashford, and L. Langley (eds), *Music and British Culture* (Oxford: Oxford University Press, 2000).
Kamenka Tchaikovsky and Pushkin Museum Guide, M. Kary, 1988.
Katz, R. and Dars, C., *The Impressionists* (Leicester: Abbeydale Press, 1991).
Kennedy, M., *Mahler* (Master Musicians) (London: J.M. Dent, 1974).
Kennedy, M., *Portrait of Elgar* (London: Oxford University Press, 1982).
Kennedy, M., *Richard Strauss* (Master Musicians) (Oxford: Oxford University Press, 1995).
Kennedy, M., *Richard Strauss: Man, Musician, Enigma* (Cambridge: Cambridge University Press, 1999).
Kenyon, N., *Musical Lives* (Oxford: Oxford University Press, 2002).
Keys, I., *Mozart: His Music in his Life* (London: Elek, 1980).
Keys, I., *Johannes Brahms* (London: Christopher Helm, 1989).
Keysler, J.G., *Travels Though Germany, Bohemia, Hungary, Switzerland, Italy and Lorrain* (London: A. Linde and F. Field, 1756).
Kiernan, V., *The Duel in European History* (Oxford: Oxford University Press, 1988).
King, R., *Henry Purcell* (London: Thames and Hudson, 1994).
Klobas, O., *Václav hrabě Kounic Šlechtic Nejen Rodem* (Brno, 1993).
Knight, F., *Beethoven and the Age of Revolution* (London: Lawrence and Wishart, 1973).
Kracauer, S., *Offenbach and the Paris of his Time* (London: Constable, 1937).
Krause, E. (trans. J. Coombs), *Richard Strauss* (London: Collet's (Publishers) Ltd., 1964).
Kupferberg, H., *The Mendelssohns* (London: W.H. Allen, 1972).
La Rue, C. Steven, in D. Burrows, *The Cambridge Companion to Handel* (Cambridge: Cambridge University Press, 1997).
La Casa di Rossini: Catalogo del Museo (Fondazione Scavolini, 1989).
Lacombe, H. (trans. E. Schneider), *The Keys to French Opera in the Nineteenth Century* (Berkeley, CA: University of California Press, 2001).
Lady Mary Wortley Montagu, *The Letters of Lady Mary Wortley Montagu, ed. by her grandson Lord Wharncliffe* (London: Richard Bentley, 1837).
Laerum, O.D., in E. Dahl and M. Jangaard (eds), *Edvard Grieg* (Troldhaugen: Edvard Grieg Museum, 2000).
Lakond , W. (trans. and ed.), *The Diaries of Tchaikovsky* (Westport, CT: Greenwood Press, 1973).
Lambert, C., *Music Ho! A Study of Music in Decline* (London: Faber and Faber, 1966).
Lang, P.H., *Music in Western Civilisation* (London: J.M. Dent, 1963).
Langford, P., *A Polite and Commercial People* (Oxford: Guild Publishing, 1989).
Larousse., *Grand Larousse Encyclopédique*, 1960.
Laver, J., *Taste and Fashion* (Edinburgh: Harrap, 1945).

Lawrence, D.H., *Sons and Lovers* (London: Penguin, 1948; first published 1913).
Lawson, W., *The History of Banking* (London: R. Bentley, 1855).
Layton, R., *Sibelius* (Master Musicians) (London: J.M. Dent, 1978).
Layton, R., *Grieg* (London: Omnibus Press, 1998).
Leaska, M., *Granite and Rainbow: The Hidden Life of Virginia Woolf* (London: Picador, 1998).
Leslie, A., *Edwardians in Love* (London: Hutchinson, 1972).
Lesure, F. (trans. D. Stevens), 'Claude Debussy after his Centenary', *Musical Quarterly*, vol. 49 (3), 1963, p. 277–288.
Lesure, F. (ed.) and Nichols, R. (trans.), *Debussy: Selected Letters* (London: Faber and Faber, 1987).
Levas, S. (trans. P.M. Young), *Sibelius: A Personal Portrait* (London: J.M. Dent, 1972).
Levine, V.L., in D. Nicholls (ed.), *The Cambridge History of American Music* (Cambridge: Cambridge University Press, 1998), p. 3.
Lewis, W. and T., *Modern Organ Building* (London: William Reeves, 1939).
Libby, D., in N. Zaslaw (ed.), *The Classical Era* (London: Macmillan, 1989).
Listowel, J., *A Habsburg Tragedy* (London: Ascent Books, 1978).
Locke, R., *Music, Musicians and the Saint Simonians* (Chicago, IL: University of Chicago Press, 1986).
Lonely Planet Guide to Finland, J. Brewer and M. Lehtipuu (Victoria, Australia: Lonely Planet Publications, 1999).
Lukowski, J. and Zawadzki, H., *A Concise History of Poland* (Cambridge: Cambridge University Press, 2001).
Macaulay, Lord (ed. H. Trevor-Roper), *Essays* (London: Fontana Press, 1965).
Macaulay, Lord., *History of England* (London: Longman, Green and co., 1880).
Macdonald, H., *Berlioz* (Master Musicians) (London: J.M. Dent, 1982).
MacDonogh, G., *Frederick the Great* (London: Weidenfeld and Nicolson, 1999).
Mack Smith, D., *Cavour* (London: Weidenfeld and Nicolson, 1985).
Maclean, F., *Bonnie Prince Charlie* (London: Weidenfeld and Nicolson, 1988).
Magee, B., *Wagner and Philosophy* (London: Allen Lane The Penguin Press, 2000).
Magnan, A. Fauchier, see Fauchier-Magnan, A.
Magraw, R., *France 1815–1915* (London: Fontana Press, 1983).
Mahler-Werfel, A. (trans. A. Beaumont), *Diaries 1898–1902* (London: Faber and Faber, 1998).
Maland, D., *Europe in the Seventeenth Century* (London: Macmillan, 1966).
Mander, R. and Mitchenson, J., *The Theatres of London* (London: Hart-Davis, 1961).
Mann, T. (trans. H.T. Lowe-Porter), *Buddenbrooks* (London: Vintage, 1999; first published 1902).
Mann, T. (trans. H.T. Lowe-Porter), *Death in Venice* (London: Penguin, 1955; first published, 1911).
Mansel, P., *Paris Between the Empires, 1814–1852* (London: John Murray, 2001).
Marek, G.R., *Beethoven: Biography of a Genius* (London: William Kimber, 1970).
Marek, G.R., *Gentle Genius: The Story of Felix Mendelssohn*, (London: Robert Hale Ltd., 1972).
Massie, R., *Dreadnought* (London: Jonathan Cape, 1992).
Matthews, D., *Beethoven* (Master Musicians) (London: J.M. Dent, 1985).
Matthews, D., 'Enriching Influence', *Times Literary Supplement*, 24 August 2001.
McCauley, M., *The Soviet Union 1917–1991* (London: Longman, 1993).
McDonald, H., in P. Bloom (ed.), *Music in Paris in the Eighteen Thirties* (New York, NY: Pendragon Press, 1987).
McPhee, P., *A Social History of France 1780–1880* (London: Routledge, 1992).
Mehling, F.N. (ed.), *Paris and the Ile de France: A Phaidon Cultural Guide* (London: Phaidon Press, 1987).
Milhous, J. and Hume, R.D., in D. Burrows (ed.) *The Cambridge Companion to Handel* (Cambridge: Cambridge University Press, 1997).
Millington, B., *Wagner* (Master Musicians) (London: J.M. Dent, 1984).
Milner, A., 'The Sacred Capons', *Musical Times*, vol. 114, 1973, pp. 250–52.
Mitford, N., *Frederick the Great* (London: Hamish Hamilton, 1970).

Mongrédien, J., in N. Zaslaw (ed.), *The Classical Era* (London: Macmillan, 1989).
Monteath, P., 'Swastikas by the Seaside', *History Today*, May 2000, pp. 31–35.
Moore, G., *Am I too loud? Memoirs of an Accompanist* (London: Hamish Hamilton, 1962).
Moore, T., *The Poetical Works* (London: Frederick Warne, 1892).
Morton, F., *The Rothschilds* (London: Secker and Warburg, 1961).
Mount, G., 'The Men who Built the Bank at Monte Carlo', *History Today*, October 1991, pp. 32–7.
Mozart Compendium, see H.C. Robbins Landon (ed.).
Müller, U. and Wapnewski, P. (trans. J. Deathridge), *The Wagner Handbook* (Cambridge, MA: Harvard University Press, 1992).
Murray, W., 'Living in Vienna 1890–1939', *History Today*, May 1996, pp. 50–55.
Musée Hector Berlioz, Guide du (La Côte St André: Association Nationale Hector Berlioz, 1991).
Musée de la Musique, Guide du, Cité de la Musique (Paris, 1997).
Musgrave, M., in C. Bashford and L. Langley (eds), *Music and British Culture* (Oxford: Oxford University Press, 2000).
Nectoux, J.-M., in P. Bloom (ed.), *Music in Paris in the Eighteen Thirties* (New York, NY: Pendragon Press, 1987).
New Grove Dictionary of Music and Musicians (ed. S. Sadie) (London: Macmillan 1980).
New Oxford Companion to Music (ed. D. Arnold) (Oxford: Oxford University Press, 1983).
Newman, E., *Memoirs of Hector Berlioz* (New York, NY: Dover Publications, 1932).
Newman, E., *The Life of Richard Wagner: Volume IV 1866–1883* (London: Cambridge University Press, 1976).
Newsome, D., *The Convert Cardinals: Newman and Manning* (London: John Murray, 1993).
Nicholls, D. (ed.), *The Cambridge History of American Music* (Cambridge: Cambridge University Press, 1998).
Nicolson, H., *The Congress of Vienna* (London: Constable, 1946).
Nicolson, N., *Napoleon 1812* (London: Weidenfeld and Nicolson, 1985).
Nye, R. and Morpurgo, J., *The Growth of the USA* (Harmondsworth: Pelican, 1965).
Okey, R., *The Habsburg Monarchy* (London: Macmillan, 2001).
Oliver, M., *Benjamin Britten* (London: Phaidon, 1996).
Olleson, P., in C. Bashford and L. Langley (eds), *Music and British Culture* (Oxford: Oxford University Press, 2000).
Opie'nski, H. (trans. E. Voynich), *Chopin's Letters* (New York, NY: Dover Publications, 1988).
Orga, A., *Chopin, his Life and Times* (London: Midas Books, 1976).
Orledge, R., 'Debussy's Musical Gifts to Emma Bardac', *Musical Quarterly*, vol. 60, 1974, pp. 544–56.
Orledge, R., *Gabriel Fauré* (London: Eulenburg, 1979).
Orlova, A., (trans. R.M. Davison), 'Tchaikovsky: The Last Chapter', *Music and Letters*, vol. 62, 1981, pp. 125–45.
Orlova, A., *Tchaikovsky: A Self-Portrait* (Oxford: Oxford University Press, 1990).
Osborne, R., *Rossini* (Master Musicians) (London: J.M. Dent, 1986).
Ostwald, P., *Music and Madness* (London: Gollancz, 1985).
Oxford Companion to Music, ninth edition (ed. P.A. Scholes) (London: Oxford University Press, 1955).
Oxford Dictionary of Quotations (Oxford: Oxford University Press, 1979).
Oxford Dictionary, The Concise, fifth edition, 1964.
Oxford History of the French Revolution, see W. Doyle.
Palmer, A., *Metternich* (London: Weidenfeld and Nicolson, 1972).
Palmer, A., *The Life and Times of George IV* (London: Weidenfeld and Nicolson, 1972).
Parker, G., *The Thirty Years War* (London: Routledge, 1984).
Parrott, I., *Elgar* (Master Musicians) (London: J.M. Dent, 1971).
Perkin, J., 'Sewing Machines: Liberation or Drudgery for Women', *History Today*, December 2002, p. 37.
Pestelli, G. (trans. E. Cross), *The Age of Mozart and Beethoven* (Cambridge: Cambridge University Press, 1984).

Phillips-Matz, M., *Verdi: A Biography* (Oxford: Oxford University Press, 1993).
Pick, C., *Embassy to Constantinople (Lady Mary Wortley Montagu)* (London: Century, 1988).
Plantinga, L., in R. Erickson (ed.), *Schubert's Vienna* (New Haven, CT: Yale University Press, 1997).
Plumb, J., *England in the Eighteenth Century* (Harmondsworth: Penguin, 1950).
Poe, E. Allan (ed. D. Galloway), *The Fall of the House of Usher and Other Writings* (London: Penguin, 1986).
Poole, R., 'Making Up for Lost Time', *History Today*, December 1999, pp. 40–46.
Porter, R., *English Society in the Eighteenth Century* (London: Penguin, 1991).
Posnansky, A., *Tchaikovsky: The Quest for the Inner Man* (London: Lime Tree (Macmillan), 1993).
Prebble, J., *Culloden* (London: Secker and Warburg, 1961).
Preston, K., in D. Nicholls (ed.), *The Cambridge History of American Music* (Cambridge: Cambridge University Press, 1998).
Přibáňová, S., 'Leoš Janáček's Memorial', Moravian Museum (Brno, 1999).
Price, R., in B. Waller (ed.), *Themes in Modern History 1830–90* (London: Unwin Hyman, 1990).
Procházková, J. and Volný, B., *Born in Hukvaldy*, Moravian Museum (Brno, 1995).
Prod'homme, J.G., 'C.A. Debussy', *Musical Quarterly*, vol. 4 (4), 1918, pp. 555–71.
Prokofiev, S. (trans. O. Prokofiev), *Soviet Diary 1927 and Other Writings* (London: Faber and Faber, 1991).
Proust, M. (trans. S. Moncrieff and T. Kilmartin, revised D.J. Enright), *In Search of Lost Time: Swann's Way* (London: Chatto and Windus, 1992; first published 1913).
Proust, M. (trans. S. Moncrieff and T. Kilmartin, revised D.J. Enright), *In Search of Lost Time: The Guermantes Way* (London: Chatto and Windus, 1992; first published 1920).
Pushkin, A. (trans. and ed. A. Myers and A. Kahn), *The Queen of Spades and Other Stories* (Oxford: Oxford University Press, 1997; first published 1834).
Raby, P., *Fair Ophelia: A Life of Harriet Smithson Berlioz* (Cambridge: Cambridge University Press, 1982).
Radcliffe P., *Mendelssohn* (Master Musicians) (London: J.M. Dent, 1954).
Redlich, H.F., *Bruckner and Mahler* (Master Musicians) (London: J.M. Dent, 1963).
Reed, J., *Schubert* (Oxford: Oxford University Press, 1997; original edition, London: J.M. Dent, 1987).
Rees, B., *Camille Saint-Saëns: A Life* (London: Chatto and Windus, 1999).
Reese, G., *Music in the Middle Ages* (London: J.M. Dent, 1968; original edition 1940).
Reich, W. (trans. L. Black), *Schoenberg* (London: Longman, 1971).
Ribeiro, A., *Dress and Morality* (London: Batsford, 1986).
Rice, J., in N. Zaslaw (ed.), *The Classical Era* (London: Macmillan, 1989).
Richards, R., *The Early History of Banking in England* (London: P.S. King and son, 1929).
Richardson, J., *The Courtesans: The Demi-Monde in 19th-Century France* (London: Weidenfeld and Nicolson, 1967).
Richardson, S., *Pamela: Or, Virtue Rewarded* (Oxford: Oxford University Press, 2001; first published 1740).
Richter, J.-P.F. (trans. R. Nichols), *Life of Quintus Fixlein* (Columbia, SC: Camden House, 1991).
Riding, J., Burrows, D. and Hicks, A., *Handel House Museum Companion* (London: The Handel House Trust, 2001).
Ridley, J., *Garibaldi* (London: Constable, 1974).
Ridley, J., *Napoléon III and Eugénie* (London: Constable, 1979).
Robb, G., *Balzac* (London: Picador, 1994).
Robbins Landon, H.C., *Mozart's Last Year* (London: Thames and Hudson, 1988).
Robbins Landon, H.C. (ed.), *The Mozart Compendium: A Guide to Mozart's Life and Music* (London: Thames and Hudson, 1990).
Robbins Landon, H.C., *Mozart and Vienna* (London: Thames and Hudson, 1991). Includes extracts from Johann Pezzl's *Skizze von Wien* (Sketch of Vienna), translated by Robbins Landon.

Robbins Landon, H.C., *The Mozart Essays* (London: Thames and Hudson, 1995).
Robertson, A., *Dvořák* (Master Musicians) (London: J.M. Dent, 1964).
Robinson, H., *Sergei Prokofiev* (London: Robert Hale, 1987).
Roose-Evans, J., *London Theatres* (London: Phaidon, 1977).
Root-Bernstein, M., 'Popular theatre in the French Revolution', *History Today*, February 1993, pp. 25–31.
Rose, K., *King George V* (London: Weidenfeld and Nicolson, 1983).
Routh, F., *Stravinsky* (Master Musicians) (London: J.M. Dent, 1975).
Rudé, G., *Revolutionary Europe 1783–1815* (London: Fontana, 1964).
Russell, C., in N. Zaslaw (ed.), *The Classical Era* (London: Macmillan, 1989).
Rykwert, J., 'The Man who Made Paris', Review of Haussmann's *Mémoires, Times Literary Supplement*, 27 April 2001, p. 11.
Sachs, J., 'Hummel and the Pirates, the Struggle for Musical Copyright', *Musical Quarterly*, vol 59 (1), 1973, pp. 31–60.
Saints, The Book of, compiled by the Benedictine Monks of St Augustine's Abbey, Ramsgate, sixth edition (London: A. and C. Black, 1989).
Samek, B., *The Monastery of Augustinians in Brno* (Brno: Augustinian Monastery, 1993).
Sams, E., 'Schubert's Illness Re-examined', *Musical Times*, vol. 121, 1980, pp. 15–22.
Samson, J., *Chopin* (Oxford: Oxford University Press, 1996).
Sand, G. (trans. S. Raphael), *Indiana* (Oxford: Oxford University Press, 1994; first published 1832).
Sand, G., *A Winter in Majorca* (Palma: Edicions Cort, 1998; first published 1842).
Sassoon, S., *Memoirs of a Fox-Hunting Man* (London: Faber and Faber, 1918).
Saunders, D., *Russia in the Age of Reaction and Reform* (London: Longman, 1992).
Saunders, D., *Authorship and Copyright* (London: Routledge, 1992).
Schorske, C., *Fin-de-Siècle Vienna* (New York, NY: Vintage Books, 1980).
Schweisheimer, W., 'Beethoven's Physicians', *Musical Quarterly*, vol. 31 (3), 1945, pp. 289–98.
Scull, T., 'More Light on Haydn's English Widow', *Music and Letters*, vol. 78, 1997, pp. 44–55.
Selden-Goth, G., (ed.) *Mendelssohn: Letters* (London: Paul Elek, 1946).
Sheehan, J., *German History 1770–1866* (Oxford: Clarendon Press, 1989).
Sibeliuksen Hämeenlinna, Hämeenlinna Historical Museum Guide (Hämeenlinnan Sibelius-Seura r.y., 1990).
Simeone, N., *Paris: A Musical Gazetteer* (New Haven, CT: Yale University Press, 2000).
Sked, A., in B. Waller (ed.), *Themes in Modern History 1830–90* (London: Unwin Hyman, 1990).
Skelton, G. (ed.), *Cosima Wagner's Diaries (an abridgement)* (London: Pimlico, 1994).
Smetana Museum Guide, *Bedřich Smetana: Time, Life, Work*, Z. Hojda, M. Freemanová, O. Mojřišsová, and R. Habánová (Prague, 1998).
Smollett, T., *The Works of Tobias Smollett* (London: Bickers and Son, 1872).
Smollett, T., *Travels through France and Italy* (London: The Folio Society, 1979; first published 1766).
Somfai, L., in N. Zaslaw (ed.), *The Classical Era* (London: Macmillan, 1989).
Spaethling, R., *Mozart's Letters, Mozart's Life* (London: Faber and Faber, 2000).
St Aubyn, G., *Queen Victoria: A Portrait* (London: Sinclair-Stevenson, 1991).
Stafford, W., *Mozart's Death* (London: Macmillan, 1991).
Stead, J., *Food and Cooking in Eighteenth-Century Britain* (London: English Heritage, 1985).
Steblin, R., Review of B. Newbould, *Schubert, The Music and the Man*, in *Music and Letters*, vol. 79, 1998, pp.128–30.
Stendhal (trans. M. Shaw), *Scarlet and Black* (London: Penguin, 1953).
Stendhal (trans. R.N. Coe), *Life of Rossini* (London: Collins, 1956; first published 1824).
Stendhal (trans. M. Shaw), *The Charterhouse of Parma* (London: Penguin, 1958; first published 1839).
Stevens, H. (ed. M. Gillies), *The Life and Music of Béla Bartók* (Oxford: Clarendon Press, 1993).
Stone, L., *The Family, Sex and Marriage* (London: Weidenfeld and Nicolson, 1977).
Strachey, L., *Eminent Victorians* (London: Penguin, 1918).
Stuckenschmidt, H. (trans. R. Rosenbaum), *Maurice Ravel* (London: Calder and Boyars, 1969).

Styan, J.L., *The English Stage* (Cambridge: Cambridge University Press, 1996).
Suter, A., 'Nimrod in the Metro', *The Elgar Society Journal*, vol. 12 (2), pp. 62–70.
Symon, J., *The Press and its Story* (London: Seeley Service and co., 1914).
Taylor, A., *English History 1914–1945* (Oxford: Oxford University Press, 1975).
Taylor, A., 'Fenimore Cooper's America', *History Today*, February 1996, pp. 21–27.
Taylor, R., *Robert Schumann: His Life and Work* (London: Granada Publishing, 1982).
Tchaikovsky House-Museum in Klin, Guide to (Moscow Region's Committee for Culture and Tourism, 1994).
Terry, C. Sandford, *Bach: A Biography* (Oxford: Oxford University Press, 1928).
Thompson, W., *Handel* (The Illustrated Lives of the Great Composers) (London: Omnibus Press, 1994).
Thomson, D., *England in the Nineteenth Century* (London: Penguin, 1950).
Tillard, F. (trans. C. Naish), *Fanny Mendelssohn* (Portland, OR: Amadeus Press, 1996).
Tolstoy, L. (trans. R. S. Townsend), *Anna Karenina* (London: J.M. Dent, 1912; first published 1873–6).
Tomalin, C., *Mrs Jordan's Profession* (London: Penguin, 1994).
Tomalin, C., *Jane Austen* (London: Viking, 1997).
Tomalin, C., *Samuel Pepys* (London: Penguin, 2002).
Touring Club of Italy Guide (Milan: Touring Editore srl, 1999).
Troyat, H., *Turgenev* (London: W.H. Allen, 1989).
Valldemossa Monastery Guide (Barcelona: Escudo de Oro, SA).
Vandereycken, W. and van Deth, R., 'The anorectic Empress', *History Today*, vol. 46 (4), April 1996, pp. 12–19.
Vergo, P., *Art in Vienna 1898–1918* (London: Phaidon, 1993).
Vitali, C., in D. Burrows (ed.), *The Cambridge Companion to Handel* (Cambridge: Cambridge University Press, 1997).
Vlaardingerbroek, K., 'A Dutch Music Lover in Italy and France 1723–4', *Music and Letters*, vol. 72, 1991, pp. 536–51.
Vlk, M., *Nelahozeves – the Castle* (Nelahozeves, 1992).
Wagner Handbook, see U. Müller and P. Wapnewski (eds).
Wagner, C., *Diaries*, see G. Skelton (ed.).
Walker, A., *Franz Liszt, Volume I: The Virtuoso Years, 1811–47* (London: Faber and Faber, 1983).
Walker, A., *Franz Liszt, Volume 2: The Weimar Years, 1848–60* (London: Faber and Faber, 1989).
Walker, A., *Franz Liszt, Volume 3: The Final Years 1861–86* (London: Faber and Faber, 1997).
Walker, E. (revised J.A. Westrup), *A History of Music in England* (Oxford: Clarendon Press, 1952).
Walker, F., *The Man Verdi* (London: J.M. Dent, 1962).
Walker, R., *Rachmaninoff: His Life and Times* (Tunbridge Wells: Midas, 1980).
Waller, B. (ed.), *Themes in Modern European History 1830–90* (London: Unwin Hyman, 1990).
Walter, B. (trans. J. Galston), *Theme and Variations* (London: Hamish Hamilton, 1947).
Wangermée, R., in P. Bloom (ed.), *Music in Paris in the Eighteen Thirties* (New York, NY: Pendragon Press, 1987).
Warrack, J., *Carl Maria von Weber* (Cambridge: Cambridge University Press, 1976).
Warrack, J., in P. Bloom (ed.), *Music in Paris in the Eighteen Thirties* (New York, NY: Pendragon Press, 1987).
Watson, D., *Liszt* (Master Musicians) (London: J.M. Dent, 1989).
Weber, Baron M.M. von (trans. J. Palgrave Simpson), *Carl Maria von Weber* (London: Chapman and Hall, 1865, and New York, Greenwood Press 1969).
Weber, W., in N. Zaslaw (ed.), *The Classical Era* (London: Macmillan, 1989).
Weber, W., in D. Burrows (ed.), *The Cambridge Companion to Handel* (Cambridge: Cambridge University Press, 1997).
Wedgwood, C.V., *The Thirty Years War* (London: Jonathan Cape, 1938).
Weinreb, B., and Hibbert, C., *London Encyclopaedia* (London: Macmillan, 1993).
Weinstock, H., *Donizetti and the World of Opera* (London: Methuen, 1964).
Weinstock, H., *Rossini: A Biography* (London: Oxford University Press, 1968).
Wharton, G. and P., *The Queens of Society, Volume II* (London: James Hogg and Sons, 1860).
Wheatcroft, A., *The Habsburgs* (London: Viking, 1995).

White, E., *Stravinsky: The Composer and his Works* (London: Faber and Faber, 1979).
Wilhelm, K., *Richard Strauss Persönlich: Eine Bildbiographie* (Berlin: Henschel, 1999).
Williams, H. Noel, *Mme Récamier and her Friends* (London: Harper Brothers, 1901).
Williams, S., in R. Erickson (ed.), *Schubert's Vienna* (New Haven, CT: Yale University Press, 1997).
Wistrich, R., *The Jews in Vienna in the Age of Franz Joseph* (Oxford: Oxford University Press, 1990).
Wolff, C., *Johann Sebastian Bach* (Oxford: Oxford University Press, 2000).
Woodfield, I., 'New Light on the Mozarts' London Visit', *Music and Letters*, 1995, p. 187.
Woodfield, I., in C. Bashford and L. Langley (eds), *Music and British Culture* (Oxford: Oxford University Press, 2000).
Woodham Smith, C., *The Great Hunger: Ireland 1845–9* (London: Hamish Hamilton, 1962).
Wroth, W.W., *London Pleasure Gardens of the Eighteenth Century* (London: Macmillan, 1896).
Wyn Jones, D. (ed.), *Music in Eighteenth-Century Britain* (Aldershot: Ashgate Publishing, 2000).
Young, A., *Travels in France During the Years 1787, 1788, 1789* (London, 1889).
Young, P., in *Of German Music: A Symposium* (London: Oswald Wolff Publishers, 1976).
Zaluski, I. and P., *Mozart's Europe: The Early Journeys* (Lewes: The Book Guild, 1993).
Zaslaw, N. (ed.), *The Classical Era* (London: Macmillan, 1989).
Żelazowa Wola Guide *Żelazowa Wola: The Place of his Birth* (2001).
Zemanová, M., *Janáček* (London: John Murray, 2002).
Zola, E. (trans. L. Tancock), *Germinal* (London: Penguin, 1954; first published 1885).
Zola, E. (trans. D. Parmée), *Nana* (Oxford: Oxford University Press, 1998; first published 1880).
Zwickau Museum Guide, *Robert-Schumann-Haus Zwickau* (Berlin, 2000).

The following are the names of contributors to New Grove whose articles were particularly consulted: G. Abraham (Balakirev, Musorgsky, Rimsky-Korsakov, Schumann); G. Abraham and D. Lloyd-Jones (Borodin); R. Angermüller (Salieri); T. Antonicek (Vienna); D. Arnold (Monteverdi); W. Ashbrook (Boito, Leoncavallo, Mascagni); W. Ashbrook and J. Budden (Donizetti); P. Banks (Mahler); R. Barr (Zelter); H. Becker (Brahms, Hamburg, Meyerbeer); R. Benton (Pleyel); A. Blyth (Pears); J. Borwick (sound recording); G. Bourligueux (Daniel); D. Brown (Tchaikovsky); M. Brown (Schubert); J. Budden (Barbaia, Carafa, Strepponi); G. Buelow (Mattheson, Scheibe, Werckmeister); D. Cairns (Furtwängler, Toscanini); M. Carner and G. Ravenni (Puccini); M. Carner and M. Schönherr (Strauss); J. Clapham (Dvořák, Smetana); D. Cooke (Bruckner); M. Cooper (Duparc, Gounod, Massenet); G. Croll and D. Heartz (Durazzo); P. Crossley-Holland (Wales); D. Brown (Glinka); W. Dean (Bizet, Cuzzoni, Gluck, Handel, Senesino); B. Deane (Cherubini); P. Dekeyser (Kalkbrenner); P. Evans (Britten); G. Favre (Boiëldieu); E. Forbes (Hérold, Pasta); J. Fuller Maitland (Sommer); E. Garden (A. Rubinstein, N. Rubinstein, Serov); P. Gossett (Rossini); P. Griffiths (Dyagilev); J. Harding (Saint-Saëns); A. Hedley and M. Brown (Chopin); E. Helm (C.P.E. Bach); E. Heron-Allen (Reményi); C. Hill (Ries); I. Holst (Holst); G. Hopkins (Ravel); J. Horton and N. Grinde (Grieg); F. Howes (Goddard); F. Hudson (Stanford); I. Kemp (Hindemith); M. Kennedy (R. Strauss); J. Kerman and A. Tyson (Beethoven); K.-H. Köhler (Mendelssohn); A. Lamb (Offenbach); V. Lampert (Bartók); J.-P. Larsen (Haydn); R. Layton (Sibelius); H. Leuchtmann (Herz); L. Lindgren (Bononcini); F. Lippmann (Bellini); R. Longyear (Auber); H. Macdonald (Berlioz, Delibes, Halévy, Holmès, Skryabin); R. Macnutt (Ricordi); R. McAllister (Prokofiev); D. McVeagh (Elgar); J.-M. Nectoux (Fauré); R. Newmarch and G. Norris (Belyayev); D. Nichols and S. Hansell (Hasse); R. Nichols (Debussy, Poulenc); G. Norris (Cui, Rakhmaninov); R. Oliver (Joachim); H. Ottaway (Vaughan Williams); N. Pirrotta and R. Meloncelli (Rome); H. Poole and D. Krummel (music printing and publishing); A. Porter (Stolz, Verdi); P. Robinson (Massol, Nourrit); J. Roche (Moscheles); A. Rodewald (Mayr); M. Rose (Mercadante); S. Sadie (Mozart); H.-H. Schönzeler (Richter); B. Schwarz (Glazunov, Paganini, Shostakovich); H. Searle (Liszt); R. Sietz (Hiller); K. Snyder (Rosenmüller); J. Spencer (Dargomïzhsky); P. Susskind (Wieck); M. Talbot (Vivaldi); J. Trevitt (Franck); J. Tyrrell (Janáček); J. Vysloužil (Křížkovský); R. Wangermée (Thalberg); J. Warrack (von Bülow, Schröder-Devrient, Sontag, Weber); H. Weber (Zemlinsky); A. Weinmann (Artaria); C. von Westerhagen (Wagner); E. White (Stravinsky); C. Wolff and W. Emery (J.S. Bach).

NOTE ON MONEY, DATES AND NAMES

Money

A reader is generally more interested in value than money, because money is a poor measure of value, except in the very short term, when it is useful for those who wish to choose what to buy or sell. Looked at over a long period, inflation makes sensible monetary comparisons very difficult. Exchange rate movements, which in theory should iron out inflationary differences between one country and another, in practice add to the confusion, as does the variety of different currencies which were in use: exchange rates at frontiers were sometimes different from bankers' exchange rates; besides, there were, for example, many different types of ducat.[1]

While these aspects could be overcome by a determined mathematician, it is not just idleness or incompetence that lead me to balk at an attempt to translate monetary amounts from the past to the present. It is simply that the resulting information becomes virtually useless, because even the largest fortune could not begin to buy what we can obtain now: the technology was not available to provide it. Thus prices and incomes expressed in terms of our purchasing power become misleading. Besides, fashions change and expenditure patterns vary: Mozart's sister spent the equivalent of two months of her father's salary on a dress for her visit to Munich in 1780–81; even the most indulgent of modern fathers would blench at this. Appearances mattered in those days, especially if you needed a husband; less perhaps now.[2]

Sometimes large or small amounts can be interesting in themselves. For example, Puccini's estate was said to be worth £800,000 when he died in 1924.[3] However, usually relative values are more interesting and they are interspersed at various points in the text.

Some interesting relative comparisons can be done, assuming that the base data is indeed accurate. For example, from 1762 Haydn was paid 600 florins per annum at the court of Prince Esterházy,[4] who reputedly had an annual income of 700,000 fl, around twice that of several of his wealthy peers.[5] At that time, 75 per cent of the population of Vienna had taxable income of less than 50 fl, and domestic servants might earn as little as 10–30 fl annually.[6] Singers were relatively well paid: Mozart's girlfriend and eventual sister-in-law, Aloysia Weber, was offered 1,000 fl to sing in Munich in 1778.[7] Such disparities of wealth may not surprise us. But we begin to wonder when we hear that Emperor Francis Stephen could cheerfully lose 30,000 ducats (there were 4.5 florins to the ducat) in a night at cards.[8]

Relative values are often surprising. In the first half of the 19th century, when a French labourer earned 2 francs for a ten-hour day, the 683-page full score of Halévy's very popular opera *La Juive* could only be bought for 250 fr.[9] A concert grand piano cost between 1,200 and 1,400 fr.*

* For those who are interested in the 'crude' monetary comparison for these figures, we are told that there were 8–9 fl to the UK£.[10] One author writing in 1998 suggests that, for the years before 1793, one should use a multiple of 60 to convert into present-day equivalents.[11] This would mean that Fräulein Weber was paid around £7,500 in modern sterling, and the overall multiple for the florin at that time would be between 7 and 8. Caveat!

Dates and times

This book is generally based on sources where the dates have been converted to the modern calendar. At the time of the composers described, the calendar was, however, not so straightforward. In Roman Catholic countries, the Julian calendar was reformed in 1582 by Pope Gregory XIII. Protestant German states (such as Hanover, the Netherlands and Denmark) only came into line in March 1700, when 18 February leapt to 1 March. The change was made in England only in 1752, and in Ireland in 1782; Russia only changed in February 1918.[12]

Before the changes in the 18th century, the beginning of the year was Lady Day, 25 March, and not 1 January. Thus a date in the first three months of the year, such as 23 February, 1685, which we now recognise as Handel's birthday, would have been thought of as arising in 1684. There was sufficient recognition of the potential confusion that, for a date falling in these first three months, the year was sometimes designated, for example, 1684/85.

Lord Chesterfield, who, as an English diplomat overseas, had the inconvenience of managing two calendars in his correspondence, was the architect of the Calendar Reform Act of 1751. When it was announced that, in the next year, the day following Wednesday 2 September should be styled Thursday 14 September, there were practical issues about the loss of eleven days' pay, and the maturity date of financial payments. So, although the Church designated Lady Day on the new '25 March', wages and taxes, etc, only became due on 5 April. There were also more emotional issues about popish calendars, the profanity of changing saints' days, and the loss of eleven days of one's life.

Standardisation, let alone 'Brussels', was not on the agenda. Times of the day must have been highly inaccurate: imagine setting the village clock accurately without a radio, and only a sundial.[13] Indeed, until the advent of rail travel in the 19th century, there was no standard time across the country; each community set its own time according to sunrise and sunset, and so it of course varied according to longitude. For train timetables to be practicable a standard time had to be brought in.[14]

Names

At the risk of irritating those who prefer consistency of language, I have deliberately used forms of names which I would use in conversation or expect to see in print: thus, Napoleon instead of Napoléon; Ludwig van Beethoven instead of Louis or Lewis, César Franck instead of Caesar. I have found some impressive spellings of Frédéric Chopin, but have not adopted them. He was known to his friends as Fritz; I would not presume to be so familiar.

Russian names present a particular difficulty because there is no straightforward English equivalent into which they transliterate (Rachmaninov, Rachmaninof, Rachmaninow, Rakhmaninoff, etc). There is a considerable risk of some usages, including some of the most modern, becoming intrusive. To err on the safe side, I have adopted familiar usages from The Oxford Companion to Music (9th edition) which was published in the middle of the 20th century. These usages do not necessarily represent 'the latest fashion', for which I make no apology. An analogy might be drawn with the concert performer who allows the body movements to become a distraction: in that case, however, the listener has the option of closing the eyes and enjoying the music; that luxury is not so available to a reader of a book.

Many modern books use the word Conservatory rather than Conservatoire when referring to a public school of music. The Concise Oxford Dictionary, however, defines a conservatory as a greenhouse for tender plants; this may be an apt term for 99.9 per cent of the students, but not for the Great Composers.

The choice of name to adopt can also be difficult when dealing with a Marienkirche or a Thomasschule; but I take a crumb of comfort from the fact that nobody would expect me to call the great cathedral in the centre of Paris 'Our Lady'. Some may feel unhappy with me referring to Emperors Francis Stephen and Franz Joseph. For that, I rely on the wisdom of Ralph Waldo Emerson, whose grandson housed Stravinsky when he first took up residence in America,[15] and who so famously wrote: 'A foolish consistency is the hobgoblin of little minds, adored by little statesmen and philosophers and divines. With consistency, a great soul has simply nothing to do.'[16]

NOTES

1 R. Halliwell, *The Mozart Family: Four Lives in a Social Context* (Oxford: Clarendon Press, 1998), p. xxxviii.
2 Ibid., pp. xxxvii, xxxviii.
3 M. Carner, *Puccini* (London: Gerald Duckworth and co., 1974), p. 240.
4 L. Somfai, in N. Zaslaw (ed.), *The Classical Era* (London: Macmillan, 1989), p. 273.
5 Ibid., p. 269.
6 Ibid.
7 H.C. Robbins Landon, *The Mozart Essays* (London: Thames and Hudson, 1995).
8 E. Crankshaw, *Maria Theresa* (London: Longman, 1969), p. 111.
9 A. Devriès, in P. Bloom (ed.), *Music in Paris in the Eighteen Thirties* (New York: Pendragon Press, 1987), p. 241.
10 H.C. Robbins Landon (ed.), *The Mozart Compendium: A Guide to Mozart's Life and Music* (London: Thames and Hudson, 1990), p. 61.
11 C. Hibbert, *George III* (London: Viking, 1998), p. 6.
12 C. Wolff, *Johann Sebastian Bach* (Oxford: Oxford University Press, 2000), p. 54; and M. Fainsod, *How Russia is Ruled* (Cambridge, MA: Harvard University Press, 1963), p. 9.
13 R. Poole, 'Making Up for Lost Time', *History Today*, December 1999, pp. 40–46.
14 *Encyclopaedia Britannica*, fifteenth edition, 1974.
15 E. White, *Stravinsky, the Composer and his Works* (London: Faber and Faber, 1979), p. 115.
16 *Oxford Dictionary of Quotations* (Oxford: Oxford University Press, 1979).

THE BOURBONS • SCHEMATIC FAMILY TREE

NB: Not all kings etc, and not all connections, shown

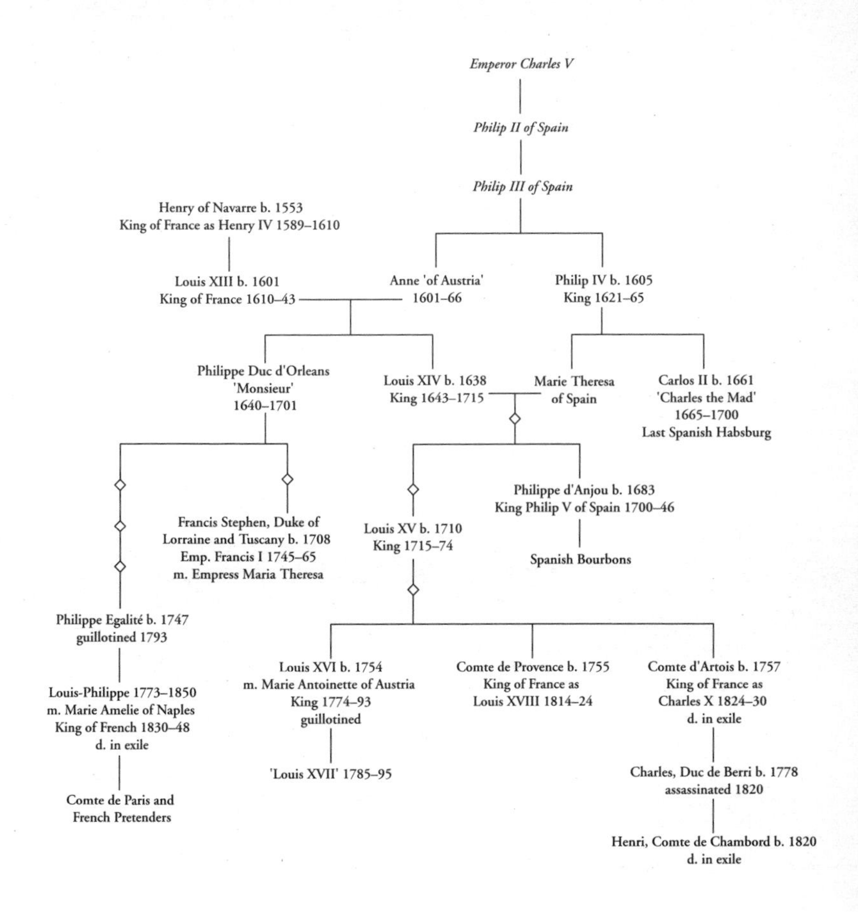

KEY TO FAMILY TREES

◇ Another generation, but less relevant
b. Born
d. Died
m. Married
Emp. Emperor

THE HABSBURGS • SCHEMATIC FAMILY TREE

NB: Not all kings etc, and not all connections, shown

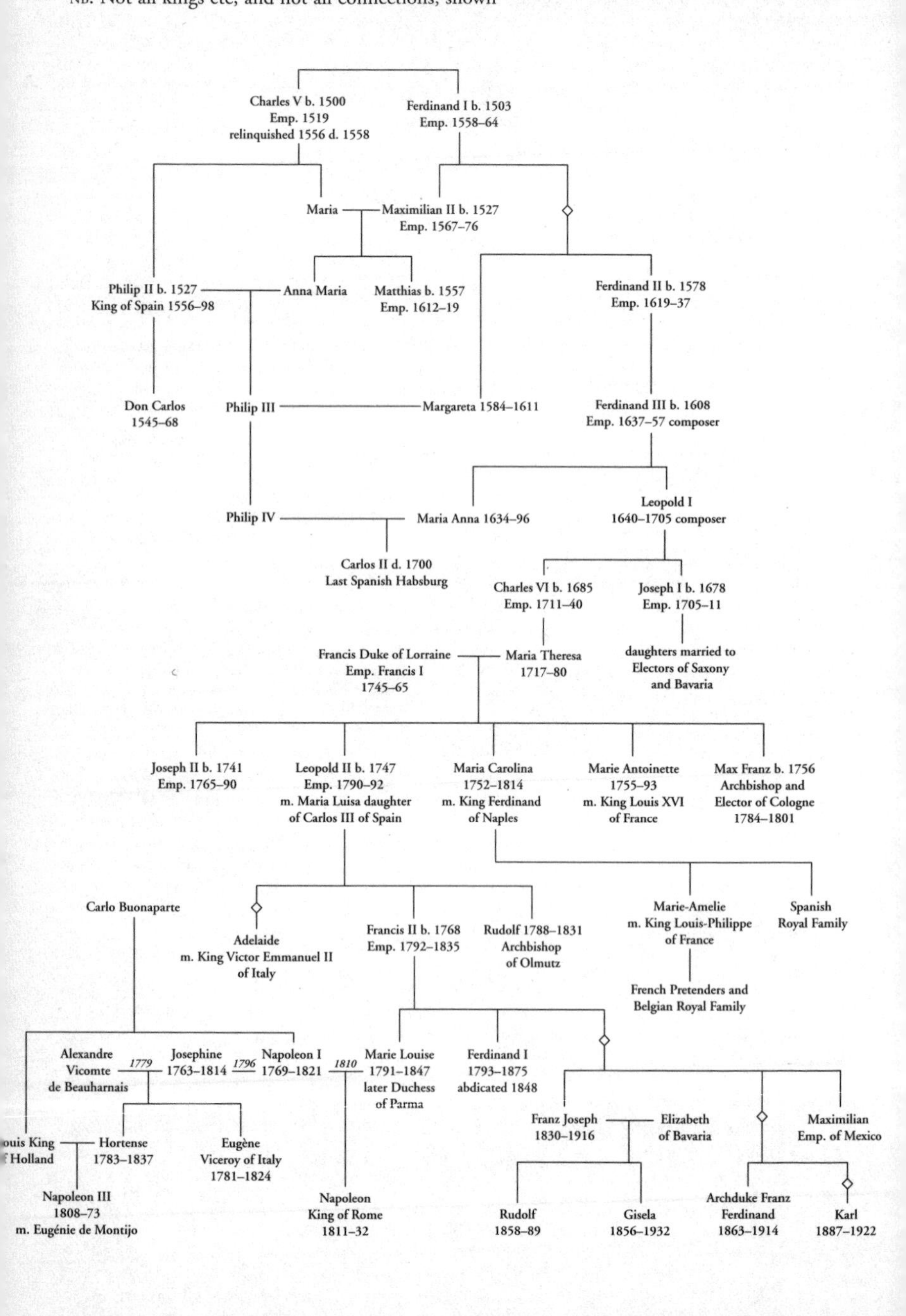

ACKNOWLEDGEMENTS

The author and publisher wish to thank the following for their permission to reprint copyright material:

E. Anderson, *The Letters of Mozart and his Family*. Reproduced with permission of Palgrave Macmillan.
W. Atwood, *The Lioness and the Little One: The Liaison of George Sand and Frederic Chopin*. Reproduced with permission from Columbia University Press.
G. St Aubyn, *Queen Victoria: A Portrait*. Reproduced with permission from Sinclair Stevenson.
S. Avins, *Johannes Brahms: Life and Letters*. Reprinted by permission of Oxford University Press.
Honore de Balzac, *Eugénie Grandet*. Reprinted by permission of Oxford University Press.
Honore de Balzac (trans. Marion Ayton Crawford), *Old Goriot*. Copyright in this translation © Marion Ayton Crawford 1951. Reproduced by permission of Penguin Books Ltd.
Honore de Balzac (trans. Sylvia Raphael), *Selected Short Stories*. Copyright in this translation © Sylvia Raphael 1977. Reproduced by permission of Penguin Books Ltd.
Honore de Balzac (trans. H.J. Hunt), *The Wild Ass's Skin*. Copyright in this translation © H.J. Hunt 1977. Reproduced by permission of Penguin Books Ltd.
P. Barbier (trans. R. Luoma), *Opera in Paris 1800–1850*. Used by permission of Amadeus Press.
J. Barrie Jones (trans. and ed.), *Gabriel Fauré: A Life in Letters*. Reproduced with permission from Chrysalis Books.
Beethoven's Letters, ed. Eaglefield Hull. Reprinted by permission of Oxford University Press.
Wilfrid Blunt, *On Wings of Song*. Copyright © Wilfrid Blunt 1974. Reproduced with permission of Curtis Brown Group Ltd., London on behalf of the Estate of Wilfrid Blunt.
Wilfrid Blunt, *The Dream King*. Copyright © Wilfrid Blunt 1970. Reproduced with permission of Curtis Brown Group Ltd., London on behalf of the Estate of Wilfrid Blunt.
J. Budden, *Verdi*. Reprinted by permission of Oxford University Press.
Alan Bullock, *Hitler and Stalin: Parallel Lives*. Copyright © Alan Bullock 1991. Reprinted with permission from HarperCollins Publishers Ltd.
D. Burrows, *Handel*. Reprinted by permission of Oxford University Press.
M. Carner, *Puccini*. Reproduced by permission of Gerald Duckworth and Co. Ltd.
William Carter, *Marcel Proust: A Life*. Copyright © 2000 by Yale University. Reproduced with permission.
Joan Chissell, *Clara Schumann: A Dedicated Spirit*. Copyright © Joan Chissell 1983. Reproduced by permission of Penguin Books Ltd.
Joan Chissell, *Schumann*. Reprinted by permission of Oxford University Press.
J. Clapham, 'Dvořák's Relations with Brahms and Hanslick'. Reprinted by permission of Oxford University Press.
D. Cooke, *The Language of Music*. Reprinted by permission of Oxford University Press.
Edward Crankshaw, *Maria Theresa*. Copyright © Edward Crankshaw 1969. Reprinted by permission of PFD on behalf of the Estate of Edward Crankshaw.
M. Curtiss, *Bizet and his World*. Reprinted by permission of The Random House Group Ltd.
M. Curtiss, 'Bizet, Offenbach and Rossini'. Reprinted by permission of Oxford University Press.
M. Curtiss, 'Unpublished Letters by Georges Bizet'. Reprinted by permission of Oxford University Press.
E. Dahl and M. Jangaard (eds), *Edvard Grieg*. Reproduced with permission from Edvard Grieg Museum Troldhaugen.
H.T. David and A. Mendel, *The Bach Reader*. Reproduced with permission from W.W. Norton and Co. Ltd.
Otto Erich Deutsch, *Mozart: A Documentary Biography*. Reproduced with permission from A. and C. Black Publishers Ltd.

Otto Erich Deutsch, *Schubert: A Documentary Biography*. Reprinted by permission of Oxford University Press.

Fyodor Dostoyevsky (trans. David Magarshack), *The Devils (The Possessed)*. Copyright in this translation © David Magarshack 1953. Reproduced by permission of Penguin Books Ltd.

A. Einstein, *Gluck*. Reprinted by permission of Oxford University Press.

A. Einstein, *Music in the Romantic Era*. Reprinted by permission of Oxford University Press.

G. Flaubert (trans. G. Hopkins), *Madame Bovary*. Reprinted by permission of Oxford University Press.

Karl Geiringer, *Haydn: A Creative Life in Music*. Copyright © 1983 Karl Geiringer. Reproduced with permission.

J.W. Goethe (trans. M. Hulse), *The Sorrows of Young Werther*. Copyright in this translation © M. Hulse 1989. Reproduced by permission of Penguin Books Ltd.

Nikolai Gogol (trans. David Magarshack), *Dead Souls*. Copyright in this translation © David Magarshack 1961. Reproduced by permission of Penguin Books Ltd.

Claire Harman, *Fanny Burney*. Copyright © 2000 Claire Harman. Reproduced with permission.

A. Hedley, *Chopin*. Reprinted by permission of Oxford University Press.

Anthony Holden, *Tchaikovsky*. Copyright © Anthony Holden, 1995. Published by Bantam. Reproduced by permission of the author c/o Rogers, Coleridge & White Ltd., 20 Powis Mews, London W11 1JN.

A. Horne, *The Fall of Paris*. Reproduced with permission from Macmillan, London, UK.

J. Horton, *Grieg*. Reprinted by permission of Oxford University Press.

M. Hurd, *Vaughan Williams*. Reproduced with permission from Faber and Faber Ltd.

H. Montgomery Hyde, *The Other Love*. Copyright © H. Montgomery Hyde 1970. Reproduced with permission of Curtis Brown Group Ltd., London on behalf of the Estate of H. Montgomery Hyde.

Christopher Isherwood, *Mr Norris Changes Trains*. Copyright © Christopher Isherwood 1935. Reproduced with permission of Curtis Brown Group Ltd., London on behalf of the Estate of Christopher Isherwood.

Belinda Jack, *George Sand*. Reprinted by permission of The Random House Group Ltd.

Burnett James, *Brahms: A Critical Study*. Reprinted by permission of Oxford University Press.

Z. Janáčková (ed. and trans. J. Tyrell), *My Life with Janáček*. Reproduced with permission from Faber and Faber Ltd.

R. Jordan, *George Sand*. Reproduced with permission from Constable and Robinson Ltd.

M. Kennedy, *Mahler*. Reprinted by permission of Oxford University Press.

M. Kennedy, *Portrait of Elgar*. Reprinted by permission of Oxford University Press.

M. Kennedy, *Richard Strauss: Man, Musician, Enigma*. Reproduced with permission from Cambridge University Press.

C. Lambert, *Music Ho!* Reproduced with permission from Faber and Faber Ltd.

P.H. Lang, *Music in Western Civilisation*. Reprinted by permission of Oxford University Press.

F. Lesure, 'Claude Debussy After His Centenary'. Reprinted by permission of Oxford University Press.

F. Lesure and R. Nichols, *Debussy: Letters*. Reproduced with permission from Faber and Faber Ltd.

A. Mahler-Werfel, *Diaries 1898–1902*. Reproduced with permission from Faber and Faber Ltd.

Thomas Mann (trans. H.T. Lowe-Porter), *Death in Venice*. Reprinted by permission of The Random House Group Ltd.

D. Matthews, *Beethoven*. Reprinted by permission of Oxford University Press.

H. Nicolson, *The Congress of Vienna*. Reproduced with permission from Constable and Robinson Ltd.

R. Orledge, 'Debussy's Musical Gifts to Emma Bardac'. Reprinted by permission of Oxford University Press.

A. Orlova, *Tchaikovsky: A Self-Portrait*. Reprinted by permission of Oxford University Press.

R. Osborne, *Rossini*. Reprinted by permission of Oxford University Press.

M. Phillips-Matz, *Verdi: A Biography*. Reprinted by permission of Oxford University Press.

S. Prokofiev, *Soviet Diary 1927 and Other Writings*. Reproduced with permission from Faber and Faber Ltd.

Marcel Proust (trans. C. Scott Moncrieff and T. Kilmartin), *In Search of Lost Time*. Reprinted by permission of The Random House Group Ltd.
Peter Raby, *Fair Ophelia: A Life of Harriet Smithson Berlioz*. Reproduced with permission from Cambridge University Press.
J. Reed, *Schubert*. Reprinted by permission of Oxford University Press.
B. Rees, *Camille Saint-Saëns: A Life*, published by Chatto and Windus. Reprinted by permission of The Random House Group Ltd.
Jasper Ridley, *Napoléon III and Eugénie*. Copyright © Jasper Ridley 1979. Reproduced with permission of Curtis Brown Group Ltd., London on behalf of Jasper Ridley.
A. Robertson, *Dvořák*. Reprinted by permission of Oxford University Press.
G. Sand, *Indiana*. Reprinted by permission of Oxford University Press.
S. Sassoon, *Memoirs of a Fox-Hunting Man*. Reproduced with permission from Faber and Faber Ltd.
D. Saunders, *Russia in the Age of Reaction and Reform*. Reproduced with permission from Pearson Education Ltd.
G. Skelton (ed.) *Cosima Wagner's Diaries (An Abridgement)*. Reproduced with permission from David Higham Associates.
R. Spaethling, *Mozart's Letters, Mozart's Life*. Reproduced with permission from Faber and Faber Ltd.
Stendhal (trans. Margaret R.B. Shaw), *Charterhouse of Parma*. Copyright in this translation © Margaret R.B. Shaw 1958. Reproduced by permission of Penguin Books Ltd.
Stendhal (trans. R.N. Coe), *Life of Rossini*. Published by Calder Publications, London. Reproduced with permission.
Stendhal (trans. Margaret Shaw), *Scarlet and Black*. Copyright in this translation © Margaret Shaw 1953. Reproduced by permission of Penguin Books Ltd.
F. Tillard (trans. C. Naish), *Fanny Mendelssohn*. Used by permission of Amadeus Press.
Peter Vergo, *Art in Vienna 1898–1918*. Copyright © Phaidon Press Ltd. Reproduced with permission.
Alan Walker, *Franz Liszt, Volumes 1–3*. Reproduced with permission from David Higham Associates.
E. Walker, *A History of Music in England*. Reprinted by permission of Oxford University Press.
Bruno Walter, *Theme and Variations*, translated by James A. Galston, copyright © 1946 and renewed 1974 by Alfred A. Knopf, a division of Random House, Inc. Used by permission of Alfred A. Knopf, a division of Random House, Inc.
E. Zola, *Nana*. Reprinted by permission of Oxford University Press.

Although every effort has been made to contact copyright holders, there are instances where we have been unable to do so. If notified, the publisher will be pleased to acknowledge the use of copyright material in future editions.

PICTURE CREDITS

c.p. = colour plate number, p. = page in text

p. 26 (1, 2), p. 29 (2, 3, 4), p. 32, p. 33, p. 67, p. 69, p. 99, p. 133, p. 153 (1, 2), p. 173, p. 174, p. 205, p. 239, p. 258 (1, 2), p. 273 (1, 2, 3), p. 277 (1, 2, 3, 4), p. 286, p. 303, p. 318, p. 356 (1), p. 387, p. 394, p. 425, p. 429 (1, 2, 3, 4, 5, 6, 7, 8, 9), p. 491 (1, 2), p. 517, p. 551, p. 553, p. 574 (1), p. 581, p. 583, p. 607 (1, 2, 3), p. 635 (1, 2, 3), p. 647 (1, 2, 3), p. 661, p. 689 (2), p. 711 (1, 2), p. 725 (1, 2), p. 743, p. 767, p. 776, p. 789, p. 799 (1, 2), p. 816 (1, 2, 3), p. 829 (1, 2, 3), p. 836 (1, 2), p. 855 (1, 2, 3), p. 858, p. 875 (1, 2), c.p. 15, c.p. 28, c.p. 43 reproduced with kind permission of the Royal College of Music, London.

c.p. 19 (copyright © Photo RMN – Ojéda/Hubert), c.p. 32 (copyright © Photo RMN – Hervé Lewandowski), c.p. 33 (copyright © Photo RMN – Hervé Lewandowski) reproduced with permission of the Agence Photographique de la RMN.

INDEX